Biology of
Amphibians

Biology of
Amphibians

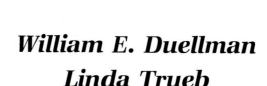

William E. Duellman
Linda Trueb

Illustrated by Linda Trueb

McGraw-Hill Book Company

New York   St. Louis   San Francisco

Auckland   Bogotá   Guatemala   Hamburg
Johannesburg   Lisbon   London   Madrid   Mexico
Montreal   New Delhi   Panama   Paris   San Juan
São Paulo   Singapore   Sydney   Tokyo   Toronto

On the cover: Adult marsupial frog *Gastrotheca aureomaculata,*
photographed in Moscapán, Colombia, by William E. Duellman.

1 2 3 4 5 6 7 8 9 0   HAHA   8 9 3 2 1 0 9 8 7 6 5

ISBN 0-07-017977-8

Library of Congress Cataloging in Publication Data

Duellman, William Edward, 1930–
    Biology of amphibians.

    Bibliography: p.
    Includes index.
    1. Amphibians.   I. Trueb, Linda.   II. Title.
QL667.D84   1985   597.6   85-14916
ISBN 0-07-017977-8

Contents

Contents

Dedication

To our graduate students—
past, present, and future

Biographical Note

William E. Duellman has been associated since 1959 with the University of Kansas, where he is now curator of the Division of Herpetology in the Museum of Natural History, and Professor in the Department of Systematics and Ecology. He teaches graduate courses in biogeography, reptile biology, and amphibian biology (with Linda Trueb). He maintains an active graduate program in herpetology, and he and his students use the extensive herpetological collections in the museum for diverse research. His studies on the systematics, ecology, and reproductive biology of amphibians have involved extensive field work in the United States, Mexico, Central and South America, as well as Australia and Africa. Born in Dayton, Ohio, he studied zoology at the University of Michigan, where he received a doctor's degree in 1956. He taught at Wayne State University before joining the University of Kansas.

Dr. Duellman's writings include more than 200 contributions to national and international journals, symposia, and museum publications. Major works are *Hylid Frogs of Middle America* (*Monogr. Mus. Nat. Hist. Univ. Kansas,* 2 vols., 1970);

Liste der Rezenten Amphibien und Reptilen: Hylidae, Centrolenidae, Pseudidae (*Das Tierreich*, vol. 95, 1977); and *The Biology of an Equatorial Herpetofauna in Amazonian Ecuador* (*Misc. Publ. Mus. Nat. Hist. Kansas*, vol. 65, 1978). He edited *The South American Herpetofauna: Its Origin, Evolution and Dispersal* (*Monogr. Mus. Nat. Hist. Univ. Kansas*, vol. 7, 1979).

Linda Trueb teaches at the University of Kansas. Her courses include scientific illustration, evolutionary morphology, and (with William E. Duellman) amphibian biology. She also maintains an active graduate program in the Department of Systematics and Ecology and in the Museum of Natural History, where she and her students are investigating diverse aspects of vertebrate morphology. She has carried out extensive field work in Central and South America and also has worked in Africa and Australia. In 1979 she was a visiting lecturer at the University of Adelaide, Australia. Originally from Pomona, California, Linda Trueb did her undergraduate work at the University of California, Berkeley, with emphasis on vertebrate zoology. At the University of Kansas she undertook research on cranial osteology of anurans for the Ph.D, which she received in 1968. She has continued investigations on amphibian morphology and systematics, especially of tropical groups of anurans, and has expanded her research to include functional morphology and the role of heterochrony in anuran osteology. Aside from her research, she is a practicing scientific illustrator.

The author of about 36 major, refereed papers, Dr. Trueb has published in both domestic and foreign symposium volumes and in a variety of national and international serials, including *Miscellaneous Publications* and *Occasional Papers of the University of Kansas, Contributions to Science of the Los Angeles County Museum of Natural History, Copeia, Herpetologica, Journal of Morphology, Journal of Zoology* (London), and *South African Journal of Science*.

Foreword

by Charles M. Bogert

Perhaps the earliest amphibians made their debut in an area with a more rigorous climate, but their initial diversification could well have occurred in tropical environments. Climatic conditions similar to those of today in the rainforests and cloud forests of the tropics presumably prevailed during the Pennsylvanian Period when amphibians were already numerous. For well over 250 million years amphibians have been exploiting habitats in moist tropical environments, where the bulk of them remain. Either most living amphibians are restricted to such environments or they belong to groups of species that have representatives with ranges extending into the tropics. In fact, the Gymnophiona, the smallest of the three orders and the one to which the only extant limbless amphibians are assigned, are known solely from moist tropical environments. These superficially wormlike amphibians, known as caecilians, include species that retain fishlike scales hidden in the skin. Fossil caecilians, unknown until recently, shed little light on their ancestry, perhaps the oldest of any amphibians extant.

Salamanders, the tailed amphibians grouped in the order Caudata, though represented in the American tropics, have the distinction of being more diversified in the United States than elsewhere. Relatively thorough investigations still in progress in this country have already revealed 115 species, almost one-third of the total now recognized. Salamanders continue to be discovered in Mexico, which may prove to support as many species as the United States. However, only 43 species are known from Europe, a thoroughly explored continent.

The third order, the Anura, the most widely represented of any group of amphibians now living, contains the tailless species known as frogs and toads. These include neary 87 percent of all amphibian species extant. During their long history they have probably exploited all but the most inhospitable environments between the poles and the Equator. Scarcely 3 percent of the species are represented in the United States. Some of these are largely tropical, with distributions that extend northward to the southern tip of Texas.

Although only one popular account of amphibians, *The Frog Book* (1906), was available until around 1940, a wealth of authoritative handbooks dealing with the frogs and salamanders in the United States began to appear. These may well have stimulated the interests of budding herpetologists, and the field expanded. A list of herpetologists, most of whom were still active when it was published in 1974, indicated about 800 in the United States, 36 in Canada, but only 1 in Mexico (where there were at least 3). Not all of these were devoting their efforts to research, but a fair percentage had published at least one report.

Until 1936 only one journal published in the United States provided an outlet for scientific contributions from herpetologists, and this journal was shared with ichthyologists. For the last 25 years, however, three journals have been available in the United States and a few in other countries. There are, of course, journals of animal behavior, ecology, and other disciplines that also publish the results of investigations dealing with amphibians. Hundreds of such reports appear annually, in addition to books restricted to specialized investigations such as the results of a 1976 symposium that dealt only with the reproductive biology of amphibians.

We need only turn back to an earlier summary to discover how much more we know about amphibians today than half a century ago. G. Kingsley Noble in his authoritative *Biology of the Amphibia* (1931) suggested that the frogs, toads, and salamanders now living included only some 1900 species. The caecilians were so poorly known that the only figure Noble mentioned represents about a third of the species now recognized. Noble's estimate, therefore, would have approximated fewer than 2000 species. When William E. Duellman and Linda Trueb completed their survey of the literature summarized in the present book, their estimate of the total was nearly double that of Noble. In other words, systematists studying the amphibians have been adding names to the roster of valid species at an average rate of 37 species per year.

Not all of the species added have necessarily been discovered or even recognized for the first time. A large percentage of them have nevertheless been diagnosed, described, and validly named since 1931. A good many others, however, had been erroneously assigned to subspecific status or even synonymized by students who had underevaluated the extent of the differentiation. In some instances, species represented by populations incapable of interbreeding had been viewed as belonging to one species. For example, tree frogs occupying similar habitats on opposite sides of the southwestern deserts in the United States and superficially similar morphologically were regarded as being conspecific for over half a century. Not until portable tape recorders became available in the 1950s had anyone attempted to subject the tree frogs' mating calls to scientific analysis using audiospectrograms. These spectrograms revealed such profound differences that no one has since doubted that two distantly related species are represented. Inevitably field studies disclosed significant differences in the species' modes of reproduction.

Satisfactory solutions to innumerable taxonomic problems awaited the introduction of new ideas, new concepts, new methods, and new or better equipment. Intensive field investigations revealed differentiation in behavioral traits as well as adaptive specializations that discouraged or prevented interbreeding between amphibians that earlier workers had regarded as being morphologically indistinct. Truly satisfactory solutions to some problems of relationships awaited the use of electrophoresis or detailed knowledge of mechanisms of inheritance. Geneticists, particularly Theodosius Dobzhansky and his students, turned their attention to species problems, and devised experiments that paved the way to significant improvements in the systematists' concept of the species. Taking their cues from Dobzhansky, systematists were soon discussing "closed systems" and carrying out field investigations to ascertain which "isolation mechanisms" discouraged or prevented interbreeding when related species were sympatric.

The more enlightened systematists realized that their predecessors had depended far too heavily on the examination of preserved specimens. Even though taxonomists had refined their techniques of measuring, recording, and evaluating morphological characters, the better systematists realized that such information could be interpreted far more effectively if correlated with the results of ecological and ethological investigations in the field. Ways were devised to supplement field studies with breeding experiments carried out under controlled laboratory conditions, perhaps more easily with some frogs than with highly specialized amphibians. Anatomical studies remained important, of course, and systematists continued to rely heavily on the maintenance of extensive collections of well-documented specimens. These are required not only to deal with the problems of variations but to document distributions. Only the most conservative taxonomists regarded collections with the philosophy of the stamp collector, who acquired only one of each kind. The acquisition of extensive broadly representative collections by large museums became the sine qua non of "the new systematics." It became important to students of evolution to find out whether populations of closely related animals lived side by side or occupied separate ranges or habitats. Ernst Mayr undoubtedly clarified the thinking of systematists and other students of evolution when he coined the terms allopatric and sympatric.

Merely pointing out that the class Amphibia proves to be represented by at least twice the number of species that an authority recognized in 1931 may seem offhand to be of limited significance. Even if systematists continued to recognize additional species of caecilians, frogs, and salamanders at current rates, which is most improbable, they would require another century to double the representation of amphibians. The new systematics, however, is not restricted to morphological descriptions. Students of evolution, perhaps more than other specialists, have contributed to the synthesis of the many fields now recognized. We have witnessed the interdigitation of anatomy, physiology, ecology, ethology, endocrinology, and paleontology, to mention only a few disciplines. There is, therefore, a sound basis for the assumption that advances in our knowledge of the biology of the amphibians in its widest sense closely parallel those that have broadened our understanding of the composition of the class Amphibia.

Paradoxically, the proliferation of humans that led to the exploitation of rainforests may already be contributing to the decline of the amphibians. We are informed that the rainforests of the world are being destroyed at rates averaging approximately 30 acres for every minute of every day. Once comprising 2.4 billion acres of prime amphibian habitat, the rainforests are being converted irretrievably into useless wasteland. The frogs, salamanders, and caecilians finely adjusted to this environment are being destroyed, and species may be extinguished.

Herpetologists must struggle with the abundance of information, old and new. Some find time to examine the more impressive "classics"—multivolumed, sometimes lavishly illustrated accounts that began to appear even before Linnaeus's day—but usually can only sample. Herpetologists feel inundated by the flood of information rolling off the presses. As early as 1950 no one could even pretend to read everything published that pertained to amphibians and reptiles, even if all such publications were accessible. At least the old card index to the literature that passed through the herpetologist's hands—a laborious system with title cards typed by the secretary and organized according to subject—can be superseded by modern retrieval systems.

Regardless of how capable, well informed, or experienced, a herpetologist is unlikely to assume the responsibility of preparing a *Biology of Amphibians* without the support and encouragement of a sympathetic institution. Fortunately William E. Duellman and Linda Trueb are among the very few, either here or abroad, who have the requisite qualifications, including the ambition and efficiency, to summarize virtually all learned thus far about the caecilians, salamanders, and frogs. At least, nearly everything confidently regarded as pertinent has been included. This account is not a compendium or an encyclopedia. Nearly every chapter could be expanded to fill an entire volume. What students as well as practicing herpetologists, biology professors, and even enlightened laypersons are likely to prefer is a reasonably complete but concise account of a fairly large, widely distributed group of animals. This is what Linda Trueb and William Duellman, after years of work in the field, in the library, and in the laboratory and classroom, have managed to produce.

The University of Kansas, which has long and faithfully supported herpetological research, along with study collections, also deserves credit. Duellman and Trueb, whether working independently or as a team, in recent decades have been among the most efficient and productive herpetologists in the United States. Anyone who makes full use of this book is unlikely to question this appraisal.

CHARLES M. BOGERT
Santa Fe, New Mexico
March 1985

Preface

More than half a century has passed since the publication of G. K. Noble's *Biology of the Amphibia,* in 1931. Noble's book has been the primary source for information on amphibians; understandably, it is out of date now. For many years we have taught a course on the biology of amphibians and have become increasingly frustrated by the lack of an adequate text. Furthermore, we have been exasperated by the number of hours spent tracking down some trivial facts, as well as synthesizing major blocks of information for use in lecture or publication.

With the urging and blessings of many of our colleagues we began early in 1980 to prepare the manuscript for this book. We have endeavored to produce a book that will serve not only as a text in a course designed for advanced undergraduate and graduate students but as a reference for amateur and professional biologists interested in diverse aspects of amphibian biology—from paleontology to physiology, from genetics to community ecology, with the coverage worldwide. We hope that we have succeeded.

In the organization, there are two lengthy chapters (2 and 3) on structure. Chapters 2 through 5 deal with diverse aspects of reproduction, and Chapters 6 and 7 are concerned with larvae and metamorphosis. Chapters 8 through 12 are concerned with the relationships of amphibians with their environment—biotic and abiotic. Chapters 13 and 14 examine the morphology of amphibians. The evolutionary history of amphibians is treated in Chapters 15 and 16, whereas Chapters 17 and 18 are concerned with the phylogeny and biogeography of the modern groups of amphibians. Chapter 19 contains a definition of each of the families, summary of the fossil history, generalized treatment of the life history, statement of geographic distribution, and a list of all recognized generic names, together with generic synonyms, numbers of recognized species, and distribution.

Some readers may be concerned that there are no chapters devoted to behavior or to locomotion. These subjects are covered in appropriate places. For example, behavior is discussed in relation to reproduction, courtship, vocalization, larvae, physiological ecology, feeding, and enemies. Likewise, not all aspects of structure are covered in Chapters 13 and 14; for example, the structure of the sound-producing mechanism of anurans is discussed in the chapter on vocalization, and the structure of the feeding mechanisms is treated in the chapter on feeding. Any of these subjects can be located through the use of the index.

Throughout the book we have stressed function and evolution. Thus, in the chapters dealing with morphology, we have tried to discuss structure with respect to functional systems. We have emphasized the evolutionary significance of aspects of reproduction, development, physiology, and ecology. Most chapters (or appropriate sections therein) begin with a discussion of the conceptual framework in which the material is presented, and most chapters terminate in a discussion relating the material to broader aspects of amphibian biology.

We have endeavored to choose appropriate examples worldwide to illustrate our points. Thus, a person knowledgeable about the amphibian fauna of Australia, Brazil, Europe, or West Africa will find as many familiar examples as will the person in North America. Of course, there are limitations. For example, most of literature concerned with endocrinology, development, or physiology deals with a relative few North American or European species.

Although we have depended heavily on our own personal knowledge of amphibians that has accumulated during a combined 60 years of experience, much of the information presented in this book has been taken from the vast and expanding literature. For those disciplines with which we were not particularly familiar we have relied on syntheses and summary papers (when available). Moreover, we have tried to include the latest information on all subjects. Thus, of the more than 2500 references (in 12 languages) cited, about one-third have appeared since we began working on the manuscript less than 5 years ago.

References are cited in the text by author and date; in cases of publications having two authors, both names are given. If there are more than two authors, only the first author is given followed by et al. Instances of different authors with the same surname are distinguished by first (and sometimes second) initials. All authors listed by name in the text are referenced in the index.

We have endeavored to update the taxonomy throughout the text. Current scientific names are used; these are not necessarily the names that were used in publications that are cited. All generic and specific names used in the text, tables, and illustrations are included in the index.

We owe a great debt of gratitude to many persons throughout the world for aiding us in innumerable ways. First and foremost we are indebted to our daughter, Dana Trueb Duellman, who while developing from an adolescent girl to a midteen tolerated our countless hours of labor and helped to manage our household.

We have shamelessly called upon many colleagues for information and references. Many persons have provided us with photographs and tape recordings; each is acknowledged in appropriate legends. Innumerable investigators have provided us with manuscripts (some unsolicited) in an effort to keep us up to date.

We are especially grateful for critical reviews of the chapters (noted in parentheses) by Kraig Adler (1), Stevan J. Arnold (3), Thomas J. Berger (6, 11, 12), James P. Bogart (16), Charles M. Bogert (1), Ronald A. Brandon (6, 7), Bayard H. Brattstrom (8), Edmund D. Brodie, Jr. (10), Daniel R. Brooks (10), David C. Cannatella (13, 15, 17, 19), Martha L. Crump (2, 12), Richard Estes (15, 17, 19), Linda S. Ford (8, 13), Darrel Frost (1, 17, 18, 19), John S. Frost (16), Sally K. Frost (2, 5, 7, 14), Carl Gans (4, 9), David M. Hillis (16), Robert Holt (12), Robert G. Jaeger (9, 11), Harvey Lillywhite (8), Murray Littlejohn (4), John D. Lynch (13, 17, 19), Linda R. Maxson (16, 18), Roy W. McDiarmid (3), Charles W. Myers (10), Ronald A. Nussbaum (17, 19), Rebecca A. Pyles (9, 13), Rodolfo Ruibal (8, 14), Stanley N. Salthe (5), Jay M. Savage (17, 18, 19), Hans-Peter Schultze (15, 18), Norman J. Scott, Jr. (12), Catherine A. Toft (9), Frederick B. Turner (11), David B. Wake (9, 13, 17, 18, 19), Marvalee H. Wake (9, 13, 14, 17, 18, 19), Richard J. Wassersug (6, 7), Kentwood D. Wells (2, 3, 4), Ernest E. Williams (15), and Richard G. Zweifel (5). In addition, Robert C. Drewes and Michael J. Tyler reviewed material on Australian and African anurans, respectively. Their efforts have greatly increased the accuracy and presentation of the material. However, any errors of omission, commission, and interpretation are our sole responsibility.

Our colleagues at the University of Kansas have suffered during the past 5 years. We are especially grateful to Sally K. Frost and Hans-Peter Schultze for the use of their personal libraries. We thank the personnel in the Science Library for aid in tracking down elusive references and in obtaining others on interlibrary loan. Production of the manuscript was made less painful by the typing skills of Rose Etta Hermann, Jennifer Volpe, and Bernard Willard. We are especially grateful to Rebecca A. Pyles for managing the computer files; the entire manuscript was processed on remote terminals to the Academic Computing Center. Nearly all of the photographs were processed by John E. Simmons, whose efforts and skills in the darkroom are greatly appreciated. Lastly, we are grateful to Patricia A. Burrowes for her assistance in compiling the index.

We would be remiss if we did not acknowledge our past and present graduate students who have contributed so much, both directly and indirectly, to the realization of this project. Basically they have provided the stimulus for our undertaking the work. They have been a continuing source of encouragement on one hand, and our most severe and exacting critics on the other. We hope that the final product meets their expectations, and we dedicate this book to them with our profound gratitude.

Sybil P. Parker, Joe Faulk, and Edward J. Fox of the Professional and Reference Division of the McGraw-Hill Book Company are professionals in the truest sense of the word. We express our appreciation to them for their continued support and expertise in bringing our efforts to fruition.

Finally, each of us owes a debt of gratitude to the persons who introduced us to the fascinating world of amphibians. For one of us (Duellman), the late Charles F. Walker of the University of Michigan provided continuous challenges and encouragement to investigate the biology of amphibians, a group of organisms that were very special for him. Perhaps it is a break in tradition to acknowledge an undergraduate zoology course, but were it not for a stimulating and comprehensive introduction to the world of vertebrate natural history at the University of California at Berkeley, the second author (Trueb) doubtless never would have pursued graduate studies in herpetology. She extends her thanks to Robert C. Stebbins who introduced the new horizon and to Daniel C. Wilhoft who, through his enthusiasm and interest, encouraged her to investigate it.

WILLIAM E. DUELLMAN AND LINDA TRUEB
Lawrence, Kansas
October 1984

Biology of
Amphibians

CHAPTER 1

Introduction to the Amphibia

These foul and loathsome animals are abhorrent because of their cold body, pale color, cartilaginous skeleton, filthy skin, fierce aspect, calculating eye, offensive smell, harsh voice, squalid habitation, and terrible venom; and so their Creator has not exerted his powers to make many of them.

Carolus Linnaeus (1758)

Since Linnaeus's early misconceptions about amphibians, biologists have discovered that these animals are among the most fascinating and numerous of terrestrial vertebrates. From the time of their remarkable feat of colonizing the land in the Mid-Devonian, nearly 350 million years ago, amphibians have evolved a wide range of morphological and ecological types. Of these, the three living groups—frogs, salamanders, and caecilians— contain more than 3900 living species, and new species (and even new genera) are being discovered each year.

THE WORLD OF AMPHIBIANS

Amphibians are intermediate in some ways between the fully aquatic fishes and the terrestrial amniotes. However, they are not simply transitional in their morphology, life history, ecology, and behavior. In the successful attainment of independence from water and colonization of land, amphibians have undergone a remarkable adaptive radiation, and the living groups exhibit a greater diversity of modes of life history than any other group of vertebrates. Their shell-less eggs have been studied extensively by developmental biologists, and much of the basic knowledge of vertebrate embryology is based on amphibians. The metamorphosis from aquatic larvae to terrestrial adults has been the subject of intensive studies, and much of what is known about the actions of thyroid and pituitary hormones has come from endocrinological studies on amphibians. Likewise, the ease of breeding amphibians in the laboratory and their relatively simple chromosome complements have provided bases for important advances in studies of hybridization and speciation. The vocalizations of frogs have provided a means for studying acoustic communication and, together with other aspects of courtship and mating, have presented the evolutionary biologists with a wealth of material for studies on sexual selection. These are but a few selected examples of the exciting ways in which studies of amphibians are contributing to knowledge of biology and our understanding of biological phenomena.

The term amphibian can be interpreted in two ways— either as an animal spending part of its life in water and then changing to an aquatic adult, or as an animal that alternates life in and out of water, such as so-called pond frogs. Actually both interpretations are valid in part but neither applies to all amphibians, some of which are aquatic throughout their lives, but others of which neither enter water nor have aquatic stages in their life histories. So, what sort of animal qualifies as an amphibian?

Essentially, amphibians can be defined as quadrupedal vertebrates having two occipital condyles on the skull and no more than one sacral vertebra. The skin is glandular and lacks the epidermal structures (scales, feathers, hair) characteristic of other groups of tetrapods. Although some

1

Paleozoic amphibians were large, plated quadrupeds, most living amphibians are small. The largest salamander attains a total length of about 1500 mm, whereas the largest frog is about 300 mm. Caecilians reach a length of about 1500 mm. Caecilians and some salamanders lack limbs and girdles, and in some other salamanders these structures are reduced. In frogs the postsacral vertebrae are fused into a single rodlike element, the coccyx, the tail is absent, and the hindlimbs are elongated and modified for jumping. Although epidermal scales are absent in amphibians, dermal scales are present in the skin of most caecilians. The skin is highly glandular and contains both mucous and granular (poison) glands. True claws are absent, but horny tips are present on the toes of some frogs and salamanders.

Internally, the structure of living amphibians is intermediate between that of fishes and amniotes. The heart has two atria, a single ventricle (which may be partially divided), and a distinct conus arteriosus with several valves. The aortic arches are symmetrical. Typically, amphibians have two lungs, but the lungs are reduced in some salamanders and absent in one entire family (Plethodontidae). The left lung is greatly reduced in most of the elongate caecilians (as it is in snakes). Living amphibians also have some unique characters. They all have pedicellate teeth and specialized papillae in the inner ear, and salamanders and anurans have green rods in the retina of the eye.

The life histories of amphibians are highly diversified. Most species of frogs have external fertilization, whereas internal fertilization occurs in the majority of salamanders and presumably in all caecilians. The classic amphibian life history of aquatic eggs and larvae, although typical of many frogs and some salamanders, is only one of many modes of reproduction, which include direct development of terrestrial eggs (no aquatic larval stage), ovoviviparity, and even viviparity. All amphibian eggs must develop in moist situations, for although they have numerous protective mucoid capsules, these capsules are highly permeable. The eggs lack a shell and the embryonic membranes (amnion, allantois, and chorion) of higher vertebrates. In those amphibians that have aquatic larvae, the larvae undergo metamorphosis into the adult form; this is an especially dramatic change in frogs.

The terms Urodela and Apoda are sometimes used instead of Caudata and Gymnophiona for salamanders and caecilians, respectively, whereas in some literature Salientia is used interchangeably with Anura for frogs. Even common English names become confusing. It is not uncommon in the literature to find "salamanders and newts" or "frogs and toads." Newts are aquatic members of the family Salamandridae, and are salamanders. Likewise, at least in the narrow sense, toads are members of the family Bufonidae, and are frogs in the broad sense. Thus, all newts are salamanders, but not all salamanders are newts, and all toads are frogs, but not all frogs are toads. To avoid confusion, the terms newt and toad are used in their narrow sense; in referring to all frogs and toads, the ordinal derivative anuran is used.

HISTORICAL RESUME

In order to place present knowledge of amphibian biology in perspective, we provide a brief history of the field of herpetology with emphasis on those workers who are major contributors to knowledge of amphibian biology. This review is biased in favor of those workers who are herpetologists and therefore neglects many of the investigators who as physiologists, embryologists, or biochemists also have made important contributions.

As biology emerged as a science in the late 1600s and early 1700s, amphibians played an important role in research. For example, the first description of cleavage in a zygote was of a frog egg by Jan Swammerdam (1738). It is noteworthy that in the same year that Linnaeus's (1758) tenth edition of the *Systema Naturae,* which represents the foundation for subsequent zoological nomenclature, was published, Rösel von Rosenhoft (1753–58) published a superbly illustrated folio on the life history of European frogs with special emphasis on *Rana esculenta* and thereby provided the first detailed documentation of the amphibian egg, aquatic larva, and morphological transformation into the terrestrial adult.

During the latter part of the 18th century and throughout most of the 19th century, the principal occupation of biologists was collecting and classifying organisms. In the late 1700s, Paris became the center for herpetological research. François Daudin (1802) published the first comprehensive account of frogs; as part of the encyclopedic "Suites de Buffon," Daudin (1803) summarized the existing knowledge on amphibians in volume 8 of *Histoire Naturelle, Génerale et Particulière des Reptiles.* The encyclopedic coverage of amphibians was expanded considerably in a later edition of the "Suites de Buffon"; Andre M. Constant Duméril, Gabriel Bibron, and Auguste H. A. Duméril (1841, 1854) covered amphibians in two volumes of the *Erpétologie Génerale ou Histoire Naturelle Complète des Reptiles.* Meanwhile in Switzerland, Johann J. von Tschudi (1838) attempted a classification of living and fossil amphibians, and in Vienna, Leopold Fitzinger (1843) proposed a classification of amphibians and reptiles; many currently used generic names were proposed by these workers. Toward the middle of the 19th century, the center of herpetology shifted to London, where Albert C. L. G. Günther at the British Museum (Natural History) published an important systematic treatise and catalogue of amphibians in that museum in 1859. Large quantities of natural history material were added to the collections of the British Museum through the energetic efforts of British explorers and collectors during Britain's great period of colonization. These formed the bases for many publications by Günther's successor, George A. Boulenger (Fig. 1-1), whose major contributions include the catalogues of the anurans (1882a)

Figure 1-1. Major workers and pioneers in various disciplines of amphibian biology: upper left, George Albert Boulenger (courtesy of the British Museum [Natural History]); upper right, Edward Drinker Cope (courtesy of the Academy of Natural Sciences of Philadelphia); lower left, Ernst Gaupp (from *Anatomische Anzeiger,* vol. 49, 1917); lower right, Gladwyn K. Noble (courtesy of American Museum of Natural History).

and of the salamanders and caecilians (1882b) and the detailed studies on the European anurans (1897–98).

Other important contributions were made in the field of amphibian taxonomy in the latter part of the 19th century by François Mocquard and Paul Brocchi in France, Wilhelm Peters and Oscar Boettger in Germany, and J. von Bedriaga in Russia. However, the preeminent student of amphibians of the time was Edward D. Cope (Fig. 1-1), who was associated with the Academy of Natural Sciences in Philadelphia. Cope's prodigious writings encompassed the fields of vertebrate paleontology and anatomy, ichthyology, and herpetology. In addition to his multitudinous papers describing new taxa, Cope's major contributions were in the utilization of internal morphological characters, particularly the skeleton, in determining the relationships of and in classifying amphibians;

these are especially evident in his works on frog classification (1865) and on the amphibians of North America (1889).

Although Cope pioneered in the use of internal morphology in the classification of amphibians, it was the German anatomists of the 19th century who provided excellent descriptive anatomy accompanied by superb illustrations. Johannes Müller (1835) discovered that caecilians had gill slits and were in fact amphibians, not snakes. Robert Wiedersheim (1879) published on the anatomy of caecilians; this was followed by the detailed work on the development and morphology of *Ichthyophis glutinosus* by Paul and Fritz Sarasin (1887–90). Probably the most detailed and copiously illustrated works on amphibian anatomy are those by C. K. Hoffmann (1873–78) that dealt with all groups of amphibians, and those of

Ernst Gaupp (Fig. 1-1) on the development and anatomy of anurans, culminating in his *Anatomie des Frosches* (1896). Also at this time in England, William K. Parker completed several major works on amphibian osteology.

By the early years of the 20th century, several centers of herpetology were established in various parts of the world, and in many of these emphasis was on amphibians. Despite two world wars, amphibian research continued to flourish in Europe. At the British Museum (Natural History) in London, Hampton W. Parker continued Cope's tradition of careful morphological studies concerned with amphibian classification, an approach subsequently maintained by Alice G. C. Grandison. At the Museum National d'Histoire Naturelle in Paris, various herpetologists under the influence of Fernand Angel and Jean Guibé pursued investigations on the amphibians of West Africa and Madagascar, and Alain Dubois is now working on Himalayan anurans, Jean Lescure on South American anurans, and Jean-Paul Risch on Asian amphibians. In Italy, Giuseppe Cei (Fig. 1-2) initiated important studies on reproductive cycles; these were followed by similar investigations on salamanders by V. Vilter and his associates in France and were extended to viviparous frogs by Maxime Lamotte and his associates. In Denmark, Arne Schiøtz (1967, 1975) has made important contributions to the knowledge of anurans in tropical Africa; these have been augmented by many important works on the amphibians of West Africa by Jean-Luc Perret in Switzerland and Jean-Luc Amiet in Cameroon. The Belgians established an intensive program on the biota of the Congo at the Musée Royal du Congo Belge in Tervuren; Raymond F. Laurent made many important contributions on the amphibians. In the Netherlands, research emphasized the amphibian faunas of the Dutch East Indies (Indonesia), especially by P. N. van Kampen (1923), and currently on Surinam by Marinus S. Hoogmoed and on Madagascar by Rose M. A. Blommers-Schlösser.

The study of amphibians, especially anurans, has flourished in South Africa in the 20th century. At Stellenbosch University, C. G. S. de Villiers and C. A. du Toit and their students carried out detailed morphological studies. Investigations on the systematics, distribution, and life histories of anurans have culminated in several important works by Walter Rose (1962), J. C. Poynton (1964), V. A. Wager (1965), and N. I. Passmore and V. C. Carruthers (1979).

The Japanese have had a long history of study of amphibians. Yaichiro Okada's (1931) beautifully illustrated work on the anurans of the Japanese Empire and Ikio Sato's (1943) work on the salamanders of Japan provided an impetus for investigations by many successors. Work on amphibian genetics and development is accomplished at the Laboratory for Amphibian Biology established at Hiroshima University in 1967 by Toshijiro Kawamura (Fig. 1-2). Other important works by biologists in eastern Asia include René Bourret's (1942) *Les Batraciens de l'Indochine,* Ch'eng-chao Liu's work on am-

phibian life histories, his *Amphibians of Western China* (1950), and his work in collaboration with Shu-quing Hu, *Tailless Amphibians of China,* published in 1961. Studies on amphibians in China are continuing, especially by Shu-quing Hu and Ermi Zhao and their associates at the Chengdu Institute of Biology. A modern account of the amphibians of Taiwan was prepared by G.-Y. Lue and S.-H. Chen (1982). In the Philippines, Angel C. Alcala at Silliman University has provided thorough studies of the life history and development of Philippine anurans.

Indian herpetologists have concentrated on morphology and development. Especially noteworthy are the studies on caecilians by L. S. Ramaswami and on anurans by Beni C. Mahendra. The only comprehensive survey of the amphibians of Sri Lanka was written by P. Kirtisinghe (1957).

Although most of the early work on Australian amphibians was done by British herpetologists, in the 1880s the Australians developed a center of study at The Australian Museum in Sydney, with J. J. Fletcher being the foremost Australian worker on amphibians. By the 1950s, A. R. Main and his students were actively studying the systematics, ecology, and life histories of frogs in Western Australia. One of Main's students, Murray J. Littlejohn, established another center at the University of Melbourne, and with his collaborators, including Angus A. Martin and Graeme F. Watson, has been innovative in the use of bioacoustics and hybridization in the study of speciation of anurans. Michael J. Tyler's tireless efforts at seeking out previously unknown frogs has resulted in the discovery of many new species in Australia and New Guinea; now at the University of Adelaide, he is collaborating with Margaret Davies on systematic revisions of the Australo-Papuan anurans.

In South America, studies on amphibians lagged behind other parts of the world. Prior to World War II, two Brazilians made important contributions. Alipio de Miranda-Ribeiro of São Paulo published a beautifully illustrated book on Brazilian frogs in 1926. Although a physician by trade and a parasitologist by profession, Adolpho Lutz contributed many works on the taxonomy of Brazilian frogs; his investigations were continued by his daughter, Bertha Lutz, whose efforts culminated in her 1973 work on the Brazilian tree frogs of the genus *Hyla.* At the Museu Nacional in Rio de Janeiro, Antenor Leitão de Carvalho made important contributions to knowledge of Brazilian amphibians, especially microhylid frogs. Knowledge of the diversity of Brazilian frogs has been increased greatly by the systematic investigations of Werner C. A. Bokermann in São Paulo and Eugenio Izecksohn in Rio de Janeiro. The fascinating frog fauna of temperate South America has been studied by José M. Gallardo and Avelino Barrio in Buenos Aires; the latter made especially important contributions to studies of anuran speciation through bioacoustic and karyological investigations. After World War II, Giuseppe Cei moved from Italy to Argentina and as José Cei established an important center at

Figure 1-2. Recent workers in the field of amphibian biology: upper left, John A. Moore (courtesy of J. A. Moore); upper right, José M. Cei (photo by W. E. Duellman); lower left, Toshijiro Kawamura (courtesy of T. Kawamura); lower right, W. Frank Blair (courtesy of University of Texas).

Mendoza, where he continued work on reproductive cycles, initiated studies on immunological relationships, and completed major works on the amphibians of Chile (1962) and Argentina (1980). Likewise, Raymond F. Laurent immigrated to Argentina and at the Fundación Miguel Lillo in Tucumán has continued to make important contributions to the systematics of frogs.

By comparison with Brazil and Argentina, the number of herpetologists in other South American countries has been relatively few. Jehan Vellard, working at the Museo Javier Prado in Lima, completed several major works on the frogs of Andean Peru. Alberto Veloso M. and Ramón Formas in Chile have been productive in studies of the taxonomy, karyology, and life histories of Chilean frogs. Pedro M. Ruíz-C. and his associates in Bogotá have initiated promising studies on the anurans of Colombia. Juan A. Rivero has made significant contributions to

knowledge of the systematics of Venezuelan (1961) and Puerto Rican (1978) frogs.

By the early part of the 20th century, several important centers of herpetology had been established in the United States. First, programs were developed at the Museum of Comparative Zoology at Harvard University and the National Museum of Natural History in Washington. At the National Museum, Leonhard Stejneger was responsible for a growing collection of international importance. He was followed by Doris M. Cochran, who devoted her life to the study of frogs from the American tropics and published major works on Hispaniola (1941), southeastern Brazil (1955), and (with Coleman J. Goin) on Colombia (1970). Currently, aspects of the systematics and behavioral ecology of neotropical anurans are being investigated at the National Museum by W. Ronald Heyer and Roy W. McDiarmid; George R. Zug is contributing studies on anuran locomotion. Biogeographic and systematic studies of amphibians flourished at Harvard under the magnanimous influence of Thomas Barbour. One of his students, Emmet R. Dunn, provided significant insights into amphibian relationships; Dunn is best known for his classic work on the plethodontid salamanders (1926b). Arthur Loveridge of Harvard wrote extensively on the amphibians of East Africa. Currently at the Museum of Comparative Zoology, Pere Alberch has an active program on the evolutionary morphology of amphibians.

Also, early in this century three other centers were developed. The establishment of the Museum of Zoology at the University of Michigan by Alexander G. Ruthven initiated one of the most active centers of graduate training in herpetology and included such important personages as Frank N. Blanchard, Helen T. Gaige, Norman E. Hartweg, Grace L. Orton, Laurence C. Stuart, Frederick H. Test, and Charles F. Walker. Present workers at the University of Michigan include Carl Gans in the field of functional morphology, Arnold G. Kluge and Ronald A. Nussbaum working on systematics and evolutionary ecology, and George W. Nace, who established a laboratory for maintaining genetic stocks of amphibians.

The American Museum of Natural History in New York has maintained an active program of studies on amphibians since the early work by Mary C. Dickerson (1906) on the frogs of North America. She was followed by Gladwyn K. Noble and Clifford H. Pope, who worked on Chinese anurans and North American salamanders. Later Charles M. Bogert was one of the pioneers in the investigation of anuran vocalizations (1960) and an important contributor to knowledge of the systematics of the amphibians of Mexico. Presently at the American Museum, Richard G. Zweifel is a leader in the field of developmental ecology of amphibians and a specialist on Australo-Papuan frogs; Charles W. Myers (with his coworker John Daly) has been innovative in the use of biochemical properties of skin toxins combined with more traditional taxonomic characters in the study of dendrobatid frogs.

Gladwyn K. Noble (Fig. 1-1) received training in herpetology, taxonomy, and biogeography under the tutelage of Thomas Barbour at Harvard University and later obtained his doctor's degree at Columbia University under the guidance of William K. Gregory. Fortunately for the institution and his chosen field, Noble became curator of the Department of Amphibians and Reptiles at the American Museum of Natural History. Noble was far ahead of his time in the application of experimental methods to problems of life history and behavior, and he founded the Department of Experimental Biology (later known as the Department of Animal Behavior) at the museum. During his relatively short career, he integrated aspects of life history into the study of phylogeny and introduced experimental methods into studies of amphibian ecology and reproduction. His *Biology of the Amphibia* (1931b) has been the standard reference on amphibian biology for more than half a century.

At Cornell University, Albert H. Wright initiated a tradition of research on the natural history of anurans; many of the students at Cornell (e.g., Sherman C. Bishop, James Kezer, Karl P. Schmidt) became well-known investigators in various disciplines of amphibian biology. An active program in physiological ecology, neurobiology, and behavior continues with research by Kraig Adler, Robert R. Capranica, and F. Harvey Pough.

Somewhat later three other herpetological centers were founded. The Field Museum of Natural History in Chicago has had an active role in amphibian systematics and biogeography initiated by Karl P. Schmidt and continued by Robert F. Inger, who has made many significant contributions to knowledge of the anurans of southeastern Asia and adjacent archipelagos. At the University of Kansas, Edward H. Taylor made prodigious contributions to the field of herpetology, including comprehensive works on amphibians of the Philippines (1920), Costa Rica (1952), Thailand (1962), and (with Hobart M. Smith) Mexico (1948); Taylor also produced the only monograph of the caecilians (1968). Present research at Kansas emphasizes anurans, with William E. Duellman working on the systematics of neotropical frogs, especially hylids (1970), and anuran communities (1978), Linda Trueb working on evolutionary morphology (1973) and systematics of anurans (1970a), and Sally K. Frost studying amphibian pigmentation. Studies on amphibians at the University of California at Berkeley have emphasized salamanders, especially in the investigations of Robert C. Stebbins and David B. Wake and their students; these studies have included diverse aspects of life history, ecology, speciation, and evolutionary morphology. The latter field is emphasized in caecilians by Marvalee H. Wake.

These long-established centers of research on amphibian biology continue to be important; graduate training programs have continued to be active at these universities. Research at other institutions has flourished and waned or has begun more recently, depending on the investigators associated with them. Sherman C. Bishop at the University of Rochester was the foremost student of eastern North American salamanders; his major works (1941, 1943) influenced a generation of students. George S. Myers had an active graduate and research program on systematics of amphibians and reptiles at Stanford University in the 1940s and 1950s; with Myers's retirement, the program terminated and the important collections were added to those at the California Academy of Sciences, where Robert C. Drewes maintains an active research program on the systematics and physiological ecology of African anurans. While at Columbia University in the 1940s and 1950s, John A. Moore (Fig. 1-2) carried out important studies on the development and physiology of amphibians, and published a pioneer treatise on the anurans of Australia (1961). At the University of Texas, W. Frank Blair (Fig. 1-2) pioneered studies of speciation of anurans using nonmorphological data, especially vocalization and hybridization; this work by Blair and his students culminated in a book on evolution in the genus *Bufo* (1972). Jay M. Savage, formerly at the University of Southern California and now at the University of Miami, has maintained an active program in the study of systematics and biogeography of amphibians for a quarter of a century. At the University of Florida, Coleman J. Goin and his students made major contributions to the knowledge of systematics and life histories of amphibians of the southeastern United States and the Caribbean region; now Martha L. Crump of the same institution is active in the field of evolutionary ecology of anurans. The morphology, physiology, and behavior of tadpoles has been studied by Richard J. Wassersug and his students formerly at the University of Chicago and now at Dalhousie University in Halifax, Canada.

Although fossil anurans and salamanders received some attention in the last century, the major research on fossils has occurred since the mid-1950s by numerous workers, particularly Walter Auffenberg, Richard Estes, Coleman J. Goin, Max K. Hecht, J. Alan Holman, Charles Meszoely, Bruce Naylor, and Joseph A. Tihen in North America; Francisco de Borja Sanchíz, Oskar Kuhn, Jean-Paul Rage, Zbynek Roček, and Zdenek Špinar in Europe; Ana Maria Báez and Osvaldo A. Reig in South America; and Eviatar Nevo in Israel. Landmark publications on fossils include the work on Tertiary frogs of Europe by Špinar (1972) and the handbook of fossil salamanders and caecilians by Estes (1981).

Early in the 1900s, Hans Spemann and his associates in Germany determined the role of the dorsal lip of the blastopore of frog embryos as an organizer, and in France, Jean Joly and his associates experimented with early development of salamanders. At about the same time in the United States, W. H. Lewis's work on the induction of the lens of the eye in *Rana* and T. H. Morgan's experiments on limb regeneration in salamanders were classic contributions to the understanding of tissue interactions during development. Tissue culturing was developed at Yale University by Ross G. Harrison using *Ambystoma maculatum,* the species for which he prepared a detailed staging table. One of his students, Victor C. Twitty (1966), integrated experimental biology with studies of speciation and behavior of newts *(Taricha)* in California. W. Gardner Lynn (1942) made important contributions through his studies on direct development in amphibians. Summaries of the use of amphibians in embryological studies were provided by one of the foremost investigators in the field, Roberts Rugh (1951, 1962). Beginning with J. F. Gundernatsche's (1912) discovery of the effect of thyroxin on metamorphosis of *Rana,* amphibians have played an important role in research on experimental endocrinology; this work has been summarized by Lawrence I. Gilbert and Earl Frieden (1981). The colony of axolotls *(Ambystoma mexicanum)* established at the University of Rochester (now maintained at Indiana University) by Rufus R. Humphrey has provided a reliable source of material for investigations in embryology, endocrinology, and genetics.

Presently, research on amphibian biology is under way by hundreds of investigators at institutions throughout the world. Many of these researchers are highly specialized, and their research varies from alpha taxonomy and descriptive morphology to feeding ecology and the biochemistry of egg capsules; in many instances the research involves only a single species. However esoteric some of this research may seem, it all contributes to an accumulation of knowledge that eventually can be interrelated and synthesized to present a more accurate, comprehensive understanding of biological phenomena and principles, with particular reference to amphibians. In recent years, the major attempts at syntheses have been the results of symposia, such as those on the evolutionary biology of anurans (Vial, 1973) and on the reproductive biology of amphibians (D. Taylor and Guttman, 1977); or of compilations of works by many specialists, such as those on amphibian physiology edited by Moore (1964) and Lofts (1974, 1976), on the amphibian visual system edited by Fite (1976), on the neurobiology of frogs edited by Llinás and Precht (1976), and on metamorphosis edited by Gilbert and Frieden (1981). The only modern comprehensive checklist of amphibians was the result of efforts by amphibian biologists worldwide (D. Frost, 1985).

PROSPECTS FOR THE FUTURE

Studies of amphibian biology promise to be exciting for many decades in the future, provided that political, environmental, and regulatory activities do not hinder investigations.

Research

Many challenges confront biologists studying amphibians. Although descriptive morphology reached its heights in the last century, much important work still needs to be done. The basic morphology of only a handful of amphibian species is known. Comparative morphological studies combined with analyses of functions will provide the data necessary for understanding the evolutionary significance of morphological features. Likewise, knowledge of the developmental programs of morphological units is necessary for a meaningful interpretation of the evolutionary sequences with respect to heterochrony.

The limited information available on water balance, temperature tolerances, and ion balance in amphibians indicates that these animals are far more complex physiologically than is generally believed. Many more studies integrating physiological tolerances, metabolic rates, and behavior are necessary before generalities can be made about metabolic levels and foraging activities or escape behavior. Most of these kinds of studies necessitate the maintenance of animals in captivity; in recent years suitable techniques have been devised for maintaining and breeding amphibians in captivity (Schulte, 1980; J. Frost, 1982; Mattison, 1982).

Since the mid-1970s, discoveries of previously unsuspected reproductive behavior suggest that many fascinating aspects of reproductive biology remain to be discovered. However, the most rewarding prospects will be the integration of diverse reproductive behavior, metabolism, and environmental factors.

Genetic studies of amphibians are still in their infancy. New techniques of protein synthesis and DNA hybridization, as well as many approaches now in use, should continue to provide new kinds of data on the transmission of traits and on the relationships of living populations. Population genetics combined with demographic data are desirable to provide an understanding of how populations exist in nature and what factors affect their stability. These kinds of data, together with information about reproductive biology, will establish a basis for meaningful ecological studies. Amphibian biologists need to shake off the dogma of community studies done on birds and approach amphibian communities with an open mind.

At one and the same time, systematic biology is considered to be the basis and the ultimate synthesis of biology; yet nowhere is the fragmentary nature of knowledge of amphibians more apparent than in the classification of amphibians that attempts to represent the phylogeny of the living groups. In part, this is because of the very incomplete fossil record, which continues to improve slowly. Nearly one-third of the known species of amphibians have been named only since the mid-1960s. Probably the numbers of recognized species will continue to increase dramatically as collectors forage in previously unknown areas of the world and as more refined techniques are used to define species.

As the research on amphibians increases, so does the literature, which has amounted to more than 1000 titles per year listed in the *Zoological Record* since 1970. It is not feasible to keep up to date on more than a small fraction of the literature. Therefore, most biologists will have to rely on papers summarizing and synthesizing recent developments in the field. Furthermore, computerized data banks are a necessity for storage and retrieval of information.

Conservation and Regulation

Throughout the history of civilization, human activities have been detrimental to the natural biota. As human populations have increased dramatically, especially in the last half century, more and more environmental destruction has eliminated natural habitat and modified the environment on such a large scale that many species are in danger of extinction. Although amphibians seldom are the subject of direct eradication, they are affected indirectly and often disastrously.

The first major threat to populations of amphibians is habitat destruction. This is particularly evident in two ways. First is the clearing of forests, especially those in the humid tropics. At the present rate of clearing, most of the humid tropical forests of the world will have been destroyed by the end of this century. It is in these forests

that the greatest diversity of anurans occurs. Second are hydrologic controls that affect wetlands, habitats used for breeding by many amphibians. Innumerable populations of amphibians in Europe and the Middle East have been decimated by the elimination of breeding sites (Honegger, 1981), and populations of amphibians have been threatened seriously in such extensive wetland areas as the Everglades in southern Florida (L. Wilson and Porras, 1983).

The second major threat to amphibians is pollution, principally the accumulation of biocides in the environment. Extensive use of insecticides and herbicides with residues that contaminate the soil and water are highly detrimental to amphibians. Aquatic eggs and larvae are particularly susceptible to these toxic substances, as well as acid rain, which may not occur in concentrations sufficient to kill adults or even embryos; nevertheless, several toxic substances do affect the development of embryos and larvae to the point of causing a high percentage of abnormalities or a decrease in the rate of development resulting in prolonged larval periods or dwarfed young (Judd, 1977; Mohanty-Hejmadi and Dutta, 1981; Dunson and Connell, 1982). The great increase in the use of fertilizers and biocides in developing countries, especially in the tropics, has potentially disastrous effects on amphibian populations. Amphibian eggs and larvae are especially sensitive to heavy metals; drainage from mines can have calamitous effects on some populations of amphibians (Porter and Hankason, 1976).

The introduction of exotic species of amphibians has been minimal in comparison with introductions of other groups of vertebrates. Too little is known about the effects of introductions, but to date no native species of amphibian is known to have become extinct because of the introduction of an exotic species. Even the introduction of the African clawed frog *Xenopus laevis* into southern California seems to have had no deleterious effect on the native biota (McCoid and Fritts, 1980). Also, there is no evidence that the introduction of *Bufo marinus* in southern Florida has been detrimental to the native toads (L. Wilson and Porras, 1983). However, these authors suggested that the introduced tree frog *Osteopilus septentrionalis*, which eats other frogs, may be affecting populations of two species of native tree frogs, *Hyla cinerea* and *H. squirella*. On the other hand, the introduction of exotic fishes can be highly detrimental to native amphibians. Tyler (1976) considered the introduction of *Gambusia* and *Tilapia* to be a major threat to the eggs and tadpoles of Australian anurans.

Ordinarily amphibians are collected for: (1) commercial purposes to be used as food, as aquarium animals, in teaching, or in zoo exhibits, and (2) scientific investigation purposes. Compared with other groups of vertebrates, relatively few amphibians are collected for commercial purposes. However, commercial collecting of some species of frogs, especially *Rana esculenta* and *R. ridibunda* in Europe, must put heavy pressures on some populations. For example, Honegger (1981) provided statistics to show that more than 2,000,000 of these frogs were exported as a luxury food item from Greece in 1975. Likewise, imports of frogs for food into Switzerland ranged from 995,000 to 1,800,000 individuals per year between 1976 and 1980. Numerous exotic species of amphibians are collected for the pet trade; commercial dealers of amphibians are principally in western Europe, where terrarists are especially plentiful.

Scientific collecting of amphibians results in far fewer individuals being taken than are gathered by commercial collectors. Most scientists are fully aware of the potential threats of overcollecting and take only the number of individuals necessary for their scientific work. Since the early 1970s, agencies in governments throughout the world, as well as international organizations, have attempted to define some of the problems regarding natural populations of animals and have passed legislation regulating the perturbation of these populations. Compared to well-known and popular big game animals and many kinds of birds and reptiles, amphibians have been nearly ignored in efforts to protect individual species. As of 1983, only 5 species of salamanders and 12 species of anurans are controlled by the Convention on International Trade in Endangered Species of Wild Fauna and Flora (CITES). However, levels of protection of various species differ from country to country, and within coun-

tries (or even states) additional species are considered to be rare or endangered, and collecting is restricted or forbidden. For example, under the Endangered Species Act of the United States, as of 1983, eight species of anurans and five of salamanders are listed as endangered and one species of anuran and two of salamanders are listed as threatened. The regulations in many countries and states or provinces within countries have little, if any, sound biological basis, and in many instances, ill-considered laws have created serious impediments to fundamental research.

There is little chance that human pressures on natural populations of plants and animals will diminish in the foreseeable future. Governments throughout the world have the resources for the establishment and maintenance of limited numbers of natural preserves. These preserves should incorporate natural areas of high endemicity and should be of sufficient size to preserve natural populations of the entire biota (Lovejoy, 1982). Furthermore, reserves should be designed not only for the protection of the habitat and the communities residing therein but also for scientific investigation. If such precautions are taken, the next generation of amphibian biologists will still be able to study frogs, salamanders, and caecilians in nature and not have to rely solely on preserved specimens and the writings of earlier generations.

PART 1

LIFE HISTORY

CHAPTER 2

Reproductive Strategies

The variation [in reproductive behavior] is a mirror of the environmental difficulties that have been overcome, and demonstrates a wide variety of success stories.

Michael J. Tyler (1976)

An essential attribute of any surviving species or population is the ability to produce a succeeding generation. Classically, ideas concerning reproduction in amphibians have centered on North Temperate species of salamanders, such as *Ambystoma* and *Triturus,* and anurans, such as *Bufo* and *Rana,* most of which undergo brief, annual periods of mating and leave unattended eggs to develop into aquatic larvae. This pattern of reproduction is unknown in caecilians and is common to probably no more than a quarter of the living species of salamanders. Although this generalized pattern occurs in a wide variety of anurans, a great diversity of reproductive patterns exists among the frogs and toads. Indeed, no general statement can be made about reproductive patterns in amphibians.

A reproductive strategy may be viewed as the combination of physiological, morphological, and behavioral attributes that act in concert to produce the optimal number of offspring under certain environmental conditions. Reproductive strategies are as significant to the survival of the species as are physiological and morphological adaptations to the environment. Patterns of reproduction are modified by natural selection so as to produce strategies with high fitness, and they reflect a compromise among many selective pressures. Some components of reproductive strategies are:

1. Endogenous and extrinsic controls of gametogenetic cycles.

2. Fecundity, including number and size of eggs, frequency of oviposition, and proportion of females breeding.
3. Duration of development, including proportion of time spent as feeding larvae.
4. Age at first reproduction and reproductive life span.
5. Reproductive effort, including parental care.
6. Quantitative and environmental constraints.

Studies on amphibians reveal considerable disparity between theory and empirical evidence. Most data are qualitative or are limited to few parameters. Very little is known about caecilians (M. Wake, 1977a). As a group, the salamanders are better known than the anurans, principally because most of the species of anurans that have diverse reproductive modes live in the tropics, where few detailed studies have been accomplished. The most comprehensive review of reproduction in amphibians is by Salthe and Mecham (1974). M. Wake (1982) reviewed the diversity of reproductive modes within morphological and physiological constraints.

REPRODUCTIVE CYCLES

Reproductive cycles in amphibians are subject to hormonal controls, which within genetic limitations respond to environmental variables and produce certain patterns; further constraints are imposed by the organism's microhabitat, size, reproductive mode, and parental care practices. General patterns are evident: (1) Caecilians reproduce biennially. (2) Salamanders reproduce annually or biennially. (3) Anurans in the wet tropics have continuous reproduction and may deposit several clutches of eggs per year; in seasonally dry or cold regions, their cycles are interrupted and the number of clutches may be as few as one per year or one every other year. (4) Definite relationships exist between body size and clutch size within reproductive modes. (5) Annual fecundity varies from one or two to potentially more than 80,000 offspring.

Gametogenesis

The development and maturation of the sex cells in amphibians are well known and adequately discussed and illustrated in most texts on embryology. A thorough, well-documented review of gametogenesis in salamanders and anurans (Lofts, 1974) was supplemented by M. Wake's (1968, 1977a) work on caecilians.

The spermatogenetic cycle is completed in the testes. The testes are simple, ovoidal structures in anurans and most salamanders, but they are composed of lobes in some salamanders (desmognathines and Neotropical plethodontids) and all caecilians. In salamanders the number of lobes may increase with age; in caecilians the number remains unchanged after sexual maturity is attained. During spermatogenesis each lobe is characterized by the presence of a number of dilated lobules. In caecilians each lobule contains sperm cells in different stages of maturation. Within a single lobule, clusters of cells may range from primary spermatogonia to maturing spermatids (M. Wake, 1968). In salamanders each of the individual locules contains sperm cells in the same stage of maturation, but along the length of the testis there is a developmental gradient representing successive zones of spermatogonia, spermatocytes, spermatids, and mature spermatozoa; the anterior lobes are least advanced sexually. In multilobed testes the developmental spectrum occurs within each testicular lobe (Lofts, 1974).

The structurally simple testes of anurans increase in size and weight during spermatogenesis. In temperate anurans the sperm cells mature uniformly throughout the testis (Lofts, 1974), but in tropical species that breed throughout the year, the testes contain sperm cells in various stages of maturation. For example, in *Rana erythraea* in Borneo, each locule contained sperm cells in only one stage of maturation, but the locules in one testis often contained cells in all stages of spermatogenesis (Inger and Greenberg, 1963). The termination of the period of spermatogenesis is characterized by various changes in the testes, including increase in interstitial tissue, disintegration of lobule stromata, degeneration of intralobular ducts, and presence of only a few spermatocytes peripherally in the lobules.

Oogenesis is basically the same in all three groups of amphibians. The developing ova lie in follicles associated with the ovary. Oogonia are derived from primordial gonocytes and give rise mitotically to successive generations of oocytes. Primary oocytes undergo meiotic division to yield secondary oocytes and the first polar bodies. A subsequent reduction division of the secondary oocyte results in an ovum and a secondary polar body. The ova are surrounded by a discrete cell membrane, a narrow zona pellucida, and a single layer of follicle cells. Previtellogenic oocytes increase in size nearly tenfold; nutrients for this growth are provided by the ovary via plasma membranes forming the follicular stalk (Wallace et al., 1970).

The process of vitellogenesis is the accumulation in the cytoplasm of the oocyte of a supply of nutrients for embryonic development (Follett and Redshaw, 1974). These nutrients, collectively referred to as yolk, consist of about 45% phosphoproteins, 25% lipids, and 8% glycogen (Barth and Barth, 1954). In *Rana temporaria* the oocyte grows during a period of three years; most of the 27,000-fold increase in size in these comparatively telolecithal eggs occurs in the six months prior to ovulation (P. Grant, 1953). The proportional increase in the macrolecithal eggs of amphibians having direct development would be much greater. In amphibians having definitive reproductive cycles, four distinct stages of oocytes and ova may be distinguished at the beginning of the breeding season (Lofts, 1974): (1) numerous cell nests that will provide the generation of follicles for the subsequent spawning; (2) previtellogenic follicles from which succeeding generations of eggs will be recruited; (3) rapidly growing vitellogenic follicles that are rapidly adding nutrients; and (4) fully grown postvitellogenic ova.

Among most amphibians, oocytes normally have only one nucleus. However, there are some exceptions among anurans. Oogenesis in *Ascaphus truei* regularly involves oocytes with eight nuclei; all but one disappear before the final stages of oogenesis (Macgregor and Kezer, 1970). Multinucleate oocytes occur in 11 of 33 species of egg-brooding hylids examined by del Pino and A. Humphries (1978); all are species that produce few eggs (all macrolecithal). In one of these, *Flectonotus pygmaeus*, small oocytes contain 1,000–3,000 nuclei; the number decreases gradually in larger oocytes until only one remains in the mature ovum. The other egg-brooding hylids have far fewer nuclei in their early oocytes. The multinucleate condition seems to develop through the disappearance of cell membranes between adjacent cells within a cyst. Nuclei in the outer shell of oocytes are larger than those in the inner part, and the larger ones contain more ribosomal DNA. Macgregor and del Pino (1982) suggested that the nucleus with the highest ribosomal DNA content may be the one to survive in the germinal vesicle.

Endogenous Factors

The seasonal development and activity of the male and female gonads are under the direct control of the adenohypophysis (pars distalis of the pituitary), which in turn is regulated by the central nervous system mediated via hypothalamic neurosecretions transported to the pituitary gland in the portal vessels (Jorgensen, 1974). The extensive literature on experimental endocrinology and amphibian productive cycles was reviewed by C. L. Smith (1955), van Oordt (1960), and Lofts (1974).

There is a positive correlation between the secretion of pituitary gonadotropin and seasonal changes in the germinal epithelium and secondary sexual characteristics in male anurans and male salamanders. Ablation of the entire pituitary or only the pars distalis results in atrophy of the reproductive organs; hypophysectomy results in atrophy of the ovaries and secondary sexual characteristics in females. Androgenic hormone production by the interstitial tissue in the testes diminishes during the reproductive season. Limited experimental data suggest that a gonadal feedback regulating gonadotropic production by the pars distalis exists in both sexes (van Oordt, 1961; Rastogi and Chieffi, 1970; Vijayakumar et al., 1971).

Three types of pituitary cells may provide hormonal control of reproductive activity: B_2 basophilic cells with luteinizing effects, B_3 basophilic cells with follicle-stimulating activity, and A_1 acidophilic cells with luteotrophic effects. In the temperate toad *Bufo bufo*, the proportions of these three kinds of pituitary cells change during the reproductive season (Obert, 1977). The A_1 cells decrease slightly in number; the number of B_2 cells is greatly reduced, and the B_3 cells become much more numerous. Androgenic hormone production by the interstitial tissue in the testes diminishes during the reproductive season. Limited experimental data suggest that a gonadal feedback regulating gonadotropic production by the pars distalis exists in both sexes (van Oordt, 1961; Rastorgi and Chieffi, 1970; Vijayakumar et al., 1971).

In oviparous amphibians, postovulatory follicles are transient and apparently have no hormonal function (Redshaw, 1972); the presence of corpora lutea in ovoviviparous salamanders and frogs and in viviparous caecilians (M. Wake, 1977a), the salamander *Salamander atra* (V. Vilter and A. Vilter, 1964), and the toad *Nectophrynoides occidentalis* (Lamotte et al., 1964) is associated with hormonal secretions differing from those in other amphibians. Extensive studies on the viviparous *N. occidentalis* reveal that the corpora lutea produce progesterone, which acts with estrogen during the follicular phase of oogenesis, but acts alone in the luteal phase; furthermore, progesterone inhibits embryonic development during maternal aestivation (Lamotte and Rey, 1954; Xavier, 1970, 1973, 1977; Xavier et al., 1970). There is evidence of ovarian control of incubation and pouch vascularization in the marsupial frog, *Gastrotheca riobambae,* in which postovulatory follicles may correspond functionally to corpora lutea in maintaining early incubation (del Pino and Sánchez, 1977). In this species, pouch formation can be induced in juvenile females by administration of estrogen (R. E. Jones et al., 1973).

Many kinds of amphibians are commonly used for developmental and endocrinological studies in laboratories.

Some valuable information has been accumulated (but not necessarily published) about reproduction of certain species in the laboratory. *Ambystoma mexicanum* will mate with no exogenous stimulation from November through early April in the Northern Hemisphere; during a given season females are capable of producing several clutches of eggs, and males produce large numbers of spermatophores. *Pleurodeles waltl* reproduces every 4 to 8 weeks in the laboratory. In the spring and fall, breeding in *Rana pipiens* can be induced by pituitary extracts, but only if the extract is from *R. pipiens* or another member of that species complex. Unsuspecting researchers that are supplied *R. berlandieri* in place of *R. pipiens* often are frustrated in their attempts to induce ovulation; *R. berlandieri* will breed only in the summer. *Bombina orientalis* can breed year-round when stimulated with anuran pituitary extracts or human chorionic gonadotropin; *Xenopus laevis* responds every 2 or 3 months to the same hormome. Injections of the synthetic hormone (D-Ala6, des-Glyl0)—LHRH ethylamide (Helix Bio-Tec Ltd.) provides a stimulus to the pituitary causing it to release hormones inducing ovulation and spermatogenesis; multiple breeding has been so induced in anurans as diverse as *Ceratophrys ornata, Bufo marinus,* and *Litoria caerulea* (E. Wagner, pers. comm.).

Experimental laboratory studies have provided substantial evidence for the hormonal control of reproductive cycles, and numerous studies have shown the correlation of environmental factors with breeding activity in amphibians. However, knowledge of how extrinsic factors influence endogenous controlling mechanisms remains limited.

Extrinsic Factors

In general, hormonal activity, such as secretion by the adenohypophysis, is correlated with environmental changes. These changes act as primary stimuli to nerve receptors and are integrated by the central nervous system, which relays appropriate impulses to the hypothalamic neurosecretory nuclei. Spermatogenetic cycles are essentially continuous in tropical and subtropical amphibians and in some cave-dwelling species in temperate regions. The cycle is interrupted or impaired during the autumn and winter in most temperate species and during the drier or colder seasons in some high montane species in the tropics. This discontinuity is correlated directly with the negative effect of lower temperatures on the secretion of gonadotropin by the pituitary and the sensitivity of germinal epithelium to gonadotropic hormones. Spermatogenetic and ovarian cycles are not necessarily synchronous and, therefore, may be influenced by different internal or external factors.

Temperature apparently is the major factor controlling gametogenesis in many salamanders. Temperatures of more than 20° are necessary to initiate spermatogenesis in *Plethodon cinereus* (Werner, 1969) or ovulation in *Cynops pyrrhogaster* (Tsutsui, 1931). Temperatures of more than 12° can cause degeneration of spermatocytes and spermatids (Ifft, 1942). The correlation of seasonal temperature variation and spermatogenesis was demonstrated experimentally in *Plethodon cinereus* (Werner, 1969) and *Paramesotriton hongkongensis* (Lofts, 1974).

Rainfall seems to be the primary factor initiating breeding activity in amphibians. Series of observations and experiments on anurans in the Chacoan region of northern Argentina, which is characterized by a distinct rainy season, revealed differential responses to temperature (see Cei, 1980, for review). Continuous spermatogenesis and mature oocytes were observed in 13 species, but lower winter temperatures inhibited gonadotropic effects on the germinal epithelium. Spermatogenesis is impaired notably during the winter in three other species; in one, the ovaries become atresic, but in the other two, mature oocytes are present throughout the year (Cei, 1949b). Similarly, spermatogenesis is retarded in *Phyllomedusa sauvagei*, in the winter, when it aestivates (Caruso, 1949). The differences in the sexual cycles exhibited by two sympatric species of *Leptodactylus* are especially significant; *L. ocellatus* shows no seasonal variation in gametogenetic activity, whereas in *L. chaquensis* both spermatogenetic and oogenetic cycles are inhibited by low temperatures (Cei, 1948, 1950). Moreover, continued exposure to high temperatures results in a cessation of spermatogenesis in *L. chaquensis* (Rengel, 1950). Some high montane frogs that are subjected to year-round cold temperatures maintain continuous spermatogenesis; this has been documented in the Andean *Hyla pulchella* (Caruso, 1949) and in the aquatic Andean *Telmatobius hauthali*, which is active at temperatures of 6–8°.

It is unlikely that photoperiod is very important in the regulation of sexual cycles in amphibians that are nocturnal or those that remain underground when inactive. However, spermatogenesis was advanced experimentally in *Plethodon cinereus* during the latter part of the quiescent period and during early spermatogenesis by increasing the daily duration of light (Werner, 1969). The lunar cycle has been implicated in the rhythm of ovulation in *Bufo melanostictus* in Java, where the species breeds throughout the year; at times of a full moon, more ovulating females are found than in darker phases of the moon (Church, 1960a). In nature, *Pachymedusa dacnicolor* breeds only in the summer, and adults maintained in a greenhouse in Tucson, Arizona, deposited multiple clutches over a period of 3 months (July–September). If day length and temperature are manipulated so as to decrease and then to increase, simulating summer conditions, the frogs breed spontaneously again in December through early February (S. Frost, pers. comm.).

The nutritional status of females may affect the numbers and sizes of eggs. Female *Plethodon cinereus* maintained on different feeding regimes for 6 months showed a significant positive correlation between oocyte size and maternal condition and between oocyte number and initial body weight (Fraser, 1980). There is evidence that a direct relationship exists between nutrition and oocyte

growth in *Xenopus laevis* (Holland and Dumont, 1975).

Evidence also exists for innate sexual rhythms that are genetically controlled and not under direct environmental-hormonal influence. In *Rana temporaria,* the germinal epithelium enters into a quiescent period that begins in late summer when temperatures are high and lasts through the winter (Witschi, 1924). The germinal epithelium remains relatively insensitive to high temperatures and high levels of gonadotropin induced experimentally during the early part of the period (van Oordt, 1956). Similar insensitivity of the germinal epithelium to increased temperatures during the early part of the quiescent period was noted in *Plethodon cinerus* (Werner, 1969). Also, autonomous spermatogenetic cycles occur in *Rana arvalis* and *R. dalmatina* (Cei, 1944). Spermatogenesis is continuous in some lowland populations of *Salamandra salamandra,* but spermatozoa are present in the Wolffian ducts only during 3 months in the summer (Joly, 1960b). In the salamandrid *Pleurodeles waltl,* maintained under constant laboratory conditions, females are capable of breeding throughout the year, but males will mate only during September through May (Pastisson, 1963). In the Upemba area of tropical West Africa, maturation of the ova in *Bufo funereus* and *B. regularis* is correlated with the rainy season, but the nuptial excrescences in males of *B. regularis* develop immediately before the beginning of the rainy season and regress before the end of the rainy season (Inger and Greenberg, 1956). Thus the cyclic development of nuptial excrescences presumably is controlled genetically.

Seasonal changes in secondary sexual characters are notable in many amphibians, but these seem to be under hormonal control. For example, Noble (1931a) reported on male hormonal control of the development of caudal glands in *Desmognathus fuscus.* Nuptial excrescences and male throat coloration were developed experimentally by hormonal injections in juveniles and female *Bufo woodhousii fowleri* (P. Blair, 1946). Testosterone control of the development of mental glands and cirri in *Eurycea quadridigitata* was shown experimentally by Sever (1976). The cyclic nature of most, if not all, secondary sexual characteristics probably is influenced by the pituitary-gonadal axis. Secondary sexual characters are discussed more fully in Chapter 3.

Annual Patterns

The innate gametogenetic cycles, acting within constraints of the local environment, produce annual patterns of reproductive cycles. Additional constraints are imposed on some species by specialized modes of reproduction and investment in parental care (see following sections: Reproductive Mode, Parental Care). The three groups of amphibians have distinctive patterns and therefore are treated separately.

Caecilians. Oviparous ichthyophiid caecilians may have extended breeding seasons or even may be aseasonally reproductive in India and the Philippines, but data are inconclusive (M. Wake, 1977a). *Ichthyophis glutinosus* breeds only during the rainy season in Sri Lanka (Breckenridge and Jayasinghe, 1979). In the viviparous *Dermophis mexicanus* in Guatemala, mating occurs at the beginning of the rainy season in May and June, and gestation requires a full year; females have at least a biennial cycle, but males have active spermatogenesis throughout most of the year (M. Wake, 1980b). These limited observations emphasize the necessity to learn much more about reproductive cycles in caecilians.

Salamanders. Two major reproductive patterns are exhibited by salamanders. The first, the classical annual pattern of aquatic breeders that begins in the spring, is characteristic of hynobiids, cryptobranchids, sirenids, amphiumids, proteiids, and most salamandrids and ambystomatids. Breeding activity is initiated primarily by the saturation of the ground by melting snow and spring rains, but temperature also is a factor, especially in aquatic species.

Within the annual patterns displayed by *Ambystoma*, it seems as though rising temperatures combined with saturation of the ground induce breeding migrations and reproductive activity in those species that breed in the spring. Spring thaws are associated with breeding activity of various species of *Ambystoma* (Bishop, 1941; Baldauf, 1952; Hassinger et al., 1970). For example, a combination of spring rains and temperatures of more than 10° is necessary for spring migrations to breeding sites by *Ambystoma* in Tennessee (Gentry, 1968). However, springlike weather in midwinter can induce reproductive activity in *A. tigrinum* (Hassinger et al., 1970), so that subsequent low temperatures result in ice-covered ponds in which both adults and eggs may be present.

The annual patterns of some other species of *Ambystoma* are different because of the seasonal differences in rainfall and temperatures throughout North America. Breeding activity is initiated by rainfall in coastal populations of *A. macrodactylum* in California, but breeding in montane populations is associated with increased temperatures (J. Anderson, 1967). In arid regions with moderate temperatures, rainfall is the primary factor inducing reproductive activity, as in *A. rosaceum* (J. Anderson, 1961). *Ambystoma annulatum, cingulatum,* and *opacum* breed in the autumn (Noble and Marshall, 1929; Noble and Brady, 1933; J. Anderson and Williamson, 1976). In Louisiana *A. talpoideum* breeds in the winter, following a cooling trend in the moderate winter temperatures (Shoop, 1960). In some primarily aquatic species that live in cold streams—e.g., *A. ordinarium* (J. Anderson and Worthington, 1971) and *Rhyacotriton olympicus* (Nussbaum and Tait, 1977)—populations reproduce throughout the year, but *Dicamptodon ensatus* has seasonal reproduction (Nussbaum, 1969).

Although annual breeding patterns, initiated by rising temperatures and spring rains, are evident in most Eurasian salamandrids and hynobiids (Thorn, 1968; Steward, 1970), there are some notable exceptions. For example, the aquatic *Pleurodeles waltl* has a prolonged breeding season through the warmer months. Annual cycles of reproduction are characteristic of the families of large, aquatic salamanders (Cryptobranchidae, Sirenidae, Proteidae, Amphiumidae), and most of these reproduce in the spring. However, *Amphiuma tridactylum* reproduces in the winter in Louisiana (Cagle, 1948); *Siren lacertina* breeds in February and March in Alabama (Hanlin and Mount, 1978); and *Andrias davidianus* breeds in the autumn in cold mountain streams in China (M. Chang, 1936).

In most salamanders exhibiting annual seasonal reproduction, fertilization is external (Cryptobranchidae, Hynobiidae, Sirenidae), or oviposition occurs within a few hours to several days after mating (Ambystomatidae and most Salamandridae). However, in some species mating occurs in the autumn, and spermatozoa are stored in the spermatheca until the following spring. This pattern is characteristic of *Necturus* (Bishop, 1926; Shoop, 1965b), *Euproctus asper* (Ahrenfeldt, 1960), *Salamandra salamandra* (Joly, 1960b), and various plethodontids.

The second major pattern is biennial reproduction and is characteristic of the terrestrial plethodontid salamanders (Plethodontinae and Bolitoglossini). Species living under similar climatic conditions usually have similar patterns of activity and reproduction, but there are some exceptions. The climatic conditions in the eastern and western United States differ from one another and from conditions in Central America, and patterns of activity and reproduction in plethodontid salamanders are different in these regions (Fig. 2-1).

In the seasonally temperate climate of eastern United States, salamanders of the genera *Aneides* and *Plethodon* are active at or near the surface of the ground from spring until autumn. Mating usually occurs in late summer or autumn and may occur again in the spring in the same populations. Oviposition takes place during a short span of time in late spring or early summer. Females attend their clutches of eggs for 2 or 3 months until hatching occurs in late summer or early autumn. In those parts of the western United States inhabited by plethodontid salamanders *(Aneides, Batrachoseps, Ensatina, Plethodon),* temperature is more equable than in the eastern part of the country, but the dry summer months restrict the activity of salamanders to autumn, winter, and spring; mating occurs throughout the period of activity. With the exception of *Batrachoseps,* oviposition takes place during a brief period at the end of spring when salamanders retreat to subterranean refuges and attend their eggs during the inhospitable summer. In Guatemala, terrestrial species of *Bolitoglossa* and *Pseudoeurycea* are active year-round. Spermatogenesis, and presumably mating, occurs throughout the year. Oviposition takes place in November at the beginning of the dry season, and females remain with their clutches in subterranean retreats until the eggs hatch near the beginning of the rainy season. Species of *Bolitoglossa* living in aseasonal high montane regions in the tropics show no seasonal patterns of activity,

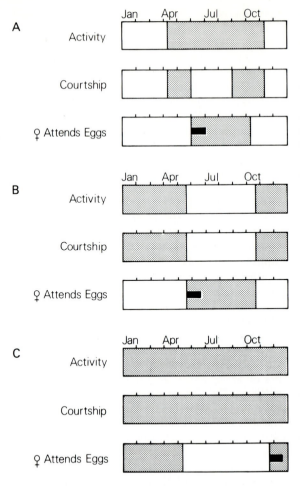

Figure 2-1. General patterns of surface activity, courtship, and egg attendance of terrestrial plethodontid salamanders in **A.** eastern North America, **B.** western North America, and **C.** Central America. The black bar indicates time when oviposition usually occurs; shading indicates time when activities usually occur. Modified from Houck (1977b).

cause of biennial cycles in *Triturus alpestris* (Joly, 1961); both of these live at high elevations and presumably require two seasons in order to obtain sufficient energy for completion of oogenesis. Long periods of gestation—up to 1 year in some montane populations of *Salamandra salamandra* (Joly, 1961) and 2 to 4 years in *S. atra* (V. Vilter and A. Vilter, 1960)—eliminate the possibility of annual reproduction. In *Amphiuma tridactylum,* lengthy attendance of eggs, possibly resulting in malnourishment, may be related to biennial cycles in some females (Cagle, 1948). Individuals of some populations of species of *Taricha* require long periods for migration to and from breeding sites; in these populations both males and females have biennial cycles (Twitty et al., 1964). Apparently not all of the females in a population of *Ambystoma maculatum* breed in any given year; a biennial or possibly triennial cycle may exist (Husting, 1965).

Most plethodontids having direct development of terrestrial eggs (plethodontines and bolitoglossines) apparently have biennial cycles in females (Houck, 1977b), but *Batrachoseps attenuatus* has an annual cycle. Considerable variation in, and/or interpretation of, data exists in desmognathodontine and hemidactyline plethodontids. Annual cycles have been hypothesized for *Desmognathus aeneus* and some populations of *D. fuscus, Leurognathus marmoratus, Stereochilus marginatus, Pseudotriton ruber,* and *Gyrinophilus porphyriticus* (see Tilley, 1977, for references). Cycles seem to be irregular in *Pseudotriton montanus* and in some populations of *Desmognathus ochrophaeus* (Bruce, 1975; Tilley, 1977). Biennial cycles have been suggested for five species of *Desmognathus* in the southern Appalachian Mountains (Organ, 1961). In most of the plethodontids with aquatic larvae, courtship is most common in the autumn but also may occur in the spring; eggs usually are deposited in the summer. Annual oogenic cycles may be normal for some populations of *Plethodon cinereus, glutinosus,* and *wehrlei,* although other populations of these species and the majority of terrestrial plethodontids apparently have biennial cycles (Houck, 1977b; Tilley, 1977).

Two factors contribute to apparent discrepancies in annual versus biennial cycles. One is simply the method of sampling. The presence of gravid or brooding females versus nonreproductive individuals at the same time of year has been interpreted as evidence for nonannual patterns, but such conclusions can be verified only by long-term capture-recapture studies of marked individuals. Second, evidence exists for geographic or altitudinal intraspecific variation in patterns of life histories, including oogenic cycles. Furthermore, the situation is complicated by the existence of cryptic species. Southern populations of *Plethodon glutinosus* have been reported to have an annual cycle, and northern ones, biennial (Highton, 1962; Organ, 1968), but now both cycles are known in the north, and apparently two species exist there (R. Highton, pers. comm.). Altitudinal differences in cycles have been found in *Pseudotriton montanus, P. ruber,* and *Desmognathus ochrophaeus* (Bruce, 1975, 1978b; Til-

mating, or oviposition, such as *B. adspersa* (Valdivieso and Tamsitt, 1965) and *B. subpalmata* (Vial, 1968). Likewise, limited data suggest that *B. peruana* is acyclic in an aseasonal lowland, tropical region (Duellman, 1978), as is *Dendrotriton bromeliacia,* an arboreal species in seasonal forest in Guatemala (Houck, 1977b).

Among the exceptions to these general patterns, *Batrachoseps attenuatus* and coastal populations of other species of *Batrachoseps* in California oviposit in the autumn; courtship presumably occurs during the summer when the salamanders are underground (Houck, 1977b). *Pseudoeuycea rex* inhabits higher elevations than the other species of salamanders studied in Guatemala; its cycle is reversed in comparison with the other species, that is, its young hatch in November and December (Houck, 1977b).

Annual female reproductive cycles seem to be the rule in the majority of non-plethodontid salamanders. However, more lengthy cycles are known for some species. A short season of activity has been implicated as the ley, 1977). Definitive evidence exists for altitudinal differences in *Salamandra salamandra* (Joly, 1961); the oogenic cycle is annual in lowland populations and biennial in montane populations (Fig. 2-2).

Under laboratory conditions, *Pleurodeles waltl* can deposit eggs at intervals of 2 months (Gallien, 1952). A captive female *Triturus cristatus* mated twice and laid two clutches of eggs in one season (Simms, 1968). Salamanders in nature apparently do not produce multiple clutches in a given season or year. Individual females are known to pick up spermatophores in successive seasons (au-

tumn and spring) but to deposit only one clutch of eggs.

In summary, most salamanders have definite seasonal reproductive cycles, which is expected of amphibians living in temperate climates. Reproductive activity is induced by increasing spring temperatures, but mating may occur in the autumn in salamanders having internal fertilization. The ability to store spermatozoa in the spermatheca over winter allows the delay of oviposition until the following spring. Rainfall also is essential for periods of activity, especially in regions having equable temperatures throughout the year. Most species inhabiting regions with seasonal rainfall oviposit and attend eggs in subterranean refuges during the dry season. Biennial oogenic cycles that seem to be associated with seasonal temperature regimes and maternal care prevail in species inhabiting aseasonal regimes on mountains in the tropics.

Anurans. Among anurans, two basic reproductive patterns are evident. Most tropical and subtropical species are capable of reproduction throughout the year; rainfall seems to be the primary extrinsic factor controlling the timing of reproductive activity. In most temperate species, reproductive activity is cyclic and dependent on a combination of temperature and rainfall.

In aseasonal, wet, tropical lowlands both sexes are reproductive throughout the year. This has been demonstrated for several species in tropical Asia and Indonesia (Hing, 1959; Church, 1960a, b; Berry, 1964; Inger and Greenberg, 1963; Berry, 1964; Inger and Bacon, 1968) and in the upper Amazon Basin in South America (Crump, 1974; Duellman, 1978). In tropical Oriental species of *Rana* and *Bufo* that have been studied, both male and female cycles

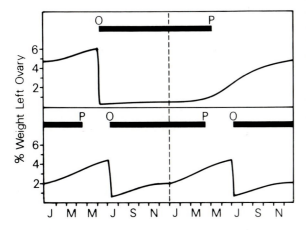

Figure 2-2. Female sexual cycle of *Salamandra salamandra* from Sarthe in western France, elevation 70 m (lower graph) and from Cauterets in the Pyrenees, 1000 m (upper graph). Lines show a 2-year cycle of weight of left ovary as percent of total weight. Bars indicate periods of gestaton. O = oviposition; P = parturition. Redrawn from Joly (1961).

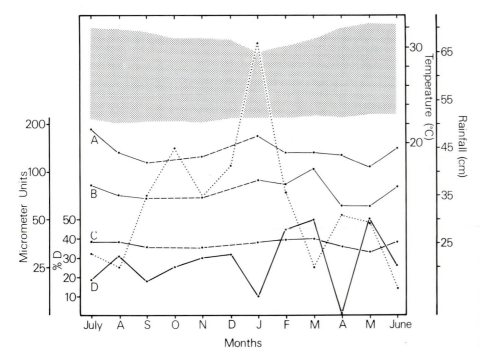

Figure 2-3. Continuous reproductive cycle of *Rana erythraea* and climatic variation at Kuching, Sarawak, Borneo. Thickness of nuptial excrescences and humeral glands measured in micrometers. **A.** Humeral glands in males. **B.** Nuptial pad glands. **C.** Nuptial pad epithelium (broken lines indicate absence of data in October and December). **D.** Percent of females with mature ova. The range of maximum and minimum temperatures is shaded; monthly rainfall is indicated by the dotted line. Data are for 1 year beginning in July 1957, as given by Inger and Greenberg (1963).

are continuous (Fig. 2-3). In the upper Amazon Basin, rainfall occurs throughout the year but is uneven and unpredictable; four patterns are evident among the 87 species of anurans in one area in Amazonian Ecuador:

1. Continuous—Breed essentially every night with the exception of clear, dry nights with intense moonlight.
2. Opportunistic—Breed regularly after heavy rains throughout the year.
3. Sporadic wet—Breed sporadically after heavy rains.
4. Sporadic dry—Breed sporadically during infrequent dry periods.

Presumably all of the species in that area are physiologically capable of reproduction throughout the year, but availability of breeding sites may limit the continuity of reproductive activity in many species. Those frogs that oviposit in ephemeral aquatic sites are dependent upon heavy rains; those that utilize streams usually breed at times of little rainfall, when the water level is low and the current is slow. Thus, even though temperature and moisture may be sufficient throughout the year, unpredictability of oviposition sites probably restricts reproductive activity.

In the seasonably dry tropics, anuran reproductive activity is closely associated with the rainy season. Analysis of breeding patterns of 13 species of anurans breeding in a pond in the llanos of Venezuela revealed a close correlation between breeding activity and the rainy season in 1974 and 1975, when the pronounced dry season occurred from January to May, but in 1976, when some rain fell during the dry season, breeding activity by some species was more or less continuous (Hoogmoed and Gorzula, 1979). These observations suggest that the frogs are capable of continuous reproduction, even though climatic conditions restrict their reproductive activity temporally. Similarly, reproductive activity associated with rainfall is evident in two species of *Ptychadena* in West Africa (Barbault and Trefaut Rodrigues, 1978) and in *Hyla rosenbergi* in central Panama (Kluge, 1981) (Fig. 2-4).

The development of mature eggs and male secondary sexual characters may precede the breeding season in some seasonal breeders; thus, such species seem to be cyclic in their innate reproductive features as well as their breeding activity. For example, at Upemba in West Africa, where there are sharply defined wet and dry seasons, males of 12 species are cyclic, and 6 are acyclic, but females of only 4 of the 18 species are acyclic (K. Schmidt and Inger, 1959). Cyclic nature of breeding associated with rainfall is evident in Australian myobatrachids of the genus *Heleioporus* (A. Lee, 1967).

In subtropical and temperate regions characterized by seasonal rainfall, breeding activity is initiated by rainfall. In the vicinity of Johannesburg, South Africa, the breeding activity of all but one species is closely associated with

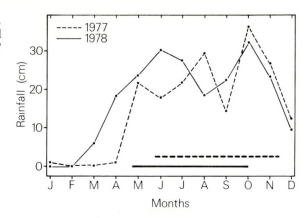

Figure 2-4. Rainfall and reproductive season (horizontal bars) of *Hyla rosenbergi* during 2 successive years in a seasonally rainy site in central Panama. Modified from Kluge (1981).

rainfall (B. Balinsky, 1969); the exception, *Bufo regularis,* breeds in streams. Spadefoot toads, *Scaphiopus,* breed only after heavy rains that completely soak the ground and form temporary pools, and when temperatures are above 11° (Bragg, 1945; Hansen, 1958). Likewise, the burrowing *Cyclorana platycephala* breeds only after rains in the spring and summer but not in the winter (van Beurden, 1979). In this species, gametogenesis is continuous throughout the year but reduced in winter; some females retain eggs over winter. Thus, in arid regions, anurans are primarily opportunistic breeders with the advent of sufficient rainfall at times of adequate temperatures.

Eurasian discoglossids exhibit a pattern of multiple breedings during the warm season of the year; *Alytes, Bombina,* and *Discoglossus* have two to six clutches per season (Knoepffler, 1962; Obert, 1977; Crespo, 1979). Reproduction is phased in periods of 2–4 weeks in the spring and summer, after which gametogenesis terminates in *Alytes* and *Bombina.* However, gametogenesis and reproduction are potentially continuous in *Discoglossus pictus;* individuals maintained in the laboratory deposited up to 10 clutches per year (Knoepffler, 1962).

Although temperate anurans respond to rainfall, temperature seems to be a major factor initiating breeding activity, as evidenced by geographic variation in the time of breeding. *Rana sylvatica* breeds in January and early February in Georgia and North Carolina (Martof and R. Humphries, 1959) but not until April–June in the northern part of its range (Herreid and Kinney, 1967). Likewise, *Scaphiopus holbrooki* and *Hyla crucifer* breed at times of winter rains in Florida but not until spring or summer in New England and Canada (A. F. Carr, 1940; Logier, 1952; Hansen, 1958). Breeding seasons may be 5 or 6 months long in southern temperate frogs, whereas in the north the season may be restricted to 1 or 2 weeks (Einem and Obert, 1956; W. Blair, 1961; Herreid and Kinney, 1967; L. Licht, 1969). Similar patterns of earlier versus later breeding seasons are associated with altitude, as evidence by coastal versus montane populations of *Rana pretiosa* (F. Turner, 1958; L. Licht, 1969) and prairie versus montane populations of *Pseudacris triseriata* (Pettus and Angleton, 1967). At high latitudes, as well as at high altitudes in temperate regions, breeding seasons are greatly restricted by temperature, as noted in *Bufo variegatus* and *Pleurodema bufonina* in southern Argentina and Chile (Cei, 1961; Hock, 1967).

A combination of a certain amount of rainfall at or above a certain temperature is known to be responsible for breeding activity in some temperate species— *Bufo bufo* (Heusser, 1960), *B. valliceps* (W. Blair, 1960), and *Rana aurora* (Storm, 1960).

Other factors stimulating reproduction include differences in light intensity over short periods of time in some pipids— *Hymenochirus boettgeri* (G. Rabb and M. Rabb, 1963a) and *Xenopus laevis* (R. Savage, 1965). Savage also demonstrated experimentally that a water-soluble substance associated with algae stimulated spawning in *Rana temporaria*. No consistent effects of temperature, rainfall, humidity, or light can be correlated with dates of breeding of that species in England (R. Savage, 1961); presumably the frogs respond to odors produced by algae, the growth of which is influenced by rainfall in the previous month.

Although it is known that populations of tropical anurans breed throughout the year, the frequency of reproduction by individual females is poorly known. *Hyla rosenbergi* (Kluge, 1981) and *Smilisca cyanosticta* (Pyburn, 1961) produce as many as six clutches in a single breeding season. *Phyllomedusa trinitatus* in Trinidad (Kenny, 1966) and *Syrrhophus marnocki* in Texas (Jameson, 1955a) produce three clutches during a season. Two clutches were produced a month apart by *Hyla rhodopepla* (Crump, 1974), and some female *Bufo typhonius* produced two clutches in 6 weeks (Wells, 1979). Frequency of breeding by captive individuals has been reported for several species: *Hyperolius viridiflavus* reproduced at intervals of 2–3 weeks for a year (Richards, 1977); *Eleutherodactylus johnstonei* reproduced every 2–3 months (Chibon, 1962); *Dendrobates auratus* produced 10 clutches in 170 days (Senfft, 1936); *Phyllobates vittatus* produced clutches at 2-week intervals (Silverstone, 1976); *Pipa carvalhoi* produced clutches 4–8 weeks apart (Weygoldt, 1976a); *Pipa parva* produced three or four clutches per year (Sughrue, 1969). *Limnodynastes tasmaniensis* may deposit clutches at 2-week intervals throughout the year (Tyler, 1976). Probably multiple clutches are the rule among tropical anurans in nature, but a lengthy breeding season is not necessarily indicative of many clutches per female; for example, although *Colostethus inguinalis* has a lengthy breeding season, females deposit only two clutches per season (Wells, 1980a). On the other hand, in the Ecuadorian Andes, brooding marsupial frogs, *Gastrotheca riobambae,* can be found throughout the year, but individual females produce only one clutch per year (del Pino, 1980).

Two clutches per breeding season are known for some temperate species: *Hyla chrysoscelis* (S. M. Roble, pers. comm.), *Pseudacris triseriata* (S. M. Roble, pers. comm.), *Rana clamitans* (Wells, 1976), *R. catesbeiana* (R. W. Howard, 1978), *Bufo valliceps* (W. Blair, 1960), and *B. woodhousii* (Thornton, 1960). *Rana sphenocephala* in central Texas deposits three clutches per year (D. M. Hillis, pers. comm.). Most female *Hyla cinerea, gratiosa,* and *regilla* breed only once per season, but some individuals have two clutches, and 5 of 248 *H. cinerea* females and 3 of 85 *H. regilla* females had three clutches in one season (Perrill and R. Daniel, 1983). The multiple clutches of discoglossids have been mentioned already.

Individuals in some populations of *Bufo* may reproduce biennially (Bragg, 1940; A. Blair, 1943); females of *Rana pretiosa* in the Rocky Mountains in Wyoming reproduce every second or third year (F. Turner, 1960), and in some populations of *Ascaphus truei* females deposit eggs in alternate years (Metter, 1964a).

In summary, anurans in tropical and subtropical enviroments tend to have continuous reproductive cycles and breed throughout that part of the year when rainfall is sufficient to provide oviposition sites. Individuals may breed many times during a season; females of some species can produce clutches only 2 weeks apart. At higher elevations and at higher latitudes, temperature becomes an important factor in the reproductive patterns, controlling time of breeding and length of breeding season. Annual reproduction by females is most common in temperate regions, but individual females in some populations deposit two or more clutches in a single season, whereas in populations existing in extremely cold environments females may not produce eggs every year.

REPRODUCTIVE MODE

Mode of reproduction as used by Salthe (1969) and Salthe and Duellman (1973) is a combination of ovipositional and developmental factors, including oviposition site, ovum and clutch characteristics, rate and duration of development, stage and size of hatchling, and type of parental care, if any.

The diversity of reproductive modes in amphibians is much greater than that observed in other groups of vertebrates, especially the amniotes. In each of the three living orders of Amphibia there are trends toward terrestriality. The variety of these trends is especially noteworthy in anurans. These reproductive adaptations have been viewed as pioneering evolutionary experiments in the conquest of terrestrial environments by vertebrates (C. Goin, 1960). Especially important is the evolution of direct development of terrestrial eggs, ovoviviparity, and viviparity that have been important in the successful invasion of montane enviroments by amphibians.

The diversity of reproductive modes is quite different in the three living groups of amphibians. Therefore, the groups are treated individually.

Caecilians

All caecilians are known, or presumed, to have internal fertilization; probably about 75% of the species bear living young (M. Wake, 1977a, 1977b). A major dichotomy in caecilian reproductive modes is that of oviparity versus viviparity. Among oviparous caecilians, ichthyophiids and probably rhinatrematids have terrestrial eggs adjacent to water; both families are characterized by aquatic larvae, as exemplified by *Caudacaecilia weberi, Ichthyophis glutinosus,* and *Epicrionops petersi.* Oviparity also occurs in members of the Caeciliidae; in some caeciliids (e.g., *Geotrypetes grandisonae* and three species of *Grandisonia*) aquatic larvae are known, whereas in others (e.g., *Grandisonia brevis* and *G. diminutiva, Hypogeophis rostratus, Idiocranium russeli,* and, presumably, *Gegeneophis* and *Uraeotyphlus*) the terrestrial eggs undergo direct development, and there is no aquatic larval stage.

Members of the aquatic family Typhlonectidae are viviparous and produce aquatic larvae. Viviparity and the absence of aquatic larvae are characteristic of many Old World species of caeciliids (e.g., *Geotrypetes angeli* and *G. seraphini, Schistometopum thomense,* and *Scolecomorphus uluguruensis*) and New World genera (e.g., *Dermophis* and *Gymnopis*).

Although the mode of reproduction is not known for many genera and species of caecilians, an evolutionary pattern does seem to be emerging. The mode of primitive families (Ichthyophiidae and Rhinatrematidae), that is, oviparity with aquatic larvae, also occurs in a few members of the Caeciliidae. In that probably composite family there is a trend toward increasing terrestriality through oviparity and direct development to viviparity. The divergent, aquatic typhlonectids are viviparous with aquatic larvae.

Salamanders

The three modes of reproduction in salamanders defined by Salthe (1969) are based primarily on oviposition site and do not take into consideration other factors incorporated into the concept of reproductive mode. The major dichotomy in salamander reproduction is external versus internal fertilization by means of a spermatophore. Six reproductive modes can be recognized among salamanders having internal fertilization. The seven modes are outlined as follows:

I. Fertilization external; eggs and larvae aquatic
II. Fertilization internal
    A. Eggs and larvae aquatic
    B. Eggs terrestrial; larvae aquatic
    C. Eggs terrestrial; larvae terrestrial, nonfeeding
    D. Eggs terrestrial; direct development
    E. Eggs retained in oviducts
        1. Ovoviviparous
        2. Viviparous

External fertilization of aquatic eggs is characteristic of

the Hynobiidae, Cryptobranchidae, and presumably the Sirenidae. Mating has not been observed in sirenids, but the absence of a spermatheca in females and cloacal glands in males seems to preclude the production of spermatophore, the only known method of internal fertilization in salamanders. External fertilization seems likely in *Siren,* which deposits eggs in clumps in water, but unreasonable in *Pseudobranchus,* which scatters its eggs singly among aquatic vegetation (Goin et al., 1978). The spermatozoa of *Pseudobranchus striatus* are large and highly motile, perhaps to facilitate the fertilization of scattered eggs (Austin and C. Baker, 1964). The eggs of cryptobranchids are unpigmented and deposited in pairs of strings under rocks in streams; the pigmented eggs of hynobiids are deposited as pairs of elliptical sacs, one from each ovary, in ponds or streams. In these families, sperm are released by the males after the eggs are deposited. An exception is the hynobiid *Ranodon sibiricus,* males of which produce spermatophores; however, fertilization is external, for females apparently deposit egg sacs on top of the spermatophores (Bannikov, 1958).

Internal fertilization exists in about 90% of the species of salamanders. Among these, aquatic eggs and larvae are characteristic of all proteiids and amphiumids, most ambystomatids, nearly all salamandrids, and aquatic plethodontids. Terrestrial eggs are deposited in depressions by *Ambystoma cingulatum* and *A. opacum;* with the advent of rains the depressions fill with water and the eggs hatch into aquatic larvae. Two plethodontids, *Hemidactylium scutatum* and *Stereochilus marginatus,* have terrestrial nests in sphagnum moss or rotting wood; upon hatching, the larvae wriggle into the water below the nest. Other salamanders having terrestrial eggs lack an aquatic larval stage. In one of these, *Desmognathus aeneus,* the eggs hatch into nonfeeding larvae that complete their development in the nest (J. Harrison, 1967). The eggs of plethodontine and bolitoglossine plethodontids have direct development.

Eggs are retained in the oviducts in four species of salamandrids. Under normal conditions, lowland populations of *Salamandra salamandra* and *Mertensiella caucasica* have aquatic larvae, but montane populations of the former and gravid females of the latter subjected to prolonged drought retain the eggs and eventually give birth to either larvae or fully developed young (Muskhelishvili, 1964; Joly, 1971; Fachbach, 1976). *Salamandra atra* and *Mertensiella luschani antalyana* are viviparous (Häfeli, 1971; Özeti, 1979).

External fertilization unquestionably is primitive in salamanders. The evolution of internal fertilization probably occurred only once in salamanders and was a precursor to direct development, which evolved independently in salamandrids and in different phyletic lines in plethodontids. The trend from aquatic eggs and larvae to direct development of terrestrial eggs is illustrated well by desmognathine plethodontids in the southern Appalachian Mountains (Table 2-1), as first pointed out by E. Dunn (1926a) and studied by Organ (1961). The fossorial

Table 2-1. Terrestrial Trends in Desmognathine Salamanders

Species	Eggs	Larvae	Adults
Leurognathus marmoratus	Large streams	Large streams	Large streams
Desmognathus quadramaculatus	Streams and seeps	Small streams	Small streams and seeps
Desmognathus monticola	Streams and banks	Small streams	Small streams and seeps
Desmognathus fuscus	Stream banks and seeps	Headwaters of small streams	Headwaters of small streams and seeps
Desmognathus ochrophaeus	Stream banks and seeps	Streams and seeps	Terrestrial
Desmognathus aeneus	Seepage areas	Terrestrial	Terrestrial
Desmognathus wrighti	Seepage areas	Direct development	Terrestrial
Phaeognathus hubrichti	Moist soil	Direct development	Terrestrial

Phaeognathus hubrichti presumably has direct development of terrestrial eggs.

Anurans

In contrast to salamanders and caecilians, practically all anurans have external fertilization; in fact, internal fertilization is known only in *Ascaphus*, the species of *Nectophrynoides, Mertensophryne micranotis* (Grandison and Ashe, 1983), and two species of *Eleutherodactylus* (Townsend et al., 1981), but internal fertilization may be more widespread in *Eleutherodactylus* and other frogs having terrestrial eggs. However, within the constraints of external fertilization, anurans have a great diversity of reproductive modes. Three major categories defined on the basis of the site of egg development contain 29 modes (Table 2-2). Modes 7, 10–11, 14, 16, and 24–27 are associated entirely with obligatory parental care and are discussed in the following section. The others, discussed here, are referenced by the numbers in Table 2-2.

The most common and phylogenetically widespread (15 of 21 families) site of oviposition is in free water—standing (Mode 1) or flowing (Mode 2), permanent or temporary. Aquatic eggs and tadpoles are characteristic of all ascaphids, rhinophrynids, Old World pipids, pelobatids, pelodytids, pseudids, and most discoglossids, bufonids, hylids, and ranids; they also occur in some groups of myobatrachids, leptodactylids, microhylids, hyperoliids, and rhacophorids. Eggs and feeding larvae in quiet water are characteristic of such diverse frog genera as *Xenopus, Pelobates, Bufo, Hyla, Rana,* and *Gastrophryne.* Similarly, in lotic sites (streams), the diversity is great, including genera such as *Ascaphus, Scutiger, Atelopus, Plectrohyla, Buergeria,* as well as some *Rana* and *Hyla.* The flowing and quiet water modes are recognized as different principally because of the adaptations of the tadpoles (see Chapter 6).

The habit of depositing eggs as a surface film in a shallow natural basin or one excavated by the male (Mode 3) is known only in a few Neotropical *Hyla*—*H. vasta* (Noble, 1927a) and members of the *H. boans* group (Kluge, 1981). Ovarian and early larval development occur in the basin; subsequent flooding results in the tadpoles dispersing into open water.

The utilization of water trapped in cavities in trees or in the axils of bromeliads for development of eggs and feeding larvae (Mode 4) is known in only a few species: the bufonids *Dendrophryniscus brevipollicatus* (Carvalho, 1949) and *Mertensophryne micranotus* (Grandison, 1980b); and the hylids *Aparasphenodon brunoi* and *Hyla perpusilla* (Lutz, 1954), *Phrynohyas resinifictrix* (B. Zimmerman and Hödl, 1983), *Phyllodytes* (Bokermann, 1966a), *Anotheca spinosa* and members of the *Hyla bromeliacia* group (Duellman, 1970), and Jamaican *Hyla* and *Calyptahyla crucialis* (E. Dunn, 1926a).

An independent preadaptation for direct development is seen in the life histories of frogs that produce eggs with sufficient yolk to provide nourishment for the developing tadpoles after they hatch from aquatic eggs (Mode 5). The only known examples of this mode are the leptodactylids *Eupsophus roseus* and *E. vittatus* in southern Chile (Formas and Vera, 1980) and the Philippine bufonids *Pelophryne albotaeniata* and *P. lighti* (Inger, 1954), in which eggs and nonfeeding tadpoles develop in water-filled depressions in the ground. Similarly, complete development of aquatic eggs and nonfeeding tadpoles in water-filled cavities in trees or axils of leaves (Mode 6) is known in three genera of Madagascaran microhylids: *Anodonthyla, Platypelis,* and *Plethodontohyla* (Blommers-Schlösser, 1975b). Likewise, eggs and nonfeeding tadpoles of the Bornean microhylid *Kalophrynus pleurostigma* develop in water-filled cavities in logs (Inger, 1966).

The construction of a foam nest on the surface of the water in ponds (Mode 8) or streams (Mode 9) is characteristic of many limnodynastine myobatrachids and most leptodactyline leptodactylids (A. Martin, 1970). The Chinese rhacophorid *Chirixalus nongkhorensis* also has foam nests on the surface of ponds (Liu, 1950). Only the Australian *Megistolotis lignarius* places foam nests in pools that become rapidly flowing streams after rains (Tyler et al., 1979).

The deposition of eggs out of water is a major step in the trend toward terrestriality in anurans. In some species, the eggs are deposited in a terrestrial nest near water; the eggs hatch when the nest floods, and the tadpoles feed and develop in ponds or streams (Mode 12). This mode is known in the Asian *Rana adenopleura* (Liu, 1950) and in species of the myobatrachid genera *Geocrinia* (Watson and A. Martin, 1973) and *Pseudophryne* (Woodruff, 1976a).

Various kinds of frogs deposit their eggs on land, rocks,

or tree roots near water, or even in burrows; when the tadpoles hatch they wriggle to, or drop into, the water and begin their feeding existence (Mode 13). Eggs are deposited on rocks or roots above streams, into which hatchlings drop, in the species of the Australian *Mixophyes* (Watson and A. Martin, 1973), in *Centrolene geckoideum* (J. D. Lynch et al., 1983), *Rana magna* (Alcala, 1962), and the African ranid *Natalobatrachus bonebergi* (Wager, 1965). Chilean leptodactylids of the genus *Batrachyla* place their eggs out of water near streams or pools, and the hatchling tadpoles either drop into or wriggle to the water (Formas, 1976a). Some hyperoliids of the genus *Leptopelis* deposit eggs in soil near water (Schiøtz, 1963); upon hatching, the tadpoles wriggle to the surface and then to water (Oldham, 1977). African *Hemisus* deposit eggs in subterranean nests attended by the females; when the eggs hatch, the female burrows to water, which may be as far as 1 m away from the nest, and the tadpoles wriggle to water to begin feeding (Wager, 1965).

The terrestrial eggs of some anurans hatch into nonfeeding tadpoles that complete their development in the nest, with nutrition provided by the yolk (Mode 15). This mode is known in two species in South America—the leptodactylid *Thoropa lutzi* (Bokermann, 1965b) and the microhylid *Synapturanus salseri* (Pyburn, 1975)—and four African species—the bufonid *Nectophrynoides malcolmi* (Grandison, 1978) and the ranids *Phrynodon sandersoni* (Amiet, 1981), *Arthroleptella hewitti* and *A. lightfooti* (Wager, 1965). Additionally, terrestrial eggs or tadpoles that hatch from terrestrial eggs are carried by adults (Modes 14, 16, 24–27) (see the following section: Parental Care).

Direct development of terrestrial eggs (Mode 17) is common among frogs inhabiting perpetually humid regions, as well as some drier areas, and occurs in eight or nine families. Reproduction in the Leiopelmatidae (B. Bell, 1978) is limited to direct development of terrestrial eggs. The large, unpigmented ovarian eggs and terrestrial habits of the adults strongly suggest direct development of terrestrial eggs in the two genera of the Brachycephalidae (Izecksohn, 1971). This mode is characteristic of the immense leptodactylid genus *Eleutherodactylus,* related genera composing the tribe Eleutherodactylini (J. D. Lynch, 1971), and Australo-Papuan microhylids of the subfamilies Asterophryinae and Genyophryninae (Zweifel, 1972a). Thus, in the leptodactylids and Australo-Papuan microhylids alone, direct development presumably occurs in more than 500 species. In addition, this is the mode of development in African ranids of at least some species of the genera *Arthroleptis* and *Anhydrophryne* (Lamotte and Perret, 1963; Wager, 1965), reported for *Rana hascheana* in Thailand (E. Taylor, 1962), and known or presumed on the basis of large, unpigmented eggs in the ranid genera *Batrachylodes, Ceratobatrachus, Discodeles, Palmatorappia,* and *Platymantis* in the Solomon Islands (W. Brown, 1952). Direct development of terrestrial eggs occurs in at least three other

families: Sooglossidae— *Sooglossus gardinerii* (Nussbaum, pers. comm.), Myobatrachidae— *Arenophryne rotunda* (Roberts, 1984), *Geocrinia rosea* (Watson and A. Martin, 1973), and *Myobatrachus gouldii* (Roberts, 1981), and Rhacophoridae—three species of *Philautus* (W. Brown and Alcala, 1983), and *Rhacophorus microtympanum* (Kirtisinghe, 1957). Also, this mode is known in one Neotropical microhylid, *Myersiella microps* (Izecksohn et al., 1971), and probably also occurs in *Syncope,* as well as the Neotropical bufonids *Oreophrynella, Osornophryne,* and *Rhamphophryne.* Eggs undergoing direct development on vegetation (Mode 20) are not common in *Eleutherodactylus* (usually in bromeliads but sometimes on leaves) and are characteristic of the arboreal species of the southern Pacific ranid genus *Platymantis* (W. Brown, 1952; Alcala, 1962).

Many kinds of arboreal frogs deposit eggs above water, into which hatchling tadpoles drop. In most of these the tadpoles develop in ponds or streams (Mode 18). Those that develop in ponds include most of the phyllomedusine hylids and members of the *Hyla leucophyllata* group (Duellman, 1970), plus most of the African *Hyperolius* (Drewes, 1984) and the Madagascaran ranids of the genus *Mantidactylus* (Blommers-Schlösser, 1979a). Eggs on vegetation above streams are characteristic of the Centrolenidae (except *Centrolene)* and for various hylids— *Phyllomedusa guttata* group (Bokermann, 1966a), *Litoria iris* (Tyler, 1963b), and *Hyla lancasteri* and *H. thorectes* (Duellman, 1970). *Rana leytensis* in the Philippines is reported to deposit eggs in strings coiled on leaves above streams, but more frequently on moss-covered roots or rocks (Alcala, 1962). Some Old World tree frogs adhere their eggs to walls of cavities in trees; the hatchling tadpoles drop into water in the cavity, where they feed and complete their development (Mode 19). This mode has been reported only in the African hyperoliid *Acanthixalus spinosus* (Perret, 1962) and three Oriental rhacophorids, *Theloderma stellatum* (Liu, 1950), *Nyctixalus pictus* (Inger, 1966), and *N. spinosus* (W. Brown and Alcala, 1983).

Terrestrial foam nests are known in three families. Some frogs construct nests in burrows or depressions that subsequently flood, and feeding larvae escape into ponds or streams (Mode 21). This is the mode known in the myobatrachid genus *Heleioporus* (A. Lee, 1967), the *Leptodactylus fuscus* group (Heyer, 1969), and some Asiatic rhacophorids— *Polypedates bambusicola* (Liu, 1950) and *Rhacophorus schlegeli schlegeli* (Okada, 1966). In others, nonfeeding tadpoles complete their development in terrestrial foam nests (Mode 22). This is known in the myobatrachids *Kyarranus* (Moore, 1961) and *Philoria* (Littlejohn, 1963) and in the leptodactylids of the genus *Adenomera* (Heyer and Silverstone, 1969) and *Leptodactylus fallax* (Lescure, 1979). Various Old World tree frogs have foam nests in trees and bushes over ponds or streams, into which the tadpoles drop, usually soon after hatching. These include Asiatic rhacophorids, such as *Philautus hosii* (Inger, 1966), various species of *Polypedates* (C. Pope, 1931; Liu, 1950; Alcala, 1962), and *Rhacophorus* (Siedlecke, 1909; Alcala, 1962; Okada, 1966). Arboreal foam nests over ponds are well known in the African rhacophorid genus *Chiromantis* (Wager, 1965; Coe, 1974) and also have been reported for the hyperoliid *Opisthothylax immaculatus* (Amiet, 1974).

The retention of eggs in the oviducts is known in only five species of frogs (M. Wake, 1978, 1980a). In three of these— *Eleutherodactylus jasperi, Nectophrynoides tornieri,* and *N. viviparus* —the eggs complete their development with nutrition provided only by the yolk; hence, they are ovoviviparous (Mode 28). However, in *N. liberiensis* and *N. occidentalis* true viviparity (Mode 29) occurs; maternal nutrition is provided to the developing young by oviducal secretions. Ovoviparity or even viviparity may be more common than is realized among frogs. The discovery of ovoviparity in one of the more than 400 species of *Eleutherodactylus* indicates the possibility that other species of this genus, as well as others that are thought to be oviparous, might produce living young, as suspected long ago in another species, *E. orcutti,* in Jamaica (Lynn and C. Grant, 1940). Furthermore, at least one oviparous species, *E. coqui,* has internal fertilization (Townsend et al., 1981).

It is generally conceded that Mode 1 (lentic eggs and tadpoles) is not only the generalized but also the primitive mode of reproduction in anurans. Assuming this to be true, there are diverse grades of specialization that can be associated with an adaptive radiation into various environments— ephemeral aquatic situations, some of which are predictably present only during a brief rainy season, and streams, which allow anurans to escape from the constraints of lentic waters characteristic of lowlands. Other trends involve terrestrial eggs with subsequent larval development taking place in water. These trends have been carried further in some groups—to the development of larvae on land, to direct development, and to ovoviviparity in a few species and eventually viviparity in two species (Fig. 2-5).

Trends toward terrestriality result in the production of larger-yolked eggs, accompanied by a reduction in the number of eggs by anurans of similar size (Salthe and Duellman, 1973). Increasingly larger yolk reserves are necessary for placing more advanced (proportionately larger) offspring in the environment. This trend is illustrated well by comparison of ovum sizes in the sequential series of those that have aquatic eggs in lentic water, aquatic eggs in lotic water, terrestrial eggs with aquatic larvae, terrestrial eggs with terrestrial larvae or direct development (see following section: Quantitative Aspects: Fecundity).

Reproductive modes associated with the construction of foam nests in the Leptodactylinae provide an excellent example of the trend toward terrestriality (Heyer, 1969). The nest is on the top of open water in the *Leptodactylus melanonotus* and *L. ocellatus* groups, placed in water in cavities adjacent to water in the *L. pentadactylus* group, and placed in a burrow on land in the *L. fuscus* group. Aquatic larvae are present in all of these groups. The derived genus *Adenomera* has nests in a terrestrial chamber, and the nonfeeding tadpoles complete their development in the nests. Within this series of adaptive types toward increased terrestriality, there is a trend for an increase in the size of the ova and a decrease in the number of eggs.

Foam nests provide protection against desiccation; the upper surface exposed to air becomes viscous and even dries to form a thin crust, while the interior remains moist. In ephemeral ponds, in which water level fluctuates, many nests may be out of water for a day or two; the interior of the nest remains moist, and even recently hatched tadpoles may remain in the nest for a day or two until the water level rises. Nests subjected to these conditions are present not only in the *Leptodactylus melanonotus* and *L. ocellatus* groups, but also in *Paludicola, Physalaemus,* and *Pleurodema.* Construction of a foam nest in an underground chamber, as exhibited by members of the *L. fuscus* group, coincides with the first heavy rains of the season. Subsequent heavy rains cause a rise in water level and flood the nest, and the tadpoles escape from the chamber. Tadpoles of *L. bufonius* may remain in the foam nest for up to 39 days after hatching; during this time they do not feed and actually may decrease in size (Philibosian et al., 1974). Experimental evidence suggests that some biological property of the foam inhibits the rate of growth (Pisano and del Río, 1968). Furthermore, tadpoles of *L. bufonius* are ureotelic (Shoemaker and McClanahan, 1973); therefore, wastes can accumulate in the nest chamber without being toxic to the tadpoles. All of these attributes are beneficial to prolonged survival in foam in the nest chamber.

Foam nests floating on open water or in water-filled depressions are subject to intense sunlight. Comparisons of temperatures within nests and of shallow, water-filled depressions show that the nests are about 5°C cooler than the water in the depressions and closely approximate the temperatures of diurnal retreats of the frogs (Gorzula, 1977). Thus, a variety of ecological, developmental, and physiological evidence points to the foam nests of leptodactylids as an adaptation to seasonally wet environments with high temperatures and fluctuating water levels. On the other hand, terrestrial foam nests in which the tadpoles complete their development *(Adenomera)* are characteristic of humid tropical forests.

Limnodynastine myobatrachids of Australia show a trend in foam nesting and development similar to that of the Neotropical leptodactylines (A. Martin, 1970). Again, the generalized foam nest floats on open water, as in *Limnodynastes, Lechriodus,* and *Adelotus;* frogs in these genera have numerous small eggs and aquatic larvae. *Limnodynastes interioris* constructs nests in water-filled burrows in the banks of streams, and the species of *Heleioporus* place nests in dry burrows that subsequently

Table 2-2. Outline of Reproductive Modes in Anurans

I. Eggs aquatic
   A. Eggs deposited in water
      1. Eggs and feeding tadpoles in lentic water
      2. Eggs and feeding tadpoles in lotic water
      3. Eggs and early larval stages in natural or constructed basins; subsequent to flooding, feeding tadpoles in ponds or streams
      4. Eggs and feeding tadpoles in water in tree holes or aerial plants
      5. Eggs and nonfeeding tadpoles in water-filled depressions
      6. Eggs and nonfeeding tadpoles in water in tree holes or aerial plants
      7. Eggs deposited in stream and swallowed by female; eggs and tadpoles complete development in stomach*
   B. Eggs in foam nest
      8. Foam nest on pond; feeding tadpoles in pond
      9. Foam nest in pool and feeding tadpoles in stream
   C. Eggs imbedded in dorsum of aquatic female
     10. Eggs hatch into feeding tadpoles in ponds
     11. Eggs hatch into froglets
II. Eggs terrestrial or arboreal
   D. Eggs on ground or in burrows
     12. Eggs and early tadpoles in excavated nest; subsequent to flooding, feeding tadpoles in ponds or streams
     13. Eggs on ground or rock above water or in depression or excavated nest; upon hatching, feeding tadpoles move to water
     14. Eggs hatch into feeding tadpoles that are carried to water by adult
     15. Eggs hatch into nonfeeding tadpoles that complete their development in nest
     16. Eggs hatch into nonfeeding tadpoles that complete their development on dorsum or in pouches of adult
     17. Eggs hatch into froglets
   E. Eggs arboreal
     18. Eggs hatch into tadpoles that drop into ponds or streams
     19. Eggs hatch into tadpoles that drop into water-filled cavities in trees
     20. Eggs hatch into froglets
   F. Eggs in foam nest
     21. Nest in burrow; subsequent to flooding, feeding tadpoles in ponds or streams
     22. Nest in burrow; nonfeeding tadpoles complete development in nest
     23. Nest arboreal; hatchling tadpoles drop into ponds or streams
   G. Eggs carried by adult
     24. Eggs carried on legs of male; feeding tadpoles in ponds
     25. Eggs carried in dorsal pouch of female; feeding tadpoles in ponds
     26. Eggs carried on dorsum or in dorsal pouch of female; nonfeeding tadpoles in bromeliads
     27. Eggs carried on dorsum or in dorsal pouch of female; direct development into froglets
III. Eggs retained in oviducts
   H. 28. Ovoviviparous
   I. 29. Viviparous

*Egg deposition site unknown; possibly have terrestrial eggs.

flood. Truly terrestrial foam nests in which nonfeeding tadpoles complete their development are characteristic of *Philoria frosti* and the species of *Kyarranus*. In this aquatic to terrestrial sequence, there are a decrease in the number of eggs, an increase in the size of the ova, and a decrease in the amount of pigmentation of the ova (A. Martin, 1967).

The foam nests are constructed in different ways by leptodactylids and myobatrachids (Tyler and M. Davies, 1979b); in the former the male kicks the foam with his feet, and in the latter the female creates currents and foam with her hands. Some Old World tree frogs construct arboreal foam nests, and at least the manner of construction in the rhacophorid *Chiromantis* differs from

that seen in the other families; the foam is kicked by the hindlimbs of both males and females (Coe, 1974). The viscosity of the nest and the hardening of the outer layer of the foam in rhacophorids are more like the condition in leptodactylid nests than in the frothy nests of myobatrachids. The habit of constructing foam nests certainly evolved independently in three groups of frogs and presumably also independently in the Hyperoliidae, in which the only species known to construct a foam nest, *Opisthothylax immaculatus,* folds a leaf over the nest (Amiet, 1974).

Direct development of terrestrial eggs may be preceded evolutionarily by nonfeeding tadpoles that complete their development in terrestrial nests. Direct development must

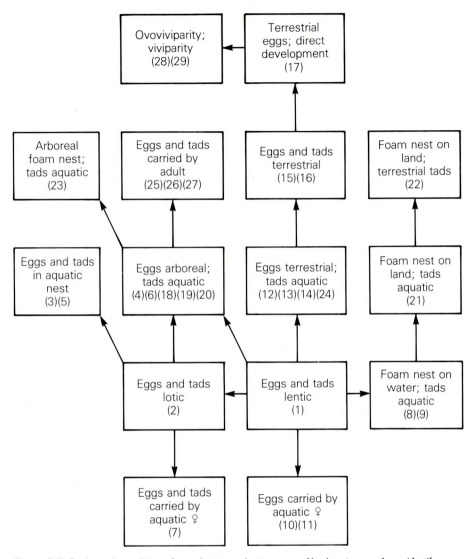

Figure 2-5. Grades in the evolution of reproductive modes in anurans. Numbers in parentheses identify modes defined in Table 2-2.

have evolved independently in at least 12 groups—minimally once each in the Leiopelmatidae, Pipidae, Sooglossidae, Myobatrachidae, Leptodactylidae, Bufonidae, Hylidae, and Rhacophoridae, and probably also in the Brachycephalidae. Presumably, direct development evolved at least twice in the Ranidae (African arthroleptines and Asiatic platymantines) and in the Microhylidae (Australo-Papuan asterophryines and genyophrynines, and Neotropical microhylines).

Stages of specialization of different reproductive modes are evident in certain groups. For example, within the egg-brooding hylid frogs there is a sequence of specialization including hatching as feeding tadpoles, as nonfeeding tadpoles, or froglets (Duellman and Maness, 1980).

Internal fertilization occurs in the species of *Nectophrynoides,* but at least one species is oviparous with nonfeeding larvae, two are ovoviviparous, and two are viviparous (Grandison, 1978; M. Wake, 1980a).

There is a great diversity of reproductive modes in some families (12 in leptodactylids, 11 in myobatrachids), whereas nine families are characterized by a single mode (Table 2-3). It is evident that the trends away from the generalized, primitive mode of eggs and tadpoles in ponds (Mode 1) does not necessarily represent increasing reproductive specialization in phylogenetically advanced groups, but rather, many independently derived reproductive modes in different phyletic lines.

The greatest diversity of reproductive modes is seen

among anurans in the tropics (Table 2-4). For example, in the United States only 4 modes are known, and 90% of the species have eggs and tadpoles in ponds. However, at Santa Cecilia in Amazonian Ecuador 10 modes occur, and only 37% of the species have eggs and tadpoles in ponds (Salthe and Duellman, 1973). Within South America, 21 reproductive modes are known, but 14 of these are restricted to the tropical part of the continent. With the exception of *Leiopelma* in New Zealand and *Rhinoderma* in southern South America, frogs at latitudes greater than 40° have aquatic eggs and larvae.

Ecologically, the generalized mode is most widespread in lowlands, whereas trends toward terrestrial modes become prevalent in highlands. Many terrestrial modes are restricted to environments with continuously high atmospheric moisture, as noted in the fidelity of so-called forest modes to rainforests and the lack of fidelity of nonforest modes (J. D. Lynch, 1979a). Within South America, the proportion of different reproductive modes changes in different climatic regimes—from atmospherically drier to wetter environments (Duellman, 1982b) (Table 2-5).

Thus, in contrast to caecilians and salamanders, the diversity of reproductive modes in anurans is more a reflection of the environmental regimes in which the frogs live than of the phylogenetic relationships of the families and higher categories.

QUANTITATIVE ASPECTS

The great diversity in patterns and modes of reproduction in amphibians is associated with differences in fecundity, duration of development, reproductive effort, and age at first reproduction. In this interface between developmental and population biology, amphibians are especially noteworthy because of their reproductive diversity and, in many species, complex life cycles.

Adequate quantitative data on various parameters of amphibian life histories are available for only a few spe-

Table 2-3. Taxonomic Diversity of Reproductive Modes in Anurans*

Mode	Leiopelmatidae	Discoglossidae	Rhinophrynidae	Pipidae	Pelobatidae	Pelodytidae	Myobatrachidae	Sooglossidae	Heleophrynidae	Leptodactylidae	Bufonidae	Brachycephalidae	Rhinodermatidae	Pseudidae	Hylidae	Centrolenidae	Dendrobatidae	Ranidae	Rhacophoridae	Hyperoliidae	Microhylidae	Total
1	–	+	+	+	+	+	+	–	–	+	+	–	–	+	+	–	–	+	–	+	+	13
2	+	–	–	–	+	–	+	–	+	+	+	–	–	–	+	–	–	+	+	–	–	9
3	–	–	–	–	–	–	–	–	–	–	–	–	–	–	–	–	–	+	–	–	–	1
4	–	–	–	–	–	–	–	–	–	+	+	–	–	–	+	–	–	–	–	–	–	3
5	–	–	–	–	–	–	–	–	–	+	+	–	–	–	–	–	–	–	–	–	–	2
6	–	–	–	–	–	–	–	–	–	–	–	–	–	–	–	–	–	–	–	–	+	1
7	–	–	–	–	–	–	+	–	–	–	–	–	–	–	–	–	–	–	–	–	–	1
8	–	–	–	–	–	–	+	–	–	+	–	–	–	–	–	–	–	–	+	–	–	3
9	–	–	–	–	–	–	+	–	–	–	–	–	–	–	–	–	–	–	–	–	–	1
10	–	–	–	+	–	–	–	–	–	–	–	–	–	–	–	–	–	–	–	–	–	1
11	–	–	–	+	–	–	–	–	–	–	–	–	–	–	–	–	–	–	–	–	–	1
12	–	–	–	–	–	–	+	–	–	–	–	–	–	–	–	–	–	+	–	+	–	3
13	–	–	–	–	–	–	+	–	–	+	–	–	–	–	–	–	–	+	–	+	–	4
14	–	–	–	–	–	–	–	–	–	–	+	–	+	–	+	–	+	–	–	–	–	4
15	–	–	–	–	–	–	–	–	–	+	+	–	–	–	–	–	–	+	–	–	+	4
16	–	–	–	–	–	–	+	+	–	–	–	–	+	–	–	–	–	–	–	–	–	3
17	+	–	–	–	–	–	+	+	–	+	+	?	–	–	–	–	–	+	+	–	+	9
18	–	–	–	–	–	–	–	–	–	–	–	–	–	–	+	+	–	+	+	+	+	6
19	–	–	–	–	–	–	–	–	–	–	–	–	–	–	–	–	–	–	+	+	–	2
20	–	–	–	–	–	–	–	–	–	+	–	–	–	–	–	–	–	+	–	–	–	2
21	–	–	–	–	–	–	+	–	–	+	–	–	–	–	–	–	–	–	+	–	–	3
22	–	–	–	–	–	–	+	–	–	+	–	–	–	–	–	–	–	–	+	+	–	4
23	–	–	–	–	–	–	–	–	–	–	–	–	–	–	–	–	–	–	+	–	–	1
24	–	+	–	–	–	–	–	–	–	–	–	–	–	–	–	–	–	–	–	–	–	1
25	–	–	–	–	–	–	–	–	–	–	–	–	–	–	+	–	–	–	–	–	–	1
26	–	–	–	–	–	–	–	–	–	–	–	–	–	–	+	–	–	–	–	–	–	1
27	–	–	–	–	–	–	–	–	–	–	–	–	–	–	+	–	–	–	–	–	–	1
28	–	–	–	–	–	–	–	–	–	+	+	–	–	–	–	–	–	–	–	–	–	2
29	–	–	–	–	–	–	–	–	–	–	+	–	–	–	–	–	–	–	–	–	–	1
Totals	2	2	1	3	2	1	11	2	1	12	9	1	2	1	8	1	1	9	8	6	5	

*See Table 2-2 for definitions of modes.

Table 2-4. Geographical Diversity of Anuran Reproductive Modes

Characteristic	Nearctic	Palearctic	Neotropical	Ethiopian	Oriental	Australo-Papuan
Number of modes	4	6	21	12	11	12
Percentage of modes	14	21	72	41	38	41
Unique modes	0	1	8	1	0	2
Percentage unique	0	17	38	8	0	17

Table 2-5. Modes of Reproduction of Anurans in Different Tropical Habitats in South America

Mode of reproduction	Savanna[a]	Seasonal rainforest[b]	Aseasonal rainforest[c]	Cloud forest[d]
Forest modes				
Eggs and tadpoles in lotic water[e]	—	—	—	10 (10.8%)
Eggs and tadpoles in tree cavities or bromeliads	—	—	1 (1.1%)	—
Eggs on vegetation above ponds; aquatic tadpoles[f]	1 (4.2%)	6 (19.4%)	15 (17.0%)	3 (3.5%)
Eggs on vegetation above streams; aquatic tadpoles	—	—	2 (2.3%)	11 (11.9%)
Eggs terrestrial; tadpoles to water on adults	—	3 (9.7%)	6 (6.9%)	9 (9.8%)
Eggs and tadpoles in terrestrial foam nest	—	1 (3.2%)	1 (1.1%)	—
Eggs terrestrial; direct development	—	1 (3.2%)	19 (21.7%)	49 (53.3%)
Eggs on dorsum of female; direct development	—	—	1 (1.1%)	8 (8.7%)
Nonforest modes				
Eggs and tadpoles in lentic water	14 (58.3%)	16 (51.6%)	34 (38.6%)	1 (1.1%)
Eggs and early tadpoles in aquatic nest	—	1 (3.2%)	1 (1.1%)	—
Eggs in foam nest; tadpoles in ponds	9 (37.5%)	2 (6.5%)	7 (8.0%)	1 (1.1%)
Eggs on dorsum of aquatic female	—	1 (3.2%)	1 (1.1%)	—
Total—forest modes	1 (4.7%)	11 (35.5%)	45 (51.1%)	90 (97.8%)
Total—nonforest modes	23 (95.8%)	20 (64.5%)	43 (48.9%)	2 (2.2%)
Total—both modes	24	31	88	92

[a]El Manteco, Venezuela (Hoogmoed and Gorzula, 1979).
[b]Belém, Brazil (Crump, 1971).
[c]Santa Cecilia, Ecuador (Duellman, 1978) with additions.
[d]Amazonian slopes of Andes in Ecuador (Duellman, 1979) with additions.
[e]Perhaps some of these species deposit eggs on vegetation above streams.
[f]Some of these—species of *Phyllomedusa*—wrap leaves around their eggs.

cies. These data are reviewed and discussed in the following paragraphs.

Fecundity

It is well known that fecundity levels are highly variable among amphibians. Generally, large species have more eggs than smaller ones. Also, species having generalized reproductive modes produce larger clutches than those that have specialized modes. This is exemplified in caecilians, in which the oviparous *Ichthyophis glutinosus* may lay as many as 54 eggs in a single clutch (P. Sarasin and F. Sarasin, 1887–90), but the viviparous *Geotrypetes seraphini* may give birth to only one to four young (M. Wake, 1977a). Among salamanders, fecundity is highest in species that deposit their eggs in water, much lower in those having terrestrial eggs, and lowest in those that give birth to living young. For example, *Siren lacertina* may deposit more than 500 eggs (Noble and Marshall, 1932), and *Cryptobranchus alleganiensis* produces up to 450 eggs in a clutch (B. Smith, 1907), whereas the largest clutches in salamanders are produced by *Ambystoma* — more than 1,000 in *A. mexicanum* (Gasco, 1881) and more than 5,000 in *A. tigrinum* (F. Rose and Armentrout, 1976). At the other extreme, *Salamandra atra* usually gives birth to only two young at a time (V. Vilter and A. Vilter, 1960). The variation in fecundity in frogs is also highly variable and is most closely associated with reproductive mode, but also correlated with body size within reproductive modes. Among species that have direct development of terrestrial eggs, the diminutive *Sminthillus limbatus* of Cuba deposits a single egg per clutch (Noble, 1931b), but other species having this mode deposit up to 100 eggs or more. The ovoviviparous *Eleutherodactylus jasperi* has only 3–5 eggs (M. Wake, 1978). Species depositing eggs in water have much larger clutches, many thousands in some of the larger species of *Bufo* and *Rana*. The largest known clutches are produced by *Rana catesbeiana;* one female having a snout-vent length of 179 mm deposited a clutch of 47,840 eggs (McAuliffe, 1978).

Size-fecundity relationships were described for salamanders by Salthe (1969) and for anurans by Salthe and Duellman (1973). Further observations and discussions were presented by Crump (1974), Kuramoto (1978a), Kaplan and Salthe (1979), and Kaplan (1980a). An ovar-

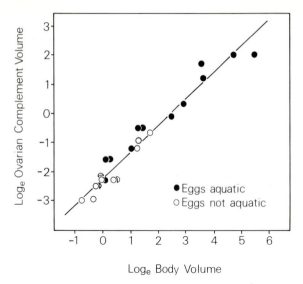

Figure 2-6. Relationship between mean body volume of gravid females and mean volume of mature ovarian complements in 23 species of anurans in Amazonian Ecuador. $Y = 2.27 + 0.903\ X$; $r = 95.1$ ($P < 0.001$). Modified from Crump (1974).

ian size factor (clutch size X ovum diameter/female snout-vent length) was proposed as an index of comparing fecundity and egg size relative to adult body size (Duellman and Crump, 1974).

The general conclusions concerning interspecific size-fecundity relationships are as follows:

1. Within a given reproductive mode, there is a positive correlation between clutch size and female body size.
2. Within a given reproductive mode, there is a positive correlation between ovum size and female body size.
3. Regardless of reproductive mode, there is a negative correlation between clutch size and ovum size.
4. Regardless of reproductive mode, there is a positive correlation between ovum size and size of hatchlings.

Other correlations are considered in the following section: Duration of Development.

The most significant conclusion is the high correlation between body size and clutch volume. Weaknesses in the relationships between fecundity and body size, and between ovum size and body size are the result of the variable negative correlation between ovum size and fecundity.

Among anurans in the upper Amazon Basin in Ecuador there is a significant positive correlation between body length and fecundity in each of three reproductive modes, and there is a significant positive correlation between body

volume and volume of the mature ovarian complement, regardless of reproductive mode (Fig. 2-6) (Crump, 1974). Likewise, a significant positive correlation exists between clutch size and female snout-vent length among species of *Eleutherodactylus* (M. Wake, 1978). Within species there are similar significant correlations in some groups: *Desmognathus* (Tilley, 1968), *Ambystoma* (Kaplan and Salthe, 1979), six species of pond-breeding frogs in Michigan (Collins, 1975), and among various Japanese amphibians (Kuramoto, 1978a). On the other hand, significant positive correlations exist in only 11 of 41 tropical species studied by Crump (1974), and no correlations exist in *Hyla rosenbergi* (Kluge, 1981). This may be because of the small ranges in sizes and/or ovarian complements of many of the species, or possibly because of variable amounts of energy available for reproduction.

There is a positive correlation between body size and clutch size and ovarian complement in temperate, terrestrial plethodontine salamanders and a similar trend in tropical bolitoglossine salamanders (Fig. 2-7), but the bolitoglossines have larger clutches than do plethodontines of similar sizes (Houck, 1977b). The ova of the tropical species generally are smaller than those of the temperate species.

Ovum-size–body-size relationships generally are not so clear as the clutch-size relationships, except that as a general rule, at a given body size there is a negative correlation between clutch size and ovum size. Nonetheless, some studies have shown significant interspecific and intraspecific correlations between ovum size and body size—various anurans (Collins, 1975), *Ambystoma* (Kaplan, 1980a), and *Eleutherodactylus* (M. Wake, 1978).

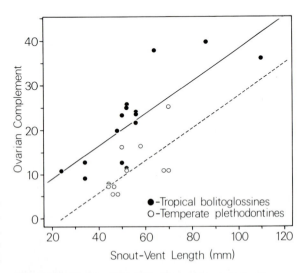

Figure 2-7. Size-fecundity relationships among plethodontid salamanders having direct development of terrestrial eggs. Among temperate species, $Y = -8.60 + 0.368\ X$; $r = 33.7$ ($0.025 < P < 0.05$). Among tropical species, $Y = -1.58 + 0.377\ X$, $r = 62.4$ ($P < 0.001$). Difference in elevation of lines, $t = 4.316$ ($P < 0.001$). Based on Houck (1977b) with additions.

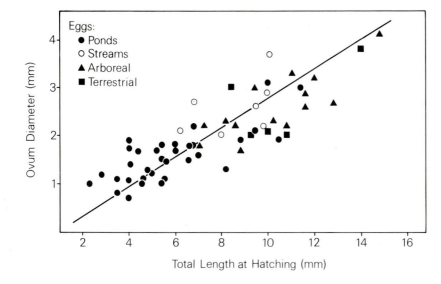

Figure 2-8. Relationship of ovum size and hatchling size in frogs. Each symbol is the mean for a species. $Y = 1.18 + 3.18\ X; r = 69.1\ (P < 0.001)$. Modified from Salthe and Duellman (1973).

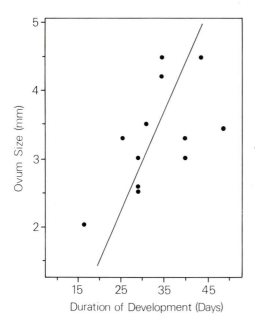

Figure 2-9. Duration of development in eggs of 12 species of anurans having direct development. $Y = 9.85 + 7.03\ X; r = 32.1$ $(P < 0.05)$.

Data on ovum size and size of hatchling are limited but show a positive correlation among species of frogs having different reproductive modes (Fig. 2-8). Also, intraspecific and intrapopulational correlations have been demonstrated in various species of *Ambystoma* (DuShane and C. Hutchinson, 1944; Kaplan, 1979, 1980a), *Triturus vulgaris* (G. Bell, 1977), and *Rhyacotriton olympicus* (Nussbaum and Tait, 1977).

Duration of Development

Within reproductive modes there are some apparent correlations between ovum size and duration of develop-

ment. For example, in species of anurans having terrestrial eggs undergoing direct development, the smaller eggs hatch much more rapidly than larger ones (Fig. 2-9). Among chorus frogs, *Pseudacris triseriata*, ovum size is significantly larger and duration of development more rapid in montane than in lowland populations (Pettus and Angleton, 1967). Conversely, among four populations of three species of *Ambystoma*, egg size does not seem to be correlated with rate of development to the feeding stage at various controlled temperatures, but larger larvae develop from larger ova and absolute differences in size become amplified with time (Kaplan, 1980a).

Basing their generalizations on frogs that deposit eggs in water and on K. Bachmann's (1969) investigations, Salthe and Duellman (1973) concluded that there is a negative correlation between ovum size and rate of development. This is an oversimplification. The eggs of most frogs develop much faster than do those of salamanders. The developmental time to hatching in aquatic eggs of salamanders ranges from about 15 days in some *Ambystoma* to 275 days in *Dicamptodon ensatus*; terrestrial eggs undergoing direct development require from 60 days in some small species of *Plethodon* to 250 days in *Bolitoglossa compacta* (Table 2-6). On the other hand, among anurans, aquatic eggs require from only 1 day in various *Bufo, Hyla,* and *Scaphiopus* to 42 days in *Rana aurora*, whereas terrestrial eggs undergoing direct development require from 15 days in *Eleutherodactylus* to 49 days in *Platymantis hazelae* (Table 2-7). Notable exceptions among frogs are the high Andean marsupial frog, *Gastrotheca riobambae*, in which the eggs require about 88 days to develop into tadpoles, and the egg-brooding *Pipa pipa*, in which 107 days on the average are required for the eggs to develop into froglets.

Rate of development and therefore duration of development are temperature-dependent. Aside from the work of K. Bachmann (1969), various studies have demonstrated the negative correlation between developmental rate and temperature. For example, *Ambystoma opacum* requires about 250 hours at 20°C from gastrula to hatching, but at 10°C this development requires about 800 hours (Kaplan, 1980a). Spadefoot toads have extremely rapid development; at 30°C, the eggs of *Scaphiopus couchii* and *S. bombifrons* hatch in 15 and 20 hours, respectively, but at 10°C, 82 and 84 hours, respectively, are required for development to hatching (Justus et al., 1977).

In the small marsupial frog, *Flectonotus pygmaeus,* the eggs are about 4.4 mm in diameter and require 24 or 25 days to develop to hatching at Stage 41 (staging according to Gosner, 1960), whereas in *Gastrotheca riobambae,* eggs are about 3.0 mm in diameter and require 88 days to hatch at Stage 25 (Duellman and Maness, 1980; del Pino and Escobar, 1981). These differences are not entirely temperature-dependent. The average temperature in the cloud forest where *Flectonotus* lives is higher than that at Quito, Ecuador, where *G. riobambae* was studied. However, eggs of *Flectonotus* developed in 29 days at Quito. Obviously, in these frogs and others having large eggs that contain sufficient yolk for development to a froglet, some mechanism or property of the egg (possibly rates of protein synthesis or enzyme activity) increases the rate of development over that of eggs developing in water.

Conflicting results were obtained by Moore (1939), who demonstrated that cold-adapted species of North American *Rana* and *Ambystoma* have faster rates of development than warm-adapted species. These results are supported by data on altitudinal variation in development of *A. macrodactylum* (J. Anderson, 1967) and *R. temporaria* (Kozlowska, 1971). Experiments by Berven et al. (1979) on development of eggs of *R. clamitans* from different elevations demonstrated that eggs from high elevations develop faster at low temperatures than do eggs from low elevations; however, in natural situations, eggs develop more slowly at high elevations because the water temperature is lower. Thus, the relationships that exist between ovum size and duration of development are affected by temperature and some other factors, which at the present time are unknown. Perhaps in the large terrestrial eggs that hatch into advanced young, part of the relatively immense caloric content of the egg helps to speed development.

Reproductive Effort

The measure of effort in terms of parental investment of time in courtship and mating, proportional weight (= energy) devoted to eggs, and amount of caloric intake required for gametogenesis and vitellogenesis are all as-

Table 2-6. Fecundity and Development in Selected Salamanders (Mean Values)

Species	Clutch size	Egg (mm)	Duration of development (days) Egg	Larva	Percent survival of young of adult female	Source
Eggs and larvae aquatic						
Hynobius nebulosus[a]	128	2.00	27	138	31.2	Thorn (1963)
Cryptobranchus alleganiensis[a]	450	6.00	76	1750	22.7	Bishop (1941)
Siren intermedia[a]	200	3.00	—	270	24.4	Noble and Marshall (1932)
Notophthalmus viridescens	302	1.50	28	84	63.1	Bishop (1941)
Triturus vulgaris	241	1.50	20	86	56.7	G. Bell and Lawton (1975)
Necturus maculosus	107	5.50	57	1750	67.8	Bishop (1941)
Ambystoma macrodactylum	307	—	25	115	—	J. Anderson (1967)
Ambystoma maculatum	134	2.75	43	87	27.8	Bishop (1941)
Dicamptodon ensatus	138	6.00	275	700	41.0	Nussbaum (1969a)
Rhyacotriton olympicus	8	3.20	250	990	80.0	Nussbaum and Tait (1977)
Leurognathus marmoratus	38	3.00	83	450	58.0	Martof (1962b)
Eurycea multiplicata	13	2.50	32	195	90.0	P. Ireland (1976)
Eggs terrestrial; larvae aquatic						
Ambystoma opacum	150	2.70	41	255	—	Bishop (1941)
Desmognathus ochrophaeus	16	3.00	71	150	25.0	Organ (1961); Tilley (1972)
Hemidactylium scutatum	50	2.75	56	42	30.0	Bishop (1941)
Eggs terrestrial; direct development						
Aneides aeneus	17	4.50	87	—	—	R. Gordon (1952)
Bolitoglossa rostrata	37	3.50	165	—	34.3	Houck (1977a)
Bolitoglossa subpalmata	23	5.00	135	—	17.3	Vial (1968)
Desmognathus aeneus[b]	11	1.90	40	15	23.9	J. Harrison (1967)
Ensatina eschscholtzi	13	3.90	120	—	29.0	Stebbins (1954)
Plethodon cinereus	9	3.00	56	—	29.3	Sayler (1966)
Plethodon glutinosus	21	4.25	60	—	20.7	Highton (1962)

[a]Fertilization external.　　[b]Nonfeeding terrestrial larvae.

pects of reproductive effort, as is the investment in parental care, if any. Theoretically, species of the same size, having the same reproductive mode, and living in the same climatic regime should devote approximately the same amount of energy to reproduction. Variables, such as the size and number of eggs and number of clutches, then would be a reflection of age (= size) and relative health of the female. Any deviations from this pattern would indicate a change in reproductive effort, and changes in reproductive mode (e.g., small aquatic eggs to large terrestrial eggs) or reproductive patterns (e.g., semelparity to iteroparity) would suggest modifications in reproductive effort.

Empirical evidence on the energetics of reproduction in amphibians is extremely limited. In *Desmognathus ochrophaeus* an estimated 68.5% of the annual secondary production in mature females is devoted to production of eggs (Fitzpatrick, 1973a). Caloric content of eggs of different species of *Ambystoma* varies independently of clutch volume (Kaplan, 1980b). Comparative studies on the energy content of eggs of Neotropical *Hyla* (Crump and Kaplan, 1979) revealed that the energy contained in each clutch (relative to female body size) is not significantly different in species depositing eggs in ponds from those placing their eggs on vegetation over ponds; small species expend proportionately the same amount of energy as larger species. However, there is a noticeable difference in the partitioning of energy within the clutches. Those species that deposit clutches in ponds have about twice the number of eggs per clutch as those that place their clutches on vegetation. The arboreal eggs contain about twice the caloric content of the aquatic eggs and require longer to hatch into larger, more advanced tadpoles.

Age and Reproduction

The age that an individual enters the reproductive population and the span of its reproductive life are important factors in a reproductive strategy. Although the existing data are limited, some patterns are evident in salamanders and anurans. Because so little information is available, it is not possible to discern patterns within the caecilians. Females of *Geotrypetes seraphini* and *Dermophis mexicanus* apparently breed for the first time at 2 years of age, whereas males of the latter species presumably do not breed until they are 3 years old (M. Wake, 1977a, 1980b). Earlier maturation by females compared with males is contrary to data for any salamanders and anurans. Females of *Dermophis* have a long gestation period and certainly do not reproduce every year, whereas males have continuous gametogenesis. Because never more than half of the females are reproductively active, early maturation of females is advantageous in maintaining a higher proportion of reproductive females in the population.

Most salamanders do not reproduce before the age of 2 years, whereas many frogs reproduce at the age of 1 year (Tables 2-8 and 2-9). In most species the females mature later than males; most of the exceptions are species in which both sexes mature early. The greatest age (5 years) at which males become reproductive are in the paedomorphic, aquatic cryptobranchids and proteiids; females require 6 years, but some males and females of *Triturus vulgaris* do not reproduce until their seventh year (G. Bell, 1977). The earliest-maturing salamander is the aquatic plethodontid *Eurycea multiplicata,* both sexes of which are sexually mature shortly after metamorphosis at an age of 5–8 months (P. Ireland, 1976). As a group, the pond-breeding *Ambystoma* mature relatively early (1–3 years), and salamandrids mature much later (3–6 years). Within the plethodontids, those species having aquatic larvae generally mature earlier (0.5–4 years for males and 0.5–5 years for females) than do those having direct development of terrestrial eggs (1.75–6 years for males and 1.75–12 years for females).

Among anurans, the greatest ages at attainment of sexual maturity are in species at high latitudes or altitudes; males may require 4 years and females as many as 6 years. On the other hand, species in aseasonal, humid tropical lowlands mature much earlier. The earliest normal maturation reported is 6–7 months in males and 9 months in females of *Rana erythraea* (W. Brown and Alcala, 1970). Quite probably, many small hylids and hyperoliids mature even faster. Precocious reproduction may occur at an age earlier than normal, such as at 80–100 days postmetamorphosis in *Limnodynastes tasmaniensis* (Horton, 1982a). Age at first reproduction in 12 tropical species of anurans is 6–15 months (mean = 10.79) in males and 8–15 months (mean = 10.99) in females, whereas in 25 midlatitude temperate species the values are 1–2.5 years (mean = 1.54) in males and 1-3 years (mean = 1.83) in females. By contrast, the ages of 8 species at high latitudes and high elevations in the temperate regions are 2–4 years (mean = 3.44) in males and 2.5–6 years (mean = 3.69) in females.

Differences in climatic regimes are reflected in age at sexual maturity in some species having broad geographic or altitudinal ranges. Latitudinal gradients show a delay in maturation of 2 years in *Bufo calamita* from Switzerland to Sweden and in *Rana pipiens* from southern to northern Michigan. Likewise, lowland populations of *Ambystoma macrodactylum* and *Desmognathus ochrophaeus* mature a year earlier than their respective highland populations. A 2- to 4-year difference in age at first reproduction occurs between lowland and highland populations of *Rana sylvatica* in Maryland.

Some of the species that require the longest time to mature have lengthy larval periods. Thus, among salamanders, *Rhyacotriton olympicus* breeds at an age of 4.5–5 years, but 3–3.5 of those years are spent as a larva in cold streams. Likewise, *Ascaphus truei* spends 3 years as a tadpole in cold streams before metamorphosing to reproduce in its fourth year. The age at first reproduction in *Rana catesbeiana* depends on the length of the larval period—one or two overwinterings; young frogs usually

Table 2-7. Fecundity and Development in Selected Anurans (Mean Values)

Species	Clutch Size	Egg (mm)	Duration of development (days) Egg	Duration of development (days) Nonfeeding larva	Duration of development (days) Feeding larva	Percent survival of young adult female	Source
Eggs and larvae aquatic							
Ascaphus truei[a]	37	4.00	30.0	—	1080	47.0	Noble and Putnam (1931)
Bombina bombina	100	2.00	12.0	—	90	36.5	Berger and Michalowski (1963)
Hymenochirus boettgeri	450	0.75	2.0	—	42	—	G. Rabb and M. Rabb (1963)
Pelobates fuscus	750	1.50	5.5	—	120	48.3	Berger and Michalowski (1963)
Macrogenioglottis alipioi	3650	1.50	2.5	—	107	—	Abravaya and Jackson (1978)
Heleophryne purcelli[a]	136	3.50	3.5	—	730	—	Wager (1965); J. Visser (1971)
Bufo canorus	1750	2.00	5.5	—	50	17.6	Karlstrom (1962)
Bufo quercicus	500	1.09	1.0	—	26	—	Volpe and Dobie (1959)
Bufo valliceps	4100	1.23	3.8	—	24	10.2	Limbaugh and Volpe (1957)
Nectophrynoides osgoodi	307	2.75	10.0	—	27	—	Grandison (1978)
Hyla avivoca	650	1.17	1.7	—	24	25.0	Volpe et al. (1961)
Hyla cinerea	700	1.20	2.0	—	35	44.0	Garton and Brandon (1975)
Hyla crucifer	900	1.10	6.0	—	45	32.2	Gosner and Rossman (1960)
Hyla rosenbergi[b]	2350	1.95	2.8	—	33	24.6	Kluge (1981)
Limnaoedus ocularis	100	0.95	3.5	—	42	48.8	Gosner and Rossman (1960)
Litoria verreauxi	731	1.23	6.1	—	90	36.2	Anstis (1976)
Phrynohyas venulosa	2920	1.60	1.0	—	42	23.6	Pyburn (1967)
Pseudacris brachyphona	646	1.60	4.6	—	55	25.0	N. Green (1938)
Pseudacris streckeri	601	1.40	4.5	—	60	32.5	Bragg (1942)
Smilisca cyanosticta	1167	1.20	1.0	—	40	22.6	Pyburn (1966)
Phrynobatrachus natalensis	650	1.00	3.5	—	28	—	Wager (1965)
Ptychadena oxyrhyncha	350	1.30	2.0	—	49	—	Wager (1965)
Pyxicephalus adspersus	3500	2.00	2.0	—	18	20.0	Wager (1965)
Rana areolata	6000	1.84	10.8	—	150	31.3	Volpe (1957c)
Rana aurora	838	3.04	42.0	—	100	26.8	Storm (1960)
Rana cancrivora	2527	1.25	3.4	—	63	20.0	Alcala (1962)
Rana everetti[a]	925	2.15	6.6	—	105	25.3	Alcala (1962)
Rana fuscigula	15,000	1.50	8.5	—	1080	—	Wagner (1965)
Rana japonica	1700	1.75	21.0	—	90	—	Okada (1966)
Rana pretiosa	539	2.40	14.0	—	85	—	F. Turner (1958)
Rana septentrionalis	509	2.30	4.0	—	360	42.8	Hedeen (1972)
Rana sylvatica	1750	1.90	20.0	—	67	30.8	Stebbins (1951)
Tomopterna delalandii	2500	1.50	3.0	—	35	19.4	Wager (1965)
Hyperolius marmoratus	350	1.30	5.0	—	49	—	Wager (1965)
Kassina maculata	300	1.50	6.0	—	270	80.0	Wager (1965)
Kassina senegalensis	400	1.20	5.5	—	90	62.0	Wager (1965)
Anodonthyla boulengeri[c]	27	2.00	8.0	18.0	—	44.7	Blommers-Schlösser (1975b)
Kaloula conjuncta	800	1.10	1.6	—	85	24.2	Alcala (1962)
Phrynomerus bifasciatus	600	1.30	4.0	—	30	—	Wager (1965)
Platypelis grandis[c]	100	4.00	19.0	16.0	—	14.4	Blommers-Schlösser (1975b)
Plethodontohyla notosticta[c]	120	3.00	14.0	14.0	—	15.0	Blommers-Schlösser (1975b)
Eggs in foam nest; larvae aquatic or in nest							
Kyarranus sphagnicola	48	3.25	10.0	20.0	—	—	Moore (1961)
Limnodynastes peroni	857	1.45	6.0	—	150	—	Moore (1961)
Megistolotis lignarius[a]	352	1.87	2.5	—	122	43.1	Tyler et al. (1979)
Philoria frosti	95	3.90	9.0	40.0	—	14.2	Littlejohn (1963)

Species							Reference
Physalaemus cuvieri	419	1.90	3.0	—	60	—	Bokermann (1962)
Chiromantis petersi[d]	325	1.00	4.0	—	157	—	Coe (1974)
Polypedates leucomystax[d]	175	1.85	3.3	1.0	90	29.7	Alcala (1962)
Rhacophorus pardalis[d]	46	3.00	7.7	1.7	83	28.1	Alcala (1962)
Eggs terrestrial or arboreal; larvae aquatic							
Alytes obstetricans[e]	63	3.10	30.0	—	360	13.7	Crespo (1979)
Nectophryne afra	26	3.50	7.0	—	28	—	Scheel (1970)
Nectophrynoides malcolmi	18	2.60	18.0	17.0	—	—	Grandison (1978)
Colostethus trinitatus[f]	12	3.50	21.0	—	56	—	Kenny (1969a)
Dendrobates femoralis[f]	23	2.00	14.5	—	48	—	Polder (1976)
Dendrobates silverstonei[f]	30	2.00	11.2	—	74	—	Myers and Daly (1979)
Phyllobates terribilis[f]	14	2.50	11.0	—	55	30.1	Myers et al. (1978)
Phyllobates vittatus[f]	14	2.50	15.0	—	25	—	Silverstone (1976)
Agalychnis callidryas	51	2.25	5.0	—	74	32.0	Pyburn (1963)
Hyla berthalutzae	52	3.00	5.0	—	50	37.5	Bokermann (1963)
Phyllomedusa trinitatus	536	3.25	7.4	—	77	28.1	Kenny (1966, 1968)
Arthroleptella hewitti	30	3.00	17.0	3.0	—	10.5	Wager (1965)
Rana magna[a]	178	2.60	6.3	—	83	17.9	Alcala (1962)
Rana microdisca[a]	47	2.00	7.5	—	55	32.7	Alcala (1962)
Mantidactylus liber	60	1.40	6.0	—	60	41.8	Blommers-Schlösser (1975a)
Afrixalus fornasinii	80	2.00	5.0	—	90	50.0	Wager (1965)
Hyperolius pusillus	310	1.00	5.0	—	42	—	Wager (1965)
Hyperolius tuberlinguis	400	1.50	5.0	—	60	—	Wager (1965)
Eggs terrestrial; development direct							
Leiopelma archeyi	9	4.50	44.0	—	—	35.5	N. Stephenson (1951b); D. Bell (1978)
Eleutherodactylus martiae	9	3.30	26.0	—	—	22.7	Crump (1974)
Eleutherodactylus planirostris	17	2.00	15.6	—	—	24.0	C. Goin (1947)
Eleutherodactylus pseudoacuminatus	7	3.50	30.0	—	—	25.6	Crump (1974)
Hylactophryne augusti	67	4.20	35.0	—	—	18.2	Jameson (1950)
Anhydrophryne rattrayi	15	2.60	28.0	—	—	25.0	Wager (1965)
Arthroleptis wahlbergi	21	2.50	28.0	—	—	16.4	Wager (1965)
Platymantis guentheri	8	3.00	39.0	—	—	33.9	Alcala (1962)
Platymantis hazelae	7	3.40	49.0	—	—	17.3	Alcala (1962)
Platymantis meyeri	27	3.30	39.0	—	—	15.0	Alcala (1962)
Breviceps adspersus	33	4.50	35.0	—	—	—	Wager (1965)
Myersiella microps	12	3.00	29.0	—	—	—	Izecksohn et al. (1971)
Eggs carried by female							
Pipa pipa[g]	83	6.00	107.0	—	—	—	G. Rabb and Snedigar (1960)
Flectonotus pygmaeus	9	4.40	24.5	13.0	—	27.7	Duellman and Maness (1980)
Gastrotheca riobambae	128	3.00	88.0	—	360	37.0	del Pino and Escobar (1981)
Eggs retained in oviducts							
Eleutherodactylus jasperi[h]	4	3.30	33.0	—	—	36.3	Drewry and K. Jones (1976)
Nectophrynoides occidentalis[h]	8	0.60	270.0	—	—	31.0	Lamotte et al. (1964)

[a]Tadpoles in streams.
[b]Eggs and early larval stages in nest.
[c]Eggs and larvae in water in tree holes or leaf axils.
[d]Foam nest arboreal.
[e]Eggs carried on legs of male.
[f]Tadpoles carried by adult from terrestrial nest to water.
[g]Aquatic.
[h]Viviparous.

Table 2-8. Age at First Reproduction in Selected Salamanders

Species	Age in years from hatching		Source
	Males	**Females**	
Ranodon sibiricus	4	4	Bannikov (1949)
Salmandrella keyserlingi	3	4	Steward (1970)
Andrias japonicus	4	5	Tago (1929)
Cryptobranchus alleganiensis	5	6	Bishop (1941)
Siren intermedia	2	2	W. Davis and Knapp (1953)
Notophthalmus viridescens (without eft)	2	2	Healy (1974)
Notophthalmus viridescens (with eft)	4–8	4–8	Healy (1974)
Pleurodeles waltl	2	3	Steward (1970)
Salamandra atra	3	4	Thorn (1968)
Salamandra salamandra	3	4	Thorn (1968)
Taricha torosa	3	3	McCurdy (1931)
Triturus cristatus	3	3	Steward (1970)
Triturus vulgaris	3–7	3–7	G. Bell (1977)
Necturus maculosus	5	6	Bishop (1941)
Ambystoma macrodactylum (coastal)	2	2	J. Anderson (1967)
Ambystoma macrodactylum (highland)	3	3	J. Anderson (1967)
Ambystoma maculatum	1	2	Husting (1965)
Ambystoma opacum	1.3	1.3	Bishop (1941)
Ambystoma tigrinum	1	1	Bishop (1941)
*Rhyacotriton olympicus**	4.5–5	4.5–5	Nussbaum and Tait (1977)
Amphiuma tridactylum	—	4	Cagle (1948)
Desmognathus fuscus	3	4	Danstedt (1975)
Desmognathus ochrophaeus (lowland)	3	4	Tilley (1973)
Desmognathus ochrophaeus (highland)	4	5	Tilley (1973)
Desmognathus quadramaculatus	3.5	5	Organ (1961)
Desmognathus wrighti	3.5	5	Organ (1961)
Leurognathus marmoratus	2	3	Martof (1962b)
Eurycea longicauda	1.5	3	J. Anderson and Martino (1966)
Eurycea multiplicata	0.5–0.7	0.5–0.7	P. Ireland (1976)
Eurycea neotenes	2	2	Bruce (1976)
Eurycea quadridigitata	0.5	0.5	J. Harrison (1973)
Hemidactylium scutatum	2.3	2.3	Blanchard and Blanchard (1931)
Pseudotriton montanus	1	4–5	Bruce (1975)
Pseudotriton ruber	4	5	Bruce (1978b)
Stereochilus marginatus	3	4	Bruce (1971)
Aneides flavipunctatus	3.3	4.3	Houck (1977b)
Batrachoseps attenuatus	2.5–3	3.5	Maiorana (1976a)
Bolitoglossa rostrata	2.5	3.7	Houck (1977a)
Bolitoglossa subpalmata	6	12	Vial (1968)
Ensatina eschscholtzi	3	3.5	Stebbins (1954)
Plethodon cinereus	1.7	1.7	Sayler (1966)
Plethodon glutinosus (Florida)	2.5	3	Highton (1962)
Plethodon glutinosus (Maryland)	4.5	5	Highton (1962)
Plethodon hoffmani	2.3	3.3	Angle (1969)
Plethodon vehiculum	2.7	3.3	Peacock and Nussbaum (1973)
Plethodon wehrlei	4	4–5	Hall and Stafford (1972)

*3–3.5 years as larva.

reach sexual maturity within a year after metamorphosis. Many temperate frogs breed for the first time in the season following hatching, so many are less than 1 year old at the time of their first reproduction.

The fossorial salamander *Batrachoseps attenuatus* may reach sexual maturity in 2.5 years, but if the subadult loses its tail, where fat is stored, or faces an adverse year, age at first reproduction may be delayed 1 year (Maiorana, 1976a).

Early versus delayed maturation can depend on certain

Table 2-9. Age at First Reproduction in Selected Anurans

Species	Age from hatching		Source
	Males	**Females**	**Source**
Ascaphus truei[a]	4 yr	4 yr	Metter (1964a)
Bombina bombina	2 yr	2 yr	Bannikov (1950)
Discoglossus pictus	2 yr	3 yr	Knoeppfler (1962)
Hymenochirus boettgeri	12–18 mo	12–18 mo	G. Rabb and M. Rabb (1963a)
Pipa carvalhoi	7–9 mo	7–9 mo	Weygoldt (1976a)
Scaphiopus holbrooki	1–2 yr	1–2 yr	P. Pearson (1955)
Helioporus eyrei	2 yr	2 yr	A. Lee (1967)
Megistolotis lignarius	10 mo	10 mo	Tyler et al. (1979)
Eleutherodactylus johnstonei	< 1 yr	< 1 yr	Chibon (1962)
Eleutherodactylus planirostris	< 1 yr	< 1 yr	Goin (1947)
Leptodactylus macrosternum	1 yr	1 yr	Dixon and Staton (1976)
Bufo americanus	2–3 yr	3 yr	Hamilton (1934)
Bufo calamita (Sweden)	4 yr	4 yr	Gislén and Kauri (1959)
Bufo calamita (Switzerland)	2 yr	2 yr	Heusser and Meisterhans (1969)
Bufo canorus	3 yr	3 yr	Karlstrom (1962)
Bufo marinus	1 yr	1 yr	G. Zug and P. Zug (1979)
Bufo quercicus	1 yr	2 yr	Hamilton (1955)
Bufo valliceps	< 1 yr	< 1 yr	W. Blair (1953)
Bufo woodhousii	2 yr	3 yr	Underhill (1960)
Phyllobates terribilis	13 mo	13 mo	Myers et al. (1978)
Acris crepitans	< 1 yr	< 1 yr	Collins (1975)
Hyla chrysoscelis	1–2 yr	2 yr	S. Roble (pers. comm.)
Hyla cinerea	< 1 yr	< 1 yr	Garton and Brandon (1975)
Hyla crucifer	1 yr	1 yr	Collins (1975)
Hyla regilla	1 yr	—	Jameson (1956)
Hyla rosenbergi	< 1 yr	< 1 yr	Kluge (1981)
Hyla versicolor	2 yr	2 yr	Collins (1975)
Pseudacris triseriata	< 1 yr	< 1 yr	S. Roble (pers. comm.)
Gastrophryne carolinensis	1 yr	1–2 yr	P. K. Anderson (1954)
Gastrophryne olivacea	1–2 yr	1–2 yr	Fitch (1956)
Ptychadena maccarthyensis	8–9 mo	8–9 mo	Barbault and Trefaut R. (1978)
Ptychadena oxyrhyncha	8–9 mo	8–9 mo	Barbault and Trefaut R. (1978)
Rana aurora	2 yr	2 yr	Storm (1960)
Rana catesbeiana[b]	2–3 yr	3 yr	Collins (1975)
Rana clamitans	1–2 yr	2 yr	Martof (1956)
Rana erythraea	6–7 mo	9 mo	W. Brown and Alcala (1970)
Rana pipiens (N. Michigan)	4 yr	4 yr	Force (1933)
Rana pipiens (New York)	2 yr	2 yr	R. Ryan (1953)
Rana pipiens (S. Michigan)	1–2 yr	1–2 yr	Collins (1975)
Rana pretiosa	4 yr	5–6 yr	F. Turner (1960)
Rana septentrionalis	2 yr	2–3 yr	Hedeen (1972)
Rana sylvatica (low Maryland)	1 yr	2 yr	Berven (1981)
Rana sylvatica (S. Michigan)	1–2 yr	2 yr	Collins (1975)
Rana sylvatica (high Maryland)	3–4 yr	3–4 yr	Berven (1981)
Rana temporaria	3 yr	3 yr	Heusser (1970b)

[a]3 years as larva.   [b]1 or 2 years as larva.

aspects of the life history. A classic example is the newt *Notophthalmus viridescens,* in which most populations have a terrestrial, subadult, eft stage lasting 2–6 years, after which the salamanders become aquatic and breed for the first time at an age of 4–8 years. Some coastal populations omit the terrestrial eft stage and reach sexual maturity at the age of 2 years (Healy, 1974).

Older females contribute more offspring than younger ones, not only because they are larger and have larger clutches, but because they may contribute more clutches in a breeding season. Females of *Rana catesbeiana* in their first breeding season produce only one clutch, whereas many older females produce two clutches (R. W. Howard, 1978b). Females of *Bombina orientalis*

breed at the age of 1 year but produce fewer and smaller eggs than older females (Kawamura et al., 1972). Females of *Discoglossus pictus* first breed at 3 years of age, when they produce one or two clutches of no more than 300 eggs each; older females produce up to six clutches, each with as many as 800 eggs, per season (Knoeppfler, 1962). Clutches of 12-year-old *Triturus vulgaris* contain four times as many eggs as those produced by 3-year-olds; furthermore, older females produce larger eggs (G. Bell, 1977).

Next to nothing is known about the reproductive life spans of amphibians. The most notable exception is *Hyla rosenbergi* in Panama, which reproduces in the rainy season following hatching at the age of less than 1 year

(Kluge, 1981). At that time females may lay up to six clutches of eggs in about 150 days; essentially no females survive for a second breeding season. The average clutch size is 2,350, so a female may produce about 14,100 eggs during her reproductive life span. Female *Rana catesbeiana* in southern Michigan have an adult life expectancy of 4 years; they deposit one clutch the first year and potentially two clutches in succeeding years (Collins, 1975; R. W. Howard, 1978b). The mean clutch size is 11,636 eggs (Collins, 1975), so one female might produce more than 80,000 eggs in her life. *Rana sylvatica* in Maryland exhibits an entirely different pattern; most females breed only once, after 2 to 4 years of growth, and deposit a single clutch of about 2,500 eggs (Berven, 1981).

Generally, salamanders live longer than frogs; a *Cryptobranchus alleganiensis* was reported to have survived for 55 years in captivity (Nigrelli, 1954). Females of this species reproduce for the first time at an age of 6 years, and they have annual clutches of about 450 eggs (Bishop, 1941). By combining the longevity record and the clutch size, we can arrive at a potential life-time fecundity of 22,500 eggs—a highly unlikely occurrence in nature. Female *Ambystoma maculatum* may breed for 5 consecutive years in southern Michigan (Husting, 1965); clutches contain about 200 eggs, giving this species a potential production of about 1,000 offspring during its life. A plethodontid, such as *Ensatina eschscholtzi*, which lives to at least 7 years but requires 3 years to reach sexual maturity, will produce three clutches of about 13 eggs each biennially, for a total of about 39 eggs during its life. *Salamandra atra* requires 4 years to reach sexual maturity and then produces two living young at intervals of usually 4 years (V. Vilter and A. Vilter, 1960). The life

span is about 16 years, so the maximum offspring expected in this species is only eight.

Very little is known about the proportion of females in a population that breed in any given season. Theoretically, in those salamanders having biennial reproductive cycles, about half of the females breed in any given year. If age at first reproduction is relatively constant within a population, then all females in a given cohort would be expected to breed in the same year. With few exceptions, female anurans breed every season, and the indication from limited data on species inhabiting aseasonal, humid tropical regions is that individuals breed frequently, as often as every 2 or 3 weeks in some species.

PARENTAL CARE

By comparison with birds and mammals, amphibians generally have been thought to exhibit little parental care. However, in recent years both field and laboratory studies have provided evidence for an astonishing array of parental care in amphibians. Parental care may be defined as any behavior exhibited by a parent toward its offspring that increases the offspring's chances of survival (Trivers, 1972); this investment may reduce the parent's ability to invest in additional offspring. Among amphibians, parental care includes attendance of the eggs, transportation of eggs or larvae, and feeding of larvae. Parental care is associated only with those species that place their eggs in single clusters, never with those that scatter their eggs in aquatic situations. Nest construction, either prior to or during oviposition, is not considered to be parental care, although in some species that construct nests, one parent may attend the eggs. Likewise, the retention of eggs in the oviducts, even though nourish-

Table 2-10. Diversity of Parental Care in Amphibians

Parental care of			Investing parent			
Eggs	Larvae	Site of care	Caecilians	Salamanders	Anurans	Remarks
+	−	Aquatic	—	4 ♂, 12 ♀	3 ♂	—
+	−	Aquatic foam nest	—	—	1 ♂	—
+	+	Aquatic foam nest	—	—	1 ♀	♀ with school of larvae
+	−	Aquatic nest	—	—	3 ♂	♂ constructs and guards nest
+	−	Terrestrial	5 ♀	3 ♀	4 ♂	Larvae aquatic
+	−	Arboreal	—	—	±11 ♂, ♀	Larvae aquatic
+	+	Terrestrial	—	1 ♀	6 ♂, ♀	Nonfeeding larvae
+	+	Arboreal	—	—	6 ♂	Nonfeeding larvae
+	−	Arboreal foam nest	—	—	1 ♀	Larvae aquatic
+	−	Terrestrial	4 ♀	±175 ♀	±50 ♂, ♀	Development direct
+	−	Aquatic	—	—	5 ♀	Eggs on dorsum
+	+	Aquatic	—	—	2 ♀	Eggs and larvae in stomach
+	−	Terrestrial	—	—	2 ♂	Carried on hindlimbs
+	−	Terrestrial/arboreal	—	—	55 ♀	On dorsum or in dorsal pouch
−	+	Terrestrial	—	—	±75 ♂, ♀	Transported to water on dorsum
−	+	Terrestrial	—	—	3 ♀	Transported to water on dorsum and subsequently fed
−	+	Terrestrial	—	—	1 ♂	Transported to water in vocal sac
−	+	Terrestrial	—	—	1 ♂	Develop in vocal sac
−	+	Terrestrial	—	—	1 ♂	Develop in inguinal pouches
−	+	Terrestrial	—	—	1 ♀	Develop on dorsum

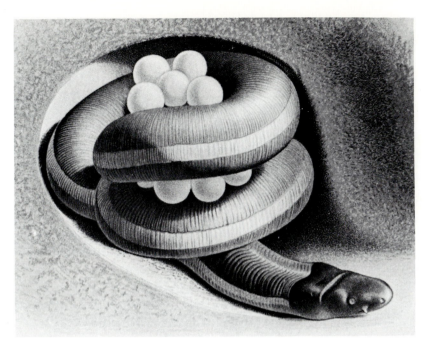

Figure 2-10. Female caecilian, *Ichthyophis glutinosus,* coiled about eggs in burrow. From F. Sarasin and P. Sarasin (1887–90).

ment is provided to the developing young, is not considered to be parental care.

In amphibians, parental care is widespread phylogenetically and is especially diverse in anurans (Table 2-10). Parental care has been reported in only about 10% of the species of frogs and in only a few caecilians (Fig. 2-10), but it occurs in the majority of salamanders. Most commonly, parental care is associated with those frogs that have prolonged breeding periods and with frogs and salamanders characterized by terrestrial modes of reproduction. In caecilians and salamanders, parental care consists solely of attendance of eggs, usually by the female. This same behavior occurs in anurans; however, compared with salamanders and caecilians, a greater number of frog species have males in the attendance of egg clutches. Attendance of eggs may be facultative— the eggs are capable of developing without the attendant parent, but survivorship may be enhanced by the presence of the parent. Only in anurans does parental care involve the transportation of eggs and larvae. Most, if not all, of the parental care involving transportation of eggs and larvae is obligatory. Complex behavior of oviposition and/or morphological and physiological modifications are associated with such parental care.

Parental care in amphibians was reviewed by Salthe and Mecham (1974); this behavior in frogs was discussed by Lamotte and Lescure (1977), McDiarmid (1978), and Wells (1981a), and in salamanders by M. Ryan (1977) and Forester (1979).

Diversity of Parental Care

Parental attendance at egg clutches has various roles in different species or at different sites. Functions include aeration of aquatic eggs, manipulation and/or moistening of terrestrial eggs, protection against predators, and removal of dead or infected eggs. Among the few species exhibiting parental care of aquatic eggs, males of *Cryptobranchus* and *Hynobius* are territorial and drive away all conspecifics except gravid females (Kerbert, 1904; B. Smith, 1907; Thorn, 1962). Captive male *Andrias japonicus* have been observed to agitate the eggs (Stejneger, 1907). Either sex of the subterranean *Proteus anguineus* may attend the eggs; these aquatic salamanders wave their tails so as to direct water currents over the eggs (Vandell and Bouillon, 1959; Durand and Vandell, 1968). In aquaria, *Necturus maculosus* jostle their eggs by periodically waving their gills near the eggs (Salthe and Mecham, 1974); females of this species also protect their eggs from conspecific oophagy (Bishop, 1926). Similar agitation of aquatic eggs by water currents generated by kicking the feet is known in the toad *Nectophryne afra* (Scheel, 1970). Agitation of aquatic eggs has been interpreted as aeration, but oscillation of the eggs may be necessary for normal embryonic development, as shown for terrestrial salamander eggs (Forester, 1979). Males of the African ''hairy'' frog, *Trichobatrachus robustus,* have been observed sitting on egg clutches in streams (Perret, 1966).

Female attendance at egg clutches in streams is known for the salamander *Dicamptodon ensatus* (Nussbaum, 1969a) (Fig. 2-11) and several plethodontid salamanders: species of *Gyrinophilus* (Bruce, 1978a), *Pseudotriton* (Bruce, 1978b), *Eurycea* (Franz, 1964), *Leurognathus* (Martof, 1962b), and *Desmognathus* (Organ, 1961). However, parental attendance of aquatic eggs is unknown in *Ambystoma* and salamandrids.

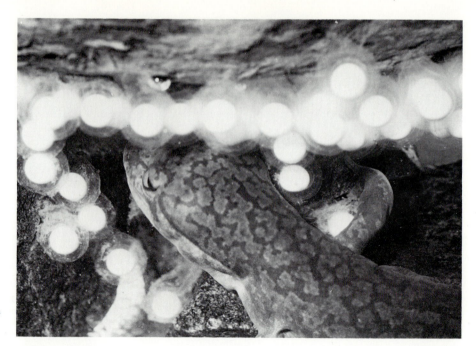

Figure 2-11. Female salamander, *Dicamptodon ensatus,* attending eggs under log in stream. Photo by E. D. Brodie, Jr.

Figure 2-12. Nest of *Hyla boans* showing surface film of eggs; the nest is scooped out by a male, which subsequently defends the nest against intruders. Photo by W. E. Duellman.

Male attendance at aquatic foam nests by the myobatrachid frog *Adelotus brevis* may be simply a consequence of territoriality, but males have long tusks on the lower jaw that might be used in effective protection of the eggs. Likewise, the presence of the male myobatrachid *Pseudophryne bibronii* in burrows containing eggs seems to be a territorial function; any protection resulting in greater survivorship of the eggs is secondary (Woodruff, 1977). Female attendance at an aquatic foam nest in *Leptodactylus ocellatus* is a precursor to protection afforded to the tadpoles. In this species the tadpoles move about in dense masses; the female remains with the tadpoles and attacks wading birds attempting to feed on the tadpoles (Vaz-Ferreira and Gehrau, 1975). The large, aggressive African ranid *Pyxicephalus adspersus* has been reported to protect tadpoles in shallow ponds by driving away potential predators (B. Balinsky and J. Balinsky, 1954). However, this apparently is only aggressive be-

Figure 2-13. A centrolenid, *Centrolenella* sp., attending an egg clutch on the underside of a leaf over a stream. Photo by W. E. Duellman.

havior, because *Pyxicephalus* will eat the tadpoles (Wager, 1965).

The best-documented study of male attendance of aquatic eggs is that of the nest-building gladiator frog, *Hyla rosenbergi* (Kluge, 1981). Males are highly territorial and aggressive, and they call from shallow basins that they scoop out of soil adjacent to water. Eggs are deposited as a surface film on water in the basin (Fig. 2-12). If the surface tension is broken, the eggs sink to the bottom of the basin and die of oxygen deprivation. Males patrol the nest areas and attack intruding conspecific males, whose entry into the nest can disrupt the surface tension. The facultative nature of this parental care is demonstrated by significantly higher rates of guarding in a year of high population density than in a succeeding year of low density.

In *Amphiuma* the habit of coiling about the eggs and holding them free of the substrate at times of drying of the nest is thought to aid in preventing desiccation of eggs (J. Weber, 1944). The terrestrial eggs of *Dendrobates auratus* and *D. pumilio* are periodically moistened by males emptying their bladders on the clutch (Wells, 1978a; Weygoldt, 1980). Presumably the ranid *Hemisus marmoratum* also provides moisture for developing eggs; the female sits on the clutch in a subterranean chamber and, subsequent to the hatching of the tadpoles, digs a tunnel to water, thereby allowing the tadpoles to escape from the nest chamber (Wager, 1965).

Attendance of developing eggs and nonfeeding larvae in terrestrial nests is a behavior common to several kinds of frogs and one salamander, *Desmognathus aeneus*. Care is exhibited by the female in *Desmognathus* (J. Harrison, 1967), in the leptodactylid *Zachaenus parvus* (Heyer and Crombie, 1979), and in the ranid *Phrynodon sandersoni*

(Amiet, 1981), but by males in the leptodactylid *Thoropa petropolitana* (Heyer and Crombie, 1979), the bufonid *Nectophrynoides malcolmi* (Grandison, 1978), in three species of the ranid genus *Petropedetes* (Amiet, 1981), and in the microhylids *Plethodontodohyla tuberata* (Blommers-Schlösser, 1975b), *Breviceps adspersus* (Wager, 1965), and *Synapturanus salseri* (Pyburn, 1975). The eggs of three Madagascaran microhylids *Platypelis grandis, Plethodontohyla notosticta,* and *Anodonthyla boulengeri*, which develop and hatch in water in tree holes or leaf axils, are all attended by males (Blommers-Schlösser, 1975b). Female *Leptodactylus fallax* remain with eggs and larvae in a terrestrial foam nest (G. Brooks, 1968; Lescure, 1979). Larvae that are essentially immobile on a disintegrated terrestrial nest or confined to a constrained aquatic situation (e.g., leaf axil or tree hole) are susceptible to many predators; thus, guarding the offspring may be the primary purpose of the attending parent. The provision of moisture to the eggs and larvae also may be a function in those species having terrestrial nests. However, parental care has not been observed in the myobatrachid genus *Kyarranus,* which has terrestrial nests and nonfeeding larvae, in leptodactylids of the genus *Adenomera* having direct development in terrestrial foam nests, or in egg-brooding hylids that place non-feeding tadpoles in leaf axils.

Centrolenid frogs of the genus *Centrolenella* breed on vegetation overhanging streams; in many species the males are territorial, and in some they attend the eggs (Fig. 2-13). *Centrolenella colymbiphyllum* and *C. valerioi* are sympatric in Costa Rica; males of the former attend egg clutches on the undersides of leaves only at night, whereas males of the latter remain with the eggs night and day (McDiarmid, 1978). The eggs are preyed upon by a small

Figure 2-14. West Indian leptodactylid, male *Eleutherodactylus hedricki,* attending a terrestrial clutch. Photo by **M. M. Stewart.**

wasp, which presumably is deterred by the presence of a male. In 112 clutches of *C. valerioi,* only 7% of the eggs were lost, compared with 23% among 152 clutches of *C. colymbiphyllum.* Females of *Hyperolius obstetricans* remain with their eggs on leaves overhanging streams; upon hatching, the female kicks the tadpoles out of the jelly (Amiet, 1974). Females of the West African ranid *Phrynodon sandersoni* attend eggs on leaves of bushes at night (Amiet, 1981). In the rhacophorid *Chiromantis xerampelina,* a female has been observed periodically moistening the arboreal foam nest (W. Rose, 1962).

The eggs of *Ambystoma opacum* develop in a terrestrial depression with an attending female, who occasionally agitates the eggs and moves about on the eggs; the area of movement is free of fungus (Salthe and Mecham, 1974). The eggs are abandoned when the nest floods and the larvae hatch. Females of the plethodontid salamanders *Hemidactylium scutatum* and *Stereochilus marginatus* attend egg clutches in sphagnum moss or rotting logs above water; upon hatching the larvae escape into the ponds (Blanchard, 1934; G. Rabb, 1956).

Parental attendance of terrestrial eggs that undergo direct development is widespread among anurans and nearly universal in terrestrial plethodontid salamanders. Male attendance occurs in some species of *Eleutherodactylus,* at least some of which (e.g., *E. coqui* and *E. hedricki)* are territorial and may attend more than one clutch at a time (Drewry, 1970; Townsend et al., 1984). In many others, females sit on, or adjacent to, eggs in leaf litter or under rocks (Fig. 2-14), or, as in *E. caryophyllaceus,* perch on top of eggs adhering to a leaf on a bush (Myers, 1969). In other leptodactylids, such as *Hylactophryne augusti,*

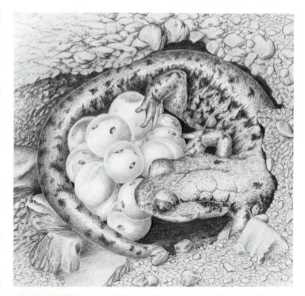

Figure 2-15. Female plethodontid salamander, *Pseudoeurycea juarezi,* attending an egg clutch originally beneath stone. Adapted from a photo by R. W. McDiarmid.

males attend the eggs (Jameson, 1950), whereas in *Geobatrachus walkeri* females are the attendants (Ardila-Robayo, 1979). Males of *Leiopelma archeyi* and perhaps also *L. hochstetteri* sit on clutches (E. Stephenson and N. Stephenson, 1957), whereas in sooglossid frogs and in the bufonid *Oreophrynella* females attend the clutches (Nussbaum, 1983; McDiarmid, pers. comm.). Among the Australo-Papuan microhylid frogs, all of which have direct development of terrestrial or arboreal eggs, only males

attend the eggs in two species of *Phrynomantis,* two of *Cophixalus,* and three of *Sphenophryne* (Méhelÿ, 1901; Tyler, 1963a; Zweifel, 1972a; M. P. Simon, pers. comm.), but both parents attend the eggs in two species of *Oreophryne* and one of *Cophixalus* (van Kampen, 1923; Zweifel, 1956; Simon, 1983). Only females of *C. riparius* attend eggs (M. P. Simon, pers. comm.). In the South American *Myersiella microps,* only the female remains with the terrestrial eggs (Izecksohn et al., 1971).

Among the terrestrial plethodontid salamanders, egg clutches are usually attended by females (Salthe and Mecham, 1974). Male attendance of some clutches and female attendance of others occurs in *Bolitoglossa subpalmata* (Vial, 1968). In all closely observed cases, the attending adult is in physical contact with the eggs, usually with the chin in contact with the clutch and the body wrapped around it (Fig. 2-15); periodically, the adult rotates the eggs in the clutch (Stebbins, 1954; Highton and T. Savage, 1961; Vial, 1968; Tilley, 1972; Forester, 1979). This parental care has been thought to contribute to the survival of the young by (1) protecting them from predation, (2) preventing or reducing their infection by phycomycete fungi, or (3) agitating them to enhance aeration and/or prevent adhesive malformation. Conspecific oophagy is common among plethodontid salamanders, and eggs also are eaten by other species of salamanders and various kinds of arthropods. Aggressive defense of clutches against predators has been observed in *Aneides, Plethodon,* and *Desmognathus* (R. Gordon, 1952; Highton and T. Savage, 1961; F. Rose, 1966). Numerous authors have noted that terrestrial eggs of plethodontid salamanders and anurans develop fungal infections in the absence of a parent, but antifungal properties have not been discovered in skin secretions (Vial and Prieb, 1966, 1967).

The contributions of parental care in *Desmognathus ochrophaeus* have been tested rigorously in field and laboratory experiments by Forester (1979). Results of these studies demonstrate conclusively that female attendance contributed significantly to survivorship of the clutches. Unattended clutches disappeared within a few days, but when attendants and clutches were protected from predators by confinement, survivorship increased by 40% over unconfined controls. Dead eggs became infected by fungus, which subsequently attacked other eggs in unattended clutches. Attendant females ate dead and infected eggs, thereby restraining the spread of fungus to other eggs. Furthermore, eggs in advanced stages of development had a higher resistance to fungal infections; possibly, as first suggested by Highton and T. Savage (1961), the embryos produce an antifungal substance. It was also noticed that an attendant female places her chin on the egg clutch, thereby subjecting the eggs to slight vibrations caused by pulsations of the throat. Clutches that were vibrated experimentally in the absence of females exhibited survivorship higher than that of controls.

Among caecilians, female *Ichthyophis glutinosus* attend terrestrial eggs that hatch into aquatic larvae (Sarasin and Sarasin, 1887–90); the eggs sometimes are infected with fungi, and attendant females will eat eggs (Breckenridge and Jayasinghe, 1979). Female *Idiocranium russeli* coil about their eggs on small mounds in a dense mat of grass (Sanderson, 1932); these eggs undergo direct development. Possibly, recently born young of some viviparous caecilians may be attended by the female; Sanderson (1932:222) reported finding a female *Geotrypes seraphini* sitting on a mound in a chamber partially filled with water and wrapped around "a bundle of smaller replicas of herself, all with their heads pointing toward her tail."

Among amphibians, all known cases of mobile parental care involve transportation of eggs and/or larvae by male or female frogs. With the exception of the aquatic pipids, all such parental care is associated with terrestrial eggs. In *Pipa* (Fig. 2-16) the eggs are carried on the dorsum of the female (G. Rabb and Snedigar, 1960; Weygoldt, 1976a). Australian myobatrachids of the genus *Rheobatrachus* are unique in that the eggs and larvae develop in the stomach of the female (Corben et al., 1974; MacDonald and Tyler, 1984), and the young froglets emerge from the mouth (Tyler and Carter, 1981). In addition to the unique trait of gastric brooding, these are the only frogs known to carry both eggs and tadpoles.

Egg-carrying by terrestrial male frogs is known only for the European *Alytes.* At the time of oviposition, the strings of eggs adhere to the hindlimbs of the male (Fig. 2-17).

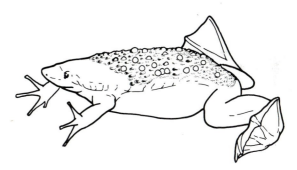

Figure 2-16. Female *Pipa carvalhoi* with eggs imbedded in dorsum.

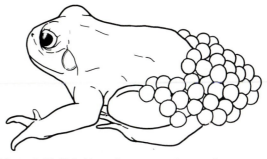

Figure 2-17. Male *Alytes obstetricians* with eggs adherent to hindlimbs.

Figure 2-18. Egg-carrying in hylid frogs. **A.** In dorsal pouch of female of *Gastrotheca cornuta*. **B.** On dorsum of female of *Hemiphractus johnsoni*.

He carries the eggs and periodically enters the water; when the larvae begin to hatch, the males sits in water and the hatchlings are released (Boulenger, 1897; Crespo, 1979). All other egg-carrying is obligatory in females of hemiphractine hylids; in some of these the developing eggs are in a dorsal pouch, and in others they are adherent to the dorsum (Fig. 2-18). In the arboreal species, development is direct in *Gastrotheca* and *Amphignathodon,* but terminates in nonfeeding tadpoles that are deposited in water in leaf axils in *Flectonotus* and *Fritziana.* In terrestrial species of *Hemiphractus, Cryptobatrachus, Stefania,* and some *Gastrotheca,* development is direct. In other high montane, terrestrial *Gastrotheca,* the eggs hatch into tadpoles; at the time of hatching the females move to ponds and release the tadpoles (Duellman and Maness, 1980). Buccal brooding of eggs in *Leptopelis brevirostris* was reported by Boulenger (1906), who found eggs equal to the size of those in the oviducts in the mouth of a female, but Noble (1926) noted that this specimen had been eviscerated through the mouth and that remnants of the ovary and ovarian eggs were present in the mouth.

External tadpole-carrying apparently is universal in the Dendrobatidae and otherwise is known in only six species. Tadpoles adhere to the dorsum of either sex in dendrobatids, males of *Rana microdisca finchi* (Inger, 1966), and females of the leptodactylid *Cyclorhamphus stejnegeri* (Heyer and Crombie, 1979) and *Sooglossus seychellensis* (Nussbaum, pers. comm.). In the last species, the tadpoles complete their development on the dorsum, whereas in all of the others the parents release the tadpoles in water. In all instances in which tadpoles have been observed attaching themselves to the dorsum of the parent, the adult sits in the remainder of the gelatinous egg clutch, and the tadpoles wriggle up the hindlimbs and onto the back. The venter of the tadpole is adherent to the dorsum by a sticky mucus; the larval mouth is not

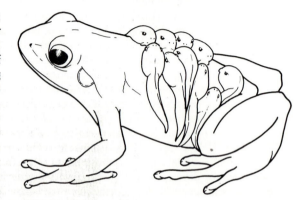

Figure 2-19. Male *Colostethus subpunctatus* carrying tadpoles; note that the ventral surfaces of the tadpoles are adherent to the parent.

involved in attachment (Stebbins and Hendrickson, 1959). In the myobatrachid *Assa darlingtoni,* nonfeeding tadpoles wriggle up the legs and into inguinal pouches in the male, which carries them until they complete their development (G. Ingram et al., 1975). Males of the two species of *Rhinoderma* transport tadpoles in their vocal sacs. In both species the hatching tadpoles are picked out of the deteriorating jelly of the terrestrial egg clutch. In *R. darwinii,* nonfeeding tadpoles complete their development in the vocal sac and emerge as froglets, whereas males of *R. rufum* simply transport tadpoles from the nest to water (Formas et al., 1975).

Parental care is complex in dendrobatid frogs, all of which are diurnal and transport tadpoles; furthermore, one or both sexes of many species are territorial and aggressive. Male attendance at clutches occurs in *Colostethus,* such as *C. subpunctatus* (Stebbins and Hendrickson, 1959). Males of *Dendrobates auratus, D. pumilio,* and *Phyllobates vittatus,* and females of *D. histrionicus, lehmanni,* and *pumilio* periodically wet their terrestrial clutches by emptying the contents of their bladders on the eggs (Wells, 1978a; Weygoldt, 1980; H. Zimmermann and E. Zimmermann, 1981). Upon hatching, the entire complement of tadpoles is carried by males of *Colostethus collaris, nubicola, palmatus, subpunctatus* (Fig. 2-19), *trinitatis, Phyllobates terribilis,* and *P. vittatus* (Stebbins and Hendrickson, 1959; Durant and Dole, 1975; Luddecke, 1976; Myers at at., 1978; Wells, 1980b, 1981a; H. Zimmermann and E. Zimmermann, 1981). Similarly, entire complements are carried by females of *C. inquinalis* and *C. pratti* (Wells, 1981a). In all of these species of *Colostethus* and *Phyllobates* the tadpoles are transported to streams or, in the case of *C. subpunctatus,* small ponds. The tadpoles of *Dendrobates* develop in water-filled leaf axils of various kinds of plants, including terrestrial and arboreal bromeliads, tree holes, or other constrained containers. Many tadpoles are transported at a time by males of *Dendrobates auratus, azureus, femoralis,* and *parvulus* (Polder, 1974; Wells, 1978a; Duellman, 1978). Paternal versus maternal transportation of tadpoles may be related to interspecific differences in territoriality (Wells, 1981a), and in some *Dendrobates* it possibly is associated with subsequent maternal care. Females of *Dendrobates pumilio, histrionicus,* and *lehmanni* carry individual tadpoles to separate water-filled leaf axils of bromeliads; no tadpole is placed in an axil already containing a tadpole. Once all of the tadpoles have been dispersed, the mother periodically oviposits unfertilized eggs in the water of the leaf axils containing her tadpoles; she can maintain as many as six tadpoles through metamorphosis, requiring 6 to 8 weeks of feeding a complement of eggs at least twice to each tadpole. The presence of an adult on the leaf of the bromeliad and subsequently entering the water in the leaf axil elicits a caudal vibration from the tadpole; this vibration presumably signals the tadpole's presence to the female (Graeff and Schulte, 1980; Weygoldt, 1980; H. Zimmermann and E. Zimmermann, 1981).

Dendrobates are the only amphibians known to feed their young, but bromeliad-dwelling tadpoles of the Central American *Hyla zeteki* (E. Dunn, 1937) and *Anotheca spinosa* (E. Taylor, 1954) eat frog eggs, presumably those of their own species (Duellman, 1970), as do four Jamaican hylids with bromeliad-dwelling tadpoles (E. Dunn, 1926a) and the African microhylid *Hoplophryne rogersi* with eggs and tadpoles in cavities in bamboo or in leaf axils (Noble, 1929a). Possibly maternal provision of unfertilized eggs for nutrition of tadpoles occurs in these species and also in a *Philautus* (Wassersug et al., 1981). The oophagous tadpoles of these taxa have relatively large beaks and reduced denticles (absent in *Hoplophryne).*

Interpretation of Parental Care

The most common form of parental care among amphibians is the attendance of the egg clutch by one parent. In some cases, it is known that the parent physically protects the eggs from potential predators, either by driving them away, as in the case of oophagous salamanders, or by eating various invertebrates that might devour the eggs. In these cases the parent actually is guarding the eggs. In terrestrial nests, attendant parents also may eat dead eggs that are infected with fungus, thereby reducing the chance of fungal infection of other eggs in the clutch. Protection from desiccation is afforded terrestrial eggs by the attendant parent actively moistening the eggs, as in *Dendrobates,* or passively by placing its body between the eggs and the dry substrate *(Amphiuma means)* or dry air *(Eleutherodactylus).* Osmotic transfer of water from parental tissue across egg capsules in *E. coqui* is regulated by differences in osmotic pressures of the parent and the eggs (Taigen, 1981). The term "brooding" might best be reserved for those frogs that carry eggs or tadpoles and provide gaseous exchange between parental and embryonic tissues. This applies to the egg-brooding hylids (del Pino et al., 1975) and pipids (Weygoldt, 1976b) and presumably to *Assa, Rheobatrachus,* and *Rhinoderma.*

In frogs, parental care usually is associated with small clutches, but there are some exceptions. The gladiator frogs of the *Hyla boans* group, males of which construct and defend nests, have clutch sizes within the range of variation of other *Hyla* of their size that do not exhibit parental care. Also, egg and tadpole attendance by females of *Leptodactylus ocellatus* is not correlated with a reduction in clutch size.

The duration of care for a given clutch of eggs is highly variable (Table 2-11). Salamanders generally have a much longer period of care than do frogs—possibly up to 8 months in *Bolitoglossa compacta* and to 9 months in *Dicamptodon ensatus* in cold mountain streams. Duration of care in frogs usually is no more than 1 month, but there are two notable exceptions. *Pipa pipa* may carry eggs for more than 4 months, but these develop directly into frogs. *Gastrotheca riobambae* lives in cool Andean habitats and carries eggs in the pouch for up to 4 months before they hatch into tadpoles; development and brooding can be reduced by half at warmer temperatures in the laboratory (Duellman and Maness, 1980).

The habit of gastric brooding in *Rheobatrachus silus* and *vitellinus* eliminates the possibility of feeding during brooding; the entire digestive system shuts down. Female salamanders attending clutches may feed on small organisms near the nests and on infected eggs; they also make short forays away from the nest, but brooding plethodontids in eastern North America are deprived of food in relation to conspecifics (Organ, 1961a; Krzysik, 1980). Dendrobatids actively feed while attending clutches and carrying tadpoles, and *Alytes* and egg-brooding hylids feed while carrying eggs. Little information is available on the energetic costs of egg attendance. There is a reduction in lipid content in fat bodies in *Desmognathus ochrophaeus* during 6 weeks of attendance of clutches (Fitzpatrick, 1976), thereby indicating that even if the salamanders are feeding, their caloric intake is not sufficient to maintain their normal metabolism. On the other hand, no significant caloric loss is evident in females of *Ambystoma opacum* attending eggs (Kaplan and Crump, 1978); however, at the time of attending eggs, no adults of this species are feeding.

The cost of investment in one clutch of eggs or group of larvae may have effects on frequency of reproduction. Annual or biennial reproductive cycles in salamanders are associated with long periods of maternal care. Likewise, females of *Gastrotheca* and *Pipa pipa* have an annual reproductive cycle (G. Rabb and Snedigar, 1960; del Pino, 1980b). but pipids that produce tadpoles reproduce several times a year (Sughrue, 1969; Weygoldt, 1976a). Females of *Colostethus inguinalis* produce two clutches per year (Wells, 1980a). The frequency of re-

production in females of other species of frogs exhibiting maternal care is unknown. However, paternal care of eggs or tadpoles commonly is associated with more than one clutch in a season or even more than one clutch at a time. Even in the cool forests of New Zealand, *Leiopelma archeyi* normally has two clutches each season that are attended by males (E. Stephenson and N. Stephenson, 1957). Adults of *Alytes obstetricans* breed two to four times each summer; the interval between breedings is peaked at about 1 month—the duration of egg-carrying by the males (Crespo, 1979). Males of *Dendrobates, Eleutherodactylus,* and *Centrolenella* are known to attend more than one clutch simultaneously (Drewry, 1970; Wells, 1978a; McDiarmid, 1978). Males of *Hyla rosenbergi* defend nests for only two or three nights, dur-

Table 2-11. Duration of Parental Care in Selected Salamanders and Anurans

Taxon	Sex	Days	Kind of care	Source
Salamanders				
Cryptobranchus alleganiensis[a]	♂	68–84	Aquatic nest	Bishop (1941)
Necturus maculosus[a]	♀	38–57	Aquatic nest	Bishop (1941)
Dicamptodon ensatus[a]	♀	275	Aquatic nest	Nussbaum (1969)
Leurognathus marmoratus[a]	♀	75–90	Aquatic nest	Martof (1962)
Eurycea bislineata[a]	♀	67–70	Aquatic nest	Bishop (1941)
Ambystoma opacum[a]	♀	41–52	Terrestrial nest	Bishop (1941)
Hemidactylium scutatum[a]	♀	52–60	Terrestrial nest	Bishop (1941)
Desmognathus ochrophaeus[a]	♀	52–69	Terrestrial nest	Tilley (1972)
Desmognathus aeneus	♀	±50	Terrestrial nest	J. Harrison (1967)
Bolitoglossa compacta	♀	250[b]	Terrestrial nest	Hanken (1979)
Bolitoglossa rostrata	♀	150–180	Terrestrial nest	Houck (1977a)
Bolitoglossa subpalmata	♀	120–150	Terrestrial nest	Vial (1968)
Ensatina eschscholtzii	♀	±120	Terrestrial nest	Stebbins (1954)
Plethodon cinereus	♀	60–65	Terrestrial nest	Highton and T. Savage (1961)
Plethodon vehiculum	♀	±60	Terrestrial nest	Peacock and Nussbaum (1973)
Anurans				
Adelotus brevis[a]	♂	6	Aquatic foam nest	J. Moore (1961)
Nectophryne afra[a]	♂	35	Aquatic nest	Scheel (1970)
Hyla rosenbergi[a]	♂	2–3	Aquatic nest	Kluge (1981)
Hemisus marmoratum[a]	♀	10	Terrestrial burrow	Wager (1965)
Breviceps adspersus[a]	♀	28–42	Terrestrial burrow	Wager (1965)
Leiopelma archeyi	♂	42	Terrestrial nest	E. Stephenson and N. Stephenson (1957)
Eleutherodactylus coqui	♂	17–26	Terrestrial nest	Townsend et al. (1984)
Hylactophryne augusti	♂	25–35	Terrestrial nest	Jameson (1950)
Thoropa petropolitana[a]	♂	10–12	Terrestrial nest	Heyer and Crombie (1979)
Nectophrynoides malcolmi	♂	35	Terrestrial nest	Grandison (1978)
Cophixalus parkeri	♂, ♀	85–100	Terrestrial nest	Simon (1983)
Myersiella microps	♀	29	Terrestrial nest	Izecksohn et al. (1971)
Dendrobates auratus[a]	♂	10–13	Terrestrial nest	Wells (1978a)
Dendrobates pumilio[a]	♂	10–12	Terrestrial nest	Weygoldt (1980)
	♀	42–56	Ovipositing for tadpoles	Weygoldt (1980)
Platypelis grandis[a]	♂	35	Eggs and tadpoles in tree hole	Blommers-Schlösser (1975b)
Plethodontohyla notosticta[a]	♂	28	Eggs and tadpoles in tree hole	Blommers-Schlösser (1975b)
Anodonthyla boulengeri[a]	♂	26	Eggs and tadpoles in tree hole	Blommers-Schlösser (1975b)
Alytes obstetricans[a]	♂	30	Eggs on hindlimbs	Crespo (1979)
Pipa carvalhoi[a]	♀	14–28	Eggs on dorsum	Weygoldt (1976a)
Pipa parva[a]	♀	30	Eggs on dorsum	Sughrue (1969)
Pipa pipa	♀	77–136	Eggs on dorsum	G. Rabb and Snedigar (1960)
Flectonotus pygmaeus[a]	♀	24–25	Eggs in pouch	Duellman and Maness (1980)
Gastrotheca riobambae[a]	♀	103–120	Eggs in pouch	del Pino et al. (1975)
Rheobatrachus silus	♀	37+	Eggs and tadpoles in stomach	Corben et al. (1974)
Assa darlingtoni	♂	7+	Tadpoles in pouch	G. Ingram et al. (1975)
Colostethus inguinalis[a]	♀	8–9	Tadpoles on dorsum	Wells (1980a)

[a]Aquatic larvae. [b]Laboratory; female not in attendance.

ing which time they do not breed; this interval of not advertising may reduce a male's chances for a successive mating (Kluge, 1981).

Communal nests, composed of eggs deposited by several females, are known in the bufonid *Nectophrynoides malcolmi* attended by a male and in the plethodontids *Batrachoseps attenuatus* and *Hemidactylium scutatum* attended by females. There is no evidence that the attending male *Nectophrynoides* is the parent of all clutches that he attends (Grandison, 1978). Aggregations of females of the microhylid frog *Sphenophryne mehelyi* attend their individual clutches of eggs (Tyler, 1967). The factors contributing to egg attendance at communal nests are not known. R. Harris and Gill (1980) suggested that successively intruding females of *Hemidactylium* could drive away and eat some existing eggs prior to ovipositing, but the selective advantages of such a behavior seem to be obscure. The communal sites for terrestrial species such as *Sphenophryne mehelyi* may provide better physical conditions than surrounding areas. *Rana sylvatica* deposits eggs in ponds, but does not attend the clutches. Most clutches are deposited communally; eggs transplanted into a pond before oviposition had begun there resulted in all subsequent egg deposition at the site of the introduced eggs (R. W. Howard, 1980).

Among frogs, paternal care is most noticeable in territorial species: dendrobatids, some *Eleutherodactylus*, some *Centrolenella*, and gladiator frogs (*Hyla boans* group). A male that defends a restricted territory can provide care for egg clutches with little additional investment. In dendrobatid frogs, different parental care is affected by males and females with respect to territorial behavior by the sexes. As emphasized by Wells (1981a), a frog transporting tadpoles is unlikely to defend a territory. Thus, in those species in which the male is highly territorial and may attend the eggs, it is the female that transports the tadpoles to water. In other species, females are territorial, and the male transports the tadpoles. Males of *Assa* and *Rhinoderma* brood tadpoles, but it is unknown if they are territorial. Egg-brooding by hylids, pipids, and *Rheobatrachus* is accomplished by females and apparently is unrelated to territoriality. With the exception of *Nectophrynoides malcolmi* and *Eleutherodactylus coqui*, in which fertilization is internal and males attend clutches, all known cases of parental care in anurans are associated with external fertilization; either sex may provide care. The only known instances of paternal care in salamanders are species that have external fertilization. Only maternal care is known in caecilians and in salamanders with internal fertilization; in these groups, oviposition may occur several months after mating.

Various hypotheses have been proposed to explain the evolution of maternal versus paternal care (see Gross and Shine, 1981, and Wells, 1981a, for reviews). G. Williams (1975) proposed that association with the developing embryos preadapts a sex for parental care. Thus, in those groups having internal fertilization, it is usually the female that is associated with the young; paternal care most often is associated with external fertilization, especially when fertilization and oviposition occur in the male's territory. This hypothesis is generally and broadly applicable to amphibians. The numerous apparent exceptions may be owing to our limited knowledge of parental care and territorial behavior, especially among anurans.

A high degree of paternal investment in care of eggs or young may lead to a reversal of the usual sex roles. The behavior in *Dendrobates auratus* is consistent with the idea of sex-role reversal; males are not territorial, attend eggs, and transport larvae, and females compete for males and produce small clutches at frequent intervals (Wells, 1978a, 1981a). Other anurans may exhibit sex role reversal, but there is no evidence for it. Attendance of eggs and transportation of larvae are restricted to males in *Assa darlingtoni* and in the two species of *Rhinoderma*, but the roles of females in these species are not known.

EVOLUTION OF REPRODUCTIVE STRATEGIES

Theories on the evolution of life-history phenomena and reproductive strategies have been expanded over the years to encompass not only fecundity but trophic level, demography, survivorship, and environmental predictability (see L. Cole, 1954; Stearns, 1976; and Wilbur et al., 1974, for reviews). Wilbur (1977a:43) summarized the ideas, as follows: "A 'reproductive strategy' is a set of 'tactics' that has been selected as the adaptations that have contributed, on the average, the greatest number of offspring to recent generations. Each strategy involves compromises in the allocation of resources between current reproduction and the potential for future reproduction. The benefit of current reproduction is balanced by its cost to adult growth, future fecundity, and adult survival. The cost may involve the direct mortality risks of current reproduction or the long-term reduction in adult longevity incurred by shifting resources from maintenance and growth to current breeding demands."

As emphasized by Crump (1982), a major factor in reproductive strategies is the predictability of the environment relative to each stage of the life history. Organisms with complex life cycles demonstrate contrasting reproductive responses in stable versus fluctuating environments, depending upon which stage is affected by the environmental instability. Thus, from theory on reproductive strategies, the general predictions are that in stable environments (1) late maturity, (2) multiple clutches, (3) fewer but larger eggs, (4) parental care, and (5) small reproductive efforts should be favored, whereas in fluctuating environments the opposite correlates should obtain. The former is the classical K-selection and the latter is r-selection in the sense of MacArthur and E. Wilson (1967) and Pianka (1970). However, life history patterns may vary depending upon age-specific mortality. If the environment of juvenile stages is unstable, resulting in high and/or unpredictable mortality, different strategies will be favored than in environments that are uncertain for adults, resulting in high and/or unpredictable mortality at that stage (see B. Low, 1976, for application to amphibians). High reproductive success in one season may result in greater density of adults in the following, or subsequent, season, in which case male-male interactions may be intensified and resources for successful reproduction may be limited.

Differences in patterns of egg deposition, fecundity, and parental investment of sympatric species of *Ambystoma* have been interpreted as adaptations to adult survival (Wilbur, 1977a). According to his analysis of populations in southern Michigan, *Ambystoma tigrinum* deposits eggs in several small clumps, in ponds that are usually permanent. Larval survivorship is relatively constant and high, but adult survivorship is low. Thus, high reproductive output is favored, and the species matures early and has high fecundity. *Ambystoma maculatum* deposits eggs in a single mass in semipermanent ponds; larval survivorship is variable, but adult survivorship is high. Therefore, it is advantageous for a female to reproduce many times; females have a relatively low reproductive effort each year but reproduce more times during a lifetime and thereby compensate for uncertain larval survivorship. *Ambystoma laterale* deposits small eggs singly in the most temporary ponds. This species has the highest reproductive effort relative to body size and has sacrificed egg size for increased fecundity. The larvae develop rapidly and metamorphose over a wide range of body sizes—an adaptation to unpredictable environments. Wilbur's model applies to populations of *A. maculatum* in Connecticut, where females breeding in permanent ponds produce more, but smaller, eggs than those breeding in temporary ponds (Woodward, 1982a). However, Kaplan and Salthe (1979) showed that smaller salamanders devote proportionately more body volume to eggs than larger salamanders; thus, Wilbur's conclusions are tenuous.

Similar adaptive modifications exist among hylid frogs in humid tropical forests (Duellman, 1978; Crump and Kaplan, 1979). In the upper Amazon Basin, most hylids breed at ponds that are subject to fluctuation in water level. Probably all of the species deposit clutches several times during the year. Species such as *Hyla parviceps,* *H. rhodopepla, Ololygon cruentomma, O. garbei,* and *O. rubra* deposit relatively large clutches in temporary ponds. Others such as *Hyla bifurca, H. sarayacuensis,* *H. triangulum, Phyllomedusa palliata,* and *P. tarsius* deposit smaller clutches on vegetation over the water. The eggs of the latter group are larger, have a higher caloric content, and hatch into larger, more advanced tadpoles. The deposition of arboreal eggs may be viewed as an adaptation to avoid the uncertainty of the aquatic environment during the period of egg development; furthermore, the placement of a larger hatchling in the larval environment may be advantageous in that the tadpole must spend less time there in order to reach metamorphosis. In the species that deposit their eggs on vegetation, clutch size has been sacrificed for increased egg size.

Early age at first reproduction usually is an indication of fluctuating or low juvenile survivorship, uncertain breeding conditions, and/or fluctuating population densities. Notable differences in life-history patterns obtain in lowland versus highland populations of *Rana pretiosa* (L. Licht, 1975). In the lowlands, where the entire reproductive effort may be lost in any given year because of drought, the females mature in 1–2 years and breed annually. At high elevations, where the environment is more certain but colder with a shorter season of activity, females require 5–6 years to mature and breed every 2–3 years. Coastal populations of newts, *Notophthalmus viridescens,* live in harsh, unstable environments compared to inland populations. The latter have a terrestrial eft stage and delay maturity until an age of 4–8 years, whereas in the coastal populations the eft stage is omitted and maturity occurs in 2 years. This difference has been interpreted as a high degree of r-selection on coastal populations (Healy, 1974); however, the difference could result from proximate environmental effects. In the aquatic plethodontid *Gyrinophilus porphyriticus,* selection has favored earlier maturity and higher size-specific fecundity in populations at low elevations subject to greater climatic fluctuation than in populations in more certain environments at higher elevations (Bruce, 1972a). Populations of *Desmognathus ochrophaeus* differ in age at first reproduction in contrasting environments (Tilley, 1973). In comparison with populations at low elevations, those at high elevations have delayed maturity accompanied by larger body size and concomitant increased age-specific fecundity.

Populations living in a fluctuating environment may be variable in their life-history strategies. The irregular breeding cycle of *Pseudotriton montanus* in the Piedmont of South Carolina may be an adaptation that favors longevity and provides for iteroparity while allowing for high fecundity (Bruce, 1975). In parts of California characterized by a variable dry season, the small fossorial salamander *Batrachoseps attenuatus* is highly flexible in its life-history strategy (Maiorana, 1976). These salamanders maximize their reproductive effort per lifetime by regulating clutch size and timing deposition according to seasonal fluctuations and available energy.

In nearly all amphibian populations that have been studied, predation pressure on eggs and larvae is high, and juvenile mortality fluctuates more than adult mortality. In situations where larval survivorship varies unpredictably in time, multiple small clutches are favored, because this strategy decreases the chances of total failure for a given breeding period. Thus, in such situations, selection favors the production of small numbers of offspring at various times or places, instead of the synchronous production of a larger number of offspring.

However, the reproductive strategies of amphibians are closely associated with general environmental conditions. Because of seasonal limitations in temperate and wet-dry tropical regions, breeding patterns are synchronous in most species. There is limited opportunity for multiple clutches in time, but females may scatter their eggs. In aseasonal, humid, tropical environments, breeding can be more or less continuous, and multiple small clutches provide a means of reducing reproductive effort per clutch and at the same time enhancing survivorship of the early stages by placing eggs in different places at different times.

One aspect of time to maturity often is overlooked. In amphibians, absolute age is not a reasonable criterion when comparing tropical with temperate species. A frog in an equatorial rainforest may reach sexual maturity in 1 year, whereas a frog of similar size in a midlatitude

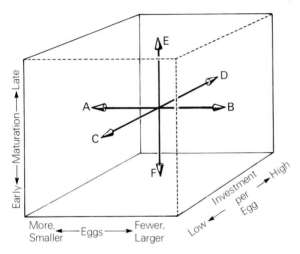

Figure 2-20. Relationship among number and sizes of eggs, investment per egg, and demography. Line A-B is the combination of egg number and egg size, line C-D is the energy allocation per egg, and line E-F is the combination of age at first reproduction and reproductive life span. See text for further explanation.

temperate region may require 2 years. However, the second frog may been inactive for 6 months of each year; therefore, in terms of actual time of active feeding and growth the two frogs are the same age. Furthermore, the reproductive life span must be considered.

Obviously, reproductive strategies are compromises among various selective pressures. Consideration of the interrelationships of selection for early versus late maturity, more and smaller versus fewer and larger eggs, and low versus high investment per egg (Fig. 2-20) presents a general view of reproductive strategies. A shift into the area A-C-E involves an increase in clutch size brought about by low investment per egg and late maturity. In the opposite area (B-D-F), clutches are small with a high investment per egg in early-maturing species. This model is applicable to comparisons among groups of closely related species or populations of the same species existing under different selective pressures. Likewise, we can compare diverse groups of amphibians in a general way. Viewing all amphibians in the model, we see that not all of the areas are filled equally. The area B-D-F is occupied by dendrobatid frogs and *Eleutherodactylus,* among others, whereas terrestrial plethodontid salamanders tend more toward the area B-D-E. Most *Hyla* and *Bufo* and deserticolous anurans like *Scaphiopus* are in the area A-C-F, whereas *Rana* tends more to the area A-C-E with tropical species in A-C-F and some stream-breeding species in B-D-E. As a group, *Ambystoma* are in the area B-C-F, and large aquatic salamanders *(Cryptobranchus* and *Necturus)* are in the area B-D-E. The relative positions of various species with respect to aspects of their reproductive strategies are an indication of the kinds of past and present selective pressures on the species (Fig. 2-21).

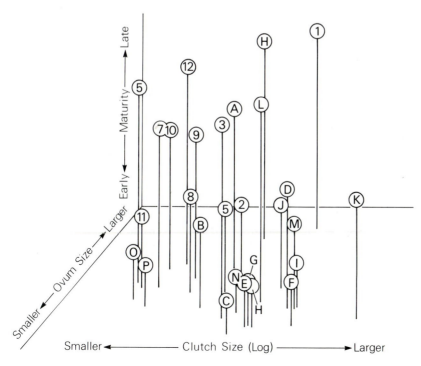

Figure 2-21. Three-dimensional plot of factors in life history strategies. Numbers are salamanders: 1. *Cryptobranchus alleganiensis,* 2. *Siren intermedia,* 3. *Triturus vulgaris,* 4. *Necturus maculosus,* 5. *Ambystoma tigrinum,* 6. *Rhyacotriton olympicus,* 7. *Desmognathus ochrophaeus,* 8. *Hemidactylium scutatum,* 9. *Bolitoglossa rostrata,* 10. *Plethodon cinereus,* 11. *Plethodon glutinosus.* Letters are anurans: A. *Ascaphus truei,* B. *Bombina bombina,* C. *Hymenochirus boettgeri,* D. *Bufo canorus,* E. *Bufo quercicus,* F. *Bufo valliceps,* G. *Hyla cinerea,* H. *Hyla crucifer,* I. *Hyla rosenbergi,* J. *Rana aurora,* K. *Rana catebeiana,* L. *Rana pretiosa,* M. *Rana sylvatica,* N. *Megistolotis lignarius,* O. *Phyllobates terribilis,* P. *Eleutherodactylus planirostris.* All are mean values.

The adaptive radiation of reproductive strategies is closely associated with the environmental histories of the groups. The life histories of generalized hynobiids may be viewed as the primitive reproductive pattern in salamanders. The deposition of numerous small eggs in ponds with subsequent fertilization limited the dispersal of salamanders. The adaptation of placing eggs in streams still had restrictions, because of inadequate means of fertilization, until the development of the spermatophore, which allowed for the deposition of eggs on preexisting sperm. Subsequent evolution of the female behavior in picking up the spermatophore opened a vast array of reproductive possibilities—increased assurance of fertilization of eggs no matter where or when they were deposited. With the advent of the spermatophore, sexual cycles could vary independently of breeding patterns, thereby resulting in adaptation to diverse environments. Occupation of moist, montane habitats probably was a precursor to the deposition of terrestrial eggs with concomitant female attendance. We can see in living species of plethodontids a continuum from small aquatic eggs that hatch into larvae requiring many months to metamorphosis, through larger eggs with short larval spans and still larger eggs with nonfeeding larvae, to large terrestrial eggs that develop directly into small salamanders. Only with internal fertilization was it possible for ovoviviparity and viviparity to evolve in salamandrids. It is surprising that these modes are so limited in salamanders.

Somewhere in their early evolution, caecilians presumably evolved internal fertilization. Their subsequent reproductive adaptations have involved the specialization of viviparity, which is associated with early maturity, long development time, low fecundity, and long adult survivorship.

Anurans presumably originated and underwent their major adaptive radiation in the humid tropics. The primitive life history probably was the deposition of a single clutch of eggs in ponds, where larvae developed. Permanent aquatic sites harbored many predators on both eggs and larvae. Modifications in life histories to avoid this predation included the placement of eggs in temporary ponds, which provided a highly uncertain environment for eggs and larvae. Deposition of numerous smaller clutches enhanced the probability of loss of all of the eggs. By placing eggs on vegetation above ponds, survivorship of the eggs was increased, and by increasing egg size (at the expense of the number of eggs), a greater proportion of the development took place in the egg, thereby shortening the time that the larva must spend in an uncertain environment. Escape from the exigencies of the aquatic environment was accomplished by packaging reproductive energy into a few large eggs that provided the caloric content necessary to carry the egg through to metamorphosis without depending upon a feeding larval stage. Many intermediate evolutionary steps are found among living anurans that have terrestrial eggs, some of which hatch as tadpoles that complete their development in water and others that do not feed and complete their development in the nest. In many cases these modes are associated with obligatory parental care. The evolution of these reproductive modes was possible in environments such as lowland tropical rainforest or humid montane forest having high atmospheric humidity. In the latter, frogs also developed modifications of oviposition and larvae for stream habitats.

Dispersal into seasonally dry tropical regions and into temperate regions necessitated other kinds of modifications in the reproduction of anurans. Sexual cycles became seasonal, and innate timing was required so that the frogs were ready to breed when the environment permitted. In predictably seasonal areas, the most notable strategy is to deposit many small eggs that develop rapidly into small offspring that can leave water at an early age. In areas where temporary ponds are of longer duration, reproductive effort can be divided into more than one clutch. The habit of depositing eggs in a foam nest is another adaptation to avoid desiccation of the eggs. In temperate regions where reproduction is limited by temperature, the general trend is to retain the generalized reproductive mode of egg and tadpole development in ponds. The major variation on this theme relates to size and fecundity, that is, large females depositing many thousands of small eggs versus fewer larger eggs resulting in larger hatchlings that spend less time in the water.

Within these general evolutionary trends in anurans there are many specializations restricted to a few species (e.g., stomach brooding and carrying tadpoles in pouches), and there are some deviations that are counter to general trends (e.g., nonfeeding tadpoles in terrestrial foam nests in humid regions). However, the major trend is clear—increased terrestriality. The available information on anuran life histories clearly shows that this evolutionary trend occurred independently in many groups of anurans. Despite the general absence of internal fertilization, many anurans have succeeded in divorcing their life histories from the aquatic environment.

The evolution of diverse reproductive strategies in amphibians is an example of many success stories. Many evolutionary experiments in amphibian life histories probably have been abandoned and their proponents are now extinct. A few probably remain to be discovered. The important thing is that amphibians have adopted diverse life-history strategies contingent upon their environmental regimes, and that the diversity of these strategies among the group as a whole and their flexibility within species and even within populations are reflected in the evolutionary and ecological diversity of amphibians, the pioneers of the terrestrial environment.

CHAPTER 3

Courtship and Mating

If it is not small enough to eat nor large enough to eat you, and does not put up a squawk about it, mate with it.

David L. Jameson (1955b)

Successful propagation of an individual's genes depends on the location of potential mates, stimulation of mates, selection of breeding site, fertilization of the eggs, and development of the eggs and young. Location of mates may be by visual, olfactory, auditory, or tactile means, or a combination of these. In some vertebrates, mating occurs with little or no specialized behavior, whereas in other groups, especially those characterized by complex, social interactions, diverse kinds of courtship are an integral part of mating and mate selection. Generally, during courtship, males are the more aggressive sex, and their courtship activities depend on female response.

In Chapter 2, the evolution of reproductive strategies was examined; here the concern is more with the interactions among individuals: (1) How do individuals locate breeding sites and mates? (2) What are the courtship behaviors? (3) How are mates selected, and what factors contribute to mating success? (4) Where are eggs deposited and how are they fertilized? These various aspects of reproduction differ not only along taxonomic lines and in different environments but also to some degree at different densities within populations.

LOCATION OF BREEDING SITE

Many amphibians, especially those that have terrestrial eggs, carry out courtship and reproductive activities within their normal home ranges; in these species, there is no congregation of individuals at particular breeding sites. This also may be true for anurans that live along mountain streams in cloud forests; the frogs are there throughout the year. On the other hand, most amphibians that deposit eggs in (or above) ponds and some that breed in streams congregate for breeding. In some instances, migrations to breeding sites cover distances up to several kilometers. The factors that initiate these movements have been discussed in Chapter 2, but here the emphasis is on the methods used by amphibians to locate breeding sites, including auditory, olfactory, and visual cues, as well as geotactic and hygrotactic stimuli.

Auditory Cues

Vocalizations clearly attract anurans to breeding sites, and there is growing experimental evidence to support auditory orientation in anurans (see Chapter 4 for details of auditory reception and response). Receptive females and males of *Bufo terrestris* responded positively at distances up to 40 m to a recording of a conspecific chorus (Bogert, 1960). Male chorus frogs, *Pseudacris triseriata,* orient at distances of 50–75 m to natural and recorded choruses (Landreth and Ferguson, 1966). An advertisement call is absent in *B. boreas,* but males and females moved toward a recording of male release calls at night (Tracy and Dole, 1969).

Although vocalization may play a role in directional movements to a breeding site in many kinds of anurans, other factors may predominate. Certainly the first calling individuals must locate the site by other cues. Furthermore, movements toward a breeding site have been observed at distances far beyond the presumed audible range of the chorus.

Olfactory Cues

Considerable evidence supports the use of olfaction in migration to breeding sites by anurans and salamanders. Odors given off by algal blooms are suspected to be the major factor in the initiation and orientation of breeding migrations in *Rana temporia* (R. Savage, 1961). Martof (1962a) placed *Pseudacris triseriata* in a T-maze and found that 71% of the individuals moved toward odors from the breeding site rather than toward odors from upland forest. Green frogs, *R. clamitans,* demonstrate directional movement to breeding sites at distances up to 550 m; this homing response is not impaired significantly by the absence of auditory, visual, hygrotactic, or geotactic stimuli, but it is reduced significantly by the ablation of the olfactory receptors (Oldham, 1967). Odor seems to be the major factor in orientation and movement in *R. pipiens;* blinded individuals orient and move toward breeding sites, as do normal frogs at distances up to 800 m (Dole, 1968).

Extensive experiments on the terrestrial newt, *Taricha rivularis,* indicate that odor is an important but not exclusive factor in orientation (Twitty, 1961, 1966; Twitty et al., 1967). Newts that were displaced 3–4 km returned to the home segment of the breeding stream before or during the next breeding season, and some individuals displaced 8 km were found in the original breeding stream the next year. Newts normally confine their breeding migration to one watershed, so homing from points beyond the stream system cannot be based on familiarity with the sites of release. Blinded newts home successfully, but those in which a section of the olfactory nerve had been removed did not home successfully until the nerve regenerated (D. Grant et al., 1968). Similar experimental results were obtained with normal, blinded, and olfactorectomized *Plethodon jordani* (Madison, 1969).

Visual Cues

Amphibians can orient to a particular compass direction when provided with celestial cues. An internal clocking mechanism presumably compensates for variations in the positions of the celestial bodies (Ferguson, 1967). The sun seems to be the most commonly used celestial cue, but ability to orient to stellar patterns or the moon is indicated in some frogs (*Acris gryllus* and *Rana catesbeiana*). Most demonstrations of this kind of mechanism have dealt with Y-axis orientation, in which a displaced animal orients in a direction at right angles to the home shoreline. The fact that blinded animals can orient to celestial cues indicates that extraoptic receptors are important (Ferguson and Landreth, 1967; D. Taylor and

Ferguson, 1970). The pineal body has been shown to be a functional photoreceptor, and covering the pineal area results in disorientation (K. Adler, 1970; D. Taylor and Ferguson, 1970).

Most migrations take place on rainy or overcast nights. Although initial orientation before sunset may influence the direction of migration, celestial cues probably are not important in long-distance migrations by amphibians in one night.

Other Factors

Geotactic and hygrotactic responses may be important in migrations, especially because breeding sites situated in depressions usually have a humidity gradient. However, such factors can be of little importance in long-distance migrations during which animals move uphill or away from one watershed to another, or cross open fields between forested areas. Furthermore, individuals often enter and leave a breeding site by the same path (Shoop, 1965a, 1968; Hardy and Raymond, 1980) or return to the same site year after year (Twitty, 1961; Oldham, 1967). A strong attachment to a particular breeding site is known in several species, and cases exist of individuals returning to the site of a pond after it has been obliterated, as for *Bufo bufo* (Heusser, 1960) and *Ambystoma talpoideum* (Shoop, 1968). Likewise, efts of *Notophthalmus viridescens,* after 2 to 4 years on land, usually return to the pond where they developed as larvae, even though other ponds are available (Hurlbert, 1969), and adults return to the same ponds yearly for breeding (Gill, 1978).

Although one factor may predominate in the orientation of a given species under certain circumstances, different factors may be important under other conditions, or one set of cues may replace another during long-distance movements. Thus, species of anurans making long-distance migrations may depend initially on celestial or olfactory cues until within auditory range of a breeding chorus. Also, some species may utilize several cues simultaneously; no single sensory cue (olfactory, visual, auditory, geotactic, or hygrotactic) is essential to orientation in *Bufo bufo,* but each may contribute to orientation (Heusser, 1960). Thus, a wide range of cues may be important in movements to breeding sites, but the relative contribution of each of these factors to breeding migrations is poorly understood.

SECONDARY SEXUAL CHARACTERS

In addition to the reproductive organs and their associated tracts, external sexual differences exist in most amphibians, including size, glandular development, skin texture, dermal ornamentation, vocal sacs, and coloration. Some differences persist throughout adult life, but others develop in response to gonadotropic hormones and therefore are present only during the active reproductive cycle. Some structures are used in courtship and others, for holding the pair in an embrace during mating or oviposition. The nature of sexually dimorphic characters is sufficiently different in the three groups of amphibians that the groups are best treated separately.

Caecilians

External sexual differences are lacking in most caecilians. In some aquatic typhlonectids, the anal region of the male is modified to form a circular depression, which E. Taylor (1968) thought could serve as a suction mechanism to facilitate copulation in water. However, in observed copulations in two typhlonectid genera—*Chthonerpeton* (Barrio, 1969) and *Typhlonectes* (Murphy et al., 1977)—the male is not attached to the female other than by the insertion of the phallodeum. Nevertheless, strong sexual dimorphism exists in the anal region of typhlonectids of the genus *Potomotyphlus;* E. Taylor (1968:18) suggested that "this area seemingly becomes a clasper, in the males being enlarged and capable of partly or wholly grasping this area in the females." This has yet to be confirmed by observation.

Salamanders

Sexual dimorphism in size of most salamanders is not great. Usually females are slightly larger-than males, but the sexes are about the same size in many species. Males are larger than females in a few species (Shine, 1979). Generally, larger body size in females has been thought to be related to egg-carrying capacity, because there is a positive correlation between female body size and clutch size. Shine (1979) interpreted large body size in males as an advantage for combat between males.

During the breeding season, the vents of males become swollen (Fig. 3-1); lobes form lateral to the vent in ambystomatids and posterior to the vent in some plethodontids. The swelling results from enlargement of the cloacal glands; the villi of the glands are visible in the cloacal aperture of some species. The enlargement of the cloacal glands is controlled by testicular hormones (Noble and Pope, 1929).

Males and females of some salamandrids, especially *Taricha* and *Cynops,* have rough skin when not breeding, but develop smooth skin during the breeding season. Presumably the skin texture functions in recognition of potentially receptive mates in these salamanders, in which many males congregate around and attempt to grasp a female.

Males of some aquatic salamanders, and also males of terrestrial salamanders that breed in water, especially ponds, develop more extensive caudal and (in newts) dorsal fins during the breeding season. This characteristic is most notable in *Triturus* (Halliday, 1977) (Fig. 3-2), but also occurs in others, such as *Notophthalmus viridescens* (Bishop, 1941) and *Ambystoma talpoideum* (Shoop, 1960). The fins in *Ambystoma* appear to function in creating disturbances in the water during tail-wav-

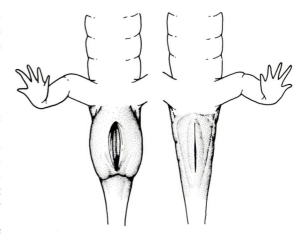

Figure 3-1. Cloacal regions of *Ambystoma jeffersonianum* showing swollen glandular area around vent and cloacal papillae in male (left) and unswollen cloacal area of female (right).

Figure 3-2. Sexual differences in fin structure and coloration in newts, *Triturus cristatus;* male above, female below.

ing. In *Triturus* this habit is combined with the development of bright colors, especially on the fins, during the breeding season; thus, the increased surface area and more extensive coloration seem to have coevolved as effective means of species recognition and provision of visual, chemosensory, and tactile cues during courtship. Although some workers have indicated an increase in color intensity, such as the spots in male *A. maculatum* and *A. tigrinum,* there is no evidence that these colors are important in sexual recognition. However, during the mating season, male *Hynobius nebulosus* develop a white gular patch, which is exposed by lifting the head and pulsating the throat in the presence of a female (Thorn, 1967).

Males of plethodontids, ambystomatids, and some salamandrids develop courtship glands (Fig. 3-3). These were termed "hedonic" glands by Noble (1927a) and most subsequent authors, but as noted by Arnold (1977:152): "Whatever functions these glands have, we will never know if they are hedonic (pleasure giving)." A series of genial glands is present in the temporal region of the head

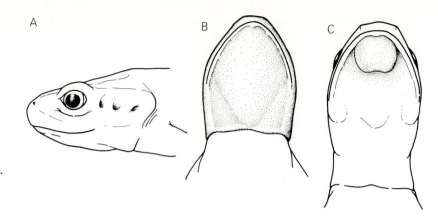

Figure 3-3. Head glands of male salamanders.
A. Genial glands on side of head of
Notophthalmus viridescens. **B.** Diffuse
submandibular glands of *Taricha torosa.*
C. Mental gland of *Pseudoeurycea smithii.*

in male *Notophthalmus* (Hilton, 1902), and other glands are present on the side of the neck and in the scapular region in *Cynops pyrrhogaster* (Tsutsui, 1931). Submandibular glands are present in male *Taricha* (R. Smith, 1941). Most male plethodontids have circular mental glands on the chin (Trufelli, 1954). Glands also are present on the sides of the head in some plethodontids (Noble, 1929b) and on the base of the tail and/or on the posterodorsal part of the body (Baird, 1951). Glands at the base of the tail also are known in some *Ambystoma* (Shoop, 1960). All of these glands come in contact with the female during courtship. The development of at least the mental and body glands is influenced by testicular hormones (Noble, 1931a; Sever, 1976).

Plethodontid salamanders exhibit sexual dimorphism in the number, size, and structure of the premaxillary teeth. In males, these are elongate, even protruding through the lip (Fig. 3-4). In males of *Desmognathus* and *Eurycea,* the premaxillary teeth are monocuspid, at least during the mating season (Stewart, 1958); females and nonbreeding males have bicuspid teeth. The development of elongate, monocuspid teeth is mediated by testicular hormones (Noble and Pope, 1929). During courtship the male uses the elongated premaxillary teeth to deliver secretions from the mental glands (Arnold, 1977).

Plethodontids also have a pair of nasolabial grooves; during the breeding season the margin of the lip encompassing the terminus of each groove becomes elongated into a cirrus in male plethodontines, but the nasolabial protuberances remain enlarged throughout the year in bolitoglossines. In male *Ensatina,* the entire upper lip becomes enlarged in the breeding season. Presumably the enlarged sensory tracts facilitate olfactory trailing of females by males and avoidance of tracts made by other males (R. Jaeger and Gergits, 1979).

In those salamanders having prolonged periods of capture, nuptial excrescences, consisting of keratinized epidermis, appear on the inner surfaces of the limbs of males during the mating season; also, the musculature of the appropriate limbs becomes hypertrophied. Nuptial adspersities are present on the hindlimbs of *Notophthalmus,*

Figure 3-4. Adult male of *Pseudoeurycea bellii* in breeding condition showing enlarged cirri and elongate premaxillary teeth protruding through upper lip.

and the forelimbs of *Pleurodeles* and *Taricha,* and on the chest and forelimbs of *Onychodactylus* in the breeding season (Fig. 3-5). Keratinized tubercles also appear on the venter in *Taricha.* These keratinized structures function in maintaining a grip on the female.

Anurans

As in salamanders, female frogs usually are larger than males, and sexual size dimorphism is great in some frogs. Females with body lengths 1.5 times the lengths of males are common in *Eleutherodactylus;* in some *Rana* (e.g., *R. andersonii),* males are only about half the length of females (Liu, 1936). However, in some species, males are equal to or slightly larger than females. Shine (1979) analyzed size dimorphism and found significant correlations between large size in males (relative to females) and (1) male-male combat and (2) presence of tusks or spines in males; he concluded that selection favored larger males in species having aggressive behavior.

Spines and Tusks. Spines or tusks are present in males of many species (Fig. 3-6). The best-documented cases of the use of spines in combat is in the gladiator frogs of the *Hyla boans* group, in which males defend their nests by grappling. Fatal wounds are inflicted by puncturing opponents with the sharp prepollical spines during wrestling bouts; this combat has been observed in *Hyla faber* (B. Lutz, 1960) and *H. rosenbergi* (Kluge, 1981). Also, use of prepollical spines has been observed in aggressive bouts between males of *Leptodactylus pentadactylus* (Rivero and Esteves, 1969). Males of the *Hyla albomarginata, granosa,* and *miliaria* groups also have projecting prepollical spines, as do males of the microhylid *Hoplophryne rogersi,* but there are no observations of combat in these frogs. Single or bifid prepollical spines are present in both sexes in species of *Plectrohyla,* but they are best developed in males, which are larger than females. Many adult male *Plectrohyla* have numerous scars, perhaps resulting from wounds received during combat with other males. Projecting spines from the proximal end of the humerus are present in males of many species of centro-

lenid frogs. Limited observations (McDiarmid, 1975; Duellman and Savitzky, 1976) indicate that male-male combat in species of *Centrolenella* involve grappling and hooking of an opponent with a humeral spine. The Papuan hylid *Nyctimystes humeralis* also has humeral spines in the male (Zweifel, 1958), and perhaps it too engages in combat.

Sharp odontoids or tusks on the lower jaw occur in both sexes of several kinds of frogs, especially carnivorous types such as *Ceratobatrachus, Hemiphractus,* and *Pyxicephalus.* Tusks are present in both sexes of the Brazilian hylid *Phyllodytes luteolus;* the much larger tusks of males are used in biting other males during combat (Weygoldt, 1981). Similarly, the tusks are much larger in males than in females of *Adelotus brevis,* an Australian myobatrachid. Males call from the midst of floating foam nests; the sexual dimorphism suggests that males may use the large tusks in defense of their nests. A similar dimorphic condition exists in the African ranid *Dimorphognathus africanus,* in which the maxillary teeth in females are moderately long and bicuspid; those in males are long and monocuspid. However, no information exists on differential use of teeth. Three species of the Oriental pelobatid genus *Leptobrachium* are unique in having a row of cornified labial spines in males (Liu, 1950;

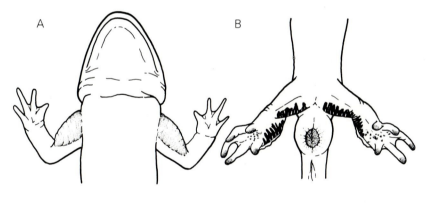

Figure 3-5. Nuptial excrescences in salamanders. **A.** Forelimbs of *Pleurodeles waltl.* **B.** Hindlimbs of *Notophthalmus viridescens.*

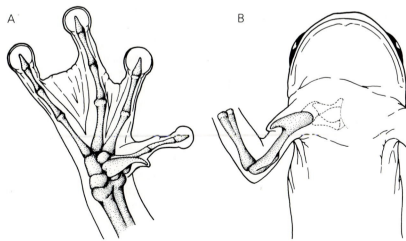

Figure 3-6. Spines on limbs of male anurans. **A.** Prepollical spine of *Hyla rosenbergi.* **B.** Humeral spine of *Centrolenella buckleyi.* Bones are stippled.

Dubois, 1980). The presence of spines (Fig. 3-7), in combination with the larger size of males compared with females, suggests the use of the spines in aggressive behavior.

Nuptial Excrescences. The most notable secondary sexual characters in anurans, except for vocal sacs, are the nuptial excrescences on the prepollices of males during the breeding season. It has been well established that the development of nuptial excrescences is influenced by testicular hormones (Greenberg, 1941; Cei, 1944), and seasonal variation in development as correlated with reproductive activities has been demonstrated by Inger and Greenberg (1956, 1963). The nuptial excrescences consist of modified dermal and epidermal tissues. The outer layer of the corium has small, conical protuberances, over which the stratum germinativum of the epidermis is thickened into a cornified covering which may be simply rugose or modified into cones or spines that usually are densely pigmented with melanin. Large mucous glands are imbedded in the corium. If present, these excrescences always are on the median surface of the prepollex.

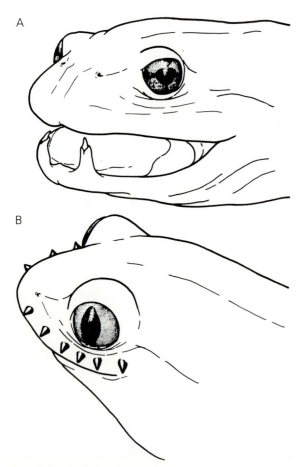

A

B

Figure 3-7. Tusks and spines of male frogs. **A.** Enlarged mandibular odontoids of *Adelotus brevis.* **B.** Labial spines of *Leptobrachium (Vibrissaphora) boringii* (modified from Liu, 1950).

In some frogs, they extend distally on the thumb and also may be present on the median or dorsal surfaces of the second and third fingers and/or on the ventromedial surface of the forearm; *Bombina* also has nuptial excrescences on its feet.

Most frogs that amplex on land or on vegetation either lack or have minimally developed excrescences. Nuptial excrescences are nearly universal in frogs that amplex in water, and they are best developed in species that breed in streams. Furthermore, males of many stream-breeding species have large clusters of spines on the prepollex, and some have excrescences or spines on the chest (Fig. 3-8). Pectoral spines also are present in some large species of pond-breeding *Leptodactylus.* Extensively developed nuptial excrescences commonly are accompanied by greatly hypertrophied forelimbs (Fig. 3-9). The increased muscle masses are anchored to broadened flanges on the humerus, as in some species of *Leptodactylus* (J. D. Lynch, 1971) and hylids such as *Plectrohyla* (Duellman, 1970). Nuptial excrescences obviously are associated with amplexus, but they also may play a role in male-male combat. The extent and spinosity of the excrescences seem to be correlated with the difficulty of maintaining amplexus, which presumably is most difficult in torrential streams. Nuptial excrescences also may be important in males holding on to mates when other males are trying to dislodge them (Wells, 1977a). Females of *Insuetophrynus acarpicus,* a stream inhabitant in southern Chile, have keratinized excrescences that are less developed than those in males (Diaz et al., 1983).

Females of limnodynastine myobatrachids that have aquatic foam nests develop broad lateral fringes on the fingers during the breeding season (Fig. 3-10). These fringes provide a much greater surface area to the hands, which are used in paddling movements for stirring water and spawn into a foam nest. Males lack the fringes, but males of some species have a knoblike medial projection on the distal end of the penultimate phalange of the first finger.

Other Phalangeal Structures. The function of other secondary sexual characters of the extremities is not known. Males of arthroleptine ranids have exceedingly long third fingers. In *Cardioglossa,* there are 15 to 20 large dermal denticles on the median surface of the finger; fewer and smaller denticles are present in *Arthroleptis,* and denticles are absent in *Schoutedenella* (Perret, 1966). Males of the hyperoliid *Acanthixalus spinosus* have many cornified spines on the posteroventral surface of the tarsus and also have much larger discs on the fingers than do the females (Perret, 1961). In males of some species of *Colostethus,* the distal part of the third finger is noticeably broadened; this may be associated with cephalic amplexus. Males of the Oriental microhylids *Kaloula rugifera, macroptica,* and *verrucosa* have 3 to 10 tubercles on the dorsal surface of the tip of each finger. Each tubercle is supported by a bony projection from the terminal phalange. Females have barely distinguishable ir-

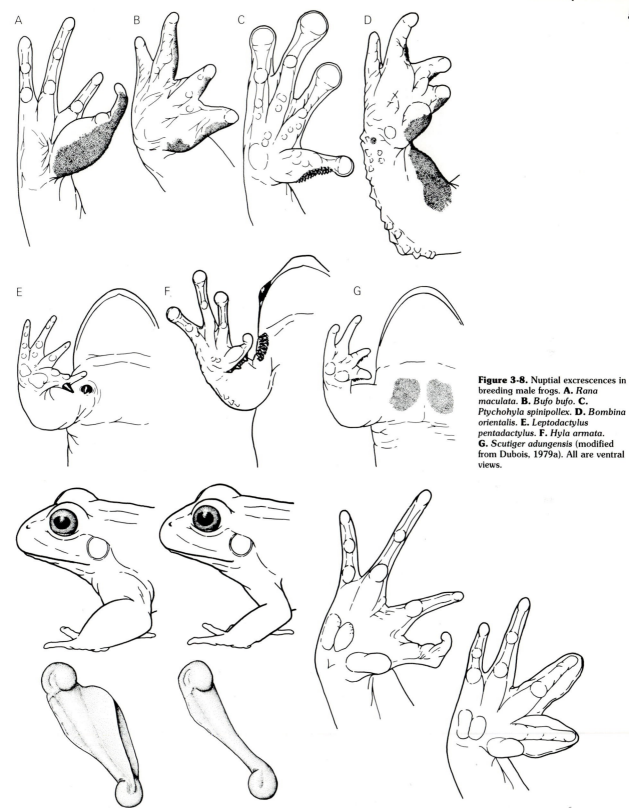

Figure 3-8. Nuptial excrescences in breeding male frogs. **A.** *Rana maculata.* **B.** *Bufo bufo.* **C.** *Ptychohyla spinipollex.* **D.** *Bombina orientalis.* **E.** *Leptodactylus pentadactylus.* **F.** *Hyla armata.* **G.** *Scutiger adungensis* (modified from Dubois, 1979a). All are ventral views.

Figure 3-9. Hypertrophied forelimb of male *Leptodactylus pentadactylus* (left) and normal forelimb of female (right) and extensive development of flanges on humerus of male as compared with female.

Figure 3-10. Sexual differences in hands of *Limnodynastes peroni*, showing projection on first finger of male (left) and dermal fringes on fingers of female (right).

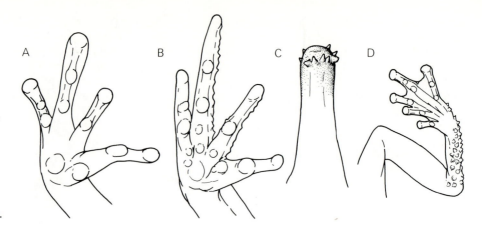

Figure 3-11. Secondary sexual characters of hands and feet of male anurans. **A.** Swollen third finger in *Colosthethus nubicola*. **B.** Elongate third finger with lateral denticles in *Cardioglossa cyanospila*. **C.** Elevations on dorsal surfaces of second finger in *Kaloula verrucosa* (redrawn from H. Parker, 1934). **D.** Tarsal spines in *Acanthixalus spinosus* (adapted from Perret, 1966).

regularities on the fingers (H. Parker, 1934; Liu, 1950) (Fig. 3-11).

Glands. Glands develop on the ventral surfaces of breeding males in many kinds of anurans (Figs. 3-12, 3-13). Abdominal glands are present in many microhylids that are excessively rotund-bodied (e.g., *Breviceps, Gastrophryne, Kaloula);* these glands secrete an adhesive substance that helps the male maintain amplexus (Conaway and Metter, 1967; Jurgens, 1978). At least in *Breviceps gibbosus,* females have similar adhesive glands on the dorsum (Visser et al., 1982). The function of the other ventral glands in male frogs is unknown, but because they are in contact with the female during amplexus, it is assumed that the secretions from these glands have some stimulating effect on ovulation or ovipositional behavior by the female. Mental (gular) glands of various shapes are present in all genera of hyperoliids, except *Leptopelis,* and in members of the Neotropical *Hyla bogotensis* and Australian *Litoria citropa* groups; these glands seem to be present throughout the year in most species. Extensive, thickened, and pigmented ventrolateral glands develop in males of all species of the Middle American *Ptychohyla.* Males of at least some species of *Leptopelis* have a pair of pectoral glands or a single transverse gland in the pectoral region; these glands consist of groups of glandules identical to those forming the nuptial pads (K. Schmidt and Inger, 1959). Round or ovoid "femoral" glands are present on the ventral surfaces of the thighs of some African ranids (*Petropedetes, Phrynodon,* and some species of *Phrynobatrachus)* and Madagascaran ranids (*Laurentomantis* and some species of *Mantidactylus).* A postaxillary gland is present in breeding males of the pipid genera *Hymenochirus* and *Pseudhymenochirus.* Other glands develop in breeding males of some ranids; these include glands on the dorsal surface of the hand in *Dimorphognathus* and *Hemisus,* "humeral" glands on the dorsal surface of the arm in some *Rana* and *Hylarana* (Fig. 3-14), a gland on the snout of *Rana macrodactyla* (also in *Polypedates dennysi),* and a large lateral

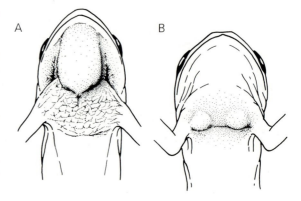

Figure 3-12. Glands of male frogs. **A.** Mental gland of *Kassina senegalensis*. **B.** Pectoral glands of *Leptopelis karissimbensis*.

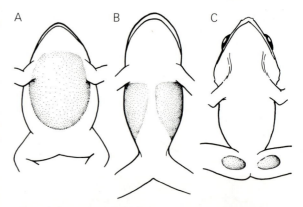

Figure 3-13. Glands of male frogs. **A.** Abdominal gland of *Kaloula verrucosa*. **B.** Ventrolateral glands of *Ptychohyla schmidtorum*. **C.** Femoral glands of *Mantidactylus pseudoasper*.

gland posterodorsal to the axilla in *Rana adenopleura* and its relatives. Males of many hyperoliids have glands on the inner surface of the forearms.

Skin Texture. Sexual differences in skin texture are common in toads and also occur in some other anurans.

In the toads of the *Bufo spinulosus* group, males have more numerous and cornified tubercles dorsally than do females (Fig. 3-15). The same is true in *Bufo regularis, Limnodynastes spenceri, Megistolotis lignarius,* and *Heleioporus australiacus,* in which the cornified spines are especially evident in the breeding season. Males of some *Centrolenella* have spicules on the dorsum. On the other hand, males of *Bufo bufo* and *B. kisoloensis,* among others, have relatively smooth skins with only low, flattened tubercles, in contrast to the more tuberculate skin of females. Males of the Neotropical tree frogs of the genus *Osteocephalus* have tuberculate skin, whereas the skin of females is essentially smooth; the size and density of the tubercles are species-specific (Trueb and Duellman, 1971). Males of the hyperoliid *Afrixalus fulovittatus* have finely tuberculate skin on the dorsum only during

the breeding season (Perret, 1966). Also, small spicules develop on the dorsum and/or venter in some species of *Ptychadena, Rana,* and *Gastrophryne* during the breeding season. In *Scutiger mammatus,* females have rugose skin on the dorsum and flanks (Liu, 1950). Any of these dermal characters may be important in sex recognition by tactile means. However, the presence of small tubercles on the margin of the jaw in some species of *Phrynobatrachus* may have some other function.

The most notable integumentary modifications occur in the African ranid *Trichobatrachus robustus* (Fig. 3-16). During the breeding season, males have long, hairlike projections on the flanks and thighs; these projections consist of vascularized epidermis (Noble, 1925a). Males are known to sit on clutches of eggs in streams (Perret, 1966), and presumably the "hairs" function to increase cutaneous respiration, thereby allowing males to remain under water for long periods of time.

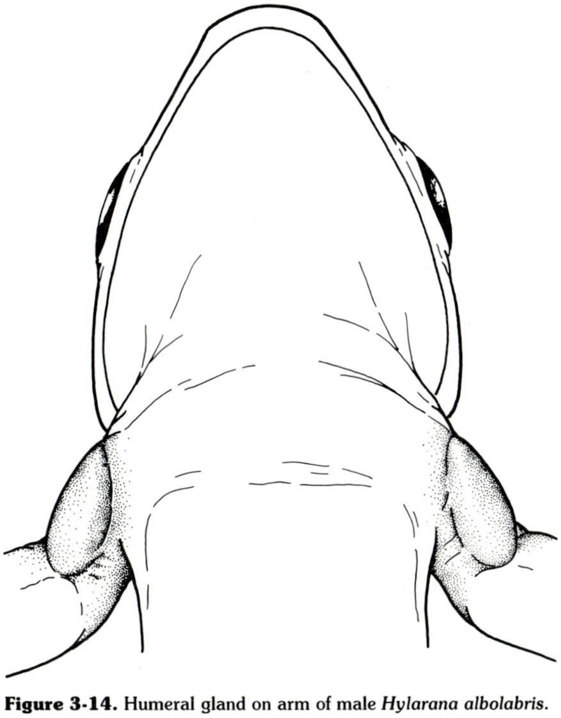

Cloacal Modifications. The most notable modification of the cloaca is the cloacal extension or "tail" of male *Ascaphus truei,* which is inserted into the cloaca of the female. Males of the small African bufonid *Mertensophryne micranotis* have protruding spiny vents; Grandison (1980b) postulated that these spines fit into furrows in the female's vent and that fertilization is internal. In most anurans, the opening of the vent is bordered by papillae or dermal folds, and there is no evident sexual dimorphism in the shape or position of these structures or of the direction of the opening. However, in *Kassina,* dermal flaps border the vent in females; perhaps these flaps function in the dispersal of the eggs as they leave the vent. In female *Pipa,* the vent of the female becomes greatly swollen just prior to oviposition.

Coloration. Males of many species of frogs develop pigmented vocal sacs during the breeding season, which may extend throughout the year. In *Bufo* the throats become gray or black, whereas in many small *Hyla* they become bright yellow. In some species of *Colostethus* the throat becomes black, but because melanin is less dense posteriorly the belly has a grayish hue; in others the throat is yellow or white. Many species of toads ex-

Figure 3-14. Humeral gland on arm of male *Hylarana albolabris.*

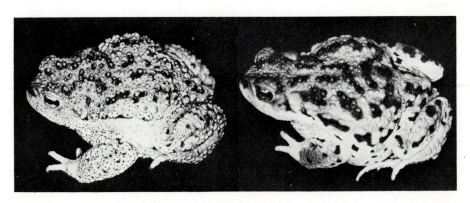

Figure 3-15. Sexual differences in skin texture in *Bufo spinulosus;* male (left), female (right). Photos by W. E. Duellman.

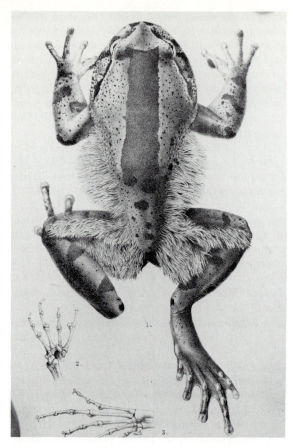

Figure 3-16. Breeding male of *Trichobatrachus robustus* showing hairlike dermal appendages. From Boulenger (1902).

Figure 3-17. Head of male *Petropedetes newtoni* showing the columella protruding through the tympanum.

hibit constant color differences between adult males and females. Usually the females are more boldly marked, as in the mottling of *Bufo canorus*, dorsolateral stripe in *B. preussi*, and broad green middorsal mark in *B. marmoreus*. *Bufo periglenes* displays striking sexual dimorphism in coloration; males are uniformly bright orange, and females are dark and rather dull except for red spots (J. Savage, 1967). Males of *Scaphiopus couchii* are plain, and females are mottled. Females of species in the *Hyla*

parviceps group have a broad diagonal pale mark dorsolaterally on the body; this mark is absent in males (Duellman and Crump, 1974). The ontogeny of sexual dichromatism of *Bufo canorus* was documented by Karlstrom (1962); juveniles of both sexes are spotted, but in older males there is a reduction of spotting, while in females the spots become accentuated with age. The seasonal development of throat color in males is under the control of testicular hormones (Greenberg, 1942), but the causes of continuous sexual dichromatism are as unknown as the functions. Male *Colostethus trinitatus* change from pale brown to black when calling; this color change occurs in a matter of 1 to 10 minutes, as does the reverse change at the end of calling (Wells, 1980b).

Tympanum.   In most anurans, the tympanum is relatively the same size in both sexes or slightly larger in females; however, in some ranids—species of *Rana* (e.g., *R. catesbeiana* and *R. clamitans)*, *Ptychadena*, *Conraua*, and *Hylarana*— the tympanum is notably larger in males. In some species of the ranid genus *Petropedetes* the columella protrudes through the tympanum in males (Fig. 3-17). The reasons for these differences are unknown. There are no correlations between tympanum size and auditory sensitivity in *Rana catesbeiana* (Frishkopf et al., 1968). The condition in *Petropedetes* would diminish the vibratory capacity of the tympanum and thus would reduce sensitivity to higher frequencies.

Linea Masculinea.   A curious sexually dimorphic character in some frogs is the linea masculinea, which consists of bands of fibrous connective tissue extending the entire length of both layers of the dorsal and ventral edges of the m. obliquus (Liu, 1935a). Lineae masculineae are known in males of many species of *Rana* and *Occidozyga* and in such diverse frogs as species of *Megophrys*, *Hyla*, *Plectrohyla*, *Polypedates*, *Philautus*, *Phrynobatrachus*, *Kaloula*, *Kalophrynus*, and *Microhyla* (Liu, 1936; K. Schmidt and Inger, 1959; Duellman, 1970). The function of this connective tissue and why it is present in some species and absent in congeners are completely unknown. In gonadectomized male *Rana pipiens,* the linea masculinea remained unchanged, thereby suggesting that its maintenance is not dependent on testicular hormones (D. Davis and Law, 1935).

COURTSHIP BEHAVIOR

The location and stimulation of potential mates are activities primarily associated with male amphibians, but some recent evidence shows that in some species females also play an active role. Courtship in salamanders has been reviewed by Joly (1966), Salthe (1967), Organ and Organ (1968), Salthe and Mecham (1974), Arnold (1976, 1977), and Halliday (1977); courtship in frogs has been reviewed by Wells (1977a, 1977b). The behavior is notably different in the three groups of living amphibians, so they are discussed independently.

Caecilians

The only observations of courtship behavior of a caecilian were of captive individuals of the aquatic typhlonectid *Chthonerpeton indistinctum,* in which the male coiled about the female and rubbed his body against her prior to copulation (Barrio, 1969). A pair of *Typhlonectes compressicauda* observed in copulation were passive for about 3 hours; no courtship was observed (Murphy et al., 1977).

Salamanders

The two major trends in salamander courtship are adaptations for female persuasion and sperm transfer (Arnold, 1977). Salamanders exhibit many modes of sperm transfer and even more differences in behavior that seem to be tactics for persuasion of females. Salthe (1976) defined five stages of courtship in salamanders:

1. The male becomes aware of a potential mate, approaches, and frequently nudges or rubs the female with his snout.
2. After ascertaining that the potential mate is a female, the male either captures her or blocks her path and continues rubbing movements or tail movements.
3. The male moves away from the female; she follows (not present in all groups).
4. The male deposits a spermatophore.
5. The male moves away from the spermatophore; the female follows him and finds the spermatophore.

These generalities are broadly applicable to salamanders having internal fertilization, but there are many deviations from the basic sequence. Hynobiids, cryptobranchids, and presumably sirenids have external fertilization in water, and there is no known courtship. Males apparently take no interest in females until eggs are visibly protruding from their vents. However, there may be some form of male behavior that entices females to males' territories, for apparently at least in *Cryptobranchus alleganiensis* (B. Smith, 1907; Bishop, 1941) and *Hynobius nebulosus* (Thorn, 1963), males select the oviposition sites. Also, some form of courtship may be present in *Ranodon sibiricus,* a hynobiid inhabiting mountain streams; females apparently deposit egg sacs on top of a previously laid spermatophore (Bannikov, 1958).

Among salamanders with internal fertilization, the proteids court and breed in water. The limited observations on *Necturus* indicate that the male swims about the female, frequently passing over and under the forepart of her body, which is elevated as she balances on her hindlimbs and tail; sperm transfer has not been observed (Bishop, 1941). In *Proteus,* which lives in subterranean waters, captive males are territorial; courtship consists of the male nudging the female's flanks with his snout and working his way anteriorly, eventually blocking her path with his cloaca near her snout and waving his tail about her head. The female then nudges the male's cloaca, and he moves forward, leading the female and fanning her with his tail. Upon depositing a spermatophore, he leads her over it, and she pauses with her cloaca over the spermatophore (Briegleb, 1962a). Courtship in *Amphiuma* also occurs in water. Unconfirmed observations on *A. tridactylum* (L. Baker, 1937; C. Baker et al., 1947) suggest that courtship may be radically different from that in other salamanders. Supposedly several females court a male simultaneously by rubbing him with their snouts from his head backward. Eventually one female enters into a mutual embrace with the male, and a spermatophore is transferred directly to her cloaca. The stream-inhabiting *Rhyacotriton olympicus* has a unique tail-wagging display with tail arched forward, just prior to deposition of a spermatophore (Arnold, 1977).

Each of the remaining families of salamanders has unique courtship behaviors; these families are discussed individually.

Salamandridae.   Courtship usually takes place in water. Salthe (1967) identified three distinct patterns of courtship in salamandrids: (1) caudal capture of the female by the male and direct transfer of the spermatophore *(Euproctus);* (2) male capture of female from below and deposition of the spermatophore on the substrate *(Chioglossa, Pleurodeles,* some *Salamandra, Tylototriton,* and presumably *Echinotriton* and *Salamandrina);* (3) dorsal capture or no capture of the female and deposition of the spermatophore on the substrate *(Cynops, Notophthalmus,* some *Salamandra, Taricha, Triturus,* and presumably in the genera *Neurergus, Pachytriton,* and *Paramesotriton).*

   1. *Caudal capture.*—Males of *Euproctus* stand on the tips of their toes with the tail directed laterally. An approaching female *E. asper* is captured by the male quickly encircling the base of her tail with his tail. Males of *E. montanus* and *E. platycephalus* capture females in their jaws and also clasp them with their hind limbs. If the captured female is quiescent, the male moves into a position to place his cloaca near hers and strokes her cloaca with his feet. Spermatophores are deposited on the female's body, and the male moves the spermatophores with his feet to the female's cloaca, after which she is released (Bedriaga, 1882).

   2. *Ventral capture.*—Most salamandrids having this pattern court in water, but courtship may begin, or even be completed, on land in *Salamandra.* In this genus the male nudges the female's flanks, belly, and throat with his snout, and in all salamandrids having this pattern, the male eventually slides under the female and encircles her forelimbs with his from below. In *Pleurodeles* the preliminary rubbing behavior is absent. The male then carries the female around on his back, presumably exposing her to secretions from glands on his dorsum (Salthe, 1967). While holding the female, the male deposits a spermatophore (Arnold, 1977). Immediately thereafter the male in *Salamandra* flexes his vertebral column laterally and

A

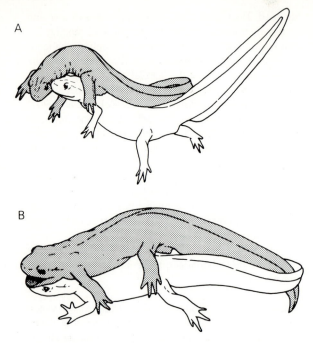

B

Figure 3-18. Capture positions in salamandrids (males shaded). **A.** *Notophthalmus viridescens* embracing female and rubbing her snout with his genial glands. **B.** *Taricha torosa* embracing female and rubbing her snout with his submandibular gland. Adapted from Arnold (1977).

pivots approximately 45° on the contralateral forelimb; this lateral displacement of the posterior part of his body allows the female's cloaca to drop onto the spermatophore (Häfeli, 1971; Joly, 1966). In *Pleurodeles* the male deposits a spermatophore and pivots 180° to face the female, who drops on the spermatophore (Arnold, 1977).

3. *Dorsal capture or no capture.*—There is considerable diversity in behavior in salamandrids having dorsal capture or no capture at all. Only in this group is there direct evidence of chemosensory sex and species identification. Twitty's (1955, 1961) experiments with *Taricha* are especially illuminating. Male *T. rivularis* were attracted to sponges soaked with skin secretions from conspecific females, but ignored sponges that lacked secretions. Females of four populations of *Taricha* (*rivularis, granulosa, torosa torosa,* and *torosa sierrae*) were anchored side by side in a stream naturally inhabited by *T. rivularis* and *T. granulosa.* Native male *T. rivularis* showed a strong attraction to conspecific females and females of *T. torosa sierrae* but a weak response to others. Blinded males of *T. rivularis* were able to distinguish conspecific females. Females of *Triturus cristatus* can distinguish secretions of males from those of females (Cedrini and Fasolo, 1971).

In *Cynops pyrrhogaster,* the male nudges the female with his snout, beginning at her cloaca and proceeding to her head; he then blocks her path with his head. From this point in the courtship, patterns vary in different geographic races. These variations include: (1) position of

the male during a tail-fanning display; (2) duration of the tail-fanning display; and (3) method of partial capture—the male placing one forelimb on shoulders of female or placing a forelimb in front of her snout and a hindlimb on her back (Kawamura and Sawada, 1959). At this stage of courtship, the male rubs the glandular side of his head on the female's snout. Subsequently the male moves away, followed by the receptive female, whose attention is focused on his cloaca. Upon deposition of a spermatophore, the female passes over the spermatophore, which adheres to her cloacal lips.

In *Taricha* and *Notophthalmus,* there is complete dorsal capture of the female; males of both genera have nuptial excrescences on the inner surfaces of the appropriate limbs. In *Taricha,* the male clasps the female with his forelimbs in her axilla and sometimes also pelvically with his hindlimbs. While holding the female directly below him, the male *Taricha* rubs his submandibular gland on the female's snout, and he may stroke her cloaca with his hindfeet. Upon dismounting, he deposits a spermatophore in front of her snout (R. E. Smith, 1941; W. Davis and Twitty, 1964). In *Notophthalmus,* after the male touches the female's cloaca with his snout, he clasps her from above and works his way forward until his hindlimbs encircle her axilla or neck (Fig. 3-18). After capture, the male arches his body laterally and rubs the side of his head (genial glands) on the snout of the female and simultaneously fans the side of her body with his tail. Subsequently the male dismounts and leads the female, who nudges his cloaca with her snout; presumably this nudging triggers spermatophore deposition (A. Humphries, 1955).

The European newts, *Triturus,* are unique in that the male does not grasp the female during courtship. The extensive fins and bright color patterns of the breeding males provide visual stimuli to the females. Extensive investigations of courtship behavior of European newts by Halliday and coworkers (summarized in Halliday, 1977) have demonstrated the primary significance of visual signals and stereotyped sequences of behavior by both sexes. Females play an important role in the timing of successive sequences, because the male is dependent on feedback from her. Furthermore, this timing is important in the completion of the courtship sequences, for if the female is not sufficiently responsive, the male must interrupt courtship and swim to the surface for breathing.

As an example of the complex courtship behavior in European newts, the following description of courtship in *Triturus vulgaris* is summarized from Halliday (1977) (Fig. 3-19). The male usually initiates sexual encounters. He walks or swims around in a pond; when he meets a female he sniffs at her cloaca and attempts to position himself in front of her. Usually the female moves away; she is pursued by the male, who again attempts to place himself in front of her. The sequences of this orientation phase are repeated several times. Once the female stops moving, the male remains in front of her and initiates a

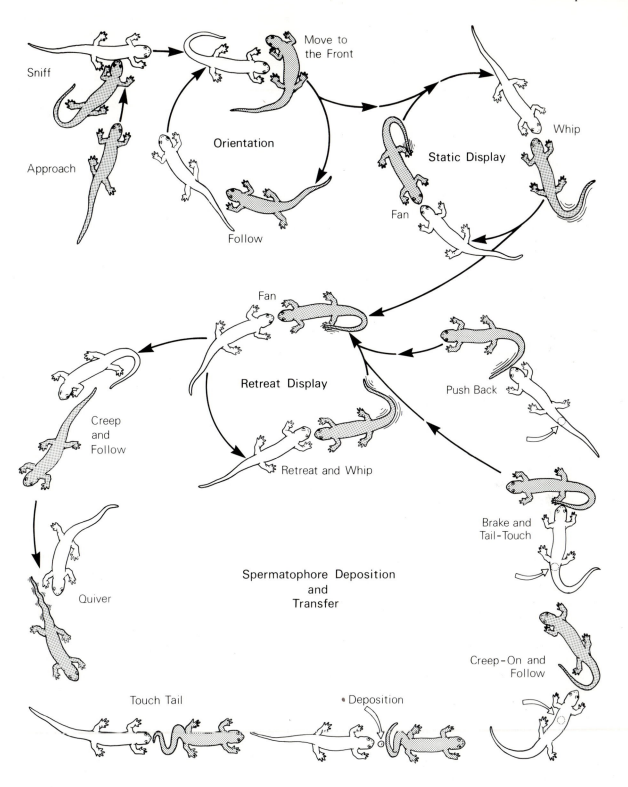

Figure 3-19. Courtship of European newt *Triturus vulgaris* (male shaded). Spatial movements indicated by solid arrows; other sequences are stationary. Open arrow indicates position of spermatophore. Redrawn from Halliday (1977).

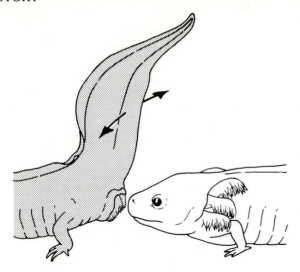

Figure 3-20. Tail-nudging walk in *Ambystoma mexicanum*, showing female nudging male's cloacal papillae while male (shaded) moves forward and waves tail laterally. Redrawn from Arnold (1977).

display of tail movements—wave, whip, and fan. These displays are not only visual but also tactile (water currents) and olfactory. The wave consists of the male holding his tail up for about 1 second, thereby giving the female a full lateral view of his body and tail. The whip is a sudden, forceful movement, in which the tail, from the wave position, is lashed against the male's flank, creating a water current of sufficient power that it may push the female backward. The fanning movement is relatively weak and sustained for periods up to half a minute; the tail is curved against the flank nearest the female, and its distal portion is vibrated at a rate of about six beats per second, generating water currents directed toward the female's snout. The wave provides a visual signal, and the whip is primarily tactile, whereas the fanning movements are thought to transmit odors from the male to the female. Bouts of stationary display are continued until the female approaches the male, who then retreats before her while maintaining his orientation and display—mostly whips with very few waves or fans. The retreat lasts 5–60 seconds, at which time the male ceases to display, turns, and moves away from the female; she follows him. He creeps for a distance of 5–10 cm, stops, and slowly quivers his tail with her snout; the male folds and raises his tail and deposits a spermatophore on the substrate. Immediately the male creeps away and turns perpendicularly with his tail folded against his flank nearest the female. She moves forward and presses against his tail, which serves to brake her progress. The male resists her pressure and may flex his body and tail so as to push her back. These maneuvers result in the female being positioned with her cloaca above the spermatophore, which becomes attached to the cloaca. From the braking position or after pushbacks, the male turns to-

ward the female and resumes his retreat display; the female approaches again. During a sexual encounter, the courtship sequence is usually performed two or three times. Apparently there is no signal from the female to the male when she picks up the spermatophore, for he is just as likely to proceed with another courtship sequence after a successful bout as he is after an unsuccessful one.

Ambystomatidae. A review of courtship patterns in *Ambystoma* by Salthe (1967) and detailed studies on *A. maculatum* and *A. tigrinum* by Arnold (1976) reveal some basic patterns and specific variations. With the exception of *A. opacum*, courtship takes place in water. Most species have rather short breeding seasons; males arrive at ponds first and are followed by females. Dorsal capture of females by males is known in only four species. In three of these (*jeffersonianum, laterale,* and *macrodactylum*), the males clasp the females anteriorly with their forelimbs, but in *A. gracile* the clasping is also with the hindlimbs around the female's axilla. In these species (except *A. gracile*) the male rubs the female's snout with his chin. Subsequently the female is released and the male leads her, and he deposits a spermatophore on the substrate.

In the other species of *Ambystoma* that have been studied, the male nudges and rubs an uncaptured female and leads her to a spermatophore, deposited immediately in front of her snout or (as in *A. maculatum*) some distance away; in the latter case the male returns to the female and leads her to the spermatophore. In most species the female follows the male with her snout close to his cloaca, and spermatophore deposition may be triggered by her prodding his cloaca with her snout (Fig. 3-20). In *A. tigrinum* the male forcefully pushes the female through the water and then initiates a tail-nudging walk. In *A. mexicanum, opacum,* and *talpoideum,* the male also focuses on the female's cloaca, sometimes resulting in a snout-to-vent circular sequence before the male leads the female forward prior to deposition of a spermatophore. Males usually deposit several spermatophores and repeat courtship sequences several times.

As a detailed example of *Ambystoma* courtship, the following account of courtship in *A. talpoideum* is summarized from Shoop (1960) (Fig. 3-21). All activities take place in shallow water, with the salamanders moving about on the bottom. Courtship is initiated by the male nudging the head of the female with his snout for about 10 seconds; then he moves his snout posterior to her cloaca, at which time the female puts her snout in the male's cloacal region. Both push with their heads, which results in a circular movement. After one or two revolutions, the male straightens his body, and the female slides her snout to the tip of his tail. At this point, the male initiates a lateral shuffling of his pelvic region and fans the posterior part of his tail, which frequently touches the female's head. Using only the forelimbs for propulsion, the male

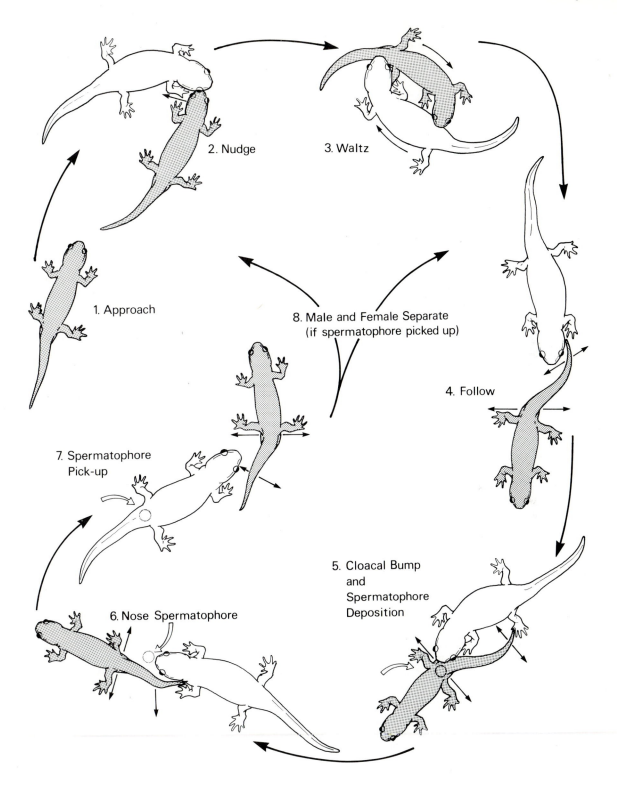

2. Nudge

3. Waltz

1. Approach

8. Male and Female Separate
(if spermatophore picked up)

4. Follow

7. Spermatophore
Pick-up

5. Cloacal Bump
and
Spermatophore
Deposition

6. Nose Spermatophore

Figure 3-21. Courtship in *Ambystoma talpoideum* (male shaded). Spatial movements indicated by solid arrows; other sequences are stationary. Open arrow indicates position of spermatophore. Adapted from Shoop (1960).

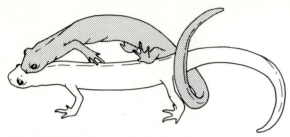

Figure 3-22. Inoculation of female by male *Eurycea bislineata* in water. Male (shaded) pulls mental gland and premaxillary teeth along dorsum of female. Redrawn from Arnold (1977).

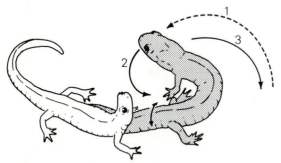

Figure 3-23. Snout-slapping of female by male (shaded) *Plethodon jordani*, as a means of applying secretions from mental gland, during the tail-straddling walk while the male undulates the base of his tail. Numbered arrows indicate sequence and direction of movements. Redrawn from Arnold (1977).

moves slowly forward while continuing the lateral shuffling and tail-fanning. The female follows, keeping her head in contact, or nearly so, with the male's tail. After she follows him for 1–11 minutes, the female moves forward and nudges the male's cloacal region one or two times. He then terminates pelvic and caudal movements, deposits a spermatophore, resumes the movements, and slowly moves forward. The female noses the spermatophore and crawls over it. Meanwhile the male continues slow forward motion, pelvic shuffling, and tail-fanning. If the female picks up the spermatophore, she terminates her association with the male; if she does not pick up the spermatophore, she continues following the male with her head in close association with his tail.

Plethodontidae.   All plethodontids, whether courting on land or in water, engage in a tail-straddling walk—a behavior unique to this family (Arnold, 1977). Males of most plethodontids have well-developed mental glands, and many have protruding premaxillary teeth. The application of mental gland secretions to the female occurs in those species having the glands. The method of application of the gland to the female is variable. In some plethodontids, the application is by "vaccination" of the female with the premaxillary teeth (Fig. 3-22). In *Desmognathus,* some small species of *Plethodon,* and some bolitoglossines, the male presses the gland against the female's dorsum and then flings himself away with a snapping motion. This motion results in the surface of

the female being abraded by the teeth of the male and the mental gland secretions being introduced directly into the female's superficial circulation. Other plethodontids, such as *Eurycea bislineata, Aneides lugubris,* and *Hydromantes platycephalus,* pull their chins in a succession of quick strokes on the dorsum of the female. Large species of *Plethodon (glutinosus, jordani,* and *yonahlossee)* deliver mental gland secretions by slapping the gland on the female's snout (Fig. 3-23). Species that lack mental glands and elongate premaxillary teeth (e.g., *Pseudotriton ruber, Ensatina eschscholtzi)* have not been observed to perform any of these kinds of actions.

As an example of plethodontid courtship behavior, the following description of the behavior of *Plethodon jordani* has been summarized from the extensive work of Arnold (1976) (Fig. 3-24). Courtship takes place on land. Upon contacting a female, the male moves along the side of her body while tapping her dorsum with his head, nudging her flanks with his snout, or sliding his chin anteriorly along her back. The male also may perform a "foot dance"—raising and lowering either forelimbs or hindlimbs one at a time. During these sequences, the male apparently identifies the sex and species by chemoreception. Upon identifying a conspecific female, the male locates her head and attempts to initiate the tail-straddling walk by nudging or sliding his mental gland along her cheek or snout and placing his head beneath her chin and lifting her head. He then crawls forward under her chin. When the female's chin comes in contact with the dorsal base of his tail, he arches the base of his tail and undulates it laterally and begins walking. If the female does not maintain contact with the base of the male's tail, he stops undulating his tail and after a few minutes turns around and initiates courtship again. The tail-straddling walk continues for several minutes to more than an hour; during this time the male apparently relies solely on tactile cues to monitor and regulate the female's position. While in the tail-straddling walk, the male may turn periodically and slap his chin (mental gland) on the female's snout. Once the female slides her chin anteriorly along the base of the male's tail, he lowers his vent and slides it along the substrate. This vent-sliding lasts for no more than 1 minute and presumably represents a tactile search for a suitable site for deposition of a spermatophore. Upon depositing the spermatophore, the male moves forward and flexes his tail laterally from beneath the female; he continues forward with the female's chin still resting on the base of his tail. He stops when the spermatophore is in contact with her vent; she makes slight lateral movements with the base of her tail, lowers her vent onto the spermatophore, and picks it up in her cloaca.

Anurans

Identification of Mates.   The major factor in anuran courtship is the production of advertisement calls by males;

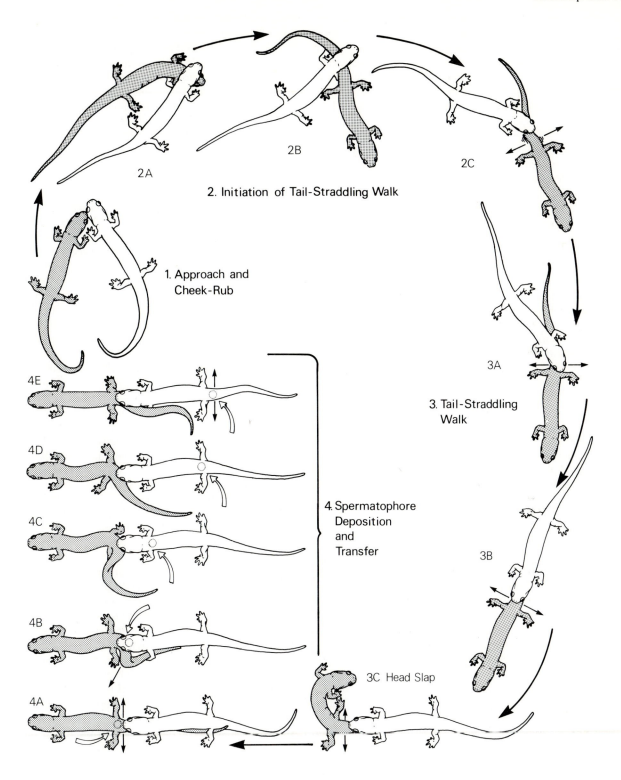

2. Initiation of Tail-Straddling Walk

2A

2B

2C

1. Approach and
Cheek-Rub

4E

4D

4C

4B

4A

3A

3. Tail-Straddling
Walk

3B

3C Head Slap

4. Spermatophore
Deposition
and
Transfer

Figure 3-24. Courtship of *Plethodon jordani* (male shaded). Spatial movements are indicated by large solid
arrows; small solid arrows indicate tail movements. Open arrow indicates position of spermatophore.
Adapted from Arnold (1976).

the complexity of vocalization and associated behavior is treated in detail in Chapter 4. Compared to salamanders, olfactory cues and visual displays seem to be unimportant in preamplectic courtship in most anurans, but some tactile cues are used by certain species. The diversity of glands developed by various male frogs in the breeding season suggests that olfactory cues may be used at least in sex recognition. This might be especially important in species that breed in water. G. Rabb and M. Rabb (1963a) suggested that secretions from the postaxillary glands in *Hymenochirus boettgeri* may repel other males or attract females; furthermore, because the glands are distinctly colored, it is possible that visual identification is made.

The absence of sexual color differences in most anurans suggests that visual cues may be unimportant in identification of potential mates, at least in nocturnal species. Experiments on species and sex identification in *Hyla cinerea* and *H. gratiosa* provided no evidence for visual cues in these nocturnally breeding species (H. Gerhardt, 1974b). On the other hand, *Bufo canorus* and *B. periglenes* breed by day and have striking sexual color dimorphism. Male ranids, *Staurois parvus,* apparently attract females by visual display; males on boulders in streams slowly and deliberately extend a leg and spread the toes, thereby exposing pale blue webbing, which contrasts with the otherwise cryptic coloration (Harding, 1982). With the exception of black throats in males, there are no pattern differences among the sexes of most dendrobatids, all of which breed by day. Visual cues to potential mates, as well as to male adversaries, may be enhanced by the posture of breeding males; usually they hold their heads high, thereby making the throat more visible.

Tactile cues probably are the most important nonvocal factors in mate identification in anurans. Differences in size and skin texture have been shown to be used in sex identification. Amplexus is stimulated by the greater girth and firmness of the female in such diverse frogs as *Rana sylvatica, Hyla andersonii, Ascaphus truei,* and *Pipa pipa.* However, in *Bufo,* males and spent females usually give release calls when clasped by a male. Size differences may be especially important in species recognition among sympatric and synchronously breeding congeners. Thus, males of *B. americanus* discriminate against females of the larger *B. woodhousii* in favor of the smaller conspecific females (A. Blair, 1942). Males of *Gastrophryne carolinensis* discriminate against the smaller females of *G. olivaceus* (A. Blair, 1950). Sexual differences in skin texture presumably are effective means of sex identification among many species of toads, especially those that do not vocalize, such as members of the *Bufo spinulosus* group.

Tactile identification probably is most important in those species that are explosive breeders, that is, species that congregate in large numbers for intense breeding activity for a short period of time (Wells, 1977b). Short-term, dense breeding aggregations are especially prevalent in highly seasonal regions, where combinations of temperature and heavy rainfall initiate migrations to breeding sites—frequently temporary ponds. Explosive breeders include *Scaphiopus* and many species of *Bufo, Gastrophryne,* and *Rana sylvatica* in North America; many species of *Cyclorana, Litoria, Limnodynastes,* and *Neobatrachus* in Australia; *Pleurodema brachyops* and many species of *Leptodactylus, Physalaemus, Bufo, Hyla,* and *Ololygon* in the llanos in northern South America; and *Pyxicephalus adspersus* and various species of *Bufo* and *Hyperolius* in South Africa. In most of these species, females are attracted to the breeding site by male vocalizations. In high densities, males usually search actively for females at the breeding site and apparently cannot discriminate visually between the sexes. However, males of some species remain in a restricted area and attempt to amplex only those frogs that approach closely; this limited-area searching is known in some species of *Bombina, Discoglossus, Pelobates, Scaphiopus, Bufo,* and *Rana* (see Wells, 1977b).

Among species having prolonged breeding seasons, females usually approach individual males and usually the male continues to call until touched by the female. Female *Hyla rosenbergi* enter, inspect, and even modify the nest in which a male is calling before she positions herself for amplexus (Kluge, 1981). Physical contact of the male by the female is not universal. For example, female *Hyla ebraccata* move to within 6–30 cm of a calling male and orient the flanks to the male, who terminates calling, tilts his head in the direction of the female, and jumps to her, positioning himself adjacent and parallel to the female before initiating amplexus (Miyamoto and Cane, 1980a). Pairs of *Agalychnis callidryas* have been observed nearly face to face on a limb; then the female turns 180° and the male mounts her (Pyburn, 1970). Female *Polypedates leucomystax* have been observed to sit perpendicularly in front of a calling male, who turns 90° and mounts the female from the side (C. Johnson and Lowery, 1968).

Some distinctive preamplectic and amplectic behaviors are known, especially among pipid and dendrobatid frogs (treated later in the section: Other Courtship Behaviors). In the terrestrial-breeding *Syrrhophus marnocki,* the female moves about the male, who scratches her dorsum with his hindfeet; when she stops moving, he mounts her in amplexus (Jameson, 1955a). Upon the initiation of amplexus, the male of the pouch-brooding hylid *Flectonotus pygmaeus* kicks the back of the female and inserts his feet into the pouch (Duellman and Maness, 1980).

Amplexus. When both the male and the female are ready to mate, the male usually grasps the female so that he is dorsal to her. This embrace, amplexus, is inguinal in the primitive frogs, including all archaeobatrachians, myobatrachids, and some telmatobiine leptodactylids (J. D. Lynch, 1973), and sooglossids (Nussbaum, 1980). With the male's forelimbs grasping the female around the waist, the vents are not juxtaposed; presumably this

Figure 3-25. Amplectic positions in anurans (males shaded). **A.** Inguinal (*Alytes obstetricans*). **B.** Axillary (*Eleutherodactylus danae*). **C.** Cephalic (*Colostethus inguinalis*). **D.** Straddle (*Mantidactylus liber*). **E.** Glued (*Breviceps adspersus*). **F.** Independent (*Dendrobates granuliferus*). Drawing C adapted from Wells (1980a); D adapted from Blommers-Schlösser (1975a), and E adapted from Wager (1965).

method of amplexus is not as efficient for ensuring fertilization of eggs as is the more forward position, axillary amplexus, which places the vents closer together (G. Rabb, 1973). Most neobatrachians have axillary amplexus. However, there are some notable exceptions in both groups (Fig. 3-25). Amplexus initially is inguinal in the European midwife toad, *Alytes obstetricans*, but as the eggs emerge, the male shifts to a cephalic embrace and draws his legs up through the eggs, which adhere to his legs (Crespo, 1979). Inguinal amplexus is a secondary adaptive condition in some neobatrachians. In the small, fossorial microhylid *Myersiella microps*, the male in inguinal amplexus does not create a larger overall diameter for the pair than that of the female, which burrows head first through mulch (Izecksohn et al., 1971). The same might be true for the African terrestrial hyperoliid *Chrysobatrachus cupreonitens*, in which the comparatively small male has short forelimbs (Laurent, 1964).

In some anurans with globular bodies and short limbs, effective axillary amplexus is not possible. Thus, the small Andean toads, *Osornophryne* exhibit inguinal amplexus (Ruiz and Hernandez, 1976). Males of the African microhylids of the genus *Breviceps* are glued to the posterior part of the dorsum of the female (Wager, 1965); in this position they both dig with their hindfeet and may

remain attached for 3 days. Although they may maintain a weak axillary amplexus, some other heavy-bodied microhylids also are adherent during amplexus; this is known in the Philippine *Kaloula conjuncta* and *K. picta* (Inger, 1954) and the North American *Gastrophryne carolinensis* (Conaway and Metter, 1967) and *G. olivacea* (Fitch, 1956). Specialized secretory cells in the dermis of the venter of the male provide the adhesive substance in *G. carolinensis* (Conaway and Metter, 1967) and presumably in the other microhylids exhibiting this behavior.

A unique, ventral inguinal amplexus occurs in two species of bufonids, *Nectophrynoides malcolmi* and *N. occidentalis*, in which fertilization is internal. Some other species of *Nectophrynoides*, two of which are known to have internal fertilization and one with external fertilization, have normal, dorsal amplexus (Grandison, 1978).

Axillary amplexus normally involves the male grasping the female in the axilla; in those species having nuptial excrescences, the pads or spines are pressed tightly into the axilla. In many tree frogs (*Phyllomedusa, Litoria, Chiromantis*), one or two fingers are placed above the arm of the female. In all cases the palms are medial. In the nest-building frog *Hyla rosenbergi*, the female is grasped by the angle of the jaw (Kluge, 1981); the sexes in this species are nearly the same size, so a more forward position of the male results in the vents being closer together.

Some dendrobatids have cephalic amplexus, in which the dorsal surfaces of the male's hands are pressed against the female's throat; this form of amplexus is known in *Colostethus inguinalis* (Wells, 1980a), *Dendrobates tricolor, Phyllobates aurotaenia,* and *P. terribilis* (Myers et al., 1978). Amplexus is absent in *Dendrobates granuliferus, D. pumilio,* and *Rhinoderma* (Crump, 1972; Limerick, 1980; Pflaumer, 1936). In some Madagascaran ranids—*Mantidactylus blommersae, depressiceps,* and *liber* —the male sits astride the head and shoulders of the female on a vertical leaf during rain; presumably sperm flow down the female's back to fertilize the eggs deposited on the leaf (Blommers-Schlösser, 1975a; 1979a). Some terrestrial Madagascaran ranids have abbreviated amplexus; *Mantella aurantiaca* has a short, loose amplexus, after which eggs are deposited amidst leaves (Arnoult, 1966), and similar abbreviated amplexus occurs in *Mantidactylus curtus,* which has aquatic eggs (Arnoult and Razariheliosa, 1967). *Discoglossus,* which deposits aquatic eggs, also are in amplexus for only a few seconds (Knoepffler, 1962).

Superimposed on the general pattern of inguinal amplexus in primitive frogs and axillary amplexus in advanced anurans are a variety of modifications relating to relative body size and shape of the sexes, parental care, and mode of oviposition. The abbreviated amplexus before, but not during, oviposition in some frogs may provide the stimulation for ovulation, but is unnecessary to ensure fertilization.

In most anurans, amplexus occurs at or near the oviposition site, and pairs remain in amplexus for only an hour or two. The duration of preovipositional amplexus probably is related to the time required for the female to find a suitable oviposition site. However, once in amplexus, female *Hyla rosenbergi* inspect and modify the nest prior to laying eggs (Kluge, 1981). Pairing of *Breviceps adspersus* takes place on the surface of the ground; subsequently the pair (male adhered to the posterior part of the female) dig a nest chamber. Pairs have been observed adhered together for 3 days prior to oviposition (Wager, 1965). Pairing in the Andean bufonid *Atelopus oxyrhynchus* takes place on the forest floor; subsequently the amplectant pair moves to a stream for egg-laying. One pair was in amplexus for 125 days (Dole and Durant, 1974a). A pair of *A. varius* was observed in amplexus for 20 days (P. Starrett, 1967). Similar long-term amplexus occurs in *A. ignescens;* pairs transported from the field to the laboratory remained in amplexus for more than a month. Females of the desert-dwelling myobatrachids *Arenophryne rotunda* and *Myobatrachus gouldii* approach calling males on the surface of the ground and then burrow deep into the ground (up to 1 m) where the pair remains together for 5 or 6 months before depositing eggs, which undergo direct development (Roberts, 1981, 1984).

Other Courtship Behaviors. Elaborate and diverse courtship behaviors are known in the diurnal, terrestrial dendrobatid frogs. The differences in courtship activities of these frogs, as compared with those of most other anurans, seem to be associated with aggressive defense of territories by either males or females and the absence of amplexus in many species. In anurans in which the pair is in amplexus prior to oviposition, the female usually chooses the oviposition site (oviposition in nests constructed by the male prior to mating, as in the *Hyla boans* group, is an obvious exception). However, in dendrobatids the male usually selects the oviposition site. The complex courtship behavior in dendrobatids was summarized by Wells (1977b, 1980a, 1980b) and H. Zimmermann and E. Zimmermann (1981). Males of all species are highly vocal. In some species that do not exhibit aggressive defense of territories, additional behavior involves tactile courtship of the male by the female (Table 3-1). For example, in *Dendrobates auratus* the female jumps on the male's back and prods him with her forelimbs. In those species in which the males aggressively defend territories, females approach males, but in species of *Colostethus* in which females aggressively defend territories, males approach females. Tactile courtship of females by males includes prodding, jumping on the back of the female, or an abbreviated cephalic amplexus. Visual displays by males include jumping up and down in front of the female, a "toe dance" in *C. collaris,* and notable darkening of color in *C. palmatus, trinitatus,* and possibly *collaris.*

Courtship and mating in pipids takes place in water. These behaviors have been described in detail for *Hymenochirus boettgeri* (G. Rabb and M. Rabb, 1963a), *Pipa pipa* (G. Rabb and M. Rabb, 1961, 1963b), and *P. carvalhoi* (Weygoldt, 1976a). In *Hymenochirus boettgeri,* calling males shuffle their feet and move their arms in a manner similar to clasping; they respond to movements of other frogs and usually approach potential mates from the flank. An attempt to clasp a male usually results in immediate release in response to an abrupt, vibratory buzz given by the other male. When clasped by a male, unreceptive females assume a tonic posture with the legs outstretched; if the male does not release her, the unreceptive female may twitch her arms, wave her feet, quiver her entire body, or lunge under an object in an apparent attempt to dislodge the male. Rejection actions by a female may be inhibited by the male pumping his arms. The stimulus for oviposition presumably is provided by the male stroking the female's head with his feet. Similar courtship activity occurs in *Pipa pipa* and *carvalhoi.* The tonic posture of an unreceptive female also occurs in *Ascaphus truei,* which mates in water (Noble and P. Putnam, 1931).

Courtship behavior during amplexus has been reported in few anurans. In addition to the pipids, arm pumping and up and down movements of the head of the male occur in *Pelobates fuscus,* the male of which

Table 3-1. Courtship in Dendrobatid Frogs, Genera *Dendrobates* and *Colostethus*[a]

Species	Territorial defense	Tends eggs	Carries tadpoles	Approaches mate	Selects site	Courtship activity
D. auratus	—	♂	♂	♀	♂	Tactile courtship of ♂ by ♀
D. azureus	—	♂	♂[b]	♀	?	Tactile courtship of ♂ by ♀
D. granuliferus	♂	?	♀	♀	♂	Tactile courtship of ♀ by ♂
D. pumilio	♂	♂	♀	♀	♂	Visual and acoustic courtship of ♀ by ♂; temporary cephalic amplexus
D. lehmanni	♂	♀	♀	♀	♀	♂ pursues ♀; tactile courtship by both
D. histrionicus	♂	♀	♀	♀	♀	♂ pursues ♀; tactile courtship by both
C. inguinalis	♂[c]	?	♀	♀	♂	Tactile and acoustic courtship by ♂; cephalic amplexus
C. palmatus	♂, ♀	♂	♂	♀	♂	Tactile and acoustic courtship by ♂
C. trinitatus	♀	♂	♂	♂	♂	Acoustic and visual courtship by ♂
C. collaris	♀	?	♂	?♂	♂	Acoustic and visual courtship by ♂

[a]Mostly summarized from Wells (1977b) and H. Zimmermann and E. Zimmermann (1981).
[b]Also sometimes by females.
[c]Females defend temporary territories.

also scratches the female's cloaca with his hindfeet while in amplexus (Eibl-Eibesfeldt, 1956). Male *Bombina variegata* also pump their arms and quiver the entire body while amplecting a female (R. Savage, 1932). While in amplexus, the male *Bufo mazatlanensis* undergoes convulsive shudderings and thumps his outer toes against the female's feet (Firschein, 1951). These diverse observations provide no insights into the significance of these actions. Apparently these movements on the part of the male provide some kinds of signals or stimuli to the female; in some instances such actions presumably induce ovulation by the female.

FERTILIZATION AND OVIPOSITION
Fertilization occurs externally at the time of oviposition in most anurans and in primitive salamanders, whereas fertilization is internal in caecilians, most salamanders, and a few anurans. In amphibians having internal fertilization, oviposition may occur from a few hours to many months after mating.

External Fertilization

Salamanders. Primitive salamanders deposit eggs in water—strings of eggs in cryptobranchids and a pair of egg sacs in hynobiids. The male moves over the eggs and releases sperm. The male of *Hynobius nebulosus* grasps the egg sac in fore- and hindfeet and crawls along the sac and rubs his cloaca over it (Thorn, 1963). The stream-dwelling hynobiid *Ranodon sibiricus* has a spermatophore but retains external fertilization. The male deposits a spermatophore, and the female places eggs on top of it (Bannikov, 1958). During oviposition, the male and female salamanders are not in contact; if any stimuli influence the timing of oviposition, they must be olfactory or visual.

Anurans. At the time of oviposition and fertilization in most anurans, the pair is in amplexus, and there is some

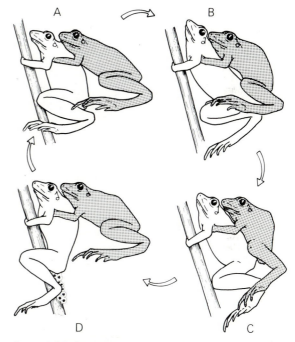

Figure 3-26. Ovipositional sequence in *Pseudacris triseriata* (male shaded). **A.** Shielding posture of male as female rests, grasping stem in water. **B.** Concave arching of back of female. **C.** Downward thrust of male as oviposition begins. **D.** Adherence of eggs to stem. Modified from Gosner and Rossman (1959).

evidence for various kinds of tactile signals between the sexes. Once the female has selected an oviposition site, peristaltic abdominal contractions in the female accompany ovulation or movement of eggs down the oviducts and may signal the male that oviposition is about to take place. Oviposition and fertilization are accomplished by synchronized movements by both partners. A male in an inguinal embrace may be able to detect abdominal movements by the female, including muscular activity of the oviduct. However, a male in axillary amplexus may not be aware of oviducal contractions.

Among anurans with inguinal amplexus, the male usually arches his back, bringing his cloaca adjacent to that of the female, and ejaculates as she releases eggs. This behavior is modified in *Alytes obstetricans,* for during oviposition the male shifts forward on the body of the female.

1. *Aquatic oviposition.*—Among anurans with axillary amplexus, the abdominal contractions of the female and positioning of the hindlimbs presumably are signals to the male that the female is ready to oviposit. Usually the female arches her back ventrally and raises her cloaca; the male arches his back dorsally, brings his cloaca into juxtaposition with hers, and ejaculates as eggs are deposited (Fig. 3-26). This pattern is essentially the same in all anurans having axillary amplexus and depositing their eggs in water. In some species, such as most species of *Rana* that deposit their eggs in a single clutch (Fig. 3-27), there are one or more massive extrusions of eggs, while the pair remains essentially stationary in the water. *Litoria splendida* forcefully expels eggs through a sperm suspension in quiet water (M. J. Tyler, pers. comm.); a similar manner of oviposition occurs in *Hyla andersonii* (Noble and Noble, 1923). Males of *L. verreauxi* cup their feet around batches of eggs as they are extruded and

Figure 3-27. Egg clutches of *Rana pipiens* in shallow water at Iris Springs, Arizona. Photo by J. S. Frost.

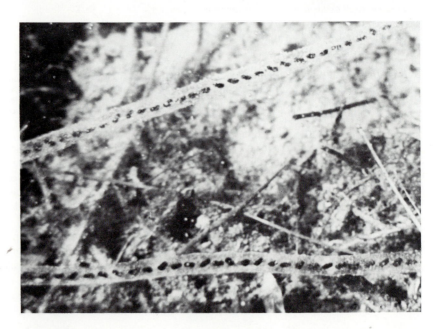

Figure 3-28. Egg strings of *Bufo americanus* in shallow water at Myersville, Maryland. Photo by K. Nemuras.

hold the eggs momentarily adjacent to their vents before pushing them to the feet of the female, which holds them for nearly 1 minute before she begins climbing around a submerged twig and wrapping the eggs around it with her feet; similar oviposition behavior occurs in *Litoria citropa, dentata,* and *glauerti* (Anstis, 1976). Female *Bufo* usually walk around in shallow water while ovipositing, so that the eggs are distributed as a pair of strings (one from each oviduct) (Fig. 3-28). Small strands of about 20 eggs are ejected during successive depositions by *Macrogenioglottis alipioi;* the male kicks the eggs, dispersing them in the water (Abravaya and Jackson, 1978). In those species that deposit their eggs as a film on the surface of the water (Fig. 2-12), the female usually is below the surface with only her vent out of water. During oviposition, the female *Pyxicephalus adspersus* moves up and down and sideways, rubbing her vent against the belly and inner surfaces of the thighs of the male; the eggs spread out in a surface film (B. Balinsky and J. Balinsky, 1954). While ovipositing, female *Phrynohyas venulosa* vibrate the vent laterally (Pyburn, 1967); this action seems to spread the eggs out on the surface of the water.

In some pipids complex oviposition maneuvers take place in water. There seems to be an evolutionary trend from ordinary midwater deposition of eggs on plants (some *Xenopus),* to upside-down oviposition on plants (some *Xenopus),* to egg-laying turnovers at the surface of the water *(Hymenochirus* and *Pseudhymenochirus),* to midwater turnovers with the adhesion of eggs on the dorsum of the female *(Pipa)* (G. Rabb, 1973). During the oviposition sequence in *Hymenochirus boettgeri* (Fig. 3-29), the pair swims to the surface; the frogs may or may not take in air, then turn over, thrust their vents above the surface and expel eggs and sperm, and turn over again

Figure 3-29. Ovipositional maneuvers in *Hymenochirus boettgeri* (male shaded). **A.** Resting on bottom. **B.** Ascent. **C.** Breathing. **D.** Turnover and oviposition on surface. **E.** Turnover and descent. In sequences in which frogs breathe (C), they usually sink slightly below the surface before turning over (D). Horizontal line is water surface. Adapted from G. Rabb (1973).

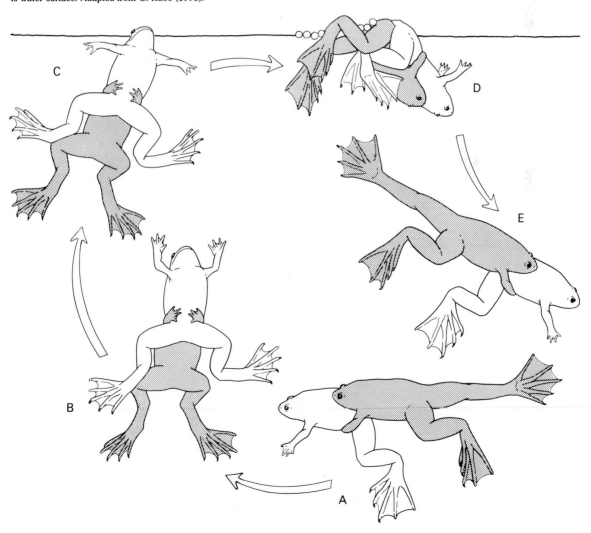

on their way to the bottom. The female leads the male through these maneuvers. While the pair is upside down at the surface of the water, the male kneads the female's abdomen, and both individuals flex their legs and move their feet forward and backward, presumably to maintain balance. As the eggs are expelled, they pass posteriorly toward the male's vent, which is simultaneously brought forward toward the eggs. The oviposition sequence is repeated until all eggs are laid. If the female slows her turnover movements, the male may initiate arm pumping and foot stroking. Four matings included 51, 143, 154, and 346 turnover sequences resulting in 20, 400, 500, and 1047 eggs, respectively (G. Rabb and M. Rabb, 1963a). Usually no eggs are expelled during the first turnover and several of the last turnovers. The duration of each oviposition sequence is about 6 seconds, and the entire oviposition process requires 1.5–7 hours.

Similar courtship activity and oviposition maneuvers occur in *Pipa pipa* (G. Rabb and M. Rabb, 1961, 1963b) and *P. carvalhoi* (Weygoldt, 1976a), but the eggs are deposited on the dorsum of the female during midwater turnovers and rotations (Fig. 3-30). During each turnover, a few eggs are extruded and are caught against the belly of the male, which then makes forward thrusts with his vent region, presumably fertilizing the eggs; as the pair settles to the bottom, the male presses the eggs to the female's dorsum, where they adhere and implant.

2. Arboreal oviposition.—Egg-laying on leaves or branches of bushes or trees is accomplished in much the same way as aquatic oviposition, except that the male maintains close contact with the dorsum of the female, and their vents are continuously juxtaposed. Two kinds of ovipositional behavior have been observed in phyllomedusine hylids (Kenny, 1966; Duellman, 1970; Pyburn, 1970, 1980a). In *Agalychnis callidryas* and *Pachymedusa dacnicolor,* the female (with the clasping male

Figure 3-30. Ovipositional maneuvers in *Pipa carvalhoi* (male shaded). **A.** Midwater swimming. **B.** Rest on bottom and push off. **C.** Ascent and turnover. **D.** Turnover and capture of eggs against belly of male. **E.** Sink to bottom and placement of eggs on dorsum of female. Horizontal line is water surface. Adapted from Weygoldt (1976a).

Figure 3-31. Oviposition by *Phyllomedusa hypocondrialis* at Belém, Brazil. Eggs can be seen just to the right of the male's right leg. Note the grasping of the edge of the leaf by the hindfeet of the male. Photo by W. E. Duellman.

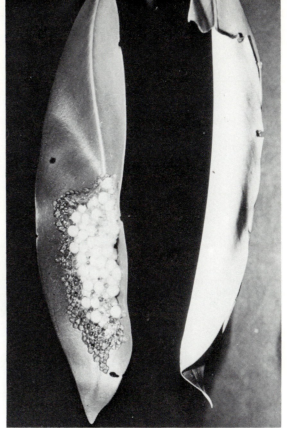

Figure 3-32. Egg clutches of *Phyllomedusa duellmani*, Departamento Amazonas, Peru. Leaf to the left has been opened to show eggs and eggless capsules, whereas leaf to the right is folded and adherent to eggs as completed by the amplectant pair. Photo by D. C. Cannatella.

on her back) descends to the pond where she takes water into her bladder; she then climbs up into overhanging vegetation and deposits a clutch of eggs, releasing water from her bladder over the eggs as they are laid. Subsequent clutches are deposited by the same pair but only after they descend to the water again. Female *Phyllomedusa* do not descend to water prior to oviposition, and some species are known to fold the leaf over the eggs as they are being deposited on it. Typically, an amplectant pair deposits eggs on the upper surface of a leaf and moves forward (upward) on the leaf as oviposition continues; the margin of the leaf is grasped by the feet of both members of the pair (Fig. 3-31). Upon completion of oviposition the leaf is entirely wrapped around the egg clutch; eggless capsules are deposited during the oviposition, and these capsules provide moisture for the developing eggs (Fig. 3-32). Similar nests are constructed by hyperoliids of the genus *Afrixalus,* some of which do so under water (Wager, 1965).

3. *Foam-nest construction.*—The habit of constructing foam nests on the surface of the water, in terrestrial

depressions or burrows, or in trees is widespread in several groups of primarily tropical anurans (see Chapter 2). In leptodactylids, the male constructs the nest with his hindfeet while in amplexus. The actual construction of the nest differs in various species. Males of *Leptodactylus pentadactylus* move both feet simultaneously in lateral motions, stirring the water and air with the eggs, jelly, and sperm as they are emitted (Heyer and Rand, 1977). In *Physalaemus pustulosus,* the male kicks his legs alternately into the mixture (Fig. 3-33). As the female *Pleurodema brachyops* releases eggs, the male holds small quantities of spawn with his hindlegs at the surface of the water and then beats the eggs into a foam by rapid crisscross motions of the feet (Hoogmoed and Gorzula, 1979). Large quantities of seminal fluid are released by males of species that have terrestrial foam nests; in *Leptodactylus bufonius,* the male vigorously whips the seminal fluid, jelly, and·eggs into a foam with his hindfeet (Pisano and del Río, 1968).

Nest construction by myobatrachid frogs that have aquatic foam nests is accomplished by the female, which

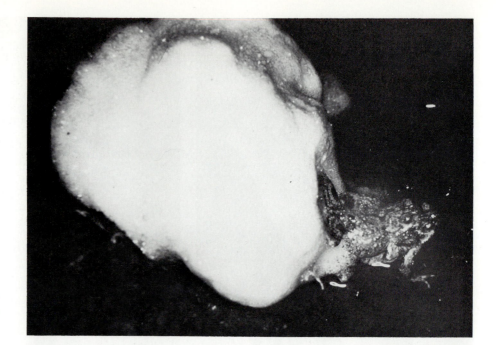

Figure 3-33. Foam-nest construction by *Physalaemus pustulosus*, Río Tuira, Panama. Note that male's feet are elevated into foam nest that is piling up on surface of water. Photo by W. E. Duellman.

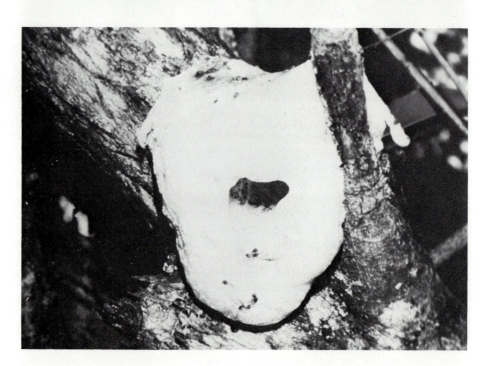

Figure 3-34. Arboreal foam nest of *Chiromantis petersi* at the Enzio River, Kenya. Photo by S. Reilly.

uses her hands (Tyler and M. Davies, 1979b). Amplexus is inguinal, and eggs are extruded below the male's belly. The female paddles with her hands in an alternating sequence. Each hand is brought forward, trapping tiny air bubbles at the surface of the water; as the hand is drawn downward and backward the water current and bubbles are directed against the male's abdomen and between his outstretched legs, where presumably the eggs are fer-

tilized as the semen, jelly, eggs, water, and rising air bubbles develop into a loose foam. The method of construction of terrestrial foam nests by myobatrachids is unknown.

Most nest-building rhacophorids construct foam nests in trees. In some species the nests are on limbs or in forks of limbs, whereas in others the nests are among leaves, some of which may be folded around the nest. In contrast to other frogs that construct foam nests, both the male and female take an active part in nest construction. While in axillary amplexus, the female selects an oviposition site above water, secretes a quantity of clear, viscous liquid, and immediately begins beating this liquid with swimming motions by the hindlimbs; the male makes the same movements. As eggs, jelly, and sperm are emitted, these are beaten into a frothy mass that adheres to the branch or leaves (Fig. 3-34). During the entire process, the female supports the pair by grasping a branch with her hands. Three or four males of *Chiromantis rufescens* have been observed completely or partially amplexing a female, with all individuals engaging in movements to whip up the foam nest (Coe, 1967, 1974). Multiple males amplexing a female also have been observed in *Polypedates dennysi* (C. Pope, 1931). In at least some species of *Polypedates* and *Rhacophorus,* a large quantity of seminal fluid is stored in modified Wolffian ducts; this fluid, in which the sperm are suspended, is discharged during amplexus and may contribute to the foam nest (Bhaduri, 1932). However, females of some species have been observed to construct a nest in the absence of males (C. Pope, 1931; Coe, 1974).

4. *Other kinds of oviposition.*—Among dendrobatids, the absence of amplexus in some species negates any continuous tactile signals for egg deposition or ejaculation. Observations indicate that at the time of oviposition members of a pair face away from one another; the male emits seminal fluid on a leaf, and the female deposits eggs on the fluid. The male may even leave the site before oviposition is completed (Weygoldt, 1980).

In some species of hylid marsupial frogs, the male takes an active part in the insertion of eggs into the pouch. However, in *Gastrotheca ovifera,* while the pair is in normal axillary amplexus, the female extends her hindlimbs and raises the posterior part of her body. In this position with the pair tilted head down, the eggs are extruded and slide anteriorly on the female's back into the large opening of the pouch. The male's cloaca is just above the opening of the pouch; presumably the eggs are fertilized as they pass below his cloaca and into the pouch (Mertens, 1957). Once in amplexus the female *G. riobambae* twists her hindlimbs so as to elevate the cloaca above the level of the small opening to the pouch; the amplectant male produces fluid presumably containing sperm from his cloaca and with his feet wipes this fluid over the area between the female's cloaca and the opening of the pouch. As the eggs are extruded, the male uses his feet to direct the eggs along the female's back to the opening of the pouch (Deckert, 1963; Hoogmoed, 1967). Complex interactions exist between male and female *Flectonotus pygmaeus* in amplexus (Duellman and Maness, 1980). The pair is tilted head down; the female's cloaca is elevated, and the male places his feet in the pouch, which has a long middorsal opening. As an egg is extruded, it slides anteriorly along the female's back; the male catches the egg between his heels, rotates the egg next to his cloaca, and with a pelvic thrust shoves the egg into the

pouch. Presumably the egg is fertilized as it is rotated at his cloacal opening.

Internal Fertilization

Caecilians and advanced families of salamanders all have internal fertilization, as do a few anurans. Sperm transfer is accomplished in different ways in these groups.

Caecilians. Male caecilians have an intromittent organ, the phallodeum; this is the eversible phallodial portion of the cloaca, which is inserted into the female's vent during copulation. Eversion is accomplished by a combination of contractions of the body wall musculature and of the cloaca. Detailed studies on the cloaca by M. Wake (1972) indicate that primitive caecilians (Ichthyophiidae) have blood sinuses that may aid in the eversion of the phallodeum, a function also attributable to blind sacs that are present in varying sizes in many caecilians but absent in others. The phallodeum is retracted by the M. retractor cloacae, which originates on the posterior body wall and inserts on the phallodeum. The morphology of the phallodeum is species-specific; the musculature and fibrous connective tissues form structural features, including longitudinal tracts possibly for the conduction of sperm, the blind sacs probably used in phallodeal eversion, and ornamentation such as knobs and transverse furrows (Fig. 3-35). The internal morphology of the female cloaca is less ornate than that of the male, but the pattern corresponds to that of the male. Adult male caecilians are unique in the retention of functional Mullerian ducts; the posterior part of the duct is an enlarged glandular structure, the lumen of which empties into the cloaca. The secretions of the Mullerian glands contain fructose, acid phosphotase, and mucopolysaccharides—constituents that provide fluid for sperm transport and probably nutrition (M. Wake, 1981). Subsequent to copulation, fertilization apparently takes place in the anterior part of the oviduct (M. Wake, 1968).

Anurans. *Ascaphus truei* is the only anuran known to have an intromittent organ. The "tail" of male *Ascaphus* is a posterior extension of the cloaca, supported in part

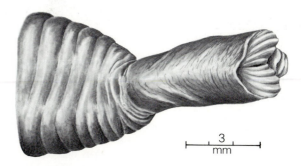

3
mm

Figure 3-35. Intromittent organ or phallodeum of a caecilian, *Geotrypetes seraphini.*

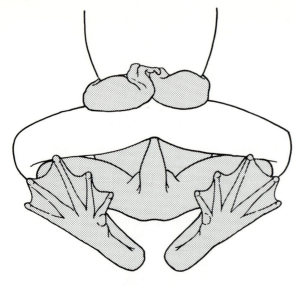

Figure 3-36. Tailpiece of cloacal extension of *Ascaphus truei* inserted into cloaca of female during inguinal amplexus. Posterior part of body viewed from below. Adapted from a photo by R. Altig.

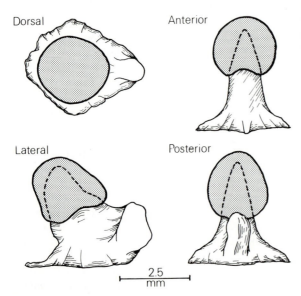

Dorsal

Anterior

Lateral

Posterior

2.5
mm

Figure 3-37. Spermatophore of *Plethodon jordani.* Sperm cap is shaded. Redrawn from Arnold (1976).

by paired Nobelian rods, which are modifications of an interfemoral ligament and connected with the prepubis (epipubis) by a tendinous sheet (van Dijk, 1955, 1959); these rods also are present in females, and in *Leiopelma* and *Xenopus*. Immediately anterior to the cloacal orifice are proctodeal glands. The cloacal epithelium changes from a mucous lining anteriorly to a cornified integument posteriorly; just within the orifice are horny spines. Vascularized tissue in the intromittent organ becomes engorged with blood making the organ turgid (Fig. 3-36). Amplexus is inguinal, and the male arches his back so

that the region posterior to the sacrum is perpendicular to the body of the female. The turgid intromittent organ is flexed another 90° by contractions of the paired mm. compressores cloacae, which insert on the Nobelian rods, and is inserted into the female's cloaca. Prior to the insertion of the organ, the females legs are extended, but after insertion her legs are drawn forward into a normal resting position; the period of copulation lasts 24 to 30 hours (Metter, 1964b). Contrary to the statement of Noble (1931b), Metter (1964b) noted that the engorgement of the organ did not result in exposure of the horny spine inside the cloacal orifice. Sperm may remain viable in the oviducts for 2 years (Metter, 1964b).

Internal fertilization is accomplished in *Nectophrynoides* and *Eleutherodactylus coqui* and *E. jasperi* simply by cloacal apposition (Grandison, 1978; Townsend et al., 1981). Modifications of the cloacal region of male *Mertensophryne micranotis* may be indicative of an intromittent function (Grandison, 1980b).

Salamanders. Salamanders (with the exception of the Hynobiidae, Cryptobranchidae, and Sirenidae) have a unique method of sperm transfer: spermatophores are deposited by males and picked up by females with subsequent storage of sperm in the spermatheca. An exception is the single hynobiid known to produce spermatophores, *Ranodon sibiricus,* in which the female presumably deposits eggs on a spermatophore that was previously deposited by a male (Bannikov, 1958).

The spermatophore is a roughly conical, gelatinous structure with a cap of sperm (Fig. 3-37); the sizes of spermatophores are correlated with the sizes of salamanders and range from 2 to 10 mm in height with about the same dimension for the greatest diameter of the base, which is ovoid. The cloacal glands in the lower walls of the male cloaca secrete a colorless, viscous material which forms the stalk of the spermatophore; the pelvic glands in the roof and upper walls of the cloaca secrete a whitish matrix, containing polysaccharides, in which the spermatozoa are imbedded to form the sperm cap (Noble and Weber, 1929). Microscopically, the matrix of the cap consists of a granular and fibrous substance and plaques of vacuolate homogeneous material concentrated near the tip of the stalk; the sperm caps of *Plethodon* have a covering of compact lamellated material resembling the plaques scattered through the sperm cap (Organ and Lowenthal, 1963). Observations on the deposition of spermatophore by plethodontids (Organ and Lowenthal, 1963) indicate that during deposition the spermatophore is nearly horizontal in the cloaca of the male; the stalk is anterior to and slightly below the cap. Upon deposition of the spermatophore, the male raises his vent and moves forward; this movement results in the change from nearly horizontal axis to vertical axis of the spermatophore with a resulting steep or vertical anterior surface and a more gently sloping posterior surface. The stalk is somewhat fluid and adhesive when first extruded, but quickly changes to a nonadhesive gel; also the base broadens as it adheres to the substance.

In females, the spermatheca is the homologue of the male pelvic gland and is in the roof of the cloaca (Beaumont, 1933). The structure of the spermatheca is variable (Noble, 1931b; Wahlert, 1953), being composed either of a number of independent simple tubules lined with columnar epithelium in salamandroids or of a common duct into which many such tubules open in ambystomatoids (Fig. 3-38). The tubules are imbedded in loose connective tissue, and they are located at the place of the opening of the oviducts into the cloaca. The loose connective tissue contains many melanophores (Dent, 1970); these melanophores may provide protection of the spermatozoa from radiation.

The spermatophore, or only the sperm cap, is grasped by the lips of the female's cloaca. The sperm cap, thus lodged in the cloaca, releases spermatozoa after it has been altered by phagocytes and leucocytes. Perhaps the sperm are attracted by some secretions of the spermatheca (Noble and Weber, 1929). The sperm arrange themselves in orderly whorls in the spermathecal tubules, where they remain until ovulation. In some salamanders sperm are stored for many months, but only for a few hours in *Ambystoma*. Sperm are stored up to 2.5 years in *Salamandra salamandra* (Joly, 1960a). In that species the sperm heads penetrate the cells of the epithelial lining of the spermathecal tubules, whereas in *Notophthalmus viridescens* the sperm heads are in contact with the epithelium (Benson, 1968). Activity of spermatozoa in the sperm cap of the spermatophore is inhibited by polysaccharides, but these polysaccharides do not persist in the spermatheca. Long-term storage of the sperm in the spermatheca necessitates their obtaining nutrients, presumably from the epithelial lining, but the exact mechanism is unknown.

At the time of ovulation, spermatozoa are expelled by contraction of muscles surrounding the spermathecal tubules, and fertilize the eggs as they enter the cloaca. In the live-bearing *Salamandra*, the sperm enter the oviducts. In *Salamandra atra*, the single egg that is fertilized in each oviduct is the first to pass through the oviduct and lodge against the oviducal opening into the cloaca; there it is readily reached by spermatozoa (Häfeli, 1971).

Salamanders with internal fertilization have the option of distributing their eggs in space and time or placing their eggs together and attending them. Salthe (1969) recognized three major oviposition sites in salamanders: open, static water (lentic sites); hidden nesting sites associated with running water (lotic); and hidden terrestrial sites.

1. Lentic sites.—Most species of *Ambystoma* are in this category. The female walks or swims to a twig or stem and grasps it with her hindfeet, pressing her cloaca to the stem and moving forward while depositing eggs on the stem. As the egg capsules swell by absorbing water, they form a clump on the stem. Only part of the ovarian complement is deposited at any one place, and as many as a dozen or so clutches may be deposited during 3 or 4 days. Two genera of plethodontids (*Hemidactylium* and *Stereochilus*) oviposit upside down at the edge of, or above, static water. Some salamandrids deposit only one egg at each site. For example, *Cynops, Notophthalmus, Paramesotriton,* and *Triturus* deposit eggs singly on leave of aquatic plants; *Cynops pyrrhogaster* deposits 1–16 eggs each day, and a female may continue laying for about 50 days, producing during that time up to 324 eggs (Tsutsui, 1931). All newts carefully wrap their individual eggs in vegetation by using their hindfeet; this behavior hides the egg, for adult newts will eat the eggs if a moving embryo is visible. Oviposition and egg-wrapping are accomplished when the female is upside down.

The attachment of eggs to stems or leaves in midwater prevents the eggs from sinking into the mud on the bottom of ponds, where the oxygen supply is very low. Normally *Triturus* and *Notophthalmus* oviposit only on young leaves; experiments by Winpenny (1951) indicated that the female has some cloacal mechanism for detecting oxygen production, which is higher in young leaves.

2. Lotic sites.—Salamanders, such as *Eurycea*, usually deposit eggs on the undersides of stones in streams so that water flows past the eggs. The eggs are stalked and deposited one at a time while the female is upside down and usually moving forward during deposition so that the eggs are close together. Females of *Euproctus asper* have a conical cloaca and scatter their eggs among cracks and recesses in rocky streams (Gasser, 1964). *Desmognathus* hide their clutches in the banks of streams. *Taricha rivularis, Dicamptodon, Rhyacotriton,* and some *Ambystoma* also lay their eggs in streams.

3. Terrestrial sites.—Terrestrial sites of oviposition are characteristic of plethodontine and bolitoglossine plethodontids. The eggs are all laid together and may be independent of one another or attached by a central stalk to the roof or wall of a cavity beneath a stone or log, or within a log. Normally the female attends the eggs.

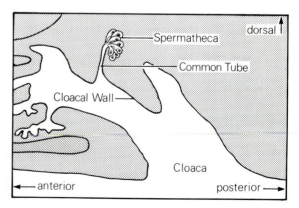

Figure 3-38. Diagrammatic sagittal section of the cloaca of a female salamander, *Desmognathus fuscus,* showing spermatheca. Modified from Noble (1931b).

SEXUAL SELECTION

Sexual selection can involve one sex choosing individuals of the opposite sex as mates (intersexual selection) or competition among individuals of one sex for access to individuals of the opposite sex (intrasexual selection). The latter can involve either direct competition for mates or competition for control of a critical resource. Generally females have a greater investment in reproduction and a higher certainty of parenthood than do males. Therefore, females would be expected to be more discriminating in their choice of potential mates. Natural selection in both sexes should favor increased genetic representation in future generations; males tend to maximize their reproductive success by increasing the number of matings, whereas females should favor higher-quality mates.

Although an abundance of theory on sexual selection has been proposed in recent years (e.g., Trivers, 1972; G. Williams, 1975; Burley, 1977; Emlen and Oring, 1977), comparatively few observations and experiments have provided empirical evidence for sexual selection in amphibians. This is not to imply that sexual selection is nonexistent in most amphibians, but rather that biologists are only now becoming aware of the phenomena and that much careful work needs to be done. The limited information on a few selected species of amphibians suggests that complex sexual interactions, some of which are density-dependent, support Berven's (1981:707) generalized contention: "The major mechanism hypothesized that underlies patterns of sexual selection is that discriminating females control the reproduction of indiscriminate males."

Mate Selection

Berven (1981) postulated four possible explanations for the patterns of anuran mating behavior:

1. Male-male competition, whereby males are competing for females, and the larger males are competitively superior to the smaller males.
2. Female choice, whereby females choose larger (or better) males.
3. Size-assortive mating, whereby females choose males of nearly equivalent or proportionately larger body size.
4. Male choice, whereby males discriminate against smaller females.

Male-male competition for mates may be by means of scramble competition, in which males actively search for mates and larger males tend to dominate the search area, forcing smaller males into areas where they are less likely to find females. This form of sexual selection is especially prevalent among anurans that have short, intense breeding seasons, such as *Rana sylvatica* (Wells, 1977b, c; R. W. Howard, 1980; Berven, 1981).

Although many male anurans that have prolonged breeding seasons maintain territories, these are commonly ephemeral in that a male uses a calling station for only one night or part thereof; such is the case in *Hyla versicolor*, in which a calling male emits encounter calls when approached by another male (Fellers, 1979b). Males of other species aggressively defend territories. Size and age are primary factors in successful occupation of preferred territories in *Rana catesbeiana* (R. W. Howard, 1978b) and *R. clamitans* (Wells, 1977c, 1978b). In *R. catesbeiana*, oviposition occurs in territories; larger males control better territories, and egg survival is highest in these territories (R. W. Howard, 1978a). Males of some species of *Centrolenella* aggressively defend calling and oviposition sites (McDiarmid and Adler, 1974; Duellman and Savitzky, 1976); successful males of *C. fleischmanni* obtain many matings (Greer and Wells, 1980). However, size may not be the major factor in sexual selection in these small arboreal frogs, because of the small range in size among calling males. Likewise, size is not a significant factor in defense of nests in *Hyla rosenbergi* (Kluge, 1981).

Territoriality may be viewed as the defense of resources needed for survival and/or reproduction. As emphasized by Wells (1977a), the attachment to a fixed site will be advantageous if it gives the occupant exclusive or priority access to limited resources. Females may be the limited resource, and they usually are not defendable except by guarding during amplexus or courtship (see the later section: Sexual Defense).

Aggressive behavior related to site-specific territoriality has been documented in a few terrestrial salamanders— *Aneides aeneus* (Cupp, 1980) and two species of *Plethodon* (R. Jaeger and Gergits, 1979)—and has been reported in aquatic cryptobranchoids having external fertilization and defending oviposition sites—*Hynobius nebulosus* (Thorn, 1962), *Cryptobranchus alleganiensis* (Bishop, 1941), and *Andrias japonicus* (Kerbert, 1904). Physical combat between male frogs frequently is preceded by agonistic vocalizations (see Chapter 4); some frogs also have postural or visual displays (Table 3-2). Territorial males of *Rana catesbeiana* and *R. clamitans* maintain high, inflated positions in the water (Emlen, 1968; Wells, 1978b). Territorial males of *Colostethus inguinalis* display their white throats (Wells, 1980a), and territorial females of *C. collaris* and *C. herminae* display their bright yellow throats (Durant and Dole, 1975; Sexton, 1960). These and other dendrobatids usually assume an erect posture with stiffened limbs when challenging intruders; a similar posture has been observed in male *Centrolenella* (Wells, 1977a). Physical combat in anurans may be simply a butting of the intruder by the territorial male, as in *Pseudophryne* (Pengilley, 1971). More physical bouts include grappling or wrestling, as in dendrobatids and *Centrolenella* (Duellman, 1966; McDiarmid and Adler, 1974; Duellman and Savitzky, 1976). In frogs that have prepollical spines, these bouts may result in injuries or fatalities (B. Lutz, 1960, 1973; Rivero and Esteves, 1969; Kluge, 1981). Duellman and Trueb have observed biting in the *Hyla microcephala;* biting also was reported for

Table 3-2. Territorial Behavior in Anurans

Species	Sex	Territory location	Site attachment	Encounter calls	Postural or other visual displays	Resident chases intruder	Jump attacks	Wrestling	Oviposition in territory	Source
*Hymenochirus boettgeri**	♂	Underwater calling site	+	+	+	+	+	+	−	G. Rabb and M. Rabb (1963a)
*Pipa carvalhoi**	♂	Underwater calling site	?	+	+	+	+	+	−	Weygoldt (1976a)
*Pipa pipa**	♂	Underwater calling site	?	+	+	+	+	+	−	G. Rabb and M. Rabb (1963b)
*Pipa parva**	♂	Underwater calling site	?	+	?	+	+	+	?	G. Rabb (1969)
Limnodynastes dumerili	♂	Pool or burrow	+	+	?	+	+	+	+	Clyne (1967)
Pseudophryne bibroni	♂	Terrestrial burrow	+	+	?	+	+	+	+	Pengilley (1971)
Pseudophryne corroboree	♂	Terrestrial burrow	+	+	?	+	+	+	+	Pengilley (1971)
Pseudophryne dendyi	♂	Terrestrial burrow	+	+	?	+	+	+	+	Pengilley (1971)
Eleutherodactylus coqui	♂, ♀	Tree hole	+	+	?	+	+	+	−	Drewry (1970)
Eleutherodactylus hedricki	♂	Tree hole	+	+	?	+	+	?	−	Drewry (1970)
Eleutherodactylus urichi	♂	Tree hole	+	+	?	+	+	?	−	Wells (1981b)
Leptodactylus bolivianus	♂	Foam nest in water	+	+	?	+	+	+	+	Sexton (1962)
Leptodactylus melanorotus	♂	Under rocks near water	+	+	−	+	−	+	+	Brattstrom and Yarnell (1968)
Leptodactylus pentadactylus	♂	Margin of pond	+	+	+	+	+	+	?	Rivero and Esteves (1969)
Colostethus collaris	♂, ♀	Rocks in stream	+	?	+	+	+	+	?	Durant and Dole (1975)
Colostethus inguinalis	♂, ♀	Rocks in stream	+	?	+	+	+	+	?	Wells (1980a)
Colostethus trinitatus	♂, ♀	Rocks in stream	+	−	+	+	+	+	−	Wells (1980b)
Dendrobates granuliferus	♂	Logs, leaves, stems	+	+	+	+	+	+	?	Goodman (1971); Crump (1972)
Dendrobates histrionicus	♂	Logs, leaves, stems	+	?	?	+	+	+	?	Silverstone (1973)
Dendrobates pumilio	♂	Logs, plants, ground	+	+	+	+	+	+	+	Duellman (1966); Bunnell (1973); Weygoldt (1980); McVey et al. (1981)
Hyla faber	♂	Excavated nest	+	?	?	?	+	+	+	Lutz (1960)
Hyla pardalis	♂	Excavated nest	+	?	?	?	+	+	+	Lutz (1973)
Hyla rosenbergi	♂	Excavated nest	+	+	+	+	+	+	+	Kluge (1981)
Pachymedusa dacnicolor	♂	Burrow	+	+	?	+	+	?	−	Wiewandt (1971)
Centrolenella fleischmanni	♂	Plant over stream	+	+	+	?	+	−	+	McDiarmid and Adler (1974); Greer and Wells (1980)
Centrolenella griffithsi	♂	Plant over stream	+	?	+	?	+	+	+	Duellman and Savitzky (1976)
Centrolenella valerioi	♂	Plant over stream	+	+	+	+	+	?	+	McDiarmid and Adler (1974)
Rana catesbeiana	♂	Vegetated area of pond	+	+	+	+	+	+	+	Emlen (1968); Howard (1978a)
Rana clamitans	♂	Margin of pond	+	+	+	+	+	+	+	Wells (1978b)

*Captive animals. Based on Wells (1977a) with additions.

Eleutherodactylus coqui (Reyes Campos, 1971) and for *Phyllodytes luteolus* (Weygoldt, 1981).

Diurnal, terrestrial dentrobatids may defend all-purpose territories that include feeding sites, shelter, and oviposition sites (Wells, 1977a, 1980a). Holes in trees that are used for shelter and oviposition sites are defended by some species of *Eleutherodactylus* (Drewry, 1970). In all of these groups, territorial behavior, typical of males, is characteristic of females of some species.

Calling sites and courtship sites are defended by many species of frogs. These include diurnal terrestrial dendrobatids, arboreal hylids, semiaquatic ranids, and aquatic pipids.

Females may choose larger males; large size and greater age are indicative of rapid growth rate and/or longevity, both of which are good indicators of fitness. Gravid female *Uperoleia rugosa* mate only with calling males and usually choose the largest male available (Robertson, 1981). Comparison of sizes of mated versus nonmated males in *Bufo quercicus* (Wilbur et al., 1978) and *Hyla marmorata* (J. Lee and Crump, 1981) revealed that mated males were larger; these results were interpreted as female choice of larger mates. How do females select larger mates? Vocalizations may provide information about the size of the calling male (see Chapter 4). Females of *Physalaemus pustulosus* discriminate against higher fundamental frequencies of the call and therefore choose larger males, which call at lower frequencies (M. Ryan, 1980). They also tend to choose males that have more complex calls (Rand and M. Ryan, 1981).

Females of *Hyla rosenbergi* apparently choose mates by the location of the nests (calling stations), preferring males that call from groups rather than isolates (Kluge, 1981). Furthermore, females enter the nests of calling males and bump the males; if a male jumps out of the nest the female will leave. Kluge (1981) interpreted these observations as female choice of male quality. A male calling as part of a group and also maintaining his position when bumped can be assessed as an individual capable of defending his nest, an important attribute in that survival of eggs and tadpoles depends on his ability to remain at the nest for several days.

Size-assortive mating presumably involves female choice of a mate that is of a size that will not interfere with her movements during oviposition but will be effective in fertilizing the eggs. Positive correlations between sizes of mated pairs have been reported for *Bufo bufo* (N. Davies and Halliday, 1978), *B. americanus* (L. Licht, 1976), and *Triprion petasatus* (J. Lee and Crump, 1981), but there is no evidence of active female choice in any of these species. Males also may choose females by size; for example, males of *Rana sylvatica* prefer larger females (Berven, 1981).

There are even fewer observations and interpretations of mate choice in salamanders. Mate choice by male and female salamanders may result from the complex olfactory, tactile, and visual cues provided during early stages of courtship; escape behavior by a female may indicate that she is not physiologically ready to mate or that she is not receptive to a particular male. For example, female newts *(Triturus)* seem to prefer large males with well-developed crests (Halliday, 1977).

Lek behavior involves a communal display area where males congregate for the sole purpose of attracting and courting females which come for breeding (Emlen and Oring, 1977). Males do not control females directly, nor do they control resources, such as oviposition sites, needed by the females. Lek behavior has been proposed for the bullfrog *Rana catesbeiana* (Emlen, 1976), but R. W. Howard (1978a) showed that males controlled territories in which the females oviposited. Likewise, even though frogs, such as *Hyla rosenbergi* and some species of *Centrolenella*, congregate for breeding, individual males defend calling sites that are also oviposition sites. Thus, in most amphibian mating systems, males seem to control either females or oviposition sites; lek behavior has yet to be demonstrated in amphibians.

Mating Success

In most amphibian mating systems, the operational sex ratio (number of ready males:number of receptive females at any given time) is highly skewed in favor of males. Ratios of seven or eight males per female are not uncommon among explosive breeders, whereas the proportion of females may be higher in long-term breeders. However, one notable exception is known; in *Dendrobates auratus,* males are occupied by attending clutches, so the number of receptive females may exceed the number of available males (Wells, 1978a).

The variance in mating success generally is much lower in males than in females. The measurement of mating success in salamanders is difficult, because in most species courtship and oviposition take place at widely separated intervals; furthermore, females may pick up more than one spermatophore, so male parentage cannot be determined. The number of spermatophores deposited per courtship and the amount of time devoted to each courtship have been used as a measure of mating success and male investment in salamanders (Arnold, 1977). As examples, *Ambystoma* deposit many spermatophores per courtship and invest only a few minutes in each spermatophore; *A. maculatum* deposits as many as 81 spermatophores per courtship with an average investment of 1.4 minutes per spermatophore (Arnold, 1976). Salamandrids usually deposit only 1–4 spermatophores per courtship, whereas the modal number is 1 in plethodontids, in which the temporal investment may be 1–5 hours per courtship (Arnold, 1977). Lengthy courtships tend to result in a higher probability of the female discovering and recovering a spermatophore (Fig. 3-39).

Although the data are extremely limited, some general patterns of mating success seem to be evident (Table 3-

3). In explosive and short-term breeders, such as *Rana sylvatica, Bufo typhonius,* and *Pseudacris triseriata,* variance in male mating success is low, whereas in species with longer breeding seasons and especially those species exhibiting male teritoriality, chances for a successful mating and multiple matings are higher. However, some males still obtain no mates.

The factors responsible for male mating success in anurans are not well understood. Most *Hyla versicolor* calling from perches, where there is the least habitat inteference with the propagation of the call, are more likely to obtain a male than mates calling from less desirable perches (Fellers, 1979b). Calling and oviposition sites, as well as the number of nights of calling, are positively correlated with mating success in *Centrolenella fleischmanni* (Greer and Wells, 1980). Males of *Hyla chrysoscelis* that spent more nights calling obtained more matings than those that were at the breeding pond only a few nights; furthermore, the probability of a male obtaining a mate increased late in the season when few males were at the pond (Godwin and Roble, 1983). Quality of males' territories clearly influences mating success in *Rana catesbeiana* and *R. clamitans* (R. W. Howard, 1978b; Wells, 1977c). Significantly more matings were obtained by more aggressive males in the territorial *Hyla rosenbergi* (Kluge, 1981). With the exception of scramble competition for females in explosive breeders, in which larger male size sometimes is advantageous, the mating success of a given male may depend on a combination of several factors—time of arrival at a breeding site, duration of stay at the breeding site, territorial behavior, aggressive behavior toward other males, effectiveness of visual displays, and in anurans the choice of a calling site and perhaps the quality of the call.

Sexual Defense

Intraspecific competition among males for mates is known in many amphibians. This is most evident in the calling behavior with respect to territories and encounters in anurans (see Chapter 4). However, nonvocal behavior at breeding sites involves ways of monopolizing females. Males of *Rhyacotriton olympicus* and several plethodontid salamanders (species of *Desmognathus, Eurycea, Plethodon,* and *Pseudotriton)* are known to bite and sometimes chase males that interfere with courtship (Arnold, 1977). Among aquatic salamanders, males may shove females away from other males, as in *Ambystoma tigrinum* (Arnold, 1976), or in cases in which the male actually captures the female, he swims away from rival males and carries the female with him—*A. laterale* (Storez, 1969), *Taricha,* and *Pleurodeles* (Arnold, 1977). The rapid courtship and multiple spermatophores of some *Ambystoma* (e.g., *A. maculatum)* may be interpreted as a form of sexual defense (Arnold, 1976). By producing many spermatophores quickly in the presence of a receptive female, the male is increasing his chances of a

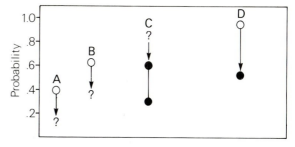

Figure 3-39. Success of individual spermatophores as a function of relative male investment per spermatophore. Open circles indicate probability of discovery by the female; solid circles indicate probability of recovery of sperm cap by female. **A.** *Ambystoma maculatum.* **B.** *Ambystoma tigrinum.* **C.** Range of variation in *Triturus cristatus, helveticus,* and *vulgaris.* **D.** *Plethodon jordani.* Modified from Arnold (1977).

successful mating prior to interference by a rival male.

Prolonged amplexus in anurans may be a strategy for monopolizing a female, especially if pairing takes place before ovulation (Wells, 1977a). Amplexus takes place at the breeding site and may last for 12 days in *Rana temporaria* (Geisselmann et al., 1971) or 14 days in *Bufo bufo* (Heusser, 1963). In *Atelopus oxyrhynchus,* pairing may occur before the frogs reach a breeding site, and pairs may be in amplexus for periods up to 125 days (Dole and Durant, 1974a). Observations of unmated males attempting to dislodge amplecting males indicate that most mated males maintain amplexus and therefore are effectively monopolizing the mated female.

Sexual Interference

Several kinds of behavior by male amphibians are directed at obtaining matings at the expense of courtship investment by another male. Arnold (1976, 1977) reviewed sexual interference in salamanders and noted that sexual interference can be accomplished by stealing a female, disrupting the spermatophore deposition of a rival male, covering the spermatophores of rival males, or duping rival males into unprofitable spermatophore depositions.

Spermatophore covering is common in *Ambystoma.* Many males vie for one female, and males deposit many spermatophores. In species such as *A. maculatum,* in which courtship involves only nudging, males not only deposit spermatophores on top of other spermatophores, including their own, but nudge females trying to pick up spermatophores and rival males depositing spermatophores. Sometimes in *A. maculatum* a male has been observed to follow another male that is depositing spermatophores and then to cover each one with a spermatophore of his own. In some instances a male has been observed to circle behind his follower and deposit another spermatophore on top of that deposited by the

Table 3-3. Mating Success in Male Anurans[a]

Species	Seasons of data	Number of males	Number of matings										Number of successful matings	Percent of males successful	Matings per successful male	Matings per male
			0	1	2	3	4	5	6	7	8	9				
Physalaemus pustulosus	1	185	119	43	16	2	4	—	1	—	—	—	103	35.6	1.56	0.557
Bufo americanus	1	129	93	33	3	—	—	—	—	—	—	—	39	27.9	1.08	0.302
Bufo bufo	1	73	58	14	1	—	—	—	—	—	—	—	16	20.5	1.07	0.219
Bufo canorus	4	795	595	165	34	1	—	—	—	—	—	—	236	25.2	1.18	0.297
Bufo exul	2	1288	952	295	38	3	—	—	—	—	—	—	380	26.1	1.13	0.295
Bufo typhonius	1	160	98	61	1	—	—	—	—	—	—	—	63	38.8	1.02	0.394
Hyla chrysoscelis[b]	1	124	81	33	8	2	—	—	—	—	—	—	55	34.7	1.28	0.444
Hyla rosenbergi	2	95	43	24	14	4	7	1	2	—	—	—	109	54.7	2.10	1.147
Hyla versicolor	1	35	26	8	1	—	—	—	—	—	—	—	10	25.7	1.11	0.286
Pseudacris triseriata[c]	2	442	366	75	1	—	—	—	—	—	—	—	77	17.2	1.01	0.174
Centrolenella colymbiphyllum	1	101	27	35	22	7	4	3	1	1	1	—	152	73.3	2.05	1.505
Centrolenella fleischmanni[d]	1	14	1	1	1	4	3	1	1	1	—	1	59	92.9	4.54	4.214
Centrolenella valerioi	1	56	15	9	9	13	5	4	1	1	—	—	112	73.2	2.73	2.000
Rana catesbeiana	3	93	45	24	12	8	2	—	1	—	—	—	93	51.6	1.94	1.000
Rana clamitans	2	46	21	17	6	1	—	1	—	—	—	—	37	54.3	1.48	0.804
Rana sylvatica	1	345	289	54	3	—	—	—	—	—	—	—	60	19.1	1.07	0.174
Rana temporaria	1	33	16	15	1	1	—	—	—	—	—	—	20	51.5	1.18	0.606

[a]Based on tabulations in Kluge (1981), except as noted.
[b]Godwin and Roble (1983).
[c]Roble (pers. comm.).
[d]Greer and Wells (1980).

follower; thus a triple spermatophore results (Arnold, 1976).

Duping of males is known in *Ambystoma tigrinum, Desmognathus ochrophaeus, Ensatina eschscholtzi, Pseudotriton ruber,* and four large species of *Plethodon* (Organ and Organ, 1968; Arnold, 1976, 1977). During the aquatic courtship of *A. tigrinum,* the female follows the male and nudges his cloaca with her snout. The continuation of his behavior and deposition of a spermatophore depend on the continual nudging of his cloaca. A rival male can replace the female and have the female follow him. The original male deposits a spermatophore, which is covered by the spermatophore of the interfering male; if the female picks up a spermatophore, it is the one deposited by the second male. Males intrude during the tail-straddling walk in plethodontid courtship and dupe other males into depositing spermatophores.

Sexual interference in anurans involves the association of silent males with calling males. This satellite behavior or "sexual parasitism" has been reported for various species of *Bufo, Hyla, Pseudacris, Rana,* and *Gastrophryne* (Axtell, 1958; L. Brown and Pierce, 1967; Wells, 1977c, 1978b; R. W. Howard, 1978a; Perrill et al., 1978; Fellers, 1979a, 1979b; Miyamoto and Cane, 1980b; Roble, pers. comm.; Godwin and Roble, 1983). Satellite males sit quietly near calling males and commonly maintain a low posture, presumably making themselves inconspicuous to the calling males, which may chase them away. Two or three satellites have been observed with one calling male in several species.

Two hypotheses have been proposed for this satellite behavior: satellite males are waiting for calling sites or territories to become available after the calling male mates; and satellite males intercept females as they move toward calling males (Wells, 1977b). These hypotheses are not mutually exclusive. The former seems to account for the satellite behavior in *Hyla versicolor,* in which there is a positive correlation between call site and mating success (Fellers, 1979b). In the territorial species *Rana catesbeiana* and *R. clamitans,* satellite males are smaller than calling males and also seem to await the vacancy of a territory. Two of 73 matings in *R. catesbeiana* were by satellite males (R. W. Howard, 1978a). Males of the small Australian myobatrachid *Uperoleia rugosa* establish territories in grass adjacent to ponds. Satellite males do not intercept females approaching calling males, but the satellites may take over a calling site when a female carries the former territory-holder to an oviposition site, or satellites may replace territory-holders that have become physically weakened after maintaining their territories for several weeks (Robertson, 1981). Convincing experimental evidence for successful interception of females by satellite males is available for two species of *Hyla.* In 13 of 30 field experiments with the release of a gravid female near a calling male–satellite association in *H. cinerea,* the satellite successfully intercepted the female (Perrill et al., 1978). In three of seven similar field experiments and

one natural observation of *H. ebraccata,* the satellite male achieved amplexus (Miyamoto and Cane, 1980b).

In the species of *Hyla* and *Pseudacris nigrita,* there is no size difference between calling and satellite males. Furthermore, in *H. cinerea, H. chrysoscelis,* and *P. nigrita,* individual males changed strategies from calling to satellite behavior or from satellite to calling behavior on different nights or on the same night (Perrill et al., 1978; Godwin and Roble, 1983; S. N. Roble, pers. comm.).

Reproductive Interference

Interference with the development of the eggs or young is another form of intraspecific competition that may enhance the reproductive success of one individual at the expense of another. Conspecific oophagy is common among female plethodontid salamanders that have terrestrial nests; females attend their own eggs and drive off potential predators, including conspecific females. Some newts *(Notophthalmus* and *Taricha)* eat conspecific eggs (J. Wood and Goodwin, 1954; Kaplan and P. Sherman, 1980). Possibly because of this behavior, the eggs of newts are concealed singly or in small clumps amidst aquatic vegetation. Moreover, it is not known if individuals recognize their own eggs, so oophagy in newts might be indiscriminate cannibalism.

The eating or destruction of eggs and larvae in conspecific clutches has been documented in two species of *Dendrobates.* Males of *D. pumilio* are territorial and attend egg clutches. When males find an unattended clutch fertilized by another male, they eat the eggs, of if the eggs are hatching, the male sits in a clutch; when a tadpole climbs onto his back, he carries it to a bromeliad axil or crevice and leaves it (Weygoldt, 1980). Because tadpoles are dependent on eggs provided by a female for food, those tadpoles transported to sites unknown to the female probably will not survive. Females of *Dendrobates auratus, lehmanni,* and *histrionicus* have been observed to eat or destroy eggs in other females' clutches (Wells, 1978a; H. Zimmermann and E. Zimmermann, 1981).

EVOLUTION OF MATING SYSTEMS

Both males and females face the same basic problem of having to form mating relationships in a way that best enhances their reproductive success. However, the mating relationship yielding maximal success is not necessarily the same for both sexes. In most amphibians, males compete among themselves for mating opportunities, and females assume noncompetitive roles, mating with winning males or choosing among courting males. Males usually are not discriminating in their choice of prospective mates, whereas females often are highly selective in choosing their mates. Male competition and female choice are the consequences of the different costs to each sex to produce offspring. Ova are energetically more costly to produce than sperm; therefore, female reproductive output is limited by resource availability and time constraints, not mate availability. Males generally produce many more sperm than needed to fertilize all of the eggs produced by available females. Thus, the availability of receptive females is limiting, and males normally compete to fertilize as many eggs as possible.

Males that exhibit paternal care increase their investment in reproduction, and it is significant that clutch sizes in such species are small. Also, salamanders that have lengthy courtships tend to produce few spermatophores. Similarly, male frogs that have a large investment in territorial defense tend to have relatively high reproductive success, but some individuals are unsuccessful.

Male mating strategies are adaptations to environmental conditions, primarily the length of the breeding season. Explosive breeding involves a short, synchronous burst of breeding activity once or a few times each year. This is characteristic of many temperate species that breed in the spring, as well as tropical anurans that breed primarily in ephemeral aquatic situations. However, some tropical species, such as *Bufo typhonius,* are explosive breeders and do not utilize ephemeral habitats (Wells, 1979); the selective advantage of synchronous oviposition in such species may be the satiation of predators by larvae and thus the survivorship of some offspring (Walters, 1975). On the other hand, prolonged breeding may last several months in temperate climates to all year in the tropics.

At high densities males of explosive-breeding anurans actively search for mates, even though many males are advertising vocally and attracting females to the breeding site. At high densities there is intense male-male competition for mates, and size and aggressiveness of males are important factors in mating success. At lower densities males of explosive-breeding anurans usually are dispersed at the breeding site; physical competition among males is reduced because advertisement calls are more effective in attracting a female to a particular male. Thus, at low densities the mating strategies of explosive-breeding anurans are more like those of prolonged breeders.

Among anurans, the establishment and defense of territories is associated only with prolonged breeders. In these frogs, mating success depends not so much on the search and scramble competition for females but on the attraction of females to the male's territory. Thus, in prolonged breeders, female choice is a major factor in mate selection. The amount of time that a male defends a territory contributes to the probability of multiple matings. However, maintenance of a territory by an advertising male does not necessarily ensure reproductive success. For example, 43 of 95 male *Hyla rosenbergi* that called from defended nests obtained no matings, whereas 28 males mated more than once (Kluge, 1981).

The energetic aspects of courtship and mating remain essentially unknown. The strictly reproductive factors can be measured energetically (Crump and Kaplan, 1979; Kaplan, 1980b). However, little information exists on the energy expenditures required for calling and courtship activities. Male salamanders that produce large quantities of spermatophores per courtship deplete their spermatophore supply after a few days, whereas plethodontids, which produce only one spermatophore, or rarely two, per courtship can continue production and therefore potentially successful courtships for many weeks (Arnold, 1977). Moreover, males require energy to develop secondary sexual characteristics and to defend territories.

Males of explosive-breeding anurans usually have empty stomachs after one day at the breeding site; apparently all efforts are directed toward mating, and these frogs generally do not feed during the brief breeding season. However, males that advertise for mates for many weeks or months must acquire nutrition during this time. Probably frogs that are absent from a breeding site for a few nights before resuming calling are taking time off for feeding. Because most anurans have a sit-and-wait feeding strategy, males of prolonged breeders may obtain some food at their calling sites; probably this is especially important to territorial species. A male that can obtain sufficient food in his territory can defend the territory and advertise consistently, thereby increasing his chances for reproductive success. But even territorial species may lose weight during the breeding season, as was noted in *Rana clamitans* by Wells (1978b).

With the exception of those species of frogs in which calling males are larger and satellite males are smaller and subordinate, the satellite behavior of males and their switching of roles may be a mechanism whereby a male can conserve energy and still possibly obtain a mate.

In summary, the mating systems of amphibians are highly complex, involving simple to elaborate courtship behavior. Some behavioral traits coincide with reproductive and morphological evolutionary trends. Courtship behavior in salamanders evolved in diverse ways once salamanders developed spermatophores, and some of the behaviors are phylogenetically related—tail and cloacal nudging in ambystomatids and the tail-straddling walk in plethodontids. Likewise, amplectic position in anurans is associated with the general phylogeny of the group, but there are exceptions. Within both salamanders and anurans, specialized courtship and mating behaviors are associated with certain specialized modes of reproduction and in some species involve complex interactions of both sexes (e.g., some pipids, foam nest-builders, some marsupial frogs). Likewise, within both groups, mating strategies differ with densities and duration of the breeding season. Existing knowledge of courtship and mating behavior and its evolutionary implications in amphibians is sufficient to titillate the imagination for much further observation and experimentation.

CHAPTER 4

Frogs feel physical joy and express it in song.

Mary C. Dickerson (1906)

Vocalization

Sound production by animals is primarily a method of advertising the presence of one individual to others of the same species. Vocalization is most common in animals that have low-density dispersal and that jump or fly, thereby leaving no continuous trail to be followed by chemosensory means. Thus, among the insects, sound production is characteristic of cicadas and (by stridulation) orthopterans. Among vertebrates, vocalization is highly developed in anurans, birds, bats, primates, cetaceans, and dolphins. In the anurans and birds the primary purpose of vocalization is advertisement, but passerine birds show a further diversity of behavioral responses associated with various kinds of vocalizations. The high-frequency sounds emitted by bats serve in echolocation and, probably secondarily, as advertisement, whereas primates and marine mammals have complex vocal communication systems.

Sound production is quite limited in salamanders (Maslin, 1950; Bogert, 1960) and has been reported in only two caecilians—*Geotrypetes grandisonae* (Largen et al., 1972) and *Dermophis mexicanus* (Thurow and Gould, 1977), but clicking sounds are produced by at least two other caecilians—*Ichthyophis* and *Siphonops* (C. Gans, pers. comm.). The various soft squeeks produced by some plethodontid salamanders, low whistles by *Siren* and *Amphiuma*, and a variety of sounds (barks, clicks, squeaks, whistles) in *Pleurodeles, Taricha, Dicamptodon,* and *Ambystoma* have been interpreted variously as defense

mechanisms (Maslin, 1950; Neill, 1952; Wyman and Thrall, 1972; L. Licht, 1973; J. Davis and Brattstrom, 1975; Brodie, 1978) or as an aid in orientation (Gehlbach and Walker, 1970). The limited information on sound production in salamanders seems to associate vocalization with defense (Chapter 10).

This chapter is devoted to anurans, most species of which have well-developed vocal structures capable of producing a variety of sounds that serve to attract mates, advertise territories, or express distress. The complex suite of morphological and behavioral characteristics associated with sound production seems to have evolved concomitantly with saltatorial locomotion. Because the force-pump breathing mechanism is an integral part of the sound production system (see Chapter 14), there is an obligate mechanical and physiological interdependence between the breathing mechanism and the vocal system. The presence of structures in the middle ear of Permian dissorophids (DeMar, 1968) and Jurassic leiopelmatid frogs (Estes and Reig, 1973) that are essentially equivalent to those of modern anurans suggests that vocalization may have existed in protolissamphibians, as well as in primitive anurans.

Early reviews of anuran vocalizations (Bogert, 1960; W. Blair, 1963; Paillette, 1971) were concerned primarily with the evolutionary significance of vocalization at population and species levels; Straughan (1973) provided an overview of evolution of vocalization in anurans. W. Mar-

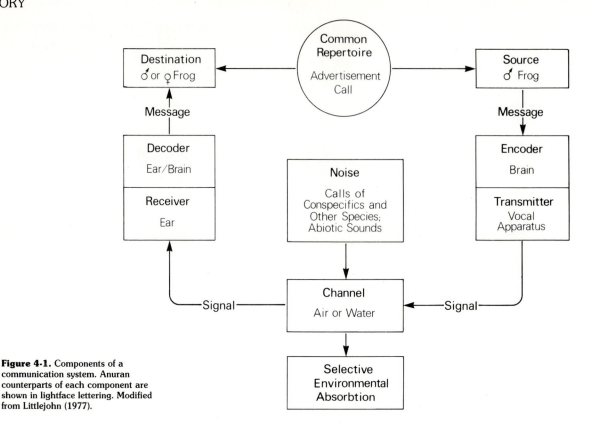

Figure 4-1. Components of a communication system. Anuran counterparts of each component are shown in lightface lettering. Modified from Littlejohn (1977).

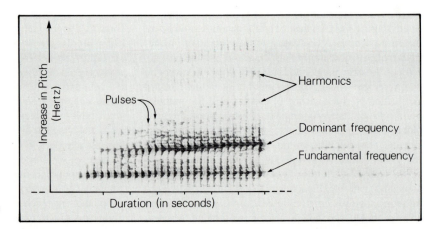

Figure 4-2. Audiospectrogram of a note from the advertisement call of the hylid frog *Triprion petasatus* showing acoustic components.

tin and Gans (1972), Gans (1973), and R. Schmidt (1973) provided insights into the mechanisms and control of vocalizations. More recent syntheses by Wells (1977a, 1977b) and Littlejohn (1977) emphasized the evolutionary and ecological interactions at the individual level.

ANURAN COMMUNICATION SYSTEM

A model communication system proposed by Shannon and Weaver (1949) was used by Littlejohn (1977) to explain the behavior significance and physical attributes of vocalization among anurans. In its simplest form, the

model requires a transmitter to emit sound and a receiver to process and respond to the signal (Fig. 4-1). By definition, sound is mechanical radiant energy that is transmitted in longitudinal pressure waves in a material medium. This mechanical perturbation of the environment is the signal that the receiver processes.

Acoustic parameters of frog calls can be described by analyzing tape recordings of the vocalizations with electronic sound analyzers. This equipment produces visual representations of the calls on an oscilloscope or as oscillographs or audiospectrographs (Fig. 4-2). Intensity (loudness) is measured in decibels (dB) on a peak-sound-level meter. The various components of anuran vocalizations are as follows:

1. *Call* or *call group* is the entire assemblage of acoustic signals produced in a given sequence. This may be a single note, a series of identical notes, or groups of notes having different acoustic characteristics.

2. *Call rate* is the frequency of production of calls or call groups; usually these are measured in calls per minute.

3. A *note* is a given individual unit of sound, whether a short, single pulse or a long series of pulses (trill).

4. *Note repetition rate* is the frequency of production of notes in a multinote call and is measured in notes per second.

5. *Pulses* are emphasized energetic impulses in the temporal spectrum of a note. In some long notes, such as the trills of toads, individual pulses are audible to the human ear. Some notes are unpulsed.

6. *Pulse rate* is the number of pulses per second or millisecond.

7. *Spectral frequency* or *spectral bandwidth* is the pitch of the call. The sound emanating from a frog has a spectrum of frequencies, measured in Hertz (Hz). In well-tuned notes, the spectrum is divided into distinct harmonics, which are masked but nevertheless present in poorly tuned notes. The oscillations resulting from air passing over the vocal cords and causing them to vibrate at a frequency primarily dependent on the mass and tension of the cords is the first (lowest-pitched) harmonic, usually referred to as the *fundamental frequency*. The frequency of sound resulting from the resonating of the fundamental frequency (or one of its harmonics) with greater emphasis than any other frequency is the *dominant frequency*. This frequency is always a multiple of the fundamental frequency. In some cases two or more harmonics may be emphasized.

The acoustic signals generated by air passing over the vocal cords and usually resonated by a vocal sac are emitted into the environment—air, water, soil, each of which has a characteristic impedance to sound transmission. The signals of most anurans are transmitted by air. Reduction of transmission range is affected by several environmental factors. For each doubling of transmission distance, the attenuation of sound waves, irrespective of frequencies, is at the rate of 6 dB; thus, the sound pressure level is reduced by half (inverse-square law). More acoustic energy is absorbed by the atmosphere at higher frequencies, higher temperatures, and lower humidities. Sound waves also are attenuated by the substrate and vegetation; these have most notable effects at higher frequencies (R. Wiley and D. Richards, 1978). Thus, Littlejohn (1977) suggested that transmission at lower frequencies (<4000 Hz) is most effective for anurans. By comparison, the range of maximum acoustic sensitivity in humans is 800–2500 Hz.

Body size and relative size of the vocal apparatus have an effect on the acoustic properties of the calls. W. Blair (1964) demonstrated that small species of toads, *Bufo*, have higher dominant frequencies than larger species. In two toads, *B. americanus* and *B. woodhousii fowleri*, intraspecific (but not necessarily intrapopulational) size differences are correlated with acoustic properties of the calls; larger individuals have higher pulse rates, longer calls, and lower dominant frequencies (Zweifel, 1968). A highly significant correlation exists between dominant frequency and body length among 81 species of Papuan frogs (Menzies and Tyler, 1977) and 39 species of neotropical hylid frogs (Duellman and Pyles, 1983). There is a significant negative correlation between body length and fundamental frequency of the secondary notes (chuck call) of the leptodactylid *Physalaemus pustulosus* (M. Ryan, 1980a). Moreover, an allometric relationship exists between larynx size and body size in *Bufo;* those species with proportionately large larynges have calls with lower dominant frequencies (W. Martin, 1972). In general, small frogs tend to call at higher frequencies and to have reduced auditory sensitivity; call frequencies of most anurans are below 5,000 Hz (Loftus-Hills, 1973).

MECHANISMS OF SOUND PRODUCTION AND RECEPTION

Sound Production Apparatus

In most tetrapods the laryngeal apparatus, or voice box, is the structure that produces sound, and in general can be visualized as a cartilaginous capsule (larynx) that houses vocal cords. The laryngeal apparatus is located between the lungs and the buccal cavity; air leaves the lungs and passes over flaps and strings of connective tissue (vocal cords) and their associated cartilages, causing these structures to vibrate. The vibration induces pulsation of the air column that is perceived as sound. The quality of the sound depends on several factors: the masses of the vibrating structures; their tensions; and the nature of the resonating chambers, through which the sound travels before leaving the body, and the way the impedance is matched to the external environment.

Although there is considerable diversity in the structure of the anuran larynx (see Trewavas, 1933; W. Martin, 1972; Schneider, 1977; Drewry et al., 1982, for more comprehensive accounts of variation), in most frogs, such as *Bufo valliceps* (described in the section: Sound Production), the larynx is composed of two arytenoid cartilages. Together, these cartilages form a compressed, hemispheric structure, the lumen of which houses the vocal cords; one vocal cord is associated with each arytenoid cartilage. The arytenoid cartilages are poised within

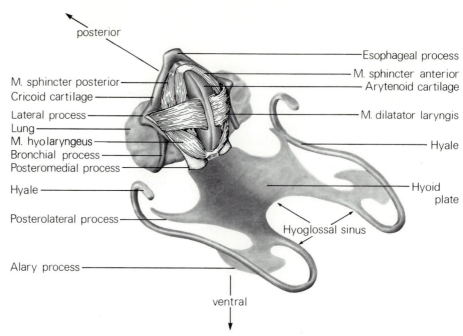

Figure 4-3. Isometric diagram of an anuran hyolaryngeal apparatus.

a ring of cartilage (cricoid cartilage) at their common base. The ring, together with its processes, the larynx, and associated musculature, composes the laryngeal apparatus that is suspended between the posteromedial processes of the hyoid (Fig. 4-3). The larynx separates the confluence of the lungs from the buccal cavity at the level of the esophagus. Viewed from the buccal cavity (Fig. 4-4), the superior or pharyngeal aspect of the larynx is marked by a vertical opening, the glottis, through which air moves between the mouth and lungs.

Movement of the arytenoid cartilages is affected by three (four according to some authors) pairs of muscles associated with the pharyngeal surfaces of the cartilages (Fig. 4-3). The m. dilatator laryngis originates lateral to the arytenoid from the posteromedial process of the hyoid and inserts near the apex of the cartilage adjacent to the glottis. Contraction of this muscle pivots the arytenoid cartilage in the cricoid ring in such a way that the pharyngeal margin of the valve is deflected laterally and the cardiac margin is moved medially, thereby stretching and increasing the tension of the vocal cord located inside the cartilage. The two remaining pairs of muscles are constrictors. The m. constrictor laryngis externus of W. Martin and Gans (1972) and Trewavas (1933) lies adjacent to the anteroventral margins of the arytenoids; this is the m. hyolaryngeus of Schneider (1977) and the m. sphincter anterior of Gaupp (1904). The m. constrictor laryngis anterior of W. Martin and Gans (1972) lies adjacent to the posteroventral margins of the arytenoids; this is the m. sphincter posterior of Gaupp (1904), mm. sphincter anterior + sphincter posterior of Schneider (1977), and mm. constrictor laryngis anterior + constrictor laryngis posterior of Trewavas (1933). Both sets of muscles origi-

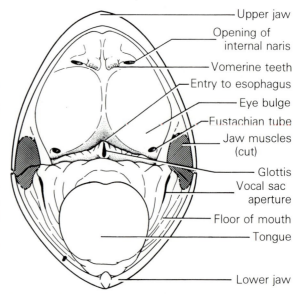

Figure 4-4. Generalized anuran buccal cavity showing principal structures.

nate from the hyoid. Rather than inserting on the arytenoid cartilages, members of each pair of muscles insert on one another. Thus, when these constrictors contract, they slide anteriorly over the arytenoid cartilages, pushing the two structures together (Gans, 1973b).

Although the cricoid cartilage, together with its processes, has extremely variable structure among anurans (see Ridewood, 1887, 1900; Trewavas, 1933), certain structural characteristics are critical to its role in suspension and support of the laryngeal system. The cricoid ring forms a firm base against which the arytenoid cartilages can be pivoted. In most anurans having a complete ring and vocal cords, the posterior (cardiac) end of each cord is attached to the inner margin of the cricoid cartilage, as well as the posterior margin of the arytenoid cartilage. As the arytenoid cartilage is pivoted, the vocal cord is stretched; the resultant tension is increased by the partial attachment of the vocal cord to the relatively rigid cricoid ring. The esophageal and bronchial processes (Fig. 4-3) of the cricoid cartilage support the proximal confluence of the lungs. The chamber thus defined is termed the posterior, or lower, laryngeal chamber (Fig. 4-5) and is overlain by the arytenoid cartilage complex. When present, the esophageal process is located at the midline on the posterior margin of the cricoid ring; thus, the process overlies and marks the confluence of the right and left lungs. One bronchial process arises from each side of the cricoid ring and curves posteroventrally beneath the anterior terminus of the right and left lung, respectively, so as to support their union as the posterior laryngeal chamber. The term "bronchial process" is misleading. With the exception of some pipids, the lungs of anurans arise directly from the posterior laryngeal chamber; bronchial and tracheal tubes (associated with the development of a neck region) are absent. The cricoid cartilage bears one remaining pair of processes: the articular processes that arise laterally from the cricoid ring and provide a pivotal point of articulation between the cricoid-laryngeal assemblage and the hyoid apparatus via the bony, posteromedial processes of the hyoid plate.

A cross-sectional view of the laryngeal complex (Fig. 4-5) illustrates the relationship of the ventral, or posterior, chamber to the dorsal, or anterior, chamber composed of the arytenoid cartilages and their associated structures. The two chambers are separated by a pair of membranes, each of which is formed by a medial extension of the lining of one of the arytenoid cartilages. These membranes are thought to direct air over the vocal cords, which lie just above them. As mentioned previously, one vocal cord is associated with each arytenoid cartilage; the anteroventral (pharyngeal) terminus attaches to the inner end of the arytenoid cartilage, whereas the posterodorsal (cardiac) end usually is connected to both the arytenoid and cricoid cartilages. The vocal cords are derived from the lining of the arytenoid cartilages and, therefore, are membranous in origin; however, their configuration is extremely variable among species. Differences include the extent and nature of the attachments between the vocal cord and the arytenoid cartilage and the size and shape of the fibrous masses that may be associated with the cord. These structural variations modify the way in which the vocal cords vibrate. This factor, in combination with the size of the organism and the shape and mass of the arytenoid cartilages, determines the fundamental frequency of sound produced by the frogs.

The pipids are sufficiently divergent to warrant special comment. In members of this tongueless group, the cricoid and thyrohyal cartilages are greatly enlarged and modified into an ossified (or partly ossified) box which partially encloses modified arytenoid elements. Vocal cords are absent, but in *Pipa* the cricoid chamber contains two bony rods that terminate and articulate with one another anteriorly via cartilaginous discs (presumably representing modified arytenoid cartilages). Each disc bears a tendinous connection to a large muscle originating from the base and covering the exterior side of the laryngeal chamber (Fig. 4-6). G. Rabb (1960) hypothesized that movements of either one of these two muscles caused the joint to open. In the course of opening, the cartilaginous disc slips or pops anteriorly, and so produces the sharp, metallic clicking noise that characterizes vocalization in these frogs. A similar mechanism is known in *Xenopus borealis* (Yager, 1982). Unlike other anurans, pipids are distinguished by the presence of bronchial tubes leading to posteriorly positioned lungs; the bronchial processes of the cricoid cartilage and the posterolateral processes of the hyoid plate are modified for support of the bronchial tubes.

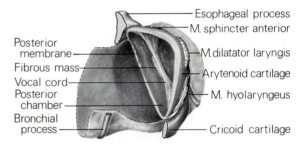

Figure 4-5. Isometric cross-sectional view of an anural laryngeal apparatus. Adapted from W. Martin (1972).

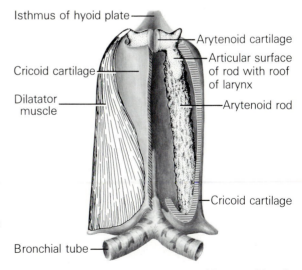

Figure 4-6. Diagram of laryngeal apparatus of *Pipa pipa*. Adapted from Ridewood (1897) and G. Rabb (1960).

Figure 4-7. Inflated external subgular vocal sac of the Mexican toad, *Bufo marmoreus.* Photo by W. E. Duellman.

Vocal Sac

Although both male and female frogs possess functional laryngeal apparatuses, the structures are better developed in males (i.e., they are larger relative to body size and have more robust musculature). Moreover, only males possess vocal sacs, which have been considered primarily as resonating chambers for sound production but may function in some species at least as sound-couplers or acoustic radiators to the air around them (Watkins et al., 1970). Acoustic energy that is transduced by the laryngeal apparatus acts on the buccal cavity and vocal sac. The vibration of these structures intensifies the acoustic signal, resonating and radiating it across the surface of the vocal sac into the air. A few male frogs that vocalize do not have vocal sacs.

In representatives of some primitive groups (e.g., discoglossids and myobatrachids), the lining of the mouth is loose and folded on either side of the tongue to form a pocket. When the buccal cavity is filled with air, the pocket is distended; Liu (1935b) viewed this as a primitive form of vocal sac. Among the majority of anurans that possess well-developed vocal sacs, the sac is formed as a diverticulum of the lining of the buccal cavity. The diverticulum lies between the superficial mandibular muscles (m. intermandibularis and m. interhyoideus of Tyler, 1971a) and the deeper geniohyoideal musculature of the lower jaw. The sac communicates with the buccal cavity via paired, round or slitlike valves (vocal slits) in the floor of the mouth; the valve lies between the m. geniohyoideus medially and the mandible laterally. Various myointegumental attachments determine the position of the inflated sac (Tyler, 1971b). Following Liu's

(1935b) scheme of classification, there are three basic kinds of muscular vocal sacs: median subgular, paired subgular, and paired lateral. The most generalized and widespread of these is the median subgular sac, which is a single sac in the throat. Derived conditions are represented by paired subgular sacs (which are completely or incompletely separated from one another) and paired lateral vocal sacs that are morphologically discrete structures located posteroventral to the angle of the jaw on either side of the head. All three types of vocal sacs may be categorized as being "internal" or "external." Internal sacs are characteristic of, but not restricted to, frogs that call from water (Fig. 4-8). Because of their effect on buoyancy, large external vocal sacs would be disadvantageous under water. Calls of frogs having internal vocal sacs, like those in which the sacs are absent, have low frequencies, presumably because of the small degree of flexibility of the resonating chamber (Littlejohn, 1977). According to Noble (1931b), if the sacs are internal, the skin covering them is unmodified; when the sac is inflated, the area assumes a "swollen" appearance. In contrast, the presence of an "external" vocal sac is indicated by modifications of the overlying skin that include: (1) the presence of discrete, inverted or everted dermal lobes to receive the underlying muscle when the sac is inflated; (2) extensive, irregular pleating or folding of the skin over the entire submandibular region; or (3) the presence of single pre- or postaxillary folds (Liu, 1935b; Tyler, 1971a). An esoteric modification of the paired subgular vocal sac occurs in African ranids of the genus *Ptychadena.* In these frogs, there are paired, submandibular gular slits (i.e., obliquely oriented invaginations of gular skin; not to be

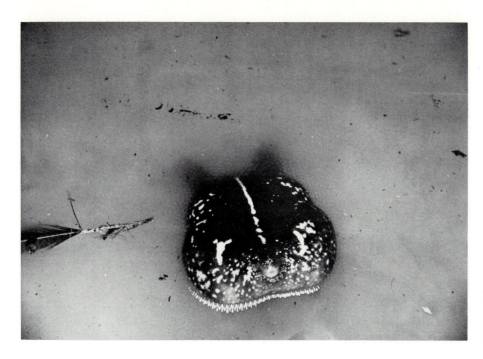

Figure 4-8. Inflated internal lateral vocal sacs of the Mexican burrowing frog, *Rhinophrynus dorsalis,* which calls from the surface of water. Photo by W. E. Duellman.

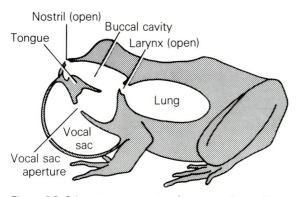

Figure 4-9. Schematic representation of an anuran showing those structures involved in vocalization.

confused with vocal slits) through which the vocal sac is everted when it is inflated (Inger, 1956a; K. Schmidt and Inger, 1959).

Sound Production

In producing sound, the anuran larynx is the transducer that converts muscular activity into acoustic energy through the manipulation of air flow by the force-pump mechanism. The patterns of air flow involved in anuran respiratory cycles and the muscular activity responsible for them were described in detail by de Jongh and Gans (1969); W. Martin and Gans (1972) subsequently explained the relationship between air-flow patterns and vocalization in the toad *Bufo valliceps.* Oscillatory cycles of respiration involve the exchange of atmospheric air with that in the buccal cavity via the nostrils. In the more complex ventilatory cycle, atmospheric air is pumped into

the lungs at two stages (interspersed among separate oscillatory cycles)—from outside to the buccal cavity prior to exhalation of pulmonary air through the larynx, and from buccal cavity to the lungs after exhalation (Figs. 4-9, 4-10). An inflation cycle involves a gradual increase followed by a decrease of inflated lung volume and pressure achieved throughout a series of ventilatory cycles. These ventilatory cycles are powered by muscle activity in the floor of the buccal cavity; some of their energy is stored in the elastic fibers and smooth muscle of the lung (i.e., pulmonary pressure). Pulmonary energy stores are released when air is expulsed from the lung. At the end of the inflation cycle, the muscular body walls, which have become distended to accommodate increased lung size, contract; this results in the forced expulsion of air from the lungs and the consequent release of pulmonary energy stores.

On the basis of electromyographic evidence, W. Martin and Gans (1972) confirmed that during vocalization the arytenoid cartilages separate to open the glottis in response to pulmonary pressure raised by contraction to the body wall rather than by direct activity of the dilatators. Prior to vocalizing, the frog uses the dilatators in combination with the constrictors to retract the laryngeal apparatus ventrally between the posteromedial processes of the hyoid; in this position the arytenoid cartilages are locked together. In most anurans the onset of vocalization is marked by (1) the culmination of the contraction of the body wall, and (2) the abrupt relaxation of the laryngeal dilatators and constrictors. The first event induces an air pressure behind the larynx that overcomes the relaxing muscles, thereby shifting the laryngeal apparatus anterodorsally and bursting open. Both the constrictors

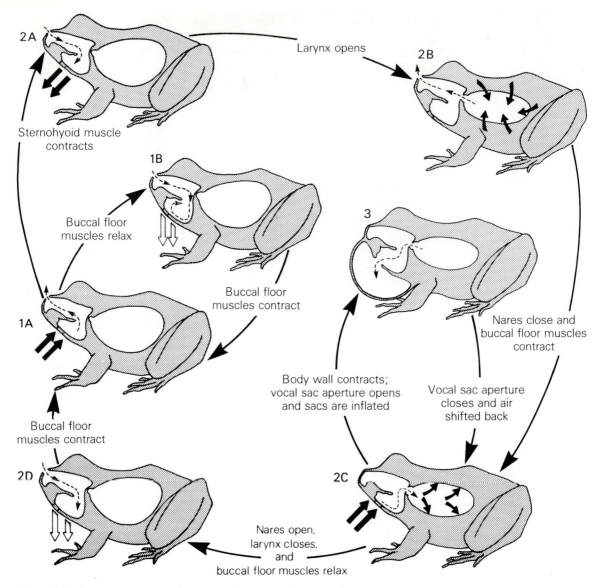

Figure 4-10. Graphic representation of anuran vocalization with respect to airflow. Peripheral figures (1A–2D) depict the ventilation cycle, and 1A and 1B show the oscillatory cycle. Vocalization is represented in Figure 4-9 as an alternative state to 2C. Major structures involved are labeled in Figure 4-9. Broken arrows show direction of air movement. Solid arrows associated with lungs and gular region indicate effective force of applied muscle activity, whereas open arrows represent movement of floor of mouth resulting from action of gravity combined with relaxation of muscles. Modified from Gans (1973b).

and dilatators are effectively inactive during sound production. Thus, as pulmonary air rushes over the vocal cords and arytenoid cartilages, these structures vibrate. They produce a sound, the frequency of which varies interspecifically depending in part on the tension of the vocal cords and effective mass of the arytenoid cartilages. These physical parameters are controlled by a pair of dilatator muscles. The resonating sound in the buccal cavity and vocal sac (if present and inflated) is transmitted across the surface of the vocal sac(s). However, *Bombina bombina* and *B. variegata* produce their calls on inspi-

ration rather than expiration (Zweifel, 1959; Lörcher, 1969).

Sound Reception

Anurans have a unique and complex receptor and peripheral nervous system for selective processing of acoustic signals. In most species, the primary sound receptors are the external ears, but the forelimbs also function in phonoreception (Hetherington and Lombard, 1982). Here the concern is how these structures function in hearing (for the details of structure, see Chapters 2 and 3). Most anurans possess a large tympanic membrane of thin, nonglandular skin. This external ear is the receptor of airborne sound waves and transfers sound pressure into vibrations of the columella in the middle ear. These vibrations, in turn, disturb the fluids in the inner ear at the interface, that is, the oval window, of the columella and the inner ear. The tympanic membrane is much larger than the oval window, and this difference in size is significant in matching the acoustic impedance of air to the higher impedance of the fluids in the inner ear; in this way sensitivity to airborne sounds is maximized (Capranica, 1976).

The oval window, the sensory opening to the inner ear, is abutted laterally not only by the footplate of the columella but also by the operculum. Each of these middle-ear bones has a muscular attachment to the ventral surface of the suprascapula. Contraction of the m. opercularis and relaxation of the m. columellaris leave the columella free to vibrate at the oval window, whereas the reverse contraction and relaxation tends to immobilize the columella and reduce transmission to the inner ear (Wever, 1979). This interlocking mechanism provides frogs with great control of acoustic reception, and (1) presumably functions to protect the receptors of the inner ear from overstimulation, and (2) possibly functions to select for reception of vibrations from different acoustic pathways, via the columella or the opercular complex.

Within the inner ear there are two separate auditory organs (papilla amphibiorum and papilla basilaris) that receive stimulation through the disturbance of the fluids in the middle ear. Each of the papillae organs possesses hair cells and a separate tectorial membrane. Motion in the perilymphatic fluid caused by vibration of the oval window is coupled with the endolymph, which causes

movements of the tectorial membranes. The exact acoustic pathways in the fluids are unknown. Possibly the disturbance is channeled through perilymphatic pathways, across the thin membranes, and then to the endolymphatic fluid around each of the auditory organs (Wever, 1973). Alternatively, the disturbance may be in a straight path to the organs, thus implying that the membranes separating the perilymphatic and endolymphatic spaces provide no selective transmission route (Capranica, 1976). In addition, the fluid pathways may be frequency-dependent, thereby affording selection of different frequencies to the two organs (Lombard and Straughan, 1974).

Various studies on acoustic reception have provided information on the function of the middle and inner ears of frogs. Capranica (1965) and Loftus-Hills and Johnstone (1969) demonstrated that frequencies below 1000 Hz are processed by the papilla amphibiorum and that higher frequencies are received by the papilla basilaris. Lombard and Straughan (1974) showed that the opercular complex conducts airborne acoustic signals at frequencies below 1000 Hz and that the tympanic-columellar complex transduces signals at higher frequencies. These conclusions were supported by Chung et al. (1978), who calculated that reception of sounds at frequencies above 1000 Hz by somatosensory and vestibular systems is ineffective, and concluded that the peripheral auditory apparatus in anurans is adapted for the detection of frequencies above 1000 Hz. Thus, the tympanic-columellar complex in the middle ear and the papilla basilaris in the inner ear, a combination of structures present in totality only in anurans, constitute the primary receiving system for advertisement calls (Fig. 4-11). Different degrees of acoustic selectivity in the inner ear have been demonstrated in various frogs. The ear of the bullfrog *Rana*

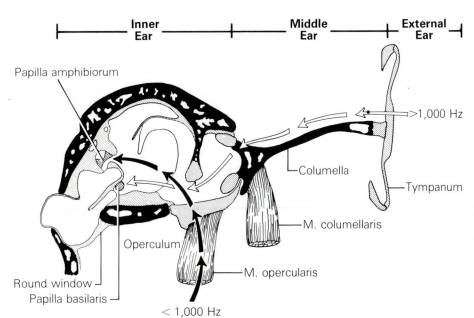

Figure 4-11. Diagram of an anuran auditory system. Solid arrows indicate transmission pathway of frequencies of less than 1000 Hz via the opercular–papilla amphibiorum complex; open arrows indicate transmission pathway of frequencies of more than 1000 Hz via the tympanic–columellar–papilla basilaris complex.

catesbeiana selects species-specific properties of the advertisement call (Capranica, 1965). In the cricket frog, *Acris crepitans,* frequency response also is geographically specific (Capranica et al., 1973). In *Eleutherodactylus coqui* there is sexual discrimination of the two notes at different frequencies in the compound advertisement call (Narins and Capranica, 1976); sexual differences exist in the sharpness of tuning and the frequency of maximum sensitivity of the papilla basilaris (Narins and Capranica, 1980).

Loftus-Hills (1973) suggested that the characteristics of the tympanic membrane (probably its area primarily) are the principal factors influencing auditory sensitivity in anurans, but Frishkopf et al. (1968) found no correlation between tympanum size and auditory sensitivity among juveniles and adults of *Rana catesbeiana,* in which tympanum size is much different in males and females.

Chung et al. (1978) and Pettigrew et al. (1978) demonstrated that the buccal cavity, to which the middle ears are connected via the Eustachian tubes, functions as a resonator. Pressure generated by the displacement of one tympanum is transmitted through the buccal cavity to the other tympanum, thereby reducing its net vibration. This tympanic coupling results in differential sound-pressure levels and enhances the ability to determine the direction of the source of the sound. Results of experiments on phonotaxis in the tree frog, *Hyla cinerea,* support the idea of differential sound-pressure levels in localization of acoustic sources in frogs (Rheinlaender et al., 1979).

The auditory role of the opercular complex and papilla amphibiorum responsible for the transmission and perception of low frequencies (Fig. 4-11) apparently is the same in anurans and salamanders, but the precise external receptors of sound waves are questionable. The presence of this system is correlated with terrestrial habits; premetamorphic amphibians and adults of some aquatic salamanders and frogs (leiopelmatids and pipids) lack the opercular complex.

In some fossorial anurans and others that live in and along streams, the tympanic-columellar system is reduced or lost. Reduction begins peripherally and proceeds medially, so that the sequential loss is tympanum, extracolumella, distal part of columella, and finally proximal part of columella. Insofar as is known, in no frog have both systems in the middle ear been reduced or lost. Both the papilla amphibiorum and basilaris are present in *Bufo bocourti* and *Ascaphus truei,* which lack columellae and tympana (R. Schmidt, 1970).

The unique auditory complex in anurans having two receptor systems (also two in crickets) allows for the inactivation of the low-frequency system, thereby enhancing the ability to perceive specific information in advertisement and territorial calls. The emphasis on peripheral hearing is important in specific acoustic recognition. But there are evolutionary constraints, as noted by Capranica (1977): "While the central nervous system of higher vertebrates may be 'plastic' and readily alterable through experience, the peripheral auditory system of anurans is likely to be more static. To change the sensitivity of a sensory receptor, particularly the ear, which is a mechanical organ, would seem to require a very gradual evolutionary process. The inadvertent introduction of a foreign species or a rapid change in the sonic and breeding environment could be disruptive."

Because temperature affects both the sound-producing mechanisms and the acoustic signals, it is only reasonable to expect that the sensitivity of the auditory receptors is temperature-dependent. Mohneke and H. Schneider (1979) and Hudl and H. Schneider (1979) obtained audiograms from the torus semicircularis of four European species of frogs at four temperatures; latencies became shorter with increased temperature and higher frequencies. The auditory receptors of three of the species functioned well at 5°C, but at that temperature the receptors of *Bombina variegata* were rather insensitive. Temperature effects are most pronounced at frequencies below 1000 Hz; thus, it seems as though temperature affects the opercularis–papilla amphibiorum pathway more than the tympanic–columellar–papilla basilaris pathway.

Central Control Mechanisms for Sound Reception and Vocalization

The papilla basilaris and papilla amphibiorum are innervated by discrete fibers of Cranial Nerve VIII (auditory); these fibers maintain their integrity as they enter the medulla oblongata and continue anteriad to the torus semicircularis, the major receiving site for auditory fibers below the optic ventricle of the midbrain. In most species of frogs examined, the auditory nerve contains three types of fibers, each having distinct excitatory frequencies; an exception is *Scaphiopus couchii,* which lacks fibers carrying intermediate frequencies (Capranica, 1976). The low- and mid-frequency fibers innervate the papilla amphibiorum, and the high-frequency fibers innervate the papilla basilaris. Pettigrew et al. (1978) demonstrated that discrete areas of neural tissue in an anterior-posterior axis of the torus semicircularis act as receptors; each receptor area is broadly tuned to a different frequency range and to sound from different directions. This "map" of auditory space in the midbrain is comparable to the visual-perceptual field on the tectal surface; one side of the brain attends to contralateral auditory space. According to Pettigrew et al. (1978), "The inner ear and the midbrain [each] are performing a separate Fourier analysis of the sound. With the low and intermediate frequency components, the animal can determine on which side its mating partners are located; once the animal orients towards the source of the sound, it can then utilize the high-frequency components of the mating call for guidance." Furthermore, it has been shown that *Rana pipiens* has a class of neurons in the central auditory system that responds selectively to particular rates of amplitude modulation (G. Rose and Capranica, 1983).

Stimuli to initiate vocalizations may be hormonal,

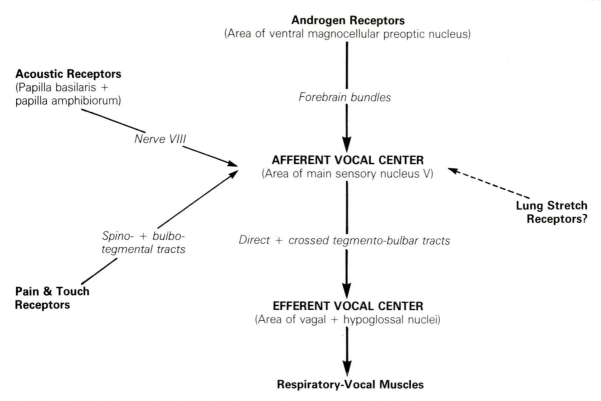

Figure 4-12. Model of the neurological basis of vocalization mechanisms in anurans. Modified from
R. Schmidt (1971).

acoustic, or tactile (R. Schmidt, 1973). Testicular development is dependent on gonadotropic hormones produced by the pituitary; activated interstitial tissue in the testes produces androgenic hormones. The androgen receptors in the ventral magnocellular preoptic nucleus in the midbrain activate a hypothesized afferent vocal center (R. Schmidt, 1971). This center may receive a variety of sensory inputs; these are analyzed, and the appropriate vocal response, if any, is transmitted posteriorly to an efferent vocal center, which generates patterns of calling movements (Fig. 4-12). Audioradiographic studies of the pipid *Xenopus laevis* indicate that androgens (dihydrotestosterone and estradiol) are concentrated in the torus semicircularis (D. B. Kelly, 1980). Appropriate tactile input into the afferent vocal center elicits release calling. The basic neurological system for vocalization apparently is present in both sexes. R. Schmidt (1966) implanted testes and anterior pituitary glands of *Rana* in the body cavities of female tree frogs, *Hyla cinerea*, and induced them to produce advertisement calls in response to taped calls of that species. D. B. Kelly (1980) suggested that hormonal concentration by laryngeal motor neurons indicates that androgens regulate the final common path for vocal behavior and that modulation of auditory sensitivity by hormones could explain seasonal variations in behavioral responses to conspecific vocalizations.

Release calls by unreceptive females of *Rana pipiens*

are initiated by stimulation of the skin of the trunk (Diakow, 1977); an internal afferent source inhibits the release call.

KINDS OF VOCALIZATIONS AND THEIR FUNCTIONS

The following classification of anuran vocalizations is based on that by Bogert (1960), as modified by Littlejohn (1977) and Wells (1977b), and emphasizes the functional aspects of the calls.

1. *Advertisement call.* Formerly known as the mating or breeding call, it is emitted by males and has two functions: (1) attraction of conspecific females, and (2) announcement of occupied territory to other males of the same or different species. In some species the advertisement call conveys only one set of information (courtship or territorial), but in other species a compound advertisement call conveys both sets of information. Three kinds of advertisement calls are recognized:

   A. *Courtship call.* Produced by males in an attempt to attract conspecific females.

   B. *Territorial call.* Produced by a resident male in response to an advertisement call received above a critical threshold of intensity.

    C. *Encounter call.* Evoked during close-range agonistic interactions between males.

2. *Reciprocation call.* Given by a receptive female in some species in response to advertisement calls of conspecific males.

3. *Release call.* An acoustic signal associated with corporal vibrations produced by a male or an unreceptive female in response to amplexus.

4. *Distress call.* A loud vocalization produced by either sex, usually with the mouth open, in response to disturbance.

Advertisement Calls

These are the primary vocalizations in anurans. Early ex-

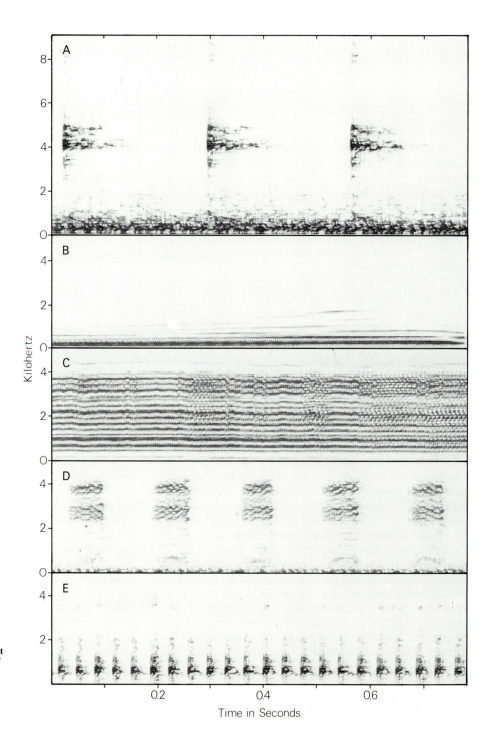

Figure 4-13. Anuran advertisement calls. **A.** *Pipa carvalhoi* (courtesy of Peter Weygoldt). **B.** *Rhinophrynus dorsalis.* **C.** *Gastrophryne olivacea.* **D.** *Dendrobates pumilio.* **E.** *Bufo valliceps.* All are narrow-band (45-Hz) displays.

periments on hylid frogs of the genus *Pseudacris* by Martof and Thompson (1958) and Littlejohn and Michaud (1959) showed that females responded positively to advertisement calls of their own species but were indifferent to calls of other species. Subsequent neurophysiological studies helped to isolate those components of the acoustic signals evoking responses by females. For example, Capranica (1965) demonstrated different responses to

acoustic signals by the bullfrog *Rana catesbeiana*. Loftus-Hills and Littlejohn (1971b) and Straughan (1975) showed that pulse repetition rate was the only component of the calls used for discrimination by two sympatric pairs of hylid frogs—respectively, *Litoria ewingii* and *L. verreauxii* in southeastern Australia and *Hyla cadaverina* and *H. regilla* in California. In contrast, females of *H. cinerea* respond only to bimodal frequency components of the

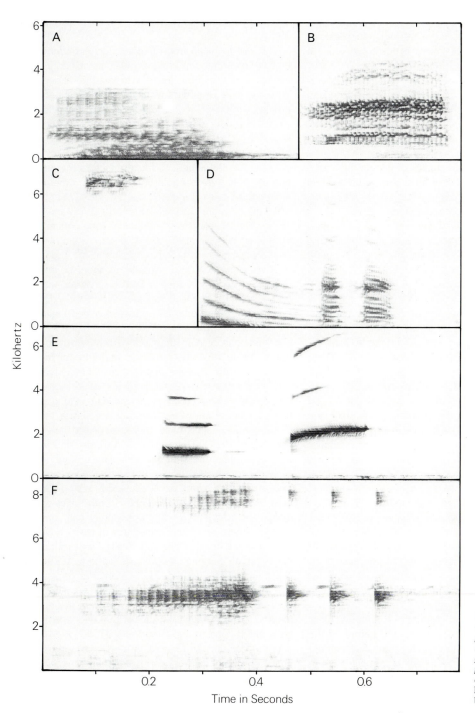

Figure 4-14. Anuran advertisement calls. **A.** *Leptodactylus pentadactylus.* **B.** *Ololygon boulengeri.* **C.** *Centrolenella grandisonae.* **D.** *Physalaemus pustulosus.* **E.** *Eleutherodactylus coqui* (courtesy of Peter M. Narins). **F.** *Hyla bokermanni.* All are narrow-band (45-Hz) displays.

advertisement call (H. Gerhardt, 1974b). In the neotropical leptodactylid, *Physalaemus pustulosus,* females selectively choose larger males by distinguishing lower fundamental frequencies in the courtship call (M. Ryan, 1980a).

The determination of species-specific call discrimination by females led to the study of the advertisement call as a premating isolating mechanism in North American toads (W. Blair, 1956), Australian myobatrachids of the genus *Crinia* (Littlejohn, 1959; Littlejohn and Watson, 1974), and Central American hylid frogs (Fouquette, 1960; Duellman, 1967b). These and many other such studies have confirmed the species-specific acoustic properties in a diversity of anurans.

Some notable cases of geographic variation in advertisement calls have been discovered in North American cricket frogs, *Acris* (Nevo, 1969); Central American hylid frogs (Duellman, 1970); neotropical poison-dart frogs, *Dendrobates* (Myers and Daly, 1976); and toads, *Bufo viridis,* in Europe and southwestern Asia (Nevo and Schneider, 1976). Detailed studies of geographic variation in advertisement calls have been completed on *Hyla regilla* (W. Snyder and Jameson, 1965), *Acris* (Capranica et al., 1973), and *H. arborea* (Schneider, 1977).

The genetic basis for the advertisement call is indicated by the production of distinctive calls by interspecific hybrids. The presence of an intermediate call in a hybrid population of the hylid frogs *Hyla cinerea* X *H. gratiosa* in Alabama was first documented by Mecham (1960); this was verified in hybrids between the same species in Georgia (H. Gerhardt et al., 1980). Natural hybrids between the spadefoot toads, *Scaphiopus bombifrons* and *S. hammondii,* have call components intermediate between those of the parental species (Forester, 1973). There are distinct differences in pulse rates between natural hybrids and parental toads *Bufo americanus* and *B. woodhousii fowleri* (Zweifel, 1968). The calls of the natural hybrids between the Australian myobatrachids *Geocrinia laevis* and *G. victoriana* contain components of both parental species and evoke positive responses from females of both species (Littlejohn and Watson, 1976). Among natural hybrids of three pairs of sympatric species of North American hylid frogs, the calls of hybrids between *Hyla avivoca* and *H. chrysoscelis,* and between *H. gratiosa* and *H. cinerea,* are intermediate between the calls of the parental species, whereas the calls of the hybrids between *H. femoralis* and *H. chrysoscelis* are more like the call of the latter; in two-way discrimination tests, females of *H. chrysoscelis, femoralis,* and *gratiosa* discriminated against the appropriate hybrid and females of *H. cinerea* showed partial discrimination (H. Gerhardt, 1974a).

Despite the limited vocal repertoire of anurans, there is much variation among species in the nature of the advertisement calls. In many species the advertisement call consists of a single note; in others the call is made up of a series of identical notes. In most toads of the genus *Bufo* and some other anurans, identical pulses are produced rapidly, so as to result in a trill (Fig. 4-13). The same is true in *Xenopus* (Vigny, 1979), in which two species *(X. laevis* and *X. ruwenzoriensis)* have harmonics reaching ultrasonic levels—80 and 150 kilohertz, respectively. In many species the call consists of two or more notes, or groups of notes, having different acoustic properties (Fig. 4-14). Such calls are common among some groups of hylids (Duellman, 1970); leptodactylids, especially *Eleutherodactylus* in the West Indies (Drewry, 1970); some species of *Rana* (Mecham, 1971); and some Australian myobatrachids (Pengilley, 1971; A. Martin et al., 1980).

The Puerto Rican frog *Eleutherodactylus coqui* has a biphasic compound call (Fig. 4-14E); the first note, "co," evokes responses from males, whereas the second note, "qui," evokes responses from females (Narins and Capranica, 1976, 1978). The aquatic South American *Pipa carvalhoi* produces an advertisement call consisting of a series of clicks (Fig. 4-13A), usually followed by a long buzz (Weygoldt, 1976a).

In the Central American *Hyla ebraccata* the buzz-like primary note evokes agonistic replies from other males, whereas the series of shorter click-like notes are produced when the frogs are in a breeding chorus (Wells and Greer, 1981). Similar responses to an initial, long note received at an intensity of more than 100 dB by males of the Australian *Geocrinia victoriana* result in the production of a territorial note and subsequent agonistic behavior (Littlejohn and P. Harrison, 1981). Likewise, males of the Australian *Uperoleia rugosa* switch from advertisement calls to a territorial call and attack males that intrude into a territory (Robertson, 1981). The same behavior has been observed in the South African *Phrynomerus annectens,* in which both resident and intruder produce aggressive calls prior to wrestling in water (Channing, 1976). South African species of the ranid genus *Ptychadena* have advertisement calls made up of long, pulsed notes; in dense choruses the notes are shortened, and these aggressive calls have greatly increased pulse rates (Passmore, 1977). The dendrobatid *Colostethus inguinalis* has an advertisement call consisting of a long series of short peeps; territorial intrusions result in an encounter call consisting of a long peep followed or not by a shorter note (Wells, 1980a). In this species both males and females also emit a close-range encounter call consisting of a low-intensity chirp. Three kinds of calls—advertisement and two kinds of encounter calls—are produced by the bufonid *Atelopus chiriquiensis* (Jaslow, 1979). The North American tree frog, *Hyla cinerea,* emits territorial calls at dusk, followed by a period of movement to ponds, during which time aggressive calls are produced; once males are situated at calling sites at ponds, courtship calls are emitted (Garton and Brandon, 1975).

In the leptodactylid *Physalaemus pustulosus,* which can emit acoustically different courtship and aggressive notes simultaneously (Drewry et al., 1982), call complexity increases as the number of males in a chorus increases and in response to (1) playbacks of a background chorus, (2) playbacks of more complex calls, (3) increased call intensity by nearby males, and (4) approach of other frogs into the visual field of the calling male (Rand and M. Ryan, 1982). These are but some of the ways of increasing the information content of the advertisement call in response to calls of other males. Other ways of increasing the information content include (1) lengthening the call, (2) increasing the note repetition rate, (3) adding notes to the call, and (4) adding new kinds of notes (Wells, 1977b). Similar modifications can be hypothesized for the evolution of compound advertisement calls from simple calls (Fig. 4-15).

Upon the approach of females, some frogs are known to change the properties of their advertisement calls. In the dendrobatid *Colostethus collaris,* calls lasting 10–20 seconds are normally produced only once every several minutes, but when a female approaches to within 10–15 cm of the male, the interval between calls is reduced to about 5 seconds (Dole and Durant, 1974b). A similar modification prevails in *Colostethus trinitatus,* which also increases the number of notes per call group (Wells, 1980b). *Centrolenella fleischmanni* intersperses soft mews amidst normal long-range courtship peeps when a female approaches (Greer and Wells, 1980). In the nest-building gladiator frog, *Hyla rosenbergi,* the advertisement call changes to a slower, softer courtship call when a female enters a nest in which a male is calling (Kluge, 1981).

Territorial calls containing agonistic signals may be incorporated into a compound advertisement call, such as in *Eleutherodactylus coqui, Physalaemus pustulosus,* and presumably *Hyla bokermanni* (Fig. 4-14), or produced independently from the advertisement call. Playbacks of conspecific advertisement trills and the mating trill of *Bufo valliceps* evoked territorial chuckle-calls from males of the sympatric *Rana berlandieri* (Gambs and Littlejohn, 1979). The Pacific tree frog, *H. regilla,* produces a diphasic advertisement call, but the approach of a female or a silent male results in a monophasic call (Whitney, 1981). Another tree frog, *H. crucifer,* has an advertisement call consisting of a single note, but a trill is emitted when another male is close by (M. Rosen and Fellers, 1974). *Rana clamitans* and *R. catesbeiana* have distinctly differ-

ent calls for advertisement and territorial encounters (Wiewandt, 1969; Wells, 1978b). Such calls are produced at times of close-range encounters and usually consist of signals with different durations or pulse rates than the advertisement calls. Agonistic signals are size-related in *R. clamitans;* calls of small males elicit strong agonistic vocalizations from small adult males, whereas calls of large males elicit agonistic responses from large males and weak responses from small males (Ramer et al., 1983). Encounter calls probably are much more common than suggested by the few documented observations by McDiarmid and Adler (1974), Weygoldt (1976a,) Wells (1977a), and Jaslow (1979). In many cases encounter calls are associated with postural or other visual displays and precede physical combat between males.

Territorial calls function as spacing mechanisms among males and are most common among species that have prolonged breeding seasons. In large concentrations of conspecific, explosive breeders, such as some pelobatids *(Scaphiopus)* and many toads *(Bufo)* among others, defense of territories is not favored; however, some explosive breeders (e.g., African ranids, *Ptychadena)* have aggressive calls (Passmore, 1977). On the other hand, what has been described as the mating calls of many species— especially tropical frogs that do not congregate for breeding (e.g., *Eleutherodactylus)*— actually may be compound advertisement calls or solely territorial calls.

Advertisement calls are involved in other intraspecific social interactions among males of many species (Wells, 1977a). Duellman (1967a) suggested different kinds of organization of choruses into duets, trios, or quartets. Like many hylids, there is synchronization of vocal activity in the European tree frog, *Hyla meridionalis,* but the chorus structure changes from duets and trios when few males are calling to no organization when many males are calling (Paillete, 1976). Alternation and synchrony of calling is best developed in species with prolonged breeding seasons and regularly spaced, repetitive calls (Wells, 1977a). Advertisement calls might be separated temporarily so as to minimize acoustic interference and thereby maximize an individual male's chances of attracting a mate (Littlejohn and Martin, 1969; M. Rosen and Fellers, 1974). Loftus-Hills (1974) suggested that anurans have

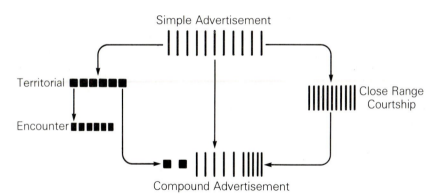

Figure 4-15. Hypothetical modifications of a simple advertisement call in the evolution of a compound advertisement call and an encounter call. Lines and squares represent different kinds of notes derived from an original common type and recombined into a complex advertisement call. Modified from Wells (1977b).

Figure 4-16. Diagrammatic representation of calling sequences of eight individuals of the hylid frog *Smilisca baudinii* (blocks 1–8). The leading edge of the plane represents time, and the lateral edge represents social organizaton into duets (A–D). Redrawn from Duellman (1967a).

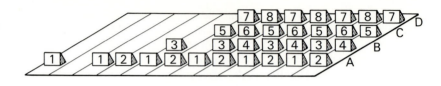

a neural pacemaker but that the basic calling rate of each individual can be altered by interactions with other calling males. Awbrey (1978) tested the hypothesis of alternation of call rates by analyzing the responses of male *Hyla regilla* to playbacks of recorded calls, and found that the observed patterns of phase shifting, inhibition of simultaneous calling, and spatial distribution of individuals within a chorus supported the hypothesis that social interractions minimize call interference among neighboring males. On the other hand, synchronous calling by numerous individuals occurs in some explosive breeders, such as *Bufo americanus* (Wells, 1977a), *Bombina bombina* and *B. variegata* (Lörcher, 1969), and *Rana esculenta* (Wahl, 1969). Rhythmic bursts of vocal activity are effective in attracting females to a breeding site where males obtain mates by active searching rather than by individual attraction by vocalization.

In choruses of some species, certain individuals may initiate choruses more frequently than do others (Fig. 4-16). Experiments with *Hyla regilla* showed that females consistently approached the loudspeaker that was used to initiate each trial of conspecific playbacks, even though the initiation of calling was varied among four speakers (Whitney and Krebs, 1975). Wells (1977a:675) cautioned against the inference of dominance in these situation: "If 'chorus leaders' do enjoy greater mating success than other frogs, this does not necessarily imply that females 'prefer' these males because they make 'better' mates. The most successful males may be those that outsignal their competitors and are therefore easiest to locate in a large chorus. . . . Chorus leaders are sometimes referred to as 'dominant' individuals, and ordered sequences of calls have been termed 'hierarchies'. . . . However, there is no evidence that call-order is determined by agonistic encounters among males, so there is no reason to suppose that organized choruses are analogous to dominance hierarchies of other animals." Nonetheless, the factors that influence certain individuals to initiate choruses remain unknown.

Little is known about the energetic costs of vocalization. Experiments on the leptodactylid *Physalaemus pustulosus* revealed rates of oxygen consumption to be four times greater in calling males than in males resting by day (Bucher et al., 1982).

Another cost of vocalization is the attraction of potential predators (M. Ryan et al., 1981). Certainly some mammals, such as raccoons *(Procyon lotor),* must be attracted to calling sites by vocalization; opossums *(Philander opossum)* are known to locate frogs acoustically (Tuttle et al., 1981). Various tropical bats are known to include frogs in their diets, and Tuttle and M. Ryan (1981) experimentally demonstrated that the Neotropical phyllostomatid bat, *Trachops cirrhosus,* not only responds to anuran vocalizations but distinguishes specific calls and avoids the distasteful *Bufo typhonius* (M. Ryan and Tuttle, 1983). The same species of bat shows greater attraction to complex than to simple advertisement calls of *Physalaemus pustulosus* (M. Ryan et al., 1982); this led Rand and M. Ryan (1981) to postulate that the complexity of advertisement calls in *P. pustulosus* evolved to allow males to effect a compromise between maximizing the ability to attract mates and minimizing the risk of predation. A similar response occurs in the hylid *Smilisca sila* to the same species of bat, but this species of frog seems to maximize its calling effectiveness by synchronized calling in the vicinity of waterfalls (Tuttle and M. Ryan, 1982). Snakes are common predators on frogs, but their most sensitive auditory reception range of 100–200 Hz (Wever and Vernon, 1960) is below the dominant frequencies emitted by most frogs; therefore snakes may not be attracted by long-distance airborne acoustic signals produced by calling frogs. However, aquatic snakes may respond to underwater vibrations caused by calling frogs, such as many species of *Rana*. Gorzula (1978) reported that *Caiman crocodilus* feeds on three species of frogs that call from the water in the Venezuelan llanos; the caimans move from large bodies of water to the temporary pools where the frogs are calling, presumably in response to their vocalization. Many large species of anurans feed on other frogs, but it is unknown if these rather sedentary species (e.g., *Ceratophrys* and *Pyxicephalus)* respond to vocalizations by potential prey. Notable exceptions are the observations of a *Bufo marinus* moving to calling *Physalaemus pustulosus* and eating them (R. Jaeger, 1976), and of a *Rana catesbeiana* being attracted to the distress calls of young individuals of *R. blairi* and *R. catesbeiana* (A. Smith, 1977).

Reciprocation Calls

These calls emitted by females are known to occur only in the European discoglossid *Alytes obstetricans* (Heinzmann, 1970) and the Mexican leptodactylid *Tomodactylus angustidigitorum* (Dixon, 1957). In both cases males respond by changing their advertisement calls—softer notes in *Alytes* and a change from peeps to a trill in *Tomodactylus.*

Release Calls

These are agonistic signals emitted by a frog when amplexed by another; they are accompanied by distinct vibrations of the body wall. These accentuated respiratory vibrations, which are produced by both males and females, expel air in short bursts; thus, the release calls usually are a series of short chirps and have notably different acoustic properties than the advertisement calls (Fig. 4-17). As noted by Aronson (1944), the release calls and warning vibrations most commonly are produced by males when amplexed by an indiscriminate male, but these release signals also are produced by spent females. Therefore, these signals may inform the amplexing male that the partner is incapable of reproducing. Rapid release presumably is advantageous, for energy is conserved and gametic wastage is prevented.

Release calls have been reported for most groups of frogs, but they are unknown in microhylids (Bogert, 1960). Release calls and vibrations are produced by many frogs that lack advertisement calls: *Pleurodema bufonina* (Duellman and Veloso, 1977), *Hemiphractus fasciatus* (Myers, 1966), and toads of the *Bufo boreas* and *B. spinulosus* groups (L. Brown and Littlejohn, 1972; Penna and Veloso, 1981).

Genetic control of the release calls is implicated by evidence that the pulse rates of the release vibration in natural hybrids between *Bufo houstonensis* and *B. woodhousii* are intermediate between those of the parental species (L. Brown and Littlejohn, 1972).

Distress Calls

The loud, explosive distress calls given in response to acute disturbance or grasping by a potential predator are produced by either sex and sometimes even newly metamorphosed young (Sazima, 1975), and are acoustically dissimilar to the advertisement calls (Fig. 4-18). Distress calls resulting from disturbance possibly provide a warning of potential danger to other individuals. A person walking along the margin of a pond in the northeastern United States might disturb a green frog, *Rana clamitans*, which emits a loud cry as it leaps into the water; usually several frogs nearby also will take refuge.

Screams are emitted by some frogs when they are grasped by predators. It is unknown if these calls convey any information to other frogs, and it is doubtful if these screams have any effect on an ophidian predator. However, loud vocalizations may sufficiently surprise a mammalian or avian predator so that the prey may be released momentarily, thereby allowing the frog to escape. This certainly is the case with uninitiated frog collectors capturing their first South American jungle frogs, *Leptodactylus pentadactylus*. Upon being seized, these large frogs sometimes emit a loud scream reminiscent of that given by a cat in distress. Australian tree frogs, *Litoria caerulea*, sleep in hollow branches by day; monitor lizards *(Varanus)* enter the hollows and disturb the frogs, which emit piercing screams (Tyler, 1976).

Distress calls usually are emitted with the mouth open, but their production with the mouth closed has been reported in *Rana catesbeiana* (J. Hoff and Moss, 1974)

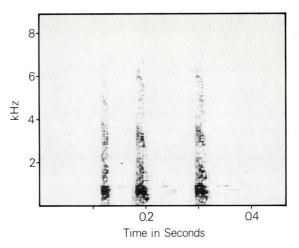

Figure 4-17. Release call of *Bufo valliceps*. Narrow-band (45-Hz) display. Compare with advertisement call in Figure 4-13E.

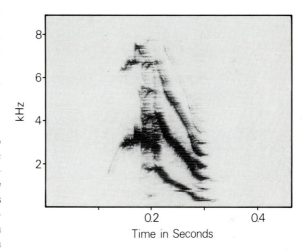

Figure 4-18. Distress call of *Leptodactylus pentadactylus*. Narrow-band (45-Hz) display. Compare with advertisement call in Figure 4-14A.

and *Bufo calamita* (E. Weber, 1978). The distress call also may be accompanied by a warning display, as noted in the Andean marsupial frog, *Gastrotheca helenae;* a disturbed female emitted a series of loud buzzes and displayed the bright bluish-green tongue and buccal lining. When disturbed, the large Chilean frog, *Caudiverbera caudiverbera*, emits a loud call and lunges forward with its mouth open (Veloso, 1977). The distress call of *Bufo calamita* is followed immediately by the appearance of a white mucous secretion over the entire dorsal surface of the body (E. Weber, 1978). Tyler (1976:143) reported that the Australian *Cyclorana cultripes* "seems to exhibit a rather nervous disposition for it screams in anticipation. When you reach to pick one up it commonly opens its mouth wide, screams piercingly and simultaneously jumps absolutely vertically high into the air to fall in a heap on the ground where it had been sitting."

ABIOTIC FACTORS
AFFECTING VOCALIZATION

Temperature

Many frogs in temperate regions breed in the early spring when temperatures are highly variable; because frogs are ectotherms, it is expected that the acoustic properties of their calls will vary with temperature. In the cricket frogs, *Acris crepitans,* call rate increases significantly at higher temperatures (A. Jackson, 1952). A statistically significant positive correlation between temperature and call rate and a negative correlation between temperature and duration of call exist in two species of chorus frogs, *Pseudacris* (Bellis, 1967). Temperature-dependent changes in pulse rate, dominant frequency, and call duration of the advertisement call of *Hyla versicolor* were demonstrated by W. Blair (1958). Similar results were obtained in analyses of release calls of several species of *Bufo* (L. Brown and Littlejohn, 1972). A high positive correlation exists between pulse rate and temperature in two species of *Bufo* and in their natural hybrids (Zweifel, 1968).

In the European tree frog, *Hyla arborea,* an increase of 10°C results in the advertisement call being shortened by about one-third of its duration and the interval between calls being reduced by about one-half (H. Schneider, 1977). Zweifel (1959) analyzed 22 recordings of one individual of *Bombina variegata* at temperatures from 16.8°C to 25.6°C, and found that repetition rate and pitch (frequency) have a significant positive correlation with temperature, but that the duration of the call is negatively correlated with temperature. These results are alike in that spectral frequencies, pulse repetition rates, and note repetition rates are directly related to temperatures, whereas durations of calls are inversely related. Thus, if a frog normally produces 10 notes in a call and those notes are produced more rapidly at higher temperatures, the duration of the call will be shorter (Fig. 4-19).

There is a positive correlation between temperature and frequency of contraction of larygeal muscles in *Hyla arborea* (Manz, 1975); thus, it seems as though temperature is affecting the basic sound-producing mechanisms of the frogs. H. Gerhardt (1978) experimented with responses by gravid females of the tree frog, *Hyla versicolor* to advertisement calls produced at different temperatures. He found that females responded to calls with temperature-dependent properties produced at temperatures similar to their own, and concluded that vocalization and recognition systems are affected by temperature in a qualitatively similar way, a phenomenon termed temperature-coupling. This conclusion is supported by Mohneke and H. Schneider (1979) and Hudl and H. Schneider (1979), who found that temperature affected auditory thresholds in four European species of frogs.

Habitat Interference

Other environmental factors also influence sound production in anurans or have an effect on the efficiency of communication. The humidity of the air and density of vegetation are important in the transmission of sound. Schiótz (1967) documented qualitative differences in the acoustic properties of anuran vocalizations in savanna and rainforest habitats in western Africa. Frogs in open habitats (e.g., deserts and grasslands) tend to have longer, more continuous, and lower-pitched advertisement calls than do those in forests. Low frequencies carry a greater distance than high frequencies, but high frequencies are easier to locate than low frequencies (Konishi, 1970). One Asiatic and three South American genera of microhylids that call from the forest floor have high-pitched calls (C. Nelson, 1973). A compromise between distance transmission and directional detectability is exhibited by several species of *Leptodactylus* that modulate frequencies over a short time span (Straughan and Heyer, 1976).

Frogs in open habitats usually have short, intense periods of breeding at the onset of the rainy season. Individual frogs may be scattered over wide areas, but suitable breeding sites may be highly localized. Vocalizations having acoustic properties enabling the sound to carry long distances are advantageous in attracting mates to these breeding sites. Bogert (1960) showed that both

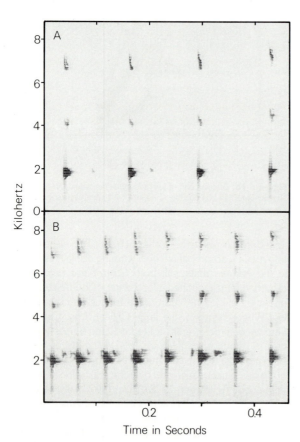

Figure 4-19. Advertisement calls of the chorus frog, *Pseudacris triseriata,* recorded at Lawrence, Kansas, at different temperatures. **A.** 3.9°C. **B.** 16.7°C. Narrow-band (45-Hz) displays.

males and females of *Bufo terrestris* oriented to recordings of choruses, and concluded that advertisement calls are significant in distance orientation and attraction of toads to breeding assemblages. Frogs in closed forest habitats tend to have softer, higher-pitched, and discontinuous advertisement calls; this was documented in Asiatic microhylids by Heyer (1971). In a tropical rainforest, it is not uncommon to be within 100 m of a breeding congregation of several species of calling frogs before the chorus can be heard. For example, the rate of attenuation of the calls of *Centrolenella fleischmanni* was doubled in vegetation as compared with open situations (Wells and J. Schwartz, 1982). This is in striking contrast to a chorus made up of *Rhinophrynus, Smilisca,* and *Phrynohyas* in open scrub forest in southwestern Mexico; what sounds like a nearby congregation may be nearly a kilometer away.

Subterranean vocalization presents some problems. Acoustic signals of high frequency are absorbed readily by soil particles, and calls are audible for only a short distance. In eight species of fossorial Papuan microhylids, the advertisement calls are characterized by a narrow band of dominant frequency at less than 1000 Hz and one or more short notes with constant amplitude. Menzies and Tyler (1977) suggested that the low frequencies are the best transmission bands through the soil and that the narrow bandwidths result in greater amplitudes by the concentration of spectral energy to counteract rapid attenuation in the soil.

Frogs that breed in, or along, torrential streams must compete acoustically with the noise generated by the rushing water. For example, short, impulsive, high-pitched calls are characteristic of centrolenids and some dendrobatids *(Colostethus);* members of both groups call from the immediate vicinity of rushing streams. Among hylid frogs in Mexico and Central America, the dominant frequencies of the advertisement calls of 19 species that call from forest ponds are 272–3578 (mean = 1726) Hz, whereas calls of 25 species that call from mountain streams are 1275-4300 (mean = 2530) Hz (data from Duellman, 1970). Some frogs that live along mountain streams have weak voices (e.g., *Atelopus, Taudactylus,* some species of *Telmatobius,* some hylids) or no voice (e.g., *Ascaphus,* some species of *Telmatobius,* some species of *Bufo,* some hylids); this may be an alternative response to the noise level of the streams.

Stream-dwelling frogs that lack voices usually remain at the edges of the streams; they do not need to vocalize in order to attract mates to the breeding sites. In multispecies associations, specific recognition may be visual, tactile, or chemosensory, whereas in monospecific situations—for example, some high montane regions inhabited by *Ascaphus,* by some *Telmatobius,* or by some *Atelopus*— critical specific recognition is not necessary. Some temperate and montane species of *Bufo* (Heusser, 1961; Schuierer, 1962; Black and Brunson, 1971; Novak and D. Robinson, 1975), *Pleurodema bufonina* (Duell-

man and Veloso, 1977), and African *Bufo, Acanthixalus,* and *Conraua* (Tandy and Keith, 1972; Schiøtz, 1973) breed in still water but lack advertisement calls. Also, some *Rana* and *Bufo* have weak advertisement calls (W. Blair and Pettus, 1954; R. Savage, 1961; Altig and Dumas, 1971; Geisselman et al., 1971). The absence of advertisement calls in such anurans possibly is related to the spatial and temporal patterns of their reproductive behavior, which includes active visual searching for mates (Wells, 1977a).

These inferences about the effectiveness and distances of sound transmission are dependent not only on the properties of the acoustic signals but also on the intensity and beaming of the calls. Little information is available on these aspects of anuran calls. Loftus-Hills and Littlejohn (1971a) found that among seven species of Australian frogs, smaller species have less intense signals than do larger species, presumably because of smaller vocal sacs and body-wall musculature. H. Gerhardt (1975) analyzed intensities of calls of 21 North American anurans and concluded that interspecific differences in intensity were not clearly related to interspecific differences in body size. Similarly, no clear relationship between body size and intensities of calls was found among calls of 17 species of African frogs (Passmore, 1981). However, body size, per se, may not be nearly so important as size of vocal sac. For example, sound intensities are about equal in *Bufo americanus* and *B. quercicus;* the former is about four times the size of the latter, but the vocal sac is proportionately much larger in *B. quercicus.*

Data on directionality of vocalizations is inconclusive. Slight reductions in sound intensities from in front of to in back of calling males of several species of North American and South African frogs were reported by H. Gerhardt (1975) and Passmore (1981). However, directionality of calls resulted from sound reflection by certain calling sites in *Eleutherodactylus coqui* (Narins and Hurley, 1982) and *Centrolenella fleischmanni* (Wells and J. Schwartz, 1982). These factors must be taken into consideration in studies of mate attraction.

Likewise, there is little information on the distances at which individuals can detect conspecific calls. According to Loftus-Hills and Littlejohn (1971a), the small Australian myobatrachid *Crinia parinsignifera* probably cannot detect conspecific advertisement calls at distances of more than 4 m, but the call of the larger hylid *Litoria ewingii* probably is detectable by conspecific individuals to distances of 100 m; the same distance of 100 m was determined for *Hyla cinerea* by H. Gerhardt (1975).

INTERSPECIFIC SIGNIFICANCE OF VOCALIZATION

Acoustic Interference

In a multispecies community, males of several species usually utilize a common site (e.g., pond) for advertisement calling. Consequently, there is the potential for acoustic interference among calling males of different species. Littlejohn (1977:279) emphasized: "Interspecific interactions will involve only the resources of communication, i.e., competition for bandwidth, temporal codes, transmission time, and calling sites. In this context, the signals of non-specifics constitute noise.... Interspecific interactions should thus lead to divergence in acoustic behavior and signal structure because of presence of these acoustic, but not reproductive, competitors."

Selection for communicative efficiency by reduction of acoustic interference might be accomplished in the following ways (Littlejohn and A. Martin, 1969):

1. Spectral stratification through the partitioning of bandwidth into numerous discrete frequencies.
2. Spatial separation through aggregation of individuals into monospecific assemblages or utilization of discrete species-specific calling sites.
3. Temporal partitioning of calling into species-specific breeding seasons, definitive discrete diel periods, or through alternation or antiphony within the same diel period.
4. Differentiation of species-specific coding patterns of advertisement calls when frequency bands and calling times broadly overlap.

Differences in acoustic properties of advertisement calls may have evolved in response to selection for minimizing acoustic interference among sympatric and synchronous breeders, thereby enhancing specific identification. However, acoustic differences may have come about incidentally or indirectly through selection for other factors, such as body size, which may affect acoustic properties of calls, such as dominant frequency.

Acoustic differences are especially important in maintaining species identities among closely related sympatric congeners. In a review of the advertisement calls of such species pairs, Littlejohn (1969) found pulse rates usually to be distinctive between pairs of species. Call differentiation in allopatric and sympatric populations of pairs of species has been documented in few cases. In the North American microhylids *Gastrophryne carolinensis* and *G. olivacea,* call durations, dominant frequencies, and pulse rates are more distinctive in sympatric than in allopatric populations (W. Blair, 1955). In the Australian hylids *Litoria ewingii* and *L. verreauxii* (Loftus-Hills and Littlejohn, 1971b) and in the North American hylids *Pseudacris nigrita* and *P. triseriata* (Fouquette, 1975) and *Hyla chrysoscelis* and *H. versicolor* (Ralin, 1968), the ranges in pulse rates do not overlap in sympatric populations, but do overlap in allopatric populations.

However, in cases of similar calls among species in a mixed chorus, vocal interactions may have important effects on the calling behavior of individual males. For example, field experiments by J. Schwartz and Wells (1983) showed that background noise generated by *Hyla microcephala* caused a shift in timing and kinds of calls given by nearby *H. ebraccata;* males of *H. ebraccata* reduced the call rate and the proportion of multinote and aggressive calls at high levels of calling by *H. microcephala.*

Acoustic Niches

Within large, multispecies communities, synchronously calling species usually have distinctive acoustic signals differing from other species in the community by frequency and/or pulse rate. Studies of such communities comprising 9 species in Florida (Bogert, 1960), 10 species (only hylids) in Costa Rica (Duellman, 1967b), 7 species in Victoria, Australia (Littlejohn, 1977), 15 species at Manáus, Brazil (Hödl, 1977), 20 species (all hylids) in Amazonian Ecuador (Duellman, 1978), and 13 species (all hylids) in Peru (Schluter, 1979) have revealed that spatial and acoustic partitioning exists in any given community at a particular time. Among 15 species in floating meadows at Manáus, overlap in dominant frequencies existed in only 4 species, but these had notably different temporal properties of the calls (Hödl, 1977). In 7 species calling at a pond in southeastern Australia, phasing of calls occurred in situations where calling sites and call frequencies were similar (Littlejohn, 1977). A stepwise discriminant functions analysis of call data from 20 sympatric hylids revealed that fundamental frequency was the best discriminator, followed by dominant frequency (highly correlated with fundamental frequency), pulse rate, and number of notes; these four properties discriminated 96% of the individuals (Duellman, 1978). In all cases, species that have the most similar calls exhibited spatial differences.

Within the limited vocal repertoire of anurans, it is expected that convergence in advertisement calls would be a common phenomenon. Striking similarities occur in geographically distant and unrelated species of frogs, such as in the North American pelobatids (*Scaphiopus*), South American leptodactylids (*Odontophrynus*), and Australian myobatrachids (*Notaden*), all of which produce structurally similar calls while floating on surfaces of temporary ponds after torrential rains. Excellent examples of convergence in advertisement calls include the African hyperoliids, *Afrixalus* and *Kassina,* with many neotropical hylids, especially members of the *Hyla microcephala, leucophyllata,* and *parviceps* groups. Also, calls of Australian species of *Limnodynastes* and of the *Litoria nasuta* group bear strong resemblances to calls of various species of *Leptodactylus* and *Ololygon,* respectively, in South America.

Moreover, at geographically separate sites in the same biogeographic realm acoustically similar calls can be heard, although the species composition of the communities is partially or completely different. Analyses of acoustic properties of 39 species of hylid frogs constituting breeding communities in Brazil, Costa Rica, and Ecuador showed that there were four groups of call types and that species from each community were included in each group (Duellman and Pyles, 1983). Acoustic properties of anuran breeding congregations are analogous to ecological resources; distinct acoustic niches are evident within anuran communities, and allopatric species tend to fill equivalent niches in different communities.

Inhibition

Inhibitory effects of the advertisement call of one species on the calling behavior of another sympatric species have been documented only in the Australian myobatrachids *Geocrinia victoriana* and *Pseudophryne semimarmorata*, which are broadly sympatric and synchronous breeders. Through playback field experiments, Littlejohn and Martin (1969) demonstrated that calling activity of males of *Pseudophryne* was inhibited upon exposure to calls of *Geocrinia*. Playback of synthetic signals indicated that pulsed notes with frequencies of 1500–2500 Hz had optimal inhibitory effects on calling by *Pseudophryne*. The inhibition of calling by *Pseudophryne* was interpreted as a mechanism of reducing acoustic interference and thereby increasing its efficiency of communication.

Similar situations undoubtedly prevail in other communities. For example, in the upper Amazon Basin *Hyla leucophyllata* and *H. sarayacuensis* are broadly sympatric and have structurally similar compound advertisement calls; they also utilize similar calling sites and oviposition sites. Both are opportunistic breeders after rains, yet choruses are discrete—not in the same ponds on the same nights (Duellman, 1978). However, silent males of one species frequently are present in congregations of calling males of the other species, and a chorus of one species may be present in a pond where a chorus of the other species existed a few nights earlier. The presence of tadpoles of both species in the same pond attests to the successful reproduction of both species there.

PHYLOGENETIC IMPLICATIONS OF VOCALIZATION

Presumably, early anuran vocalizations functioned primarily for the attraction of mates. As frogs dispersed into diverse habitats, environmental factors exerted new kinds of selective pressures that influenced acoustic signals—modification of frequency bands, temporal components, or intensity—for more effective communication. Furthermore, frogs in multispecies communities were faced with the problem of interspecific acoustic interference; thus, effective communication might have necessitated modifications in the calls. These selective pressures have resulted in the diversity of advertisement calls that now exist among anurans. Despite this diversity of modifications, it is possible to utilize vocalizations in some limited analyses of phylogenetic relationships.

Systematic studies of various genera of frogs have shown that species sharing morphological and/or biochemical attributes also have structurally similar advertisement calls. In some cases, limitations are imposed on the vocalizations by the morphology of the frogs. For example, the laryngeal apparatus of pipids is unique, and their vocalizations are unlike those of any other frogs (G. Rabb and M. Rabb, 1963). Atrophy of the middle ear structures is associated with reduced vocalization in some lineages, such as in some species of the bufonid genus *Atelopus* (McDiarmid, 1971).

With some genera that have been studied acoustically as well as morphologically, call structure parallels the morphological groups. Among Mexican and Central American hylids, some genera and species groups have characteristic advertisement calls, but intergroup relationships, as defined on morphological characters, are not always paralleled by the vocalizations (Duellman, 1970). Generic and intergeneric groups of neotropical microhylids are supported by call structure (C. Nelson, 1973b), but the advertisement calls of Asiatic microhylids have limited usefulness in determining higher phylogenetic relationships (Heyer, 1971). Morphological groups of South American *Leptodactylus* have distinctive advertisement calls (Straughan and Heyer, 1976). Two groups of species of *Dendrobates* in Central America and northwestern South America are distinctly different in morphology, skin toxins, and call structure, which also is correlated with differences in aggressive behavior in the two groups (Myers and Daly, 1976).

The most exhaustive study of the phylogenetic significance of vocalization has been on species of *Bufo* (W. Martin, 1972). Three patterns of amplitude modulation are unique to *Bufo* and to the South American leptodactylid *Odontophrynus*. These types of amplitude modulation are closely correlated with phylogenetic groups based on nonvocal characters. The primitive type of modulation occurs in *Odontophrynus* and most species of *Bufo* in South America, the postulated center of origin of the genus. Among African *Bufo* the phylogenetic groups defined on morphological and biochemical evidence are supported by data on call structure (Tandy and Keith, 1972; Tandy and Tandy, 1976).

Straughan (1973) argued that certain similarities in vocal characteristics could be indicative of relationships at the family level. He pointed out that some primitive groups of frogs (e.g., *Cyclorana*) have advanced types of calls, in the sense that they have well-developed tuning and temporal partitioning, whereas North American species of *Rana* have simple calls. Straughan (1973:326) noted: "Simplifications of a necessary functional system without passing through some peculiar adaptive zone during evolutionary development...is not very probable." Thus, he suggested an early divergence of ranids from primitive anurans. The complex interactions of acoustic and abiotic environments and morphological constraints on the vocal and auditory systems in the evolution of the major groups of frogs render such arguments tenuous at best.

CHAPTER 5

It is clear that in the Amphibia there exist patterns of development which transcend the taxonomic boundaries and appear to be adaptations in themselves....

Stanley N. Salthe and
John S. Mecham (1974)

Eggs and Development

The three previous chapters have dealt with the reproductive biology of amphibians from the internal control mechanisms of the reproductive cycles through courtship and egg deposition. This chapter treats the developmental aspects from fertilization through hatching or birth. The morphology, ecology, and behavior of larvae are treated in Chapter 6.

Amphibian development has been investigated extensively by embryologists, who have taken advantage of the development of relatively large external eggs for both descriptive and experimental studies. In fact, entire books have been devoted to amphibian development (e.g., Rugh, 1951, 1962; R. Harrison, 1969). Fox (1984) provided a thorough account of amphibian morphogenesis. The most comprehensive treatment of amphibian development within a broad biological context is the work of Salthe and Mecham (1974). This chapter summarizes amphibian development, including egg and clutch structure, embryonic metabolism, rates and patterns of embryonic development, and the process of hatching. Emphasis is placed on those aspects that have evolutionary and ecological significance. Throughout the chapter, reference is made to developmental stages, which are described in detail in the section: Normal Stages of Development.

The bulk of the research on embryonic development has been with species that have aquatic eggs; actually, the vast majority of the literature deals with the development and experimental manipulations of *Xenopus laevis*

and a few species of *Rana, Bufo, Triturus,* and *Ambystoma* (commonly, but erroneously, spelled *Amblystoma*). The comparatively small amount of work on amphibians having specialized modes of development has revealed many fascinating aspects of development that need to be pursued.

SPERMATOZOA AND FERTILIZATION

Production and release of spermatozoa have been discussed in Chapters 2 and 3. Here are treated the structure of spermatozoa and the actual processes by which they penetrate the egg capsules and ova.

Spermatozoan Structure

The basic morphology of an amphibian spermatozoon consists of the following structures in a linear, anteroposterior sequence (Fig. 5-1).

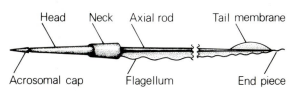

Figure 5-1. Generalized amphibian spermatozoon showing morphological structures.

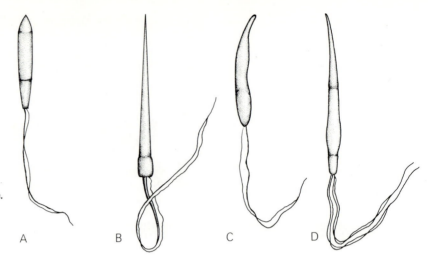

Figure 5-2. Amphibian spermatozoa. **A.** *Ichthyophis glutinosus.* **B.** *Triturus marmoratus.* **C.** *Bufo bufo.* **D.** *Ololygon fuscovaria.* Not drawn to scale. A adapted from F. Sarasin and P. Sarasin (1887–90); B and C from Angel (1947); D from Fouquette and Delahoussaye (1977).

Acrosome. The tip of the head piece is formed by transformation of laminar parts of Golgi bodies during spermatogenesis. This is properly referred to as an acrosomal cap.

Head. The head and acrosome may not be entirely distinct externally in amphibians. The head contains closely packed chromosomes covered by a thin layer of cytoplasm.

Neck or Middle Piece. Formed from cytoplasmic material, the neck contains one (in salamanders) or two (in anurans) centrosomes (centrioles) anteriorly next to the nuclear material of the head and at the proximal end of the axial rod or filament. Mitochondria spiral around the axial rod.

Tail. The tail is long, usually vibratory, and consists of an axial rod or filament covered by a very thin layer of cytoplasm, which does not reach to the tip of the tail. The axial rod consists of several longitudinal fibers with another fiber spiraled around them and contains the usual vertebrate microtubule arrangement (nine pairs surrounding a single median pair). Cytoplasm is expanded into a finlike structure, the flagellum, but the distal part of the axial rod, the end piece, is always naked. The cytoplasm may be differentiated into a tail membrane posteriorly. The spermatozoa of salamanders and caecilians have single tails, but in anurans the tail may be single or double. This normal pattern is modified in *Bombina bombina* and *B. variegata,* in that the tail is truncated and the flagellum is present on the head as well as on the tail (Broman, 1900; Furieri, 1975).

The morphology of spermatozoa is highly variable in anurans and salamanders (Fig. 5-2); too little is known about their morphology in caecilians to make any generalizations. Among the kinds of variation in salamander spermatozoa is the presence of a tail membrane in ambystomatids that is unknown in other salamanders (Martan and Wortham, 1972). A cytoplasmic droplet containing mitochondria migrates from the head to the neck in plethodontids but remains in the head in other salamanders. Also, apparently there is a barb on the acrosome in all salamander spermatozoa, but its length and position are variable (Wortham et al., 1982). There are interspecific differences in lengths of parts of spermatozoa in *Ambystoma,* and spermatozoa of hybrids are intermediate between those of parental species (Brandon et al., 1974); the same is true for species of *Hynobius* and their hybrids (Kawamura, 1953). Proportional differences in lengths of different parts of spermatozoa of plethodontids are consistent with the taxonomy of the group (Wortham et al., 1977). The structure of the junction of the head and neck in spermatozoa is different among genera of salamandrids (Fawcett, 1970; C. Werner, 1970) and among the species of *Ambystoma* (Brandon et al., 1974). Similar differences among plethodontids are consistent with the subfamilial groupings, except for *Aneides* (Wortham et al., 1977).

Striking differences occur in tail structure among anurans (Fouquette and Delahoussaye, 1977). Two or more tail filaments are present in all primitive anurans studied (discoglossoids, pipoids, and pelobatoids). Two tail filaments occur in some members of the Hylidae and Leptodactylidae and in nearly all centrolenids and bufonids. Many leptodactylids, most hylids, all pseudids, and nearly all ranids and microhylids have a single tail. Careful study of the structure of the spermatozoa of the species of the hylid genus *Ololygon* revealed interspecific differences in the shapes and proportional lengths of the head and neck, plus variation in tail structure.

Results of these studies on spermatozoa of relatively few taxa suggest that certain morphological characters are consistent with classification and that characters of the spermatozoa may contribute to understanding of the phylogenetic relationships among groups of amphibians.

Proteins. The protein structure of amphibian spermatozoa is highly variable, like that in fishes and unlike that in reptiles, birds, and mammals. Interspecific differences in histones were noted for a variety of anurans (Kasinsky et al., 1978). Different species of *Xenopus* and their interspecific hybrids can be distinguished by their histones (Kasinsky et al., 1981). Even intraspecific differences occur in proamines in salamanders (Ando et al., 1973). Kasinsky et al. (1978) hypothesized that histone diversity in spermatozoa declines in vertebrate evolution as sex determination becomes increasingly chromosomally based. However, this does not explain the diversity of histones in anurans. Histone variation does not seem to be correlated with reproductive modes in anurans, for all species studied so far have the generalized mode of aquatic eggs and larvae. On the other hand, there may be some phylogenetic significance, for species of *Rana* are grouped together, *Scaphiopus* is clustered with *Bufo*, and *Xenopus* is closest to *Notophthalmus* (Kasinsky et al., 1978).

The biological significance of differences in size and structure of spermatozoa is unknown. Species-specific differences in spermatozoa may be correlated with differences in the structures of egg membranes (Kawamura, 1953; C. Nelson and R. Humphrey, 1972). Because there is a positive correlation between spermatozoan head length and the amount of nuclear material in plethodontid salamanders (Macgregor and M. Walker, 1973), Wortham et al. (1977) suggested that the long heads (more nuclear material) of plethodontine spermatozoa may be related to the evolutionary plasticity of that subfamily.

Fertilization

The complex interactions of ova and their mucoid capsules with the spermatozoa are both enzymatic and mechanical in the processes of insemination and fertilization. In amphibians having aquatic eggs, 10 to 15 minutes elapse between the first contact of a spermatozoon with the egg capsule and fertilization.

Proteolytic enzymes produced by the acrosome of a spermatozoon digest the egg capsule and permit mechanical penetration of the spermatozoon into the ovum (Penn and Glenhill, 1972). Differences in the size of holes digested in egg capsules in various species of *Rana* and *Bufo* indicate that enzymatic or substrate traits are species-specific (Elinson, 1974).

The site of entry of the spermatozoon into the ovum determines the future plane of bilateral symmetry, and this site eventually comes to be on the ventral side of the embryo. Penetration is effective only in the animal hemisphere. The gray crescent forms opposite the point of entry; gastrulation is initiated at the gray crescent. In those anurans studied, spermatozoa entering the ovum cause a localized change in the surface of the ovum, as a clump of microvilli develop; this cytoplasmic differentiation reaches

its maximum development in about 2 hours after penetration (Elinson and Manes, 1978). In salamanders the site of spermatozoan entry is marked by a sperm pit (Fankhauser and C. Moore, 1941).

Penetration of the ovum by the spermatozoon serves three functions. First, the egg is activated; second, the diploid chromosome complement is formed; and third, cleavage is initiated. Activation involves elevation of the vitelline membrane, rotation of the ovum within the vitelline membrane, changes in the turgidity of the ovum, and changes in the surface of the ovum (that is, formation of microvilli or a "pit" where entry was achieved) and elimination of the second polar body. Cortical contraction is associated with turgidity and serves to bring the nuclei of the spermatozoon and ovum closer together, thereby bringing about chromosomal association (Elinson, 1975, 1977). Apparently cleavage is initiated by the presence of a centriole from the spermatozoon (Maller et al., 1976); the action of the centriole in organizing a spindle or aster is dependent on activated egg cytoplasm. Also, the sperm aster is important in formation of the gray crescent (Manes and Barbieri, 1976, 1977). The fate of the centrioles produced by the ovum is unknown. Eggs of some species can be stimulated to develop parthenogenetically without spermatozoa, and these form normal blastulae.

Amphibian eggs normally are fertilized after reaching Metaphase II. When eggs are inseminated prior to that phase, several spermatozoa may enter, but entry does not activate the ovum. In anurans the changes in egg surface in response to activation apparently result in part from the breakdown of cortical granules; these mucopolysaccharides are discharged into the perivitelline fluid and seem to block the entrance of more spermatozoa. Cortical granules apparently are absent in salamander eggs, but changes in some of the mucoid capsules upon hydration seem to block the entrance of additional spermatozoa (McLaughlin and A. Humphries, 1978).

As a result of the rapid propagation of the first surface reaction of the egg followed by the second, slower cortical reaction and elevation of the vitelline membrane, only one spermatozoon normally penetrates to the ovum in those anurans studied. If more than one spermatozoon enters the anuran egg, development inevitable is abnormal and the embryo is not viable. Several spermatozoa may enter the ovum in salamanders, but only one of these participates in the development of the zygote; the others degenerate. The distinction of monospermy in anurans and polyspermy in salamanders may be artificial, for the polyspermic condition is common to large-yolked eggs, such as those of some mollusks, reptiles, and birds. The number of spermatozoa entering large-yolked eggs of anurans that have direct development is unknown.

EGG STRUCTURE

Although all amphibian eggs are basically the same in possessing layers of semipermeable membranes surrounding the ovum, there is much interspecific variation in the disposition of individual eggs within clutches, such as sizes, and number and arrangement of capsules. Furthermore, various physicochemical properties of the eggs are important to their development under different environmental conditions.

Clutch Structure

Eggs laid in water may be in the form of large clumps representing the entire ovarian complement (e.g., most *Rana* and many *Ambystoma*), or the clumps may represent only part of the ovarian complement, in which case the female deposits small parcels of eggs at different sites (e.g., some *Hyla* and some *Ambystoma*). Commonly clumps of eggs are attached to sticks or vegetation in the water; this serves to maintain the position of the clutch in the pond or stream.

The clutches of hynobiid salamanders are deposited as two sacs, one from each oviduct (Thorn, 1968), whereas the aquatic salamanders *Cryptobranchus* and *Amphiuma* deposit paired strings of eggs with a constriction of the jelly between each egg (Bishop, 1941; Cagle, 1948). Similar strings of eggs with constrictions are attached to undersides of rocks in streams by *Ascaphus truei* (Noble and P. Putnam, 1931). Toads of the genus *Bufo* characteristically deposit eggs in paired strings, one from each oviduct, as do the bufonids *Atelopus varius* and *Dendrophryniscus minutus* (P. Starrett, 1967; Duellman and J. D. Lynch, 1969) and myobatrachids of the genus *Neobatrachus* (Watson and A. Martin, 1973). Clutches in the form of a film with all of the eggs at the surface of the water are characteristic of many kinds of frogs that deposit in still, shallow water. These include hylids of the *Hyla albomarginata* and *H. boans* groups and species of *Litoria, Osteocephalus, Osteopilus, Phrynohyas,* and *Smilisca* (Duellman and A. Schwartz, 1958; Bokermann, 1965a; Tyler and M. Davies, 1978a); ranids such as *Rana catesbeiana, clamitans, cancrivora, limnocharis, Ptychadena oxyrhyncha, Ptychadena porosissima,* and *Phryno-*

batrachus natalensis (C. Pope, 1931; A. H. Wright and A. A. Wright, 1949; Alcala, 1962; Wager, 1965); and some species of the microhylid genus *Kaloula* (Alcala, 1962).

Single aquatic eggs are deposited on the surface of the water by the pipid *Hymenochirus boettgeri* (Sughrue, 1969) and the bufonid *Melanophryniscus moreirae* (P. Starrett, 1967); underwater by *Bufo punctatus* (Livezey and A. H. Wright, 1947) and the ranids *Hildebrandtia, Pyxicephalus,* and *Tomoptema* (Wager, 1965); or are attached to submerged vegetation by many kinds of newts (Bishop, 1941; Thorn, 1968), sirenids (Noble and Marshall, 1932), and frogs such as *Xenopus laevis, Kassina senegalensis* (Wager, 1965), *Hyla crucifer* (Gosner and Rossman, 1960), and *H. cadaverina* (Gaudin, 1965). The attachment of groups of single eggs or small clumps of eggs by means of gelatinous stalks to the undersides of rocks or logs is common among salamanders inhabiting streams, including *Necturus maculosus* (Bishop, 1941), *Dicamptodon ensatus* (Nussbaum, 1969a), and plethodontids such as *Eurycea bislineata, Gyrinophilus porphyriticus, Pseudotriton ruber* (Bishop, 1941), and various species of *Desmognathus* (Organ, 1961). Other aquatic or semiaquatic salamanders, such as *Rhyacotriton olympicus* (Nussbaum, 1969b) and *Eurycea multiplicata* (P. Ireland, 1976), deposit unstalked single eggs under rocks or in crevices.

The terrestrial eggs of some bolitoglossine plethodontids are in strands with constricted jelly between each egg (McDiarmid and Worthington, 1970), whereas the terrestrial eggs of other bolitoglossines, some plethodontines, and *Ambystoma* are unstalked and adherent to one another, as are the terrestrial eggs of anurans. Strands of terrestrial eggs with constrictions are characteristic of some caecilians (M. Wake, 1977a) and *Alytes obstetricans* (Boulenger, 1897). Many plethodontine salamanders have stalked eggs attached to the roof or walls of underground chambers; stalked terrestrial eggs are unknown in anurans.

Egg clutches of anurans also include foam nests; these are on land or in water in many genera of myobatrachids and leptodactylids and in trees among rhacophorids and hyperoliids. Centrolenid and phyllomedusine hylids, plus some other frogs, have clutches of eggs adherent to vegetation above water (see Chapter 2 for discussion and references).

Egg Morphology

The ovum of all amphibians is enclosed in a thin, tough membrane—the vitelline membrane (fertilization membrane or chorion of many embryologists). The vitelline membrane is proteinaceous and semipermeable and is produced by the ovary (Townes, 1953; Wartemberg and W. Schmidt, 1961; Salthe, 1965). It is surrounded by a series of concentric capsules secreted by the oviducts (Lofts, 1974) (Fig. 5-3). The egg capsules are composed of acidic or neutral mucopolysaccharides and mucoproteins (A.

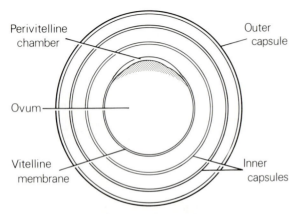

Figure 5-3. Diagrammatic generalized amphibian egg showing membranes and capsules. The mucoid capsules vary in number, thickness, and viscosity.

Humphries, 1966; Freeman, 1968); in some species sulfated mucopolysaccharides are present in some capsules—only the innermost ones in *Notophthalmus viridescens* and *Rana pipiens* (A. Humphries, 1970; Steinke and Benson, 1970). Histochemical tests have revealed that various regions can be distinguished in the oviducts of some anurans (Shaver et al., 1970) and some salamanders; each of these regions produces a different egg capsule (see Salthe and Mecham, 1974, for examples and references). The number of oviducal regions and resultant number of egg capsules vary interspecifically (Salthe, 1963).

The innermost capsule of salamander eggs liquefies soon after deposition; thus, the ovum, surrounded by the vitelline membrane, floats freely in a capsular chamber. In most frogs the ovum is restrained by the viscosity of the innermost capsule (Salthe, 1963). Rotation of the ovum occurs almost instantaneously in salamanders, whereas in anurans without a capsular chamber, rotation requires several minutes. Eggs of several anurans (*Alytes, Discoglossus, Pipa,* and *Eleutherodactylus*) are like those of salamanders in that a liquid capsular chamber develops soon after deposition (Salthe, 1965); a similar chamber is present in the caecilian *Ichthyophis glutinosus* (Breckenridge and Jayasinghe, 1979). In plethodontid salamanders, *Pipa,* and *Eleutherodactylus* the chamber is small at first and increases in size only late in development, but in other salamanders, *Discoglossus,* and *Alytes* the chamber is essentially expanded fully shortly after deposition.

Salthe (1963) identified as many as eight capsules in salamander eggs and noted that firm capsules existed between soft ones. Homologous capsules identified among salamanders indicate that the eggs of *Ambystoma* are like those of *Hynobius,* except that the two outermost capsules of the latter are absent in *Ambystoma.* The eggs of other salamanders have fewer capsules. With the exception of some primitive frogs, such as *Alytes* and *Pipa,* anurans have fewer capsules than salamanders (Fig. 5-4). The greatest variation is among aquatic anurans, and in some species (e.g., *Rana catesbeiana)* the egg consists solely of an ovum, vitelline membrane, and one capsule. The eggs of egg-brooding hylids, which hatch into tadpoles or froglets, lack a liquefied inner chamber, have only two capsules, and retain a vitelline membrane until hatching. Salthe (1963) was unable to find any obvious correlations between detailed structure of the eggs and environment, except that nonaquatic eggs tend to have thinner but fewer capsules. Terrestrial eggs also tend to have tougher outer capsules; many of these are sticky.

The sizes of ova and the capsules are highly variable. The largest amphibian eggs known are those of the caecilian *Ichthyophis glutinosus,* which attain diameters of 35 mm and lengths of 42 mm (Breckenridge and Jayasinghe, 1979). Among salamanders, the ova of *Cryptobranchus alleganiensis* are 6 mm and the capsules 18 mm (Bishop, 1941). Most other salamanders with

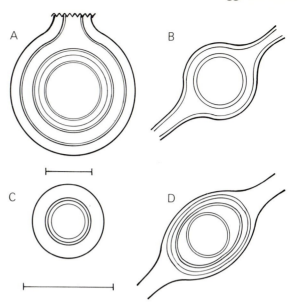

Figure 5-4. Diagrammatic representation of amphibian eggs. **A.** *Dicamptodon ensatus* (Nussbaum, 1969a). **B.** *Pseudoeurycea nigromaculata* (McDiarmid and Worthington, 1970). **C.** *Scaphiopus bombifrons* (Hoyt, 1960). **D.** *Alytes obstetricans* (Salthe, 1963). Redrawn from sources cited. Scale = 5 mm. Small scale refers to A; large scale refers to B, C, and D.

large eggs have direct development; the largest of these are the eggs of *Aneides lugubris,* in which the ovum may be 7.4 mm and the outer capsule 9.5 mm in diameter (Stebbins, 1951), and *Batrachoseps wrighti* in which capsules are 9 to 10 mm in diameter in later stages (Stebbins, 1949a). Eggs of *B. wrighti* in early stages of development have ova 5 to 6 mm and capsules about 8.5 mm in diameter (Tanner, 1853). Ovarian eggs of *Phaeognathus hubrichti* are 5 to 7 mm in diameter (Brandon, 1965). The smallest eggs among salamanders are those of newts (*Notophthalmus viridescens* and *Triturus vulgaris),* in which the ova are 1.5 mm in diameter and the ovoid capsules 2.4 by 3.6 mm (Bishop, 1941; G. Bell and Lawton, 1975).

The largest known anuran ovum is 12 mm in diameter with a capsular diameter of 14 mm in the hylid marsupial frog, *Gastrotheca cornuta,* which has direct development (Duellman, 1970). Some frogs having direct development have proportionately large capsules; for example, *Pipa pipa* has an ovum diameter of 6 mm and a capsule of 10 to 12 mm (G. Rabb and Snedigar, 1960). The largest capsules known among aquatic eggs are 15 mm, produced by *Rana spinosa,* in which the ovum is only 3.37 mm in diameter (Dubois, 1975). The smallest known amphibian eggs are produced by the pipid *Hymenochirus boettgeri,* in which the capsule is 1.5 mm and the ovum 0.75 mm in diameter (G. Rabb and M. Rabb, 1963a) and by the tiny hylid *Limnaoedus ocularis;* the aquatic eggs of the latter have ova 0.95 mm and capsules 1.57 mm in diameter (Gosner and Rossman, 1960). Other frogs, such as some leptodactylids of the genera *Physa-*

laemus, Pleurodema, and *Pseudopaludicola,* have equally small ova but capsules that are up to 3 mm in diameter. Hylid frogs producing surface-film clutches also have small eggs—ova of 1.3 and 1.2 mm and capsules of 1.5 and 1.8 mm in *Smilisca baudinii* and *S. cyanosticta,* respectively (Duellman and Trueb, 1966; Pyburn, 1966).

Amphibian eggs deposited in sites exposed to sunlight have melanin deposits over the animal hemisphere, whereas most eggs deposited in places not exposed to sunlight lack the pigment. Terrestrial eggs that undergo direct development and that are deposited in concealed sites lack pigment, as do the eggs deposited on vegetation above water by some species of *Hyla, Phyllomedusa, Centrolenella, Afrixalus,* and *Hyperolius.* In each of these, the eggs are adherent to the undersides of leaves or wrapped in leaves, so that the eggs are not exposed to sunlight. Species in the *C. fleischmanni* group deposit unpigmented eggs on the undersides of leaves, whereas other species of *Centrolenella* have pigmented eggs on the tips or upper surfaces of leaves. Likewise, all species of *Phyllomedusa* that wrap their eggs in leaves have unpigmented eggs but the species that have exposed clutches have pigmented eggs. Leptodactylids that construct foam nests in open water have pigmented eggs but those that have nests in concealed sites have unpigmented eggs. Not all eggs in concealed sites lack pigment. The eggs of some salamanders that are deposited in dark places have some pigment in the animal hemisphere, such as *Euproctus asper* (Gasser, 1964), *Taricha rivularis* (Riemer, 1958), and *Hemidactylium scutatum* (Bishop, 1941). The same is true for some frogs, such as *Heleioporus eyrei* (A. Lee, 1967), *Notaden nichollsi* (Slater and Main, 1963), *Colostethus subpunctatus* (Stebbins and Hendrickson, 1959), *Rana everetti* (Alcala, 1962), and *R. spinosa* (C. Pope, 1931). Intraspecific variation in the amount of pigmentation occurs in eggs of newts wrapped in leaves in water exposed to sunlight, such as *Notophthalmus viridescens* (Bishop, 1941), *Triturus palmatus,* and *T. vulgaris* (Hamburger, 1936).

The occurrence of melanin in eggs exposed to sunlight suggests that the melanin may function to protect the embryo from ultraviolet radiation or to increase the temperature of the egg through greater heat absorbtion. Certainly, pigmented eggs will absorb more heat when exposed to sunlight than will unpigmented eggs but the latter are never deposited in areas exposed to sunlight. Furthermore, heat retention seems to be correlated with the shape of the egg mass (see following section). Experimental exposure of eggs of *Ambystoma mexicanum* (Sergeev and Smirnov, 1939), *Triturus alpestris* (Kraft, 1968), *Xenopus laevis* (Gurdon, 1960), and *Rana pipiens* (Higgins and Sheard, 1926) to intense ultraviolet irradiation caused mortality and abnormal development of the eggs. The darkly pigmented eggs of *Rana temporaria* are more resistant to radiation than the paler eggs of *R. esculenta* (Beudt, 1930).

Amphibian yolk usually is creamy yellow or pale grayish yellow. Some frogs that deposit their eggs on leaves have pale green yolks; these yolks may be protectively colored. This is true for centrolenids, phyllomedusine hylids, and some hyperoliids.

Physicochemical Properties

The structure of amphibian eggs in combination with their biochemical properties provides a fascinating glimpse at apparently adaptive phenomena. Unfortunately, these kinds of developmental data are available for few species representing even fewer reproductive modes, so neither generalizations nor evolutionary trends can be proposed at this time.

The vitelline membrane and perivitelline chamber of *Rana pipiens* have been studied in detail by Salthe (1965). During development there is an increase in the volume of the perivitelline chamber. This increase is primarily an osmotic phenomenon with the vitelline membrane acting as a semipermeable membrane. The rate of increase of the volume of the chamber appears to be specific to developmental stages, but the permeability of the vitelline membrane to ions does not change during development, although permeability is modified by changes in the pH. The elastic modulus of the vitelline membrane decreases at about Stage 15 when the major increase in volume begins. Excess pressure in the perivitelline chamber decreases from Stage 15 to hatching. Osmotic pressure in the perivitelline chamber increases owing to excretory products and secretions by the embryo; primarily these are proteins associated with the hatching enzymes produced by the frontal glands beginning in Stage 15.

The mucoid capsules surrounding the ovum and vitelline membrane protect the developing embryo from injury, fungal infestation, and ingestion; the outermost capsule provides support for the ovum by fastening it to some object. It has been suggested that the capsules act as lenses, focusing rays of the sun on the ovum, thereby increasing the temperature of the eggs (Bragg, 1964). However, measurements of the refractive indices of the capsules of *Ambystoma maculatum* and *Rana sylvatica* revealed no significant refraction at the water-capsule surface or between capsules (Cornman and Grier, 1941).

Immediately after egg deposition, the capsules swell by the uptake of water. The ionic concentration of the water affects the rate and extent of capsular swelling. In the eggs of *Rana temporaria,* there is a strong negative correlation between the size of the capsules and ionic concentration (Beattie, 1980). Similar results were obtained for *R. pipiens* (T. Lee, 1964) and for *Bufo bufo* (Kobayashi, 1954). The optimum pH for swelling of eggs of *R. temporaria* is 6.5 and for those of *B. bufo,* 6.4 to 6.8.

The aquatic eggs of *Rana sphenocephala, sylvatica,* and *temporaria* retain heat more effectively than the surrounding water (Hassinger, 1970; Beattie, 1980). In *R. temporaria,* heat retention is much greater in larger eggs than in smaller ones. If this correlation prevails interspecifically, it may account in part for the variation observed in the sizes of capsules relative to the ova in many amphibians. Thus, species that deposit their eggs in cold water tend to have proportionately much larger capsules than those in warm water. For example, calculations of the ratio of total egg diameter to ovum diameter from measurements given in the literature show a range in *Rana* from 1.60 for *R. cancrivora,* which deposits its eggs in a surface film on lowland ponds in the Philippines (Alcala, 1962), to 4.06 in *R. japonica,* an early breeder in cold ponds in Japan (Okada, 1966), and 4.75 in *R. spinosa,* which places its eggs in cold Himalayan streams (Dubois, 1975). Similarly, within hylids the ratios are comparable—1.5 for *Smilisca cyanosticta* and 1.6 for *Hyla rosenbergi,* which deposit eggs as surface films on warm water in the American tropics (Pyburn, 1966; Kluge, 1981) to 4.4 for *Pseudacris brachyphona,* which deposits clumps of eggs in cold ponds (N. Green, 1938).

Distinctly different thermal properties exist between globular and surface-film egg clutches. The globular egg masses deposited in still, cold water by some *Rana* retain heat and consequently are warmer than the surrounding water. Temperatures of egg masses of *R. temporaria* and *R. sphenocephala* were 0.63°C warmer than the water (R. Savage, 1961; Hassinger, 1970); masses of *R. sylvatica* in Alaska were 1.0°C, and in New Jersey, 1.6°C, warmer than the water (Herreid and Kinney, 1967; Hassinger, 1970). However, in the absence of insolation, temperature differences become much less (Zweifel, 1968b). If heat retention is dependent on the size of the mass, communal egg deposition, as reported for *R. temporaria* and *R. sylvatica* by R. Savage (1961) and R. D. Howard (1980), respectively, would result in higher temperatures for the developing eggs. Actually, egg masses in the center of communal masses deposited by *R. sylvatica* are warmer than peripheral masses and have greater survivorship to hatching (Waldman, 1982a). Conversely, the surface film clutches of *R. catesbeiana* and *Hyla rosenbergi* dissipate heat, and their temperatures are 0.84°C and 0.40°C lower than the surrounding water (M. Ryan, 1978; Kluge, 1981).

Oxygenation of eggs is critical to their development, and there is a continual increase in oxygen consumption during development (Salthe and Mecham, 1974). However, in *Rana temporaria* at least, there is no correlation between the rate and extent of swelling of the egg capsules and the amount of dissolved oxygen in the water (Beattie, 1980). Eggs deposited as a surface film are adaptive with respect to meeting the oxygen needs of the embryos (Moore, 1940). Cool water contains more dissolved oxygen, and the eggs in the middle of a globular but porous mass obtain sufficient oxygen, but in warm water with a low oxygen tension, surface films provide maximum exposure for each egg. The small egg masses of *Scaphiopus* and strings of eggs produced by *Bufo* also are adapted to warm water because they allow more exposure of individual eggs to surrounding water (Zwei-

fel, 1968b). The importance of the development on the surface of the eggs of *Hyla rosenbergi* was demonstrated by Kluge (1981), who found that survivorship of eggs was extremely low when eggs were placed on the mud at the bottom of nests where the oxygen tension was low.

Despite the relatively tough outer capsule of terrestrial amphibian eggs, the eggs are readily susceptible to dehydration. Eggs take up moisture from the damp substrate and lose moisture to the drier air. Moisture contained within the egg capsules provides a reservoir for the developing embryos. Terrestrial egg masses of *Plethodon cinereus* and *Eleutherodactylus portoricensis* can lose up to 12% of their hydrated weight without affecting viability (Heatwole, 1961; Heatwole et al., 1969). The size of the capsules relative to the ovum and therefore the amount of water contained in the egg seem to be important factors in the ability of terrestrial eggs to withstand dehydration. Larvae of the myobatrachid frog *Geocrinia victoriana* can survive up to 4 months within the capsules of the terrestrial eggs before the nests are flooded (A. Martin and A. Cooper, 1972). These eggs can lose up to 90% of their hydrated weight without affecting larval viability. In egg masses that are not flooded for several weeks after Stage 26 is reached, the individual capsules break down and fuse into one homogeneous jelly mass. This large mass presents less surface area proportional to entire volume than do individual eggs, and this reduces dehydration. Presumably the breakdown of the capsules is caused by accumulations of hatching enzymes produced by the frontal glands of the embryo.

The arboreal egg masses of some tree frogs of the genus *Phyllomedusa* are encased in leaves, and each group of embryonated eggs is supplemented by many eggless capsules containing metabolic water (Agar, 1910; Pyburn, 1980a). Experiments with eggs of *P. hypochondrialis* by Pyburn revealed that the leaves protect the eggs from desiccation and that the eggless capsules provide water for the embryonated eggs.

In the aquatic foam nests of some leptodactylid and myobatrachid frogs, the outer capsules of the eggs are shared in common with water, air, and seminal fluid. In some cases the outer surface of the foam nest exposed to air becomes dry and crustlike. Terrestrial and arboreal foam nests commonly have dry outer surfaces that provide an effective protection against dehydration of eggs in the moist interior of the nest (Coe, 1974). The foam nest also may be effective in maintaining lower developmental temperatures in otherwise warm water, as noted for *Physalaemus enesefae* by Gorzula (1977).

The mucoid capsules seem to provide some protection against ingestion by predators. Larger, firmer capsules seem to be a deterrent to predation by small fish (Grubb, 1972). Experiments on predation of eggs of *Ambystoma maculatum* by D. Ward and Sexton (1981) showed a significant increase in predation associated with the removal of the capsules. Some amphibian eggs have toxic and noxious properties. Eggs of *Taricha* and *Atelopus* contain an effective neurotoxin, tarichatoxin (tetrodotoxin) (Mosher et al., 1964; Pavelka et al., 1977), and those of some species of *Bufo* are highly toxic to reptiles and mammals (L. Licht, 1968), as well as to fishes and other anurans. Fishes tend to avoid most toad eggs in nature; thus, some noxious quality seems to be associated with the toxicity.

Egg capsules must be present for fertilization and hatching to occur. Eggs taken from the coelom or proximal part of the female reproductive tract are not capable of being fertilized in *Bufo bufo* (Kambara, 1953), *B. melanogaster* (K. Low et al., 1976), and *Cynops pyrrhogaster* (Nadamitsu, 1957). The rate of fertilization increases as the number of jelly layers accumulates on the ova as they pass down the oviduct in *Notophthalmus viridescens* (McLaughlin and A. Humphries, 1978) and *B. melanogaster* (K. Low et al., 1976). Furthermore, experimental envelopment of ova (removed from the upper part of the tracts) with jelly resulted in eggs capable of being fertilized in *Taricha torosa* (Good and J. Daniel, 1943) and *Rana pipiens* (Subtely and Bradt, 1961). The innermost capsules are necessary for fertilization in *Hyla japonica* (Katagiri, 1963) and various North American *Bufo, Hyla,* and *Rana* (Aplington, 1957). In *B. arenarum* at least, substances diffused from the egg capsules into the surrounding water result in a positive reaction by conspecific sperm (Barbieri, 1976).

Egg capsules also are important to the ability of eggs to hatch. This ability depends on the number of jelly coats. Although the jelly might provide a mechanical foothold enabling sperm to penetrate to the ova (Kambara, 1953), substantive evidence points to antigen-antibody-like reactions between jelly and sperm. Regional differences in antigens in anuran oviducts are correlated with the effective fertilization of the eggs (Barch and Shaver, 1963). The jelly also may affect the maturation of the eggs and may have mechanical and possibly even nutritive significance during cleavage (A. Humphries, 1966). The progressive increase in fertilization and ability to hatch as eggs descend the reproductive tract seems to be attributable to the increase in the amount and composition of jelly on the eggs. The limited information on the histochemical complexity of oviducal secretions and the antigenic materials in the jelly layers suggests that: (1) some components in the jelly layers are essential for fertilization; (2) these include both species-specific attributes and components shared with congeners; and (3) there is a regional distribution of these components in the oviduct (Shaver et al., 1970).

EGG DEVELOPMENT

The development of amphibian eggs has been the subject of study and experimentation by embryologists for more than a century. The massive amount of literature is summarized adequately in texts, such as B. Balinsky (1960). Anuran development is described thoroughly by Rugh (1951), who also treated experimental embryological work on amphibians in detail (Rugh, 1962). This section is concerned with those comparative aspects of amphibian development that have evolutionary and ecological significance.

Figure 5-5. Fetal teeth of a caecilian, *Gymnopis multiplicata,* that function as scraping organs in the oviduct. Photo by M. H. Wake.

Table 5-1. Comparison of Caloric Utilization Between Fertilization and Hatching in Four Species of Amphibians*

Species	Calories	Total length of hatchlings (mm)	Hours of development	Percent of lipids in yolk
Bufo bufo	0.528	4	82	20
Rana pipiens	0.560	6	—	10
Ambystoma mexicanum	1.710	11	204	29
Andrias japonicus	136.450	14	650	35

*Data from Salthe and Mecham (1974).

Embryonic Metabolism

Amphibian embryonic metabolism was summarized by Salthe and Mecham (1974). The emphasis here is on nutrition, respiration, and elimination of nitrogenous wastes.

Nutrition. With the exception of most viviparous taxa, amphibian embryos obtain all nutrients for their development, at least to hatching, from the egg yolk. Although *Eleutherodactylus jasperi* gives birth to live young, which develop entirely within the oviducts, the nutrients for the entire embryonic development are provided by the yolk and not maternal tissues (M. Wake, 1978). Likewise, pipid and hylid frogs that carry developing eggs on their backs or in pouches provide no nutrients to the embryos; maintenance of the same dry weights of eggs throughout development indicates that there is no addition of nutrients (del Pino et al., 1975; Weygoldt, 1976b).

The majority of viviparous amphibians are caecilians; three of the five families contain species known to bear living young (M. Wake, 1977b). Fetuses of caecilians quickly exhaust their yolk supply, hatch from the egg membranes, and obtain nourishment from the female by ingesting secretions and epithelial tissue from the lining of the oviduct. Fetal caecilians have deciduous teeth that are specialized for scraping the lining of the oviduct (M. Wake, 1976) (Fig. 5-5).

Maternal nutrients are supplied by the epithelial walls of the oviduct in viviparous *Salamandra*. In *S. atra* only 1 or 2 eggs in each oviduct are fertilized; another 20 to 30 eggs degenerate into a mass of yolk, which is ingested by the developing fetuses after their own yolk reserves are exhausted; subsequently the fetuses are nourished by secretions from the oviducal walls (Wunderer, 1910; Vilter and Vilter, 1960, 1964). Likewise, maternal nutrients are supplied via epithelial secretions in the oviducts by the viviparous frog *Nectophrynoides occidentalis* (Vilter and Lugand, 1959; Xavier, 1973); fetuses have fine papillae around the mouth, but their function in feeding, if any, is unknown (Lamotte and Xavier, 1972).

Caloric utilization has been calculated for few species. From data on two species of anurans and two of salamanders (Table 5-1), it seems evident that far more energy is required to produce a larger hatchling than a smaller one and that this requires considerably more time. Thus, increased amounts of energy are required simply to maintain an embryo having a longer duration of development. Lipids are a major source of energy during development; the longer duration of development and larger hatchlings in salamanders, as compared with anurans, are the result of not only larger yolks but proportionately more lipids in the yolk. However, caloric contents of eggs of three species of *Ambystoma* vary intrapopulationally; the range is 16.5 to 29.0 calories per egg in *A. tigrinum* (Kaplan, 1980b). Embryos of all three species require 1.45 calories to hatch, regardless of ovum size, hatchling size, or temperature.

During the development of *Ambystoma mexicanum*, fats appear to be utilized early in development, with carbohydrates becoming increasingly important through gastrulation stages, after which fats are utilized again; only during the later stages are proteins the primary energy source (Løvtrup and Werdinius, 1957). However, temperature influences differential utilization of energy sources; at lower temperatures, embryos of *A. mexicanum* tend to utilize proteins, whereas at higher temperatures fats are the primary energy source. There is virtually no utilization of glycogen in *Bufo arenarum* (Barbieri and Salomón, 1963) or *Rana temporaria* (Brachet and Needham, 1935) until gastrulation, at which time glycogen is used at an ever-increasing rate.

Respiration. The presence of external gills in some amphibian embryos enhances respiratory capabilities. Three pairs of external gills develop in salamanders and caecilians. Among caecilians, the gills are triradiate, elongate, and plumose in groups exhibiting diverse reproductive modes—oviparity, ovoviviparity, and viviparity—but they are expanded sheets in typhlonectids (M. Wake, 1969) (Fig. 5-6).

In most species of salamanders that develop in ponds, the gills of the larvae have moderately long fimbriae and a general bushy appearance. The gills are more robust and have shorter fimbriae in those that develop in streams; however, prior to hatching the gills of all aquatic salamanders have only small fimbriae. Two different kinds of gills are present in the encapsulated larvae of terrestrial plethodontids undergoing direct development. In most plethodontids the gill rami are fused and the fibriae are moderately long—the "staghorn" type of gill; there is variation in the number and lengths of the fimbriae (Vial, 1968; McDiarmid and Worthington, 1970), and the fim-

Figure 5-6. Gills of fetal caecilians. (Left) Triradiate gills of *Dermophis mexicanus*. (Right) Sheetlike gills of *Typhlonectes compressicauda*.

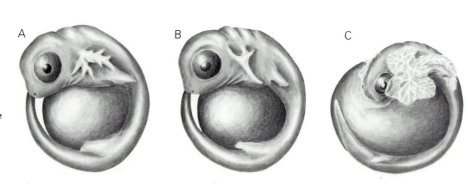

Figure 5-7. Gills of embryos of terrestrial plethodontid salamanders. **A.** Staghorn type in *Pseudoeurycea nigromaculata* (McDiarmid and Worthington, 1970). **B.** Elongate type in *Batrachoseps pacificus* (J. Davis, 1952). **C.** Leaf type in *Ensatina eschscholtzi* (Stebbins, 1954). Redrawn from sources cited; not to scale.

briae are absent on fairly long rami in *Batrachoseps attenuatus* and *B. pacificus* (Emmel, 1924; J. Davis, 1952). However, in *Aneides lugubris, Hydromantes shastae,* and *Ensatina eschscholtzi* the gills are flattened and leaflike (Ritter and L. Miller, 1899; Gorman, 1956) (Fig. 5-7), whereas those of *Aneides aeneus* are intermediate between the staghorn and leaf types (Bishop, 1943). No environmental or developmental factors seem to be correlated with these different types of gills in terrestrial eggs of plethodontid salamanders. The gills of the viviparous species of *Salamandra* have numerous and very long fimbriae (Gasche, 1939), presumably as an adaptation to obtain oxygen in the oviducts.

Compared with other amphibians, external gills are poorly developed in anuran embryos, but the larvae do have well-developed internal gills. With the exception of the egg-brooding hylid frogs, external gills are transitory, if present at all, and usually do not persist after hatching. However, tadpoles of gladiator frogs of the *Hyla boans* group have large filamentous gills (Noble, 1927b). The gills develop soon after hatching (Stage 17) in *Hyla rosenbergi* (Kluge, 1981); by Stage 19 the gills are large

and branched, and the tadpoles hang from the surface of the water with their gills outspread until Stage 24, when the gills are reduced and the operculum closes. External gills persist for a while after hatching in some species, the eggs of which develop in foam nests, such as *Physalaemus pustulosus* (Noble 1927b) and *Polypedates leucomystax* (Alcala and W. Brown, 1956). External gills are especially well developed in embryos of some species that have eggs attached to vegetation over water, such as *Phyllomedusa* (Pyburn, 1980a) and *Centrolenella* (Noble, 1927b; P. Starrett, 1960), but external gills are absent from embryos in the arboreal eggs of *Mantidactylus liber* (Blommers-Schlösser, 1975a).

In the egg-brooding hylid frogs, the eggs undergo direct development on the dorsum of the female or in a dorsal pouch; in some species carrying eggs in a pouch, hatching occurs at a larval stage. The developing embryos of all seven genera are characterized by extensive bell-shaped gills that partially or completely envelop the embryo and yolk sac. These gills are associated with only the first gill arch in *Flectonotus* and *Cryptobatrachus,* which have only one pair of gills partially covering the embryo, or with the first and second gill arches in *Fritziana, Hemiphractus,* and *Stefania,* which have two pairs of gills that completely envelop the embryo in all but *Fritziana* (del Pino and Escobar, 1981). Only one pair of gills is present in *Gastrotheca* and *Amphignathodon,* but these have two pairs of stalks; the large single gill apparently is the result of fusion of two pairs (Fig. 5-8).

In aquatic frogs of the genus *Pipa,* eggs are imbedded in the dorsal skin of the female; small gills are present in embryonic *P. carvalhoi* (Weygoldt, 1976b). In that species the implantation of the eggs involves extensive reorganization of the epidermis and dermis of the female's dorsum. The egg chambers are well supplied with capillaries, and the single jelly capsule of the egg adheres to the wall of the chamber. The lining of the pouches of brooding females of egg-brooding hylids is highly vascularized and also has extensions of vascularized tissue between the eggs (del Pino et al., 1975). The gills of the embryos are separated from the maternal tissue by a thin jelly capsule. It is evident that embryonic respiration is

accomplished by gaseous exchange between the embryonic gills and vascularized maternal tissue.

In some other anurans having direct development of terrestrial eggs, respiration presumably is enhanced by the development of vascularized tissue other than gills. The tail is greatly expanded and pressed against the vitelline membrane in the Papuan microhylid *Phrynomantis robusta* (Méhelÿ, 1901) and in many species of *Eleutherodactylus* (Fig. 5-9), including *E. optatus* (Noble, 1927b), *nubicola* (Lynn, 1942), *guentheri* and *nasutus* (Lynn and B. Lutz, 1946a, b), and *johnstonei* (Lamotte and Lescure, 1977). The tail develops into a thin membrane that almost completely envelops the embryo in *Hylactophryne augusti* (Jameson, 1950; Valett and Jameson, 1961). However, in other species of *Eleutherodactylus* (e.g., *E. planirostris,* Goin, 1947) the tail is not expanded. In most species of *Eleutherodactylus* that have been studied, external gills are absent, but they do appear for a brief period of time in at least three species—*E. inoptatus, johnstonei,* and *portoricensis;* in the last species the gills are associated with the third gill arch (Gitlin, 1944). The gills presumably function in respiration before the highly vascularized caudal tissue expands and assumes this function.

External gills are absent or transitory in other frogs having direct development. The tail is vascularized but not greatly expanded in embryos of frogs such as *Leiopelma* (E. Stephenson and N. Stephenson, 1957), the microhylid *Myersiella microps* (Izecksohn et al., 1971), and the ranid *Anhydrophryne rattrayi* (Wager, 1965). Platymantine ranids of the genera *Discodeles* and *Platymantis* have direct development of terrestrial eggs. Their embryos have vascularized, thin-walled, lateral, abdominal sacs that presumably function in respiration (Fig. 5-9); in these embryos the tail is small and external gills are absent (Boulenger, 1886; Atoda, 1950; Alcala, 1962).

Among the viviparous species of *Nectophrynoides,* the tail is relatively long and thin but well vascularized (Lamotte and Lescure, 1977), and it may serve respiratory functions. The tail in the ovoviviparous *Eleutherodactylus jasperi* is greatly expanded (M. Wake, 1978).

In summary, embryonic respiration in both aquatic and terrestrial eggs of caecilians and salamanders and vivi-

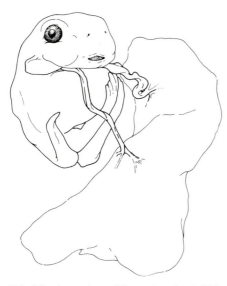

Figure 5-8. Gills of an embryo of the egg-brooding hylid frog *Gastrotheca cornuta.*

Figure 5-9. Respiratory structures of embryos of anurans having direct development of terrestrial eggs. (Left) Expanded vascularized tail in *Tomodactylus nitidus.* (Right) Expanded abdominal folds in *Platymantis guentheri.*

parous species of caecilians is accomplished by external gills. Other tissues (tail or abdominal walls) perform this function in the embryos of some terrestrial anurans, whereas gills are the primary respiratory organs in embryos of some other anurans. The smaller total surface area of gills of embryonic salamanders as compared with those in most aquatic larval salamanders suggests that less oxygen is consumed per unit time as embryos than as active free-swimming larvae. However, no comparable measurements of respiratory rates of eggs of diverse developmental modes and corresponding larvae are available. Gill growth in embryos of *Rana pipiens* and *R. temporaria* can be suppressed by elevated oxygen tension and promoted by high carbon dioxide pressure (Løvtrup and Pigon, 1969).

The rate of oxygen consumption is known to increase during intracapsular development in some amphibians: *Bufo* (Wills, 1936), *Rana temporaria* (Brachet, 1934), *Ambystoma* (Hopkins and Handford, 1943), *Taricha* (Connon, 1947), *Ascaphus* (H. Brown, 1977), and various species of Japanese anurans (Kuramoto, 1975). This increase occurs in two phases, at pre- and postneurulation, with a plateau during early stages of neurulation in *Rana* (Barth and Barth, 1954) and later stages of neurulation in *Ambystoma* (Løvtrup and Werdinius, 1957). Except for the earliest developmental stages, the embryos of anurans have higher levels of oxygen consumption and more rapid rates of increase than do salamanders (Atlas, 1938; Fischer and Hartwig, 1938). However, the total amount of oxygen consumed during neurulation is about the same even though they respire at different rates (Spirito, 1939), because neurulation is a longer process in species having comparatively low respiratory rates than in those having faster rates. Interspecifically, there is a positive correlation between rapid development and high rates of oxygen consumption (Connon, 1947). Within species, larger ova consume more oxygen at a given stage than do smaller ones (Barth and Barth, 1954), but this correlation does not hold between species (Connon, 1947). The large ova of *Ascaphus truei* have extremely low rates of oxygen consumption; this is related to the low temperatures at which they develop and suggests the presence of a large amount of inactive cytoplasm in the developing embryos (H. Brown, 1977).

Nitrogenous Wastes.   Amphibian embryos and larvae generally excrete nitrogenous wastes in the form of ammonia (J. Balinsky, 1970). In an aquatic environment large quantities of toxic ammonia can be diluted by continual diffusion of water into the perivitelline fluid. Thus, although aquatic amphibian eggs are primarily ammonotelic, small amounts of urea are produced by aquatic eggs, and the total amount of ammonia and urea increases during development. For example, urea amounts to 10 to 20% of the total amount of excretory products in *Rana temporaria, Bufo bufo,* and *Xenopus laevis*. The amount of urea produced by eggs of these three species,

respectively, is 0.172, 0.046, and 0.046 mg per 100 eggs per day at the neurula stage, but increases to 0.721, 0.525, and 0.242 mg per 100 eggs per day just before hatching (Munroe, 1953). However, ureotelism may be common in terrestrial and arboreal eggs, for which large quantities of water are not available for the ready disposal of ammonia. Urea accounts for as much as 86% of the nitrogenous wastes in the terrestrial eggs of *Geocrinia victoriana* (A. Martin and A. Cooper, 1972). Furthermore, urea accumulates at a much faster rate than ammonia in the terrestrial foam nests of *Leptodactylus albilabris* and *L. bufonius* (Candelas and Gomez, 1963; Shoemaker and McClanahan, 1973). The accumulation of whitish crystalline deposits within the egg capsules and on the tail during late intracapsular development in *Batrachyla taeniata* suggests the possibility that these embryos might be excreting uric acid (Cei and Capurro, 1958).

Although relative concentrations of ammonia and urea have not been measured in arboreal eggs, such as those of *Phyllomedusa hypocondrialis,* probably the majority of nitrogenous wastes is in the form of urea. Embryos of such frogs have a limited external water supply—the eggless capsules. As noted by Pyburn (1980a), in early developmental stages, the increasing osmotic pressure of the perivitelline fluid causes water to diffuse from the adjacent eggless capsules into the perivitelline space, diluting the concentration of nitrogenous wastes. Because of the limited supply of water in the eggless capsules, eventually the rate of dilution becomes less than the rate of waste concentration in the perivitelline fluid. Accumulation of metabolites in late embryonic stages is evident by the amber color of the perivitelline fluid.

A green alga (*Chlamydomonas* sp.) occurs symbiotically in the perivitelline fluid of the eggs of *Ambystoma gracile* (Goff and Stein, 1978). The alga removes ammonia from the perivitelline fluid and stores the excess nitrogen as membrane-bound proteinaceous bodies; this symbiotic relationship apparently affects the rate of development and survivorship, which is higher in the presence of the alga than in its absence.

Temperature and Development

Various environmental factors influence the development of amphibian embryos. These will develop normally only within certain limits of salinity and pH (see Dobrowolski, 1971, for review). The most extensive work has been with the relationship of temperature and development. The pioneering quantitative work of Lillie and Knowlton (1897) demonstrated the negative correlation between developmental time and temperature, within the thermal limits of the eggs, in amphibians. Subsequent work, principally initiated by Moore (1939), showed a correlation between breeding habits and geographic distribution on one hand and temperature tolerances and rates of embryonic development on the other. Experiments on *Rana pipiens* and *R. temporaria* by Atlas (1935) and Svinkin

(1962), respectively, demonstrated that later embryonic stages have broader temperature tolerances than do earlier stages.

Bêlehrádek (1957) noted that viscosity varies with temperature, as does the developmental rate, but reaction rates do not; therefore, he concluded that biochemical rates in intact organisms are diffusion-restricted. Data on embryos of *Rana pipiens* suggest that shifts in temperature responses may be related to changes in viscosity (McLaren, 1965). Salthe and Mecham (1974) attempted to show that as ovum size, altitude, or latitude increases, the rate of development at a given temperature increases. However, interspecific comparisons between ovum size and developmental rate are the inverse (see Chapter 2).

Most amphibian embryos that have been studied develop normally with a temperature range of about 15 to 20°C; the upper and lower limits of this range are species-specific or in some cases are variable between intraspecific populations living in different environmental regimes. At temperatures near the upper limit, development proceeds much faster than at temperatures near the lower limit, and this temperature-dependent acceleration is the same for all embryonic stages. Therefore, K. Bachmann (1969) concluded that within the normal range of temperatures for a species or population, a general rate of development can be determined as the inverse of the time interval between any two developmental stages. In view of the complex timing relations of inductive processes in amphibian embryology, the temperature independence of the relative timing of developmental progress appears to be an important specific or populational adaptive feature. Furthermore, at temperatures only a little above or below the range of 100% normal development, the relative timing begins to vary, resulting in abnormal embryos, and at extreme temperatures no development at all. For example, at 20 to 33°C nearly all embryos of *Bufo valliceps* develop normally, but normal gastrulation does not occur at 15 or 36°C (Volpe, 1959a) (Fig. 5-10A). Temperature ranges for normal development vary among species. However, within that range of temperature the overall rate of development is the only feature that varies with temperature. K. Bachmann (1969) suggested that developmental rate is a linear function of temperature throughout the range of 100% survival (Fig. 5-10B), but McLaren and Cooley (1972) questioned the linearity of the relationship.

The intercept of the rate-temperature line with the temperature axis (T_0) usually lies below the range in which normal development occurs. However, the temperature 10°C above T_0 not only lies near the middle of the adaptive temperature range of every species but also is the temperature at which the temperature coefficient (Q_{10}) of the development rate is equal to 2. Therefore, (T_0 + 10) is a constant relating the temperature effect on developmental rate to the temperature range to which the embryos are adapted. Cold-adapted amphibians typically have values of (T_0 + 10) between 10 and 15°C, whereas

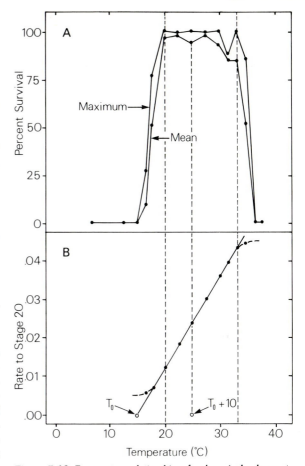

Figure 5-10. Temperature relationships of embryonic development in *Bufo valliceps*. **A.** Maximum and mean survival of batches of eggs at different temperatures. **B.** Rate of development (reciprocal of time in hours between first cleavage and gill circulation × 10³) to Stage 20 (gill circulation) at different temperatures. Note the correspondence between 100% possible survival in A and the linear part of the rate curve in B. See text for definitions of T_0 and (T_0 + 10). Adapted from K. Bachmann (1969); data from Volpe (1957a).

the values are between 20 and 25°C for most warm-adapted species (K. Bachmann, 1969).

Comparison of embryonic developmental rates independent of temperature necessitates the measurement of the product of the time interval between two comparable stages. Usually these are the two-celled stage (Stage 3 of R. Harrison, 1969, for *Ambystoma,* and Gosner, 1960, for anurans) and the closure of the neural tube (Stage 21 of R. Harrison, 1969, for *Ambystoma;* Stage 16 of Gosner, 1960, for anurans). Using (16) as a standard for completion of neural tube formation, K. Bachmann (1969) measured the progress of development as

$$(16) = \Delta t(16)(T - T_0)$$

where $\Delta D(16)$ is the developmental interval between the two-celled stage and closure of the neurula, $\Delta t(16)$ is the time interval between the two stages, T is the developmental temperature, and T_0 is a constant.

Comparison of data on various amphibians reveals that adaptive temperatures ($T_0 + 10$) vary from 10 to 27°C, and that the relative rates are highly variable (Table 5-2); the temperature tolerances are measured from first cleavage at constant temperatures. The relative developmental rates of *Bufo* in warm waters is much faster than *Rana* in cold waters or than aquatic salamanders. In comparison with anurans, most salamanders have much narrower ranges of adaptive temperatures; however, *Ambystoma gracile* has developmental temperature tolerances of 5 to 22.5°C (H. Brown, 1976a). Furthermore, salamander embryos require about half again as much time to reach a given stage of development as do anurans. These generalizations are based on data on relatively few species, all of which have aquatic eggs and larvae. Comparable kinds of data are needed on salamanders and anurans having direct development and anurans having other diverse reproductive modes.

Still, it is obvious that different species have different developmental rates at the same temperatures. For example, embryos of *Ambystoma gracile* require about half as much time to reach the stage of gill circulation as do those of *A. tigrinum; A. jeffersonianum* develops even faster (Table 5-3). Studies on cold-adapted species reveal similar ranges of thermal tolerances but notably different rates of development at constant temperatures. For example, three amphibians breeding in the same pond in extreme northwestern Washington, have embryonic temperature tolerances of 4–21°C *(Rana aurora),* 5–22.5°C *(Ambystoma gracile),* and 6–28°C *(Hyla regilla),* but at 10°C gill circulation is reached in 16 and 19 days respectively in *H. regilla* and *R. aurora* but not until 36 days in *A. gracile* (H. Brown, 1976a). The embryos of *Ascaphus truei* in streams in the same area tolerate temperatures of only 5–18°C and require 27 days at 10°C to attain gill circulation (H. Brown, 1975a). The ranges of temperature tolerances of these cold-adapted species (13.5–17.5°C) is slightly more than the range

Table 5-2. Values for the Adaptive Temperature ($T_0 + 10$) and the Relative Developmental Time from the Two-celled Stage to Closure of the Neurula for Various Amphibians[a]

Species	$T_0 + 10$ (°C)	ΔD (16) (°C × hours)	Reference
Salamanders			
Cynops pyrrhogaster	17.2	1287	K. Bachmann (1969)
Notophthalmus viridescens	17.3	1092	K. Bachmann (1969)
Triturus alpestris	15.0	1222	Knight (1938)
Ambystoma maculatum	15.8	1335	K. Bachmann (1969)
Ambystoma mexicanum	18.2	861	K. Bachmann (1969)
Ambystoma tigrinum	17.8	822	Moore (1939)
Ambystoma tigrinum	19.0	860	Tamini (1947)
Proteus anguineus	18.0	(5000)[b]	Briegleb (1962b)
Anurans			
Ascaphus truei	14.4	1817	H. Brown (1975a)
Xenopus laevis	20.5	252	Nieuwkoop and Faber (1956)
Scaphiopus hammondii	23.3	183	H. Brown (1967b)
Scaphiopus multiplicatus	24.5	137	H. Brown (1967b)
Bufo americanus	24.2	250	Volpe (1953)
Bufo bufo bufo	15.5	912	Douglas (1948)
Bufo bufo japonicus	10.2	1650	Hasegawa (1960)
Bufo terrestris	24.5	(200)[b]	Volpe (1953)
Bufo valliceps	24.8	(200)[b]	Volpe (1957a)
Bufo woodhousii fowleri	24.9	250	Volpe (1953)
Bufo woodhousii woodhousii	25.0	(250)[b]	Volpe (1953)
Hyla arborea	19.2	556	Tamini (1957)
Rana berlandieri (Veracruz)	22.3	379	Ruibal (1955)
Rana berlandieri (Texas)	21.6	438	Moore (1949)
Rana catesbeiana	24.3	357	Moore (1939)
Rana clamitans	21.0	475	Moore (1939)
Rana esculenta (Germany)	18.0	602	Hertwig (1889)
Rana esculenta (Italy)	21.6	430	Tamini (1947)
Rana esculenta (England)	24.0	350	Douglas (1948)
Rana palustris	19.0	703	Moore (1939)
Rana pipiens (New Jersey)	20.0	500	Moore (1949)
Rana pipiens (Wisconsin)	20.8	451	Moore (1949)
Rana pipiens complex (Costa Rica)	22.0	500	Volpe (1957b)
Rana septentrionalis	22.4	525	Moore (1952)
Rana shenocephala	23.0	344	Moore (1949)

[a]Extracted from K. Bachmann (1969).
[b]Interpolated data.

Table 5-3. Comparative Rates of Embryonic Development of Five Species of *Ambystoma* to Different Developmental Stages from First Cleavage*

| | Time in hours to | | | |
Species and temperature	Gastrula	Muscular response	Heart-beat	Gill circulation
A. jeffersonianum (19.9°C)	18	83	103	120
A. tigrinum (19.9°C)	24	105	122	146
A. maculatum (20°C)	45	165	175	195
A. mexicanum (18°C)	52	155	165	197
A. gracile (20°C)	36	262	283	305

*Adapted from H. Brown (1976a).

Table 5-4. Comparative Rates of Embryonic Development of Six Species of Anurans in a Desert Region in Southeastern Arizona at Different Temperatures[a,b]

| | Constant temperature | | | Range of tolerance (°C) |
Species	21°C	26°C	32°C	
Bufo cognatus	86	43	25.5	16.0–33.5
Bufo debilis	88	39	24	18.2–33.8
Bufo punctatus	76	40.5	22.5	16.0–33.0
Scaphiopus bombifrons	41	27	19.5	13.0–31.5
Scaphiopus couchii	57.5	25	16.5	15.5–34.0
Scaphiopus multiplicatus	42	29	28	15.6–32.5

[a]Adapted from Zweifel (1968b).
[b]Time is given in hours to reach gill circulation.

(17.0–19.5°C) of six species of anurans studied in an area of sympatry is southeastern Arizona (Zweifel, 1968b). The lowest temperature at which normal development occurred was in *Scaphiopus bombifrons* (13.5°C), whereas *Bufo debilis* required temperatures of 18.2°C. The highest temperatures tolerated were 33.8 and 34.0°C by *B. debilis* and *S. couchii,* respectively, whereas *S. bombifrons* could tolerate temperatures of only 31.5°C. Within the ranges of temperature tolerances the rates of development were notably faster at higher temperatures (Table 5-4).

No geographic variation in temperature tolerances is evident in such widely distributed species as *Rana catesbeiana, clamitans, sylvatica,* or *Scaphiopus couchii* (Moore, 1939, 1942; Herreid and Kinney, 1967; Zweifel, 1968b). But geographic variation is known in at least three species of anurans—*Bufo americanus, B. woodhousii,* and *Hyla regilla* (Volpe, 1953; H. Brown, 1975b)—and two of salamanders—*Ambystoma maculatum* and *A. macrodactylum* (DuShane and C. Hutchinson, 1944; J. Anderson, 1967). Apparent geographic variation in *Scaphiopus hammondii* (H. Brown, 1967b) reflects the inclusion of two species (H. Brown, 1976b). Geographic variation in *Rana pipiens* (Moore, 1949) is explained, in part, by the inclusion of several sibling species (Pace, 1974).

In nature, developing eggs of *Rana aurora* are known to survive short exposures to freezing temperatures (Storm, 1960), but the differential survival of different developmental stages exposed to varying durations of low or freezing temperatures is unknown. Likewise, little information is available on the tolerance levels of embryos exposed to high temperatures for varying periods of time or on tolerance changes during ontogeny. The only thorough experiments of this type have dealt with North American (H. Brown, 1967a; Zweifel, 1977) and Japanese (Muto and Kawai, 1960; Kuramoto, 1978) anurans. Among most species studied, the maximum temperature tolerated is inversely related to the duration of exposure (Table 5-5). *Bufo cognatus* is an exception in that the duration of exposure had no obvious effect on maximum tolerance, which was less than 40°C (Zweifel, 1977); also, exposure of embryos of *R. limnocharis* to temperatures of 43°C for 2 and 6 hours had no effects on maximum tolerance (Kuramoto, 1978). Embryos of all species studied increase their temperature tolerances as they grow; a marked increase takes place early in development during the first several cleavages. *Rana sylvatica,* a cold-adapted species, does not attain maximum tolerance until gastrulation is complete, or nearly so; *Scaphiopus couchii,* which develops in warm water, achieves more than 90% of its total tolerance before the beginning of gastrulation (Fig. 5-11). Experiments with American anurans were terminated at Stage 20, but those on Japanese anurans by Kuramoto (1978) were continued until Stage 25; immediately after hatching the temperature tolerances are much lower than in stages 11–20.

Amphibians are adapted to temperature regimes of the breeding habitat in two ways. One is a behavioral ad-

Table 5-5. Maximum Temperatures (°C) Tolerated by Anuran Embryos for Different Periods of Exposure[a,b]

Species	Base level	2 hours	4 hours	6 hours	10 hours
Rana sylvatica	24.0	34.6 (10.6)	33.7 (9.2)	32.9 (8.9)	32.6 (8.6)
Hyla regilla	29.6	38.0 (8.4)	—	—	—
Rana chiricahuensis	31.5	37.7 (6.2)	37.6 (6.1)	37.5 (6.0)	36.8 (5.3)
Scaphiopus bombifrons	32.5	40.0 (7.5)	39.2 (6.7)	39.2 (6.7)	39.2 (6.7)
Scaphiopus multiplicatus	32.5	40.4 (7.9)	40.0 (7.5)	39.0 (6.5)	—
Scaphiopus couchii	34.0	40.3 (6.3)	39.8 (5.8)	39.8 (5.8)	39.5 (5.5)
Bufo cognatus	33.5	>40.5 (>7.0)	>40.5 (>7.0)	>40.5 (>7.0)	—

[a]Adapted from Zweifel (1977).
[b]Figures in parentheses represent increase over base-level tolerance.

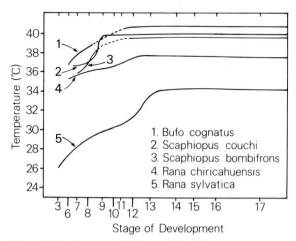

Figure 5-11. Ontogenetic changes in 2-hour temperature tolerances in embryos of five species of anurans. Stages of development follow Gosner (1960); the developmental axis is adjusted to be approximately linear with respect to time. Adapted from Zweifel (1977).

justment; the time and/or place of breeding are governed by temperatures suitable for embryonic development. Thus, there is a close correspondence between temperature tolerances and the temperatures encountered in the breeding sites (Kobayashi, 1963; Ballinger and McKinney, 1966). Also, temporal differences prevail at given localities; temperature tolerances of species breeding later in the summer in central Texas are higher than those of species breeding earlier in cooler water at the same localities (Hubbs et al., 1963).

A second adaptation involves modifications of embryonic temperature responses. If a species is sufficiently conservative in its selection of times and places of breeding, or if the habitat is extremely stenothermic, there is no need for embryonic adaptation to a broad range of temperatures. For example, populations of the *Rana pipiens* complex living in environments with relatively little fluctuation in temperature during the year have relatively narrow embryonic temperature ranges compared with populations living in environments with great fluctuations in temperature (Ruibal, 1962). Such conservativeness restricts the successful breeding of a species should the environment change. On the other hand, there seem to

be physiological limitations that prevent early embryos from being adapted to both extremely cold and extremely warm temperatures. "Given a restricted range of temperature tolerance at the beginning of life and having no way of actively avoiding detrimental temperatures should they occur, the obvious adaptive change is for the embryo to widen its range of tolerance as it grows" (Zweifel, 1977:14). Rapid changes in tolerances may be an adaptation to shorten the period in which an embryo is sensitive to high temperatures. For example, the temperature of the water in shallow ponds is within the range of tolerance of early embryos of *Scaphiopus* when they deposit their eggs at night. By midday the temperature of the water frequently is above the level of tolerance of early embryos, but by that time the rapidly developing embryos have reached a point where their tolerance incorporates the higher temperatures (Zweifel, 1968b, 1977). Thus, the critical thermal maxima, rate of change of tolerance, and developmental rate may have been modified by selective pressures directly relating to environmental temperature.

The mechanism of embryonic temperature tolerance is unknown. Genetic control has been questioned, because the early temperature tolerance of hybrid embryos is not intermediate between the parents but maternal in nature. For example, hybrid embryos of *Bufo americanus* X *B. woodhousii* are maternal in their temperature tolerance (Volpe, 1952). Kuramoto (1978) suggested the participation of cytoplasmic factors in determining the level of temperature tolerance of early embryos; a relatively sharp increase of tolerance during early cleavage stages may be the result of progressive partitioning of cytoplasm or may be mediated by maternal messenger RNA transcribed in oogenesis. Some of the maternal contribution to the level of tolerance may be provided by the mucopolysaccharide capsules. Certainly the number, thickness, and viscosity of the capsules are important in providing the early embryo with some protection from rapid changes in temperature.

Patterns of Development

Although much has been written about amphibian development, most of these investigations have not been concerned with the evolutionary or ecological aspects of development. This section discusses briefly the patterns of development that seem to be evident on the basis of comparative embryology. Details of the development of the skeletal system in posthatching larvae are given in Chapter 6.

Early Development. Cleavage in amphibian eggs is holoblastic and unequal; in large ova, many divisions may occur on the animal hemisphere before the first cleaves through the vegetal pole. *Ichthyophis glutinosus* is the only caecilian for which cleavage has been described (P. Sarasin and F. Sarasin, 1887–90). In that species cleavage is nearly meroblastic, that is, as a result of incomplete cleavage the egg is divided into numerous separate blastomeres and a residual multinucleate mass of cytoplasm. Cleavage through the blastula stage is essentially identical among those amphibians that have been studied. The blastocoel occupies a relatively small area near the animal pole in larger ova.

Differences in gastrulation seem to be associated with the amount of yolk. In most salamanders and anurans the entire yolk is covered as the blastopore closes, but in caecilians the blastopore becomes circular while the yolk still is mostly uncovered. In this way the blastopore becomes surrounded by the blastodisc on the upper surface of the partly divided egg. Also, a blastodisc is formed in the marsupial frog, *Gastrotheca riobambae* (Elinson and del Pino, 1982).

In embryos of anurans and salamanders that develop from large-yolked eggs, development takes place on the surface of the animal hemisphere, and the bulk of the yolk is not incorporated into the gut but instead forms a kind of yolk sac. In most eggs having small amounts of yolk, as is characteristic of aquatic eggs, the yolk is incorporated into the gut at early stages. Notable exceptions are embryos developing in aquatic (*Physalaemus pustulosus,* Noble, 1927b) and arboreal (*Rhacophorus schlegeli,* Ichikawa, 1931; *Chiromantis petersi,* Cherchi, 1958) foam nests and those developing on vegetation above water—phyllomedusine hylids and centrolenids. The eggs of these frogs are reasonably small, but their development is like those of telolecithal eggs.

At the tail-bud stage, caecilians and salamanders have relatively long necks incorporating the gill plates and projecting forward from the yolk mass, but have only a short tail bud. In anurans, the gill plate region is above the yolk mass with only a small portion of the head projecting beyond the yolk, but a relatively long tail bud is present. These differences, first pointed out by Kerr (1919), are generally consistent regardless of ovum size or subsequent mode of development. The relative length and freedom of the gill plate region may be indicative of the comparatively greater degree of development of external gills in caecilians and salamanders as contrasted with anurans. However, the neck region is exceedingly long in embryos of *Eleutherodactylus* (Lynn, 1942; Lynn and B. Lutz, 1946a, 1946b). During the development of these terrestrial eggs, internal gills are absent, and external gills are absent or poorly developed and transitory.

Beginning at the neurula stage, amphibian embryos are ciliated. The motions of the cilia keep the embryo constantly rotating in the perivitelline fluid. There is some evidence that prolonged contact of the embryo with the vitelline membrane results in cytolysis; motion of the perivitelline fluid may aid in the dispersal of oxygen prior to the development of specialized respiratory structures (Bayley, 1950).

Operculum Development. The operculum, that sheath of tissue covering the branchial chambers, arises from the hyoid arch anterior to the first branchial slit. The posterior growth of the paired opercula results in the eventual covering of the branchial chambers and fusion of the bilateral extensions midventrally. In salamanders and caecilians, gill slits persist and external gills protrude from the posterolateral margins of the opercular sheaths, while internally a single, median branchial chamber exists.

The development of the operculum in anurans is more complex, and the differences in opercular development among anurans are associated with the buccal pump mechanism and the internal gills. The covering of the gills necessitates the development of an outlet for water pumped over the gills. This outlet, the spiracle, is single in all but the pipoid frogs, in which it and the branchial chambers are paired. In some embryos having direct development, an operculum and branchial chambers never develop (e.g., *Eleutherodactylus;* Lynn, 1942), but in otheers (e.g., *Leiopelma)* an operculum develops but does not cover the forelimbs (N. Stephenson, 1951b).

Gill Development. Embryos of caecilians and salamanders develop three pairs of external gills (Branchial arches III, IV, V), whereas anuran embryos lack gills or have as many as three pairs of external gills. Usually only two pairs of gills appear in anurans (Branchial arches III and IV). In most frogs hatching occurs after the development of the gills, but the embryos of some others (e.g., *Xenopus, Discoglossus,* some *Scaphiopus,* and some *Bufo)* hatch before the gills develop. In any case, gills are transient in anurans having aquatic larvae. Three pairs of gills develop in the African bufonid *Schismaderma carens* (B. Balinsky, 1960). Gills develop only from the third branchial arch in some egg-brooding hylid frogs and from Branchial arches III and IV in other species. Gills are absent in embryos of many frogs that have direct development of terrestrial eggs, but external gills may be present briefly in some species of *Eleutherodactylus.* Also, both internal and external gills are absent in the viviparous *Nectophrynoides occidentalis* (Lamotte and Xavier, 1972b).

The absence of external gills in aquatic feeding stages of anuran larvae is associated with the presence of filter feeding and the buccal-pump mechanism in tadpoles, in which water is pumped over well-developed internal gills. Internal gills are developed on all four gill arches in primitive frogs having aquatic larvae; no patterns are evident in the absence of gills on certain arches in other anurans (Sokol, 1975). Moreover, the presence of internal gills in anurans and their absence in salamanders are mostly a difference in position. There is developmental (E. Gerhardt, 1932) and morphological (Schmalhausen, 1968) evidence that the internal gills in anurans are merely ventral extensions of the external gills. The latter do not develop at all or disappear soon after hatching in frogs, in contrast to aquatic salamander larvae.

Limb Development. Vestigial limb buds appear in *Ichthyophis glutinosus* (P. Sarasin and F. Sarasin, 1887–90) but not in other oviparous caecilians that have been studied: *Hypogeophis* (Brauer, 1899) and *Siphonops* (Goeldi, 1899).

In embryos of aquatic salamanders there is a definite anteroposterior wave of limb development, and the digits appear sequentially on both sets of limbs. In species developing in still water, only the forelimbs develop before hatching, and these have partially undifferentiated digits. Differential timing of development of forelimbs and hindlimbs in embryos of stream-inhabiting salamanders is decreased. The hindlimb buds appear relatively sooner, and more of the digits appear simultaneously on both sets of limbs. At hatching most of these larvae have forelimbs and hindlimbs with most of the digits developed. In plethodontid embryos undergoing direct development, the hindlimb buds appear almost simultaneously with the forelimbs, and all of the digits appear at the same time.

In most anurans having free-swimming larvae, limbs do not develop until after hatching. The hindlimb appears as a bud, as it does in salamanders, and undergoes growth and differentiation externally, while the forelimb develops within the branchial chamber, only to appear outside the body during metamorphic climax. Among anurans having terrestrial eggs without a free-living larval stage, the forelimbs may develop externally and nearly at the same time as the hind limbs, as in *Eleutherodactylus* (Salthe and Mecham, 1974), or they may develop simultaneously, as in *Leiopelma* (N. Stephenson and de Beer, 1951). However, hindlimbs appear before forelimbs in the viviparous *Nectophrynoides occidentalis* and the ovoviviparous *N. tornieri* (Lamotte and Xavier, 1972a, 1972b).

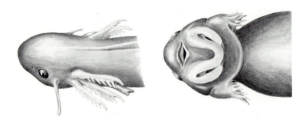

Figure 5-12. Embryonic structures in amphibians. (Left) Balancer in *Pleurodeles waltl*. (Right) Adhesive organ in *Bufo calamita*. Both structures develop in late embryos and degenerate shortly after hatching.

The ecological correlates of limb development in salamanders also are influenced by the amount of yolk available to the developing embryos (Salthe and Mecham, 1974). Salamander larvae hatching from small eggs have only the forelimbs present and continue their development and differentiation as feeding larvae. Stream-inhabiting larvae require limbs to maintain their position in flowing water; at hatching these larvae have hindlimbs, and the energy for the development is supplied by the larger amount of yolk in their eggs. Terrestrial plethodontids, which must be capable of locomotion on land upon hatching, have fully developed limbs, and all of the energy for their development is supplied by yolk.

The same ecological and energy correlates apply to anurans. Tadpoles that hatch in an early stage of development live in still water and obtain energy from the environment for their continued development, whereas those that develop directly into terrestrial froglets obtain all of the energy for their development from large quantities of yolk.

Balancers and Adhesive Organs. In pond-dwelling salamanders of the Hynobiidae, Salamandridae, and Ambystomatidae, ectodermal projections, known as balancers, develop from the mandibular arch shortly after the appearance of the forelimb buds. These rodlike structures, one on each side of the head, contain nerves and capillaries and produce a sticky, mucous secretion (Fig. 5-12). Balancers prevent early larvae from sinking into the sediment and also help them to maintain their balance until the forelimbs develop. At that time the balancers break off or gradually degenerate.

The adhesive organs (cement organs or suckers) in anuran embryos and early larval stages also are ectodermal in origin, but these structures are derived from the hyoid arch, rather than the mandibular arch. Morphological and histological studies of balancers and adhesive organs led Lieberkind (1937) to conclude that they are not homologous.

Adhesive organs develop at about the same time as the tail bud. In discoglossoids and pipoids the organ is bipartite, but the two halves function as a single structure. In *Pelobates,* it is Y-shaped. In all higher frogs, adhesive organs are single median structures until the opercular folds close; at this stage the adhesive organ is divided into two parts (Fig. 5-12). The adhesive organ secretes a sticky mucus, which may result in a threadlike conection between a recently hatched tadpole and the egg capsule (Fig. 5-13), or the recently hatched tadpoles may adhere to vegetation. By means of the adhesive organ, a tadpole that hatches at an early developmental stage may stabilize its position in the environment until its tail, muscular coordination, and mouth have developed to the point that the larva can swim and feed. Embryos that have a long intracapsular development and hatch at later stages may have transient adhesive organs. Once tadpoles begin feeding, the adhesive organs degenerate. In

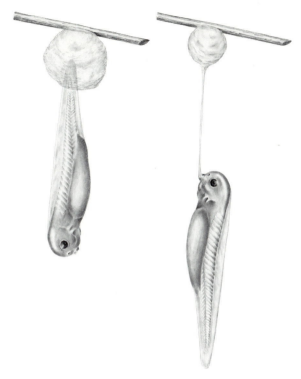

Figure 5-13. Function of adhesive glands in *Xenopus laevis*. (Left) Hatching tadpole leaving egg capsule attached to twig in water; a thread of mucus from the adhesive gland to the egg is obscured by the tadpole. (Right) The same tadpole a few seconds later hanging by a thread of mucus to the shrinking egg capsule. The tadpole remains in this suspended position until it has developed an effective tail and mouth. Redrawn from Bles (1905).

some frogs that have direct development of terrestrial eggs (e.g., *Eleutherodactylus)* adhesive organs never appear.

Normal Stages of Development

The changing appearance of embryos, especially during organogenesis, necessitates a method of quantifying the progress of development. Tables of normal stages of development have been worked out for a number of species (Table 5-6). Complete tables of development are necessary for accurate comparison of developmental stages in different organisms. Each stage must be identified as to age at a given temperature; the stages then can be identified mostly by external features. During cleavage, the stages are determined from the number and size of the blastomeres; during gastrulation, the shape of the blastopore is used, and just after gastrulation the neural plate provides easily recognizable features. During organogenesis, the progress in the formation of the tail, limbs, gills, and mouth are convenient characteristics. Development is, of course, continuous, and the designated stages gradually grade into one another. The amount of time between successive stages varies. For example, neu-

rula stages are rapid, whereas successive larval stages may be separated by several days or even weeks.

Normal stages in salamanders and anurans are quite different after gastrulation, especially the timing of neurulation and limb and gill formation. Furthermore, there is some variation within these groups.

In recent years, R. Harrison's (1969) numbered stages of normal development in *Ambystoma maculatum* have been considered the standard for salamanders, and Gosner's (1960) generalized table is accepted as a standard for anurans. These tables are basically applicable to taxa that have aquatic eggs and larvae; interspecific comparisons can be made and differences noted readily.

Illustrations and brief descriptions of the standard stages of salamander and anuran development follow.

Salamanders. This account is based on the stages of development of *Ambystoma maculatum* (R. Harrison, 1969) (Figs. 5-14, 5-15); hours given in parentheses after the stage number are for development at 20°C.

1. (0) Single cell; second polar body released.
2. (6.5) First cleavage; 2 blastomeres.
3. (8.0) Second cleavage; 4 blastomeres.
4. (9.5) Third cleavage; 8 blastomeres.
5. (11.0) Fourth cleavage; 16 blastomeres.
6. (13.5) Fifth cleavage; 24 blastomeres by division of only those in animal hemisphere.
7. (17.5) Irregular cleavage into about 100 blastomeres.
8. (22.0) Early blastula.
9. (29.0) Late blastula; animal hemisphere consisting of several layers of cells.
10. (42.0) Invagination of dorsal lip of blastopore.
11. (58.0) Dorsal lip of blastopore expands into semicircle.
12. (65.0) Blastopore formed, surrounding yolk plug; blastopore elevated to point of posterior axis of embryo.
13. (72.0) Blastopore is narrow vertical opening; neural keel on dorsal surface; body begins to elongate.
14. (75.0) Dorsal flattening; neural plate forms.
15. (80.0) Neural plate shield-shaped, bordered by low neural folds.
16. (84.0) Neural folds elevated.
17. (88.0) Neural folds further elevated; one pair of somites.
18. (92.0) Neural folds elevated still further; fore- and hindbrain vesicles evident; two somites.
19. (93.5) Neural folds approximate; mandibular arch marked by shallow groove; three somites.
20. (95.0) Neural folds fused, except anteriorly; four somites.
21. (97.0) Neural folds closed to form neural tube; four somites.

22. (98.5) Head with optic vesicles distinct; hyomandibular groove appears; five somites.

23. (100) Head more prominent; mandibular arch forming low ridge from neural cord ventrally to behind eye; six somites.

24. (104) Hyobranchial groove appears; pronephros pear-shaped; depression of otic capsule visible; nine somites.

25. (107) Head prominent; ear spot dorsal to hyomandibular groove; nine somites.

26. (110) Tail bud present; body begins to lengthen; gill plate definite with shallow pit indicating formation of first branchial groove; 10 somites.

27. (115) Stomodeum appears; 12 somites.

28. (119) Further elongation of body; greater prominence of head; first branchial groove distinct; 14 somites.

29. (123) Tail bud well defined; head more prominent; gill plate more distinct; 16 somites.

30. (133) Beginning of straightening of head curvature and lengthening of trunk; 18 somites.

31. (140) Gill folds become distinct ventrally; lens pit and nasal pit visible; 19 somites.

32. (150) Pericardial cavity present; straightening of head curvature about half complete; 20 somites.

33. (158) Muscular response; heart tube present; 21–22 somites.

34. (167) Heart tube more distinct; 24–25 somites.

35. (169) Body curvature practically eliminated; heart beat; three external gill nodules present; balancer bud forms; chromatophores appear.

36. (180) Gill buds definite; balancer bud prominent.

37. (192) Gill circulation; forelimb bud.

Table 5-6. Tables of Normal Development of Amphibians

Current name	Name used in publication	Reference
Caecilians		
Ichthyophis glutinosus	*Ichthyophis glutinosus*	P. Sarasin and F. Sarasin (1887–90)[a]
Salamanders		
Hynobius nigrescens	*Hynobius nigrescens*	Usui and Hamsaki (1939)
Onychodactylus japonicus	*Onychodactylus japonicus*	Iwasawa and Kera (1980)
Andrias japonicus	*Megalobatrachus japonicus*	Kudo (1938)
Cynops pyrrhogaster	*Triturus pyrrhogaster*	P. L. Anderson (1943); Okada and Ichikawa (1946)
Echinotriton andersoni	*Tylototriton andersoni*	Y. Utsunomiya and T. Utsunomiya (1977)
Euproctus asper	*Euproctus asper*	Gasser (1964)
Notophthalmus viridescens	*Triturus viridescens*	M. Grant (1930b)[b]; Fankhauser (1967)
Pleurodeles waltl	*Pleurodeles waltlii*	Gallien and Durocher (1957)
Salamandra atra	*Salamandra atra*	Wunderer (1910)
Taricha torosa	*Triturus torosus*	Twitty and Bodenstein (1948)
Triturus alpestris	*Triton alpestris*	Knight (1938); Fischberg (1948)
Triturus cristatus	*Triton cristatus*	Glücksohn (1931)
Triturus helveticus	*Triturus helveticus*	Gallien and Bidaud (1959)
Triturus vulgaris	*Molge vulgaris*	Gläesner (1925)
	Triton taeniatus	Glücksohn (1931)
	Triturus taeniatus	Rotmann (1940)
Tylototriton verrucosus	*Tylototriton verrucosus*	Ferrier (1974)
Necturus maculosus	*Necturus maculosus*	Eycleshymer and J. Wilson (1910)
Proteus anguineus	*Proteus anguineus*	Briegleb (1962b)
Ambystoma jeffersonianum	*Ambystoma jeffersonianum*	M. Grant (1930a)
Ambystoma maculatum	*Ambystoma punctatum*	R. Harrison (1969); Hara and Boterenbrood (1977)
Ambystoma mexicanum	*Ambystoma mexicanum*	Schreckenberg and Jacobson (1975); Bordzilovskaya and Dettlaff (1979)
Ambystoma opacum	*Amblystoma opacum*	M. Grant (1930a)[b]
Eurycea bislineata	*Eurycea bislineata*	I. Wilder (1925)[b]
Plethodon cinereus	*Plethodon cinereus*	Dent (1942)
Anurans		
Ascaphus truei	*Ascaphus truei*	H. Brown (1975a)
Xenopus laevis	*Xenopus laevis*	Weisz (1925); Nieuwkoop and Faber (1967); Deuchar (1975)
Alytes cisternasii	*Alytes cisternasii*	Crespo (1979)
Alytes obstetricans	*Alytes obstetricans*	Cambar and Martin (1959); Crespo (1979)
Bombina orientalis	*Bombina orientalis*	J. Michael (1981)
Discoglossus pictus	*Discoglossus pictus*	Gallien and Houillon (1951)
Scaphiopus bombifrons	*Scaphiopus bombifrons*	Trowbridge (1941, 1942)
Caudiverbera caudiverbera	*Calytocephalella gayi*	Jorquera and Izquierdo (1964)

[a]Incomplete; temporal scale not included.
[b]Primarily dealing with metamorphic stages.

38. (210) Gills reach to base of forelimb bud; filaments developing on ventral ramus of each gill ramus.
39. (228) Gills reach to tip of forelimb bud; balancer club-shaped.
40. (252) Gills feathery, curved dorsally; forelimb bud slightly flattened distally; operculum distinct across venter; cornea transparent; pigmentation of iris visible.
41. (315) Median notch of operculum evident; forelimb bud notched distally.
42. (330) Forelimb with deeper bifurcation distally and slight bulge marking beginning of elbow joint; gall bladder present.
43. (410) Mouth opens; hindlimb buds appear.
44. (455) Forelimb longer, bowed slightly; first movements of forelimb.
45. (500) Third digit of forelimb distinct; yolk still present in intestine.
46. (525) Yolk completely absorbed; fourth finger bud distinct; hatching.

The development of *Ambystoma maculatum* at 20°C can be summarized, as follows: Stages 2–7 are times of cleavage and require about 17.5 hours. The blastocoel is formed in stages 8 and 9 (11.5 hours). Stages 10–12 are gastrulation and require about 36 hours. Neurulation (stages 13–20) requires about 30 hours. Stages 21–29 involve rapid growth of the head region including sensory capsules and require about 28 hours. In stages 30–35, the body is straightened and the tail bud elongates; these changes require about 46 hours. During stages 36–40, the gills and balancers develop, and the forelimb bud takes on a paddle shape (83 hours). Stages 41–46 involve further development of the forelimbs, appearance of hindlimb buds, development of the digestive system, absorption of the yolk, and hatching; this is the longest period of development, requiring about 273 hours.

Current name	Name used in publication	Reference
Heleioporus eyrei	*Heleioporus eyrei*	Packer (1966)
Eleutherodactylus coqui	*Eleutherodactylus coqui*	Townsend and Stewart (1984)
Eleutherodactylus nubicola	*Eleutherodactylus nubicola*	Lynn (1942)
Physalaemus biligonigerus	*Paludicola fuscomaculata*	Bles (1907)[a]
Pleurodema brachyops	*Pleurodema brachyops*	J. León and Donoso-Barros (1970)
Bufo andersonii	*Bufo andersonii*	Bhati (1969)
Bufo arenarum	*Bufo arenarum*	del Conte and Sirlín (1952)
Bufo bufo	*Bufo vulgaris*	W. Adler (1901)
	Bufo bufo	Cambar and Gipouloux (1957); Michniewska-Predygier and Pigón (1957); A. Rossi (1959)
Bufo maurantiacus	*Bufo maurantiacus*	Siboulet (1971)
Bufo melanostictus	*Bufo melanostictus*	Khan (1965)
Bufo regularis	*Bufo regularis*	Sedra and M. Michael (1961)
Bufo valliceps	*Bufo valliceps*	Limbaugh and Volpe (1957)
Nectophrynoides occidentalis	*Nectophrynoides occidentalis*	Lamotte and Xavier (1972)
Rhinoderma darwinii	*Rhinoderma darwini*	Jorquera et al. (1972)
Rhinoderma rufum	*Rhinoderma darwini*	Jorquera et al. (1974)
Gastrotheca riobambae	*Gastrotheca riobambae*	del Pino and Escobar (1981)
Hyla regilla	*Hyla regilla*	Eakin (1947)
Hyla avivoca	*Hyla avivoca*	Volpe et al. (1961)
Phyllomedusa hypocondrialis	*Phyllomedusa hypochondrialis*	Budgett (1899)[a]
Phyllomedusa trinitatus	*Phyllomedusa trinitatus*	Kenny (1968)[a]
Hemisus marmoratum	*Hemisus marmoratum*	Bles (1907)[a]
Rana arvalis	*Rana terrestris*	Michniewska-Predygier and Pigón (1957)
Rana breviceps	*Rana breviceps*	Mohanty-Hejmadi et al. (1979)[a]
Rana brevipoda	*Rana brevipoda*	Iwasawa and Morita (1980)
Rana chalconota	*Rana chalconota*	Hing (1959)[a]
Rana cyanophlyctis	*Rana cyanophlyctis*	Ramaswami and Lakshman (1959)
Rana dalmatina	*Rana dalmatina*	Cambar and Marrot (1954)
Rana esculenta	*Rana esculenta*	Michniewska-Predygier and Pigón (1957)
Rana japonica	*Rana japonica*	Tahara (1959, 1974)
Rana nigromaculata	*Rana nigromaculata*	Chu and Sze (1957)
Rana pipiens	*Rana pipiens*	Shumway (1940); A. Taylor and Shumway (1946)[b]
Rana sylvatica	*Rana sylvatica*	Pollister and J. Moore (1937)
Rana temporaria	*Rana fusca*	Moser (1950); Kopsch (1952)
	Rana temporaria	Michniewska-Predygier and Pigón (1957)
Rana tigerina	*Rana tigrina*	Khan (1969); Bhadi (1969); Agarwal and Niazi (1977)
Rhacophorus arboreus	*Rhacophorus arboreus*	Iwasawa and Kawasaki (1979)
Uperodon systoma	*Uperodon systoma*	Mohanty-Hejmadi et al. (1979)[a]

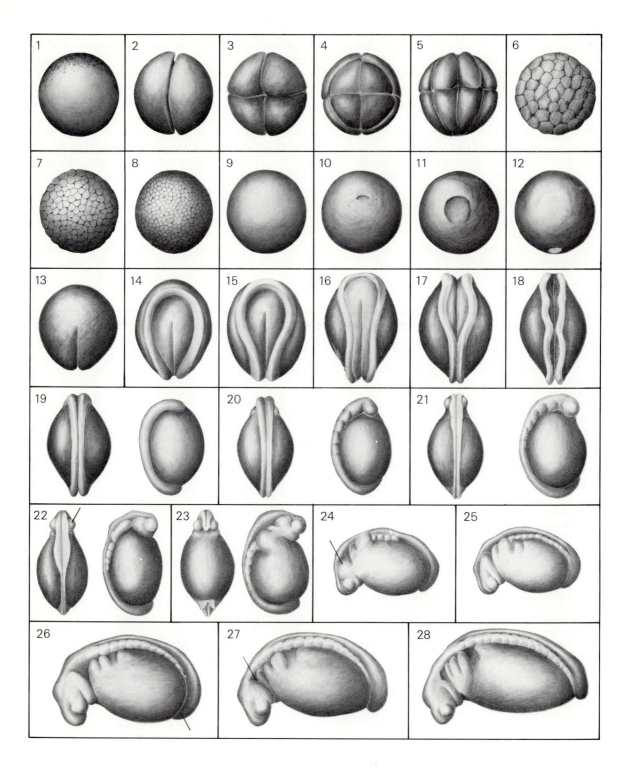

Figure 5-14. Early stages of normal development of a salamander, *Ambystoma maculatum*. Stages are according to R. Harrison (1969). Guidelines indicate major features mentioned in text.

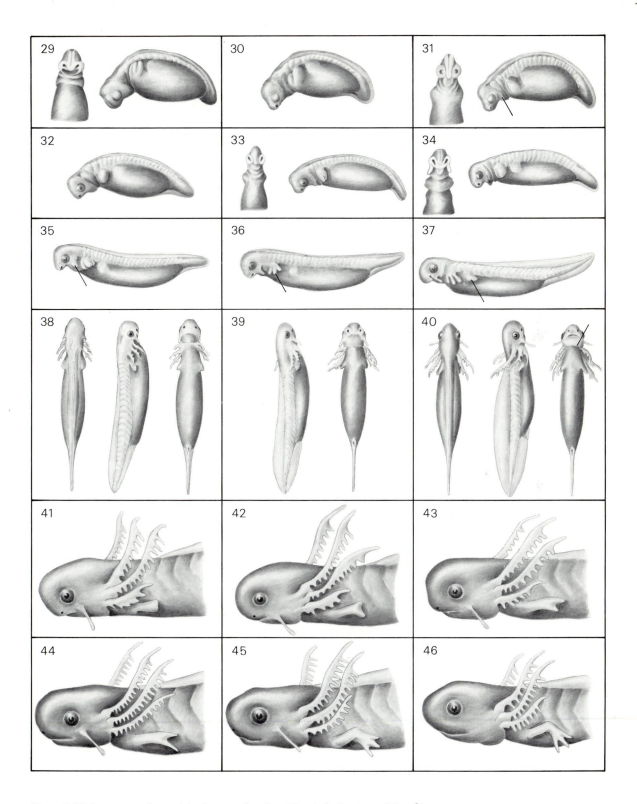

Figure 5-15. Later stages of normal development of a salamander, *Ambystoma maculatum*. Stages are according to R. Harrison (1969). Pigmentation is not shown. Guidelines indicate major features mentioned in text.

The staging of salamander development generally is not carried through to metamorphosis, as is characteristic of the staging of anurans. However, 56 stages through metamorphosis have been defined in two European salamandrids: *Pleurodeles waltl* (Gallien and Durocher, 1957) and *Triturus helveticus* (Gallien and Bidaud, 1959). I. Wilder (1925) recognized four stages in the larva of *Eurycea bislineata:*

1. Postembryonic: the brief period between hatching and feeding.
2. Typical larval: the typical feeding stage.
3. Premetamorphic: development of nasolabial grooves but no vesicular glands in skin.
4. Metamorphic: morphological changes associated with metamorphosis.

Most developmental tables are for species having aquatic eggs and larvae. A developmental table is available for only one species having direct development of terrestrial eggs, *Plethodon cinereus* (Dent, 1942). Detailed descriptions and illustrations of postneurula development are available for two other plethodontids having direct development: *Batrachoseps wrighti* (Stebbins, 1949a) and *Ensatina eschscholtzi* (Stebbins, 1954).

Rates of development are notably different between species of *Ambystoma* and salamandrids of the genera *Cynops* and *Taricha* (Fig. 5-16). According to the staging tables for *Pleurodeles waltl* (Gallien and Durocher, 1957) and *Triturus helveticus* (Gallien and Bidaud, 1959), these salamandrids are like *Cynops* and *Taricha*. Perhaps patterns of development reflect phylogenetic relationships, but before any generalizations can be made, many other species, especially plethodontids, need to be studied in detail and staged in a standard way.

Anurans. The anuran stages (Figs. 5-17, 5-18) follow Gosner (1960); hours given in parentheses after the stage number are for *Bufo valliceps* at 25°C (Limbaugh and Volpe, 1957).

1. (0) Single cell; at fertilization egg rotates so that animal hemisphere is dorsal.
2. (0.25) Second polar body released; gray crescent evident.
3. (0.50) First cleavage; 2 blastomeres.
4. (1.00) Second cleavage; 4 blastomeres.
5. (1.50) Third cleavage; 8 blastomeres.
6. (2.00) Fourth cleavage; 16 blastomeres.
7. (3.00) Fifth cleavage; 32 blastomeres; cleavage furrows irregular; dorsal cells (animal hemisphere) smaller and completely cleaved; ventral cells (vegetal hemisphere) larger and incompletely cleaved.
8. (4.50) Midcleavage, characterized by continued irregular cleavage and intrusion of pigmented area over pale area.
9. (6.50) Late cleavage; cells in animal hemisphere are small, pigmented and extend well down toward vegetal pole.
10. (8.00) Involution at dorsal lip of blastopore; beginning of gastrulation.
11. (9.00) Dorsal lip of blastopore expands into semicircle; involution along semicircular surfaces; balance of embryo shifts, raising blastopore.
12. (10.5) Blastopore formed, surrounding yolk plug; blastopore elevated to point of posterior axis of embryo.
13. (13.0) Dorsal flattening; formation of dorsal plate.

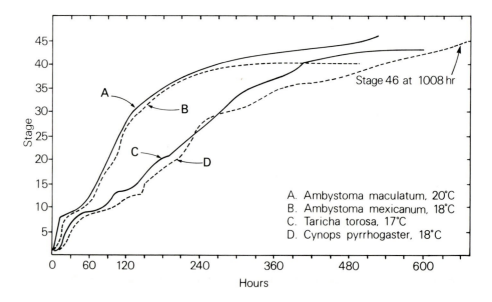

Figure 5-16. Comparative rates of development to the same stages (R. Harrison, 1969) in four species of salamanders. Data for *Ambystoma maculatum* from R. Harrison (1969), for *A. mexicanum* and *Taricha* from Schreckenberg and Jacobson (1975), and for *Cynops* from P. L. Anderson (1943).

A. *Ambystoma maculatum*, 20°C
B. *Ambystoma mexicanum*, 18°C
C. *Taricha torosa*, 17°C
D. *Cynops pyrrhogaster*, 18°C

Stage 46 at 1008 hr

14. (16.5) Neural folds form as ridges lateral to neural groove.
15. (19.0) Neural folds coalesce; body begins to elongate; embryo begins to rotate.
16. (22.0) Closure of neural folds, except anteriorly, to form neural tube; gill plates distinct; body elongated.
17. (28.0) Tail bud; adhesive organs may begin to develop.
18. (33.5) Muscular response; differentiation of gill arches; olfactory pits form.
19. (38.0) Heart beat; external gill buds, if present at all, conspicuous.
20. (41.5) Gill circulation begins.
21. (51.5) Cornea transparent; mouth opens; adhesive organs begin to disappear.
22. (58.5) Tail fins become transparent; circulation begins in fins.
23. (71.0) Opercular fold covers base of gills; lips and denticles begin to differentiate.
24. (81.5) Opercular fold closes on right side.
25. (91.0) Opercular fold closes on left; spiracle forms.
26. (115) Hindlimb bud appears; length of limb bud less than half of its diameter.
27. (139) Hindlimb bud equal to or slightly greater than half of its diameter.
28. (163) Hindlimb bud equal to or slightly greater than its diameter.
29. (188) Hindlimb bud equal to or slightly greater than 1.5 times its diameter.
30. (235) Hindlimb bud equal to twice its diameter.
31. (259) Foot paddle-shaped; no interdigital indentations.
32. (283) Margin of foot indented between fourth and fifth toes.
33. (306) Margin of foot indented between third and fourth, and fourth and fifth toes.
34. (332) Margin of foot indented between second and third, third and fourth, and fourth and fifth toes.
35. (356) Margin of foot slightly indented between first and second toes.
36. (379) First and second toes joined; others separated.
37. (403) All five toes separated.
38. (415) Inner metatarsal tubercle formed.
39. (427) Pigment-free patches on ventral surfaces of toes where subarticular tubercles will develop.
40. (451) Subarticular tubercles formed; cloacal tail-piece present.
41. (475) Skin over forelimbs thin and transparent; larval mouthparts begin to break down; cloacal tail-piece lost.

42. (499) Forelimbs protrude; angle of mouth (lateral view) anterior to nostril; labial denticles lost; horny beaks disappear.
43. (546) Angle of mouth between nostril and midpoint of eye; jaws and tongue formed; tail begins to regress.
44. (596) Angle of mouth between midpoint and posterior margin of eye; tail greatly reduced.
45. (643) Angle of mouth at posterior margin of eye; tail reduced to stub.
46. (667) Tail resorbed; metamorphosis complete.

In summary, stages 1–7 are continuous cleavage, and in stages 8 and 9 the blastocoel forms. Gastrulation occurs during stages 10–12 and neurulation during stages 13–16. Stages 17–21 involve the elongation of the body and development of the tail bud, adhesive organs, and gills. Stages 21–25 mark the transition from a relatively immobile embryo sustained by yolk to a feeding and free-swimming tadpole. Mouthparts begin to develop in Stage 23 and are essentially complete by Stage 25. The initial formation of patterns of pigmentation and the development of the operculum generally occur in stages 23–25. Stages 26–40 involve growth of the larva and development of the hind limbs. Metamorphosis begins in Stage 41 and is completed in Stage 46.

The pattern of development of embryos developing into aquatic larvae is generally the same in stages 1–16. Rates of development to different stages may be dependent primarily on temperature and secondarily on ovum size (Fig. 5-19). Hatching may occur at any time after Stage 16.

Caecilians. The development of the caecilian *Ichthyophis glutinosus* has been described and beautifully illustrated by P. Sarasin and F. Sarasin (1887–90), but comparison with salamanders and anurans is difficult because no times were given for the duration of the various stages. However, some similarities and differences are apparent. During neurulation, the embryo elongates tremendously, so as to be curved over the top of the large yolk sac. The anterior ends of the neural folds close, and regions of the brain begin to differentiate before the neural tube is closed posteriorly (Fig. 5-20A). Nasal, optic, and otic capsules form at about the same time as the mandibular and hyoid arches and the gill buds (Fig. 5-20B). By the time the mouth is open, the eyes, gills, and lateral-line system are well developed (Fig. 5-20C).

HATCHING AND BIRTH

Embryonic amphibians enter the external environment by escaping from the egg capsules either as larvae or as miniature replicas of the adults, or by leaving the body of the parent.

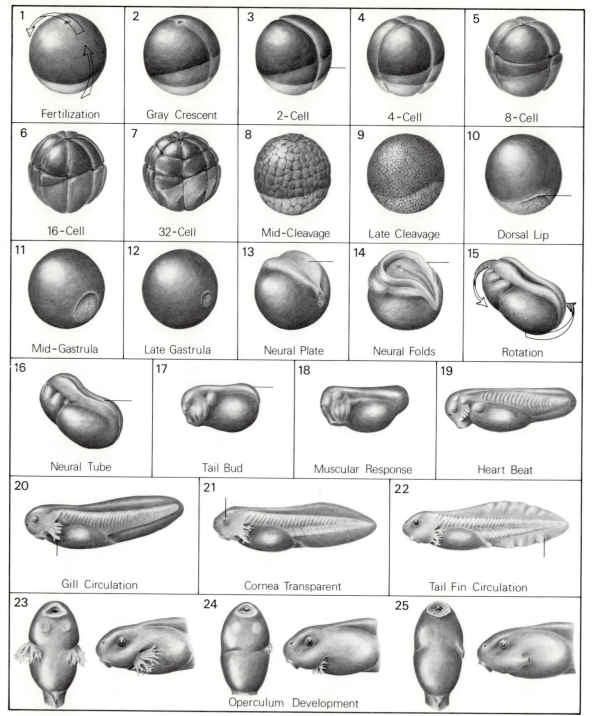

Figure 5-17. Standard early stages of development of anurans. Stages are according to Gosner (1960). Guidelines indicate major features mentioned in text.

Hatching

Two basic mechanisms are associated with hatching. One of these, the egg tooth, is mechanical; so far it is known only in frogs of the genus *Eleutherodactylus*. This small, usually bifid, structure on the median margin of the upper lip (Fig. 5-21) is effective in cutting the tough egg capsules while sharp movements are made by the head. Once the egg capsules have been cut, the froglet pushes its head through the incision, then pulls its forelimbs free, and climbs out of the egg.

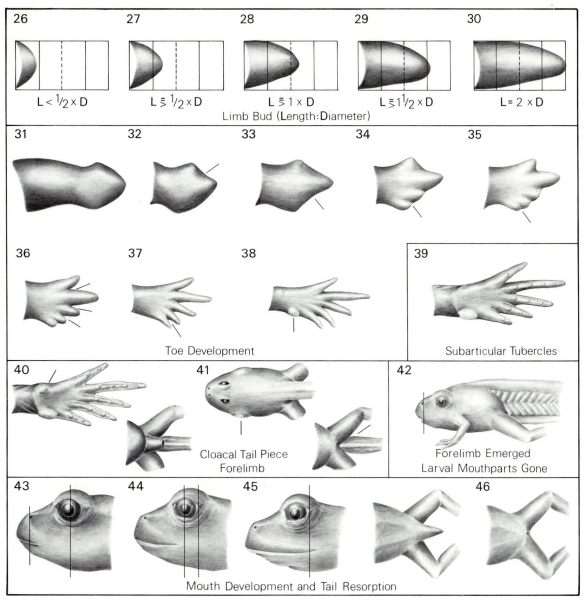

Figure 5-18. Standard later stages of development of anurans. Stages are according to Gosner (1960). Pigmentation is not shown. Guidelines indicate major features mentioned in text.

The second, and more widespread, hatching mechanism is chemical. Frontal glands are scattered over the snout and nape or concentrated on the snout of embryos. These glands produce hatching enzymes, which are proteinaceous proteases capable of digesting gelatin and other proteins but not active against mucopolysaccharides (Miganti and Azzolina, 1955). Antiproteolytic factors identified in embryos by Wu and Wang (1948) presumably protect the embryos from their own hatching enzymes. Possibly there is more than one kind of hatching enzyme produced at different times by a given species, for different electrophoretic components were identified in hatching enzymes at different stages of development in *Rana pipiens* (Salthe, 1965).

A dual hatching process occurs in salamanders, except plethodontids. Hatching from the vitelline membrane occurs just after neurulation; thus, the embryo comes to lie in the capsular fluid formed by previous dissolution of the inner mucoid capsule (Salthe, 1963). Hatching from the egg capsules occurs much later, at a stage when at least the forelimb buds are present. The vitelline membrane remains intact until hatching in plethodontids.

Anurans in which later development occurs in a capsular chamber *(Alytes, Discoglossus, Pipa,* and probably *Eleutherodactylus)* hatch first from the vitelline membrane and much later from the capsules (Salthe, 1963). Possibly the first hatching is accomplished by hatching enzymes in *Eleutherodactylus,* while only the escape from

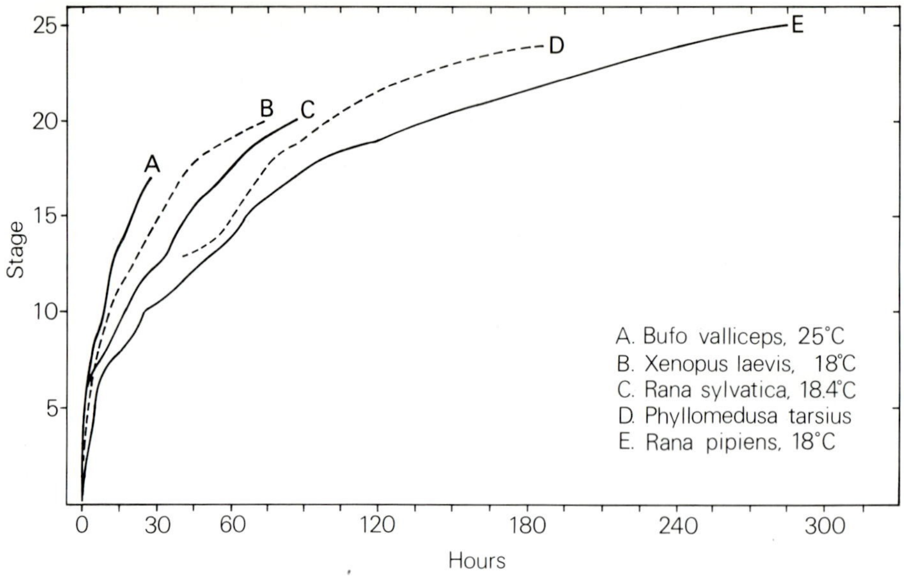

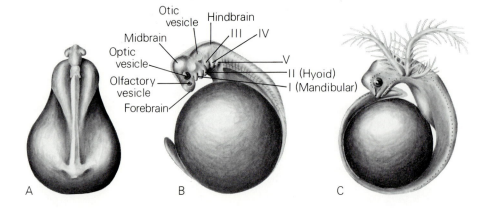

Figure 5-19. Comparative rates of development to hatching in five species of anurans. Developmental stages follow Gosner (1960). Data for *Bufo valliceps* from Limbaugh and Volpe (1957), for *Xenopus laevis* from Weisz (1945), for *Rana sylvatica* from Pollister and Moore (1937), for *Phyllomedusa trinitatis* from Kenny (1968), and for *Rana pipiens* from Shumway (1940).

A. Bufo valliceps, 25°C
B. Xenopus laevis, 18°C
C. Rana sylvatica, 18.4°C
D. Phyllomedusa tarsius
E. Rana pipiens, 18°C

Figure 5-20. Stages in the development of the caecilian *Ichthyophis glutinosus:* **A.** Neurulation. **B.** Early organogenesis. **C.** Late development. Branchial arches are designated by roman numerals. Redrawn from F. Sarasin and P. Sarasin (1887–90).

the egg capsules is accomplished by the egg tooth, a structure not present at the time of hatching from the vitelline membrane.

Two other patterns of hatching are known in anurans. In some bufonids, leptodactylids, and hylids, the outermost capsules split open and the inner capsules emerge from them prior to the hatching of the embryo. This type of hatching occurs in various kinds of aquatic eggs, such as those of *Xenopus laevis* (Bles, 1905), and may result from differential swelling of capsules. At least in *Bufo bufo,* this type of hatching occurs before the frontal glands develop (Kobayashi, 1954). In other anurans, hatching occurs first through the vitelline membrane and then through the capsules; the entire process is continuous and rapid.

Final escape from the capsules is accomplished by gliding through the degenerating membranes in at least some *Bufo* and *Hyla,* in which the outer capsules rupture first; ciliary action has been suggested as the mechanism for this relatively passive escape (Kobayashi, 1954; Volpe et

Figure 5-21. Egg tooth on margin of upper lip in *Eleutherodactylus rugulosus.* Rapid movements of the head result in the egg tooth cutting through the egg capsules.

al., 1961). In other frogs, the weakened membranes are ruptured by violent muscular actions of the embryos. Hatching of the arboreal eggs of *Phyllomedusa trinitatus* is rather explosive (Kenny, 1968); presumably such a high hydrostatic pressure develops in the eggs that when the vitelline membrane is weakened by hatching enzymes the membrane bursts, hurling the tadpole free of the leaves.

The mode of hatching is known for relatively few species of amphibians. The ways in which amphibian eggs hatch seem to be more closely associated with their mode and site of development than with their phylogenetic relationships. The trigger for activation of hatching enzymes may be reduced oxygen pressure, as noted in aquatic eggs of some salamanders and anurans (Petranka et al., 1982).

Birth

Embryonic development and metamorphosis are completed in the uterine portions of the oviducts in *Salamandra atra* and *Mertensiella luschani,* one species of *Eleutherodactylus (jasperi),* several species of *Nectophrynoides,* and many species of caecilians. In these animals, the young emerge from the cloaca as miniature replicas of the adults, although in caecilians the newborn young may be 40% of the length of the mother.

The young of several kinds of frogs are carried by their parents and develop in specialized brooding pouches. The aquatic frogs of the genus *Pipa* carry eggs imbedded in the dorsum of the female. Upon completion of development, the froglets push their way out of the aperture of the dermal chamber and swim away (Fig. 5-22). Similarly, tadpoles emerge from the chambers in *Pipa carvalhoi.*

Among the egg-brooding hylid frogs, hatching of the eggs carried on the dorsum by female *Hemiphractus* results in froglets attached to the dorsum of the female by pairs of gill stalks; those parts of the gills that are adjacent to the female are adherent to the thin egg capsule, which remains fastened to the female. Subsequently, the stalks are broken; the froglets depart, and the gills and stalks are sloughed from the female. In those egg-brooding hylids in which the eggs are brooded in a dorsal pouch on the female, the eggs hatch into tadpoles or froglets in the pouch. Parturition from the pouch may be simply by pressure exerted by the female flexing her shoulders and breathing deeply (Duellman and Maness, 1980). As the young emerge, the large external gills are broken off and lost (Fig. 5-23). In those species of *Gastrotheca* having small pouch apertures, the female aids in the parturition of tadpoles or froglets by inserting her hindfeet into the pouch and digging out the young.

Males of *Assa darlingtoni* carry tadpoles in paired inguinal pouches, where they develop into froglets (Straughan and Main, 1966). There is no evidence that the male aids in the escape of the young. The tadpoles of *Rhinoderma darwinii* develop into froglets in the vocal sac of the male. These froglets crawl from the vocal sac into the mouth and then to the exterior. Obviously the escape of the young requires the cooperation of the male, who presumably opens his mouth in response to the movement of the froglets.

Certainly the most bizarre example of egg brooding and birth in amphibians is that of *Rheobatrachus silus* and *R. vitellinus.* Tadpoles develop in the female's stomach. Birth is accomplished by the female opening her mouth and greatly dilating the esophagus. The young are almost propelled out of the stomach into the mouth, and they hop away (Tyler and Carter, 1981) (Fig. 5-24).

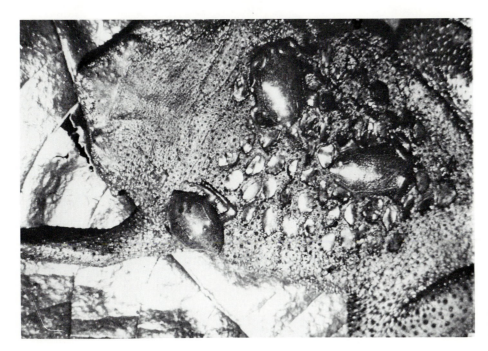

Figure 5-22. Young of *Pipa pipa* emerging from dorsum of female. Photo by J. Lescure.

Figure 5-23. Young emerging from the pouch of a female *Gastrotheca ovifera*. The external gills surrounding the embryo are either broken off during parturition or sloughed soon after birth. Photo by S. J. Maness.

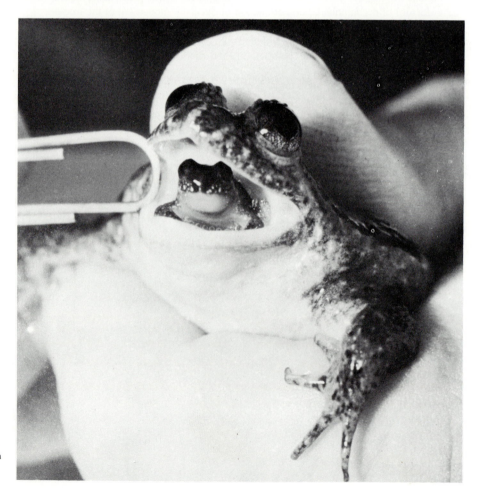

Figure 5-24. Oral birth of *Rheobatrachus silus*. Young develop in the stomach and are expelled from the mouth. Photo courtesy of M. J. Tyler.

DEVELOPMENT AND AMPHIBIAN DIVERSITY

The three living orders of amphibians have the same basic egg structure and development, but different kinds of adaptations and specializations are evident in each group. Some of these adaptations and specializations seem to be correlated with highly specialized reproductive modes, whereas others seem to be associated with, and perhaps responsible for, broad ecological tolerances and wide geographic distributions.

The common occurrence of polyspermy in salamanders having a spermatheca is understandable when it is realized that the eggs pass by a concentration of captive spermatozoa. This method of insemination insures a high percentage of fertilization and necessitates immediate swelling of the egg capsules to block the entrance of additional sperm. Monospermy is the rule in anuran eggs, in which the eggs are placed in water and capsular swelling begins immediately prior to insemination. Penetration of the ovum by a single spermatozoon results in the breakdown of cortical granules into the perivitelline fluid and prevention of the entrance of additional spermatozoa. It is doubtful if any anuran eggs are ever subjected to the concentration of spermatozoa that await the passage of eggs by the spermatheca in salamanders, although this might be true in those ovoviviparous and viviparous anurans having internal fertilization.

The absence of cortical granules in salamander eggs may be related to the early liquefication of the innermost capsule in these eggs, as opposed to retention of a highly viscous inner chamber in most anurans. Likewise, the sequence of degeneration of capsules seems to be related to the method of hatching. However, these attributes of amphibian eggs are known for few species, most of which have aquatic eggs.

Embryonic respiratory structures and mechanisms are relatively simple in salamanders. The degree of development of the external gills in species having aquatic larvae seems to be associated with the environmental conditions in which the larvae will develop, but for the most part, the same conditions prevail for the developing eggs—different oxygen tensions in stagnant versus flowing water. The significance of the different structural types of external gills in embryos of terrestrial plethodontid salamanders is unknown. Developing caecilians have external gills, but these function solely within the egg or maternal oviduct, for the gills are resorbed immediately after hatching in those that have free-swimming larvae or immediately before birth in oviparous and viviparous caecilians. External gills are absent or transient in embryos of most anurans; those that have aquatic tadpoles have well-developed internal gills. However, anuran embryos developing on land have either large external gills or other respiratory tissues—expanded tails or lateral folds. The diversity of embryonic respiratory structures is a reflection of the different environmental conditions in which embryos develop, as well as precursors to larval respiratory mechanisms—external gills in salamander larvae and internal gills in anuran larvae.

Information on basic metabolic rates of amphibian embryos is very fragmentary. Salamander eggs seem to require more nutrients and more time to develop than do those of anurans. At the present time there is no reasonable explanation for these differences. However, the relatively rapid rate in anuran embryos is partially reflected in their ability to tolerate higher temperatures than salamander eggs. The wide range of developmental tolerance levels in anuran embryos also is associated with a diversity of clutch structure, which is important in heat retention and dissipation.

Some members of all three orders of living amphibians are viviparous. The methods of obtaining maternal nutrients are different in the three groups and are especially well developed in caecilians, in which viviparity is common. In this respect caecilians may be regarded as the most highly derived group developmentally, but their highly specialized morphology and mode of existence have limited their evolutionary and geographic diversity.

Salamanders seem to have the simplest patterns of development and the fewest modifications of the generalized amphibian development. This conservativeness is reflected in the relatively narrow ecological and geographic diversity of the group, as compared with anurans. Probably, the great diversity of anurans, both ecologically and geographically, is associated with their developmental plasticity, as evidenced by their diversity of egg and clutch structure, temperature tolerances, respiratory mechanisms, metabolic excretory products, and hatching processes.

Given the recent emphasis on the importance of ontogeny to the understanding of adaptations and phylogeny (e.g., S. Gould, 1977), much more must be learned about patterns of development and embryonic metabolism in order to support or falsify many of the hypotheses being advanced. Descriptive embryology has been out of vogue for many years, during which time developmental biologists have emphasized molecular and biochemical aspects of development. However, the answers to many fascinating problems of amphibian development are dependent on many more comparative embryological studies in an evolutionary context of the development of the embryo in its natural environment.

CHAPTER 6

In patterns of adaptive radiation, the larvae of a taxonomic unit share certain major characters, but in other respects they show divergent modifications that adapt them to different ecological conditions or different ways of life.

Grace L. Orton (1953)

Larvae

Amphibian larvae represent posthatching developmental stages that are morphologically distinct from the adults and are nonreproductive. Most larvae obtain nutrients from the environment for further development and growth. The majority are aquatic and thus are subjected to different selective pressures than the adults. Larvae of salamanders and caecilians more closely resemble their respective adults morphologically, physiologically, and trophically than do anuran larvae.

This chapter treats the morphology, physiology, ecology, feeding, growth, and social behavior of amphibian larvae. Most of the material on larval morphology is covered here, but early embryonic development is covered in Chapter 5 and most aspects of metamorphosis are treated in Chapter 7. Population dynamics and community ecology of larvae are discussed in chapters 11 and 12, respectively.

MORPHOLOGY OF LARVAE

Operationally, a vertebrate usually is described by its external characteristics—that is, its general size and shape, presence or absence of obvious features, and relative proportions of parts of the body. Most of these characteristics reflect differences in the structure of the musculoskeletal system that supports and protects vital organs and provides for locomotory and feeding movements.

The habitus of amphibian larvae are as diverse as their life styles. Typically, anuran tadpoles are found in streams and ponds or ephemeral situations such as puddles and roadside ditches, where they glean food by scraping it off the substrate or feeding on particles suspended in the water. Their specialized feeding habits require mouthparts and a digestive system that is dramatically different from those characterizing the adult frog. The adult is short-bodied and tailless, but the larva possesses a tail and usually well-developed caudal fins in order to propel itself through the water. Salamander and free-living caecilian larvae also are found in aquatic situations, but unlike short-bodied tadpoles, these larvae are elongate. The presence of a fin along the tail, and on the back of some as well, enables them to swim effectively; moreover, the larvae, like the adults, are active predators. Consequently, larval salamanders and caecilians have functional jaws, teeth, and an adult-like digestive system at the time of hatching, or shortly thereafter.

The similarity of salamander and caecilian larvae to their respective adult morphs may account for their protracted embryonic development prior to hatching in contrast to that of most anuran larvae. Although the timing of hatching varies considerably among anurans, it can occur as early as the tail-bud stage (early post-neurulation; e.g., *Bufo*). In salamanders, hatching occurs subsequent to development of the mouth and internal organs; gills are present and the digits on the forelimb are differentiating, but the hindlimb is present only as a bud. When caecilians hatch, they are distinguished externally from adults only by the presence of a tail fin posteriorly on the body, an open gill slit, and external gills in some.

The disparities in the timing of hatching, both within and among the orders of amphibians, make it especially difficult to describe larval morphology that changes continuously. Nonetheless, there are certain commonalities of developmental form and function among all three groups that are worthy of comment. For example, all amphibian larvae are elongate and usually not well ossified. The brain and primary sensory organs are protected by cartilage—the chondrocranium that is composed of olfactory and auditory capsules and the cartilaginous precursors of the sphenethmoid, prootic, and exoccipital that protect the brain. The mandibular arch is developed and variably ossified depending on larval feeding habits, but it is always present. All amphibian larvae possess a cartilaginous hyoid arch and branchial arches, although the latter may be modified for special feeding and respiratory functions. Lateral-line sensory organs are present. The skin is thin and the eyes lack any protective covering. There are some striking differences as well as similarities among the orders of amphibians in the development and adult morphology of the skin, and in the urogenital and digestive systems. Because these are described elsewhere in association with metamophosis, emphasis is placed here on ectodermal and mesodermal derivatives that give rise to the musculoskeletal system and, therefore, determine the overall, external appearance and body plan of the larva. Although a discussion of organogenesis is in the province of developmental biology (and early organogenesis is described in Chapter 5), the following description provides information relevant to an understanding and appreciation of the development of the larval musculoskeletal system in particular.

Basic Pattern of Development

Despite the readily recognized differences among fully formed, premetamorphic amphibian larvae, the course of primary organogenesis of ectodermal and mesodermal components is remarkably similar in its pattern. At the completion of neurulation (the earliest stage at which any amphibian is known to hatch and therefore be classified as a larva), the neural tube overlies the notochord and

is flanked laterally by mesoderm that gives rise to somites. Concomitant with the formation of the neural tube, a group of uniquely important cells—the neural crest cells—migrate from the external surface of the epidermis to its internal surface. Here they lie between the epidermis and

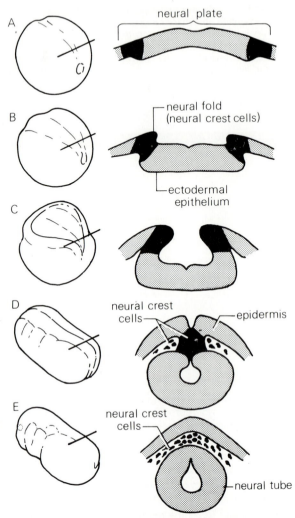

Figure 6-1. Stages in the formation of the neural plate and neural tube in anurans. On the left are diagrammatic representations of embryos and the plane of section (heavy line) corresponding to the schematic transverse sections on the right (neural crest cells are black). Embryos designated A–E approximate Gosner's (1960) stages of development 12F–13, 14, 15, and 17, respectively.

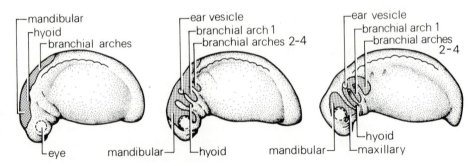

Figure 6-2. Three successive stages (left to right) in the migration of neural crest cells in the salamander *Ambystoma maculatum*. Redrawn from B. Balinsky (1960).

the mesoderm (Fig. 6-1). As they migrate throughout the developing embryo or larva, neural crest cells give rise to a variety of important structures. Some produce pigment cells and thereby establish the basic color and pattern of the larva. Others that come to lie in the head region produce the visceral skeleton (i.e., quadrate, Meckel's cartilage, hyoid, and first branchial arch), the papillae of the teeth, and the rudiments of the anterior half of the chondrocranium. The action of neural crest cells in association with the formation of primary brain vesicles and the rudiments of the eyes from the anterior part of the neural tube establishes the generalized, early amphibian embryonic or larval form in which the body is subdivided into a head and trunk separated by visceral clefts and arches posteroventral to the head (Fig. 6-2).

Subsequent development involves interactions of ectodermal and mesodermal components that produce the larval chondrocranium, visceral skeleton, axial and appendicular skeletons, mouth, fin, external gills and balancers, and somatic musculature. Owing to the complexity of these events and structures, they are described separately.

Chondrocranium. The chondrocranium and anterior elements of the first visceral arch (palatoquadrate and Meckel's cartilage) house and protect the brain and primary sensory organs, and provide a mechanism for larval feeding. Earliest development (Figs. 6-3, 6-4) is marked by the appearance of a procartilage bar (the palatoquadrate) anterior to the second visceral pouch (which becomes the tympanic cavity). The dorsal, vertical component of this bar is the quadrate, the element that suspends the mandibular arch from the neurocranium. A horizontal component, Meckel's cartilage, extends forward from the base of the palatoquadrate and, in the adult, forms the lower jaw in combination with dermal investing bones. Subsequent to the appearance of the palatoquadrate, longitudinal bars of procartilage arise medial to it. The bars (cranial trabeculae) increase in length and mass. Anteriorly, the bars fuse medially; their various outgrowths eventually give rise to the cartilaginous components of the nasal capsule. Posterior to the nasal capsule, the sphenethmoid will form in the trabecular cartilage; in the adult, this bone forms the posterior walls of the nasal capsule and the anterior braincase. The cranial trabeculae extend posteriorly and attach to the sides of the anterior tip of the notochord. As the posterior trabeculae increase in mass, they become integrated with the developing auditory capsules and connected to the palatoquadrate laterally by means of a lateral outgrowth. In this way, the cartilaginous precursors of the prootic and exoccipital, which form the posterior end of the braincase in the adult, are established. Integration of the cartilaginous auditory capsules laterally completes the rudiments of the posterior region of the skull, and the establishment of a connection with the palatoquadrate assures the continuity of the suspensorium—the mechanism by which the jaws are connected to the braincase.

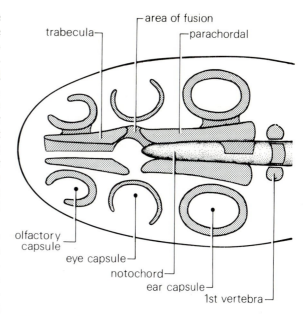

Figure 6-3. Schematic representation of the components of an amphibian chondrocranium in dorsal view. Initial stages of cartilaginous components are stippled. Areas in which cartilaginous elements eventually will fuse are indicated by hatching in upper or right-hand side of diagram. Redrawn from B. Balinsky (1960).

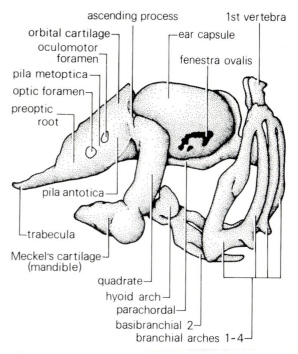

Figure 6-4. Lateral view of the chondrocranium and visceral skeleton of a salamander larva. Structures labeled ascending process and quadrate compose the palatoquadrate; see text for further explanation. Redrawn (in part) from B. Balinsky (1969).

Visceral Skeleton. The branchial region of all amphibian larvae is pierced by a series of five or six clefts, or visceral pouches. The first and most anterior of the series lies between the developing Meckel's cartilage and hyoid and is incorporated into the tympanic cavity. This pouch never opens to the outside in salamanders and frogs; in caecilians, however, it is open briefly, during which time it acts as a spiracle. Posteriorly, four (salamanders and frogs) or five (caecilians) more pouches form. The pharyngeal wall between these clefts is supported by bars of cartilage that represent the hyobranchial apparatus (Fig. 6-4). The most anterior and generally the most substantial of these elements is the ceratohyal (hypohyal) that lies between Pouches I and II (see Fig. 6-7). The lateral components either articulate with, or are fused to, a midventral, longitudinal element or series of elements known as copulae or basibranchials. The ceratohyals and their associated midventral basibranchials form the hyoid plate and its anterior processes which, in the adult, represent the skeletal platform from which various tongue muscles originate. Posterior to the ceratohyals is a series of four pairs of ceratobranchials (I–IV), cartilaginous bars that separate Pouches II, III, IV, and V. These either are fused midventrally or articulate with basibranchials to form the posterior part of the hyolaryngeal apparatus.

Axial Skeleton. The vertebral column is mesodermal in origin and formed from the association of the somites that flank the neural tube and notochord (Fig. 6-5). The cells composing each somite are differentiated into three types. The most dorsal type is the dermatome that is continuous with, and gives rise to, the connective tissue layer of the skin. A somatic cavity (the myocoele) internally separates this outer layer from the internally that produces the somatic musculature. The ventromedial portion of each somite is composed of the sclerotome. This portion breaks up into mesenchyme cells that migrate and continuously envelop the notochord and spinal cord. Subsequently, the mesenchyme cells differentiate into cartilaginous nodules, the arcualia, to form the centra, transverse processes or ribs, and the neural arches of the developing vertebrae.

Appendicular Skeleton. Among those amphibians that have limbs (i.e., salamanders and anurans), the limb buds are the first trace of the appendicular skeleton. Aside from nerves and blood vessels, the primary components of limb buds are lateral plate mesoderm, epidermis, and somites. Initial limb-bud formation involves migration of mesenchyme cells from the upper edge of the parietal surface of the lateral plate mesoderm to the inner surface of the overlying epithelium in two areas—one just posterior to the branchial region and a second just anterior to the anus. As the mesenchyme proliferates internally and the overlying epidermis thickens, the limb bud protrudes. Once the limb bud has grown to the point that it is longer than broad, subordinate parts of the limb begin to differentiate in a proximodistal sequence. Thus, the upper arm and leg (stylopodium) are established before the lower segments (zeugopodium), and the latter prior to the distal elements (autopodium). Among the distal elements, however, the proximodistal scheme of development does not prevail; larger skeletal elements (i.e., metatarsals and metacarpals) differentiate prior to smaller ones (i.e., carpals, tarsals, and phalanges). Proximal phalangeal elements form before distal ones. Thus, digits I and II develop before III, IV, and V (when present), and the latter form in the sequence of their numbers. Because fusion of individual cells into masses (myoblasts) provides the rudiments from which the limb muscles eventually develop, limb muscles presumably are formed by the migration of these cells from the myotomes into the developing limb.

Of the mesenchyme cells that migrate from the parietal surface of the lateral- plate mesoderm, the central cells are destined to form the limb bud proper, whereas the peripheral cells give rise to the pectoral and pelvic girdles. Thus, development of girdles is associated closely with that of limbs, but it is independent because girdle formation proceeds independently of the direct mesenchymal-epidermal interaction that is essential to limb development. However, normal formation of articular facets of the girdles is dependent on the formation and presence of upper limb elements.

Characteristic Epidermal Structures. During neurulation the epidermis is separated from other ectodermal components (i.e., neural plate and neural crest). In addition to the skin, several other important structures are

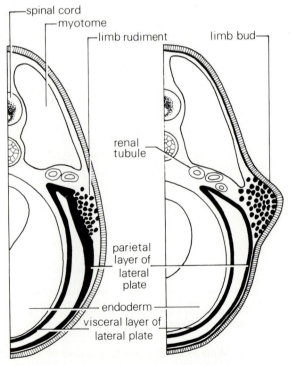

Figure 6-5. Diagram of the origin of limb bud mesoderm in an amphibian embryo. Redrawn from B. Balinsky (1960).

derived from the epidermis. Among these are the lens of the eye, the cornea, cranial ganglia, the ear, and nasal organ. By a series of complicated inductions involving the developing brain and sensory organs, protective cartilaginous capsules are laid down and eventually incorporated into the developing chondrocranium.

Other epidermal structures are simple protrusions. These include the fin, external gills, balancers and barbels, and the paired limbs described above. A depression in the superficial ectodermal epithelium, the stomodeum, marks the invagination of the mouth. When the internal, endodermal epithelium of the alimentary canal fuses with the external epithelium, the pharyngeal membrane is formed. The mouth opens when this membrane disappears. A similar membrane is formed between the ectoderm and endoderm at the base of the tail bud. As the tail lengthens, the cloacal membrane produces a diverticulum (post-anal gut) that enters the tail rudiment. Depression of the superficial epithelium in this area produces the proctodeum; once the cloacal membrane ruptures, the cloaca is open to the exterior.

Nomenclature of Chondrocranial and Visceral Elements. The descriptive accounts of chondrocranial and visceral components of caecilians, salamanders, and anurans that follow are generalized. Sufficient information is provided so that the reader can grasp the basic architectural plan of each group in order to appreciate their gross similarities and differences, but details of variation are beyond the scope of this book. The descriptions present the basic architecture and terminology applied to amphibian chondrocrania, so that a better understanding may be gained from technical papers and monographs, such as de Beer (1937), that deal exhaustively with the structure and development of the skull.

Except for the old and rare review paper of Gaupp (1906), no one person has dealt with the cranial development of all three orders of amphibians. Thus, terminology of elements frequently is not the same across the three orders, and at this point, knowledge is so incomplete that it is not possible to solve the existing problems of homology. In many cases, terms have been used interchangeably in the literature. In order to simplify the following descriptions, the following nomenclatural conventions have been adopted:

Alary cartilage = cupular cartilage of caecilians
Anterior trabecular plate = internasal plate, ethmoid plate, planum internasalis, planum trabecula anterior
Basal plate = planum basalis
Basibranchials I–II = Copulae I–II
Basitrabecular process = basipterygoid process, ? otic process of some authors
Ceratobranchial = branchial
Ceratohyal = hyale
Cranial trabecula = cornua trabecula
Hypochordal commissure = planum hypochordialis

Orbital cartilage = orbital cartilage + taenia marginalis of caecilians
Palatoquadrate = quadrate + ascending process + otic process + pterygoid process
Planum terminale = lamina orbitonasalis of caecilians
Posterior basicapsular commissure = occipital arch of caecilians
Pterygoid process = basal process

Caecilians

The striking feature that characterizes caecilian larvae in contrast to salamander and frog larvae is the advanced stage at which they hatch. Superficially, larvae are distinguished from adults only by their smaller size, the presence of a gill slit, and a fin in those larvae that metamorphose into terrestrial adults (ichthyophiids, rhinatrematids, and some caeciliids). Any discussion of caecilian larval morphology is hampered by a lack of knowledge; the only caecilians having aquatic larvae for which there are developmental observations are *Ichthyophis glutinosis* (P. Sarasin and F. Sarasin, 1887–1890; Peter, 1898), *Typhlonectes obesus* (M. Wake, 1977), and *Gegeneophis carnosus* (Ramaswami, 1948). The work of Brauer (1897, 1899), H. Marcus (1909, 1910, 1922), Gewolf (1923), H. Marcus et al. (1933, 1935), and Lawson (1963) described *Hypogeophis rostratus* and *Grandisonia alternans;* M. Wake (1980a, 1980b) and M. Wake and Hanken (1982) have contributed substantially to understanding the development of *Dermophis mexicanus*. But *Dermophis* is viviparous and *Hypogeophis* and *Grandisonia* are oviparous with direct development. It remains to be demonstrated that the developmental observations on these species are applicable to those taxa having aquatic larvae, although M. Wake (1977a) suggested that they are.

External Features. Free-living larval caecilians are proportionally shorter than adults. They are characterized by thin skin, long triramous gills, a lateral-line system, adult dentition, and a moderate tail fin that extends onto the posterodorsal surface of the body. The eyes of "mature" larvae are covered by skin and bone. The tentacle, which does not appear until metamorphosis, is absent.

Chondrocranium and Mandible. In comparison with the chondrocrania of salamanders and anurans, that of caecilians is highly fenestrated and delicate (Fig. 6-6). The floor of the chondrocranium lacks a basal plate between the auditory capsules; the capsules are united posteriorly by a bar—the hypochordal commissure that incorporates the anterior tip of the notochord medially and the poorly developed auditory capsules laterally by means of a lateral outgrowth, the posterior basicapsular commissure. Paired, anterior extensions (cranial trabeculae) that unite anteromedially behind the olfactory capsule enclose an immense ventral fenestra that represents a union of the anterior and posterior basicranial fenestrae.

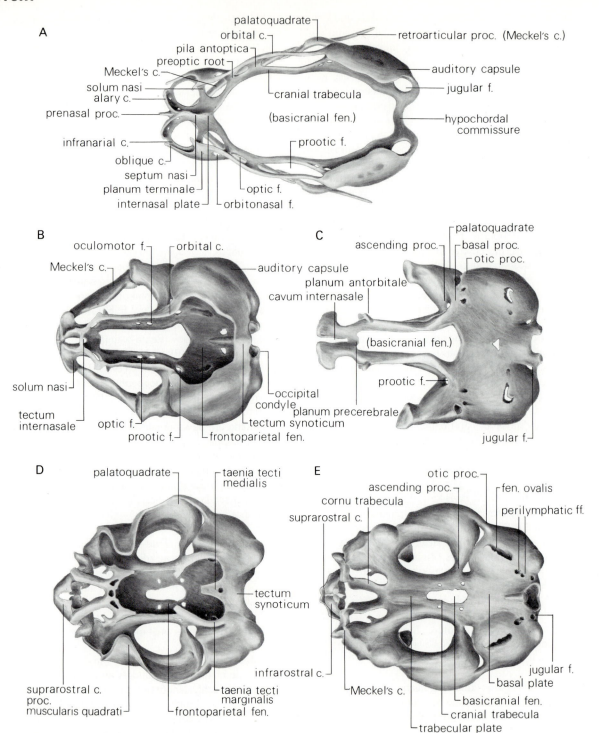

Figure 6-6. Chondrocrania of amphibian larvae. **A.** Dorsal view of *Ichthyophis glutinosus*. **B.** Dorsal view of *Salamandra salamandra* (total length 20 mm). **C.** Ventral view of same (without mandible). **D.** Dorsal view of *Rana temporaria* (total length 29 mm). **E.** Ventral view of same. Abbreviations: c = cartilage; f = foramen; fen = fenestra; ff = foramina. Redrawn from Gaupp (1906).

Dorsal extensions from each trabecula, the pila antoptica (posterior) and preoptic (anterior) root, unite the trabecula with a slim dorsolateral rod, the orbital cartilage (taenia marginalis), thus forming the scant side wall of the chon-drocranium. The chondrocranium lacks a roof entirely.

The auditory capsule is particularly poorly developed in caecilians, having large gaps in its walls. These represent the fenestra ovalis (lateral), basicapsular fenestra (ventral), and the perilymphatic, endolymphatic, and acoustic foramina (medial). Internally, there are three slender septae for the semicircular canals. The fenestra ovalis contains a rodlike columella that attaches laterally with the posterior face of the quadrate. Functionally, an operculum is absent, although some individuals (e.g., de Beer, 1937; Ramaswami, 1948) claimed that the opercular cartilage is incorporated into the proximal stapes.

In contrast to the rest of the chondrocranium, the nasal capsule is moderately well formed, although it lacks a roof (tectum nasi) and a cartilage (planum antorbitale) between the posterolateral wall, lamina orbitonasalis, and the medial septum nasi that separates the olfactory organs. The anterior union of the cranial trabeculae forms a ventral trabecular, or internasal, plate. This bears a vertical, medial plate of cartilage, the septum nasi, that extends anteriorly as the prenasal process. Lateral extensions from the ethmoid plate fuse with the side wall of the nasal capsule (planum terminale) to form the floor of the nasal capsule (solum nasi) and the anterior borders of the choanae. The anterior wall of the nasal capsule is formed by the alary cartilage that arises from the anterolateral region of the septum nasi. Anterolateral continuity between the alary cartilage and the planum terminale (side wall) is affected by the oblique cartilage. Together, the alary and oblique cartilages form the medial and dorsal margins of the external naris. A ventral strut of cartilage (infranarial cartilage) that extends anteromedially from the side wall of the nasal capsule to the anteromedial corner of the septum nasi forms the ventral border of the external naris.

The quadrate cartilage (palatoquadrate) bears various connections to the central chondrocranium. In the anteroventral auditory region it is connected to the basitrabecular (basipterygoid) process by a ligament *(Ichthyophis)* or a cartilaginous basal process (pterygoid process) in *Gegeneophis, Siphonops,* and *Hypogeophis.* Dorsally, the processus ascendans of the quadrate is attached to the orbital cartilage by fibrous tissue, and a small otic process projects toward the otic capsule and establishes a connection with the distal end of the columella. Ventrally, the quadrate is united with Meckel's cartilage of the lower jaw which characteristically bears a long retroarticular process.

Ossification Sequence of the Cranium. Among the significant features of larval caecilians in contrast to larval anurans and salamanders are the lack of a sclerotic cartilage and the early onset of ossification; by the time metamorphosis occurs, nearly the entire cartilaginous neurocranium has been replaced by bone. This probably is correlated with the reduced structure of the chondrocranium which would afford minimal protection and support. Based on *Dermophis mexicanus* (M. Wake, 1982), the ossification sequence is as follows. Elements of the mandible (mentomeckelian bones, articular and angular components, and retroarticular process) appear first (29-mm foetus). Subsequently (33–36-mm foetuses) and

more or less contemporaneously, the upper jaw (with mineralized teeth) forms. Endochondral ossification involves the exoccipitals, basisphenoid, and quadrate at this stage. At the same time, various investing bones appear—frontals, parietals, palatines, squamosals, and, in the lower jaw, the splenial. In a 44.5-mm foetus, the orbitosphenoid has begun to ossify along with the parasphenoid, vomer (prevomer), and pterygoid. Fusion of the palatine and maxilla has occurred in a 51.8-mm foetus. The last bones to appear are the septomaxilla and columella in a 54.5-mm foetus. Subsequent development involves elaboration and fusions of bony cranial elements.

Branchial Arches. The hyobranchial skeleton of larval caecilians is robust and chondrifies early with respect to the rest of the skull (Fig. 6-7); de Beer (1937) suggested that this precocious development was associated with the hyobranchial skeleton's function in supporting the long external gills. The stout ceratohyals articulate ventrally with a median basibranchial. The second median basibranchial unites ceratobranchial pairs I and II midventrally. Ceratobranchial pair III are fused midventrally but separated from anterior hyobranchial elements. The fourth pair of ceratobranchials are rudimentary and articulate distally with the third pair.

Axial Skeleton. The larval vertebral column is differentiated regionally, but the vertebrae are more homogeneous in their sizes and proportions than are those of the adult caecilian (M. Wake, 1980c). Apparently this results from a differential growth pattern in which midbody vertebrae grow more rapidly than anterior and posterior vertebrae. It is the midbody vertebrae and their associated ribs and muscles that are critical to the organism's locomotor activities (Gans, 1973a); therefore, it is not surprising that these are the most fully developed in the actively swimming larvae.

Salamanders

The larval structure of *Necturus, Amphiuma, Cryptobranchus, Triturus, Salamandra,* and *Ambystoma* are the best known (Francis, 1934; de Beer, 1937), but these larvae are as morphologically diverse as the adult morphotypes into which they may metamorphose (see Chapter 13). Consequently, it would be misleading to describe the larval morphology of any one species as typical for the order as a whole.

External Features. Although the general morphology of larval salamanders is similar to that of their adult counterparts, a number of features serve to distinguish the larvae from the adults—smaller size, external gills, a tail fin, distinctive larval dentition, a rudimentary tongue (little more than a muscular thickening of the floor of the mouth that allows prey to be held and manipulated against the palatal dentition), and the presence of a scleral cartilage that disappears at metamorphosis. The shape of the head

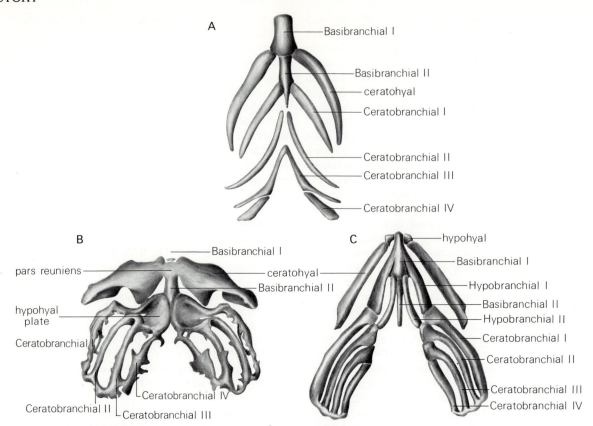

Figure 6-7. Hyobranchial skeletons of amphibian larvae. **A.** Dorsal view of *Ichthyophis glutinosus*. **B.** Ventral view of *Rana temporaria*. **C.** Corsal view of *Salamandra salamandra*. Redrawn from Gaupp (1906).

is less angular owing to the absence of parotoid glands, poorly developed jaw musculature, and incompletely developed maxillary arcade. The nostrils are wide, immobile, and not distinctly elevated. The eyes lack lids, and the lens is convex and protuberant. Larval salamanders (except sirenids) possess four fully developed limbs and begin to feed soon after hatching.

Chondrocranium and Mandible. The cartilaginous cranium is robust, and although less fenestrate than that of caecilians (Fig. 6-6), it is more delicate than are anuran chondrocrania. Unlike frogs, the salamander chondrocranium does not undergo extensive modifications at metamorphosis; thus, the larval skull can be thought of as a well-developed cartilage framework from which the adult skull arises by ossification of cartilaginous elements and deposition of dermal bones on their surfaces. The floor of the chondrocranium bears one or two extensive basicranial fenestrae. The anterior basicranial fenestra is invariably present and formed by the cranial trabeculae, which border it laterally and fuse anteriorly to form the transverse internasal plate—the anterior margin of the fenestra. The posterior basicranial fenestra, if present, lies in the basal plate uniting the auditory capsules and is defined posteriorly by a narrow transverse bar of carti-

lage, the hypochordal commissure, and anteriorly by a second narrow transverse cartilaginous bar, the crista stellaris, which separates the anterior and posterior fenestrae (e.g., in *Salamandra*). In some species (e.g., *Ambystoma maculatum)*, the crista breaks down; thus, the fenestrae are confluent and the chondrocranium virtually floorless. In others (e.g., *Triturus*), the posterior chondrocranial floor is invaded by mesotic cartilage, and the posterior fenestra thus is obliterated. Three stout dorsal extensions arise from each cranial trabecula and unite with the dorsolateral orbital cartilage to form the sides of the braincase. The pila antotica is the most posterior; the oculomotor foramen lies between it and the second dorsal extension, the pila metoptica. The optic foramen separates the pila metoptica and the preoptic root. The braincase is open dorsally. The immense frontoparietal fenestra is margined posteriorly by a transverse bridge of cartilage, the tectum synoticum, that unites the auditory capsules. The orbital cartilages form the lateral margins, and the tectum internasale the anterior border of the frontoparietal fenestra.

The auditory capsules, which flank the parachordal plate laterally and are connected dorsally by the tectum synoticum, are well developed and lack the basicapsular fenestra typical of caecilians. The medial wall is chondrified except for the anterior and posterior acoustic foramina and perilymphatic and endolymphatic foramina. Laterally, the capsule wall is perforated by the fenestra ovalis, which in turn is occluded by a columella and, in most species, an operculum. The relationships of the columella and the origin of the operculum are variable (de Beer, 1937). The columella arises as an independent plate of cartilage that partially or wholly occludes the fenestra ovalis and may or may not fuse with its margin. A rod or stylus develops from the plate; the stylus projects anterodorsally from the lateral wall of the auditory capsule and bears one of several relationships with elements of the suspensory and visceral apparatus. In *Necturus*, there is a ligamentous attachment of the distal end of the columella to the squamosal; during development, the attachment shifts to the posterior surface of the quadrate. *Ambystoma, Salamandra,* and some plethodontids are characterized by a synchondrotic union of the quadrate and columella, whereas *Triturus* lacks any connection. In neotenic taxa, such as *Cryptobranchus* and *Amphiuma*, the columella bears a ligamentous attachment to the squamosal or quadrate and the ceratohyal; none of these species has an operculum. In those species that metamorphose, an operculum arises in either of two ways, or by a combination of both. It may chondrify in the membrane of the hind part of the fenestra ovalis and grow forward (e.g., plethodontids), or it may originate from the otic capsule (e.g., *Hynobius*). Kingsbury and Reed (1909) believed that the operculum originated from the auditory wall posteroventral to the columella, whereas Reinbach (1950) suggested that it formed from cells liberated from the otic capsule. At metamorphosis, the columella is united synchondrotically with the lateral wall of the auditory capsule, and the operculum, located in the fenestra ovalis, is a free cartilaginous disc that is connected to the suprascapula of the pectoral girdle by the opercularis muscle. The internal ear initially bears cartilaginous septa for the anterior, lateral, and posterior semicircular canals, but in later stages of development, the posterior septum disappears.

Among amphibians, the nasal capsules of salamanders are unique in not sharing a medial wall (i.e., the septum nasi of caecilians and anurans). Instead, the ventral trabecular plate gives rise to two vertical components, each of which forms the anterior and medial walls of its respective nasal capsule; the intervening space is termed the cavum internasale. Posteromedially, the two capsules are joined by a transverse plate of cartilage (planum precerebrale) that arises between the olfactory nerves. The planum precerebrale, together with the planum antorbitale (a lateral outgrowth of the trabecular plate), completes the posterior and lateral walls of the nasal capsule. A small cartilaginous process (inferior prenasal process) protrudes anteromedially (against the overlying premaxillary bone) from the anteromedial wall of each capsule. The capsule thus formed is rigid but fenestrate. The large ventral fenestra choanalis encloses the internal choana. The side wall bears the large fenestra lateralis through which the lateral ramus of the nasal branch of the profundus nerve exits. The dorsum of the capsule is unroofed, bearing the large fenestra dorsalis, which is separated from the anterolateral fenestra narina by a slim bridge of cartilage, the oblique cartilage; the fenestra narina marks the position of the external naris and entrance of the nasolacrimal duct to the nasal capsule. The foramen apicale lies anteromedial to the fenestra narina and provides an exit for the medial ramus of the nasal branch of the profundus nerve.

The quadrate (palatoquadrate) articulates ventrally with Meckel's cartilage, which forms the cartilaginous framework of the mandible. Otherwise, the quadrate is fused to the central chondrocranium at three or four positions. Among primitive salamanders (e.g., *Cryptobranchus* and *Hynobius)*, the quadrate is connected to the braincase by means of the ascending process that fuses with the pila antotica, and to the auditory capsule by means of the basitrabecular, or otic, process of the basal plate. Anteroventrally the quadrate develops the pterygoid process that extends forward and fuses with the posterolateral wall (planum terminale) of the nasal capsule. The process is absent in some salamanders (e.g., *Necturus),* but present in most; however, in more advanced salamanders (e.g., ambystomatids), the pterygoid process projects forward and ends freely, lacking the connection to the nasal capsule typical of more primitive salamanders. The quadrate also may bear a synchondrotic or syndesmotic association with the columella, as discussed above.

Ossification Sequence of the Cranium. There have been surprisingly few studies of the process of ossification in salamander crania—a mechanism that is so extraordinary that it deserves more attention. The most complete accounts are of *Triturus vulgaris* (Erdmann, 1933), *Salamandra salamandra* (Stadtmüller, 1924), *Ambystoma mexicanum* (R. Keller, 1946), *Ambystoma texanum* (Bonebrake and Brandon, 1971), and *Aneides lugubris* (T. Wake et al., 1983). Aside from these few comprehensive studies, there is considerable anecdotal information, much of which was summarized by de Beer (1937) and Larsen (1963).

The fully developed salamander larva has a skull less extensively ossified than that of a caecilian, but far better developed than that of anuran larvae. Salamander larvae are unique in that the entire bony palate is remodeled at metamorphosis, and in contrast to caecilians, the main component of the upper jaw, the maxilla, does not appear until late in larval development. Ossification commences before larvae begin to feed, and is marked by the appearance of the vomers, palatines, dentaries, coronoids (splenials), and premaxillae—all of which bear simple, conelike larval teeth. The parasphenoid, prearticulars, squamosals, and precursors of the pterygoids appear at a time approximately coincident with the opening of the larval mouth. The prearticular, coronoid, and dentary invest Meckel's cartilage to form the mandible. The maxillary arch is abbreviated, being composed of only the premaxillae (or a fused premaxillary complex). The palatal bones (vomers and palatines) form longitudinally oriented dental arcades that laterally flank the parasphenoid, which forms a floor to the fenestrate chondrocranial braincase. This configuration of elements forming the jaws and palate allows the larva to open its mouth rapidly and to suck in prey. Once in the buccal cavity, prey can be adpressed against the palate by the rudimentary tongue, and swallowed.

Subsequent to the appearance of bones involved in larval feeding, the major dermal roofing bones—the frontals and parietals—begin to ossify. These are followed by endochondral ossifications of the chondrocranium representing the paired exoccipitals, prootics, opisthotics, quadrates, and the orbitosphenoid (sphenethmoid), and the initial appearance of the maxilla. Generally, the last elements to ossify in the larvae are the columella and various dermal elements that occur spuriously in salamanders—namely, prefrontals, lacrimals, nasals, septomaxillae, and quadratojugals.

Branchial Arches.   The hyobranchial skeleton of salamander larvae is a good deal more complicated than that of caecilians (Fig. 6-7), owing to its role in food capture by the carnivorous larvae. Although there is considerable variation in the structure of the skeletal unit, in the fully formed larva the hyobranchial apparatus basically consists of a median basibranchial series of one or two elements. If two elements are present, the anterior basibranchial is the larger, and the posterior is a slim rod of cartilage. When only one element is present, it usually bears a posterior projection, suggesting that the two copular elements have fused to form one plate. The anterior margin of the hyobranchial apparatus is composed of the anterior tip of the basibranchial that is flanked laterally by small hypohyal and large ceratohyal elements. Together, these components form a broad cartilaginous arc that comes to rest against the lower jaw when the hyobranchial apparatus is protracted during feeding.

The larger of the basibranchial plates (if two are present) bears two pairs of posterolateral processes, Hypobranchials I and II (Branchial Arches I and II). The first pair usually is fused to the basibranchial, whereas the second pair normally articulates with it. Distal to the hypobranchials are three or four pairs of ceratobranchials (termed epibranchials by some authors). Ceratobranchials I and II articulate with the distal ends of Hypobranchials I and II, respectively. In turn, the ceratobranchials are united to one another proximally and distally by delicate cartilaginous connections.

The entire apparatus bears a ligamentous connection to the skull. The complexity of its design accommodates movement in the dorsoventral and anteroposterior planes as well as a certain degree of rotation around the longitudinal axis. Movement of the hyobranchial skeleton changes the volume of the oropharyngeal cavity and controls the opening and closing of the gill slits. As described by Severtzov (1968), the floor of the buccal cavity is depressed at the same time that the mouth is opened and the gill arches are closed. This forces a stream of water (along with prey) into the mouth. Closure of the mouth and lifting of the floor of the buccal cavity forces most of the ingested water out through the gill slit as it opens. When the gill slit closes and as the floor of the buccal cavity continues to be elevated, the increasing pressure forces the contents of the buccal cavity to the esophagus where it is swallowed.

Axial Skeleton.   There are limited ontogenetic data on the postcranial anatomy of salamanders and no studies similar to that on caecilians by M. Wake (1980c). Apparently, most workers (except T. Wake et al., 1983) have assumed like I. Wilder (1925:92) that postcranial elements in general and the appendicular skeleton in particular of larval salamanders are unimportant because "larval appendages are examples of adult characters which make an anachronistic appearance."

Anurans

Of the three orders of amphibians, anuran larvae are the most deviant from their adult counterparts and the most specialized of the three larval types. Moreover, among those anurans having free-swimming larvae, there is an astounding array of morphological variation relative to that observed in either caecilians or salamanders. This diversity is related to several evolutionary phenomena. Morphologically, anurans are more specialized than salamanders (and specialized in a different way than caecilians)—that is, their body plan has deviated the most strikingly from the short-limbed attenuate body plan of the more generalized, and presumed primitive, ancestral form. They alone are capable of saltatorial movement between and within terrestrial and aquatic habitats. This is facilitated, of course, by their long hindlimbs and short trunk. Thus, it is not surprising that their larvae deviate from the generalized morphological and developmental mode observed in the other orders. Anurans have undergone phylogenetic and ecological diversification that far surpasses that observed in salamanders and caecilians; anuran larvae reflect this diversification and differ strikingly from their adult counterparts in their habits, ecology, and morphology. Because of this complexity it is exceedingly difficult to draft a "generalized" account of anuran larvae comparable to that presented for caecilians and salamanders. Consequently, this section is organized on a slightly different scheme than the preceding ones. A general morphological account of the body plan and chondrocranial, visceral, and axial elements is provided before accounts of basic types of anuran larvae, with details of the buccopharyngeal morphology and the functional interrelationships of feeding and respiration.

Basic Body Plan.   At hatching, a tadpole seems to resemble a fish. However, this superficial similarity belies striking differences. The body is short (approximately 25–35% of the total length) and generally ovoid. The long tail is laterally compressed and composed of a central axis of caudal musculature provided with dorsal and ventral "fins." The ventral fin is continuous from the vent at the posterior end of the body to the tip of the tail. The dorsal fin extends from the top or end of the body to the tip of the tail. The union of dorsal and ventral fins distally assumes a variety of terminal shapes depending on the adaptive type of the larva. Similarly, the shapes and sizes of the dorsal and ventral fins vary.

The body of the tadpole is characterized by slightly protuberant, lidless eyes, wide nares, and a terminal mouth, which is highly variable in form and position. In its most simplistic state (e.g., pipoids), the mouth is wide and slit-like. Most anuran larvae have more complex mouths characterized by fleshy, papillose or funnel-shaped "lips." Internal to the lips, the mouth usually bears rows of fine, keratinous denticles and a prominent beak, beyond which lies the buccopharyngeal cavity. Although absent in most anuran larvae, sensory barbels border the mouth in some pipoid larvae. Early in development, anuran larvae have external gills, anterior to which lies a fold of skin. The opercular fold grows posteriad to enclose the gills in all amphibians that metamorphose; however, this occurs much earlier in the development of anurans than in salamanders and caecilians. Thus, in young anuran larvae, the gills come to be enclosed in an opercular chamber that opens to the outside via a funnel-shaped spiracle or pair of spiracles. The position and number (one or two) of spiracles vary depending on the species.

Whereas larval salamanders are characterized by functional fore- and hindlimbs, anuran larvae are not. The forelimbs develop within the opercular chamber and erupt through the body wall just prior to the completion of metamorphosis. The hindlimbs first appear as buds that emerge from the posterior margin of the body and develop adpressed to the tail. Thus, throughout its larval life, the tadpole maintains a hydrodynamically efficient, fusiform shape, with the limbs becoming functional only toward the completion of metamorphosis when the organism moves from an aquatic to a terrestrial environment.

In contrast to salamanders and caecilians, the digestive system of anuran larvae is strikingly different from that of the adults. Owing to the microphagous, herbivorous food habits of most anuran larvae, they require a large intestinal surface area for absorbing nutrients; thus, the intestine is long and coiled on itself. The stomach is undeveloped, but near the cardiac portion of the presumptive stomach is a structure known as the manicotto gland; presumably secretions of this gland aid in the digestion of food.

Chondrocranium and Mandible.   Contrasted to the chondrocrania of salamanders and caecilians, that of anurans is robust and boxlike (Fig. 6-6). Fenestration is reduced. The palatoquadrate lies in a horizontal rather than a vertical position, and the anterior chondrocranial cartilages are modifed to form structural support for the tadpole mouth. During metamorphosis, these parts of the chondrocranium are restructured and repositioned totally to provide for the mandibulae and suspensory apparatus of the adult—an architectural system similar to that of adult and larval salamanders and caecilians.

The floor of the anuran chondrocranium bears one relatively small fenestra, the basicranial fenestra, which is bordered laterally by the cranial trabeculae and anteriorly by the trabecular plate. Posterior to the fenestra, the floor of the chondrocranium is composed of a broad sheet of cartilage, the basal plate. From this ventral framework three pillars of cartilage extend dorsally to form the sides of the braincase. The most posterior is the pila antotica, which fuses with the roof of the otic capsule dorsally, thereby forming the prootic foramen through which the trigeminal, facial, and abducens nerves exit the chondrocranium. A second strut of cartilage, the pila metoptica, lies anterior to the pila antotica. Fusion of these two pilae dorsally encloses the foramen for the oculomotor nerve and opthalmica magna artery. The optic and trochlear nerves emerge between the pila metoptica and a third, more anterior pillar of cartilage, the preoptic root, which forms the anterior corner of the braincase. A fourth set of cartilage pillars, the pilae ethmoidalis, arise from the anterior floor of the chondrocranium to form the anterior wall of the braincase (Fig. 6-4). This wall has a medial fenestra between the pilae ethmoidalis, the fenestra precerebralis, and a pair of anterolateral foramina, the foramen olfactorium, formed between the pila ethmoidalis and the preoptic root. The olfactory nerve exits the braincase via the foramen olfactorium. The fenestra precerebralis is obliterated in early metamorphosis by the development of a medial septum that extends anteriorly to separate the nasal capsules and provide a complete anteromedial wall to the braincase. The dorsal ends of the lateral pilae are united by the orbital cartilages, and the anterior pilae are joined dorsally by the tectum internasale. Together, these cartilages form the anterolateral and anterior margins, respectively, of the frontoparietal fenestra in the roof of the braincase.

Dorsal fenestration of the anuran chondrocranium is variable, depending on the degree of development of the roofs of the auditory capsules. If the auditory capsules are united only by a single, posterior bridge, the tectum synoticum, then the frontoparietal fenestra is extensive. If the capsules are united anteriorly by the taenia tecti transversalis, as well as posteriorly, the dorsal fenestration is subdivided into the anterior frontoparietal fenestra separated from the posterior parietal fenestra by the taenia tecti transversalis. Occasionally the latter is developed incompletely, thereby effecting only partial separation between the fenestrae. Appearance of a dorsomedial (i.e., longitudinal) bridge of cartilage, the taenia tecti medialis, between the taenia tecti transversalis and tectum synoticum subdivides the posterior parietal fenestra into two smaller fenestrae.

The auditory capsules flank the posterior floor of the braincase; thus, their ventral aspect is complete. In this respect anurans and salamanders are alike and differ from caecilians, which have a basicapsular fenestra. In contrast to salamanders and caecilians, each of which lacks the taenia tecti transversalis and taenia tecti medialis, the auditory capsules of anurans tend to be roofed more completely. The lateral wall of the auditory capsule has an opening, the fenestra ovalis. Associated with this fenestra is a plate of cartilage, the operculum, that occludes the posterior part of the opening. A second cartilage, the rodlike stapes, or columella, arises independently of the auditory capsule, but fuses with its ventral margin and has ligamentous attachments to the quadrate anterolaterally and the operculum posteriorly. The medial wall of the auditory capsule is perforated by one to three acoustic foramina and two perilymphatic foramina (superior and inferior). The posteromedial wall of the auditory capsule is completed by the occipital arch of the posterior end of the chondrocranium. The union of these two structures accommodates two foramina, the posterior jugular foramen through which the glossopharyngeal and vagus nerves exit the cranium, and a third perilymphatic foramen.

The anterior end of the chondrocranium of anurans is unlike that of salamanders and caecilians. The nasal capsules characteristic of the latter organisms do not develop in anurans until metamorphosis owing to the structure and function of the larval mouthparts and their role in larval respiration. With the exception of microhylids in which the nares do not open until just before metamorphosis, the external nares of tadpoles remain open permanently and communicate with the internal nares by means of a short passage through the buccal roof; parts of the passage are lined by olfactory epithelium, but a discrete olfactory organ does not develop until metamorphosis.

The floor (planum trabeculae anterior) of the anterior end of the braincase bears a pair of anterolateral projections, or cornua. Each cornu is deflected ventrally and fused anteriorly with the suprarostral cartilage, which supports the upper beak of the larva. Posterolaterally, the cornua bear a ligamentous connection (quadratocranialis ligament) with the anteromedial margin of the quadrate cartilage. The lower beak is supported by paired, medial chondrifications, the infrarostrals. Medially, these elements articulate with one another; posterolaterally each articulates with Meckel's cartilages. The latter, in turn, articulate laterally with the palatoquadrate. The palatoquadrate is massive and aligned horizontally in lateral view, and lateral and parallel to the neurocranium in dorsal view. Posteriorly, it is connected to the pila antotica via the ascending process of the quadrate and to the auditory capsule via the larval otic process. Anteriorly, the processus quadrato ethmoidalis forms a massive strut between the anterolateral corner of the neurocranium and the anterior end of the palatoquadrate. Anterolaterally, the palatoquadrate bears a dorsal process, the processus muscularis quadrati, from which the depressor muscles originate; these muscles insert on the ceratohyal ventrolaterally.

Ossification Sequence of the Cranium.   Owing to the dramatic structural and functional changes in the anuran skull at metamorphosis, cranial ossification is delayed for the most part until the onset of metamorphosis. A discussion of these aspects of development follows in Chapter 7.

Branchial Arches.   There is considerable diversity among anurans in the structure of their branchial apparatus, but basically each consists of a pair of robust anterior plates, the ceratohyals, that underlie the floor of the buccal cavity and that usually unite ventromedially to one another (Fig. 6-7). Anterolaterally the ceratohyals articulate with the palatoquadrate, and posteromedially they are fused to a basibranchial cartilage. Presumably the latter is homologous with the second basibranchial of salamanders and caecilians, the first basibranchial having been lost or reduced in anurans. The basibranchial articulates posteriorly with two broad cartilages, the hypobranchial plates, from which four ceratobranchials arise on each side. The ceratobranchials are united distally, forming a basketlike framework which supports the larval gill filters. The structure of the larval branchial apparatus is associated intimately with buccal pumping and feeding mechanisms described below. With the shift in feeding mechanisms at metamorphosis, the branchial apparatus undergoes profound modifications to form the adult hyoid apparatus, which supports the laryngeal structures and serves as a base for the tongue.

Morphological Types of Anuran Larvae.   Orton (1953) recognized four basic kinds of tadpoles, which she designated as Types I–IV depending on the structure of the opercular chamber and its opening(s) from the body, and the nature of the larval mouth (Fig. 6-8). Type I includes the peculiar pipids and rhinophrynids that have paired spiracles (one opening from each of two spiracular chambers), that lack keratinous mouthparts, and some of which possess sensory barbels bordering the simple, slitlike mouth. A single family, the Microhylidae, is represented in Orton's Type II tadpoles. Like Type I larvae, Type II tadpoles lack mouthparts. They also lack barbels and have a single opercular chamber with a single, median posterior spiracle. Types III and IV larvae have mouthparts. Orton distinguished Type III larvae (ascaphids and discoglossids) from Type IV larvae (all remaining families) on the basis of the midventral spiracle in the former and the sinistral spiracle of the latter.

As originally proposed, Orton's scheme was phenetic and provided a convenient, shorthand way of classifying tadpole morphotypes. Subsequent workers sought to arrange these types in a phylogenetic sequence. Thus, P.

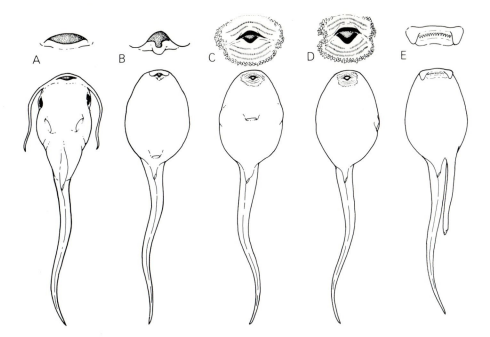

Figure 6-8. Morphological types of anuran larvae; mouths and ventral views of bodies showing positions of spiracular openings. **A–D.** Orton's (1953) types 1–4, respectively. **E.** *Otophryne robusta.*

Starrett (1973) elaborated Orton's work and proposed names for the morphological types, and the names were applied to suborders of frogs by some workers (e.g., J. Savage, 1973). As more recent research (Sokol, 1975) has shown, Orton's classification is vastly oversimplified. Moreover, ontogenetic studies suggest the possibility of "primitive" types of tadpoles (Types I and II) being derived through developmental truncation from "advanced" types (Types III and IV) (Wassersug, 1984; Wassersug and Duellman, 1984). The types, as defined below, still provide a useful framework within which to describe tadpoles, but too little is known about the distribution and variation of the characters within and between types to warrant a phylogenetic assessment.

Type III tadpoles.—This type was termed the Lemmanura by P. Starrett (1973) and Discoglossoidea by Sokol (1975). There are a number of features of ascaphid and discoglossid tadpoles that seem to be primitive. The tadpoles have a shallow opercular chamber similar to that of salamanders. The chamber is provided with a single, midventral opening to the exterior. This opening, or spiracle, is formed by a single hiatus in the fusion of the opercular skin to the body wall; thus, a siphon is absent. So far as is known, Type III tadpoles are unique among anurans in having separate trigeminal and facial ganglia (C.N. V and VIII), a condition characteristic of salamanders (Sokol, 1975). Branches of these nerves exit the cranium through the prootic foramen and the palatine foramen, which are separated by a bar of cartilage, the prefacial commissure. The palatine foramen and hence the prefacial commissure are absent in all other tadpoles. Type III tadpoles possess a shearing beak and rows of keratinous denticles. Internal gills are present, and the

anterior filter valve of the buccopharyngeal cavity is unpaired, extending across the glottis in the midline.

Type III tadpoles are characterized by a "high" suspensorium similar to that of salamander larvae and differing from the "low" suspensoria of other tadpoles (Sokol, 1975). The suspensorium involves the structures that suspend the main portion of the palatoquadrate from, or attached to, the braincase. In tadpoles having a "high" suspensorium, the anterior end of the palatoquadrate is deflected ventrally, whereas in those having a "low" suspensorium, the long axis of the palatoquadrate is nearly level owing to the attachment of the posterior end of the lower aspects of the braincase. In Type III tadpoles, the ascending process of the palatoquadrate fuses to the neurocranium at the dorsal end of the pila antotica (the dorsal column of cartilage that separates the oculomotor and trigeminal foramina just in front of the auditory capsule). A second process of the palatoquadrate, the otic process, bears a ligamentous attachment to the anterior end of the auditory, or otic, capsule. In tadpoles having a "high" suspensorium, the anteromedial margin of the dorsal aspect of the otic capsule bears a projecting shelf or ledge that connects the otic capsule with the taenia tecti marginalis. This ledge overlies the upper end of the ascending process.

Other morphological complexes of Type III larvae are perceived as showing one or more derived features (Sokol, 1975). For example, in the hyobranchial apparatus, the branchial basket is composed of two complete septa and a third, incomplete septum. A septum is defined as the aortic arch complex (afferent and efferent vessels), an interbranchialis muscle, and the surrounding tissues associated with each ceratobranchial and its internal gills.

Type III tadpoles lack the third interbranchialis muscle. In salamanders, the ceratobranchials bear a ligamentous attachment to the hypohyals. Similarly, in some Type III tadpoles, the ceratohyals have a ligmentous connection to the hypohyal plate; this presumably represents a derived condition from the primitive ligamentous connection between these elements in salamanders and some other tadpoles.

Type IV tadpoles.—This is the Acosmanura of P. Starrett (1973) and the Ranoidea of Sokol (1975). Type IV tadpoles include the majority of anurans—all except the ascaphids, discoglossids, microhylids, pipids, and rhinophrynids. They show fewer primitive features than do Type III larvae, but nonetheless are characterized by a melange of primitive and derived characters. Like Type III larvae, Type IV tadpoles possess a shearing beak and usually rows of keratinous denticles. Internal gills are present, and the anterior filter valve of the buccopharyngeal cavity is unpaired. In contrast to Type III tadpoles, the branchial basket is composed of three complete septa, and the attachment between the second basibranchial and the hypohyal plate is ligamentous. The ceratobranchials are ligamentously attached to the hypohyal plate in some Type IV tadpoles and fused in others.

The suspensoria of Type IV tadpoles generally are "lower" than those of Type III larvae because the otic process lies posteroventral to the most anterior margin of the otic capsule; thus, the palatoquadrate lies in a plane almost paralleling that of the floor of the neurocranium. The ascending process of the palatoquadrate either slopes downward toward the otic process from its point of fusion with the dorsum of the pila antotica or, in the absence or reduction of the pila antotica, extends in a lateral plane from the wall of the neurocranium to the palatoquadrate. Type IV tadpoles lack an otic ledge or shelf connecting the otic capsule to the taenia tecti marginalis.

Other, apparently derived features of Type IV larvae include the following. The opercular chamber is deep and provided with a single spiracle with a tubular siphon opening to the exterior. Secretory tissue in the branchial food traps is organized into ridges. The spiracle is sinistral in all Type IV tadpoles, except in the larvae of *Flectonotus* and *Fritziana,* two genera of egg-brooding hylids in which the spiracle is midventral (Griffiths and Carvalho, 1965; Duellman and Gray, 1983). The trigeminal and facial ganglia are fused; thus, the palatine foramen and prefacial commissure are absent.

Type II tadpoles.—This is the Scoptanura of P. Starrett (1973) and the Microhyloidea of Sokol (1975). Type II tadpoles include only a single family, the Microhylidae, which is characterized by only two primitive features. Like Type III and IV larvae, the microhylids have internal gills, and like Type IV tadpoles, they have branchial baskets composed of three complete septa.

The suspensorium is "low" because the otic process is fused with an extension of the crista parotica of the otic capsule. The pila antotica is absent; thus, the as-cending process of the palatoquadrate extends lateral to the palatoquadrate from the ventral margin of the neurocranium (the region of the cranial trabecula).

A host of derived features characterize Type II larvae. These include the two that are shared with Type III and/or Type IV tadpoles: (1) presence of a single prootic ganglion and loss of the palatine foramen and prefacial commissure; (2) fusion of ceratohyal and hypohyal elements; (3) fusion of the second basibranchial with the hypohyal plate. They are distinguished from Type III and IV larvae by the presence of a paired anterior filter valve and glottis that is displaced anteriorly. The opercular chamber is greatly enlarged and bears a single spiracle with a siphon. In all known microhylids except *Otophryne robusta* (Fig. 6-8E) and *Pseudohemisus granulosum,* the spiracle is midventral and located beneath the vent. Similarly, all microhylids except *O. robusta* and *P. granulosum* lack keratinous mouthparts. In *O. robusta,* the mouth is simple and lacking oral papillae like those of other microhylids; however, *O. robusta* has a single row of sharp, fanglike, cornified "teeth" along the upper and lower jaws (Fig. 6-9) (Pyburn, 1980b). These "teeth" are not homologous with true teeth and are unique insofar as is known; no one has speculated as to their possible homology with the denticular structures of Type III and IV larvae. The spiracle of *O. robusta* also is bizarre. The opercular chamber is enlarged, and the spiracle is posterior, as is typical of microhylids, but the spiracle is sinistral instead of midventral, and the siphon is elongated into an enormously attenuate tube that extends from the body caudad about half the length of the tail.

Type I tadpoles.—This is the Xenoanura of P. Starrett (1973) and Pipoidea of Sokol (1975). All features used to distinguish the Type I pipid and rhinophrynid tadpoles from Type II, III, and IV larvae seem to be derived. The opercular chamber is shallow and divided into two parts of reduced size. Each chamber bears a ventral and hiatal opening; thus, the spiracles are said to be paired and lacking siphons. The trigeminal and facial ganglia are fused, so Type I tadpoles lack a palatine foramen and prefacial commissure. The mouth bears neither a beak nor keratinous denticles. Internal gills are absent, and the anterior filter valve of the buccopharyngeal cavity is paired with a median hiatus. The branchial basket of the hyobranchial apparatus is composed of only two complete septa; thus, the third interbranchialis muscle and aortic arch complex are absent. The ceratohyals are reduced in number and fused to the hypohyal plate in *Hymenochirus* and *Pseudhymenochirus.* The second basibranchial is fused to the hypohyal plate.

The suspensorium of Type I tadpoles is "high," but structured in such a way that it bears little resemblance to the "high" suspensorium of Type III larvae and salamanders. Because the palatoquadrate is short, its otic process does not reach the anterior end of the otic capsule. The ascending process of the palatoquadrate attaches to the dorsal end of the pila antotica but is not

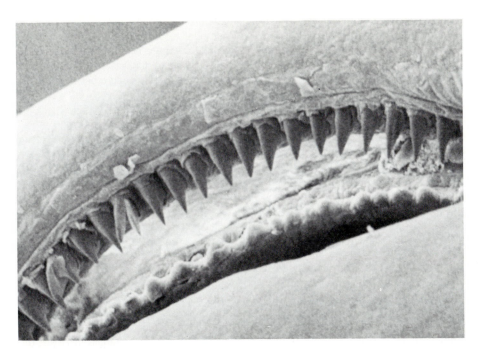

Figure 6-9. Part of the mouth of the tadpole of *Otophryne robusta*. The sharp "denticles" are on the margin of the upper jaw; "denticles" on the margin of the lower jaw are obscured by a fleshy fold. Note the shedding of the outer layer of the third "denticle" from the left. Scanning electron micrograph by W. R. Fagerberg provided by W. F. Pyburn.

overlain by an otic ledge of the auditory capsule, because that structure is absent. Furthermore, the gap between the ascending and otic processes is filled by a cartilaginous plate that is fused to the otic capsule. The nerves (ramus mandibulomaxillaris of the trigeminal and ramus ophthalmicus of the facial) that pass behind the ascending process pierce the otic plate through two foramina.

Functional Interrelationships Between Respiratory and Feeding Mechanisms. Two major distinctions between anuran larvae and those of caecilians and salamanders are the presence of internal gills and specialized larval mouthparts lacking true teeth in tadpoles. It is implicitly clear from their morphology that anuran larvae, unlike the larvae of the other orders, must have evolved mechanisms for (1) irrigating their internal gills, and (2) obtaining food in the absence of jaws provided with teeth that, together, act to grasp and manipulate food. The processes are related functionally and are dependent on a complex morphological system that is restructured completely at metamorphosis.

The tadpole mouth, or opening to the buccal cavity, is supported by three cartilaginous elements. Dorsally there is a suprarostral cartilage that pivots on the ends of the cranial trabeculae, and ventrally the paired infrarostrals that articulate with the distal ends of Meckel's cartilages. A complex set of ligaments and visceral musculature (Gradwell, 1972a, 1972b) effects movement of these labial cartilages through movement of the larval hyoid. In all anuran larvae, except microhylids and pipoids, the mouth is provided with a keratinous beak (supported by labial cartilages) and various configurations of rows of keratinous denticles and labial papillae on the fleshy area

of the mouth circumdistal to the beak. The larvae use their jaws and these keratinous structures to chop food into sizes that can pass through the small gape of the mouth and/or to scrape or rasp food from surfaces. The mouth also acts as a valve in a buccal-pump system in which water flows into the buccal cavity via the oral aperture, caudally to the pharyngeal cavity, and then over the gills in the branchial baskets to emerge to the exterior via the spiracle(s). Simultaneously, food particles are trapped and gases are exchanged from this flow of water.

The morphological components of the buccal pump system consist of two internal chambers—the buccal and pharyngeal cavities—through which water flow is controlled by three valves—the mouth, as described above, aided by the choanae and ventral velum. Each choana has a flaplike, semilunar valve of the mucosa along its posterior border. During aqueous ventilation, hydrostatic pressure inside the buccal cavity closes the valve, thereby preventing a backflow of water through the nasal chamber (Gradwell, 1969). The ventral velum is an epithelial flap that arises from the floor of the buccal cavity and separates this chamber from the more posterior branchial baskets of the pharynx. A ventral velum is possessed by all anuran larvae except pipids. In this family, backflow of water is prevented by flaplike covers of the paired opercular openings (Gradwell, 1971). The final morphological component of this system is the larval hyobranchial apparatus and its associated musculature. Depression of the ceratohyals results in expansion of the buccal cavity; thus, water flows through the mouth and nares into the buccal cavity. When the medial portions of the ceratohyals are elevated and the mouth closes, the buccal cavity is contracted, the choanae closed by hydrostatic pressure, and the water forced from the buccal cavity over the ventral velum and into the branchial baskets of the pharynx. Contraction of the branchial baskets drives the water through the gill slits and then out via the spiracle or opercular opening. Details of this mechanism are given by De Jongh (1968), Kenny (1969b), Gradwell (1968, 1970, 1972a, 1972b), Severtzov (1969), and Wassersug and K. Hoff (1979).

As anuran larvae pump water through their buccopharyngeal cavities, they extract food particles suspended in the water. Their ability to do so depends on the presence of secretory epithelium and on the configuration of the buccal cavity, which bears species-specific configurations of papillae (Wassersug, 1976, 1980). Food particles that are small enough to enter the mouth are sorted mechanically in the buccal cavity. Larger particles are shunted directly posterior into the esophagus, whereas smaller particles move over the ventral velum into the pharynx. There, the larger of these small particles are trapped by direct interception and inertial impaction on the gill filters and smaller particles are aggregated in mucus on the branchial food traps (Kenny, 1969b; Wassersug, 1972, 1980). Aggregates of small particles of food are moved posterolaterally from the gill filters to the ciliary groove that marks the margin of the roof of the pharynx on each side. Once in the ciliary groove, food is transported posteriorly to the esophagus. Food is entrapped and aggregated by mucous strands produced by zones of specialized epithelium (Kenny, 1969c). A zone of pitted, secretory epithelium is present as a transverse, crescentic band at the posterior margin of the buccal roof, and often along the posterior edge of the ventral velum (Wassersug, 1976). A second kind of secretory epithelium, ridged epithelium, forms secretory ridges on the ventral surface of the ventral velum. From the velum, the ridged epithelium may extend ventrally into each filter chamber to form branchial food traps.

ADAPTIVE TYPES OF LARVAE

Many of the structural differences among larvae in the three groups of living amphibians are associated with the different environments in which they live. These differences may not be correlated with the systematic relationships of the taxa. Similar selective pressures on larvae of diverse phylogenetic lineages has resulted in many examples of convergence of morphological features in larvae of unrelated taxa in similar habitats. Conversely, entirely different adaptive types of larvae exist among closely related taxa.

In salamanders the major structural differences are associated with respiration and locomotion, whereas among anurans the adaptations seem to be associated with feeding and locomotion (or maintaining their position in the environment). Free-living larvae of ichthyophiid and rhinatrematid caecilians have slight fins on their tails and

at hatching have external gills that are resorbed within a few days. Their eel-like locomotion is in quiet water or in mud. Essentially there are no adaptive modifications of the larvae, which are distinguished from adults primarily by having an open gill slit and a better-developed lateral-line system.

Salamanders

Three adaptive types of salamander larvae are recognized (Valentine and Dennis, 1964). These types have differences in their gills, in opercular covers (Fig. 6-10), and in the degree of development of caudal fins. In general, larvae that develop in quiet water have laterally compressed bodies, high caudal fins, balancers, and large gills, as contrasted with larvae that develop in streams.

The size and surface area of the gills are dependent on the oxygen content of the water. Furthermore, observations and experiments suggest that the large bushy gills in pond-type larvae are important in respiration at higher temperatures, at which time the oxygen content of the water is low, and also at times of activity (Whitford and R. Sherman, 1968; Guimond and V. Hutchinson, 1972). Extensive surface area of the gills increases respiratory efficiency in water with low oxygen content and thereby enables these salamanders to survive in stagnant ponds—a habitat occupied by many kinds of pond larvae (Fig. 6-11). Stream larvae, on the other hand, live in cool water with a high oxygen content; probably much of their respiration is cutaneous. The atrophied gills of the mountain brook-type of larvae are indicative of primarily cutaneous respiration. The small gills in such species also allow these salamanders to crawl into underwater cracks and crevices.

The extent of the caudal fin and lateral compression of the body and tail are correlated with the nature of the larval habitat. Pond-dwelling larvae walk about on the bottom of ponds, but at least some of them commonly feed near the surface at night (J. D. Anderson and Graham, 1967), at which time they maintain their positions and move about by gentle movements of their thin but deep tails. Moreover, the deep tails are effective in rapid acceleration in quiet water, when the larvae are disturbed. Proportionately more muscular tails with shallower and less extensive fins are characteristic of larvae that develop in streams. Locomotion in streams is accomplished primarily by crawling on the substrate. The tail may be used for balance or for short bursts of swimming, and if movement is against the current, the strong musculature and shallow fleshy fins are more effective in propulsion than the deeper but comparatively weak tails of pond-type larvae. Caudal fins are reduced further in mountain brook-type larvae; these move almost exclusively by crawling. The surface area of the caudal fins also may be important in respiration; thus, the increased surface area of the tails of larvae in ponds facilitates cutaneous respiration. Reduced fins in stream-dwelling larvae may facilitate their taking refuge in crevices.

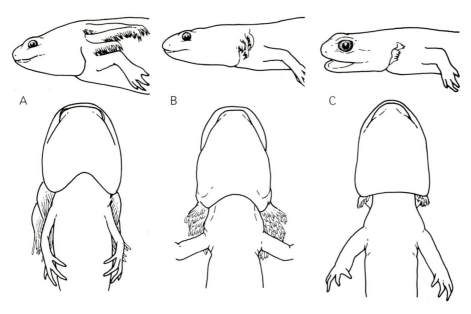

Figure 6-10. Adaptive types of salamander larvae. **A.** Pond type—*Ambystoma tigrinum*, with large bushy gills and high caudal fin. **B.** Stream type—*Gyrinophilus porphyriticus*, with shorter, less filamentous gills and low, fleshy caudal fin. **C.** Mountain brook type—*Rhyacotriton olympicus*, with short, stubby gills and reduced caudal fin.

Figure 6-11. Pond larva of *Ambystoma opacum* from Centreville, Virginia. The large, filamentous gills provide extensive respiratory surfaces for survival in ponds with low oxygen content. Photo by K. Nemuras.

Balancers are paired, rodlike lateral projections that develop on the head of many pond-type larvae (Fig. 5-12). In some species they are resorbed before the larvae hatch. In others they persist until the developing forelimbs have become fully functional. During this interim, the balancers (along with the extended forelimbs) seem to keep the larva from sinking into the muddy substrate and help the larva to maintain its balance during its first, feeble attempts at locomotion using the forelimbs. The absence of balancers in some pond-type larvae (e.g., sirenids) is unexplained at present. Although most stream-type larvae hatch with well-developed forelimbs and lack balancers, *Salamandrina* has rudimentary balancers.

The three adaptive types of salamander larvae are defined as follows.

Pond-type larvae have an operculum forming a gular fold that is deeply incised midventrally (Fig. 6-10A). The gill rami are long and tapering, and each ramus has two rows of long fimbriae with many other fimbriae intercollated between the rows. Gill rakers, long conical projections on the inner surface of the rami, are present. Balancers usually are present in early larval stages (absent in some *Hynobius* and *Taricha*, and rudimentary in *Salamandra* and plethodontids). The dorsal and ventral caudal fins are thin and deep. The dorsal fin extends well onto the body, and in young larvae the ventral fin may bifurcate around the vent and continue anteriorly onto the belly. This type of larva is characteristic of most *Hynobius*, *Necturus*, various salamandrids *(Notophthalmus, Pleurodeles, Taricha, Triturus,* and *Tylototriton),* most *Ambystoma,* and some plethodontids *(Hemidactylium, Stereochilus,* and *Eurycea quadridigitata).* All of these develop in ponds, but *Taricha rivularis* does occur in quiet pools in streams. Neotenic salamanders of the family Sirenidae also have pond-type adaptations.

Stream-type larvae have a gular fold that is only slightly indented midventrally (Fig. 6-10B). The gill rami are long and tapering, and each ramus bears two rows of moderately long fimbriae. Gill rakers are short and few in number. Balancers are absent. The dorsal and ventral caudal fins are low and fleshy and extend the full length of the tail. In many of these larvae the body is depressed. This type of larva is characteristic of some *Batrachuperus, Ranodon, Cryptobranchus, Proteus, Euproctus, Dicamptodon, Rhyacosiredon, Ambystoma ordinarium,* and stream-dwelling plethodontids, such as *Gyrinophilus, Pseudotriton, Typhlotriton,* and most species of *Desmognathus* and *Eurycea.*

The mountain brook-type of larva has a gular fold with no medial indentation (Fig. 6-10C). The gill rami are short and bear a single row of small fimbriae; gill rakers are absent or present only as small protrusions on the

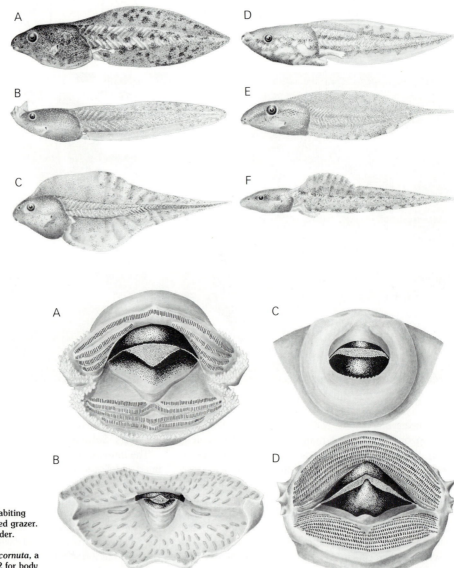

Figure 6-12. Adaptive types of tadpoles in quiet water. **A.** *Rana palmipes,* a generalized grazer. **B.** *Megophrys montana,* a surface feeder. **C.** *Ololygon nebulosa,* which lives amidst vegetation in midwater. **D.** *Gastrophryne carolinensis,* a midwater, microphagous type. **E.** *Hyla microcephala,* a midwater, macrophagous type. **F.** *Occidozyga lima,* a bottom-feeding type.

Figure 6-13. Mouths of tadpoles inhabiting ponds. **A.** *Rana palmipes,* a generalized grazer. **B.** *Megophrys montana,* a surface feeder. **C.** *Hyla microcephala,* a midwater, macrophagous type. **D.** *Ceratophrys cornuta,* a predaceous carnivore. See Figure 6-12 for body shapes of A–C.

rami. Balancers are absent. Dorsal and ventral caudal fins are low, fleshy, and present only on the distal half of the tail. Examples of this type of larva include *Onychodactylus,* some *Batrachuperus,* and *Rhyacotriton olympicus.*

Anurans

The adaptive radiation among anuran larvae is far more diverse than in salamanders. Orton (1953) defined seven adaptive types (including direct development) of tadpoles based on position and size of the mouth, shape of the body, and development of the caudal musculature and fins. These adaptive types should not be confused with the basic morphological types of tadpoles presented earlier. Orton (1953) derived various adaptive types of tadpoles from a generalized pond-type with an anteroventral mouth and moderately developed caudal fins.

The generalized pond-type of tadpole is an aquatic organism with a roughly ovoid body, a tail about twice as long as the body with dorsal and ventral caudal fins each about as deep as the caudal musculature, and an anteroventrally directed mouth (Fig. 6-12A). The mouth usually is bordered laterally and ventrally by one or two rows of small papillae. The upper lip bears two or three rows of keratinized denticles, and there are three or four rows on the lower lip. The jaws bear keratinized beaks with fine serrations (Fig. 6-13A). This is the pond-type of tadpole common to many genera within the families Discoglossidae, Pelobatidae, Myobatrachidae, Leptodactylidae, Bufonidae, Pseudidae, Hylidae, Ranidae, Hyperoliidae, and Rhacophoridae.

The adaptive radiation within pond-type tadpoles involves modifications for life in different strata and feeding on different-sized particles of food. Among the most strikingly different adaptive types are the funnel-mouthed surface feeders occurring in the genera *Megophrys, Microhyla,* and *Phyllomedusa* (Figs. 6-12B, 6-13B). These tadpoles suspend from the surface tension of forest ponds (quiet pools in streams in the case of *Phyllomedusa)* and feed on various-sized particles of floating material. In such tadpoles, the broad mouth possibly provides not only a larger surface area for suspension from the surface but a larger food-gathering surface; denticles are greatly reduced or absent. Some pond tadpoles have laterally compressed bodies and very deep caudal fins, perhaps best exemplified by some species of the hylid genus *Ololygon* (Fig. 6-12C). These tadpoles swim amidst dense vegetation. The generalized pond-type and laterally compressed tadpoles graze on periphyton, leaves, and detritus.

A variety of *Hyla* and *Occidozyga,* among others, are macrophagous in ponds. Many of these tadpoles have terminal mouths, lack denticles, and have either few large or no labial papillae (Fig. 6-13C). Various shapes of bodies and tails correspond to the strata in ponds where they feed; tadpoles with rounded bodies, ventral spiracles, and normal caudal fins, such as those of many microhylids (Fig. 6-12D) live in midwater. Those tadpoles with de-

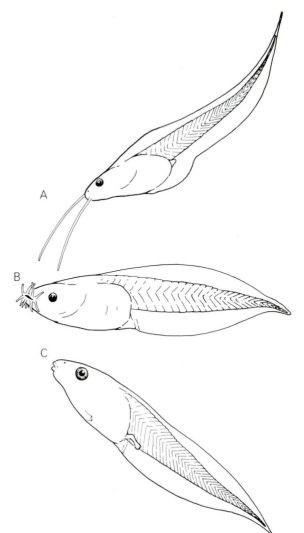

Figure 6-14. Midwater filter-feeding types of tadpoles shown in characteristic planes of orientation. **A.** *Xenopus laevis.*
B. *Rhinophrynus dorsalis.* **C.** *Agalychnis spurrelli.* Denticles and beaks are absent in *Xenopus* and *Rhinophrynus;* two upper and three lower rows of denticles and horny beaks are present in *Agalychnis. Xenopus* and *Rhinophrynus* have paired ventrolateral spiracles, and *Agalychnis* has a single spiracle just to the left of the midventral line.

pressed bodies, lateral spiracles, and elongate tails are bottom feeders or live amidst dense aquatic vegetation (Figs. 6-12E, 6-12F).

Nectonic filter-feeding tadpoles that characteristically feed in midwater have terminal mouths and thin caudal fins that may be moderately low and long or shorter and deeper. Nectonic tadpoles of *Xenopus* and *Rhinophrynus* (Fig. 6-14) lack denticles and beaks and have elongate barbels at the border of the mouth. These tadpoles are obligate filter-feeders, whereas the facultative filter-feeders of the hyperoliid *Kassina* and phyllomedusine hylids have denticles and beaks but no barbels. Many,

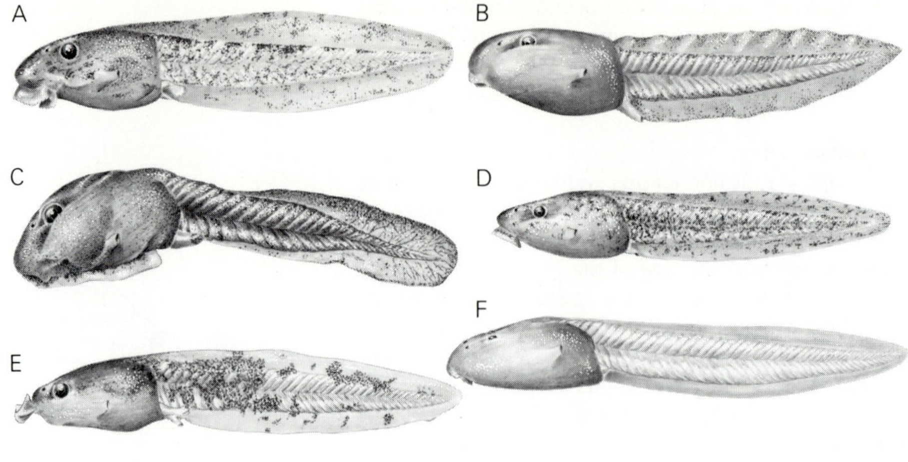

Figure 6-15. Adaptive types of tadpoles in streams. **A.** *Hyla rivularis,* a riffle inhabitant. **B.** *Hyla lindae,* a riffle inhabitant. **C.** *Atelopus ignescens,* with suctorial disc for clinging to stones. **D.** *Hyla uranochroa,* an inhabitant of pools. **E.** *Colostethus nubicola,* with upturned terminal mouth for clinging to lee sides of stones. **F.** *Centrolenella griffithsi,* with an elongate body and reduced fins for living in litter or gravel.

and perhaps all, of these filter-feeders form conspecific aggregations in midwater and have characteristic orientations—level in *Rhinophrynus,* head down at about a 45° angle in pipids, and head up at about a 45° angle in *Kassina* and phyllomedusine hylids. The tadpoles maintain their positions by constantly fluttering the tips of their tails.

Tadpoles of many groups of frogs inhabit streams. Some of these remain in quiet pools and exhibit no particular morphological adaptations to life in flowing water, although some have proportionately longer tails and shallower caudal fins than is characteristic of tadpoles inhabiting ponds. Most stream-adapted tadpoles have ventral mouths, depressed bodies, long muscular tails, and shallow fleshy fins (Fig. 6-15). These tadpoles usually remain on or near the substrate, and they characteristically maintain their position in the current by facing upstream and maintaining constant caudal movement. However, in quiet pools they orient in various directions and may feed amidst accumulated leaf litter or other detritus. Most stream tadpoles are grazers on algae growing on rocks in the streams. These tadpoles have enlarged mouths, usually completely bordered by two or more rows of labial papillae, but in some stream tadpoles the median part of the upper lip is bare. The number of rows of denticles is highly variable; in some it is the same as in many pond tadpoles (i.e., 2 upper and 3 lower rows), but the denticles are large and the rows long, extending to the labial papillae (Fig. 6-16). Some stream tadpoles have many rows of denticles, as many as 9 upper and 14 lower rows in *Hyla claresignata* (B. Lutz and Orton, 1946) and 4 upper and 17 lower rows in *Heleophryne purcelli,* which lacks beaks (Wager, 1965). The multiplication of rows of denticles in a large mouth occurs in tadpoles of many families of anurans, including the pelobatids of the genus *Scutiger,* the myobatrachid *Megistolotis,* the African *Heleophryne,* many hylids (some species of *Hyla, Litoria, Nyctimystes,* and *Ptychohyla),* and many ranids *(Conraua, Petropedetes, Trichobatrachus,* and some Asian *Rana).* Commonly these tadpoles, as well as many stream-adapted

tadpoles with no multiplication of rows of denticles, have robust beaks with large serrations.

Some stream-inhabiting tadpoles are able to survive in torrential streams, but a clear distinction cannot be made between stream and torrent tadpoles. Many of the tadpoles that have large mouths and many rows of denticles not only use these buccal structures for scraping moss off rocks but also use their mouths for holding onto rocks and thereby maintaining their positions in the strong current. However, some torrent-adapted tadpoles have developed a suctorial ventral disc with which they adhere to rocks. Such a disc is present in the tadpoles of *Ascaphus,* the bufonids *Ansonia* and *Atelopus,* and the ranid *Amolops* (Fig. 6-16C). Their suctorial discs are sufficiently effective that the tadpoles have to be pried off rocks; tadpoles of *Atelopus* even adhere to the undersides of rocks (Duellman and Lynch, 1969). The ventral musculature is highly modified in the tadpoles of *Amolops* (Noble, 1929a) and presumably so in the other genera; furthermore, the lungs are small and develop late in larval life. The mouths of these torrent-adapted tadpoles apparently function in the same way as those stream tadpoles that lack suctorial discs, except that the scraping action of the denticles takes place within the oral discs. Tadpoles of *Ascaphus truei* can extract food particles from suspension (Altig and Brodie, 1972), but, as noted by Gradwell (1973) and Wassersug (1980), there is no support for Noble's (1927b) suggestion that these tadpoles take in food through their nares.

Some stream-inhabiting tadpoles have funnel-shaped mouths (Fig. 6-16D). Tadpoles of this type (e.g., pelobatids of the genus *Leptobrachium* and members of the *Hyla uranochroa* and *Ptychohyla schmidtorum* groups) inhabit relatively quiet pools in streams and feed on loose particles of food. The reduction of the denticles suggests that they do not scrape moss or algae from rocks like those stream tadpoles with large mouths and well-developed denticles. The dendrobatid *Colostethus nubicola* has a terminal funnel mouth (Fig. 6-15E) and feeds along the lee and undersides of rocks in streams. Tadpoles of

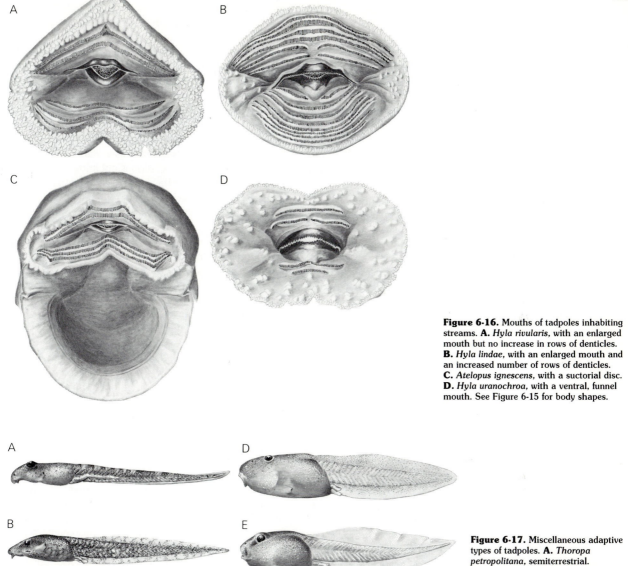

Figure 6-16. Mouths of tadpoles inhabiting streams. **A.** *Hyla rivularis*, with an enlarged mouth but no increase in rows of denticles. **B.** *Hyla lindae*, with an enlarged mouth and an increased number of rows of denticles. **C.** *Atelopus ignescens*, with a suctorial disc. **D.** *Hyla uranochroa*, with a ventral, funnel mouth. See Figure 6-15 for body shapes.

Figure 6-17. Miscellaneous adaptive types of tadpoles. **A.** *Thoropa petropolitana*, semiterrestrial. **B.** *Leptopelis hyloides*, terrestrial to aquatic. **C.** *Hyla bromeliacia*, an inhabitant of arboreal bromeliads. **D.** *Anotheca spinosa*, oophagous. **E.** *Ceratophrys cornuta*, carnivorous. **F.** *Stephopaedes anotis*, with fleshy crown surrounding eyes and nares.

centrolenid frogs have relatively small, unmodified mouths but greatly elongated bodies and tails with reduced, fleshy fins (Fig. 6-15F). Although they develop in fast-flowing streams, these tadpoles generally do not live in open water. Instead they are in the gravel or under rocks on the bottom of the streams and thus are not subjected to the rigors of flowing water. Their morphology seems to be an adaptation for movement within the gravelly substrate.

This same type of morphology is even more extreme in the semiterrestrial larvae of some South American leptodactylids. Tadpoles of *Cycloramphus fuliginosus* and species of *Thoropa* wriggle though mud and creep over wet rock faces (Wassersug and Heyer, 1983). In these tadpoles the fins are greatly reduced on the extremely long, muscular tail; the body is elongated and depressed, and the ventral part of the body may be flattened and expanded (Fig. 6-17A). The mouth is slightly enlarged, and there is no proliferation of denticles. These tadpoles are very much like those of the closely related *C. stejnegeri,* which have reduced mouthparts and complete their development with nutrients provided by the yolk (Heyer and Crombie, 1979).

Other kinds of tadpoles have long, muscular tails and reduced fins as adaptations for movement across wet ground, in shallow cracks, or on leaves. Also the long tails may be important as respiratory structures. Tadpoles of the hyperoliid genus *Leptopelis* have relatively long tails and reduced fins (Fig. 6-17B); these tadpoles wriggle from a terrestrial nest to ponds (Oldham, 1977). Tadpoles of *Leptodactylus rugosus* also have long, muscular tails with reduced fins; these slender tadpoles live in shallow cracks on granitic rock and can move from one water-filled crack to another by violently flipping the tail and thus propelling themselves across rock. Some tadpoles that live in bromeliads, such as *Osteopilus brunneus* and *Hyla marianae* in Jamaica (E. Dunn, 1926a) and *H. bromeliacia* and *H. dendroscarta* in Middle America (Duellman, 1970) also have elongate bodies and muscular tails with low fins (Fig. 6-17C). These tadpoles move about on the wet leaves of arboreal bromeliads.

Various tadpoles that develop in bromeliads or tree-holes eat anuran eggs. Oophagous habits are known for some Jamaican and Central American *Hyla* (E. Dunn, 1926a, 1937), *Anotheca* (E. Taylor, 1954), some species of *Dendrobates* (Weygoldt, 1980; H. Zimmerman and E. Zimmerman, 1981), *Philautus* (Wassersug et al., 1981), and *Hoplophryne* (Noble, 1929a). The mouths of these tadpoles are terminal or subterminal and have large beaks but few or no denticles (Fig. 6-17D).

Many kinds of tadpoles are facultatively carnivorous and are cannibalistic under crowded conditions or with a limited food supply. Tadpoles of *Dendrobates auratus* developing in a water-filled cavity in a log have been observed to grow at different rates, with the larger individuals eventually eating their smaller siblings. Carnivory, especially cannibalism, is common among tadpoles that develop in temporary ponds in arid regions; this has been noted especially for *Rhinophrynus, Scaphiopus, Lepidobatrachus,* and *Pyxicephalus. Lechriodus* not only feeds on tadpoles but carcasses of dead frogs (A. Martin, 1968). The tadpoles of *Leptodactylus pentadactylus* are notorious predators on other kinds of tadpoles (Heyer et al., 1975; Kluge, 1981). However, most of these tadpoles do not exhibit any specific adaptations for carnivory like those of *Ceratophrys* that have anterior mouths, relatively massive jaw musculature, and large," strongly serrated beaks (Figs. 6-13D, 6-17E).

The presumably predaceous tadpole of the microhylid *Otophryne robusta,* which develops in sand bars in streams, is unique among known tadpoles in having a long, sinistral spiracular tube that extends posteriorly to the midlength of the tail and a single row of long, pointed denticle-like structures on the margin of each jaw (Pyburn, 1980b). Beaks and normal labial denticles are absent, and the sharp "denticles" protrude from the upper jaw and are concealed by a fleshy fold on the lower jaw (Fig. 6-9). Each "denticle" is composed of thin, hard layers of cornified tissue; the outer layers apparently are shed as the "denticle" grows.

The same feeding mechanisms are involved whether the food eaten is phytoplankton, periphyton, small aquatic organisms, or amphibian larvae. Thus, the hyobranchial pump mechanism operates more or less continuously in nektonic *Xenopus* tadpoles, but it is this same pumping mechanism that is used in the ingestion of small aquatic invertebrates by *Hymenochirus* (Sokol, 1962, 1969). Oophagous tadpoles apparently ingest entire anuran eggs, but the mechanism of ingestion is not known. Two genera of African bufonids have tadpoles that differ from all others by having a thick crown surrounding the eyes and nostrils, with the mouth opening just below the ventral edge of the crown (Fig. 6-17F). The tadpoles of *Stephopaedes anotis* were observed in a stagnant pool between tree buttresses; the crown was in contact with the air while the tadpoles clung to the bark in a tail-down position (Channing, 1978). The crown, composed of spongy connective tissue, may be an accessory respiratory surface or may function to keep surface scum away from the nostrils (Channing, 1978). In *Mertensophryne micranotis* the crown is used to suspend the tadpole at the surface (Grandison and Ashe, 1983).

The recent discoveries of peculiar modifications of some African bufonids and the tadpole of *Otophryne robusta* reveal that there still is much to be learned about the structural modifications and their functional significance in tadpoles.

PHYSIOLOGY AND ECOLOGY

Amphibian larvae develop in a great variety of aquatic habitats. Some occur in environmentally stable habitats having nearly constant temperature and oxygen concentrations, whereas others develop in environmentally less stable aquatic situations that are subject to considerable variations in temperature and therefore oxygen concentrations. Some of these environmental variables affect respiratory and growth rates and provide constraints on the adaptive types of larvae that can develop successfully in different aquatic habitats. Moreover, some combinations of these environmental variables may influence the behavior of the larvae. Population dynamics of larvae are treated in Chapters 2 and 11, and interspecific interactions are discussed in Chapter 12.

Phototaxis

Although most adult amphibians are negatively phototactic, larvae exhibit a variety of responses to light. Generally salamander larvae in ponds and anuran larvae in streams are negatively phototactic, whereas the opposite is true in salamander larvae in streams and anuran larvae in ponds. However, there are exceptions and even ontogenetic shifts in phototactic responses.

Observations on activity cycles of *Ambystoma* reveal

that larvae developing in ponds at low elevations, where temperatures are relatively warm, are negatively phototactic (J. Anderson and Graham, 1967; J. Anderson and Williamson, 1974; Marangio, 1975). However, larvae developing in montane streams or lakes, where temperatures are comparatively cooler, are positively phototactic (J. Anderson and Worthington, 1971; J. Anderson, 1972). A notable exception is *A. maculatum,* which is positively phototactic in warm ponds (C. Schneider, 1968). Abrupt changes in light intensity have the most noticeable effect in phototactic response of *A. opacum;* normally larvae migrate into open water of ponds on dark nights. This is especially so on dark nights following bright, sunny days; there is less noticeable activity on cloudy days or moonlit nights, but a total eclipse of the moon resulted in rapid migration of larvae to open water (Hassinger and J. Anderson, 1970). Nocturnal activity by *Ambystoma* larvae does not result in distinct stratification of larvae in the water column (L. Branch and Altig, 1981). The floating behavior by *A. tigrinum* larvae is dependent on buoyancy; air breathing and availability of pelagic prey are correlated with floating (Lannoo and M. Bachmann, 1984b).

Positive phototaxis has been demonstrated or observed in tadpoles of many species of the genera *Bufo, Hyla,* and *Rana,* plus *Xenopus laevis* and *Agalychnis callidryas* inhabiting warm ponds (Ashby, 1969; Duellman, 1970; R. Jaeger and Hailman, 1976; Beiswenger, 1977). Likewise, tadpoles of *B. canorus* and *R. pretiosa* inhabiting cold montane ponds are positively phototactic (Mullally, 1953; L. Licht, 1975). Also, Duellman and Trueb have observed positive phototaxis in tadpoles of *B. spinulosus, Pleurodema marmorata, Gastrotheca marsupiata,* and *G. riobambae* in cold ponds at high elevations in the Andes.

Tadpoles inhabiting cool montane streams seem to be negatively phototactic; this conclusion is based on the observations of *Ascaphus truei* by deVlaming and Bury (1970) and Duellman and Trueb's extensive observations on many species of *Hyla, Plectrohyla, Ptychohyla,* and *Telmatobius.* If tadpoles of these species are active at all by day, they tend to be in shaded areas of the streams. Pools in streams that seem to be devoid of tadpoles by day may contain many individuals at night.

Limited data are available on ontogenetic changes in phototaxis during the larval stages. Larvae of *Ambystoma opacum* are positively phototactic until their hindlimbs are fully developed; subsequently they are negatively phototactic (Marangio, 1975). Young larval *Eurycea bislineata* are less sensitive to light than older larvae (J. Wood, 1951). Ontogenetic spectral shifts in phototaxis have been demonstrated in *Xenopus laevis, Bufo americanus, Rana pipiens,* and *R. temporaria* (Muntz, 1963b; R. Jaeger and Hailman, 1976). At early stages the response was strongly toward green light; at midstages response to blue and green were nearly equal, but preference for blue predominated after the eruption of the forelimbs. There is an ontogenetic spectral shift to shorter wavelengths in

absorption by visual pigments (Liebman and Entine, 1968), and this could account for the ontogenetic changes in phototactic responses.

Investigations on compass orientation in larval amphibians have shown that there is a Y-axis orientation. Celestial orientation in tadpoles of *Bufo woodhousii, Rana catesbeiana, R. clamitans,* and *Gastrophryne carolinensis* is away from the shoreline toward deeper water until metamorphosis, when orientation shifts 180° toward land (Goodyear and Altig, 1971; Justis and D. Taylor, 1976). Larvae of *Ambystoma maculatum, opacum, talpoideum* and *tigrinum* use solar cues in Y-axis orientation and also have the same 180° shift in orientation at metamorphosis (Tomson and Ferguson, 1972; D. Taylor, 1972). Larvae of *A. tigrinum* and *R. catesbeiana* can perceive solar cues extraocularly for sun-compass orientation and for synchronization of their biological clocks; experimental results suggest that the pineal body and/or frontal organ are involved in extraocular photoreception (D. Taylor, 1972; Justis and D. Taylor, 1976).

Some of the observed phototactic behaviors of amphibian larvae may be partial responses to temperature gradients. Vertical migration and interspecific stratification in ponds at night by *Ambystoma* larvae may be initiated by darkness with subsequent stratification dependent on different preferred temperatures. Because the larvae are feeding in open water at night, their vertical migration and stratification also could be influenced by the spatial distribution of prey in the water column (J. Anderson and Graham, 1967). In pond-dwelling tadpoles, response to increasing light intensity rather than to more slowly increasing temperature would give larvae additional time in the morning for feeding and moving into optimal areas; positive phototaxis also allows the tadpoles to anticipate heating of shallow areas and to move into them just as they are beginning to warm, thus providing maximum use of the heat for metabolism and growth. Therefore, tadpoles aggregating in warm shallow water may have responded initially to light (Beiswenger, 1977). Likewise, negative phototaxis among stream-inhabiting tadpoles may be important in the avoidance of pools in which temperatures exceed their thermal preferences.

However, not all phototactic responses may be so simple. The Y-axis orientation away from shore seems to contradict the general observations of the influences of light and temperature on aggregation in warm shallow water. Therefore, this orientation may be more closely associated with escape behavior, for when tadpoles in shallow water are disturbed they invariably flee away from shore. The green spectral preference of tadpoles without hindlimbs can be associated with green plants (Muntz, 1963b); perhaps color vision, along with olfaction, is important in locating food (R. Jaeger and Hailman, 1976).

Thermal Preferences and Tolerances
It is well known that aquatic ectotherms adopt various behavioral, biochemical, and physiological strategies to minimize the effects of varying ambient temperature on

their metabolic processes. The difficulty in assessing the temperature responses of amphibian larvae in nature and the variation in experimental design of laboratory studies lead to difficulty in ascertaining the effects of temperature on the larvae in nature. Consequently, different studies have provided conflicting results. Metabolic compensation may be determined from a rate-temperature curve of temperature-dependent rate functions; in ectotherms this curve may be modified by the organism's previous thermal experience.

Thermal preferences in larvae of *Ambystoma tigrinum, Rana catesbeiana,* and *R. pipiens* are dependent on their previous acclimation (Lucas and Reynolds, 1960). Heat resistance in tadpoles of *Scaphiopus couchii, S. hammondii, Hyla regilla,* and *Osteopilus septentrionalis* can be increased by warm thermal histories (H. Brown, 1969). These observations suggest compensatory abilities. However, experiments on tadpoles of *R. pipiens* (G. Parker, 1967) and *Limnodynastes peroni* (B. Marshall and Grigg, 1980) showed an absence of ability to acclimate metabolically.

Most experiments with temperature adaptations of amphibian larvae have emphasized critical thermal maxima with respect to thermal acclimation. Larvae acclimated at higher temperatures have greater heat resistance and therefore higher thermal maxima than larvae acclimated to lower temperatures (Fig. 6-18). The tadpoles of most anurans succumb at temperatures of 38 to 40°C, but some species that develop in shallow ponds in xeric or tropical regions tolerate higher temperatures—above 41°C in *Scaphiopus couchii* and *Osteopilus septentrionalis* (H. Brown, 1969), 39.2°C in *Cyclorana cultripes, C. platycephala,* and *Litoria rubella* (Main, 1968), 40.4°C in *Leptodactylus albilabris* (Heatwole et al, 1968), 42°C in *Rana cancrivora* (Dunson, 1977), and 41.8°C in *Bufo terrestris* (Noland and Ultsch, 1981). However, amphib-

ians that live in cooler environments usually have notably lower tolerances to heat. The highest temperatures tolerated (LD_{50}) by *Rana sylvatica* in Alaska is 36°C (Herreid and Kinney, 1967), and larvae of newts, *Taricha rivularis,* tolerate temperatures of only 34°C (P. Licht and A. Brown, 1967).

Different species living under the same climatic regime exhibit differences in tolerances to rates of heating. In Puerto Rico, tadpoles of *Leptodactylus albilabris* heated at a rate of 1°C/minute died at temperatures of 39.5 to 41.0°C, whereas those heated at 1°C/5 minute survived until temperatures of 40 to 42°C; tadpoles of *Bufo marinus* heated at the two rates all died at 44 to 45.6°C (Heatwole et al., 1968).

However, in nature and in laboratory experiments providing a thermal gradient, larvae demonstrate preferred temperatures. These range from 9 to 29°C in *Rana sylvatica* with a mode of 19 to 20°C (Herreid and Kinney, 1967), whereas the mode is 30°C in *Bufo terrestris* (Noland and Ultsch, 1981), but only 23 to 24°C in *Taricha rivularis* (P. Licht and A. Brown, 1967) and 25°C in *Ambystoma tigrinum* (Lucas and Reynolds, 1960).

In most studies in which developmental stage has been associated with temperature, the results show that younger larvae have greater heat resistance and broader ranges of tolerance than older larvae. However, first-year tadpoles of *Ascaphus truei* prefer temperatures below 10°C, whereas second-year tadpoles prefer temperatures of 10 to 22°C (deVlaming and Bury, 1970).

Intraspecific geographic and altitudinal differences in heat tolerances are known for a few larvae. Montane larvae of *Ambystoma tigrinum* acclimated at 20°C tolerated significantly higher critical maximum temperatures than larvae from low deserts, but larvae from both sites acclimated at 10°C showed no significant differences (Delson and Whitford, 1973). This is the opposite of the gradient observed in *Pseudacris triseriata,* in which tadpoles from lower elevations had higher critical thermal maxima than those from the high mountains (Hoppe, 1978). On the other hand, no significant differences were found in heat resistance between lowland and highland tadpoles of *Leptodactylus albilabris* (Heatwole et al., 1968).

Studies on the role of temperature adaptation in the ecology and distribution of amphibians generally support Ushakov's (1964) contention that differences in temperature tolerances are important in speciation. This idea is supported further by the intermediate temperature tolerances of hybrids between parental species *Scaphiopus hammondii* and *S. multiplicatus* (H. Brown, 1969).

Respiration

Respiration by amphibian larvae may be branchial, cutaneous, and/or pulmonary. Thorough studies have involved only a few species of *Ambystoma, Xenopus, Bufo,* and *Rana.* From the results of these limited investigations, some generalities seem to be apparent, but application of them to the broad spectrum of amphibian larvae must

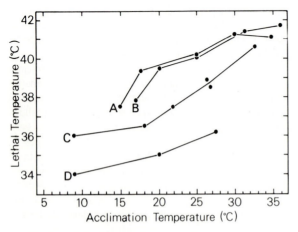

Figure 6-18. Relationships between incipient lethal temperature (LD_{50}) and acclimation temperature in tadpoles. **A.** *Scaphiopus couchii.* **B.** *Osteopilus septentrionalis.* **C.** *Scaphiopus hammondii.* **D.** *Hyla regilla.* Adapted from H. Brown (1969).

be done with caution and necessarily should include careful comparative studies.

Among salamander larvae, at high oxygen concentrations the gills perform only a small part of the total respiration; the majority is cutaneous. At low oxygen concentrations, larvae of *Ambystoma maculatum* that have had their gills removed have lower respiratory rates than larvae with gills (Boell et al., 1963). Experiments on unaltered larvae of the same species show that during their development larvae become progressively less tolerant of low oxygen concentrations (L. Branch and D. Taylor, 1977). In experiments by Bond (1960), the fimbrial area of gills of *A. jeffersonianum, A. opacum,* and *Salamandra salamandra* increase in size in response to lowered oxygen concentrations. These changes involve an increase in number and size of cells in the fimbrae; however, the changes are reversible, depending on the oxygen concentration. The mudpuppy, *Necturus maculosus,* relies largely on cutaneous respiration at low temperatures, but at higher temperatures (and therefore lower oxygen concentrations) or when the salamanders are disturbed, the gills assume the dominant role in respiration (Guimond and V. Hutchinson, 1972). Likewise, at 25°C larval *A. tigrinum* take in about 59% of their total oxygen from the water; the rest is acquired via the lungs by gulping air (Whitford and R. Sherman, 1968).

Respiratory rates for larval anurans were summarized by Feder (1981), who demonstrated that body size, trophic state, diel cycles, and experimental stress all influenced rates of oxygen consumption by tadpoles of *Xenopus laevis* and *Rana berlandieri;* he concluded that the results of much of the earlier work on metabolic rates of tadpoles must be viewed with caution because most investigators had not recognized the effects of these variables. Experiments with larvae of *Hymenochirus boettgeri, X. laevis, Bufo woodhousii,* and *R. berlandieri* (Feder, 1981, 1982c) have shown that at a constant temperature body size accounts for most of the variance in rates of oxygen consumption in these tadpoles and that reported differences in rates at different developmental stages are related to size. There is an increased rate of oxygen consumption with increased size; however, in late developmental stages of some *X. laevis,* oxygen consumption decreases, presumably because of their reduced physical activity. Rates of oxygen consumption increase with higher temperatures in tadpoles of *R. pipiens* (G. Parker, 1967) and *Limnodynastes peroni* (B. Marshall and Grigg, 1980).

Amphibian larvae with lungs respond to low concentrations of oxygen by increasing the rate of pulmonary ventilation (Wassersug and Seibert, 1975). They also may increase the rates of branchial irrigation (N. West and Burggren, 1982) and anaerobic metabolism (Weigmann and Altig, 1975).

As the amount of dissolved oxygen decreases, most tadpoles can consume more oxygen by gulping air. This behavior is especially conspicuous in pond-inhabiting tadpoles that develop lungs early in their larval life. Lungs do not develop until just before metamorphosis in stream-adapted larvae and in *Bufo;* thus, these tadpoles cannot effectively consume oxygen by gulping air. Gulping air is unnecessary by tadpoles in well-oxygenated streams; furthermore, air bubbles would increase their buoyancy, which would be detrimental to hydrodynamics. At low concentrations of oxygen, *Bufo* tadpoles swim at the surface of the water; at such times these tadpoles may supplement branchial respiration with cutaneous respiration.

The relationships among oxygen content, body size, respiratory behavior, and locomotor stamina in tadpoles of *Xenopus laevis, Bufo americanus,* and *Rana berlandieri* were investigated by Feder (1983a), who demonstrated that respiratory patterns may have major effects on locomotor capacities and that locomotion may alter respiratory patterns. The problems of gas exchange are associated with those of hydrodynamics and locomotion in the following ways: (1) locomotor activity increases the demand for oxygen either during activity, after activity ceases (oxygen debt), or both; (2) aerial and aquatic respiratory surfaces are important in meeting this increased oxygen demand; (3) irrigation of aquatic respiratory surfaces (gills) is in part counterproductive because it increases drag and therefore locomotor effort; (4) ventilation of aerial respiratory surfaces (gulping air) is in part counterproductive because it increases buoyancy and promotes hydrodynamic instability (at least in flowing water); and (5) any increase in respiratory activity may increase the demand for oxygen.

Tadpoles of some species are capable of existing out of water in moist terrestrial environments, but respiratory rates of such tadpoles have not been studied. Tadpoles of *Leptodactylus albilabris* hatch from eggs laid in terrestrial chambers that subsequently are flooded. These tadpoles have been maintained on moist cotton in the laboratory for up to 40 days; under these conditions the respiratory rates declined greatly but returned to normal when the tadpoles were replaced in water (Candelas et al., 1961).

Salt Balance

Most amphibian larvae are intolerant of saline conditions, and their nitrogenous wastes are almost exclusively ammonia, which is readily diluted in water. However, there are exceptions to both of these generalities.

In Sweden, *Bufo viridis* frequently breeds in brackish water, and tadpoles survive in water that is 15% of the salt concentration of sea water (Gislén and Kauri, 1959). *Rana cancrivora* is a common inhabitant of brackish mangrove swamps in southeastern Asia, and its tadpoles are capable of development in brackish water. Experiments by Dunson (1977) showed 100% survival of tadpoles in concentrations up to 40% sea water and more than 50% survival in concentrations of 80% sea water.

The tadpoles of some species of leptodactylids that develop in foam nests have high tolerances to urea. Tadpoles of *Leptodactylus albilabris* (Candelas and Gomez,

1963) and *L. bufonius* (Shoemaker and McClanahan, 1973) initiate a high level of urea production as embryos (see Chapter 5); throughout their larval development they have rates of nitrogen excretion essentially equivalent to those of other kinds of tadpoles, but in these species of *Leptodactylus* the level of ammonia excretion remains nearly constant while the rate of urea excretion increases with age, only to decline at metamorphosis. Possibly the ratio of urea to ammonia is determined by the total rate of nitrogen excretion, but the percentage of total nitrogen excreted as ammonia also may be related to the availability of water.

Feeding

Most salamander larvae feed indiscriminately on aquatic invertebrates of appropriate sizes. However, some larval newts *(Notophthalmus* and *Triturus)* feed on algae (C. Pope, 1924; Creed, 1964). In some populations of *Ambystoma tigrinum,* larvae have a coiled gut, perhaps indicative of herbivory (Tilley, 1964). The limited evidence on ontogenetic changes in food and foraging strategies of salamander larvae suggests that these differences are partly associated with gape-limited predation. Young larval *A. macrodactylum* are rather sedentary and simply snap at prey passing by, whereas older larvae are much more agile and stalk prey (J. Anderson, 1967). Likewise, young larval *A. opacum* feed on the bottom of ponds, whereas larger larvae actively forage in the water column (J. Anderson and Graham, 1967; Marangio, 1975). A similar ontogenetic shift in feeding behavior occurs in larvae of *Triturus vulgaris,* for which G. Bell (1975) suggested that an exponential rate of weight gain forces larger larvae to switch from passive to active foraging, thus enabling them to catch larger prey but at the expense of incurring a higher rate of mortality. In the stream-dwelling *Leurognathus marmoratus,* diets of larvae are composed of nearly the same diversity of insects as the aquatic adults, except that the adults eat larger prey (Martof and D. Scott, 1957). On the other hand, learned microhabitat

selection may be important in the selection of prey types. Henderson (1973) showed that larval *A. gracile* selected particular microhabitats through increased encounter rates of prey types in association with a particular microhabitat.

Larvae of many kinds of salamanders are known to prey on smaller amphibian larvae, especially under laboratory conditions when the food supply is inadequate, but there also are documented cases of this behavior in nature. The large larvae of *Dicamptodon ensatus* are especially predatory. At one site, tadpoles of *Ascaphus truei* formed 14% of the diet (Metter, 1963), and at another site 39% of the stomach contents were larvae of *Ambystoma gracile* (C. Johnson and Schreck, 1969). Larvae of *Ambystoma tigrinum* feed on larvae of *Rana sylvatica* and other species of *Ambystoma* (Wilbur, 1972). Larvae of *Triturus alpestris* prey on tadpoles of several sympatric anurans—*Bombina variegata, Rana ridibunda,* and *R. temporaria,* but not on *Bufo calamita* (Heusser, 1971). In alpine ponds, larger larvae of *Salamandra salamandra* feed on smaller conspecifics (Parâtre, 1894); the same occurs in *Typhlotriton speleaus* in subterranean waters (C. C. Smith, 1959). Cannibalism in these populations may be the result of low incidence of other kinds of food.

In some populations of *Ambystoma tigrinum* three larval and adult morphs are found. A large morph inhabits permanent ponds and commonly does not metamorphose; a small morph inhabits ephemeral ponds and metamorphoses. The larvae of these two morphs are normal in their morphology and feeding habits for pond-dwelling *Ambystoma*. Cannibal morphs are like the small morphs in habitat and life history, but they have disproportionately large heads, wide mouths, and elongate teeth (Fig. 6-19), and they prey on conspecific larvae (F. Rose and Armentrout, 1976). Slight differences in allozyme frequencies exist between cannibals and noncannibals, but these are less than the magnitude of differences between subspecies of *A. tigrinum* (Pierce et al., 1981). Experiments by Collins and Cheek (1983) suggest that

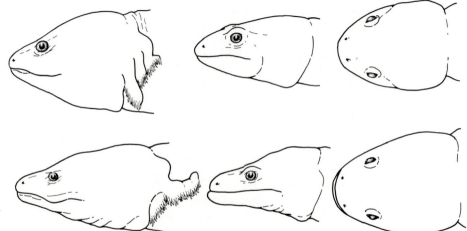

Figure 6-19. Normal and cannibalistic morphs of *Ambystoma tigrinum.* Upper row—larval and adult normal morph. Lower row—larval and adult cannibalistic morph. Adapted from F. Rose and Armentrout (1976).

larval density stimulated expression of cannibalistic traits. The adaptive significance of the cannibalistic morphs involves not only greater prey availability because of increased gape but also more rapid growth and therefore earlier metamorphosis (Lannoo and M. Bachmann, 1984a).

In contrast to the larvae of salamanders, anuran larvae are primarily highly specialized filter-feeders. Tadpoles have a mechanism for extracting suspended particles of food from water (Kenny, 1969b, Severtzov, 1969; Wassersug, 1972). The following synthesis of feeding is summarized from Wassersug (1980).

Most of the internal oral structures of tadpoles make up a multitiered, particle-entrapping system that is capable of sorting particles by size. Direct interception and inertial impaction are used to different extents on various surfaces. The mucous surfaces of the branchial food traps, together with the gill filters of the pharynx, can trap the smallest particles ingested by typical pond larvae. Large particles are strained from the water by buccal papillae and funneled directly into the esophagus, thereby bypassing most of the pharynx. This size-sorting mechanism protects the delicate pharyngeal surfaces from clogging or damage by large particles.

From the size, shape, number, and arrangement of buccal and pharyngeal structures, it is possible to infer the size of the particles on which a species feeds most efficiently. Intraspecific differences in these structures presumably reflect differences in size distribution of food particles in the microhabitats of the tadpoles. Compared with generalized tadpoles, in extreme macrophagous larvae (e.g., *Hyla leucophyllata* and *H. microcephala* groups and *Occidozyga*) all pharyngeal structures associated with planktonic entrapment are reduced. Larvae that are obligate microphagous suspension feeders in midwater (e.g., *Xenopus* and many phyllomedusine hylids) have the opposite extreme; they have large branchial baskets and dense gill filters that effectively entrap small phytoplankton. Stream-inhabiting tadpoles are benthic and thigmotactic (e.g., *Ansonia, Atelopus,* and *Plectrohyla*). By scraping periphyton with their keratinized mouthparts, they create a coarse suspension of particles; they have closely spaced, supernumerary buccal papillae for straining coarse particles but highly porous gill filters not suited for the entrapment of ultraplankton. Umbrella-mouthed tadpoles (e.g., *Megophrys* and some *Microhyla*) feed selectively on large particles floating on the surface of the water; instead of buccal papillae, they have ridges that sort coarse particles.

Developmental differences among siblings of *Scaphiopus bombifrons* result in some individuals developing normally as scraping suspension feeders and others developing larger and more serrate beaks, enlarged jaw muscles, and modifications of the denticles (Orton, 1954; Bragg, 1965). The latter are highly predaceous on tadpoles of other species of *Scaphiopus* and are even cannibalistic.

Further details about feeding and foraging strategies in tadpoles are included in the foregoing section: Adaptive Types of Larvae. In addition to the oophagous species discussed there, other species have been observed to ingest amphibian eggs. This facultative habit is known for tadpoles of *Rana temporaria,* which eat conspecific eggs, as well as those of six other anurans (Heusser, 1970a). A tadpole of *Leptodactylus labyrinthicus* ate eggs of *Hyla albopunctata* (Cardoso and Sazima, 1977).

Growth

Growth rates are dependent primarily on temperature and food availability. Most pond-dwelling larvae have a sigmoidal growth curve, whereas the rate in stream-dwelling salamander larvae is more nearly curvilinear. There is a positive correlation between growth rate and ovum size in *Ambystoma maculatum* (DuShane and C. Hutchinson, 1944). Growth studies of *Ambystoma* summarized by Salthe and Mecham (1974) show that larvae of *A. tigrinum* grow faster than those of *A. maculatum* and that larvae of *A. mexicanum* grow faster than those of *A. opacum*. Also, growth rates in a cohort of *A. tigrinum* were found to be more variable than the rates in a cohort of *A. maculatum* (C. Hutchinson and Hewitt, 1935). Higher respiratory rates of *A. tigrinum* larvae, as compared with *A. maculatum* (Hopkins and Handford, 1943), correlate with the differences in growth rates in these two species.

Growth rates within cohorts of anuran larvae are known to be highly variable. This variation has been attributed to the availability of food and to a growth inhibition substance. However, Travis (1983) showed that in *Hyla gratiosa* the duration of the larval period was inversely related to early larval growth and that this relationship appeared to be strengthened slightly at increased densities. Observations and experiments on tadpoles of European species of *Rana* and *Bufo* (R. Savage, 1952) showed that larger, more aggressive larvae outcompeted smaller siblings for food. Similar results were obtained in studies of *B. americanus* and *R. sylvatica* (Wilbur, 1977b, 1977c).

A "crowding effect" resulting in inhibition of growth of smaller tadpoles by a chemical substance was observed in *Rana pipiens* larvae (C. Richards, 1958; S. Rose, 1960; L. West, 1960). The growth rate of small tadpoles is inhibited when they are raised in water in which larger tadpoles have lived. The growth-inhibiting substance is a proteinaceous compound produced by larger tadpoles (Runkova et al., 1974; Stepanova, 1974). Most laboratory experiments have dealt with intraspecific inhibition effects, but growth rates of young tadpoles of *Bufo calamita* are inhibited when the tadpoles are raised in water conditioned by large tadpoles of *R. temporaria* and *B. bufo,* and especially by older conspecifics (Heusser, 1972a). Moreover, different inhibitory effects were noted for the different members of the *Rana esculenta* complex (Heusser and Blankenhorn, 1973). Intra- and interspecific effects also were found with *Bufo woodhousii* (L.

Licht, 1967) and *R. temporaria* (Heusser, 1972b). Inhibition seems to occur in some natural populations of *R. temporaria* (Pikulik, 1977). However, laboratory experiments on that species (Hodler, 1958) and on *R. pipiens* (Gromko et al., 1973), in which the tadpoles were always provided with an excess of food, showed no growth inhibition. Experiments on the tadpoles of *Scaphiopus holbrooki* by Semlitsch and Caldwell (1982) revealed differential growth rates at high densities. Those tadpoles reared at high densities that gained an early growth advantage presumably metamorphosed at the minimum size possible so as to escape the density stress. This relieved density stress on smaller tadpoles, which then increased their growth rates and size at metamorphosis. These results support Steinwascher's (1978) contention that larger tadpoles of *R. sphenocephala* outcompete smaller ones for food (exploitative competition) and that as the relative level of food decreases, chemical inhibition (interference competition) supplants exploitative competition. Steinwascher suggested that in nature, exploitative and interference mechanisms could be complementary, and a switch to interference mechanisms at low food levels might be common. This suggestion needs to be tested both intra- and interspecifically.

The duration of larval development varies from about 2 weeks in some anurans to as long as 5 years in some salamanders. The most rapid development occurs in anuran larvae developing in temporary ponds in arid environments. North American spadefoots, *Scaphiopus*, are among the most rapidly developing tadpoles—*S. bombifrons* 13–15 days (King, 1960; Voss, 1961), *S. couchii* and *S. holbrooki* 14–15 days (A. H. Wright and A. A. Wright, 1949). The South African ranids *Cacosternum nanum* and *Pyxicephalus adspersus* may metamorphose in 15 and 18 days after hatching, respectively (Wager, 1965). The Australian myobatrachid *Notaden nichollsi* may spend as few as 14 days as a tadpole (Slater and Main, 1963). Although most tropical species of anurans require 3 weeks to 2 months, and temperate species 2 to 3 months, there are some notable exceptions. The North American *Hyla avivoca* requires only 24 days (Volpe et al., 1961).

Tadpoles of some species of *Rana* in North America and Eurasia overwinter in ponds—*R. catesbeiana* (Viparina and Just, 1975), *R. pretiosa* (F. Turner, 1958), *R. rugosa* (Okada, 1966), *R. septentrionalis* (Hedeen, 1971). Tadpoles of *R. clamitans* developing in temporary ponds metamorphose during their first summer, whereas those in permanent water may overwinter (Richmond, 1964). Tadpoles of the large leptodactylid *Caudiverbera caudiverbera* in austral South America commonly require 2 years to metamorphose (Cei, 1962). Tadpoles that develop in cold mountain streams also have long larval development—3 years in *Ascaphus truei* (Noble and P. Putnam, 1931), 2 years in *Heleophryne purcelli* (Wager, 1965), and presumably more than 1 year in *Plectrohyla glandulosa* (Duellman, 1970). Tadpoles of the South Af-

rican *R. fuscigula* may spend 3 years in ponds before metamorphosing (Wager, 1965).

The duration of larval development in salamanders varies from 42 days in *Hemidactylium scutatum* to 5 years in *Cryptobranchus alleganiensis* and *Necturus maculosus* (Bishop, 1941). Larvae of most ambystomatids and salamandrids that develop in ponds require 2 to 5 months from hatching to metamorphosis, but developmental times are longer for species developing in streams—3.5 years in *Rhyacotriton olympicus* (Nussbaum and Tait, 1977) and *Gyrinophilus porphyriticus* (Bishop, 1941), 2 to 3 years in *Eurycea bislineata* (Duellman and J. Wood, 1954), 2 years in *Desmognathus quadramaculatus,* and 1 year in *D. fuscus, monticola,* and *ochrophaeus* (Organ, 1961). Larvae of some *Ambystoma* that breed in the spring overwinter; this is an exception in *A. maculatum* in Maryland (Hillis and R. Miller, 1976) and elsewhere, but it is common in montane populations of *A. macrodactylum* (J. Anderson, 1967), *A. gracile* (Eagleson, 1976), and *A. tigrinum* (Bizer, 1978).

With the exception of food availability, temperature seems to be the major external factor controlling the duration of development and differentiation. Larval development in *Rana catesbeiana* ceases at temperatures of 12.8°C or lower (Viparina and Just, 1975). Low temperatures halt metamorphic processes by depressing neuroendocrine and thyroid activity (Voitkevich, 1963), thereby preventing a rise in circulating thyroid hormones occurring in natural metamorphosis (Just, 1972) and prohibiting tissue responses to existing circulating hormones (Ashley et al., 1968).

Another facet of larval development is the amount of yolk reserve when the larvae hatch. Of course, some larvae have a sufficient amount of yolk to reach metamorphosis (see Chapter 2 for examples). Others are provided with a small amount of yolk that is utilized before the larvae begin to feed. For example, larvae of *Pseudotriton ruber* spend 6 to 10 weeks in streams before they begin to feed (R. Gordon, 1966). Back-riding tadpoles of *Colostethus inguinalis* have a small yolk reserve and grow slightly while adhering to the mother's back (Wells, 1980c).

In general, larvae that reach a large size have a longer larval period than those that metamorphose at a smaller size, but there are numerous exceptions. The aquatic South American frog *Pseudis paradoxa* is renowned for its giant tadpole, which on Trinidad attains a length of 230 mm, whereas adult female frogs are no more than 73 mm long; the tadpoles reach their full size in 4 months (Kenny, 1969a). A great size discrepancy exists between adults and tadpoles of the South African hyperoliid *Kassina maculata;* tadpoles require 8 to 10 months to attain lengths of about 130 mm before metamorphosing into frogs that attain lengths of about 60 mm (Wager, 1965).

The amount of nuclear DNA is negatively correlated with the duration of larval development in a wide variety of anurans (O. Goin et al., 1968). The amount of DNA is positively correlated with metabolic activity. Thus, species that have higher metabolic activity have shorter larval periods.

Therefore, the rate of larval growth and duration of the larval stage is influenced by a number of intrinsic (DNA content, metabolic rate, yolk reserves) and extrinsic factors (temperature, food, inhibitory compounds), as well as absolute size to be reached at metamorphosis. In most amphibians, especially anurans, females are larger than males. In some cases the larger size may be attained by females' utilizing more time from metamorphosis to sexual maturity. On the other hand, in those, as well as species in which both sexes require about the same amount of time to reach sexual maturity, larvae metamorphose at different sizes. It is not known if the larger larvae are destined to become females.

SOCIAL BEHAVIOR

The kinds of cues and responses existing among larval amphibians are poorly known. Although aggregative behavior in anuran larvae has been known for several years, few observations are available for salamanders.

Salamanders

Size-dependent spacing behavior is known to occur in larval and neotenic *Ambystoma* (J. Taylor, 1983). However, most aggregations of larval salamanders seem to result from the diminution of the aquatic habitat; larvae simply congregate in areas of remaining water or moisture. Aggregations of 10 to 50 larvae of *A. tigrinum* were observed in shallow water in a montane pond in Wyoming (Carpenter, 1953); when these aggregations were disturbed, individual larvae scattered, only to reform in a few minutes. Similar aggregations of this species have been interpreted as feeding aggregations (Gehlbach, 1968), but there is no evidence that the individuals in these groups are attracted to any particular food source or that individuals benefit from association with other larvae. Aggregations of metamorphosing individuals of *A. macrodactylum* (J. Anderson, 1967) may be in response to environmental conditions instead of metamorphic synchronization that might result in greater survivorship of young in the face of predation.

Anurans

Tadpoles of many species of anurans are known to be gregarious. Aggregations of tadpoles have been interpreted as simple feeding aggregations, metamorphic aggregations, clusters in response to environmental gradients, and social schools. Since the review and classification of social behavior of tadpoles by Lescure (1968), new observations and experiments suggest some highly organized social interactions among some kinds of tadpoles. Wassersug (1973) classified tadpole aggregations into two broad categories—simple aggregates based on biotaxis other than biosocial mutual attraction and schools based on biosocial attraction. Beiswenger (1975) classified tadpole aggregations according to their functional characteristics.

Aggregations of tadpoles in shallow parts of ponds by day apparently are the result of individual tadpoles' responding to temperature gradients in the water. Experiments by Brattstrom (1962) showed that aggregations of tadpoles actually raised the temperature of surrounding water. However, the diel cycle of tadpoles of *Bufo americanus* is more directly correlated with changes in light rather than temperature (Beiswenger, 1977); the immediate importance of light probably has evolved through the relation between light and temperature. Usually an increase in light intensity in a shallow pond will be followed closely by an increase in temperature. Quite possibly, aggregations of tadpoles of other species also respond primarily to light, as noticed in *Agalychnis callidryas* (Duellman, 1970).

Aggregations of metamorphosing individuals are common in species of *Scaphiopus* (Bragg, 1965) and *Bufo* (Beiswenger, 1975; Arnold and Wassersug, 1978; G. Zug and P. Zug, 1979). Metamorphic synchrony in these species may have evolved as a defense against predation at metamorphosis, a time when anurans are especially vulnerable to predation. Presumably this synchronous metamorphosis satiates predators and results in higher survivorship than if metamorphosis were asynchronous.

The sibling relationships of tadpoles in these observations are not known, but recent experiments with *Bufo americanus* (Waldman, 1981) and *Rana cascadae* (Blaustein and O'Hara, 1981) show that tadpoles recognize their siblings and tend to associate with them rather than with nonsiblings.

Moving schools of tadpoles have been observed in *Rhinophrynus dorsalis* (Stuart, 1961), *Scaphiopus bombifrons* (Bragg, 1965), *Scaphiopus holbrooki* (Richmond, 1947; Bragg, 1968), *Leptodactylus ocellatus* (Vaz-Ferreira and Gehrau, 1975), *Bufo americanus* (Beiswenger, 1975), *Schismaderma carens* (van Dijk, 1972), *Hyla geographica* (Duellman, 1978), *Osteocephalus taurinus* (Duellman and Lescure, 1973), *Phyllomedusa vaillanti* (L. Branch, 1983), *Pyxicephalus adspersus* (van Dijk, 1972), *Rana cascadae* (O'Hara and Blaustein, 1981), and *Phrynomerus annectens* (Channing, 1976).

Essentially stationary schools of tadpoles have been observed in two species that are midwater filter-feeders—*Xenopus laevis* (Wassersug and Hessler, 1971) and *Phyllomedusa tarsius* (Duellman, 1978). In these tadpoles, groups maintain their midwater positions by constantly fluttering the tips of the tails while body axes remain parallel to one another.

Schooling behavior has been interpreted as a mechanism to avoid predation or to enhance feeding. Certainly individuals in large aggregations would be less vulnerable to predation by small potential predators, such as insects and small fishes, than they would be as individuals. This notion has been documented in *Scaphiopus bombifrons,* in which Black (1970) observed that the tadpoles only aggregate in the presence of predaceous cannibalistic congeners or hydrophilid beetle larvae. Avoidance of predation by aggregative behavior in tadpoles of *Leptodactylus ocellatus* is enhanced by the presence of the mother with the tadpoles; she attacks potential predators, such as birds (Vaz-Ferreira and Gehrau, 1975). However, gregariousness in shallow water can result in greater vulnerability to predators; Ideker (1976) observed high rates of predation on such aggregates of *Rana berlandieri* by birds.

Schooling may facilitate feeding. Moving aggregations of *Scaphiopus* and *Bufo* stir up much bottom detritus, thereby creating a rich mixture of suspended particles of food (Richmond, 1947; Bragg, 1965; Beiswenger, 1975). In moving schools of *Osteocephalus taurinus,* the tadpoles circulate within the school so that those at the rear of the school move forward along the bottom of the group and back along the top (Duellman and Lescure, 1973); in this way all individuals come in contact with the substrate, where food is most abundant. Likewise, circulation of tadpoles within moving schools of *B. americanus* results in different individuals' being at the leading edge (Beiswenger, 1975). Groups of midwater filter-feeding tadpoles utilizing parallel orientation may generate more currents than individuals do; consequently they increase the flow of suspended food particles. This idea is substantiated by the fact that weights of tadpoles of *Xenopus laevis* at metamorphosis were positively correlated with the densities at which they had been raised (Katz et al., 1981). Also, tadpoles of *Rhinophrynus dorsalis* raised in isolation grew at a slower rate than those raised in groups (Foster and McDiarmid, 1982).

The mechanisms of tadpole schooling have been investigated experimentally by Wassersug and his associates (Wassersug and Hessler, 1971; Wassersug, 1973; Wassersug et al., 1981; Katz et al., 1981; Breden et al., 1982). These studies have shown that tadpoles of various species can and do orient visually but that other cues also are important, at least in some species. For example, tadpoles of *Xenopus laevis* show parallel orientation in both light and darkness, but in light the uniformity of orientation is greater; also distances between individuals are less in darkness than in light. These observations suggest that orientation is maintained by input into the lateral-line system in darkness and that this is augmented by vision in light. Different sizes are included in the same schools, except that in *Xenopus* parallel orientation is better developed in larger tadpoles and the distances between individuals is proportional to their size.

The results of these experiments partly confirm observations in nature. Vision seems to be the primary mechanism for schooling in tadpoles of *Phrynomerus annectens,* for the tadpoles scatter at night and reform by day (Channing, 1976). Individuals in schools of midwater filter-feeding tadpoles of *Phyllomedusa vaillanti* disperse at night; experiments involving lights at night showed that

in the presence of artificial light the schools remained intact (L. Branch, 1983). However, schools of other midwater filter-feeders (e.g., *Rhinophrynus dorsalis, Phyllomedusa tarsius)* and at least some bottom-feeders (e.g., *Osteocephalus taurinus* and various *Bufo)* maintain their integrity at night, presumably by stimuli other than vision.

Species-specific selection of substrate patterns by tadpoles of *Rana aurora* and *R. cascadae* (Wiens, 1970, 1972) and experimental evidence that tadpoles of *Kaloula pulchra* associate with substrate patterns based on early experience (Punzo, 1976) suggest that visual cues may be most important in maintaining schools. This may be further substantiated by the existence of color vision in tadpoles (R. Jaeger and Hailman, 1976). Vision may be the primary mechanism by which groups of sibling tadpoles of *Hyla rosenbergi* return to their basin-nest after they have been washed out of the nest by high water (Kluge, 1981).

However, vision apparently is not an important factor in sibling recognition. Laboratory experiments with tadpoles of *Bufo americanus* (Waldman and K. Adler, 1979; Waldman, 1981) and *Rana cascadae* (Blaustein and O'Hara, 1981; O'Hara and Blaustein, 1981) have demonstrated conclusively in these species, both of which aggregate in nature, that siblings preferentially associate with one another rather than with nonsiblings. Postembryonic experience with conspecifics is not a prerequisite for sibling preference, because tadpoles of both species raised in isolation later preferentially associated with unfamiliar siblings over unfamiliar nonsiblings. However, tadpoles of both species that were reared with siblings and nonsiblings did not show preferential association, whereas tadpoles raised only in the presence of siblings subsequently showed a preferential association with siblings instead of nonsiblings. Tadpoles of *B. americanus* raised in isolation later preferentially associated with full siblings and maternal siblings over paternal siblings. These findings strongly suggest that tadpoles recognize siblings by some innate mechanism and that the mechanism of recognition may be olfactory. Tadpoles of *R. cascadae* reared in groups from different clutches showed no preferential association with siblings, whereas tadpoles raised only with siblings and later placed in mixed groups preferentially associated with siblings. Thus, tadpoles raised in mixed groups might assimilate and temporarily retain an "odor" of a composite group and be unable to distinguish siblings. Preferential association with maternal over paternal half-siblings in *B. americanus* suggests that the recognition factor is contributed by the mother. Possibly this factor (pheromone or metabolite) is associated with the egg capsules; the attraction to any substance in the egg capsules may be enhanced by the continued association of recently hatched tadpoles with the capsules.

Possibly sibling recognition is a phenomenon characteristic of all tadpole aggregations; if so, this may partially explain the association of tadpoles of the same size in

Bufo woodhousii (Breden et al., 1982) and higher degree of parallel orientation among tadpoles of similar sizes in *Xenopus laevis* (Katz et al., 1981). However, not all aggregations of tadpoles contain individuals of only one size. For example, tadpoles of different sizes compose individual schools of *Rhinophrynus dorsalis* (Stuart, 1961) and *Phrynomerus annectens* (Channing, 1976). Unless there is considerable discrepancy in growth rates, it seems unlikely that all tadpoles in such schools are siblings. Waldman (1982) suggested that in some situations, individuals in schools may increase their inclusive fitness by associating with kin through aposematic advertisement, alarm signaling in response to predation, or kin-influenced growth regulation. Clearly, there is much to learn about tadpole aggregations—their cause, maintenance, and effect on survivorship.

EVOLUTIONARY SIGNIFICANCE OF LARVAE

Amphibians lead two lives—at least, those that have aquatic larvae and are terrestrial as adults have two very different lives. The larvae and adults differ from one another in their modes of respiration and locomotion and also in their diets and feeding—especially anurans. These differences are reflected in the behavior of the organisms and their responses to environmental factors. By utilizing two independent sets of resources, larvae are not in competition with adults for food or shelter.

Therefore, it is obvious that selective pressures are quite different on larvae and adults. For example, two species of tree frogs that live in the same montane rainforest might face nearly the same selective pressures as adults, but if the larvae develop in different kinds of aquatic situations (e.g., temporary ponds versus torrential streams), the tadpoles of the two species face highly different problems. One must have a rapid rate of development in warm water with a low oxygen content, whereas the other must be able to maintain its position and feed in cool, flowing water. Both larvae and adults must be successful in order for the species to survive.

Most amphibians, especially anurans, that have aquatic larvae are r-strategists, in that they have many offspring that undergo rapid development (see Chapter 2). Coincidence of anuran breeding with high productivity in both temporary and permanent ponds provides larvae with an abundance of food. Because of this resource availability, niche overlap among coexisting species can be high and the competitive interactions weak; thus, predation may be a major regulator of larval density (Wassersug, 1975). However, many anurans breed in ephemeral ponds, and desiccation of these ponds can be an important regulator of the abundance of the species, for entire cohorts are eliminated.

Wassersug (1975) emphasized that the suspension-feeding habits and mechanisms of anuran larvae were especially well adapted for highly eutrophic waters in seasonal environments, habitats in which most, if not all, anurans have free-swimming aquatic tadpoles. Moreover, he noted that the amphibious life cycle of anurans constitutes one of the few biotic mechanisms for transport of excessive nutrients out of eutrophic bodies of water into terrestrial ecosystems.

Salamander larvae are essentially aquatic equivalents of the adults. They operate at the same trophic level and undergo comparatively few gross changes at metamorphosis. Thus, salamander larvae probably are most like the larvae of primitive amphibians. The varying degrees of metamorphosis of obligate neotenic salamanders and the facultative neoteny of other species reinforces the structural similarity of larvae and adults. Salamander larvae seem to be evolutionary prisoners, temporarily incarcerated in the aquatic environment because of the necessity that the eggs develop there. Of course, many salamanders, especially plethodontids, have direct development of terrestrial eggs—not necessarily in aseasonal environments, but development taking place in humid microhabitats.

On the other hand, the morphologically and ecologically distinctive anuran larvae represent an adaptive radiation for utilization of the aquatic environment. Their diversification, which goes back at least to the Cretaceous (Nevo, 1968) and probably to the Triassic (Estes and Reig, 1973), probably has been an important part of the overall radiation of anurans. Thus, the coevolution of anurans and their larvae is unique among the vertebrates.

CHAPTER 7

Metamorphosis

Amphibian metamorphosis is commonly envisioned as ... a long-tailed, round-mouthed, fat-bodied polliwog swimming sluggishly among vegetation of a pond and then undergoing extensive alterations without any interruption to business to become a tailless, pop-eyed, insect-eating participant in long-distance jumping contests.

W. Gardner Lynn (1961)

Although ontogenetic metamorphosis occurs in many groups of animals, it is best known in insects and amphibians. Metamorphosis can be defined as a series of abrupt postembryonic changes involving structural, physiological, biochemical, and behavioral transformations. Recent summaries of amphibian metamorphosis are by Gilbert and Frieden (1981) and Fox (1984); earlier important reviews are by Etkin and Gilbert (1968) and M. Dodd and J. Dodd (1976). Three major kinds of changes occur during amphibian metamorphosis: (1) regression of structures and functions that are significant only to the larvae; (2) transformation of larval structures into a form suitable for adult use; and (3) development of structures and functions de novo that are essential to the adult.

Three metamorphic stages defined by Etkin (1932) are referenced commonly by experimental biologists: (1) premetamorphosis, characterized by considerable growth and development of larval structures but not metamorphic changes; among amphibians this phase is unique to anurans; (2) prometamorphosis, a period of continued growth, especially of limbs, and initiation of minor metamorphic changes; and (3) climax, the period of radical changes that culminate in the loss of most larval characters; in anurans the beginning of this period is marked by the initiation of tail regression, and complete resorption of the tail marks the end of the period. All of the events of larval growth and metamorphosis are controlled ultimately by hormones.

ENDOCRINE CONTROL

Throughout the stages of metamorphosis there is a finely tuned integration of the endocrine glands, the products of which influence the morphological and physiological changes (Table 7-1). Gundernatsch (1912) discovered that metamorphosis in tadpoles of *Rana temporaria* was precipitated by feeding the tadpoles on thyroid glands of horses. This observation marked the beginning of the science of experimental endocrinology and the initiation of studies of the endocrine control of amphibian metamorphosis.

Nearly all of the experimental work on amphibian metamorphosis has dealt with only three species of anurans: *Xenopus laevis, Rana catesbeiana,* and *R. pipiens.* Far less extensive studies have been with the salamanders *Ambystoma gracile* and *A. tigrinum,* and the anurans *Bufo bufo* and *R. temporaria.* Consequently, realistic comparisons among taxa are not possible. The material presented here is only a brief synthesis of the extensive experimental work on the hormonal control of amphibian metamorphosis. Much more comprehensive coverage is presented by M. Dodd and J. Dodd (1976) and A. White and Nicoll (1981).

Thyroid

Because of the obvious action of its products on metamorphosis in experimental animals (Table 7-2), the thy-

173

roid commonly is considered to be the keystone of amphibian metamorphosis. The primary products of the thyroid are two hormones—tetraiodothyronine (T_4, thyroxin) and triiodothyronine (T_3). The paired thyroid glands are composed of aggregates of spherical, cystlike follicles. Each follicle is lined with a secretory epithelium that sur-

rounds the follicular cavity. The thyroid increases in size during larval development, both by the proliferation of follicles and by an increase in the volume of the entire follicle. Both T_3 and T_4 are made and stored within the thyroid gland. Synthesis of both hormones occurs by the iodination of tyrosine residues that are present on a spe-

Table 7-1. Endocrine Levels and Their Shifts During Amphibian Metamorphosis

Structure or factor	Premetamorphosis	Prometamorphosis		Climax
		Early	Late	
Brain (hypothalamus)				
Median eminence	Undeveloped	Developing	Well developed	Fully developed
Production of TRH	None	Slight	Great	Great
Aminergic fibers	Undeveloped	Developing	Well developed	Disappear
Effect on prolactin	None	Slight inhibition	Increased inhibition	None
Effect on TSH	None	Slight enhancement	Increased enhancement	None
Pituitary secretions				
Prolactin	High	Decreasing	Low	Surge followed by maintenance of steady low level
TSH	Low	Increasing	High	High until end of climax
Thyroid hormones (T_3, T_4)				
Rate of secretion	Low	High	High	High
Plasma levels	Low	Low	High	Low
Interrenal steroids				
Aldosterone	Low	Low	Low	Increase to adult level
Corticosterone	Low	Increasing	High	Decreases, then surges to adult level
Cortisol	Low	Slowly increasing	Rapidly increasing	High, then drops to adult level

Table 7-2. Major Morphological and Functional Changes Induced by Thyroid Hormones During Amphibian Metamorphosis*

Skin
Formation of dermal glands
Degeneration of skin on tail
Proliferation of skin on limbs
Formation of skin "window" for forelimb (anurans)
Degeneration of operculum
Formation of nictitating membrane
Differentiation of Leydig cells
Sodium transport (? indirect)
Changes in skin pigments and pigment patterns

Connective and supportive tissues
Degeneration of tail (anurans)
Degeneration of gill arches
Restructuring of mouth and head
Calcification of skeleton

Muscle
Degeneration of caudal muscle (anurans)
Growth of limb muscles
Growth of extrinsic eye muscles

Nervous and sensory systems
Reduction of Mauthner cells
Growth of mesencephalic V nucleus

Growth of cerebellum
Growth of lateral motor column cells
Growth of hypothalamic nucleus preoticus
Development of hypophysial portal system and median eminence
Increase in retinal rhodopsin
Fusion of internal and external retinas
Growth of dorsal root ganglia
Degeneration of Rohon-Beard cells

Kidney
Resorption of pronephros
Induction of prolactin receptors

Respiratory system
Regression of gills

Gastrointestinal tract and associated structures
Regression and reorganization of intestinal tract
Reduction and restructuring of pancreas
Induction of urea-cycle and other enzymes in liver

*Adapted from A. White and Nicoll (1981).

cific protein, thyroglobulin. When the thyroid gland is stimulated to produce thyroid hormones, T_3 and T_4 are released from the large thyroglobulin molecule and move into the bloodstream.

Amphibians, like other organisms, acquire iodine solely from dietary sources. As metamorphosis proceeds, certain histological changes occur within the thyroid gland. The secretory epithelial cells become progressively more columnar, reaching a peak at metamorphosis, only to regress in adults. Furthermore, during metamorphosis the thyroid gland in anurans undergoes an increase in the amount of rough endoplasmic reticulum and Golgi apparatus—changes presumably associated with the synthesis and secretion of thyroid hormones.

There is an apparent surge in the production of all thyroid hormones at metamorphic climax (Stages 41–44) in *Rana catesbeiana* (A. White and Nicoll, 1981). However, in *Xenopus laevis,* the level of T_4 rises gradually from late premetamorphic stages to a peak at midclimax; T_3 is not detectable until late prometamorphosis, reaching a maximum earlier than the peak of T_4 (Leloup and Buscaglia, 1977). Likewise, in *Ambystoma gracile* levels of T_4 are greater in metamorphosing animals than in larvae or transformed individuals (Eagleson and McKeown, 1978). These conclusions are all based on measurements by radioimmunoassay of the relative amounts of plasma protein-bound iodine, T_3, and T_4 in the blood.

Several reasons could account for the observed temporal differences in circulatory hormone levels among these species. For example, undoubtedly there is a lag time between the actual secretion and subsequent binding of thyroid hormones, the extent of which may vary interspecifically. Moreover, in many cases circulating plasma levels of hormones do not accurately reflect intracellular concentrations. Cells apparently retain T_3 better than T_4 as evidenced by the fact that in target cells, T_3 binding to cytoplasmic receptor proteins is about 250 times greater than binding by T_4 (Kistler et al., 1977). Consequently, it has been proposed that the actual role of intracellular receptor molecules for thyroid hormones in amphibian larval tissues may be to ensure adequate retention of T_3 by the cells during metamorphosis. Unfortunately, attempts to explain the observed differences in potencies between T_3 and T_4 in amphibians by measured differences in receptor binding have not led to consistent results. Apparently the sensitivity of tissues to thyroid hormones changes during development. Cells that once were less responsive to T_4 may gradually (or abruptly) acquire the ability to respond (i.e., bind) to this hormone. Such changes unquestionably play an important role in the ability of a tissue to complete the process of metamorphosis. Why tissues respond to the various thyroid hormones in different ways and at different times is not clear. Perhaps insights into the control of metamorphosis may be obtained by better understanding how cells selectively bind T_3 and T_4 to intracellular receptor molecules.

Interrenals

Like the thyroid, these small glands, consisting of cords of cells surrounded by connective tissue and lying under the dorsal aorta, also undergo ultrastructural changes during development. For example, in *Xenopus laevis* the interrenal tissue apparently is inactive during premetamorphosis but shows an increase in activity through prometamorphosis, reaching a peak at early metamorphic climax and then regressing (Rapola, 1963). Three interrenal steroids have been identified by radioimmunoassay in serum of tadpoles of *Rana catesbeiana* (Krug et al., 1978). Aldosterone is first detectable in premetamorphosis and remains at a low level until completion of metamorphosis, when it occurs at the slightly higher level characteristic of adults. Corticosterone is present at a low level during late premetamorphosis and rises rapidly in early prometamorphosis to reach a peak at about Stage 40; the level declines somewhat to midclimax and then increases rapidly to the concentration occurring in adults. Cortisol is present in small amounts in early premetamorphic stages and increases slowly until midprometamorphosis, from which point there is a rapid increase to midclimax and then a decline to the low concentrations characteristic of adults. Not surprisingly, the results of radioimmunoassay of serum of *Rana* indicate earlier production of steroids than was suspected originally from histological examination of interrenals in *Xenopus.* It is likely that the sensitive radioimmunoassay procedure more accurately reflects the synthetic capabilities of the interrenal glands.

The activity of the interrenal cells can be stimulated by adrenocorticotropic hormone (M. Dodd and J. Dodd, 1976), thereby suggesting that the activity of these glands is under the control of the pars distalis of the pituitary. The exact influence of interrenal steroids on metamorphosis is unknown. The rise in corticosterone levels during prometamorphosis is associated with regression of the intestine, which is induced by thyroid hormones. The profile of cortisol levels in serum coincides with the pattern of growth of the hindlimbs in *Rana catesbeiana,* and the peak level of cortisol is associated with the beginning of rapid resorption of the tail. Because interrenal steroids presumably act synergistically with thyroid hormones to promote tail regression, it has been suggested that cortisol and corticosterone facilitate thyroid-induced metamorphosis.

Adenohypophysis

The anterior lobe or pars distalis of the pituitary is the source of many hormones. The secretions that are active during larval development and metamorphosis are hormones that stimulate other endocrine glands or promote growth. Prolactin and possibly a growth hormone seem to direct growth and development by acting on peripheral endocrine organs and by controlling the activity of the thyroid gland. There is disagreement as to whether both prolactin and a growth hormone are present in amphibians. It has been suggested that a single hormone with prolactin- and growth hormone-like properties acts as the somatotropic agent in larval amphibians. Generally, this hormone is referred to as amphibian prolactin.

Although the evidence for a somatotropic role of prolactin among different species is not consistent, indirect but compelling evidence exists that an endogenous prolactin-like hormone is responsible for suppressing metamorphosis in *Ambystoma, Bufo,* and *Rana.* Prolactin apparently is a potent anabolic and somatotropic agent in specific tissues (e.g., caudal tissue in tadpoles and gills in salamander larvae), but it may do little to drive general metabolism in a direction most suitable for overall growth. Perhaps, as suggested by Frye et al. (1972), there is a selective advantage provided by the employment of a hormone that promotes growth in certain tissues but does not mobilize important energy stores, such as fat bodies, for the promotion of body growth, because growth is followed by a considerable expenditure of energy for structural transformation. Prolactin may favor growth in larval amphibians by stimulation of intestinal absorption of amino acids and glucose.

Prolactin antagonizes the actions of thyroid hormones in certain larval organs. For example, prolactin reduces tail regression and antagonizes thyroid promotion of hindlimb growth, gill regression, water and sodium loss in certain larval tissues, and nitrogen excretion (A. White and Nicoll, 1981). However, prolactin does not inhibit several other responses to thyroid hormones, including pancreatic resorption, increased urea-cycle enzymes, hepatic dehydration, or retinal dehydrogenase activity. Furthermore, prolactin also may exert a direct inhibitory action on the thyroid gland. Because metamorphosis proceeds at the expense of growth, it might be expected that antimetamorphic and growth-promoting actions of hormones are intimately related. There is no evidence for the separation of these actions. Prolactin antagonizes the action of thyroid hormones at the level of the target organ. This organ specificity of prolactin antagonism may be an important factor in determining the correct sequence and rate of tissue regression or differentiation during metamorphosis.

The pituitary gland of amphibians, like all vertebrates, is directly controlled by the hypothalamus in the brain. Dopamine, secreted by the hypothalamus, is a regulator of prolactin secretion. Dopamine lowers circulating levels of prolactin and therefore accelerates metamorphosis in larval amphibians. There is evidence for an inhibitory effect of a dopamine agonist on prolactin secretion in the viviparous *Nectophrynoides occidentalis* (Zuber-Vogeli, 1968). It has been suggested that aminergic fibers regulate (possibly by tonic inhibition) the release of prolactin during prometamorphosis; the surge of prolactin secretion in late climax may be caused by release from the inhibitory influence of these fibers, which regress at the onset of metamorphic climax.

Newts (*Notophthalmus* and *Triturus*) undergo a second metamorphosis when the terrestrial efts return to water. However, in contrast to the clear prolactin-thyroid antagonism that exists in the metamorphosis of larvae to subadults, there is no consistent evidence for a prolactin-thyroid synergism in the control of the second metamorphosis in newts (M. Dodd and J. Dodd, 1976).

The pituitary control of the thyroid gland is accomplished by thyroid-stimulating hormone; this hormone in *Rana catesbeiana,* as in other vertebrates, is a glycoprotein (MacKenzie et al., 1978). The early development of the thyroid in larval amphibians seems to be partially independent of the pituitary. The follicular arrangement in the thyroid epithelium develops in late embryonic stages independently of pituitary stimulation. The onset of thyroglobulin and thyroid hormone synthesis, which first occurs in late embryonic stages, also is independent of thyroid-stimulating hormone. However, this changes in early larval stages when normal thyroid function first shows signs of dependence on thyroid-stimulating hormone.

The developmental pattern of pituitary-controlled thyrotropic activity during the larval period is not so well delineated as the developmental changes in the thyroid gland itself. In *Xenopus laevis,* a high level of thyroid-stimulating hormone occurs during early climax, and the level declines by midclimax (M. Dodd and J. Dodd, 1976). This decline correlates with the sharp rise in circulating thyroid hormone (T_3) observed by Leloup and Buscaglia (1977). Measurements of thyroid-stimulating hormone correlate directly with the observed changes in activity of thyrotropic cells; also, this activity generally is associated with changes in the function of the thyroid gland during metamorphosis. The action of thyroid-stimulating hormone may be confounded by thyroid response to other pituitary hormones, especially prolactin. The thyroid and pituitary act in close association, and there is a direct negative feedback of thyroid hormone on the synthesis and/or secretion of thyroid-stimulating hormone by the pituitary.

The adenohypophysis secretes another substance, adrenocorticotropic hormone (ACTH). As mentioned previously, this hormone stimulates the activity of the interrenal glands.

Hypothalamus

Ultimately, it is the hypothalamus within the brain itself that controls the release of pituitary hormones. Within the paired preoptic nucleus of the hypothalamus are a number of neurosecretory cells. These cells are the source of small peptides, which function as pituitary releasing (or inhibiting) factors, and hormones of the neurohypophysis, such as oxytocin and vasotocin. Axons originating within the preoptic nucleus terminate either in the median eminence of the hypothalamus or in the neurohypophysis of the pituitary gland. Hypothalamic releasing factors enter the hypophysial portal system by way of an arterial plexus within the median eminence. Once in the hypophysial portal system, releasing factors are transported directly to the adenohypophysis.

There seems to be a clear-cut developmental sequence

to the establishment of hypothalamic-pituitary control. In *Xenopus laevis* neurosecretory neurons appear during early larval stages (Goos, 1978), at about the same time that the thyroid epithelium assumes a follicular arrangement. The median eminence in *Rana pipiens* begins to develop in early prometamorphosis. During late prometamorphosis capillary connection is made with the pars distalis (Etkin, 1968). Thus, in the case of the thyroid gland, ultimate activation of thyrotropic activity requires a stimulus from the hypothalamus. This stimulus is thyrotropin-releasing hormone, which acts directly on the pituitary to initiate release of thyroid-stimulating hormone. There is positive feedback between the thyroid and the hypothalamus, because an increase in thyroid hormone promotes further development of the median eminence. As mentioned in the preceding section, the secretion of prolactin is also ultimately controlled by the hypothalamus.

Ultimobranchial Bodies

In anurans these glands are paired, but in salamanders there is a single gland. The glands form at the same time as the operculum (early premetamorphosis). They develop as thickenings in the floor of the fifth branchial (last pharyngeal) pouch. Subsequently, secretory cells of neural crest origin migrate into the pharyngeal epithelium. Eventually the glands separate from the original pouch area and acquire a definite lumen. At the beginning of metamorphic climax the epithelium becomes entirely stratified, and the ultimobranchials increase in size. This period of activity coincides with the period of calcium mobilization from the endolymphatic sacs. These sacs are associated with the auditory organs and have posterior extensions along the vertebral column. Calcium carbonate, in the form of aragonite, is stored in these paravertebral "lime sacs" and in the endolymphatic sacs. During larval life, the endolymphatic sacs enlarge. Ultimately the accumulated calcium is utilized at metamorphosis for completion of the calcification of the skeleton. The ultimobranchial bodies and "lime sacs" are retained in most postmetamorphic anurans, with the exception of *Xenopus laevis* (M. Dodd and J. Dodd, 1976).

Thus, the ultimobranchial bodies serve to sequester calcium salts in special storage sacs during development,

probably by preventing mobilization of the salts and thereby ensuring an adequate supply of calcium for calcification during metamorphosis. Relationships of the ultimobranchial bodies to other endocrine glands have not been clearly established; possibly there is a prolactin-ultimobranchial relationship.

Other Glands

Evidence is contradictory concerning the possible role, if any, of the pineal gland in amphibian metamorphosis. Pineal extracts have no effects on metamorphosis of *Taricha torosa, Ambystoma tigrinum,* and *Rana pipiens,* but accelerate metamorphosis in *Bufo americanus* (M. Dodd and J. Dodd, 1976). If pineal secretions, such as melatonin, do have an effect on amphibian metamorphosis, it probably is indirect.

In addition to the pineal gland, there are metamorphic changes associated with the endocrine pancreas. Differences in insulin sensitivity and glucose tolerances between larvae and adults are related to the action of the endocrine pancreas. Presumably these differences become established during metamorphic climax and are accounted for by hormone-mediated activation or intensification of insulin-antagonistic functions; changes in growth hormone and glucocorticoid secretions and their metabolic effects are believed to be responsible for these changes (M. Dodd and J. Dodd, 1976).

Hormonal Integration

A model for the control of anuran development and activation of the metamorphic climax proposed by Etkin (1968) has been modified by M. Dodd and J. Dodd (1976) and A. White and Nicoll (1981). This model can be outlined, as follows (Fig. 7-1):

1. During premetamorphosis, the median eminence of the hypothalamus is undeveloped, and the brain exerts little or no control over adenohypophysial functions. Consequently, secretion of prolactin is high and secretion of thyroid-stimulating hormone (and thus thyroid hormone levels) is low. Therefore, prolactin can promote larval growth without interference from thyroid hormones. Negative

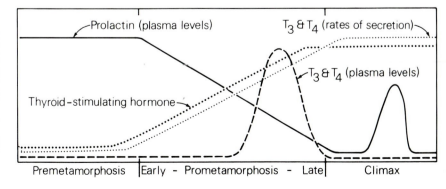

Figure 7-1. Hypothetical relative levels of pituitary and thyroid hormones in *Rana catesbeiana* during metamorphosis.

feedback of thyroid hormone on secretion of thyroid-stimulating hormone is operative.

2. During early prometamorphosis, the rate of secretion of thyroid hormone is high, but this is not reflected in increased plasma protein-bound iodine or by radioimmunoassay-detectable plasma T_3 or T_4 levels, probably because of the rapid clearance of the thyroid hormones. The increased secretion of thyroid hormones presumably results from rising levels of thyroid-stimulating hormone; this increase probably reflects gradual development of hypothalamic influence on the adenohypophysis. The rate of secretion of thyroid hormones continues to increase, so that late in prometamorphosis the capacity of tissues to bind and utilize thyroid hormones is saturated. Consequently, the continually increasing output of thyroid hormones results in a surge in plasma levels of these hormones.

3. The rising level of thyroid hormones also promotes development of the median eminence and the establishment of portal vascular connections between the hypothalamus and the adenohypophysis. As this process progresses, more thyrotropin-releasing hormone is able to reach the pituitary to stimulate increased secretion of thyroid hormones. The increase in thyroid hormones promotes further development of the median eminence. Thus, a positive feedback loop is established.

4. While hypothalamic control of pituitary function is developing, secretion of prolactin comes under inhibitory control, and the circulating levels of prolactin decrease progressively. Thus, prolactin antagonism of thyroid hormone action on peripheral tissues is reduced, allowing development to proceed more rapidly.

5. Late in prometamorphosis, the median eminence and its vascular connections with the hypophysis have developed substantially. The saturation of tissues with thyroid hormones results in rapid and complete transformation (climax). Blood levels of prolactin are greatly reduced during this period, reflecting maximum hypothalamic inhibition. Thus, at this stage of development the prolactin-mediated inhibition of thyroid hormone action is minimized.

6. During metamorphic climax, the positive feedback interactions of the hypothalamo-hypophysial-thyroid axis presumably are lost. It is not clear how this comes about. Possibly the aminergic fibers that "innervate" the adenohypophysis in larvae are involved in both the positive and negative feedback loops. These fibers disappear during metamorphic climax. Thus, rising levels of thyroid hormones during late prometamorphosis may act on the hypothalamus and cause these fibers to increase secretion of thyroid-stimulating hormone, thereby accounting for the positive feedback. Rising levels of thyroid hormones also may cause the eventual degeneration of these fibers. Thus, neural stimulation of secretion of thyroid-stimulating hormone is lost, and the inhibitory action of thyroid hormone directly on the pituitary can operate unopposed.

OTHER BIOCHEMICAL CHANGES

The morphological and physiological changes that take place during metamorphosis are accompanied by, if not driven by, nonhormonal biochemical changes. Electrophoretic and radioimmunoassay investigations indicate that marked changes take place in the blood in late prometamorphosis and during metamorphic climax (Broyles, 1981), and numerous biochemical changes also occur during organ differentiation and maturation (Smith-Gill and Carver, 1981; Atkinson, 1981). The changes in hormone levels in the blood have been discussed in the preceding section.

Serum Proteins

One important function of serum proteins is to maintain osmotic equilibrium between blood and tissue fluids. An increase in the total protein concentration at metamorphosis serves to increase the osmotic pressure of the blood and hence its water-retaining capacity, an important adaptive switch considering the transition from the aquatic environment of larvae to the terrestrial environment of postmetamorphic amphibians. Albumin, with its lower molecular weight, exerts two to three times the osmotic pressure per unit weight in comparison with the globulins. Not surprisingly, albumin increases proportionately more than globulins during metamorphosis. At normal blood pH, albumin has great ion-binding capacity. An increase in the ion-binding capacity per unit volume of blood at metamorphosis fulfills the greater transport needs associated with metabolism and excretion in the terrestrial environment (Frieden, 1961).

The concentration of serum proteins more than doubles during metamorphosis in various *Rana* (Just et al., 1977), and at least 20% of the increase in *R. catesbeiana* is due to an increase in serum albumin, which rises more than 10-fold (Feldhoff, 1971). At least part of the increase in serum albumin during metamorphosis is due to an increased rate of synthesis in late prometamorphosis in *R. catesbeiana* (Ledford and Frieden, 1973); serum albumin peaks at early climax and declines at late climax to just about the same level as in midprometamorphosis. Albumin levels remain high in froglets, indicating a decreased rate of albumin degradation. In species of ambystomatid salamanders (Nussbaum, 1974), there are increases in the albumin/globulin ratio and total protein concentrations. However, in the aquatic *Cryptobranchus alleganiensis* there are no changes in serum proteins (Nickerson and Mays, 1973).

The hypothesis that the increase in albumin attendant with metamorphosis is designed by natural selection to meet the osmotic needs of the organism in the terrestrial environment (Frieden et al., 1957) was proposed as an adaptive aspect of amphibian metamorphosis. Subsequent investigations on *Bufo arenarum* from humid and arid habitats (Bertini and Cei, 1960) and various ambystomatid salamanders (Nussbaum, 1974) demonstrated that there is both interspecific (*Ambystoma macrodactylum* and *Rhyacotriton olympicus*) and intraspecific (*Dicamptodon ensatus* and *B. arenarum*) evidence that higher concentrations of albumin are characteristic of transformed individuals of populations adapted to more arid environments.

The absence of metamorphic changes in serum protein concentrations in *Cryptobranchus* is understandable. However, the aquatic *Xenopus laevis* exhibits a marked change in albumin/globulin ratio and total protein concentration between larvae and adults. In comparison with *Rana,* this change is slow and steady and continues after morphological metamorphosis. The differences between *Rana* and *Xenopus* are reasonable in that a rapid change in serum proteins in *Rana* is necessary for the froglet to survive in the terrestrial environment, whereas *Xenopus* remains aquatic. Then, why should concentrations of serum proteins change in *Xenopus* and not in *Cryptobranchus?* The latter lives in permanent rivers, whereas *Xenopus* lives in ponds that may dry up during droughts; the frogs aestivate in the soil during droughts and thus are confronted with the osmoregulatory demands faced by terrestrial frogs such as *Rana*.

Iron Transport, Metabolism, and Storage

Ceruloplasmin is the principal copper protein of serum and is important in donating copper to cells for the synthesis and assembly of cytochrome oxidase; also it is a molecular link between iron and copper metabolism. The ferroxidase activity of ceruloplasmin is important in the mobilization of iron from ferritin, an intracellular iron-storage protein. Levels of ceruloplasmin increase gradually through premetamorphosis and rapidly during prometamorphosis to peak at the beginning of metamorphic climax in *Rana grylio* (Frieden, 1968). There is a significant increase in ferritin reducing activity in the liver in early metamorphic climax (Osaki et al., 1974), which undoubtedly plays a role in the mobilization of iron from the liver. The marked increase in ceruloplasmin is probably important in mobilization of iron from both the liver and larval red blood cells and the transfer of iron to serum transferrin. Transferrin is required as a donor of iron to

the immature, differentiating cells that synthesize hemoglobin.

Red Blood Cells and Hemoglobins

Morphological differences between larval and adult red blood cells have been noted in numerous species of anurans (Broyles, 1981). During metamorphosis, larger larval red blood cells are replaced by smaller adult red blood cells; the midpoint of this transition is at midclimax. The red blood cell count and whole blood hemoglobin concentration are greater in adults than in larvae. The mature, differentiated red blood cell retains its nucleus in both larval and adult blood cells, but the nuclei of larval cells have a greater amount of endoplasmic reticulum than do adult red blood cells.

Differences in the nuclei and cytoplasm support the view that adult red blood cells are more mature cells and less active in the synthesis of amino acids and proteins, as compared with larval red blood cells. Circulating red blood cells of premetamorphic tadpoles of *Rana catesbeiana* and *R. pipiens* have a greater ability than the red blood cells of froglets or adults to incorporate amino acids, uridine, and thymidine (Benbassat, 1970). Thus, there are both morphological and biochemical differences between larval and adult red blood cells. Of course, of major importance is the difference in the types of hemoglobins that they contain.

A notable transition in hemoglobins takes place at metamorphosis. Extensive work on *Rana catesbeiana* (Frieden, 1968) illustrates the adaptive significance of the transition. Hemoglobins of tadpoles have higher affinities for oxygen and are well suited for an aquatic environment where oxygen tensions are low. Adult hemoglobins have a lower affinity for oxygen. Although it requires a greater oxygen tension to load the adult hemoglobins, they will release oxygen more readily at the oxygen tensions that prevail in the various tissues of the animal. Thus, adult hemoglobins are well suited for an air-breathing animal that requires a more active metabolism to support its greater muscular activity.

The four major hemoglobins (I–IV) in tadpoles of *Rana catesbeiana* are different from the four major hemoglobins (A–D) in adults. The change from one set to another occurs during larval life. In early premetamorphic larvae, about 90% of the total hemoglobin is made up of components I and II, whereas in late premetamorphic stages about two-thirds of the hemoglobin is composed of components III and IV (Broyles, 1981). Of the four adult hemoglobins, A and D are relatively minor, and component C has a higher oxygen affinity than B. Component C is the first to appear during metamorphosis and comprises essentially all of the hemoglobin in froglets.

In *Rana catesbeiana* the switch in hemoglobins occurs rapidly, mostly in midclimax, but some adult hemoglobin is detectable in late prometamorphic stages. Similar hemoglobin transitions are known in several other species of *Rana* (Broyles, 1981). The hemoglobin transition begins much earlier and ends much later in *Xenopus laevis* (Maclean and Jurd, 1971) and especially in *Bombina variegata* (Cardinelli and Sala, 1979). The lengthy duration is understandable in *Xenopus,* adults of which are aquatic. The functional significance of the lengthy period of transition in *Bombina* is unknown, but it simply may represent a primitive condition of prolonged metamorphosis.

Three major types of hemoglobin have been identified in larvae and three others in adults of the salamander *Dicamptodon ensatus* (S. Wood, 1971). The ontogenetic changes in hemoglobins in *Dicamptodon* are similar to those in anurans with respect to oxygen affinity. The transition from larval to adult hemoglobins occurs at the time of morphological metamorphosis in *Ambystoma tigrinum;* a similar transition occurs at about the same age (100–150 days) in the neotenic *A. mexicanum* but is not accompanied by morphological metamorphosis (Ducibella, 1974).

A distinctly different kind of ontogenetic shift in oxygen equilibrium has been described for the aquatic, viviparous caecilian *Typhlonectes compressicauda* (Garlick et al., 1979). Developing fetuses of this species have large external gills (Fig. 5-6) that function in gaseous exchange with maternal oviducal tissue. Oxygen affinity of fetal blood is higher than that of adult blood, but the hemoglobins of fetuses and adults are essentially the same structurally and have the same oxygen-binding capacities. The differences in binding properties are the result of a threefold increase in the level of adenosine triphosphate in the blood of adults.

A general scheme of changes in erythropoiesis and hemoglobin synthesis during anuran development was presented by Broyles (1981), as follows:

1. The first red blood cells arise in the ventral blood islands of the embryo. The type of hemoglobin synthesized in these embryonic red blood cells is unknown.

2. Both pronephric and mesonephric kidneys are erythropoietically active in larvae and represent the second ontogenetic site(s) of formation of red blood cells. In *Rana pipiens* the pronephros becomes hemopoietically active in early premetamorphosis and is mainly a granulocyte producer during the larval period. Erythropoiesis constitutes less than 10% of the hemopoietic activity of the pronephros in early premetamorphosis. The relative number of different types of hemopoietic cells in the mesonephros at different stages of early development is unknown. However, in late premetamorphic stages the intertubular regions of the mesonephric kidneys are producing red blood cells of a defined morphol-

ogy (type 1) containing larval hemoglobin (type IV).

3. Liver erythropoiesis begins in early premetamorphic stages in *Rana pipiens* and continues through metamorphosis in *R. catesbeiana.* In *R. pipiens* macrophages are the predominant hemopoietic cell type in the liver in early premetamorphic stages, and erythroblasts dominate in midpremetamorphic stages. It is not known whether mesonephric kidney erythropoiesis and liver erythropoiesis begin simultaneously or at different developmental stages. In tadpoles of *R. catesbeiana* liver erythropoiesis produces red blood cells that differ in cell morphology (type 2) and hemoglobin type from red blood cells emanating from the kidneys.

4. As development progresses toward metamorphosis in *R. catesbeiana,* the relative contribution of the kidneys and liver to total erythropoiesis changes—kidney erythropoiesis predominates at earlier stages, whereas liver predominates at later stages.

5. During metamorphic climax in *R. catesbeiana,* liver erythropoiesis switches from production of larval to adult hemoglobins. Presumably kidney erythropoiesis declines. The molecular and cellular events that occur in the liver to mediate the metamorphic switch in hemoglobins are largely unknown. There is disagreement as to whether both larval and adult hemoglobins occur in the same red blood cells during the transition.

6. In froglets the liver is the primary erythropoietic site. The red blood cells produced there are uniform morphologically and apparently contain only adult hemoglobins. However, there may be a low level of larval hemoglobins in the circulating blood of froglets and adults.

7. During maturation of the froglet into an adult, erythropoiesis shifts from the liver to one or more other sites. Apparently the spleen is the principal erythropoietic organ in adult frogs. However, in temperate species red blood cells also are produced by the bone marrow in the spring of the year.

Liver

The changes in the liver that accompany metamorphosis encompass a panorama of biochemical differentiation events. These include DNA synthesis, synthesis and accumulation of a stable amount of transcriptional RNA with an associated enumeration of nucleoli, lipid synthesis, elaboration of the rough endoplasmic reticulum, and a change in the structure and an increase in the number of mitochondria. Newly synthesized proteins include the enzymes of the ornithine-urea cycle, which develop in association with the transition from ammonotelism to ureotelism. Regulation of the rates of protein synthesis seems to be at both the transcriptional and posttranscriptional levels. During metamorphosis, periods of DNA synthesis precede the appearance of new proteins, and cell death may accompany liver metamorphosis. Presumably, significant cellular turnover precedes biochemical differentiation, and differentiation of adult function occurs in proliferating populations of cells. However, a functional relationship between proliferation and liver metamorphosis has not been established experimentally.

Intestine

In anurans regression of the gut occurs during late prometamorphosis and metamorphic climax, and is characterized by shortening of the gut and loss of the primary epithelium. This loss seems to be initiated by the mobilization of lysosomes and release of hydrolases into the cytoplasm of the epithelial cells. Alkaline phosphatase activity, which is correlated with a functional larval epithelium, decreases during regression of the gut.

Integument

Several biochemical changes occur in the skin during metamorphosis. Thyroid hormones presumably are responsible for the proliferation of epidermal cells, sodium-phosphorus-adenosine triphosphate synthesis, and at least one protein involved in keratinization. Other functions of the skin, such as osmoregulation, are influenced by prolactin. Development and regulation of the active sodium transport system may be mediated by different hormones.

During metamorphosis, chromatophore densities, associations, and morphologies typical of the adult pigmentary pattern develop, although additional changes in pigmentation may occur in later postmetamorphic life. Complex interactions among pigment cells, their biochemical products, and their tissue and endocrine environments mediate pattern formation and pigment synthesis. Morphological transitions include migrations and rearrangements of existing chromatophores, mitosis of chromatoblasts and existing differentiated chromatophores, and differentiation of new chromatophores (Smith-Gill and Carver, 1981). Pigment synthesis and chromatophore differentiation are essential to expression of the color pattern and may involve the production of new pigments and/or the development of new organelles. Also, specific classes of pigments may be degraded. Both thyroid hormone and melanocyte-stimulating hormone may be important in the development of the pigmentary pattern. However, much of the evidence linking thyroid hormone action with changes in pigment patterns at metamorphosis is circumstantial and is based on the temporal association of pigment changes with other aspects of metamorphosis.

Eye

The principal biochemical change in the eye is the conversion of photopigments. Two systems of photopigments are contained in the retinal rods of amphibians. Most adult amphibians have rhodopsin, a red-photosensitive pigment in cycle with vitamin A_1, and larvae have porphyropsin, a purple-photosensitive pigment in cycle with vitamin A_2. Each photopigment is a conjugated protein (opsin), containing as the prosthetic group retinal$_1$ or retinal$_2$, which are aldehydes of vitamins A_1 and A_2, respectively.

The transition from porphyropsin to rhodopsin occurs during metamorphosis, and the retinas of partially metamorphosed larvae contain a mixture of the two types of photopigments. At least one species that is aquatic as an adult, *Xenopus laevis,* retains porphyropsin as the visual pigment (Bridges et al., 1977). Newts (*Notophthalmus* and *Triturus*) that undergo a second metamorphosis from terrestrial subadults to aquatic adults have a porphyropsin-rhodopsin-porphyropsin sequence (Grüsser-Cornehls and Himstedt, 1976). Whether thyroid or one or more other hormones subsequently induce a particular visual pigment during metamorphosis is a function of prior evolutionary selection. Depending on the life history of the species, thyroid hormones may coordinate the change in larval photopigment to that of the adult. However, in newts prolactin has been identified as inducing the change from rhodopsin in terrestrial subadults to porphyropsin in aquatic adults.

Tail and Gills

During amphibian metamorphosis the gills and tail (anurans only) undergo complete degeneration. Experimental studies (summarized by Atkinson, 1981) of spontaneous and thyroid-induced anuran gill and tail atrophy suggest that degeneration in these organs encompasses at least three discrete phases of cellular activity. In the first phase a selective decrease in the rate of protein synthesis occurs; the second phase is highlighted by enhanced histolytic activity; and in the final phase cellular debris produced during the second phase is eliminated. Each tissue of these organs participates in each phase in a characteristic manner.

Lungs

In *Rana catesbeiana,* rates of incorporation of amino acids and thymidine into the lung tissues increase and their rates of incorporation in the degenerating gill tissues decrease during metamorphic climax (Atkinson and Just, 1975). It may seem that the lung tissue prepares biochemically to assume a respiratory role before it actually begins its major respiratory function. However, many kinds of tadpoles, including those of *R. catesbeiana,* swim to the surface and gulp air when oxygen concentrations of the water are low. Thus, biochemical preparation for respiratory function of differentiating lung tissue is necessary prior to the lungs becoming the major respiratory structures in froglets.

MORPHOLOGICAL CHANGES

The most obvious changes during metamorphosis are in the structure of amphibians. The changes are most extensive in anurans, in which the aquatic larva undergoes a drastic transformation into a terrestrial adult.

Metamorphosis in caecilians seems to involve the fewest changes, but this group has been studied far less thoroughly than the others. From the works of P. Sarasin and F. Sarasin (1887–1890), Brauer (1899), H. Marcus (1939), and E. Taylor (1968), it is possible to summarize existing knowledge, based mostly on *Hypogeophis rostratus* and *Ichthyophis glutinosus*. Gill degeneration occurs during late embryonic, larval, or fetal life. In those caecilians having aquatic larvae, the gills are lost (either by resorption or breakage) soon after hatching, leaving only a single gill slit on either side. Upon metamorphosis the gill slits close. A dorsal caudal fin is present in larval ichthyophiids and rhinatrematids; this degenerates during metamorphosis. Sometime during fetal life the eyes of most caecilians become covered with skin or bone, and certain muscles and nerves associated with the eyes either do not develop or degenerate. During fetal or larval life, the sensory tentacles develop in front of the eyes. In late stages of metamorphosis, the skin thickens, skin glands form, and small scales develop in the skin. The lungs probably are not functional until after birth, and therefore metamorphosis also entails lung maturation. The fetal teeth are lost, and adult dentition develops immediately after birth.

Although the transition from larva to adult is not nearly so dramatic in salamanders as it is in anurans, definite changes take place during metamorphosis. The morphological changes in salamanders detailed for *Eurycea bislineata* by I. Wilder (1925) and summarized for salamanders in general by M. Dodd and J. Dodd (1976) include locomotor, sensory, respiratory, and feeding structures. The caudal fin is resorbed, and the skin thickens with the development of dermal glands. Gills are resorbed and gill slits close; associated branchial circulation is modified as lungs develop (except in plethodontids). Eyelids develop, and the simple flap of connective tissue that acts as a valve to close the internal nares in larvae may be replaced by a more sophisticated valve operated by smooth muscle fibers. The larval labial folds shrink, and the mouth takes on a different appearance with a wider gape. Maxillary bones are formed, and teeth develop on the maxillaries and parasphenoid. A tongue develops, and associated changes occur with the hyobranchial apparatus.

Because larval and adult anurans are such divergent organisms morphologically and ecologically, it is not surprising that the transition from tadpole to froglet is abrupt and dramatic. The hindlimbs grow and mature; forelimbs develop in the branchial chambers, from which they erupt in late metamorphosis. The internal gills and associated blood vessels degenerate; lungs and pulmonary ventilation develop. The tail is resorbed, and the skin thickens with the development of dermal glands. Larval mouthparts degenerate, and the adult mouth is formed. A tongue (except in pipids) and associated hyolaryngeal structures develop. The intestine shortens, and the digestive tract differentiates. The eyes enlarge and undergo structural modifications; eyelids develop.

In all groups of amphibians, changes occur in the urogenital system. The pronephric kidney degenerates, and an opisthonephric or mesonephric kidney forms. The gonads and associated ducts develop. Comprehensive summaries of morphological metamorphosis by M. Dodd and J. Dodd (1976) and Fox (1981, 1984) are discussed here by organ systems.

Skeleton

Whereas the appearance of limbs, resorption of the tail, and development of eyelids are obvious corollaries of the shift from an aquatic to a terrestrial mode of life in anurans, less apparent but no less dramatic changes involve the restructuring of the larval skull and hyobranchial apparatus. These changes (1) accommodate the transition from larval feeding and respiratory modes to those of the adult, and (2) house newly developed sensory organs that serve the organism's needs in the terrestrial environment. Skeletal changes are much less conspicuous in salamanders and caecilians and are discussed in Chapter 6, which contains a discussion of terminology and illustrations.

The formation of the adult mouth involves a restructuring of the anterior end of the chondrocranium and a complete reorganization and realignment of the larval palatoquadrate. The suprarostral cartilage, which supported the upper beak of the tadpole, disappears along with the distal ends of the cranial trabeculae that supported it. The infrarostrals supporting the lower beak fuse with Meckel's cartilage, which is lengthened to accommodate the vertical rotation of the quadrate and the posterior shift of the jaw articulation (between Meckel's cartilage and the quadrate) from the region of the olfactory foramen to the auditory capsule. The formation of the adult maxillary arch also involves the disappearance of larval neurocranial braces and the formation of new struts to brace the upper jaw against the skull. Thus, the quadratojugal commissure, ascending process, and larval otic process break down. The muscular process of the quadrate fuses dorsally with the crista parotica of the auditory region by means of the adult otic process. Posteroventrally the quadrate is braced against the auditory capsule via the pseudobasal process, a block of cartilage that arises beneath the anterior end of the auditory capsule. The pterygoid process lengthens to attach to the developing nasal capsule anteriorly (via the posterior maxillary process), and the auditory capsule posteromedially.

The ceratobranchials that form the larval branchial baskets disappear as the hyobranchial apparatus assumes its flattened adult shape that serves as a framework for the tongue. The first basibranchial is resorbed, whereas the second is incorporated with the hypohyal plates to form the corpus or hyoid plate of the adult. The large ceratohyals lose their connection with the larval palato-quadrate and become long slender elements (anterior cornua or hyalae) that extend anterolaterally and then recurve posteriorly to fuse with the ventral aspect of the auditory capsules.

In the ethmoid region, the anterior neurocranial wall and cornua trabeculae undergo an elaborate transformation that results in the paired nasal capsules composed of a variety of cartilaginous supports (described in Chapter 13) that protect the olfactory organs. In the larva, the external naris cannot be closed, and closure of the narial canal is affected through hydrostatic pressure against a valvular flap covering the internal choana. This flap is missing in adults, and the narial passage is closed instead by movement of the cartilages supporting the external naris. Posterior to the ethmoid region, in the orbitotemporal area, the basicranial fenestra closes and the neurocranial walls proliferate so that the optic and trochlear nerve foramina are delimited. Depending on the species, the pilae antoticae may be united dorsally by the taenia tecti transversalis, and a medial element, the taenia tecti medialis, may connect the transverse tectum to the tectum synoticum posteriorly. Laterally, the eye is protected by a saucer-shaped sclerotic cartilage.

In the auditory region, the roof of the otic capsule is proliferated into a lateral extension, the crista parotica, to which the quadrate is attached by the otic process. The fenestra ovalis, which lies ventral to the crista parotica, is occluded by two cartilaginous structures that arise independent of the wall of the otic capsule—the operculum posteriorly, and the pars interna plectri of the columella anteriorly. The rodlike columella fuses with the ventral edge of the fenestra ovalis and bears two transient ligamentous connections—proximally with the operculum and distally with the posterior surface of the quadrate. Eventually, synchondrotic connection of the proximal portion of the columella with the margin of the fenestra ovalis is replaced with a ligamentous one, and upon ossification the operculum and columella are fused. The tympanic ring originates from cells derived from the quadrate. Subsequent to metamorphosis it chondrifies and fuses dorsally to the crista parotica; coincidentally, the ring seems to act as an organizer in the formation of the tympanic membrane. The cartilaginous distal portion of the columella (pars externa plectri) extends from the crista parotica to the distal end of the pars interna plectri and fuses with the latter once the proximal columella has lost its ligamentous connection with the quadrate.

In the occipital region, the notochord is incorporated into the basal plate by chondrification and encroachment of the parachordal cartilages, the posterior ends of which articulate with the first presacral vertebra via the occipital condyles.

The surprisingly sparse information on sequences of ossification in anurans was summarized by Trueb (1985). This is most nearly complete for species of *Rana* and *Xenopus laevis*. Because the timing of metamorphosis is highly variable, it is impossible to draft a generalized schedule of ossification applicable to all frogs. Thus, in some species, the organism may be quite well ossified before it transforms, whereas in others the greatest part of ossification occurs during or after metamorphosis. Ossification proceeds cephalocaudally in those species for which there are data; thus, elements of the skull begin to ossify before vertebral elements, and limb bones ossify in a proximodistal sequence. Only the most generalized scheme of ossification can be outlined for cranial components. Usually the first bones to appear before metamorphosis are neurocranial roofing and flooring elements (frontoparietal and parasphenoid) and the exoccipitals, which form the back end of the skull. During late prometamorphosis and metamorphic climax, the auditory area of the braincase (prootic) ossifies along with the roof of the nasal capsule (nasal), the septomaxilla internal to the nasal capsule, and the upper jaw (maxilla and premaxilla). During the latter part of metamorphic climax, the main elements of the mandible (dentary and angulosplenial) appear along with the bracing elements of the maxillary arch (pterygoid and squamosal) and the vomer. The last bones to ossify are the mentomeckelians at the mandibular symphysis, the palatine, quadratojugal, columella, and sphenethmoid, which forms the anterior end of the braincase. As pointed out by Trueb and Alberch (1985), those elements that frequently are absent from the skulls of some anurans (i.e., vomer, palatine, quadratojugal, and columella) are among the last cranial components to appear.

Integument

Amphibian skin is a dynamic cellular system adapted to a complex and changing life cycle. The larval epidermis and dermis are composed of many different cellular components, each of which differs in structure, function, and topographic relationships; also some kinds of cells differ in their times of origin and duration of existence. The skin becomes progressively more elaborate in its cellular composition as development proceeds. However, some kinds of epidermal cells originate early in larval life and disappear prior to prometamorphosis. Other kinds exist throughout larval and adult life. Although the ultimate fate of some specialized cells is unknown, it is likely that apart from the germinative layer, most if not all epidermal cells and much of the dermis ultimately degenerate and disappear; some of these are replaced regularly throughout life.

The epidermis proper is formed when the outer epithelial layers of the skin are delimited by a basement membrane. Larval epidermis consists of two or three layers of cells; these increase to five or six layers at metamorphic climax. In early larvae the epidermis lies on the thin, unstructured basement membrane and a thicker collagenous lamella. In addition to epithelial cells, larval epidermis contains some specialized cells (Table 7-3). These include:

1. Merkel cells constitute only about 0.3% of the number of epidermal cells and have reciprocal synapses with nerve terminals; possibly they function as mechanoreceptors. Apparently they originate from interstitial cells in the epidermis, and they persist in adults.
2. Leydig cells are specialized epithelial cells that probably secrete mucus into subsurface extracellular compartments of the epidermis. Although they occur in tadpoles, they are far more abundant in salamander larvae. The Leydig cells disappear at metamorphosis.
3. Stiftchenzellen are possibly chemoreceptor cells in the epidermis of anuran larvae; they are unknown in adults and presumably degenerate at metamorphosis.
4. Mitochondria-rich cells that possibly function in osmoregulation or ion transport have been

identified in the epidermis of anuran larvae; cells of the same type occur in the epithelium of the bladder and palate of some adults but not in the epidermis of adults.
5. Flask cells, which are rich in mitochondria in adults, first appear in situ in the epidermis at metamorphic climax.
6. Goblet cells are mucous surface cells known in tadpoles of *Xenopus*.
7. Mucous surface cells are mucus-producing cells that appear in early larval stages and persist after metamorphosis.
8. Ciliary cells develop in embryos and function in embryonic movements; some of these persist as vestiges in early larval stages.
9. Neuromast cells are the sensory cells in the lateral-line system characteristic of all amphibian larvae, aquatic adult salamanders, and adult pipid frogs. The lateral-line organs originate from pre- and postauditory placodes and subsequently migrate and differentiate. Each neuromast cell has a surface kinocilium and stereocilia. Lateral-line systems are fully developed at the time of hatching. Their development has been described for a newt, *Cynops pyrrhogaster* (Sato and Kawakami, 1976). The changes that take place at metamorphosis in *Xenopus laevis* affect the histology and innervation of the neuromast cells (Shelton, 1970). In *Xenopus*, the individual sensory plaques sink inward; tactile structures develop between the organs, and some rows of larval plaques are reduced or lost. At metamorphosis the innervation of the lateral line is augmented by the appearance of a small myelinated inhibitory nerve, which possibly switches off the lateral-line organs while the frog is swimming.

Table 7-3. Cellular Components of Skin in Larval and Adult Amphibians[a]

Component	Larva[b] Tail	Larva[b] Body	Adult Body[b]
Epithelial cells	E	E	E
Surface keratinocytes	E	E	E
Keratinized beak cells	—	E	—
Hatching gland cells	—	E	—
Cement gland cells	—	E	—
Ciliary cells	E	E	E
Mucous surface cells	E	E	E
Merkel cells	E	E	E
Stiftchenzellen (anurans)	E	E	E
Mitochondria-rich cells	E	E[c]	E
Flask cells	—	E	E
Goblet cells (*Xenopus*)	E	E	—
Leydig cells (salamanders)	E	E	—
Melanophores	D, E	D, E	D, E
Xanthophores	—	D	D
Iridophores	D	D	D
Mesenchymal macrophages	D, E	D, E	D, E
Mesenchymal fibroblasts	D	D	D
Granulocytes	D, E	D, E	D, E
Polymorphonuclear leucocytes	D, E	D, E	D, E
Nerve fibers	D, E	D, E	D, E
Schwann cells	D	D	D
Neuroblast organs	E	E	E[d]
Striated muscle tissue	D	D	D
Smooth muscle tissue	D	D	D
Mucous and granular glands	—	D	D

[a]Adapted from Fox (1981).
[b]E is Epidermis, D is dermis.
[c]Bladder (*Bufo*) and palate (*Rana*).
[d]*Xenopus* and obligate neotenic salamanders.

Some specialized cells develop into adhesive glands ventral to the mouth in anuran embryos, and elongate, bottle-shaped cells form hatching glands on the head of embryos; both of these kinds of cells degenerate shortly after hatching. In anurans some epidermal cells are keratinized to form the beaks and denticles of tadpoles; these structures degenerate at metamorphic climax. Other epidermal structures include immigrant melanophores, polymorphonuclear neutrophils, granulocytes, mesenchymal macrophages, and nerve fibers.

During larval life the dermis becomes organized and many structures appear by metamorphic climax. These include melanophores, xanthophores, iridophores, granulocytes and other leucocytes usually in capillaries, mesenchymal fibroblasts and macrophages, and multicellular mucous and granular (serous) glands. These glands open by means of ducts at the surface of the skin at climax. Also there are muscle fibers and nerve components, in-

Figure 7-2. Adult and recently metamorphosed young of *Ambystoma opacum* from Centreville, Virginia, showing differences in color pattern. Photo by K. Nemuras.

cluding Schwann cells (nucleated neurosheaths) (Table 7-3).

Thus, during larval development and metamorphosis the dermis is continually becoming more complex and approaching the condition in adults, whereas the epidermis undergoes various stages of appearance and disappearance of cellular structures before assuming the adult condition. In general, cellular degeneration of larval epidermis occurs by autolysis, demonstrated by autophagy and the presence of cytolysosomes (Fox, 1981). Some necrotic cells, such as those of hatching glands and adhesive glands, probably are phagocytosed by neighboring macrophages. Likewise, probably most of the remnants of autolysed cells of the external gills suffer phagocytosis. Epidermal cells autolyze, keratinize, and are shed.

There is variable influence of thyroid hormones on the origin, development, and subsequent degeneration of dermal and epidermal structures. The life cycles of ciliary cells, and the cells comprising hatching glands, adhesive glands, and epithelial gill filaments probably are independent of thyroid hormones, as are the origin and differentiation of Stiftchenzellen, Merkel cells, chromatophores, mitochondria-rich cells, neuromast cells, and mesenchymal fibroblasts (Fox, 1981). The origin and differentiation of epidermal flask cells and skin glands and also the ultimate loss of beaks and denticles in tadpoles and keratinized lips in salamander larvae seem to depend on a threshold level of thyroid hormone.

The adult conditions of glandular development or pigmentation are not necessarily attained at metamorphosis. The development of dermal glands continues after the froglet assumes a terrestrial life; this is particularly noticeable in those anurans that have thick, glandular skin as adults (e.g., *Bufo*). Many recently metamorphosed amphibians have color patterns unlike those of the adults (Fig. 7-2); the adult pattern usually develops within a few days after the completion of morphological metamorphosis. The striking blue and yellow bars on the flanks of the hylid *Agalychnis callidryas* only become apparent several weeks after metamorphosis, during which time the iris changes from gold to red (P. Starrett, 1960).

Musculature

Head and body muscles present in larvae undergo remodeling during metamorphosis. In *Rana pipiens* exposure of the m. rectus abdominis to hormonal changes, which presumably are similar throughout the muscle, elicits proliferation of fibers medially and degeneration of fibers laterally (K. Lynch, 1984). This contrasts with the remodeling of the jaw musculature during metamorphosis, which entails the loss of larval muscle fibers and their simultaneous replacement by new fibers that form the adult muscles (Alley and Cameron, 1983).

Tail

Upon metamorphosis the caudal fins of salamander and caecilian larvae are resorbed. Presumably the resorption of the fins is accomplished in the same way as the degeneration of the entire tail in anuran tadpoles. In anurans the degeneration of the tail begins with the fins, followed by the distal musculature, and finally the proximal musculature. Resorption of tissues in salamanders terminates with the caudal fins, but the controlling factors that halt degeneration at that point are not known. As summarized by M. Dodd and J. Dodd (1976), tail resorption is a remarkable example of controlled cell death. Presumably this is genetically programmed, and the proximate controlling agent is thyroxin. Autolysis and phagocytosis are the main agents responsible for tail resorption, but lysosomes may play a role. Caudal tissues become increasingly acidic during metamorphic climax, as various acid hydrolases accumulate in the tissues; these are the principal enzymes associated with tissue degeneration. Apparently just prior to the initiation of tail resorption, there is a thyroxin-stimulated synthesis of hydrolytic enzymes, possibly by macrophages.

Limbs

The growth of the limbs of all amphibians that have them is a continuous process from early limb-bud stages with no dramatic changes during metamorphosis. The hindlimbs of anuran larvae develop in much the same way as those of salamander larvae, but in late prometamorphosis certain structures, such as subarticular and metatarsal tubercles, toe pads, and webbing, develop. The forelimbs of anurans that have aquatic larvae develop in peribranchial sacs within the branchial chamber and emerge well developed at the beginning of metamorphic climax. The skin covering the developing forelimbs becomes thin and transparent before the eruption of the limbs. In at least some frogs having direct development (e.g., *Eleutherodactylus)*, the forelimbs develop externally. Subsequent to metamorphosis, tubercles and other structures, such as toe pads, continue to differentiate and develop into the adult form. Webbing between the toes of recently metamorphosed frogs commonly is much less extensive than in adults. Limb growth and development are dependent on thyroxin, as is the eruption of the forelimbs in anurans.

Alimentary Canal

The gross structure of the alimentary canal does not change much during metamorphosis in salamanders and caecilians, although the small intestine in at least one salamander, *Ambystoma tigrinum*, is about 25% shorter in adults than in larvae (Tilley, 1964). However, in anuran tadpoles the digestive tract consists mainly of a long, coiled intestine, which undergoes drastic changes at metamorphosis. Other changes also occur.

The epithelium in the buccal cavity retains the goblet cells present in larvae, but other structures develop de novo, including: (1) intermaxillary glands posterior to the premaxillae and between the nasal capsules; (2) palatine glands associated with the prevomerine teeth; (3) cilia, which are especially numerous and active in the vicinity of the outlets of the intermaxillary glands; and (4) a tongue derived from muscle tissue in the floor of the mouth. In salamanders, and presumably in caecilians, the adult tongue incorporates a "primary" tongue that develops in larvae, whereas the tongue in anurans is a completely new structure.

The digestive tracts of salamander and caecilian larvae are much the same as in adults; in fact, the most noticeable changes in the gastrointestinal tract in salamanders occurs just before the young larvae begin to feed. At that time the last of the yolk is absorbed, and peristalsis begins. Subsequent changes in the gut involve the increase in the surface of the epithelial lining by folding and the development of microvilli.

Whereas a true pepsin-secreting stomach is present in larval salamanders (Kunz, 1924) and presumably in caecilians, a true stomach is absent in anuran larvae. Instead, the presumptive stomach region of the gut usually is not enlarged and has associated with it a manicotto gland in most anuran larvae. The gland is absent in pelobatids and bufonids, and its occurrence is sporadic in some other groups (Griffiths, 1961). The manicotto gland develops in late embryonic stages and is formed from elements of the ventral pancreatic anlage, which proliferates within the wall of the gut. In most tadpoles a connection between the pancreas and the manicotto gland persists only until early premetamorphosis. Typically the manicotto gland surrounds the foregut; the gland consists of long cords arranged in a complex pattern of branching crypts that communicate with the lumen of the gut, not by definitive ducts, but through irregular gaps in the epithelium. In most kinds of tadpoles, the lumen of the foregut in the region of the manicotto gland is lined with ciliated epithelium enclosed in a sheath of circular muscle. There are some notable deviations from the typical development and structure. Tadpoles of *Xenopus, Rana macrodactyla,* and *Heleophryne rosei* retain a connection between the pancreas and the manicotto gland until metamorphosis. Carnivorous tadpoles of *Ceratophrys* and *Occidozyga* have a thick muscular coat surrounding the gland, no cilia in the lumen of the foregut, and a greatly reduced number of epithelial perforations. In microhylid tadpoles the pattern of the crypts is more complex, and the crypts are more extensive than those of other tadpoles. The manicotto gland is limited to the pancreatic side of the gut in *Alytes obstetricans,* but the gland encircles the foregut in other discoglossids that have been studied. In the tadpoles of the rhacophorid *Philautus gryllus* the manicotto gland is modified into a muscular diverticulum connected to the lumen of the foregut by two ciliated canals and another opening that permits only discharge into the foregut. These various modifications might be correlated with the dietary habits of the tadpoles (Griffiths, 1961).

The postesophageal part of the foregut that is associated with the manicotto gland apparently has no digestive functions and serves only for the storage of food. During metamorphosis the cells of the manicotto gland degenerate and are replaced by new cells incorporated into the gut; the new cells secrete pepsin, so it is at this time that a functional stomach is formed. The midgut or intestine shrinks greatly; the luminal cilia are replaced by microvilli. The major changes in the alimentary canal begin prior to the emergence of the forelimbs. During this dramatic shift in the digestive system to change from the digestion of small particles of plant material to large pieces of animal tissues, the metamorphosing froglet is incapable of digesting any kind of food for several days.

Pancreas

In late prometamorphosis, the exocrine pancreas begins to decrease in size; this seems to be caused in part by the degeneration of acinar cells and tissues and also by dehydration. Degeneration occurs by autolysis, but probably some phagocytosis ensues. Absolute reduction in volume of the pancreas may be as much as 80%. Immediately after metamorphosis the pancreas increases in size, with a relatively larger increase in the endocrine tissue because of proliferating islets of specialized types of cells. New RNA is synthesized as the pancreas regenerates; perhaps some predetermined cells need to degenerate in order to permit the remaining rudimentary pancreas to develop into the adult pancreas (Fox, 1981). These changes in the pancreas are induced by thyroxin.

Urogenital System

Larval amphibians have a relatively primitive type of kidney that functions primarily in the excretion of water and ammonia, whereas in terrestrial adults the kidney functions to conserve water and excrete urea. Concomitant with the morphological metamorphosis of the kidney is the development and differentiation of the gonads (Fig. 7-3).

The larval kidney is the pronephros which forms from the anterior nephrostomes and persists throughout larval life only to regress and disappear by the end of metamorphosis in salamanders and anurans. Degeneration starts at about the time of the onset of metamorphic climax and is complete by the end of metamorphosis. Degeneration involves autolysis and phagocytosis; lysosomes in the form of degeneration bodies also may be important. Pronephric growth, differentiation, and ultimate degeneration are controlled mainly by circulating thyroid hormones. Structurally the pronephros is a tightly arranged mass of tubules with ciliated nephrostomial ducts leading to the coelom. Anurans have three nephrostomial ducts; primitive salamanders (cryptobranchids) have five, and more advanced salamanders, only two. Caecilians, in which the pronephros is greatly elongate, have 8 to 12 nephrostomial ducts. The nephrostomial tubules join to form a common tubule, the Wolffian duct. Evaginations of the dorsal aorta form paired glomeruli, which are partially surrounded by outpocketings of the nephrostomial ducts (Bowman's capsules).

In caecilians the anterior part of the kidney remains intact and, together with differentiating nephric tissue from the middle and posterior nephrostomes, persists in adults as an elongate opisthonephros connected by tubules to the Wolffian duct throughout its entire length. Prior to the degeneration of the pronephros, the middle and posterior nephrostomes differentiate into functional kidneys

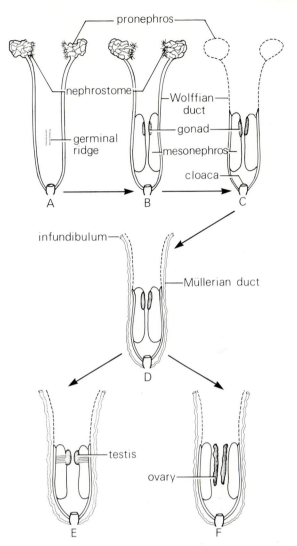

Figure 7-3. Diagrammatic representation of the development of the urogenital system in anurans. **A.** Young larva with three nephrostomes, Wolffian ducts, and germinal ridges. **B.** Late larva with functional pronephros and mesonephros. **C.** Metamorphosis with degeneration of pronephros and anterior part of the Wolffian duct. **D.** Undifferentiated state of genital tract. **E.** Sexually differentiated male. **F.** Sexually differentiated female. Gonads are shaded. Based on Gallien (1958).

in salamanders, whereas only the posterior nephrostomal tissues persist in anurans. In these mesonephric kidneys, along with the opisthonephric kidneys of caecilians, the tubular connections with the coelom have been lost, and the glomeruli are contained within Bowman's capsules.

Genital ridges are formed by sexually undifferentiated primordia in the peritoneal cavity in close association with the nephrostomes. Parts of these ridges give rise to the gonads; the anterior parts form the fat bodies (Franchi et al., 1962). The genital ridges develop in a posterior direction, and two areas become distinct—a peripheral cortex derived from proliferation of the peritoneal epithelium, and an inner medulla. Concomitant with the development of the genital ridges, primordial germ cells, which originate from extragonadal sources, migrate into the ridges by passive movements induced by differential growth of the embryonic tissues. In anurans the germ cells are derived from presumptive endoderm, but those in salamanders are thought to originate from lateral-plate mesoderm (Franchi et al., 1962). The origin of germ cells in caecilians is unknown. Later differentiation of the gonads follows different patterns in males and females. Proliferation of the cortex with a concomitant regression of the medulla forms hollow ovaries by folding of the germinal ridge; the internal lining of the ovaries is medullary in origin. The reverse is true in males; the medulla develops into testes, while the cortex regresses. In the undifferentiated gonads, mesenchyme cells separate the medullary tissue from the cortex; these cells eventually give rise to the tunic ensheathing the testes. In the Bufonidae, cortical remnants of the germinal ridge form Bidder's organs in males. These round structures on the anterior ends of the testes consist of a compact mass of small oocytes surrounding a vestigial ovarian cavity; these oocytes remain in an immature state.

During development two pairs of ducts are derived from primitive kidney ducts and develop in both sexes to become the forerunners of the adult genital ducts. These are the Müllerian and Wolffian ducts; each pair extends from the primordial gonads to the cloaca. Commonly both sets of ducts are present in larvae; upon metamorphosis the Müllerian ducts tend to degenerate in males, whereas in females they become the functional oviducts. The Wolffian ducts persist in both sexes. In larval amphibians the Wolffian ducts first function as the primary nephric ducts draining the pronephric tubules, and later they become the mesonephric ducts. In females the Wolffian ducts retain their exclusively excretory function, but in males they also serve as genital ducts after the efferent ductules of the medullary cords join the mesonephric tubules. Unlike the Müllerian ducts, the Wolffian ducts retain no connection with the nephric tubules. There is variable regression of the Müllerian ducts in male anurans; usually they regress to small rudiments, but in some members of the *Rana pipiens* complex they persist throughout life as complete ducts.

The gonads and their products differentiate and develop continuously during larval life in caecilians and salamanders, whereas in anurans the testes may differentiate and mature well before metamorphic climax (e.g., *Pleurodema cinerea)*, shortly before metamorphic climax (e.g., *Ceratophrys ornata* and *Rana catesbeiana),* or long after metamorphosis (e.g., *Bufo arenarum)* (Lofts, 1974). In anurans the ovaries do not mature until well after metamorphosis.

Nervous System

The general transitions in the nervous system during metamorphosis have been summarized by Kollros (1981) and Fox (1984). Changes in the nervous system have been demonstrated to be effected directly by increased amounts of thyroid hormone (T_4). However, many neural structures have yet to be studied with respect to modifications that occur during development, particularly during or near metamorphic climax.

Gross changes in the central nervous system, which is well developed by prometamorphosis, include (in anurans) reduction in size but thickening of the walls of the ventricles of the cerebellum and medulla oblongata, widening and shortening of the diencephalon, and narrowing and shortening of the fossa rhomboidalis of the medulla. In tadpoles the cerebellum remains in a relatively early developmental stage during premetamorphosis, and has a more rapid development during prometamorphosis and a rapid maturation during metamorphic climax. Some of the changes are associated with corresponding modifications of the shape of the chondrocranium as it ossifies. By comparison, changes in the gross morphology of the brains in salamanders are slight.

The spinal cord differentiates proximodistally and enters the tail in early premetamorphosis, and incipient dorsal root ganglia are evident at that time. During metamorphic climax there is selective degeneration of some cellular components of the spinal cord and ganglia in the body, whereas there is complete degeneration of those in the tail of anurans.

Studies on some special cells in the nervous system have revealed notable modifications during metamorphic climax. Paired Mauthner cells, on each side of the medulla, have long axons extending through the trunk cord to the tail. These cells are considered to be adaptations to aquatic life and disappear in anurans at or shortly after metamorphic climax. They persist for as long as 2 months after metamorphosis in *Xenopus* and are unknown in *Bufo* (Moulton et al., 1968). The development and growth of the Mauthner cells is controlled by increasing levels of circulating thyroid hormones in pre- and postmetamorphosis, and their disappearance seems to be associated with the dramatic decrease in circulating thyroid hormones at metamorphic climax.

Rohon-Beard cells are primary sensory cells located on either side of the dorsal midline of the spinal cord in tadpoles. They develop anteroposteriorly in the body and then the tail. They are present in maximal numbers in early premetamorphosis. Thereafter, cell loss proceeds gradually anteroposteriorly, and by late prometamorphosis only a few degenerating cells remain. Degeneration of Rohon-Beard cells occurs earlier in *Xenopus* than in *Rana* (Nieuwkoop and Faber, 1976). Because cell loss occurs so early in larval life, it is unlikely that the loss is related directly to thyroid hormones; more likely the loss is related to the early development of the spinal ganglia, which take over the sensory functions initially assumed by the Rohon-Beard cells (Kollros, 1981). However, final degeneration at metamorphic climax may be influenced by changing levels of thyroid hormones (Stephens, 1965).

The cells of the lateral motor column provide motor innervation to the limbs. The development of the lumbar cells occurs in late embryonic stages, and the brachial cells in prometamorphosis. The number of cells increases to a maximum and then declines gradually to metamorphic climax, when the number stabilizes. Thyroid hormones are essential for the growth and differentiation of the lateral motor column neurons, but increased levels of circulating thyroid hormones in late prometamorphosis apparently stabilize the number of cells.

The maturation changes in the cerebellum include a reduction in the number of external granule cells, the migration of most of these cells into the internal granular layer, and the conversion of small, immature Purkinje cells into large, mature ones. Purkinje cells are flask-shaped cells forming an incomplete layer between the molecular and nuclear layers of the cerebellar cortex. The growth and maturation of the Purkinje cells is dependent on thyroid hormones.

The proprioceptors of the jaw musculature, the cells of the mesencephalic nucleus of the trigeminal nerve, appear in the optic tectum just as feeding begins in larval *Ambystoma* and *Rana*. The number of cells increases rapidly during development, and in *Rana* the number of cells is highest just prior to metamorphic climax; this suggests that some cells die during climax. In *Ambystoma* the size of the cells decreases with time, but in *Rana* the size remains small throughout most of the larval period, begins to increase in prometamorphosis, increases more rapidly during metamorphic climax, and increases more slowly after metamorphosis. The observed differences between *Rana* and *Ambystoma* may be related to the modifications of the suspensorium and associated musculature in anurans, whereas few changes occur in these structures in salamanders. The mesencephalic nucleus cells are insensitive to thyroid hormones at the time of their appearance and also again several months after metamorphosis; in the meantime, sensitivity to thyroid hormones begins early in larval life and increases rapidly through metamorphosis.

Sensory Structures

Most sensory structures undergo changes during metamorphosis; changes in the lateral-line system are discussed in the section Integument, and the development of the ear is discussed in the section Skeleton.

In larval amphibians, internal and external corneas are separated by intraorbital fluid. These cornea fuse at metamorphic climax to form the single adult cornea. In late premetamorphosis and during metamorphic climax the relatively thin and weakly developed extrinsic ocular muscles grow enormously and simultaneously shift their points of origin mediad on the parasphenoid. The eye itself increases in size, and this growth, in combination with the growth of the extrinsic ocular muscles, produces the bulging eyes characteristic of most amphibians (except caecilians and obligate neotenic salamanders). During metamorphic climax in most salamanders and anurans, accessory structures—upper and lower eyelids, nictitating membrane, and conjunctival sacs—develop from

epidermal folds. Also, at metamorphic climax the tendon of the nictitating membrane and the lacrimal duct develop. These structures do not develop, or develop only partially, in obligate neotenic salamanders and pipid frogs. In caecilians the eyes degenerate and are covered by a thin layer of bone and/or skin.

Changes in the optical properties of the eyes of *Salamandra salamandra* and *Pelobates syriacus* were documented by Sivak and Warburg (1980, 1983), who found that during metamorphosis there is change from a spherical lens to a flattened lens. This change is much more gradual in *Pelobates* than in *Salamandra;* in fact, the refractory power of the lenses of tadpoles in late prometamorphosis is poor in the aquatic environment. Moreover, the alignment of the eyes changes from a lateral plane to an anterolateral plane; this takes place during metamorphic climax at the time of the development of the sclerotic ring that supports the eye in metamorphosed amphibians.

Eyes are poorly developed in subterranean salamanders. In *Proteus, Haideotriton,* and *Typhlomolge,* lenses and retinal structures fail to develop completely, and in juveniles the vestiges of these structures degenerate. However, in *Typhlotriton* the eye structures develop fully, but in juveniles there is partial degeneration (Besharse and Brandon, 1974).

The chemosensory organs of Jacobson develop as ventromedian grooves in the floor of the nasal sacs. With the exception of *Siren* (Jurgens, 1971), the nasal sacs rotate on their longitudinal axes so that the organs of Jacobson lie in a lateral position. During metamorphic climax, the epithelial lining differentiates into the glands composing the organs.

During late prometamorphosis and metamorphic climax, the nasolacrimal duct is formed from rodlike thickenings of epidermal cells. According to Schmalhausen (1968), the duct has two origins—partly from the posterior nostril and partly from tissues that gave rise to the infraorbital seismosensory canal of crossopterygian fishes. At about the same time in development, orbital (or Harderian) glands develop as thickenings of epidermal cells immediately anterior to the eye.

In caecilians, the tentacle develops in late embryos and is evident in young free-swimming larvae. The tentacular sheath probably represents the enlarged common duct of the orbital glands, which in caecilians function to lubricate the tentacular sheath rather than the degenerate eyes. The tentacle develops from a longitudinal epithelial fold in the wall of the duct (Badenhorst, 1978). The retractor muscle of the tentacle is homologous with the m. retractor bulbi of anurans and salamanders.

NEOTENY

The phenomenon of attaining reproductive maturity while retaining the larval external morphology has been known in salamanders since the middle of the last century. The multiplicity of terminology referencing aspects of delayed somatic maturity and precocious reproductive maturity has hampered effective communication. Well-entrenched terms such as neoteny, paedogenesis, and paedomorphosis have been variously redefined (e.g., Pierce and H. Smith, 1979); new terms such as progenesis (S. Gould, 1977) and parthenopaedogenesis (Dubois, 1979b) have been introduced.

Neoteny is used here in the sense of Gould (1977), who summarized the evidence that larval reproduction in salamanders is the result of delayed somatic development and not precocious reproductive development. Thus, it seems that paedogenesis is not a common cause of larval reproduction in salamanders, and the general phenomenon of reproduction by salamanders in their larval state may be justifiably termed neoteny in both the broad and narrow sense of the term. Paedogenesis should be ap-

Table 7-4. Taxonomic Occurrence of Neoteny in Salamanders

Taxon	Reference
Hynobiidae	
Hynobius lichenatus	Sasaki (1924)
Cryptobranchidae	
*Cryptobranchus alleganiensis**	Nickerson and Mays (1973)
Andrias	
*davidianus**	Liu (1950)
*japonicus**	Stejneger (1907)
Sirenidae	
*Pseudobranchus striatus**	Martof (1974)
Siren (2 species)*	Martof (1974)
Salamandridae	
Notophthalmus	
perstriatus	Bishop (1943)
viridescens	Brandon and Bremer (1966)
Triturus	
alpestris	Rocek (1974)
cristatus	Dely (1967)
helveticus	Gabrion et al. (1977)
Amphiumidae	
Amphiuma (3 species)*	Salthe (1973)
Proteidae	
Necturus (5 species)*	Hecht (1958)
*Proteus anguinus**	Briegleb (1962a)
Ambystomatidae	
Ambystoma	
*dumerilii**	Brandon (1970a)
gracile	Sprules (1974b)
*lacustris**	Tihen (1969)
*lermaense**	Tihen (1969)
*mexicanum**	Brunst (1955)
ordinarium	J. Anderson and Worthington (1971)
*subsalsum**	Tihen (1969)
talpoideum	A. F. Carr and C. Goin (1943)
tigrinum	Gehlbach (1967)
Rhyacosiredon altamirani	Brandon and Altig (1973)
Dicamptodontidae	
Dicamptodon ensatus	Nussbaum (1976)
Plethodontidae	
Eurycea	
*latitans**	B. Brown (1967a)
multiplicata	Dundee (1965a)
*nana**	B. Brown (1967b)
neotenes	Sweet (1977a)
*tridentifera**	Sweet (1977b)
*troglodytes**	J. Baker (1966)
*tynerensis**	Dundee (1965b)
*Gyrinophilus palleucus**	Brandon (1966a)
*Haideotriton wallacei**	Brandon (1967b)
Typhlomolge	
*rathbuni**	Potter and Sweet (1981)
*robusta**	Potter and Sweet (1981)
Typhlotriton spelaeus	Brandon (1970b)

*Obligate neotenes in nature.

Table 7-5. Comparative Patterns of Metamorphosis in Genera of Obligate Neotenic Families of Salamanders

Genus	Cerato-branchials	Maxillae	Septo-maxillae	Lacrimals	Gills	Gill slits	Skin
Andrias	2	+	−	−	0	0	Adult
Cryptobranchus	4	+	−	−	0	1	Adult
Pseudobranchus	4	+	+	+	1	1	Larval
Siren	4	+	+	+	3	3	Adult
Necturus	3	−	+	+	3	2	Larval
Proteus	3	−	+	+	3	2	Larval
Amphiuma	4	+	+	+	0	1	Adult

plied only when direct evidence suggests that larvae are sexually mature as the result of accelerated reproductive development.

Occurrence of Neoteny

All members of four families of salamanders are neotenic, and at least some populations of salamanders in all other families have neotenic individuals (Table 7-4). Aquatic larvae are highly transitory in caecilians, and it is most unlikely that any are neotenic. Although "neotenic" anuran larvae have been described from time to time, these all have been individuals with abnormal thyroid glands that resulted in failure to metamorphose completely, and these fail to reproduce (Wassersug, 1975). Space for the gonads and especially for the storage of eggs does not become available until metamorphosis of anuran larvae.

The fifteen species of obligate neotenic salamanders constituting all of the living species of four families exhibit different patterns of partial metamorphosis (Table 7-5). These range from the failure of certain cranial and jaw elements to develop to the retention of larval skin containing Leydig cells. Salamanders of the genera *Andrias, Cryptobranchus,* and *Amphiuma* resorb their gills, and in *Andrias* the gill slits close. Three pairs of external gills are retained in adults of all of the others, except *Pseudobranchus,* which retains only one pair.

Five species of *Ambystoma* and nine species of hemidactyline plethodontids are obligate neotenes in nature, whereas fifteen species in four families are known to be facultatively neotenic. The most famous neotenic salamander is the Mexican axolotl, *A. mexicanum* (Fig. 7-4);

it was referenced in 3311 books and articles from 1615 to 1970 (H. Smith and R. B. Smith, 1971). Much of this literature has dealt with experimental embryology and endocrinology of laboratory-reared animals in the United States and Europe. The largest of the neotenic *Ambystoma* is *A. dumerilii* (Fig. 7-4).

Spontaneous metamorphosis has been reported for *Ambystoma dumerilii* and *A. mexicanum* (Brandon, 1976; H. Smith and R. B. Smith, 1971), but in each case the animals were stressed during shipment or manipulation in the laboratory, or they survived for only short periods of time. There are no substantiated reports of either of these species undergoing metamorphosis in their natural habitat. Four species of *Ambystoma* are facultatively neotenic; some populations normally metamorphose, whereas others do not unless their aquatic environment becomes uninhabitable. The best known of these facultative *Ambystoma* are *A. gracile* and *A. tigrinum* (Fig. 7-5). Likewise, one *Hynobius* and five newts have populations that sometimes do not metamorphose, whereas other populations do metamorphose into terrestrial adults. Only three of twelve neotenic species of hemidactyline plethodontids are known to metamorphose in nature. The most specialized of the obligate neotenes among the plethodontids are *Haideotriton wallacei* and the two species of *Typhlomolge* (Fig. 7-6).

Endocrine Aspects of Neoteny

The discovery of neotenic salamanders provided experimental biologists with ideal laboratory animals for determining the endocrinological control of metamorphosis;

Figure 7-4. Two neotenic species of *Ambystoma.* (Left) *A. mexicanum* from Lago Texcoco, Mexico. (Right) *A. dumerilii* from Lago de Pátzcuaro, Mexico. Both of these species are confined to lakes on the southern part of the Mexican Plateau and normally do not metamorphose in nature. Photos by H. B. Shaffer.

Figure 7-5. A neotenic, subterranean plethodontid salamander, *Typhlomolge rathbuni,* from Ezell's Cave, Texas. The eyes are degenerate, and the skin lacks pigment. Photo by E. J. Maruska.

most of the knowledge is based on two species— *Ambystoma mexicanum* and *A. tigrinum.* However, experimental work also has involved some of the neotenic plethodontids, as well as other species of *Ambystoma.*

In obligate neotenes, such as *Necturus, Proteus,* and *Amphiuma,* the major cause for cessation of metamorphosis seems to be insensitivity of tissues to thyroid hormone (J. Harris, 1956); treatment of these salamanders with thyroid hormone may result in some initial changes, such as sloughing of skin or reduction of gills, but prolonged treatment is lethal. Some neotenic plethodontids (*Haideotriton* and *Typhlomolge*) undergo partial metamorphosis when treated with thyroxin (Dundee, 1957, 1961), whereas others (*Eurycea tynerensis* and *Gyrinophilus palleucus*) can be induced to complete metamorphosis (Kezer, 1952; Dent and Kirby-Smith, 1963).

Experiments with facultatively neotenic *Ambystoma* have demonstrated that thyroid hormone (T_4) readily induces metamorphosis and that the thyroids of these salamanders are sensitive to thyroid-stimulating hormone (Taurog, 1974). Similar results were obtained from experiments on newts— *Notophthalmus viridescens* (Dent, 1968) and *Triturus helveticus* (Gabrion and Sentein, 1972). There is a low rate of uptake of labeled iodine by the thyroids of neotenic salamanders; the rates of facultative neotenes is intermediate between the rates of obligate neotenes and those of species that normally metamorphose (D. Norris and Platt, 1974).

Nearly all of the evidence indicates that in facultatively neotenic salamanders the level of activity in the hypothalamo-pituitary-thyroid axis is very low, and most results support the view that the primary failure is at the hypothalamic level (e.g., D. Norris and Platt, 1973; Taurog et al., 1974). Whether external or internal cues, which activate the axis, are lacking, or whether, for genetic or some other reasons, some individuals are insensitive to them is not known for certain. However, natural selection may be operating to select genotypes for neoteny in areas of harsh terrestrial environments.

ECOLOGICAL AND EVOLUTIONARY SIGNIFICANCE OF METAMORPHOSIS

Theoretically, the ranges of body sizes at metamorphosis and the duration of the larval stage (and therefore time of metamorphosis) of individuals in a given population are determined by a minimum body size that must be attained and a maximum body size that cannot be exceeded at metamorphosis (Wilbur and Collins, 1973). Between these two size thresholds, the endocrinological initiation of metamorphosis is expected to be related to the recent growth history of the individual larva. Species that exploit ephemeral aquatic environments, such as temporary ponds, will have a wide range of possible sizes at metamorphosis, whereas those developing in relatively stable environments will have a narrow range.

According to Wilbur and Collins' (1973) interpretation of their extensive observations and experiments on *Ambystoma maculatum* and *Rana sylvatica,* the large variation in the length of the larval period and body size at metamorphosis cannot be explained solely by differences in dates of hatching or egg sizes. Therefore, they proposed that as development proceeds, variation in exponential growth coefficients causes a trend from a normal to a skewed distribution of body sizes. The degree of skewing increases, and the median of the distribution decreases, with increasing initial densities of populations. The relative advantages of the largest members of a cohort may arise from a variety of mechanisms including the production of growth inhibitors, interference competition, and size-selective feeding behavior. These mechanisms result in a nonnormal distribution of competitive ability, a possible source of the density-dependent competition coefficient found in many species (Wilbur, 1972).

As noted by Wilbur and Collins (1973), teleologially the decision to initiate metamorphosis is an educated (adaptive) guess that the risk of metamorphosis is less than the risk of remaining in the aquatic habitat. Lack of food and/or desiccation of the aquatic habitat are two major factors that may "force" larvae to metamorphose, if they have reached the critical minimum size and necessary hormonal levels. Because the larval stage is a period of intense feeding and rapid growth, early metamorphosis may result in small, malnourished young that have low survivorship, and those that do survive may require more time to reach reproductive maturity than those that metamorphose at larger sizes.

However, availability of food and stability of the aquatic habitat are not the only factors that may be responsible for the initiation of metamorphosis. In high-elevation populations of *Ambystoma tigrinum* in the Rocky Mountains, temperature of the aquatic habitat determines the size at, and time of, metamorphosis (Bizer, 1978). Growth rates of larvae increase at higher temperatures, whereas sizes of larvae at metamorphosis decrease at higher temperatures. Thus, there is a negative correlation between growth rate and size at metamorphosis in these high-elevation populations.

Temperature-dependent rates of development have been established for various species of amphibians (Chapter 5), but although endocrine production also is correlated with temperature in amphibian larvae, the rates of production and circulation of hormones and the degree of sensitivity of target tissues to the hormones with respect to temperature remain essentially unknown. Therefore, the proposed minimum size at metamorphosis is only one facet of the developmental problems that must be overcome before metamorphosis can be completed successfully. The endocrinological aspects of metamorphosis need to be studied under diverse environmental conditions to arrive at an understanding of possible synergistic effects of hormones and environmental factors (temperature, light, crowding), as well as nutritional state.

The transition from larvae to terrestrial adults in salamanders is a gradual change during which the animals are feeding continuously and seem to have no period of locomotor inhibition. In contrast, metamorphosis in anurans involves a period of degeneration of larval mouthparts and development of adult jaws, during which time the animal is unable to feed. By this time, larval growth has ceased, and all nutrition is provided by the resorption of the tail. Moreover, the period of transformation from a tadpole that propels itself through water by means of its tail to a frog that propels itself through air by means of jumping is a critical period in the survivorship of the animal. It has been demonstrated experimentally (in *Pseudacris triseriata*) that metamorphosing tadpoles cannot sustain swimming nearly as effectively as tadpoles that do not have visible forelimbs; furthermore, froglets that still have a tail are ineffective hoppers as compared with those that have resorbed their tails completely (Wassersug and Sperry, 1977). Analysis of stomach contents of garter snakes (*Thamnophis*) reveals that these snakes are most effective preying on metamorphic stages of several species of anurans (Wassersug and Sperry, 1977; Arnold and Wassersug, 1978). Vulnerability to predation is an ecological obstacle that can be minimized by undergoing metamorphosis rapidly and by synchrony of metamorphosis in cohorts of tadpoles.

The occurrence of either facultative or obligate neoteny among species in the Hynobiidae, Salamandridae, Ambystomatidae, and Plethodontidae is primarily restricted to populations inhabiting permanent aquatic habitats in high montane or arid environments, and usually where fishes are rare or absent. Thus, neotenic populations of *Hynobius lichenatus* and populations of various species of *Triturus* and *Ambystoma* are neotenic in such habitats, whereas at lower elevations or in more mesic habitats populations of the same species characteristically metamorphose.

With respect to *Ambystoma*, Sprules (1974a) summarized evidence on the occurrence of neoteny in permanent aquatic situations. In regions where there exist harsh terrestrial conditions, such as severe temperature fluctuations, lack of suitable cover or food, and low humidity, neoteny will evolve because salamanders that spend their entire lives in the larval form in the water have an adaptive advantage over those that metamorphose and become primarily terrestrial. These conclusions specifically apply to several species of *Ambystoma* and *Triturus*. The facultative response to environmental conditions provides an intraspecific flexibility that certainly is adaptively advantageous over being locked into either obligate neoteny or normal metamorphosis.

There is a high correlation between the presence of facultatively neotenic *Ambystoma* and *Notophthalmus* and the absence of fishes (Sprules, 1974a; Petranka, 1983); yet the obligate neotene *A. dumerilii* coexists with numerous species of fishes in Lake Pátzcuaro in Mexico. Perhaps coexistence is possible because of the large size of the salamanders and/or their nocturnal habits.

Populations of neotenic *Triturus* in Europe have not been studied as thoroughly as *Ambystoma* in North America, but in each species neoteny occurs in populations living in permanent water in harsh terrestrial environments. On limestone plateaus in southern France, the ponds inhabited by *T. helveticus* have no iodine deficiency; furthermore, there is a significant positive correlation between the frequency of neoteny and the concentrations of calcium, magnesium, and phosphorus (Gabrion et al., 1978). The importance of these ions to the maintenance of neoteny, if any, is unknown.

Neoteny in hemidactyline plethodontids is associated with subterranean species living in limestone regions. Those species that are restricted to deep subterranean waters are obligate neotenes, whereas those species that inhabit surface waters, as well as subterranean waters, commonly are facultatively neotenic. Thus, *Haideotriton* and *Typhlomolge* are examples of the obligate extreme, and *Eurycea neotenes* and *Typhlotriton spelaeus* are facultative neotenes intermediate ecologically between the obligate neotenes and those species of *Eurycea* that undergo normal metamorphosis in surface waters. The origin of neoteny in *Eurycea* on the Edwards Plateau in central Texas is related to the limitation of suitable habitat (Sweet, 1977a). During periods of drought when the discharge of surface springs diminishes, salamanders must retreat underground via spring channels. The selective disadvantages of metamorphosis may be most pronounced under conditions of unreliable spring flow; in this situation neotenic individuals can feed while they are underground, but adaptations for terrestrial feeding in metamorphosed individuals are ineffective underwater and in darkness.

On the basis of the foregoing ideas regarding the adaptive significance of facultative neoteny, it is tempting to hypothesize that all cases of neoteny in salamanders evolved in response to unfavorable terrestrial environments. Permanence and stability of aquatic habitats, such as subterranean streams and rivers in ancient positive land masses, could result in salamanders that live in those habitats losing the ability to metamorphose through the insensitivity of tissues to thyroid hormone. Thus, obligate neotenes, such as proteids, sirenids, and amphiumids, may have become neotenic in response to unfavorable terrestrial environments in the Cretaceous, whereas the neotenic plethodontids may have adapted to subterranean aquatic habitats at the time of the developing grasslands in the Miocene. The distribution and generally facultative neoteny of newts and *Ambystoma* suggest that neoteny in these salamanders may be more recent, possibly adaptive responses to Pleistocene and Recent climatic changes.

PART 2

ECOLOGY

CHAPTER 8

Relationships with the Environment

Pity the poor frog, his behavioral and physiological problems are so complicated and interrelated, it is amazing that we can understand them and he is alive at all!

Bayard H. Brattstrom (1979)

Amphibians, especially those that have left the water, generally inhabit environments that are hostile to their basic physiology. Because they are ectotherms and have a permeable body covering, they are more susceptible to the vicissitudes of the environment than any other tetrapods. Nevertheless, by combinations of many unique morphological structures, physiological mechanisms, and behavioral responses, they have adapted to life in nearly all terrestrial habitats, ranging from Arctic tundra to some of the driest deserts in the world, and from elevations of more than 5000 m to sea level, even to brackish mangrove swamps. However, when the diversity of amphibians is examined, physiological limitations are apparent, because the majority of species inhabit regions having high ambient moisture and moderate to warm temperatures.

Because of their abundance and physiological characteristics, some amphibians, especially frogs of the genus *Rana* and salamanders of the genera *Ambystoma, Triturus, Salamandra,* and *Necturus,* have been favorite experimental animals for laboratory physiologists for many decades. This chapter deals with the environmental physiology of amphibians. The major purpose of the material presented herein is a synthesis of the ways amphibians exist with respect to their abiotic environment. Terrestrial conditions are emphasized, for most of the physiological problems associated with the aquatic environment were discussed in relation to the physiology of larvae in Chapter 6.

Although for purposes of organization the material in this chapter is discussed under specific headings of water economy, temperature, etc., it must be kept in mind that the mechanisms involved in one aspect of the organism's physiology cannot be dissociated entirely from another. The physiological interaction of amphibians with their abiotic environment is a complex, dynamic system of related processes.

WATER ECONOMY

Aquatic species are bathed constantly by water; thus they encounter no difficulties with water loss. However, terrestrial amphibians have had to evolve adaptations to cope with the inevitable loss of body water while maintaining a moist skin for gas exchange. Their success is exemplified best in the capability of some amphibians to inhabit demanding, inhospitable deserts, where life poses two major physiological problems—scarcity of water and environmental conditions that accentuate water loss by evaporation.

Water generally makes up 70–80% of the body mass of amphibians; the higher percentages are for aquatic species (Thorson, 1964). Water is exchanged readily with the environment, and water conserving mechanisms could function potentially at several sites:

1. Wherever oxidation takes place throughout the body, metabolic water is produced. This is

added to the watery medium of the protoplasm and is subject to loss from the body only, indirectly, as is water from other sources. However, production of metabolic water amounts to less than 0.01% of the body mass per 24 hours at 20°C (Adolph, 1943). Thus, the amounts of production and loss of metabolic water apparently are of minor importance in the overall water economy of amphibians.

2. Adult amphibians do not drink, except under certain physiological stresses in a laboratory. Thus, the alimentary canal is not an important site of water exchange, except in the degree to which water is ingested as a component of (or incidental to) food. Some of this water may be absorbed in the large intestine, but most is eliminated with the fecal matter.

3. In air-breathing amphibians, the lungs dissipate a small and probably fairly constant quantity of water into the atmosphere. In habitats of high atmospheric moisture, this loss would be negligible. In dry environments, the loss could be considerable over a long period of time.

4. Aquatic amphibians excrete comparatively large quantities of dilute urine; practically all water loss is via the kidneys. Terrestrial amphibians produce urea, and some terrestrial anurans produce uric acid.

5. The vast majority of water lost by terrestrial amphibians is by evaporation from the skin. Rehydration through the skin may occur from free water or from the substrate.

6. Body water can be stored in the urinary bladder and in lymph sacs. Such water provides a supply for body tissues as required because of loss by evaporation, excretion, or respiration.

From these generalities, it is obvious that the significant water-conserving mechanisms must involve (1) the curtailment of water loss through the skin, (2) modifications of the excretory products of the kidneys, and (3) storage of water in vesicles and tissues. Furthermore, survival in terrestrial environments necessitates mechanisms for rehydration.

Because anurans inhabit a wide variety of environments and also occur in arid regions, studies on water economy have been more extensive on anurans than on salamanders. Little is known about caecilians.

Behavioral Adaptations

With a few exceptions among the anurans, terrestrial amphibians generally are nocturnal, thereby avoiding higher daytime temperatures and lower atmospheric humidity. Diurnal retreats of these animals usually have a higher moisture content than surrounding areas exposed to in-

solation and air currents. Thus, the undersides of stones, interiors of logs, depths of leaf mulch, shaded crevices, and axils of leaves of aroids and bromeliads, as well as burrows in the soil, are common diurnal shelters for terrestrial and some arboreal amphibians. Ensconced in a bromeliad with water in the axils of the leaves or within a moist, rotting log, an amphibian can rehydrate during the day. If sufficient water is taken in during the day, the animal can afford to lose water during nocturnal forays. For example, the Australian burrowing frog *Heleioporus eyrei* experiences an average water loss equivalent to 22.3% of its body mass while it is foraging each night (A. Lee, 1968).

Although many kinds of amphibians may become active during and immediately after heavy rains by day, normally they are active only at night; however, the young of some anurans, particularly bufonids, tend to be diurnal and heliothermic in contrast to conspecific adults. On the other hand, some groups of anurans characteristically are active only by day. All of these live in habitats of high atmospheric humidity or those in which water is readily available. For example, the diurnal *Dendrobates* and *Phyllobates* live in forested regions having high atmospheric humidity, as do most species of *Colostethus*. Other species of *Colostethus* that live in areas of lower atmospheric humidity are active only in the vicinity of streams, which they enter frequently. Other stream-dwelling frogs may be rehydrated continuously from the spray of waterfalls or by entering the streams frequently; these include New World bufonids (*Atelopus*), Asiatic ranids (*Staurois*), and Australian myobatrachids (*Taudactylus*). Many other anurans living in cool temperate or montane habitats may be active by day, but only when there is a sufficiently positive moisture gradient to overcome evaporative water loss, unless there is some compelling reason (e.g., feeding, mating, basking) wherein the anuran risks evaporative water loss and even death to accomplish some goal.

Reduction of the amount of surface area exposed to evaporation is an important way of reducing water loss. Several elongate plethodontid salamanders and *Amphiuma* curl their bodies and tails into tight coils and thereby reduce evaporative water loss (Ray, 1958). Many arboreal anurans pass the day on branches or leaves of trees. By selecting a shaded site and tucking the limbs close to the body, and fingers and toes between the body and the substrate, tree frogs reduce the surface area exposed to the air and thereby reduce evaporative water loss (Fig. 8-1). Such frogs characteristically are quiescent; presumably the slowing of metabolic processes results in a slower rate of breathing and thus less loss of moisture through respiration. *Eleutherodactylus coqui* assume water-conserving postures on dry nights but are not quiescent (Pough et al., 1983).

Aggregations of recently metamorphosed toads, *Bufo* and *Scaphiopus,* and subadult salamanders, *Ambystoma,* occasionally are found in shelters in dry areas.

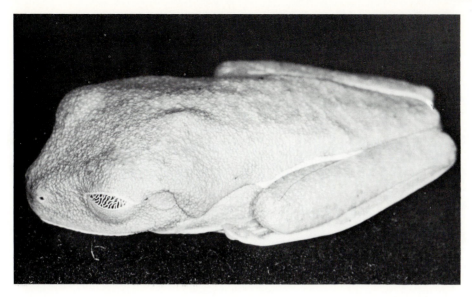

Figure 8-1. Diurnal sleeping posutre of *Agalychnis callidryas,* Puerto Viejo, Costa Rica. Photo by W. E. Duellman.

Closely packed individuals provide comparatively less surface area, overall, for evaporative water loss than do single individuals; Gehlbach et al. (1969) found that isolated individuals of *A. tigrinum* lost water at a significantly higher rate than individuals in aggregations. Significant differences were found between dehydration rates of single individuals versus aggregates of two to four individuals of *A. macrodactylum* (Alvarado, 1967) and between single versus aggregates of two to five juveniles of three species of myobatrachid frogs, *Limnodynastes* (C. Johnson, 1969).

Many salamanders and anurans utilize burrows made by other animals for diurnal retreats; a few salamanders, some anurans, and all caecilians create their own burrows. Such burrowing behavior is best exemplified by anurans in arid habitats. In Arizona, the spadefoot toad, *Scaphiopus multiplicatus,* spends about 9 continuous months underground in self-made burrows to depths of 90 cm (Ruibal et al., 1969). By maintaining an osmotic concentration equal to the soil moisture tension, the toads may remain in these burrows for long periods of time without losing water to the soil. During the rainy season, these spadefoot toads burrow only about 4 cm for diurnal retreats; they emerge each evening. Many anurans burrow to equal or greater depths during droughts; the deepest known burrows are those of the Australian *Heleioporus eyrei* at 80 cm (Bentley et al., 1958).

Morphological Adaptations
Some notable morphological modifications, principally of the skin, but also of the bladder, are important in water economy.

Skin and Cutaneous Vascularization. The skin of amphibians is highly permeable; the presence of mucous glands in the dermis and the vascularization of the dermis is highly variable (see Chapter 14). Actually, the epidermal sculpturing is important in hydration. Most salamanders and all frogs that live in aquatic and riparian situations have smooth skin on the ventral and lateral surfaces of the body. Most terrestrial and arboreal anurans have granular skin on the belly and proximal ventral surfaces of the thighs, and many have granular or areolate skin on the flanks. The irregular ventral surfaces provide a greater surface area that can be in contact with the substrate for greater rates of water absorption, but probably more important is the habit of flattening the body on a moist surface, thereby spreading the skin and exposing the thin skin between the granules to moisture. There seems to be a general correlation between granular ventral surfaces and habitats of frogs. Thus, frogs that characteristically are in the vicinity of free water (e.g., *Rana, Ptychadena, Discoglossus, Leptodactylus*) have smooth venters, whereas those that are primarily terrestrial or arboreal (e.g., *Bufo, Hyla, Rhacophorus, Hyperolius*) have granular venters. In some large groups inhabiting diverse environments, both types of venters are found in different species. For example, most species of *Eleutherodactylus* are terrestrial or arboreal and have granular venters, but members of some groups that characteristically inhabit margins of streams have smooth venters. Most hylid frogs have coarsely granular venters, but the ventral surfaces are smooth in *Acris,* which is semiaquatic. There are some exceptions to the general correlation; the most notable is *Scaphiopus,* species of which have smooth venters and are terrestrial in xeric habitats. Also, dendrobatids have smooth venters, but these terrestrial frogs live in humid forests or along streams.

The ventral pelvic region has been identified as the area primarily responsible for water uptake in anurans (Dole, 1967; R. Baldwin, 1974; McClanahan and R. Baldwin, 1969). Comparative studies on the vasculari-

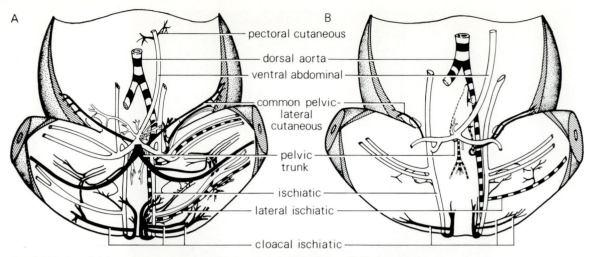

Figure 8-2. Vascularization of ventral pelvic regions in anurans. **A.** *Bufo alvarius.* **B.** *Xenopus laevis.* Adapted from J. Roth (1973). Banded vessels are arteries; open vessels are veins; solid vessels are those associated with the integument.

zation of the ventral pelvic region of diverse anurans by J. Roth (1973) and Christensen (1974) revealed that (1) the ventral pelvic integument is hypervascularized compared to other regions of the body in terrestrial anurans, and (2) terrestrial anurans, such as *Bufo,* have more vascularization in the pelvic region than semiaquatic *Rana,* which are more vascularized than the aquatic *Xenopus* (Fig. 8-2). The increased surface area of the integument and increased vascularity in the ventral pelvic region coincide with behavioral observations and laboratory experiments indicating that this region of the body is most important in rehydration (Fig. 8-3). Water movement across amphibian skin is affected by various hormones, of which vasotocin probably is the most significant. The skin on the ventral pelvic region of anurans is more responsive to vasotocin than is skin elsewhere on the body (Bentley and Main, 1972). No comparable regional differentiation of the integument has been identified in salamanders. Moreover, terrestrial and arboreal anurans, such as *Bufo* and *Litoria,* respectively, have greater responses to vasotocin than does the aquatic *Xenopus.* However, in at least *Scaphiopus couchii,* responsiveness to vasotocin is seasonal (Hillyard, 1976b); animals captured during most of the year (and tested immediately) showed no response.

Experiments by Lillywhite and P. Licht (1974) on *Bufo* demonstrated that cutaneous channels on the flanks and dorsum function to move water in all directions over the surface of the skin; movement seems to occur by capillarity. Experiments by Lopez and Brodie (1977) revealed that costal grooves function in much the same manner; when dry salamanders were placed on a wet substrate, water moved dorsally in the costal grooves and along the minute cutaneous channels interconnecting the costal grooves.

Water absorption should be facilitated by cutaneous

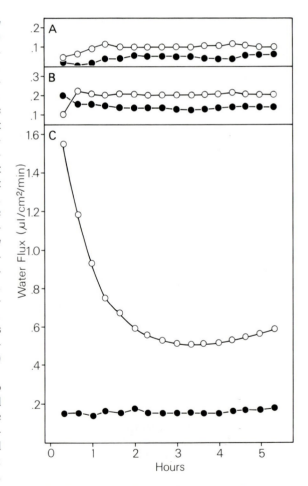

Figure 8-3. Net water flux through isolated pelvic and pectoral skin of anurans. **A.** Pelvic skin of *Xenopus laevis* (pectoral skin is essentially the same). **B.** Pectoral skin of *Bufo bufo.* **C.** Pelvic skin of *Bufo bufo.* Solid circles are normally hydrated animals; open circles are dehydrated animals. Adapted from Christensen (1974).

channels in three ways (Lillywhite and P. Licht, 1974): (1) Any sculpturing increases the surface area of the skin potentially available for absorbing water. (2) Channels induce wetting of an area of skin that is larger than that in contact with the water source. (3) Forces of capillarity attributable to skin structure actually may increase the total force with which the integument can extract water from a moist surface with which it is in direct contact.

Movement of water to the dorsal surfaces of amphibians suggests the importance of cutaneous channels in preventing desiccation of integumentary surfaces that are exposed to an ambient atmosphere of relatively low vapor pressure. Any mechanism that supplies water to the integumentary surface at rates equal to or exceeding evaporative water losses should be advantageous when pressure gradients from the skin to the ambient atmosphere are steep.

Highly vascularized skin results in quantities of blood passing near the surface and therefore increased evaporative water loss. Several genera of casque-headed hylid frogs have the skin co-ossified with the dermal bones of the skull; in these frogs the dermis and its vascularization are greatly reduced (Trueb, 1970a). These frogs back into crevices, tree holes, or bromeliads and plug the holes with their heads (Fig. 8-4); thus, only the skin on the head is exposed to the air. Evaporative water loss from the skin on the head is much less than that from other surfaces of the body (Siebert et al., 1974).

Some other hylid frogs (e.g., *Gastrotheca weinlandii* and *Phyllomedusa bicolor*) that inhabit the canopy in rainforests have osteoderms in the skin on the dorsum of the body. Possibly these osteoderms function to decrease evaporative water loss when the frogs are at rest high in the trees during the day. Atmospheric humidity during the day is much lower in the canopy than it is near the ground in rainforests.

Evaporative water loss is extremely low in two African rhacophorid frogs (*Chiromantis petersi* and *C. xerampelina*) that survive long, dry seasons while perched on limbs, trunks, or buildings. These frogs are unique among anurans in having chromatophore units containing multiple iridophores in the skin of surfaces exposed to desiccation when the frogs are at rest (Drewes et al., 1977). A similar chromatophore arrangement is known in the African *Hyperolius nasutus,* which also has a low rate of evaporative water loss (Withers et al., 1982). In the absence of other known morphological structures or physiological mechanisms to retard evaporative water loss, the unique chromatophore arrangement has been suggested as the mechanism for reducing water loss, but how this might function is not known.

Urinary Bladder and Lymph Sacs. The urinary bladders in amphibians are baglike structures, but in anurans they become distended into bilobate structures when they are filled with dilute urine. In salamanders, the bladders usually are comparatively smaller than they are in anurans; the largest bladder reported in a salamander is that of *Salamandra salamandra,* which contains fluid equal to about 35% of the body weight (Bentley, 1966a). The bladder of the aquatic *Xenopus laevis* is small, containing fluid equal to only about 1% of the body weight. How-

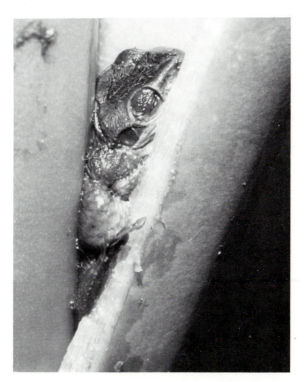

Figure 8-4. Blocking of opening between axils of leaves of a bromeliad by the head of *Gastrotheca fissipes,* Santa Teresa, Brazil. Photo by I. Sazima.

ever, bladders of anurans that inhabit arid environments can store large quantities of water. Ruibal (1962b) found that *Bufo cognatus* can store up to 30% of its body weight as water in the bladder. Australian tree frogs, *Litoria latopalmata* and *L. moorei,* can store water equal to 20–30% of their body weight, and this value in the desert burrowing frogs, *Notaden nicholsi* and *Neobatrachus wilsmorei,* is about 50% (Main and Bentley, 1964).

The subcutaneous lymph sacs of anurans possibly are another site for water storage. In some burrowing frogs, the sacs are bloated before the frogs enter the soil for long periods of time. The central Australian frog *Cyclorana platycephala* is called the water-holding frog: "It becomes surrounded by loose, floppy bags of water" (Tyler, 1976:126). However, the lymph sacs are more extensive in aquatic anurans than in terrestrial species, so the major function of the lymph sacs may be the collection of water from the body tissues (Carter, 1979).

Physiological Adaptations

The physiological mechanisms associated with water economy in amphibians involve reduction of evaporative water loss through the skin, increased permeability of the skin at times of favorable moisture tension, modification of the excretory products, and osmoregulation. Ionic concentrations and excretory products are controlled largely by the kidneys, which are regulated by neurohypophysial and adrenal secretions.

Moisture Exchange with the Environment.

There have been many studies on the rates of water loss and water uptake in amphibians, especially anurans. However, the results of these studies are not necessarily readily comparable because of differences in experimental design. For example, water loss (usually determined as weight loss) has been measured in still air or at relatively rapid rates of convection; also, bladder contents were emptied in some experimental animals and not in others. In experiments dealing with rehydration, the absorptive capabilities of the skin on different regions of the body and the moisture tension of the substrate were not always taken into consideration. Nevertheless, some patterns are evident, and some generalities can be made.

Unless the skin of amphibians is protected by some special coating essentially "waterproofing" the skin or contains structures that reduce the permeability, the skins of amphibians, irrespective of taxonomic group or habitat, give up water at approximately the same rate when exposed to equivalent conditions of desiccation. On the other hand, rehydration rates are highly variable and depend on structural differences and absorptive properties of the skin; these seem to be related to habitat—terrestrial and arboreal species have faster rates of rehydration than semiaquatic and aquatic species (see Mullen and Alvarado, 1976, and P. Brown et al., 1977, for reviews). However, aquatic species can tolerate prolonged hydration better than terrestrial species.

Although semiaquatic species normally have access to free water and all amphibians have access to abundant moisture during rains, the critical aspects of moisture exchange with the environment are at times of absence of free water. During these times, amphibians must rely primarily on the moisture content of the substrate. For arboreal species the source of moisture may be the condensation on leaves of bushes and trees, but in terrestrial species the exchange is with the soil.

Soil and moisture availability.—The moisture tension of the soil was shown to determine the amount of moisture available to the salamander *Plethodon cinereus* by Heatwole and Lim (1961), who introduced three concepts: (1) Absorption threshold, which is the level of substrate moisture above which there is a net gain in body weight (uptake of water) by dehydrated amphibians and below which there is a net loss. (2) Critical level, which is the level of substrate moisture below which water loss in amphibians increases markedly. (3) Limiting range, which includes all values of substrate moisture between levels 1 and 2.

Absorption of soil moisture involves movement of water through the soil and transfer of soil-bound water to the skin; this transfer requires close adsorption of soil particles to the skin (Hillyard, 1976a). With a favorable water potential gradient, water will move across the skin where contact allows water movement from soil to skin. With a given absorptive area, water movement across the skin will be determined by the hydraulic conductivity of the soil and of the skin. The hydraulic conductivity of subsaturated soil increases as the water content (and water potential) increases. In wetter soils, the hydraulic conductivity of the soil is greater than that of the skin, and water movement will be greatest across the skin having the greatest conductivity. In drier soils, the hydraulic conductivity of the soil is lower than that of the skin, and water movement in either direction across the skin is greatly diminished. However, over a long period of time, even a slow rate of water loss would be lethal. Amphibians that pass many months burrowed into relatively dry soil can elevate the osmolarity of their body fluids and thereby decrease water loss, or some form a waterproof cocoon.

Some experiments have related soil particle size and the affinity of the soil particles for water (soil matric potential) with water absorption rates. The effect of soil matric potential on the water economy of spadefoot toads, *Scaphiopus couchii* and *S. multiplicatus,* was examined by Ruibal et al. (1969), Shoemaker et al. (1969), and McClanahan (1972). Soils of fine particle size have a higher affinity for water than do sandy soils with identical water content. Therefore, it is more difficult for anurans to obtain water from silty soil than sandy soil when the water content is low.

Absorption thresholds have been determined for few species. Heatwole and Lim (1961) found the absorption threshold for *Plethodon cinereus* to be very low, 1.0 to 1.5 atmospheres of soil moisture tension. Six species of salamanders studied by Spight (1967a) had absorption thresholds of about 2 atm (Fig. 8-5), but Spotila (1972) in a study of 14 species of plethodontid salamanders found that thresholds varied from 1.2 to 2.8 atm. R. Walker and Whitford (1970) reported thresholds of three fossorial anurans (including *Scaphiopus multiplicatus*) to be about 2.5 atm, *Bufo americanus* 1.5 atm, *Hyla cinerea* 1.2 atm, and *Rana pipiens* 0.8 atm. However, Ruibal et al. (1969) reported the absorption threshold of *S. multiplicatus*, which spends about 9 consecutive months burrowed in soil, to be above 10 atm, and it may be as high as 15 atm; the absorption threshold varies depending on the soil moisture tension and the animal's internal osmotic concentration. Thus, it seems that absorption thresholds are highest for amphibians that are subjected to water stress in nature.

Dole's (1967) work on *Rana pipiens* showed that these semiaquatic frogs could absorb water from wet soils and from sand having a water content of 20%, but frogs that were rehydrated on sand containing only 10% water could not regain all of the water that they lost by dehydration. The arid-adapted Australian anuran *Heleioporus eyrei* absorbs water from sand containing 13% water (Packer, 1963), and *Scaphiopus multiplicatus* can do the same in soils containing only 3% water (Ruibal et al., 1969).

Temperature and moisture exchange.—Most experiments dealing with dehydration and rehydration were performed at constant temperatures. Claussen (1969) found no correlations between rehydration rates and temperature in six species of North American anurans. Although hormonal release and rate of blood circulation increase with temperature, other properties of anurans, especially differential uptake of water by the skin in different regions of the body, seem to negate the effect of temperature. Experimental design has affected the results of many experiments. Animals usually are rehydrated from a moist substrate; at higher temperatures evaporative water loss may balance or exceed the rehydration rate.

Spotila (1972) demonstrated significant differences in both dehydration and rehydration rates at different temperatures in species of plethodontid salamanders. Dehydration was accomplished in desiccators and rehydration in culture dishes partially filled with water, both maintained in environmental chambers at 5, 15, and 25°C. Both rates were positively correlated with temperature, and the rehydration rate showed a greater response to temperature, except for one species that had the same rates (Fig. 8-6).

Dermal mucous glands discharge secretions more frequently at higher temperatures, and the layer of mucus on the skin increases the rate of evaporative water loss, whereas dry skin forms a diffusion barrier and a decrease in the rate of evaporative water loss (Lillywhite, 1971a). Dehydrating amphibians at high temperatures seem to be faced with conflicting physiological demands—how to decrease the rate of evaporative water loss and also lower body temperatures (see section: Thermoregulation).

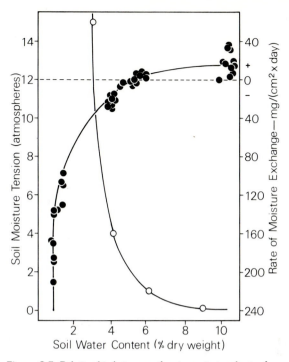

Figure 8-5. Relationship between soil water content and rate of water exchange by six species of salamanders (solid circles). The soil moisture tension at various water contents is shown by open circles (each is the mean of three values). Based on data in Spight (1967).

Size, surface area, and moisture exchange.—Intraspecific differences in tolerance to water loss do not seem to be related to size in some species. For example, no significant correlations between size (measured as standard weight) and tolerance to water loss were found in individuals among several species of North American hylids and ranids (W. Schmid, 1965; Farrell and MacMahon, 1969; Ralin and Rogers, 1972). However, differences in rates of evaporative water loss probably relate most closely to surface-area/volume ratios. With the exception of a few species of frogs having integumentary modifications that reduce the rate of evaporative water loss, this rate per unit area of skin seems to be about the same in all species subjected to equivalent experimental conditions. Passage of dry air over an amphibian results in evaporation from all exposed surfaces; small amphibians have proportionately more surface area and, therefore, have higher rates of evaporative water loss. This was demonstrated among species of plethodontid salamanders by Spotila (1972). For example, the dehydration rate of *Plethodon cinereus* (mean weight 0.62 g) was 10 mg · cm^{-2} · h^{-1}, whereas in *P. glutinosus* (mean weight 3.93 g) subjected to the same experimental conditions the rate was 3 mg·cm^{-2}·h^{-1}. Heatwole et al. (1969) subjected *Eleutherodactylus portoricensis* to various experiments and found a significant negative correlation between body size and rate of evaporative water loss. Also, a significant

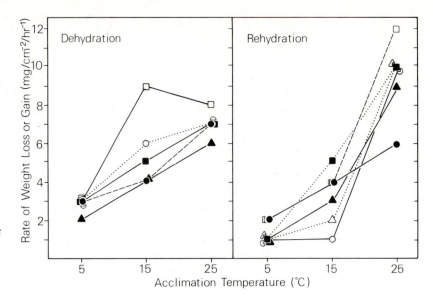

Figure 8-6. Dehydration and rehydration rates of plethododontid salamanders acclimated to three temperatures. Open circles = *Eurycea lucifuga;* open squares = *Plethodon caddoensis;* solid triangles = *P. glutinosus;* solid circles = *P. jordani;* solid squares = *P. ouachitae;* open triangles = *P. yonahlossee.* In the dehydration graph *P. yonahlossee* is the same as *P. glutinosus.* Adapted from Spotila (1972).

negative correlation was found to exist between the rate of evaporative water loss and body mass among species of "waterproof" frogs (Withers et al., 1982).

Activity and moisture exchange.—A dehydrating amphibian faces conflicting drives. In order to escape desiccating conditions, it must increase its activity at the cost of increasing its evaporative water loss. If the animal assumes a water-conserving posture, it can reduce evaporative water loss and prolong its ability to survive, but it will not be able to escape if the desiccating conditions persist. In at least one anuran, *Notaden bennetti* (Heatwole et al., 1971), and one salamander, *Plethodon cinereus* (Heatwole, 1960), activity (mostly escape behavior or movements along moisture gradients) increases during progressive dehydration until a peak is reached, after which activity declines (burrowing or moisture-conserving postures) until just before death, when a brief, secondary burst of activity (escape movements) occurs. Heatwole et al. (1969) showed that activity greatly influences the rate of evaporative water loss in *Eleutherodactylus portoricensis.* In that species, activity increases evaporative water loss up to 200% above the rate for individuals at rest, largely by changes in exposed surface area (maximum effect 130%) and gradient modifications (maximum effect 30%); effects of elevated metabolism probably account for the rest.

R. Putnam and S. Hillman (1977) showed a progressive increase in activity levels in *Bufo boreas* and *Xenopus laevis* during dehydration, up to 35% and 25% loss in body weight, respectively. Experiments by Heatwole and Newby (1972) on 12 species of anurans showed that peak activity levels occurred at the loss of 31 to 40% of body weight to dehydration in 11 species, but that the peak for juvenile *Bufo marinus* was 41 to 50%. Furthermore, *Bufo marinus* maintained activity when its body water content had been decreased to 30 to 39% of nor-

mal. Nocturnal species had the peak of activity at night, whereas diurnal species had a peak of activity by day. A notable exception was *Litoria caerulea,* in which diurnal and nocturnal peaks were nearly identical.

Waterproofing. Some amphibians have developed novel ways of "waterproofing" the skin, either by the formation of a cocoon that encases the body during long periods of dormancy or by the secretion of a coating having low permeability that covers the animal during the day, when it is inactive.

One salamander, *Siren intermedia,* and several species of anurans living in xeric habitats are known to form cocoons encasing the body while the animal is in a subterranean burrow. *Siren intermedia* burrow into the mud at the bottom of drying ponds; once ensconced in their burrows, sirens form a parchmentlike cocoon that completely envelops the animal, except for the mouth (Reno et al., 1972).

Burrowing anurans that form cocoons include *Pternohyla fodiens* in North America (Ruibal and S. Hillman, 1981), *Ceratophrys ornata* and *Lepidobatrachus llanensis* (Fig. 8-7) in South America (McClanahan et al., 1976), *Pyxicephalus adspersus* and *Leptopelis bocagei* in South Africa (Loveridge and Craye, 1979), and *Limnodynastes spenceri, Neobatrachus pictus,* and several species of *Cyclorana* in Australia (A. Lee and Mercer, 1967).

The cocoon, composed of layers of statum corneum, is dry, parchmentlike, and encases the entire frog, with openings at the nostrils. In *Pternohyla fodiens* the cocoon is about 0.05 mm thick and is formed by multiple sheddings of the epidermis (Fig. 8-8); as many as 43 layers of epidermal cells, each layer separated by an intracellular space representing the original subcorneal space, were observed (Ruibal and S. Hillman, 1981). The cocoon of *Lepidobatrachus llanensis* may contain as many

Figure 8-7. South American burrowing frog *Lepidobatrachus llanensis* in a cocoon (left) and emerging from a cocoon upon rehydration (right). Photos by L. L. McClanahan.

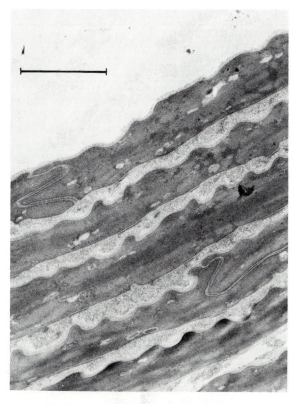

Figure 8-8. Electron micrograph of a section through the cocoon of *Pternohyla fodiens*. Scale = 1 μm. Photo courtesy of R. Ruibal.

nohyla and *Lepidobatrachus* are immobile during cocoon formation. This immobility allows the detached stratum corneum to remain in place and the next, and subsequent, sheddings also to remain and to adhere to each other by means of the secreted subcorneal mucus, thus providing the multilayered, protective cocoon.

Experimental passage of dry air over cocooned individuals of *Pyxicephalus adspersus* and *Leptopelis bocagei* showed that weight loss (water loss) was reduced to 50% and 20%, respectively, of the loss by noncocooned frogs (Loveridge and Craye, 1979). Comparable figures for *Lepidobatrachus llanensis* are 7–14% (McClanahan et al., 1976). Equivalent rates of water loss were calculated for cocooned individuals of *Pternohyla fodiens* and Australian myobatrachids (A. Lee and Mercer, 1967; Ruibal and S. Hillman, 1981). Rates of evaporative water loss in nature certainly are lower than those obtained in the laboratory. The experimental conditions of passing dry air over cocooned frogs are far more severe than those encountered in subterranean burrows (Fig. 8-9). Experiments with the salamander *Siren intermedia* by Gehlbach et al. (1973) revealed that individuals in cocoons lost 25–28% of their body weight during a 16-week period; sirens die if they lose 40–60% of their body weight.

As more epidermal layers are added, the cocoon becomes thicker and less permeable. Laboratory experiments with the frog *Lepidobatrachus llanensis* by McClanahan et al. (1983) showed that individuals add an epidermal layer daily for 40 days, and that there is an inverse relationship between the number of layers and the rate of water loss. During 35 days the evaporative water loss dropped from 8.0 mg·g^{-1}·h^{-1} to 0.9 mg·g^{-1}·h^{-1}.

In some tree frogs of the genus *Phyllomedusa*, dermal secretions provide a covering that reduces evaporative water loss to 5–10% of that of most other anurans and comparable to that of a desert-adapted lizard (Shoemaker et al., 1972; Shoemaker and McClanahan, 1975). These frogs (*P. boliviana, hypocondrialis, iheringi,* and *sauvagei*) inhabit subhumid Bolivia, and arid areas in

as 60 layers (McClanahan et al., 1976), and that of *Pyxicephalus adspersus,* 36 layers (Loveridge and Craye, 1979). Reno et al. (1972) suggested that the cocoon of *Siren* was formed by the hardening of mucus secreted by the dermal mucous glands. However, the microscopic structure of the cocoon is the same as that of cocoons of anurans.

Normal shedding in anurans is arrested by hypophysectomy (Budtz, 1977); hypophysectomized toads develop a multiple-layered stratum corneum. At least *Pter-*

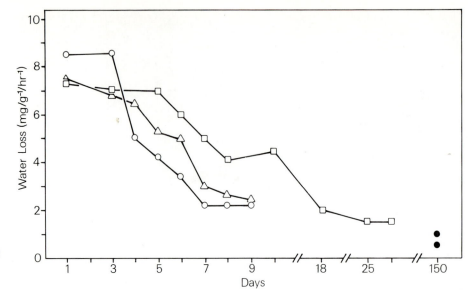

Figure 8-9. Comparison of rates of evaporative water loss in three individuals of the South American frog *Lepidobatrachus llanensis* removed from water on day 1 and maintained in open containers (open symbols) with two individuals having intact cocoons and excavated from dry soil (solid symbols). Redrawn from McClanahan et al. (1976).

Argentina, Paraguay, Bolivia, and southern Brazil. They perch in bushes and trees by day, where they are subject to desiccation by the dry air. Desiccation is avoided by the secretion of lipids; the frogs methodically spread this secretion over their entire bodies by wiping motions with the hands and feet (Fig. 8-10). Once the wiping is completed, they close their eyes and remain in a torpid state on the perch for the day.

The secretion of lipids and wiping behavior have been described for four species of *Phyllomedusa* (Blaylock et al., 1976). These species are unique among amphibians in having lipid glands, in addition to the usual mucous and poison glands, in the skin. The secretions of the lipid glands form a thin, nearly impermeable covering when wiped over the surface of the frog and allowed to dry. The chemical composition of the lipids consists of triglycerides and smaller amounts of wax esters.

Nitrogen Excretion. Most amphibians lack the means for excreting nitrogen or salts economically with respect to water because they cannot produce hyperosmotic urine, do not possess salt glands, and excrete nitrogen in a soluble form. Some aquatic amphibians normally excrete most of their nitrogenous wastes in the form of ammonia (ammonotelism); because of the high toxicity of ammonia, this excretory product is possible only in aquatic situations where the ammonia is diluted immediately and carried away from the animal. For example, among anurans, the aquatic pipids are primarily ammonotelic; representative species of *Hymenochirus, Pipa,* and *Xenopus* excrete 60 to 80% of their nitrogenous wastes as ammonia (Cragg et al., 1961). A few other aquatic and most terrestrial and arboreal amphibians produce urea (ureotelism), and a few tree frogs produce uric acid (uricotelism). In the sequence ammonotelism-ureotelism-uricotelism, less water is needed as uricotelism is approached.

The production and storage of urea is not limited to nonaquatic amphibians. Experimental studies with the aquatic *Xenopus laevis* by J. Balinsky (1970) revealed that frogs deprived of water and then placed in water excreted urea that had been stored in body fluids; subsequently, the frogs shifted to excreting ammonia again. *Xenopus* survive underground when their ponds dry up; during these dormant periods they become ureotelic, and urea accumulates in their body fluids. When kept under moderately saline conditions, *Xenopus* increase the production and storage of urea (Funkhouser and Goldstein, 1973). *Xenopus laevis,* acclimated to saline solutions of

Figure 8-10. Wiping behavior by *Phyllomedusa sauvagei*. Photos by R. Ruibal.

570 to 625 milliosmoles per liter, increased the concentration of body fluids to as much as 60 mOsm/liter greater than the medium primarily by storing urea in the body fluids (Schlisio et al., 1973). The similar physiological responses of *Xenopus* to drought and to hypersaline media is expected, for under both conditions the frogs are faced with low water potentials and the possibility of water loss.

Because many aquatic anurans seem to be able to store urea in the absence of free water, McClanahan (1975) suggested that anurans were preadapted to invade environments having low water potentials. Many anurans living in xeric habitats utilize this same physiological pattern to survive underground for long periods of time. The only difference may be that arid-adapted anurans can produce and store more urea than aquatic anurans. Spadefoot toads, *Scaphiopus couchii* and *S. multiplicatus,* are capable of storing up to 300 millimoles per liter of urea in body fluids. The rate at which urea is produced and stored is inversely proportional to soil water potential. If the soil in which they are burrowed dries and the soil water potential decreases, the toads store urea and lower their body water potential to retard cutaneous water loss to the soil (McClanahan, 1967, 1972; Shoemaker et al., 1969). Tiger salamanders (*Ambystoma tigrinum*) in the Chihuahuan Desert spend up to 9 months in underground burrows and store urea and electrolytes in body fluids at levels comparable to those of *Scaphiopus;* probably *Ambystoma* also use urea storage to offset the low water potential in soil around their burrows (Delson and Whitford, 1973b).

Two groups of tree frogs are known to be primarily uricotelic: two African rhacophorids (*Chiromantis petersi* and *C. xerampelina*) and four South American hylids (*Phyllomedusa boliviana, hypocondrialis, iheringi,* and *sauvagei*). Approximately 60 to 80% of the dry weight of excreted urine is uric acid in *C. xerampelina* (Loveridge, 1970), and uric acid amounts to 97% in *C. petersi* (Drewes et al., 1977). Uric acid comprises 80% of the excreted nitrogenous wastes in *P. sauvagei,* about 45% in *P. boliviana* and *P. iheringi,* and 24% in *P. hypocondrialis* (Shoemaker and McClanahan, 1975).

It is obvious that patterns of nitrogen excretion within the amphibians are diverse and that these patterns are related to the availability of water. Furthermore, there are ontogenetic and seasonal changes in the excretory patterns. During their larval development, some species of *Leptodactylus* produce more urea than ammonia and thus become ureotelic as tadpoles; this phenomenon is even more noticeable in tadpoles of *Phyllomedusa sauvagei* that begin producing urates, as well as urea, as larvae (see Chapter 6).

Seasonal or even short-term shifts in the components of the nitrogenous wastes have been identified in several kinds of amphibians. When many kinds of aquatic amphibians are deprived of free water by dehydration or acclimation to saline media, urea accumulates in their body fluids as a result of increased urea production and/or decreased glomerular filtration rates in the kidneys (Goldstein, 1972). On the other hand, some species of *Rana* seem to be obligatorily ammonotelic (Shoemaker and McClanahan, 1980). Changes occur in terrestrial species as well. For example, most *Bufo* are ureotelic, but *B. quadriporcatus,* a terrestrial species in forests in southeastern Asia, is ammonotelic in water and ureotelic with the deprivation of water (Shoemaker and McClanahan, 1980).

Jungreis (1976) explained the partitioning of excretory nitrogen in amphibians by the physiological radiation hypothesis originally proposed by Florkin and Schoffeniels (1965). In so doing, Jungreis concluded: (1) Little ammonia is present in the blood, and the ammonia in the urine is formed and secreted in the kidneys, presumably as a means of conserving blood sodium. (2) Urea normally represents a passive component of blood and serves an unknown function. (This is interpreted to mean to the blood per se, for the presence of urea in the blood increases its concentration and thereby reduces evaporative water loss.) (3) Under conditions of dehydration, elevated levels of serum and body urea result initially from reductions in urine formation and subsequently in response to increased amino acid metabolism.

Osmoregulation. The maintenance of the osmotic pressure of the body fluids involves not only the amounts of water but also the amounts of specific solutes. The input and output of these solutes are extremely important in the water-, electrolyte-, and nitrogen-budgets of amphibians. The maintenance of plasma concentrations that are greater than, or at least equal to, the immediate environment is essential for the survival of terrestrial amphibians and those few species that exist in saline environments. The subject of osmoregulation in amphibians was reviewed by Shoemaker and Nagy (1977).

The concentrations of urea in the plasma and urine are generally lower in aquatic than in terrestrial amphibians; for example, in normally active *Xenopus laevis,* the concentrations are 10 mOsm/liter in the plasma and 15 mOsm/liter in the urine (M. Ireland, 1973), as compared with 39.3 and 40.5 mOsm/liter in *Scaphiopus couchii* (McClanahan, 1967) and 40 and 60 mOsm/liter in *S. multiplicatus* (Shoemaker et al., 1969).

At times of water stress, increased amounts of urea are stored in the plasma and tissues, and the concentration becomes higher in the urine. Plasma concentrations are increased about 3 to 6 times during dehydration in terrestrial amphibians, such as in the anurans *Scaphiopus, Bufo, Rana, Pyxicephalus,* and the salamander *Batrachoseps,* and 4.5 to 13.6 times in the aquatic anuran *Xenopus laevis* and the salamander *Ambystoma tigrinum,* respectively (Scheer and Markel, 1962; Shoemaker et al., 1969; M. Ireland, 1973; M. Ireland and Simons, 1977; R. M. Jones and S. Hillman, 1978; Loveridge and Withers, 1982). Greater increases seem to be

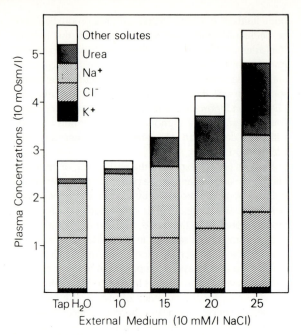

Figure 8-11. Mean contributions of measured osmolytes to plasma osmotic concentration in *Xenopus laevis* adapted to various concentrations of salt water. Redrawn from Romspert (1976).

characteristic of arboreal anurans—9.5 to 21 times the concentration in various hylids and the rhacophorid *Chiromantis petersi* (Shoemaker and McClanahan, 1975; Drewes et al., 1977). The greatest increase reported is in *A. tigrinum;* individuals increased the urea concentration from 10 mOsm/liter of urea in hydrated controls to 100 to 330 (mean = 220) mOsm/liter in individuals dehydrated in soil for 9 months (Delson and Whitford, 1973). Spadefoot toads, *S. couchii,* also store urea in muscle tissues (McClanahan, 1964), and muscle tissue of the euryhaline *R. cancrivora* is able to tolerate high concentrations of urea (Thesleff and Schmidt-Nielsen, 1962).

Concentration of electrolytes varies considerably among hydrated amphibians, with levels of sodium (Na$^+$) and chloride (Cl$^-$) always at least 10 times greater than the level of potassium (K$^+$). In animals subjected to water stress, the concentrations of sodium and chloride show marked increases, but that of potassium may increase or decrease (Fig. 8-11). For example, among aquatic and semiaquatic anurans (*Xenopus laevis, Bufo viridis, Rana cancrivora*) exposed to concentrations of 40 to 50% sea water for 3 to 7 days, sodium showed an increase of 39 to 61%, chloride 51 to 119%, and potassium 3 to 50% (M. Gordon et al., 1961; M. Gordon, 1962; M. Ireland, 1973). The increases in various hylids and *Chiromantis petersi* generally are comparable to the foregoing figures: sodium 22 to 90%, chloride 17 to 94%, and potassium 41 to 93% (Shoemaker and McClanahan, 1975; Drewes et al., 1977). In hydrated versus cocooned *Pyxicephalus adspersus,* sodium increased 42% and potassium 59%

(Loveridge and Withers, 1981). Although data are available for few species, it is evident that the water economy of amphibians subjected to dehydration benefits from increased concentrations of certain electrolytes, especially sodium and chloride.

These electrolytes also are stored in body tissues. Shoemaker (1964) found that the concentration of potassium was much higher in the skeletal muscle and liver than in the plasma of *Bufo marinus* and that the concentrations of sodium and potassium increased at about the same rates in tissues and plasma in dehydrated individuals, but there was an initial decrease in the concentration of potassium in the blood. Experiments on physiological adaptations of *Rana cancrivora* to salinity by M. Gordon and Tucker (1968) revealed that much greater amounts of potassium were stored in skeletal muscle than in plasma, and concentrations of all electrolytes in plasma and muscle tissue increased at about the same rates at higher salinities of the external medium. However, changes of concentrations of intracellular urea and free amino acids are primarily responsible for increases in osmotic concentrations in skeletal muscle. Subsequent experiments on *Ambystoma tigrinum* (Delson and Whitford, 1973b) showed that there were two major alterations of body fluid concentrations during long-term dehydration—an initial increase in concentrations of electrolytes and a subsequent increase in urea.

Numerous studies have demonstrated the ability of amphibian skin in situ or in vitro to take up sodium and chloride from an aquatic medium (see Salibián, 1977, for review). Apparently urea must be present in the plasma for ion transfer to take place and build up the concentration of electrolytes; the changes in the electrical properties of isolated amphibian skin in the presence of urea presumably activate an inward cation pump or an outward anion pump (M. Gordon and Tucker, 1968).

The source of urea and electrolytes in feeding amphibians is from the metabolism of the proteins in their food, but individuals that are resisting desiccation by remaining in burrows or cocoons for long periods of time or are faced with increasing salinity but no food must catabolize body proteins (Shoemaker and McClanahan, 1975; Romspert, 1976). Water stored in the urinary bladder also can aid in osmoregulation, for the bladder walls are permeable to urea and also transport sodium (Bentley, 1966b).

Renal Function. Amphibian kidney function has been investigated thoroughly (Deyrup, 1964). Because of pressure differentials, fluid is filtered from the blood plasma through capillary walls in the glomerulus and into the kidney tubule. By a combination of pressure and ciliary action, the fluid is forced down the tubule. Cells lining the lumen resorb water and solutes; these pass back into the blood flowing through capillaries surrounding the tubule. Simultaneously, urea and other solutes are secreted from the blood into the tubular fluid. Water resorption occurs primarily in the proximal convoluted tubule. Coelomic fluid can enter the renal tubules via ciliated nephrostomes in salamanders and thus may add to the glomerular filtrate. In anurans the nephrostomes connect to the renal veins, and they may play a role in water resorption from the bladder. Peritubular circulation is derived from the efferent glomerular arterioles and from renal portal veins. The kidneys are not capable of producing hypertonic urine.

This type of structure is admirably suited for life in fresh water, for all amphibians can produce dilute urine at very high rates ($10–25$ ml·kg^{-1}·h^{-1}) when maintained in fresh water (Shoemaker and Nagy, 1977). In this situation glomerular filtration rates are high ($20–50$ ml·kg^{-1}·h^{-1}) and can be considerably higher in experimentally water-loaded animals. In anurans, only about half of the water is resorbed in the tubules, but resorption of sodium and chloride may be about 99% complete (Garland and I. Henderson, 1975). In larval salamanders, glomerular filtration rates tend to be lower ($8–16$ ml·kg^{-1}·h^{-1}), but only 10 to 30% of the filtered water and 90 to 95% of the filtered sodium are resorbed when the animals are in fresh water (Kirschner et al., 1971; Stiffler and Alvarado, 1971). When the concentration of the environmental medium is increased or the animals are deprived of water, glomerular filtration rates are reduced drastically, fractional water resorption increases markedly, and the concentration of the urine approaches that of the plasma. Renal water conservation is well developed in amphibians because they can become completely anuric after loss of only a small fraction of their body water. Generally it is assumed that glomerular filtration ceases, but analysis of kidney function is difficult when no urine is produced.

Energetically, ammonia is the most economical vehicle for nitrogen excretion, but its toxicity precludes this product when water turnover is low. On the basis of equivocal evidence, Jungreis (1976) suggested that the main advantages of excretion of ammonia by aquatic amphibians are in cation conservation and pH regulation. Most amphibians are ureotelic, but they excrete appreciable amounts of ammonia when they are in water and become completely ureotelic when water influx is low. Reduction or cessation of urine production leads to an accumulation of urea, which places the animal in a more favorable situation for obtaining water from soil or saline solutions. Accumulated urea is eliminated rapidly by the kidneys when the animals are rehydrated. There is active, tubular secretion of urea, but when plasma levels of urea are high, urinary urea concentrations usually approximate those in the plasma. This is true even for *Rana cancrivora* adapted to saline conditions, where active tubular resorption of urea would be beneficial (Schmidt-Nielsen and P. Lee, 1962). In this situation urine flow rates are reduced greatly (matching osmotic influx) by reducing the glomerular filtration rate by about 75% and resorbing more than 90% of the filtrate.

Several hylid frogs of the genus *Phyllomedusa* and two rhacophorid frogs of the genus *Chiromantis* are uricotelic (Shoemaker and McClanahan, 1975; Drewes et al., 1977). In these anurans the partitioning of water into various products is independent of water turnover, and most of the nitrogen is excreted in the form of precipitated urate salts. When uricotelic frogs are maintained out of water and fed, precipitated urate accumulates in the bladder, thereby indicating continued renal function during water deprivation. At least in *Phyllomedusa sauvagei,* urate excretion prevents the rapid concentration of urea in the body fluids and also aids in electrolyte excretion; 45% of the sodium input and 22% of the potassium input are secreted in urate form. Uricotelism combined with low rates of evaporative water loss places these arboreal anurans in a position similar to that of insectivorous lizards in terms of their ability to osmoregulate without access to fresh water.

J. Balinsky et al. (1976) determined differences in enzymes of urea and uric acid metabolism between the uricotelic anuran *Chiromantis xerampelina* and ureotelic amphibians. They concluded that the adaptation to uricotelism involves three kinds of enzymatic changes: (1) Levels of the enzymes of the urea cycle are lowered; this evidently is correlated with the decreased output of urea and presumably represents an economy measure, reducing the synthesis of enzymes not needed for metabolism. (2) Levels of the enzymes for uric acid degradation are lowered; this is vital because it ensures that the uric acid formed in the kidneys and liver is not degraded into urea. (3) There is an increase in the level of at least one enzyme for uric acid biosynthesis (PRPP amidotransferase). This model of urea and uric acid metabolism requires the acquisition of no new enzymes but only a change in existing enzymatic pathways.

Hormonal Effects. The neurohypophysis produces two identified hormones (arginine vasotocin and oxytocin) that affect osmoregulation directly. These hormones (and also mammalian neurohypophysial peptides) increase the permeability of the skin and membranes of the urinary bladder and kidney tubules, thereby accelerating the diffusional uptake of free water and hypotonic urine in the urinary bladder and kidney tubules (Deyrup, 1964). However, some aquatic salamanders (*Necturus, Amphiuma, Siren,* and *Desmognathus quadramaculatus*) have limited responses to arginine vasotocin; not all aquatic salamanders respond in the same way, for the aquatic newts (*Notophthalmus* and *Triturus*) have a strong response (P. Brown et al., 1972). *Xenopus laevis* is unique among anurans studied in that arginine vasotocin increases water uptake by the skin but apparently does not suppress urine formation (Ewer, 1952).

Adrenaline stimulates active transport of chloride from the inside to the outside of isolated frog skin and also affects glomerular circulation and filtration. Interrenal secretions of aldosterone and cortisol effect renal sodium excretion and sodium transport by the urinary bladder

(Chester Jones et al., 1972). Deoxycorticosterone glucoside enhances sodium transport by the skin of *Bufo* (Pasqualini and Riseau, 1951).

The release of all of these hormones initially involves the preoptic nucleus of the hypothalamus, which stimulates the neurohypophysis. This stimulation results in the release of the neurohypophysial hormones that directly effect osmoregulation and the secretions that activate the adenohypophysis, causing it to release adrenocorticotropic hormone (ACTH). This hormone stimulates the interrenal bodies to release aldosterone and cortisol. In at least some anurans, dehydration causes the release of the neurohypophysial secretions (Bentley, 1974), but the specific neurophysiological mechanisms that initiate hypothalamic activity are not known.

TEMPERATURE

Amphibians are ectotherms, and generally have body temperatures close to that of their immediate surroundings, especially the substrate. There is no evidence of internal heat-production mechanisms that increase the body temperatures of amphibians above that of the environment. The amount of metabolic heat produced is so small that it is lost immediately to the environment (Fromm, 1956). Some anurans bask and thereby raise their body temperatures; however, basking creates problems of evaporative water loss. In warm environments, most amphibian behavior seems to be associated with maintaining low body temperatures, but cryptic and nocturnal activity (in places or at times of lower temperatures) more likely is a response to problems of water economy than to temperature.

In cryptic or nocturnal amphibians the thermal relationships with the environment involve (1) convective heat loss or gain from the atmosphere, (2) heat conduction to or from the substrate, (3) thermal radiation to the environment, and (4) evaporative heat loss. A basking anuran also receives heat from direct sunlight and from thermal radiation from the atmosphere, substrate, and vegetation nearby.

Thermal Tolerance

Amphibians as a group have a wide range of thermal tolerances; differences in tolerances reflect the different thermal regimes in their habitats. However, individuals can be acclimated to different thermal regimes that result in modifications of their tolerances.

Thermal Requirements. The temperatures at which amphibians are active in the field are known for many species of salamanders and anurans, especially species in North and Central America (Brattstrom, 1963; Feder et al., 1982). As a group, anurans usually are active at temperatures exceeding the activity temperatures of salamanders (Table 8-1). On the basis of the data on North and Central American amphibians, the range of temperatures for salamanders is − 2.0 to 30.0°C (mean = 13.9°C), compared with 3.0 to 35.7°C (mean = 21.7°C) in anurans. This difference becomes even more evident if the data for the cold-adapted *Ascaphus* are not included; the mean temperatures for anurans, exclusive of *Ascaphus,* is 23.6°C.

Complex relationships exist between body temperatures and latitude and altitude. For example, Feder and J. F. Lynch (1982) found that ambystomatid and plethodontid salamanders in the temperate zone experience lower minimum temperatures than neotropical salamanders. The tropical salamanders show similar rates of decline in mean body temperatures with increasing altitude, but the temperatures of ambystomatids at high altitudes are significantly higher than those of plethodontids at the

Table 8-1. Temperatures of North and Central American Amphibians Recorded in the Field*

Group	Number		Temperatures (°C)	
	Species	**Individuals**	**Range**	**Mean**
Salamanders				
Cryptobranchids, amphiumids, sirenids	5	12	8.0–28.0	20.1
Salamandrids	4	109	4.5–28.4	16.0
Temperate ambystomatids	9	933	1.0–26.7	14.5
Tropical ambystomatids	12	56	10.5–30.0	19.0
Temperate aquatic plethodontids	9	261	2.0–22.0	11.3
Temperate terrestrial plethodontids	28	2065	− 2.0–26.3	13.5
Tropical plethodontids	43	1660	1.8–30.0	14.2
Anurans				
Ascaphus	1	5	4.4–14.0	10.0
Scaphiopus	2	11	12.2–25.0	21.4
Leptodactylids	5	11	22.0–28.0	24.7
Bufo	17	474	3.0–33.7	24.0
Hylids	14	507	3.8–33.7	23.7
Gastrophryne	2	108	15.5–35.7	26.5
Rana	12	299	4.0–34.7	21.3

*Based on Brattstrom (1963) and Feder et al. (1982).

same altitudes. Because they are aquatic, the ambystomatids presumably are not subjected to temperatures as variable as those encountered by the terrestrial plethodontids. Brattstrom (1968, 1970) found that tropical anurans have a higher thermal regime than do anurans in the temperate zone and that species (or populations) at high altitudes have lower thermal regimes than do those at low altitudes. Intraspecific differences in thermal tolerances may occur over short geographical distances with a drastic change of altitude, as noted for populations of the chorus frog, *Pseudacris triseriata,* on the eastern face of the Rocky Mountains in Colorado, by K. Miller and Packard (1977).

Seasonal variation in body temperatures is greater among temperate amphibians than among tropical species. However, at a given time and place, variation in body temperatures among members of a population is similar for temperate and tropical amphibians. Species living at high altitudes are subjected to highly variable temperatures daily, whereas those in warm tropical regions have relatively little daily variation in temperature. Species living at high altitudes in the low latitudes experience diel temperature variations approximating the annual variation.

The majority of field data suggest that amphibians seldom maintain a constant body temperature in the manner of some reptiles (Huey and Slatkin, 1976), but rather are at whatever temperatures are available within suitable microhabitats. The covariance of body temperatures with the environment is evident at the level of individuals, populations, and species (Carey, 1978). Therefore, most amphibians seem to maintain a constant body temperature from day to day only when the prevailing environmental conditions do not vary. For example, the similar body temperatures of amphibians living in bromeliads in the tropics (Feder, 1982a; Feder and J. F. Lynch, 1982) are the result of minimal thermal diversity within the bromeliads. Likewise, the body temperatures of the leptodactylid frog *Somuncuria somuncurensis* are limited to the nearly constant temperatures (20–22°C) of the thermal springs in which it lives (Cei, 1969).

A few salamanders have been found active at temperatures near 0°C; these include *Hydromantes platycephalus* at −2°C (Brattstrom, 1963), *Eurycea multiplicata* at 0°C (P. Ireland, 1976), *Ensatina eschscholtzi* at 1°C (Stebbins, 1954), and *Ambystoma jeffersonianum* and *A. maculatum* at <1°C (Feder et al., 1982). The lowest temperatures for anurans are 3.0°C for *Bufo boreas* (Brattstrom, 1963) and 3.5°C for *B. bocourti* (Stuart, 1951). Mullally (1952) determined that −2°C was the lethal minimum temperature for *B. boreas.*

Many physiologists discounted the possibility of amphibians surviving if frozen. However, W. Schmid (1982) reported that three species of anurans (*Hyla crucifer, H. versicolor,* and *Rana sylvatica*) could tolerate temperatures of −6°C for 5 days, at which time approximately 35% of their body fluids was frozen. He demonstrated

the presence of relatively large quantities of glycerol in body tissues and fluids in these frogs in the winter; glycerol was not present in the frogs in the summer, nor at any time of the year in *Rana septentrionalis* and *R. pipiens,* two species that cannot survive freezing temperatures.

In nature, many amphibians seem to be active at characteristic levels of body temperature, and it is commonly assumed that these levels invariably represent the actual thermal preferences of particular species. However, the range of body temperatures over which at least some species are active in nature markedly exceeds or differs from those observed in thermal gradients in the laboratory. Consequently, field measurements may not define levels of body temperature actually preferred for activity. For example, Feder (1982b) found that the mean temperatures selected on a thermal gradient by six species of plethodontid salamanders were 1.1 to 5.7°C (mean = 3.7°C) lower than the mean temperatures of individuals from the same localities in nature, as given by Feder et al. (1982). Not all data are in agreement; for example, Lillywhite (1971a) found that preferred body temperatures of juvenile *Rana catesbeiana* on a thermal gradient in the laboratory were essentially the same as those in nature.

Although amphibians seem to avoid extremes and exhibit thermal preferenda, the preferred body temperatures may be altered by trophic state, acclimation temperature, developmental stage, environmental moisture, oxygen availability, reproductive state, time of day, and availability of appropriate environmental temperatures (Feder (1982b). Of all these factors, moisture probably has the most notable effect. In Spotila's (1972) study, salamanders selected the highest relative humidity in thermal and relative humidity gradients. Thus, there seems to be a definite interplay between thermal and moisture responses.

Preferred body temperatures usually are nearer the upper than the lower extremes of temperature tolerated. Brattstrom (1968) recorded the critical thermal maxima for six species of North and Central American anurans to be greater than 40°C, notably higher than the temperatures at which these species are active in nature (Brattstrom, 1963); preferred temperatures were far above the minimum temperatures tolerated. For example, temperatures of 19 active *Smilisca baudinii* were 21.2 to 28.8°C (mean = 24.3°C), whereas the critical thermal maximum and minimum were 40.4 and 5.0°C, respectively. Comparable temperatures for 25 *Bufo marinus* were 22.0 to 27.0°C (mean = 25.2°C) with critical thermal maximum and minimum of 41.8 and 11.0°C, respectively. The highest critical thermal maximum for salamanders (38°C for *Ambystoma mabeei;* V. Hutchinson, 1961) is 8°C above the highest temperatures recorded in the field (see Table 8-1); a similar difference is found in anurans, the highest critical thermal maximum for which is 42.5°C for *Hyla smithii* (Brattstrom, 1968).

Table 8-2. Comparison of Critical Thermal Maximum Temperatures Determined by the Onset of Spasms of Anurans from Temperate North America and Tropical Middle America Acclimated to Different Temperatures for 2 or 3 Weeks[a]

Group	Number of species	Acclimation temperature (°C)	Critical thermal maximum (°C)[b]	Range of variation (°C)
Temperate anurans	27	5	28.1–3.74 (32.6 ± 2.47)	9.3
	15	23	31.3–40.0 (35.3 ± 2.57)	8.7
	18	30	33.6–40.3 (36.3 ± 1.92)	6.7
Tropical anurans	4[c]	5	31.5–36.7 (34.3 ± 2.20)	5.2
	6	23	31.4–40.0 (37.2 ± 3.15)	8.6
	6	30	39.5–42.5 (40.7 ± 1.20)	3.0

[a]Based on data in Brattstrom (1968).
[b]Numbers in parentheses are means ± 1 standard deviation.
[c]Individuals of 15 additional species died at this acclimatory temperature.

Thermal Acclimation. Amphibians usually respond to a prolonged change in ambient temperature by adjusting their thermal tolerances accordingly. This compensatory change is known as thermal acclimation. Numerous investigators of thermal acclimation in amphibians have used the critical thermal maximum (CTMax) or (far less commonly) minimum (CTMin) as the measure of temperature tolerance at which 50% of the animals survive. For data on salamanders, see V. Hutchinson (1961), Claussen (1977), Layne and Claussen (1982), and references cited therein; for data on anurans, see Brattstrom (1968, 1970, 1979) and references cited therein. Most investigators have been concerned primarily with the magnitude of thermal acclimation, but acclimation rates have been considered by some workers, notably Brattstrom and Lawrence (1962), Brattstrom and Regal (1965), V. Hutchinson and Rowlan (1975), Claussen (1977), and Nietfeldt et al. (1980).

The experimental approach usually consists of acclimating individuals to a constant temperature and then increasing or decreasing the temperature to determine the critical thermal maximum or minimum that the animals can tolerate. Critical temperatures usually are determined by the onset of spasms, loss of righting response, and heat or cold vigor. Equivocal results obtained by various investigators may be due to experimental design—aquatic versus terrestrial test chambers, photoperiod, starvation versus feeding—or intraspecific variation in the animals tested because of differences in size, maturity, sex, or place or season of origin.

Magnitude of acclimation.—It is generally assumed that amphibians living in regions of high temperatures tolerate higher temperatures than those living in cooler regions. Comparison of critical thermal maxima of tropical and temperate species shows that amphibians living in the tropics typically have higher critical or lethal temperatures than ones living in the temperate zones (G. Snyder and Weathers, 1975), but amphibians from both regions are similar in their abilities to undergo acclimation to high temperatures (Table 8-2). In both regions the upper thermal tolerances of amphibians increase within certain limits of thermal acclimation, as shown for various

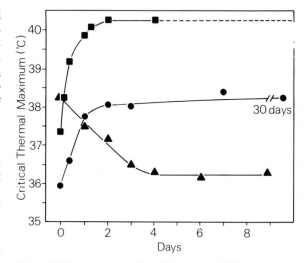

Figure 8-12. Comparison of rates of thermal acclimation of newts, *Notophthalmus viridescens.* Symbols are means of samples. Circles are for individuals transferred from 4 to 20°C; squares from 19.5 to 32°C; triangles from 20 to 4°C. Redrawn from V. Hutchinson (1961).

salamanders (e.g., *Notophthalmus viridescens;* Fig. 8-12) and anurans.

Not all amphibians in either tropical or temperate regions have equally broad ranges of thermal tolerance; in fact, some species in both regions have limited acclimatory abilities. Such species are physiologically less plastic because of a small gene pool, low heterozygosity, or much inbreeding (i.e., the total morphological and physiological variability is less than in wide-ranging species); thus, should local climatic conditions change, these species are likely to become extinct. For example, Brattstrom (1970) found that two species of anurans (*Kyarranus sphagnicola* and *Philoria frosti*) living on mountaintops in eastern Australia, where there is little environmental fluctuation, have essentially no ability to undergo thermal acclimation. Likewise, *Bufo exsul,* restricted to one small valley in California, has limited temperature tolerances in comparison with its wide-ranging relative *B. boreas. Centrolenella fleischmanni* in montane forests in Costa Rica has a very limited ability to adjust to changing temperatures (Brattstrom, 1968). Microhabitat temperatures may differ considerably from general ambient temperatures, as in the case of the interiors of bromeliads and banana plants inhabited by various anurans and bolitoglossine salamanders in the Neotropics (Feder, 1982b).

Limited data on salamanders (V. Hutchinson, 1961) and anurans (Brattstrom, 1968, 1970; G. Zug and P. Zug, 1979) show that in species with broad geographical ranges, especially latitudinally, there is geographic variation in temperature tolerance; altitudinal effects corresponding to latitudinal gradients have been demonstrated in *Bufo boreas* (Brattstrom, 1968) and *Pseudacris triseriata* (K. Miller and Packard, 1977).

Only a few investigations on temperature tolerances have been concerned with critical minimum temperatures. Brattstrom (1968, 1970) provided data on minimum lethal temperatures for many kinds of anurans and concluded that high-tatitude species are more cold-tolerant than tropical species (Fig. 8-13).

Rates of acclimation.—Acclimation rates are highly variable but usually follow a hyperbolic curve (Fig. 8-12). There seems to be no correlation with latitude or altitude. However, Claussen (1977) suggested that there is a correlation between the magnitude and rate of thermal acclimation. He proposed an acclimation response ratio of $ARR = \Delta CTM/ZT$ as being the change in the critical thermal maximum (ΔCTM) per degree Celsius change in acclimation temperature (ΔT). Because this ratio assumes a linear relationship between the critical thermal maximum and the acclimation temperature and because acclimation rates usually follow a hyperbolic curve, Claussen suggested using the time required for 50% acclimation (1/2AT). Acclimation is quite rapid (1/2AT of 2 days or less in most species), yet highly variable in magnitude (Table 8-3). Calculated acclimation response ratios in salamanders vary from 0.12 for *Desmognathus fuscus* to 0.19 for *Cryptobranchus alleganiensis* and *Necturus maculosus*; ratios have a broader range in anurans—from <0.01 for *Philoria frosti* to 0.40 for *Scaphiopus holbrookii*, *Cyclorana brevipes*, *Hyla cadaverina*, and *Rana clamitans* (Claussen, 1977).

Although ΔCTM values for acclimation to lower temperatures are similar to values for acclimation to higher temperatures (Table 8-3; Figs. 8-12, 8-14), reverse acclimation is markedly slower in some species (e.g., *Notophthalmus viridescens*, *Chiropterotriton multidentatus*, and *Eurycea bislineata*) and slightly faster in the large aquatic salamanders, *Cryptobranchus alleganiensis* and *Necturus maculosus*. Acclimation to maximum and minimum temperatures seems to be decoupled in magnitude as well as in rate. Consequently, a considerable degree of independence seems to exist between the acclimation to critical thermal maxima and critical thermal minima. As noted by Layne and Claussen (1982), this may have adaptive value in allowing differential heat- versus cold-

tolerance responses to an altered thermal environment. An organism might thus change its heat resistance without necessarily modifying its cold tolerance, or vice versa.

Factors affecting thermal acclimation.—Differences in the magnitude of thermal acclimation in wide-ranging species have been noted already; no evident trends seem to be apparent in rates of acclimation by individuals of a given species from different geographic regions. Limited data suggest seasonal differences in magnitude and rates of thermal acclimation in two salamanders, *Notophthalmus viridescens* (V. Hutchinson, 1961) and *Eurycea bislineata* (Fig. 8-14; Layne and Claussen, 1982).

Size possibly affects the critical thermal maximum. V. Hutchinson (1961), Gatz (1973), and Claussen (1977) found no significant intraspecific size effect in various kinds of salamanders, nor did Heatwole et al. (1965) with two species of frogs of the genus *Eleutherodactylus*. However, Sealander and B. West (1969) found a slight, although insignificant, tendency for smaller individuals of species of salamanders to be more resistant to temperature than larger conspecifics, and Seibel (1970) found that larger individuals of *Rana pipiens* have higher critical thermal maxima than smaller conspecifics. In larval amphibians, younger individuals usually have greater heat resistance and broader ranges of tolerance than older larvae. Recently hatched larvae of *Ambystoma maculatum* and *Taricha rivularis* either do not respond to temperature differences, except extremes, or have notably slower responses than older larvae (P. Licht and A. Brown, 1967; Keen and Schroeder, 1975). The latter authors found that among the larvae of three species of *Ambys-*

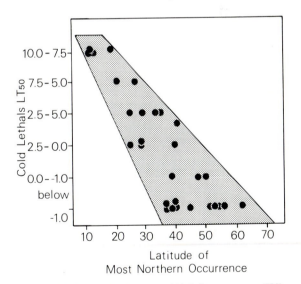

Figure 8-13. Relationship between cold lethal temperatures (50% survival) and latitude of northernmost occurrence of species of anurans in North and Central America. Symbols are means of temperatures for a given species at a given latitude. Redrawn from Brattstrom (1968).

toma, temperature selection is positively correlated with size and acclimation histories. On the other hand, the thermal responses of larval *T. rivularis* are similar to those of the adults (P. Licht and A. Brown, 1967), the magnitude and rates of acclimation of larval *A. tigrinum* parallel those of adults (Nietfeldt et al., 1980).

The available data on the effect of water balance on thermal acclimation are equivocal, although temperature acclimation has an effect on rates of dehydration and rehydration (Fig. 8-6). Dehydration decreases the critical thermal maximum of juvenile *Ambystoma maculatum* (Pough and R. Wilson, 1970) and adults of *A. jeffersonianum* and *A. tigrinum* (Claussen, 1977). On the contrary, V. Hutchinson (1961) and Feder and Pough (1975) found that dehydration increased thermal tolerance in *Notophthalmus viridescens.* The negative influence of dehydration on critical thermal maxima of *Ambystoma* does not support the free-radical hypothesis advocated

Table 8-3. Rate and Magnitude of Thermal Acclimation in Amphibians*

Species	Initial temperature (°C)	Final temperature (°C)	ΔT (°C)	½ΔT (Days)	ΔCTM (°C)	ΔCTM/ΔT	ΔCTM/½ΔT
Salamanders							
Cryptobranchus alleganiensis	5	25	20	2.80	4.30	0.20	1.44
Cryptobranchus alleganiensis	25	5	−20	2.15	4.52	0.23	−2.10
Necturus maculosus	5	25	20	1.54	4.16	0.21	2.70
Necturus maculosus	25	5	−20	1.18	−3.20	0.16	−2.71
Notophthalmus viridescens	4	20	16	0.17	2.53	0.16	9.37
Notophthalmus viridescens	20	4	−16	2.24	−2.78	0.17	−1.24
Ambystoma jeffersonianum	5	25	20	0.57	1.47	0.07	2.58
Chiropterotriton multidentatus	5	20	15	0.39	2.56	0.17	6.56
Chiropterotriton multidentatus	20	5	−15	1.00	−2.89	0.19	−2.89
Eurycea bislineata (spring)	5	25	20	0.12	1.37	0.07	11.42
Eurycea bislineata (summer)	5	25	20	0.60	2.27	0.11	3.78
Anurans							
Scaphiopus holbrooki	5	23	18	0.69	7.92	0.44	11.48
Pseudophryne bibronii	5	25	20	0.27	6.44	0.32	23.85
Bufo americanus	10	30	20	1.20	1.87	0.09	1.56
Bufo debilis	5	23	18	1.42	4.71	0.26	3.32
Bufo marinus	5	23	18	2.10	3.46	0.19	1.65
Bufo woodhousii	5	23	18	0.08	2.86	0.16	35.75
Hyla cadaverina	5	30	25	1.39	10.73	0.43	7.72
Litoria ewingi	10	20	10	1.42	3.13	0.31	2.20
Rana catesbeiana	5	23	18	0.12	2.00	0.11	16.67
Rana clamitans	5	23	18	2.17	7.82	0.43	3.60
Rana palustris	5	23	18	2.50	2.70	0.15	1.08
Rana pipiens	5	7	2	0.82	0.64	0.32	0.78
Rana pipiens	5	12	7	0.40	2.65	0.38	6.63
Rana pipiens	5	23	18	0.35	3.48	0.19	9.94
Rana pipiens	5	29	24	0.18	4.26	0.18	23.67
Rana pipiens	15	25	10	1.75	2.20	0.22	1.26
Rana pipiens	23	5	−18	0.43	−3.79	0.21	−8.81

*Based on Claussen (1977) and Layne and Claussen (1982).

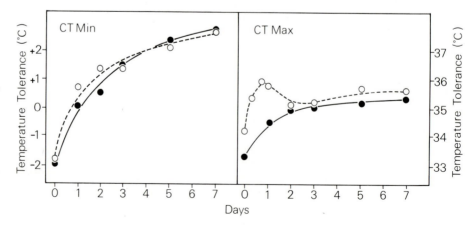

Figure 8-14. Comparison of rates of thermal acclimation in the salamander *Eurycea bislineata* at different seasons following transfer from 5 to 25°C. Open symbols connected by broken lines are means for six individuals collected in April; solid symbols connected by continuous lines are means for seven individuals collected in August. Adapted from Layne and Claussen (1982).

by Feder and Pough (1975) as a control mechanism of thermal acclimation.

Photoperiod has an effect on thermal acclimation in some amphibians, at least in some heliothermic anurans. Brattstrom (1968) determined that *Bufo boreas*, especially toads that had been acclimated at higher temperatures, modified their critical thermal maximum in response to 8 and 16 hours of light. Comparisons of *Hyla labialis* and *Rana pipiens* revealed significant variation in the critical thermal maximum over a 24-hour period in *H. labialis* acclimated at 25°C, light:dark (LD) 12:12, and *R. pipiens* at 25°C, LD 8:16, and at 15°C, LD 12:12 (Mahoney and V. Hutchinson, 1969). In both of these species, times of highest thermal tolerance are in the late morning and early afternoon, and lowest tolerance is during the dark period; this 24-hour rhythm of tolerance is consistent with the basking habits, which would expose the frogs to the highest temperatures at about midday. Part of the seasonal variation in critical thermal maxima for *Notophthalmus viridescens* may be controlled by photoperiod. V. Hutchinson (1961) found that if these newts were maintained on a 7-hour photoperiod centered on noon, the critical thermal maxima were significantly lower than for those kept in constant light or constant dark. Obviously, the interaction between light and temperature in controlling biological rhythms is complex and poorly understood.

Thermoregulation

As emphasized by Brattstrom (1979), the study of temperature regulation in amphibians is complicated by the requirement of amphibians to maintain a moist skin. Thermoregulation may be compromised by demands of water economy, whereas in other situations thermoregulatory demands may predominate.

Behavioral Thermoregulation. Field and laboratory studies have provided sufficient information to demonstrate that at least some species of amphibians exert behavioral control over their body temperatures within the range of ambient temperatures available to them and in some cases actually exceed ambient temperatures. Exposure of amphibians to thermal gradients in the laboratory shows that individuals select temperatures by moving to preferred parts of the gradient. This has been demonstrated most effectively in plethodontid salamanders (Spotila, 1972; Feder, 1982b) and in *Ambystoma* larvae (Keen and Schroeder, 1975). In the latter study, it was shown that selection was accomplished by recurrent avoidance reactions, as in *Taricha rivularis* (P. Licht and A. Brown, 1967). However, in *Ambystoma* larvae, the accuracy with which body temperature is maintained is less than that in juvenile *Rana catesbeiana* reported by Lillywhite (1971b).

Behavioral thermoregulation in diurnal anurans usually involves moving into or out of sunlight or water, thereby changing the magnitude and direction of heat flux be-

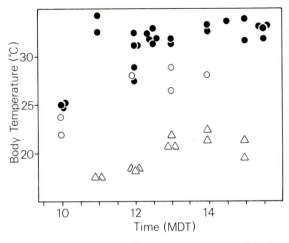

Figure 8-15. Relationships of body temperature to time of day in *Bufo debilis* while basking (solid circles), hopping in sun (open circles), and sitting in shade (triangles). Redrawn from Seymour (1972).

tween themselves and the environment. This was shown for *Acris crepitans* and *Rana pipiens* by Brattstrom (1963). Lillywhite (1970) found that bullfrogs, *R. catesbeiana*, thermoregulate behaviorally not only by changing locations but also by altering their posture. Bullfrogs can remain exposed to insolation all day as long as a source of moisture is available. Evaporative cooling, augmented by postural changes and periodic rewetting of the skin, serves to stabilize the body temperature at levels lower than would be possible without the evaporative mechanism, and enables these frogs to remain relatively stationary for periods under radiant heat loads that otherwise would be lethal (see following section: Physiological Thermoregulation).

Seymour (1972) found distinct differences in body temperatures of basking individuals of toads, *Bufo debilis*, and those that were hopping in sunlight or sitting in the shade (Fig. 8-15); mean body temperatures were 30.9, 25.8, and 19.5°C, respectively. These toads also selected slopes that exposed them to the most direct insolation, and during the day moved from one slope to another in response to the direction of insolation; body temperatures of toads basking on slopes facing toward the sun were significantly higher than those of toads on the level or on slopes facing away from the sun (means = 32.6 versus 29.5°C). Seymour (1972) suggested that in view of the lower body temperatures of toads hopping in the sun, the choice of basking sites minimized convective and evaporative heat losses. Lillywhite (1970) noted that *Rana catesbeiana* hold the ventral surface off the ground when they are heat-stressed, which increases evaporative cooling via convection, and lie prostrate under cool conditions.

Many amphibians living at high altitudes increase their body temperatures by exposure to insolation. *Ambystoma tigrinum* in ponds at high elevations in the Rocky

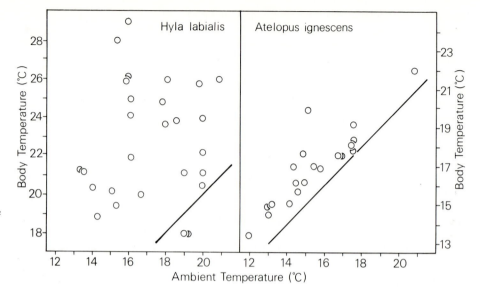

Figure 8-16. Body temperatures of basking frogs in relation to ambient temperatures (air temperatures in shade 5 mm above ground for *Hyla labialis;* substrate temperature at site of frog for *Atelopus ignescens*). Diagonal lines connect isothermal points. Data for *H. labialis* from Valdivieso and Tamsitt (1974); data for *A. ignescens* collected by W. E. Duellman and L. Trueb.

Mountains move into shallow water on sunny days; at night they retreat to the depths of the ponds, where the water is warmer than that at the surface being cooled by the night air (Heath, 1975). Basking behavior has been reported for several anurans that live in temperate regions (Brattstrom, 1963). Additionally, basking behavior has been reported in two montane hylid frogs; *Plectrohyla glandulosa* basks on rocks in and along streams in the mountains of Guatemala (Duellman, 1970), and the Andean *Hyla labialis* basks on the ground or on bushes (Valdivieso and Tamsitt, 1974). Neither species seems to employ postural modifications with respect to insolation. Basking *H. labialis* elevate their body temperatures well above the ambient temperature (Fig. 8-16). The high Andean *Bufo spinulosus* basks and actively moves about during the day and seeks shelter when insolation ceases (O. Pearson and Bradford, 1976).

Bufonids of the genus *Atelopus* are diurnal, and at least some high montane species (*A. ebanoides, ignescens,* and *oxyrhynchus*) bask. Duellman and Trueb's observations on *A. ignescens* in the paramos of Ecuador show that on bright sunlit days after rains, great numbers of these frogs move about; subsequently individuals remain stationary, usually in the sun on lee sides of clumps of bunch grass, where they are exposed to insolation and protected from cold winds. These black frogs are able to raise their body temperatures rapidly; within half an hour after emergence, 20 individuals had body temperatures of 0.5 to 4.6°C (mean = 1.45°C) above the temperature of the adjacent substrate (Fig. 8-16).

Probably many kinds of high-altitude amphibians seek shelters that have higher temperatures than surrounding areas. This has been demonstrated for the diminutive plethodontid salamander *Thorius narisovalis*. These salamanders select the smallest possible crevices under the bark on logs; these small crevices have higher tempera-

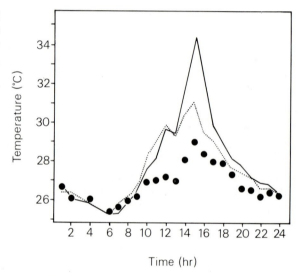

Figure 8-17. Daily temperature regime of unrestrained *Bufo marinus*. Circles are mean body temperatures of one to four individuals; dotted line = mean air temperature; solid line = mean substrate temperature. Redrawn from G. Zug and P. Zug (1979).

tures than do large crevices or the interiors of the logs (Feder, 1982b).

The body temperatures of nocturnal amphibians coincide closely with the ambient temperatures during periods of activity. In these animals, regulation of body temperature, if it occurs at all, is restricted to those times when the animal is in its diurnal retreat. The daily fluctuation of body temperature of *Bufo marinus* is less than that of the ambient temperatures (Fig. 8-17); during the night the body temperature is nearly equivalent to that of the ambient temperature, but during the day body temperature remains well below ambient temperature (G.

Zug and P. Zug, 1979). The lower temperature is the result of evaporative cooling of the body surface.

Physiological Thermoregulation. It is evident that there is an interplay between behavioral thermoregulation and water balance, but there has been only one in-depth investigation of the mechanisms. In a study of the thermal parameters associated with evaporative water loss in the bullfrog, *Rana catesbeiana*, Lillywhite (1971a) found that the periodic and synchronous discharge of the cutaneous mucous glands onto the integumentary surface occurs in response to sympathetic nervous stimulation. The frequency of discharge depends on central nervous impulses and increases with higher temperatures. Experimental results implicate the anterior hypothalamus in the control of the activity of the mucous glands; apparently peripheral afferents modify central impulses determining the frequency of discharge. Thermal modulation of mucous discharge seems to function to maintain a moist (and therefore permeable) integument during terrestrial basking, thereby stabilizing body temperature. A slow rate of discharge results in drier (and less permeable) integument, so that at lower temperatures evaporative cooling is minimized.

This type of mechanism allows amphibians to raise their body temperatures by basking and to control the body temperature by evaporative cooling. Obviously, such a mechanism is associated with diurnal basking and is an adaptation for cooling the body. There are no known physiological mechanisms by which an amphibian can increase its body temperature. Brattstrom (1970) suggested that basking Australian hylids, *Litoria caerulea*, may have some control over the rate of water loss through the skin, thereby allowing this anuran to control the rate of evaporation and hence maintain a sublethal body temperature under otherwise lethal conditions.

Significance of Thermoregulation. In contrast to reptiles in which basking (and therefore attainment of preferred body temperature) commonly is a prelude to foraging activity, the reverse seems to be true in amphibians, most of which have relatively broad ranges of thermal activity. Lillywhite et al. (1973) found that when juvenile *Bufo boreas* are well fed, they prefer temperatures of 26 to 27°C, but in the absence of food, they prefer temperatures of 15 to 20°C. Feder (1982b) noted that subsequent to feeding, plethodontid salamanders (*Pseudoeurycea smithi*) had preferred body temperatures of 3 to 5°C greater than those of unfed salamanders. These observations are corroborated by field observations on *Rana catesbeiana* (Lillywhite, 1970), *B. woodhousii* (Hadfield, 1966), and *B. spinulosus* (O. Pearson and Bradford, 1976). Three aspects of thermal metabolism seem to be evident in relation to behavioral thermoregulation. (1) By increasing their body temperatures, amphibians increase their digestive rates. (2) Increased digestive rates maximize growth in juveniles. (3) In-creased rates of digestion result in the deposition of more fat, which is essential for survival during long periods of dormancy.

GAS EXCHANGE

With the possible exception of cloacal tissues, amphibians utilize every type of respiratory gas exchange known in vertebrates—gills, lungs, skin, and buccopharyngeal. Adults of most kinds of amphibians, whether they be caecilians, salamanders, or anurans, use skin, lung, and buccopharyngeal respiration, but the lungless salamanders of the family Plethodontidae use only buccopharyngeal and cutaneous gas exchange. Gills are common in the larval stages of most amphibians and cease to function at metamorphosis, but in some neotenic salamanders gill respiration is retained in the adults.

Since the reviews of amphibian respiration by Foxon (1964) and by Chugunov and Kispoev (1973), much new information has become available that provides a basis for the interpretation of patterns of respiration displayed by amphibians. However, too little is known about the details of the morphology of respiratory structures, and even less is known about their functions in all but a few species.

Gas Transportation

The exchange of gases between an amphibian and its environment is dependent on several structural features—respiratory surfaces, circulatory system, and properties of the blood.

Respiratory Surfaces. The contribution of each of the four kinds of respiratory surfaces to total gas exchange depends on the organism's structure, stage of life history, and habitat, as well as environmental variables, especially temperature.

Cutaneous gas exchange is highly important in all active (as contrasted with resting or dormant) amphibians and may account for more than 90% of the exchange in the lungless plethodontid salamanders, whereas in anurans and other salamanders the lungs account for varying amounts of the total gas exchange (Table 8-4). With increasing temperatures, the lungs and buccopharyngeal mucosa play an increasing role in oxygen uptake (see section: Factors Affecting Gas Exchange). Because oxygen uptake through the skin or gills is passive, it is dependent on the proximity of capillaries to the surface, density of capillaries, blood flow through the capillaries, the affinity of the hemoglobin to oxygen, and in the case of the skin a moist surface. Uptake of oxygen through the pulmonary and buccopharyngeal tissue is dependent on these same factors and also the depth and rate of breathing movements. Increased utilization of the lungs in respiration can be correlated with lung size and complexity and with the tidal volume and breathing rates.

Comparison of the vascularity of the different respi-

Table 8-4. Contributions of Different Respiratory Surfaces to Gas Exchange in Various Amphibians[a]

Species	Oxygen[b]			Carbon dioxide[c]		
	Cutaneous	Pulmonary	Branchial	Cutaneous	Pulmonary	Branchial
Salamanders						
Necturus maculosus	30.4	8.4	61.2	31.6	8.5	59.9
Siren lacertina	33.1	61.6	5.3	53.9	27.7	18.4
Ambystoma maculatum	68.4	31.6	—	79.6	20.4	—
Taricha granulosa	49.4	50.6	—	86.8	13.2	—
Desmognathus quadramaculatus	9.7	90.3[d]	—	88.9	11.1[d]	—
Anurans						
Xenopus laevis	58.5	41.5	—	90.3	9.7	—
Scaphiopus bombifrons	32.4	67.6	—	74.3	25.7	—
Eleutherodactylus portoricensis	23.2	76.8	—	80.3	19.7	—
Bufo boreas	44.4	55.6	—	79.0	21.0	—
Hyla gratiosa	35.9	64.1	—	73.4	26.6	—
Rana pipiens	45.8	54.2	—	76.0	24.0	—

[a]Based on data in Guimond and V. Hutchinson (1976), V. Hutchinson et al. (1968), and Whitford and V. Hutchinson (1963, 1965).
[b]Percentages of total oxygen exchange at 15°C.
[c]Percentages of total carbon dioxide exchange at 15°C.
[d]Buccopharyngeal only.

Table 8-5. Percentages of Capillaries in Different Respiratory Structures in Various Amphibians[a]

Group	Skin	Buccal cavity	Lungs
Salamanders			
Siren intermedia[b]	38.7	0.9	58.1
Amphiuma means	31.3	0.5	68.2
Salamandra salamandra	41.4	1.3	57.3
Triturus (3 species)	74.5	2.0	23.5
Taricha granulosa	64.5	4.5	31.0
Notophthalmus viridescens	72.8	3.9	23.3
Rhyacotriton olympicus	85.6	5.3	9.1
Dicamptodon ensatus	54.0	3.5	42.5
Ambystoma (2 species)	56.1	3.0	40.9
Plethodontids (7 species)	93.2	6.8	—
Anurans			
Xenopus laevis	33.9	0.2	65.9
Leiopelma hochstetteri	65.1	3.0	31.9
Bombina (2 species)	47.6	1.2	51.2
Pelobates fuscus	48.3	2.4	49.3
Bufo (5 species)	27.8	1.4	70.8
Hyla arborea	24.2	1.1	74.7
Rana (3 species)	34.4	0.8	64.8

[a]Summarized from Czopek (1962) and Foxon (1964).
[b]Plus 2.3% in gills.

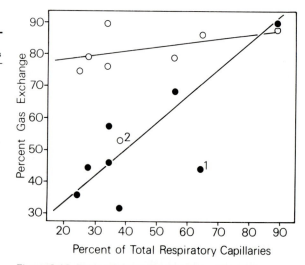

Figure 8-18. Relationship of relative amounts of cutaneous vascularization and cutaneous gas exchange in various amphibians (see Tables 8-4 and 8-5). Solid circles are oxygen exchange; $Y = 21.7 + 0.72\,X$, $r = 0.748$ ($P < 0.05$). Open circles are carbon dioxide exchange; $Y = 74.0 + 0.169\,X$, $r = 0.241$ (not significant). Outliers (1 = *Taricha*; 2 = *Siren*) not included in regression analyses.

ratory surfaces shows that the percentage of capillaries in the buccal cavity is usually minute compared to those in the skin or lungs (Table 8-5). Exceptions are the lungless plethodontid salamanders and *Rhyacotriton olympicus*, a salamander that dwells in cold water. The skin of terrestrial anurans is more vascularized, relative to the lungs, than that of aquatic or semiaquatic anurans; this suggests that pulmonary ventilation is more important in the aquatic and semiaquatic anurans, but the high degree of integumentary vascularity in terrestrial anurans may be indic-

ative of increased need for water uptake. Nevertheless, there is a positive correlation between the relative amounts of cutaneous oxygen uptake and cutaneous vascularization, although no such correlation exists for the relative amount of carbon dioxide exchange (Fig. 8-18).

The lungs vary in size from very small in some amphibians that dwell in cold water (e.g., the salamander *Rhyacotriton olympicus* and the leptodactylid frog *Telmatobius culeus* in Lake Titicaca in the high Andes) to large in most terrestrial anurans, ambystomatid salamanders, and neotenic salamanders, such as *Siren* and *Amphiuma,* that live in poorly oxygenated water (see Chapter 14 for details of pulmonary structure).

The ventilation of the lungs is accomplished by a force-pump mechanism (de Jong and Gans, 1969). In *Rana catesbeiana,* buccopulmonary ventilation comprises three kinds of cyclic phenomena: (1) Oscillatory cycles consist of rhythmic raising and lowering of the buccal floor with the nares open; in this way fresh air is introduced into the buccal cavity. (2) Ventilatory cycles consist of opening and closing the glottis and nares and the renewal of pulmonary air. (3) Inflation cycles consist of a series of ventilatory cycles interrupted by an apneic pause. This respiratory mechanism depends on the activity of a buccal force pump, which determines pulmonary pressure; elevated pulmonary pressure is responsible for the expulsion

of pulmonary air during the second phase of the next ventilation cycle (Fig. 8-19). Pressure is maintained by the elastic fibers and smooth muscles of the lungs. This basic respiratory mechanism is not very efficient, but it is characteristic of all living amphibians. Even the lungless plethodontid salamanders may obtain up to 24% of their oxygen through the buccal mucosa (Whitford and V. Hutchinson, 1965). Anurans are locked into this respiratory mechanism, for it is an integral part of the vocalization mechanism (see Chapter 4).

Circulatory System.   Circulation of oxygenated and deoxygenated blood in amphibians is not completely separate because of mixing in the heart (see Chapter 3 for details of structure). Although there is some mixture of the blood in the heart, differential blood pressure caused

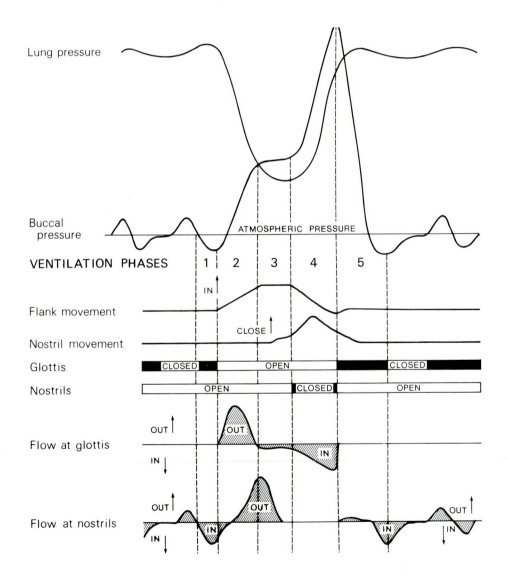

Figure 8-19. Diagrammatic representation of buccal pump respiration in *Rana catesbeiana* showing temporal relationships among lung pressure, buccal pressure, nostril and flank movements, and airflow. Adapted from de Jong and Gans (1969).

by vasoconstriction of certain vessels helps to regulate the flow. For example, *Xenopus laevis* breathes aerially at the surface of the water and depends on cutaneous respiration when below the surface; approximately 58% of its oxygen uptake is cutaneous under experimental conditions at 15°C (V. Hutchinson et al., 1968). Monitoring of respiratory cycles and circulation by Shelton (1976) revealed that gas exchange occurs at a high rate in the lungs when the frog is using aerial ventilation, but the rate decreases rapidly when it submerges. The amount of blood flowing to the lungs is related to the extent that they are ventilated. When *Xenopus* is not breathing, vasoconstriction of the lung vessels reduces blood flow in the pulmonary artery to low levels, so that patterns of blood flow and pressure in the arterial arches can be interpreted in terms of the constantly changing vasomotor state of the lung vessels. Shelton (1976) hypothesized that the selective distribution of blood leaving the heart is achieved by maintenance of more or less separate streams of oxygenated and deoxygenated blood; the separation of these streams is affected considerably by the degree of vasoconstriction of the lung vessels. Measurements of the relative amounts of oxygen and carbon dioxide in vessels entering and leaving the heart in *Bufo paracnemis* also indicate a physical separation of oxygenated and deoxygenated blood (Johansen and Ditada, 1966).

On the other hand, in a study of the lungless salamander, *Desmognathus fuscus*, Piiper et al. (1976) concluded that arterial and venous blood probably are completely mixed in the heart. Of the cardiac output of 0.11 to 0.19 ml·min·g body weight of this salamander, less than 50% of the blood is directed to the skin, where gas exchange occurs; the majority of the cardiac output is directed to other tissues and organs, where oxygen is delivered. Partial pressures of oxygen in arterial blood is 57 to 75 torr, in venous blood 31 to 37 torr, and in mixed blood 40 torr. The different interpretations of patterns of flow of oxygenated and deoxygenated blood in a lungless salamander as contrasted with that in anurans possibly are associated with lunglessness, or there may be a basic difference between salamanders and anurans.

Characteristics of Blood. Oxygen transport by the blood depends on several hematological factors—number and volume of red blood cells (erythrocytes), hematocrit (percent of blood that is red blood cells), hemoglobin content, and pH of the blood. The affinity between oxygen and red blood cells varies with environmental factors, such as temperature and partial pressure of oxygen; the latter commonly is measured as P_{50} (50% saturation of the red blood cells with oxygen).

Blood characteristics with respect to oxygen transportation are known for only a few amphibians (Table 8-6). Surveys of amphibian bloods by Lenfant and Johansen (1967) and by Johansen and Lenfant (1972) show a clear trend toward lower oxygen affinities in the bloods of amphibians that rely mostly on their lungs as contrasted with aquatic amphibians that accomplish oxygen uptake by means of gills, skin, and buccopharyngeal mucosa.

Activity also has an effect on blood characteristics, especially in the case of dormant versus resting or active animals. In dormant spadefoot toads (*Scaphiopus*), P_{50} values are lower than in resting individuals, but hemoglobin levels and hematocrit are not significantly different; Seymour (1973c) suggested that hemoglobin may function mainly for oxygen storage during dormancy. However, in cocooned *Pyxicephalus adspersus*, hemoglobin concentration and hematocrit increase significantly as compared with nondormant frogs, reflecting dehydrational hemoconcentration (Loveridge and Withers, 1981).

Table 8-6. Characteristics of the Blood of Some Species of Amphibians[a]

Species	RBC[b] volume [ml/(100 ml blood)$^{-1}$]	RBC[b] volume (μ³)	Hemoglobin [g/(100 ml blood)$^{-1}$]	Concentration [g/100 ml (RBC)$^{-1}$]	RBC[b] Hb content (pg)	O₂ capacity [ml O₂/(100 ml blood)$^{-1}$]	P_{50} (mmHg)
Caecilians							
Boulengerula taitanus	40.0	588	10.3	25.7	151	14.00	28.0
Salamanders							
Cryptobranchus alleganiensis	49.0	7,425	13.3	27.1	2,010	—	20.0
Necturus maculosus	21.4	10,070	4.6	21.4	2,160	6.26	17.7
Amphiuma means	40.0	13,857	9.4	23.5	3,287	7.26	30.0
Taricha granulosa	36.7	3,336	9.5	13.2	837	9.70	36.5
Dicamptodon ensatus	24.2	4,938	4.4	15.6	880	5.60	31.6
Anurans							
Telmatobius culeus	27.9	394	8.1	28.1	281	8.02	15.6
Rana catesbeiana	29.3	670	7.8	26.9	179	10.43	49.8
Rana esculenta	27.3	659	7.8	28.9	187	—	39.7
Rana pipiens	24.6	768	6.7	27.2	208	11.70	—

[a]Data from S. Wood et al. (1975) and V. Hutchinson et al. (1976).
[b]RBC = red blood count.

Factors Affecting Gas Exchange

Respiratory rates, principally oxygen consumption, vary with properties of the animals (activity, surface area, and body size) and environmental variables (temperature, oxygen pressure, moisture, and photoperiod).

Body Size and Surface Area. As expected, larger amphibians consume more oxygen than smaller ones, but the rate of oxygen consumption has a negative curvilinear relationship with body size, at least in anurans (Fig. 8-20). V. Hutchinson et al. (1968) concluded that the lungs are the most important respiratory structures in anurans and that, in general, there is an inverse relationship between body size and ventilatory rate and a direct relationship between tidal volume and weight. The lungs also are the most important respiratory structures in adult caecilians (A. Bennett and M. Wake, 1974).

In salamanders the respiratory surface area differs between lunged and lungless salamanders; at weights of more than 0.44 g, lunged salamanders have greater respiratory surface areas than lungless salamanders of the same weight (Ultsch, 1974), and this discrepancy increases with body size (Whitford and V. Hutchinson, 1967). The expected differences between lunged and lungless salamanders in rates of oxygen consumption are evident in salamanders in hypoxic or aquatic media (Beckenback, 1975; Ultsch, 1976). In atmospheric air the rate of oxygen consumption is similar for resting lunged and lungless salamanders under standard conditions (Feder, 1976). However, the reduced respiratory surface area in large lungless salamanders apparently results in reduced capacity for oxygen exchange at postactivity times compared to lunged salamanders (Feder, 1977; Withers, 1980).

Temperature. The effects of temperature on respiration were reviewed by Whitford (1973), who concluded that in temperate zone amphibians, except plethodontid salamanders, pulmonary oxygen uptake increases with temperature and that tropical anurans have a rate of oxygen consumption equivalent to that of temperate amphibians at temperatures of 10°C or more. In plethodontid salamanders the rate of cutaneous gas exchange increases with temperature, and aquatic salamanders have a lower rate of oxygen consumption than other temperate amphibians (Fig. 8-21).

The rates of oxygen consumption in relation to temperature in plethodontid salamanders apparently are the result of decreased respiratory surface area (absence of lungs). The lower rates in tropical anurans, relative to temperate anurans and lunged terrestrial salamanders, indicate lower resting metabolic rates in tropical anurans (Weathers and G. Snyder, 1977), a conclusion also reached by Feder (1978b) regarding tropical versus temperate plethodontids. These correlations suggest that tropical anurans and plethodontid salamanders not only have lower metabolic rates but should have less capacity for thermal acclimation of metabolism.

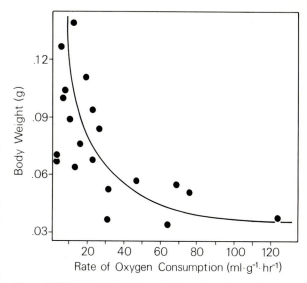

Figure 8-20. Relationship between body weight and rate of oxygen consumption in 20 species of anurans at 15°C. Based on data in V. Hutchinson (1971).

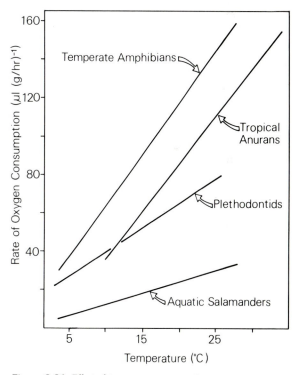

Figure 8-21. Effect of temperature on rate of oxygen consumption in various groups of amphibians. Redrawn from Whitford (1973).

Feder (1978a, 1982a) summarized existing data on acclimation of amphibians. Acclimation temperatures altered standard metabolic rates of two temperate zone salamanders (*Batrachoseps attenuatus* and *Taricha torosa*) but not of two tropical salamanders (*Bolitoglossa occidentalis* and *Pseudoeurycea smithi*). Also, acclima-

Figure 8-22. Aquatic leptodactylid frog *Atelognathus patagonicus* from Laguna Blanca, Argentina, 1275 m elevation. The extensive flaps of skin provide a greatly increased surface area for respiration in cold water. Photo by W. E. Duellman.

tion temperature had a greater effect on several measures of postactivity oxygen consumption in the temperate zone species than in the tropical species. Investigations on tropical and temperate anurans have provided similar results; all temperate zone species show significant acclimation of metabolism, and all tropical species, except *Rana erythraea,* show no acclimation. Moreover, differences in the abilities of tropical versus temperate species to undergo thermal acclimation of rates of oxygen consumption are contrary to the pattern for acclimation of critical thermal maxima, in which tropical and temperate species show no consistent differences (Brattstrom, 1968; Feder, 1978a).

Oxygen Pressure. Differential partial pressure of oxygen at different altitudes seems to be reflected in the oxygen-carrying capacity of the blood. As early as 1951, Stuart noted that *Bufo bocourti* in the highlands of Guatemala had 22% more hemoglobin than *B. marinus* in the lowlands. The only detailed work on a high altitude amphibian deals with the aquatic *Telmatobius culeus,* which lives in perpetually cold water (10°C) at an elevation of 3812 m in Lake Titicaca (V. Hutchinson et al., 1976). This anuran has extensive flaps of skin that increase its surface area for greater cutaneous respiration, a condition also characteristic of some other inhabitants of cold waters (e.g., *Cryptobranchus alleganiensis* and *Atelognathus patagonicus;* Fig. 8-22). In *Telmatobius* and *Cryptobranchus,* at least, capillaries penetrate to the epidermis. When submerged in water with a low oxygen pressure, *T. culeus* periodically sways from side to side

so as to break up the boundary layer between the water and skin, thereby ventilating the cutaneous surfaces. This habit also is characteristic of *C. alleganiensis* (Guimond and V. Hutchinson, 1973).

Oxygen transport characteristics in *Telmatobius culeus* include the smallest erythrocyte volume known in amphibians and the highest erythrocyte count and lowest P_{50} known for anurans. The oxygen capacity, hemoglobin concentration, and hematocrit values are higher than in most amphibians. During a 10-week period of acclimation from 3800 to 335 m, the erythrocyte count, hemoglobin concentration, and hematocrit declined steadily, thereby indicating that these characteristics are subject to environmental influence. Comparable kinds of data on terrestrial amphibians from high elevations are lacking, so it is unknown if all of these characteristics of *T. culeus* are associated strictly with lower oxygen pressure or with cold water.

Moisture. The moisture coating the skin is important in diffusion. The only experimental data on the relationship of dehydration and oxygen consumption are from the Puerto Rican frog *Eleutherodactylus coqui* (Pough et al., 1983). The metabolic rates of resting frogs increase and the maximum metabolic rates decrease as the frogs become more dehydrated.

Photoperiod and Seasonality. There are few data on the effects of photoperiod on metabolic activity, as measured by oxygen consumption, and the experimental results and interpretations are inconsistent (see review by

Turney and V. Hutchinson, 1974). Endogenous metabolic rhythms were reported in temperate but not tropical amphibians; however, Weathers and G. Snyder (1977) demonstrated rhythmic metabolism in three species of tropical *Rana* subjected to different photoperiods. One aspect of rhythmic behavior that does seem to be apparent is the increase in metabolism at times of normal increase in activity in nature. F. Brown et al. (1955) reported that amphibians have endogenous rhythms correlated with daily changes in ambient atmospheric pressure, but V. Hutchinson and Kohl (1971) found no such correlation in *Bufo marinus.*

Knowledge of seasonal variation in metabolic rates is very limited. Vernberg (1962) reported seasonal differences in the salamanders *Plethodon cinereus* and *Eurycea bislineata;* at 10°C the highest metabolic rates of both species were in May and June, and the lowest were in October and November. Fitzpatrick and A. V. Brown (1975) found that *Desmognathus ochrophaeus* have adaptive patterns of partial metabolic compensation over a range of seasonally encountered temperatures—i.e., inverse metabolic compensation at a temperature commonly encountered during winter dormancy, and temperature-insensitive acute metabolic rates during short-term changes in temperatures similar to those encountered during early spring and autumn.

Natural seasonal differences in metabolism, as measured by rates of oxygen consumption, may reflect differences in activity levels (see following section), energy metabolism, or reproductive effort, especially during vitellogenesis (see Chapter 2). Endogenous rhythms are evident in reproductive cycles in temperate and some tropical amphibians. Furthermore, as concluded by Lagerspetz (1977), the seasonal variation of metabolism in amphibians is controlled largely by the central nervous system with the thyroid and the autonomic nervous system as principal mediators.

Activity Levels. Resting amphibians consume less oxygen and therefore have lower metabolic rates than active animals (Fig. 8-23). Feder (1978b) demonstrated these differences in 18 species of salamanders. Oxygen consumption increases dramatically after short bursts of activity. Moreover, in lungless salamanders the rate of maximum oxygen consumption is less than in lunged salamanders, especially in larger salamanders and at higher temperatures. Few data are available on rates of oxygen consumption in active versus resting anurans. Oxygen is consumed at rates 3 to 10 times greater in active individuals than in resting ones at the same temperature (Seymour, 1973a; S. Hillman and Withers, 1979). *Pyxicephalus adspersus* is an exception in that the rate of oxygen consumption during activity is similar to that of other anurans, but the rate at rest is much lower, about 5% of that during activity (Loveridge and Withers, 1981).

There is a great reduction in metabolic rate in dormant amphibians. Dormant *Siren intermedia* (Gehlbach et al., 1973) and *Scaphiopus couchii* and *S. multiplicatus* (Seymour, 1973b) consume oxygen at a rate equal to about 20% of that of resting individuals, and *Cyclorana platycephala* has a rate of about 30% of resting individuals (van Buerden, 1980). In dormant and cocooned *Pyxicephalus adspersus,* the rate is equal to 16% of that of resting individuals (Loveridge and Withers, 1981). There is a corresponding decrease in heart rate in dormant amphibians.

The mechanism by which the metabolic rate of dormant amphibians is lowered to substantially less than the standard metabolic rate is unknown. The low rate of oxygen consumption of dormant *Scaphiopus couchii* is not associated with tissue acidosis (Withers, 1978), whereas the tissues of *Pyxicephalus adspersus* are acidotic. This acidosis probably is associated with cocoon formation rather than with dormancy per se and is not responsible for the decline in the rate of oxygen consumption that

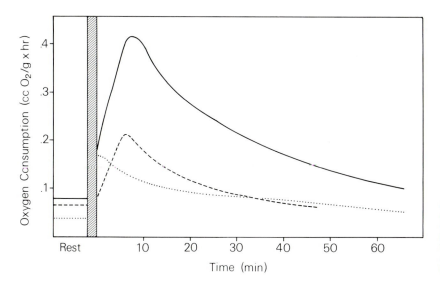

Figure 8-23. Oxygen consumption before, during, and after activity at 20°C by *Hyla regilla* (solid line), *Batrachoseps attenuatus* (broken line), and *Geotrypetes seraphini* (dotted line). The hatched vertical bar is a brief period of activity stimulated by an electrical current. Redrawn from A. Bennett and M. Wake (1974).

accompanies dormancy but precedes cocoon formation (Loveridge and Withers, 1981).

ENERGY METABOLISM AND ENERGY BUDGETS

Energy production in amphibians has been reviewed by A. Bennett (1978) and Brattstrom (1979).

Energy Metabolism

The relative contributions made by aerobic and anaerobic pathways to activity metabolism is dependent on work output. At low-level sustainable locomotion, aerobic catabolism of carbohydrates and fats probably accounts for all of the work output. A certain amount of anaerobic metabolism, causing a rise in blood lactate, may occur at the initiation of exercise until oxygen supply systems catch up with oxygen requirements. This initial anaerobiosis makes little contribution to overall energetics if activity is prolonged and remains at a low level. As long as no lactate accumulates or is excreted, oxygen consumption accounts for the total energy output. Lactate may be formed in muscle or other tissue, may enter the blood, and be catabolized aerobically elsewhere.

In general, aerobically supported metabolism functions at low rates of locomotion; this is supplemented by anaerobic metabolism during burst speeds. However, amphibians cannot sustain burst speed for more than 1 or 2 minutes, after which they become fatigued and unresponsive. Burst activity is fueled mainly, or almost exclusively, by anaerobic metabolism. During 2 minutes of activity, lactic acid formation accounts for two-thirds or more of the total adenenosine triphosphate production (A. Bennett and P. Licht, 1973). Because of the large and rapidly mobilized anaerobic potential and the relative low levels of oxygen consumption, burst activity is essentially oxygen-independent. The temperature independence of lactate formation in comparison with aerobic scope (A. Bennett and P. Licht, 1974) provides the functional basis for the temperature independence of burst activity. The anaerobic metabolic mode exerts an even greater influence on total metabolism at low body temperatures. Although recovery from activity requires much more time at lower temperatures, anaerobic metabolism provides the capacity for rapid activity.

Aerobic and anaerobic capacities of amphibians are correlated inversely in various species (A. Bennett and P. Licht, 1973; J. Baldwin et al., 1977; Harlow, 1978); the total energy output during activity is similar but the component factors are highly variable. For example, species having the greatest aerobic scopes (e.g., *Taricha*, *Bufo*, and *Scaphiopus*) do not produce large quantities of lactic acid during activity, whereas those that produce large amounts (e.g., *Batrachoseps*, *Hyla*, and *Rana*) have low aerobic scopes. These differences seem to have an enzymatic basis; reaction rates of two regulatory glycotylic enzymes (phosphofructokinase and lactate dehydro-

genase) are twice as great in *R. pipiens* (primarily anaerobic during activity) as in *Bufo boreas* (primarily aerobic) (A. Bennett, 1974). Species that rely on burst activity for rapid escape utilize anaerobic metabolism. The more aerobically competent amphibians are physiologically incapable of this rapid activity and rely on static defense mechanisms (Taigen et al., 1982).

Most studies on fatigue in amphibians have emphasized lactate removal with recovery. In *Batrachoseps attenuatus,* Feder and L. Olsen (1978) noted that a major synchrony between recovery from fatigue and lactate removal occurs during the first 30 minutes after exhaustion, and for the next 4.5 hours, recovery parallels lactate removal. The relationships among oxygen concentration, recovery from fatigue, and lactate elimination suggest that oxygen debt is an important aspect in recovery from exhaustion. Therefore, rates of postactivity oxygen consumption may limit rates of recovery. There are intraspecific size differences in rates of fatigue. For example, juvenile toads, *Bufo americanus,* become exhausted much more rapidly than adults (Taigen and Pough, 1981).

Energy Budgets

There are few studies on the energy budgets of amphibians. Fitzpatrick (1973b) studied energy budgets in *Eurycea bislineata,* and G. Smith (1976) produced an energy budget for *Bufo terrestris*. Assuming a digestive assimilation efficiency of 74% for that species, approximately half of that energy goes into metabolic costs and half into production (Fig. 8-24). The amount of energy devoted to reproduction will depend on the age and sex of the toad and on the season of the year.

In terms of energy metabolism, and thus costs of various functions, it is important to know how amphibians partition the utilization of energy seasonally. Lillywhite et al. (1973) suggested that behavioral thermoregulation and energy partitioning in juvenile toads, *Bufo boreas,* maximize growth, thereby shortening the time to reach adult size. Also, many kinds of amphibians must accrue energy reserves for survival of long periods of dormancy. In species having a short period of activity because of brief rainy seasons or brief summer temperatures, energy must be partitioned between reproduction and reserves.

Marked seasonal changes occur in liver and muscle glycogen, blood glucose, and body lipids in amphibians living in seasonal environments. For example, Byrne and R. J. White (1975) found that in *Rana catesbeiana* lipid reserves become exhausted from the time of emergence through the breeding season. Lipid reserves increase prior to and into dormancy, whereas levels of blood glucose rise during the breeding season and are lowest upon emergence from dormancy. Presumably these levels of body composition are in response to seasonal environmental changes and associated activities on the part of the frogs. Seasonal changes in carbohydrate, protein nucleic acid, body lipid, and fat-body lipid levels during dormancy in *Cyclorana platycephala* indicate that fat-body lipids provide most energy for larger individuals (fat bodies account for up to 20% of the weight in large individuals), whereas smaller frogs have proportionately smaller fat bodies and draw on other energy reserves (van Buerden, 1980). No comparable studies have been conducted on amphibians in aseasonal environments.

ECOLOGICAL SYNTHESIS

The interrelationships of physiological mechanisms with one another and with the environment are complex. With the exception of Tracy's (1975, 1976) model of moisture and temperature relationships for terrestrial amphibians, no broad models of temperature-moisture-respiration-activity have been generated. Tracy's models do take into account that evaporative heat losses tend to offset radiative heat gain in basking anurans, but basking anurans may rest on substrates that are much warmer than the values used in the model. Therefore, it is fairly easy for an anuran to elevate its body temperature by basking. However, Tracy suggests that amphibian thermoregulation is crude or nonexistent because of the constraint of evaporation on the rise in body temperature. In fact, this effect actually facilitates thermoregulation.

Most efforts have been directed toward seeking correlations between two variables, such as temperature versus rate of evaporative water loss, or temperature versus metabolic rate. The time is ripe for a multivariate approach to physiological responses. Unfortunately, complete data sets for diverse taxa are not available. Furthermore, differences in experimental design have resulted in noncomparable measurements.

Until such analyses have been performed, precise predictions about the collective physiological responses of diverse amphibians to different environmental conditions are impossible. Nevertheless, based on the available data and correlations, it is possible to make some generalizations about the ecological physiology of amphibians.

The physiological attributes of animals are among the principal factors that dictate how a species survives under a given set of environmental conditions, and therefore influence the habitats utilized and the activity patterns. In most cases it is not possible to pinpoint one physiological mechanism that is responsible for the ecological limitations of a particular species; instead, a combination of interacting mechanisms results in a suite of attributes that adapt a species for existence under a set of environmental variables.

Moisture is the principal factor affecting the ecological distributions of amphibians. Rates of evaporative water loss and water uptake from the environment must be balanced with respect to activity. An amphibian may be able to sustain considerable water loss during periods of activity if it can replenish water between these periods. If the animal cannot tolerate much water loss, it can be active only in areas where, or at times when, ambient moisture content is high.

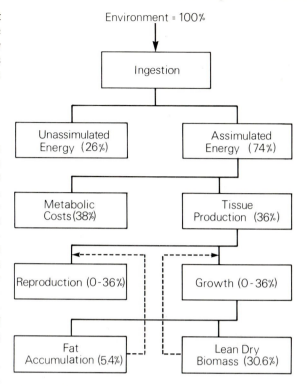

Figure 8-24. Energy budget of a toad, *Bufo terrestris*, weighing 33 g and maintained in the laboratory at 25°C. Broken lines indicate feedback mechanisms. Adapted from G. Smith (1976).

The ability to obtain moisture from soil having relatively low water content and the ability to concentrate solutes (thereby increasing water uptake) and to store water in vesicles enable many kinds of amphibians to live in subhumid areas. Thus, these physiological features are characteristic of desert inhabitants, such as *Scaphiopus*, *Cyclorana*, and *Bufo*. Furthermore, these attributes allow these animals to survive long periods of dormancy, during which their metabolism is lowered and respiration is primarily by ventilation of the lungs. In contrast, plethodontid salamanders have much lower capacities for water uptake from such soils, water storage, and solute concentrations, and the absence of lungs necessitates cutaneous respiration; these characteristics preclude plethodontids from inhabiting xeric areas, except where suitable local microhabitats (e.g., spring seepages) exist. The absorption of water from soil probably is unique to amphibians; no other vertebrates have this ability. The general impression that the permeable skin is a detriment to survival in dry conditions is incorrect, for actually the permeable skin is an important factor in water uptake.

Generally, amphibians that live in subhumid environments are moderately large, have relatively short limbs, and therefore have relatively small surface-area/volume ratios. These animals have relatively low amounts of surface area for evaporative water loss, and ventilation of the lungs is the primary means of gas exchange. Furthermore, it seems that these animals characteristically have a high aerobic scope of metabolism allowing sustained low levels of activity without building up an oxygen debt. In contrast, small amphibians with relatively long limbs (and tails in salamanders) are inhabitants of humid environments, where rates of evaporative water loss are relatively low. Constant moisture on the skin allows for effective cutaneous respiration. In these animals, high anaerobic scopes of metabolism may be the rule.

The combination of available moisture and ambient temperature may greatly restrict the distribution of some species. Thermal tolerances of some montane species are quite narrow, and these in combination with moisture requirements presumably are the factors that restrict the distributions of such species to specific microhabitats within limited geographical areas. Other species have broad tolerances to temperature and moisture and consequently may have broad ecological and geographical distributions. Perhaps the best example of a broadly tolerant species of amphibian is *Bufo marinus,* which lives in rainforests and semideserts from sea level to elevations of more than 2000 m. In at least some species that have broad ecological tolerances, there are interpopulational differences in physiological tolerances, for example, in critical thermal maxima for example, in *B. marinus* (G. Zug and P. Zug, 1979), rate of evaporative water loss in *B. arenarum* (Cei, 1959), and rehydration rate in *Eleutherodactylus coqui* (van Berkum et al., 1982).

The local distributions of amphibians may be determined by their tolerances of moisture or temperature. For example, the local distributions of two salamanders in the Appalachian Mountains seem to be the result of different moisture requirements (R. Jaeger, 1971). *Plethodon cinereus* requires the moisture in the deep soils, whereas *P. richmondi* can tolerate the drier slopes. Water absorption rates in Puerto Rican frogs *Eleutherodactylus antillensis* and *E. coqui* seem to limit the distribution of the smaller *E. antillensis* as compared with the populations of *E. coqui* that have larger body sizes (van Berkum et al., 1982). Studies on four other Puerto Rican *Eleutherodactylus* (Pough et al., 1977) showed interspecific differences in microhabitats and activity patterns with respect to rates of evaporative water loss, resistance to desiccation, temperature selection, and critical thermal maxima.

Combinations of some physiological and behavioral mechanisms apparently have coevolved so as to permit the existence of some species in otherwise uninhabitable environments. The most striking of these combinations is that of lipid waterproofing, skin wiping, high osmoconcentration, uricotelism, and quiescence exhibited by some species of *Phyllomedusa* in arid regions in South America (Shoemaker and McClanahan, 1975; Blaylock et al., 1976). Prolonged survival in dormancy apparently is enhanced by formation of cocoons in burrowed anurans

(e.g., *Lepidobatrachus* and *Pyxicephalus*) with its attendant modifications of water loss, osmoconcentration, and metabolism (Loveridge and Withers, 1981; McClanahan et al., 1983). Few amphibians can tolerate saline conditions, but osmoregulatory adaptations allow *Rana cancrivora* to inhabit brackish water, where it has no other anuran competitors (Gordon and Tucker, 1968). The accumulation of glycerol in body tissues provides an antifreeze for some anurans, thereby allowing them to survive subfreezing temperatures during hibernation (W. Schmid, 1982).

The diel and seasonal activities of amphibians are regulated by environmental conditions, principally moisture and temperature. The interaction of these variables, especially as it affects condensation of moisture, is extremely important in the timing of diel activity by amphibians. For example, on rainless nights many nocturnal tree frogs do not emerge from their diurnal retreats until the dew point has been reached and moisture condenses on the leaves. Other arboreal frogs may emerge when the leaves are dry, but the frogs assume moisture-conserving postures and do not call (Pough et al., 1983).

The seasonal differences in temperature at high latitudes and in soil moisture at all latitudes have obvious limiting effects on amphibian activity, especially reproduction. Within this broad framework of seasonality, subtle differences in physiological tolerances can influence the times of activity in different species. Thermal tolerances of two species of salamanders and three of anurans in the northeastern United States are related to their times of emergence and utilization of a breeding pond (Gatz, 1971). Of course, successful reproduction also depends on the physiological tolerances of the embryos (see Chapter 7).

The inverse correlation of aerobic and anaerobic metabolic scopes found in those few amphibians that have been examined may have broad ecological implications, not only in escape behavior, as emphasized by A. Bennett (1978), but also in habitat selection and foraging behavior. If burst activity is possible only in those species having high anaerobic scopes, it is most likely that tree frogs that leap from branch to branch will have high anaerobic scopes, as will amphibians that pursue their prey. On the other hand, those that have slow, deliberate movements are expected to be primarily aerobic.

Behavioral thermoregulation probably is far more common among amphibians than has been realized. The subtle changes in temperature preferences among cryptic species and the more obvious differences among basking species may be correlated with digestive efficiency. Because there is a direct correlation between temperature and metabolic rates, digestion will be facilitated at higher temperatures. In the presence of an abundance of food, rapid digestion permits increased rates of ingestion, and the resulting intake and assimilation of energy will result in increased rates of growth and/or accumulation of fats.

Although there are definite physiological limitations characteristic of amphibians, especially permeability of the skin, absence of an internal thermoregulatory mechanism, and incomplete segregation of oxygenated and deoxygenated blood, many physiological adaptations have evolved so that amphibians as a group are capable of various kinds of activities in diverse environments. Thus, we should not "pity the poor frog" as jested by Brattstrom (1979); instead, we should marvel at the diverse physiological adaptations of amphibians.

Food and Feeding

The different manners of capturing prey would account for such differences as exist between the diet of adult frogs and urodeles.

G. K. Noble (1931b)

The feeding strategies of amphibians include their choice of prey and the ways in which they locate, capture, and ingest prey. Amphibians generally are considered to be feeding opportunists with their diets reflecting the availability of food of appropriate size. This may be true for some, but results of field and laboratory studies show that some species are selective in their feeding. Many constraints influence the diets and feeding habits of amphibians, including extrinsic factors such as seasonal abundance of food and presence or absence of competitors, and intrinsic factors such as ecological tolerances and morphological constraints that relate to ontogenetic stage, size, and specializations. Ultimately, feeding must be efficient—i.e., more energy must be gained from the food than is expended in obtaining it, thereby maximizing energy gain. These factors, as they pertain to adult amphibians, are discussed in this chapter. The food and feeding of larval amphibians, especially tadpoles, are treated in Chapter 6, and the intraoviducal feeding by viviparous species is discussed in Chapter 5.

PREY SELECTION

Most accounts of amphibian feeding are anecdotal and involve only a few taxa. Consequently, little is known about prey selection and foraging strategies; the latter are discussed in the last section of this chapter: Evolution of

Prey-Capturing Mechanisms and Strategies. The limited information on amphibian diets indicates that all adult amphibians are carnivores; most feed principally on insects, although many species eat a wide variety of invertebrates.

Herbivory is characteristic of anuran larvae, but it may occur in other amphibians; for example, the aquatic salamanders of the genus *Siren* have been reported to have large quantities of vegetable matter in their digestive tracts and to eat *Elodea,* as well as aquatic invertebrates (Ultsch, 1973). *Bufo marinus* may eat vegetable scraps and canned dog food (Alexander, 1964; Tyler, 1976).

Some anurans are especially voracious eaters. Large anurans, such as *Ceratophrys ornata, Discodeles guppyi, Pyxicephalus adspersus,* and *Rana catesbeiana,* commonly feed on large prey items, such as small mammals, birds, turtles, snakes, and other anurans (Fig. 9-1). *Discodeles,* found in the Solomon Islands, eats land crabs (Boulenger, 1884). W. Branch (1976) reported a *Pyxicephalus adspersus* that had eaten 17 newly born cobras (*Hemachatus haemachatus*) and another that had attacked a young chicken. Some large salamanders also capture relatively large vertebrates; *Dicamptodon ensatus* eat plethodontid salamanders, frogs, snakes, mice, and shrews (Bury, 1972). These prodigious gastronomic feats are exceptions, as are the feeding on marine crabs by *Rana cancrivora* (Elliott and Karunakaran, 1974), on ma-

229

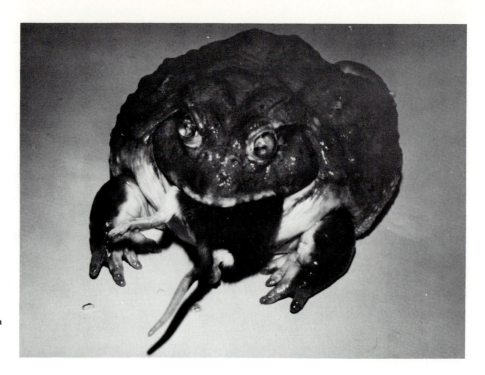

Figure 9-1. A captive South African bullfrog, *Pyxicephalus adspersus,* engulfing a rat. Photo by W. E. Duellman.

rine invertebrates by the leptodactylid *Thoropa miliaria* (Sazima, 1972), and on terrestrial gastropods by hyperoliid frogs of the genus *Tornierella* (Drewes, 1981).

Prey Availability

General availability of prey of the appropriate size and type seems to be a basic constraint on th diets of amphibians. For example, analyses of stomach contents of five species of salamanders in New England (T. M. Burton, 1976), *Acris crepitans* in Indiana (Labanick, 1976), and terrestrial eft stages of *Notophhalmus viridescens* in New York (MacNamara, 1977) revealed that the abundance of food items in the stomachs was correlated with the relative prey abundance in the habitat.

Ontogenetic Changes

As individuals become larger, the kinds of prey that they select may change. Ontogenetic changes in diets of larval salamanders were reported by Brophy (1980); as they grew, larvae of *Ambystoma tigrinum* and *Notophthalmus viridescens* increased their predation on snails and decreased their predation on smaller items (ostracods and cyclopoid copepods). In addition, there was a significant increase in the variety of prey taxa in larger *Ambystoma* larvae. Larval *Triturus vulgaris* feed primarily on small zooplankton (chydorids, daphniids, and cyclopoid copepods); as they grow and develop more teeth, the larvae pursue and capture larger prey (principally chironomid larvae), although larger larvae do not select larger individuals of a given prey species (G. Bell, 1975). During postmetamorphic growth, hylid frogs (*Acris crepitans,* Labanick, 1976; *Pseudacris triseriata,* Christian, 1982) in-

gest increasingly larger prey items as well as a broader spectrum of prey sizes. Likewise, at least some terrestrial plethodotid salamanders show the same trends in increasing the size, in addition to the diversity, of their prey among larger individuals—e.g., *Plethodon wehrlei* (Hall, 1976) and *Batrachoseps attenuatus* (Maiorana, 1978).

An ontogenetic shift in the size of prey selected by larval salamanders may be a function of developmental changes (e.g., increased number of teeth or increased mobility) as well as increased gape (e.g., in postmetamorphic anurans). Gape is known to be a factor in the size of prey eaten by various species of anurans (Toft, 1980a) and at least one salamander (R. L. White, 1977).

Habitat

Individuals of a particular species may exhibit significant differences in the kinds and amounts of prey eaten in different habitats; this mainly reflects differences in prey availability among habitats. Thus, Inger and Marx (1961) found noticeable differences in stomach contents of several species of anurans at different elevations in the Upemba National Park in Zaire, and Barbault (1974) noted differences in diets of anurans in savanna and forest habitats in the Ivory Coast.

Differences on a more local scale also are evident. For example, in freshwater habitats, the diet of *Rana cancrivora* consists mainly of insects, but in nearby brackish water the frogs eat mostly crustaceans (Elliott and Karunakaran, 1974). Newts (*Taricha granulosa*) in a permanent pond eat a greater diversity of prey than do individuals in a temporary pond (R. L. White, 1977). Different diets of individuals of the Argentine leptodactylid *Pleurodema cinerea* are correlated with terrestrial and aquatic feeding (Hulse, 1979).

Seasonality

Seasonal differences in diets have been reported for various species of amphibians (e.g., *Rana pretiosa,* F. Turner, 1959; *Notophthalmus viridescens,* T. M. Burton, 1977; and *Plethodon glutinosus* and *P. jordani,* Powers and Tietjen, 1974). Surveys of diets of many anurans in a seasonal tropical environment in West Africa revealed noticeable differences throughout the year (Inger and Marx, 1961). Among 13 species of anurans dwelling on the forest floor in Amazonian Peru, the diversity of food eaten by some species was greatest in the dry season (Toft, 1980a). Moreover, a comparison of diets among forest-floor anurans at a drier site and a wetter site in Panama revealed greater differences between sites than between seasons at any one site (Toft, 1980b).

Seasonal differences in diets reflect availability of prey and, in some cases, seasonal differences in selectivity by amphibians (e.g., certain forest-floor anurans; Toft, 1980a). This selectivity may be "forced" on the amphibians by factors other than food, especially by the necessity of foraging under physiologically tolerable moisture conditions. For example, the plethodontid salamander *Desmognathus fuscus* demonstrates a selection for larger prey with increased precipitation (Sites, 1978). *Plethodon cinereus* forages in moist leaf litter; when the leaf litter is dry, the salamanders are confined to feeding on limited amounts and kinds of prey occurring under rocks or logs (R. Jaeger, 1980). On foggy or rainy nights, *P. cinereus* climbs on vegetation and feeds on kinds of insects not present on the ground, actually ingesting more food than conspecifics on the forest floor (R. Jaeger, 1978).

The seasonal activity of certain species is determined, in part, by the activity of their prey. This is especially evident among prey specialists. The activity of the termite-eating anuran *Breviceps verrucosus* in South Africa is timed to the swarming of termites (Poynton and Pritchard, 1976). The period of feeding activity by the spadefoot, *Scaphiopus couchii,* in southwestern North America also is correlated with the swarming of termites (Dimmitt and Ruibal, 1980).

Diel activity of prey may account for the predator's feeding activity and, therefore, kinds of prey taken. For example, peak surface activity of three species of streamside plethodontid salamanders is highly correlated with the activity of potential prey at dusk or shortly after dark (Holomuzki, 1980). Freed's (1980) analysis of prey behavior and feeding selectivity by the tree frog *Hyla cinerea* suggested that the frogs selected prey in relation to the proportion of time that the prey species was active and the kind of activity displayed by the prey. Thus, increased frequency of prey activity resulted in a perceived increase in the density of that prey species for the predator, thereby resulting in greater predation. When prey selection was limited to prey types having similar activity patterns, size of the prey species became an important factor in prey selection, with the larger prey being selected. Analysis of stomach contents of the Malaysian ranid *Amolops larutensis,* and activity patterns and abundance of prey species throughout the year led Berry (1966) to conclude that diet selection by this frog is associated most closely with activity of the prey.

LOCATION OF PREY

Basically two kinds of foraging strategies are utilized by amphibians. Most anurans have adopted a sit-and-wait strategy, whereas active foraging seems to be more common among some salamanders and apparently is characteristic of caecilians. However, the strategy used by an individual may vary with the abundance of prey. The method of monitoring prey abundance may depend on the sensory mechanism employed by the predator. Predators using olfactory or tactile stimuli to detect prey may not be able to perceive either relative or absolute abundances of different kinds of prey without actually capturing them. Conversely, encounter rates may be used more commonly by species that search for prey visually.

Visual Detection

The vast majority of anurans and salamanders use vision in the final encounter with a prey item, although preliminary location of prey also may involve other cues. Several studies embracing field observations and laboratory experiments indicate that vision is of primary importance in locating prey. This has been demonstrated for such diverse salamanders as *Salamandra* (Luthardt and G. Roth, 1979), *Triturus* (Margolis, 1976), *Notophthalmus* (J. Martin et al., 1974), *Ambystoma* (Lindquist and M. Bachmann, 1982), *Hydromantes* (G. Roth, 1976), and *Plethodon* (R. Jaeger et al., 1982), as well as various anuran species of the genera *Bufo* (Brower et al., 1960; Heatwole and Heatwole, 1968; Ewert, 1976; Borchers et al., 1978) and *Rana* (Maturana et al., 1960; Kramek, 1976).

Visual detection is most common in those species that have adopted a sit-and-wait strategy. Once a prey item is sighted, it may be pursued for a short distance before capture. For example, the tree frog *Hyla cinerea* obtains only 12% of its prey without pursuit; 88% of the prey items are captured after visual detection and a short pursuit (Freed, 1980).

Recent experiments on the elicitation of feeding responses in amphibians that use visual cues (Borchers et al., 1978; G. Roth, 1978) indicate a complex interrelationship among stimulus parameters of velocity, size, and orientation with respect to the direction of movement of the prey. For example, in order to elicit maximal prey-catching behavior by *Salamandra salamandra,* it seems that stimuli of a certain orientation must move at a certain velocity and in a certain manner (Luthardt and G. Roth, 1979). Elongation of the prey image along the axis of movement facilitates prey capture by *Bufo marinus;* the toad strikes mainly at the leading object when stimuli travel orthogonally to the toad's optic axis (Ingle and McKinley, 1978).

Visual cues also can be important in identifying kinds of prey, such as those that may be optimal in energy content or that may be distasteful. Experiments with *Bufo terrestris* (Brower et al., 1960) revealed that the toads learned to reject bumblebees (*Bombus americanorum*) and their robberfly mimics (*Mallophora bomboides*) by sight alone.

Olfactory Detection

Chemosensory cues for the location of prey have been inferred in various aquatic salamanders— *Notophthalmus viridescens* (J. Wood and Goodwin, 1954), *Gyrinophilus porphyriticus* (Culver, 1973), and *Haideotriton wallacei* (Peck, 1973). Heusser (1958) showed that *Bufo calamita* could find prey solely on the basis of olfactory cues. Experiments with *Bufo boreas* (Dole et al., 1981), *B. marinus* (J. Rossi, 1983), *Rana pipiens* (Shinn and Dole, 1978), *Ambystoma tigrinum* (Lindquist and M. Bachmann, 1982), *Plethodon cinereus* (David and R. Jaeger, 1981), and two species of *Triturus* (Margolis, 1976) have demonstrated that these species are capable of locating prey by olfactory cues alone.

The role of olfaction in prey detection probably is much more common among amphibians than indicated by available observations and experiments. The role of olfaction in prey location, particularly in trailing prey, is strongly inferred by specialized chemoreceptors in some amphibians—protrusible tentacles, in which the lumen opens to Jacobson's organ, in caecilians (Badenhorst, 1978, and references cited therein) and nasolabial grooves in plethodontid salamanders (C. Brown, 1968). The location of termitaria by fossorial anurans such as *Rhinophrynus dorsalis* (Trueb and Gans, 1983) and *Myobatrachus gouldii* (Calaby, 1956) may involve olfactory detection.

Experiments on *Ambystoma tigrinum* (Lindquist and M.. Bachmann, 1982) and on *Triturus* (Margolis, 1976) show that the efficiency of detecting, locating, and capturing prey is greatest when both visual and olfactory cues are used. However, the type of prey may dictate which cues are more effective. The location of pill clams (*Musculium rosaceum*) by the newt *Notophthalmus viridescens* apparently is accomplished by olfaction alone (J. Wood and Goodwin, 1954). Although visual cues predominate in the detection of moving insects by many terrestrial salamanders, immobile prey such as insect pupae are located by olfaction in *Plethodon cinereus* (David and R. Jaeger, 1981). Olfaction is strongly implicated in the ability of *Hydromantes* to project its tongue at prey in total darkness (G. Roth, 1983).

Auditory Detection

Few observations are available on auditory stimuli in location of prey by amphibians. Martof (1962) found that

Bufo woodhousii were alerted to the presence of insects by the sounds they produced. R. Jaeger (1976) observed that *B. marinus* were attracted to calling frogs, *Physalaemus pustulosus,* which they consumed. Large carnivorous anurans that prey on smaller anurans also may utilize auditory cues to locate prey.

CAPTURE OF PREY

In addition to differences in kinds of prey and foraging strategies, amphibians exhibit striking differences in feeding mechanisms. All terrestrial amphibians except caecilians use the tongue in capturing prey; the tongueless pipid frogs and aquatic salamanders have entirely different mechanisms. Even among terrestrial anurans and salamanders there are notably different methods of prey capture. These differences are reflected in the diversity of the the structure of the tongue and its supportive hyobranchial apparatus and associated musculature.

Many caecilians and some large, carnivorous anurans have long, fanglike teeth that may be curved posteriorly; these teeth serve to hold struggling prey. In larval and most neotenic salamanders, the teeth are unicuspid and lack the weak planes of the typically bicuspid pedicellate teeth of adult salamanders and anurans. Teeth are absent from the lower jaws of most anurans, and some anurans (e.g., all bufonids) also lack teeth on the upper jaw. Many frogs have a few vomerine teeth in the palate, whereas salamanders characteristically have patches of vomerine teeth that may extend posteriorly as a parasphenoid series.

The tongues of amphibians possess glands that produce a sticky secretion that serves to adhere the prey to the surface of the tongue. Presumably in all amphibians except caecilians the tongue is used in prey capture. In all groups it is used to hold the prey against the roof of the mouth and to manipulate food in the buccal cavity; this is facilitated by secretions of the intermaxillary glands. In anurans and salamanders, food is pushed posteriorly by the contraction of the m. retractor bulbae, which depresses the eye into the buccal cavity. Once food passes the ciliated pharynx, ingestion is completed by peristaltic action of the esophageal walls. Secretions of mucous glands in the buccal cavity facilitate food transport by lubricating the mouth and pharynx.

Caecilians

Terrestrial caecilians feed primarily on elongate prey, such as earthworms, located on the surface of the ground or, probably more commonly, in burrows. Prey capture involves a slow approach to the prey until contact is almost effected, at which time the prey is seized by a powerful bite. Caecilians tend to bite the prey broadside; they move the head past the prey and bite laterally. If a caecilian has not completely emerged from its burrow when the prey is seized, it retreats into the burrow, spinning in a corkscrew fashion around its body axis. This action creates friction between the prey and the sides of the bur-

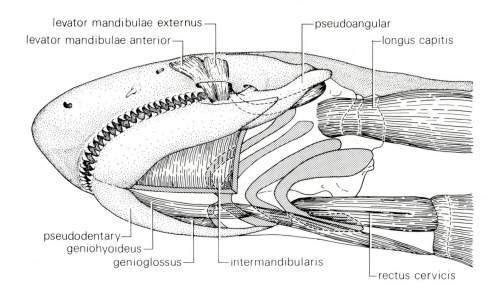

levator mandibulae externus

levator mandibulae anterior

pseudoangular

longus capitis

pseudodentary

geniohyoideus

genioglossus

intermandibularis

rectus cervicis

Figure 9-2. Ventrolateral view of cranial, hyoid, and anterior trunk musculature of a caecilian, *Dermophis mexicanus*. Redrawn from Bemis et al. (1983).

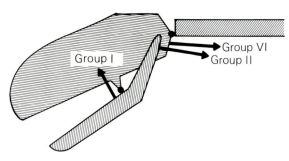

Group I

Group VI
Group II

Figure 9-3. Diagram of the jaw-closing mechanism of a caecilian. Three distinct sets of muscles affect this unique mechanism. Dots are fulcra; arrows are direction of muscular contraction.

row, constricting and shearing the prey to approximately the width of the gape of the caecilian.

The tongue is not protrusible, but interspecific variation exists in the amount of free margin of the tongue and the extent of the glandular field on its dorsal surface. The m. genioglossus forms the body of the tongue; it originates at the mandibular symphysis and from the connective tissue overlying the m. geniohyoideus, and inserts on the surface epithelium of the tongue. The muscle fibers in the body of the tongue are dispersed vertically among extensive blood sinuses and the bases of lingual glands. Contraction of these fibers (1) depresses the tongue pad, thereby increasing pressure in the blood sinuses, (2) facilitates extrusion of lingual gland secretions by compressing the bases of these glands, and (3) aids in food transport (Bemis et al., 1983).

Adult caecilians are unique among amphibians in lacking a m. hyoglossus and in having a completely roofed skull, a fixed quadrate, and a lower jaw with a long retroarticular process (Fig. 9-2). Associated with this bony structure are muscles that provide a unique jaw-closing mechanism (Bemis et al., 1983; Nussbaum, 1983). This

is a double-lever system with the quadrate functioning as the fulcrum. As in other gnathostomes, contraction of the m. levator mandibulae (m. adductor mandibulae) results in the lower jaw being pulled upward. The novel component in caecilians is that contraction of the m. interhyoideus posterior, which originates on the fascia of the ventral and lateral body wall and inserts on the ventral surface of the retroarticular process, pulls the retroarticular process back and down, thereby causing the anterior jaw ramus to pivot upward around the quadrate. A third muscle that acts synergistically to produce a strong bite is the m. longis capitis, a large ventral trunk muscle that originates on the basapophyses of the anterior vertebrae and inserts on the cranium ventral to the cranioverterbal articulation; this muscle is a powerful flexor of the neck and cranium (Fig. 9-3).

Motion analyses and electromyography of feeding by the caeciliid *Dermophis mexicanus* (Bemis et al., 1983) revealed that during prey capture the lower jaw is pressed against the substrate and the mouth is opened as the cranium is raised as a result of activity of the m. depressor mandibulae and the dorsal trunk musculature. Jaw closing is rapid and involves simultaneous contractions of the m. levator mandibulae and m. interhyoideus posterior and presumably the m. longis capitis. A single bite requires about 0.5 second. Holding onto struggling slippery prey is facilitated by the presence of two rows of long, recurved teeth in the upper jaw.

Salamanders

Although the basic structures are the same in the feeding mechanics of all salamanders, functional and developmental constraints have played an important role in the modification of the hyobranchial apparatus for different kinds of feeding mechanisms. These were summarized by D. Wake (1982) and are grouped into three categories.

Aquatic Salamanders. In larval salamanders, neotenic adults such as proteiids, and terrestrial salamanders (when in water during breeding), the hyobranchial apparatus functions to (1) support and move the gill filaments for respiration (not so in terrestrial adults in the water temporarily), and (2) expand and contract the buccal cavity during feeding. These movements are accomplished by the hyoid musculature in association with the depressor mandibulae. During feeding, most salamanders lunge toward the prey; the buccal cavity is expanded and, almost simultaneously, the rather weak jaws are opened. However, in *Amphiuma tridactylum,* there are two different types of suction feeding (Erdman and Cundall, 1984) depending on the size and activity of the prey. If the prey is small or relatively immobile, the salamander does not thrust its head forward; once the mouth is opened, buccal expansion induces an inward flow of water which sucks the prey into the mouth. The lunge or rapid strike mechanism is used to capture actively moving prey. In this strategy, mouth-opening and buccal expansion are synchronous, and buccal expansion is greater than in stationary feeding. Water and prey are sucked into the mouth by the action of the buccal pump. The rudimentary tongue manipulates the prey against the teeth on the roof of the mouth. The jaws have limited use; their small teeth are used to secure large prey during manipulation (Matthes, 1934).

Generalized Terrestrial Salamanders. In metamorphosed, terrestrial salamanders having lungs (Hynobiidae, Dicamptodontidae, Ambystomatidae, and generalized salamandrids) the tongue is attached anteriorly, is protrusible, and plays an important role in prey capture. The hyobranchial apparatus has a dual role as a buccal pump mechanism in respiration and as the main mechanism of tongue protrusion. Cinematographic investigations coupled with morphological studies (Severtzov, 1971, 1972; Larsen and Guthrie, 1975) provided an interpretation of the feeding mechanisms of these salamanders, but electromyographic evidence is absent.

In their analysis of the feeding mechanisms of adult *Ambystoma tigrinum* in the laboratory, Larsen and Guthrie (1975) noted that after an initial lunge the lower jaw is immobilized as it is pressed against the substrate by the contraction of the m. geniohyoideus and m. rectus cervicis superficialis. The cranium is elevated by the contraction of the m. cucullaris major and the m. depressor mandibulae. The gape is increased further as the salamander rocks forward, keeping its lower jaw stationary. The tongue is elevated and protruded up to 8% of the body length beyond the margin of the lower jaw. These complementary actions seem to be accomplished by (1) initial propulsion of the tongue by the medial divisions of the m. genioglossus pulling the copula of the hyoid anteriorly, (2) forward projection of the hyobranchial apparatus by the contraction of the m. subarcualis rectus I acting on the tips of the ceratobranchials (epibranchials of Larsen and Guthrie, 1975), (3) concomitant contraction of the m. geniohyoideus drawing the m. rectus cervicis superficialis and second basibranchial (Copula II) anteriorly, (4) buckling of the anterior radial cartilages providing the form of the outgoing tongue, (5) subsequent shaping of the front and lateral rims of the tongue by the otoglossal cartilage and second radial cartilages, respectively, and (6) turgidity of margins of the tongue increased by fluids forced from the sublingual sinuses posterolaterally into sinus pockets.

When the prey is struck by the posterior half of the tongue, the lingual divisions of the m. genioglossus contract, resulting in the expulsion of a sticky secretion that adheres the prey to the tongue; the m. rectus cervicis profundus then contracts causing the partial collapse of the anterior rim of the tongue, entrapping the prey in a sticky trough (Fig. 9-4). Tongue retraction is accomplished primarily by the m. rectus cervicis profundus and lateral divisions of the m. rectus cervicis superficialis. Small prey is brought within the range of the vomerine teeth, but larger prey commonly escape from the sticky trough during retraction and are held only by the marginal teeth. Once the tongue has retracted completely, the mouth is closed by depressing the cranium sharply through the contraction of the m. levator mandibulae. Immobilization of the lower jaw and opening of the mouth requires 0.05–0.09 second, during which time the tongue protrudes; retraction of the tongue and prey requires 0.03 second and closure requires 0.02–0.03 second. Thus, the entire sequence of prey capture lasts 0.10–0.15 second; subsequent swallowing requires about 0.07 second.

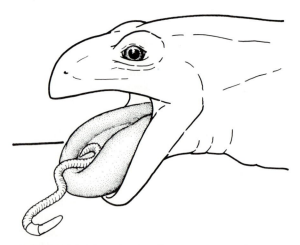

Figure 9-4. Terrestrial prey capture by the salamander *Ambystoma tigrinum.* Note the slight protrusion of the tongue with a noticeable trough and the adpression of the mandibular symphysis to the substrate. Drawn from a photograph in Larsen and Guthrie (1975).

Lungless Salamanders. Lungs are absent in salamanders of the family Plethodontidae and two genera of salamandrids, *Chioglossa* and *Salamandrina*. In these salamanders, the hyobranchial apparatus no longer functions as a buccal pump to force air into the lungs, and the hyobranchium is modified to project the tongue from the mouth. Not only is the cranium elevated during feeding, but the lower jaw is dropped and is not adpressed against the substrate. Morphological evidence indicates that tongue projection evolved independently in salamandrids and plethodontids, and within the latter group, highly projectile tongues evolved independently in the hemidactylines and the bolitoglossines (D. Wake, 1982). The morphology of the feeding mechanisms and their functions have been described for salamandrids by Özeti and D. Wake (1969) and for plethodontids by Lombard and D. Wake (1976, 1977). Electromyography of the tongue protrusion in one plethodontid, *Bolitoglossa occidentalis,* was accomplished by Thexton et al. (1977).

In those plethodontids with highly projectile tongues, the "projectile" consists of the tongue pad trailed by an elongate bundle of folded cartilages, retractor muscles, nerves, and vessels enclosed in a mucosal sheath (Fig. 9-5). In many plethodontids, the tongue pad either has lost the anterior attachment or has a rather elastic connection to the lower jaw. The hyobranchial apparatus is composed of elongated mobile subunits. A pair of ceratohyals that are attached posteriorly by hyoquadrate ligaments to the suspensoria lie on the floor of the mouth; they are not in contact with one another, nor do they articulate with any other, elements of the hyobranchium. The posterior part of each ceratohyal is cylindrical and hooked, and the anterior part is flattened and expanded. The cartilages that move out of the mouth with the tongue are articulated to form a single complex unit. The principal element of this unit is the unpaired, median basibranchial or copula. The anterior end of the basibranchial has a projection that is either continuous with the basibranchial proper or united with it by connective tissue. If detached, the element is called the lingual cartilage. A pair of radial cartilages also is attached anteriorly to the basibranchial, and two pairs of hypobranchials articulate with the posterior part of the basibranchial. The first pair of hypobranchials are the longest elements; they articulate with the basibranchial just posterior to its midpoint. The second pair of hypobranchials articulate with the basibranchial at its posterior end. The first and second hypobranchials on each side approximate each other posteriorly, and both articulate with the ceratobranchial, a tapered element of varying length. The median second basibranchial (Copula II) lies at the juncture of the m. rectus cervicis superficialis and m. geniohyoideus; it has no connections with other elements and is lost in bolitoglossine plethodontids.

The tongue pad is large, and its base is supported by the anterior end of the basibranchial. The radial and lingual cartilages extend into the pad. The principal muscles associated with the hyobranchium are the m. rectus cervicis profundus and the m. subarcualis rectus I. The for-

Figure 9-5. Highly projectile tongue of the plethodontid salamander *Hydromantes italicus* in the capture of an insect. Drawn from a photograph in Lombard and D. Wake (1976).

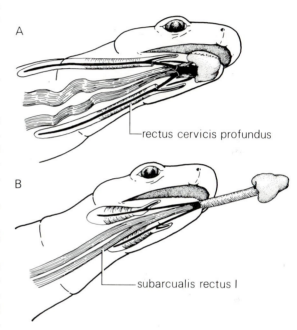

Figure 9-6. Diagrammatic representation in ventrolateral view of the tongue projection mechanism in the plethodontid salamander *Bolitoglossa occidentalis.* **A.** Tongue retracted. **B.** Tongue projected. Modified from Thexton et al. (1977).

mer is an anterior continuation of a muscle that arises on the ischium and inserts principally into the muscular body of the tongue. The m. subarcualis rectus I originates on the ventral surface of the ceratohyal and wraps around the epibranchial (sensu D. Wake) in a complex spiral, forming a muscular bulb.

Analysis of muscle action in *Bolitoglossa occidentalis* (Thexton et al., 1977) showed that the tongue and hyoid apparatus are projected by contraction of the m. subarcualis rectus I. Upon contraction of these protractors, the epibranchials are forced out of the cavity within the subarcualis muscles (Fig. 9-6). Simultaneously the entire muscle shortens, and the posterior end moves toward the gular region. The forward-moving ceratobranchials conduct force via the first and second ceratobranchials to the median basibranchial and thence to the tongue

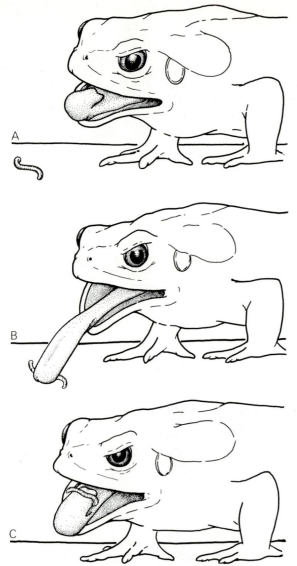

small prey and is accomplished rapidly (<50 milliseconds). Salamanders with highly projectile tongues can capture prey at distances equal to 44–80% of their body length.

Anurans

The feeding mechanism of most advanced anurans involves a lingual flip during which the posterodorsal surface of the retracted tongue becomes the anteroventral surface of the fully extended tongue (Regal and Gans, 1976). In such anurans the hyobranchium provides the mechanical base for the forceful flipping of the tongue; as such, it has a limited amount of anteroposterior movement and is not projected as in salamanders. The hyobranchium also functions as part of the buccal pump mechanism, as it does in generalized terrestrial salamanders.

The adductor musculature is similar to that of salamanders, except that the m. adductor mandibulae posterior is a single slip in anurans instead of two as in salamanders (Salomatina, 1982). A unique feature among most anurans is the ability to depress the mandibular symphysis during the lingual flip. This is possible because of the flexibility afforded to the jaw by the presence of mentomeckelian cartilages and bones at the mandibular symphysis (Fig. 9-7). Contraction of the m. submentalis, a median muscle extending transversely just posterior to the symphysis, rotates the anterior parts of the dentaries downward and brings them closer together, thereby depressing the anterior margin of the lower jaw (Gans and Gorniak, 1982a).

Cinematographic and electromyographic studies on the toad *Bufo marinus* (Gans and Gorniak, 1982b) show the sequential steps in what is assumed to be the generalized feeding mechanism of most anurans. During the tongue-flipping movement, the tongue is supported by the m. genioglossus medialis, which stiffens the tongue when contracted. Simultaneous contraction of the m. genioglossus basalis provides a wedge under the anterior tip of the rodlike m. genioglossus medialis. In addition to depressing the mandibular symphysis, the m. submentalis acts on the wedge of the m. genioglossus basalis to raise and rotate the rod of the m. genioglossus medialis over the symphysis. The tip of this lingual rod carries along the pad and soft tissues of the tongue. Contraction of the long, parallel fibers of the m. hyoglossus retracts the medial sulcus of the tongue pad and holds the prey by a cuplike effect, which is enhanced by the sticky secretion of the glands in the lingual pad. The extensibility of the buccal membranes allows the pad to be retracted first; the pad reaches the posterior part of the buccal cavity before the still-rigid, backward-rotating m. genioglossus medialis reaches the level of the symphysis. During this process, protraction of the hyoid facilitates the extension of the m. hyoglossus; the m. sternohyoideus retracts and stabilizes the hyoid when the tongue starts to retract; it does not function in tongue protrusion.

Figure 9-7. Lingual flipping feeding mechanism in the toad *Bufo marinus*. **A.** Initiation of the lingual flip. **B.** Fully extended tongue contacts prey. **C.** Partially retracted tongue with prey. Note depressed anterior part of jaw. Adapted from Gans and Gorniak, 1982a, *Science* 216:1335. Copyright 1982 by the AAAS.

pad. The retractors (m. rectus cervicis profundus and m. rectus abdominis profundus) are lax and lie in loops when the tongue is in the mouth. When the tongue is projected, the retractor muscles become taut; as their tension becomes greater than that of the protractors, the tongue is retracted into the mouth.

When the sticky tongue pad is projected and contacts a prey item, adhesion permits retraction of the prey into the mouth. As the mouth closes, the tongue presses the prey against the teeth in the roof of the mouth and permits it to be manipulated and swallowed. This feeding mechanism is most effective for the capture of relatively

There is considerable diversity in tongue structure among anurans (Magimel-Pelonnier, 1924; Horton, 1982b), principally involving modifications of the m. genioglossus. In the archaic families, Leiopelmatidae and Discoglossidae, there is little free margin to the tongue. In *Bombina* the tongue can be protruded slightly, as in *Ambystoma*, but presumably it cannot be flipped as in most other anurans (Regal and Gans, 1976). The m. genioglossus is rather poorly developed in some myobatrachids, and in the aquatic *Rheobatrachus* the tongue is firmly attached to the floor of the mouth (Horton, 1982b). Some of the carnivorous frogs (e.g., *Ceratophrys* and *Hemiphractus*) that feed on large prey have exceedingly strong mandibular symphyses with dorsally directed odontoids that hold prey. Most likely, these anurans do not depress their mandibular symphyses during feeding. Some megophrine pelobatids, myobatrachids, and microhylids have variously modified tongues, but no functional studies have been performed. However, feeding mechanisms have been studied in two groups of anurans that differ significantly from the tongue-flipping mechanism.

Pipids. The completely aquatic pipids are unique among anurans in lacking tongues. The hyobranchial apparatus and associated musculature are quite different from that in anurans which have tongues (Chaine, 1901; Trewavas, 1933). The aquatic feeding mode of pipids (*Hymenochirus, Pipa,* and *Xenopus*) is accomplished by transportation of the food into the mouth with water currents produced by hyobranchial pumping movements (Sokol, 1969); essentially these are the same movements characteristic of anuran larvae. Compression of the buccopharyngeal cavity results from the protraction of the hyobranchial apparatus by the m. geniohyoideus and by the flattening of the buccal floor by the m. interhyoideus and m. intermandibularis posterior.

Essentially, these aquatic frogs suck in food and water; the water is expelled before the mouth is closed completely. This is an effective mechanism for feeding on zooplankton. *Pipa* and *Xenopus* sometimes take larger prey, using their long fingers to push the food into the mouth.

Fossorial Anurans. Many kinds of fossorial anurans are known, or presumed, to feed underground; most of these frogs feed on ants, termites, and worms. Obviously, tongue-flipping is not a useful mechanism underground unless the frog is in an open burrow. *Rhinophrynus dorsalis*, a fossorial anuran that feeds on ants and termites, not only differs structurally from other frogs but has a unique method of tongue protrusion (Trueb and Gans, 1983). The contraction of one intrinsic tongue muscle, m. hyoglossus, results in reshaping the tongue from a flat, triangular structure to a rodlike tube by stiffening the tongue and exerting hydrostatic pressure on the fluids in the lingual sinus. Actual protrusion of the tongue is accomplished by a forward shift of the hyoid plate and cornua, from which the m. hyoglossus originates. This forward movement is accomplished by contraction of the m. geniohyoideus and apparently is facilitated by contraction of the m. mandibulomentalis, which elevates the buccal floor. Retraction of the tongue is accomplished by contraction of the m. sternohyoideus, which retracts the hyoid, and the subsequent relaxation of the m. hyoglossus.

Presumably *Rhinophrynus* positions itself with its highly glandular, elongate snout just penetrating the wall of a termitarium or termite tunnel (Fig. 9-8). As termites are

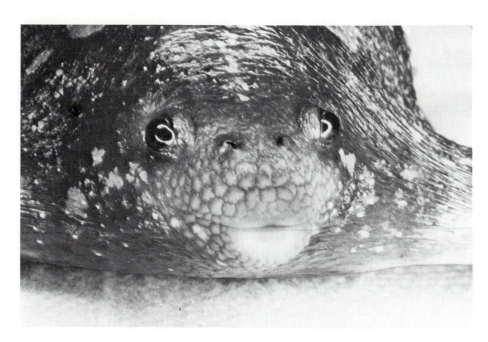

Figure 9-8. Burrowing toad, *Rhinophrynus dorsalis,* showing the calloused tip of the snout and the opening of the buccal groove through which the tongue protrudes. Photo by L. Trueb.

detected, the tongue is protruded through a groovelike vault in the buccal ceiling. Prey are enfolded by the cup-shaped, villous lingual tip and withdrawn into the mouth.

EVOLUTION OF PREY-CAPTURING MECHANISMS AND STRATEGIES

The feeding mechanisms of living amphibians have evolved in response to natural selection and phylogenetic constraints, and are limited somewhat by the involvement of the hyobranchial apparatus in both feeding and ventilation. Moreover, striking differences exist in the metabolism and energy budgets among amphibians. The dual function of the hyobranchial apparatus leads to interrelationships that affect the foraging strategies of amphibians, but these aspects of amphibian biology are poorly understood.

Morphological Constraints on Foraging Tactics

Various evolutionary lineages of amphibians have evolved specialized feeding mechanisms that are effective in obtaining prey of certain sizes and/or shapes under given environmental conditions. How do these functional specializations correspond with (1) the kind of prey that are eaten and (2) the tactics used to obtain the prey?

The size of the gape is an important factor; obviously, smaller amphibians are limited to smaller prey than species that are much larger, but within size classes, some species have much smaller gapes than others. This is especially evident in comparing ant-eating specialists, such as many microhylid and dendrobatid frogs, with terrestrial leptodactylids and ranids that feed on other kinds of prey. The former have relatively small gapes and are limited to small prey, of which ants are the most abundant. The larger gapes of other anurans allow ingestion of larger prey; these frogs have a more diversified diet including large as well as small prey.

The generalized feeding mechanisms of some terrestrial salamanders (hynobiids, ambystomatids, most salamandrids, and desmognathine and plethodontine plethodontids) and archaic frogs (leiopelmatids and discoglossids) involve only slight protrusion of the tongue, subsequent manipulation of the prey by the tongue against the vomerine teeth, and use of the jaws. The size of the prey seems to be limited solely by the gape. In caecilians, gape is a major factor when feeding on the surface, but positioning and shearing the prey also are important when feeding underground. Most anurans that capture prey by a lingual flip and salamanders that have a projectile tongue have a further constraint—the load-bearing capacity of the extended tongue. Thus, amphibians that extend the tongue may be limited in the size of the prey that they can hold and retract. Carnivorous frogs that ingest large prey lunge at their prey while extending the tongue and use their jaws to secure the prey; thus, they do not rely solely on the tongue as the prey-capturing mechanism.

The opposite is true in *Rhinophrynus dorsalis,* in which the tongue and its protrusion mechanism are highly specialized for the ingestion of small prey.

With some notable exceptions, amphibians that have generalized feeding mechanisms are active foragers with highly diverse diets, whereas those that have specialized feeding mechanisms tend to use a sit-and-wait strategy. The latter include many kinds of semiaquatic, terrestrial, and arboreal anurans and hemidactyline and bolitoglossine salamanders. Most of these amphibians are cryptic and nocturnal. Because of their ability to extend the tongue for moderate to great distances, these amphibians can afford to sit and wait until suitable prey come within striking distance of the tongue, or sufficiently close that the amphibian needs to move only a short distance before capturing its prey and returning to its feeding site. Selection of a suitable feeding site is a critical aspect of success as a sit-and-wait predator. Observations on *Rana pipiens* by Dole (1965) and on *R. septentrionalis* by Kramek (1976) showed that these frogs would move farther from the feeding site for a large prey item than they would for a small one. Moreover, if feeding success was low, the frogs moved to a different site. Capture success in *R. septentrionalis* was higher (84%) for slow-moving aphids and chrysomelids than for aerial insects (16% for dragonflies and damselflies).

Among the notable exceptions are various groups of anurans that are ant specialists (Toft, 1980a). These include many dendrobatids and bufonids, all of which have noxious or toxic skin secretions (see Chapter 10). These active foragers with their effective antipredator mechanism are "released" from the constraints of the cryptic, innoxious anurans that use the sit-and-wait strategy to obtain food. However, other ant specialists, notably some microhylids, are cryptic and seem to search for ant trails; presumably these trails are located by olfaction. Once an ant trail is found, these anurans tend to sit and wait and pick up ants as they pass by. A similar strategy presumably is used by fossorial ant and termite specialists such as *Rhinophrynus* and *Hemisus*. Most large predatory frogs also have adopted a sit-and-wait strategy. At least in *Ceratophrys* this behavior may be enhanced by pedal luring, the habit of vibrating and undulating the fourth and fifth toes of the elevated hindfoot, thus attracting smaller amphibians toward the *Ceratophrys* (Murphy, 1976).

Physiological Constraints on Foraging Tactics

Two aspects of physiology are important in feeding—energy metabolism and energy budgets. In some amphibians, such as *Bufo,* lactate production is low (see Chapter 8), so these animals are capable of long periods of sustained activity. Other amphibians, such as *Hyla* and *Rana,* produce large amounts of lactic acid and are capable of bursts of activity over short periods of time. As first pointed out by Toft (1980a), these metabolic attributes may be correlated with foraging strategies. Thus, active foragers are species that are capable of sustained, low levels of activity, whereas sit-and-wait strategists are capable of bursts of activity. The few species that have been studied metabolically conform to this dichotomy, but a wide range of taxa need to be examined before any generalizations can be made.

Little is known about energy budgets of amphibians. G. Smith (1976) assumed an assimilation efficiency of 74% for *Bufo terrestris* with approximately half of the energy going into metabolic costs. In the salamander *Plethodon cinereus,* digestive efficiency does not change with size or sex, but caloric intake increases with size (Crump, 1979). Also, digestive assimilation is negatively correlated with temperature in this species and in *P. shenandoah* (Bobka et al., 1981). However, assimilation efficiency also varies with the kind of food. Assimilation efficiency by *Scaphiopus couchii* is 90% when fed on *Tenebrio* larvae but only 69% when fed on *Tenebrio* beetles, which contain proportionately more indigestible chitin (Dimmitt and Ruibal, 1980).

Rates of food consumption are highly variable. The semiaquatic hylid frog *Acris crepitans* is active for about 7 months and feeds by night and day (B. Johnson and Christiansen, 1976). These frogs contain an average of 6.74 prey items in the stomach, and the rate of food passage through the digestive system is about 8 hours. Thus, it was calculated that each frog consumes about 20 prey items per day. Food consumption was greater in larger individuals, females, breeding individuals, and frogs with small fat bodies. It seems that this small frog must feed nearly continuously throughout its activity season in order to maintain a positive energy budget. This is in striking contrast to some desert anurans that are active for only short periods of time during the year. On the basis of diet, stomach capacity, and energy budgets, Dimmitt and Ruibal (1980) concluded that *Scaphiopus couchii* (which may consume termites equal to 55% of its body weight at one feeding) is capable of consuming enough food at a single feeding to provide it with energy reserves for 1 year. Other desert-dwelling anurans are not so efficient; *S. multiplicatus* requires 7 feedings, and various species of *Bufo* require 11–22 feedings in order to accumulate sufficient fat reserves and other necessities (e.g., trace elements and electrolytes) for 1 year. Because of fluctuating availability of prey or environmental limitations (e.g., dry weather), amphibians may not be able to feed effectively throughout their season of activity. Thus, R. Jaeger (1980) found that some individuals of *Plethodon cinereus* were existing on negative energy budgets during hot, dry weather.

Interrelationships of Foraging Strategies and Constraints

An animal must maintain a positive energy budget in order to grow, reproduce, and survive periods of inactivity. Optimal foraging behavior of predators varies when they have a choice of prey differing in quality and/or

varying in abundance, either temporally or spatially (Pyke et al., 1977; Krebs, 1978). Optimal diet includes the kinds of prey which, if eaten whenever encountered, will maximize the intake of caloric value per unit time. Optimal prey choice depends on the predator's ability to distinguish among prey of varying profitability and to choose the more profitable kinds. Ideally, the predator needs information about six more or less constant values in order to evaluate the caloric profitability of a kind of prey (R. Jaeger and Barnard, 1981): (1) gross calories per prey; (2) predator's assimilation efficiency; (3) rate of digestion of prey; (4) calories expended in pursuit of the prey once encountered; (5) probability of capturing the prey once pursued; and (6) calories expended in handling the prey once captured. The most profitable kind of prey gives maximum values for 1, 2, 3, and 5, and minimum values for 4 and 6. When the most profitable kind of prey is abundant and easy to capture, the energy expended per search time is low, so theoretically the predator can maximize net energy gain by specializing on that kind of prey. As the abundance of that prey decreases and energy per search time increases, the predator can maximize net energy gain by expanding its diet to include the next most profitable kind of prey. When all kinds of prey are scarce, the predator must be indiscriminate in its choice of diet in order to maintain a positive energy budget.

The only empirical tests of these ideas using an amphibian are included in R. Jaeger and Barnard's (1981) study on *Plethodon cinereus.* They found that the salamanders had an indiscriminate diet at low prey densities and specialized on larger prey at high densities, but at such times the salamanders did not exclude small prey. Also, salamanders switched from pursuit to sit-and-wait tactics with increasing prey density. R. Jaeger and Barnard (1981) concluded that the salamanders compromise between maximizing net energy while foraging and minimizing the time for passage of prey through the digestive tract; small prey (in this case, flies) take longer to digest than larger flies because of their proportionately larger exoskeletons. Experiments on feeding of *Bufo marinus* by Heatwole and Heatwole (1968) revealed that hungry toads selected larger prey, but as the toads became satiated they selected smaller prey.

Therefore, digestive time, as well as assimilation efficiency, is important in regulating the net energy gain from a given amount of food in a given amount of time. The energy gained from any feeding sequence determines the amount of energy available for a subsequent (although not necessarily sequential) feeding without drawing on fat reserves. In this context, a sit-and-wait strategist capable of ingesting large prey uses very little energy in obtaining food and obtains large quantities of energy from a given prey. Therefore, amphibians such as *Ceratophrys* and *Pyxicephalus* need to eat infrequently. Feder (1983) suggested that low metabolic rates, relatively large energy reserves, and thus profound resistance to starvation enable plethodontid salamanders to survive indefinite periods between feedings. On the contrary, amphibians that actively search for prey and consume small prey items (e.g., *Dendrobates*) must maintain a continuous feeding schedule in order to maximize fitness. Those amphibians that have evolved highly specialized feeding mechanisms specialize on small prey, of which ants are the most abundant; many feeding specialists have diets composed entirely of ants. In at least three species of dendrobatids, predation on ants is correlated with high aerobic activity, low anaerobic capacity, and high resting metabolism, as contrasted with the sit-and-wait strategist, *Eleutherodactylus coqui* (Taigen and Pough, 1983).

The different feeding mechanisms that evolved in diverse lineages of amphibians, whether these be the highly projectile tongues of bolitoglossine plethodontid salamanders or the paedomorphic conditions of pipid frogs, simultaneously increase the effectiveness of capturing particular prey and impose morphological constraints. The more complex a morphological mechanism, the more rigid its associated physiological attributes and behavioral traits. The foraging strategies of species may be affected by proximal temporal variation in both prey abundance and the physical environment. Ultimately, the feeding tactics employed by any organism are constrained by the morphological mechanisms available to the species.

CHAPTER 10

Enemies and Defense

It appears that almost anything will eat an amphibian!

Kenneth R. Porter (1972)

Amphibians, like all other animals, are subject to a great variety of predators, parasites, and diseases. Little information is available on the debilitating effects of pathogens or parasites on individual amphibians or on populations in nature. On the other hand, amphibians are known to be important components of the diets of many kinds of predators. This must have a profound regulatory effect on populations of these amphibian prey species.

This chapter summarizes briefly the existing knowledge of amphibian diseases, parasites, and predators and discusses more thoroughly the defensive mechanisms of amphibians.

DISEASES

Amphibians are subject to many diseases—viral, bacterial, and fungal, including forms of tuberculosis and cancer. Amphibian diseases were reviewed by Reichenbach-Klinke and Elkan (1965), Elkan (1976), L. Marcus (1981), and G. Hoff et al. (1984).

Viral Infections

Since Lucké's (1934) discovery of a renal adenocarcinoma in *Rana pipiens,* numerous workers have investigated the viral nature of amphibian tumors (see Elkan, 1976, for review). Herpes-like and other viruses have been associated with some cases of carcinoma. A lymphosarcoma was described in *Xenopus laevis* and in some salamanders; causative agents have not been identified. Also, causes are unknown for many kinds of benign tumors that arise mainly in soft tissues.

Bacterial Infections

Diverse bacteria infect amphibians. At least among laboratory specimens, the most virulent bacterial infection is caused by *Pseudomonas* (Pseudomonaceae). These bacteria commonly are associated with *Bacillus, Proteus,* haementerococci, and various staphylococci. All of these infect amphibians primarily by way of polluted water and secondarily by way of infected food. Septicemia or "redleg" is caused by *Pseudomonas;* this fatal inflammation is not restricted to the skin but also affects the lungs, spleen, intestine, and kidneys. There is some evidence that *Pseudomonas* and other aerobic bacteria are facultatively psychrophilic and are especially detrimental to hibernating amphibians (A. H. Carr et al., 1976).

Amphibians living in association with human habitations in the tropics may become infected with *Salmonella.* As many as seven species of *Salmonella* were found in the toad *Bufo marinus* in Panama (Kourany et al., 1970).

Mycobacteria cause lesions in amphibians; the lesions are analogous to human tuberculosis. Those mycobacteria that infect amphibians are ubiquitous saprophytes commonly present on the moist skin. Infections seem to occur only in debilitated or injured animals. External lesions may develop at the sites of wounds; in the case of lesions on the extremities, the infection spreads via the lymphatic channels to the visceral organs, especially the kidneys. Infections of mycobacteria resulting from injuries to the mouth may develop into tuberculosis of the bronchi and lungs.

Fungal Infections

Many kinds of fungi apparently enter amphibians' bodies via minor abrasions or through the nostrils. Once established in the body, the fungi spread and eventually transform vital parenchymatous organs into fungal granulomata, resulting in death. The principal fungi infecting adult amphibians are strains of *Basidiobolus, Cladosporium, Hormiscium,* and *Phialophora* (Elkan, 1976).

Various fungi are saprophytic on dead amphibian eggs, but two species are parasitic on nonaquatic eggs of neotropical anurans (Villa, 1979). Tadpoles also are subject to lethal infections of fungi; Bragg (1962) noted the parasitic fungus *Saprolegnia* infecting three species of tadpoles in temporary ponds. The yeast *Candida humicola* seems to be parasitic in young tadpoles of the green frog, *Rana clamitans,* and a mutualistic symbiont of large tadpoles (Steinwascher, 1979).

PARASITES

Many kinds of external and internal parasites are associated with adult and larval amphibians, and some insect larvae parasitize amphibian eggs. No review of amphibian parasites exists, but Elkan (1976) summarized some of the literature concerning endoparasites of adult amphibians. The following account is organized taxonomically by parasites.

Protozoa

According to Elkan (1976), amphibians invariably have some degree of infestation by protozoans, which may cause debilitation or death if they penetrate vital organs or become too abundant. However, protozoans commonly live symbiotically with amphibian hosts. Nevertheless, massive infections by sporozoans can be catastrophic to amphibian populations, as in the case of the microsporidian *Pleistophora,* normally a parasite of insects and fishes, which was responsible for a lethal epidemic among populations of the toad *Bufo bufo* in southern England (Canning et al., 1964). Infestations of the sporozoan *Charchesium* cause clogging of the gills and spiracle in tadpoles, resulting in developmental retardation and death.

Several genera of flagellate protozoans occur in the intestinal tracts of amphibians. Most of these are commensals, and by far the most abundant and widespread are species of the multiflagellate *Opalina.* Metcalf's (1923a) work on the group resulted in his (1923b) suggesting that these protozoans provided evidence for the "southern dispersal" of some groups of anurans, a hypothesis soundly criticized by Noble (1925b). However, in the light of evi-

dence from plate tectonics, Metcalf's ideas now seem far more plausible; a modern review of the distribution of opalinids and their hosts might provide support for Metcalf's early theory.

Entamoeba occur in the digestive tracts of amphibians and occasionally encyst in the liver.

Trypanosoma are common blood parasites of amphibians, and hemogregarine parasites are known to occur in the bloodstream of amphibians. The former may be transmitted by blood-sucking leeches, and the latter are transmitted by blood-sucking insects. Malaria (*Plasmodium*) has not been reported in amphibians, although the vectors, *Anopheles* mosquitoes, have been observed biting anurans.

Helminths

Intestinal worms of the phyla Platyhelminthes, Nemata, Nematomorpha, and Acanthocephala are common parasites of amphibians. Yamaguti (1959–63, 1971) and Tuff and Huffman (1977) provided compilations of hosts and distributions of helminth parasites in amphibians. Prudhoe and Bray (1982) provided a review of platyhelminth parasites of amphibians, and D. Brooks (1984) summarized the biology, hosts, and distributions of platyhelminth parasites of amphibians.

One genus of monogenetic trematode, *Polystoma,* is highly host-specific in anurans worldwide; usually it inhabits the urinary bladder. Many kinds of digenetic trematodes parasitize amphibians. Intermediate larval forms (cercaria or metacercaria) commonly encyst in the skin or internal organs, especially in aquatic amphibians, including larvae. Common intestinal trematodes include *Opisthoglyphe, Glypthelmins,* and *Dolichosaccus* in anurans and *Batrachocoelium* in salamanders. Species of *Brachycoelium* were reported in 25 species of North American salamanders (Dyer and Brandon, 1973). The pulmonary trematode *Haematoloechus* has a worldwide distribution in anurans. Trematodes either share the host's food or live on desquamated epithelium, mucus, blood, or body fluids. Apparently the hosts have neither humoral nor cellular defenses against these parasites. Once the parasite has invaded the body of the host, walling off the parasite seems to be the only protection. Encysted cercaria remain viable and resume their life cycles when the amphibian has been eaten by a predator. The diversity of digenetic trematodes parasitizing amphibians is suggestive of coevolution of hosts and parasites, as suggested for plagiorchoid trematodes and anurans by D. Brooks (1977).

Cestodes are uncommon but persistent gastrointestinal parasites of amphibians. *Nematotaenia* is common among Eurasian anurans, and larvae of several species of *Diphyllobothrium* infect anurans and salamanders in North America, where *Batrachotaenia* and *Proteocephalus* also parasitize salamanders. *Chlamydocephalus* is a common intestinal cestode in *Xenopus laevis.* Tyler (1976) noted that in Australia anurans are second intermediate hosts for spargana larvae of tapeworms of the genus *Spiro-metra.* The life cycle of this cestode involves (1) eggs passed from carnivorous mammals, (2) aquatic development of a coracidium larva that is eaten by an aquatic crustacean, (3) a procercoid stage in the haemocoel of the crustacean, (4) ingestion of the crustacean by a frog, in which the parasite develops into a sparganum stage in muscle or connective tissue, and (5) ingestion of the frog by a mammal, in which the life cycle is completed as a tapeworm.

Numerous nematodes probably are the most common helminth parasites of amphibians. Some, such as the larvae of *Filaria,* are microscopic, but most, such as the lungworm (*Rhabdias),* are macroscopic. Nematodes are found in the gastrointestinal tract, lungs, blood vessels, and lymphatic channels; the worms encyst in the intestinal wall, skeletal muscle, or any parenchymatous organ. Host specificity may be much lower in nematodes than in digenetic trematodes and cestodes. For example, a cosmocercid nematode, *Cosmocerca brasiliensis,* is known to parasitize 15 species of South American anurans (Dyer and Altig, 1976), and another species, *Cosmocercoides dukei,* is known from 14 salamander hosts in North America (Dyer and Brandon, 1973).

Adult acanthocephalans attach themselves to the mucous lining of the stomach or intestine. The most common adult form in amphibians is *Acanthocephalus ranae.* The first intermediate hosts of acanthocephalans are small crustaceans or insects; adult or larval amphibians become infected upon ingesting these intermediate hosts. However, some acanthocephalans have a second intermediate stage. This encysted stage of *Porrochis* is known in some Australian anurans; the adult stage is known only in birds.

Annelids

Blood-sucking leeches (Hirundinoidea) are common external parasites on amphibians that live in or enter water to breed; these leeches also attach themselves to aquatic larvae. Terrestrial leeches parasitize terrestrial anurans in the wet tropics from southeastern Asia to northern Australia. In most cases parasitism is temporary and probably does not interfere drastically with the health or activity of the host. However, in some cases many leeches attached to an individual can be debilitating, as noted by Waite (1925) for the frog *Limnodynastes dumerili* during the breeding season in South Australia, and by Gill (1978) for the newt *Notophthalmus viridescens* in North America.

Some other leeches gain access to the subcutaneous lymph sacs and remain as endoparasites. Leeches of the genus *Batrachobdella* are common ectoparasites of aquatic anurans, but occasionally the leeches do enter the lymph sacs of *Rana catesbeiana* at least. Leeches of the genus *Philaemon (Cedbdella)* are unique in entering the cloaca of terrestrial and arboreal frogs in New Guinea (Mann and Tyler, 1963); once inside the body they reside in lymph sacs or the body cavity, where they feed on blood in the liver and heart.

Arthropods

Several groups of arachnids parasitize terrestrial amphibians. Ereynetid mites of the subfamily Lawrencarinae occur only in the nasal passages of anurans (Fain, 1962). Chigger mites (Trobiculidae) and ticks (Ixodidae), especially *Amblyomma,* are common blood-sucking ectoparasites of terrestrial amphibians, especially those in dry forests. Habitat selection by amphibians may be associated with the degree of infestation by chiggers. Or, differential toxic or mucous secretions of the skin may have an effect on chiggers. For example, among three syntopic species of salamanders, two species (*Plethodon dorsalis* and *P. glutinosus*) are rarely infested by chiggers of the genus *Hannemania,* whereas *P. ouachitae* is infested heavily (Duncan and Highton, 1979). Toads (*Bufo*) commonly have many ticks. As noted for *B. marinus* by G. Zug and P. Zug (1979), *Amblyomma* are attached mostly on the head, particularly on or adjacent to the parotoid glands. When the ticks fall off, they leave small lesions.

Parasitic copepods of the genus *Argulus,* or fish lice, are common ectoparasites on fishes. They have been reported on two North American aquatic amphibians—the salamander *Pseudobranchus striatus* and tadpoles of *Rana heckscheri* (C. Goin and Ogren, 1956).

The peculiar vermiform arthropods of the order Pentastomida (tongue worms) occur in the intestinal tract of amphibians.

The only group of insects that parasitize amphibians is Diptera. Several groups of flies deposit their eggs on the bodies of anurans or on terrestrial eggs, and the larvae parasitize the frogs or the embryos. Tachinid flies lay their eggs on the bodies of anurans. Upon hatching, the larvae of *Batrachomyia,* endemic to Australia, burrow under the skin of the back (Tyler, 1976). Larvae of *Lucilia* move to the anuran's head and enter the body by way of the eyes or nostrils and devour the host. Of 14 cases of *Lucilia* infections in four species of European anurans reported by Meisterhans and Heusser (1970), only one frog survived.

Larvae of some flies of the families Calliphoridae, Chironomidae, Drosophilidae, Ephydridae, Phoridae, and Psychodidae parasitize the eggs of amphibians (Villa, 1980; Villa and Townsend, 1983; Yorke, 1983). In all cases the eggs are nonaquatic, although larvae of the ephydrid *Gastrops* feed on embryos of *Leptodactylus pentadactylus* and *Physalaemus* in foam nests floating on the water. These parasitic flies lay their eggs immediately below the surface of the amphibian egg mass. Timing of hatching of the fly larvae must coincide with early stages of embryonic development of the host, for advanced anuran embryos are capable of muscular movements thwarting attacks by the fly larvae. The larvae pupate in the egg mass. These flies are known to parasitize the egg clutches of various tropical anurans, including the arboreal clutches of *Agalychnis, Centrolenella, Polypedates,* and two species of *Hyla* and the terrestrial clutches of *Dendrobates* and *Eleutherodactylus*. Also, phorid larvae are known to parasitize the terrestrial eggs of one plethodontid salamander, *Aneides aeneus*. The presence of psychodid, chironomid, and phorid larvae in developing amphibian egg clutches probably is peripheral to their usual life cycle, but the life cycles of some ephydrid and drosophilid flies may be dependent upon amphibian egg clutches (Villa, 1980). Infestations of larvae in egg clutches may be very high at some places; 80% of the egg masses of *Physalaemus cuvieri* and up to 100% of those of *Centrolenella fleischmanni* were infested.

PREDATORS

Because amphibians are numerous, small to moderate in size, and have soft skin, they are common prey for a great variety of predators of all classes of vertebrates, as well as some arthropods; small anurans even fall prey to a carnivorous plant, the Venus flytrap (*Dionaea muscipula*). Because adults of many species aggregate during the breeding season and tadpoles and metamorphosing young often are concentrated, at such times these amphibians provide sustenance for many kinds of predators that aggregate for easily acquired meals. No attempt has been made to document the predation on amphibians by all of the numerous kinds of predators. Instead, major predators, especially those that specialize on amphibians—eggs, larvae, or adults—are emphasized in the following discussion.

Eggs

Aquatic eggs of amphibians are subject to predation primarily by fishes and aquatic invertebrates. In permanent ponds and streams, amphibian eggs are susceptible to fishes and aquatic invertebrates; in temporary ponds, aquatic invertebrates are probably one of the most important predators. Aquatic invertebrate predators on salamander eggs include the leech, *Macrobdella decora,* feeding on the eggs of *Ambystoma maculatum* (Cargo, 1960) and caddisfly larvae (Trichoptera: *Ptilostomis* sp.) feeding on the eggs of the same species and on those of *A. tigrinum* (Dalrymple, 1970). Aquatic salamanders also feed on amphibian eggs. Larval and adult newts (*Notophthalmus viridescens*) and larval *A. opacum* eat eggs of several species of anurans and salamanders (Walters, 1975).

Terrestrial eggs of plethodontid salamanders and various groups of anurans are eaten by a variety of insects, especially carabid and tenebrionid beetles. Furthermore, plethodontid salamanders feed on the eggs of other plethodontids. Eggs in the terrestrial foam nests of *Leptodactylus latinasus* are eaten commonly by a lycosid spider, *Lycosus pampeana* in Argentina (Villa et al., 1982). The arboreal eggs of centrolenid frogs are consumed by phalangids, graspid crabs, and crickets (Hayes, 1983).

The arboreal eggs of phyllomedusine frogs are eaten by nocturnal colubrid snakes of the genus *Leptodeira* (Duellman, 1958). These snakes manipulate their jaws around part of a clutch of eggs and continue to engulf the cohesive clutch.

Larvae

Larval amphibians are the prey of numerous kinds of fishes, turtles, wading birds, and small mammals. Even passerine birds feed on tadpoles, as evidenced by Beiswenger's (1981) observations of gray jays (*Perisoreus canadensis*) feeding on aggregations of *Bufo boreas* tadpoles. Some snakes feed on larvae; the South American colubrids *Liophis epinephelus* and *L. reginae* are common predators on pond tadpoles, and the North American *Thamnophis sirtalis* and *T. couchii* commonly feed on tadpoles and salamander larvae.

Numerous aquatic insects prey on tadpoles. Larval odonates (*Anax* and *Pantala*) are important predators (Heyer et al., 1975; Caldwell et al., 1981), as are the predaceous diving beetles, especially their larvae, of the genera *Acilius* and *Dystiscus* (Young, 1967; Neill, 1968). Water bugs (*Belostoma*) and water scorpions (*Nepa* and *Ranatra*) suck the body fluids from captured tadpoles, their chief prey (Wager, 1965).

Perhaps some of the most significant predators on amphibian larvae are other amphibians. This is especially true in temporary ponds, although in streams larval salamanders, *Dicamptodon ensatus,* prey on the tadpoles of *Ascaphus* (Metter, 1963). Studies by Heusser (1971) and Cooke (1974) in Europe and by Wilbur (1972), Calef (1973), Walters (1975), Morin (1981), and Caldwell et al. (1981) in North America have shown that adult and larval newts (*Notophthalmus* and *Triturus*) and larval *Ambystoma* are selective predators on a wide range of anuran larvae. Tadpoles of a few species, such as *Ceratophrys cornuta,* seem to be obligate carnivores and feed chiefly on tadpoles of other species, whereas other kinds of tadpoles (e.g., *Leptodactylus pentadactylus*) are facultative predators on tadpoles (Heyer et al., 1975). *Xenopus laevis* commonly feeds on tadpoles and small frogs (Wager, 1963).

Adults

As noted by Porter (1972), practically anything will eat an amphibian, but the subterranean habits of most caecilians preclude their exposure to most predators except fossorial snakes, such as coral snakes (*Micrurus*).

Various species of predaceous spiders feed on amphibians (see Formanowicz et al., 1981, for review). In some cases the amphibians are caught in webs and subsequently killed and eaten, but crab spiders, tarantulas, and other hunting spiders spring on amphibian prey, grasp them, and kill by injection. Formanowicz et al. (1981) demonstrated a negative correlation between successful predation by the crab spider (*Olios*) and body size of the frog *Eleutherodactylus coqui*. Freshwater crabs seem to prey on small frogs. In Panama we observed a crab grasping the foreleg of a *Colostethus inguinalis;* many frogs of this genus along streams in the Neotropics inhabited by crabs are missing limbs. Larvae of horseflies (*Tabanus punctifer*) burrow tail first into mud at the margins of ponds; these larvae have hooked mandibles and seize recently metamorphosed spadefoot toads (*Scaphiopus multiplicatus*). The larvae pull the toads into the mud and kill them by feeding on their body fluids (Jackman et al., 1983).

Among vertebrates, fishes, turtles, and crocodilians are major aquatic predators on anurans, whereas various kinds of snakes, birds, and mammals are terrestrial or aquatic-margin predators. Also, some anurans feed on other frogs. Large, carnivorous frogs, such as *Cyclorana australis, Pyxicephalus adspersus, Rana catesbeiana, Rana tigerina,* and species of *Ceratophrys* and *Lepidobatrachus,* are notorious for their voracious appetites, which include any available smaller frogs. The carnivorous hylid frogs *Hemiphractus* commonly eat anurans; stomachs of 10 specimens of *H. proboscideus* contained 15 frogs of 12 species (Duellman, 1978).

Lizards are not important predators on amphibians, although monitors (*Varanus*) are known to eat anurans (Wager, 1965). Many kinds of snakes feed on amphibians, and some species specialize on certain kinds of amphibians. The colubrid *Diadophis punctatus* and various species of *Thamnophis* prey on plethodontid salamanders, and the semiaquatic natricines *Natrix, Nerodia,* and *Thamnophis* prey on frogs. The aquatic colubrid *Farancia abacura* feeds almost exclusively on *Amphiuma.* Some snakes specialize on heavy-bodied anurans, especially *Bufo.* North American colubrid snakes of the genus *Heterodon* and South American colubrids of the genus *Xenodon* specialize on *Bufo,* and the latter also eats large frogs, such as *Leptodactylus pentadactylus* (Fig. 10-1). These snakes have large gapes and long, grooved teeth on the maxillae; they are capable of piercing the tough skin of the inflated toads and killing them with venom. Although most viperids specialize on warm-blooded prey, juveniles of many species of vipers feed on amphibians; adults of *Agkistrodon* commonly feed on anurans, and the African *Causus rhombeatus* feeds exclusively on toads (*Bufo*).

In the tropics, where the diversity of anurans is highest, there are many species of snakes that feed on anurans, and some eat anurans almost exclusively. In Africa, colubrid snakes of the genus *Philothamnus* specialize on *Hyperolius,* and species of *Lycodontomorphus* feed exclusively on *Rana* (Wager, 1965). Many neotropical colubrid snakes feed primarily or exclusively on anurans. In the Amazon Basin, nocturnal tree snakes *Leptodeira annulata* and *Imantodes lentiferus* feed on active, arboreal frogs at night, and diurnal arboreal snakes *Leptophis ahuetulla* and *Oxybelis argenteus* ferret out the frogs by day (Duellman, 1978). In the same region, snakes of the genera *Chironius, Liophis,* and *Xenodon* actively forage for anurans on the ground by day.

Wading birds, such as egrets, herons, and ibises, are known to prey heavily on anurans in, and at the edges of, ponds, especially on species of *Rana.* Passerine birds are important predators on amphibians. R. Jaeger (1981a) observed which foraging passerines which scratch in leaf litter for prey are more efficient at finding prey when the

Figure 10-1. A colubrid snake, *Xenodon severus,* an anuran specialist, 1050 mm in body length, swallowing a *Leptodactylus pentadactylus,* 173 mm in snout-vent length. Santa Cecilia, Ecuador. Photo by W. E. Duellman.

Figure 10-2. A phyllostomatid bat, *Trachops cirrhosus,* about to capture a hylid frog, *Agalychnis callidryas.* Barro Colorado Island, Panama. Photo by M. D. Tuttle.

leaves are dry than when wet; plethodontid salamanders, which are suitable prey for these birds, are more common in the leaf litter when it is wet. Some birds may have developed specialized search images or behaviors for preying on certain amphibians. For example, the South American hawk *Geranospiza caerulescens* apparently uses its long legs and talons to extract anurans from their diurnal retreats in the axils of leaves of arboreal bromeliads (Bokermann, 1978).

Nocturnal mammals, especially raccoons (*Procyon),* skunks (*Mephitis),* night monkeys (*Aotus),* and various kinds of opossums, prey on amphibians. Also, two genera of bats feed on anurans. *Megoderma* in the Old World and the neotropical *Trachops cirrhosus* are attracted by anuran vocalizations (Fig. 10-2) (see Chapter 4).

Cannibalism

Feeding on conspecifics has been documented in several larval amphibians, particularly among tadpoles of *Scaphiopus bombifrons* and the larvae of *Ambystoma tigrinum,* in both of which cannibalistic morphs have evolved (see Chapter 6). The feeding on conspecific eggs and juveniles by adult anurans and salamanders seems to represent only a predator taking advantage of an available food source. There is no evidence that the predator can distinguish conspecifics. Cannibalism by many kinds of tadpoles is the result of crowding and/or a limited food supply.

ANTIPREDATOR MECHANISMS

Generally, amphibians are viewed as rather defenseless creatures that are consumed readily by a great variety of predators. However, amphibians have evolved various morphological, physiological, and behavioral features, which alone or in combination provide varying degrees of protection from potential predators.

Escape Behavior

Predation can be avoided by escaping from a potential predator prior to an actual encounter; this usually involves the prey sensing the presence of a predator. Escape may be affected by rapid movement, hiding, or a combination thereof.

Movement. Active escape depends on the locomotor capabilities of the organism. Terrestrial caecilians are seldom active aboveground, and unless they happen to be on an impenetrable surface, they are capable of burrowing into the soil quickly. Most salamanders move rather slowly, but some salamanders are capable of rapid protean movements resulting in changes in the shape, position, or location of the salamander. These flipping movements are accomplished by (1) propelling the body by a series of rapidly alternating coiling and uncoiling movements, (2) propelling the body by flipping the tail while the salamander is running, or (3) lateral writhing resembling serpentine locomotion. The last type of movement is especially developed in the extremely elongate plethodontids of the genus *Oedipina.*

The saltatorial locomotion of most anurans is an excellent mechanism for escaping potential predators, especially those that depend on chemosensory cues for trailing prey, for the trail is interrupted by jumping in anurans. This escape behavior may involve any one of several strategies depending on the anuran and its environment:

(1) a single, long leap carrying the frog to shelter, as is characteristic of many *Rana,* which leap from land to water; (2) a single, long leap and subsequent immobility with the anuran relying on cryptic coloration to avoid subsequent discovery, as is characteristic of many terrestrial frogs (e.g., some species of *Eleutherodactylus);* (3) a leap from one branch to another, as is characteristic of many tree frogs and is carried to an extreme in a few species that are capable of "parachuting" or gliding (e.g., *Agalychnis moreletii, Hyla miliaria,* and various species of *Rhacophorus);* (4) a series of long leaps that carry the frog a sufficient distance from the predator, as in the Australian rocket frog, *Litoria nasuta;* (5) a prolonged series of short, unidirectional hops and subsequent immobility, as in many *Bufo;* (6) a series of short, multidirectional hops, as in *Acris* at the margin of a pond or *Colostethus* on the forest floor or in a stream bed.

Cryptic Coloration and Structure.   The colors, patterns, and structural features of many amphibians are important to their avoidance of visual recognition by predators, or create optical illusions that confuse predators.

Concealing coloration.—Many species of amphibians have colors and patterns that tend to match those of the substrates on which they live (K. Norris and Lowe, 1964). These colors may be pale, lichenous markings on the dorsum that blend with rocks or tree trunks, as in the salamanders *Hynobius lichenatus* and *Aneides aeneus* or the tree frog *Hyla arenicolor* (Fig. 10-3). The dull browns, grays, and blacks of many terrestrial amphibians that inhabit the forest floor are effective concealing colors, as are the mottled patterns of bottom-dwelling aquatic salamanders and the uniform or mottled green patterns of tree frogs that perch on leaves. Countershading, as in adult newts (*Notophthalmus),* also is important in concealment. Some tree frogs that perch on leaves (e.g., species of *Centrolenella* and *Agalychnis*) reflect near-infrared light (Schwalm et al., 1977); infrared reflectance may be crytic coloration in that leaves also reflect infrared.

Disruptive coloration.—The visual search image of a predator can be confused by color patterns that do not conform to the outline of the prey. Many terrestrial and some arboreal anurans have a dark stripe along the side of the head (even continuing through the eye), thereby disrupting the image of the head; also, dark diagonal marks on the hindlimbs and chevron-shaped marks on the dorsum of the body break up the outline of many terrestrial anurans (Fig. 10-4). A middorsal pale line is a common disruptive color pattern in many species of *Eleutherodactylus, Physalaemus, Bufo,* and *Rana.* Likewise, irregular dorsal markings, such as pale-colored proximal segments of limbs, of many terrestrial salamanders are thought to be disruptive. Tadpoles of *Acris crepitans* that develop in ponds have black tips to the tails, whereas those that develop in lakes and streams have no distinctive caudal markings; the black-tipped tail seems to be an important deflective mechanism to divert attacks by dragonfly larvae that occur in ponds (Caldwell, 1982).

Confusing coloration.—Elongate organisms that rely on speed to escape predators often have linear color patterns that presumably create an optical illusion when the animal is moving. Color patterns of this type are uncommon in amphibians but do occur in caecilians of the genus *Rhinatrema* and in a few salamanders (e.g., *Eu-*

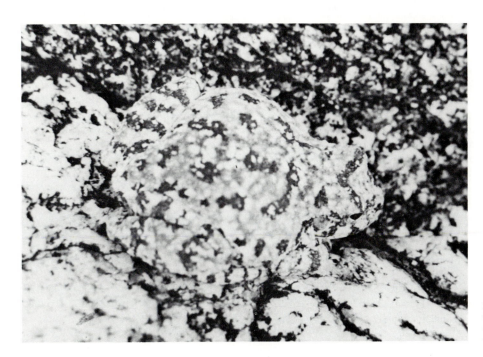

Figure 10-3. Concealing coloration in a hylid frog, *Hyla arenicolor.* Sabino Canyon, Arizona. Photo by J. S. Frost.

Figure 10-4. Disruptive coloration in a leptodactylid frog, *Eleutherodactylus w-nigrum.* Chiriboga, Ecuador. Photo by W. E. Duellman.

rycea and *Pseudobranchus).* A pattern of longitudinal stripes is not common among anurans but does occur in some species of *Rana, Hyla, Hyperolius,* and *Ptychadena,* all of which have rather slender bodies. Among anurans, a more common, confusing coloration may be so-called flash colors on the flanks and thighs, surfaces that are concealed when the frog is at rest but that are visible when the frog leaps. These flash colors usually are vivid and contrast strikingly with the dorsal surfaces (Fig. 10-5). Flash colors are visible only momentarily to a predator while the frog leaps; the frog then assumes a resting position and may be cryptically colored. Flash colors are especially prevalent among tree frogs.

Cryptic structure.—Some structural features of anurans present a disruptive pattern and therefore are useful in concealment from predators. Bony extensions of the squamosal provide anurans, such as *Ceratobatrachus, Hemiphractus,* and *Bufo typhonius,* with a disruptive outline to the head. These and features such as dermal flaps on the eyelids and heels, scalloped dermal folds on the limbs, and tubercles on the body all aid in concealment. Anurans such as *Megophrys nasuta* with tan colors and irregular outlines to the body and *Edalorhina perezi* with longitudinal dermal ridges and brown streaks on the body are camouflaged among leaves on the forest floor, whereas *Hyla lancasteri* with spinous tubercles and mottled green coloration is cryptic on moss-covered branches in cloud forest. Cryptic structure and/or coloration are most common among species that either are rather sedentary or tend to escape potential predators by a single leap.

Encounter Behavior

Predators that encounter amphibians may be faced with a variety of defense mechanisms that allow the amphibian to escape, although it may suffer wounds in the process. Faced with a potential predator, some amphibians have rather stereotyped postures in which they (1) feign death, (2) present a larger image to the predator, (3) confuse the predator by changing the characteristic shape of the body, (4) present the predator with the least palatable part of the body (areas of concentrations of granular glands), (5) present aposematic coloration, or (6) physically attack the predator.

The data on defensive behavior in terrestrial salamanders were discussed by Brodie (1977, 1983 and papers cited therein), whereas the data presented here on anurans are from a variety of sources, including the early work by Hinsche (1928), experiments by Marchisin and J. Anderson (1978), and brief reviews by Lescure (1977) and Perret (1979); C. Dodd (1976) provided a cross-indexed bibliography of anuran defense mechanisms.

Although some similarities exist between the behaviors of salamanders and anurans, the differences and unique attributes of each group are sufficient so that the groups are treated best individually.

Caecilians. The only reported defensive behavior by a caecilian is Sanderson's (1932:221) statement about *Geotrypetes seraphini:* "...it spat a small blob of water at me with considerable force. This it continued to do while I gathered it up." However, when caecilians are grasped they exude copious quantities of mucus, which makes

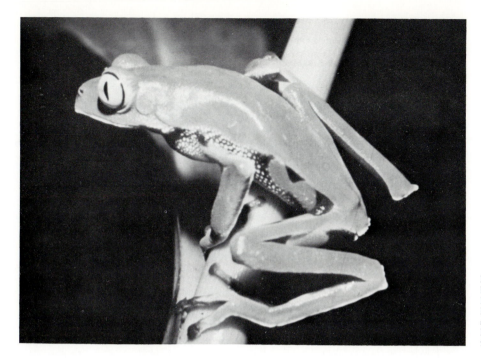

Figure 10-5. Flash colors in the hylid frog *Phyllomedusa perinesos.* Río Salado, Ecuador. The dorsum is leaf green, and the flanks and hidden surfaces of the thighs are purple with large orange spots and small white flecks. Photo by W. E. Duellman.

them extremely difficult to hold while they writhe strenuously. Large caecilians are capable of inflicting painful bites and deep lacerations with their teeth. Furthermore, at least some caecilians have toxic secretions (De Lille, 1934; Sawaya, 1939; Moodie, 1978).

Salamanders. Brodie (1983) listed 29 antipredator mechanisms in terrestrial salamanders (Table 10-1) and identified four suites of correlated antipredator mechanisms that act together (probably synergistically) to protect salamanders from predators (Table 10-2; Fig. 10-6):

Unken reflex.—The term comes from the onomatopoetic German name for *Bombina,* which produces a call sounding like "unk, unk, unk," and which exhibits the reflex named after it. This is a rigid, immobile posture with the chin and tail elevated so as to display bright ventral coloration. All salamanders exhibiting this behavior are salamandrids with toxic skin secretions that emanate from glands more or less evenly distributed on the dorsum. The toxicity and associated noxiousness protect salamanders with this suite of characters from being eaten by most predators, but do not prevent predators from attacking. The bright coloration and distinctive posture displaying the ventral coloration are cues that are associated with noxiousness by predators. The immobility characteristic of the Unken posture reduces the intensity of predator attack, which increases the probability that a predator will reject an inedible salamander without inflicting serious wounds. Salamanders exhibiting the Unken reflex have bony frontosquamosal arches and expanded neural arches on the vertebrae; this increased ossification

presumably reduces the probability of injury by a predator that has yet to learn that the salamander is inedible (Naylor, 1978a).

Tail lashing.—Salamanders that lash their tails at a predator have well-developed caudal musculature and a concentration of enlarged granular glands on the dorsal surface of the tail. Aposematic coloration, if present, is confined to the dorsum. This active antipredator behavior involves lashing the tail laterally and forcefully toward a predator. Tail-lashing normally takes place with the pelvic region elevated by the extension of the hindlimbs. Movement of the tail attracts the predator to the area of concentration of glands; any attack on the tail, the most dispensable part of the salamander, results in the predator encountering noxious secretions.

Tail undulation.—This is a passive antipredator behavior in which the tail is moved in a sinuous manner while the body is immobile; usually the tail is held vertically while undulating and the body is coiled with the head under the base of the tail. The tail is long and slender with a concentration of granular glands on the dorsal surface; most species have specializations for caudal autotomy. Aposematic coloration, if present, is restricted to the dorsum. This behavior directs the predator's attention to the tail, which produces large quantities of distasteful secretions and in most cases can be autotomized. The predator is attracted to the autotomized tail, which continues to undulate; during this distraction, the salamander has a chance to escape.

Head butting.—Some heavy-bodied salamanders with concentrations of granular glands in the parotoid region

Table 10-1. Antipredator Mechanisms of Terrestrial Salamanders[a,b]

Taxon	Noxious skin secretions	Toxic skin secretions	Parotoid glands	Glandular warts laterally	Dorsum of tail glandular	Venter of tail glandular	Middorsum of body glandular	Secretion sprayed	Aposematic coloration on dorsum	Aposematic coloration on venter	Pseudoaposematic coloration	Immobile posture	Body coiled	Body flipped	Venter exposed, tail up	Venter exposed, chin up	Rolls onto dorsum	Body arched	Head butting	Tail lashed	Tail wagged	Tail undulated	Ribs pierce skin	Hook on quadrate	Vocalize	Bite	Tail autotomy	Frontosquamosal arch	Expanded neural spines
Hynobiidae	·	·	+	−	+	·	·	·	−	−	·	·	·	·	·	·	·	·	·	·	·	·	−	−	·	·	−	−	−
Batrachuperus	+	·	+	−	+	+	−	−	+	−	·	−	+	·	−	−	−	−	−	+	+	·	−	−	·	·	−	−	−
Hynobius	·	·	−	−	+	−	−	−	−	−	·	·	·	·	·	·	·	·	·	·	·	·	−	−	·	·	−	−	−
Onychodactylus	·	·	−	−	+	−	−	−	−	−	·	·	·	·	·	·	·	·	·	·	·	·	−	−	·	·	+	−	−
Ranodon	·	·	+	−	+	·	·	·	−	−	·	·	·	·	·	·	·	·	·	·	·	·	−	−	·	·	−	−	−
Salamandridae	·	·	+	−	+	−	−	−	+	+	−	+	+	−	+	+	−	−	−	·	·	·	−	−	·	·	−	+	+
Chioglossa	+	+	+	−	+	−	−	−	+	+	−	+	+	−	+	+	−	−	−	·	·	·	−	−	·	·	−	+	+
Cynops	+	·	+	+	+	+	+	−	+	+	−	+	+	−	+	+	−	−	−	+	+	+	+	+	·	·	−	+	+
Echinotriton	+	·	+	+	+	+	+	−	+	+	−	+	−	−	+	+	−	−	−	−	−	−	+	−	·	·	−	+	−
Euproctus	·	+	−	−	+	+	+	−	+	+	−	+	+	−	+	+	−	−	−	·	·	·	−	−	·	·	−	−	+
Neurergus	+	+	+	−	−	+	−	−	+	+	−	+	+	−	+	+	−	−	−	·	·	·	−	−	+	·	−	+	−
Notophthalmus	+	+	+	+	+	+	+	−	+	+	−	+	+	−	+	+	+	+	+	+	+	+	+	−	+	·	−	+	+
Pachytriton	+	+	+	+	+	+	+	−	+	+	−	+	+	−	+	+	−	+	+	+	+	+	−	−	−	+	−	+	−
Paramesotriton	+	·	+	−	+	+	+	−	−	+	−	+	+	+	+	+	+	−	−	−	−	−	−	−	·	·	−	−	+
Pleurodeles	+	+	+	+	+	−	+	−	+	+	−	+	+	−	+	+	−	−	−	+	+	+	+	−	+	·	−	+	−
Salamandra	·	·	+	+	−	−	+	−	+	+	−	+	−	−	+	+	−	−	−	−	−	−	−	−	+	·	−	+	+
Salamandrina	+	+	+	+	−	−	+	−	+	+	−	+	+	−	+	+	−	−	−	−	−	−	−	−	+	·	−	−	−
Taricha	+	+	·	−	−	−	+	−	+	+	−	+	+	−	+	+	−	−	−	+	+	+	+	−	+	·	−	+	+
Triturus	+	+	+	−	+	−	+	−	+	+	−	+	+	−	+	+	−	−	−	+	+	+	−	−	+	·	−	+	−
Tylototriton	+	+	+	+	+	+	+	−	+	+	−	+	+	−	+	+	+	+	+	+	+	+	+	−	·	+	−	+	+

Dicamptodonidae	
Dicamptodon	
Rhyacotriton	
Ambystomatidae	
Ambystoma	
Rhyacosiredon	
Plethodontidae	
Aneides	
Batrachoseps	
Bolitoglossa	
Chiropterotriton	
Desmognathus	
Ensatina	
Eurycea	
Gyrinophilus	
Hemidactylium	
Hydromantes	
Lineotriton	
Oedipina	
Parvimolge	
Phaeognathus	
Plethodon	
Pseudoeurycea	
Pseudotriton	
Thorius	
Typhlotriton	

[a] Modified from Brodie (1983).

[b] + = present in at least one species; − = unknown in genus; · = no data.

Table 10-2. Defensive Behavior in Terrestrial Salamanders*

Genus	Unken reflex	Tail lashing	Tail undulation	Head butting
Hynobius	−	+	−	−
Cynops	+	−	−	−
Echinotriton	+	−	−	−
Notophthalmus	+	−	−	−
Paramesotriton	+	−	−	−
Pleurodeles	−	+	−	+
Salamandra	+	−	+	+
Taricha	+	−	−	−
Triturus	+	+	−	−
Tylototriton	+	+	−	+
Dicamptodon	−	+	−	−
Rhyacotriton	−	+	−	−
Ambystoma	−	+	+	+
Rhyacosiredon	−	+	−	−
Aneides	−	−	+	−
Bolitoglossa	−	−	+	−
Chiropterotriton	−	−	+	−
Ensatina	−	+	−	−
Eurycea	−	−	+	−
Gyrinophilus	−	−	+	−
Hemidactylium	−	−	+	−
Hydromantes	−	−	+	−
Oedipina	−	−	+	−
Plethodon	−	+	+	−
Pseudoeurycea	−	−	+	−
Pseudotriton	−	−	+	−
Thorius	−	−	+	−
Typhlotriton	−	−	+	−

*Data from Brodie (1983).

flex the head downward and swing the head toward, or lunge at, a predator. The body is held off the substrate, and the head and anterior part of the body are inclined toward the predator. Some species vocalize while engaging in this behavior. Aposematic coloration, if present, is dorsal and may be centered on the parotoid glands. This behavior presents the predator with the most distasteful part of the salamander.

Other mechanisms.—Salamanders may defend themselves actively once they are grasped by a predator. This, most commonly, is by biting, and *Pleurodeles, Dicamptodon, Desmognathus,* and some species of *Ambystoma* bite strenuously. *Amphiuma* is notorious for its capability to inflict deep lacerations. Species in three genera of salamandrids utilize their ribs in defensive behavior (Brodie et al., 1984). The blunt-tipped ribs of *Tylototriton* elevate the lateral concentrations of granular glands. The ribs are rotated, elevated, and penetrate the skin in *Pleurodeles waltl* and *Echinotriton andersoni* and *E. chinhaiensis;* in *Echinotriton* the ribs pierce concentrations of granular glands. Also in *Echinotriton* a hook on the quadrate pierces a concentration of granular glands (Fig. 10-7). Two other ultimate defense mechanisms by *Batrachoseps attenuatus* were described by Arnold (1982). Some of these salamanders grasped by small garter snakes (*Thamnophis*) escaped either by looping the tail around the snake's neck, thereby thwarting ingestion or by im-

mobilizing the snake by means of adhesive secretions (Fig. 10-8). Observations by Arnold (1982) of attacks by snakes on various plethodontid salamanders indicate that the defensive value of their skin secretions may be adhesive rather than toxic; the secretions produced by large individuals of various plethodontids can completely immobilize a small snake by gluing coils together or gluing the snake's mouth closed.

Feigning death may be an effective defense mechanism because many predators tend to take only living prey. The salamandrid *Paramesotriton chinensis* feigns death by rolling onto its back, thereby exposing its brightly colored venter (Brodie, 1983).

Anurans. Most anurans seem to rely on escape behavior to avoid predation, but some, especially species that are incapable of rapid escape, have developed various defensive behaviors in response to encounter by predators.

Death feigning is widespread in anurans. Among hylids, some species of *Hyla* and *Phyllomedusa* tuck the limbs in close to the body and remain motionless on their back. Other anurans stretch their limbs out (Fig. 10-9); in some of these, such as *Proceratophrys appendiculata* and *Stereocyclops parkeri*, a stiff-legged motionless posture combined with cryptic coloration may be especially effective against visually oriented avian predators that

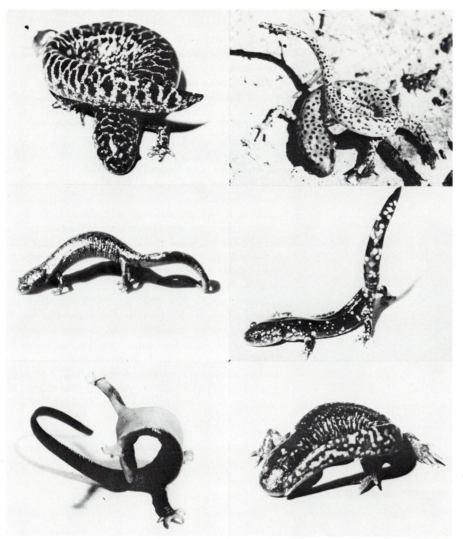

Figure 10-6. Types of antipredator postures by terrestrial salamanders. (Upper left) *Ambystoma cingulatum;* the tail is held across the head. (Middle left) *Bolitoglossa franklini;* the middle portion of the body is elevated and the tail is undulated. (Bottom left) *Taricha rivularis;* the chin, belly, and tail are elevated so as to display the bright red ventral color. (Upper right) *Eurycea lucifuga;* the tail is undulated from this position. (Middle right) *Ambystoma laterale;* the tail is undulated from this elevated position. (Bottom right) *Ambystoma lacustris;* the tail is lashed from this position. Photos by E. D. Brodie, Jr.

Figure 10-7. Salamanders that use their ribs in protection. (Left) *Echinotriton andersoni* protrudes sharply pointed ribs through concentrations of granular glands on the flanks. (Right) *Tylototriton verrucosus* has blunt-tipped ribs that elevate the concentrations of granular glands on the flanks. Both species elevate the tails so as to display bright ventral colors. Photos by E. D. Brodie, Jr.

disturb leaf litter for food (Sazima, 1978). The hyperoliid *Acanthixalus spinosus* crouches with its limbs tucked against the body, closes its eyes, and protrudes its orange tongue (Perret, 1962).

A common defensive behavior among heavy-bodied anurans is the inflation of the lungs, thereby puffing up the body and presenting a larger image to a potential predator. In species of *Scaphiopus, Limnodynastes, Lep-*

Figure 10-8. Defensive behavior by the salamander *Batrachoseps attenuatus* toward garter snakes, *Thamnophis.* (Upper) Thwarting ingestion by wrapping the tail around the snake's neck. (Lower) A *Thamnophis* immobilized by adhesive skin secretions. Photos by S. J. Arnold.

todactylus, and *Bufo,* inflation of the lungs usually is accompanied by lifting the body off the substrate. Some species of *Bufo* also tilt the body laterally toward the predator (Hanson and Vial, 1956). Many kinds of anurans elevate the posterior part of the body and flex the head downward toward the predator (Fig. 10-10). In *Bufo,* this posture presents the parotoid glands toward the predator, but the other anurans that exhibit this posture do not have concentrations of granular glands in the parotoid region.

Leptodactylids of the genera *Physalaemus* and *Pleurodema* have large inguinal glands, and in some of these the glands are elevated and brightly colored. Some species of *Pleurodema* and *Physalaemus* assume a defensive posture of lowering the head and elevating the pelvic region, thereby presenting the glands to the predator (Fig. 10-11). The ocelli-like markings on the glands have been interpreted as "eyespots" with the suggestion that the broad pelvic region with elevated "eyes" gives the image of a much larger organism.

Some anurans gape when faced with a predator. Hyperoliids of the genus *Leptopelis* simply open their mouths in an apparently threatening pose (Perret, 1966). The hylid *Hemiphractus fasciatus* tilts the head up, opens the mouth widely displaying an orange tongue, turns toward the predator, and sometimes snaps at it (Fig. 10-12); a pair of sharp odontoids on the lower jaw inflict deep punctures as the frog maintains a tenacious grip (Myers, 1966). The leptodactylid *Caudiverbera caudiverbera* inflates the lungs, elevates the body, opens the mouth, emits loud vocalizations, and jumps at a potential preda-

Figure 10-9. Death feigning by *Eleutherodactylus curtipes;* the limbs are outstretched, and the frog remains motionless. Photo by J. E. Simmons.

Figure 10-10. Elevation of the posterior part of the body and inclination of the head toward a predator by *Phrynomerus bifasciatus*. Photo by E. D. Brodie, Jr.

Figure 10-11. Defensive posture by *Physalaemus nattereri*, elevating inguinal glands toward a predator. Photo by E. D. Brodie, Jr.

tor (Veloso, 1977); this behavior also is characteristic of *Megophrys montana*.

The Unken reflex posture of arching the back with the head and posterior part of the body elevated while remaining motionless and displaying the brilliantly colored venter is well known in *Bombina* (Fig. 10-13). Two spe-

cies of South American bufonids of the genus *Melanophryniscus* also exhibit this behavior (Cei, 1980). Like *Bombina*, these small toads have brightly colored venters and many granular glands on the dorsum.

Vocalization may be used in defense (see Chapter 4). However, advertisement calls may attract predators, in

Figure 10-12. Mouth gaping by the horned hylid frog, *Hemiphractus fasciatus*, exposing the bright orange tongue. Photo by C. R. Schneider; courtesy of C. W. Myers.

Figure 10-13. Unken reflex in *Bombina variegata*, showing frog resting on its belly with chin elevated and palms and soles, which are bright orange, upturned. Photo by E. D. Brodie, Jr.

which case some species of anurans have modified calling behavior in response to the presence of predators; for example, chorusing *Physalaemus pustulosus* detect predatory bats visually and terminate calling within a second after the arrival of a bat over the pond (Tuttle et al., 1982). Some frogs produce odors that are disagreeable (to humans); these are well known in *Rana septentrion-*

alis and *Scaphiopus* and also have been reported in various other anurans, including *Pelobates fuscus, Litoria aurea,* and various species of *Phyllomedusa*. There is no experimental evidence on the effects, if any, of these odors on potential predators; possibly the odors are associative cues.

Ultimate defense mechanisms include biting, which can

be most effective in some large-headed species with strong jaws, such as *Pyxicephalus adspersus* and species of *Ceratophrys*. Also, some African ranids of the genus *Ptychadena* have the terminal phalange of the third toe modified as a spine that protrudes through the skin; possibly this is used in defense, because kicking by the frog could result in lacerations of the predator. There have been many reports of anurans emptying their bladders when grasped by a predator; this may be a reaction to extreme stress, and there is no evidence that the bladder water causes the predator to release its grasp.

Noxiousness and Toxicity

Presumably, all amphibians have two kinds of glands in the skin, namely mucous and granular glands. Mucous glands are distributed throughout the integument, and their secretions provide the moist coating necessary for cutaneous respiration (see Chapter 8). Granular glands, also referred to as serous or poison glands, may be distributed evenly or concentrated in certain areas of the body; in some species the granular glands secrete substances that are noxious or even toxic, thereby rendering the amphibian unpalatable to some predators. Some of these secretions also might be effective against bacterial and fungal infections (Bachmeyer et al., 1967), because at least some of them contain antimicrobial activity (Pruesser et al., 1975). Pharmacologically active substances in the skin of amphibians range from simple amines (and derivatives) such as norepinephrine and histamine to biologically active peptides, piperidine, and steroidal alkaloids, bufodienolides, and tetrodotoxin (see reviews by Michl and Kaiser, 1963; Erspamer, 1971; Daly and Witkop, 1971; Daly et al., 1978; Daly, 1982).

Evidence for the noxious and toxic properties of secretions from the granular glands has been derived from observations on predator-prey interactions (e.g., Brodie et al., 1979; DiGiovanni and Brodie, 1981) and from the isolation of compounds from the secretions and the determination of the toxicity of compounds by the injection of compounds into laboratory mice (e.g., Daly et al., 1978; Brandon and Huheey, 1981). Human taste is a sensitive indicator of the presence of pharmacologically active substances in amphibian skin (Myers and Daly, 1976; Myers et al., 1978). Noxious secretions of at least some species apparently have postingestional consequences that produce conditioned taste aversions (Mason et al., 1982).

Noxious properties are far more widely distributed among amphibians than are toxins. Even the eggs of some species have noxious properties, and those of *Taricha, Atelopus,* and at least some species of *Bufo* contain toxins (see review by Brodie et al., 1978). Larger tadpoles of some species (e.g., *Rana chalconota,* K. Liem, 1961; *Gastrophryne carolinensis,* Garton and Mushinsky, 1979) are unpalatable to predators presumably because of the development of granular glands in late larval stages. Formanowicz and Brodie (1982) showed experimentally that noxious qualities of several anurans and salamanders

appeared at metamorphosis and that in at least one species, *Rana sylvatica,* noxiousness was correlated with the development of granular glands.

Skin Toxins. The taxonomic distribution and biochemical composition of the skin toxins of amphibians only now are being discovered, although the toxic properties of some dendrobatid frogs and salamandrids have been known for more than 100 years.

Caecilians.—Sawaya (1940) demonstrated toxic properties of a compound (siphonopsina) in the skin of *Siphonops annulatus*. Experiments with the aquatic caecilian *Typhlonectes compressicauda* by Moodie (1978) revealed that the secretions were toxic to a coexisting predatory fish, *Hoplias malabaricus.*

Salamanders.—Most salamanders having toxic secretions are members of the family Salamandridae. The major toxin in *Taricha* and *Notophthalmus* is the neurotoxic tetrodotoxin (tarichatoxin); salamandarin alkaloids causing muscle convulsions are present in *Salamandra*. The secretions of tarichatoxin from *T. granulosa* are highly toxic; an adult *T. granulosa* has sufficient toxin to kill approximately 25,000 white mice (Brodie et al., 1974). The two species of the plethododontid genus *Pseudotriton* are the only nonsalamandrids known to produce toxins (Brandon and Huheey, 1981). The proteinaceous toxin of *Pseudotriton* has a high molecular weight, unlike the weights of other salamander toxins, except the heavy proteinaceous toxin of *Triturus cristatus* (Jaussi and Kunz, 1978), although Brandon and Huheey (1981) noted heavy toxins in other North American salamandrids. The effect of pseudotritontoxin on mice is primarily severe hypothermia.

Anurans.—A wide variety of toxins of relatively low molecular weights have been identified in numerous anurans, although a toxin with a high molecular weight has been found in *Bombina variegata* (Bachmeyer et al., 1967). Substances such as bradykinin, caerulin, leptodactylin, physalaemin, phyllokinin, sauvagine, and serotonin have been isolated from the skins of a wide variety of anurans (Erspamer, 1971; Erspamer and Melchiorri, 1980; Nakajima, 1981). These compounds may serve a defensive function when present in large quantities. Some of these have vasoconstrictive or hypotensive actions.

Bufonids possess numerous bufodienolides (Flier et al., 1980; Habermehl, 1981), which are cardiotoxic steroids. Some of these, such as bufotoxin and bufogenin, are strictly cardiotoxic, whereas others have diverse effects. A serotonin derivative, O-methyl-bufotenin, from *Bufo alvarius,* is a potent hallucinogen. Tetrodotoxin-like compounds, zetekotoxin and chiriquitoxin, have been isolated from the skins of *Atelopus* (Pavelka et al., 1977).

Dendrobatid frogs of the genus *Dendrobates* and especially *Phyllobates* have extremely toxic steroidal alkaloids in the skin (Daly et al., 1978; Myers and Daly, 1983). More than 200 alkaloids representing five distinct classes of compounds have been discovered in species of *Den-*

Figure 10-14. Aposematic coloration in amphibians: predominantly red in *Pseudotriton ruber* from Ash Cave, Ohio (upper left), and *Dendrobates pumilio* from the Río Changuinola, Panama (upper right); predominantly yellow in *Phyllobates terribilis* from the upper Río Saija drainage, Colombia (middle left) and *Atelopus zeteki* from El Copé, Panama (middle right); contrasting patterns of yellow and black in *Salamandra salamandra* from Europe (lower left) and orange-red and dark brown in *D. histrionicus* from El Valle, Chocó, Colombia (lower right). Photos of anurans by C. W. Myers, of salamanders by W. E. Duellman.

drobates and *Phyllobates,* all of which have aposematic coloration. The molecular structure of the large majority of dendrobatid alkaloids consists of a simple piperidine ring of one nitrogen atom and five carbon atoms; piperidine rings occur in all groups of toxic dendrobatids. However, in *Phyllobates* the biosynthesis of piperidine alkaloids has been suppressed in favor of batrachotoxins, which are extraordinarily toxic alkaloids.

Batrachotoxins are among the most potent, naturally occurring, nonprotein toxins. These compounds selectively increase the permeability of the outer membranes of nerve and muscle fibers. Batrachotoxin prevents the normal closing of sodium channels in the cell membranes with the result that cells become depolarized because of massive influxes of sodium. Thus, nerve cells cannot transmit impulses, and muscle cells remain in an activated, contracted state. This results in heart arrhythmias, fibrillation, and failure. An individual of the largest species of highly toxic dendrobatid, *Phyllobates terribilis,* (Fig. 10-14) contains enough toxin to kill about twenty thousand 20-gram white mice, extrapolated to be sufficient to kill several adult humans (Myers et al., 1978).

The other dendrobatid toxins are simpler in structure and much less toxic. Histrionicotoxins, first isolated from *Dendrobates histrionicus,* interact with acetylcholine receptors and block the transmission of signals from nerves to muscles and also block potassium channels in cell membranes. Pumiliotoxin-B, first isolated from *D. pumilio,* affects the transport of calcium ions. Pumiliotoxin-C and gephyrotoxin also block ions and prevent acetylcholine from triggering muscle contraction. Little is known about self-immunity to these toxins. In *Phyllobates terribilis,* a sodium-channel regulatory site in nerve and muscle seems to have been altered minimally, so that these frogs are insensitive to their own toxins but not to similarly acting plant toxins, to which they are never exposed in nature (Daly et al., 1980).

Aposematic Coloration. Amphibians that have toxic skin secretions tend to have aposematic colors or patterns. These so-called warning colors supposedly function in providing visual warning, a learned response on the part of the predator. For this reason, noxious qualities presumably are associated with toxic properties, although the former may be present without the latter. A predator that finds a certain kind of amphibian to be distasteful will associate the warning color with the bad taste and after one or more such experiences will recognize the distasteful species and refrain from attacking.

Aposematic coloration usually involves red, orange, or yellow. The animal may be predominantly or uniformly one of these colors, such as *Dendrobates pumilio* and *Pseudotriton ruber* (red), and *Phyllobates terribilis* and *Atelopus zeteki* (yellow), or it may bear these colors against a contrasting background, usually black, as in *Salamandra salamandra* and *D. histrionicus* (Fig. 10-14). In most anurans and many salamanders, aposematic coloration is present on the dorsum; some salamanders and a few anurans have aposematic coloration ventrally, and some of these exhibit the Unken posture in which the ventral color is displayed.

Some amphibians have striking patterns that may be aposematic, but neither the presence of toxins nor correlative behavior has been observed. Included here are the "bull's-eye" black and white ventral patterns in some African *Phrynobatrachus* and the white spot on the brown chest of some neotropical *Phyllomedusa*.

Mimicry. There are few examples of mimicry among amphibians. The palatable *Eleutherodactylus gaigeae* has a color pattern closely resembling the highly toxic *Phyllobates aurotaenia* and *P. lugubris,* with which it occurs in sympatry (Myers and Daly, 1983) (Fig. 10-15). However, there is no experimental evidence to support this presumed Batesian mimicry, or that of the presumably palatable *Lithodytes lineatus* and the slightly toxic *Dendrobates femoralis* (C. Nelson and G. Miller, 1971).

Several examples of Batesian mimicry (noxious model and palatable mimic) are known among North American salamanders. The red phase of *Plethodon cinereus* is a mimic of the toxic eft stage of *Notophthalmus viridescens* (Brodie and Brodie, 1980). In parts of its range in the southern Appalachian Mountains, populations of the distasteful, black *Plethodon jordani* have red markings. In the area where *P. jordani* has red cheeks, some individuals of the palatable *Desmognathus imitator* mimic this pattern. In areas where *P. jordani* has red legs, some individuals of *D. ochrophaeus* are mimetic (R. R. Howard and Brodie, 1973). In each of these cases, the mimics are polymorphic. Experimental feeding trials of models, mimics, and nonmimic conspecifics resulted in significantly higher survival of mimics than nonmimics.

The aposematic coloration of the toxic *Pseudotriton* was interpreted by Brandon and Huheey (1981) as a case of Müllerian mimicry with the coloration of the highly toxic *Notophthalmus viridescens*. In this situation the effectiveness of the model is reinforced by the presence of a toxic mimic. There is a size-correlated degree of toxicity in *P. ruber;* it is most toxic when it is the size of the efts of *Notophthalmus,* and its level of toxicity declines with larger size.

EVOLUTION OF DEFENSE MECHANISMS

Among terrestrial vertebrates, amphibians are unique in possessing two kinds of integumentary glands: mucous and granular. These glands produce at least two kinds of substances: mucus for maintaining a moist surface for cutaneous respiration and, in some species, toxins for protection against predators. Basic similarities in the morphology of granular glands in diverse amphibians (see Chapter 14 and Neuwirth et al., 1979) suggest that the granular glands probably served an original function other than poison synthesis, but the glands may have been a

Figure 10-15. Highly toxic model *Phyllobates lugubris* from Isla Colón, Panama (left), and the Batesian mimic *Eleutherodactylus gaigeae* from the Río Concepción, Panama (right). Photos by C. W. Myers.

convenient preadaptation for producing the diverse toxins that evolved independently in several groups of amphibians. In fact, Flier et al. (1980) demonstrated that various bufonids contain high levels of compounds in the skin that inhibit sodium- and potassium-dependent adenosinetriphosphatase as well as the binding of ouabain to the enzyme; they hypothesized that the toxins in bufonids may have originated from compounds that regulate enzymes involved in maintaining salt and water balance.

As concluded for salamanders by Brodie (1983) and also emphasized in the preceding discussion, Skin Toxins: Anurans, the basic factor underlying the evolution of the various antipredator mechanisms is the distribution of granular glands on the body and the degree of development of noxious or toxic secretions of these glands. Thus, there has been considerable convergence in defensive behavior in independent lineages of anurans as well as in salamanders, but some salamandrids and dendrobatids have developed highly toxic secretions that are unique to those groups. These secretions can be viewed as the ultimate in secretory defense mechanisms, which are associated with aposematic coloration. Many potential predators quickly learn to avoid these amphibians (R. R. Howard and Brodie, 1973; Hensel and Brodie, 1976). Even invertebrate predators (diving beetles, *Dytiscus*) and possibly parasitic leeches learn to avoid the noxious skin secretions of newts, *Notophthalmus viridescens* (Pough, 1971; Brodie and Formanowicz, 1981).

Some predators, especially certain snakes, seem to be immune to amphibian toxins. For example, colubrid snakes of the genera *Heterodon* and *Xenodon* feed almost exclusively on *Bufo*, adults of which are avoided by most other snakes. The colubrid *Liophis epinephelus* is immune to a variety of potent toxins, even batrachotoxins, for captive snakes have fed on *Atelopus*, *Dendrobates*, and even the highly toxic *Phyllobates terribilis* with no apparent ill effects (Myers et al., 1978). *Thamnophis sirtalis* is resistant to the strong toxins of *Taricha* and eats the salamanders without apparent ill effects (Brodie, 1968).

Although eggs and larvae of some amphibians have noxious or even toxic properties, these defense mechanisms develop in the metamorphic stages of some amphibians (Brodie et al., 1978). Metamorphosing anurans are subject to heavy predation (Wassersug and Sperry, 1977; Arnold and Wassersug, 1978), possibly not only because of their inability to escape but also because of incomplete development of the granular glands.

Tail autotomy is common among plethodontid salamanders and also occurs in the salamandrid *Chioglossa lusitanica*— all of which have wound-healing properties. Autotomy may have evolved independently in three different ways among plethodontids, and D. Wake and Dresner (1967) suggested that selection has been for behavior and structural adaptations for control of tail loss, rather than for tail loss per se. This suggestion is supported by the tail undulation behavior of some plethodontids and the attraction of predators to the tail, which not only is dispensable but also contains the highest concentration of granular glands. Salamanders that exhibit caudal autotomy lose the tail upon being grasped by a predator; under these conditions salamanders that are tailless at the time of an attack have a lower survival rate than those with a tail (Ducey and Brodie, 1983).

There seems to be a relationship between aerobic and anaerobic capacities of amphibians on one hand and normal escape behavior on the other; species that rely on burst activity for rapid escape utilize anaerobic metabolism (A. Bennett and P. Licht, 1973; J. Baldwin et al., 1977). Amphibians that do not utilize burst activity commonly have noxious or toxic secretions; thus, slow-moving anurans (e.g., *Bufo*, *Scaphiopus*, *Atelopus*) and salamanders (e.g., *Salamandra*) that have high aerobic scopes rely on their noxious skin secretions to avoid predation. Anaerobic metabolism is associated with struggling with a predator; in the salamander *Plethodon jordani*, lactate concentrations arising from anaerobic metabolism during escape from snakes reached 880% of the resting level (Feder and Arnold, 1982).

Although almost any kind of predator may try to eat an amphibian, amphibians are able to survive because they have evolved a diverse suite of antipredator mechanisms. Morphological and metabolic features are correlated with these mechanisms; aside from flight and concealment, the basis for most defensive behavior is the presence of granular glands, the diverse secretions of which make many amphibians distasteful to predators.

CHAPTER 11

Population Biology

The disparity between theory and empiricism is particularly conspicuous in anuran ecology and behavior, where detailed studies of natural populations are rare.

Arnold G. Kluge (1981)

Populations are made up of conspecific individuals of different sexes, sizes, and age classes. Each individual has a history of growth and, upon reaching sexual maturity, reproduction. Characteristics such as growth rates, size, and longevity of individuals are integral aspects of the demographic features of populations. These factors, plus movements, interactions with conspecific individuals, and environmental constraints, constitute the main elements of population dynamics.

Although various aspects of population biology have been studied in numerous species of amphibians, comprehensive data are available for only a few species, and there have been no recent summaries or syntheses of existing data. In this chapter, data on individual characteristics, movements, and demography are summarized and synthesized with respect to the factors regulating population densities. Material on the reproductive aspects of population biology is included in Chapter 2 (see especially Tables 2-6 through 2-9), whereas information on larval growth and developmental periods is presented in Chapter 6.

CHARACTERISTICS OF INDIVIDUALS

Individuals are the constituents of populations. Important individual demographic characteristics include growth rate and longevity, with the latter being especially important with respect to the individual's age at first reproduction

and reproductive life span. Furthermore, absolute size is important with respect to fecundity (see Chapter 2). All of these factors are interrelated (Stearns, 1976).

Growth Rates

Amphibians presumably have indeterminate growth. Most information on growth rates is for temperate zone species of anurans that have restricted growing seasons (Table 11-1). For example, the postmetamorphic growth rate of the bullfrog *Rana catesbeiana* is rapid at early ages and tends to level off with increased age (Fig. 11-1). Most importantly for temperate zone species, the time to reach adult size and to become sexually mature is a function not just of the growth rate but of the duration of the individual's seasonal activity period. F. Turner (1960a) summarized data on postmetamorphic growth in anurans, but there has been no equivalent summary of salamanders.

Geographic differences in growth rates probably are influenced by differences in the physical environment. For example, bullfrogs (*Rana catesbeiana*) metamorphose at a mean length of 40 mm in Louisiana and grow to a mean length of 69 mm before hibernating and to a mean length of 129 mm the next year; in New York the frogs are larger at metamorphosis (mean = 45 mm) but grow to only 53–55 mm before hibernating and to 93–100 mm the next year (F. Turner, 1960a). A similar difference exists between populations of the slimy salamander

Table 11-1. Postmetamorphic Growth Rates of Temperate Zone Anurans as Revealed by Studies of Natural Populations*

Species	Maximum size		Size at metamorphosis	Size at hibernation	Age				Reference
	Male	Female			1 yr	2 yr	3 yr	4 yr	
Ascaphus truei	55	56	26	—	32	38	44	49	Daugherty and Sheldon (1982a)
Bombina bombina	56	56	17	22	35	45	—	—	Bannikov (1950)
Scaphiopus holbrooki	77	71	10	—	42	50	53	—	P. Pearson (1955)
Bufo americanus	100	115	10	30	70	88	—	—	Hamilton (1934)
Bufo bufo	75	83	10	17	30	47	60	—	Heusser (1970c)
Bufo quercicus	26	30	7	18	27	—	—	—	Hamilton (1955)
Hyla regilla	44	—	14	21	34	—	—	—	Jameson (1956)
Rana catesbeiana	—	155	45	53	93	123	138	—	Raney and W. Ingram (1941)
Rana clamitans	103	105	32	38	66	83	89	—	Martof (1956)
Rana pipiens	82	93	25	47	67	73	—	—	R. Ryan (1953)
Rana pretiosa	61	72	16	25	35	42	48	—	F. Turner (1957)
Gastrophryne olivacea	37	42	15	20	31	—	—	—	Fitch (1956)

*All sizes are in millimeters for snout-vent length and represent mean or modal values.

(*Plethodon glutinosus*) in Florida and Maryland (Houck, 1982); in Florida the growth rate is about 21 mm the first year, compared to 16 mm in Maryland.

Similar patterns of growth rate are shown by several species of salamanders. For example, data on four species of *Plethodon* summarized by Peacock and Nussbaum (1973) show that 28–33% of posthatching growth occurs during the first year; in these small salamanders the rate of growth is 10–15 mm (snout-vent length) dur-

ing their first year. Rates of 14–18 mm during the first year are known for three species of tropical plethodontid salamanders (Houck, 1982). The most rapid growth rate in a plethodontid is by *P. glutinosus* in Florida, which grows an average of 21 mm during the first year (Highton, 1956). Juvenile *P. jordani* do not appear aboveground until they are 1 year old; during their second year, average growth in snout-vent length is 13.92 mm, whereas during the next season of activity average growth is 9.26 mm and growth rate declines in subsequent years (Hairston, 1983a). Growth rates of newts are comparable to those of plethodontids; most growth occurs during the terrestrial eft stage in *Triturus vulgaris* (G. Bell, 1977; Fig. 11-2) and *Notophthalmus viridescens* (Gill, 1978). In the White River of Missouri, U.S.A., the hellbender (*Cryptobranchus alleganiensis*) adds about 68 mm to total length during the first year after metamorphosis to a length of 125 mm; large adults (400 mm) grow at a rate of about 1 mm per year (Peterson et al., 1983).

Many tropical anurans apparently grow throughout the year and thus attain their adult sizes rapidly. Data on introduced populations of the toad *Bufo marinus* indicate extremely rapid growth. In Hawaii, metamorphosing young of 8–12 mm attain lengths of 60–75 mm in 3 months and 90–120 mm at the age of 6 months (Pemberton, 1934). The large neotropical tree frog, *Hyla rosenbergi,* grows at a rate of 0.21 mm per day and reaches adult size in less than 1 year (Kluge, 1981). The growth rates of the tropical *Rana erythraea* in the Philippines is much more rapid than that of temperate species (W. Brown and Alcala, 1970). Females grow about 11 mm during the first month after metamorphosis, reach 76–83% of their maximum size in 1 year, and maintain a growth rate of about 1 mm per month after about 7 months of age. Males grow about 6 mm during the first month after

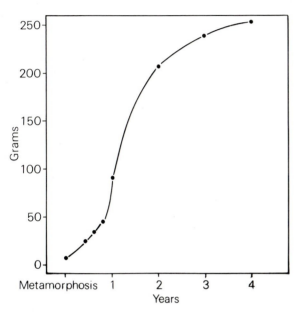

Figure 11-1. Growth curve for the bullfrog *Rana catesbeiana* in Illinois. The points are average weights of marked frogs of known ages in a natural population. Data from Durham and G. Bennett (1963).

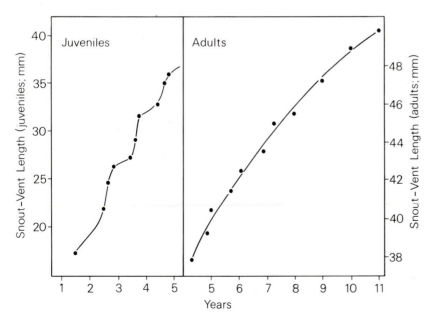

Figure 11-2. Growth curves for juvenile (terrestrial) and adult stages of the newt *Triturus vulgaris*. The points are average lengths of cohorts in a natural population. Adapted from G. Bell (1977).

metamorphosis, reach 96% of their maximum size in 1 year, and maintain a growth rate of about 1 mm per month after 6 or 7 months of age. These growth rates are comparable to those of three Bornean species of *Rana* reported by Inger and Greenberg (1966). Growth to sexual maturity within the first year is the rule in tropical anurans and also occurs in some temperate zone species (see Table 2-9).

Few data on growth rates of caecilians are available. M. Wake's (1980b) analysis of a population of *Dermophis mexicanus* in Guatemala showed that newly born individuals have lengths of 108–155 mm and that the smallest reproductive females are 2 years old and have lengths of 320–335 mm; thus, this caecilian grows at a rate of nearly 100 mm per year for the first 2 years. Determination of age classes in a sample of *Geotrypetes seraphini* from Ghana by M. Wake (1977a) implies rapid rates of growth; newly born individuals have lengths of 70–81 mm, whereas at the age of 2 years the caecilians are 180–240 mm long.

Many factors affect growth rates, including the availability of an abundance of essential food. However, different food items vary in their quality (caloric content and digestibility), so that the kinds of prey eaten (Fig. 11-3A), the efficiency of capture rates, and energy used in capturing prey all potentially contribute to the growth rate (see Chapter 12). Moreover, abiotic factors may influence growth rate, especially among young amphibians. For example, Lillywhite et al. (1973) suggested that behavioral thermoregulation in young *Bufo boreas* was important in raising body temperatures to increase digestive rates. C. Richards and Lehman (1980) demonstrated that constant light has a positive effect on growth rates of postmetamorphic *Rana pipiens* (Fig. 11-3B). The results of these laboratory studies need to be incorporated into investigations of growth rates in natural populations.

Size

There is great disparity in the maximum sizes attained by different species in the three living orders of amphibians. Several species of caecilians in the South American genus *Caecilia* exceed 1 m in total length; the largest known caecilian is a *C. thompsoni* having a length of 1515 mm. The smallest caecilians are the West African *Idiocranium russeli* and the Seychellean *Grandisonia brevis,* which attain lengths of only 114 and 112 mm, respectively; a female of the former was sexually mature at a length of only 90 mm (E. Taylor, 1968).

The giant Asiatic salamanders of the genus *Andrias* are the largest living salamanders. *Andrias davidianus* attains a total length of 1520 mm, and *A. japonicus* attains a total length of 1440 mm, much larger than the next largest salamanders— *Amphiuma tridactylum* (1015 mm) and *Siren lacertina* (950 mm). A living *Andrias japonicus* having a length of 1440 mm weighed 40 kg (Flower, 1936). The smallest salamanders are members of the plethodontid genus *Thorius*. In an unnamed species of *Thorius* from Cerro Pelon, Oaxaca, Mexico, the smallest sexually mature male has a snout-vent length of 15.7 mm and a total length of 26.9 mm (J. Hanken, pers. comm.).

The largest anuran is the West African ranid *Conraua goliath* with a snout-vent length of 300 mm and a weight up to 3.3 kg. This immense size is approached (but not very closely) by the South American *Bufo blombergi,* which reaches 250 mm, and by *Bufo marinus* in the Guianan region of South America; there, the toads attain snout-vent lengths of 240 mm. The smallest anurans are the Brazilian brachycephalid *Psyllophryne didactyla* (the most diminutive known tetrapod) reaching only 9.8 mm in snout-vent length and the Cuban leptodactylid *Sminthillus limbatus* attaining a length of 11.5 mm.

Longevity

Little is known about the longevity of amphibians in nature. On the basis of records of captive individuals, it is evident that many kinds of amphibians have the potential to live for two or more decades (Table 11-2). Generally, the longest-lived amphibians are the large aquatic salamanders, although a record of 50 years for a *Salamandra salamandra* (Bohme, 1979) approaches the record of 55 years for *Andrias japonicus*. Moreover, it seems that larger species tend to live longer than smaller ones, and that

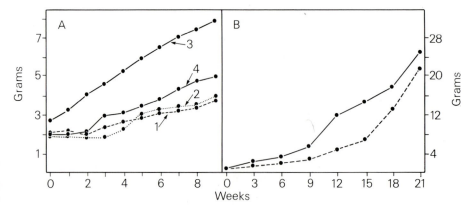

Figure 11-3. Growth rates of recently metamorphosed anurans. **A.** Effects of diet on *Bufo woodhousii.* Curve 1 = diet of crickets (*Acheta domestica*); 2 = diet of cabbage loopers (*Trichoplusia* sp.); 3 = diet of mealworms (*Tenebrio molitor*); 4 = combined diet. The points are mean weights of 15 toads in each group. Adapted from Claussen and Layne (1983). **B.** Effects of photoperiod on *Rana pipiens.* Solid line = constant light; broken line = 8 hours of light per day. The points are mean weights for 13 individuals at 21 weeks and 40 individuals at the beginning. Adapted from C. Richards and Lehman (1980).

salamanders are longer-lived than anurans. The correlation with size may be an artifact because zoos tend to maintain larger species for display. Nonetheless, in nature larger amphibians probably are less prone to predation than smaller ones and therefore might have a greater life expectancy, but because larger individuals require more food, their life expectancy or fitness might be reduced.

Notable discrepancies exist between longevity records in captivity and life expectancy in nature. For example, Bowler (1977) reported that five adult male *Hyla rosenbergi* lived for 3.5 years in captivity, but Kluge (1981) found no males that survived 2 years in nature. The records of 4–5 years for many plethodontid salamanders in captivity (Bowler, 1977) do not reflect the potential longevity of these salamanders in nature, because many of the species do not reach sexual maturity until they are 4 years of age (see Chapter 2). On the other hand, some estimates of age of individuals in nature correspond well with longevity records for captive individuals; for example, Peterson et al. (1983) estimated the largest individuals in a population of *Cryptobranchus alleganiensis* to be 25 years old, only 4 years less than the record for a captive (Flower, 1936).

MOVEMENTS AND TERRITORIALITY

Movement patterns of individuals are fundamental components of the ecology and population biology of a species. Movement patterns probably reflect age-specific variation in life history strategies with subsequent differences in ecological requirements. Among amphibians, migrations are associated mostly with reproductive aggregations (see Chapter 3), but dispersal of recently metamorphosed young also may involve movements over long distances. Young of *Bufo marinus* move about 150 m away from their natal ponds (G. Zug and P. Zug, 1979), and young of *Hyla regilla* move up to 237 m from a natal pond (Jameson, 1956). The young of *Syrrhophus marnocki* move 112 to 300 m (mean = 211 m) from their terrestrial nest sites before establishing residency (Jameson, 1955a).

Movements of individuals have been ascertained by capture-recapture studies of animals that have been marked by toe-clipping, branding, tags, or dyes. Movements of individuals can be monitored more accurately when the animals have been tagged with radioactive isotopes, because then continuous monitoring of individuals provides an hour-by-hour or day-by-day schedule of movements, whereas most capture-recapture studies do not provide such accuracy.

Home Range

Home range is considered to be the area in which an individual carries out its normal daily activities. Migrations to breeding sites outside the area of daily activity should not be considered to occur within the home range. However, many kinds of amphibians do not migrate to breed-

Table 11-2. Selected Longevity Records for Captive Amphibians*

Species	Age (years)
Caecilians	
Typhlonectes compressicauda	5
Salamanders	
Hynobius boulengeri	5
Andrias japonicus	55
Cryptobranchus alleganiensis	55
Siren lacertina	25
Necturus maculosus	9
Proteus anguinus	15
Cynops pyrrogaster	25
Pleurodeles waltl	20
Salamandra salamandra	50
Taricha torosa	21
Triturus vulgaris	28
Amphiuma means	27
Ambystoma mexicanum	25
Various plethodontids	5
Anurans	
Xenopus laevis	15
Bombina bombina	20
Scaphiopus holbrooki	12
Ceratophrys ornata	13
Leptodactylus pentadactylus	15
Bufo bufo	36
Dendrobates auratus	8
Hyla arborea	14
Litoria caerulea	16
Osteopilus septentrionalis	13
Rana catesbeiana	16
Kaloula pulchra	6

*Based mainly on Flower (1936) and Bowler (1977).

ing sites; reproduction occurs within the home ranges of terrestrial amphibians such as eleutherodactyline frogs and plethodontine salamanders.

Home range requirements differ among species, but shelter and food are mandatory components. The home range usually encompasses a preferred shelter and one or more feeding sites, and, for many kinds of male anurans it may include a suitable calling site.

For amphibians, the sizes of home ranges generally can be correlated with the size of the animal. For example, G. Zug and P. Zug (1979) determined the average size of the foraging area (as a main component of the home range) to be 160 m^2 in the large toad *Bufo marinus* on Barro Colorado Island, Panama. The home range of *Rana clamitans* is 20 to 200 m^2 (mean = 60 m^2) (Martof, 1953) and that of *Leptodactylus macrosternum*, 9.4 to 134 m^2 (Dixon and Staton, 1976). In the terrestrial, montane bufonid *Atelopus oxyrhynchus*, home ranges are larger in males (mean = 56.2 m^2) than females (32.6 m^2) (Dole and Durant, 1974a). Males of the small *Dendrobates pumilio* have home ranges of only 20 m^2 (McVey et al., 1981). However, *Syrrhophus marnocki* is an exception; Jameson (1955a) calculated the size of the home ranges of this relatively small terrestrial leptodactylid to vary from 267 to 700 m^2.

Among salamanders, *Ambystoma maculatum* have home ranges of 3.3 to 29.4 m² (mean = 9.83 m²) (Kleeberger and J. Werner, 1983); in *Salamandra salamandra*, the average home range of males is 9.8 m² and of females 12.8 m² (Degani and Warburg, 1978). The sizes of home ranges among terrestrial plethodontid salamanders vary greatly. For example, in *Ensatina eschscholtzi*, the average home range of males is 1194 m² and of females only 314 m² (Stebbins, 1951). In contrast, male *Plethodon cinereus* have smaller home ranges (mean = 10.8 m²) than females (mean = 19.9 m²) (Kleeberger and J. Werner, 1982). Representative sizes of home ranges in other terrestrial plethodontids in which there are no significant differences between the sexes are: *Batrachoseps attenuatus*, 7.1 m² (Hendrickson, 1954); *Bolitoglossa subpalmata*, 44 m² (Vial, 1968); *Plethodon glutinosus*, 34 to 75 m² (Merchant, 1972); and *P. jordani*, 6.7 to 55 m² (Madison and Shoop, 1970).

The shape of the home range obviously depends on the habitat of the animal. Although not defined formally, shapes of home ranges have been described as linear, two-dimensional, or three-dimensional. These are generalized and, at the best, loose descriptive terms. Linear is understood to be a point-to-point distribution, whereas a two-dimensional home range can be construed as an animal's distribution in a planar space (e.g., surface of the forest floor). A three-dimensional home range implies that the organism is active in more than one plane; for example, salamanders may utilize the forest floor by day and arboreal perches at night.

Most terrestrial salamanders and anurans have planar ranges, but many salamanders descend below the surface in times of drought; little attention has been paid to this third dimensional component of home ranges. Using radioisotopes, Semlitsch (1981) tracked individual *Ambystoma talpoideum* in the underground burrows that constitute their summer home ranges; he found that within their home ranges each individual had several activity centers with areas from 0.02 to 0.21 m². On the other hand, the home ranges of stream-inhabiting amphibians usually are linear, as shown in *Desmognathus fuscus* by Ashton (1975), who found that individuals move 0.3 to 10.2 m (mean = 0.49 m) along a small stream, and in *D. ochrophaeus* by Holomuzki (1982), who determined that the average linear movement was 0.71 m. During the period of summer activity, adults of the stream-breeding tree frog *Hyla cadaverina* move only 1 to 5 m away from the stream, and juveniles are even more sedentary, moving only 0.5 to 2 m away (R. T. Harris, 1975). *Bombina variegata* move more than 200 m to a breeding stream in the Balkan Mountains in Bulgaria, and during the breeding season, males move an average of 63.8 m and females only 20.0 m along the stream (Beshkov and Jameson, 1980). Likewise, the stream-inhabiting frog *Ascaphus truei* has linear home ranges (Daugherty and Sheldon, 1982b). Arboreal frogs that move vertically to calling sites along streams at night and back to diurnal perches by day have a third dimension to their home ranges, but these have not been measured.

Many other studies have provided information on distances moved by amphibians during their daily activities, but they have not quantified home ranges as such. These data suggest that the home ranges of some amphibians may be greater than those already mentioned. For example, Heusser (1968) noted that *Bufo bufo* forages for distances of 50 to 150 m, and Pyburn (1958) reported that *Acris crepitans* move 15 to 100 m along the margin of a pond. Some amphibians may not have definable home ranges, but instead move about arbitrarily in favorable habitat, as in *Notophthalmus viridescens* (R. N. Harris, 1981).

Homing Behavior

In response to reduced food supply, lack of available shelter, or lack of mates, individuals may extend or shift their home ranges. The ability to return to the home range is defined as homing behavior, and it provides a means for returning to known haunts from breeding activities or other searches. Moreover, in species that attend their eggs, the ability to return to the nest site is important for the survival of the eggs. Some species use visual cues to locate specific sites, whereas olfactory cues seem to be the primary stimuli for salamanders (see Chapter 3).

Many species exhibit a high degree of fidelity to their home range; in fact, some long-distance displacements have resulted in individuals returning to exactly the same place where they had been living. For example, individuals of *Bufo bufo* displaced 3 km returned to their home sites (Heusser, 1969), and newts, *Taricha rivularis*, that were displaced 8 km returned to their home stream within 1 year (Twitty et al., 1967). Terrestrial plethodontids can return to their home ranges when displaced for moderate distances. For example, *Plethodon jordani* returned when displaced up to 150 m (Madison, 1969); 90% of *P. cinereus* displaced 30 m returned to their home sites, but only 25% of those displaced 90 m returned (Kleeberger and J. Werner, 1982). Of 83 tree frogs, *Hyla regilla*, which were displaced 275 m from a breeding site, 43 (76%) of 56 recovered frogs returned to the site within 1 month, but none of 414 frogs that was moved 914 m to another pond returned to the original site within 1 month (Jameson, 1957).

Both European newts, *Triturus vulgaris*, and American newts, *Notophthalmus viridescens*, have high fidelities to their breeding ponds; although these newts move about arbitrarily in the terrestrial environment, they usually return to the same ponds to breed (G. Bell, 1977; Gill, 1978). Colonization of new ponds and formation of new demes in a metapopulation of *Notophthalmus* is dependent on the dispersal of efts (Gill, 1978).

In prairies in Minnesota, *Bufo hemiophrys* breeds in shallow ponds, and there is no evidence of fidelity to particular ponds by the toads; however 88 to 95% of the toads return to the same mound for hibernation in successive years (Kelleher and Tester, 1969).

Territoriality

Because territoriality is best understood in the context of competition for limited resources, a territory can be defined as an area coincident with, or included within, the home range that is defended against intruders. Territoriality is best understood in the context of competition for limited resources. Fidelity to, and defense of, a particular site is advantageous if it provides the occupant exclusive, or priority, access to resources needed for the individual's survival or reproduction. Aggressive behavior related to site-specific territoriality has been reported for numerous kinds of amphibians. Most of these observations relate to courtship (see Chapter 3), and vocalization is an important aspect of territoriality in many anurans (see Chapter 4). Aggressive defense of territories also is associated with some kinds of parental care, especially among terrestrial plethodontid salamanders and anurans that guard their eggs (see Chapter 2). As yet, there is no evidence that male amphibians defend territories that include female harems and their offspring, as is the case in some lizards and mammals.

Laboratory observations by Thurow (1976) demonstrated that intraspecific social dominance occurred in several salamanders of the genus *Plethodon*. Although juveniles interacted competitively among themselves, a strong, size-related dominance exists, so that in contests between individuals of different sizes the larger animal won 22% of the time; in most of the other contests there was no clear winner. R. Jaeger and Gergits (1979) showed that *P. cinereus* mark their territories by pheromones and that neighboring individuals recognize each other's pheromones. In a series of laboratory experiments, R. Jaeger (1981b) showed that adult male and female *P. cinereus* employed "dear enemy" recognition. Individuals were less aggressive and more submissive toward familiar territorial neighbors than toward strangers, and pheromones were used to distinguish familiar from unfamiliar individuals. R. Jaeger concluded that this behavior reduces the likelihood of escalated aggressive contests between neighbors. When combat occurs, bites usually are directed at two vulnerable parts of the body—the tail, which can lead to caudal autonomy and therefore loss of fat reserves, or the nasolabial grooves, scarring of which impairs their chemosensory function, which results in a reduced prey-capture rate during foraging and possibly reduced ability to locate mates and to defend a territory.

Many terrestrial dendrobatid frogs defend all-purpose territories that include feeding sites, calling sites, shelter, and oviposition sites (Wells, 1977a). Both males and females of *Eleutherodactylus coqui* defend tree holes that are used as diurnal shelters and may be used as oviposition sites, and at least some females defend their feeding sites (Drewry, 1970). Defense of shelters against conspecifics possibly is widespread in anurans; such behavior has been reported in the defense of burrows by the Mexican hylid *Pachymedusa dacnicolor* (Wiewandt, 1971) and several species of *Pseudophryne* in Australia (Pengilley, 1971). Defense of feeding sites probably is much more common than reported in the literature, because many anurans (e.g., *Eleutherodactylus* and *Centrolenella*) use the same perch for calling and feeding (also for oviposition by some species); thus, the defense of that resource can be for several reasons.

With the exception of the few observed cases of size-related dominance in defense of territories, there is little evidence of hierarchical behavior in amphibians. Studies on captive anurans have produced conflicting results. Tracy (1973) noted a feeding hierarchy among young *Bufo boreas* but was unable to ascertain aggression. Boice and Witter (1969) commented that there was no linear dominance in a feeding hierarchy of *Rana pipiens*. Haubrich (1961) concluded that in *Xenopus laevis* there were no absolute displays of dominance of one individual over another in groups of individuals, but in experiments with various pairs definite aggression and dominance were observed. It is unknown if aggressive intraspecific dominance occurs in nature, and if so, whether such behavior may be related to the abundance of food, density of conspecifics, or other factors.

DEMOGRAPHY

In nearly all amphibian populations that have been studied, predation pressure on eggs and larvae is high, and juvenile mortality varies more than adult mortality. Unpredictable environmental conditions, such as a drought-related disappearance of ponds, would affect survivorship of eggs and larvae more than adults. Survivorship of eggs and larvae also may be correlated with the amount and kind of parental care, if any. Thus, determination of demographic parameters, such as fecundity, natality, recruitment, age at first reproduction, reproductive life span, and age-specific mortality, are contingent on density-independent factors such as environmental stability and mode of life history, including parental care, as well as the usual density-dependent factors—available resources for shelter, oviposition sites, and sufficient food to maintain a positive energy budget.

Fecundity and natality have been discussed with respect to reproductive modes and parental care in Chapter 2. The other demographic parameters as they relate to the population dynamics of larval and postmetamorphic amphibians are treated here.

Survivorship

Most of the published data on survivorship is obfuscated by diverse methodologies that tend to make a synthesis

Table 11-3. Survivorship of Amphibian Eggs and Larvae

| Species | Percent survival | | | Reference |
	Eggs	Larvae	Eggs and larvae	
Salamanders				
Triturus vulgaris	2.6	8.8	0.23	G. Bell and Lawton (1975)
Ambystoma maculatum	22.2	71.2	15.80	Shoop (1974)
Ambystoma tigrinum	—	—	3.30	J. Anderson et al. (1971)
Anurans				
Rana aurora	91.0	5.3	4.82	L. Licht (1974)
Rana pretiosa	71.0	7.3	5.18	L. Licht (1974)
Rana sylvatica	—	—	4.00	Herreid and Kinney (1966)

difficult. Consequently, the following selected data are summarized so as to provide a range of variation of survivorship of different stages in the life histories of various kinds of amphibians.

Eggs. Survivorship of aquatic eggs to hatching ranges from a low of 2.6% in *Triturus vulgaris* to a high of 91% in *Rana aurora* (Table 11-3). In the nest-building gladiator frog, *Hyla rosenbergi,* only 24% of 49 nests suffered little or no mortality, and no eggs survived in 22% of the nests (Kluge, 1981); survivorship of eggs to hatching was only about 48%. In the arboreal foam nests of *Polypedates leucomystax,* survivorship of eggs is 0 to 100% (mean = 34%) (Yorke, 1983). Terrestrial eggs, especially with parental care, have greater survivorship; for example, more than 95% of the eggs survive to hatching in three species of *Pseudophryne* (Woodruff, 1976).

Larvae. The survivorship of most larvae is rather low (Table 11-3), although there are some exceptions, especially among stream-inhabiting salamander larvae. Nussbaum and Clothier (1973) calculated that 43% of *Dicamptodon ensatus* survive their first year of larval life; this survival rate is similar to those determined for the stream larvae of *Ranodon sibiricus* (42.7%; Bannikov, 1949) and *Pseudotriton ruber* (50%; Bruce, 1972b). Survivorship of *Rana* larvae in ponds generally is less than 10%. Calef (1973) found that there is higher mortality among tadpoles of *Rana aurora* during the first 4 weeks after hatching; then mortality gradually declines, so that only 5% survive to metamorphosis 11 to 14 weeks after hatching. In contrast, 11.8 to 17.6% of the tadpoles of *Rana catesbeiana* survive to metamorphosis (Cecil and Just, 1979).

Postmetamorphics. Little information is available on the numbers of metamorphosing young that survive to sexual maturity. G. Zug and P. Zug (1979) extrapolated that only about 0.5% of young *Bufo marinus* survive to sexual maturity; this rate of survivorship would still result in an expansion of population size. This may be the approximate survivorship in species that produce large

numbers of eggs, but survivorship must be much greater in order to maintain population sizes in those species that produce few offspring (e.g., terrestrial plethodontid salamanders and dendrobatid frogs).

Survivorship of adult newts from their first to their second breeding year is about 50%, but the percentage differs between sexes. In *Notophthalmus viridescens,* the rate of survival of males is 51%, of females 43% (Gill, 1978), whereas in *Triturus vulgaris* the rates are 45% for males and 55% for females (G. Bell, 1977). Presumably the bright courtship colors of male *T. vulgaris* result in higher rates of predation than on females, even though these newts have noxious skin secretions.

Annual adult survivorship among anurans varies from 0 to 69% (Table 11-4). Limited data suggest that survivorship is much lower in the tropics than in temperate regions. Of course, in the humid tropics the frogs are active throughout the year and thus are susceptible to continuous predation pressure, whereas in many temperate species the season of activity is 6 months or less each year. In *Hyla rosenbergi,* the average length of residency in the breeding population is only 18.3 days for males and 23.2 days for females; only 3 of 109 marked females returned to breed a second year, and none of 178 males returned. Therefore, Kluge (1981) concluded that annual population turnover was nearly 100%.

Survivorship of temperate salamanders ranges from intermediate between the extremes calculated for anurans to much greater than that of anurans. In the most comprehensive study of survivorship, Organ (1961) calculated life tables for five species of *Desmognathus* and showed that there is a progressive increase in early survival rate from the most aquatic species, *D. quadramaculatus,* to the most terrestrial, *D. wrighti* (Table 11-5). The annual survival rates of these salamanders are approximated by those of *Bolitoglossa subpalmata* (21%; Vial, 1968) and *Plethodon jordani* (36% in the second year and 48% in the third year; Hairston, 1983a). On the other hand, Bruce (1976) showed that annual survivorship in the epigean *Eurycea neotenes* is about 10% in the first year; survivorship increases among older salamanders, particularly males.

Table 11-4. Annual Survivorship of Some Adult Anurans

Species	Sex	Percent survival	Reference
Bufo hemiophrys	♂, ♀	34	Kelleher and Tester (1969)
Bufo woodhousii	♂, ♀	22	R. Clarke (1977)
Hyla rosenbergi	♂	0	Kluge (1981)
Hyla rosenbergi	♀	3	Kluge (1981)
Rana aurora	♂, ♀	69	L. Licht (1974)
Rana cascadae	♂	59	Briggs and Storm (1970)
Rana cascadae	♀	46	Briggs and Storm (1970)
Rana erythraea	♂, ♀	2–5	W. Brown and Alcala (1970)
Rana pretiosa	♂	45	L. Licht (1974)
Rana pretiosa	♀	67	L. Licht (1974)

Table 11-5. Life Tables of Five Species of Plethodontid Salamanders of the Genus *Desmognathus* Arranged from the Most Aquatic to the Most Terrestrial*

Species	Percent survival — Males	Percent survival — Females	Age (years)
D. quadramaculatus	100.00	100.00	0–1
	20.30	13.00	3–4
	3.75	5.30	5–6
	0.56	0.08	7–8
	0.14	0.01	9–10
D. monticola	100.00	100.00	0–1
	21.40	14.00	3–4
	5.70	4.90	5–6
	1.56	0.75	7–8
	0.26	0.01	9–10
D. fuscus	100.00	100.00	0–1
	28.80	15.60	3–4
	11.40	3.40	5–6
	1.90	0.24	7–8
	0.14	0.01	9–10
D. ochrophaeus	100.00	100.00	0–1
	35.20	28.50	3–4
	19.50	12.00	5–6
	6.30	2.70	7–8
	0.67	0.05	9–10
D. wrighti	100.00	100.00	0–1
	62.00	47.00	3–4
	51.00	20.00	5–6
	4.25	3.50	7–8
	0.43	0.12	9–10

*Based on Organ (1961).

Population Structure

Populations generally are made up of individuals of different ages and sexes. The timing of recruitment of young into the population depends on the duration of the breeding season and variation in the length of the larval period; the amount of recruitment depends on the effective size of the breeding population and the survivorship of the eggs and larvae. Thus, the recruitment of young in populations of *Rana sylvatica* is high for a short period of time in early summer, because the breeding season of that species lasts for only a few days. Likewise, in mid to late summer, metamorphosing young of highly seasonal breeders, such as *Scaphiopus couchii* and *Bufo boreas*, are recruited in large numbers. Conversely, species that have long breeding seasons or highly variable larval periods may recruit young into their populations during much of their activity seasons. Thus, temperate anurans that have multiple clutches and/or overwintering of some of the tadpoles, as well as many tropical anurans that breed throughout the year, may have nearly continuous recruitment. However, not all tropical anurans follow this pattern. For example, *Bufo typhonius* has a short breeding season with a mass metamorphosis of young (Wells, 1979). Many savanna-inhabiting species have distinct seasonal recruitment of young (e.g., species of *Ptychadena;* Barbault and Trefaut Rodrigues, 1978). Likewise, some salamanders having lengthy aquatic larval periods may recruit metamorphosing young into the population at various times of the year; for example, recruitment of young of the plethodontid *Stereochilus marginatus* occurs from April through November (Bruce, 1971)

Most evidence points to an initial 1:1 sex ratio in amphibians, even though in most explosive breeders the number of males is much greater than that of females at any given time at breeding sites. However, in many cases this is owing to the fact that males tend to remain at the breeding sites, whereas once females have spawned, they leave. This apparently is not the case in *Ambystoma maculatum,* in which captures of adults entering and leaving a breeding pond revealed a much higher percentage of males during a period of 5 years (Husting, 1965). In some amphibians, differences in age-specific mortality between the sexes results in skewed sex ratios. For some unknown reason, survivorship is lower in females than in males of the newt *Notophthalmus viridescens,* so although the sex ratio is 1:1 in recruits, the breeding population consists of about two males for each female (Gill, 1978). The opposite is true in *Triturus vulgaris,* in which age-specific mortality affects males more significantly, with the result that more older breeding adults are females (G. Bell, 1977). Also, in some anurans in which male survivorship is greater than females (e.g., *Rana aurora;* Briggs and Storm, 1970), males outnumber females in the breeding population, whereas the sex ratio is 1:1 in immatures.

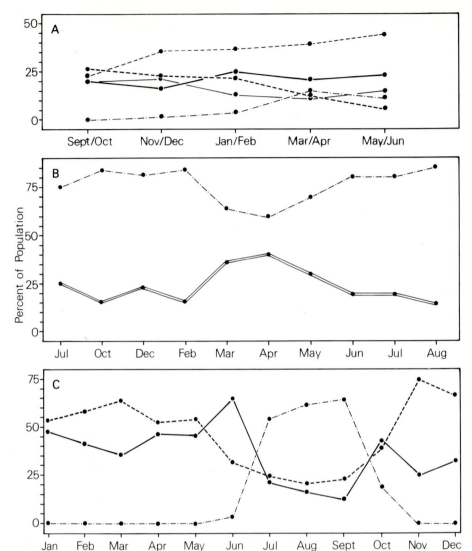

Figure 11-4. Population structure in amphibians. **A.** A plethodontid salamander, *Plethodon richmondi,* in eastern Tennessee, in which small numbers of young are recruited into the population over several months (data from Nagel, 1979). **B.** An anuran, *Eleutherodactylus coqui,* in humid forest in Puerto Rico, in which young are recruited throughout most of the year (data from Stewart and Pough, 1983). **C.** An anuran, *Ptychadena maccarthyensis,* in the seasonally wet savannas of the Ivory Coast, in which young are recruited only after a short breeding season (data from Barbault and Trefaut Rodrigues, 1978). Heavy lines = adults; light lines = subadults; solid lines = males; broken lines = females; double lines = both sexes; dashes-and-dots = juveniles.

By determining the numbers of individuals in different size (age) classes, growth rates, and size or age at sexual maturity of each sex, it is possible to quantify the structure of populations. For example, among pond-breeding *Rana,* sexually mature frogs constituted 50.6% of the population of *R. pretiosa* in Wyoming (F. Turner, 1960b), whereas somewhat lower percentages prevailed in tropical species having year-round recruitment—47.7% in *R. blythi,* 47.0% in *R. macrodon,* and 27.6% in *R. ibanorum,* all in Borneo (Inger and Greenberg, 1966), and 15 to 33% in *R. erythraea* in the Philippines (W. Brown and Alcala, 1970).

Some plethodontid salamanders are relatively long-lived and do not reach sexual maturity until they are at least 2 to 4 years old; furthermore, females produce relatively small numbers of young only biennially. At any given time, populations of these species consist primarily of adults. In contrast, in species of tropical anurans in which the adult life span is short and breeding occurs through-

out the year, the population always contains a high percentage of juveniles. However, in those species that have short breeding seasons, juveniles are absent during part of the year but tend to make up a large percentage of the population after a period of metamorphosis (Fig. 11-4). In the first case annual population turnover is low, whereas in the last two examples population turnover may be moderate or approach 100%, depending on the survivorship of the adults.

Population Density

Most studies of amphibian populations include information on the size of the population only as total numbers without regard to area. Thus, actual densities are impossible to determine from many of the data. Moreover, many studies involving species that aggregate for breeding include data only on the number of breeding individuals. These data are useful in determining the size of breeding congregations but provide no real idea of the density of the species throughout the habitat.

As examples, Husting's (1965) study of *Ambystoma maculatum* revealed the presence of 234 to 315 males and 69 to 155 females annually for each of 5 years in a pond with an area of about 1,250 m^2 in Michigan. In each of five ponds of about 150 m^2 area in the mountains of Virginia, Gill (1978) found breeding populations of *Notophthalmus viridescens* during a period of 3 years to be as low as 6 to 44 (mean = 25) in one pond and as high as 1867 to 2637 (mean = 2195) in another. In Costa Rica, the tree frog *Agalychnis spurrelli* was found breeding in incredible numbers; N. Scott and A. Starrett (1974) estimated about 200 frogs per meter of shoreline around a pond of about 3500 m^2 area and estimated a total of 13,000 frogs in the pond on one night. Gadow (1908) estimated a minimum of 45,000 tree frogs (*Smilisca baudinii*) in a pond of about 750 m^2 in southern Veracruz, Mexico.

The most meaningful estimates of densities of anurans are from censuses taken when the animals are not breeding or of species that do not congregate for breeding. For example, seven species of *Eleutherodactylus* inhabiting cloud forest leaf litter at San Vito, Costa Rica, have densities of 0.0017 to 0.459/m^2 (mean = 0.0775/m^2), but the most abundant of these, *E. stejnegerianus,* has a density of only 0.043/m^2 in the Osa Peninsula of Costa Rica (N. Scott, 1976). Estimated densities of other terrestrial frogs range from 0.00029/m^2 for *Syrrhophus marnocki* in Texas (Jameson, 1955a) to 0.010/m^2 for *Eleutherodactylus lynchi* and 0.016/m^2 for *Atelopus ebenoides* in a páramo in the Colombian Andes, and 0.0152/m^2 for *Pleurodema marmorata* on the Altiplano of Bolivia (Péfaur and Duellman, 1980). The highest densities have been reported for the bufonid *Nectophrynoides occidentalis* on Mont Nimba in West Africa, where on one date the total density was 5.92/m^2 (1.64/m^2 for adults and 4.28/m^2 for juveniles) and at another time, 4.72 adults/m^2 (Lamotte, 1959).

There is great variation in the densities of local populations of plethodontid salamanders (Table 11-6). Several population estimates are available for *Plethodon cinereus* (see T. M. Burton and Likens, 1975, for references). A surface census in Michigan provided an estimate of 0.0496/m^2, whereas digging up of plots of dry and wet litter resulted in estimates of 0.0900 and 0.8900/m^2, respectively. Mark-recapture data from Pennsylvania provided an estimate of 0.2118/m^2, and a surface census after a rain in Virginia gave an estimate of 0.210 to 0.250/m^2. R. Jaeger (1980c) estimated a surface density of 2.2/m^2 in Virginia; density did not vary significantly over 22 days of sampling. Salamander densities in a forest in New Hampshire are extremely high; T. M. Burton and Likens (1975) estimated that populations of four species (*Desmognathus ochrophaeus, Eurycea bislineata, Gyrinophilus porphyriticus,* and *Plethodon cinereus*) consisted of 106,508 individuals in 36.1 hectares. Of these, *P. cinereus* comprised 93.5% with 95,000 individuals having a biomass of 59.85 kg (1.65 kg/ha). These estimates are even more impressive when compared to those of other groups of animals in the same forest; not only are there more salamanders than all birds and mammals combined, but the biomass of salamanders is 2.6 times higher (wet weight) than that of birds during the peak of the breeding season and is about equal to that of shrews and mice combined.

Population densities are dependent on many factors, such as available resources or variation in predator pressure. Thus, the two- to fivefold increase in densities of *Batrachoseps attenuatus* on islands in San Francisco Bay over those on the mainland (P. K. Anderson, 1960) may be the result of lower predation pressure on the islands. Differences in densities may be owing to local microenvironmental conditions (e.g., *Plethodon cinereus*) or time of the year (e.g., *Nectophrynoides occidentalis*). Minor differences in habitat may affect densities; for example, in New Guinea, *Bufo marinus* occurs in densities of 0.0001 to 0.0003/m^2 in undisturbed savannas and 0.0030/m^2 in

Table 11-6. Estimated Densities of Populations of Plethodontid Salamanders

Species	Individuals/m^2	Reference
Aneides aeneus	0.2500–0.1000	R. Gordon (1952)
Aneides lugubris	0.4051–0.4989[a]	P. K. Anderson (1960)
Batrachoseps attenuatus	0.4516	Hendrickson (1954)
Batrachoseps attenuatus	0.9500–2.0155[a]	P. K. Anderson (1960)
Bolitoglossa subpalmata	0.7560–0.9097	Vial (1968)
Desmognathus fuscus	0.4000–1.4000	Spight (1967b)
Desmognathus ochrophaeus	0.0170	R. Gordon et al. (1962)
Ensatina eschscholtzi	0.1482–0.1729	Stebbins (1954)
Plethodon cinereus	0.0496[b]	Test and Bingham (1948)
Plethodon cinereus	2.3670–2.5830[b]	T. M. Burton and Likens (1975)
Plethodon glutinosus	0.0040	R. Gordon et al. (1962)
Plethodon glutinosus	0.4180–0.8440	Semlitsch (1980)
Plethodon jordani	0.0220	R. Gordon et al. (1962)
Plethodon yonahlossee	0.0070	R. Gordon et al. (1962)

[a]Island populations.
[b]Extremes of estimates from Michigan and New Hampshire; other estimates are intermediate (see text).

the vicinity of human habitation, where food presumably is more abundant (G. Zug et al., 1975). The habitat of *Eleutherodactylus coqui* in Puerto Rico was altered experimentally by placing bamboo retreats in some study plots; after 1 year the experimental plots contained significantly more frogs than did the control plots (Stewart and Pough, 1983). The highest reported density of an amphibian is 116/m² for the spring-dwelling salamander *Eurycea nana,* which reaches these densities in mats of algae that serve as shelter and contain an abundance of food (Tupa and W. Davis, 1976).

FACTORS REGULATING POPULATIONS

Although much has been learned since F. Turner's (1962) review of anuran demography, some of his same basic questions need to be addressed more specifically in the field and laboratory. What are the causes of age-specific mortality? How are growth rates and reproductive success reflected in population densities and structures? Are particular populations regulated by density-dependent factors or affected by density-independent factors?

Density-independent factors, particularly climatic variability, are especially important in the survivorship of amphibian larvae. After a 4-year study of a population of *Ambystoma tigrinum,* Semlitsch (1983) concluded that environmental factors affecting the drying rate of ponds were the most important mechanisms controlling larval population size; in some years, no young were recruited into the postmetamorphic population, but in a year with favorable climatic conditions, more than 1000 young survived and left one pond. Shoop (1974) also implied that climatic variation was responsible for yearly fluctuations in the recruitment of young of *A. maculatum,* and desiccation of ponds is the primary cause for larval mortality in *Triturus vulgaris* (G. Bell and Lawton, 1975).

Amphibian larvae developing in temporary ponds seem to be far more susceptible to mortality because of drought than are those that develop in permanent bodies of water. However, these larvae, too, may not survive some climatic perturbations, as evidenced when all *Ambystoma opacum* larvae and nearly all *Rana clamitans* tadpoles overwintering in a pond in Maryland were killed by the pond freezing during a severe winter (Heyer, 1979a). Exceedingly heavy rains or snow melt can cause flash floods in streams and thereby eliminate or at least greatly reduce larval populations, such as noted for populations of *Ascaphus truei* by Metter (1968a).

The net effect of these environmental fluctuations is to reduce or eliminate a cohort of offspring and thereby reduce the size of the postmetamorphic population and to modify the age structure of the population. For example, Bannikov (1948) showed that population density of *Rana temporaria* was significantly higher in years following breeding seasons with favorable climates than in those years following droughts. The population of *Hyla*

rufitela on Barro Colorado Island, Panama, remained more or less constant and confined to one or two breeding sites for nearly 50 years; the population expanded greatly and dispersed over much of the island in 1980, possibly as a result of favorable conditions (short dry season) in 1979–80 (Rand et al., 1983).

Variable climatic conditions also affect adults. During unusually severe winters, shallow ponds may freeze to the bottom and result in the deaths of anurans hibernating there, as noted for *Rana pipiens* by Manion and Cory (1952). Also, floods can be devastating to adults. We found only two individuals of the small bufonid *Atelopus mindoensis* along a 200-m stretch of a mountain stream in Ecuador after a flash flood had scoured away nearly all streamside vegetation. Before the flood we had observed 77 individuals along the same stretch of stream. A 28-day drought resulted in 99% mortality in a population of *Plethodon shenandoah* on talus slopes in Virginia, but had no perceptible effect on the population of *P. cinereus* living in adjacent habitats with deep soils (R. Jaeger, 1980b).

Different reproductive strategies also are important density-independent factors. This is especially evident in the different survivorship curves among five species of *Desmognathus;* Organ (1961) showed that the series— *D. quadramaculatus, monticola, fuscus, ochrophaeus, wrighti*— is not only one of progressively greater terrestrialism but also one of progressive increase in survivorship through the early years of sexual maturity (Table 11-5). The variability in survivorship of aquatic eggs and larvae is much greater than that of adults. Therefore, reproductive strategies that involve the removal of eggs and/or larvae from water might enhance survivorship. In an analysis of reproductive strategies of tropical anurans, Duellman (1978) emphasized that ephemeral ponds were "preferable" to permanent ponds for egg and larval development because of the absence of predatory fishes. One way of increasing survivorship in temporary ponds is the production of multiple small clutches; in this way, anurans in humid tropical environments do not put all of their reproductive energy into a single large clutch, which may desiccate. Moreover, placement of eggs on vegetation above water or in floating or arboreal foam nests seems to be an adaptation for increasing survivorship of eggs associated with temporary ponds. Hatching at relatively advanced larval stages and rapid growth to metamorphosis minimize the duration of the aquatic stage and maximize survivorship (see Chapter 2 for more extensive discussion).

Maximizing growth rates is important not only for larval stages but also for postmetamorphic individuals. Predation pressure is exceedingly high on recently metamorphosed young anurans, especially by snakes (Tester and Breckenridge, 1964; Arnold and Wassersug, 1978) and even by tabanid fly larvae (Jackman et al., 1983).

Larval stages of both salamanders and anurans are

subject to heavy predation in permanent ponds by fishes and in temporary ponds by insects, such as diving beetles and dragonfly larvae (see Chapter 10). In temporary ponds in the American tropics, tadpoles also are eaten by the carnivorous tadpoles of *Ceratophrys* and *Leptodactylus pentadactylus* (Heyer et al., 1975). Natural mortality among larvae of *Ambystoma tigrinum* was caused mainly by predation (J. Anderson et al., 1971). Calef (1973) attributed most of the mortality of tadpoles of *Rana aurora* in British Columbia to predation, because (1) tadpoles kept in the laboratory on starvation diets survived for many weeks, even though they did not grow; (2) tadpoles living in densities up to 100 times normal could survive and grow to metamorphosis in the absence of predators; and (3) predation rates observed in the field and simulated in the laboratory were sufficient to account for much of the mortality observed in the natural population.

However, other studies have concluded that density-dependent intraspecific competition is the factor controlling survivorship of larvae. Thus, on the basis of field and laboratory experiments, survivorship is negatively density-dependent in *Ambystoma maculatum* (Wilbur, 1972), *Bufo americanus* (Wilbur, 1977b), *Rana tigerina* (Dash and Hota, 1980), and *Scaphiopus holbrooki* (Semlitsch and Caldwell, 1982). Not all species respond in the same way to increased densities. Comparable field experiments on three species of *Ambystoma* in Michigan by Wilbur (1972) showed that *A. laterale* increased both the number of survivors and the percentage survivorship when the density of conspecifics was increased, presumably by dividing available food among smaller larvae and by increasing the larval period. An increase in density of *A. tremblayi* resulted in a higher number of survivors without a higher percentage of survivorship, but the larvae were smaller and required a longer time to reach metamorphosis. At high densities, only a few larvae of *A. maculatum* survived, but these were large and grew rapidly. Wilbur concluded that the effect of larval density on *A. maculatum* occurred early in their development and that the few larvae which survived this competition were able to exploit the food supply and grow rapidly; on the other hand, the plastic growth rates and variable sizes at metamorphosis of *A. laterale* and *A. tremblayi* are adaptations to the uncertain environment of temporary ponds.

Factors regulating survivorship of amphibian larvae may change temporally and spatially, even in adjacent ponds, as demonstrated for *Bufo americanus* by Brockelman (1969). In one of his experimental ponds, time of metamorphosis, individual growth variability, and mortality were related directly to initial tadpole density, and size at metamorphosis was related inversely to initial tadpole density. In a second experimental pond, there was a lack of significant density effects; high mortality rates were affected by an abundance of predators, chiefly dragonfly nymphs

and leeches. A more complex situation was described for *Pseudacris triseriata* by D. Smith (1983). In temporary pools on the rocky shore of Isle Royale, Michigan, pools near the lake shore frequently do not persist for the duration of the larval period. In other pools, predation by dragonfly nymphs (*Anax*) eliminates most or all tadpoles. In other pools that persist and lack *Anax,* competition exists for food, and survivorship of tadpoles is density-dependent. In some aquatic sites, especially temporary ones, density-independent factors, such as unfavorable climatic conditions, can be most important in determining survivorship, whereas in these same sites during periods of favorable climatic conditions and in permanent ponds, resource availability and competition can be major controlling factors. The importance of predation can be negated by adverse environmental conditions, and the importance of competition may be negated by intense predation.

Although the interactions of these factors are complex, an understanding of the regulation of larval populations is emerging. However, the mechanisms controlling the populations of adults are not so well understood. It is assumed that most adult amphibians are lost to the population through predation or disease, but adequate documentation is lacking. Catastrophic, density-independent events (e.g., effects of drought on *Plethodon shenandoah* and floods on *Atelopus mindoensis*) are unpredictable and can cause crashes of local populations.

Few studies document density-dependent effects on populations of adult amphibians. Tyler (1976) reported that a population of *Bufo marinus* in New Britain had increased to the point that available insects became scarce and emaciated toads died daily. The increase in numbers of *Eleutherodactylus coqui* in study plots provided with bamboo retreats, which are defended and used as oviposition sites (Stewart and Pough, 1983), suggests that shelter and oviposition sites may be a limited resource and therefore a density-dependent factor regulating populations of that frog. Although predation probably is the major mortality factor in adults of *Hyla rosenbergi,* Kluge (1981) suggested that injuries resulting from male-male combat in the defense of nests might be an important factor in regulating the number of males.

The accumulating data on the dispersion of juveniles, fidelity to breeding ponds, limited home ranges of non-aggregative breeders, and shapes of home ranges suggests that populations are made up of demes that have individual characteristics of growth, survivorship, and structure. This phenomenon has been documented best in *Notophthalmus viridescens* (Gill, 1978). These populational or demic parameters have genetic implications. Inger et al. (1974) found that genetic homogeneity was negatively correlated with the degree of movement for breeding purposes (see Chapter 16). Samallow (1980) noted distinct temporal changes in allele and/or genotype frequency distributions within cohorts of young *Bufo bo-*

reas and concluded that mortality among young toads was not genetically random. These studies emphasize the necessity of integrating ecological and genetic studies of natural populations.

If real progress is to be made in understanding the population dynamics of amphibians, it is essential that investigators standardize the parameters and their measurements. The usefulness of many of the existing data is extremely limited because comparisons cannot be made, and a meaningful synthesis is impossible.

CHAPTER 12

Community Ecology and Species Diversity

To fully understand an assemblage or a community, not only must its structure be known but the flow of energy and materials among species must be assessed. Both these aspects are in their infancy as far as herpetofaunal assemblages are concerned.

Harold Heatwole (1982)

Coexisting species of organisms constitute a community or assemblage, within which interactions may occur among species. Basically this chapter addresses the structure of amphibian communities and examines the patterns of assemblages in different parts of the world. Adequate studies of amphibian communities are pitifully few, and only in a few cases have the mechanisms regulating community structure been demonstrated.

COMMUNITY STRUCTURE

Until recently, theoretical community ecology has been dominated by the assumption that interspecific competition is of primary importance in the determination of species composition in most communities (Roughgarden, 1983; Schoener, 1983). Most inferences about interspecific competition concern exploitative competition—use of the same resource by two or more species of organisms—but some studies have demonstrated interference competition—one organism limiting another species' access to a resource. However, predation may affect differentially the relative abundance of coexisting species and thereby have a profound effect on the outcome of interspecific competition; also predation may affect the species composition of communities. Recent reevaluations of earlier descriptive studies of vertebrate communities (e.g., Strong et al., 1979) have questioned the sta-

tistical validity of much of the indirect evidence that has been cited in support of the role of competition in structuring communities. Strong et al. (1979) and Simberloff (1983) suggested that much of the purported structural pattern in vertebrate communities simply reflects interspecific variation in ecological attributes usually associated with resource utilization, rather than a systematic partitioning of resources consistent with competition and niche theory.

Studies of amphibian communities have been uneven in their approaches and thoroughness. Most studies of salamanders have emphasized the ecological relationships of two or just a few sympatric or parapatric species, whereas many anuran communities have been studied in their totality but in less detail. Nothing is known about caecilian communities.

It is necessary to distinguish between experimental and observational studies of amphibian communities. In experimental studies (e.g., Inger and Greenberg, 1966; Hairston, 1981; Morin, 1983a) the numbers of one or more species are directly altered, and changes in the abundance or behavior of other species are monitored. Such experiments can demonstrate unequivocally the existence of interspecific interactions. However, without a detailed knowledge of natural history, the mechanistic basis of the interaction may be obscure (e.g., Hairston, 1981), thereby making it difficult to assess the generality

275

of the experimental results. Moreover, for obvious logistical reasons, experimental manipulations usually involve only a few species, may extend through only a fraction of a generation, and may be conducted at spatial scales inappropriate for understanding community dynamics.

Most observational studies emphasize resource partitioning—the differential utilization of the physical and/or biotic environment by different species. Commonly this has been accomplished by measurements of a resource matrix (niche breadth) of a species and of the association of two or more species with respect to one or more resources (niche overlap) (see Hurlbert, 1978, for discussion and formulas). These measurements form the bases for the determination of the community structure.

Because of the different approaches used in their respective studies, communities of terrestrial salamanders, terrestrial anurans, and aquatic larvae are discussed separately. Much of the material has been taken from Toft's (1985) review of resource partitioning in amphibians. The study of amphibian communities is difficult because of potential interactions at different stages in the life cycle. Furthermore, it should be kept in mind that much of the structure of amphibian communities may result from interactions between amphibians and other organisms (e.g., bat predation on anurans; Tuttle and M. Ryan, 1981) rather than from interspecific interactions among amphibians alone.

Terrestrial Salamanders

Plethodontid salamanders have been the subjects of many ecological studies. Hairston's (1949) pioneering work on several species of *Plethodon* in the Applachian Mountains documented elevational and macrohabitat differences and food-size partitioning; the patterns were interpreted as the result of interspecific competition. Subsequent intensive studies on pairs of species of *Plethodon* were performed by various workers—Dumas (1956) on *P. dunni* and *vehiculum,* R. Jaeger (1971, and papers cited therein) on *P. cinereus* and *shenandoah,* and Hairston (1983b, and papers cited therein) on *P. glutinosus* and *jordani.* Field experiments showed that closely related species of *Plethodon* can compete strongly under natural conditions. Sharp habitat partitioning—narrow elevational sympatry in *P. jordani* and *glutinosus* and microhabitat parapatry in *P. cinereus* and *shenandoah*— results from this intense competition. These are examples of interference competition for space under logs on the forest floor. *Plethodon* are territorial, and in defense of their territories they may inflict wounds on intruders. In the case of *P. cinereus* and *shenandoah,* the former is more aggressive and is expanding its range, whereas *P. shenandoah,* which can tolerate drier conditions than *P. cinereus,* is becoming restricted to dry talus slopes that are uninhabitable by *P. cinereus.* In the Smoky Mountains, *P. jordani* and *glutinosus* have only slight elevational sympatry in a narrow zone where fluctuating environmental conditions alternately favor *P. jordani* (cooler and moister)

or *P. glutinosus* (warmer and drier). However, in the Balsam Mountains the two species are more broadly sympatric, apparently because of less intense interspecific competition.

Salamanders of the genus *Desmognathus* occur in a variety of sympatric assemblages and display interesting patterns of microhabitat partitioning. In the southern Appalachian Mountains, three to five species form an array from aquatic to terrestrial habitats. Both moisture and predation gradients exist along this habitat gradient. Although Hairston originally interpreted the microhabitat partitioning of these salamanders as the result of interspecific competition, he (1980) hypothesized that predation is the primary factor structuring salamander niches along the gradient. Alternatively, differences in habitat and food size resulting in differences in body size may be interpreted as the results of interspecific competition. Evidence for the occurrence of interspecific competition includes niche shifts between allopatry and sympatry among three species of *Desmognathus* in Pennsylvania (Krzysik, 1979) and in two species in Florida (Means, 1975). Presumably different factors—competition, predation, and physiological tolerances—vary in importance in different communities.

Anurans

Studies of anuran communities have analyzed habitat-specific assemblages—forest-floor, stream-edge, and breeding-pond communities— as well as entire tropical communities.

Forest-Floor Communities. Assemblages of anurans living amidst leaf litter on the forest floor are much like those of salamanders in that the same species inhabit the area throughout the season of activity. The numbers of species and densities of anurans inhabiting the leaf litter in tropical forests have been summarized by N. Scott (1982), who noted that the numbers of litter-inhabiting anurans are much higher in the American tropics than in Africa, Borneo, or the Philippines, but diversities are similar in wet forests of Costa Rica and Borneo (Table 12-1).

Toft's (1982 and citations therein) work on anurans living in the litter in tropical forests in Gabon, Panama, and Peru showed that resources are partitioned in different ways depending on the species and on environmental conditions. For example, litter-inhabiting anurans have specific local distributions along moisture gradients between ridges and ravines in Panama, but in homogeneous locations in Peru and Gabon, anurans do not partition the microhabitat. Seasonal and diel activities are partitioned in all tropical forest habitats; in the American tropics this is especially evident in comparing diurnal dendrobatids with the mostly nocturnal *Eleutherodactylus* (Duellman, 1978; Toft and Duellman, 1979).

Among tropical litter inhabitants, food is partitioned by both prey size and type. As emphasized by Toft (1985),

Table 12-1. Comparative Numbers of Species of Anurans Inhabiting the Leaf Litter in Lowland Tropical Forests

Locality	Latitude	Rainfall (mm) [dry months]	Number of species	Reference
Lombé, Cameroon	4°N	±4000 [3]	12	N. Scott (1982)
Makokou, Gabon	1°N	±1700 [?]	4*	Toft (1982)
Sakaerat, Thailand	14°N	±1500 [6]	8	Inger and Colwell (1977)
Negros Island, Philippines	9°N	1430 [4]	11	W. Brown and Alcala (1964)
Nanga Tekalit, Borneo	1°N	5000 [0]	19	Lloyd et al. (1968)
Guanacaste, Costa Rica	10°N	1670 [6]	7	N. Scott (1976)
La Selva, Costa Rica	10°N	±3600 [1]	20	N. Scott (1976)
Rincón de Osa, Costa Rica	9°N	±4000 [2]	19	N. Scott (1976)
Silugandi, Panama	9°N	2000 [3]	19	Heatwole and Sexton (1966)
Barro Colorado island, Panama	9°N	2700 [4]	12	Myers and Rand (1969)
Río Canclón, Panama	8°N	2000 [5]	9	Heatwole and Sexton (1966)
Santa Cecilia, Ecuador	0°N	4400 [0]	30	Duellman (1978)
Belém, Brazil	2°S	2860 [6]	9	Crump (1971)
Río Llullapichis, Peru	10°S	2220 [2]	25	Toft and Duellman (1979)

*Dry season only.

there are two adaptive peaks of foraging modes—sit-and-wait foragers and widely ranging, searching foragers. These peaks are not exclusive, for some species are intermediate in their foraging strategies. Moreover, differences in physiological, morphological, and behavioral attributes exist among species using these adaptive strategies. Sit-and-wait foragers usually are cryptically colored and are capable of activity bursts to capture a few large prey or to escape predation. Active foragers concentrate on small, common prey and are capable of sustained, low levels of activity (A. Bennett and P. Licht, 1973; Taigen and Pough, 1983). Also, many active foragers are highly toxic and aposematically colored. Because of the coevolution of physiological, morphological, and behavioral traits leading to these adaptive peaks, these differences would exist in the absence of interspecific competition. However, interspecific competition seems to be evident within feeding guilds of these anurans. For example, patterns of food-size partitioning among the ant-eating guild in homogeneous forests in Peru show that there is considerable overlap in food, but this overlap diminishes during the season of lower food abundance (Toft, 1980a). The same is true for species of *Eleutherodactylus* in the non-ant-eating guild in Panama (Toft, 1980b). Similar trophic partitioning exists among four species of West Indian *Eleutherodactylus* (K. Jones, 1982). Syntopic species pairs differ in the size of the prey eaten; three species are sit-and-wait foragers on foliage and one is an active diurnal forager.

Although competition may play a role in microhabitat partitioning in litter anurans, specific physiological tolerances also are involved (and may be more important). For example, those species most resistant to desiccation, such as the bufonids *Atelopus* and *Bufo,* inhabit drier ridges in Panama, whereas those species that are least resistant— *Colostethus,* small *Eleutherodactylus,* and *Dendrobates auratus*— are in ravines. However, on Taboga Island, *D. auratus* has no anuran competitors and forages in dry areas; this suggests that perhaps competition may be more important and that the species has broader physiological tolerances than recognized previously (Toft, 1985). Pough et al. (1977) observed a similar physiological basis for habitat partitioning among Jamaican *Eleutherodactylus.*

Stream-side Communities. Some species of anurans are restricted to riparian habitats and other species move to streams for breeding. Three streams in Sarawak in northern Borneo supported 24 species of anurans (Inger, 1969). The nine most abundant species were grouped into four ecological types: (1) four large species that are strictly terrestrial, riparian, and weakly clustered in their distributions; (2) two small to large species that are partially arboreal, riparian, and weakly clustered; (3) two small to large species that are partially arboreal, riparian, and strongly clustered; and (4) one large, mainly arboreal, strongly clustered species that is not restricted to stream banks. Populations of *Rana blythi, ibanorum,* and *macrodon* were manipulated by the removal of one species from one stream and of a second species from another stream. The removal of a species resulted in an increase in numbers of individuals of the other two species; thus, Inger and Greenberg (1966) concluded that interspecific competition affected population size.

Breeding Ponds. Many species of anurans migrate to temporary ponds for breeding; during the time that they are at the ponds the potential exists for interspecific interactions. Because of different species-specific tolerances to temperature and responses to rainfall, different species enter the breeding community at different times. This succession provides a temporal partitioning of the pond (Wiest, 1982, and references therein; Fig. 12-1). Moreover, a diel pattern is evident among some species. In a temporary pond in Kenya, six species were most abundant in the pond early in the evening and four were most abundant in the middle of the night (R. Bowker and M. Bowker, 1979).

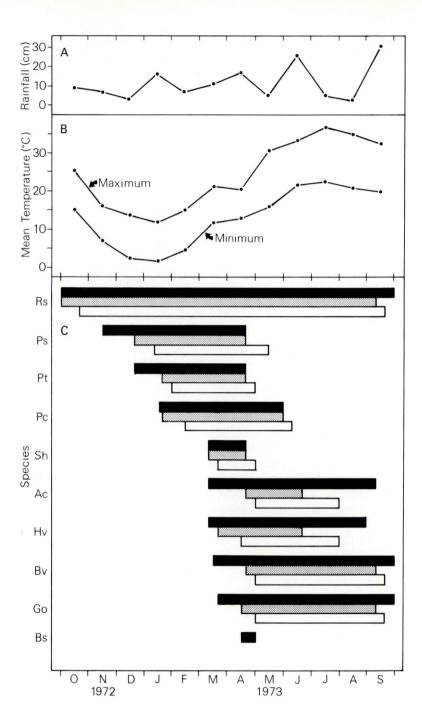

Figure 12-1. Anuran succession in a temporary pond in Brazos County, Texas. **A.** Monthly rainfall (October 1972–September 1973) in centimeters. **B.** Mean monthly maximum and minimum temperatures (°C). **C.** Anuran succession. Solid bars = calling males; shaded bars = breeding; open bars = larvae. Abbreviations for species: Ac = *Acris crepitans*, Bs = *Bufo speciosus*, Bv = *B. valliceps*, Go = *Gastrophryne olivacea*, Hv = *Hyla versicolor*, Pc = *Pseudacris clarki*, Ps = *P. streckeri*, Pt = *P. triseriata*, Rs = *Rana sphenocephala*, Sh = *Scaphiopus holbrooki*. Based on Wiest (1982).

Among tropical anuran breeding assemblages, vocalization was deemed to be the primary factor separating species, followed by calling sites and oviposition sites, for 10 species of hylids in Costa Rica (Duellman, 1967b) and for 5 species of hylids in Brazil (Cardoso, 1981). Results of analyses of calls of hylid frogs in breeding communities in Costa Rica, Brazil, and Ecuador led Duellman and Pyles (1983) to suggest that the acoustic environment is partitioned in particular anuran communities and

that the pattern of acoustic partitioning is similar in disjunct communities of like habitat but with different species compositions.

Resource partitioning among synchronously breeding species also involves calling sites and oviposition sites, but the most important factor seems to be advertisement calls (see Chapter 4). As examples, Creusere and Whitford (1976) concluded that among five synchronously breeding species of anurans in the Chihuahuan Desert in

New Mexico, advertisement call was the primary ecological factor allowing for species recognition, and the second factor was calling site. R. Humphries (1981) noted that the presence or absence of other species did not affect the timing, intensity, or duration of breeding activity by a given species in a breeding community of 11 species of anurans using a pond in Australia. He hypothesized that distinct advertisement calls are important in resource partitioning by anurans.

Tropical Communities. Because of their abundance and diversity in the wet tropics, anurans have been the subjects of several community studies. The most comprehensive of these is Duellman's (1978) analysis of the herpetofauna at Santa Cecilia on the Equator in Amazonian Ecuador, where temperature and photoperiod are relatively stable throughout the year and rainfall is more or less evenly and abundantly distributed throughout the year. Eighty-one species of anurans occur at Santa Cecilia. These were analyzed with respect to macrohabitat (primary forest, secondary forest, clearings), microhabitat (terrestrial, bush, tree), diel activity (nocturnal, diurnal), and food.

Eleven of the 69 species in the primary forest are restricted to that habitat; 58 of these are among the 68 species occurring in the secondary forest (3 restricted there). Eighteen of the species in the primary forest and 25 in the secondary forest are among the 26 species occurring in clearings (1 restricted there). Therefore, 18 species are macrohabitat generalists and 15 are macrohabitat specialists. In the primary forest, 24 species occur in trees (more than 1.5 m above ground), 46 in bushes, and 39 on the ground or amidst leaf litter (some species occur in more than one microhabitat). The same categories in the secondary forest have 20, 48, and 31 species, and in the clearings 0, 14, and 16 species. The only diurnal frogs are on the forest floor; 7 species there are entirely diurnal, 9 are both diurnal and nocturnal, and 13 are completely nocturnal.

Four major feeding guilds were recognized. Actively foraging terrestrial species that specialize on ants include five dendrobatids, four bufonids, and five microhylids; in addition, one *Eleutherodactylus* and two hylids (*Sphaenorhynchus*) specialize on ants. The terrestrial leptodactylid *Physalaemus petersi* eats only termites. Two species are carnivores and feed on frogs—the terrestrial *Ceratophrys cornuta* and the arboreal *Hemiphractus proboscideus*. The other species of anurans in this community are sit-and-wait foragers and eat a variety of prey, of which orthopterans are the most abundant items, followed by coleopterans, lepidopterans, and homopterans.

In this community, the macrohabitat is only weakly partitioned; the secondary forest contains a slightly depauperate assemblage of the primary forest. The subcommunity in clearings primarily is made up of a few species that also occur in the forests. By contrast, within the forest there is striking vertical stratification of species

from the ground to bushes and to trees. All bush- and tree-dwelling species are nocturnal. The terrestrial subcommunity in the forest consists of species that are associated with swamps and those in the leaf litter; this subcommunity is further divided into nocturnal and diurnal species.

Although 81 species occur at Santa Cecilia, differences in activity cycles, microhabitat preferences, and feeding habits result in numerous guilds that have little or no overlap. Furthermore, these anurans have diverse reproductive modes, so they are using different oviposition sites, and their tadpoles (if present in the mode of life history) develop in diverse aquatic habitats (Fig. 12-2). Duellman (1978) concluded that this large number of species could coexist because of the absence of, or little pressure from, interspecific competition and that the absence of interspecific competition was the result of: (1) the abundance of available resources; (2) structural heterogeneity of the environment; (3) climatic equability of the environment; and (4) differential spatial and temporal utilization of resources by the fauna. Furthermore, he suggested that populations were controlled by unpredictable environmental fluctuations and by predation, so abundances are kept in check below the level where competition might be important.

Similar patterns of resource utilization were documented for 53 species of anurans in a seasonally dry rainforest in Amazonian Peru (Toft and Duellman, 1979) and for 37 species at Belém, Brazil (Crump, 1971). A comparison of anuran communities in adjacent areas of broadleaf evergreen forest, deciduous dipterocarp forest, and agricultural land in northeastern Thailand (Inger and Colwell, 1977) revealed that in that seasonally dry region only 24 species of anurans occurred. Nineteen species were found in the evergreen forest, 20 in the deciduous forest, and 19 in the agricultural land, with the greatest faunal overlap between the evergreen and deciduous forests. Larger and more distinct guilds existed in the evergreen forest (most predictable habitat) than in the other habitats. Inger and Colwell (1977) suggested that unpredictable environments tend to prevent the formation of distinct guilds, which are an expression of specialization in resource use; therefore the greater species richness of more predictable habitats may be a function of guild formation.

Aquatic Larvae

Most studies of larval communities have been concerned with anuran tadpoles, but the effects of salamander larvae of some salamanders, principally *Ambystoma* and *Notophthalmus,* on tadpoles also have been investigated (e.g., Wilbur, 1972; Morin, 1981). Amphibian larvae lend themselves to field and laboratory manipulations, and numerous experimental studies have provided an understanding of the mechanisms of community structure in these organisms. However, the resulting interpretations are not always consistent. For example, an *Ambystoma-*

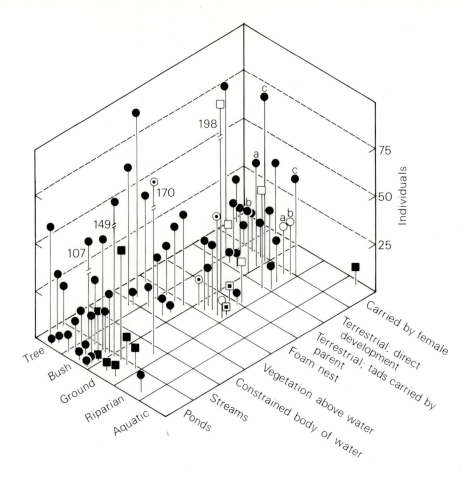

Figure 12-2. Community structure of 69 species of anurans inhabiting primary lowland rainforest at Santa Cecilia, Ecuador. Each cell in the grid represents a combination of microhabitat and site of egg development. Circles are sit-and-wait foragers; squares are active foragers feeding primarily on ants. Solid symbols are nocturnal species; open symbols are diurnal species; open symbols with dark centers are diurnal and nocturnal species. Lengths of lines leading to the symbols represent the numbers of individuals collected. Symbols noted a, b, and c indicate three species that are active in one habitat by day and another by night. Based on data in Duellman (1978).

Rana community in Michigan was considered to be structured primarily by interspecific competition (Wilbur, 1972), but the structure of tadpole communities in Maryland, Panama, and Thailand were considered to be the result of adaptive modifications of the tadpoles, environmental fluctuations, and predation (Heyer, 1976, and references therein).

Amphibian larvae, especially tadpoles, exploit the extraordinarily rich, but sometimes highly transient, aquatic environments that are at least seasonally available. Anuran larvae have been shown to partition resources in these temporally fluctuating environments. This partitioning is evident with respect to macro- and microhabitat within a temporal framework. Temporal partitioning is conspicuous within tadpole communities, as shown for temperate forest ponds by Heyer (1976), Seale (1980), and Wiest (1982), for tropical ponds by Dixon and Heyer (1968) and Heyer (1973), and for a tropical stream by Heyer (1976) (see Fig. 12-1). For example, among 10 species of anuran larvae developing in each of two ponds in Thailand, no more than 5 were found at the same time in one pond and 6 in the other (Heyer, 1973). Furthermore, densities of synchronously developing tadpoles showed temporal differences; at one pond, tadpoles of

Glyphoglossus molossus and *Polypedates leucomystax* contributed most heavily to the biomass, but the peak of the former was in April and of the latter in June.

Anuran larvae are highly specialized "feeding machines." Tadpoles have distinct interspecific differences in mouth structures and thus differ in their abilities to gather food in different macro- and microhabitats. Moreover, structural differences are related to their abilities to inhabit flowing or still water, as well as their positions in the water column (see Chapter 6). Macro- and microhabitat partitioning is primarily a result of the adaptive modifications of the tadpoles. For example, in a stream community in Panama, the tadpoles of *Colostethus nubicola* have an anterodorsal mouth and feed on the surface; tadpoles of *Centrolenella fleischmanni* have ventral mouths and long, muscular tails and feed amidst the detritus on the bottom, and tadpoles of *Smilisca sila* have anteroventral mouths and weak tails and feed on the bottom of quiet pools (Heyer, 1976). The tadpoles of *Colostethus* are present throughout the year, *Centrolenella* in the rainy season, and *Smilisca* in the dry season when water flow is minimal.

Macrohabitat partitioning in the choice of types of ponds or streams is a matter of choice by the adults; survival of the larvae is dependent on their hatching (or being placed) in a suitable aquatic habitat. Heyer et al. (1975) argued effectively that predation influences tadpole survival and larval community structure in ponds in the tropics; because of differing risks of predation, similar kinds of habitat partitioning occur in temperate ponds (Heusser, 1970a; Woodward, 1982b). Avoidance or reduction of predation is accomplished by larvae inhabiting ephemeral ponds, where aquatic predators are few or absent. Larvae that inhabit permanent aquatic environments also inhabited by aquatic predators have mechanisms to avoid predation. For example, in Panama, tadpoles of *Bufo typhonius* have noxious skin secretions and survive in large pools in streams inhabited by the predatory tadpoles of *Leptodactylus pentadactylus* (Wells, 1979). Tadpoles of *Hyla geographica* move about in large schools in lakes inhabited by many species of predatory fish (Duellman, 1978); schooling presumably reduces predation.

Microhabitat partitioning by larvae that develop synchronously is accomplished principally by the positioning of the larvae in the water column, as noted for tadpoles by Heyer (1973) and *Ambystoma* larvae by J. Anderson and Graham (1967). Presumably, partitioning of food by tadpoles is a function of, first, the abilities of various species to ingest particles of different sizes and, second, the position of the tadpole in the water column (Heyer, 1974c). Although exploitative interspecific competition for food among tadpoles has not been demonstrated convincingly, the diversity of foraging behavior and buccal structures for ingesting particles of food of specific sizes suggests that food is partitioned, and that the more generalized feeders may be able to overlap with several other species. On the other hand, the tadpoles of *Gastrotheca* commonly are the only tadpoles in ponds at high elevations in the Andes; these tadpoles have extremely generalized buccal structures that allow them to ingest a wide spectrum of particle sizes (Wassersug and Duellman, 1984).

The factors regulating larval communities in temporary ponds are correlated with the duration of larval development. Environmental uncertainty and predation put absolute limits on the maximum time that larvae can remain in the pond before metamorphosing (Wilbur and Collins, 1973). The probability of the pond drying up increases with the time of residency in the pond. Also, the longer a pond is in existence, the greater will be the accumulation of predators and the risk of predation. Invasion of small ponds by predators may result in the extinction of all larvae in the pond (Morin, 1983a; D. Smith, 1983). Both intra- and interspecific competition is correlated with relative limits of time in temporary ponds. In the absence of predation, or even in the presence of predation (Woodward, 1982c), population sizes of larvae can increase to the point of intense competition. Field studies have documented that tadpoles can have an extreme impact on food density (principally algae) in natural ponds, and suggest that competition for food can

occur under natural conditions (Seale, 1980). Density-dependent interspecific competition for food has been demonstrated primarily in experimental conditions (Morin, 1983b, and references therein).

Exploitative competition for food is the ultimate threat at high densities, but the proximate competitive factor is interference, which is mediated by growth inhibition, both intra- and interspecifically (see Chapter 6). By inhibiting the growth of another species, the superior competitor decreases its own time to metamorphosis while increasing that of the inferior competitor. Because of differential rates of predation on different sizes of larvae and at different times during the season, the outcome of interspecific competition can be altered by such inhibition (Morin, 1981).

It is evident that the structure and maintenance of larval communities are dependent on complex interrelationships of physical factors, predation, and intra- and interspecific competition. Furthermore, the effects of these factors change with respect to temporal utilization of the environment by different species with respect to the duration of development.

SPECIES DIVERSITY

The concept of species diversity as a unitary measure involving both the numbers of species (richness) and relative numbers of individuals per species (equitability) has received considerable attention (see Pianka, 1977, for review). Species richness is simply the number of species, whereas equitability indicates how individuals in a community are distributed among species. If all species in a community contain the same number of individuals, the apportionment is maximally equitable. If some species are abundant and some rare, the distribution is inequitable. Several ecologists (e.g., Peet, 1975) have argued that the concept of species diversity is biologically meaningless, because it encompasses two separate concepts (species richness and equitability). Therefore, these components of species diversity of amphibians are discussed separately.

Species Richness

Generally it is known that the number of species of ectothermic vertebrates is higher in the tropics than at high latitudes. Although this is not necessarily true of salamanders, it is true of anurans (Table 12-2). General, broad patterns of species richness in amphibians as a group show latitudinal trends, such as an increase from 10 to 40 species between Maine and Florida in eastern United States (Fig. 12-3). However, integrated with the latitudinal trend are trends along moisture gradients. For example, in North America, the greatest numbers of species are in areas of high rainfall, principally in southeastern United States and secondarily in the northwest.

Comparisons of amphibian species richness among

Table 12-2. Latitudinal Gradient in Anuran Species Diversity in the New World

Site	Degrees N. latitude	Number of species	Reference
George Reserve, Michigan	42	8	Collins (1975)
University of Kansas Reservation	39	9	Fitch (1965)
Brazos County, Texas	31	11	Wiest (1982)
Tehuantepec, Mexico	16	17	Duellman (1960)
Barro Colorado island, Panama	9	19	Myers and Rand (1969)
Santa Cecilia, Ecuador	0	81	Duellman (1978)

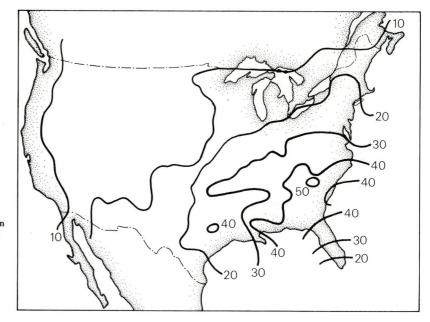

Figure 12-3. Species densities of amphibians in North America constructed from compilation of numbers of species in grids of 100 miles square (160 kilometers square). Note the increase in number of species to the southeast and less so to the northwest, both areas characterized by high rainfall. A peninsula effect (diminishing number of species) is evident in peninsular Florida. Redrawn from Kiester (1971).

various regions in the tropics emphasize the importance of moisture to the richness of the amphibian fauna. For example, a strong gradient in the number of species from south (high number) to north (low number) in the Yucatan Peninsula is strongly correlated with the amount of rainfall (J. Lee, 1980). A latitudinal gradient corresponding to decreasing moisture is evident in the numbers of species of amphibians in supratreeline habitats in the Andes; the moist páramos in Colombia and Ecuador support up to five species, whereas only one species is present in the dry parts of the Altiplano in northern Argentina (Péfaur and Duellman, 1980). Even at the same latitude, this moisture gradient is apparent. At Belém, Brazil, at the mouth of the Rio Amazonas, rainfall amounts to about 2800 mm annually but is unevenly distributed, so that most of the rain falls in one 6-month season; 37 species of anurans are known from the vicinity of Belém (Crump, 1971). At Santa Cecilia, Ecuador, in the western part of the Amazon Basin, about 4400 mm of rain falls throughout the year; 81 species of frogs are known from Santa Cecilia (Duellman, 1978). Within anuran communities inhabiting leaf litter in tropical forests, species richness is

positively associated with the amount of rainfall and negatively associated with the number of dry months (Table 12-1).

Among anurans, generally there is a decrease in the number of species with altitude, although local environmental conditions may alter this gradient. A transect essentially along the Equator from the Amazon Basin to the eastern crest of the Andes reveals that at 340 m in the tropical rainforest as many as 81 species of anurans exist in one community. At elevations of 1400–1600 m in cloud forest, the largest community consists of 23 species, and at elevations of 2500–2700 m only 17 species coexist. Richness diminishes to only 5 species in subparamo habitats at elevations of 3000–3200 m and to 4 species in páramo above 3500 m (Fig. 12-4).

Salamanders not only require moist conditions like anurans but also prefer cooler temperatures. Accordingly, altitudinal gradients in salamanders commonly differ from those of anurans. For example, among 15 species of plethodontid salamanders recorded along a transect in southwestern Guatemala (D. Wake and J. F. Lynch, 1976), only 4 species occur in tropical forest below 1000 m; 6

occur at elevations of 1000–2000 m, and 10 live between 2000 and 3000 m.

Abundance and Equitability

Few sufficiently quantitative studies have been carried out to permit evaluation of the abundance of amphibians in different regions, although some individual species, such as the salamander *Plethodon cinereus,* have been studied in detail (see Chapter 11).

The only detailed comparisons of amphibian abundance are the works of M. Lloyd et al. (1968) and Inger (1980a) among communities in tropical forests in southeastern Asia and the analyses of forest floor communities in Central America, Africa, and southeastern Asia (N. Scott, 1976, 1982; Inger, 1980b). These comparisons showed that both terrestrial amd arboreal anurans were far more abundant in diurnal and nocturnal samples from forests in northern Borneo and peninsular Malaya than in the seasonally dry forests in northeastern Thailand. For example, the average number of terrestrial, nonriparian frogs captured per day at Sakaeret, Thailand, was 0.12 in dry evergreen forest and 0.27 in deciduous forest, as compared with 1.31 per day at Nanga Tekalit in Borneo. However, these figures are extremely low in comparison with those from Central America—11.6 for Rincón de Osa, Costa Rica, 14.7 for La Selva, Costa Rica, and 29.8 for Silugandi, Panama.

Altitudinal changes in abundance have been noted for forest-floor anurans in Costa Rica (N. Scott, 1976); at two lowland sites the numbers of amphibians on the forest floor were $0.12/m^2$ and $0.15/m^2$, whereas at 1200 m there were $0.55/m^2$. A similar increase in abundance was noted among samples of anurans taken at elevations of 1010, 1200, and 1425 m on the slopes of Cuernos de Negros in the Philippines (W. Brown and Alcala, 1961). On the slopes of Volcán San Marcos in Guatemala, the overall abundance of salamanders increases at higher elevations (D. Wake and J. F. Lynch, 1976).

It has been well documented that in many groups of organisms, species richness is high in tropical forests, but a fallacy that has persisted in the literature is that in tropical forests no one species is common, thereby implying that equitability is high. As recently as 1976, Maiorana stated, "There are many species in the tropics, but generally individuals of any one of them are rare." This may be true for some organisms, such as trees, but considerable evidence indicates that this is not true for amphibians. For example, in large samples of anurans inhabiting the leaf litter in tropical forests in Borneo, the Philippines, and Central America (reviewed by N. Scott, 1976), the most abundant species was represented by at least twice the number of individuals of the second-most abundant species, and in some cases the most abundant species was represented by more individuals than all of the other

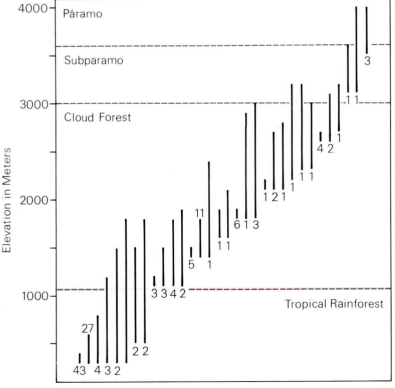

Figure 12-4. Patterns of altitudinal distribution of anurans along an equatorial transect from the crest of the Andes (Paso de Guamaní) to the Amazon Basin (Santa Cecilia) in Ecuador. Numbers denote the number of species having the altitudinal distribution indicated by the vertical bars. Based on data in Duellman (1978, 1979).

Table 12-3. Equitability of Anurans in Leaf Litter at Different Elevations in Costa Rica*

Locality	Elevation (m)	Number of plots	Number of species	Number of individuals	Most abundant (%)	Second-most abundant (%)
La Selva	100	19	15	165	42	19
Rincón de Osa	20	20	24	135	37	18
San Vito	1200	10	8	266	83	6

*Based on N. Scott (1976).

species combined. In an aseasonal tropical rainforest at Santa Cecilia, Ecuador, 5665 anurans representing 81 species were collected (Duellman, 1978). The 5 most abundant species represented 22% of the total number of individuals, whereas the five least abundant species (4 with one individual each, and 1 with two) represented only 0.1% of the total. These figures are biased in that sampling was not complete; not all individuals of common species were collected.

Comparable data are available from Lost Lake, South Carolina, in the eastern United States (S. Bennett et al, 1980). Among five species of salamanders sampled over 2 years, *Notophthalmus viridescens* composed 85% and *Ambystoma opacum* only 0.1% of 3641 individuals. Among 11 species of anurans, *Gastrophryne carolinensis* and *Bufo terrestris* were the most abundant, composing 36% and 29%, respectively, of 11,381 individuals, whereas 2 species, *Hyla squirella* and *H. versicolor,* were each represented by only a single individual. The figures for temperate-zone anurans are not greatly different from those for tropical environments.

The decline in species richness but increase in abundance of individuals with increasing altitude results in lower equitability at higher elevations. This was demonstrated by N. Scott's (1976) analysis of litter plots at different elevations in Costa Rica (Table 12-3), which shows a twofold difference in relative abundance of the most common species at a montane site as compared with lowland sites. This comparison is especially meaningful between one lowland site, Rincón de Osa, and the montane site, San Vito, because the same species, *Eleutherodactylus stejnegerianus* (listed as *E. bransfordi* by N. Scott, 1976), is the most abundant anuran at both sites, but the relative abundance increases from 37% to 83% from Rincón de Osa to San Vito. The second-most abundant species (*E. longirostris*— 18%) at Rincón de Osa does not occur at San Vito, but the second-most abundant species (*E. ridens*— 6%) at San Vito composes only 0.7% of the fauna at Rincón de Osa.

The available data indicate that among anuran communities, equitability generally is low in both temperate and tropical communities and that equitability decreases with altitude in tropical regions

EVOLUTION OF AMPHIBIAN COMMUNITIES

Several hypotheses have been proposed to explain the numbers of species and individuals making up communities and the differences among communities, especially between those in the tropics and in the temperate regions (see Pianka, 1966, for review). These are the: (1) evolutionary time theory, (2) ecological time theory, (3) climatic stability theory, (4) spatial heterogeneity hypothesis, (5) productivity hypothesis, (6) competition theory, and (7) predation theory. The following discussion of these concepts emphasizes their applicability to amphibian communities and assemblages.

The evolutionary time theory advocates that community diversity increases with the age of the community. From that premise it has been argued that temperate communities are impoverished because of geologically recent glaciations or other disturbances, whereas tropical communities are older (more mature) and hence more diverse. However, the idea of the antiquity and immutability of equatorial rainforests has been challenged effectively by paleoclimatological and geological evidence in support of drastic climatic changes in equatorial regions during the Quaternary (see Prance, 1982, for review). In fact, this climatic-ecological fluctuation has been used to explain the richness of the rainforest biotas, including the diversity of anurans (Duellman, 1982a). Vicariance models of three groups of anurans are correlated with the patterns of Quaternary ecological changes in the Amazon Basin and provide a historical explanation for the coexistence of closely related species in the upper Amazon Basin.

The concept of ecological time deals with shorter time spans than the theory of evolutionary time and emphasizes the time required for the dispersal of species into newly opened areas of suitable habitat rather than the time necessary for the evolution of new species or for the adaptation of existing species. Ecological time would seem to be an important determinant of diversity only in cases where there are pronounced barriers to dispersal. This idea is most applicable to insular biotas and may explain the absence of some continental species on nearby islands, but in general the theory has little applicability to continental amphibian communities.

Stability of climate and vegetation creates a stable environment for animals and allows them to specialize on food and microhabitat. Thus, regions with stable climates allow the evolution of finer specializations and adaptations than do regions with more erratic climates, because of the relative constancy of resources. Klopfer and MacArthur (1961) proposed that more species can occupy the unit of habitat space, and niches are smaller (i.e., organisms more specialized) in stable environments.

The mechanism suggested for the control of diversity by the theory of climatic stability also can apply to climatic predictability; thus, a region with a highly predictable but variable annual climatic pattern conceivably could allow species to specialize on those resources that are predictable from year to year.

It has been shown that many reproductive specializations in anurans are associated with highly stable environments (see Chapter 2); therefore, the presence of anurans having such specialized reproductive modes in a given assemblage is dependent on the climatic stability of the region. For example, generally the successful development of terrestrial or arboreal eggs is dependent on continuous high atmospheric humidity; there is a high degree of fidelity of such anurans to regions with high atmospheric humidity (Duellman, 1982a). The patterns of the complex timing of breeding, gestation, and oviposition by plethodontid salamanders differs in eastern and western North America and in the highlands of Central America; these differences correspond to different but predictable climatic patterns in the three regions (see Chapter 2). Thus, climatic stability is considered to be a major factor in the structuring of amphibian communities and to be an important component of diversity.

Everything else being equal, more complex habitats should support more species than simpler ones because each species can live on a different part of the environmental mosaic. Spatial heterogeneity may exist at several levels. Macrospatial heterogeneity involves topographic relief, and it is obvious that topographically diverse regions contain more habitats (and thus more species) than topographically simple areas. This aspect of spatial heterogeneity is important in between-habitat diversity, and the differences in amphibian assemblages in diverse habitats were discussed earlier in this chapter.

Microspatial heterogeneity is significant in explaining within-habitat diversity. Microspatial complexity includes horizontal, vertical, and qualitative heterogeneity of physical and biotic elements in the environment. Complex habitats contain more microhabitats than homogeneous habitats and may contain subcommunities that are absent in less complex habitats. For example, bromeliads in cloud forests in the American tropics provide a microhabitat that is used by many salamanders and anurans, and some of these species are restricted to that habitat. Therefore, such species are present only in communities in which that microhabitat is available.

All other things being equal, regions of greater productivity can support more species than regions of lesser productivity, because each species uses less of the total range of resources. Furthermore, a greater number of individuals can be supported in highly productive environments. Productivity is known to be correlated with rainfall. Regions of the world having high amounts of rainfall annually support the richest amphibian assemblages. However, another component of productivity may be important for terrestrial amphibians inhabiting the leaf litter on the forest floor. In Costa Rica, leaf fall is continuous throughout the year both in montane cloud forest and in lowland rainforest, but in the former the leaf litter is about twice as deep as in the lowland forests, and the montane forests support a greater number of individuals of litter-inhabiting anurans (N. Scott, 1976). The higher temperature in the lowlands results in a more rapid rate of leaf decay, thereby reducing the amount of the microhabitat.

Many plants store the products of their primary production and expend this stored energy in one great bloom of flowering and seeding; this tends to reduce the stability of the system. In attempting to explain the depauperate numbers of species and individuals of amphibians in the leaf litter on the forest floor in Indo-Malayan forests as compared with neotropical forests, Inger (1980b) suggested that the primary causal factor was the seasonality of fruiting by the dominant trees. The Bornean and Malayan forests are dominated by dipterocarps, trees characterized by the synchronous fruiting of more than 100 species with intervals between such reproductive explosions exceeding 1 year. The synchronized fruiting should lead to reduction in abundance of an entire group of arthropod primary consumers during nonfruiting years; this should affect the total size of the insect population and therefore the numbers of insectivorous secondary consumers, such as anurans.

The theoretical basis for the role of interspecific competition in community structure was discussed previously. However, this concept has been broadened and modified with respect to latitudinal gradients in species diversity. Dobzhansky (1950) suggested that natural selection is controlled largely by the exigencies of the physical environment in the temperate zones, whereas inter- and intraspecific competition is more important in determining the course of evolution in the tropics. Presumably, natural selection would proceed in a different direction in aseasonal tropical environments because density-independent mortality factors such as drought and cold seldom occur there. According to Dobzhansky's reasoning, catastrophic mortality usually causes selection for increased fecundity and/or accelerated development and reproduction, rather than selection for competitive abilities and interactions with other species. These ideas have been expanded by various theoreticians to argue that in comparison with temperate species, tropical species (1) are more highly evolved, (2) possess finer adaptations, (3) have more restricted diets, and (4) have more specific habitat requirements.

The component arguments of the competition hypothesis imply that the latitudinal gradient in competition allows more species to coexist in a given environment; therefore competition for resources is keener and niches are smaller. Thus the competition hypothesis makes many of the same predictions as the theory of climatic stability. However, there is one major difference. The competition hypothesis implies that more individuals occupy the same unit of habitat space in more diverse communities, whereas the theory of climatic stability predicts that the same number of individuals will be supported by a unit of habitat, regardless of the diversity, but there are fewer individuals of more species in tropical habitats.

It has been shown that diversity of reproductive modes in anurans contributes to increased species richness in humid tropical habitats, but this apparently is in response to climatic stability. Furthermore, it is generally conceded that spatial heterogeneity provides more microhabitats in aseasonal tropical habitats than elsewhere. But does this higher number of species in tropical environments mean that there is more competition? In order to address this issue it is necessary to consider (1) the spectrum and abundance of available resources, (2) the stability of the resources, (3) the extent of resource utilization by members of the community, (4) the amount of overlap in resource utilization by members of the community, and (5) the degree to which resources are limiting, rather than other factors (e.g., predation). A tenet basic to the entire theory of competition is that one or more required resources must be limited (demand being greater than supply) for effective competition to occur. There is no evidence that interspecific competition is greater in amphibian communities in the tropics than in temperate habitats.

Advocates of the predation hypothesis suggest that there are proportionately more predators (individuals and/or species) in the tropics and that by limiting various prey populations to low densities, predators reduce the level of competition among and between prey species. Presumably this lower level of competition then allows the addition and coexistence of new intermediate types of prey. As noted by Pianka (1966), two predictions may be drawn from the predator hypothesis: (1) Competition among prey species will be less in more diverse communities than in simpler communities. (2) There should be an increase in the proportion of predatory individuals and/or species as communities become more diverse.

There is no available evidence relating to the first prediction, but Arnold (1972) demonstrated a latitudinal gradient in the number of species of frog-eating snakes corresponding to the gradient in the number of species of frogs.

It is evident from the limited data on amphibian communities that no single factor universally explains the structure of these communities. Furthermore, in a given community the regulating factors may change temporally.

Most of the literature dealing with community structure and species diversity omits consideration of the history of the region and the biota. Each community is an assemblage of species, each one of which has had a separate phylogenetic history. Although the component species of an existing community are subjected to the same environmental variables, prior to the formation of this community, some of the component species may have been subjected to different environmental conditions and may not have been in the same community. Thus, those species may have evolved prior to coexistence and the evolution of some of the attributes that allow them to exist in the present community. It is most unlikely that the component species evolved syntopically and that the various adaptations of each species evolved in response to other species in the present community. Actually the adaptations, ecological tolerances, and basic resource utilization probably were established at the time and place of origin of the species, which probably was not in the present community. Therefore, an understanding of community structure and of the differences among communities in different regions necessitates not only a knowledge of the factors regulating the present assemblage of species but also a knowledge of the history of component species.

MORPHOLOGY

Musculo-skeletal System

Substantial portions of this book deal with aspects of the biology of amphibians that could be described and analyzed only with the advent of modern technological methodology. Among the oldest studies of amphibians are morphological descriptions of the macro- and micro-structure of selected organs or organ systems. Observation and description are the morphological premises on which interpretations are founded—interpretations that might address the phylogenetic history of form, its functional significance, ontogenetic development, or variation. Although the species (or populations thereof) is the operational unit of evolution, the morphology of a species represents its observable interface with the environment. Thus, knowledge of the structure of an organism is prerequisite to an understanding of its phylogenetic relationships, behavior, and relationship with biotic and abiotic aspects of the environment.

Although various details of amphibian morphology are described throughout this book in order to elucidate particular subjects (e.g., vocalization, feeding, and so on), two chapters have been allocated to the treatment of general structural patterns. The present chapter is dedicated to basic architecture—that is, the musculoskeletal system that constitutes the framework of support for the various organ systems described in the following chapter.

The musculoskeletal system of adult amphibians can be divided into three convenient units—the cranium in-cluding the hyobranchial apparatus, the axial component, and finally the appendicular musculoskeletal system. Because salamanders are, in most respects, the most generalized morphologically of the three orders, they are discussed first in each subsection. Myological descriptions of salamanders are the most detailed and nearly complete, and in this chapter they serve as the base to which the muscle complexes of caecilians and anurans are compared. The ways in which the three units are integrated to produce the distinctive Bauplan of each order are discussed at the end of the chapter.

SKULL AND HYOBRANCHIUM

The cranium and hyobranchial apparatus is a complex and diverse architectural unit in amphibians. As in all vertebrates, it is the seat of the central nervous system and the primary sense organs of sight, olfaction, hearing, and equilibrium. In anurans laryngeal cartilages derived from the larval hyobranchial apparatus allow for vocalization. The hyobranchial apparatus lying in the floor of the mouth between the pectoral girdle (anurans and salamanders) and the mandible is the foundation for the attachment of mandibular, branchial, and tongue muscles; this musculoskeletal unit is the mechanical system for ventilation as well as securing, manipulating, and ingesting food.

The skull is composed of endochondral and membranous, or dermal, bones. Endochondral elements are formed by the development of osteoblasts in cartilage that is formed in the chondrocranium of the larval or prehatching organism. Endochondral bones form the neurocranium and auditory capsules of amphibians, the middle ear bones, the bony portions of the hyobranchium, the jaw articulation, and usually the symphysis of the lower jaw.

The more numerous dermal components form intermembranously in a connective tissue precursor and may be categorized as investing bones of various types. Roofing and flooring bones cover the neurocranium and olfactory capsules to varying degrees. The primary osseous components of the upper and lower jaws are dermal. A variety of dermal bones brace the upper jaw against, and help to suspend it from, the braincase; these bones, as well as those of the jaws, invest cartilage that is derived from the chondrocranium. Only one dermal bone is internal in some amphibians. This is the septomaxilla in anurans, which is involved in protection and support of nasal cartilages and the nasolacrimal duct in the olfactory region. The septomaxilla is largely external in caecilians and salamanders, and there is evidence that it is of dual endochondral and dermal origin in salamanders. Anurans are unique among amphibians in two other respects. They have fewer cranial bones and a simplified hyobranchial apparatus. A few taxa are characterized by neomorphic bones that have no known homologues in other vertebrates; all such elements described thus far are intermembranous in origin.

Classically, the skull and hyobranchial structure have been discussed relative to the classes or origins of the bones. But complex structures are explained more readily in terms of functional units or complexes. Accordingly, the following accounts are organized into discussions of the bones and associated musculature of (1) the neurocranium (including the auditory capsule and middle ear bones), (2) the nasal capsule, (3) neurocranial investing and bracing bones (including those of the auditory and olfactory capsules), (4) upper and lower jaws, (5) the suspensorium, and (6) the hyobranchial apparatus. Most details of chondrocranial structures internal to the osseous skull retained in adults are not discussed here but are included in the accounts of larval structure in Chapter 6.

As any student of comparative anatomy quickly realizes, there is no satisfactory and totally logical way in which to deal with cephalic musculature. It is an anatomical morass of muscles of mixed origins, uncertain homologies, and variable names (see Francis, 1934, for a list of synonyms of salamander muscles, as an example). In general, the following descriptions follow the nomenclature of Edgeworth (1935). Two of the most common schemes of muscle descriptions are based on (1) patterns of innervation and (2) embryonic origins of the muscles.

Embryonic origin (i.e., somatic origin innervated by spinal nerves versus visceral origin innervated by cranial nerves) provides no category for muscles that presumably are somatic (e.g., eye muscles) but are innervated by cranial nerves. Insofar as possible, the following descriptions are grouped functionally in association with the appropriate architectural unit of the skull.

Three types of voluntary muscles are involved with the cranium. Somatic or parietal muscles are derived embryologically from the myotomes of the epimere (i.e., the dorsal plate of the mesothelial wall) and are innervated primarily by spinal nerves. Somatic cranial musculature includes the eye muscles and epaxial (dorsal) and hypaxial (ventral) muscles of the trunk that attach to the back of the head and constitute the neck musculature. Visceral or branchial muscles are derived embryologically from the mesoderm of the hypomere (i.e., the lateral plate of the mesothelial wall) and are innervated by dorsal-root homologues of cranial nerves. The latter category includes some hyoid arch muscles as well as one or two muscles that originate on the head and insert on the pectoral girdle. The remaining cranial musculature is hypobranchial; embryologically it is derived from myotomes behind the gills that grow downward, turn forward, and extend anteriorly to the jaw. Hyobranchial muscles generally are innervated by ventral-root homologues of cranial nerves.

The organization of cephalic muscle descriptions is as follows. The section on the neurocranium includes the eye muscles, major trunk muscles of the head and neck region, and muscles extending between the ear and pectoral girdle. Except for the eye muscles, the association of these muscles with the cranium is arbitrary and a matter of convenience. Both cervical and ear muscles are derived from somatic musculature of the trunk, but the actions of these muscles affect the opercular-columellar apparatus or movement of the head as a whole. Moreover, the muscles insert on endochondral elements derived from the larval chondrocranium that give rise to the adult neurocranium; thus they are described in this unit. Musculature associated with the nasal capsule is treated in that section. Muscles that open and close the jaws are described in the section on the suspensorium, and those involved in swallowing and moving the hyoid and tongue are treated in the section dealing with the hyobranchial apparatus.

Salamanders

Although the skulls of many species of salamanders have been described in the literature in the last 100 years, to date no synthesis exists that summarizes the cranial diversity of the group. Early contributions include the descriptions of W. Parker (1877, 1882), that of E. Emerson (1905) on the general anatomy of *Typhlomolge rathbuni,* Francis's (1934) anatomical monograph on *Salamandra salamandra,* and the works of H. Wilder (1894) and I.

Wilder (1925) on plethodontids. Many useful papers were published by students from the University of Stellenbosch in South Africa. Among the most useful of these descriptive papers based on histological preparations are Rÿke (1950) on *Onychodactylus japonicus,* Theron (1952) on *Ambystoma maculatum,* and Papendieck (1954) on *A. macrodactylum.* Less detailed descriptions of many plethodontids are available in Hilton (1945, 1946a, 1946b). D. Wake (1963, 1966) has provided extensive information on plethodontids. A substantial part of the recent literature deals only with particular parts of the skull—for example, the sound-conducting apparatus (Monath, 1965), the inner ear (Lombard, 1977), and the nose (Jurgens, 1971). Paedomorphic taxa (e.g., *Cryptobranchus, Necturus*) are the most frequently illustrated owing to their use as laboratory specimens. Broader, comparative treatments are available in D. Wake (1966) for the plethodontids, Özeti and D. Wake (1969) for salamandrids, and Larsen (1963) who described some aspects of the cranial osteology of neotenic and transformed salamanders of a variety of taxa. Carroll and Holmes (1980) illustrated the skulls of a number of salamanders in their paper on the ancestry of the group. Lebedkina (1968, 1979) contributed to an understanding of the development and evolution of the amphibian skull with an emphasis on salamanders.

The skulls of salamanders generally are less compact than those of caecilians and more robust than those of most anurans. Dermal roofing bones are relatively small and often few in number (Table 13-1). The temporal fossae are open, the orbits large, and commonly the nasal region is poorly roofed. The maxillary arcade is incomplete, and the neurocranium poorly developed. The cranial architecture of salamanders is diverse and reflects adaptations to a variety of terrestrial and aquatic habitats.

The literature dealing with the cephalic myology of salamanders is extensive and was summarized by Francis (1934). Work previous to this tended to concentrate on comparative studies of particular muscle systems (e.g., Walter, 1887, on visceral muscles of salamanders, anurans, and reptiles; Lubosch, 1913, 1915, and Luther, 1914, on the muscles innervated by the trigeminal nerve in amphibians; Edgeworth, 1935, on the cephalic musculature of vertebrates). Comparative studies on salamanders are rare and limited in scope. One example is the work of Drüner (1901, 1903, 1904), who compared the muscles supplied by Cranial Nerves (C.N.) VII, IX, and X, and the hypoglossal nerve in several species. There has been no synthesis of the diversity of cranial musculature of salamanders. Because of the different approaches to myological studies and the diversity of species studied (albeit limited with respect to the total diversity of salamanders), a thorough synthesis is not attempted here. Francis's (1934) account of the myology of the generalized, terrestrial species *Salamandra salamandra* is

the most nearly complete, and unless otherwise specified, the myological descriptions that follow are based primarily on that work.

Neurocranium.   The neurocranium, housing the brain and auditory organs, extends from the posterior limits of the nasal region to the occiput. In salamanders, the neurocranium is composed of four elements, only two of which can be distinguished in the mature organism (Fig. 13-1). The anterior part is the orbitosphenoid (= orbitotemporal), which probably is a partial homologue of the sphenethmoid of caecilians and anurans. The auditory capsule is composed primarily of the prootic. Posterior portions may arise from separate centers of ossification (Bonebrake and Brandon, 1971, and references therein), but in the adult these centers of ossification fuse with the exoccipital to form the occipital region of the neurocranium. This posterior unit is referred to as the occipito-otic by most authors.

Auditory apparatus.—The auditory apparatus of salamanders is highly variable and has attracted considerable attention since Kingsbury and Reed's (1909) original investigations. More recent contributions are those of Lombard (1977) on the inner ear and Monath (1965, and included references) on the opercular apparatus. The sound-conducting apparatus is composed of two structures. The columella (= stapes) develops first and is predominant during larval stages, whereas the operculum appears relatively late in the life cycle among those taxa that possess it and, generally, is considered to be a terrestrial adaptation for sound transmission.

According to Monath (1965), in the generalized and primitive condition characteristic of some hynobiid and ambystomatid salamanders, the opercular apparatus consists of two discrete elements—an operculum and columella—both of which are associated with the fenestra ovalis (= fenestra vestibuli of some authors) in the lateral wall of the otic capsule (Fig. 13-2). The columella is bony and bears a distal stylus. The operculum is cartilaginous or bony, and forms at metamorphosis in the fenestra ovalis posterior to the columella. In both the hynobiids and ambystomatids, there is a trend toward reduction or fusion of the operculum with the lateral wall of the otic capsule. The salamandrids exhibit a derived condition in which the columella is lost and the cartilaginous or bony operculum fills the fenestra ovalis. In the plethodontids, the operculum probably is fused with the columella. The latter is a rod-shaped element that is fused proximally to the operculum, which appears as a plate that fills nearly all of the fenestra ovalis.

Muscles of the auditory region.—Just as the bony structure of the opercular apparatus varies, so do muscle connections between this region and the pectoral girdle (Fig. 13-2). The majority of salamanders have a so-called opercularis muscle, but this muscle is absent in some hynobiids and ambystomatids, and in all cryptobran-

Table 13-1. Probable Homologies of Cranial and Hyobranchial Elements in the Three Recent Orders of Amphibians

Salamanders	Caecilians	Anurans
Orbitotemporal [= orbitosphenoid]	Os sphenethmoidale	Sphenethmoid
———	!Orbitosphenoid	———
———	!Mesethmoid [= prenasal process, presphenoid]	———
———	!Basisphenoid	
———	!Supraethmoid [= infrafrontal, dermethmoid]	*Dermal sphenethmoid
Occipito-otic	Os basale	Otoccipital
!Prootic	!Prootic	″Prootic
!Opisthotic	!?Opisthotic	———
	!?Pleurosphenoid	———
!Exoccipital	!Exoccipital	″Exoccipital
Parasphenoid	!Parasphenoid	′Parasphenoid
*Columella [= stapes]	Columella [= stapes]	*Columella [= stapes]
*′Operculum	!?Operculum	′Operculum
	*Nasopremaxilla	———
*Nasal	!Nasal	Nasal
Premaxilla [= intermaxilla]	!Premaxilla	Premaxilla
*Septomaxilla	″Septomaxilla [= turbinale, nariale]	Septomaxilla [= intranasal]
———	Maxillopalatine	
*Maxilla	!Maxilla	Maxilla
*Prefrontal	*′Prefrontal	———
*Palatopterygoid	———	
″Palatine	!Palatine	*Palatine
	Pterygoquadrate [= pterygoid process of quadrate]	———
*Pterygoid [= palatopterygoid]	!Pterygoid	Pterygoid
Palatoquadrate	!Quadrate	Quadrate
*Lacrimal [= ectethmoid]		
———	*Ectopterygoid [= pterygoid]	———
!Quadratojugal	———	*Quadratojugal
Squamosal [= paraquadrate]	Squamosal	Squamosal
———	′*Orbital [= ocular, postfrontal]	———

* = Element not present in all taxa.
! = Fused in all taxa to form compound element.
″ = Fused in most taxa to form compound element.
′ = May be fused in a few taxa to form compound element.
? = Occurrence of center of ossification questionable, or homology uncertain.

chids, amphiumids, sirenids, proteids, and the plethodontid *Typhlomolge*. As Monath (1965) discussed in detail, there actually are two different muscles that may originate from the fenestral plate; both are referred to as the m. opercularis and both function to transmit vibrations from the substrate and pectoral limb to the perilymph of the inner ear. In hynobiids, salamandrids, and ambystomatids, the m. opercularis inserts on the suprascapular cartilage and is derived from a trunk muscle, the m. levator scapulae. In plethodontids, the m. opercularis inserts of the bony scapulocoracoid of the pectoral girdle; in this family, the muscle is derived from the m. cucullaris major, a visceral muscle of the branchial arch that is innervated by C.N. XI. In one plethodontid (*Pseudotriton montanus*), parts of three muscles attach to the fenestral plate; the m. cucullaris major takes its origin from the plate, whereas the m. levator scapulae (a muscle of the pectoral girdle) and the m. intertransversarius capitis in-

ferior (part of the dorsal trunk musculature) insert on the plate.

Eye muscles.—The eye musculature is composed of three groups of muscles. The four recti muscles have tendinous origins from the orbital walls of the neurocranium, insert on the eye, and act to turn the eyeball in the horizontal and vertical planes at right angles to its own optical axis. The mm. rectus superior, rectus inferior, and rectus anterior are innervated by C.N. III (oculomotor), whereas the m. rectus posterior is innervated by C.N. VI (abducens). Additional rotation of the eyeball is provided by the oblique muscles. The m. obliquus superior arises by a tendon from the antorbital cartilage (wall separating nasal capsule and orbit) and is innervated by C.N. IV (trochlear). The m. obliquus inferior also arises from the antorbital cartilage, but this muscle is innervated by C.N. III (oculomotor). The two remaining eye muscles are the mm. retractor bulbi and levator

Salamanders	Caecilians	Anurans
Frontal	Frontal	Frontoparietal
Parietal	Parietal	
Vomer	Vomer [= prevomer]	'*Vomer
————	Pseudodentary	————
Dentary	!Dentary	Dentary
————	!Splenial	————
————	!Coronoid	————
————	!Supraangular	————
Mentomeckelian	!Mentomeckelian	*Mentomeckelian
[= mentomandibular]		
————	Pseudoangular	
————	!Angular	Angulosplenial [= angular, goniale]
Prearticular [= goniale, coronoideum]	!Prearticular	?
*Articular	!Articular	?
————	!?Complementale	
Ceratohyal [= anterior cornua of hyoid]	Ceratohyal	*Anterior cornua of hyoid
Copula I [= Basibranchial I]	Basibranchial I [= Copula I]	Copulae, hypobranchials, and ceratobranchials fuse to form hyoid plate and associated process of anurans
Copula II [= Basibranchial II]	Basibranchial II [= Copula II]	
Hypobranchial I	?	
*Hypobranchial II	?	
Ceratobranchial I [= Epibranchial I]	Ceratobranchial I	
'Ceratobranchial II [= Epibranchial II]	Ceratobranchial II	
'Ceratobranchial III [= Epibranchial III]	!Ceratobranchial III	
*'Ceratobranchial IV [= Epibranchial IV]	!Ceratobranchial IV	
————	!Ceratobranchial V	————

bulbi. The retractor muscle originates from the orbitosphenoid, inserts on the medial surface of the eyeball, and bears a tendinous connection to the eyelids. This muscle, which is innervated by C.N. VI (abducens), retracts the eyeball medially and closes the eyelids. The m. levator bulbi is a thin muscular sheet that lies between the eyeball and the roof of the mouth. The muscle is innervated by C.N. V (trigeminal) and has the dual function of elevating the eye and thus simultaneously enlarging the buccal cavity.

Neck muscles.—Derivatives of the dorsal muscle mass (m. dorsalis trunci) attach the posterior end of the skull to the axial skeleton and provide for lateral flexion of the skull on the vertebral column. Superficially, the m. intertransversarius capitis superior (= m. longissimus capitis) arises from the dorsal side of the transverse processes of the second and third vertebrae and inserts over the posterolateral surface of the auditory capsule. Medial and deep to this muscle is the m. rectus capitis posterior

(= m. occipitalis), which arises from the neural spine and neural arch of the first vertebra and inserts over the dorsal surface of the occipital region of the skull. The third muscle, the m. intertransversarius capitis inferior, is a continuation of the subvertebral trunk musculature that arises from the transverse process of the second vertebra and inserts on the ventral surface of the occiput of the skull. A number of other muscles originate on the posterior aspect of the skull and insert on the pectoral girdle. Because their action involves movement of the girdle rather than the head, they will be considered in the appendicular musculoskeletal system.

Nasal Capsule. The rostral region of salamanders differs from those of caecilians and anurans in being wide and usually having distinctly separated nasal capsules (see Francis, 1934, or Jurgens, 1972, for a discussion of this feature) (Fig. 13-1).

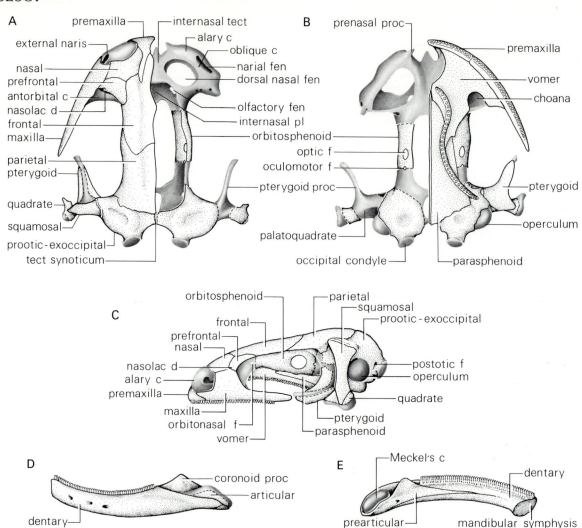

Figure 13-1. Skull of *Salamandra salamandra* redrawn from Francis (1934). **A.** Dorsal. **B.** Ventral. **C.** Lateral. **D.** Mandible in lateral aspect and **E.** medial aspect. Bones are stippled; cartilage is gray. Abbreviations: c = cartilage; f = foramen; fen = fenestra; nasolac d = nasolacrimal duct; pl = planum; proc = process; tect = tectum.

The capsules are enclosed by the premaxillae and maxillae as well as various other dermal investing bones such as the vomers, nasals, prefrontals, frontals, and lacrimals. The protection afforded by these cranial elements in salamanders is somewhat less than that typical of caecilians and greater than that of anurans. Thus, the cartilaginous components of the nasal capsule tend to be more extensive than those of caecilians, and less well developed than those of anurans. The septomaxilla is sporadic in occurrence (present in hynobiids, dicamptodontids, ambystomatids, and many plethodontids); however, its absence in salamanders is not associated with fusion to adjacent elements as it is in caecilians.

The medial walls of the nasal capsules are formed by the septum nasi which is synchondrotically united with the orbitosphenoid bone. Generally, the septum is short and thick. Anteriorly, the nasal capsule walls diverge from one another to produce an internasal cavity that contains the intermaxillary gland. The posterior wall of each capsule is formed by a lateral, cartilaginous extension from the orbitosphenoid bone, the lamina orbitonasalis. The roof (tectum nasi) of the capsule is fenestrate, as is the floor (solum nasi). The anterior end of the capsule is formed by a cup-shaped cartilaginous structure (alary cartilage).

Narial muscles.—Opening and closing of the external naris in salamanders is controlled by three smooth muscles described by Bruner (1896, 1901). The m. constrictor naris arises around the posterior edge of the narial opening and inserts on the alary cartilage anteriorly. The m. dilatator naris arises from a cartilaginous portion of the nasal capsule posterior to the naris and extends forward to insert on the cutaneous wall of the posterior border of the naris. The m. dilatator naris accessorius (absent in some taxa) arises from the maxilla and from cartilage lateral to the naris and extends obliquely in an anteromedial direction to insert on the posterolateral margin of the naris.

Dermal Investing Bones and Braces. The skulls of salamanders have unroofed temporal regions and, therefore, are gymnokrotaphic. However, the neurocranium and nasal capsule generally are well protected by dermal investing bones.

Dorsal components.—As many as five pairs of bones are involved in the dorsal skull roof; these are the prefrontals, nasals, and lacrimals in the nasal region, and the frontals and parietals posteriorly (Figs. 13-3, 13-4). Of these components, only the frontals and parietals are found in all salamanders. The frontals invest the anterior part of the orbitosphenoid bone and in some taxa (e.g., *Cryptobranchus, Salamandra, Necturus,* and *Siren*) extend forward to roof part of the nasal capsule. The paired parietals lie posterior to the frontals and primarily invest auditory capsule. In some taxa the parietal may be ex-

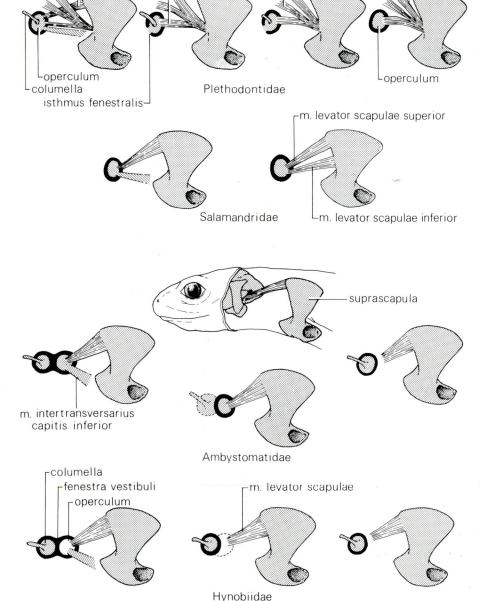

Figure 13-2. Schematic summary of conditions of ear ossicles and associated muscles in four families of salamanders (adapted and redrawn from Monath, 1965). Bony elements are stippled. The fenestra ovalis (= fenestra vestibuli) is black. Dashed outlines indicate elements that have fused with the prootic bone within which the fenestra ovalis lies. Families are arranged in a primitive to advanced sequence from bottom to top, respectively. Among hynobiids, the operculum always is cartilaginous; however, in ambystomatids, salamandrids, and plethodontids, the operculum may be cartilaginous or bony.

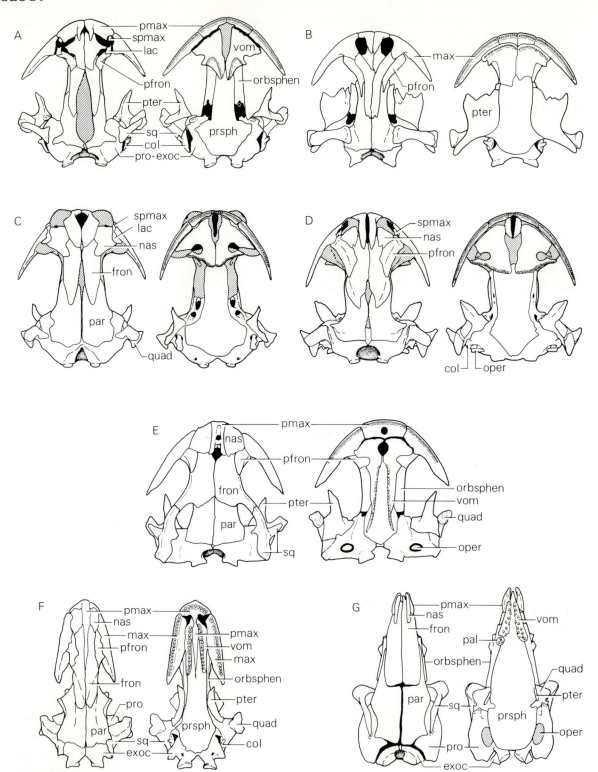

Figure 13-3. Dorsal (left) and ventral (right) views of salamander skulls. **A.** *Salamandrella keyserlingii.* **B.** *Cryptobranchus alleganiensis* **C.** *Rhyacotriton olympicus.* **D.** *Ambystoma maculatum.* **E.** *Taricha granulosa.* **F.** *Amphiuma means.* **G.** *Pseudobranchus striatus.* Skulls are not drawn to relative scale. Stippled pattern indicates cartilage; dorsal fenestrae are hatched. Cartilaginous pterygoid processes are not shown. A, B, E, and G redrawn from Larsen (1963), C from Cloete (1960), D from Theron (1952), and F from Erdman and Cundall (1984). Abbreviations listed in Fig. 13-4.

panded laterally over the exoccipital and prootic to artic-
ulate with the squamosal (e.g., *Hynobius, Batrachuperus,
Amphiuma, Salamandra,* and *Cryptobranchus,* but not
Necturus, Ambystoma, or *Notophthalmus).*

Nasals are present in all salamanders except the proteiids (*Necturus* and *Proteus*) and some plethodontids
(e.g., *Haideotriton* and *Typhlomolge*). Loss of this element is presumed to be an expression of paedomorphosis. When present, the nasal roofs the nasal capsule
and, in association with the prefrontal, helps to brace the

maxilla against the central part of the skull. The nasal is
variable in its configuration and association with adjacent
bones (Figs. 13-1, 13-3, 13-4). In *Siren,* the nasal is long
and slender, and lies medially adjacent to the alary process
of the premaxilla; thus, it provides only a minimal roof
to the olfactory capsule and braces the premaxilla, instead of the maxilla, against the skull. The nasals always
lie anterior to the prefrontals (if present) and the frontals;
however, their relationship with the alary processes of
the premaxillae is variable. In primitive taxa, such as

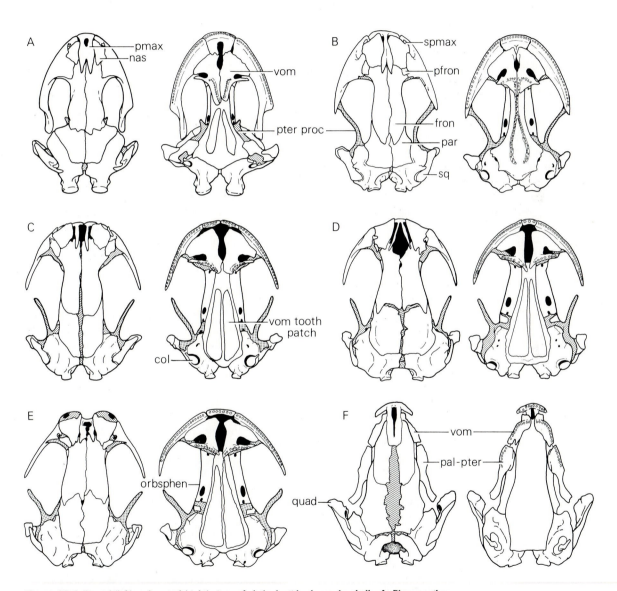

Figure 13-4. Dorsal (left) and ventral (right) views of plethodontid salamander skulls. **A.** *Phaeognathus
hubrichti.* **B.** *Stereochilus marginatum.* **C.** *Plethodon jordani.* **D.** *Bolitoglossa subpalmata.* **E.** *Bolitoglossa
hartwegi.* **F.** *Eurycea neotenes.* Stippled pattern indicates cartilage; dorsal fenestrae are hatched.
A—D redrawn from D. Wake (1966), E from D. Wake and Brame (1969), and F from Larsen (1963).
Abbreviations: col = columella; exoc = exoccipital; fron = frontal; lac = lacrimal; max = maxilla; nas =
nasal; oper = operculum; orbsphen = orbitosphenoid; pal-pter = palatopterygoid; par = parietal; pfron =
prefrontal; pmax = premaxilla; pro = prootic; pro-exoc = prootic-exoccipital; prsph = parasphenoid;
pter = pterygoid; pter proc = pterygoid process; quad = quadrate; spmax = septomaxilla; sq =
squamosal; vom = vomer; vom tooth patch = vomerine tooth patch.

Cryptobranchus and *Hynobius,* the nasals articulate with one another medially and lie posterior to the premaxillae, whereas in more advanced taxa (e.g., *Salamandra, Necturus, Amphiuma, Ambystoma,* and some of the plethodontids), the nasals are separated medially by the alary processes of the premaxillae.

The prefrontal is a small bone located at the anterior margin of the orbit, usually in articulation with the nasal and frontal (Fig. 13-1). Prefrontals are present in all salamanders except the sirenids, proteids, and some plethodontids (Fig. 13-4); loss in these groups is thought to be paedomorphic. When present, the bone forms part of the roof of the nasal capsule and acts with the lacrimal (if present) to brace the maxilla against the frontal. In the absence of a lacrimal bone, the prefrontal bears a groove or tube that supports the nasolacrimal duct.

The lacrimal is present only in the hynobiids and dicamptodontids (Fig. 13-3). The bone forms part of the anterior margin of the orbit, thereby bracing the maxilla against the prefrontal. A tube in the lacrimal encloses the posterior part of the nasolacrimal duct.

Ventral components.—Salamanders have three ventral investing bones—paired vomers anteriorly and a median parasphenoid posteriorly (Fig. 13-1). Generally, the vomers are large palatal bones that lie adjacent to the premaxillae and maxillae anteriorly (except in *Necturus,* in which the vomer functionally forms part of the upper jaw). The posterolateral margin of each vomer usually forms the bony margin of the internal choana, and the vomer, as a whole, floors nasal capsule. The relationship of the vomer to the parasphenoid is highly variable. The bone overlaps the anterior part of the parasphenoid to some degree in all taxa, and depending on the configuration of the vomerine teeth, may have an attenuate dentigerous process that extends nearly the entire length of the parasphenoid (e.g., some plethodontids).

The parasphenoid invests the braincase ventrally and is present in all salamanders. Although usually it is broader in the prootic region than in the orbitosphenoid region, the parasphenoid usually lacks distinct posterolateral alae. Unlike the parasphenoid bones of caecilians and some anurans, the parasphenoid of salamanders is not incorporated into the ossification of the braincase.

The morphogenesis and development of the two remaining palatal elements—the palatine and pterygoid—are controversial. Most authors (e.g., Larsen, 1963) seem to think that the centers of ossification of the palatine and pterygoid are consolidated to form a single palatoquadrate bone, but Lebedkina (1960) reported that the two bones begin to ossify separately in *Hynobius* and *Pleurodeles* but fuse soon after their appearance. Whatever the case, the palatine functionally is lost in all adult salamanders, except *Siren* and *Pseudobranchus* (Fig. 13-3), in which the bone is a small, quadrangular element lying posterolateral to the vomers near the anterior end of the parasphenoid. The pterygoid (palatopterygoid of some authors) is present in all salamanders except fully metamorphosed plethodontids (Fig. 13-4) and large *Siren.* The pterygoid articulates with the inner side of the quadrate and the anterior wall of the prootic posteriorly. An anterior ramus extends forward to, but does not bear a bony articulation with, the posterior end of the maxilla. In the proteiid *Necturus,* which lacks a maxilla, the pterygoid bears teeth, articulates with the vomer, and functionally forms the posterior half of the upper jaw.

Lateral component.—The squamosal is present in all salamanders (Fig. 13-1). The bone articulates either with the posterolateral edge of the parietal or with the prootic bone and invests the quadrate laterally.

Upper and Lower Jaws. In most salamanders, the upper jaw is composed of a premaxilla (paired or unpaired) anteriorly and paired maxillae posteriorly (Fig. 13-1). These dermal bones are dentate in all taxa, except the sirenids, most *Thorius* and some *Bolitoglossa.*

Premaxilla.—The premaxillae (= intermaxillae of some authors) are paired in all transformed and nontransformed cryptobranchids, ambystomatids, proteids, and sirenids. Among the remaining salamanders, the premaxillae may be separate (e.g., *Ambystoma,* most hynobiids, and some plethodontids) or fused (Figs. 13-3, 13-4), as in one hynobiid (*Hynobius nebulosus*) and many salamandrids and plethodontids (e.g., *Taricha, Batrachoseps,* and *Eurycea).* In *Amphiuma* (Fig. 13-3A), the premaxilla arises from a single center of ossification. The premaxilla is composed of three parts. The primary component of the premaxilla that is involved with the maxillary arcade is the tooth-bearing pars dentalis (= pars alveolaris of some authors). The dorsal ramus that arises from the pars dentalis to form a skeletal roof and anterior abutment for the nasal capsule is termed the pars praenasalis (= pars dorsalis, pars frontalis, frontal spine, or alary process of some authors). These portions of the premaxillae are highly variable in size among salamanders; they may be small (as in most hynobiids) or large (e.g., *Ambystoma maculatum*). The processes are adjacent to one another in some taxa (e.g., *Ambystoma*) or separated. The pattern of separation also is variable. For example, the partes praenasali are separated by the nasals in *Salamandrella keyserlingii* and by the frontals in *Salamandra salamandra.* Among the plethodontids, the partes are separated by a so-called fontanelle in some taxa (e.g., *Plethodon cinereus),* whereas in others the partes are fused distally (e.g., *Desmognathus* and *Stereochilus*) to enclose the fontanelle. The third portion of the premaxilla is the pars palatina, a ledge of bone along the lingual side of the pars dentalis. The pars palatina is absent in proteiids, sirenids, and neotenic plethodontids; it is poorly developed in cryptobranchids, amphiumids, and ambystomatids. Among the remaining taxa, it forms the anterior part of the bony palate, but varies from small to large in size.

Maxilla.—In most salamanders, the maxilla completes the upper jaw laterally (Fig. 13-1). It is absent in the proteiids, *Pseudobranchus,* and *Typhlomolge,* vestigial in

Siren, and reduced or sometimes absent in other paedomorphic species (Fig. 13-3). As with the premaxilla, the main part of the maxilla is the pars dentalis. Along the anterior margin of the bone, there is a vertical process known as the pars facialis that forms the lateral wall of the nasal capsule. The lingual pars palatina is variably developed among different species and, when present, articulates medially with the vomer. The posterior end of the maxilla bears ligamentous connections with two elements—the quadrate and the pterygoid.

Mandible.—Basically, the mandible of salamanders consists of two dermal bones that invest Meckel's cartilage, a rod of cartilage that extends the length of the jaw, and ossifies anteriorly as the mentomeckelian (= mentomandibular of some authors), that forms in Meckel's cartilage in the area of the mandibular symphysis (Fig. 13-1). The tooth-bearing portion of the lower jaw is the dentary (and the coronoid in the proteid *Necturus).* The dentary is synostotically united with the mentomeckelians anteriorly and extends along the lateral and ventral surfaces of Meckel's cartilage. The lingual side of Meckel's cartilage is invested by the prearticular (= gonial or coronoideum of some authors). The prearticular is elaborated in the articular region to form a coronoid flange which approximates the pterygoid and serves for the attachment of masticatory muscle fibers. Posteriorly, in the articular region, part of Meckel's cartilage may ossify as the articular. Cryptobranchoids have an angular bone in the mandible, and most paedomorphic salamanders have a tooth-bearing coronoid. Adult *Dicamptodon* have an edentate coronoid.

Dentition.—The teeth of most salamanders are short and bicuspid (Fig. 15-20A). However, in a few male plethodontids the maxillary teeth are elongate, monocuspid, and directed anteriorly; in some species of *Eurycea* the teeth of both jaws are elongated and monocuspid. Replacement teeth on the jaws and all other toothed elements are formed interior to the older rows of teeth; the replacement teeth move peripherally to replace older teeth as they are resorbed (Regal, 1966; Lawson et al., 1971).

Suspensorium. The suspensory apparatus is a complex of cartilaginous, bony, and muscular elements that act to suspend and brace the jaws against the central part of the skull, and owing to muscle origins and insertions enable the organism to open and close the mouth.

Skeletal components.—The central element of the apparatus that suspends and braces the jaws against the skull in salamanders is the palatoquadrate, which lies nearly perpendicular to the long axis of the skull and is deflected in an oblique, downward direction (Fig. 13-5). The palatoquadrate consists of two major parts, a dorsal or proximal cartilaginous portion, known as the pars quadrata, and a ventral or distal part that is the ossified quadrate. The quadrate is situated dorsal to the pars articular, the cartilaginous area that articulates with the lower jaw, or the ossified articular if present.

Proximally, the pars quadrata bears three cartilaginous connections with the auditory capsule. These connections are arranged in a tripod-like fashion so that a cavity with three exits is enclosed between the palatoquadrate and the auditory capsule. The dorsal process lies beneath the squamosal and is known as the otic process. It is synchondrotically united (i.e., fusion of two cartilaginous structures) with the crista parotica of the otic capsule in most taxa, although the connection is reduced or lost in some (e.g., *Cryptobranchus* and *Rhyacotriton).* The ascending process is anterior and ventral to the otic process and is fused to the otic capsule. The third and largest process is the basal process which lies directly ventral to the otic process. The basal process is fused completely with the larval skull and remains so in adults of most salamanders (e.g., *Triturus, Salamandra,* and *Plethodon),* although in some species the basal process is separated from the auditory capsule by an outgrowth of connective tissue (e.g., *Ambystoma maculatum* and *Hynobius).* Because this separation occurs slightly lateral to the point of original fusion, a portion of the primitive basal process remains fused to the auditory capsule. The basitrabecular process (or secondary basal process) is connected to the skull by a joint—a condition generally characterizing primitive salamanders. In addition to these

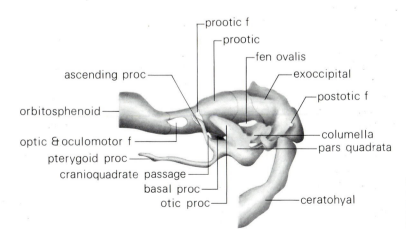

Figure 13-5. Palatoquadrate and suspensorium of the dicamptodontid salamander *Rhyacotriton olympicus,* redrawn from the graphic reconstruction of Cloete (1961). Abbreviations: f = foramen; fen = fenestra; proc = process.

synchondrotic connections and articulation, the pars quadrata is attached to the sound-conducting apparatus by the suspensorio-columella ligament.

In adult salamanders, the palatoquadrate bears a fourth process at its distal end, the pterygoid process. This process arises from an independent chondrification but is continuous with the palatoquadrate of the adult, where it protrudes from this element in an anterolateral direction toward the posterior end of the maxilla. The pterygoid process is overlain by the pterygoid in all taxa except adult plethodontids which lack the pterygoid.

Two dermal investing bones, the pterygoid and the squamosal, are associated with the palatoquadrate (Figs. 13-1, 13-3, 13-4). Although adult plethodontids lack a pterygoid, in all other salamanders this bone extends from the posterior end of the pars quadrata toward the maxilla. A groove in its dorsal surface accommodates the cartilaginous pterygoid process. The bony pterygoid does not articulate with the maxilla. The squamosal invests the palatoquadrate laterally and articulates with the crista parotica of the prootic and, in some salamanders, the parietal dorsally.

Suspensory muscles.—The primary muscles responsible for the opening and closing of the jaws are the mm. levator (= adductor) mandibulae and depressor mandibulae, both of which are visceral muscles (Fig. 13-6). The adductor musculature is a complex of mandibular arch muscles that are innervated by C.N. V (trigeminal), arise from the skull roof and insert on the lower jaw, and act to elevate or close the lower jaw. Variation in this muscle complex was discussed by Carroll and Holmes (1980). The m. levator mandibulae is composed of two major muscle masses—the mm. levator mandibulae anterior (= internus) and levator mandibulae externus. The m. levator mandibulae anterior lies medial to the mandibular branch of C.N. V and is divided into superficial and deep layers. The superficial portion arises from the skull roof and the dorsal fascia that extends from the skull to the neural spine of the first vertebra; the muscle then traverses the otic region and extends ventrally anterior to the auditory capsule to insert via a tendon on the coronoid process of the mandible. The deep portion of the m. levator mandibulae anterior is a fan-shaped muscle that originates from the skull roof and inserts on the dorsal margin of the mandible just anterior to the jaw articulation. The m. levator mandibulae posterior arises from the squamosal, quadrate, and pterygoid to a fleshy insertion on the articular portion of Meckel's cartilage and, via a tendon, on the coronoid process just anterior to the insertion of the superficial part of the m. levator mandibulae anterior. The fourth part of the levator musculature is the m. levator mandibulae externus which lies anterior to the m. levator mandibulae posterior and lateral to the trigeminal nerve. The muscle originates from the squamosal and anterior wall of the auditory capsule and inserts on the posterior end of the dentary and lateral surfaces of the coronoid process of the mandible.

The antagonist of the levator mandibulae series is the m. depressor mandibulae, which is innervated by C.N. VII (facial) and acts to open the jaw. This muscle originates from the posterior part of the squamosal, the auditory capsule, and the superficial dorsal fascia of the head and shoulder, and inserts on the posterior end of the mandible at its articulation with the quadrate (Fig. 13-6). The origin of the m. depressor mandibulae is variable among taxa; moreover, it may become separated into superficial and deep parts, or antero- and posterolateral parts.

Hyobranchial Apparatus.   The hyobranchial apparatus consists of the hyobranchial skeleton, which lies in the floor of the mouth and serves as a structural base for the tongue. The hyobranchium bears muscular and ligamentous attachments to the lower jaw, skull, and pectoral girdle.

Skeletal components.—In most adult salamanders, the hyobranchial apparatus consists only of portions of the hyoid and the first two branchial arches, the remainder having disappeared during metamorphosis. Although the configuration of the hyobranchium varies considerably among salamanders (Fig. 13-7), the basic structure is as follows. Usually there is one medial, longitudinal element termed the copula or basibranchial, to which other parts of the hyobranchial apparatus are attached. Some paedomorphic salamanders such as *Proteus* and *Siren* have two median elements. Anterolaterally, the copula usually bears a pair of horns (also termed anterior radials) that are imbedded in the tongue musculature. In an anterior to posterior sequence, the copula(e) is flanked by the following pairs of elements: the ceratohyals and one or two pairs of hypohyals. The ceratohyals (anterior cornua of the hyoid) usually are relatively massive elements (except in the plethodontids) that lie ventral to the hypobranchials and curve dorsally from their medial articulation with the copula toward the suspensorium. The ceratohyals bear a ligamentous connection with the suspensorium distally. The hypobranchials may be thought of as connecting rods between the copula medially and the ceratobranchials distally.

It seems useful to insert a parenthetical statement here regarding the use of the terms ceratobranchial and epibranchial for the terminal elements of the posterior branchial arches in salamanders. In the literature dealing with plethodontid salamanders beginning with Wiedersheim (1877), continuing through H. Wilder (1894) and I. Wilder (1925), and culminating with the many recent contributions by D. Wake and his colleagues, the ceratobranchials have been referred to as epibranchials. Use of this nomenclature is based on the interpretation that the hyobranchial and ceratobranchial elements of fishes are represented by only one element in salamanders, a bone termed the ceratobranchial. Distal elements then are termed epibranchials. If one assumes that epibranchials are lost in amphibians and other tetrapods [although Ea-

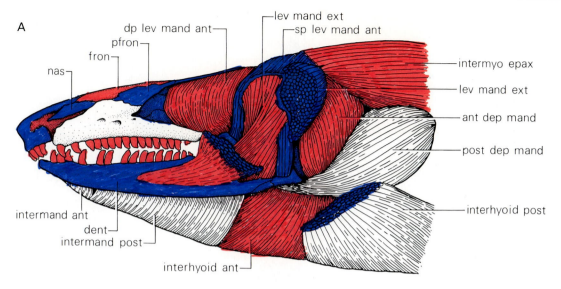

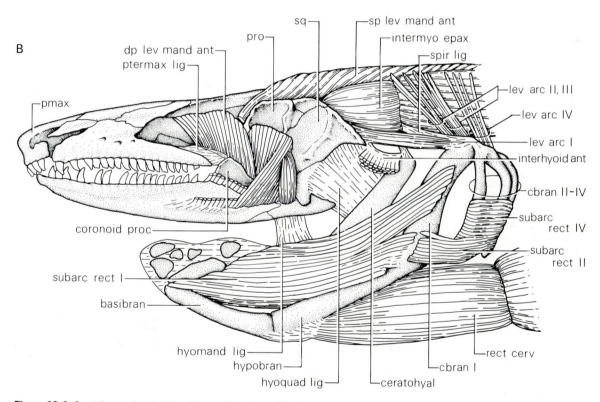

Figure 13-6. Cranial musculature of *Amphiuma tridactylum* in lateral view. **A.** Superficial. **B.** Deep. Redrawn from Erdman and Cundall (1984). Abbreviations: ant dep mand = m. depressor mandibulae anterior; basibran = basibranchial; cbran I—IV = Ceratobranchials I—IV; dent = dentary; dp lev mand ant = deep m. levator mandibulae mandibulae anterior; fron = frontal; hyomand lig = hyomandibular ligament; hyoquad lig = hyoquadrate ligament; hypobran = hypobranchial; interhyoid ant = m. interhyoideus anterior; interhyoid post = m. interhyoideus posterior; intermand ant = m. intermandibularis anterior; intermand post = m. intermandibularis posterior; intermyo epax = m. intermyoseptal epaxial; lev arc I—IV = mm. levatores arcuum I—IV; lev mand ext = m. levator mandibulae externus; max = maxilla; nas = nasal; pfron = prefrontal; pmax = premaxilla; post dep mand = m. depressor mandibulae posterior; pro = prootic; proc = process; ptermax lig = pterygomaxillary ligament; rect cerv = m. rectus cervicis; sp lev mand ant = m. levator mandibulae anterior superficialis; spir lig = spiracular ligament; sq = squamosal; subarc rect I, II, IV = m. subarcualis rectus I, II, or IV.

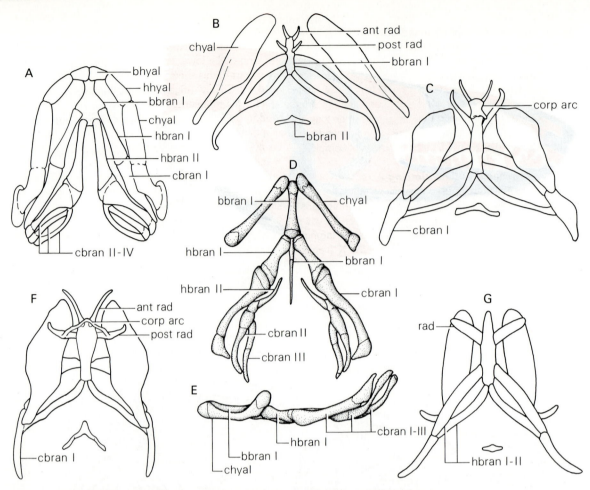

Figure 13-7. Hyoid apparatus of some representative salamanders. **A.** *Cryptobranchus allenganiensis*, ventral view. **B.** *Salamandra salamandra*, ventral view. **C.** *Rhyacotriton olympicus*, dorsal aspect. **D.** *Proteus anguinus* in ventral and **E.** lateral views. **F.** *Ambystoma macrodactylum*, dorsal view. **G.** *Aneides* sp., ventral aspect. Drawings adapted from following sources: A—Jollie (1962); B—Francis (1934); C—Cloete (1960); D—E—Marche and Durand (1983); F—Papendieck (1954); G—Hilton (1947). Abbreviations: ant rad = anterior radius; bbran I—II = Basibranchials I—II; bhyal = basihyal; cbran I—IV = Ceratobranchials I—IV; chyal = ceratohyal; corp arc = corpus arcuata; hbran I—II = Hypobranchials I—II; hhyal = hypohyal; post rad = posterior radius; rad = radius.

ton (1933) suggested that an epihyal might be present between the ceratohyal and its connection to the palatoquadrate in *Ambystoma macrodactylum*], then it follows that the terminal hyobranchial elements of salamanders would be ceratobranchials. For the time being, this issue is unresolved, but the term ceratobranchials is used in this text.

Usually there are two pairs of hypobranchials and between one and four pairs of ceratobranchials. Reduction by loss and/or fusion of the posterior elements of the hyobranchial apparatus is common among salamanders. *Necturus*, *Proteus*, and *Amphiuma*, as examples, have only one pair of hypobranchials. Most salamanders show some degree of reduction in the number of ceratobranchials. If four pairs are present (e.g., *Pseudobranchus* and

Siren) fusion usually is evident; thus in *Siren*, Ceratobranchials II–IV are fused proximally and articulate with Hypobranchial II. Some taxa (e.g., most plethodontids and *Proteus*) develop only three branchial arches instead of the usual four, thereby eliminating the possibility of having four pairs of ceratobranchials. In the majority of salamanders, the ceratobranchials are either fused or lost so that only one distal element remains to articulate with the ends of Hypobranchials I and II.

Hyobranchial muscles.—The musculoskeletal system of the hyobranchial apparatus is complex. The muscles and bones of the floor of the mouth are involved in ventilation and in feeding, which involves the complete cycle of procuring prey, manipulating food in the buccal cavity, and then swallowing it. Capture of prey is accomplished by one of several mechanisms (see Chapter 9), depending on the age of the salamander and on the species. Thus, the musculoskeletal system of a gape-and-suck feeder such as the neotenic *Necturus* would be expected to be considerably different from that of terrestrial feeders such as *Salamandra* and *Bolitoglossa*, which use their tongues to obtain food. In some plethodontids (e.g., *Hydromantes*), the salamanders are able to project the tongue far beyond the mouth (Fig. 9-5); this ability depends on a highly derived and specialized hyobranchial complex.

Laryngeal and swallowing muscles

The principal muscles used in swallowing are the mm. dilatator laryngis, constrictor laryngis, intermandibularis, interhyoideus, cephalodorsosubpharyngeus, and levator bulbi. The mm. dilatator laryngis and constrictor laryngis are antagonistic muscles innervated by C.N. X (vagus) that open and close the larynx and glottis. The dilatator is single, arising from the hyobranchial skeleton and inserting on the arytenoid cartilage. There may be two sets of constrictors—the constrictor laryngei dorsalis, anterior to the insertion of the dilatator, and the c. laryngis, posterior to the insertion. The c. laryngei dorsalis is lost at metamorphosis in some salamanders such as *Salamandra* and *Triturus,* but apparently is retained in all neotenic

salamanders such as *Cryptobranchus* and *Amphiuma.* Plethodontid salamanders lack a larynx and all laryngeal muscles. A superficial sheet of musculature lies between the rami of the lower jaw (Figs. 13-6A, 13-8A). The anterior part of this sheet is the m. intermandibularis, supplied by C.N. V (trigeminal); the posterior part of the sheet is the m. interhyoideus that originates mainly by a tendon from the quadrate. Contraction of the m. intermandibularis results in elevation of the floor of the buccal cavity. Contraction of the anterior part of the m. interhyoideus (innervated by C.N. VII, facial) constricts the hyobranchial skeleton and the posterior part of the mouth. Action of the posterior part of the m. interhyoideus constricts the pharynx, and depresses the head and moves it sideways. The m. levator bulbi is a sheet of muscle lying between the eye and the roof of the mouth. Innervated by C.N. V (trigeminal), this muscle contracts to raise the eye, thereby enlarging the buccal cavity. The m. cephalodorsosubpharyngeus is supplied by C.N. X (vagus) and derived from gill muscles of the larva. It arises from the posterolateral area of the skull and passes ventrally between the m. depressor mandibulae and the m. cucullaris to insert along the midline dorsal to the pharynx anterior to the larynx. Contraction of this muscle causes constriction of the pharynx.

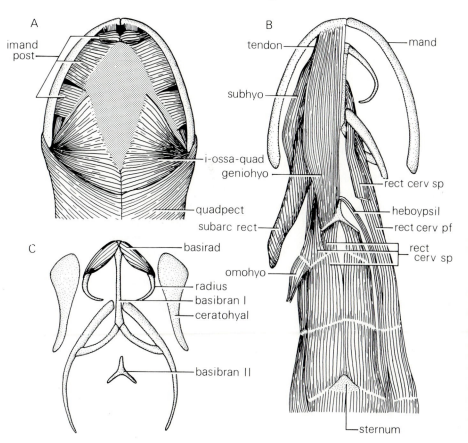

Figure 13-8. Throat muscles of the salamandrid *Chioglossa lusitanica.* **A.** Superficial musculature. **B.** Deep longitudinal muscles. **C.** Deep muscles of hyobranchial apparatus. Nomenclature follows Özeti and D. Wake (1969) from whom drawing is adapted. Abbreviations: basibran I—II = Basibranchials I—II; basirad = m. basiradialus; geniohyo = m. geniohyoideus; heboypsil = m. hebosteoypsiloideus; imand post = m. intermandibularis posterior; i-ossa-quad = m. interossa quadrata; mand = mandible; omohyo = m. omohyoideus; quadpect = m. quadratopecoralis; rect cerv pf = m. rectus cervicis profundus; rect cerv sp = m. rectus cervicis superficialis; subarc rect = m. subarcualis rectus; subhyo = m. subhyoideus.

Mm. rectus cervicis and geniohyoideus

Movement of the hyoid and tongue is affected by a complex of muscles, some of which are derived from the ventral trunk musculature (Figs. 13-6A, 13-8A, 13-8B). The m. rectus cervicis, an anterior continuation of the m. rectus abdominis, is divisible into superficial and deep layers that arise from the sternum. Because the m. rectus abdominis profundus bypasses the sternum in plethodontids, the m. rectus cervicis profundus is a direct continuation of this muscle. Both portions are innervated by the first three spinal nerves. The deep portion inserts on the dorsal side of the copula or basibranchial of the hyoid in some taxa, but the usual insertion is into the substance of the tongue pad. The superficial part is a broad sheet of muscle that passes dorsal to the coracoid to insert on the ventral surface of the hyoid. The m. rectus cervicis retracts the hyoid and, therefore, the tongue. The m. geniohyoideus is a strap-like muscle that lies deep to the m. intermandibularis. In some taxa (e.g., species of *Salamandra, Triturus, Eurycea, Pseudotriton*), the m. geniohyoideus also has a lateral component that originates from the inner edge of the lower jaw anteriorly and inserts on the ceratohyal posteriorly. Its insertion is associated with the anterior end of the m. rectus cervicis. The m. geniohyoideus is innervated by the hypoglossal nerve; contraction of this muscle depresses the lower jaw or the entire head if the jaws are kept closed by the masticatory muscles, and pulls the hyoid apparatus forward. The m. transversus ventralis is a deep branchial muscle, innervated by C.N. X (vagus), and originating from the terminal ceratobranchial and inserting on a median raphe. In some salamanders (e.g., *Pseudotriton*), the muscle forms the subpharyngeal part of the m. cephalodorsosubpharyngeus.

Mm. subhyoideus and subarcualis rectus I

Two deep visceral muscles are associated with tongue movement (Fig. 13-8B). The m. subhyoideus (absent in ambystomatids and plethodontids) is supplied by C.N. VII (facial) and arises from the posterior end of the ceratohyal and inserts on the dorsal surface of the aponeurosis of the m. intermandibularis. When the muscle contracts, the dorsal margin of the ceratohyal is deflected anteroventrally and the tongue above is elevated. The m. subarcualis rectus I (Fig. 13-6B), innervated by C.Nn. IX and X, arises from the dorsal side of the posterior end of the first ceratobranchial cartilage. The muscle arises from a pinnate raphe from which fibers radiate around the end of the cartilage to enclose it in a muscular cup and then inserts on the anteroventral border of the ceratohyal. The action of the m. subarcualis complements that of the m. subhyoideus. Thus, the m. subhyoideus rotates and secures the anterior element of the hyoid (ceratohyal), thereby elevating the tongue slightly. Contraction of the m. subarcualis rectus I pulls the posterior end of the first ceratobranchial ventrally while forcing the branchial arches to rotate forward about the median co-

pula or basibranchial. The effect of this combined action is to project the tongue forward and out of the mouth (see discussion of this mechanism in Chapter 9).

Mm. genioglossus and hyoglossus

The tongue is composed of the m. genioglossus (absent in at least *Siren* and *Pseudotriton*) and the m. hyoglossus, both of which are innervated by the hypoglossal nerve. In most salamanders the bulk of the tongue is made up of the m. genioglossus which originates from the mandibular symphysis and consists of two parts. A medial bundle of parallel fibers inserts in the base of the tongue and in a ligament that also connects to the basibranchial of the hyoid and the insertion of the deep portion of the m. rectus cervicis. The second part consists of a fan-shaped group of fibers that spread out over the floor of the mouth, where they insert at the sides of the tongue. The fibers of the m. hyoglossus arise from the dorsal surface of the hyoid and extend into the tongue (Fig. 9-6). The projectile tongues of some salamandrids and plethodontids are possible because of considerable modification of the hyobranchium (see Chapter 9).

Caecilians

Caecilians have remarkably compact, well-ossified skulls that are stegokrotaphic (skull completely roofed except for narial, orbital, and tentacular openings) or zygokrotaphic (presence of a zone of weakness or a narrow kinetic suture between the squamosal and parietal bones in the temporal region). The temporal regions of most anurans and salamanders are unroofed, a condition referred to as gymnokrotaphic. The origin of the solidly roofed skull in caecilians has been a focal point of continued controversy regarding the origins of the group. Some individuals consider caecilians to have been derived secondarily from an ancestor with a reduced skull typical of other Recent amphibians, whereas others favor the idea of a caecilian descent from Paleozoic microsaurs. The most recent reviews of these conflicting hypotheses can be found in Carroll and Curie (1975), Nussbaum (1977, 1983), and M. Wake and Hanken (1982). Despite this debate, there is consensus that the configuration of the caecilian skull is associated with functional demands imposed by their fossorial mode of existence. Earlier descriptions of caecilian skulls are cited by M. Wake and Hanken (1982). The only broad comparative treatment is that of E. Taylor (1969). Perusal of the latter and Carroll and Curie's (1975) summary documents variation in the numbers of dermal investing and bracing bones owing to apparent fusion of elements. Because of the lack of comparative developmental data (only *Dermophis mexicanus* is well documented by M. Wake and Hanken, 1982), the homologies of cranial elements among caecilians are sometimes questionable; the homologies of many caecilian cranial components with those of salamanders and anurans constitute a subject that has yet to be addressed. As a consequence, the terminology of osseous elements among the groups frequently is inconsistent and confusing. A provisional scheme of equivalent terms is presented in Table 13-1.

The literature dealing with cephalic musculature of caecilians was reviewed by Bemis et al. (1983). Among the works that include comparisons with other amphibians are Luther (1914), Edgeworth (1935), and Nishi (1938). Descriptive morphology is provided by Wiedersheim (1879), H. Norris and Hughes (1918), de Jager (1939a, 1939b), and Lawson (1965). Bemis et al. (1983) and Nussbaum (1983) were the first authors to provide functional analyses and/or interpretations of the cranial muscles of caecilians. The former work is especially useful because the authors presented a provisional list of synonyms of cephalic muscles.

Neurocranium. The caecilian braincase is composed of two complex units—the os sphenethmoidale anteriorly (i.e., anterior to the optic foramen) and the os basale posteriorly. In the adult, the sphenethmoid is a single bone that houses the anterior end of the brain and forms the medial, posterior, and posterolateral walls of the nasal capsule. The bone is endochondral in origin and formed from five ossification centers, the names of which frequently are used to designate various parts of the sphe-

nethmoid in the adult (Table 13-1)—the orbitosphenoid areas laterally, the mesethmoid (or prenasal process) anteromedially, the basisphenoid ventromedially, and the supraethmoid dorsomedially. The sphenethmoid is obscured ventrally and laterally by dermal investing bones, but its dorsal exposure varies. In some species (e.g., *Hypogeophis rostratus, Scolecomorphus uluguruensis)*, the bone is covered completely (Figs. 13-9, 13-10), whereas in others (e.g., *Schistometopum thomensis, Idiocranium russeli*) the dorsomedial, or supraethmoidal portion, of the bone is exposed and sometimes termed the infrafrontal or dermethmoid.

The posterior braincase, the os basale, is represented by a unit of complex origins—the exoccipitals posteriorly, the otic capsules laterally, and the parasphenoid ventrally—all of which are synostotically fused in adults. The exoccipitals ossify in cartilage around the foramen magnum and form the occipital condyles and posteromedial walls of the auditory capsule. The remainder of the auditory capsule also is endochondral in origin. M. Wake and Hanken (1982) reported that ossification arose from a single center (? the prootic) in *Dermophis,* but earlier workers (summarized in De Beer, 1937) recorded as many as three separate centers of ossification (prootic, opisthotic, and pleurosphenoid) in other caecilians. Ventrally, the parasphenoid, an investing bone of membranous or-

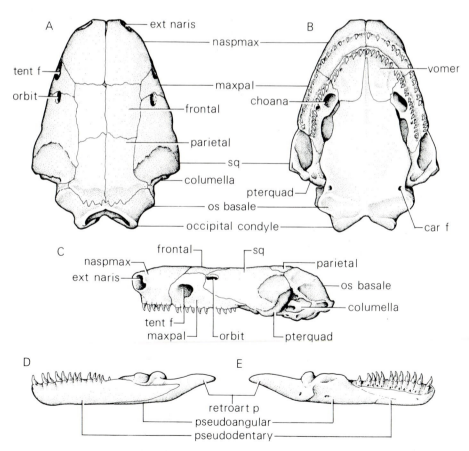

Figure 13-9. Skull of *Dermophis mexicanus.* **A.** Dorsal. **B.** Ventral. **C.** Lateral. **D.** Mandible in lateral view and **E.** medial view. Redrawn from M. Wake and Hanken (1982). Abbreviations: car f = carotid foramen; maxpal = maxillopalatine; naspmax = nasopremaxilla; pterquad = pterygoquadrate; retroart p = retroarticular process; sq = squamosal; tent f = tentacular foramen.

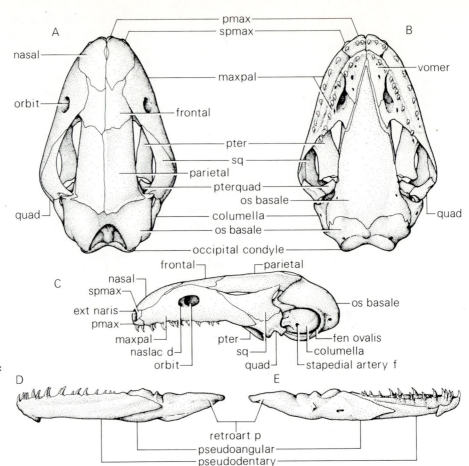

Figure 13-10. Skull of *Epicrionops petersi*. **A.** Dorsal. **B.** Ventral. **C.** Lateral. **D.** Mandible in lateral view and **E.** medial view. Redrawn from Nussbaum (1977). Abbreviations: ext = external; f = foramen; fen = fenestra; maxpal = maxillopalatine; naslac d = nasolacrimal duct; pmax = premaxilla; pter = pterygoid; pterquad = pterygoquadrate; quad = quadrate; retroart p = retroarticular process; spmax = septomaxilla; sq = squamosal.

igin, extends anteriorly from the occipital area to the anterior palate. The bone forms a broad floor to the neurocranium, uniting the posterior exoccipital and otic ossifications to the sphenethmoid anteriorly. Posteriorly the ossification is integrated completely with that of the exoccipitals and auditory capsules in the adult.

Auditory apparatus.—Although not strictly a part of the auditory capsule, the middle ear bones are associated laterally with this structure in the region of the fenestra ovalis. In caecilians, the middle ear bones are represented by a single element, the columella or stapes, which is present in all caecilians except *Scolecomorphus* (Brand, 1956; E. Taylor, 1969b). The columella is a robust endochondral element composed of a spheroid footplate and a distal style that extends rostrad from the anterior end of the footplate to articulate with the quadrate (Figs. 13-9, 13-10). Apparently, an operculum is absent in caecilians, although H. Marcus (1935) suggested that it has been incorporated into the stapedial footplate, as it is in plethodontid salamanders. However, it should be noted that, insofar as is known, the columella in caecilians forms from a single center of ossification.

Muscles Associated with the Neurocranium. In contrast to salamanders and anurans, caecilians lack a

pectoral girdle and, therefore, lack an opercularis muscle extending between the auditory apparatus and the girdle. As summarized by Wever and Gans (1976), the broad footplate of the columella (= stapes) lies in the fenestra ovalis of the otic capsule, to which it is bound by an annular ligament. The distal stylus of the columella articulates with the quadrate. The skin and muscles covering the auditory apparatus constitute the receptive surface for sound waves.

Eye muscles.—The eye muscles of caecilians consist of the four recti and two oblique muscles as described for salamanders. The m. retractor tentaculi, innervated by C.N. VI (abducens), retracts the tentacle and is the homologue of the m. retractor bulbi of other amphibians. According to Badenhorst (1978), the m. levator bulbi has been lost in caecilians. This muscle is not homologous with the m. compressor glandulae orbitalis of caecilians, as had been assumed previously, because the two muscles are innervated by different branches of the trigeminal nerve.

Neck muscles.—Derivatives of both dorsal and ventral trunk musculature insert on the posterior surface of the skull in caecilians. The skull is bound tightly by ligaments, and movement is restricted mostly to the dorsoventral plane. Three pairs of muscles are derived from the dorsal trunk musculature—the mm. rectus capitis superior, intertransversarius capitis superior, and intertransversarius capitis inferior. These muscles insert on either side of the base of the skull above and below the occipital condyles and are responsible for raising the head and a small amount of lateral movement. Some additional lateral movement is affected by the m. longus capitis, which is derived from the ventral trunk musculature and inserts near the craniovertebral joint.

Nasal Capsule.   Relative to other Recent amphibians, the nasal capsules of adult caecilians are structurally simple (Fig. 13-11). The lack of internal, cartilaginous support probably is correlated with the extensive development of rostral dermal bones (i.e., nasals, premaxillae, maxillopalatines, septomaxillae, and vomers).

Structure of nasal capsule.—The medial and posterior walls of the nasal capsule are formed by the mesethmoid portion of the sphenethmoid. The floor of the capsule is composed of lateral extensions from the mesethmoid, the palatal processes of the maxillae and premaxillae, and the vomers. The olfactory organs lying within the nasal capsule are supported internally by struts arising from the vomers, septomaxillae, and maxillopalatines in combination with various cartilaginous structures. The anterior end of each nasal capsule is formed by a cup-shaped cartilage (cartilago cupularis, or alary cartilage of anurans and salamanders), which also supports the terminal nares. Anteromedially the alary cartilages rest against the premaxillae,

and are united posterodorsally with their shared medial wall (septum nasi) via a process known as the oblique cartilage. Posteroventrally an oblique cartilage (infranarial cartilage) unites the alary cartilage with the floor (solum nasi) of the nasal capsule.

Narial muscles.—Bruner (1914) reported the occurrence of a constrictor and dilatator muscle of the external nares of *Siphonops.* Although the presence of these muscles has not been documented in other taxa, it is likely that they are present in order to close the nares when the organism burrows.

Dermal Investing Bones and Braces.   The numbers and configurations of dermal investing and bracing elements among caecilians are highly variable (Figs. 13-9, 13-10, 13-12), and the nomenclature of the elements is inconsistent. Ichthyophiid and rhinatrematid caecilians have the greatest number of cranial elements.

Dorsolateral components.—Dorsally, the nasal capsules and sphenethmoid are invested by three pairs of bones—the nasals are anterior and flanked posterolaterally by the frontals (= lacrimals of some authors); the frontals lie posterior to the nasals. The posterior braincase is roofed by paired parietals. Among advanced caecilians, the nasal and premaxilla are fused into a single bone, the nasopremaxilla. Similarly, the prefrontal is incorporated into the facial process of the maxillopalatine. The lateral wall of the nasal capsule is composed of the septomaxilla (or the nasopremaxilla with which the septomaxilla is fused

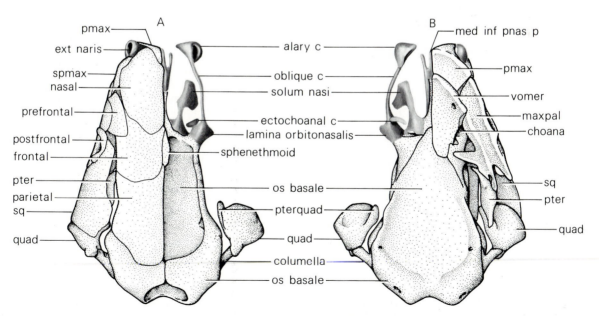

Figure 13-11. Skull of *Ichthyophis glutinosus* with dermal bones removed from right side to show underlying chondrocranial elements; bones are stippled and cartilaginous structure shown in gray. **A.** Dorsal. **B.** Ventral. Redrawn from a graphic reconstruction by M. Visser (1963). Abbreviations: c = cartilage; ext naris = external naris; maxpal = maxillopalatine; med inf pnas c = medial inferior prenasal cartilage; pmax = premaxilla; pter = pterygoid; pterquad = pterygoquadrate; quad = quadrate; spmax = septomaxilla; sq = squamosal.

in some caecilians) anteriorly and the facial process of the maxillopalatine. The tentacular foramen or groove lies in this facial process. The association of the posterior margin of the facial process of the maxillopalatine with other elements varies depending on the presence or ab-

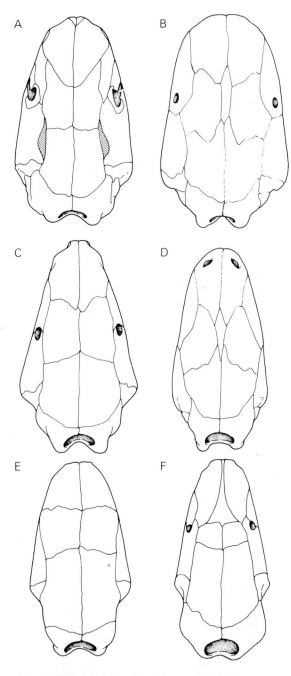

Figure 13-12. Dorsal views of caecilian skulls redrawn from photographs in E. Taylor (1969) showing a variety of skull shapes and dispositions of cranial roofing bones. B—F are examples of stegokrotaphic species of the family Caeciliidae, whereas A is a zygokrotaphic representative of the family Ichthyophiidae. **A.** *Ichthyophis kohtaoensis.* **B.** *Caecilia nigricans.* **C.** *Hypogeophis rostratus.* **D.** *Oscaecillia ochrocephala.* **E.** *Afrocaecilia uluqurensis.* **F.** *Idiocranium russeli.*

sence of an orbit, the relationship of the tentacular and orbital openings, and the configuration of bone surrounding the orbit (Fig. 13-13). In species of *Ichthyophis* and *Uraeotyphlus* there is a discrete orbital (= ocular or postfrontal of some authors). This bone forms either the entire orbit except for a small portion of its ventral margin, or only the posterior half of the orbit; portions of the orbit not formed by a circumorbital bone are formed by the facial process of the maxillopalatine, which forms the subocular facial bone that articulates posteriorly with the squamosal. Most caecilians lack a discrete circumorbital element; the component may be lost entirely, or it may have fused posteriorly with the squamosal or ventrally with the maxilla. Thus, in most species the margin of the orbit is formed by the maxillopalatine anteriorly and anteroventrally and the squamosal dorsally and posteriorly. In some caecilians (e.g., *Epicrionops petersi* and species of *Caecilia),* the entire orbit lies within the facial process of the maxillopalatine.

The squamosal is a broad, posterolateral investing bone of the temporal region. In most caecilians, which are stegokrotaphic as adults, the bone articulates dorsally with the frontals and parietals (Fig. 13-9). In species that are slightly zygokrotaphic, the squamosal has an incomplete articulation with both roofing elements (Fig. 13-10). The more marked the zygokrotaphy, the greater the temporal opening between the squamosal and the cranial roofing bones. Absence of an articulation of the squamosal with the parietal seems to be more common than absence of an articulation with the frontal (Fig. 13-12). In extreme zygokrotaphy (e.g., *Epicrionops petersi),* the squamosal lacks any articulation with dermal roofing bones and instead forms an arch between its remaining articulations with the auditory capsule and quadrate posteriorly and the facial process of the maxillopalatine anteriorly (Fig. 13-10).

Ventrolateral components.—In all caecilians, the maxilla is fused to the palatine to form the maxillopalatine, a multifunctional bone (Figs. 13-9, 13-10). The facial process of this bone is a lateral covering bone for the cheek, and the dental ridge serves as a primary element of the upper jaw. The palatine portion is a ventral, shelf-like element that forms the lateral and posterolateral portion of the palate, bears a row of teeth, and braces the upper jaw via medial articulations with the vomer and sphenethmoid and a posterolateral articulation with the ectopterygoid (if present as a separate element), pterygoid, or pterygoquadrate. Similarly, the premaxilla (or nasopremaxilla, if the premaxilla is fused with the nasal) serves several functions. Its rostral portion supports the anterior end of the nasal capsule, whereas its dental ridge completes the maxillary arcade of the upper jaw. The palatine shelf of the premaxilla forms the anterior end of the palate, articulating with the palatine posterolaterally and the vomer posteriorly.

Ventral components.—The central elements of the caecilian palate are the paired vomers (= prevomers of some authors). These dermal elements underlie the nasal capsule and sphenethmoid, bear an inner row of teeth contiguous with those of the maxillopalatines, and, together with these latter elements, form the margins of the choanae. The extent of the medial articulation of the vomers is variable. Apparently the anterior ends of the vomers articulate with one another in nearly all species. However, in many taxa the medial margins diverge posteriorly from one another to articulate with the dagger-like cultriform process of the parasphenoid medially. Although the parasphenoid is considered to be an integral part of the os basale (i.e., posterior braincase) in caecilians, its anterior half clearly is also a major component of the palate.

In some caecilians (e.g., species of *Grandisonia, Schistometopum, Herpele, Geotrypetes, Siphonops, Gymnopis*), a so-called ectopterygoid has been identified (Fig. 13-10). This bone (= pterygoid of some authors) braces the posterior palatal portion of the maxillopalatine against the pterygoid (= pterygoid process of the quadrate of some authors).

Upper and Lower Jaws. The upper jaw of caecilians is composed of the premaxilla (or nasopremaxilla if fusion has occurred) anteriorly and the maxillopalatine posteriorly (Figs. 13-9, 13-10). The mandible consists of two broadly overlapping dermal elements, the pseudodentary and pseudoangular, which are attached to each other by fibrous connective tissue and, in a few species, a remnant of Meckel's cartilage. As described by Bemis et al. (1983), the mandibular symphysis is a butt joint. The pseudoangular bears a U-shaped facet which articulates with the

quadrate and a long retroarticular processs that serves as an attachment site for three major jaw muscles.

Dentition.—All jaw bones bear teeth in caecilians. In addition, there is an inner, palatal series on the vomer and the palatine portion of the maxillopalatine. Because of the relative positions of the upper and lower jaws, the mandibular teeth fit between the two rows of upper teeth. Caecilian teeth are pedicellate and generally recurved (Fig. 15-20B). The shape of the crown, while consistent within a species, is highly variable among species (M. Wake and Wurst, 1979). The cusp may be monocuspid or bicuspid, recurved or subconical, and may bear lateral flanges of varying degrees of development. Replacement teeth develop interior to the older rows of teeth in an alternate sequence; as older crowns are lost and pedicels resorbed, the younger teeth move peripherally to replace them (M. Wake, 1976, 1980d).

Suspensorium. The suspension and bracing of the jaws in caecilians is a highly integrated, robust mechanism that differs from the suspensory apparatus of salamanders and anurans in the pattern of masticatory muscles and in the involvement of the columella (= stapes) in the mechanism.

Skeletal components.—The central suspensory element is the pterygoquadrate (so named because the pterygoid arises as a flange from the quadrate). The quadrate (= palatoquadrate of salamanders) portion of this bone articulates with the neurocranium and, distally, the pseudoangular of the mandible; it also articulates posteriorly with the columella and is overlain by the squamosal. The

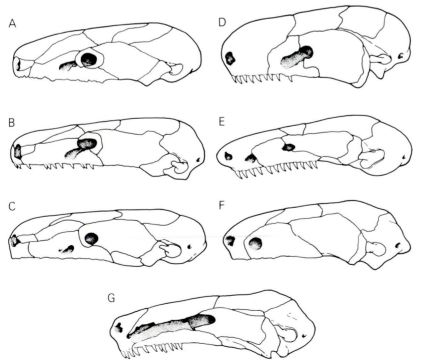

Figure 13-13. Lateral views of caecilian skulls redrawn from photographs in E. Taylor (1969). Teeth are shown only if they were present in the specimen. **A.** *Ichthyophis beddomei* (Ichthyophiidae). **B.** *Ichthyophis kohtaoensis.* **C.** *Caudacaecilia larutensis* (Ichthyophiidae). **D.** *Siphonops annulatus.* (Caeciliidae). **E.** *Idiocranium russeli* (Caeciliidae). **F.** *Gegeneophis ramaswamii* (Caeciliidae). **G.** *Geotrypetes seraphini* (Caeciliidae). In A—C note presence of separate premaxillae, septomaxillae, and prefrontals. A and B have separate orbital bones. D—F illustrate fusion of rostral bones and variation in the development of the facial process of the maxillopalatine and its association with the orbit and/or tentacular opening.

latter bone articulates to varying degrees with the frontal and parietal dorsally, and anteriorly is attached firmly to the maxillopalatine; thus, the squamosal serves as a cheek bone as well as completing the maxillary arcade and serving as a suspensory element. The pterygoid portion of the quadrate provides an internal strut between the posterior end of the maxillopalatine and the lower end of the quadrate. If an ectopterygoid is present, it lies between the pterygoid flange and the maxillopalatine.

Suspensory muscles.—The masticatory musculature of caecilians has been reviewed most recently by Bemis et al. (1983) and Nussbaum (1983). As one would suspect from the configuration of the skull in this group, the pattern of the levator and depressor muscles is quite different from that of salamanders and anurans. On the basis of their study of *Dermophis mexicanus,* Bemis et al. subdivided the levator muscles into two groups—internal and lateral. The four internal levators arise from the lateral wall of the braincase, the inner surface of the dermatocranium (primarily from the squamosal), and the pterygoquadrate (Fig. 9-2). The m. levator mandibulae anterior fills most of the dorsal portion of the adductor cavity. Posterior to the latter muscle is the m. levator mandibulae externus. Both of these muscles function as a unit to raise the lower jaw on which they insert. There

is some evidence that the levator mandibulae externus also acts to close and protract the lower jaw. The third muscle in this series is the m. levator mandibulae posterior, which originates on the ventromedial surface of the quadrate and exits the skull through the subtemporal fenestra to insert on the ventromedial surface of the retroarticular process of the mandible. The fourth internal levator is the m. levator quadrati, a straight, parallel-fibered muscle that extends from the wall of the neurocranium to the pterygoid process of the quadrate. This muscle may act to restrict downward rotation of the quadrate during periods of contraction of the other three levators. There is no known homologue of the m. levator quadrati in salamanders or anurans.

In caecilians the m. interhyoideus has assumed a totally different function than in salamanders and anurans. Instead of being a member of the mandibular musculature, it is a levator of the jaw in caecilians. The muscle arises from the fascia of the ventral and lateral surfaces of the body and inserts by means of a tendon on the ventral surface of the retroarticular process of the mandible. The muscle is single in some caecilians but may be separated into anterior and posterior components in others (Nussbaum, 1983). The m. interhyoideus (or m. interhyoideus posterior in those caecilians with anterior and posterior

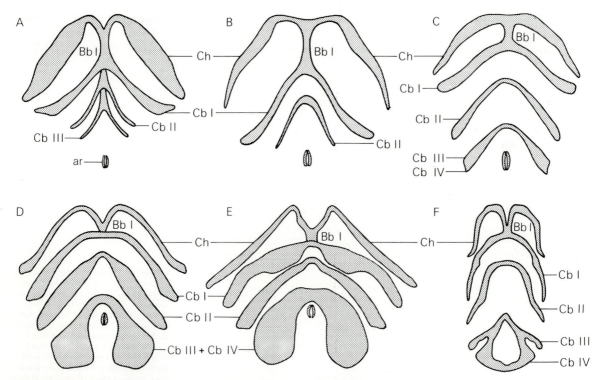

Figure 13-14. Hyobranchial skeletons of caecilians in ventral view redrawn from Nussbaum (1977).
A. *Epicrionops* (Rhinatrematidae). **B.** *Rhinatrema* (Rhinatrematidae). **C.** *Ichthyophis* (Ichthyophiidae).
D. *Gymnopis* (Caeciliidae). **E.** *Typhlonectes* (Typhlonectidae). **F.** *Scolecomorphus* (Scolecomorphidae).
Abbreviations: ar = arytenoid cartilages; Bb I = Basibranchial I; Cb I—IV = Ceratobranchials I—IV;
Ch = ceratohyal.

components) pulls the retroarticular process back and down, thereby causing the jaw to rotate upward from an open position. It is the major muscle of jaw elevation in caecilians, and, so far as is known, its function in this group is unique among tetrapods.

The m. depressor mandibulae is a massive muscle that originates on the posterolateral surface of the skull. Fibers of the fan-shaped muscle converge ventrally to insert on the dorsal surface of the retroarticular process. Contraction of this muscle pulls the process forward and up, causing the jaw to rotate downward from a closed position.

Hyobranchial Apparatus. The hyoids of adult caecilians are relatively unchanged from the larval condition and much less specialized than those of most salamanders and anurans. This doubtless is associated with the minimal use of the tongue in feeding by caecilians.

Skeletal components.—The hyoid of most caecilians consists of a series of flat, cartilaginous, recurved elements to which muscles attach in the gular region (Figs. 9-2, 13-14). The most anterior elements, the ceratohyals and first pair of ceratobranchials (I) are united midventrally by Basibranchial I, occasionally termed the copula. Posterior to this unit is Ceratobranchial II which sometimes bears a small, anteromedial extension that represents the remnants of Basibranchial II. Ceratobranchials III–V are fused posteriorly into a single, broad element. The larynx lies within the arc of this posterior element.

Mandibular and hyoid muscles.—The principal muscles used in swallowing are the mm. dilatator laryngis, two groups of constrictors, and the m. intermandibularis. The m. cephalodorsosubpharyngeus of salamanders and the levator bulbi of salamanders and anurans are not present.

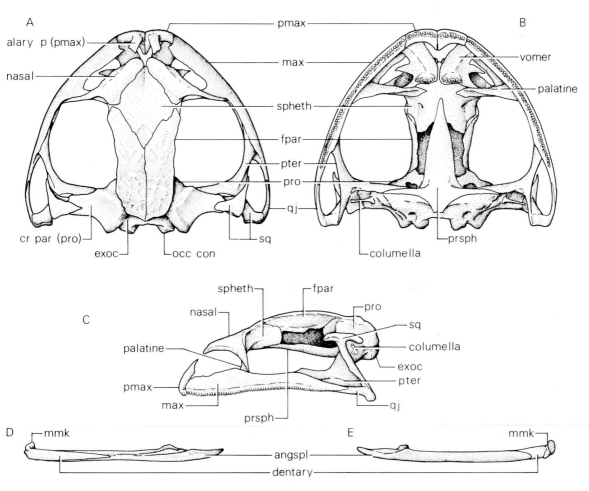

Figure 13-15. Skull of *Gastrotheca walkeri*. **A.** Dorsal. **B.** Ventral. **C.** Lateral. **D.** Mandible in lateral view. **E.** Mandible in medial view. Abbreviations: alary p = alary process; anglspl = angulosplenial; cr par = crista parotica; exoc = exoccipital; fpar = frontoparietal; max = maxilla; mmk = mentomeckelian bone; occ con = occipital condyle; pmax = premaxilla; pro = prootic; prsph = parasphenoid; pter = pterygoid; qj = quadratojugal; spheth = sphenethmoid; sq = squamosal.

Mm. interhyoideus and dilatator laryngis

If single, the m. interhyoideus posterior acts to close the lower jaw rather than to elevate the hyobranchial apparatus. In most caecilians, which have a m. interhyoideus anterior, the latter muscle elevates the hyobranchial apparatus, whereas the m. interhyoideus posterior adducts the jaw. The laryngeal muscle complex acts to open and close the glottis. The m. dilatator laryngis arises from the fused third and fourth ceratobranchials and inserts on the laryngeal cartilage. Most caecilians have two sets of constrictors, one that inserts on the arytenoid cartilage anterior to the insertion of the m. dilatator laryngis and a second set that inserts posterior to this muscle. The anterior set of constrictors is absent in *Siphonops* (Edgeworth, 1935). The m. intermandibularis is represented by a thin, superficial sheet of transverse muscle fibers that originate along the medial edge of each mandible and insert on a narrow, medial raphe. Contraction of this muscle elevates the hyoid and buccal floor.

Mm. rectus cervicis, geniohyoideus, levator arcus branchialis, and transversalis i and iv

Muscles involved in the movement of the hyoid and the limited movement of the tongue are the mm. rectus cervicis, geniohyoideus, levator arcus branchiales, and transversalis ventralis i and iv (Fig. 9-2). The m. rectus cervicis is a forward continuation of the posterior ventral trunk musculature (m. rectus abdominis) that inserts on the posterior ceratobranchials. The latter muscle has a serial connection with the strap-like m. geniohyoideus that inserts on the first ceratobranchial and arises from the anterior margin of the mandible. Contraction of these muscles retracts and protracts the hyoid, but does not depress the jaw as it does in other amphibians. The m. levator arcus branchiales (not present in metamorphosed salamanders or anurans) has a fan-shaped origin from the dorsal fascia of the trunk musculature. The muscle passes ventral, deep to the m. interhyoideus, and inserts onto the hyoid, which it elevates. Two deep visceral muscles that may act to move the hyoid are the mm. transversalis ventralis i and iv which extend between the hyoid and a median raphe that underlies the trachea.

M. genioglossus

Apparently the tongues of caecilians are composed solely of the m. genioglossus; the hyoglossus of salamanders and anurans seems to be absent.

Anurans

In comparison to salamanders and caecilians, there is a great deal more literature on anuran cranial osteology, a summary of which appears in Trueb (1973). The appar-

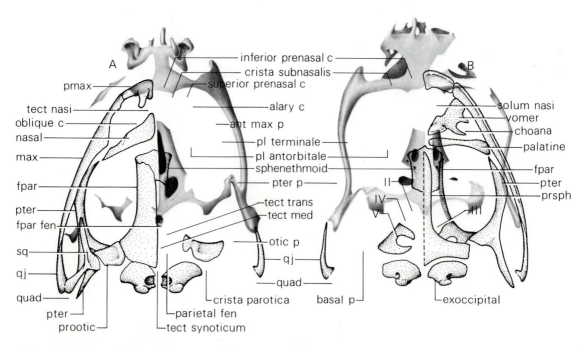

Figure 13-16. Skull of *Rana esculenta* with dermal bones removed from right side to show underlying chondrocranial elements; bones are stippled and cartilaginous structures are shown in gray. **A.** Dorsal. **B.** Ventral. Redrawn from Gaupp (1896). Abbreviations: ant = anterior; c = cartilage; fen = fenestra; fpar = frontoparietal; max = maxilla; p = process; pl = planum; pmax = premaxilla; prsph = parasphenoid; pter = pterygoid; qj = quadratojugal; quad = quadrate; sq = squamosal; tect = tectum; tect med = tectum medialis; tect trans = tectum transversalis.

ent richness of this resource is deceptive because of the great number of species of anurans (more than 3400 as contrasted to 350 of salamanders and 160 of caecilians) and the anatomical diversity of anurans. Trueb (1973) provided a synthesis of the major evolutionary trends in anuran osteology. Synonyms for the names of various bones and an extensive list of the literature are provided in that paper. The terminology used in the following accounts follows that of Trueb except where noted. Readers wishing more detailed descriptions of internal features of the anuran skull should consult Trueb (1968, 1970a) and references cited therein.

Because of the diversity of cranial architectural types characterizing anurans, it is difficult to make generalizations about them relative to caecilians and salamanders. Typically, the skulls of anurans are broad and fenestrate (Figs. 13-15, 13-17, 13-18). The number of cranial elements is reduced relative to other amphibians, and the suspensorium (i.e., jaw articulation) usually is located toward the posterior limit of the skull. Those parts of the skull involved with sensory systems (e.g., olfaction, hearing) tend to be much more elaborate than those of salamanders and caecilians. The palate is poorly developed, and dentition is reduced.

Many of the same general works cited for the cephalic musculature of salamanders also apply to anurans. The one exhaustive summary exclusive to anurans is that of Gaupp (1896) on the anatomy of *Rana esculenta*. Although the summary is detailed, in many cases it is difficult to reconcile myological homologies between anurans and salamanders because Gaupp frequently applied names derived from the study of human anatomy to the muscles of anurans. General descriptions of cephalic musculature are available for *Rheobatrachus silus* (M. Davies and T. C. Burton, 1982), *Phrynomantis stictogaster* and other microhylids (T. C. Burton, 1983a, 1983b); these are among the most complete descriptions since that of Gaupp.

Neurocranium. The braincase of anurans can be thought of as a T-shaped box (Fig. 13-16). The leg of the T extends posteriorly from the nasal region to the auditory region, and the auditory capsules form the head of the T. The neurocranium is composed of only five bones—the sphenethmoid, and the paired prootics and exoccipitals. In the orbital and preorbital regions, the sphenethmoid forms the braincase and contributes to the medial and posterior walls of the nasal capsule. Its posterior limit lies at the level of the optic foramen, the anterior margin of which is formed by the sphenethmoid. The sphenethmoid always has a large dorsal fenestra that is covered to varying degrees by dermal investing bones (Figs. 13-17, 13-18). Ossification of this endochondral element is highly variable among anurans. Among poorly ossified species (e.g., *Ascaphus, Notaden,* and some microhylids), the two halves of the sphenethmoid fail to unite in bone dorso- and ventromedially, and ossification

may be limited to the anterior part of the orbit, just behind the nasal capsules. In the majority of taxa (e.g., *Rana, Bufo, Hyla),* the sphenethmoid is ossified anteriorly to form the posteromedial wall of the nasal capsule, and to encircle completely the anterior part of the brain throughout the orbital region. In a few hyperossified taxa (e.g., pipids, *Brachycephalus),* ossification of this element may invade cartilage separating the orbit from the nasal capsule, and the bone may be fused with adjacent dermal investing elements such as the nasals, frontoparietals, and parasphenoid.

The prootic lies posterior to the sphenethmoid. In most anurans its anterior margin forms the posterior edge of the optic foramen. Posterolateral ossification of the prootic gives rise to the auditory capsules. Like the sphenethmoid, the prootic always bears a large dorsal fenestra that is contiguous with that of the sphenethmoid. In most anurans, the ossified portions of the prootic are united medially, and posteriorly are fused indistinguishably with the exoccipitals to form one massive element that houses the posterior end of the brain and the otic organs; this element has been referred to as the otoccipital by some authors. In hypo-ossified anurans, ossification of the prootic may be limited to the anterior wall of the auditory capsule and to the posterior area of the orbit (e.g., *Notaden),* in which case fusion with the exoccipital does not occur.

The posterior end of the neurocranium is formed by the exoccipitals that flank the foramen magnum and form the occipital condyles. The exoccipitals sometimes fuse with one another dorsally and ventrally and with the prootics anteriorly to complete the auditory capsule.

Auditory apparatus.—Most anurans possess a complete auditory apparatus composed of a plectrum and an operculum (Fig. 4-11). The operculum is a small, cartilaginous element that lies in the posterior portion of the fenestra ovalis—a lateral opening in the auditory capsule. The plectrum lies anterior to the operculum and consists of an expanded, ossified footplate and an ossified stylus (together called the columella or stapes), and distal cartilaginous elements. The footplate fills the anterior portion of the fenestra ovalis, and the columellar stylus extends anterolaterally from the auditory capsule toward the side of the head. The distal end of the stylus bears cartilaginous elements that are synchondrotically united with the tympanic ring, which lies beneath the skin on the side of the head and supports the tympanic membrane that is visible externally. In many anurans, the sound-conducting apparatus is reduced (e.g., *Telmatobius*) or lost (e.g., *Rhinophrynus).* Frequently, the tympanum, tympanic annulus, and the entire plectrum are lost, leaving only the operculum in the fenestra ovalis (e.g., *Rhinophrynus).* Insofar as is known, the operculum always is retained; however, in pipid frogs, the operculum may be incorporated into the footplate of the columella (de Villiers, 1932).

Muscles of the auditory region.—Most anurans, like salamanders, have muscles that originate from the pec-

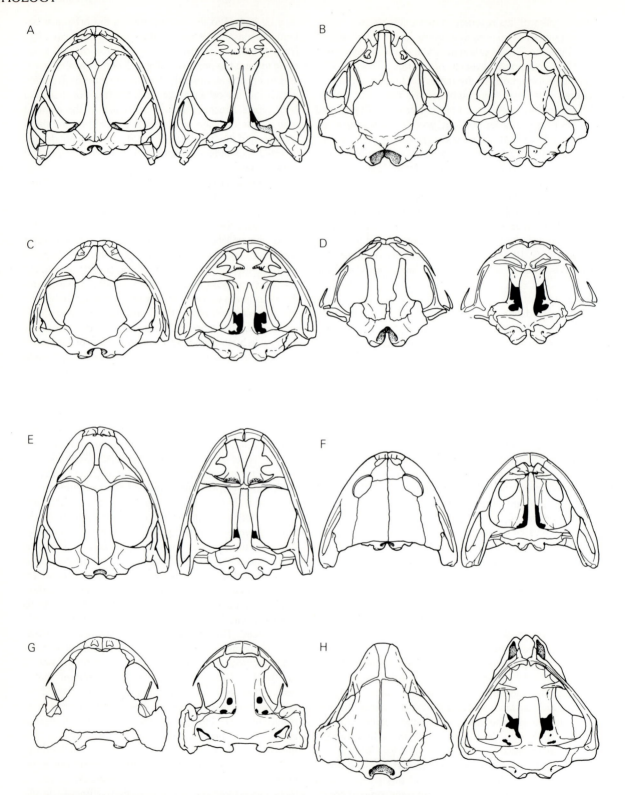

Figure 13-17. Dorsal (left) and ventral (right) views of anuran skulls. **A.** *Barbourula busuquanensis* (Discoglossidae). **B.** *Rhinophryus dorsalis* (Rhonophyrnidae). **C.** *Pelobates fuscus* (Pelobatidae). **D.** *Notaden nichollsi* (Myobatrachidae). **E.** *Leptodactylus bolivianus* (Leptodactylidae). **F.** *Caudiverbera caudiverbera* (Leptodactylidae). **G.** *Brachycephalus ephippium* (Brachycephalidae). **H.** *Rhamphophyrne festae* (Bufonidae).

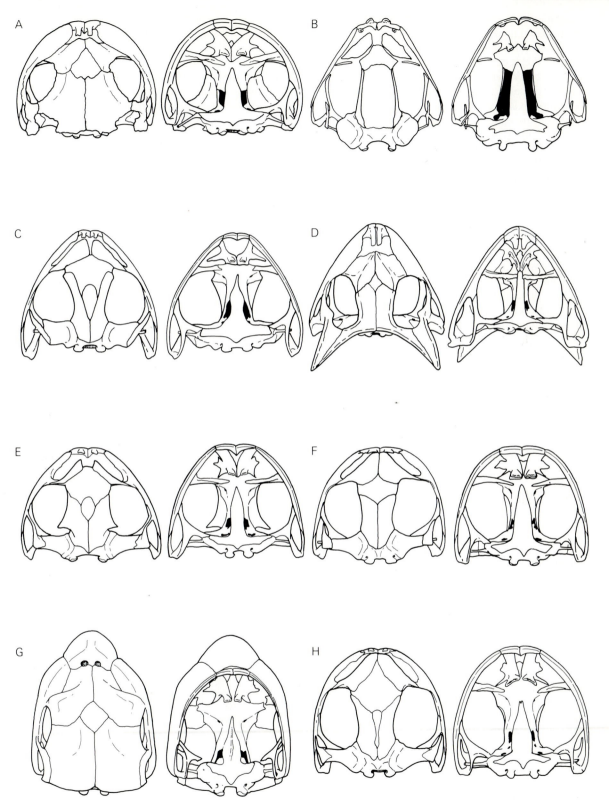

Figure 13-18. Dorsal (left) and ventral (right) views of skulls of hylid frogs. **A.** *Gastrotheca ovifera.*
B. *Pseudacris clarkii.* **C.** *Phyllomedusa venusta.* **D.** *Hemiphractus proboscideus.* **E.** *Smilisca baudinii.*
F. *Phrynohyas venulosa.* **G.** *Triprion petasatus.* **H.** *Osteocephalus leprieurii.*

toral girdle and insert on the opercular-plectral apparatus. The so-called m. opercularis of anurans seems to be homologous with the muscle of the same name in salamanders that is derived from the m. levator scapulae. As depicted by Wever (1979, Fig. 1), the m. opercularis is the most dorsal of a series of three muscles; it arises from the anteromedial, ventral surface of the suprascapula and inserts on the operculum in all anurans examined thus far except the pipids, which lack a discrete operculum (Fig. 4-11). The muscle was shown by Becker and Lombard (1977) to have distinctive fibers that are small. The m. columellaris is inferior to the m. opercularis; it arises on the suprascapula posterolateral to the opercularis and inserts by means of a ligament to an extended process of the footplate of the columella (Fig. 4-11). The derivation of this muscle is not known, although it would seem reasonable that it might have been derived from the m. levator scapulae also; it has no homologue in salamanders. The m. levator scapulae lies beneath the auditory muscles; it originates from the medial surface of the suprascapula and inserts on the sides of the nasal capsule. Functionally, it is not a cephalic muscle and therefore will be dealt with in the section: Appendicular Skeleton. The actions of the opercular and columellar muscles are discussed in Chapter 4.

Eye muscles.—The eye muscles of anurans are the same as those described for salamanders.

Neck muscles.—The skulls of anurans, like those of salamanders, are attached to the vertebral column by derivatives of the dorsal trunk musculature, specifically the mm. intertransversarii capitis superior and inferior. The anterior interspinalis (= m. intercrurales of Gaupp, 1896) extends from the neural arch of the first vertebra anteriorly to the occiput in the region of the foramen magnum.

Nasal Capsule   Of the Recent amphibians, anurans probably have the most complex nasal capsules. The nasal organ consists of a complicated series of nasal sacs and ducts that, in the absence of a well-developed palate and rostral roof, are supported internally by the septomaxillae and a variety of cartilages.

Structure of nasal capsules.—The capsules lie anterior to the sphenethmoid within the area enclosed by the premaxillae and maxillae (Fig. 13-19). These latter elements, along with the nasals and vomers (= prevomers of Trueb, 1973, and other authors), provide support and protection for an intricate system of nasal cartilages. The anterior and anterolateral walls of the nasal capsule are formed by the cup-shaped alary cartilage that supports the anterolateral margin of the external naris. A small rod of cartilage (the superior prenasal cartilage) extends from the alary cartilage anteriorly to abut the posterior face of the premaxilla. The floor (solum nasi), roof (tectum nasi), and the medial wall (septum nasi) separating the nasal capsules are formed in sphenethmoidal cartilage and may be ossified to varying extents. The only other bony elements internal to the nasal capsule are the septomaxillae, a pair of bones present in all anurans. The septomaxilla is dermal in origin but lies imbedded in cartilage medial to the maxilla and supports the anterior end of the nasolacrimal duct which extends from the nasal organ posteriorly to the region of the eye. The posterolateral and posterior walls of the nasal capsule are formed by two

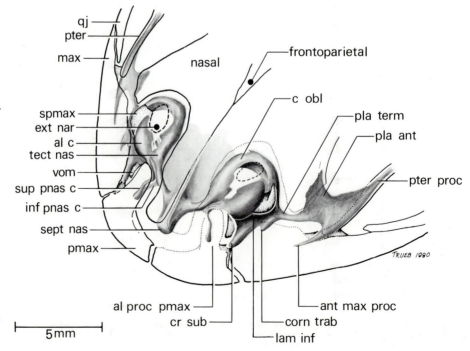

Figure 13-19. Isometric view of anterior cranium of *Rhinophrynus dorsalis* to show cartilaginous components of nasal capsule and their relationships to overlying bones. Cartilage is shown in gray, the septomaxillae are stippled in black, and the positions of the maxillary arch and dermal investing bones are indicated by outlines. Abbreviations: al c = alary cartilage; al proc pmax = alary process of premaxilla; ant max proc = anterior maxillary process; c obl = oblique cartilage; corn trab = cornu trabeculae; cr sub = crista subnasalis; ext nar = external naris; inf pnas c = inferior prenasal cartilage; max = maxilla; pla ant = planum antorbitale; pla term = planum terminale; pmax = premaxilla; pter = pterygoid; pter proc = pterygoid process; qj = quadratojugal; sept nas = septum nasi; spmax = septomaxilla; sup pnas c = superior prenasal cartilage; tect nas = tectum nasi; vom = vomer. Reproduced from Trueb and Cannatella (1982).

qj
pter
max
nasal
frontoparietal
spmax
ext nar
al c
tect nas
vom
sup pnas c
inf pnas c
sept nas
pmax
c obl
pla term
pla ant
pter proc
TRUEB 1980
al proc pmax
cr sub
ant max proc
corn trab
lam inf
5mm

cartilaginous walls, the planum terminale and planum antorbitale, respectively. There is a variety of other internal cartilaginous struts and braces associated with the nasal capsule. Details about these structures are available in Trueb (1968, 1970a) and Jurgens (1971) and references in those publications.

Narial muscles.—The occurrence of narial muscles in anurans is a matter of dispute that was reviewed most recently by Gans and Pyles (1983). According to these authors, who examined more than 40 species of anurans, striated muscle is absent in the narial region. Although a smooth muscle (m. lateralis narium) may be present in some taxa (e.g., *Rana),* it is not present in all (e.g., *Hyla crucifer);* if present, smooth muscle could not be involved in narial closure.

Edgeworth (1935) reported the presence of a smooth muscle (m. labialis superior) along the upper lip in anurans.

Dermal Investing Bones and Braces. Relative to both salamanders and caecilians, most anurans have fenestrate skulls with open temporal regions (i.e., gymnokrotaphic) which afford only minimal protection to the neurocranium and nasal capsules. As might be anticipated, the number of dermal investing and bracing elements has been reduced. Lacrimals, pre- and postfrontals, and separate parietals are absent. The usual complement of dorsal roofing bones consists only of paired nasals and frontoparietals. A squamosal bone always invests the lateral part of the suspensorium, and a parasphenoid and paired pterygoids invariably are present ventrally. Vomers and palatines may be reduced or absent.

Dorsal components.—The paired nasals lie anterior to the ossified portion of the sphenethmoid (Figs. 13-15–13-18). They provide a dermal roof to the nasal capsule, although the extent of protection afforded obviously depends on the size of the nasals. Minimally, nasals are slim, diagonally oriented slivers of bone that cover only the posterior portions of the nasal capsules (e.g., *Ascaphus* and many small, arboreal hylids and centrolenids). In many anurans, the nasals are more extensive quadrangular elements that approximate one another medially, cover most of the nasal capsule, and bear a posterolateral process (the maxillary process) that articulates with the maxillae to brace it against the neurocranium. Obvious elaboration of the nasals occurs in two groups of anurans— hyperossified, casque-headed species (discussed separately) and some pipoid frogs. In the case of the latter (e.g., *Xenopus*) the nasals fuse medially and grow downward to form part of the medial partition (septum nasi) between the olfactory organs.

The second pair of dermal roofing bones lies posterior to the nasals; these are the frontoparietals that represent the fusion of the frontal and parietal elements of other amphibians. In their minimal configuration, the frontoparietals are long, slender elements that flank the fron-

toparietal fenestra (the dorsal neurocranial fenestra formed in the sphenethmoid and prootic) in the orbital region (e.g., centrolenids). In most anurans, the frontoparietals are larger elements that cover at least the posterior part of the fenestra and the medial area of the prootics in the auditory region. Frequently the medial margins of the frontoparietals articulate with one another throughout their lengths (e.g., *Rana, Bufo*) to roof the neurocranium completely. Depending on the degree of hyperossification, the frontoparietal may be elaborated to produce a supraorbital flange over the orbit and/or a temporal flange that extends posterolaterally over the otic capsule toward the side of the skull. In some anurans (e.g., pipoids and *Pelobates*) the frontoparietal is azygous (i.e., single), completely covers the sphenethmoid, and overlaps the posterior margins of the nasals (Fig. 13-17).

Three additional dermal roofing elements are present in a few species. Among hyperossified, casque-headed anurans (e.g., *Triprion* and some *Gastrotheca*) there frequently is a dermal sphenethmoid that lies above the sphenethmoid between the nasals and frontoparietals (Fig. 13-18). One peculiar, burrowing, casque-headed hylid (*Pternohyla fodiens*) has an internasal element protecting the median part of the rostrum in front of the nasals. Finally, the primitive discoglossid *Bombina orientalis* has an interfrontal bone that lies above the frontoparietal fenestra medially between the anterior ends of the frontoparietals.

Ventral components.—Anurans usually have three ventral investing bones—paired vomers anteriorly and a single parasphenoid posteriorly (Figs. 13-15, 13-17, 13-18). Vomers frequently are absent (e.g., *Pipa* and many other taxa), reduced, or undergo fusion in one of two ways. The vomers may be reduced or fused medially (some species of *Xenopus),* or fused with the palatines to form a vomeropalatine (some microhylids). When present, the vomers form part of the palate and floor the nasal capsules, and usually are associated with the premaxillae and maxillae anteriorly and the sphenethmoid posteriorly. They usually bear teeth on a dentigerous process or, occasionally, as in *Hemiphractus,* odontoids (projections of bone resembling teeth).

The parasphenoid invests the braincase ventrally and is present in all anurans. In most taxa, the bone is T-shaped; thus, the posterolateral alae (wings) cover the auditory capsules laterally, and the anterior ramus (cultriform process) extends from the prootic region forward to terminate at the anterior margin of the orbital region. The single deviation from this plan is found among pipoid frogs in which the parasphenoid lacks posterolateral alae. A few taxa (e.g., *Pseudis paradoxa*) bear odontoids on the parasphenoid. In hyperossified frogs (e.g., *Brachycephalus,* Fig. 13-17G), the ossification of the parasphenoid may be incorporated with that of the neurocranium.

Of the two remaining pair of palatal elements—the palatines and pterygoids—the former frequently are reduced, lost, or fused (see discussion of vomer above), whereas the latter always are present. The palatine is absent in leiopelmatids, discoglossids, pipoids, and possibly pelobatids and pelodytids; in most other anurans it is present as a slim, transverse element that braces the upper jaw against the neurocranium. Reduction of the palatine occurs in a medial to lateral direction so the palatine always is associated with the maxilla laterally. True teeth never are present on the palatine, but the bone frequently bears a distinct ridge that may be serrate.

The pterygoid is a triradiate element in all but two genera of anurans. The bone basically has an inverted Y shape. The anterior leg of the Y articulates with the maxilla, and the two posterior arms articulate laterally with the quadrate of the suspensorium and medially with the auditory capsule, respectively. The pterygoid acts as a brace between the suspensorium and upper jaw and the neurocranium. In several species, the pterygoid does not serve as a medial brace because its medial arm is reduced so that it does not articulate with the auditory capsule, and in one taxon (*Rhinophrynus*, Fig. 13-17B) it is absent. In *Hymenochirus*, the anterior arm of the pterygoid is absent and along with other pipids, the posterior arms of the pterygoid are expanded greatly to form a plate that covers the otic capsule ventrally.

Lateral components.—Paired squamosal bones that invest the quadrates laterally and articulate medially with the crista parotica of the auditory capsule are present in all anurans, although the elements vary considerably in their degree of development. Among hypo-ossified anurans (e.g., *Notaden*, Fig. 13-17D), the squamosal may be reduced to a sliver of bone applied laterally to the quadrate. In most anurans, the squamosal is triradiate, bearing a ventral arm along the quadrate perpendicular to the maxilla and two dorsal arms oriented horizontally (Fig. 13-15). The posterior, or otic, ramus articulates with the prootic bone of the auditory capsule, thereby participating in the suspension of the jaws from the skull. The otic ramus frequently is expanded into an otic plate that overlaps the prootic. In hyperossified anurans (e.g., *Triprion*, Fig. 13-18G), the head of the otic ramus may be elaborated to form a temporal arch that extends medially to articulate with the temporal flange of the expanded frontoparietal. Most anurans bear an anterior, or zygomatic, ramus on the squamosal that extends from the head of the squamosal toward the maxilla ventrally. In some taxa it articulates with the maxilla, whereas in most it bears a ligamentous connection with the upper jaw. In pipids, the squamosal has undergone a most peculiar transformation. During development, ossification of this element is incorporated with ossification of the tympanic annulus, so that in adults the squamosal consists of a vertical element flanking the quadrate and an anterior conch-shaped element that surrounds the distal portion of the columella.

Hyperossification.—Hyperossification is a phenomenon commonly observed among anurans. It is unrelated to size; thus, a species as small as *Brachycephalus ephip-*pium (about 16 mm snout-vent length, Fig. 13-17G) is ossified more heavily than a large *Bufo marinus* (about 150 mm snout-vent length). Hyperossification can affect the structure of the skull in several ways. In the pipids, nearly all cartilaginous parts of the skull are replaced by bone, and synostosis of dermal and endochondral elements tends to result in solid fusion of the braincase—the parasphenoid and frontoparietals are fused with the sphenethmoid and prootics. Hyperossification also can affect the external dermal investing bones of the skull. This development can be seen in most bufonids, many hylids (e.g., *Aparasphenodon*, *Corythomantis*, *Gastrotheca*, *Hemiphractus*, *Pternohyla*, and *Triprion*, Figs. 13-17, 13-18), and some pelobatids, leptodactylids (e.g., *Caudiverbera*, Fig. 13-17F), and ranids (*Ceratobatrachus*), among others. In most anurans the first sign of hyperossification is the appearance of sculptured patterns on the surfaces of the dermal bones, a condition termed exostosis. In its most generalized state, exostosis is expressed as a poorly organized reticulate pattern. This generalized pattern may be retained in the adult (e.g., *Bufo*) or may undergo modification during development to produce intricate patterns of radial ridges such as those found in the hylid *Triprion petasatus*. Further hyperossification is expressed by the hypertrophy of dermal elements to increase their overall size and produce extensive marginal flanges. In extreme examples (e.g., *Triprion*, *Ceratobatrachus*), the gymnokrotaphy of the basic skull is disguised because only the orbital region of the skull remains open. The most extreme expression of hyperossification involves co-ossification of the dermal bones with the overlying skin. Bone forms in the dermis of the skin during development and then fuses with the underlying cranial bone so that in the adult the skin is united completely to the bone below. This condition is typical of many bufonids and hylids.

Upper and Lower Jaws. The upper jaw of most anurans is composed of two or three pairs of bones— the premaxillae, maxillae, and quadratojugals (Fig. 13-15). The latter may be reduced or absent, but the former two always are present.

Premaxilla.—The paired premaxillae are located anteromedially and syndesmotically united to one another medially and to the maxillae laterally. Typically, a premaxilla is composed of three parts. The pars dentalis bears the dental ridge. A vertical strut, the alary process, provides an abutment for supporting cartilages of the nasal capsule. A lingual shelf, the pars palatina, varies in its degree of development among anurans and serves as the site for attachment of the soft tissue lining of the buccal cavity. Generally, the premaxilla simply abuts the maxilla laterally, but in some taxa (e.g., some microhylids and *Peltophryne*) the maxilla overlaps the premaxilla laterally.

Maxilla.—The maxilla bears the same three basic parts as the premaxilla, although its vertical component is termed the pars facialis. The pars facialis forms the lateral wall of the nasal capsule anterior to the orbit and may provide support to the upper jaw if the nasal articulates with it. When present and complete, the quadratojugal completes the upper jaw posteriorly. The bone articulates with the maxilla anteriorly, and posteriorly it is integrated with the pars articularis of the quadrate. If reduced, the quadratojugal bears a ligamentous connection with the posterior end of the maxilla.

One genus of hylid frog, *Triprion,* bears special mention owing to its bizarre nature. The basic configuration of the upper jaw is like that of other anurans except that the maxillae bear broad, upturned lateral flanges that articulate with a single, large rostral element—the prenasal. This triangular, neomorphic dermal bone (Fig. 13-18G) lies anterior to the partes dentalis of the premaxillae. The alary processes of the premaxillae are rotated forward so that they lie within the prenasal. Thus, *Triprion* is the only frog known to have an additional element in its upper jaw.

Dentition.—Maxillary and premaxillary dentition is sporadic in occurrence. For example, all bufonids lack such dentition, but all hylids (except *Allophryne*) possess it. When present, the teeth usually are spatulate and bicuspid; however, in the pipid frog *Xenopus,* the teeth are monocuspid, nonpedicellate, and fused to the maxillae and premaxillae (Katow, 1979). In many carnivorous taxa (e.g., *Ceratobatrachus, Hemiphractus, Xenopus, Ceratophrys),* the teeth are modified to form fangs that may be recurved (Fig. 15-20C). Replacement teeth on all dentate elements form interior to the older teeth in either an alternate or successive pattern. As older teeth are resorbed, the younger teeth move peripherally to replace them (Gillette, 1955; C. Goin and Hester, 1961; Shaw, 1979).

Mandible.—The lower jaw of anurans is composed, maximally, of three pairs of elements (Fig. 13-15). Except in pipoids, a pair of mentomeckelian bones forms anteromedially in Meckel's cartilage; the bones bear a syndesmotic connection with one another medially. In pipids and rhinophrynids the two halves of the jaw lack a symphysis. The dentary invests Meckel's cartilage anterolaterally and the angulosplenial invests the medial and posterior surfaces of Meckel's cartilage. Occasionally (e.g., some microhylids) the dentaries articulate anteromedially. The angulosplenial articulates with the quadrate posteriorly. Mandibular teeth are known to occur in only one species of anuran, *Amphignathodon guentheri,* and these are borne on the dentary. In some other taxa (e.g., *Adelotus, Ceratobatrachus, Hemiphractus),* the margin of the dentary is modified to form toothlike serrations and anteriorly it bears a single large, fanglike odontoid.

Suspensorium. The anuran suspensory apparatus usually is much less robust than that of either caecilians or salamanders owing to the extreme gymnokrotaphy of the skull. There is considerable variation in both the development of the skeletal components and the nature of the associated musculature as elaborated below.

Skeletal components.—The central element that sus-

pends and braces the jaws against the skull in anurans is the quadrate (= palatoquadrate of salamanders), which usually is not visible in adults because it is covered by the ventral arm of the squamosal laterally and the lateral ramus of the pterygoid medially and posteromedially. The orientation of the quadrate coincides with that of the ventral arm of the squamosal; thus, in most anurans the long axis of this cartilaginous element is more or less vertical and its upper end deflected slightly anteriorly. In histological preparations, it is possible to see that the upper end of the quadrate is attached to the otic capsule via a small process, termed the otic process. Basally, two other cartilaginous processes provide support for the quadrate. The pterygoid process is invested by the pterygoid bone ventrally and then extends forward from the quadrate to fuse with a cartilaginous support of the maxilla which parallels and lies medial to this process. The pseudobasal process extends posteromedially from the quadrate to articulate with the anteroventral edge of the otic capsule, although this union is fused in a few taxa (e.g., *Bufo).* Leiopelmatids differ from all other anurans (for which data are available) in lacking a pseudobasal process. In this family, medial support of the quadrate is accommodated by two processes—the basitrabecular and basal processes—in much the same manner as in salamanders. The basitrabecular process is produced from the basal plate of the neurocranial floor and abuts the basal process which arises as a medial outgrowth of the quadrate. Ventral support of these cartilaginous processes is provided by the medial arm of the pterygoid. Although the quadrate remains largely cartilaginous, perichondral ossification may occur along its medial margin, and the ventral end (pars articularis) that articulates with the mandible usually is ossified. Ossification of the quadratojugal (if present) is integrated with ossification of the pars articularis. The three dermal investing bones involved with the suspensorium (pterygoid, squamosal, and quadratojugal) are discussed above with other investing and bracing elements.

Suspensory muscles.—Anuran jaw musculature is a great deal more complex and variable than that of salamanders, and has attracted considerable attention over the years with respect to its condition and its developmental history. Sedra (1950) produced a monograph on the metamorphosis of the jaws and jaw muscles in *Bufo regularis,* and de Jongh (1968) wrote on the functional morphology of the musculoskeletal system in larval and metamorphosing *Rana temporaria.* Luther's (1914) study of muscles innervated by the trigeminal nerve in amphibians is still one of the most complete accounts of anuran jaw musculature, although it is based on only eight species representing six families. P. Starrett (1968) emphasized the variability of these muscles among anurans in her discussion of the phylogenetic significance of the jaw musculature. This variability has become increasingly apparent based on morphological studies such as that of Limeses (1965) on ceratophryine leptodactylids, M. Davies and T. C. Burton (1982) on *Rheobatrachus*

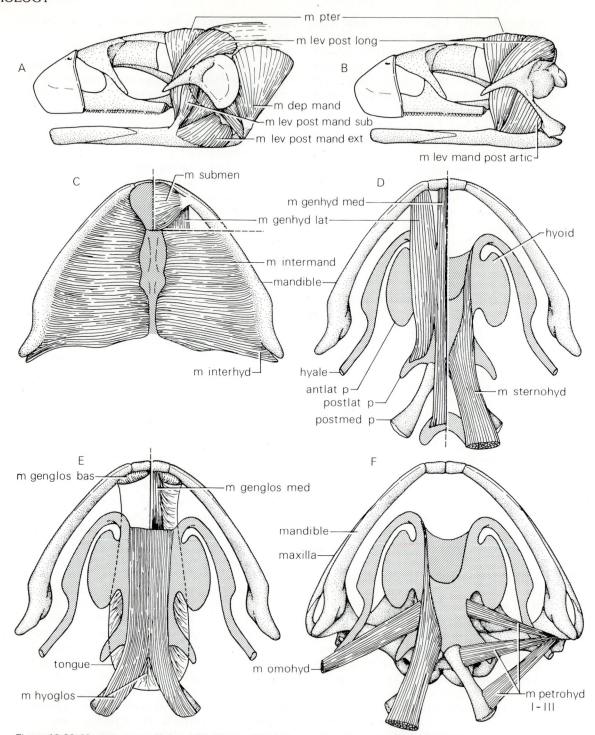

Figure 13-20. Masticatory, mandibular, and hyoid musculature of representative anurans. **A.** Superficial adductor muscles and **B.** deep adductor muscles of *Rana temporaria*, redrawn from Luther (1914). **C.** Superficial mandibular musculature of *Bufo marinus* with medial raphe removed in upper right quadrant to expose deeper muscles. **D.** Superficial (left) and deeper (right) hyoid musculature of *B. marinus*. **E.** Tongue muscles of *B. marinus*. **F.** Deep hyoid muscles of *B. marinus*. Cartilage is stippled; raphes and membranes are hatched. Abbreviations: antlat p = anterolateral process of hyoid; m dep mand = m. depressor mandibulae; m genglos bas = m. genioglossus basalis; m genglos med = m. genioglossus medialis; m genhyd lat = m. geniohyoideus lateralis; m genhyd med = m. geniohyoideus medialis; m hyoglos = m. hyoglossus; m. interhyd = m. interhyoideus; m intermand = m. intermandibularis; m lev mand post artic = m. levator mandibulae posterior articularis; m lev post long = m. levator posterior longus; m lev post mand = m. levator posterior mandibulae; m lev post mand sub = m. levator posterior mandibulae subexternus; m omohyd = m. omohyoideus; m petrohyd = m. petrohyoideus; m pter = m. pterygoideus; m sternohyd = m. sternohyoideus; m submen = m. submentalis; postlat p = posterolateral process of hyoid; postmed p = posteromedial process of hyoid.

silus, and T. C. Burton (1983a, 1983b) on microhylids. The work that has been done is primarily descriptive, and to date little is known about the functional correlates of the variation.

Anurans apparently have a basic complex of six adductor muscles (Fig. 13-20). Although they vary in relative size and areas of origin and insertion, these muscles can be divided into three topographic groups (Luther, 1914)—an internal levator, two external levators, and three or four posterior levators. The internal levator is the m. levator mandibulae anterior longus (= m. pterygoideus of Gaupp, 1896, and Luther, 1914). This muscle generally arises from the dorsal surface of the skull roof and from the lateral surface of the neurocranium, lies anterior to the trigeminal nerve, and inserts via a tendon on the medial margin of the angulosplenial of the mandible. The m. levator mandibulae anterior longus may be homologous with the m. levator mandibulae anterior of salamanders, based on its forward position with respect to the fifth cranial nerve. Posterior to this nerve lies the massive m. levator mandibulae posterior longus

(= m. temporalis of Gaupp, 1896), a member of the posterior group of adductors. This muscle arises from a median raphe on the skull roof, the lateral aspect of the frontoparietal, and the dorsal and anterior surfaces of the prootic. Its fibers converge on a tendon that inserts on the medial margin of the angulosplenial. In some taxa, it is divided into superficial and deep layers. Another member of the posterior group is the m. levator mandibulae posterior lateralis that arises from the ventral arm of the squamosal and inserts on Meckel's cartilage and the lateral surface of the angulosplenial. The last of the posterior muscles is the m. levator mandibulae posterior articularis which arises from the quadrate and inserts on the mandible. The two remaining muscles belong to the external group. These are the m. levator mandibulae externus which arises from the zygomatic process of the squamosal and inserts laterally on the mandible, and the m. levator mandibulae posterior subexternus which also arises from the zygomatic ramus and inserts on the upper surface of the mandible. The homologies of these muscles with those of salamanders are not certain.

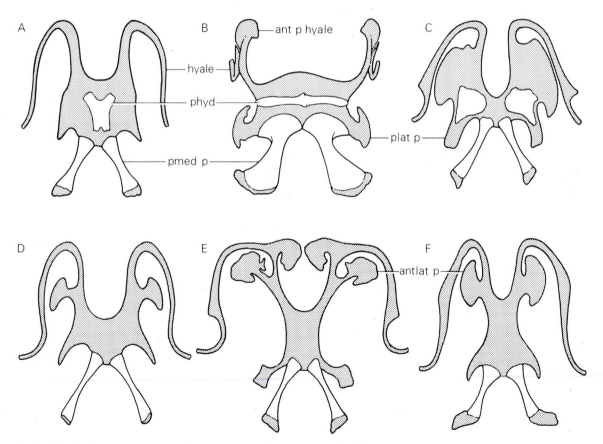

Figure 13-21. Hyobranchial skeletons of anurans in ventral view. Bone is white and cartilaginous structure are stippled. **A.** *Leiopelma hochstetteri* (Leiopelmatidae). **B.** *Rhinophrynus dorsalis* (Rhinophrynidae). **C.** *Bombina variegata* (Discoglossidae). **D.** *Leptodactulus ocellatus* (Leptodactylidae). **E.** *Heleioporus albopunctatus* (Myobatrachidae). **F.** *Bufo himalayanus* (Bufonidae). Abbreviations: ant p hyale = anterior process of hyale; antlat p = anterolateral process of hyoid plate; phyd = parahyoid bone; plat p = posterolateral process of hyoid plate; pmed p = posteromedial process of hyoid plate.

The m. depressor mandibulae is a massive muscle that is composed of several slips, the number and origins of which vary among species. The depressor is broad dorsally at its origins which may include the dorsal fascia, the skull roof, otic region, and the squamosal. Ventrally, the fibers converge into a tendinous insertion at the posterior end of the mandible.

Hyobranchial Apparatus.   Anurans have the most highly derived hyobranchial apparatus of any amphibians with the possible exception of plethodontid salamanders. Moreover, there is marked variation in the structure of this part of the musculoskeletal system; for the most part, the significance of this variation is poorly understood.

Skeletal components.—The anuran hyoid consists of a central cartilaginous plate that has a shallow V-shape in cross section (Figs. 4-3, 13-21). Two pair of attenuate, doubly recurved structures—the cornua or anterior hyale—arise from the anterolateral corners of the hyoid plate and curve posterodorsally above the plate to attach to the ventral surface of the otic capsule. The cornua are missing in some anurans (e.g., pelodytids) and discontinuous in some others (e.g., *Rhinophrynus).* The hyoid plate usually bears three additional pairs of processes. Anteriorly on the plate, the anterolateral processes flank the cornua laterally. Posteriorly, there are posterolateral processes and a pair of long, bony posteromedial processes. The anterior cornua and posteromedial processes are invariably present; however, the anterolateral and posterolateral pairs vary in both their presence and shape. A few taxa (*Rhinophrynus, Pelodytes,* and leiopelmatids) have parahyoid bones associated with the central hyoid plate; these vary in number, position, and size, and their homologies, function, and histological derivation are uncertain. The hyoid lies in the floor of the mouth and serves as the site of insertion for a variety of muscles associated with movement of the tongue and as the origin of the m. hyoglossus which constitutes the main body of the tongue.

The laryngeal apparatus is derived from the larval hyobranchial skeleton, In most anurans, it is composed of a pair of arytenoid cartilages that are supported by the cricoid ring (Figs. 4-3, 4-5). which is complete in most species. It is incomplete dorsally in a few (e.g., pelobatids), ventrally incomplete in myobatrachids and sooglossids, and bears lateral gaps in at least one species of *Dendrobates.*

Mandibular and hyobranchial muscles.—Since 1970, a great deal has been learned about the mandibular and hyoid musculature of anurans, which is considerably more complex and derived than that of salamanders. In anurans, the hyobranchial musculoskeletal system is involved in vocalization as well as ventilation and feeding, as the majority of anurans feed by flipping the tongue anterior to the snout (Gans and Gorniak, 1982a). The mechanisms of tongue protrusion in salamanders and anurans is described in Chapter 9. Trewavas (1933) remains the classic reference on variation in the anuran hyoid and its associated musculature. Tyler, in several papers (e.g., 1971a, 1972), described variation in the superficial mandibular musculature and discussed its probable phylogenetic significance within various groups of anurans. Magimel-Pelonnier (1924) described the tongues of many amphibians, especially anurans. Attention was focused on the functional aspects of this variation by Regal and Gans (1976), and the diversity and systematic significance of the anuran tongue musculature was discussed by Horton (1982b).

Laryngeal and swallowing muscles

As in salamanders, the principal muscles used in swallowing are the mm. dilatator laryngis, constrictor (= sphincter) laryngis, intermandibularis, interhyoideus, and levator bulbi. The m. dilatator laryngis (Figs. 4-3, 4-5), present in all anurans, originates from the posteromedial process of the hyoid and inserts on the arytenoid cartilage. The constrictor or sphincter encircles the arytenoid cartilage (Figs. 4-3, 4-5). Usually it is separated into anterior and posterior parts, and from its origin on the hyoid plate inserts on a raphe. Many bufonids lack the posterior constrictor, and the muscle also is absent in *Bombina.* In pipids the muscle is not divided into anterior and posterior portions.

The mandibular musculature of anurans is especially variable in that many supplemental slips apparently have arisen from the main muscle masses in various taxa (Tyler, 1971a, 1972, 1974). The basic configuration of this sheet of muscles in anurans consists of the mm. submentalis, intermandibularis, and interhyoideus in an anterior to posterior sequence (Figs. 13-20, 13-22). The m. submentalis is a small bundle of short, transverse fibers that unite the mandibular rami most anteriorly. Contraction of this muscle rotates the jaw symphysis by moving the mentomeckelian bones. This action is linked to closing the external nares (Gans and Pyles, 1983) and is involved in the depression of the lower jaw in the initial stages of feeding. The m. intermandibularis consists of long, more or less transverse fibers that insert on a medial aponeurosis and raphe, and unite the margins of the mandibular rami usually almost to their posterior ends. Posterior to the m. intermandibularis, and sometimes overlapping it, is the m. interhyoideus. The diversity of the size and structure of this muscle is associated with variation in the structure of the vocal sac, which may be internal (Fig. 4-8) or external, single and median (Fig. 4-7), or paired lateral or posterolateral (see Chapter 4). Depending on the disposition of the vocal sac, the muscles may take the form of a relatively flat sheet, or have a single, large posterior lobe or some degree of bilobate development. If the vocal sacs are internal and lateral, the m. interhyoideus is elaborated into a tubular extension that lies posterolateral to the head. Obviously the function of the m. interhyoideus in anurans is modified from that in salamanders.

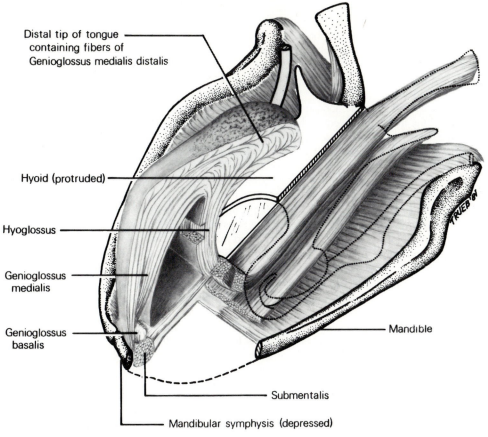

Distal tip of tongue
containing fibers of
Genioglossus medialis distalis

Hyoid (protruded)

Hyoglossus

Genioglossus
medialis

Genioglossus
basalis

Mandible

Submentalis

Mandibular symphysis (depressed)

Figure 13-22. Cutaway of mandibular, hyoid, and tongue musculature of *Bufo marinus* at the beginning of a tongue-flip sequence. Bones are stippled, cartilage is white, and muscles are gray. Reproduced from Gans and Gorniak (1982a) with permission of the AAAS.

Mm. geniohyoideus, omohyoideus, and petrohyoidei

Muscles that move the hyoid and tongue lie deep to the mandibular series (Fig. 13-20). The most superficial of these is the strap-like m. geniohyoideus that arises from the anterior margin of the mandible and inserts on the posterolateral processes of the hyoid. In most anurans, the m. geniohyoideus is composed of medial and lateral components, although it is single in *Leiopelma* and the discoglossids. The muscle protracts the hyoid and is associated intimately with the m. sternohyoideus (a derivative of the m. rectus abdominis of the ventral trunk musculature) which arises from the sternum, inserts along the posterolateral edge of the hyoid, and acts to retract the hyoid plate. Movement of the hyoid plate also is affected by the m. omohyoideus and the mm. petrohyoidei. The m. omohyoideus is unique to, and present in most, anurans; it arises from the ventral margin of the scapula and inserts on the edge of the hyoid plate. The mm. petrohyoidei are derived from the branchial arch musculature; they arise from the venter of the skull in the auditory region and attach to the lateral edge and the

posteromedial process of the hyoid. The number of pairs of petrohyoids varies. Some anurans possess four, whereas others have only three, in which case the m. petrohyoideus iii is missing. Pipids have only one petrohyoid; the identity of this muscle is unknown. Petrohyoid muscles are not present in salamanders.

Mm. genioglossus and hyoglossus

The tongue is composed of two muscles in anurans, the m. genioglossus and m. hyoglossus (Fig. 13-22). The m. genioglossus basalis is a small muscle that lies in the area of the mandibular symphysis above the m. submentalis at the anterior root of the tongue. The m. genioglossus medialis arises just behind the mandibular symphysis, dorsal to the m. genioglossus basalis, and is composed of parallel fibers that diverge slightly posteriorly and insert on hyoglossal fibers. This muscle forms the upper surface of the tongue. The m. hyoglossus arises from the ventral surface of the posteromedial processes of the hyoid, extends along the ventral surface of the hyoid plate, and turns posterodorsally into the floor of the mouth at the anterior edge of the hyoglossal sinus.

Fibers of the m. hyoglossus insert on the fibers of the m. genioglossus medialis. The point of its flexion represents the posterior root of the tongue; distal to this root, the m. hyoglossus forms the free ventral surface of the tongue.

AXIAL SYSTEM

The axial skeleton provides a rigid, but flexible, longitudinal brace for the support of the head and viscera and suspension of the appendicular skeleton, and serves as a conduit for the spinal cord. If a tail is present, it is supported by the posterior part of the vertebral column. The vertebral column is composed of varying numbers of individual vertebrae, each of which consists of a cylindrical body of bone known as a centrum which is round or oval in cross section. The neural arch is located on the dorsal side of each centrum; the spinal cord passes dorsal to the centra through the neural arches of the vertebrae. The neural arch may bear a dorsal projection known as the neural spine to which muscles and ligaments attach.

Each vertebra except the first (the atlas, which is located behind the skull) bears two pairs of processes for articulation with adjacent vertebrae; the prezygapophyses located at the anterior end of the vertebra articulate with the postzygapophyses located at the posterior end of the next anterior vertebra. In addition, amphibian vertebrae may bear various lateral projections—namely, diapophyses for the attachment of the upper head of two-headed ribs, parapophyses for the attachment of the lower head of two-headed ribs, and pleurapophyses representing the rib attachments of the vertebra plus the fused rib. The first postcranial vertebra or atlas of all amphibians is modified anteriorly to articulate with the skull. The atlas bears two cup-shaped atlantal cotyles that form condyloid joints with the occipital condyles of the skull. Ribs in amphibians are either present or absent, and if present, may bear a double-headed or single-headed articulation with the vertebra, or be fused to the vertebra. The ribs of amphibians are unique among tetrapods (including labyrinthodont amphibians) because they do not extend beyond the vertebral musculature into the flank musculature (with the exception of some salamanders, e.g., *Euproctus* and *Triturus)*. As pointed out by Cox (1967), the presence of short ribs probably is correlated with the mechanism of breathing in amphibians which involves a buccal pump rather than expansion of the coelom for inflation.

In addition to various articulations between adjacent vertebrae described above, successive vertebral centra articulate with one another via condyloid joints. Although the centra of all Recent amphibians are monospondylous, the formation and the appearance of the centra, as well as the nature of the articulation between them, are variable. The origin of this variation as well as its functional and phylogenetic significance continue to be issues of debate. Various schemes have been devised to categorize the observed variation. Thus, Griffiths (1959b) proposed that on the basis of development, anuran vertebral centra could be classified as ectochordal (spool-shaped with an open center in which the notochord lies), holochordal (spool-shaped with solid center), or stegochordal (depressed dorsoventrally and solid). Taking issue with Griffiths's scheme, Kluge and Farris (1969) suggested that based on developmental evidence provided by Mookerjee (1930) and Mookerjee and Das (1939), anuran centra are either perichordal or epichordal. Perichordal centra are formed from ossification around the notochord; the resulting centrum thus is cylindrical in cross section. Epichordal centra are formed from ossification associated with the dorsal part of the notochord; the resulting centrum tends to be depressed in cross section. On the basis of rather limited evidence, Kluge and Farris also noted that there is considerable variation in the degree of epichordy among anurans; thus some centra are less depressed than others because ossification extends farther down the sides of the notochord. On the basis of their review of the literature and their own observations, Kluge and Farris concluded that anuran vertebrae should be classed as either epichordal or perichordal, and that Griffiths' term holochordal should be reserved to describe any centrum that is solid, as opposed to one which is ringlike (i.e., hollow in the center).

Griffiths (1959b) and Kluge and Farris (1969) were concerned with vertebral development and morphology as it applied to anurans primarily. Other authors, notably E. Williams (1959), D. Wake (1970), and most recently Gardiner (1983) have taken broader views. Gardiner provided a summary of the literature relating to vertebral development among fishes and tetrapods, and concluded that in all Recent amphibians the vertebrae are formed chiefly by membrane bone with only the ends of the centra and the cores of the neural and haemal arches being formed of cartilaginous bone. According to Gardiner (1983), initially the vertebra is formed from bone produced from the notochordal mesenchyme (perichordal) that spreads in the perichondrium, the fibrous membrane that covers cartilage. He argued that cartilage between adjacent vertebrae forms between the two sheaths of the notochord and therefore is chordacentral. Thus, in Gardiner's view, the vertebral centra of amphibians are perichordal with some chordacentral additions. This conclusion contrasts with those of Schmalhausen (1958), E. Williams (1959), D. Wake (1970), and D. Wake and Lawson (1973), all of whom claimed that in salamanders the husklike centrum was the result of perichondral ossification.

Amphibian vertebrae also are classified on the basis of their intervertebral relationship. Thus, the term amphicoelous is used to describe amphibians having centra that are biconcave terminally and separated by intervertebral cartilage which may or may not be independent of the adjacent centra. Opisthocoelous denotes a condition wherein the intervertebral cartilage is confluent with the anterior end of the centrum; thus, a condyloid joint that allows movement in two planes is formed between the anterior end of one centrum and the posterior end of the anteriorly adjacent centrum. Procoely is the reverse of opisthocoely; thus, the intervertebral cartilage is associated with the posterior end of each centrum.

The axial musculature is composed of somatic or parietal muscles that are derived from the myotomes of the epimere (dorsal muscle plate) and innervated by spinal nerves. Somatic muscles are constituted by an axial succession of muscle segments or myotomes, each of which is separated from the adjacent myotome by a connective tissue partition known as a myoseptum. Myotomes are divided in dorsal and ventral halves by a horizontal skeletogenous septum; the dorsal half comprises the epaxial musculature, whereas the ventral half is the hypaxial musculature.

In amphibians, the epaxial musculature consists of a single, segmented sheet, the m. dorsalis trunci, from which many deeper fiber tracts arise that span two or more successive vertebrae. These muscles facilitate angular movement between vertebrae in the horizontal plane; such movement is associated with lateral undulations of the body.

The hypaxial musculature is composed of three series—the subvertebral, flank (i.e., lateral), and abdominal muscles. The subvertebrals are the most dorsomedial and flex the spinal column. The flank muscles, or oblique series, are composed of three sheets of muscles superimposed on one another. The abdominal muscles extend from the shoulder to the pelvis; the right and left halves of this series are separated by an aponeurosis, the linea alba. The abdominal and flank muscles provide support for the viscera, flex the vertebral column ventrally, and in some cases retract the hyoid apparatus.

Salamanders

Axial Osteology. Most early descriptions of the axial skeletons of salamanders as exemplified by Francis (1934) and Hilton (1948, and references cited therein) are typological. Interest has been rekindled recently owing to D. Wake's (1970) and D. Wake and Lawson's (1973) descriptions of the various kinds of centra and their development in salamanders, especially as this relates to relationships among Recent amphibia (see also Gardiner, 1983, and included references).

Vertebral regions.—The vertebral column consists of five, poorly differentiated regions—namely, cervical, trunk, sacral, caudal-sacral, and caudal regions (Fig. 13-23). The cervical region is represented by a single vertebra, the atlas, that lacks ribs. Unlike other amphibians, in salamanders the atlas bears four points of articulation with the posterior end of the skull (Fig. 13-23). There are two, large, cup-shaped atlantal cotyles that articulate with the occipital condyles. Ventromedially, between the atlantal cotyles is an anterior process, the odontoid process or tuberculum interglenoideum, that projects into the fora-

men magnum of the skull and bears articular facets that articulate with the lateral walls of the foramen.

The trunk region lies between the atlas and the sacrum, and is composed of 10–60 vertebrae depending on the species of salamander. Unlike most other vertebrates, the spinal nerves of salamanders often pass through foramina in the vertebrae, but many salamanders (e.g., hynobiids, cryptobranchids, and proteiids) also retain intervertebral nerves (Edwards, 1976). Trunk vertebrae generally are similar to one another (Fig. 13-23), although the centrum length of midtrunk vertebrae is greater than that of vertebrae at the anterior end of the column and behind the sacrum. The functional significance of this and other variation in vertebral proportions is discussed by Worthington and D. Wake (1972). Zygapophyses are well formed and broad, a neural spine is present, and ribs are present on all but the most posterior trunk vertebrae. Ribs usually are bicapitate, with the ventral head (capitulum) articulating with the parapophysis projecting from the dorsal part of the centrum, and the dorsal head (tuberculum) articulating with the diapophysis which arises near the midpoint of the neural arch. The diapophyses tend to be posterolaterally oriented and robust (e.g., *Salamandra*), and sometimes are termed transverse processes. In some salamanders (e.g., some hynobiids, cryptobranchids, and plethodontids), the two heads of the rib have fused to produce a unicapitate rib. The ribs of the anterior trunk vertebrae (second and third) tend to bear cartilaginous expansions at their distal extremities for the attachment of muscles suspending the pectoral girdle to the vertebral column.

The sacrum is an enlarged trunk vertebra with transverse processes (diapophyses) and ribs that are elaborated for support of the pelvic girdle (Fig. 13-23). The ilia of the girdle are bound to the sacrum by fibrous tissue.

The caudal-sacral region consists of two to four vertebrae posterior to the sacrum (Fig. 13-23). These vertebrae usually do not bear ribs. The last vertebra of the series is distinguished by its possession of a well-developed but nonspinous haemal arch ventrally. This vertebra supports the posterior part of the cloaca and marks the posterior limit of the trunk of the salamander.

Depending on the species of salamander, the caudal or tail region may consist of 20 to more than 100 vertebrae. These vertebrae exhibit a gradual reduction in the sizes of their transverse processes and zygapophyses, but these structures never are entirely absent. All caudal vertebrae bear a ventral haemal arch that forms a bony canal for the protection of the caudal artery and vein.

Tail autotomy is characteristic of most salamanders under conditions of stress. The process has been reviewed and studied by D. Wake and Dresner (1967). Breakage occurs in an intervertebral plane and subsequently another tail is regenerated. If the salamander has a thick-based tail (e.g., *Desmognathus),* breakage usually is limited to the posterior, thinner part of the tail. In species with slender-based tails (e.g., *Chioglossa),* breakage can

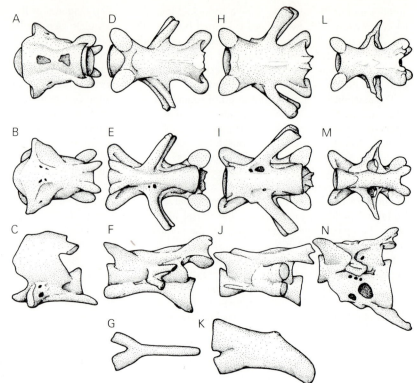

Figure 13-23. Vertebrae of the salamander *Ambystoma opacum*, redrawn from Worthington (1971). **A.** Atlas in dorsal, **B.** ventral, and **C.** lateral views. **D.** Seventh trunk vertebra in dorsal, **E.** ventral, and **F.** lateral views. **G.** Anterior view of seventh rib drawn to slightly larger scale than vertebra. **H.** Sacral vertebra in dorsal, **I.** ventral, and **J.** lateral views. **K.** Anterior view of sacral rib drawn to slightly larger scale than sacral vertebra. **L.** First caudal vertebra in dorsal, **M.** ventral, and **N.** lateral views.

occur anywhere throughout the length of the tail, but it does so in a specialized manner. The break in the skin occurs one segment posterior to the break in the muscle; thus, the skin covers the wound to facilitate healing. Most plethodontid salamanders have constricted-based tails. In these species, tail breaks usually occur in the basal, constricted area, at the end of the first caudal segment where the muscle is thinner and the skin weaker. After autotomy, tail regeneration proceeds rapidly with all tissue except the notochord being regenerated.

Centra.—The centra of salamander vertebrae typically have been described as either amphicoelous (i.e., biconcave) or opisthocoelous (bearing a condyle at the anterior end of the centrum that articulates with a concavity in the posterior end of the next anterior centrum). Based on developmental and histological studies, D. Wake (1970), Worthington (1971), and D. Wake and Lawson (1973) have shown that the structure and relationships of vertebral centra in salamanders are a great deal more complex than has been assumed in the past. The centra have a dual origin from both cartilaginous and membranous components. Gardiner (1983) provided a controversial summary based on the work of other individuals (see Schmalhausen, 1958, and additional references) in which he stated that formation of salamander vertebrae begins with the appearance of paired, cartilaginous anlagen in the position of the myosepta. The dorsal elements fuse to form a neural arch dorsally, whereas the ventral elements fuse to form a haemal arch in the tail ventrally. The process of ossification commences with the appearance of an acellular sheath in the mesenchyme around the developing centrum. The sheath rapidly increases in thickness, and becomes cellular as it encloses connective tissue cells. Bone first appears in the angles between the bases of the neural arch and then spreads over the surface of the notochordal sheath in the connective tissue mesenchyme. In the majority of salamanders the bone spreads from the notochordal mesenchyme into the perichondrium of the neural and haemal arches. Because ossification never separates the cartilaginous arches from the notochordal sheath, the cartilaginous core of the neural arch rests directly in the notochord. In the hynobiid *Ranodon,* bone penetrates beneath the bases of the neural arches, thereby completely removing the cartilaginous arch from the notochord beneath (Schmalhausen, 1958).

According to Gardiner (1983), while ossification of the centrum and neural arch is progressing, cartilaginous intervertebral rings form and become enclosed within the ends of two, adjacent centra. However, Schmalhausen (1958), E. Williams (1959), D. Wake (1970), and D. Wake and Lawson (1973) reported that the husklike centrum of salamanders is a perichondral ossification rather than a perichordal ossification as stated by Gardiner. His conclusion is based on the fact that the centrum ossifies prior to formation of intervertebral chordacentral cartilage that forms between the two sheaths of the notochord—a process not observed by D. Wake (1970) or D. Wake and Lawson (1973).

Once formed, the cartilaginous ring may remain narrow, or it may widen to fill the intervertebral gap. Ultimately, two intervertebral configurations are possible in salamanders. The cartilaginous ring may remain undivided and the notochord unconstricted, or the ring may thicken and contrict the notochord intervertebrally. If the ring is segmented transversely, an opisthocoelous joint is formed between adjacent vertebrae. Thus the cartilage, which may become mineralized or ossified (D. Wake and Lawson, 1973), adheres to the anterior end of the centrum. The resulting vertebra is composed primarily of membrane bone with the cores of the neural and haemal arches, and some parts of the centrum having been formed of cartilage bone, according to Schmalhausen (1958) and D. Wake (1970).

Primitively, a large notochord persists in salamanders. Thus the vertebrae of cryptobranchids, for example, are described as notochordal because the spool-shaped centrum is hollow, allowing for the passage of the notochord. In more advanced species (e.g., ambystomatids) the notochord remains continuous throughout life but can be rather constricted intervertebrally. The cartilage is attached to the anterior end of each vertebra, and a joint is formed by a disk of fibrocartilage with the anteriorly adjacent centrum. Because a kind of condylar joint is formed, these vertebrae are considered to be functionally opisthocoelous, but owing to the persistence of the notochord, they are considered to be notochordal (or amphicoelous) structurally. In more advanced salamanders such as salamandrids and plethodontids, the notochord may be disrupted almost completely and replaced by large amounts of inter- and intravertebral cartilage. The intervertebral cartilage is highly differentiated and a distinct zone of fibrocartilage marks the articular region between adjacent centra. The posterior part of the intervertebral cartilage forms a condyle that is fused to the centrum behind to produce a truly opisthocoelous vertebra.

Axial Myology. Among the earliest works dealing with the axial musculature of salamanders are those of Maurer (1892, 1911) and Nishi (1916). Francis (1934) included a detailed description of *Salamandra salamandra* in his monograph. More recently, Naylor (1978) dealt with variation in the vertebral column and trunk musculature as it relates to the systematics of fossil and Recent salamanders. The description that follows is based primarily on Francis's work.

Epaxial musculature.—The epaxial, or dorsal trunk, musculature is composed of a superficial, segmented sheet termed the m. dorsalis trunci (Fig. 13-24). Both this sheet and the deeper tracts that are derived from it are innervated by dorsal rami of the spinal nerves. There are two deeper tracts that can be distinguished. The m. interspinalis lies on the dorsal side of the vertebrae. Fibers arise from the posterodorsal edge of the postzygapophysis of one vertebra and insert along the dorsal surface of the neural arch of the posteriorly adjacent vertebra. the mm. intertransversarii lie between adjacent transverse processes

where they arise from, and insert on, bone. In the region of the neck, the m. intertransversarius is differentiated into three muscles that attach to the back of the skull and that are described above with the neurocranium of salamanders. These muscles are the mm. transversarius capitis superior, posterior, and inferior.

Hypaxial musculature.—The hypaxial, or so-called ventral trunk musculature consists of both dorsal and ventral components that are subdivided into three categories—subvertebral, flank, and abdominal muscles—all of which are innervated by spinal nerves (Fig. 13-24). The subvertebral muscles lie ventral to the vertebral column, and are composed of at least two sets of muscles. The most dorsomedial of these is the pars subvertebralis that is associated with the ventral aspect of successive vertebrae. Lateral to these muscles lies the pars transversalis, a band of vertical fibers that are attached to the ventral surfaces of the ribs.

The flank musculature is composed of the oblique muscles, a series of three muscular sheets that are superimposed on one another. The most superficial sheet is the m. obliquus externus. The fibers of this muscle slant downward posteriorly and arise dorsally from the ribs and the tendinous inscriptions to insert on the next posteriorly adjacent inscription. Beneath this sheet lies the m. obliquus internus. The fibers of this muscle run in right angles to those of the m. obliquus externus—that is, they slant downward anteriorly. Fibers are attached to adjacent myosepta that are continuous with the ribs. This layer of flank musculature generally is absent in hynobiid salamanders (e.g., *Batrachuperus, Hynobius,* and *Ranodon*) (Naylor and Nussbaum, 1980). The third and deepest layer of the flank musculature is the m. transversus, the fibers of which run in a dorsoventral direction and form a band along the flanks. The primary function of the oblique musculature is to provide support for the vicera, and to exert a ventral force on the axial column.

The abdominal trunk musculature is represented by the m. rectus abdominis and its derivatives. This system of muscles extends between the pectoral and pelvic girdles and is divided into right and left halves that are separated ventromedially by the linea alba. The most superficial layer is the m. rectus abdominis superficialis, an extensive flat sheet that covers the venter of the abdomen from the anterior edge of the pubis to the sternum. The muscle is interrupted by tendinous inscriptions, each of which is firmly attached to the overlying skin and each of which corresponds to a costal groove. The anterior fibers of the m. rectus abdominis insert primarily on the posterolateral edge of the sternum and the anterior fibers of the m. rectus abdominis superficialis on the pericardium; a few fibers extend forward to insert on the hyoid. Posteriorly, a few fibers insert on the ypsiloid cartilage if it is present. The deeper layer of the m. rectus abdominis (profundus) arises from the anterior edge of the pubis in *Salamandra,* but from the ischium in plethodontids. The muscle also is characterized by the presence of tendinous inscriptions, the most posterior of which

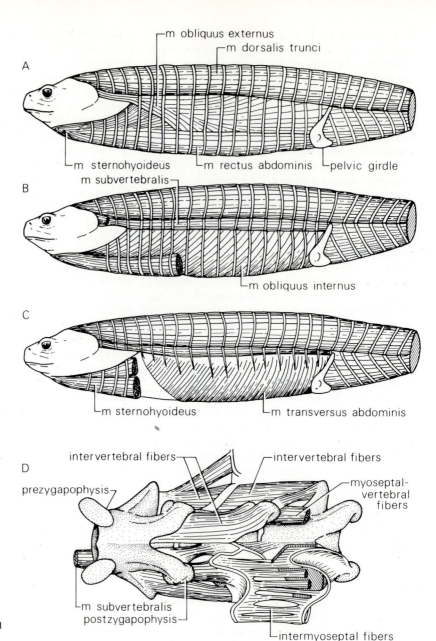

A

—m obliquus externus
—m dorsalis trunci

—m sternohyoideus ——m rectus abdominis —pelvic girdle

B

—m subvertebralis

—m obliquus internus

C

—m sternohyoideus ——m transversus abdominis

D

intervertebral fibers— —intervertebral fibers

prezygapophysis— —myoseptal-
vertebral
fibers

—m subvertebralis
postzygapophysis—

—intermyoseptal fibers

Figure 13-24. Diagrammatic illustration of
salamander trunk musculature. **A.** Superficial.
B. Deep to mm. obliquus externus and rectus
abdominis. **C.** Deep to m. obliquus internus.
D. Dorsal view of epaxial musculature. Adapted
from K. Liem (1977).

are attached to the superficial layer of the muscle
(m. rectus abdominis superficialis) in most salamanders;
anteriorly, the two layers of muscle are not attached. The
m. rectus abdominis profundus extends anteriorly to the
sternum. At this level one portion of the muscle forms a
neck muscle, the m. rectus cervicus profundus, whereas
the remaining fibers (m. hebosteoypsiloideus) pass forward to insert on the urohyal. The primary functions of
the rectus abdominis muscles are to provide support for
the viscera, retract the hyoid, and flex the vertebral column ventrally.

Salamanders possessing an ypsiloid cartilage (see discussion under Appendicular System) have two additional

derivatives of the rectus abdominis muscles, namely the
mm. ypsiloideus anterior and ypsiloideus posterior. The
former muscle is composed of a few fibers that originate
from the anterior edge of the lateral processes of the
ypsiloid cartilage and insert on the anteriorly adjacent
inscription. Contraction of this muscle elevates the ypsiloid cartilage. The m. ypsiloideus posterior is a much
larger muscle that arises from the anterodorsal edge of
the pubis deep to the m. rectus abdominis profundus and
spreads anteriorly in a fan shape to insert on the lateral
edges of the shaft and the posterior edges of the lateral
processes of the ypsiloid cartilage. Contraction of this
muscle depresses the ypsiloid cartilage.

The caudal muscles of salamanders are similar to those of the body. The anterior part of the caudal musculature is distinguished as the m. iliocaudalis. The fibers of this muscle arise from the first two or three caudal vertebrae and insert on the ilium. A tough ligament attaches the spines of the haemal arches of the caudal vertebrae to the skin below, thereby separating the musculature of each half of the tail. Dorsally, there is a deep longitudinal groove in the caudal musculature that accommodates cutaneous skin glands.

Caecilians

Axial Osteology. The only summary of the caecilian axial skeleton is that of M. Wake (1980c) in which she reviewed the pertinent literature, and based on her examination of *Dermophis mexicanus, Ichthyophis glutinosus,* and *Typhlonectes compressicauda,* discussed interspecific variation as well as regional, ontogenetic, and populational variation in the vertebral column of *Dermophis.* Caecilians have an atlas and 95–285 trunk vertebrae; all caecilians lack a vertebra differentiated as a sacrum, and most lack a tail. All vertebrae except the atlas and the terminal 3–6 vertebrae bear double-headed ribs. The diapophysis with which the dorsal head (tuberculum) of the rib articulates is borne on the anterior part of the neural arch, whereas the parapophysis for the articulation of the ventral head (capitulum) of the rib usually lies at the extreme anterior end of the centrum.

Vertebral regions.—There is regional variation in the features and proportions of the vertebrae (Fig. 13-25). The atlas bears large atlantal cotyles for articulation with the occipital condyles of the skull. The centrum and neural arch of this vertebra are shorter than those of posterior vertebrae, and usually this vertebra lacks a nuchal and ventral keel, transverse processes and elongate parapophyses. The remaining cervical (i.e., next 19 or 20) vertebrae have a longitudinal nuchal keel for the attachment of dorsal head musculature. The parapophyses are shorter and more expanded, and the pre- and postzygapophyses broader and flatter than those of more posterior vertebrae. Midbody vertebrae have well-extended rib-bearers, narrower zygapophyses, and a greater length than anterior vertebrae. Toward the posterior end of the animal, overall vertebral dimensions decrease, and in the cloacal region transverse processes (and ribs), parapophyses, and the ventral keel are absent. The most posterior vertebrae consist of rings (composed of the much-reduced centrum and neural arch) around the terminal fibers of the spinal cord. These vertebrae are shaped irregularly and usually fused into sets of two or three vertebrae.

Centra.—The centra of caecilian vertebrae are spool-shaped and amphicoelous. Centrum development is initiated by the appearance of a series of paired, cartilaginous anlagen (i.e., basidorsals) resting above the notochord on its outer sheath; the basidorsals may fuse basally in an anterior-to-posterior sequence to give rise to two continuous, cartilaginous rods. Subsequently, a

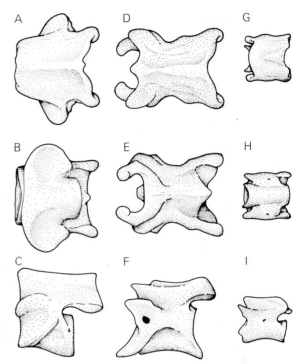

Figure 13-25. Vertebrae of the caecilian *Dermophis mexicanus.* **A.** Atlas in dorsal, **B.** ventral, and **C.** lateral views. **D.** Tenth vertebra in dorsal, **E.** ventral, and **F.** lateral views. **G.** Near-terminal vertebra in dorsal, **H.** ventral, and **I.** lateral views. Redrawn from M. Wake (1980c).

medial cartilaginous rod appears beneath the notochord and becomes divided to form the basiventrals. Accounts of the development of the caecilian vertebral column are provided by Marcus and Blume, Mookerjie, and Ramaswami, as cited by M. Wake (1980c). Presumably the process is similar to that described for salamanders. A peripheral cartilaginous ligament joins successive vertebral centra in some taxa. Naylor and Nussbaum (1980) suggested that the intercentral ligaments, which have no muscle fibers associated with them, seem to provide automatic realignment of the vertebrae after flexion and strengthen the intervertebral joints.

Axial Myology. Early contributions to knowledge of caecilian trunk musculature includes Wiedersheim (1879), Nishi (1916), Marcus (1934), and von Schnurbein (1935). There are three basic, recent works that deal with caecilian trunk musculature in some detail—Lawson (1965) on *Hypogeophis,* and Naylor and Nussbaum (1980) and Nussbaum and Naylor (1982) on comparative studies of several taxa. The last work is particularly helpful because the authors summarize variation among 28 species of caecilians, summarize early work, provide a table of synonyms of muscle names, and compare the trunk musculature of caecilians with that of salamanders and anurans. The major difference between caecilians and other amphibians with respect to axial musculature is that all of the hypaxial components except the subvertebral musculature form an external muscular sheath that is attached firmly to the skin by fibrous connective tissues and virtually disassociated from vertebral musculature; thus, the skin and superficial muscles move as a unit. In caecilians having only primary annuli, or primary and secondary annuli (Caeciliidae, Scolecomorphidae, Typhlonectidae, Uraeotyphlidae), the positions of the primary annuli correspond to the positions of the myosepta in this sheath. This congruency is absent in species having tertiary annuli (Rhinatrematidae, Ichthyophiidae).

Epaxial musculature.—The epaxial musculature consists of a thick dorsal mass of V-shaped flexures that extend posteriorly, the m. dorsalis trunci (Fig. 13-26). Deep to this are series of paired hyperapophyseal muscles that originate over the neural arch of one vertebra and insert by a broad aponeurosis to the hyperapophysis of the anteriorly adjacent vertebra in a manner characteristic of salamanders.

Hypaxial musculature.—The hypaxial components of the muscular body wall sheath are the mm. obliquus externus superficialis, rectus lateralis, obliquus externus profundus, rectus abdominis, obliquus internus, and transversus (Fig. 13-26). The m. obliquus externus superficialis forms a narrow, longitudinal band of muscles on the dorsolateral edge of the body; the fibers are arranged in an oblique plane, and may or may not be segmented. This band covers the junction of the two deeper components of the sheath—the m. rectus lateralis dorsally, and the m. obliquus externus profundus ventrally. The former is a longitudinal, segmented band of muscles, whereas the latter is a sheetlike muscle having fibers that extend longitudinally between the myosepta. Ventromedially, the sheath is composed of the segmented m. rectus abdominis. This muscle is continuous with the m. obliquus externus profundus dorsally, and separated into right and left halves by the linea alba mid-

ventrally. Deeper elements of the sheath are the m. obliquus internus laterally and the m. transversus ventrolaterally. The m. obliquus internus usually is unsegmented, lies between the m. obliquus profundus and m. transversus, and has nearly vertical fibers. The m. transversus is a deep, sheetlike, unsegmented muscle with dorsoventral fibers.

The most dorsal part of the hypaxial musculature is the m. subvertebralis which is separable into three parts. The uppermost layer consists of basapophyseal muscles that connect successive vertebrae. Each muscle blends laterally and ventrally into its associated subvertebral myomere, and these myomeres represent a series of overlapping units divided by myosepta deep to the external sheath. The most ventral part of the subvertebral musculature, the pars ventralis, is a series of muscles that attach midventrally to the vertebral centra and subcentral keels, and extend anterolaterally to insert on the external muscular sheath. This layer of subvertebral muscles is unknown in salamanders and anurans.

Although the trunk musculature is basically similar to that of salamanders, it is much better developed in caecilians. Moreover, caecilians possess a derivative of the m. subvertebralis unknown in salamanders, and the vertebral musculature is largely independent of the body wall muscles in contrast to all salamanders except *Amphiuma means*. Nussbaum and Naylor (1982) correlated these differences with the locomotory habits of caecilians that involve serpentine and vermiform action, both of which are possible only if the vertebral column is supple and the trunk muscles well developed.

Anurans

Axial Osteology. The axial skeleton of anurans is highly modified in comparison to those of salamanders and caecilians; moreover, there is a great deal of variation in centrum structure. Doubtless, it was this variation that attracted the attention of many earlier workers. Thus,

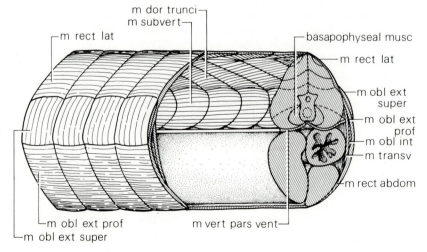

Figure 13-26. Schematic illustration of caecilian trunk muscles redrawn from Nussbaum and Naylor (1982). Abbreviations: m dor trunci = m. dorsalis trunci; m obl ext prof = m. obliquus externus profundus; m obl ext super = m. obliquus externus superficialis; m obl int = m. obliquus internus; m rect abdom = m. rectus abdominis; m rect lat = m. rectus lateralis; m subvert = m. subertebralis; m transv = m. transversus; m vert pars vent = m. subvertebralis pars ventralis; musc = muscle.

Cope (1865) and Noble (1922) used vertebral characters in their major classifications of anurans. Nicholls (1916), Mookerjee (1931), and Griffiths (1963) investigated the morphology and development of anuran centra, and developed a scheme of classification of vertebral types that subsequently was amended by Kluge and Farris (1969). Most recently, Gardiner (1983) has reviewed vertebral development in anurans as part of his review of gnathostome vertebrae and the classification of the Amphibia. Despite these efforts, there is still a great deal to be learned about the ontogenetic and adult variation in anuran vertebrae and its functional and phylogenetic significance.

Vertebral regions.—The anuran vertebral column customarily is divided into three regions—presacral, sacral, and postsacral (Fig. 13-27). The presacral region consists of five to eight vertebrae, the most anterior of which is the atlas or cervical vertebra (also designated as Presacral I). The atlas lacks transverse processes in most anurans, and bears a pair of atlantal cotyles that articulate with the occipital condyles of the skull. The odontoid process of salamanders is lacking in anurans.

Each presacral vertebrae posterior to the atlas bears a pair of pre- and postzygapophyses on the neural arch, and a pair of transverse processes (parapophyses) that extend laterally from the pedicel. The transverse processes of Presacrals II–IV or V are expanded and more robust than those of the posterior presacrals, and bear muscular attachments for the suspension of the pectoral girdle.

There is considerable variation in the development of the neural arches of presacral vertebrae. In poorly ossified species (e.g., *Notaden*) the halves of the neural arch may fail to unite on anterior vertebrae, but in most anu-

rans the arch is complete and bears a neural spine. Generally, neural spines are best developed on anterior presacrals and gradually diminish in size posteriorly. Depending on the posterior elaboration of the neural arch, the presacral vertebrae may be nonimbricate (i.e., nonoverlapping as in *Ascaphus*) or imbricate (i.e., overlapping as in pipids).

In many anurans, there is a tendency to reduce the number of presacral vertebrae through fusion. The centra of Presacrals I and II fuse (e.g., *Pipa*, Fig. 13-27B), and the atlas comes to bear a pair of transverse processes. Fusions can involve as many as the first four presacrals (e.g., some dendrobatids). The number of presacral vertebrae also is reduced by incorporation of posterior vertebrae into the sacrum. When this occurs (e.g., the pipids *Hymenochirus* and *Pseudhymenochirus)*, it is evidenced by the presence of additional spinal nerve foramina in the sacrum.

Ribs occur in only three Recent anuran families—leiopelmatids, discoglossids, and pipids—and usually are limited to three pairs that are associated with the transverse process of Presacrals II, III, and IV (Fig. 13-27). Occasionally, the leiopelmatids have a fourth pair of ribs associated with Presacral V. The ribs are free in the leiopelmatids and discoglossids, but ankylosed to the transverse processes in adult pipids.

The sacrum usually is a single, specialized vertebra (but see discussions of vertebral fusions above) from which the pelvic girdle is suspended. It is located between the presacrals anteriorly and the rodlike coccyx (= urostyle) posteriorly. The sacrum bears a pair of prezygapophyses which articulate with the postzygapophyses of the last

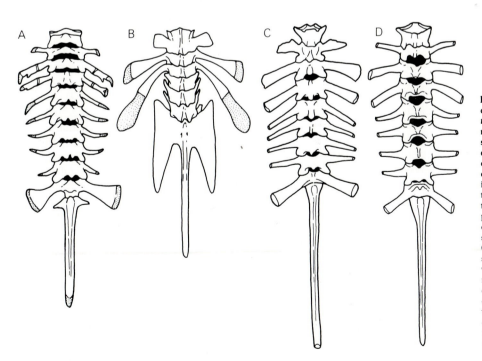

Figure 13-27. Anuran vertebral columns in dorsal view. **A.** *Ascaphus truei* illustrating a frog with nonimbricate vertebrae, free ribs, a sacrum with moderately expanded diapophyses, and vestigial processes on the coccyx. **B.** *Pipa myersi,* an example of a species having only six imbricate presacral vertebrae with the first two presacrals fused, ribs that are ankylosed to the transverse processes, a sacrum with widely expanded diapophyses, and the sacrum fused to the coccyx. **C.** *Leptodactylus pentadactylus,* a species with eight presacral vertebrae, most of which are nonimbricate, a sacrum bearing diapophyses that are scarcely expanded, and moderately broad transverse processes. **D.** *Rana esculenta,* an anuran with nearly round, posterolaterally oriented sacral diapophyses.

presacral vertebra, but postzygapophyses are absent on the sacra of almost all anurans (Fig. 13-27). The transverse processes of the sacrum are expanded to form sacral diapophyses that articulate with the ilia of the pectoral girdle. The sacral diapophyses are broadly expanded in some anurans (e.g., pipids and some pelobatids), moderately dilated (e.g., bufonids, hylids) in many, and round or cylindrical in some (e.g., ranids, pseudids).

The terminal element in the anuran axial column is the coccyx (Fig. 13-27), a rodlike element that represents the fusion of postsacral vertebral elements. The coccyx lies between the shafts of the ilia of the pelvic girdle and bears muscular attachments to these elements. In most anurans the coccyx bears a bicondylar articulation with the sacrum, although in some (e.g., pipids) it is fused or bears a monocondylar articulation (e.g., *Rhamphophryne*). In leiopelmatids, the coccyx lacks a distinct articulation with the sacrum, and instead, the two components are connected by fibrocartilage. A dorsal crest and lateral expansions are variably developed on the urostyle, and in some anurans (e.g., pelobatids, and some leptodactylids and bufonids) the anterior end may bear a pair of vestigial transverse processes.

Centra.—The structure of the vertebral centra in anurans is highly variable, and although several schemes have been devised to categorize this variation, none is particularly amenable to phylogenetic, functional, or ontogenetic interpretation. The terms most frequently encountered in the literature describing anuran centra are amphicoelous, anomocoelous, opisthocoelous, procoelous, and diplasiocoelous, especially as these were promulgated by Noble (1922, based on the work of Nicholls, 1916) in his classification of frogs. Amphicoelous has been applied to primitive anurans (e.g., leiopelmatids) in which the bony centrum is terminally flat or biconcave, remnants of the notochord persist, and the intervertebral joint (including that between the sacrum and urostyle) is formed by a combination of hyaline and fibrocartilage. The term anomocoelous has been used to describe the pelobatids, in reference to the relationship of the coccyx and sacrum which either are fused or have a monocondylar articulation in this family. The presacral centra have a variety of configurations in pelobatids. They may be biconcave with a free intervertebral disc that remains cartilaginous or is mineralized. The disc may tend to adhere to the posterior end of the centrum without actually being fused to it, or it may be united synostotically with the centrum to form a procoelous vertebra (see definition below). Opisthocoely refers to a condition in which the presacral centra are concave posteriorly and bear a condyle formed from intervertebral cartilage on their anterior ends for articulation with the anteriorly adjacent centrum. This pattern is typical of discoglossids and pipids. In procoelous anurans (the fossil palaeobatrachids, some pelobatids, and all other more advanced frogs), the presacral centra are concave anteriorly and bear a condyle on their posterior end for articulation with the posteriorly adjacent

centrum. The term diplasiocoelous has been used to describe the condition typical of most microhylids, ranids, hyperoliids, and rhacophorids in which all but the last presacral vertebra are procoelous. The last presacral is biconcave; thus, it bears a normal procoelous relationship with the anteriorly adjacent vertebra, but articulates with a condyle produced at the anterior end of the sacrum posteriorly.

Based on developmental evidence, Griffiths (1959a, 1963) proposed another classification of anuran vertebral centra. In the embryo, sclerotomic cells aggregate around the notochord to produce a perichordal tube. The centra and intervertebral bodies develop as thin (centra) and thick (intervertebral bodies), alternating, cylindrical segments along the length of the continuous perichordal tube surrounding the notochord in all anurans. Subsequent development occurs in one of four ways to produce three different types of centra. If the entire perichordal sheath is converted to cartilage and then bone, the resulting centrum is an ossified cylinder that encloses a persistent notochord. This condition is termed ectochordal and characterizes leiopelmatids and *Rhinophrynus*. In some pelobatids and some advanced frogs, the notochord is replaced completely by bone so that the centrum is cylindrical and solid; such vertebrae are described as holochordal. Stegochordal vertebrae, in which the centra are transversely flattened rather than cylindrical, arise in one of two ways according to Griffiths. In pipids and some pelobatids, a cartilaginous perichordal sheath is formed in the same manner as for ectochordal and holochordal vertebrae, but ossification is limited to the dorsal part of the cylinder. The lateral and ventral parts of the cartilaginous perichordal tube degenerate. In discoglossids, both chondrification and ossification are limited to the dorsal part of the perichordal tube; the rest of the tube remains fibrous and finally degenerates at metamorphosis.

Griffiths's work was based in part on that of Mookerjee (1931) and Mookerjee and Das (1939), who defined two primary modes of centrum development—perichordal and epichordal. Perichordal formation includes (1) condensation of sclerotomic cells around the notochord to form a notochordal sheath that subsequently chondrifies, and (2) partial or entire replacement of the notochordal cartilage by bone. This mode of development thus would include Griffiths's ectochordal and holochordal vertebral types. Mookerjee's epichordal vertebral development is equivalent to Griffiths's stegochordy in the discoglossids because chondrification and ossification occur only in the dorsal and dorsolateral areas of the perichordal tube of sclerotomic cells. The relative merits of these two systems of anuran vertebral classification were discussed at length by Kluge and Farris (1969) who preferred to designate centra as either epichordal or perichordal (sensu Mookerjee, 1931), and retain Griffiths's term holochordal in reference to vertebrae in which the notochord is replaced entirely by bone. Logic suggests that the term notochordal (as used by D. Wake, 1970) could be used to describe vertebrae in which remnants of the notochord persist.

The most recent contribution to this controversy was made by Gardiner (1983). He pointed out that, as in salamanders, centrum formation in anurans begins with the appearance of paired basidorsal cartilages in the position of the myosepta. From this point there are two possible courses for further development that result in perichordal or epichordal vertebrae, respectively. In the case of perichordal vertebrae, the basidorsal cartilages fuse basally to form two continuous longitudinal rods, whereas the basiventrals take the form of a median rod of cartilage or a hypochord. The rod may subdivide (as it does in caecilians), but often it persists in the coccygeal region. Rings of bone develop in the membrane investing the notochord. Ossification of the centra and neural arches proceeds separately. Large transverse processes grow out from the side of the neural arch and extend into the septa between myomeres. According to Gardiner, in epichordal development the basidorsals are the only cartilaginous elements that are formed; he noted, however, that E. Williams (1959) and D. Wake (1970) claimed that both lateral and ventral cartilages are present, but that they degenerate to varying degrees and in some cases the basiventrals disappear altogether. Ossification encloses the notochord in a membrane bone cylinder which subsequently grows up over the neural arches and transverse processes. As in salamanders and caecilians, Gardiner claimed that intervertebral cartilage forms in the notochordal sheath and grows inward to constrict and eventually obliterate the notochord. Subsequently, the cartilage is divided in a transverse, arc-like plane at its anterior or posterior end. The cartilage then ossifies to form an articular end that fuses with either the anterior end of the centrum (opisthocoelous) or the posterior end (procoelous).

By referring to Kluge and Farris's (1969) summary of anuran vertebral characteristics as well as the summary presented in Table 17-3, it is obvious that there is a distressing lack of concordance among the various schemes that have been proposed to classify frog vertebrae. Moreover, one must take care to understand precisely the sense in which various authors are applying descriptive terms. Until much more descriptive morphology based on histological examination of adult and developing anuran vertebrae has been completed, it will not be possible to speculate on the evolutionary significance of the variation that has been observed.

Axial Myology. With the exception of Ritland's (1955) account of the postcranial myology of *Ascaphus,* and the recent work of T. C. Burton (1983a, 1983b) on microhylids and M. Davies and T. C. Burton (1982) on *Rheobatrachus silus,* the axial musculature of anurans largely has been overlooked since Gaupp's (1896) and Grobbelaar's (1924) monographs on *Rana* and *Xenopus,* respectively. As pointed out by Nussbaum and Naylor (1982), anurans have relatively inflexible vertebral columns and greatly reduced vertebral and body wall musculature as compared with caecilians and salamanders. These differences in the axial musculoskeletal system seem to be correlated with the development of saltatorial locomotion in anurans whereby the organisms rely on powerfully developed hindlimbs for progression in both terrestrial and aquatic environments. Obviously, undulatory movements are not involved in saltatorial locomotion; therefore, spinal flexion is of minimal importance to the animal. Moreover, too much axial flexibility would be detrimental to an organism that relies on trajecting its rigid, fusiform body forward by means of the hindlimbs.

Epaxial musculature.—The epaxial, or dorsal trunk, musculature is represented by a series of long muscles in contrast to the relatively homogeneous m. dorsalis trunci of caecilians and salamanders. The m. longissiumus dorsi is a segmented muscle that originates along the anterior part of the coccyx and extends forward along the neural spines of the presacral vertebrae to insert on the neural spines and transverse processes of the anterior presacrals (Fig. 13-28). Posteriorly, the m. coccygeosacralis origi-

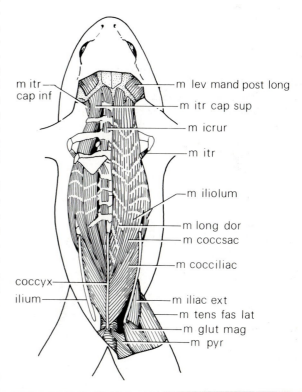

Figure 13-28. Dorsal view of the back muscles of *Rana esculenta,* redrawn from Gaupp (1896). Superficial muscles removed on left side. Abbreviations: m cocciliac = m. coccygeoiliacus; m coccsac = m. coccygeosacralis; m glut mag = m. gluteaus magnus; m icrur = m. intercrurales; m ileolum = m. ileolumbaris; m iliac ext = m. iliacus externus; m itr = m. intertransversarius; m itr cap inf = m. intertransversarius capitis inferior; m itr cap sup = m. intertransversarius capitis superior; m lev mand post long = m. levator mandibulae posterior longus; m tens fas lat = m. tensor fasciae latae.

nates from the lateral surfaces of the anterior half of the coccyx and passes forward to insert on the neural arch of the sacrum and the sacral diapophyses. The m. coccygeoiliacus also originates from the lateral surfaces of the coccyx, but its fibers insert along the medial margins of the ilia. The final long muscle of the back is the m. iliolumbaris which originates from the anterior extremity of the ilium and extends forward to insert on the transverse processes of Presacrals IV–VII.

Deeper epaxial muscles include the mm. intertransversarii dorsi that extend between adjacent transverse processes of the vertebrae and anteriorly form the two cervical muscles, the mm. intertransversarii capitis superior and inferior. The mm. interspinales (= mm. intercrurales of Gaupp, 1896) pass between the neural archs of adjacent vertebrae.

Hypaxial musculature.—The hypaxial musculature is limited to flank and abdominal muscles (Fig. 13-29). In

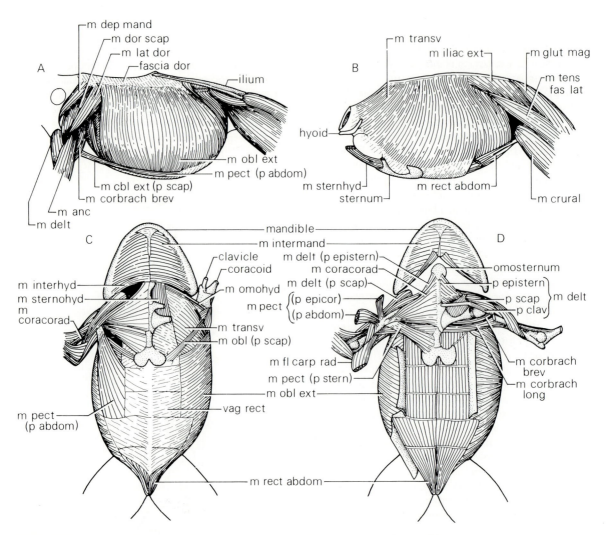

Figure 13-29. Body wall and pectoral girdle musculature of *Rana esculenta*, redrawn from Gaupp (1896). **A.** Lateral view, superficial. **B.** Lateral view with shoulder muscles and superficial lateral and ventral muscles removed. **C.** Ventral view with pectoral muscles removed on frog's left side. **D.** Ventral view showing deep pectoral musculature on frog's left side and deeper body wall musculature. Abbreviations: fascia dor = fascia dorsalis; m anc = m. anconeus; m corbrach brev = m. coracobrachialis brevis; m corbrach long = m. coracobrachialis longus; m coracorad = m. coracoradialis; m crural = m. cruralis; m delt = m. deltoideus; m dep mand = m. depressor mandibulae; m dor scap = m. dorsalis scapulae; m fl carp rad = m. flexor carpi radialis; m iliac ext = m. iliacus externus; m interhyd = m. interhyoideus; m intermand = m. intermandibularis; m lat dor = m. latissimus dorsi; m obl ext = m. obliquus externus; m omohyd = m. omohyoideus; m pect = m pectoralis; m rect abdom = m. rectus abdominis; m sternhyd = m. sternohyoideus; m tens fas lat = m. tensor fasciae latae; m transv = m. transversus; p clav = pars clavicularis of m. deltoideus; p epistern = pars episternalis of m. deltoideus; p scap = pars scapularis of m. deltoideus; p abdom = portio abdominalis of m. pectoralis; p epicor = portio epicoracoidea of m. pectoralis; p stern = portio sternalis of m. pectoralis; vag rect = vagina recti.

contrast to salamanders and caecilians, anurans lack any subvertebral musculature. There are two layers of flank muscles, the m. obliquus externus and m. transversus; the middle layer of other amphibians, the m. obliquus internus, is absent. The m. obliquus externus originates from the posterior margin of the suprascapula, and the fascia ensheathing the epaxial musculature. The broad sheet of muscle extends posteroventrally to insert along the lateral margin of the fascical sheath that invests the ventrolateral surface of the rectus muscle and the ilium. The deeper m. transversus arises from the transverse process of Presacral IV and the fascia covering the mm. intertranversarii. This muscle inserts ventrally on the sheath of the m. rectus abdominis anterior to the level of the sternum and then by a fascical sheet that lies along the internal surface of the coracoid and scapula.

The longitudinal fibers of the m. rectus abdominis are separated midventrally by the linea alba. Each half of the muscle arises by a strong tendon from the ventral border of the pubis and passes forward. Anteriorly, the m. rectus abdominis widens to cover the abdominal region, and in the pectoral region the muscle splits into medial and lateral portions. The medial part inserts on the dorsal surface of the sternum and a tendinous inscription lateral to the sternum and gives rise to the m. sternohyoideus. The m. sternohyoideus arises from the deep surface of the sternum and attaches to the hyoid anteriorly. In a few anurans (e.g., discoglossids) there is a second derivative from the medial portion of the m. rectus abdominis, the m. sternoepicoracoideus, which arises from the style of the sternum and passes medial to the epicoracoid plate of the pectoral girdle. The lateral part of the m. rectus abdominis forms the lateral portion of the m. pectoralis abdominalis, a muscle of the shoulder girdle. In *Ascaphus,* which possesses an epipubis, the m. rectus abdominis is differentiated into a prepubic segment that has a broad, fleshy origin from the cartilaginous ledge of the pubis just dorsal to the epipubic plate. This muscle inserts on the surface of the prepubis and supports the epipubis.

Cutaneous musculature.—As T. C. Burton (1980) pointed out in his review of cutaneous muscles in microhylid frogs, anurans are unique among tetrapods in having loose skin that is attached to the body wall only at intervals. One of the forms of attachment is by thin, sheetlike cutaneous muscles that insert on the skin. These muscles are associated with both dorsal and ventral trunk musculature. In many species of anurans, the lateral portion of the m. rectus abdominis adheres directly to the skin. However, in some microhylids the lateral portion of the m. pectoralis abdominalis is a flat, rectangular slip of muscle that originates from the skin; in others this slip of muscle is absent, but the entire m. pectoralis abdominalis is bound to the skin by connective tissue. Two additional cutaneous muscles are associated with the ventral musculature in some microhylids and ranids. The m. rectus abdominis pars anteroflecta arises from the pubis anterior to the origin of the m. rectus abdominis and passes lat-

erally, dorsal to the m. rectus abdominis. At the lateral edge of the m. rectus abdominis the muscle folds around the abdominal muscle or folds on its own ventral surface so that the fibers pass anteriorly over the ventral surface of the abdominal muscle, or along the lateral edge of the m. rectus abdominis. In the latter case the muscle inserts on the lateral body wall, and in the former the muscle inserts on the skin medially about half way between the pectoral and pelvic girdles. Dorsally, the m. coccygeocutaneus originates from the posterior extremity of the coccyx; apparently this muscle is connected with the rectal musculature from which it passes outward to insert on the skin. This muscle is known to occur in *Rana;* its distribution among other anurans is unknown. A second muscle, the m. cutaneus dorsalis, arises from the fasciae attached to the pubic symphysis, passes dorsally through the gap between the belly and thigh muscles, and then radiates anteriorly to insert on the skin. This muscle is known in microhylids, ranids, hyperoliids, rhacophorids, and some leptodactylids (T. C. Burton, 1980).

APPENDICULAR SYSTEM

The pectoral and pelvic girdles together with their associated limbs constitute the appendicular skeleton. The girdles are suspended from the axial skeleton, and the limbs, in turn, articulate with the girdles. The girdles of modern amphibians are much reduced from those of primitive tetrapods, and in some cases (caecilians) lacking completely.

The pectoral girdle lies just behind the head and is divisible into three general areas. The bladelike suprascapular portion lies dorsolateral in the shoulder region above the glenoid cavity and bears muscle attachments to the first three or four vertebrae. Laterally, the glenoid cavity for the articulation of the forelimb is formed by the scapula and coracoid (and the clavicle in anurans). The ventral (i.e., abdominal) portions of the pectoral girdle can be defined as zonal elements that support the viscera in part and serve as an attachment site for muscles of the head and trunk regions.

The pelvic girdle lies at the end of the trunk and articulates with the sacral vertebra of the axial column. It is composed of three pairs of elements—the ilia, ischia, and pubes. The ilium articulates with the sacrum proximally. Its distal portion forms one facet of the acetabulum for the articulation of the proximal hindlimb bone laterally. The ventral portion of the girdle in salamanders and the posterior part in anurans is composed of the ischia and pubes.

Five basic segments compose the tetrapod limb; in a proximal to distal sequence these are the propodium, epipodium, mesopodium, metapodium, and phalanges. In amphibians, the propodium is represented by the humerus (forelimb) and femur (hindlimb). These are associated, in turn, with the radius and ulna, and the tibia and fibula—the epipodial elements of the fore- and hindlimb, respectively. The radius and tibia are located on the inner or preaxial (i.e., primitively anterior) sides of the limbs. Mesopodial components form the wrist (i.e., carpus) and ankle (i.e., tarsus), and are composed of several series of small bones. Proximally, these include the ulnare, intermedium, and radiale of the hand and the fibulare, intermedium, and tibiale of the foot. There is a central row of bones, the centralia, and a distal row of carpalia (hand) or tarsalia (foot). The palm of the hand and the sole of the foot are composed of metapodial elements—four metacarpals in the hand and either four or five metacarpals in the foot. The terminal elements are the phalanges, longitudinal series of small bones that form the digits of the hand and foot. Digits are designated by Roman numerals with the first being the preaxial or inner digit, and the last the postaxial or outer digit. Reduction in the number of digits occurs postaxially; thus, when fewer than five digits are present (hands of all amphibians and the feet of some salamanders), one can assume that reduction has occurred through loss of the fifth, or outer, digit.

As Radinsky (1979) pointed out, the occurrence of girdles and paired appendages interrupts the series of axial myotomes, and the musculature that is associated with these skeletal elements is derived from muscle buds sent out by adjacent myotomes. This musculature tends to spread over the segmented, axial musculature. This is especially true of muscles associated with the pectoral girdle. Because the girdle lacks a solid attachment to the vertebral column, robust hypaxial muscles extend from the ribs and/or transverse processes and the skull to suspend the pectoral girdle from the axial column. The pelvic girdle, in contrast, bears strong fibrous attachments to the axial column, and although hypaxial muscles extend between the pelvis and the femur, their function is to move the femur in the hip joint rather than support the girdle.

The primary function of the forelimbs in amphibians is to raise and stabilize the body, although they also help to control movement and velocity, and supplement the power of forward movement supplied by the hindlimbs. The primary function of the hindlimbs is to provide force for forward progression. Owing to these functional differences, the basic arrangements of the limbs are different. Thus, the elbow joint of the forelimb is directed backward, whereas the knee joint of the hindlimb is directed forward in order to provide better purchase for the hindlimb on the substrate. In the case of both the fore- and hindlimb, the musculature is composed of basically two groups—dorsal and ventral. In the forelimb, with the elbow joint directed posteriorly, the dorsal or preaxial muscles are the extensors, whereas the ventral or postaxial muscles are the flexors. The situation is reversed in the hindlimb in which the knee joint is directed anteriorly. The dorsal, preaxial muscles form the flexors, whereas the ventral postaxial muscles constitute the extensors. This functional distinction chiefly affects the proximal elements (i.e., upper and forearm, and thigh and shank) of the limbs; distal muscles are affected little and, in fact, are similar in the fore- and hindlimbs. The musculatures of the fore- and hindlimbs are generally similar to one another in being composed of short, deep muscles that extend over one limb joint, and of longer, more superficial muscles that extend over two or more limb segments.

Salamanders

The most complete description of the appendicular musculoskeletal system of a salmander probably is that of Francis (1934) on *Salamandra salamandra;* earlier literature is cited in this work. The descriptions of muscles and their patterns of innervation that follow are based on *Salamandra*. More recent contributions include those of Hilton (1945, 1946a, 1946b) on ambystomatids, dicamptodontids, and plethodontids, and D. Wake (1966), Hanken (1982, 1983), Alberch (1983), and Alberch and Gale (1985) on plethodontids. Hilton's and Wake's works are largely descriptive, whereas that of the other authors deals with variation in mesopodial and phalangeal elements. Aspects of limb development and a review of the literature on this subject was provided by de Saint-Aubain (1981). The limbs and girdles are complete in all salamanders except the sirenids and amphiumids. In the latter, girdles are retained, but the limbs are vestigial. Sirenids have a pectoral girdle and small forelimbs, but the pelvic girdle and hindlimbs are absent.

Pectoral Girdle Structure. The pectoral girdle of salamanders is largely unossified and lacks dermal components (i.e., clavicle of anurans). Each half of the girdle forms a single skeletal element that consists of three areas—the scapular, procoracoid, and coracoid regions—and the halves of the girdle overlap and move freely over one another midventrally (Fig. 13-30). The scapular region lies dorsolateral to the glenoid fossa (for articulation of the forelimb), and consists a proximal, bony scapula and a distal cartilaginous plate, the suprascapula. The suprascapula is fan-shaped and attached to the axial skeleton by muscles and connective tissue. The scapula forms the lateral facets of the glenoid cavity, and is united synostotically with the coracoid that forms the anterior and medial margins of the glenoid cavity in adult salamanders.

The ventral portion of the girdle can be divided into the procoracoid and coracoid regions. The procoracoid is a spatulate element extending anteriorly from the glenoid fossa. If it is ossified, it is fused to the scapula in the region of the fossa, but cartilaginous anteriorly. The anteromedial margin of the girdle bears a deep notch, the incisura coracoidea, that separates the cartilaginous regions of the procoracoid and coracoid. The coracoid region lies posterior to this notch. The coracoid is ossified

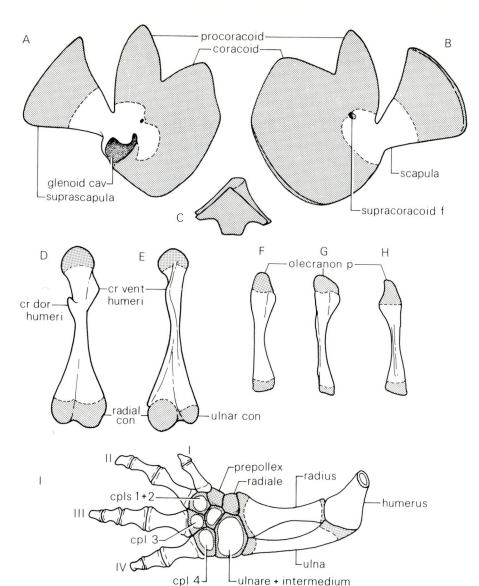

Figure 13-30. Anterior appendicular skeleton of *Salamandra salamandra*, redrawn from Francis (1934). **A.** Right half of pectoral girdle in ventrolateral view and **B.** dorsomedial view. **C.** Ventral aspect of sternum. **D.** Right humerus in dorsal aspect and **E.** ventral aspect. **F.** Right ulna illustrated from dorsal, **G.** postaxial, and **H.** ventral surfaces. **I.** Left forearm and hand in dorsal view. Cartilage is stippled. Abbreviations: cav = cavity; con = condyle; cpl(s) = carpal(s); cr = crista; dor = dorsalis; f = foramen; p = process; vent = ventralis.

around the glenoid fossa, but its largest, medial portion is a cartilaginous plate that overlaps its complement on the opposite half of the girdle. The ossifications of the scapular, procoracoid, and coracoid regions are fused completely in adults; thus, many authors refer to the single bone as the scapulocoracoid. The bone bears a single foramen (supracoracoideum) through which the supracoracoideus nerve and its corresponding artery and vein pass. The glenoid fossa is bony except for its ventral, posteromedial edge that is formed by the coracoid cartilage.

The sternum is a small, ventral, cartilaginous plate that lies posterior to the pectoral girdle (Fig. 13-30). The sternum is diamond-shaped. The anterior edges of the sternum are grooved to receive the posteromesial margins of the coracoid plates; these plates are bound to the sternum by connective tissue. The sternum provides some support for the overlying viscera and serves for the attachment of muscles.

Forelimb Structure. The forelimb of salamanders consists of a humerus proximally, and radius and ulna distally (Fig. 13-30); usually the epiphyses of these long bones fail to ossify. The number of mesopodial elements tends to be reduced through loss and fusion, and many of those that remain are cartilaginous. Four metapodial elements (metacarpals) are present in association with the four digits. The most common phalangeal formulae of the digits is 1-2-3-2 or 2-2-3-3 for Digits I–IV, respectively, but in some salamanders (notably the plethodon-

338

tids) reduction occurs. Reduction involves the length of the digit, not the number of digits, and is the result of shortening of the phalangeal elements and occasionally the loss of an element.

Musculature of Pectoral Girdle and Forelimb. The muscles of the shoulder and forelimb can be separated into three groups for discussion—those which attach the pectoral girdle to the skull and axial column, and the extensors and flexors of the forelimb.

Suspensory muscles of the pectoral girdle.—Among the muscles that attach the pectoral girdle to the skull and vertebral column are the m. levator scapulae (see discussion under Neurocranium in Skull and Hyobranchium), the m. cucullaris, and the m. thoraciscapularis (Fig. 13-31). Although the m. levator scapulae arises from the otic region and inserts on the suprascapula, it seems to be involved in the auditory apparatus. Thus, its structure is discussed in association with the neurocranial elements of the skull.

M. cucullaris

The major muscle attaching the pectoral girdle to the skull is the m. cucullaris which is innervated by C.N. XI (accessory) and divided into two heads (Fig. 13-31). The posterior head (m. cucullaris minor) arises from the dorsal fascia of the head and inserts on the lateral border of the procoracoid and scapula. The anterior head (m. cucullaris major) arises in part from the dorsal fascia and in part from the posterodorsal surface of the skull; it inserts on the lateral face of the procoracoid, near the shoulder joint, and along the ventral edge of the scapula. Contraction of this muscle turns and depresses the head unless the head is immobilized by contraction of trunk musculature that attaches to the posterior end of the skull. In the latter case, contraction of the m. cucullaris pulls the pectoral girdle toward the skull.

M. thoraciscapularis

The m. thoraciscapularis arises by a series of bundles from the first five ribs and inserts on the medial face of

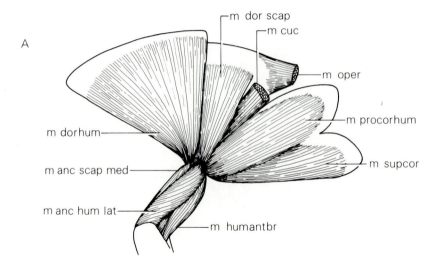

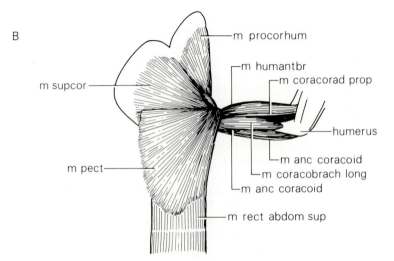

Figure 13-31. Shoulder and pectoral girdle musculature of the salamander *Salamandra salamandra,* redrawn from Francis (1934). **A.** Superficial extensor muscles of the right shoulder and upper arm in dorsolateral view. **B.** Superficial flexor muscles of pectoral region and left upper arm in ventral aspect. Abbreviations: m anc coracoid = m. anconeus coracoideus; m anc hum lat = m. anconeus humeralis lateralis; m anc hum med = m. anconeus humeralis medius; m anc scap med = m. anconeus scapularis medialis; m coracobrach long = m coracobrachialis longus; m coracorad prop = m. coracoradialis proprius; m cuc = m. cucullaris; m dor scap = m dorsalis scapulae; m dorhum = m. dorsohumeralis; m humantbr = m. humeroantibrachialis; m oper = m. opercularis; m pect = m. pectoralis; m procorhum = m. procoracohumeralis; m rect abdom sup = m. rectus abdominis superficialis; m supcor = m. supracoracoideus.

the scapula. The general function of this muscle is to attach the pectoral girdle to the axial column thereby forming an elastic suspension for the anterior end of the body. However, the m. thoraciscapularis is separable into two parts. The straight portion inserts on the dorsomedial border of the suprascapula; contraction of this part depresses the scapula and, as a consequence, expands the ventral portions of the girdle. An oblique portion inserts on the posterodorsal angle of the suprascapula and retracts the scapula. The m. thoraciscapularis is innervated by S.Nn. 2–4.

Forelimb extensors and abductors.—Among the shoulder muscles are three, the mm. dorsalis scapulae, latissimus dorsi, and subscapularis, that act as forelimb extensors— that is, they are responsible for moving the humerus backward.

M. latissimus dorsi

The m. latissimus dorsi (= m. dorsohumeralis of Francis, 1934) is a triangular plate of muscle that is situated behind the shoulder (Fig. 13-31). It originates from the dorsal facia, and its fibers converge to a superficial, tendinous attachment with the head of the humerus. Contraction of this muscle pulls the upper arm backward. The m. latissimus dorsi is innervated by the dorsohumeralis nerve which emerges from the anastomosis of S.Nn. 3 and 4.

M. dorsalis scapulae

The m. dorsalis scapulae (= m. deltoides of some authors) is a fan-shaped muscle that arises from the dorsolateral surface of the cartilaginous suprascapula (Fig. 13-31). Its fibers converge to a tendinous insertion on the crista ventralis of the humerus. Contraction of this muscle, which is innervated by S.N. 3, abducts the humerus.

M. subscapularis

The m. subscapularis arises from the dorsal surface of the procoracoid and inserts on the humerus. It is innervated by S.N. 3 and acts along with the m. latissimus dorsi to extend or draw the upper arm backward toward the flank.

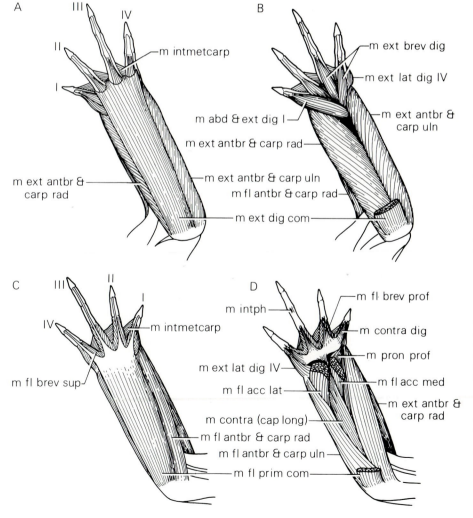

Figure 13-32. Muscles of the right forearm and hand of the salamander *Salamandra salamandra,* redrawn from Francis (1934). **A.** Extensor muscles of dorsal surface in superficial view and **B.** deep view. **C.** Flexor muscles of ventral surface in superficial view and **D.** deep view. Abbreviations: m abd & ext dig I = m. abductor et extensor digiti I; m contra (cap long) = caput longum of m. contrahentium; m contra dig = m. contrahentes digitorum; m ext antbr & carp rad = m. extensor antibrachii et carpi radialis; m ext antbr & carp uln = m. extensor antibrachii et carpi ulnaris; m ext brev dig = m. extensor brevis digiti; m ext dig com = m. extensor digitorum communis; m ext lat dig IV = m. extensor lateralis digiti IV; m fl acc lat = m. flexor accessorius lateralis; m fl acc med = m. flexor accessorius medialis; m fl antbr & carp rad = m. flexor antibrachii et carpi radialis; m fl antbr & carp uln = m. flexor antibrachii et carpi ulnaris; m fl brev prof = m. flexor brevis profundus; m fl brev sup = m. flexor brevis superficialis; m fl prim com = m. flexor primordialis communis; m intmetcarp = m. intermetacarpalis; m intph = m. interphalangeus; m pron prof = m. pronator profundus.

M. anconeus

The major and proximal extensor of the forearm is the m. anconeus (= m. triceps) which lies along the dorsal surface of the humerus (Fig. 13-31). This muscle originates from the humerus and the pectoral girdle via four heads which unite distally to insert on the olecranon process of the ulna. The muscle is innervated by S.N. 3 and it acts to extend or straighten the elbow joint.

Distal forearm extensors.—Distal forearm extensors include the mm. extensor digitorum communis, extensor antibrachii et carpi radialis, and extensor antibrachii et carpi ulnaris, all of which arise from the humerus and are innervated by branches derived from S.N. 3 or the anastomosis of S.Nn. 3 and 4 (Fig. 13-32).

The m. extensor digitorum communis is the most superficial and prominent of the three muscles. It separates into four to six separate tendons which insert on the dorsal surfaces of the digits, and acts to extend the wrist joint and, therefore, the hand as a whole. The mm. extensor antibrachii et carpi ulnaris and extensor antibrachii et carpi radialis act in tandem to extend the forearm by straightening the elbow joint. The former muscle inserts on the distal end of the ulna, whereas the latter inserts on the distal end of the radius.

In addition to the extensor muscles described above, there are four more groups innervated by branches of the same spinal nerves that extend and rotate the digits. They originate from the wrist and extend to the metacarpals or phalanges. They are the mm. abductor and extensor digiti primi, extensores breves digitorum, and extensor lateralis digiti quadrati.

Forelimb flexors and extensors.—Four pectoral, or chest, muscles are involved in the ventral musculature that acts as flexors of the forelimb (Fig. 13-31); these are the mm. pectoralis, procoracohumeralis, supracoracoideus, and coracobrachialis.

M. pectoralis

The m. pectoralis is a superficial, fan-shaped muscle that originates from the fascia of the m. rectus abdominis and covers the posterior region of the breast. The fibers converge to a tendinous insertion on the posterior surface of the humerus along with the m. latissimus dorsi, an extensor muscle. The muscle is innervated by branches of S.Nn. 4 and 5, and acts to adduct the arm, or draw it inward toward the body and backward.

M. procoracohumeralis

The m. procoracohumeralis orginates from the dorsal surface of the procoracoid cartilage and inserts near the head of the humerus. It is innervated by branches of S.Nn. 2 and 3, and is antagonistic to the m. latissimus dorsi, because the m. procoracohumeralis flexes the shoulder joint thereby drawing the upper arm forward.

M. supracoracoideus

The m. supracoracoideus is superficial and lies anterior to the m. pectoralis. The muscle originates from the coracoid cartilage. Its fan-shaped fibers converge to a tendon that inserts along with the m. pectoralis on the posterior face of the humerus. The m. supracoracoideus is innervated by S.Nn. 2 and 3, and it is antagonistic to the dorsal extensor, the m. dorsalis scapulae, because the m. supracoracoideus adducts the humerus, thereby drawing the arm toward the body, and flexes the elbow joint.

M. coracobrachialis

The m. coracobrachialis arises by two heads, both of which originate from the ventral surface of the coracoid. The m. coracobrachialis inserts along the posterior face of the humerus and flexes the shoulder joint, thereby drawing the arm backward.

M. humeroantibrachialis

There is one major muscle responsible for flexion or bending of the elbow joint. This is the m. humeroantibrachialis (= m. biceps), which is innervated by branches of S.N. 4 (Fig. 13-31). The muscle arises from the flexor side of the humerus; its fibers, which parallel the humerus, insert on the proximal end of the radius.

Distal forearm flexors

Distal forearm flexors include the mm. flexor antibrachii et carpi radialis, flexor carpi ulnaris, flexor antibrachii ulnaris, and flexor digitorum communis, which are supplied by branches of S.N. 4 (Fig. 13-32). Each of these muscles orginates from the lateral epicondyle of the humerus and inserts in the areas of the lower forearm and hand. The m. flexor antibrachii et carpi radialis inserts along the external face of the radius and the radiale, whereas the m. flexor antibrachii ulnaris inserts along the outer edge of the ulna and the m. flexor carpi ulnaris on the lateral surface of the ulnare. These three muscles flex the wrist joint, tending to close the angle between the forearm and the hand. The m. flexor digitorum communis is a thin, flat sheet of muscle that arises from the humerus; distally, in the palm of the hand the muscle passes into a flat tendon that divides into four parts and passes along the digits to insert on the terminal phalanges. This muscle is responsible for flexing the wrist and hand as a whole. There is a series of deep, ventral muscles that are responsible for flexing the wrist and the digits, and for adducting the digits. For further details about these, see Francis (1934).

Forelimb Movement.   As explained by K. Liem (1977), movements of the forelimb can be subdivided into two locomotory phases—propulsive and recovery. The propulsive phase consists of backward movement of the humerus accompanied by flexion of the elbow joint and carpus. The retraction of the humerus is caused by contraction of the mm. latissimus dorsi, pectoralis, procoracohumeralis, and coracobrachialis, which act on the shoulder joint. Concurrently, the elbow and carpometacarpal joints are flexed by the mm. humeroantibrachialis, flexor antibrachii et carpi radialis, flexor carpi ulnaris, and flexor antibrachii ulnaris. The contraction of these muscles, along with the flexor digitorum communis and other small flexors of the digits, acts to straighten the arm and press the digits against the substrate. Thus, friction is increased and the chance of backward slip diminished. In this position, the forelimb forms a weight-support column that transmits the propulsive force supplied by the hindlimb to the ground.

The recovery phase of the forelimb begins when the digits are lifted from the ground. The humerus is protracted forward and upward by the contraction of the mm. dorsalis scapulae and procoracohumeralis. The elbow and wrist remain flexed during the first part of the

recovery phase but toward the end of the phase, the m. extensor digitorum communis contracts to extend the wrist and hand as a whole. The elbow joint never is extended completely; however, a decrease in its angle of flexion and a general stabilization of the joint is accomplished through the action of the forearm extensors, and the mm. anconeus, extensor antibrachii et carpi radialis, and extensor antibrachii et carpi ulnaris.

Pelvic Girdle Structure.   The pelvic girdle of salamanders consists of a ventral puboischiac plate and a dorsal, club-shaped pair of ilia that are attached dorsally to the sacral diapophyses of the sacral vertebra by fibrous tissue (Fig. 13-33). Ventrally, the ilium of each half of the

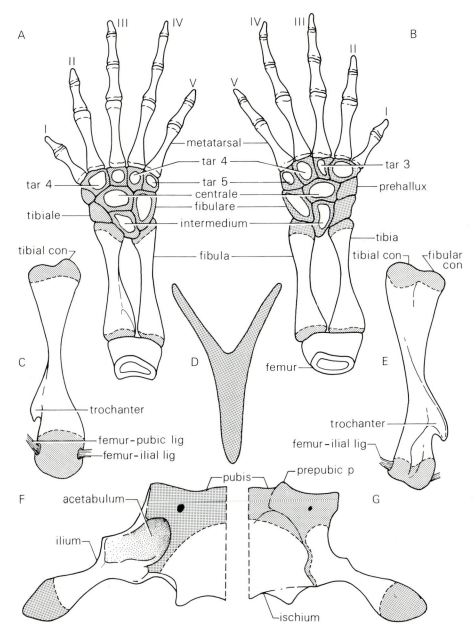

Figure 13-33. Posterior appendicular skeleton of *Salamandra salamandra*, redrawn from Francis (1934). **A.** Dorsal view of right foot. **B.** Ventral view of right foot. **C.** Extensor surface of right femur. **D.** Ventral aspect of ypsiloid cartilage. **E.** Flexor surface of right femur. **F.** Pelvic girdle in ventrolateral and **G.** dorsomedial (G) aspects. Cartilage is in stippled pattern. Abbreviations: con = condyle; lig = ligament; p = process; tar = tarsal.

pelvic girdle joins the ischium posteriorly and the pubis anteriorly to form the acetabulum laterally for the articulation of the femur. The ischia are represented by a pair of rounded ossifications in the posterior portion of the puboischiac plate; the anterior cartilaginous part of the plate is the pubic cartilage which is perforated by a small obturator foramen for the passage of the obturator nerve. The halves of the girdle are united by a symphysis. All salamanders except the sirenids, proteids, amphiumids, and plethodontids have an ypsiloid cartilage in association with the pelvic girdle. This Y-shaped structure lies in the midline dorsal to the m. rectus abdominis and anterior to the puboischium with which it articulates. The ypsiloid cartilage has been associated with hydrostatic function of the lungs. By elevating the cartilage, the salamander is thought to compress the posterior end of the body cavity and force air in the lungs forward, thereby causing the head to rise in the water. Conversely, when the ypsiloid cartilage is depressed, air is thought to move posteriorly in the lungs, thereby reducing the buoyancy of the head so that it tends to sink in the water.

Hindlimb Structure. Proximally, the femur articulates with the pelvic girdle by means of a ball-and-socket joint. The shank (or crus) consists of a pair of bones, the tibia and fibula (Fig. 13-33). The mesopodial elements tend to be reduced through both loss and fusion and are largely cartilaginous. Usually there are four metapodial elements (metatarsals) associated with the five digits with a phalangeal formula of 1-2-3-3-2 (Fig. 13-33). Occasionally (e.g., plethodontids) the lengths of the digits are modified by reduction in the sizes of the phalangeal elements or by loss of a terminal element on Digit IV. A number of salamanders that otherwise have normal hindlimbs have lost the fifth (i.e., outer or postaxial) toe; among these are *Hynobius* and *Batrachuperus* (hynobiids), *Salamandrina* (salamandrid), *Necturus* (proteid), and *Batrachoseps*, *Hemidactylium*, and some *Eurycea* (plethodontids).

Musculature of Pelvic Girdle and Hindlimb. Unlike the muscles of the forelimb and shoulder of salamanders, those of the hindlimb do not tend to spread out over the axial musculature (Fig. 13-34). The primary reason for this is that the pelvic girdle is anchored firmly to the axial column by way of a fibrous connection between the ilia and the sacral vertebra; therefore, additional suspensory muscular support is unnecessary. Given this fact, derivatives of axial musculature are not specialized for support of the pelvis and movement of the upper part of the limb as they are in the forelimb.

The hindlimb musculature can be separated into two general groups—those that are derivatives of dorsal or epaxial musculature, and those that are derivatives of ventral or hypaxial musculature. Generally, derivatives of the dorsal musculature are flexors, whereas ventral derivatives are extensors, in contrast to the functions of these respective muscle complexes in the forelimb. In the hip joint, the femur is capable of wide, elliptical excursions, which are greater in the horizontal than in the vertical plane. Movement of the knee and ankle joints is restricted for the most part to flexion and extension, although some rotation takes place.

Hindlimb extensors.—Extension of the hip joint is powered by one major derivative of the dorsal musculature and one derivative of the ventral musculature.

M. iliofemoralis

The m. iliofemoralis is innervated by branches of S.Nn. 16 and 17. It is the deepest of the thigh muscles, originating on the posterolateral face of the ilium and the dorsal (i.e., inner) face of the ischium and inserting along the middle of the posterior surface of the femur. The m. iliofemoralis extends the hip joint and draws the thigh backward.

M. ischiofemoralis

A derivative of the ventral musculature, the m. ischiofemoralis extends the hip joint thereby pulling the femur backward. This short muscle arises from the inner side of the ischium and inserts on the posterior face of the head of the femur (Fig. 13-34). The muscle is innervated by branches of S.Nn. 16 and 17.

Mm. iliotibialis, iliofibularis, and ilioextensorius

Three dorsal muscles are responsible for extension of the knee (i.e., lower part of hindlimb), and all are innervated by branches of S.Nn. 16 and 17 (Fig. 13-34). The m. iliotibialis arises from two heads from the dorsolateral surface of the ilium and passes superficially along the dorsal, extensor surface of the thigh and over the knee to a tendinous insertion on the tibia. The m. iliofibularis arises from the lateral face of the ilium, posterior to the origin of the m. iliotibialis, and extends along the posterodorsal border of the thigh to a tendinous insertion on the proximal end of the fibula. In conjunction with the m. iliotibialis, the m. iliofibularis acts to extend, or straighten, the knee joint and, therefore, extend the lower leg; however, in combination with the ventral flexor, the m. pubotibialis (see below), contraction of this muscle flexes the shank. Contraction of a third muscle, the m. ilioextensorius, also extends the knee joint, moving the shank forward. The m. ilioextensorius originates from the ilium, runs parallel with, and posterior to, the m. iliotibialis.

Mm. extensor digitorum communis, e. tarsi tibialis, and e. cruris tibialis

There are three primary dorsal extensor muscles that originate from the lateral epicondyle of the femur and extend beyond the knee; each is innervated by branches of S.Nn. 16 and 17 (Fig. 13-34). The m. extensor digitorum communis is the most superficial muscle. From its origin, it spreads out into a thin, fan-shaped muscle that

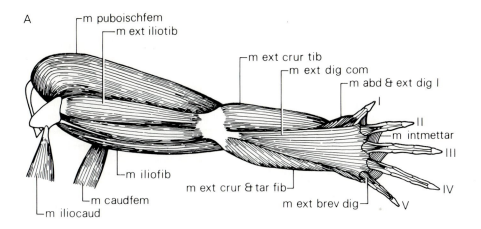

A

m puboischfem
m ext iliotib
m ext crur tib
m ext dig com
m abd & ext dig I
I
II
m intmettar
III
IV
V
m iliofib
m caudfem
m ext crur & tar fib
m ext brev dig
m iliocaud

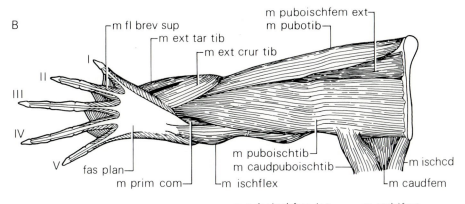

B

m fl brev sup
m ext tar tib
m ext crur tib
m puboischfem ext
m pubotib
I
II
III
IV
V
fas plan
m prim com
m puboischtib
m caudpuboischtib
m ischflex
m ischcd
m caudfem

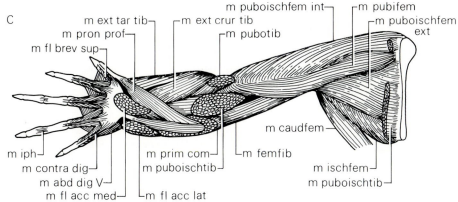

C

m ext tar tib
m pron prof
m fl brev sup
m ext crur tib
m pubotib
m puboischfem int
m pubifem
m puboischfem ext
m caudfem
m iph
m contra dig
m abd dig V
m fl acc med
m prim com
m puboischtib
m fl acc lat
m femfib
m ischfem
m puboischtib

Figure 13-34. Musculature of the right hindlimb of the salamander *Salamandra salamandra*, redrawn from Francis (1934). **A.** Superficial extensor muscles in dorsal aspect. **B.** Superficial flexor muscles in ventral view. **C.** Deep flexor muscles in ventral aspect. Abbreviations: fas plan = fascia plantaris; m abd dig V = m. abductor digiti V; m abd & ext dig I = m. abductor et extensor digiti I; m caudfem = m. caudalifemoralis; m caudpuboischtib = m. caudalipuboischiotibialis; m contra = caput longum of m. contrahentium; m contra dig = m. contrahentis digitorum; m ext brev dig = m. extensor brevis digitorum; m ext crur tib = m. extensor cruris tibialis; m ext crur & tar fib = m. extensor cruris et tarsi fibularis; m ext dig com = m. extensor digitorum communis; m ext iliotib = m. extensor iliotibialis; m ext tar tib = m. extensor tarsi tibialis; m femfib = m. femorofibularis; m fl acc lat = m. flexor accessorius lateralis; m fl acc med = m. flexor accesorius medialis; m fl brev sup = m. flexor brevis superficialis; m iliocaud = m. iliocaudalis; m iliofib = m. iliofibularis; m intmettar = m intermetatarsalis; m iph = m interphalangeus; m ischcd = m. ischiocaudalis; m ischfem = m. ischiofemoralis; m ischflex = m. ischioflexorius; m prim com = m. primordialis communis; m pron prof = m. pronator profundus; m pubifem = m. pubifemoralis; m puboischfem ext = m. puboischiofemoralis externus; m puboischfem int = m. puboischiofemoralis internus; m puboischtib = m. puboischiotibialis; m pubotib = m. pubotibialis.

extends down the shank and onto the dorsum of the foot. At the bases of the digits, nine tendons arise from this muscle; eight insert on either side of the bases of the metatarsals, whereas the ninth inserts on the lateral, or fibulare, side of the first metatarsal. The extensor digitorum communis is the chief extensor of the foot. The m. extensor tarsi tibialis is a small muscle that shares a common origin with, or arises close to, the extensor digitorum communis. It is spindle-shaped and passes along the m. extensor cruris tibialis to insert on the ventral surface of the tibiale and prehallux cartilage. The primary action of the extensor tarsi tibialis is to turn the foot into

a supine position. The third muscle is the m. extensor cruris tibialis, which inserts along the entire lateral border of the tibia and extends to the tibiale and prehallux cartilage, and extends the ankle joint.

Distal extensors

The distal, dorsal extensors of the digits are the mm. extensores digitorum breves. This complex is divisible into many muscles associated with the individual digits (see Francis, 1934, for explanation), but is composed primarily of superficial and deep strata. The muscles generally arise from the tarsal elements and insert by tendons at the base of the terminal phalanx of each digit (Fig. 13-34). Each tendon is attached to the other, more proximal phalanges by means of small, lateral slips at the interphalangeal joints.

Hindlimb flexors.—One derivative of the dorsal musculature, the m. puboischiofemoralis internus, along with several ventral muscles of the hip and thigh act chiefly to flex the hip joint, adduct the femur, and flex the knee joint.

M. puboischiofemoralis

The m. puboischiofemoralis internus is a large, powerful muscle (innervated by branches of S.Nn. 15–16 in *Salamandra*) that arises from the entire dorsal side of the pubis and parts of the ischium and ilium (Fig. 13-34). It bends around the anterior edge of the pubis and extends along the anterior surface of the thigh to insert on the anterior end of the shaft of the femur. Contraction of this muscle flexes the hip joint, moving the femur forward. The action of the m. puboischiofemoralis internus is antagonistic to that of the m. iliofemoralis described above.

The m. puboischiofemoralis externus arises from the ventral surface of the pelvic girdle at the anterior end of the pubis and inserts along the middle of the ventral surface of the femur. This muscle is innervated by branches of S.Nn. 15–17 and, on contraction, it serves as a flexor of the hip joint moving the femur forward.

M. puboischiotibialis

The most superficial ventral muscle is the m. puboischiotibialis which arises lateral to the puboischiadic symphysis of the pelvic girdle and extends down the ventral surface of the thigh to insert along the shaft of the tibia (Fig. 13-34). It bears a tough, fibrous connection with the next muscle to be discussed, the m. pubotibialis, and serves as the site of insertion of one of the tail muscles (m. caudalipuboischiotibialis). Acting alone, contraction of this muscle flexes the knee, but acting in antagonism to dorsal extensors, it causes flexion at the hip and depression of the foot toward the substrate.

M. pubotibialis

The m. pubotibialis has a tendinous origin from the anteroventral edge of the pelvic girdle and extends along the ventrolateral border of the thigh to insert on the anterior face of the proximal end of the tibia (Fig. 13-34). Its contraction adducts the hindlimb and tends to flex the knee.

M. ischioflexoris

The m. ischioflexoris is a strap-like muscle that originates from the ventrolateral angle of the ischium just posterior to the origin of the m. puboischiotibialis (Fig. 13-34). The m. ischioflexoris passes along the posteroventral border of the thigh and inserts into the aponeurosis of the m. flexor primordialis communis on the plantar surface of the foot.

Caudal muscles

There is a group of three tail muscles that arise from the ventral surface of the fourth and fifth caudal vertebrae. One of these, the m. caudalifemoralis (Fig. 13-34), inserts on the femur and exerts a powerful backward pull on the thigh while flexing the tail at the same time. Although the two remaining muscles are associated with the pelvic girdle and thigh musculature, their function is limited to flexion of the tail. From its posterior origin, the m. caudalipuboischiotibialis extends anterolaterally to insert by a flat tendon into the posterior edge of the superficial ventral flexor, the m. puboischiotibialis. The m. ischiocaudalis passes forward from its origin between the m. caudalipuboischiotibialis and the cloaca to insert on the posterior border of the ilium.

M. flexor primordialis communis

The primary flexor of the foot is the m. flexor primordialis communis that arises mainly from the lateral surface of the fibula; a few fibers originate from the lateral epicondyle of the femur. The course of this muscle parallels the shank axis and passes into the plantar aponeurosis. Distally, the aponeurosis divides into five tendons which extend along the flexor side of the digits and insert on the proximal end of the terminal phalanx of each toe. Each tendon of the flexor primordialis communis sends small, lateral slips to the proximal ends of the other phalangeal elements. In addition to flexing the entire foot, contraction of this muscle tends to turn the foot forward.

There is a variety of accessory digital flexors (see Francis, 1934) that act in concert with the flexor primordialis communis. These small muscles arise primarily from the distal ends of the tibia and fibula and insert on the tarsals and metatarsals; some extend between the tarsals and metatarsals. The chief action of these muscles is to abduct the digits.

M. flexor accessorius

Two additional muscles, the mm. flexor accessorius lateralis and flexor accessorius medialis (Fig. 13-34), are involved in pronation of the foot. The lateral muscle arises from the lateral edge of the fibulare and passes obliquely across the middle of the tarsus to insert on the plantar aponeurosis. The medial muscle originates from the distal two thirds of the fibula along its ventromedial surface and from the tarsal elements. It inserts on the dorsal surface of the plantar aponeurosis.

M. interosseus cruris

The final muscle to be considered is the m. interosseus cruris, which is a thin sheet of muscle that joins the inner sides of the tibia and fibula. It arises along the proximal surface of the fibula, inserts on the distal surface of the tibia, and functions as an elastic ligament between the two bones.

Hindlimb Movement. Movements of the hindlimb, like those of the forelimb, are divisible into propulsive and recovery phases. According to K. Liem (1977), the propulsive phase is initiated at the time the sole of the foot contacts the substrate and consists of backward movement of the femur (i.e., the thigh) accompanied by flexion of the shank and foot. Retraction of the thigh chiefly results from contraction of the ventral, caudal muscle, the m. caudalifemoralis, in association with two ventral thigh muscles, the mm. iliofemoralis and pubois- chiofemoralis externus. Coincident flexion of the knee and ankle joints is powered by contraction of the m. ischioflexoris. Action of the m. flexor primordialis communis presses the foot and digits against the sub- strate, preventing the foot from slipping backward. In the propulsive phase, the femur acts as a driving lever that propels the body forward as it swings back in a horizontal plane. The force is transmitted from the thigh to the ground via the flexed limb, of which the foot and lower leg rep- resent a stationary pivot on which the femur rotates.

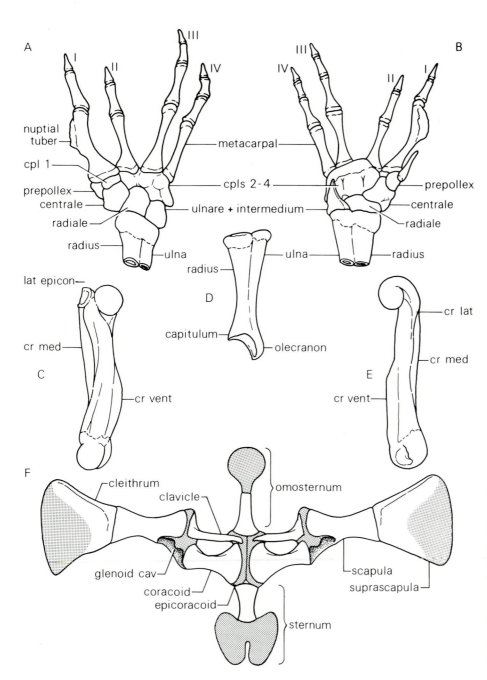

Figure 13-35. Anterior appendicular skeleton of *Rana esculenta* redrawn from Gaupp (1896). **A.** Dorsum of right hand. **B.** Venter of hand. **C.** Medial view of right humerus. **D.** Dorsal view of right radioulna. **E.** Lateral view of right humerus. **F.** Pectoral girdle in ventral view with scapula and suprascapula deflected ventrally into abdominal plane. Stippled areas are cartilaginous. Abbreviations: cav = cavity; cpl(s) = carpal(s); cr lat = crista lateralis; cr med = crista medialis; cr vent = crista ventralis; lat epicon = lateral epicondyle; tuber = tuberosity.

The recovery phase begins as the foot rolls gradually off the substrate. At this time the upper and lower portions of the hindlimb are protracted forward as a unit through the combined action of several muscles. The m. puboischiofemoralis acts on the thigh, whereas the mm. iliotibialis, ilioextensorius, iliofibularis, extensor tarsi tibialis, and extensor cruris tibialis protract the shank. When the hindlimb is protracted to a position slightly beyond a right angle to the body, the knee is flexed. The limb then is protracted further forward while the m. extensor digitorum communis extends the foot. When the foot is placed on the substrate, another propulsive phase begins.

Anurans

Relative to that of primitive tetrapods and salamanders, the appendicular morphology of anurans is highly derived and modified to provide for their saltatorial mode of locomotion. Features of pectoral girdle morphology have been used in the major classification of anurans since Cope (1864, 1865); consequently, many systematic papers include descriptions of the pectoral girdle. Similarly, because the ilia of the pelvic girdle frequently are found as fossils, there exists considerable miscellaneous information on this unit. The most important morphological literature relating to the appendicular skeleton was summarized by Trueb (1973). Significant contributions include those by S. Emerson (1983, 1984) on the pectoral girdle and T. Green (1931), Whiting (1961), S. Emerson (1979, 1982), and S. Emerson and De Jongh (1980) on functional aspects of the pelvic girdle. Andersen (1978) surveyed the carpus and tarsus of anurans, and Alberch and Gale (1985) described digital reduction in amphibians.

Pectoral Girdle Structure. In contrast to salamanders, most anurans retain two dermal bones in their pectoral girdles—the clavicle and cleithrum (Fig. 13-35). Endochondral components include the scapula and coracoid. For purposes of discussion, it is easiest to consider each half of the pectoral girdle to consist of two areas—the scapula-suprascapula area above the glenoid fossa and the zonal area below it (Fig. 13-35). The dorsal half of the glenoid fossa is formed by the proximal end of the scapula. Distally, the scapula is expanded and articulates with the bony base of the suprascapula. The suprascapula varies from a blade shape to a fan shape. At least a part of the leading edge is bony, and this ossification represents the cleithrum. Ossification from the cleithrum invades the suprascapular cartilage to varying degrees in different species of anurans; thus, ossification of the suprascapula might be limited to the anterior and ventral margins, or as is more commonly the case, one-third to two-thirds of the blade may be ossified. In some hyperossified frogs (e.g., *Brachycephalus*) the entire blade is ossified (Fig. 13-36). The scapulae of primitive anurans (e.g., leiopelmatids, discoglossids, and pipids) tend to be short (i.e., one-third or less the length of the clavicle) and proximally uncleft or unicapitate. Among more advanced anurans, the scapula is relatively longer and bicapitate.

The zonal area of the pectoral girdle can be defined as all those parts ventral and medial to the glenoid fossae (Fig. 13-35). These, in turn, are classified as prezonal, zonal, and postzonal elements in an anterior to posterior sequence. If present, the prezonal element is termed the omosternum (= episternum). Zonal components include the clavicles (present in all anurans except some microhylids), coracoids, and the cartilaginous arc that unites the clavicle and coracoid of each half of the girdle in the midline. The medial part of the cartilage is known as the epicoracoid cartilage, whereas the anterolateral portion that may be associated with the clavicle is termed the procoracoid cartilage. The division between these two areas of cartilage in adults is arbitrary. The postzonal part of the pectoral girdle is the sternum, which is subdivided in some frogs into a mesosternum proximally and a xiphisternum distally.

Arcifery and firmisterny.—Basically, there are two kinds of pectoral girdles in anurans depending on the relationship of the zonal elements (Griffiths, 1959a). The most widespread pattern is arcifery in which the epicoracoid cartilages are elaborated into posteriorly directed epicoracoid horns (Fig. 13-36). The latter articulate with the sternum by means of grooves, pouches or fossae in the dorsal surface of the sternum and provide a surface for the insertion of a pair of muscles derived from the m. rectus abdominis. Most arciferal anurans also are characterized by fusion of the epicoracoid cartilages in the interclavicle region. Posterior to the clavicles, the epicoracoids usually are free and overlapping.

The firmisternal girdle characteristic of ranids, microhylids, and dendrobatids lacks epicoracoidal horns (Fig. 13-36). The sternum is fused to the pectoral arch, and the epicoracoidal cartilages of each half of the girdle are fused to one another. The midzonal length of the girdle is shorter than that of an arciferal girdle, but pre- and postzonal elements tend to be much longer.

A few anurans have pectoral girdles that are modified to produce so-called pseudofirmisternal or pseudoarciferal conditions from arciferal and firmisternal girdles, respectively. For example, in some bufonid genera (e.g., *Atelopus, Oreophrynella, Dendrophryniscus),* and leptodactylids (e.g., *Sminthillus, Geobatrachus, Phrynopus)* the fusion of the epicoracoid cartilages in the region of the epicoracoid bridge is extended posteriorly. Thus, the cartilages no longer overlap freely, and functionally, a partially firmisternal condition is created. The pipid frog *Hymenochirus* represents an extreme of pseudofirmisterny in which the epicoracoid cartilages are fused throughout their lengths so that no movement of one half the girdle on the other is possible. Pseudoarcifery is known to occur only in a few species of ranids and the sooglossids in which the epicoracoid cartilages are partly

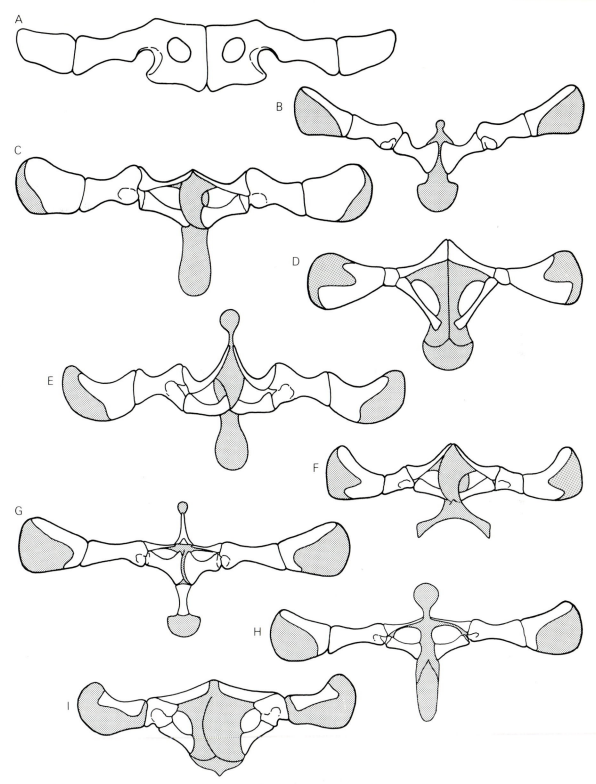

Figure 13-36. Diagrammatic ventral views of pectoral girdles of anurans. Scapulae and suprascapulae are deflected ventrally into abdominal plane. Cartilaginous areas are stippled. **A.** *Brachycephalus ephippium.* **B.** *Kaloula pulchra.* **C.** *Bufo coccifer.* **D.** *Xenopus laevis.* **E.** *Scaphiopus hammondii.* **F.** *Alytes obstetricans.* **G.** *Rana rugulosa.* **H.** *Rhinoderma darwini.* **I.** *Ascaphus truei.*

free and overlapping; however, the epicoracoids are fused to one another and the sternum posteromedially.

Prezonal structure.—The occurrence of prezonal elements is irregular. Omosterna are usually present in firmisternal anurans (Fig. 13-36). In its simplest state, the omosternum is a simple disc of cartilage that lies anterior to the precoracoid bridge or the medial articulation of the clavicles. In some anurans (ranids especially), the omosternum is elaborated into a long style with a terminal cartilaginous disc, and the style may be ossified. Arciferal anurans frequently lack omosterna, and when present, this prezonal element usually is small.

Postzonal structure.—All anurans except *Rhinophrynus* and the brachycephalids have a sternum. The sternum has a variety of shapes (Fig. 13-36). Among firmisternal anurans, it tends to be long (except in microhylids with reduced girdles) and to be elaborated into an ossified stylus (mesosternum) with an expanded cartilaginous end (xiphisternum). The majority of arciferal anurans have a broad, ovoid sternum that is proportionately shorter than that of firmisternal anurans. By comparison with all other anurans, pipids of the genus *Pipa* especially, have the largest sterna. In these frogs, the sternum covers most of the abdominal region and is flanked anterolaterally by the epicoracoid cartilages that have expanded posterolateral to the coracoid bones. Because the sternum serves as a site of muscle attachments, it would seem that this structural variation must have some functional significance. But this, along with any functional differences that might exist between the arciferal and firmisternal conditions, is undetermined as yet.

One anuran genus, *Leiopelma,* has so-called abdominal or inscriptional ribs that lie in the myosepta of the ventral trunk musculature, the m. rectus abdominis; these are similar to structures that are found in the proteid salamander *Necturus.* There are three pairs of cartilaginous elements posterior to the sternal horns. The posterior two pairs may or may not be united medially; the halves of the anterior pair are fused medially and may be united synchondrotically with the sternum. According to de Vos (1938), the ribs may be serially homologous with the posterior horns of the sternum, but they are not associated in any way with the ribs which are of dermal origin.

Forelimb Structure. The proximal, or propodial, element of the anuran forelimb is the humerus (Fig. 13-35), which in males frequently is modified by the proliferation of large crests for the attachment of hypertrophied musculature (Fig. 3-9). The radius and ulna are fused to form the compound epipodial bone—the radio-ulna. Although there may be as many as 12 mesopodial elements, there is great variation in their number and configuration in anurans, and a tendency toward loss and fusion. The following description is based on the leiopelmatid *Ascaphus truei.* There are two large elements associated with the radio-ulna. These are assumed to be the radiale (perhaps fused with one of the centrale series) preaxially and the fused intermedium and ulnare postaxially. Distal to these two large elements are the prepollex (preaxial) and three centrales, the homologies of which are uncertain. Two small distal carpals lie between the centrales and the series of four metacarpals. All anurans have four digits on the hand, and the normal phalangeal formula is 2-2-3-3 (Digits I–IV, respectively). Reduction in the lengths of the phalanges (e.g., some species of the bufonid genus *Rhamphophryne,* and the brachycephalids) or loss of a phalangeal element (e.g. some *Atelopus*) can result in one or more shortened digits, although all anurans retain at least the vestiges of four digits so far as is known. Several groups of frogs—the hylids, centrolenids, hyperoliids, rhacophorids, pseudids, mantelline ranids, and phrynomerine microhylids—are characterized by the presence of an additional element, the intercalary cartilage or bone, between the penultimate and ultimate phalanges. Among leptodactylids, bufonids, hyperoliids, hylids, centrolenids, and microhylids, the terminal or ultimate phalanges frequently are modified into a variety of different shapes.

Forelimb Movement. Myologically, the pectoral region of anurans is highly modified and variable in comparison with the generalized pattern characteristic of most salamanders. The modification of the anterior appendicular skeleton from a more generalized scheme obviously is associated with the saltatorial habits of anurans. The mechanics of the hindlimb have been analyzed by Gans (1961) and Calow and R. Alexander (1973), but aside from S. Emerson's (1984) paper on some mechanical properties of arciferal and firmisternal girdles, nothing specific is known about the role of the pectoral girdle and forelimbs in anuran locomotion. Based on personal observations and Gans's (1961) stop-frame photographs of *Rana catesbeiana* jumping, it is evident that the forelimb of anurans is positioned differently than that of salamanders and fulfills a different functional role in locomotion. At rest, the shoulder joint tends to be extended with the upper arm lying against the flank raher than held at a right angle to the body as it is in salamanders. The elbow joint is flexed and the forearm directed in an anteromedial direction rather than directly forward. Thus, the entire lower arm and hand are rotated inward toward the center of the body. As the animal thrusts itself forward in a leap, it probably rolls off the palmar surface of the hand while straightening the elbow and wrist joints. Thus, the forelimb lies parallel to the body for maximum streamlining. After full thrust has been developed from the hindlimbs, the forelimb is flexed at the elbow, and the upper arm is pulled as far forward as possible. Subsequent flexion of the wrist allows the animal to land on its hands, the force of landing presumably being absorbed by the pectoral girdle.

Musculature of Pectoral Girdle and Forelimb. Given the differences in locomotion and the structure of the pectoral girdle between salamanders and anurans, it is not surprising that anuran pectoral musculature is quite different. Moreover, the marked variability of pectoral girdle structure in anurans is paralleled by an equivalent amount of variation in the muscles associated with the girdle. Thus, it is difficult to present a generalized description. Among the most useful descriptions available are those of Gaupp (1896) for *Rana esculenta,* Ritland (1955) for *Ascaphus truei,* T. C. Burton (1983a, 1983b) for microhylids, M. Davies and T. C. Burton (1982) for *Rheobatrachus silus,* S. Liem (1970) for rhacophorids and hyperoliids, and Grobbelar (1924) for *Xenopus laevis.* De

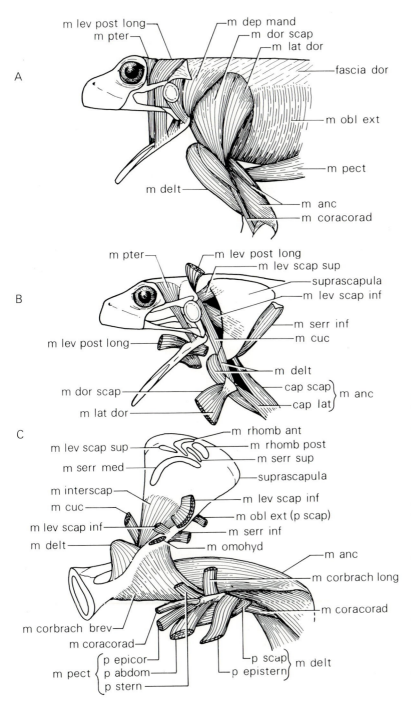

Figure 13-37. Shoulder girdle musculature of *Rana esculenta* redrawn from Gaupp (1896). **A.** Superficial lateral view. **B.** Deep lateral view. **C.** Medial view of inner side of right side. Abbreviations: cap lat = caput laterale of m. anconeus; cap scap = caput scapulare of m. anconeus; fascia dor = fascia dorsalis; m anc = m. anconeus; m coracorad = m. coracoradialis; m corbrach brev = m. coracobrachialis brevis; m corbrach long = m. coracobrachialis longus; m cuc = m. cucullaris; m delt = m. deltoideus; m dep mand = m. depressor mandibulae; m dor scap = m. dorsalis scapulae; m interscap = m. interscapularis; m lat dor = m. latissimus dorsi; m lev post long = m. levator mandibulae posterior longus; m lev scap inf = m. levator scapulae inferior; m lev scap sup = m. levator scapulae superior; m obl ext = m. obliquus externus; m omohyd = m. omohyoideus; m pect = m. pectoralis; m. pterygoideus; m rhomb ant = m. rhomboideus anterior; m rhomb post = m. rhomboideus posterior; m serr inf = m. serratus inferior; m serr med = m. serratus medius; m serr sup = m. serratus superior; p epistern = pars episternalis of m. deltoideus; p scap = pars scapularis of m. deltoideus; p epicor = portio epicoracoidea of m. pectoralis; p stern = portio sternalis of m. pectoralis.

Villiers (1922) produced a monograph that concentrated primarily on the structure and development of the breast-shoulder apparatus in *Bombina variegata,* and E. Jones (1933) and Hsaio (1933–1934) provided comparative studies of the pectoral regions of some anurans. There is an appalling lack of concordance in the names applied to various pectoral muscles. Because Gaupp's (1896) descriptions are the most thorough and well documented, his nomenclature is adopted here, and unless otherwise stated, the following descriptions are based on *Rana esculenta.*

As in salamanders, the muscles of the anuran shoulder and forelimb are separable into three groups—muscles that chiefly are suspensory in function, and those that extend and flex the forelimb. A fourth category that exists in anurans are intrinsic muscles that move one part of the pectoral girdle with respect to another.

Suspensory muscles of girdle.—The extrinsic suspensory muscles are of two types—those that arise in association with the vertebral column or the axial musculature and insert on the suprascapula, and those that arise from the posterior part of the skull and extend to the suprascapula (Fig. 13-37).

M. rhomboideus anterior

The m. rhomboideus anterior is a thin, broad, rhomboidal muscle that is innervated by S.N. 3 and originates from the posterior part of the frontoparietal bone and the anterior part of the dorsal fascia. It is superficial in position and extends posteriorly from the skull to insert on the ventral surface of the anteromedial corner of the suprascapula. Contraction of the rhomboideus anterior pulls the suprascapula forward. The muscle is enlarged in many species of *Bufo* and arises from the dorsal surface of the prootic and the posteromedial part of the squamosal, as well as the frontoparietal.

Mm. levator scapulae and opercularis

The levator scapulae complex is composed of three muscles that originate from the prootic-exoccipital region of the skull and insert on the medial side of the suprascapula (Fig. 13-37). The m. levator scapulae superior arises from the lateral part of the otic capsule and is innervated by S.Nn. 2 and 3. A dorsal derivative of this muscle, the m. opercularis (see discussion of neurocranial head musculature above), extends between the operculum and the suprascapula in all anurans except pipids. The m. levator scapulae inferior has a broad origin from the prootic and exoccipital bones. The inferior muscle is innervated by S.N. 2 and inserts on the posteroventral corner of the suprascapula, whereas the superior portion inserts on the anterodorsal corner. Both muscles protract the suprascapula.

M. cucullaris

The only muscle extending between the skull and the pectoral girdle in anurans for which there is an obvious homologue in salamanders is the m. cucullaris, which is similarly innervated in both groups by C.N. XI (accessory). From its origin on the prootic and the otic ramus of the squamosal, the m. cucullaris extends posteroventrally to insert on the anterior border of the suprascapula. It lies anterior and external to the m. levator scapulae inferior. Contraction of this muscle depresses the head, unless the head is immobilized by contraction of trunk musculature that attaches to the posterior end of the skull, in which case the muscle pulls the suprascapula forward.

M. rhomboideus posterior and serratus

There are four extrinsic muscles in anurans that suspend the pectoral girdle from the axial column and generally are antagonistic in action to the extrinsic muscles arising from the skull (Fig. 13-37). This group of muscles probably is homologous with the m. thoraciscapularis of salamanders. These muscles lie deep to the mm. latissimus dorsi and dorsalis scapulae (described below). The two most posterior members of the series are the mm. rhomboideus posterior and serratus superior, both of which are innervated by branches of S.N. 3. The m. rhomboideus posterior is dorsal in position and derived from the epaxial musculature. From its broad origin from the transverse process of Presacral IV, the muscle fibers converge as the m. rhomboideus posterior extends anteriorly to insert on the dorsomedial surface of the suprascapula. Contraction of this muscle pulls the suprascapula backward. The m. serratus superior originates from the transverse process of Presacral IV distal to the origin of the m. rhomboideus posterior. This muscle extends anteriorly to insert on the dorsomedial surface of the suprascapula beneath the point of insertion of the m. rhomboideus posterior. The m. serratus superior retracts the suprascapula in a posterolateral direction. The two remaining members of this series of dorsal suspensory muscles are the mm. serratus medius and serratus inferior; the former is innervated by S.N. 3, whereas the latter is innervated by S.N. 4. The m. serratus medius arises from the transverse process of Presacral III and extends forward to insert on the central, medial surface of the suprascapula. Contraction of this muscle pulls the suprascapula in a lateral direction. The m. serratus inferior arises from two heads. The posterior head is associated with the transverse process and cartilaginous epiphysis of Presacral IV, whereas the anterior head is associated with these parts of Presacral III. From its origins, the muscle gradually decreases in size as it extends anteriorly and ventrolaterally to insert on the medial surface of the suprascapula near the posteroventral edge of this element. The m. serratus inferior draws the ventral portion of the suprascapula posteromedially.

Forelimb extensors and adductors, and intrinsic pectoral muscles.—Forelimb extension is powered by two shoulder muscles and a variety of distal muscles (Figs. 13-37, 13-38). Intrinsic pectoral muscles also are consid-

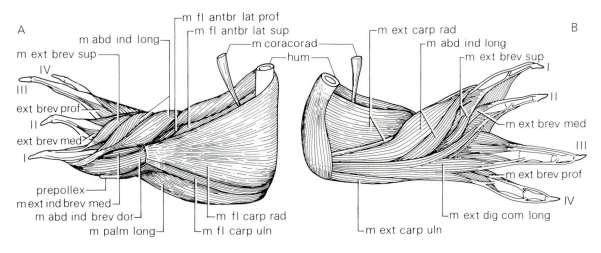

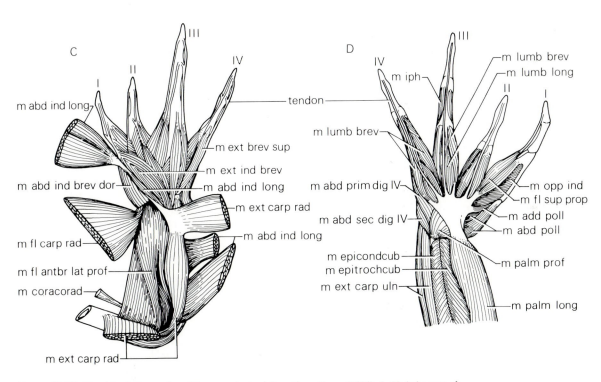

Figure 13-38. Distal forelimb muscles of *Rana esculenta*, redrawn from Gaupp (1896). **A.** Medial aspect of right hand and forearm. **B.** Lateral aspect of right hand and forearm. **C.** Dorsal surface of right hand and forearm with superficial muscles removed. **D.** Ventral aspect of right hand and forearm. Abbreviations: aponeur palm = aponeurosis palmaris; hum = humerus; m abd ind brev dor = m. abductor indicis brevis dorsalis; m abd ind long = m. abductor indicis longus; m abd poll = m. abductor pollicis; m abd prim dig IV = m. abductor primus digiti IV; m abd sec dig IV = m. abductor secundus digiti IV; m add poll = m. adductor pollicis; m coracorad = m. coracoradialis; m epicondcub = m. epicondylocubitalis; m epitrochcub = m. epitrochleocubitalis; m ext brev med = m. extensor brevis medius; m ext brev prof = m. extensor brevis profundus; m ext brev sup = m. extensor brevis superficialis; m ext carp rad = m. extensor carpi radialis; m ext carp uln = m. extensor carpi ulnaris; m ext dig com long = m. extensor digitorum communis longus; m ext ind brev = m. extensor indicis brevis; m ext ind brev med = m. extensor indicis brevis medius; m fl antbr lat prof = m. flexor antibrachii lateralis profuncus; m fl antbr lat sup = flexor antibrachii lateralis superficialis; m fl carp rad = m. flexor carpi radialis; m fl carp uln = m. flexor carpi ulnaris; m fl sup prop = m. flexor superficialis proprius; m iph = m. interphalangealis; m lumb brev = m. lumbricalis brevis; m lumb long = m. lumbricalis longus; m opp ind = m. opponens indicis; m palm long = m. palmaris longus; m palm prof = m. palmaris profundus.

ered here, although they do not affect extension of the forelimb directly.

Mm. latissimus dorsi and dorsalis scapulae

These shoulder muscles are innervated by a branches of S.N. 3 and probably are homologous with the muscles of the same names in salamanders. In most anurans the m. latissimus dorsi is superficial, thin, and triangular and arises from the ventral surface of the dorsal fascia; however, in some species of *Bufo* the muscle is narrow and thick and arises from the cartilaginous epiphysis of the transverse process of Presacral IV. Its fibers converge to a flat tendon that inserts on the deltoid crest (= crista ventralis) of the humerus. Contraction of the m. latissimus dorsi extends the shoulder joint by pulling the upper arm backward.

The m. dorsalis scapulae lies anterior to the m. latissimus dorsi; it arises from the outer (i.e., lateral) surface of the suprascapula. From its broad origin, the muscle converges into a flat tendon that unites with the tendon of the m. latissimus dorsi to insert on the deltoid crest of the humerus. The primary action of the m. dorsalis scapulae is to adduct, or raise, the humerus. In conjunction with the m. latissimus dorsi, this muscle acts to circumduct the humerus dorsally and backward.

Mm. interscapularis and sternoepicoracoideus

There are two intrinsic muscles associated with the pectoral girdle in anurans—the mm. interscapularis and sternoepicoracoideus (= m. sternocoracoideus of some authors). The m. interscapularis arises from the ventromedial surface of the suprascapula and extends ventromedially to insert on the ventral surface of the scapula. It is innervated by a branch of C.N. X (vagus). Contraction of this muscle closes the angle between the suprascapula and the scapula. Although all anurans possess this muscle, it varies in size and configuration. It is bifurcate in discoglossids, but single in most other anurans, and varies from large in bufonids to small in ranids. The second intrinsic muscle, the m. sternoepicoracoideus, is found only in discoglossids and *Leiopelma*. It is innervated by S.N. 3 and arises from the anterior border of the distal part of the sternal horn. From their broad origin, the muscle fibers converge to a narrow tendon that inserts anteromedially on the dorsal surface of the epicoracoid cartilage near its posterior margin. The m. sternoepicoracoideus is thought to be derived from the m. rectus abdominis. Its function is unknown.

M. anconeus

The major extensor of the elbow joint is the m. anconeus which lies along the dorsal surface of the upper arm. This muscle, along with all the other forearm extensors, is innervated by branches of S.N. 2. The anconeus bears three heads, the longest of which originates from the posterior border of the scapula at the upper border of the glenoid cavity where it is attached to the joint capsule. The inner head arises from the proximal,

medial surface of the humerus, and the outer head from the lateral surface of the humerus. The fibers of these three heads unite to form a robust muscle that covers the upper, inner, and outer surfaces of the humerus and converge on a tendon that inserts on the proximal end of the olecranon process of the radio-ulna. On contraction, this muscle straightens the elbow, thereby extending the forearm.

Distal forearm extensors

Distal forearm extensors include the mm. extensor carpi radialis, extensor carpi ulnaris, epicondylocubitalis, epitrochleocubitalis, extensor digitorum communis longus, and abductor indicis longus (Fig. 13-38). Each of these muscles takes its origin, at least in part, from the lateral epicondyle of the humerus.

The m. extensor carpi radialis arises by two heads. The superior head originates from the lateral crest of the humerus, whereas the more distal head arises from the lateral epicondyle of the humerus and the elbow joint. Although the two heads are separated throughout the greater part of their lengths, they unite distally to cross the radio-ulna and insert on the carpals. The m. extensor carpi radialis extends the wrist in a dorsal direction.

The m. extensor carpi ulnaris is a narrow muscle that originates from the lateral epicondyle of the humerus, extends down the forearm, and inserts on the outer surface of the carpus; contraction of this muscle extends the wrist joint.

The m. epicondylocubitalis arises by two heads; one is located on the lateral epicondyle of the humerus, whereas the other is on the medial epicondyle. This muscle unites medially with the m. epitrochleocubitalis, which arises from the medial epicondyle, to form a pinnate muscle that extends distally to cover the olecranon process of the radio-ulna and insert on the dorsal border of the ulnar portion of the radio-ulna. The muscle acts to rotate the forearm medially.

The m. extensor digitorum communis longus lies on the outer border of the forearm. It originates from the lateral epicondyle of the humerus and passes down the forearm into an aponeurosis on the dorsum of the hand. The aponeurosis is continuous with tendons of the m. extensor brevis digitorum that insert on the phalangeal elements; thus, the muscle is an extensor of the wrist and Digits II–IV. The superior head of the m. abductor indicis longus has a common origin with the m. extensor digitorum communis longus, whereas its lower head arises from the lateral surface of the radio-ulna. The muscle fibers unite to extend obliquely down and across the radio-ulna and insert on Metacarpal I. Contraction of this muscle extends the wrist and abducts the first, or inner, digit.

In addition to the extensor muscles described above, there is a multiplicity of muscles that act to extend and abduct the digits. The primary muscle is the m. extensor digitorum communis brevis that arises from the wrist and inserts on the terminal phalanx of Digits II–IV. Smaller abductors and extensors are associated with each separate digit. Gaupp (1896), S. Liem (1970), Andersen (1978), and T. C. Burton (1983a) provided detailed descriptions of these muscles.

Forelimb flexors and adductors.—Five pectoral muscles are involved in the ventral musculature that acts as flexors of the shoulder and elbow joints (Fig. 13-37). The most superficial of these are the mm. pectoralis, coracoradialis, and deltoideus. The mm. coracobrachialis longus and coracobrachialis brevis lie deep to these muscles.

M. deltoideus

The m. deltoideus (not homologous with the muscle of the same name applied by some authors to the m. dorsalis scapulae of salamanders) is the most anterior of the three superficial muscles, and is innervated by branches of S.N. 3.The m. deltoideus is composed of three parts—the partes episternalis, clavicularis, and scapularis. The pars episternalis arises from the lateral border of the omosternum and inserts on the distal portion of the humerus. The pars clavicularis is a small muscle that originates from the lateral end of the ventral surface of the clavicle. This muscle unites with the third part of the m. deltoideus, the pars scapularis, to insert on the deltoid crest of the humerus. The pars scapularis arises from the lateral end of the clavicle, the precoracoid cartilage, and the anterior and ventral surfaces of the scapula. Contraction of the various parts of the m. deltoideus, flexes the shoulder joint by pulling the humerus forward.

M. coracoradialis

The m. coracoradialis lies posterior to the m. deltoideus. It is a broad, fan-shaped muscle that overlies part of the m. deltoideus anteriorly, and is partially covered posteriorly by the anterior part of the m. pectoralis. The m. coracoradialis has a broad origin from the omosternum and epicoracoid cartilage. The fibers converge laterally to a tendon that inserts on the proximal end of the radio-ulna. This muscle, which is innervated by S.N. 3, is a powerful flexor of the elbow joint and, therefore, is antagonistic to the action of the m. anconeus.

M. pectoralis

The last and most posterior of the three superficial pectoral muscles is the m. pectoralis which is composed of three parts and innervated by branches of S.Nn. 2 and 3. The most anterior section is the portio epicoracoidea which has a broad origin from the epicoracoid cartilage and overlies the posterior part of the m. coracoradialis. The fibers of this part of the m. pectoralis converge laterally to a tendon that inserts on the deltoid crest of the humerus. The portio sternalis arises from the sternum posterior to the portio epicoracoidea; its fibers converge anterolaterally and insert into the groove beside the deltoid crest of the humerus. The most posterior and largest part of the m. pectoralis is the portio abdominalis. This muscle is derived from the m. rectus abdominis. From its broad, posterior origin, the muscle extends anteriorly to insert on the deltoid crest of the humerus. Contraction of the m. pectoralis adducts the upper arm downward.

Mm. coracobrachialis longus and brevis

The two deep muscles, the mm. coracobrachialis longus and brevis, are innervated by branches of S.N. 3. The m. coracobrachialis longus is a long, narrow muscle that arises from the dorsal surface of the coracoid near the sternum and extends laterally to insert on the middle of the humerus. The m. coracobrachialis brevis arises from the dorsal surface of the coracoid and scapula and inserts on the deltoid crest of the humerus. Contraction of these two muscles pulls the arm posteroventrally; therefore, they are antagonistic to the m. deltoideus.

Variation in ventral pectoral musculature

Given the great amount of variation in the structure of the ventral parts of the pectoral girdle among anurans, one would anticipate correlative variation in the ventral pectoral musculature. Hsiao (1933–1934) and E. Jones (1933) demonstrated that the mm. deltoideus, pectoralis, and coracoradialis are the most variable. In anurans having a small omosternum or lacking this prezonal element, the origins of the anterior components of the mm. deltoideus and pectoralis tend to be narrowed and shifted posteriorly, and in some cases (e.g., some microhylids) these muscles may fuse. The clavicular portion of the m. deltoideus is absent in many microhylids. The clavicular portion of the m. coracoradialis varies with respect to its attachment to the clavicle, and with reduction of this element, the origin of the muscle may shift posteriorly to the procoracoid cartilage. In general, there is less variation in the posterior muscles, although the portio sternalis of the m. pectoralis tends to diminish in size in association with smaller sterna, and in some microhylids the m. pectoralis portio abdominalis is divided into medial and lateral parts.

Distal forearm flexors

The distal forearm flexors are complex; for convenience, they are broken into two groups—those that lie on the medial surface of the forearm and those that lie on the lateral surface (Fig. 13-38). All are innervated by branches of S.N. 2.

The m. flexor carpi radialis is a superficial muscle that takes a broad origin from the inner border of the humerus above the medial condyle. The fibers of this muscle converge distally on the forearm and insert on the carpus. The m. flexor carpi ulnaris lies along the inner side of the m. flexor carpi radialis. The muscle originates from the median condyle of the humerus, and like the m. flexor carpi radialis, it inserts on the carpus. Together, these two muscles serve as the main flexors of the hand. Typically, the m. flexor carpi radialis is better developed in males than in females owing to the use of the forearm in males to grasp the female during amplexus. The third superficial muscle of the medial side is the m. palmaris longus. This muscle arises from the medial epicondyle of the humerus and the medial surface of the elbow joint. It extends down the forearm and passes into the triangular palmar aponeurosis. Tendons arise from the distal margin of the aponeurosis of the m. palmaris longus and extend to each digit where they are inserted on the phalangeal elements. Through the association of the m. palmaris longus with the m. palmaris profundus, the m. palmaris longus flexes the digits. The mm. flexor antibrachii medialis and ulnocarpalis lie deep to the foregoing muscles on the median side of the forelimb. The former muscle arises by a tendon from the medial epicondyle of the humerus and inserts on the radial side of the radio-ulna; it pulls the forearm in a medial direction. The m. ulnocarpalis lies deep to the m. palmaris longus where it arises

along the distal third of the ulna and extends around the wrist and inserts on the ulnare. Contraction of this muscle flexes the wrist thereby pulling the hand downward.

On the lateral side of the forearm, the m. flexor antibrachii lateralis superficialis arises by two heads. The superior head lies on the outer edge of the humerus, whereas the lower originates from the lateral epicondyle. Fibers of the heads unite and pass into a tendon that runs over the radio-ulna–carpal articulation; distally, the tendon inserts on the carpus and on the tendon of the extensor of the first digit. Contraction of this muscle flexes the elbow, and extends and supinates the hand. The m. flexor antibrachii lateralis profundus arises deep to the superficial antibrachial muscle from the lateral epicondyle of the

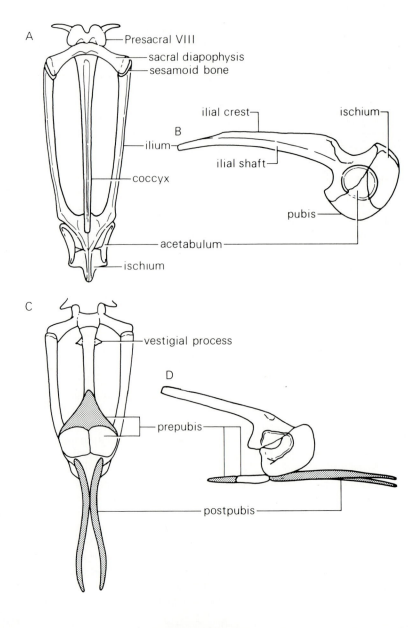

Figure 13-39. Anuran pelvic girdle structure. **A.** Dorsal view of pelvic girdle of *Rana esculenta* articulated with posterior part of vertebral column. **B.** Lateral view of pelvic girdle of *R. esculenta*. **C.** Ventral aspect of pelvic girdle of *Ascaphus truei* showing pre- and postpubic elements. **D.** Lateral view of pelvic girdle of *A. truei*. Cartilaginous elements are shown in stippled pattern. A—B redrawn from Gaupp (1896), and C—D from Ritland (1955).

humerus. The muscle inserts along the length of the lower ridge of the radio-ulna and acts to flex the elbow and supinate the hand.

In the hand, the m. palmaris profundus arises from the ulnar border of the radio-ulna and extends obliquely to insert on the palmar aponeurosis. Detailed descriptions of the balance of the palmar musculature associated with the prepollex and each of the four digits in various taxa were provided by Gaupp (1896), Andersen (1978), S. Liem (1970), and T. C. Burton (1983a).

Pelvic Girdle Structure.   The pelvis of frogs consists of three paired elements that unite in a medial symphysis; these are the ilium, ischium, and pubis (Fig. 13-39). The primary elements are the ilium and ischium, because in most anurans the pubis is reduced. The ilium consists of an anterior shaft that articulates with the sacral diapophyses and an expanded posterior end that forms the anterior half of the acetabulum. Variation in this element involves its length, the presence and nature of crests along the shaft, the kinds of protuberances for muscle attachment that may be located anterodorsal to the acetabu-

lum, and the nature of its articulation with the sacral diapophysis. Proportionately longer ilia are associated with anurans that are more saltatorial, whereas shorter ilia are characteristic of terrestrial or fossorial species that tend to walk rather that jump.

The ilium articulates with the ventral surface of the sacral diapophysis in one of three ways according to S. Emerson (1979) (Fig. 13-40). In anurans having broadly expanded sacral diapophyses with more or less straight lateral margins, a superficial, transverse ligament unites the anterolateral ends of the ilia across the body. This configuration (Emerson's Type I) maximizes anterior-posterior movement of the pelvic girdle in a horizontal plane and minimizes lateral and dorsal-ventral rotation. In the Type II iliosacral articulation, each ilium is attached to its adjacent sacral diapophysis by a ligament deep to the dorsal back musculature, and a well-developed joint capsule is present. There are two kinds of Type II articulations. In anurans having moderately expanded sacral diapophyses with convex lateral margins, the ilium is attached to the diapophysis by a broad, transverse ligament and articulates with its cartilaginous margin via a groove.

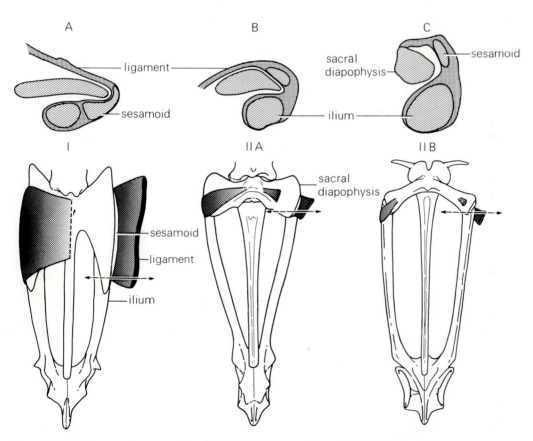

Figure 13-40. Diagrammatic representation of the three major types of iliosacral articulations in anurans. Dorsal views of pelvic girdles and posterior vertebral columns with ligamentous attachments are illustrated below schematic sections; levels of sections are indicated by section lines in lower figures. **A.** Type I with broad, transverse ligament. **B.** Type IIA with broad, medially interrupted ligament. **C.** Type IIB with narrow, distal ligament. Adapted from S. Emerson (1979).

According to S. Emerson, the Type IIA iliosacral articulation allows a certain amount of lateral rotation of the pelvis in the horizontal plane, and is characteristic of the majority of anurans. Anurans having a Type IIB iliosacral articulation have round sacral diapophyses that are oriented posterolaterally. The ilium is attached to the sacral diapophysis by a narrow, transverse ligament, but lacks the groovelike articulation with the distal cartilage found in Type IIA. S. Emerson proposed that the Type IIB iliosacral articulation accommodated dorsoventral excursion of the pelvis in a vertical plane, and she associated it with anurans such as *Rana* that are accomplished, long-distance leapers.

The ischium forms the posterior half of the acetabulum and varies considerably in its shape, presumably in correlation with the muscles that originate from this area of the girdle. The pubis usually is present as a cartilaginous element ventral to the acetabulum and located between the anteroventral margin of the ischium and the posteroventral margin of the ilium. In some anurans, the element calcifies so that its articulations with adjacent elements are difficult to distinguish.

Two ancillary structures are associated with the pelvic girdle in some frogs. These are pre- and postpubic elements (Fig. 13-39C, D). The leiopelmatids and the pipids *Xenopus* and *Pseudhymenochirus* possess a prepubic element known as an epipubis. This small plate of cartilage is synchondrotically united with the pubis, and may be calcified in adults. De Villiers (1934) suggested that the epipubis is homologous in these anuran genera and that it probably is a derivative of the linea alba. Further, he proposed that it might be a morphological or functional homologue to the ypsiloid cartilage of salamanders. Postpubic, or Nobelian, bones occur only in *Ascaphus truei* where they lie within the copulatory organ (or so-called tail) and are attached to the posteroventral part of the pelvic girdle. According to de Villiers (1934), these postpubic elements are incorporated into the phallic organ and possibly act as an os penis.

Hindlimb Structure. The anuran hindlimb is elongated relative to the forelimb. The proximal thigh element that articulates with the pelvic girdle is the femur (Fig. 13-41). The shank (or crus) is represented by a compound bone, the tibiofibula. The mesopodial or tarsal elements of anurans are modified significantly. The preaxial fibulare (= astragalus) and postaxial tibiale (= calcaneum) are elongate bones that are fused medially at their proximal and distal ends. Fusion of the fibulare and tibiale throughout their entire lengths to form a compound bone occurs only in the centrolenids and pelodytids. The remaining mesopodial elements consist of a prehallux (preaxial), a centrale, and one distal tarsal. Insofar as is known, all except two species of anurans have five toes, and, thus, a series of five metatarsals and phalanges with the typical formula of 2-2-3-4-3 (Digits I–V, respectively). *Psyllophryne didactyla* (brachycephalid) and *Didynamipus sjoestedti* (bufonid) have only four toes on the foot.

In contrast to salamanders in which digital reduction occurs through the loss of the last (i.e., postaxial) toe, in anurans it is the first preaxial digit that is lost (Alberch and Gale, 1985). Reduction in the length of individual digits can occur through the loss of one or more phalanges. Intercalary structures are present between the penultimate and ultimate phalanges of the hylids, centrolenids, pseudids, rhacophorids, hyperoliids, mantelline ranids, and phrynomerine microhylids.

As summarized by Nussbaum (1982), three heterotopic skeletal elements are known to occur in association with tendons in the tarsal segment of anurans. The cartilago plantaris of *Pipa, Rana esculenta,* and some petropedetine ranids lies in the subarticular region of the foot. A variety of anurans has a heterotopic element, the cartilago sesamoides, in the ligamentum calcanei. The third element is the os sesamoides tarsale which lies in the proximal part of the aponeurosis plantaris in sooglossids, species of *Pipa,* and some petropedetine ranids. Generally these heterotopic elements occur at stress points in tendons where the tendon transmits a force of a powerful muscle across a joint. According to Nussbaum, their presence and calcification is presumed to strengthen a tendon, help to maintain its shape, and increase the mechanical advantage of force translation.

Hindlimb Movement. Not all anurans are equally accomplished at leaping. Some short-legged terrestrial forms (bufonids such as *Osornophryne*) tend to walk. Aquatic species such as *Xenopus* or *Pipa pipa* are agile swimmers, and when on land, essentially utilize the splayed limbs to swim across the substrate. Nonetheless, all anurans are capable of some form of saltatorial locomotion, be it by a sequence of short hops or longer-ranging leaps, and even anurans that primarily swim do so in a saltatorial fashion (Calow and R. Alexander, 1973). As pointed out by Gans (1961), this pattern is unique to anurans among lower tetrapods. It represents a fundamental departure from the generalized mode of progression by alternating limb movement characteristic of salamanders and primitive tetrapods, because anuran saltation is powered by simultaneous activation of both hindlimbs. Some of the morphological modifications that accommodate this locomotory habit in anurans are familiar (e.g., the short, fusiform body and attenuate hindlimbs), but others involving the musculature of the pelvic girdle and hindlimb are less so.

In a resting position, the several sets of long bones in the anuran hindlimb are folded against one another. As the animal leaps, the joints are extended more or less simultaneously, powered by muscles that lie on opposite (i.e., anterior and posterior) sides of each leg segment so that each bone can be shifted upon the one lying next closer to the body. The straightening of the legs transmits a propulsive force through the sole of the foot to the substrate. It is this force that reaches its peak just before the foot leaves the ground and provides the power enabling anurans to leap forward.

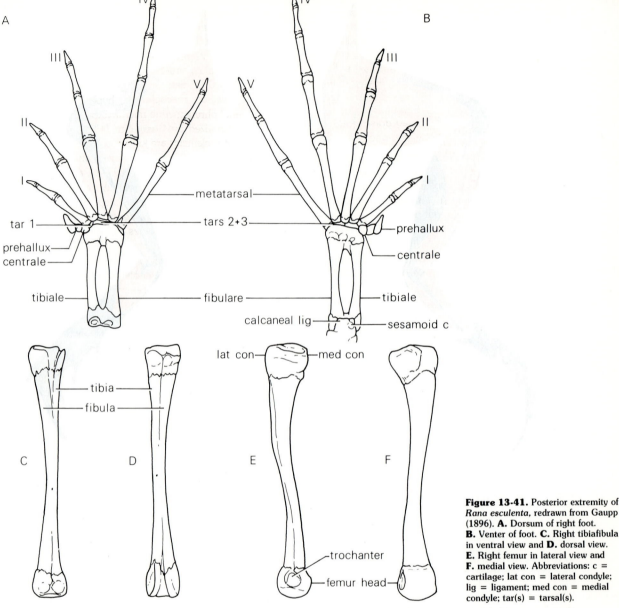

Figure 13-41. Posterior extremity of *Rana esculenta*, redrawn from Gaupp (1896). **A.** Dorsum of right foot. **B.** Venter of foot. **C.** Right tibiafibula in ventral view and **D.** dorsal view. **E.** Right femur in lateral view and **F.** medial view. Abbreviations: c = cartilage; lat con = lateral condyle; lig = ligament; med con = medial condyle; tar(s) = tarsal(s).

Musculature of Pelvic Girdle and Hindlimb. As mentioned above, anurans demonstrate a wide variety of locomotory habits such as walking, hopping, burrowing, and climbing that can be viewed as specializations. These derived patterns of movement are associated with morphological modifications of the musculoskeletal system that involve the iliosacral articulation, the construction of skeletal components, and the nature and arrangement of associated muscles. This variation in pelvic and hindlimb musculature (principally that of the thigh) has attracted a great deal of attention since Noble's (1922) monograph on the phylogeny of the Salientia in which he utilized characteristics of thigh muscles in his classifi-

cation of anurans. In this work, Noble provided a summary of earlier literature. Aside from the general myological works cited previously in the description of the forelimb musculature, the single most informative paper since Noble's, is that of Dunlap (1960) on the comparative myology of the hindlimb in anurans. The nomenclature used below follows Gaupp (1896) as modified by Dunlap (1960). The descriptions are based primarily on *Rana catesbeiana* and *R. pipiens* with some notes on the major variation in other anurans that have been studied. Details of this variation are provided by Dunlap (1960).

The structure and orientation of the anuran hindlimb deviates markedly from the more generalized pattern ob-

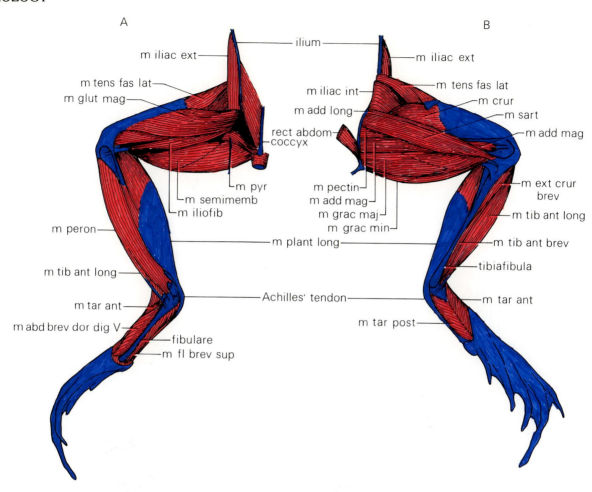

Figure 13-42. Left hindlimb musculature of *Rana esculenta,* redrawn from Gaupp (1896). **A.** Dorsal aspect.
B. Ventral aspect. Abbreviations: m abd brev dor dig V = m. abductor brevis dorsalis digiti V; m add
long = m. adductor longus; m add mag = m. adductor magnus; m crur = m. cruralis; m ext crur brev =
m. extensor cruris brevis; m fl brev sup = m. flexor brevis superficialis; m glut mag = m. glutaeus magnus;
m grac maj = m. gracilis major; m grac min = m. gracilis minor; m iliac ext = m. iliacus externus; m iliac
int = m. iliacus internus; m iliofib = m. iliofibularis; m pectin = m. pectineus; m peron = m. peroneus;
m plant long = m. plantaris longus; m pyr = m. pyriformis; m rect abdom = m. rectus abdominis; m
sart = m. satorius; m semimemb = m. semimembranosus; m tar ant = m. tarsalis anticus; m tar post =
m. tarsalis posticus; m tens fas lat = m. tensor fasciae latae; m tib ant brev = m. tibialis anticus brevis; m
tib ant long = m. tibialis anticus longus; m tib post = m. tibialis posticus.

served in salamanders in which extensors tend to be located on the dorsum of the limb and flexors on the venter. While it surely would be a useful academic excercise
to organize the muscle descriptions by function, in the
case of the anuran hindlimb the structure is understood
more easily with regional, topographic descriptions. The
accounts describe the animal as though it were laid out
for dissection, that is, prone with the thigh at a right angle
to the midline of the body and the shank and foot extended. All references to medial, lateral, anterior, etc.
should be interpreted accordingly.

Thigh musculature.—The well-developed thigh muscles of anurans originate on the pelvic girdle (Figs.
13-42, 13-44) and are responsible for moving the femur
in the hip joint in all directions, and in some cases, flexing
the knee joint. Because these muscles are complex and

numerous, they will be described relative to their size and
topographical position. Thus, long muscles originating on
the pelvic girdle are subdivided into three groups—(1)
prefemoral muscles that occur on the anterior edge of
the thigh, (2) postfemoral muscles that are posterior and
ventral, and (3) postfemoral muscles that are posterior
and dorsal. A description of the short thigh muscles that
originate on the pelvic girdle follows the description of
the long muscles. All of these muscles are innervated by
branches of the lumbosacralis plexus formed by S.Nn.
7–10.

Mm. triceps femoris and tensor fasciae latae

The prefemoral thigh musculature is composed of the
mm. triceps femoris and tensor fasciae latae. The m. triceps femoris forms the outer border of the thigh, ex-

tending onto both dorsal and ventral surfaces, and is a compound muscle that is homologous with the m. ilioextensorius of salamanders. The m. cruralis constitutes the dorsal head of the m. triceps femoris. It arises from the ventral margin of the acetabulum and extends along the anterior margin of the thigh; the fibers converge on a tendon at the knee. The tendon extends over the knee and bifurcates. One branch inserts at the base of the epiphysis on the tibial side of the tibiofibula, and the other, smaller tendon inserts inside the belly of the m. plantaris longus (see description below). The posterior head of the the m. triceps is the m. glutaeus magnus. This muscle arises anterodorsal to the acetabulum along the dorsolateral surface of the ilium and extends along the dorsal surface of the thigh to unite in a common tendon with the m. cruralis. The m. tensor fasciae latae arises along the ventral margin of the posterior part of the ilial shaft and extends posterolaterally to insert on the fascia covering the m. cruralis on the anterodorsal aspect of the thigh. Together, this complex of muscles extends the knee joint and flexes the hip joint.

Mm. sartorius and semitendinosus

The mm. sartorius and semitendinosus (= m. sartoriosemitendinosus of some authors) form a compound muscle that abducts the femur and pulls it ventrally and flexes the knee. These are two of a group of seven muscles that constitutes the postfemoral, ventral thigh musculature. The m. sartorius is a wide, thin muscle that arises from the anteroventral margin of the preacetabular zone of the pelvis (ilium) and extends across the ventral surface of the thigh. The fibers converge on a tendon at the knee; the tendon inserts on the aponeurosis of the m. cruralis and the tendon of the m. semitendinosus and the insertion of the m. gracilis major.

The second member of this complex, the m. semitendinosus, has a double, tendinous origin from (1) the posteroventral pelvic rim near the union of the ischium and pubis, and (2) the posterodorsal pelvic rim. The muscle extends along the ventromedial surface of the thigh and inserts on the ventral surface of the tibiofibula. In more primitive frogs (e.g., leiopelmatids, most discoglossids, pipids, and pelobatids), the mm. sartorius and semitendinosus are united into a common muscle with two heads that unite about half way down the thigh; both muscles insert on the ventral surface of the tibiofibula. In most bufonids, the muscles are separate; however, the m. sartorius may insert on the tendon of the m. semitendinosus. The mm. sartorius and semitendinosus are considered to be homologues of the m. puboischiotibialis of salamanders.

Mm. pectineus and adductor longus

The mm. pectineus and adductor longus compose a compound muscle that adducts the femur. The m. pectineus is a short muscle of the thigh, from which the m. adductor longus is thought to have differentiated. Both muscles are homologues of the m. puboischiofemoralis internus of salamanders, are considered together here. The m. adductor longus is a wide, thin muscle that lies ventral to the m. cruralis and is partially covered ventrally by the m. sartorius. It arises via a tendon from the anteroventral part of the preacetabular rim between the mm. sartorius and the pectineus. The m. adductor longus bears a fleshy insertion on the lateral face of the distal part of the m. adductor magnus (see description below), and sometimes bears a tendinous insertion on the knee aponeurosis. The m. pectineus has a fleshy origin from the ventrolateral ilium and anterior part of the pubis. This short, fan-shaped muscle has a fleshy insertion on the proximal half of the ventral surface of the femur. It is bordered anteriorly by the m. cruralis and posteriorly by the m. obturator externus, and lies deep to the m. sartorius. The m. adductor longus is absent in some frogs (e.g., Ascaphus, Leiopelma, Alytes, Bombina, and some pipids, pelobatids, and bufonids); its absence may have resulted from loss or lack of differentiation from the m. pectineus. The latter is assumed to be the case in primitive frogs.

M. adductor magnus

The m. adductor magnus is a large muscle that extends along the superficial and proximal ventromedial surface of the thigh, and is covered by the mm. sartorius and gracilis major distally. The primary action of this muscle is to adduct the hip joint. The m. adductor magnus arises by two heads which are separated from each other by the ventral tendon of the m. semitendinosus. The ventral head, which arises via a tendon from the ventral border of the pubic part of the pelvic rim, is considered a homologue of the m. pubotibialis of salamanders. The dorsal head has a fleshy origin from the ischiatic border of the pelvic rim beneath the origin of the m. gracilis major, and is the homologue of the m. puboischiofemoralis of salamanders. The dorsal and ventral heads unite to form a single muscle that inserts one-fourth to three-quarters down the length of the femur on its medial side. Variation involves the level of insertion of this muscle and the presence or absence of two heads. In those anurans in which the m. semitendinosus has a superficial origin (primarily primitive anurans), an accessory head is absent; it is present in most advanced anurans in which the semitendinosus has a deep origin.

Mm. gracilis major and minor

The mm. gracilis major and minor form a muscle complex that flexes the knee joint and extends the hip joint by pulling the upper limb backwards; both muscles are considered to be homologous with the m. ischioflexoris of salamanders. The gracilis major is a broad, flat muscle on the medioventral surface of the thigh. It bears a tendinous inscription at its midlength and is bordered dorsally by the m. semimembranosus (see description below), laterally by the m. semitendinosus, and ventrolaterally by the m. adductor magnus. The m. gracilis major bears a tendinous origin from the posterior border of the pelvic rim of the ischium. It inserts by means of two tendons; one broad tendon inserts on the knee aponeurosis and medial side of the head of the tibiofibula, and the other tendon attaches to the posterior surface of the tibiofibula just distal to the head. Variation in this muscle involves its origin (fleshy versus tendinous) and the position of its insertion with respect to that of the m. semitendinosus. The m. gracilis minor is a thin, narrow muscle that lies beneath the skin along the medial surface of the thigh and bears a tendinous inscription. It bears a tendinous origin from the ischiatic region of the pelvic rim just ventral to the cloaca. The muscle unites with the gracilis major distally prior to the formation of a common tendon. Variation in this muscle involves its origin which may be primarily from the pelvis, chiefly from the skin, or via two heads—one from the pelvis and the second from the skin.

Mm. iliofibularis and semimembranosus

Two muscles compose the postfemoral dorsal thigh musculature—- mm. iliofibularis and semimembranosus. The m. iliofibularis is a long, slender, subcylindrical muscle that lies on the dorsal surface of the thigh between the mm. glutaeus magnus and semimembranosus, and is homologous with the muscle of the same name in salamanders. The muscle has a tendinous origin from the dorsolateral surface of the base of the ilial crest just posterior to the origin of the m. glutaeus magnus. Its tendinous insertion on the knee aponeurosis is covered by the aponeurosis of the m. triceps femoralis and the origin of the m. plantaris longus. Contraction of the m. iliofibularis flexes the knee joint and abducts the femur.

The m. semimembranosus is a large muscle that covers the dorsomedial surface of the thigh and bears a tendinous inscription near its midlength. The muscle originates from the posterior surface of the ischium, along the pelvic rim and below the cloaca. It inserts via a tendon on the ventral surface of the femur and the adjacent surface of the head of the tibiofibula and acts to flex the knee joint and adduct the femur. Variation includes origin by two heads rather than one, and a tendinous instead of a fleshy origin. Like the mm. gracilis major and minor, the m. semimembranosus is thought to be a homologue of the m. ischioflexoris of salamanders.

M. iliacus internus

The m. iliacus internus is one of eight short muscles (exclusive of the m. pectineus described above) involved in the thigh musculature, among the most superficial of which are the mm. iliacus internus, iliacus externus, iliofemoralis, and pyriformis. The m. iliacus internus is homologous with the m. puboischiofemoralis of salamanders. This broad, flat muscle passes under the ventral border of the pelvis anterior to the origin of the m. cruralis from its fleshy origin along the margin of the ilium in the angle formed between the ilial shaft and the preacetabulum. It extends dorsally between the mm. cruralis and

iliacus externus to a broad, fleshy insertion along the proximal two-thirds of the femur on its dorsomedial surface. Contraction of the m. iliacus internus abducts the femur.

M. iliacus externus

The m. iliacus externus is also thought to be homologous with the m. puboischiofemoralis of salamanders. From its broad, fleshy origin on the lateral surface of the posterior half of the ilial shaft, this muscle extends ventrolaterally to insert on the dorsal surface of the head of the femur by a tendon, and acts to flex the hip joint, drawing the femur forward. There is considerable variation in the m. iliacus externus. It is absent or undifferentiated from the m. iliacus internus in *Leiopelma*. In the other anurans that possess this muscle, it may originate by either one or two heads, and its origin varies from the posterior half to the entire length of the ilial shaft.

M. iliofemoralis

The m. iliofemoralis is homologous with the muscle of the same name in salamanders. The muscle originates in part from the ilium ventral to the origin of the m. iliofibularis and in part from the tendon of origin of the m. iliofibularis. The fibers of the m. iliofemoralis parallel those of the m. iliacus internus to their fleshy insertion along the proximal third of the dorsomedial border of the femur. Contraction of this muscle draws the femur dorsally.

M. pyriformis

The m. pyriformis is a long, slender, subcylindrical muscle that has a fleshy origin from the dorsolateral border of the distal end of the coccyx. The muscle extends distally, ventral and between the mm. glutaeus magnus and iliofibularis on one side and the m. semimembranosus on the other, and has a fleshy insertion on the dorsal surface of the femur, which it abducts. The m. pyriformis is absent in *Pipa* and *Xenopus*, and varies in the position of its insertion along the femur in other anurans. It is considered to be a homologue to the m. caudalifemoralis of salamanders.

The m. obturator internus is one of four additional, deeper muscles of the thigh. It extends ventrolaterally over the hip joint from its fleshy origin that covers the entire lateral surface of the pelvic rim. The muscle inserts via a tendon on the dorsomedial surface of the femur head, and ventral fibers extend posterodorsally to insert on the heavy tendon to the head of the femur. The muscle is considered to be a homologue of the m. ischiofemoralis of salamanders. On contraction, it pulls the femur dorsally and rotates it.

Mm. obturator externus, quadratus femoris, and gemellus

The remaining three deep, short muscles—the mm. obturator externus, quadratus femoris, and gemellus—

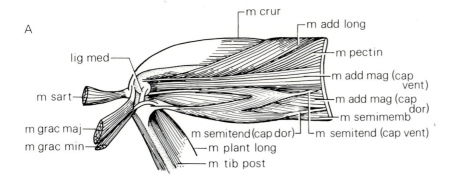

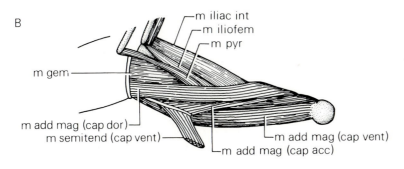

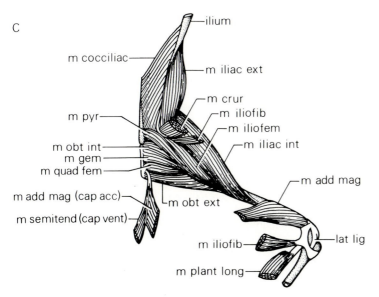

Figure 13-43. Thigh musculature of right limb of *Rana esculenta*, redrawn from Gaupp (1896). **A.** Ventral aspect with some superficial muscles removed. **B.** Dorsal aspect with superficial muscles removed. **C.** Dorsal view showing deep muscles of thigh. Abbreviations: cap acc = caput accessorium; cap dor = caput dorsalis; cap vent = caput ventralis; lat lig = lateral ligament; med lig = medial ligament; m add long = m. adductor longus; m add mag = m. adductor magnus; m cocciliac = m. coccygeoiliacus; m crur = m. cruralis; m gem = m. gemellus; m grac maj = m. gracilis major; m grac min = m. gracilis minor; m iliac ext = m. iliacus externus; m iliac int = m. iliacus internus; m iliofem = m. iliofemoralis; m iliofib = m. iliofibularis; m obt ext = m. obturator externus; m obt int = m. obturator internus; m pectin = m. pectineus; m plant long = m. plantaris longus; m pyr = m. pyriformis; m quad fem = m. quadratus femoris; m sart = m. sartorius; m semimemb = m. semimembranosus; m. semitend = m. semitendinosus; m tib post = m. tibialis posticus.

form a single muscle complex that pulls the femur ventrally. The m. obturator externus (a homologue of the m. pubifemoralis of salamanders) is a short, triangular muscle that has a fleshy origin from the lateral surface of the pelvic rim in the area posteroventral to the acetabulum near the pubis. The fleshy insertion of the muscle lies on the ventral surface of the proximal half of the femur.

The m. quadratus femoris is a short, triangular muscle homologous with the m. pubifemoralis of salamanders. Its fleshy origin from the ventrolateral border of the is-

chium is separated from that of the m. obturator externus by the ventral head of the m. semitendinosus. The m. quadratus has a fleshy insertion on the ventromedial surface of the femur near the head of this bone.

The last deep, short muscle is the m. gemellus, a homologue of the m. ischiofemoralis of salamanders. This slender muscle has a fleshy origin from the dorsal margin of the ischium dorsal to the origin of the m. quadratus femoris. Its fleshy insertion lies on the medial surface of the femur at the base of the head. This complex muscle is variable in the degree of separation and fusion of the

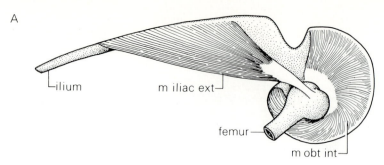

A

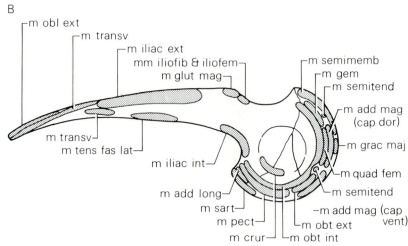

B

Figure 13-44. Muscles associated with the pelvic girdle of *Rana esculenta,* redrawn from Gaupp (1896). **A.** Lateral view of pelvic girdle and head of femur. **B.** Diagram showing positions of muscle origins from pelvic girdle. Abbreviations: m add long = m. adductor longus; m add mag (cap dor) = m. adductor magnus (caput dorsalis); m add mag (cap vent) = m. adductor magnus (caput ventralis); m crur = m. cruralis; m gem = m. gemellus; m glut mag = m. glutaeus magnus; m grac maj = m. gracilis major; m iliac ext = m. iliacus externus; m iliac int = m. iliacus internus; m iliofem = m. iliofemoralis; m iliofib = m. iliofibularis; m obl ext = m. obliquus externus; m obt ext = m. obturator externus; m obt int = m. obturator internus; m pectin = m. pectíneus; m quad fem = m. quadratus femoris; m sart = m. sartorius; m semimemb = m. semimembranosus; m semitend = m. semitendinosus; m tens fas lat = m. tensor fasciae latae; m transv = m. transversus.

three muscles that compose it. For example, the mm. obturator externus and quadratus femoris are fused in *Ascaphus,* and the mm. gemellus and quadratus femoris are partly united in *Bufo.* There is also considerable variation in the insertion of the complex.

Lower hindlimb musculature.—The shank (tibiofibula) bears eight muscles. of which are associated with the medial, or flexor, side of this element. These are the mm. plantaris longus and tibialis posticus (Figs. 13-43, 13-45).

Mm. plantaris longus and tibialis posticus

The m. plantaris longus (= m. gastrocnemius of some authors) is a large, thick-bellied muscle that extends the foot. It is one of two muscles which are associated with the medial, or flexor, side of this element; the other is the m. tibialis posticus. The m. plantaris longus originates by two tendinous heads—one a long, slender dorsal tendon from the distal border of the aponeurosis covering the knee, and the second, a short, cylindrical tendon formed by the union of two branches of the heavy, tendinous arc along the medial surface of the knee joint. The m. plantaris longus inserts distally by a thick, flat tendon that spreads out on the plantar surface of the foot to form the aponeurosis plantaris, from which numerous tarsal and foot muscles originate. The m. tibialis posticus is covered for the most part by the m. plantaris longus. This muscle has a fleshy origin along the medial surface of the shaft of the tibiofibula and inserts on the tibiale via

a long, slender tendon that extends from the distal part of the tibiofibula. Contraction of the mm. plantaris longus and tibialis posticus results in straightening the ankle joint.

M. peroneus

The m. peroneus is one of four muscles on the lateral side of the tibiofibula. It is a long, thick muscle that originates from a short, heavy ligament on the external surface of the knee joint via a long tendon that extends deep to, and penetrates, the aponeurosis. The muscle has a tendinous insertion on the dorsal surface of the distal end of the tibiofibula, and acts to extend the knee joint.

M. tibialis anticus longus

The m. tibialis anticus longus is a second, lateral muscle of the tibiofibula. It is a large, tapering muscle located on the lateral surface of the shank that arises via a tendon that passes over the knee from the ventral surface of the medial condyle of the femur. Approximately two-thirds the distance down the shank, the m. tibialis anticus longus divides into two bellies, the heads of which insert (1) laterally, on the dorsolateral surface of the proximal end of the fibulare, and (2) medially, on the medial border of the proximal end of the tibiale. Contraction of this muscle extends the ankle joint.

M. extensor cruris brevis

A third lateral tibiofibula muscle, the m. extensor cruris brevis is slender and lies deep to the m. tibialis anticus

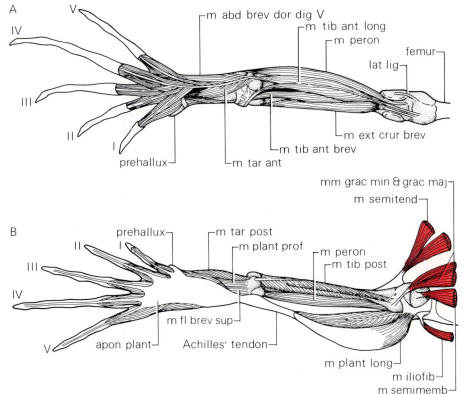

Figure 13-45. Distal musculature of right hindlimb of *Rana esculenta,* redrawn from Gaupp (1896).
A. Dorsomedial aspect.
B. Ventrolateral aspect.
Abbreviations: apon plant = aponeurosis plantaris; lat lig = lateral ligament; m abd brev dor dig V = m. abductor brevis dorsalis digiti V; m ext crur brev = m. extensor cruris brevis; m fl brev sup = m flexor brevis superficialis; m iliofib = m. iliofibularis; m peron = m. peroneus; m plant long = m. plantaris longus; m plant prof = m. plantaris profundus; m semimemb = m. semimembranosus; m. semitend = m. semitendinosus; m tar ant = m. tarsalis anticus; m tar post = m. tarsalis posticus; m tib ant brev = m. tibialis anticus brevis; m tib ant longus = m. tibialis anticus longus; m tib post = m. tibialis posticus; mm grac min & grac maj = mm. gracilis minor et gracilis major.

longus along the ventrolateral margin of the tibiofibula. The muscle originates from a long, slender tendon that passes over the external surface of the knee from the ventral surface of the medial condyle of the femur. It bears a fleshy insertion along the proximal one-half to two-thirds of the ventrolateral surface of the tibiofibula and on contraction extends the knee joint.

M. tibialis anticus brevis

The final muscle of the shank is the m. tibialis anticus brevis which pulls the foot dorsally and supinates it. This long, slender muscle is covered partially by the m. tibialis anticus longus, but is visible along the medial margin of the latter. The m. tibialis anticus brevis has a fleshy origin from the dorsolateral surface of the middle third of the tibiofibula and inserts by a short tendon on the proximomedial surface of the tibiale.

Dorsal tarsal muscles

The anuran tarsus bears three muscles dorsally. The m. tarsalis anticus arises by a tendon from the lateral aspect of the distal end of the tibiofibula and has a fleshy insertion along the distal half of the dorsal surface of the tibiale. Contraction of this muscle flexes the ankle joint and supinates the foot. The m. extensor longus digiti IV is a long, narrow muscle that lies on the dorsal surface of the foot between the m. tarsalis anticus, with which it shares a common origin, and the m. adductor brevis dorsalis digiti V. It has tendinous insertions on the distal ex-

tensors. The m. adductor brevis dorsalis digiti V is a relatively large, fleshy muscle that lies along the dorsolateral surface of the tarsus. It originates along the entire length of the fibulare and has a fleshy insertion on Metatarsal V.

Ventral tarsal muscles

Six or seven muscles are associated with the ventral, or plantar, surface of the tarsus. Superficially, the tendinosus aponeurosis plantaris is a continuation of the distal tendon of the m. plantaris longus of the shank. Tendons arise from the distal border of the aponeurosis and extend to the prehallux and each digit where each tendon is connected to the phalangeal elements. The m. tarsalis posticus is a large, fleshy muscle that extends the tarsus. It shares its origin with, and lies dorsal to, the m. plantaris profundus. The m. tarsalis posticus inserts along the distal three-quarters of the ventral surface of the tibiale. The m. plantaris profundus arises from the medial half of the ligamentum calcanei and has a fleshy insertion that extends along the distal two-thirds to three-quarters of the tarsus to base of the prehallux. The m. flexor digitorum brevis superficialis arises from the lateral half of the ligamentum calcanei, and inserts by a tendon on the aponeurosis plantaris. The mm. transversus plantae proximalis and distalis are distal transverse muscles of the tarsus that are not always distinct from one another. The m. intertarsalis lies between the tibiale and fibulare. It has a fleshy origin along the lateral margin of the proximal two thirds of the tibiale and the medial margin of the fibulare, and a tendinous insertion on the centrale.

For details of the foot musculature, the reader is referred to Dunlap (1960) and Andersen (1978) as well as the several myological descriptions of particular groups of anurans cited above. The dorsal musculature is composed primarily of the mm. extensores breves medii and profundi. The former is a group of thin muscles that originate from near the middle of the distal fused extremities of the tibiale and fibulare. The muscle mass extends distomedially and subdivides into two or more muscular slips per digit. The mm. extensores breves profundi consists of a series of 10 muscles, one of which lies on the lateral and one on the medial border of each digit. These muscles originate from the metatarsal and insert on the base of the terminal phalanx. Significant features of the plantar musculature include the tendines superficiales that arise from the aponeurosis plantaris and the mm. lumbricales, a group of small muscles that flex the digits. Distally, there are additional flexors, as well as muscles that connect adjacent metatarsal elements and adjacent, basal phalangeal bones.

INTEGRATION OF FUNCTIONAL UNITS

As mentioned in the introductory remarks to this chapter, the overall morphology of a species, or its Bauplan, represents the observable interface of the organism with its environment. In this respect, the Bauplans of the three living orders of amphibians are remarkably different from one another—a fact that suggests that each group has had a long evolutionary history. The following paragraphs attempt to summarize how the various functional units described in the preceding text are combined to produce the architectural plan characteristic of each of the orders of amphibians.

Salamanders

In contrast to caecilians and anurans, most salamanders are characterized by a lack of specialization marked by possession of relatively small heads, attenuate bodies, four limbs, a tail, and a sprawling gait. The skulls of most terrestrial salamanders are rather arched and narrow, and not especially well roofed despite the fact that they are composed of more separate elements than the crania of either caecilians or anurans. However, in contrast to these groups, salamander skulls bear an additional set of articulations with the vertebral column. Possibly, this modification of the primitive tetrapod condition may relate the need to stabilize the head on the axial skeleton in terrestrial situations in the absence of specialized trunk musculature that accomplishes this task in the other orders of amphibians. The modification also might reflect the independent evolution of a craniovertebral joint in this group.

The hyoid apparatus of salamanders allows them to protrude their fleshy tongues from the buccal cavity to obtain food. The majority are only able to roll the tongue forward over the margin of the lower jaw to contact the prey. Once in the buccal cavity, food is held and manipulated by the teeth and tongue. Such a system does not require specializations of mandibular and jaw musculature or possession of robust, specialized teeth—features that salamanders generally lack. However, it does involve sensory perception. Thus, salamanders are characterized by well-developed eyes and nasal organs. In the absence of significant vocal abilities, their ears are rather poorly developed in contrast to those of frogs.

Owing to the lack of specialization of the postcranial musculoskeletal system of most salamanders, they are limited to somewhat primitive modes of locomotion. The axial skeleton is relatively undifferentiated, the trunk musculature well developed, and the girdles neither well developed nor especially firmly attached to the vertebral column. This allows most salamanders, if startled, to move quickly across the substrate by undulating their bodies; thus, the limbs are not used, and the organism is propelled forward by a series of successive undulations on opposite sides of the long body and tail. Under other circumstances, salamanders are able to move by a deliberate, diagonal pattern of limb movement whereby each limb moves alternately, and the trunk and body are thrown into a curve to advance the stride of the forelimb.

Most deviations from the general pattern occur in aquatic salamanders. These animals that are supported by their aquatic environment may attain much larger sizes than their terrestrial counterparts. In some cases the limbs are lost. Such salamanders depend on undulatory movements to propel themselves through the water, but those with limbs are capable of crawling on the bottom.

Caecilians

Of the three orders, caecilians probably are the most narrowly specialized. Although some are aquatic, most are adapted for a burrowing, subterranean existence. They also are the most limited distributionally and have fewer representatives than either salamanders or anurans. The external morphotype of caecilians is remarkably uniform and wormlike in appearance. The head is compact and well ossified. Many centers of ossification have fused to provide a robust, spatulate cranium which the organisms use to push through the soil. The compact nature of the skull necessarily limits the size and development of jaw musculature; thus, in caecilians the lower jaw bears a retroarticular process to which the main adductor of the jaw attaches external to the cranium. The hyomandibular apparatus is modified only slightly from the larval condition because the tongue in caecilians is rudimentary and cannot be protruded from the oral cavity. The eyes of caecilians are reduced, but their chemosensory perception is enhanced by the development of a tentacle in addition to their well-developed nasal organ. Hearing probably is less acute in caecilians than in salamanders and and anurans. The operculum, if present, is incorporated into the columella, a compact bone that articulates with the auditory capsule and quadrate.

The axial musculoskeletal system is highly modified for subterranean locomotion and feeding. The axial muscles are firmly attached to the overlying skin, and together these elements form a tough sheath that surrounds the attenuate body and extends onto the posterior part of the skull. Because the vertebral column is extremely flexible within this myointegumental sheath, caecilians are capable of propelling themselves forward through the soil by a process known as concertina locomotion. As explained by Gans (1974, and references therein), part of the body is folded so that it is in static, frictional contact with the substrate; adjacent parts of the body are pushed or pulled forward at the same time. This results in an alternation of folding and extending that travels the length of the body.

Although caecilians are known to feed on the surface, presumably most usually feed in subterranean burrows in which there may not be much latitude for movement. They seem to utilize their powerful jaw musculature and anterior trunk musculature to seize and immobilize prey with sharp, recurved teeth. If the prey cannot be ingested whole, they shear it against the walls of the burrow by rotations of the body (Bemis et al., 1983).

Anurans

The locomotory, feeding, and reproductive specializations of anurans have enabled them to exploit a broader range of habitats than either salamanders or caecilians. They are more widespread, diverse, and numerous than either of those groups. The basic body plan of anurans is characterized by a broad, flat head that is nearly as wide as the body. The trunk is short and largely inflexible except in the area of the sacrum; thus, the head and trunk form a fusiform structure that is propelled forward in a trajectory by the long, powerful hindlimbs. Because of their saltatorial habits, anurans have more elaborate pectoral and pelvic girdles than salamanders. The pectoral girdle bears an elastic, muscular suspension to both the skull and the vertebral column, and is designed to absorb the shock of the anuran's landing on its forelimbs. Unlike the pelvic girdles of salamanders, those of anurans lie in a horizontal plane flanking the coccyx, the bony rod that represents the posterior end of the vertebral column. The pelvic girdle is attached to the coccyx, sacrum, presacral vertebrae, and proximal part of the hindlimb by muscles and ligaments so that when the animal leaps, the girdle lies in the same plane as the axial column, but when it sits at rest, the posterior end of the girdle is deflected ventrally.

Despite the specialization of this morphological system for jumping, many anurans have evolved adaptations that facilitate burrowing or arboreal habits. This primarily involves changes in the relative proportions of the limbs and the iliosacral articulation. One group in particular, the pipids, are aquatic specialists. In *Pipa* the entire body is depressed, and the axial skeleton constructed in such a way that little or no flexibility is possible. Thus, the animals utilize their strong hindlimbs to thrust their flat, fusiform bodies through water.

The vast majority of anurans have well-developed tongues which they are able to catapult from their mouths in order to pick up prey. This complicated mechanism involves a complex system of mandibular and hyoid muscles that are associated with a specialized hyoid apparatus. Given the locomotory and feeding habits of anurans, there obviously is a premium on visual acumen; thus, it is not surprising that, in general, these animals have large, well-developed eyes. Most anurans vocalize as part of their mating and territorial behavior; thus, their ears are more highly developed than those of salamanders, and most have an external tympanum—a feature unknown in either salamanders or caecilians.

It is often pointed out that anurans are the most specialized of the amphibians. Obviously, they are derived relative to salamanders, but the comparison is less clearcut with respect to caecilians owing to the nature of the specializations of each order. In general, caecilians are adapted to a subterranean mode of life. Although some are aquatic, the order as a whole now seems to be restricted in its evolutionary options. The specializations that resulted in the anuran morphotype, in contrast, seem to have opened up a plethora of adaptive avenues that anurans have pursued. The current success of this order is reflected in some measure by their greater numbers relative to salamanders and caecilians. Taken together, however, the evolutionary diversity of modern amphibians must be regarded as nothing short of of spectacular, given the physiological constraints that tie them to their environment in contrast to the relative independence achieved by amniotes.

CHAPTER 14

An animal is a highly integrated machine and, because it is, it is convenient rather than analytical to regard it in pieces, as a collection of separate characters and adaptations.

Thomas H. Frazzetta (1975)

Integumentary, Sensory, and Visceral Systems

As was demonstrated in Chapter 13, the gestalt of an organism is determined by its musculoskeletal organization, which dictates how the animal can feed and move and, to a certain extent, determines its utilization of the physical environment. The musculoskeletal system, together with the integument, also protects and supports the soft anatomical components of the sensory, nervous, circulatory, respiratory, digestive, urogenital, and endocrine systems. The nervous system coordinates the activities of all other systems. Sensory structures are the receptors of environmental stimuli. Perceived sensory cues are transmitted to the central nervous system and thence to the peripheral and/or visceral nervous systems. Signals transmitted via the peripheral nervous system affect the musculoskeletal system directly, whereas those transmitted via the sympathetic (= efferent) and parasympathetic (= autonomic) portions of the visceral nervous system affect visceral organs of the circulatory, digestive, urogenital, exocrine, and endocrine systems.

The respiratory, digestive, excretory, exocrine, endocrine, and circulatory visceral systems are involved with the maintenance of the internal environment. Thus, metabolic requisites are introduced via the respiratory, integumentary, and digestive systems, and metabolic products are disposed of by the excretory, respiratory, and integumentary systems. Metabolic and endocrine products are transported throughout the body by the circulatory system to maintain a stable internal environment.

Only one visceral system is not involved in the maintenance of the internal environment; this is the reproductive system. Anatomically it is associated intimately with the excretory system; hence, the two usually are discussed as the urogenital system. The reproductive system acts in response to the internal environment and cues from the external environment, but its function obviously is to ensure the transmission of the parental genotype to a succeeding generation.

INTEGUMENT

Although the integument is the structural and functional interface between the organism and its environment, the morphological and functional complexity of amphibian skin is incompletely understood (see Lindemann and Voûte, 1976, and Whitear, 1977, for reviews). The skin of amphibians generally is described as being naked, that is, lacking the covering of scales, feathers, or hair characteristic of most other classes of vertebrates. Furthermore, amphibian skin is permeable to water and as such is important in respiration, osmoregulation, and to a limited degree, thermoregulation; these functional aspects are treated in Chapter 8. Also, the general appearance of amphibians is the result of integumentary structures; color and pattern are determined by the chromatophores, and texture is the result of integumentary modifications.

367

Structure

As in all vertebrates, the integument consists of an outer layer, the epidermis of ectodermal origin, and an underlying layer, the dermis. Most of the latter is of mesodermal origin, but the pigment cells are derived from the neural crest and thus are ectodermal; also, the glands imbedded in the dermis are derived from the ectoderm.

The outermost layer of the epidermis, the stratum corneum, consists of a single layer of flattened cells. The stratum corneum is keratinized in most adult amphibians, but it is not keratinized in obligate neotenic salamanders, such as *Necturus*. The keratinized stratum corneum is separated from the underlying stratum germinativum by irregular intercellular spaces that are interrupted by interconnecting filaments (desmosomes). The fibers of these keratinized cells form a double horizontal network reinforced by vertical bundles of filaments (tonofilaments) (Le Quang Trong and Bouligand, 1976) (Fig. 14-1). Underlying the stratum corneum is the stratum germinativum which normally is 4–8 cells thick; the innermost cells are columnar and the outer ones are progressively shorter. Lying within the stratum germinativum are specialized mitochondria-rich cells and flask cells of unknown function. The epidermis is separated from the dermis by a basement membrane of collagenous fibers.

The stratum corneum is sloughed (shed or molted) periodically. The duration of the intermolt period varies from 4–5 days in *Ambystoma* to 3–19 days in *Bufo* (Ling, 1972). In both salamanders and anurans, the stratum corneum splits middorsally beginning on the head; the splitting of the dorsal skin progresses posteriorly. Most amphibians use their limbs to loosen and remove the slough either in patches or in one large piece; usually the slough is eaten. During the sloughing cycle, the intercellular subcorneal space between the stratum corneum and the underlying stratum germinativum is filled with mucus thought to be secreted by the mitochondria-rich cells. During actual sloughing, the desmosomal connections between the cells of the stratum corneum and the underlying replacement layer, derived from the stratum germinativum, are broken, and the desmosome fragments adhere to the sloughed stratum corneum. According to Budtz (1977), sloughing in *Bufo* is arrested by hypophysectomy; adrenocorticotrophic hormone (ACTH) and corticosteroids are the only hormones that elicit sloughing in hypophysectomized toads, but neither hormone has an effect on sloughing in normal toads. The formation of cocoons by aestivating amphibians is the result of multiple sloughs (see Chapter 8).

The dermis also consists of two layers. The outer stratum spongiosum is made up of areolar connective tissue with interlacing fibers and various types of cells, including the pigment-bearing chromatophores. The underlying stratum compactum is composed of compactly arranged collagenous fibers. Mucous and granular (= poison) glands of epidermal origin are imbedded in the stratum spongiosum, as are the scales in caecilians. Other structures in the dermis include capillaries, nerve fibers, and smooth muscles.

In salamanders and especially caecilians, there is a

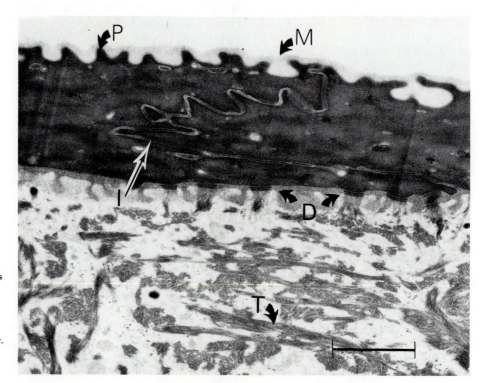

Figure 14-1. Electron micrograph of the surface layer of the epidermis of an anuran, *Phyllomedusa sauvagei*. D = desmosomes, I = intercellular junction, M = mucoid coat, P = protuberances on outer surface of epidermis, T = tonofilaments. Bar = 1 micrometer. Photo courtesy of R. Ruibal; reproduced with permission from *Copeia.*

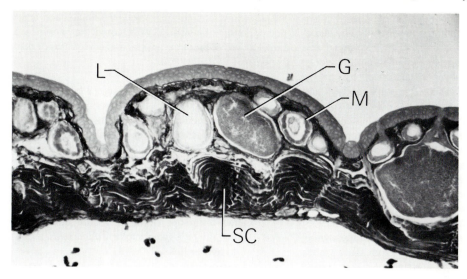

Figure 14-2. Photomicrograph of a vertical section of the ventral integument of an anuran, *Phyllomedusa sauvagei.* G = granular gland, L = lipid gland, M = mucous gland, SC = stratum compactum. Photo courtesy of R. Ruibal; reproduced with permission from *Copeia.*

practically imperceptible transition from the collagenous fibers of the stratum compactum of the dermis to the connective tissues covering the underlying bones and muscles. However, anurans are unique in having a loose skin attached to the body wall only at discrete places in one of the following ways: (1) by lymphatic septa which are thin, transparent sheets of connective tissue that divide the space between the skin and the muscles into separate compartments, the lymphatic sacs; (2) by fibers of transparent connective tissue commonly aggregated to hold a particular part of the skin close to the body wall; (3) by co-ossification of the skin with underlying dermal bones; (4) by direct attachment of the skin to muscles, as in the vocal sacs of some hylids (Tyler, 1971a); and (5) by cutaneous muscles that insert on the skin. T. C. Burton (1980) summarized previous work on cutaneous muscles and suggested that two cutaneous muscles, the m. rectus abdominis pars anteroflecta and the m. cutaneus dorsalis, may aid in the adoption of a defensive posture and in the secretion of fluids from integumentary glands in some microhylids.

Integumentary Glands. The epidermal glands imbedded in the dermis of amphibians have received considerable attention from morphologists. Important descriptive works on the glands in salamanders are those by Dawson (1920) on *Necturus,* Theis (1932) on *Salamandra,* and McManus (1937) on *Desmognathus.* Some earlier workers (e.g., Muhse, 1909) believed that only one kind of integumentary gland was present in amphibians, even in toads. It is now known that all amphibians have both mucous and granular (= poison or serous) glands.

Contrary views exist on the development of the glands. For example, Bovbjerg (1963) indicated that in *Rana pipiens* the two types of glands and secretory cells develop independently without intermediate or transitional types. On the other hand, McManus (1937) found that the granular cells and glands of *Desmognathus fuscus* pass through a mucoid stage during histogenesis. During their development, some glands contain both mucus and granular material at the same time; intermediate stages could be traced from mucous to granular cells. In studies of *Ambystoma mexicanum* and *Nectophrynoides occidentalis,* Le Quang Trong (1966, 1967) noted that some glands have granular cells basally and mucous cells in or below the neck region.

Neuwirth et al. (1979) concluded that the granular glands are shared primitive characters among amphibians and their original function probably was other than poison synthesis, but the glands were a preadaptation for producing the diverse toxins that evolved separately in some groups of amphibians.

All of the glands are alveolar. Typical mucous glands are smaller than granular glands and enclosed completely in the stratum spongiosum (Fig. 14-2). In some salamanders and anurans, the mucous glands lack a distinct myoepithelium, but a distinct myoepithelium is present in caecilians (Fox, 1983). The bases of granular glands may project into the stratum compactum; the glands have one or two types of myoepithelial cells, and at least in some dendrobatids there is a layer of melanophores around the lateral and superficial surfaces of the glands (Neuwirth et al., 1979).

The numbers of mucous and granular glands vary throughout the body; generally mucous glands are more abundant in the dorsal skin than ventrally. Interspecific distribution of the glands, as shown in various ranids by Le Quang Trong (1971, 1975a, 1975b), may be related to differences in habitat. Also, mucous glands are more numerous and widely distributed throughout the integument than are granular glands, which tend to be aggregated at specific sites in many species (e.g., head and neck of many anurans and some salamanders and dorsal surface of tail in other salamanders).

Mucopolysaccharides secreted spontaneously and continuously serve to keep the skin moist (see Chapter 8). Granular glands secrete only following sympathetic nervous or humoral stimulation. Various substances (e.g., peptides and alkaloids) in these secretions commonly are noxious and in some cases highly toxic; these secretions are important defense mechanisms (see Chapter 10). Three other kinds of integumentary glands are known in amphibians. Rather large, elongate glands are present in the skin in the dermal folds of caecilians; E. Taylor (1968) noted that these glands are associated with the dermal scales and suggested that secretions from these glands may form the scales. Blaylock et al. (1976) discovered lipid glands in the skin of *Phyllomedusa*, hylid frogs that secrete an impervious coating that protects them from desiccation (see Chapter 8). Lipid glands are slightly larger than granular glands, usually are in contact with the stratum corneum basally, and have a distinct myoepithelium. Breeding glands in the skin of the chest region of the microhylid *Gastrophryne carolinensis* were described by Conaway and Metter (1967); similar glands have been noted in other microhylids (see Chapter 3). The breeding glands are about the same size as the granular glands. The secretion is released by the fragmentation of the superficial part of the gland, and the sticky secretion adheres the male to the dorsum of the female. Histochemically, the secretion is similar to that of the mucous glands, but it lacks the sulfate groups characteristic of mucus (Holloway and Dapson, 1971).

Clusters of mucous or granular glands form obvious integumentary structures (macroglands) in many anurans and in some salamanders. Many of these structures develop only in males in response to testicular hormones; these structures are present only in the breeding season (see Chapter 3). The most widespread of these are nuptial excrescences, which are highly keratinized clusters of mucous glands, on the thumbs of many kinds of anurans and on the limbs of some salamanders. Clusters of granular glands may be present only in males (e.g., mental glands in plethodontid salamanders), and although these glands may become enlarged during the breeding season and therefore be affected by testicular hormones, they are not strictly seasonal in their presence. Other clusters of granular glands, such as the dorsal warts and parotoid glands of bufonids and some salamandrids, the lumbar glands of several genera of leptodactylids, the tibial glands of some myobatrachids and bufonids, and the dorsolateral and dorsal ridges of ranids, are permanent structures. The secretions of many of these macroglands are known to be important in defense against predators (see Chapter 10).

The secretions produced by the integumentary glands include numerous complex biogenic amines and active polypeptides. Erspamer (1971) noted the presence of three groups of aromatic amines and five groups of polypeptides. The amines are:

1. Indolealkylamines, including 5-hydroytryptamine (5-HT), which is present in most families and genera of amphibians, and N-methylated derivatives such as bufotenin and bufotenidine, which are found in pipids, leptodactylids, bufonids, hylids, ranids, and some salamanders.
2. Imidazolealkylamines known from *Leptodactylus labyrinthicus* and *L. pentadactylus*. Related histimines occur in several unrelated genera (e.g., *Leptodactylus*, *Taudactylus*, and *Litoria*).
3. Hydroxyphenylalkylamines, including leptodactylin known from various leptodactylids, and epinephrine and norepinephrine known from *Bufo*.

The active polypeptides include numerous toxins (see Chapter 10) and other, less toxic substances:

1. Eledosine-like polypeptides, such as physalaemin isolated from *Physalaemus*, phyllomedusin from *Phyllomedusa*, and uperolein from *Uperoleia*.
2. Bradykinin and bradykinin-like polypeptides, including bradykinin isolated from *Rana temporaria* and phyllokinin from *Phyllomedusa*.
3. Caerulein and caerulein-like polypeptides, including caerulein known from *Xenopus laevis* and various species of *Litoria* and *Leptodactylus*, and phyllocaerulein from *Phyllomedusa*.
4. Three types of alytesin and alytesin-like polypeptides: I from *Alytes obstetricans*, II from *Bombina bombina* and *B. variegata*, and III from *Rana pipiens*.
5. Miscellaneous polypeptides, including several other kinds, the chemical nature of which is not yet known.

The taxonomic distribution of many of these compounds generally corresponds to the classification based on other criteria, as noted for many South American anurans by Cei and Erspamer (1966) and for Australo-Papuan anurans by Roseghini et al. (1976) and Erspamer (1984). Some groups of anurans (e.g., phyllomedusine hylids) contain large amounts of unique polypeptides, and each species has its own characteristic polypeptide spectrum (Cei, 1963). The dendrobatids are well known for their strong toxins; *Phyllobates* produce mainly batrachotoxins, which are extraordinarily toxic steroidal alkyloids, whereas *Dendrobates* secretes a variety of less

Figure 14-3. A hylid frog, *Amphignathodon guentheri*, from Quebrada de Zapadores, Ecuador, showing supraciliary processes and calcars. Photo by W. E. Duellman.

toxic and chemically simpler piperidine alkyloids (Myers et al., 1978). Thus, the biochemical differences in the genera of dendrobatid frogs seem to have phylogenetic significance. Analyses of biogenic amines (Cei et al., 1972) and secretions of the parotoid glands (B. Low, 1972) of *Bufo* from throughout the world showed that trends in these biochemical traits corresponded to morphological groups of toads presumably representing different evolutionary lineages.

Too little is known about the factors affecting the biochemistry of granular glands to allow meaningful generalizations. For example, Myers et al. (1978) noted a decline in the toxicity of secretions produced by *Phyllobates terribilis* maintained in captivity. There even may be differences in the presence of a substance in secretions from glands on different parts of the body in the same species. Serotonin was identified in the secretions of parotoid glands of *Bufo alvarius*, but that compound was absent in secretions from the macrogland on the hindlimb (Cannon et al., 1978).

Texture and Integumentary Structures. Although the skin of many amphibians appears to be smooth, usually it has a texture owing to various dermal and/or epidermal modifications. Detailed macroscopic and histological studies of the amphibian integument by Rabl (1931) and H. Elias and Shapiro (1957) have shown that the epidermis varies in thickness and may have projections or indentations, and that there are elevations and thickenings of various kinds in the dermis, especially in anurans. H. Elias and Shapiro (1957) provided definitions and a terminology of the fine structures of anuran integ-

ument and noted that in many taxa, verrucae (warts) or coni (pointed projections) have the apex covered with keratin. These structures give a roughened, sandpaper-like structure to the skin.

Caecilians have dermal folds or annuli encircling or partly encircling the body. These annuli reflect body segmentation. Primary annuli overlie the vertebrae and myotomal septa, whereas secondary annuli (when present) lie between the septa (M. Wake, 1975). The costal grooves in salamanders also reflect body segmentation; the grooves overlie the myotomal septa and mark the position of the ribs.

Some integumentary structures, such as costal grooves in salamanders, granular ventral skin and lateral cutaneous channels in anurans, dermal flaps in some aquatic salamanders (e.g., *Cryptobranchus*) and anurans (e.g., *Telmatobius culeus*), and the hairlike projections on the flanks and hindlimbs of the aquatic ranid *Trichobatrachus robustus*, are associated with increased cutaneous vascularity. Increased surface area and vascularity function to increase water uptake in terrestrial amphibians, whereas increased surface area in aquatic amphibians provides for increased respiration (see Chapter 8).

Some kinds of integumentary structures seem to be associated with disruptive outlines and thereby aid in concealment (see Chapter 10). Such structures include small, irregular ridges, supraciliary processes, scalloped folds on the outer edges of limbs, and calcars (Fig. 14-3). The latter are elongated triangular flaps on the heels of some anurans. The presence of calcars in many kinds of arboreal frogs living in rainforests and their absence in other anurans invites the speculation that they might serve as points for runoff of water, much the same as drip tips on leaves, or they may mimic drip tips.

Local thickenings of keratinized epidermis are present on the feet of various amphibians. The tips of the digits of some stream-dwelling salamanders of the families Hynobiidae, Ambystomatidae, and Plethodontidae have keratinized caps, and these are pointed and clawlike in the hynobiid *Onychodactylus japonicus*. Keratinized digit tips are present on the forefeet of *Siren*. Keratinized, pointed, clawlike tips also are present on the inner three toes of frogs of the genus *Xenopus*. The inner, and sometimes outer, metatarsal tubercles of several kinds of fossorial anurans (e.g., *Rhinophrynus, Scaphiopus*) are enlarged and covered with thick layers of keratin.

The webbing between the fingers and toes of anurans is entirely integumentary. Webbing commonly is absent on the hands; it is most extensive on the feet of many aquatic frogs (e.g., pipids, *Telmatobius, Pseudis,* and many *Rana)*; in these frogs the extensive webbing obviously provides greater surface area for the feet in propelling the animal through the water. Several arboreal anurans (some species of *Agalychnis, Hyla,* and *Rhacophorus*) have fully webbed hands and feet. These frogs are capable of parachuting or gliding because of the great surface area present when the fingers and toes are spread (D. Davis, 1965); one species is able to attain a gliding angle of 55° (Table 14-1).

Also related to locomotion is the grasping ability of the toes of many kinds of arboreal frogs that have expanded adhesive toepads. Light and electron microscopical studies by Ernst (1973a, 1973b) and D. Green (1979) have shown that the epidermal cells in the toepads are structurally different from other epidermis on the body. The toepads of arboreal frogs of the families Hylidae, Hyperoliidae, and Rhacophoridae are nearly hemispherical structures on the ventral surfaces of the distal segments of the fingers and toes. The pad is bordered, except proximally, by a circumferal groove (transverse groove or circummarginal groove of some authors). The epidermal

cells of the toepad are columnar, usually hexagonal in shape, and clearly separated from one another at their apices (Fig. 14-4). The outermost surfaces of these cells are flat but covered with small, round hemidesmosome plaques. Epidermal cells elsewhere on the digits are squamous, except in an area of transition where the circumferal groove is absent; in this area the cells are cuboidal. In some frogs, cuboidal epidermis also is present on the subarticular tubercles. Interspersed among the columnar cells are mucous pores; these are numerous and bordered by unmodified cells in hyperoliids and rhacophorids, and less numerous and bordered by modified cells in hylids. The mucous glands imbedded in the dermis are large, convoluted, and surrounded by a thin myoepithelium of smooth muscle. The toepads are offset from the plane of the digit by an intercalary element between the distal and penultimate phalanges; this allows the entire surface of the toepad to be in contact with the substrate. Experiments by S. Emerson and Diehl (1980) and D. Green (1981) provided evidence that surface tension (capillarity) enhanced by mucous secretions is the principal means by which anurans adhere to smooth surfaces. Adhesion by toepads is supplemented by adhesion of the skin of the belly, also by surface tension. On rough surfaces, the structure of the epidermis allows interlocking of the toepad with the substrate.

Many species of the plethodontid salamander genus *Bolitoglossa* are arboreal and have thick interdigital webbing and shortened digits so that the hand and foot are padlike with a continuous smooth margin; the epidermis on the plantar and palmar surfaces is exceptionally smooth. Microscopical and experimental studies by Alberch (1981) and by D. Green and Alberch (1983) have shown that the principal mechanism of adhesion to smooth surfaces is suction created by the careful placement of the feet, the smooth perimeters of which adhere to the substrate while the middle part is lifted above the substrate. The suction requires moisture which is provided by the mucous glands in the palmar and plantar dermis.

Table 14-1. Results of Jumping Tests and Total Hindfoot Area of Gliding or Parachuting Frogs[a]

Snout-vent length (mm)	Number of trials	Total area of hindfeet (mm^2)	Height of release (m)	Horizontal length of jump (m)	Angle of glide (degrees)
Rhacophorus otilophus					
86	2	53	5.4	3.0–4.0	30–38
72	1	39	5.4	3.7	35
Rhacophorus pardalis					
43	2	38	5.4	3.2	33
42	1	38	5.4	2.5	26
Rhacophorus nigromaculatus					
89	3	221	5.4	4.8–7.3	42–55
Phrynohyas venulosa					
—	—	—	42.7	27.4	34
Agalychnis spurrelli					
46–67	—	—	4.5	1.5–4.0	18–41
50[b]	—	—	4.5	2.2[b]	23[b]

[a]Adapted from N. Scott and A. Starrett (1974).
[b]Median values.

Figure 14-4. Scanning electron photomicrograph of the epidermal surface of a toepad of *Hyla versicolor*. Photo by D. B. Green.

The only other major modifications of the integument are associated with the brooding of eggs or tadpoles. The dorsal pouch in hylid marsupial frogs (*Gastrotheca*) is formed as an invagination of the integument (del Pino, 1980a). In comparison with the normal skin, the lining of the pouch is less keratinized and has numerous mucous glands. At the time of incubation the lining of the pouch becomes highly vascularized and forms partitions between the embryos. Eggs of some other hylids (*Cryptobatrachus, Hemiphractus, Stefania*) are carried openly on the back; mucous glands on the dorsum secrete a matrix that forms a pad to which the eggs adhere. The dorsal skin of female *Pipa* becomes thin prior to breeding; eggs adhere to the dorsum and sink into the skin, which subsequently thickens and encapsulates the embryo. The lateral pouches in which tadpoles of *Assa* develop are integumentary invaginations like those of *Gastrotheca*.

Dermal Ossicles and Co-ossification. The skin of several kinds of anurans contains bony structures. The dermis of the dorsal skin on the body of some hylid frogs (*Gastrotheca weinlandii, Phyllomedusa bicolor, P. vaillanti*) contains small, vascularized bony plates (osteoderms) from which bony lamellar spines protrude into the epidermis. The pelobatid *Megophrys nasuta* and the leptodactylid *Hylactophryne augusti* have avascular osteoderms composed of calcified bundles of collagen. In all of these frogs the collagen fibers of the stratum compactum often are continuous with the ossified lower surface of the osteoderms (Ruibal and Shoemaker, 1984).

Brachycephalus and leptodactylids of the genera *Ceratophrys* and *Lepidobatrachus* have large dermal plates in the dorsal skin (Fig. 14-5). These vacularized bony shields are separated from the epidermis by loose connective tissue, except that rugosities on the outer surface of the shield lie adjacent to the epidermis in *Brachycephalus*. In the latter, the plates of the shield are fused to the neural spines of the vertebrae.

The skin on the head is co-ossified with the dermal roofing elements of the skull in several groups of anurans, particularly in *Bufo* and several genera of hylids. In such cases, the stratum germinativum of the epidermis is compacted. The collagenous fibers in the dermis become ossified with the underlying bone, and the mucous glands and capillaries in the dermis are greatly reduced or absent, as the dermis becomes co-ossified with the underlying bones (Trueb, 1966). Co-ossification is associated with exostosis of the dermal bones (see Chapter 13).

Among amphibians, caecilians are unique in that many species have dermal scales; these are small, flat discs set in pockets in the transverse folds (= annuli). The scales arise in the pockets, and the basal part of each scale is attached to connective tissue in the deep part of the pocket. The scales have three principal layers. The basal layer is cellular. The middle portion is composed of bundles of parallel collagenous fibers arranged in two or three layers of different orientations. The superficial layer consists of mineralized squamulae separated from one another by concentric and radial furrows lacking mineralization. The most superficial of the fibrous layers is unmineralized and

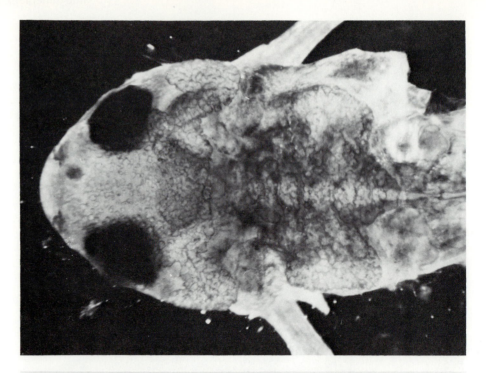

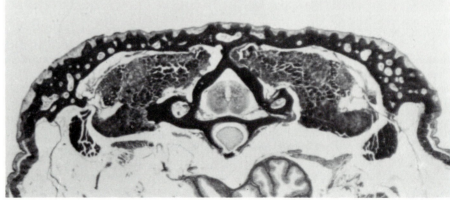

Figure 14-5. *Brachycephalus ephippium.* **A.** Dorsal view of cleared and stained adult (snout-vent length 16 mm) showing hyperossification of skull and presence of a broad dermal plate overlying vertebral column. **B.** Transverse cross section of midbody vertebra showing fusion of dermal spine with overlying dermal shield. Bones are black. Photos by L. Trueb.

is contiguous with the mineralized squamulae; mineral deposits are present on those fibers that extend into the squamulae (Zylberberg et al., 1980).

E. Taylor (1972) provided an atlas of caecilian scales in which he noted that the patterns of concentric and radial furrows were different among taxa. The question of independent origin of caecilian scales versus homology with osteichthyan scales is unresolved (see Zylberberg et al., 1980, for discussion). Although the scales may provide some protection, the large number of scales arranged in specific circular and overlapping repetitive patterns along the body and associated with the musculature may have a role in locomotion by providing requisite rigidity while permitting a wide range of body movements. Such a function might explain their usual absence in the aquatic typhlonectids, but scales also appear to be

absent in scolecomorphids and some caeciliids, both of which are fossorial.

Chromatophores and Pigmentation

The chromatophores and pigments in amphibians have been studied extensively, particularly by Bagnara and his associates—Bagnara and Ferris (1971), Bagnara and Hadley (1969, 1973), Bagnara et al. (1969, 1973, 1978, 1979), Hadley and Bagnara (1969), S. Frost and Bagnara (1979a, 1979b), and S. Frost and S. Robinson (1984). The synthesis that follows is derived primarily from these works.

Structure and Function. Amphibian chromatophores are located in either the epidermis or dermis. Melanophores are the predominant type of epidermal chromatophores, although erythrophores have been observed in the epidermis of some amphibians (e.g., *Notophthalmus viridescens,* Forbes et al., 1973). Epidermal melanophores are thin, elongate cells with long dendritic processes that extend between surrounding cells. For example, in tadpoles of *Bombina orientalis,* epidermal melanophores form an elaborate orthogonal network composed of melanophores each with four dendritic processes radiating symmetrically from a central cell body (Ellinger, 1980). Epidermal melanophores are characteristic of larval amphibians; upon metamorphosis these may be lost or their number reduced as the dermis thickens and dermal chromatophores develop. Epidermal melanophores, like those in the dermis, produce pigments known as eumelanins, which are deposited within organelles known as melanosomes. An epidermal melanophore unit consists of a melanophore and surrounding epidermal cells (Malpighian cells) that act as receptors of melanin donated by the melanophores through cytocrine activity.

In the dermis of most amphibians that have been studied there usually are three types of chromatophores that are arranged in what has been termed a dermal chromatophore unit (Fig. 14-6). In this unit, xanthophores (or erythrophores) are the most superficial cells; they lie just below the basement membrane separating the epidermis and dermis. Xanthophores impart yellow, orange, or red colors primarily because of the presence of pteridine pigments. In some cases the red, yellow, or orange colors observed in amphibian skin are caused by the presence of carotenoid pigments that are concentrated in carotenoid vesicles in cells best described as erythrophores. Some anurans, such as *Bombina orientalis,* have chromatophores that contain both pteridines and caro-

tenoids in discrete pigment organelles (Fig. 14-7A). Such cells are best termed xantho-erythrophores.

Iridophores underlie xanthophores; these cells (also called guanophores) are white or silvery in appearance and have the capacity to reflect light of specific wavelengths through the overlying xanthophores. Together, the xanthophores and iridophores interact to produce bright colors. Iridophores reflect light by virtue of the arrangement of their pigment-containing organelles (i.e., reflecting platelets). These organelles commonly are arranged in parallel stacks which thus function as a multilayer interference reflector (i.e., a "mirror," S. Frost and S. Robinson, 1984). The principal pigments in these cells are purines (e.g., guanine, hypoxanthine, adenine).

Often, the iridophore layer in amphibian skin is only one cell layer thick. An exception occurs in the arid-adapted species of African rhacophorid frogs, *Chiromantis,* which have chromatophore units containing 3–5 layers of iridophores; presumably this results in increased reflectance, which might be correlated with reducing evaporative water loss (Drewes et al., 1977). In a blue morph of *Dendrobates pumilio,* xanthophores are lacking and iridophores are stacked in layers above the underlying melanophores (Fig. 14-7B; S. Frost, unpubl. data). In this case the iridophores reflect blue light, which, in the absence of overlying red or yellow pigments, imparts a structural blue color to the skin.

Melanophores are the basal-most chromatophores; dendritic processes extend upward to terminate on the upper surfaces of iridophores, between these cells and the overlying xanthophores. The principal pigment of dermal melanophores is eumelanin. In phyllomedusine and some pelodryadine hylids (Bagnara and Ferris, 1975;

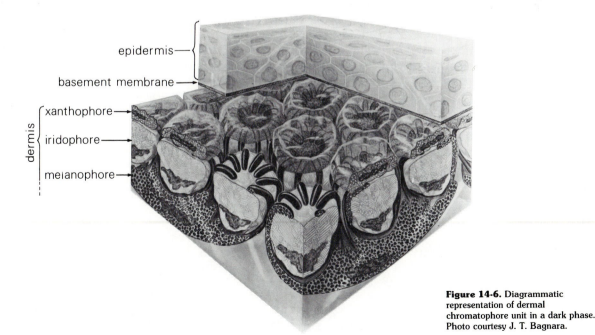

epidermis —
basement membrane —
dermis
xanthophore —
iridophore —
melanophore —

Figure 14-6. Diagrammatic representation of dermal chromatophore unit in a dark phase. Photo courtesy J. T. Bagnara.

376

Tyler and M. Davies, 1978b), melanosomes are extremely large and contain, in addition to a eumelanin core, a red pigment, pterorhodin, which is a pteridine dimer. This pigment and unusual type of melanosome are unknown in other vertebrates (Misuraca et al., 1977).

Characteristically in adult amphibians, the dermal chromatophore unit responds to physiological changes by affecting a change in color, usually manifested as a darkening or lightening of the skin. It is only when dermal chromatophore units contain two or more chromatophore types, with melanophores residing deepest within the unit, that color changes are affected.

In amphibians, blue skin is primarily a structural phenomenon resulting from both the reflecting and scattering (i.e., Tyndall scattering) properties of iridophores and the absence of xanthophores or bright-colored xanthophore pigments. When yellow pigments are present in the xanthophore layer, the pigments act as filters such that blue light reflected from the underlying iridophores and passing through the yellow layer will appear green. This, in fact, is the basis for the observed green skin color of many amphibians, although shades and intensity of green colors may vary tremendously.

According to S. Frost and S. Robinson (1984), there are three major factors contributing to green color in frog skin: (1) the kind of yellow pigment (i.e., carotenoids or pteridines) in xanthophores, (2) the quantity of yellow pigment in xanthophores, and (3) the arrangement of pigment organelles in the iridophores below the xanthophores. The first two factors presumably account for differences in the intensity of green color, whereas the last probably affects the quality (shade or tone) of green. In their studies of *Bombina orientalis,* these investigators noted that the structural arrangement of reflecting platelets in the green dorsal skin is such that these organelles function as refractosomes (i.e., multiple-layer interference reflectors). Furthermore, the red color on the venter of *Bombina* is explained easily because ventral skin lacks iridophores, only a few melanophores are present, and the xanthophores contain only carotenoid vesicles. The pigment in these vesicles is densely concentrated carot-

enoid which appears red-orange. Thus, differences in location and composition of chromatophores result in the different colors and patterns observed in amphibians (see reflectance model of Nielsen and Dyck, 1978).

In addition to the presumably genetically based color dimorphism observed in many species of amphibians, there are occasional examples in nature of melanism and albinism (Dyrkacz, 1981). The genetic basis for the color variants has been studied in species of *Rana* and in the axolotl, *Ambystoma mexicanum* (C. Richards and Nace, 1983; S. Frost et al., 1984, and references therein). Peculiar blue variants are known in *R. catesbeiana* and *R. clamitans.* The problem in these frogs seems to reside in the xanthophores, which have abnormal pterinosomes and lack bright-colored pteridine pigments (Bagnara et al., 1978).

Bagnara, Matsumoto et al. (1979) proposed that the different chromatophore types are derived from a common stem cell containing a primordial organelle. Cues present in the tissue milieu dictate the fate of this organelle. Thus, differentiation of the stem cell into a specific chromatophore may be controlled genetically, hormonally, or environmentally. Developmentally, pigmentary changes may occur at various stages in the life cycle. C. Richards (1982) determined that chromatophore pigments change ontogenetically with the development of sex hormones in the African treefrog *Hyperolius viridiflavus.* During and subsequent to metamorphosis, the majority of pterinosomes in xanthophores are replaced by carotenoid vesicles in the dorsal skin of *Bombina orientalis* (S. Frost and S. Robinson, 1984) and *Notophthalmus viridescens* (Forbes et al., 1973). Thus, the chromatophores and pigment compositions of the amphibian integument represent a highly dynamic system.

Color Change. Two kinds of color change can be affected by the chromatophore units of amphibians. Rapid color changes involving intracellular mobilization of pigment-containing organelles are referred to as physiological color changes; this change results from hormonal stimulation. These changes may require only seconds to

Figure 14-7. Photomicrographs of amphibian chromatophores.
A. Epidermal melanophore pattern in dorsal skin of a tadpole of *Bombina orientalis.* The melanophores form a highly organized, reticulate network within the epidermis. Bar = 25 μm.
B. Stacked iridophores in the dermis of *Dendrobates pumilio.* The skin of this specimen was a deep blue-black. Two layers of reflecting pigment cells (iridophores) are located immediately below the epidermis. Melanophores lie beneath the iridophore layer. Abbreviations: E = epidermal cell, I = iridophore, M = melanophore process. Bar = 1 μm. Photos by S. K. Frost.

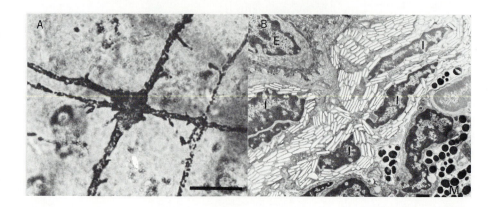

accomplish and commonly are of short duration (minutes to hours). Color changes that are evoked slowly and that involve the accumulation or reduction of the amount of pigment are referred to as morphological color changes. This is a slow process because it involves the synthesis or destruction of relatively large amounts of pigment as a result of either the persistence or continuous lack of stimulation of the chromatophores. Such changes are of long-term duration (days to months).

Epidermal melanophores undergo morphological changes. Some anurans subjected to continuous stimulation deposit so much melanin in adjacent epidermal cells that practically the entire epidermis becomes melanized. Within the dermal melanophore unit, increases in melanin may be accompanied by a decrease in guanine in iridophores. Thus, the morphological effects elicited by iridophores and melanophores are supplemental to one another.

Morphological color changes usually are preceded by physiological color changes, but morphological color change is not a necessary consequence of physiological color change. Morphological color change involving an increase in the amount of pigment contained in a chromatophore seems to be related to the dispersion of the pigment-containing organelles in the cell, just as a decrease in pigment content is accompanied by an aggregation of the organelles in the middle of the cell. The occurrence of morphological color change in the absence of physiological change was noted by J. D. Taylor (1969) for *Hyla cinerea;* when the frogs were treated with MSH (melanocyte-stimulating hormone; intermedin) there was diminution of purines in the iridophores, but the organelles remained aggregated.

Physiological color changes in the dermal chromatophore unit involve the dispersion and aggregation of melanosomes and reflecting platelets. In a pale color phase, melanosomes are aggregated in a perinuclear position, and the melanophores contribute little to the color of the animal. Concomitantly, the iridophores are not obscured by overlying melanin and the reflecting platelets are fully dispersed (in those iridophores that show physiological color change). Xanthophores, which apparently do not undergo cellular rearrangement during physiological color change, play only a passive role by serving as a yellow filter. Thus, the net effect of these iridophore and melanophore responses is that the animal becomes paler in color. In a dark color phase, there is an aggregation of iridophore pigments thereby reducing the reflecting surface area and a dispersion of melanosomes into the melanophore projections that cover the iridophores.

Nielsen's (1978a) ultrastructural studies of color change in *Hyla arborea* also demonstrated that during the change from a pale to dark color phase: (1) dermal melanophore projections partly surround the xanthophores as well as the iridophores, (2) iridophores change from a cup shape to a cylindrical or conical shape, with a simultaneous reorientation of platelets from being parallel to the upper surface to being irregular, and (3) xanthophores change from a lens shape to a plate shape. During intermediate darker stages, xanthophores migrate down between iridophores and may even go beneath iridophores; the pterinosomes gather in the periphery of the cell, and carotenoid vesicles aggregate around the nucleus.

Color change in adult amphibians seems to be mostly, if not exclusively, controlled by circulating levels of MSH which disperses melanosomes in melanophores and causes aggregation of reflecting platelets within iridophores and dispersion of pigmentary organelles in some xanthophores. The secretion of MSH is under inhibitory regulation, possibly by the hypothalamus. Electrophysiological studies by Oshima and Gorbman (1969) indicated the presence of two types of active electrical units in the pars intermedia of anurans; one of these neurons is inhibited by light, and the other is indifferent to illumination. Thus, it was proposed that these two nervous elements are in balance and regulated by the influence of light on one of them. The light-inhibitable neuron is considered to stimulate the release of MSH under conditions of low illumination.

Amphibian larvae become pale when subjected to prolonged darkness; the melanosomes aggregate in the middle of the melanophores. Experiments by Bagnara (1960) revealed that this change was negated by pinealectomy, but administration of pineal hormones induced the aggregation of melanosomes. The hormone melatonin, secreted by the pineal gland, is a melanosome-aggregating agent. The release of melatonin is regulated by light receptors in the pineal body.

Controversy exists whether color change in adult amphibians is caused solely by levels of MSH or involves other hormones. In vitro, the contraction of iridophores by MSH can be counteracted by the administration of norepinephrine or acetylcholine (Bagnara et al., 1969). Nielsen and Dyck (1978) observed differential dispersion of organelles in the three types of chromatophores in *Hyla cinerea* and concluded that MSH could not be the only agent influencing color changes; they did not rule out the possibility of nervous control of the chromatophores, as did Bagnara and Hadley (1973). Moreover, chromatophores may be sensitive to light, as shown in *Pachymedusa dacnicolor* by Iga and Bagnara (1975).

Observations on numerous kinds of amphibians indicate that color change can be affected by changes in illumination and also by temperature. Moreover, in at least some species color change is affected by background color; the animals become darker on dark backgrounds. However, this is not a generality. For example, Nielsen (1979) experimented with two color phases of *Rana esculenta;* the green color phase changed in response to a pale background, whereas the brown phase did not. Experiments with *Hyla arborea* and *H. cinerea* by Nielsen (1978b) revealed that both species became pale when treated with epinephrine; also, stress (frogs pressed into a plastic box) affected the hue and purity of the dorsal color of *H. arborea* and the paleness of *H. cinerea*.

The dilemma expressed by Bagnara and Hadley (1973:74) remains unresolved: "... chromatophores may be affected by either hormonal or neurohormonal agents as well as by direct environmental influences. ... Certain hormones may be inhibited from being released under conditions of illumination, whereas others may be released under conditions of darkness, or vice versa. In either situation the chromatic responses may appear similar, although their regulatory basis may be quite different."

Integumentary Sensory Receptors

As the interface between the organism and its environment, the integument receives stimuli that must be trans-

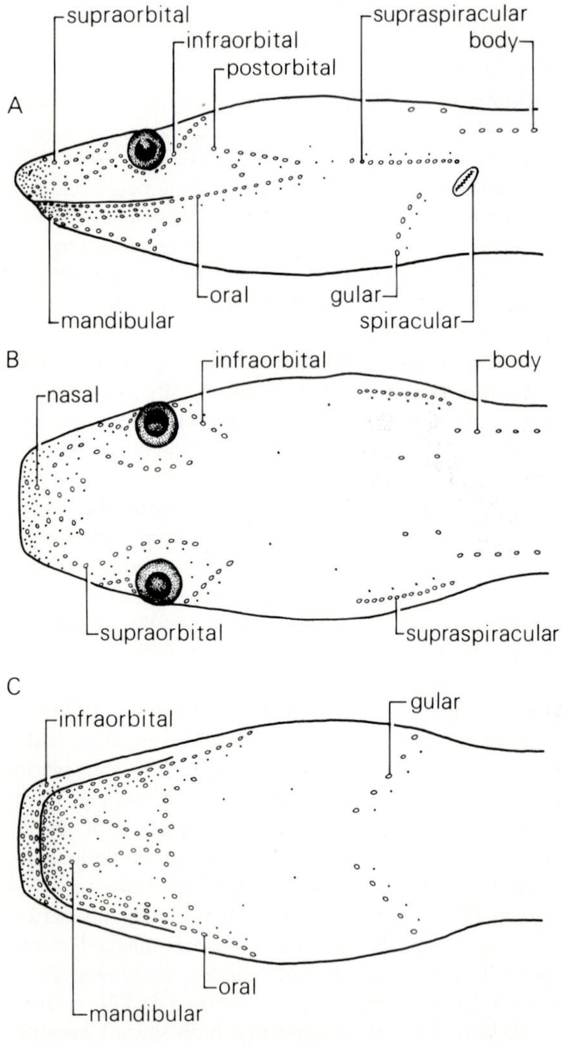

Figure 14-8. Distribution of lateral-line organs in *Ichthyophis*. **A.** Lateral. **B.** Dorsal. **C.** Ventral. Open structures are neuromasts; solid structures are ampullary organs. Redrawn from Hetherington and M. Wake (1979).

mitted to the brain so that the organism may respond appropriately.

Lateral-line System. The lateral-line system is a collection of epidermal sense organs distributed over the head and along the body in aquatic amphibians. Lateral-line organs are present in aquatic larvae, aquatic adult salamanders (e.g., *Cryptobranchus*, *Necturus*, *Amphiuma*, and *Siren*), adult pipid frogs, and adult salamandrids that are aquatic after a terrestrial stage (e.g., *Notophthalmus*) or remain aquatic (e.g., *Neurergus*).

The biology of lateral-line receptors in salamanders and anurans was reviewed by Russell (1976) and in caecilians by Hetherington and M. Wake (1979). Also, new information was provided on salamanders (*Neurergus*) by Gorgees et al. (1977). Earlier work on the lateral-line system involved only the identification of mechanoreceptors, the neuromasts. The identification of ampullary organs that are electroreceptors has been more recent— Hetherington and M. Wake (1979), Fritzsch (1981), Münz et al. (1982), Himstedt et al. (1982), and Fritzsch and Wahnschaffe (1983).

The structure and arrangement of the lateral-line organs (neuromasts) are similar in different amphibians. The organs are distributed singly (*Siren*) or in small groups along the lateral or dorsolateral surface of the body and especially on the head, where distinct patterns are evident on dorsal, lateral, and ventral surfaces (Fig. 14-8).

Each neuromast consists of a pear-shaped group of cells imbedded in the epidermis and resting on the basement membrane. Each organ is constructed of three types of cells: (1) mantle cells forming the periphery, (2) supporting cells internal to the mantle cells and extending from the basement membrane to the surface, and (3) sensory cells or hair cells in the apical half of the organ. The organs protrude beyond the surface of the skin in larvae but usually are recessed in a small pit in adults. The apical surface supports a thin, ribbonlike projection, the cupula. On the apical end of each sensory cell is a single, long kinocilium and a group of much shorter steriocilia, which decrease in length with increasing distance from the kinocilium (Fig. 14-9). Neuromasts are innervated by one efferent and two afferent nerve fibers. Most neuromasts on the head are innervated by the anterior lateral-line nerve (lateralis anterior of C.N. VII), and all remaining neuromasts by the posterior lateral-line nerve (lateralis posterior of C.N. X). Fibers from these two nerves enter the area of the acousticolateralis in the dorsolateral wall of the medulla.

In *Notophthalmus viridescens* the neuromasts are normal during the aquatic larval and adult stages, but during the subadult terrestrial stage the cells in the neuromasts dedifferentiate until they are alike cytogenetically (Dawson, 1936). In the adult aquatic stage, the sensory cells are replicated by division of both sensory and supporting cells. It is not known if there are changes in the nerve fibers innervating the neuromasts of *Notophthalmus*, but in the terrestrial stage of *Triturus cristatus*, which under-

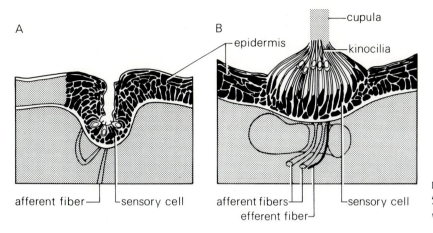

A

B

cupula

epidermis

kinocilia

afferent fiber — sensory cell

afferent fibers — sensory cell

efferent fiber

Figure 14-9. Comparative structure of **A.** ampullary organs and **B.** neuromasts in *Triturus alpestris*. Redrawn from Fritzsch and Wahnschaffe (1983).

goes similar dedifferentiation of neuromast cells, the nerves degenerate (Russell, 1976). Some neuromasts in aestivating *Siren intermedia* dedifferentiate and sensory cells loose the cilia, as they are overgrown by epidermis (Reno and Middleton, 1973).

Ampullary organs are present in larval caecilians and aquatic salamanders; there is no trace of these organs in anurans or in plethodontid salamanders that undergo direct development. The ampullary organs are restricted to the head, where they are less numerous than neuromasts but commonly are associated in parallel fashion with rows of neuromasts. The ampullary organs are like neuromasts in general structure except that they are sunken in the epidermis, lack a cupula, have a long neck, and have reduced capillarity. Moreover, ampullary organs have one cluster of microvilli per sensory cell and no kinocilium or steriocilia, and they have only one afferent nerve fiber and no efferent nerve fibers. Hetherington and M. Wake (1979) suggested that ampullary organs are derived from sunken neuromasts.

Neuromasts function as mechanoreceptors; they are sensitive to water currents and probably also to pressure (Russell, 1976). Ampullary organs are electroreceptors (Münz et al., 1982).

Other Integumentary Receptors. The dermis contains many unmyelinated nerve fibers, and some of these axons extend into the epidermis. Investigations of these receptors were summarized by Catton (1976) and Spray (1976). The free nerve endings are thought to be the transduction elements for various stimuli. Various experimental studies indicate that cold and heat receptors and tactile receptors are located in the epidermis, whereas pain receptors and pressure receptors are situated in the dermis.

SENSORY RECEPTOR SYSTEMS

As in all terrestrial vertebrates, three major sensory receptor systems are present in amphibians. The eye and its associated structures receive visual signals; the nares and associated structures receive olfactory signals, and the ears receive acoustic signals and vibrations. The pineal organ also is a photoreceptor. The morphology and function of each of these systems are discussed in this section; the integumentary receptors, including the lateral-line system, are discussed in the foregoing section: Integument.

Visual System

The eyes of terrestrial amphibians show numerous advances over those of fishes. The lens is flattened and it lies behind the iris; muscles of accommodation are present, and protective lids and glands are present in terrestrial forms. The eyes of amphibians, especially those of anurans, have been studied morphologically and electrophysiologically (Walls, 1942; Fite, 1976).

Structure. The eyes of living amphibians vary greatly in size. Those of terrestrial and arboreal anurans and terrestrial salamanders, especially plethodontids, are proportionally largest, whereas those of aquatic and fossorial species are smaller; the eyes of subterranean salamanders and caecilians are very small. In the case of salamanders (*Proteus, Haideotriton, Typhlomolge, Typhlotriton,* and one species of *Gyrinophilus*), the eye undergoes normal development until a certain stage when growth and differentiation cease and degeneration begins (Schlampp, 1892; Eigenmann, 1900; Brandon, 1968; Besharse and Brandon, 1973, 1974). In the case of some small species of terrestrial salamanders (e.g., *Thorius* and *Batrachoseps*), miniaturization has been achieved by reduction or loss of cranial elements, accompanied by a relative increase in the size of the sense organs (G. Roth et al., 1983).

The eyeball is nearly spherical. Distally the eyeball is covered by a transparent membrane, the cornea (Fig. 14-10A). The remainder is covered by a dense fibrous layer, the sclera, which is strengthened by a cup or ring of cartilage in anurans, most larval salamanders, and adults of paedomorphic salamanders. The scleral cartilage is greatly hypertrophied in crytobranchid salamanders, in

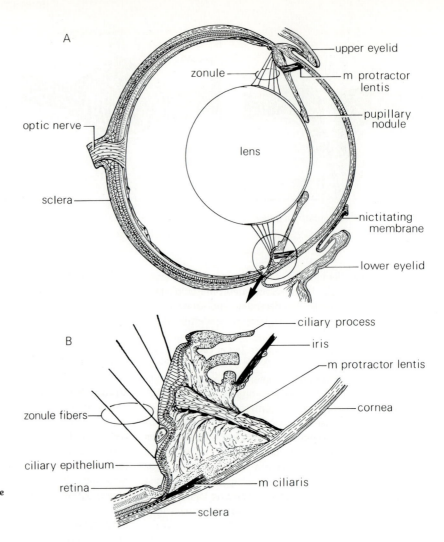

A

upper eyelid

zonule

m protractor
lentis

pupillary
nodule

optic nerve

lens

sclera

nictitating
membrane

lower eyelid

B

ciliary process

iris

m protractor lentis

cornea

zonule fibers

ciliary epithelium

retina

m ciliaris

sclera

Figure 14-10. Semidiagrammatic views of the
eye of *Rana pipiens.* **A.** Cross section of eye.
B. Ventral ciliary process and associated
structures. Adapted from Walls (1942).

some terrestrial salamanders (e.g., *Ambystoma*), and in
the microhylid frog *Stereocyclops incrassatus* (Walls, 1942).

In most salamanders and anurans, eyelids develop at
metamorphosis; they are absent in obligate neotenic salamanders and in pipid frogs. The upper eyelid is merely
an integumentary fold with limited independent movement. The lower eyelid is much more movable and is
variously modified in some salamanders and many anurans. According to Noble (1931b), the upper part of the
lower eyelid is thin, translucent, and folded on itself to
form an N-shaped structure; the translucent upper portion is the nictitating membrane. It arises from a small
mass of undifferentiated tissue at the anterior corner of
the eye in larvae. In some anurans (e.g., *Agalychnis* and
Nyctimystes), both parts of the lower eyelid are translucent or even transparent with a pigmented reticulated
pattern. A tendon that encircles the eyeball is attached
to either end of the upper edge of the nictitating membrane. When the eyeball is retracted into the orbit, the
tendon draws the membrane up over the cornea. The
nictitating membrane is withdrawn and the lower lid is

folded again partly by protrusion of the eyeball but chiefly
by a slip of the m. levator bulbi which inserts on the
ventral side of the posterior end of the lower eyelid. Eyelids are absent in caecilians, in which the eye is covered
by translucent skin, undifferentiated skin, or bone.

The orbital glands that lubricate the eye are present
along the length of the lower eyelid in primitive salamanders. Numerous ducts open onto the conjunctiva,
the mucous membrane that lines the eyelids and extends
onto the sclera of the eyeball. In some salamanders (e.g.,
Salamandra), the glandular tissue is differentiated into an
anterior Harderian gland and a posterior lacrimal gland.
Only the anterior (Harderian) gland is present in anurans
and caecilians. The Harderian gland is greatly hypertrophied and occupies most of the orbit in caecilians; its
secretions lubricate the tentacle. The lacrimal duct leads
from the orbit to the nasal chamber; in salamanders the
duct opens on the conjunctiva near the anterior corner
of the eye, whereas it opens on the middle of the lower
eyelid in anurans.

The lens is large and flattened; it is more nearly spherical in obligate neotenic salamanders, and it is clouded in caecilians. The chorioid coat is thinner in anurans than in salamanders, and it is pigmented (xanthophores and iridophores) in both groups. In caecilians, the chorioid coat is thinner than in anurans and lacks pigment. The ciliary body is largest and most complex in anurans. The body is roughly triangular (Fig. 14-10B). The zonule area is formed by crescentric fibers of the ciliary muscles. These fibers suspend the lens. Accommodation is accomplished by protraction of the lens by the protractor lentis muscles. One large ciliary fold (= ciliary process) is present midventrally, and there are two or three large folds dorsally. The ciliary bodies are smaller in salamanders, and ciliary muscles usually are present dorsally and ventrally; only a midventral ciliary fold is present. Caecilians lack ciliary bodies and have no means of accommodation.

The iris surrounds the lens; it is pigmented, and it can be dilated or contracted to control the size of the pupil and thus the amount of light that strikes the retina. The iris consists of two retinal layers and one stroma layer in salamanders and anurans. The epithelial layers are pigmented; both iridophores and melanophores are present, and in some anurans xanthophores also are present. The irises of salamanders and some anurans are black or dull brown, but those of many anurans are brilliantly colored or have a concealing coloration blending in with the facial color pattern. Thus, many species of *Rana* and *Eleutherodactylus,* as examples, have a dark streak through the eye that is continuous with a stripe of the same color extending from the snout at least to the posterior end of the head. Many anurans (e.g., some *Hyla* and *Bufo*) have brilliant gold reticulations on the iris, and other hylids (e.g., *Agalychnis* and some *Hyla*) have a bright uniform red or orange iris, and some *Phyllomedusa* have a pale silvery-gray iris. In caecilians, the iris consists of only two epithelial layers, only one of which contains pigment.

Dilation and contraction of the iris is accomplished in salamanders and anurans by actions of the mm. dilatator pupillae and sphincter pupillae, respectively. In anurans with a horizontal pupil, contraction is correlated with the presence of large dorsal and ventral pupillary nodules; these nodules are absent in salamanders. Salamanders have round pupillary apertures, but the shape is variable among anurans—round, triangluar, vertically elliptical, or horizontal. These shapes have some systematic consistency (see Chapter 17), but the differences in the patterns of muscle fibers have not been investigated.

The vast amount of information on the retina in amphibians was summarized by Dowling (1976), J. Gordon and Hood (1976), and Grüsser Cornhels and Himstedt (1976). The retina is a thin, complex structure consisting of five layers: (1) pigment epithelium, (2) outer nuclear layer containing receptor nuclei, (3) outer plexiform layer, (4) inner nuclear layer containing nuclei of horizontal, bipolar, and amacrine cells, and (5) inner plexiform layer.

There are four types of receptors in amphibians. These consist of two kinds of rods and two types of cones, receptor cells so designated because of the shapes of their

outer segments. The presence of two kinds of rods is unique to amphibians, the only group to possess green rods. However, green rods are absent in caecilians and in some subterranean and obligate neotenic salamanders. Red rods maximally absorb wavelengths of 502 nm and have long outer segments and short myoids. Green rods maximally absorb wavelengths of 432 nm and have short outer segments and long, thin myoids (Fig. 14-11). Cones are single or double. Single and primary members of double cones maximally absorb wavelengths of 580 nm, and the smaller accessory members of the double cones maximally absorb wavelengths of 502 nm. The nuclei of the rods lie next to the outer limiting membrane, whereas the nuclei of the cones are more proximal to the outer nuclear layer. Both kinds of rods and cones show marked photomechanical movements, except that accessory cones are immobile.

Electron microscopic studies by Nilsson (1964) re-

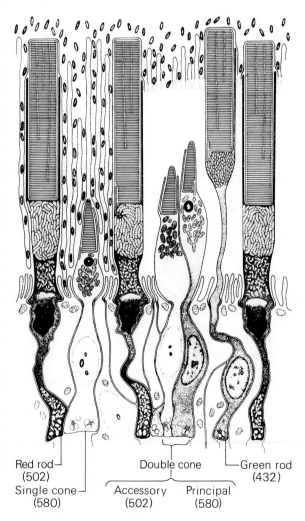

Red rod (502)
Single cone (580)
Double cone
Accessory (502)
Principal (580)
Green rod (432)

Figure 14-11. Schematic drawing based on an electron micrograph of the receptor layer in the retina of *Rana pipiens.* Numbers in parentheses are peak sensitivities (nanometers). Adapted from Nilsson (1964).

vealed that the outer segments of the rods are made up of a series of discs that are stacked vertically within the plasma membrane. These discs originate as invaginations at the base of the outer segment; subsequently, the discs are pinched off and become separated from the plasma membrane. The outer segments of cones are made up of a stack of discs of decreasing diameter, but cones differ from rods in that the discs are a series of invaginations of the plasma membrane. In rods, new discs are formed continuously at the base of the outer segment; the discs move up the outer segment until they finally detach terminally and are absorbed by the pigment epithelium. Shedding of the terminal discs is synchronous in about 25% of the rods daily; shedding occurs with the onset of light (Basinger et al., 1976). Thus, rods constantly are renewing themselves, but cones do not renew themselves in this manner.

The outer segments of all receptors are attached to their inner segments by a thin cilium. The inner and outer segments intedigitate with long strands from the pigment epithelial cells. The inner segments of single cones and principal members of double cones contain an oil droplet in their ellipsoids that is essentially transparent to visible light. The numbers of different kinds of rods and cones vary in relation to the amount of light to which the species normally is exposed. In *Rana pipiens,* the proportion of different receptors is: green rods 8%, red rods 50%, single cones 18%, principal members of double cones 12%, and accessory members of double cones 12% (Liebmann and Entine, 1968).

The outer plexiform layer contains the receptor terminals; behind this layer is the inner nuclear layer containing three kinds of cells and synapses. Processes of bipolar cells ramify in the outer plexiform layer and synapse with the receptors; others extend into the inner plexiform layer. The horizontal cells lie distally in the inner nuclear layer; the processes of these cells extend laterally in the outer plexiform layer and end in the vicinity of the receptor terminals. The amacrine cells are proximal in the inner nuclear layer; their processes end in the inner plexiform layer, which is thicker and more complex than the outer plexiform layer. It is the region where bipolar cells and amacrine cells synapse with ganglion cells from the optic fibers.

Pigments. The principal visual pigment in terrestrial amphibians is the red-photosensitive rhodopsin contained in the red rods. The same pigment is present in cones but the absorption peak is 580 nm in single cones and principal members of double cones versus 502 nm in red rods and accessory members of double cones. The lower absorption peak of 432 nm in green rods suggests that green rods have a yellow pigment (Donner and Reuter, 1976).

The visual pigment in larval amphibians and those that remain aquatic as adults is the purple-photosensitive porphyropsin. The change in visual pigments takes place during metamorphosis (see Chapter 7). However, in at least one species, *Rana catesbeiana,* the retina in adults contains as much as 30–40% porphyropsin, all of it concentrated in the upper third of the retina (Reuter et al., 1971). In this species which commonly sits in water with only the upper half of the eye above water, the upper part of the retina receives images from below the water and the lower part receives images from above the water.

Perception. Vision plays an important role in environmental sensing in anurans and most salamanders. The degenerate eyes of caecilians and subterranean salamanders allow them to distinguish between light and dark at best, and in those taxa in which the optic nerves have no connection with the eye, obviously no signals are transmitted to the brain, so the eyes do not have a sensory function. Various behavioral and neurophysiological studies have provided important data on visual perception in anurans and salamanders.

Light intensity and spectral sensitivity.—Classically, animals have been classified as photopositive or photonegative. Furthermore, amphibians generally have been considered to lack color vision. Muntz (1962) showed that *Rana temporaria* was photopositive to white light intensities and responded to blue light. The same results were obtained for *Triturus cristatus* (Muntz, 1963a), but *Salamandra salamandra* was photonegative to white light intensities and responded strongly to the two ends of the visual spectrum (a U-shaped spectral response peaking in red or violet).

In a series of experiments on 121 species of anurans, Hailman and R. Jaeger (1976, and other papers cited therein) showed that each species has a preferred white light intensity (optimal ambient illumination) to which it responds phototactically. Most species prefer illuminance above 90 lux, a few less than 0.01 lux, and the rest between these values. Hailman and R. Jaeger suggested that the response to blue light is based on true color vision, but that the U-shaped spectral response probably is a function of spectral selectivity. They proposed the following relationship between responses by anurans to intensity and spectral cues: (1) When the ambient illumination is brighter than the optimal ambient illumination for a given species, the individual responds photonegatively and exhibits the U-shaped spectral response, because the ends of the visible spectrum appear dimmest to the eyes. (2) When ambient light is dimmer than the optimal ambient illumination, the individual responds photopositively and exhibits the blue response based on true color vision. (3) When ambient light is at the optimal level, the individual attempts to maintain that intensity and is indifferent to colors. This model proposes that phototaxis is merely a means by which anurans of different species seek the ambient illumination that is optimal for their visual system.

The experiments by Hailman and R. Jaeger indicate that phototactic behavior is associated with four related physiological mechanisms which contribute to the diversity of behavioral responses to light of different intensities and wavelengths: (1) possession of different kinds of photoreceptors having different absorption levels, (2) pupillary responses that control the amount of light reaching the retina, (3) migration of pigment epithelium controlling the amount of light striking individual receptor cells, and (4) dark- and light-adaptation of photoreceptor cells which increase sensitivity in darkness and increase it in light.

Himstedt's (1972) experiments on selection of colored prey dummies by *Salamandra* and *Triturus* indicate that these salamanders exhibit a U-shaped spectral response like that reported for anurans by Hailman and R. Jaeger (1974). All experimental evidence indicates at least a limited distinction of different wavelengths of light, but so far there is no solid evidence for the ability to perceive the differences in colors evident in so many species of anurans or the breeding coloration in male newts (*Triturus*).

The presence of different photopigments in the retinas of larval amphibians presumably is the primary factor for tadpoles responding to green light instead of blue light (Muntz, 1963b; R. Jaeger and Hailman, 1976; see Chapter 6).

Depth perception and stereopsis.—Among vertebrates two major mechanisms are known for depth perception and stereopsis. One of these, binocular vision, is absent in amphibians that have small, lateral eyes. However, because of their large, protuberant eyes, many anurans and some salamanders have visual fields of nearly 360°. The right and left fields broadly overlap in some anurans, especially centrolenids, and in some plethodontid salamanders. Experiments with *Rana* and *Bufo* by Ingle (1976, and papers cited therein), Collett (1977), and Lock and Collett (1980) demonstrated that binocular vision (stereopsis) is important for depth perception and accurate movements toward prey and avoidance of barriers. Anurans with one ablated eye are less accurate in striking a prey.

The other mechanism is accommodation. This takes place by a change in the position of the lens within the eye. accommodation for near objects is accomplished by contraction of the m. protractor lentis, which moves the eye toward the cornea. Anurans have two protractor muscles, whereas salamanders have only one. accommodation may be essential only in monocular vision, because the overall effect of accomodative mechanisms is small (< 5 diopters); furthermore, Jordan et al. (1980) showed that depth estimation in *Bufo* with suppressed lens accommodation was nearly as precise as that of normal toads. G. Roth et al. (1983) suggested that accommodation plays a minor role in depth perception in many plethodontid salamanders, which have an extremely large lens proportional to the size of the eye and a short focal length. Moreover, the length of the outer segments of the photoreceptors might be sufficient to compensate for variations in object distance (Grüsser and Grüsser-Cornhels, 1976).

Pattern discrimination.—Lettvin et al. (1959) demonstrated that the output of the retina in anurans is composed of four facets of the visual images: (1) local sharp edges and contrast, (2) movement of edges, (3) local dimmings produced by movement or general rapid darkening, and (4) the curvature or the edge of a dark object. The fibers involved respond best when an object smaller than the receptive field enters the field, stops, and moves about. The response is not affected by changes in lighting or by moving the background. Thus, the eyes of amphibians are excellent at visually isolating potential prey of a correct size.

Experimental work on anurans summarized by Ingle (1976) and Ewert (1976) was expanded by Ingle and McKinley (1978), Ewert et al. (1978), and Burghagen and Ewert (1983). Experiments were performed on salamanders by G. Roth (1978), Luthardt and G. Roth (1979), and Finkenstädt and Ewert (1983). Studies on toads show that elongation of the prey along the axis of movement facilitates capture; there is a stronger effect for black stimuli than for white objects of the same size, and toads strike mainly at the leading object when the prey moves orthogonally to the toad's optic axis. Extensive neurophysiological work on visual sensitivity to prey stimuli by Ewert et al. (1978) showed that neurons with sensitivity to particular moving configurational stimuli occur in the retina and retinal projection fields, and that corresponding behavior occurs in a class of tectal neurons. However, no neurons are known to have specific responses to a stimulus of only a certain configuration. Also, inhibitory thalamic networks play an important role in discrimination between object motion and self-induced motion. Highly complex interactions between visual stimuli and somatic motor coordination are involved in prey capture (see Chapter 9).

Extraoptic Photoreception

Although a well-differentiated parietal eye such as known in the tuatara and in lizards is absent in amphibians, a homologous pineal end organ is present in anurans. Earlier work on the pineal end organ and its function was summarized by K. Adler (1970) and Eakin (1973), and the structures were reviewed by Dodt and Meissl (1982).

Structure. The morphology of the pineal end organ (= frontal organ or stirnorgan) and associated neurological features has been described by Oksche (1965), Van de Kamer (1965), D. E. Kelly (1971), and Ueck et al. (1971). The pineal end organ is present in adults of some anurans (e.g., *Rana*) although it is present in tadpoles of others (e.g., *Hyla regilla*). The end organ appears as a nearly pigmentless spot medially between the anterior edges of the eyes.

The pineal end organ and the pineal body develop from a common dorsal pouch of the diencephalon. In

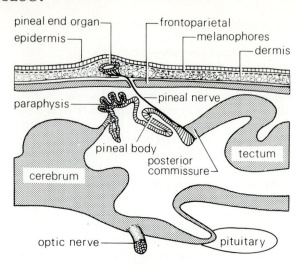

pineal end organ
epidermis
frontoparietal
melanophores
dermis
paraphysis
pineal nerve
pineal body
posterior
commissure
tectum
cerebrum
optic nerve
pituitary

Figure 14-12. Diagrammatic medial sagittal section through the brain of *Rana temporaria* showing the pineal complex and associated structures. Adapted from Van de Kamer (1965).

those anurans with a persistent end organ, the extracranial portion of the pouch is pinched off from the pineal body and comes to lie in the dermis, whereas the pineal body (= epiphysis) remains in the neurocranium. The pineal body lies immediately posterior to the paraphysis, a secretory pouch on the dorsal wall of the diencephalon (Fig. 14-12). The pineal end organ and the pineal body are hollow; in salamanders the lumen of the the pineal body is obliterated during development.

Both the pineal end organ and the pineal body have receptor cells. The ultrastructure of these cells resembles that of the photoreceptors in the retina of the eye; their outer segments contain a complex of lamellae resembling the discs of retinal rods, and the inner segments contain mitochondria-packed ellipsoids. The pineal end organ is innervated by the pineal nerve from the posterior commissure of the brain; this nerve apparently is absent in some species (e.g., *Hyla arborea;* Dodt and Heerd, 1962). The pineal nerve contains both afferent and efferent fibers. Both the pineal end organ and the pineal body are sensitive to light intensity and to different wavelengths (Dodt and Heerd, 1962; Dodt and Jacobson, 1973).

Function. The pineal body and in anurans also the pineal end organ have been implicated experimentally in pigmentary adaptation, synchronization of circadian locomotor rhythms, sun-compass orientation, and polartaxis.

The photoreceptor cells in the pineal body are inhibited by light and stimulated by its absence; stimulation of the receptors results in the release of melatonin which contracts dermal melanophores. Thus, the blanching of the skin resulting from melanophore contraction seems to be controlled by the pineal body, and the stimulus is the amount of light received by the the photoreceptors

in the pineal body or end organ (Bagnara and Hadley, 1970).

Phase shifts of the locomotor rhythm is accomplished in salamanders (*Plethodon glutinosus*) with or without eyes; experiments by K. Adler (1969) strongly implicated the pineal body as the receptor and regulator for this circadian rhythm.

Behavioral experiments with many species of anurans and salamanders have established that (1) orientation can be accomplished by celestial cues, (2) the organisms must know the local time in order to orient, and (3) eyeless animals respond in a manner similar to that of normal animals. This compass orientation has been associated with pineal photoreception and effectively demonstrated in *Acris gryllus* (D. Taylor and Ferguson, 1970) and *Ambystoma tigrinum* (D. Taylor, 1972). Further experiments with *A. tigrinum* (K. Adler and D. Taylor, 1973) revealed that both normal and eyeless salamanders trained under linearly polarized light orient to the bearing of the plane (*e*-vector) of linearly polarized light, but when the top of the head is covered with opaque plastic orientation is random.

Olfactory System

Structure. More is known about the anuran olfactory system than that of either salamanders or caecilians, but morphologically the organs of the three orders are sufficiently similar to suggest that they function in the same way. The only comparative morphological study is Jurgens (1971). A review of the olfactory system by Scalia (1976a) is restricted to anurans.

Amphibians possess a dual olfactory system—the olfactory system proper, and the accessory olfactory system or the vomeronasal organ (= Jacobson's organ). Each component arises from separate receptor organs, follows parallel but distinct neural channels in the cerebral hemisphere, and probably involves different central mechanisms in the diencephalon. Thus, afferent nerves of the olfactory system proper originate in the olfactory epithelium of the nasal organ and terminate upon postsynaptic neurons in the olfactory bulb, whereas afferents of the accessory system arise from the sensory epithelium of Jacobson's organ and form the vomeronasal nerve which terminates in the accessory olfactory bulb.

The nasal organ lies within, and is supported and protected by, the rostral part of the skull. If dermal roofing and palatal bones are well developed (e.g., caecilians), internal cartilaginous support of the olfactory organ is minimal. In salamanders and in anurans especially, the chondrocranium is elaborated into a complicated framework that supports the tissues of the principal nasal cavity (cavum principale), its accessory chambers, and the nasolacrimal duct.

Basically, the olfactory organ can be thought of as a system of saclike chambers. The largest of these is the cavum principale, which opens anteriorly at the external naris and posteriorly into the buccal cavity at the choana. Accessory chambers are located ventrally and laterally; their numbers and positions are variable and will be described in more detail below. The nasolacrimal duct generally is associated with the lateral part of the cavum principale, although it may open into an accessory chamber rather than into the cavum principale directly.

The ciliated epithelium lining the nasal chambers is organized into two anatomically distinct types—respiratory and sensory—that are supported in places by glandular tissue. Respiratory epithelium generally is found on medial and lateral surfaces of the cavum principale. The motile cilia of these cells maintain a continuous flow of mucous secretion over the entire epithelium. There are three distinct areas of sensory epithelium. The most widespread occurs on the medial wall, roof, and anterior end of the cavum principale. Nerve fascicles found in the lamina propria beneath the epithelium converge posteriorly to give rise to the dorsal division of the olfactory nerve. The sensory epithelium covering the elevated portion of the floor of the cavum principale, the eminentia olfactoria, is separated from the remaining sensory epithelium of the cavum principale by a perimeter of nonsensory epithelium. Sensory epithelium of the eminential olfactoria gives rise to the ventral division of the olfactory nerve. The third area of sensory epithelium is Jacobson's organ which is located in an accessory chamber to the cavum principale. This epithelium gives rise to the vomeronasal nerve.

The cilia of the sensory epithelia presumably are sensitive to chemical materials that are in solution in the mucous covering of the nasal epithelium, but little is known about actual olfactory behavior or function.

Salamanders.—Of the three orders of amphibians, the olfactory system is simplest in salamanders (Jurgens, 1971, and references cited therein). The organ consists primarily of a large chamber (cavum principale) that lies between the external naris and the choana. The cavum principale has a ventrolateral extension (Fig. 14-13) known as the lateral diverticulum that extends beyond the level of the choana as a fold, the sulcus maxillo-palatinus. The lateral diverticulum can be subdivided into anterolateral and posterolateral parts. The nasolacrimal duct runs from the eye to the anterolateral portion of the lateral diverticulum where it opens in the area of sensory epithelium of Jacobson's organ. The posterolateral portion of the lateral diverticulum that communicates with the buccal cavity lacks sensory epithelium. There is considerable variation in the complexity of the olfactory organ among salamanders. It is the least complex in aquatic taxa, and tends to be more complex in more terrestrial species. Thus, *Amphiuma* and *Siren* lack a nasolacrimal duct, and in *Amphiuma*, the proteids, and *Cryptobranchus*, Jacobson's organ is reduced. In contrast, terrestrial species are characterized by greater differentiation of the cavum principale into a main chamber and lateral diverticulum, of which the anterior end is specialized by the presence of a well-developed Jacobson's organ.

Caecilians.—Early descriptions of the nasal organ include the works of Wiedersheim (1879) and P. Sarasin and F. Sarasin (1887–90). The development of Jacobson's organ and the tentacular apparatus of *Ichthyophis glutinosus* was investigated by Badenhorst (1978), and Jurgens (1971) briefly compared the structure of the caecilian olfactory system with that of salamanders and anurans. A nasal tube leads from the external naris to a long, depressed nasal sac, the cavum principale. The cavum is divided into medial and lateral halves throughout the posterior two-thirds to three-quarters of its length by the olfactory eminence, a longitudinal, ridgelike structure in the floor of the cavity. Posterolaterally, the principal chamber is differentiated into two distinct ventral chambers—Jacobson's organ and the *Choanenschleimbeutel* (Fig. 14-13). Jacobson's organ is tubular, and lies nearly perpendicular to the long axis of the nasal sac. The glands of Jacobson's organ are located near the distal end of the structure. The nasolacrimal duct is composed of paired tubes which arise from the tentacular sheath, pass through the glands of Jacobson's organ, and unite into a short, single tube before terminating in the distal end of Jacobson's organ. The *Choanenschleimbeutel* lies between Jacobson's organ and the choana and ventral to the lateral part of the cavum principale. The *Choanenschleimbeutel* is not connected to Jacobson's organ; instead, it communicates by means of a so-called communal cavity with the lateral part of the cavum principale. The epithelial lining of these structures corresponds to that of the cavum principale and is composed of simple, ciliated columnar cells interspersed with numerous goblet cells.

The tentacular apparatus lies lateral to the nasal sac with its posterior end directed dorsally and its anterior end directed ventrally. The apparatus consists of the tentacular sheath and tentacle anteriorly and a retractor muscle posteriorly. The sheath extends posteriorly from the external orifice to the orbit where it encloses the orbital or Harderian glands that fill the orbit. The tentacle is formed from the wall of the sheath, and consists of an inner mass of connective tissue that is surrounded by an epithelial layer. The distal end of the tentacle is free; thus, it can be moved in and out of the sheath by the retractor muscle that arises from the lateral wall of the neurocranium. This muscle is homologous with the m. levator bulbi of salamanders and anurans and is innervated by C.N. VI (abducens). According to Jurgens (1971), the tentacle is lubricated by secretions from the Harderian glands as it moves in and out of the tentacular sheath. Chemical substances are transported from the tentacle via the sheath to the nasolacrimal ducts and thence to Jacobson's organ. Thus, when caecilians are burrowing and their nostrils presumably are closed, they are capable of chemosensory perception. Air routed through the nostrils probably

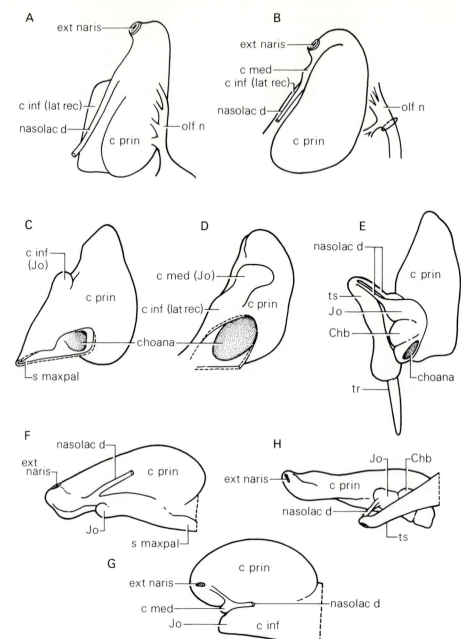

Figure 14-13. Schematic drawings of amphibian nasal organs. **A.** The salamander *Triturus alpestris* in dorsal view. **B.** The anuran *Ascaphus truei* in dorsal view. **C.** The salamander *Ambystoma maculatum* in lateral view. **D.** *Ascaphus truei* in lateral view. **E.** The caecilian *Ichthyophis glutinosus* in lateral view. **F.** *Ambystoma maculatum* in ventral view. **G.** *Ascaphus truei* in ventral view. **H.** *Ichthyophis glutinosus* in ventral view. Abbreviations: c med = cavum medium, c inf (lat rec) = cavum inferius (lateral recess), c. prin = cavum principale, Chb = Choanenschleimbeutel, ext naris = external naris, Jo = Jacobson's organ, naslac d = nasolacrimal duct, olf n = olfactory nerve, S maxpal = sulcus maxillopalatinus, tr = tentacular refractor muscle, ts = tentacular sheath. All redrawn from Jurgens (1971).

is shunted directly through the cavum principale and into the buccal cavity through the choana via the common chamber and the *Choanenschleimbeutel*.

    Anurans.—The structure of the nasal organ in anurans was investigated by Helling (1938), and summarized by Jurgens (1971; see included references). In contrast to salamanders, the organ is differentiated into three distinct chambers (Fig. 14-13). The largest, the cavum principale, extends from the level of the external naris to the choana. The diverticulum laterale is differentiated as the cavum inferius in anurans, and is subdivided into medial and lateral portions. The medial part (diverticulum mediale of the cavum inferius) represents Jacobson's organ, whereas the lateral part (diverticulum laterale of the cavum inferius) lacks olfactory epithelium and opens into the choana and buccal cavity. The diverticulum laterale is assumed to be homologous with the sulcus maxillo-palatinus of salamanders. The cava inferius and principale are joined anterolaterally by a small chamber, the cavum medium, which lacks olfactory epithelium. The nasolacrimal duct extends from the eye to open into the cavum medium. In primitive anurans (e.g., leiopelmatids and discoglossids), the cavum medium and the eminentia olfactoria tend to be smaller than in advanced anurans. All anurans possess a nasolacrimal duct.

Function. The olfactory receptors function in chemoreception (see review by Madison, 1977). The caecilian tentacle probably is the primary receptor used in locating food and also may play a role in locating mates. Numerous studies have shown that anurans use olfactory cues for orientation, especially to familiar breeding sites (see Chapter 3) and to recognize the odor of particular prey (Martof, 1962b; Kmelevskaya and Duelina, 1971; Gesteland, 1976; K. Müller and Kiepenheuer, 1976).

Olfactory communication is well developed among plethodontid salamanders, which have a nasolabial groove leading from the margin of the upper lip (commonly included in an elongate cirrus) to the nares (C. Brown, 1968). These salamanders are capable of picking up olfactory cues from the substrate. Experimental studies on various species of *Plethodon* have shown that these salamanders can identify conspecifics as well as individuals of other species (see R. Jaeger and Gergits, 1979, for review).

Auditory System

Amphibians have evolved an auditory apparatus that is unique among vertebrates; it contains a combination of structures that function in the transmission of substrate vibrations and, especially in anurans, airborne sound waves. The ears of salamanders have been studied by Monath (1965) and Lombard (1977), and those of caecilians by Wever (1975) and Wever and Gans (1976). Anurans vocalize, and their ears have been the subject of many kinds of investigations (see Chapter 4); the principal morphological studies have been by Wever (1973, 1979) and E. Lewis (1984).

Structure. Generally the tetrapod ear consists of three parts. The outer ear consists of the tympanum (or tympanic membrane), which receives airborne vibrations. These are directed toward the tympanum by fleshy reflectors in mammals. Most anurans have a distinct tympanic membrane, a thin layer of integument stretched over a cartilaginous annulus in a drumlike manner. In some anurans the tympanic annulus is absent. In such aurans and in salamanders and caecilians there is no differentiated tympanum.

A middle ear, or tympanic cavity, is present only in anurans. The columella (= stapes), which is homologous to the hyomandibular of fishes, transmits vibrations from the tympanic membrane to the membrane covering the oval window (= fenestra ovalis or fenestra vestibuli), which separates the middle ear from the inner ear. The columella has an expanded proximal end, or footplate, against the membrane of the oval window, a space that is shared by the operculum, part of the system for transmitting substrate vibrations to the inner ear. The columella is reduced or absent in some anurans that lack a tympanum. A canal (Eustachian tube) connects the middle ear with the pharynx in anurans; airflow in the Eustachian tube equalizes pressure on either side of the tympanic membrane. The middle ear and Eustachian tube are absent in salamanders and caecilians. In the latter the columella articulates with the quadrate; proximally it is fused with the operculum, or an operculum is absent. In salamanders the columella articulates distally with the squamosal in larvae, and its articulations are variable in adults (see Chapter 13).

The inner ear, or membranous labyrinth, is suspended within the otic capsule by loose connective tissue. The labyrinth consists of a perilymphatic (= periotic) fluid system and an endolymphatic fluid system, each contained within distinct sets of membranes (Fig. 14-14). The perilymphatic system consists of a large cistern against which the operculum and footplate of the columella rest in the oval window. The perilymphatic system is connected by a duct to the perilymphatic sac which lies in the neurocranium. Branches of the perilymphatic duct

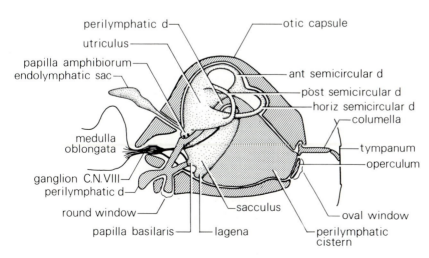

Figure 14-14. Schematic diagram of the ear of the bullfrog, *Rana catesbeiana;* posterior view of right ear. Bone and cartilage are hatched; the perilymphatic system is coarsely shaded, and the endolymphatic system is finely shaded. Adapted from Frishkopf and Goldstein (1963).

perilymphatic d
utriculus
papilla amphibiorum
endolymphatic sac
medulla oblongata
ganglion C.N. VIII
perilymphatic d
round window
papilla basilaris
lagena
sacculus
otic capsule
ant semicircular d
post semicircular d
horiz semicircular d
columella
tympanum
operculum
oval window
perilymphatic cistern

abut the chambers of the papilla amphibiorum and papilla basilaris of the sacculus of the endolymphatic system.

The endolymphatic system consists of the receptor organs of the inner ear. The basic structure of the endolymphatic system consists of two large vesicles, the dorsal utriculus and the ventral sacculus. The lagena is a pouch off the posteroventral surface of the sacculus. Two other small pouches off the sacculus are the dorsal chamber of the papilla amphibiorum and the ventral chamber of the papilla basilaris. Two vertical semicircular ducts (canals) diverge from the terminus of a dorsal extension of the utriculus, the cruz commune, and the horizontal semicircular duct diverges from its base. All three ducts enter the utriculus via ampullae containing receptor cells.

An endolymphatic duct leads from the sacculus to the endolymphatic sac in the neurocranium. This sac is small in most salamanders, but the sacs are expanded in some salamandrids, and those on either side coalesce dorsal to the brain in *Ambystoma*. In anurans, the endolymphatic sacs are fused and consist of a ring around the brain, a posterior extension into the vertebral canal, and in many species an anterior intercerebral portion (Dempster, 1930).

The neuroepithelium of the inner ear is located in well-defined areas, and these receptors are innervated by branchlets of the posterior branch of the auditory nerve (C.N. VIII). Neuroepithelial cells are like neuromast cells. Each cell has many stereocilia and one kinocilium. The neuroepithelial cells in the ampullae (cristae ampullae) of the semicircular ducts have their cilia imbedded in a gelatinous membrane, or cupula, as do the cells in a sensory patch in the utriculus called the crista neglecta (in amphibians, present only in caecilians). Other patches in the neuroepithelium in the utriculus, sacculus, and lagena are referred to as maculae; structurally these cells are like those in the cristae, except that inorganic crystals (otoliths) are present in the cupula.

The papilla basilaris and papilla amphibiorum are patches of neuroepithelium contained in separate pouches; the papilla amphibiorum is unique to amphibians.

The basilar chamber contains hair cells arranged circumferentially around the lumen of the chamber that opens directly into the sacculus on one end and on the other terminates in a thin contact membrane separating it from the perilymphatic system. The cells sit on a basilar membrane. Each hair cell has numerous stereocilia and one kinocilium; all are oriented with the kinocilium toward the contact membrane. The cilia are attached to an overlying gelatinous tectorial membrane which partially fills the cross section of the chamber. The papilla basilaris is innervated only by afferent nerve fibers. The papilla basilaris is present in all three living orders of amphibians, but it is reduced in size in some salamanders and absent in all sirenids, proteids, and plethodontids, and in some salamandrids (Lombard, 1977).

The amphibian chamber also terminates in a thin contact membrane against the perilymphatic fluid. The size and arrangement of the papilla amphibiorum are highly variable, as are the number and polarization of the hair cells. In advanced anurans, such as *Rana catesbeiana*, there are about 600 hair cells, each containing 70–80 stereocilia and one kinocilium. The tips of the cilia approach a gelatinous tectorial membrane that is suspended from the sensory surface of the chamber and covers the full extent of the papilla. The cells do not sit on a basilar membrane; instead, they are imbedded in the labyrinth wall. The amphibian papilla receives both afferent and efferent nerve fibers. The general topography of the sensory surface consists of a single patch of hair cells in caecilians and salamanders. In most anurans the sensory surface seems to consist of two contiguous patches, the more posterior of which is conspicuously elongated and curved. E. Lewis (1984) demonstrated that there is a grade in elongation and complexity of the surface of the neuroepithelium and that this grade corresponds to the general scheme of anuran phylogeny.

E. Lewis (1981, 1984) summarized the morphological features distinguishing the papilla amphibiorum of salamanders and that of anurans. The typical anuran structure consists of two patches of neuroepithelium, each innervated by a separate branchlet of the auditory nerve and each having two populations of oppositely polarized hair cells; the salamander structure consists of a single patch innervated by one branchlet of the auditory nerve with a single pair of populations of oppositely polarized hair cells. In anurans the perilymphatic duct is in contact with the posterior end of the amphibian chamber, whereas in salamanders the duct is in contact with the medial surface of the chamber. The tectorial membrane is thick where it is adjacent to the anterior patch of neuroepithelium and thin adjacent to the posterior elongation in anurans; in salamanders it is of a uniform intermediate thickness over the entire papilla. The kinocilia in anurans terminate in a bulb, whereas the kinocilia in salamanders lack a bulb. Limited observations on caecilians indicate that the structure of the papilla amphibiorum is like that in salamanders.

The results of E. Lewis's (1981, 1984) ultrastructural studies have phylogenetic significance. Leiopelmatid frogs are like salamanders in having a single patch of neuroepithelium with a single pair of populations of oppositely polarized hair cells (Fig. 14-15), the perilymphatic duct being in contact with the median surface of the chamber, the tectorial membrane being of uniform thickness, and the kinocilia lacking terminal bulbs. In anurans, other than leiopelmatids, the kinocilia of the hair cells in the lagena, sacculus, and papilla basilaris also have terminal bulbs (E. Lewis, 1981). The development of kinociliary bulbs is an ontogenetic phenomenon in *Rana catesbeiana* (E. Lewis and Li, 1973). Also, the confluence of the anterior and posterior patches of neuroepithelium seems to be an ontogenetic phenomenon; in *Xenopus laevis* and

R. catesbeiana, the two patches are not contiguous in early larval stages but gradually merge in later larval stages (Li and E. Lewis, 1974).

Function. The neurophysiology of the inner ear, especially that of anurans, has been the subject of intensive study. The inner ear functions to maintain equilibrium and to transmit vibrations from the air or substrate to the brain. The receptor organs in the inner ear are characterized by innervated epithelial surfaces studded with sensory receptor cells and an acellular mechanical network consisting of both fluid and solid elements. Electrophysiological evidence indicates that the stereocilia of the receptor cells are sensitive to strain and that the acellular mechanical network serves as part or all of a filter that selects particular mechanical stimuli, translates them into stereociliary strain, and rejects other mechanical stimuli. In this way, the acellular networks are partly or totally responsible for the efficient stimulus selectivity of the inner ear.

The stereocilia are immersed in the endolymphatic fluid, and the stimulation of these receptor cells is by means of mobilization of the perilymphatic and endolymphatic fluids. The perilymphatic fluid is mobilized by vibrations of the operculum or the footplate of the columella against the membrane at the oval window. These vibrations may originate from the substrate and are transmitted via tonic responses of the opercularis muscle extending between the pectoral girdle and the operculum. In most anurans, airborne sound waves are transmitted via the tympanum and columella to the oval window. Sensitivity to airborne sounds is maximized by the large size of the tympanum compared with the size of the oval window; in this way the acoustic impedance of the air is matched with the higher impedance of the fluids in the inner ear (Capranica, 1976). Oscillation of the perilymph is transmitted to the endolymph via common membranes.

The displacement of fluids in the inner ear occurs in different ways in anurans, caecilians, and salamanders (Wever, 1978). Anurans have a round window in the otic capsule which is bounded by the perilymphatic membrane. Vibratory sound pressures exerted against the oval window oscillate the perilymph between the oval window and the round window; the inward displacement at the oval window is accompanied by an outward displacement of equal volume at the round window. Caecilians and salamanders lack a round window. In caecilians, vibrations against the oval window set the perilymph in motion along a roundabout course back to the oval window; the fluid surges back and forth along this pathway. In salamanders, pressure exerted against the oval window produces fluid displacements that traverse a complex path across the head to the contralateral oval window. The pathway leads through three different fluids beginning with that in the perilymphatic cistern and then to the endolymph in the sacculus, where the motion passes

over the papillae basilaris and amphibiorum. From the latter, a membranous window leads to the perilymphatic duct and on to the perilymphatic sac within the neurocranium. Thereafter, the pathway traverses the arachnoid membrane to the cerebrospinal fluid and extends across the midline, mainly beneath the brain, and continues through a reverse order through the same structures to the contralateral oval window. Thus, in salamanders reception invariably is binaural.

Auditory reception.—The sensory receptors in the inner ear of all amphibians are sensitive to seismic (substrate) vibrations, and those in anurans are sensitive to a wide range of airborne frequencies. Electrophysiological studies on salamanders by Ross and J. Smith (1980) revealed that receptors in the sacculus are sensitive to frequencies of 20 to 450 hertz (Hz) and that sensitivity seems to be related to the habitat. For example, peak sensitivity in terrestrial efts of *Notophthalmus viridescens* is 150–250 Hz, whereas that of aquatic adults is 150 Hz. Terrestrial *Plethodon cinerus* have a peak sensitivity of 200–250 Hz, but larvae of *Ambystoma maculatum* have a peak of only 200 Hz. Wever and Gans (1976) reported a peak sensitivity of 200 Hz in the caecilian *Ichthyophis glutinosus.*

A high degree of sensitivity to seismic vibrations has been reported in anurans. Receptors in the sacculus and lagena of *Rana catesbeiana* are sensitive to frequencies of 15–200 Hz (Koyama et al., 1982); low frequencies (20–160 Hz) produced by *Leptodactylus albilabris* and transmitted by the substrate are selectively received by the sacculus in other individuals (E. Lewis and Narins, 1985).

Airborne sound waves are transmitted via the tympanum and columella to the inner ear, where mobilization of the perilymph is coupled with the endolymph to create motion of the tectorial membranes and stereociliary strain on the receptor cells of the papilla amphibiorum and papilla basilaris. The receptors of these auditory epithelia are sensitive to different frequencies. Electrophysiological evidence (Capranica, 1965; Chung et al., 1978; Koyama et al., 1982) shows that the greatest sensitivity of the receptors in the sacculus is 20–150 Hz in most anurans. Hence, these receptors have a low sensitivity to airborne sounds but a high sensitivity to seismic vibrations. The greatest sensitivity of the papilla amphibiorum is from 100 to 1000 Hz and that of the papilla basilaris is from 1000 to 5000 Hz. The presence of both kinds of papillae, the impedance-matching system of the middle ear, and the interlocking columellar-opercular mechanism provides anurans with an efficient mechanism for acoustic reception (see Chapter 4).

Selection of frequencies in anurans also is accomplished by tonotopic organization of the sensory patches of the papilla amphibiorum (E. Lewis, 1981; E. Lewis et al., 1982). Frequencies are sorted by a combination of two patches of neuroepithelium with separate innerva-

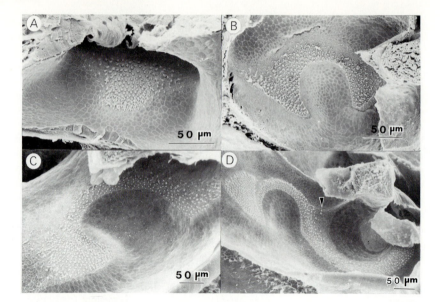

Figure 14-15. Scanning electron micrographs of neuroepithelial surface of the papilla amphibiorum in the inner ear; the sensory surface is identified by the presence of projecting hairlike tufts. **A.** *Ascaphus truei.* **B.** *Pipa pipa.* **C.** *Pelobates fuscus.* **D.** *Kassina senegalensis.* Photos courtesy of E. R. Lewis.

tions, a tectorial membrane with spatially graded bulk, the position of the contact membrane at the posterior end of the chamber instead of along its medial margin, and possibly by the polarization of the hair cells. In anurans, such as *Ascaphus truei* (Fig. 14-15A), and presumably in salamanders and caecilians with a single patch of papilla amphibiorum, the frequency range of sensitivity is 100–600 Hz. Extension of this frequency range beyond 600 Hz seems to depend on the posterior elongation of the posterior patch of hair cells. This was shown to be the case in the elongate patch in *Rana catesbeiana* by E. Lewis et al. (1982), who determined the best excitatory freqencies for auditory stimuli of 29 afferent axons of the auditory nerve innervating the papilla amphibiorum. Fourteen axons with frequencies at or below 300 Hz terminated in the anterior region of the papilla; ten axons with frequencies of 400–550 Hz terminated in the central region; and five axons with frequencies of more than 550 Hz terminated in the posteriormost region.

Equilibrium.—The neuroepithelia and associated gelatinous cupulae of the crista ampullae and the maculae of the utriculus, sacculus, and lagena are equilibrium receptors. According to the summary by E. Lewis and Leverentz (1983), in the semicircular ducts the viscosity and inertia of the endolymph apparently combine with the viscoelasticity of the cupulae to translate rotational motions about particular axes into stereociliary strain; at the same time, rotational motion about the orthogonal axes and linear motion along any axis are rejected. The calcariferous masses of the otolithic maculae and the viscoelastic gelatinous membrane associated with each sensory patch apparently combine to translate linear motion into stereociliary strain. Directional selectivity in the maculae appears to be provided by the polarization patterns

of the hair cells. Apparently the crista neglecta in caecilians also is a receptor for head motions (Wever and Gans, 1976).

NERVOUS SYSTEM

Although the nervous system of amphibians is somewhat more highly developed than that in fishes, amphibians retain the primitive pattern of nerve-cell bodies around the ventricles of the brain. In contrast to the everted forebrain of fishes, there is an invagination of the hemispheres in amphibians; this construction is like that of amniotes, which, unlike amphibians, have a definitive cerebral cortex. Amphibians have two meninges, a vascularized pia mater attached to the brain and spinal cord and a tough, outer dura mater adjacent to the bones.

Herein the classic regions of the nervous system are discussed in the following order—brain, cranial nerves, spinal cord and spinal nerves, and autonomic nervous system. Some developmental aspects of the nervous system are discussed in Chapter 7. Neurophysiology and ultrastructure are treated only in a general way; an extensive literature is available on these subjects (see Jørgensen, 1974; Llinás and Precht, 1976; and Oksche and Ueck, 1976).

Brain

The morphology of the brain has been studied in *Rana esculenta* by Gaupp (1896); nearly all modern treatments of the gross morphology of the anuran brain are based on that work. Kuhlenbeck (1922) provided a detailed description of the brain of the caecilian *Hypogeophis rostratus,* and Kuhlenbeck et al. (1966) presented additional information on the forebrain of caecilians. The brain of

Salamandra salamandra was described by Francis (1934), and the most exhaustive study is that by Herrick (1948) on *Ambystoma tigrinum*. Noble (1931b) made general comparisons of the brains of the three living orders of amphibians.

Forebrain. The forebrain is differentiated into the telencephalon and diencephalon (Fig. 14-16). The telencephalon is composed of a pair of bilateral olfactory bulbs and cerebral hemispheres; it is shorter but farther invaginated in anurans than in salamanders and caecilians. The olfactory nerve (C.N. I) exits from the anteroventral surface of the olfactory bulb in anurans and hynobiid salamanders and from the anterolateral surface in other salamanders and caecilians; in the latter, the base of the

nerve is comparatively massive. Each cerebral hemisphere is divided into a dorsal pallium and ventral subpallium; their distinction is marked by a sulcus on the inner surface of the ventricles and in anurans by a groove on the outer surface. In the subpallium, a medial septum is distinguished from lateral basal ganglia. Also, the pallium is differentiated into an internal hippocampus and external pyriform primordium.

Differentiation of an accessory olfactory lobe in the anterior part of the cerebral hemisphere occurs in caecilians and anurans; it is poorly developed in most salamanders and is absent in obligate neotenes. The degree of development of the accessory olfactory lobe is positively correlated with development of Jacobson's organ, which is absent in neotenic salamanders. The amygdaloid

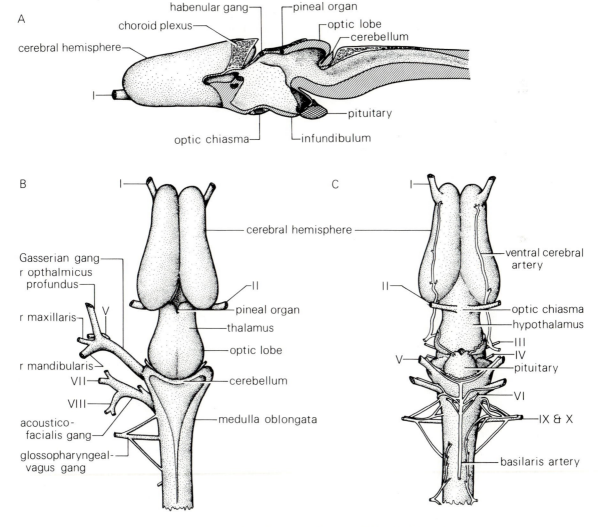

Figure 14-16. Brain of *Salamandra salamandra*. **A.** Lateral (midsagittal section). **B.** Dorsal. **C.** Ventral. Cranial nerves are indicated by roman numerals. Abbreviations: gang = ganglion, r = ramus. Adapted from Francis (1934).

nucleus (a prominence on the lower surface of the cerebral hemisphere) is correspondingly well developed in anurans and caecilians, as is the striatum (external tissue of the subpallium). The relative development of the latter also seems to be correlated with an increase in exteroreceptive tracts.

The telencephalon is the receptor for sensory impulses derived from the olfactory epithelium of the nasal sacs and from Jacobson's organ. Although there is a concentration of olfactory fibers in the olfactory bulbs (and accessory olfactory lobes when present), all parts of the cerebral hemispheres receive impulses from the olfactory fibers. The septum and striatum are synaptic stations where olfactory fibers join with fibers from the thalamus and midbrain. A peripheral wandering of cells from the hippocampus and pyriform areas is most extensive in anurans. In amniotes, these cells lead to the development of cell laminae in the pallium separate from the periventricular cells; these laminae cells differentiate into correlation centers, whereas the periventricular cells remain pathways for relatively simple reflexes.

The unpaired posterior part of the forebrain, the diencephalon, consists of three major parts—epithalamus, thalamus, and hypothalamus. The epithalamus is composed of the habenular ganglia, a choroid plexus (a vascularized invagination into the third ventricle), and the pineal organ. The habenular ganglia receive fibers from the telencephalon. A tract of olfactory fibers, the fasciculus retroflexus, extends posteroventrally from the habenular ganglia to the interpeduncular nucleus in the mesencephalic tectum; in salamanders, this nucleus projects posteriorly into the medullary tectum, but this projection has not been noted in anurans or caecilians.

The pineal organ (= epiphysis) is a small projection, best developed in anurans, attached to the dorsomedian surface of the epithalamus by a few fibers. These fibers contain the frontal and pineal tracts (parietal nerve), fibers of which enter the pretectal region in the posterior part of the epithalamus. The lateral and ventral walls of the diencephalon are constituted by the thalamus, which contains a web of connecting fibers with all contiguous parts of the brain, which make the thalamus an important center for sensory correlation. For example, even though the optic nerves enter the neurocranium and have a chiasma under the thalamus, these optic tracts pass posterodorsally to the optic lobes of the midbrain. However, on their way to the midbrain the optic tracts give off collateral fibers which synapse in the thalamus with fibers of other sensory systems.

Posteroventrally, the hypothalamus is a bilobate projection of the diencephalon. The hypothalamus is divided into preoptic and tuberoinfundibular regions. In addition to numerous connecting fibers with the ventral thalamus, the magnocellular preoptic nucleus is connected with the ventral lobe of the hypophysis, and distinct areas of the parvocellular tuberoinfundibular nuclei are connected with the hypophysial portal vessels. The hypothalamus is an important center for control of the autonomous nervous system.

Midbrain. The midbrain, or mesencephalon, is made up of the dorsal tecta (optic lobes) and the basal tegmental or peduncular portion. The latter transmits motor impulses. The peduncular region receives fibers from practically all parts of the brain anterior to the medulla; its primary function is to control mass movements of the body and limbs. Also, this is the site of origin of two eye muscles (C.Nn. III and IV).

The optic lobes and tissues composing the optic tectum are best developed in anurans and least developed in caecilians. In anurans, the tectum has white and gray strata. Fibers from the optic tract spread throughout the tectum. The function of the optic tectum is the visual control over movements of the body as a whole, and particularly the orientation of the body and conjugate movements of the eyeballs with reference to objects in the visual field.

Just below the optic lobes is the torus semicircularis. This subtectal cluster of cells is the principal receptor site for afferent auditory fibers from the bulbotectal tract in the cerebellum.

Hindbrain. The posterior part of the brain consists of the cerebellum and the medulla oblongata (rhomboencephalon), which is continuous with the spinal cord. The cerebellum consists of paramedian dorsal protrusions and a more lateral pair of auricular lobes that are an anterior continuation of the acousticolateralis system of the medulla. The histological structure of the cerebellum of anurans is more complex than that of other amphibians. Anurans have a cerebellar nucleus and tracts to the peduncular region of the midbrain. Also, in anurans there is true lamination of cells and fibers, and the Purkinje cells (interlaminar flask-shaped cells) have a more definitive structure than in other amphibians.

In comparison with other vertebrates, the cerebellum is small, especially in terrestrial adult amphibians. It is the center for motor coordination, and the small size presumably is correlated with the comparatively simple locomotor activities of amphibians. The degree of development of the auricular lobes is correlated with the presence of a lateral-line system. Thus, larvae and neotenic salamanders have proportionately larger auricular lobes.

Situated between the cerebellum and the medulla is the isthmus, a region which is distinct in early development, but which becomes incorporated into the anterior part of the medulla in adults. Afferent fibers coming from practically all parts of the brain terminate in the isthmus. Here, too, is the chief sensory nucleus of the trigeminal nerve (C.N. V). Efferent fibers from many centers converge in the isthmic tegmentum. The isthmic region is the chief regulator of the jaw musculature.

The medulla is the widened and flattened anterior part of the spinal cord, from which it differs by having a largely membranous dorsal surface with a cluster of blood vessels, which forms as the choroid plexus a vascular diverticulum extending into the ventricle of the medulla. Like the spinal cord, the medulla is divided into a ventromedian motor region and a dorsolateral sensory region. The later is the acousticolateralis region, which merges with the auricular lobes of the cerebellum. Between the dorsal and ventral portions of the medulla is a region of synaptic junction of sensory and motor fibers. In the anterior part of this region in salamanders are the giant Mauthner cells which have axons that extend the length of the spinal cord to the caudal musculature; these fibers function in the regulation of swimming movements. Vestibular and (in larvae) lateral-line fibers have synapses with Mauthner cells.

In primitive tetrapods, more of the medulla was contained within the skull than in living amphibians, so that all 12 cranial nerves exited from the skull. In living amphibians, the hypoglossus nerve (C.N. XII) is associated with the first spinal nerve. Of the 11 cranial nerves exiting from the skull, 7 (C.Nn. V–XI) enter the medulla and send afferent and efferent fibers to specific locations within the medulla. In the ventral motor portion of the medulla, the nuclei of the cranial nerve fibers are arranged in numerical order; this separation (particularly nuclei of C.Nn. VII, IX, and X) is more evident in anurans than in other amphibians. The sensory nuclei of C.Nn. V and VII are anastomosed in salamanders but not in anurans.

The medulla controls actions of swallowing, digestion, heartbeat, and respiration, as well as jaw action and some locomotor responses.

Fibers of the auditory nerve (C.N. VIII) enter the medulla as discrete branches through a dorsal root and a ventral root, where they become associated with a dorsal medullary nucleus of small cells and a ventral nucleus of large cells, respectively. Anurans are unique among anamniotes in having a pair of superior olivary nuclei, located on the ventral side of the medulla. Cells of the superior olivary nucleus receive input from the dorsal medullary nucleus and the contralateral superior olivary nucleus. Fibers from the dorsal medullary and superior olivary nuclei form the lateral bulbotectal tract which extends anteriorly to the torus semicircularis of the midbrain. Anurans also have a large nuclear mass, the nucleus isthmi, in the tegmentum; it may have some auditory function. The function of the complex auditory receptor system in anurans is discussed in Chapter 4.

Finally, the medulla exits the cranium through the foramen magnum and becomes the spinal cord. Although there are nerve fibers from the medulla anteriorly into the midbrain and fibers from the forebrain posteriorly into the midbrain, there is no uninterrupted pathway from the forebrain to the spinal cord.

Cranial Nerves

The cranial nerves of amphibians have received only cursory attention for more than 50 years. In the most recent review of anurans, Nieuwenhuys and Opdam (1976:813) stated: "In this survey we have relied heavily on the exhaustive analysis of Gaupp (1896)." Gaupp's work was on one species of anuran, *Rana esculenta*. Basic descriptive morphology of the cranial nerves of salamanders was done by Coghill (1902) on *Ambystoma tigrinum* and by H. Norris (1908, 1913) and by Francis (1934) on *Amphiuma means, Siren lacertina,* and *Salamandra salamandra,* respectively. The work of earlier authors is reviewed by H. Norris and Hughes (1918) in their description of the nerves in a few species of caecilians.

In the following synopsis, which is based entirely on the literature concerning a few species, the cranial nerves (C.N.) are described; unless specified otherwise, the description is applicable to all three living orders.

C.N. I (Olfactory). The first visceral sensory nerve leaves from the ventrolateral border of the olfactory lobe and passes through the fenestra olfactoria into the nasal capsule where it divides into the ramus profundus and the ramus dorsalis. Fibers of the ramus dorsalis enter the olfactory lobe proper and are connected via olfactory tracts with secondary olfactory centers in the cerebral hemisphere. The fibers of the ramus profundus extend posteriorly into the accessory olfactory bulbs. The ramus dorsalis innervates the olfactory epithelium of the nasal sac. The main branch of the ramus profundus innervates the vomeronasal epithelium of Jacobson's organ, and the ramus medialis nasi pierces the roof of the nasal capsule to supply the skin of the dorsal snout. Various other branches of the ramus profundus seem to be homologous in the living orders, although different names have been used (Jurgens, 1971). The principal variations in these are: (1) the branches in *Xenopus* are similar to those of salamanders (Paterson, 1939), (2) *Cryptobranchus* is different from other salamanders in that the ramus lateralis nasi does not enter the nasal capsule secondarily, and (3) in caecilians the ramus lateralis nasi innervates the tentacular sheath, and the ramus medialis nasi is divided into two main branches.

C.N. II (Opticus). This somatic sensory element actually is part of the brain. It enters the floor of the diencephalon where it crosses with its contralateral counterpart to form the optic chiasma. After crossing, the nerve ascends the lateral wall of the diencephalon as an external bundle of fibers, the tractus opticus. Most of these fibers spread in the superficial layer of the roof of the midbrain, but smaller contingents terminate in the thalamus, hypothalamus, and tegmentum of the midbrain. The optic nerve exits the neurocranium via the large optic foramen (or fenestra), which is an hiatus between the sphenethmoid and prootic. The nerve is covered by a fibrous connective-tissue sheath and is continuous with the layer of nerve cells on the inner surface of the eye. In caecilians in which the eye is covered by skin (e.g., *Dermophis, Geotrypes, Ichthyophis*), the optic nerve is rudimentary; it passes from the optic foramen, along the retractor muscle of the tentacle, and through the orbital glands to the eye. In caecilians in which the eye is vestigial and covered by bone (e.g., *Caecilia, Oscaecilia*), the optic nerve is absent. The optic nerve is greatly reduced in diameter in subterranean salamanders; the nerve is continuous with the brain in *Proteus* and *Haideotriton* but usually not in *Typhlotriton* (Brandon, 1968).

C.N. III (Oculomotorius). The fibers of the third nerve emerge from the ventral surface of the mesencephalon and exit the neurocranium via the oculomotor foramen just posterior to the optic foramen. The bulk of the nerve consists of somatic efferent fibers that innervate four eye muscles. Within the orbit the nerve divides into two rami; the ramus superior innervates the m. rectus superior, and the ramus inferior innervates the m. obliquus inferior and the mm. rectus inferior and anterior. Close to the point of division of the somatic rami, a smaller bundle of fibers belonging to the visceral afferent category forms the ramus communicans to the ramus ophthalmicus profundus (C.N. V); after synaptic interruption in the ganglion ciliare, the fiber bundle innervates the intrinsic eye muscle, the smooth m. sphincter pupillae. In caecilians having the eye covered by skin, the efferent nerves are reduced (*Dermophis*) or vestigial (*Ichthyophis*), whereas they are absent in caecilians in which the eyes are covered by bone. There is no connection of the oculomotor with the trigeminal (C.N. V) in caecilians.

C.N. IV (Trochlearis). This somatic efferent nerve originates ventromedially in the posterior part of the mesencephalon, passes dorsally in a deep groove (cerebellomesencephalic fissure), crosses with its contralateral counterpart in the anterior medullary vellum, and exits the cranium via the optic foramen or a small, oblique foramen anterodorsal to the optic foramen. This nerve supplies a single eye muscle, the m. obliquus superior. Francis (1934) discussed variation in this nerve in salamanders, noting that in *Salamandra* the nerve divides before or after leaving the cranium; the smaller branch innervates the m. obliquus superior, and the larger one anastomoses with the ramus ophthalmicus profundus (C.N. V). In at least some caecilians with the eye covered by skin (e.g., *Dermophis, Hypogeophis*), a thin trochlear nerve is present, but it has not been observed in others.

C.N. V (Trigeminus). The trigeminal originates from the lateral surface of the medulla and exits the cranium via the large prootic foramen, which contains the Gasserian ganglion, from which branches of the trigeminal nerve arise. The largest branch, the sensory ramus ophthalmicus profundus, contains somatic afferent fibers. This ramus actually arises from a second ganglion (ophthalmic ganglion) in caecilians; in all amphibians it bifurcates into six major branches that innervate the skin on the snout, top of the head, and facial region, as well as penetrate the eyeball (superior and inferior ciliary rami).

A ventral branch anastomoses with the ramus palatinus (C.N. VII) and innervates the tissues of the mouth under the nasal organs; this anastomosis is absent in caecilians. Shortly after leaving the Gasserian ganglion, the ramus maxillo-mandibularis, which contains both visceral motor fibers and somatic sensory fibers, bifurcates. The ramus maxillaris has three major branches; two of these supply the skin of the eyelids and the temporal region of the head, whereas motor fibers innervate the eye muscle, m. levator bulbi (except in caecilians, all of which lack this muscle). The ramus mandibularis also contains somatic sensory and visceral motor fibers; it divides into three major branches. One of these supplies the m. levator mandibulae, and another innervates the skin over the angle of the jaw and the posterior mandible. The primary mandibular branch divides into a ramus mentales, which innervates the dentary and skin along the anterior part of the mandible, and the ramus intermandibularis, which supplies sensory fibers to the skin between the rami of the jaws and motor fibers to the mm. intermandibularis and submentalis. In the caecilians, the m. compressor glandulae orbitalis is innervated by the ramus mandibularis (Badenhorst, 1978), which is partially anastomosed with the ramus maxillaris. A branch of the latter innervates the tentacular sheath in caecilians.

C.N. VI (Abducens). This somatic motor nerve arises from the ventral surface of the medulla and exits the neurocranium via the optic foramen in anurans and caecilians and via a separate foramen abducentis in salamanders. In the orbit the nerve bifurcates, each ramus innervating one of two eye muscles, the mm. rectus lateralis and retractor bulbi. In caecilians, the nerve innervates the retractor muscle of the tentacle, which is homologous with the m. retractor bulbi of other amphibians. In those caecilians having the eye covered by skin (e.g., *Ichthyophis*), the m. rectus lateralis is present and innervated by the abducens, whereas in those caecilians in which the eye muscles are degenerated, that branch of the abducens is absent.

C.N. VII (Facialis). The slender facial nerve originates on the ventrolateral surface of the medulla and exits the neurocranium through a foramen into the cavity formed by the tripodial attachment of the palatoquadrate (salamanders) or quadrate (anurans and caecilians). It is composed of branchiomotor and visceral efferent fibers. The facial nerve is closely associated with the auditory nerve (C.N. VIII) within the neurocranium. Outside the neurocranium the nerve passes anteriorly to the Gasserian ganglion. From that point the ramus palatinus extends anteriorly and innervates the roof of the mouth; it is anastomosed with the ramus ophthalmicus profundus (C.N. V) in salamanders and anurans. Also, the Harderian glands in the orbit and the intermaxillary gland in the roof of the mouth are innervated by the ramus palatinus. The major part of the facial nerve consists of the truncus hyomandibularis, which exits between the otic and basal processes of the (palato)quadrate and gives rise to three branches: (1) ramus alveolaris, sensory fibers that run along the lingual side of the lower jaw and innervate the epithelial lining of the floor of the mouth; (2) ramus muscularis (or mandibularis), motor fibers that innervate the m. depressor mandibulae; and (3) ramus jugularis, motor fibers that innervate the m. interhyoideus and (in salamanders) the m. subhyoideus.

C.N. VIII (Auditory). The auditory nerve is made up primarily of special somatic afferent fibers, but it also contains some efferent axons that exert an inhibitory influence on the spontaneous activity of the vestibular afferent fibers in anurans. Although these different fibers leave the lateral surface of the medulla, they maintain their integrity anteriorly to the torus semicircularis below the optic ventricle of the midbrain. In salamanders and caecilians, the auditory nerve is intimately associated with the facial nerve in the otic capsule. In salamanders, the two nerves have a common acoustico-facialis ganglion, but in caecilians the auditory nerve seems to have a separate but poorly developed ganglion. In anurans, the auditory nerve remains distinct from the facial. The auditory nerve trifurcates and enters the auditory capsule via three foramina in salamanders, but has only two rami (and foramina) in anurans and caecilians. The ramus anterior innervates the utriculi and ampullae of the anterior and lateral canals (also the sacculus in anurans). The ramus posterior innervates the ampullae of the posterior canal, the papilla lagenae, and the papilla amphibiorum in all three orders; in caecilians, this branch also innervates the sacculus, and in anurans, the papilla basilaris. The sacculus is innervated by a ramus medianus in salamanders.

C.N. IX (Glossopharyngeus). This small nerve consisting of branchiomotor and visceral efferent and afferent fibers arises directly in front of the first root of the vagus (C.N. X) on the lateral wall of the medulla. Both nerves exit the neurocranium via the postotic foramen immediately posterior to the otic capsule, where they form a large glossopharyngeal-vagus ganglion. Except in caecilians, one branch of the glossopharyngeal passes anteriorly to communicate with the facial nerve (C.N. VII). Branchiomotor fibers of the ramus muscularis innervate the m. subarcualis rectus I. The dorsal buccal mucosa is innervated by visceral afferent fibers of the ramus pharyngeus, and the tongue by the same kind of fibers in the ramus lingualis, which also probably supplies special visceral afferent fibers to the taste buds of the tongue.

C.N. X (Vagus). The origins of the vagus, glossopharyngeal, and accessory nerves are difficult to distinguish in amphibians. Different authors recognize two to four roots of the vagus, but apparently only two exist; the others represent the roots of the glossopharyngeal and accessory nerves. The vagus and glossopharyngeal (C.N. IX) exit the neurocranium via the postotic foramen; once outside the cranium the two nerves form a common

glossopharyngeal-vagus ganglion (also apparently incorporating the accessory nerve). The vagus consists of branchiomotor and visceral efferent fibers; the latter constitute the main peripheral path of the parasympathetic system. The branchiomotor fibers innervate three throat muscles—mm. transversus ventralis, cephalodorsosubpharyngeus, and subarcualis rectus I. Sensory fibers supply the mucosa of the mouth and pharynx. A ramus auricularis provides afferent fibers to the tympanic region in anurans and salamanders. Various branches of the main part of the vagus, the laryngeus ventralis, innervate the smooth muscles and glands of the esophagus and stomach, as well as the muscles of the lungs and heart.

C.N. XI (Accessorius). This small motor nerve emerges from the lateral wall of the medulla with the roots of the vagus. It innervates a single pectoral suspensory muscle, the m. cucullaris.

C.N. XII (Hypoglossus). The primordia of this nerve are in the first and second spinal nerves, but this nerve contains fibers which represent the hypoglossal nerve in amniotes; therefore, it can be considered with the cranial nerves. It exits from the spinal cord either through a foramen in Presacral I (salamanders and caecilians) or through an intervertebral foramen between Presacrals I and II (anurans). This nerve innervates the muscles associated with the tongue— mm. geniohyoideus, genioglossus, hyoglossus, and rectus cervicis.

Lateral-line Nerves. The lateral-line organs of larval amphibians and certain ones that are aquatic as adults (pipid frogs and obligate neotenic salamanders) are innervated by branches of cranial nerves. Except for those groups mentioned, these nerves degenerate at metamorphosis. The ampullary organs and neuromasts of the snout are innervated by the ramus lateralis anterior of the facial nerve (C.N. VII), and the other parts of the lateral-line system of the head by the ramus lateralis posterior (and its many branches) of the vagus nerve (C.N. X). The fibers of these nerves enter the medulla at the same point as those of the auditory nerve (C.N. VIII).

Spinal Cord and Spinal Nerves

Details of the morphology and ultrastructure of the spinal cord in anurans were provided by Ebbesson (1976) and Sotelo and Grofova (1976), respectively. The gross morphology of the spinal nerves in anurans is based on Gaupp's (1896) work on *Rana esculenta*, whereas that of *Salamandra salamandra* was described by Francis (1934) and that of caecilians by H. Norris and Hughes (1918).

Spinal Cord. The basic structure of the anterior part of the spinal cord is similar in the three living groups of amphibians. The cord is contained in the neural canal of the vertebrae and completely covered by bone of the imbricate neural arches, except in some anurans, in which nonimbricate neural arches leave portions of the spinal cord exposed. The dorsal surface is formed by nuclei where somatic afferent fibers terminate; the lower part of the cord is formed by visceral efferent cells, below which are somatic efferent cells. Axons from the medulla extend for varying distances along the cord. For example, in anurans, fibers from C.Nn. IX and X extend to the second and third spinal segments, from C.N. VIII to the sixth segment, and from C.N. V to the seventh segment. In salamanders, fibers of Mauthner cells extend from the medulla throughout the length of the spinal cord.

The spinal cord is uniform in size anterior to the sacrum except for the slight brachial and lumbar enlargements in the regions of the brachial and sciatic plexuses in anurans and salamanders. Postsacrally, the spinal cord diminishes in size in salamanders. In anurans, the cord terminates as such at the level of the sixth spinal nerve; succeeding nerves extend independently in the neural canal, and a slight, median cord terminates in the coccyx.

Spinal Nerves. Each body segment is supplied with a pair of spinal nerves. In anurans, each nerve exits the spinal cord intervertebrally, except the tenth and eleventh (if present) which exit via foramina in the coccyx. Vertebal fusion in some anurans (e.g., pipids and bufonids) results in the nerves exiting via foramina in the fused vertebrae. In caecilians, the nerves exit via foramina in the anterior vertebrae (vertebrae 1–3 in *Typhlonectes* to 1–20 in *Ichthyophis*) (M. Wake, 1980c). The first spinal nerve always exits through a foramen in the first vertebra of salamanders, but the exits of the nerves in other vertebrae are variable (Edwards, 1976). In some salamanders (e.g., hynobiids), all other spinal nerves exit intervertebrally, whereas in plethodontids all nerves exit through foramen in the vertebrae, and members of some other families are intermediate—some nerves are intravertebral and others are intervertebral.

With the exception of the first spinal nerve (S.N. 1), which has no dorsal root in adults (dorsal root and ganglion atrophy at metamorphosis), all spinal nerves have a dorsal root with a large dorsal root ganglion and a ventral root which fuses with the dorsal root just peripheral to the ganglion. At this point the small dorsal branch of the spinal nerve passes dorsally to innervate the skin and muscles of the dorsal trunk (also, dorsal lymph sacs in anurans). The large ventral branch of each spinal nerve innervates ventral and lateral skin and muscles of the body and the limbs. A ramus communicans extends from each ventral branch to the sympathetic nerve cord.

The number of body segments, and therefore the number of vertebrae is highly variable in amphibians. Most anurans have only 10 pairs of spinal nerves, although more than 20 are present in tadpoles; all but 1 or 2 postsacral pairs atrophy during the absorption of the tail at metamorphosis. A small nerve, the occipital nerve, anterior to S.N. 1 is uncommon in anurans and salamanders, but in caecilians it has dorsal and ventral

branches, as well as an anastomosis with the hypoglossal (C.N. XII). In all three groups, S.N. 1 innervates neck musculature, and the hypoglossal fibers (C.N. XII) innervate the tongue muscles.

Spinal nerves in the thoracic region are interconnected to form the brachial plexus. In *Salamandra,* the plexus is formed primarily by S.Nn. 3 and 4 with some contributions from S.Nn. 2 and 5. S.N. 2 in salamanders primarily innervates muscles of the pectoral girdle, but a branch connects with S.N. 3. Prior to this fusion, S.N. 3 gives off the ramus supracoracoideus which innervates pectoral muscles. S.N. 3 receives a branch from S.N. 4 and becomes the extensor nerve, which bifurcates into two branches that innervate the extensor muscles of the forelimb. S.N. 4 has branches to thoracic muscles and to the m. rectus abdominis. After receiving a branch from S.N. 3, S.N. 4 gives off a branch to the m. pectoralis. Subsequently there is a fine branch from S.N. 5, after which the main branch of S.N. 4 enters the ventral part of the forelimb as the brachial nerve to innervate the flexor muscles.

The arrangement of nerves forming the brachial plexus is different in anurans. In *Rana,* the plexus is formed by S.Nn. 2 and 3, which have a connecting ramus; both nerves have branches to muscles of the pectoral girdle. The brachial nerve supplying the flexor muscles of the forelimb is derived from S.N. 2, and the extensors of the forelimb are innervated by S.N. 3. Thus, in the course of shortening the trunk region, a rearrangement of spinal nerves has occurred, with S.N. 2 in anurans assuming the brachial nerve that is a branch of S.N. 4 in salamanders.

Numerous experiments have shown that during development peripheral nerves will develop in transplanted limb buds (see Saxen and Toivonen, 1962, for review). For example, Detwiler (1927) showed that in salamander larvae a primordium transplanted to a more posterior portion of the body became innervated by the segment of the spinal cord juxtaposed to the transplant.

The sciatic or crural plexus of nerves that innervate the hindlimb is formed in the vicinity of the sacral vertebra in salamanders. In *Salamandra,* which has 16 presacral vertebrae, the plexus is formed by S.Nn. 16 and 17 with a contribution from S.N. 15. The latter has an obturator branch to the m. puboischiofemoralis, an iliohypogastric branch to the muscles of the lateral and ventral body wall, and a branch which anastomoses with S.N. 16. After receiving this branch, S.N. 16 gives off a branch to S.N. 17 and becomes the femoral nerve which innervates the extensor muscles of the hindlimb. S.N. 17 exits from the sacral vertebra and after receiving the branch from S.N. 16 becomes the sciatic nerve which innervates the flexor muscles of the hindlimb. Small rami of S.Nn. 14 and 18 also make contributions to the sciatic plexus.

Three spinal nerves form the sciatic plexus in anurans. In *Rana,* these are S.N. 7 which exits between Presacrals VII and VIII, S.N. 8 which exits between Presacral VIII and the sacrum, and S.N. 9 which exits between the sacrum and the coccyx. S.N. 7 gives off an iliohypogastric branch to muscles of the lateral and ventral body wall; thus, it seems to be homologous with S.N. 15 in *Salamandra*. S.Nn. 7–9 extend posterior under the m. iliococcygeus to the base of the hindlimb, where they form the sciatic plexus. S.Nn. 7 and 8 fuse, and this bundle anastomoses with S.N. 9, which receives a branch from S.N. 10. Just after the fusion of S.Nn. 7 and 8, the cruralis nerve branches off and enters the hindlimb to innervate the extensor muscles. The main branch from the plexus is the sciatic nerve, which with its many branches innervates the flexor muscles of the hindlimb.

Brachial and sciatic plexuses are absent in caecilians.

The ventral branches of the spinal nerves between the brachial and sciatic plexuses are rather uniform; each gives off branches to the lateral and ventral musculature and to the skin. The same general pattern exists throughout the length of the body in caecilians and in the tail of salamanders. In anurans, S.N. 10 fuses with a branch of S.N. 9 to form an ischiococcygeal plexus, from which nerves pass to the bladder, cloaca, oviducts, and posterior lymphatic hearts. In primitive anurans, S.N. 11 anastomoses with the ischicoccygeal plexus.

Autonomic Nervous System

The autonomic nervous system is essentially the same in the three living orders of amphibians. Detailed descriptions of the system are given by Gaupp (1896) for *Rana esculenta* and by Francis (1934) for *Salamandra salamandra*. A brief description of the system in caecilians is provided by H. Norris and Hughes (1918).

The autonomic part of the peripheral nervous system innervates smooth muscles and glands; it has its own set of ganglia separate from the central nervous system but connected with it by communicating rami. Unlike the peripheral nerves of the central nervous system, motor neurons do not extend from the central nervous system to the innervated organs. Instead, the neurons terminate in peripheral ganglia where they synapse with the dendrites or cell bodies of the peripheral neurons that continue to the organs.

The autonomic nervous system consists of two parts—sympathetic and parasympathetic. Neurons of the sympathetic system leave the central nervous system via spinal nerves. A pair of sympathetic trunks ventrolateral to the vertebral column receive neurons from the central nervous system via communicating rami to sympathetic ganglia along this trunk; numerous communicating fibers exist between the two trunks. Synapses of the preganglionic and peripheral neurons occur in these ganglia. Small nerves leave the sympathetic trunk and follow major arteries to the visceral organs. These nerves tend to form intricate plexuses, such as the solar plexus formed by branches from Sympathetic Ganglia III–V and supplying the stomach and adjacent parts of the alimentary canal.

Neurons of the parasympathetic system leave the central nervous system via cranial nerves. Rami extend from the Gasserian ganglion of C.N. V and the glossopharyngeal-vagus ganglion of C.Nn. IX and X to the first sympathetic ganglion. A separate branch of C.N. X, the laryngeus ventralis (= pneumogastric), innervates smooth muscles in the lungs, heart, and stomach.

Sympathetic and parasympathetic fibers are carried in the same nerves, as are sensory fibers from the viscera to the central nervous system. The impulses of the sympathetic and parasympathetic fibers are antagonistic in their effects. For example, sympathetic impulses act to halt peristalsis in the gut, to tighten the sphincters in the gut, and to increase the rate of heartbeat; parasympathetic impulses have the opposite effects.

Interrelationships of Components

The complexities of the nervous system are becoming better understood through electrophysiological, developmental, and behavioral studies (see Llinás and Precht, 1976, for review). The reception of external stimuli has been discussed in the previous sections: Integument; Sense Organs. Reception of stimuli involves pathways from the cranial or spinal nerves to correlation centers in the brain, which respond via motor pathways to the peripheral system. Both sensory and motor pathways of the brain arise from, and terminate on, a limited set of neurons in the spinal cord. These spinal neurons form the basic reflex arcs and are the only elements other than cranial nerves that transmit sensory information to the brain. Furthermore, the efferent pathways of the brain can affect organs of the body only via these spinal elements.

The pathways in the brain are numerous and complex; they are discussed in detail by Nieuwenhuys and Opdam (1976), Scalia (1976a, 1976b), and Sotelo (1976).

CIRCULATORY AND RESPIRATORY SYSTEMS

The transportation of oxygen and metabolic products through the body is dependent on an effective system of ion binding, a pumping mechanism, and an efficient vascular system. These are the blood, heart, and the blood and lymph vessels, respectively. In contrast to other vertebrates, amphibians have diverse modes of respiration—pulmonary, branchial, or buccopharyngeal. Each of these modes involves different vascular systems to provide effective transport of oxygen from and carbon dioxide to the respiratory surfaces. Consequently, the circulatory and respiratory systems are discussed together.

Blood

The blood of amphibians is composed of plasma containing erythrocytes, leucocytes, and thrombocytes. Except for the erythrocytes, the other constituents are capable of passing out of the blood vessels into the lymphatic system. A thorough account of the structural and physiological properties of the blood in amphibians by Foxon

(1964) is summarized here. In adults, hematopoiesis takes place mainly in the spleen, but in anurans erythrocytes also are formed in the marrow of the long bones at metamorphosis and upon emergence from hibernation. Granular leucocytes are formed in the liver in some adult salamanders and in the kidneys in proteids. Considerable differences exist in sites of hematopoiesis, as do physiological properties of the blood, between larvae and adults (see Chapter 7).

The red blood cells, erythrocytes, typically are nucleated and elliptical. There is a great range in size, and amphibians have the largest known erythrocytes. The greatest length is 40–70 qm in obligate neotenic salamanders; the largest are in *Amphiuma* (erythrocytes are larger in larvae than in metamorphosed amphibians). In anurans the length is 17.7–26.5 qm. Enucleated erythrocytes (erythroplastids) are rare in anurans, but as many as 5% of the erythrocytes are enucleated in plethodontid salamanders, and erythroplastids make up 95% of the total in *Batrachoseps attenuatus* (Emmel, 1924).

Counts of erythrocytes are roughly proportional to the size of the cells. In *Amphiuma means* the erythrocytes are 70 qm in length, and there are about 30,000/mm³, whereas comparable figures for some other species are: *Proteus anguinus* 58 qm, 36,000/mm³; *Necturus maculosus* 54 qm, 51,000/mm³; *Rana catesbeiana* 25.5 qm, 460,000/mm³; and *Hyla versicolor* 20.7 qm, 900,000/mm³ (Szarski and G. Czopek, 1966).

Distinct biochemical differences exist between hemoglobins in larvae and those in adults (see Chapter 7:

Other Biochemical Changes). Hemoglobins in metamorphosed amphibians have a lower affinity for oxygen than larval hemoglobins, but they release oxygen more readily at the oxygen tensions that prevail in the tissues of terrestrial adults.

The white cells are made up of agranular leucocytes (lymphocytes and monocytes) and granular leucocytes (basophils, neutrophils, and eosinophils). Normally all of these cells are nucleated, but enucleated cells occur in salamanders. The ratio of leucocytes to erythrocytes is 1:20–70. The size of leucocytes is relatively constant at a length of 30–32 qm. Foxon (1964) noted that comparative counts of the number of granular and agranular leucocytes is known for only a few species; he listed *Bombina variegata* as having 25% granular and 75% agranular leucocytes, and *Salamandra atra* as having 65% granular and 35% agranular leucocytes.

Thrombocytes or spindle cells typically are nucleated, but enucleated cells (thromboplastids) have been reported in some species of salamanders. These cells presumably function like the platelets in mammals.

Heart and Aortic Arches

The structure and function of the heart have been discussed in detail by J. Simons (1959), Foxon (1964), and Kumar (1975). Usually the heart of amphibians has been described as being composed of three chambers—two atria and one ventricle. However, a septum dividing the ventricle into right and left chambers is known in some salamanders (*Siren* and *Necturus*) (J. Putnam and J. Dunn,

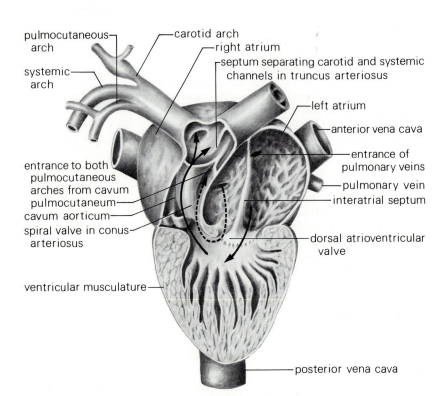

Figure 14-17. Ventral view of the heart of an anuran, *Rana catesbeiana*, partly sectioned in the frontal plane to show internal structure. The circulatory pathway of oxygenated blood is indicated by solid arrows and that of deoxygenated blood by broken arrows. Adapted from W. Walker (1967).

1978), and some caecilians (e.g., *Ichthyophis* and *Hypogeophis*) have extensive trabeculae in the ventricle (Ramaswami, 1944; Lawson, 1966).

Although the hearts of the three living orders of amphibians are similar in gross morphology (Fig. 14-17), there are differences in relative proportions and in the internal structure. In most salamanders and anurans the left atrium is much smaller than the right, but in some anurans (e.g., *Xenopus*) the two atria are about equal in size. In caecilians the right atrium is much smaller than the left. Anurans have a complete interatrial septum, and the septum is fenestrated in caecilians and all salamanders except *Siren*. In plethodontid salamanders the atrial division consists of a membranous septum and a sino-atrial valve (J. Putnam and D. L. Kelly, 1978). The sinus venosus is divided into right and left portions by indentations of the wall of the sinus or by a pair of transverse valves in caecilians, and by constrictions of the inner wall in anurans; there is no division of the sinus venosus in salamanders. A sinoventricular fold is present in salamanders but not in caecilians or anurans.

A conus arteriosus receives blood from the left atrium and becomes the median truncus arteriosus. Within the conus is the spiral valve which is absent in at least some plethodontid salamanders (Nel, 1970). The aortic arches divide from the truncus arteriosus. The truncus is short in salamanders, exceedingly short in anurans, and greatly elongate in caecilians. The aortic arches of adults are derived from the visceral arches (V.A.) of larvae; the first two visceral arches are lost. Only some salamanders have a full complement of aortic arches as adults. The carotid arch (V.A. III) delivers blood to the head. The systemic arch (V.A. IV) delivers blood to the body, including parts of the head but excluding the pharynx and lungs (and to a varying extent the skin). The third arch (V.A. V) is separate proximally but becomes confluent with the systemic arch in *Salamandra* and with the pulmonary arch in *Necturus;* it is small and not connected to other arches in *Cryptobranchus* and *Amphiuma,* and it is absent in adult plethodontids (J. Putnam and Sebastian, 1977). The pulmonary arch (V.A. VI) supplies the lungs and the walls of the pharynx; cutaneous branches also supply skin, but this branch is reduced or absent in plethodontid salamanders. Only three arches persist in anurans; the third arch is absent.

Elongation of the body and reduction of the left lung have resulted in some major modifications of the aortic arches of caecilians. Only two arches persist; the third is absent, and the carotid and systemic are fused. Usually two systemic-carotid arches and two pulmonary arteries arise from the long truncus arteriosus. After the divergence of the carotid arteries, the systemic arteries extend posteriorly to merge into the median dorsal aorta in most caecilians (Fig. 14-18). In others (e.g., *Dermophis*) the two systemic arteries unite anterior to the heart to form the dorsal aorta. Asymmetrical reduction of the arches is known in some genera. For example, only the right sys-

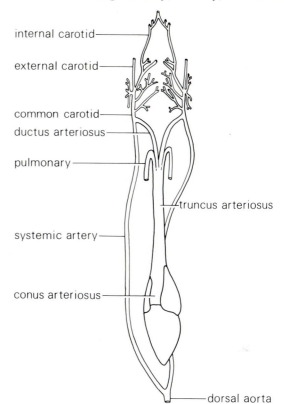

Figure 14-18. Ventral view of the heart and principal arteries in the anterior part of the body in a caecilian, *Ichthyophis glutinosus.* Redrawn from P. Sarasin and F. Sarasin (1887–90).

temic arch persists in *Herpele* and *Chthonerpeton* and only the left in *Hypogeophis.* In some caecilians, such as *Ichthyophis,* the right pulmonary artery is larger than the left. In *Gegeneophis* the left pulmonary artery is absent; the small left lung is supplied by a branch from the right pulmonary artery.

The tissues of the heart obtain nutrients and oxygen from the blood passing through the organ. In addition, caecilians have a network of coronary veins covering the ventricle; blood in these veins is derived from the cavity of the ventricle and passes into the sinus venosus. Foxon (1964) suggested that these veins supply the muscular wall of the ventricle and that this system of coronary veins argues for a mixing of oxygenated and deoxygenated blood in the ventricle.

Major modifications of the aortic arches take place during metamorphosis with the change from branchial to pulmonary or cutaneous respiration; these changes are more dramatic in the lungless plethodontid salamanders and far less noticeable in the perennibranchiate neotenic salamanders (Fig. 14-19). In larvae, the carotid arch supplies the internal gills; it and the systemic and third arches also supply the external gills. In crytobranchid and proteid salamanders a carotid duct exists between the affer-

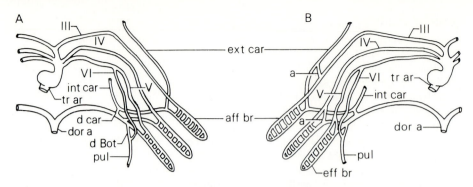

Figure 14-19. Metamorphic changes in branchial circulation in *Desmognathus fuscus*. **A.** Young larva, ventral view of left side. **B.** Early metamorphic stage, ventral view of right side. The aortic arches are identified by their visceral arch numbers; III, IV, V, and VI are carotid, systemic, third, and pulmonary arches, respectively. Abbreviations: a = anastomoses (one for each branchial arch), aff br = afferent branchial artery, d Bot = ductus Botalli, d car = ductus caroticus, dor a = dorsal aorta, eff br = efferent branchial artery, ext car = external carotid artery, int car = internal carotid artery, pul = pulmonary artery, tr ar = truncus arteriosus. For the adult condition in salamanders, see Figures 14-20 and 14-21. Adapted from McMullen (1938).

ent branches of the carotid and systemic arches. The pulmonary arch does not enter a gill, but it may be connected to the third arch by a duct (ductus Botalli). This duct is variably present in salamanders; it is present in cryptobranchids, present or reduced in salamandrids and ambystomatids, and absent in proteids and plethodontids (McMullen, 1938). During metamorphosis, anastomoses form between the efferent and afferent branches of each branchial arch; as the gills are resorbed, the anastomoses take over the entire blood flow.

In amphibians blood leaves the single ventricle by routes which may lead to the head, body, skin, or lungs (except in the lungless plethodontid salamanders). Blood returning from the head, body, and skin enters the left atrium via the sinus venosus, and that from the lungs enters the left atrium via the pulmonary vein (Fig. 14-17). The skin is an important respiratory surface in many amphibians, but blood that has been oxygenated there is mixed with blood from the body in the right atrium. Thus, as emphasized by Foxon (1964), the circulatory arrangement in amphibians may be expected to show marked specialization correlated with their peculiar respiratory methods.

The detailed description of cardiac respiration of *Rana temporaria* provided by J. Simons (1959) shows that little mixing takes place as blood passes from the atria to the ventricle. The destination of any particular blood corpuscle on leaving the ventricle is determined largely by its position in the ventricle. Thus, blood from the left side of the ventricle passes up one side of the spiral valve in the conus arteriosus into the carotid arteries and the right systemic arch; simultaneously, blood from the right side of the ventricle passes mainly up the other side of the spiral valve and into the left systemic arch. During the early part of ventricular systole, a stream of blood flows over the spiral valve from the cavum aorticum into the cavum pulmocutaneum and on into the left systemic arch;

thus, some oxygenated blood goes into that arch. The slight differences in pressure among the aortic arches are insufficient to regulate the flow of blood from the ventricle.

The foregoing account of the flow of blood in the heart and aortic arches may be typical of terrestrial anurans, but a different pattern is evident in the aquatic *Xenopus*, which relies more on pulmonary than on cutaneous respiration (De Graaf, 1957). In *Xenopus* blood returning from the lungs passes to all parts of the ventricle. Upon ventricular contraction, the blood is distributed to carotid, systemic, and pulmocutaneous arches. Despite this apparent mixing in the ventricle, most blood returning to the right atrium passes into the pulmocutaneous artery, which has a much lower diastolic pressure than the carotid and systemic arteries.

Studies on cardiac circulation in salamanders have provided conflicting interpretations. Segregation of oxygenated and deoxygenated blood takes place in *Amphiuma tridactylum*, but no differential distribution occurs in *Salamandra salamandra* or *Triturus cristatus* (Foxon, 1964). Differential distribution may be especially important in aquatic salamanders (e.g., *Amphiuma* and *Siren*) living in poorly oxygenated water, and presence of a ventricular septum in *Siren* (also a complete interatrial septum) and in *Necturus* indicates that differential distribution may be complete in those salamanders. The presence of a sinoatrial valve that controls blood flow between the atria seems to be associated with the loss of the pulmonary vein in plethodontid salamanders.

No experimental data are available on cardiac circulation in caecilians, but on the basis of morphology it seems most likely that mixing of oxygenated and deoxygenated blood takes place in the ventricle. However, the extensive ventricular trabeculae may function in partial segregation of the blood as it is pumped out of the ventricle.

Vascular System

The arrangement of arteries and veins has been described for *Rana esculenta* by Gaupp (1896), *Xenopus laevis* by Millard (1941), and *Salamandra salamandra* by Francis (1934); some general patterns in caecilians were given by Wiedersheim (1879). Obviously, only gross differences and similarities in the vascular systems of the three orders can be addressed here; furthermore, with the exception of the components of the aortic arches, little is known about the variation in the pattern of vessels within groups. For example, Millard (1941) pointed out differences in the vessels in the pelvic region between *X. laevis* and *R. esculenta,* and Szarski (1948) noted numerous interspecific differences in the vessels of the facial and pelvic regions among anurans. The presence of adequate descriptions of only a few species is complicated further by a duplicity of names and inadequate knowledge of homologies. Consequently, the following commentary is very general and is intended only to serve as an introduction to the major aspects of the vascular system.

Arteries.   As noted in the preceding discussion of the heart and aortic arches, profound differences exist in the number and arrangement of the aortic arches. The arteries are discussed in relation to the aortic arches from which they are derived (Fig. 14-20).

Carotid system.—The left and right common carotids originate from their corresponding systemic-carotid arches in caecilians, or from the persisting arch in those taxa in which one of the arches has been lost. The common carotids originate from their corresponding arches in salamanders and primitive anurans (leiopelmatids, discoglossids, and pipids); both carotid arteries originate in association with the left systemic arch in other anurans. Immediately before the divergence of the internal and external carotid arteries there is an enlargement of the common carotid in anurans and salamanders. This enlargement, the so-called carotid gland, contains a membranous labyrinth and apparently functions to divert blood into the external carotid artery which diverges at an obtuse angle from the common carotid. No carotid gland exists in caecilians, in all of which the two carotid arteries diverge in an anterior direction.

The external carotid artery delivers blood to the muscles of the tongue and the floor of the mouth via four major branches: (1) muscular artery to the mm. rectus cervicis and interhyoideus posterior, (2) thyroid artery to the thyroid gland, (3) sublingual artery to the the tip of the snout where branches go to the tongue and the m. geniohyoideus, and (4) lingual artery to the tongue.

The internal carotid artery supplies the upper jaw and cranium, which it enters by way of the carotid canal and the basicranial fenestra. The major branches are: (1) cerebral artery with many branches supplying the chorioid plexuses of the brain, (2) lateral pretrosal (= stapedial) artery to the ear with branches to the eye-lids (temporal artery) and to the roof of the mouth (mandibular artery), and (3) ophthalmic artery. The latter exits the cranium via the oculomotor foramen; branches supply the eye, the eye muscles, and the eyelids. An anterior branch of the ophthalmic anastomoses with a branch of the occipital (= palatonasal) artery and enters the nasal capsule.

Systemic system.—The systemic arches extend anterodorsally and then posteromedially to unite in the dorsal aorta; this unification is anterior to the heart in salamanders and usually just posterior to the heart in anurans. Several arteries diverge before the arches meet to form the dorsal aorta. The cutaneous artery supplies the thymus and parotoid region. In salamanders the pharyngeal artery supplies the jaw muscles and the hyoid muscles; the mandibular branch supplies the lower jaw. In most anurans these structures are supplied by the auricular branch of the cutaneus magnus artery which originates from the pulmonary arch. The occipital-vertebral artery in anurans divides into an occipital artery that extends anteriorly into the head and the vertebral artery that bifurcates and extends posteriorly on either side of the vertebral column. The occipital is the same as the palatonasal in salamanders, in which it and the vertebral artery have separate origins from the systemic arch. The occipital has several branches: (1) pharyngeal to walls of the pharynx, (2) pterygoid to the roof of the mouth, (3) maxillopalatine to the roof of the mouth and posterior region of the maxilla, and (4) anterior and posterior palatines to the palate. A final branch of the occipital artery is the orbitonasal, which passes below the eye muscles in salamanders and dorsal to those muscles in anurans. The orbitonasal has three nasal branches to the nasal capsule, two maxillary branches to the upper jaw, and an anterior orbital branch which anastomoses with a branch of the ophthalmic branch of the internal carotid artery. Posteriorly, the vertebral arteries have numerous small branches to the dorsal trunk musculature and to the skin on the dorsum.

The arteries supplying the organs in the coelom normally all emerge from the dorsal aorta. The large coeliaco-mesenteric artery originates just posterior to the confluence of the systemic arches; however, it emerges from the left systemic arch in most anurans but from the dorsal aorta in leiopelmatids, discoglossids, and pipids. This artery has many branches that have been given diverse names and seem to be variable in their arrangement; the terminology of Francis (1934) is followed here. The three major branches are: (1) gastrico-linealis to the spleen and dorsal wall of the stomach, (2) duodeno-hepatic with many branches to the liver, duodenum, ventral wall of stomach, and gall bladder, and (3) duodeno-pancreatic to the pancreas and duodenum. Four to eight (in *Salamandra*) anterior mesenteric arteries originate from the dorsal aorta and supply the distal part of the small intestine, and three posterior mesenteric arteries deliver blood to the large intestine.

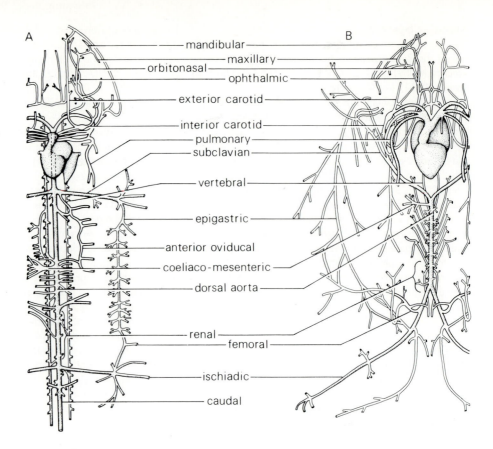

A

B

mandibular
maxillary
orbitonasal
ophthalmic
exterior carotid
interior carotid
pulmonary
subclavian
vertebral
epigastric
anterior oviducal
coeliaco-mesenteric
dorsal aorta
renal
femoral
ischiadic
caudal

Figure 14-20. Semidiagrammatic ventral views of the arterial system in amphibians. **A.** *Salamandra salamandra,* left side (adapted from Francis, 1934). **B.** *Xenopus laevis,* right side (adapted from Millard, 1941). Only major vessels are labeled.

The arteries supplying the urogenital system consist of numerous small vessels to the gonads, oviducts, and kidneys. Each kidney is supplied by numerous, short renal arteries from the dorsal aorta to its dorsal surface, whereas its ventral surface is supplied by the superficial renal artery which emerges from the posterior oviducal artery just posterior to the kidney. Three oviducal arteries deliver blood to the anterior, middle, and posterior parts of the oviduct. The mesial and posterior oviducal arteries originate from the dorsal aorta, whereas the anterior one emerges from the dorsal aorta, subclavian artery, or vertebral artery. The oviducal arteries are smaller in males in which they supply the Müllerian ducts. Four or five ovarian (or spermatic) arteries diverge from each side of the dorsal aorta and carry blood to the gonads and fat bodies.

A large subclavian artery branches off from each systemic arch in anurans or from either side of the dorsal aorta just posterior to the heart in salamanders. Numerous small branches deliver blood to the muscles of the shoulder region, and a major branch, the brachial artery, supplies the forelimb. The epigastric artery branches off at the point of origin of the brachial artery in salamanders; it supplies the ventral pectoral region and the ventral body wall. In anurans this artery is part of the pulmo-

cutaneous system. In both groups it continues posteriorly to connect with the femoral artery.

The arrangement of arteries in the pelvic region and hindlimb differs from the pattern in salamanders. The dorsal aorta bifurcates to form a pair of common iliac arteries in anurans, whereas a trifurcation includes a caudal artery in salamanders. After giving off the femoral artery, which has an anastomosis with the epigastric artery, the common iliac continues on as the ischiadic artery. This is the major vessel entering the hindlimb; posterior and ventral thigh muscles are supplied by a major branch, the cutaneus femoral artery.

Pulmocutaneous system.—In caecilians and salamanders (except plethodontids) the pulmonary arches curve posterolaterally from the truncus arteriosus to enter the lungs. Along this short route, dorsal and ventral esophageal arteries emerge and pass anteriorly to deliver blood to the floor of the mouth, pharynx, and esophagus before the major vessel, the pulmonary artery, turns to enter the lungs. In lungless plethodontid salamanders in which the pulmonary arch is present, the pulmonary artery supplies the skin of the neck and dorsum and in some species it anastomoses with the epigastric artery. The pulmonary arch in anurans is much more important in delivering blood to the skin. The main vessel, the pul-

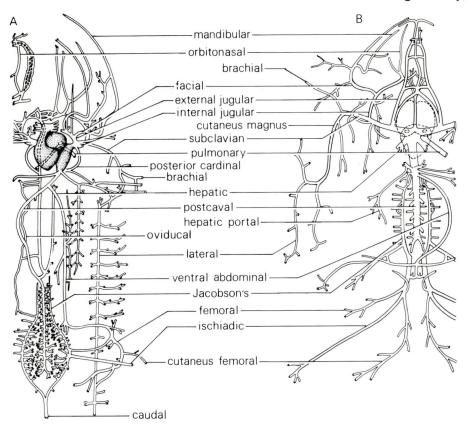

A
mandibular
orbitonasal
brachial
facial
external jugular
internal jugular
cutaneus magnus
subclavian
pulmonary
posterior cardinal
brachial
hepatic
postcaval
hepatic portal
oviducal
lateral
ventral abdominal
Jacobson's
femoral
ischiadic
cutaneus femoral
caudal

B

Figure 14-21. Semidiagrammatic ventral views of the venous system in amphibians. **A.** *Salamandra salamandra*, left side (adapted from Francis, 1934). **B.** *Xenopus laevis*, right side with position of heart outlined (adapted from Millard, 1945). Only major vessels are labeled.

monary artery, delivers blood to the heart, but the large cutaneus magnus artery originates from the pulmocutaneous arch and supplies the skin of the dorsal and lateral body wall; a branch of the cutaneus magnus, the auricular artery, supplies the jaw muscles, hyoid muscles, and tissues of the lower jaw.

Veins. The venous system is more variable, especially peripherally, than the arterial system. A major difference exists among the living orders with respect to the receptacle of the systemic veins, the sinus venosus, from which blood passes into the right atrium via the sinoatrial opening on the dorsal side of the atrium. The sinus venosus is transversely elliptical in caecilians; the left portion is separated from the slightly smaller right portion by an internal indentation of the walls or by transversely situated valves. The sinus in salamanders is approximately triangular and is situated to the left of the midline; it is the same shape but medial in position in anurans.

Systemic veins.—The veins that enter the sinus venosus from all regions of the body are grouped into this category. The sinus venosus receives three major veins, the postcaval which enters the posterior part of the sinus, and the paired precaval veins (ducts of Cuvier) which enter the lateral corners of the sinus. The left precaval is

exceedingly short because the juncture of the veins on the left side is adjacent to the sinus venosus; on the other hand, the right precaval extends across the dorsal surface of the heart to the dextral corner of the sinistrally offset sinus venosus.

Three major veins, the internal and external jugulars and the subclavian, enter the precaval vein (Fig. 14-21). A postcardinal vein is present in larvae and in adults of caecilians, salamanders, and leiopelmatid and discoglossid frogs. The internal jugular receives many veins draining the palate, brain, and the orbital, nasal, and auditory regions; the vertebral vein collects blood from the muscles of the neck and drains into the internal jugular. The external jugular vein with its major confluents (facial, lingual, and thyroid veins) collects blood from the muscles of the head and tongue and the thyroid gland. The subclavian vein collects blood from the forelimb via the brachial veins, from the muscles and skin of the trunk via the anterior epigastric and lateral veins; the anterior part of the latter also is known as the cutaneus magnus vein. The postcardinal veins (when present) originate as a single vessel from the posterior part of the postcaval vein; shortly after the origin a bifurcation results in the two postcardinals that pass anteriorly on either side of the dorsal aorta to enter the precaval veins. The postcardinals provide an alternate route for blood from the region of the kidneys to the sinus venosus.

The postcaval originates near the posterior end of the kidneys by the fusion of a large renal vein from each kidney. The postcaval receives various vessels from the kidneys and gonads and passes through the liver to the sinus venosus. In anurans, right and left branches of the hepatic vein from corresponding lobes of the liver coalesce before entering the postcaval vein.

Hepatic-portal system.—A major vessel, the ventral abdominal vein, is formed by the coalescence of veins in the pelvic region. The pelvic veins fuse to form the ventral abdominal in anurans, but in salamanders the coalescence also includes the median cloacal and posterior vesicle veins from the cloaca and bladder, respectively. The ventral abdominal vein passes forward along the ventral midline and thence through the liver to the postcaval. In the region of the liver it receives vesicles from the gall bladder and the portal vein with branches from the stomach and intestines.

Renal-portal system.—The veins of the hindlimb combine (also with the caudal vein in salamanders) to form the paired Jacobson's veins which pass anteriorly on the dorsolateral surface of the kidney, from which they receive many small vesicles. Jacobson's vein also receives blood from the oviducal vein and then passes anteriorly to enter the postcaval vein.

There are distinct differences in the veins of the pelvic region and hindlimb among anurans and between anurans and salamanders. For example, in *Salamandra* and *Xenopus* the major vessel from the hindlimb is the ischiadic vein, whereas the femoral vein is the major vessel in *Rana*. Also, there are differences in the anastomoses of the femoral and Jacobson's veins.

Pulmonary system.—The pulmonary veins arise from the mesial surfaces of the lungs, fuse near the midline, and enter the left atrium. A few small vesicles are received from the esophagus.

Lymphatic System

A third series of vessels, the lymphatics, extends throughout the body of amphibians; these vessels collect blood (exclusive of erythrocytes) that seeps through the walls of the capillaries and return it to the veins. The intestinal lymphatics also collect fats, which are not absorbed by the capillaries entering the veins.

The lymphatic system of *Salamandra* was described by Francis (1934), who noted the fine subcutaneous network of vesicles, especially laterally on the body and the lymphatic sinuses in the head and at the bases of the limbs. The subcutaneous lymphatics in salamanders empty into the postcardinal veins or various cutaneous vessels. The visceral lymphatics parallel the digestive tract and empty into the subclavian veins. Lymph is pumped through the system by a series of contractile vesicles, the lymph hearts. In *Salamandra* there are 15 pairs of lateral hearts— 4 postsacrally and 11 presacrally. Associated with the

lymph hearts are valves that restrict a unidirectional flow of lymph in the vessels. Lymph is received in the hearts from the cutaneous network and from branches from the subvertebral vessels that collect lymph from the body cavity. A central lymph heart associated with the truncus arteriosus receives lymph from the head and neck and delivers it to the lingual vein.

Caecilians differ from salamanders by having more than 200 lymph hearts situated intersegmentally under the skin (H. Marcus, 1908); these hearts pump lymph into intersegmental veins.

Anurans have few lymph hearts; an anterior pair is located beneath the scapulae, and one to five posterior pairs are situated along the coccyx. Anurans differ from other amphibians by having extensive subcutaneous lymph spaces. These are separated by fine septa and are most extensive in aquatic anurans. The spaces store water absorbed from the environment. Carter (1979) proposed that excess water is excreted by the posterior lymph hearts pumping water from the lymph spaces into the renal portal vein and thence to the kidney.

Respiratory System

Amphibians have diverse modes of respiration. Larvae have gills that are the primary respiratory structures, but cutaneous respiration also takes place (see Chapter 6). Most postmetamorphic amphibians have lungs; these and the buccopharyngeal surfaces are the internal respiratory structures; however, considerable gas exchange takes place cutaneously in terrestrial amphibians (see Chapter 8). Herein the structures associated with buccopharyngeal and pulmonary respiration are discussed.

Nares. The nostrils (external nares) and the narial duct are intimately associated with the olfactory system (see earlier section: Sensory Receptor Systems). The narial duct opens into the buccal cavity via the choana (internal naris). The nares are closed by means of smooth muscles in salamanders and caecilians; in anurans the nares are closed by an upward swelling of the m. submentalis (Gans and Pyles, 1983).

Buccopharyngeal Cavity. The mouth and pharynx are lined with mucoid and ciliated epithelium that is highly vascularized. In the floor of the pharynx is a longitudinal slitlike aperture, the glottis, which leads to the larynx. The glottis is bounded by the arytenoid cartilages, and the glottis is opened and closed by the mm. dilatator laryngis and constrictor laryngis, respectively.

Larynx. The larynx is a narrowly triangular chamber; an elongated posterior tube, the trachea, is present in salamanders, caecilians, and pipid frogs. The larynx is supported by a series of semicircular cartilages, the so-called lateral cartilages. The anterior pair is modified as the arytenoid cartilages, which support the glottis and are an integral part of the sound-production system in anurans (see Chapter 4). The second pair, the cricoid cartilage, forms a complete ring in most adult amphibians. A ventral evagination forms a tracheal lung in some caecilians (*Typhlonectes compressicauda* and *Uraeotyphlus oxyurus);* in these caecilians the ciliated tracheal mucosa is replaced by respiratory epithelium and the walls of the tracheal lung are infiltrated by cartilage and served by the tracheal artery. In salamanders, caecilians, and pipid frogs, the trachea bifurcates posteriorly into the bronchi, paired short tubes with ciliated epithelium leading into the lungs; bronchial tubes are absent in other anurans.

Lungs. Basically the lungs are paired organs. Although they are variable in size (small in *Ascaphus*) and especially large in some aquatic taxa (e.g., pipids and *Telmatobius*), paired lungs are invariably present in anurans. In pipids the lungs are reinforced by cartilage. Most salamanders (including the obligate neotenes) have well-developed, paired lungs, but in some taxa that inhabit mountain streams (e.g., *Salamandrina* and *Rhyacotriton*) the lungs are greatly reduced in size. Lungs are absent in all plethodontid salamanders. The lungs of caecilians are extremely elongate; the right and left lungs are approximately equal in length in some caecilians (e.g., *Typhlonectes* and *Ichthyophis monochrous*). In most caecilians the left lung is reduced, in some to about 10% of the length of the right lung, and the left lung is absent in *Uraeotyphlus narayani* (Baer, 1937).

Structurally, the lungs of terrestrial salamanders are conical sacs, more or less pointed posteriorly. The pulmonary membrane is folded to form internal septa, and each lung has two longitudinal compartments, one containing the pulmonary artery and the other the pulmonary vein. The septa are highly vascularized and covered with a thin epithelium except along their inner edges where ciliated and mucous cells cover the sheaths of smooth muscle. In obligate neotenic salamanders and some aquatic salamandrids (e.g., *Notophthalmus* and *Triturus*) the lungs have few septa and are comparatively poorly vascularized. In caecilians the elongate lung is infiltrated by cartilage; the inner surface is divided by a network of blood vessels, connective tissue, and smooth muscle which form alveoli. The lungs of terrestrial anurans are short but similar in structure except that they lack cartilage (except pipids) and the septa form more and smaller chambers.

In aquatic amphibians (especially obligate neotenic salamanders, some adult newts, pipid frogs, and possibly typhlonectid caecilians) the lungs seem to function more as hydrostatic organs than as respiratory organs. Some of these aquatic salamanders (e.g., *Cryptobranchus, Amphiuma,* and *Triturus*) breathe air through the nares, but *Siren* and *Necturus* take air in through the mouth (Atz, 1952), as pipid frogs do commonly.

Breathing. Observations and experiments on salamanders and anurans by Willem (1924), on a caecilian (*Siphonops annulatus*) by Mendes (1945), and sophis-

ticated experiments by De Jongh and Gans (1969) on *Rana catesbeiana* have demostrated that all amphibians studied breathe by means of a force-pump mechanism. Action of the throat musculature elevates and depresses the floor of the buccal cavity; this is analogous to the piston of the pump. When the nostrils are open and the buccal floor is depressed, air is drawn into the buccal cavity; closure of the nostrils and elevation of the buccal floor concomitant with the opening of the glottis forces air into the lungs. The cycle is reversed by the depression of the buccal floor while the glottis is open and the nares are closed; air is drawn out of the lungs into the buccal cavity. Subsequent closure of the glottis and opening of the nares combined with elevation of the buccal floor forces air out of the mouth. This mechanism is modified during vocalization in anurans (see Chapter 4).

Pulmonary respiration and buccopharyngeal respiration are complemented by cutaneous respiration in most terrestrial amphibians, and by cutaneous and branchial respiration in many aquatic amphibians. The differential rates of gas exchange are dependent on the degree of capillarity of the different respiratory surfaces as well as temperature and moisture of the skin. These functional aspects of respiration are discussed in Chapter 8.

UROGENITAL SYSTEM

The excretory and reproductive systems are closely associated in amphibians, as they are in all vertebrates, although these structures originate from different embryonic tissues (see Chapter 7). The urogenital system of salamanders was described in detail by Francis (1934), who based his work on *Salamandra salamandra.* Bhaduri (1953) and Bhaduri and Basu (1957) provided comparative descriptions of the system in anurans. The comparative morphology of the system in caecilians was described in detail by M. Wake (1968, 1970a, 1970b, 1972), and early development was treated by Fox (1963).

In this section the morphology of adults is described (Fig. 14-22). The ontogeny of the urogenital structures is covered in Chapter 7. The production of sperm and ova is discussed in relation to sexual cycles in Chapter 2, and kidney function is discussed in relation to water and ion balance in Chapter 8.

Kidneys

The kidneys in adult amphibians are paired structures lying on either side of the dorsal aorta. They develop from larval nephrostomes. In caecilians, anterior and posterior nephrostomes persist in the formation of the kidney; thus, caecilians have an opisthonephric kidney, in which some evidence of segmentation is retained in adults. The anterior part of the larval kidney (pronephros) is lost in adult anurans and salamanders; only the middle and posterior nephrostomes persist in adults, which therefore have a mesonephric kidney (Fig. 7-3).

The gross morphology of the kidneys differs in the

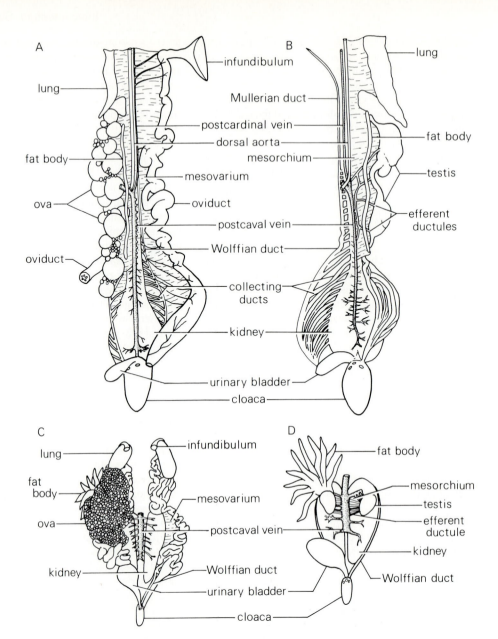

Figure 14-22. Ventral views of urogenital structures in salamanders and anurans. **A.** *Salamandra salamandra*, female. **B.** Same, male. **C.** *Rana catesbeiana*, female. **D.** Same, male. Some structures have been omitted from one side of each drawing. A and B adapted from Francis (1934); C and D adapted from W. Walker (1967).

three living orders of amphibians. The kidneys are long and slender in caecilians, in which they extend from the region of the heart nearly to the cloaca. In hynobiid and cryptobranchid salamanders, the kidneys also are elongate and there is no obvious sexual dimorphism in shape. In other salamanders the kidneys are proportionately shorter, and those in males are narrow anteriorly. The kidneys in anurans vary from long and slender, six to eight times as long as broad (e.g., *Ascaphus, Heleophryne,* and *Dendrobates*) to only about three to four times as long as broad (most anurans).

The kidney is highly vascularized from numerous renal arteries from the dorsal aorta which branch to form innumerable clusters of capillaries or glomeruli. Each glo-

merulus is surrounded by an expanded end of a kidney tubule; this structure, Bowman's capsule, is the major site of filtration. The kidney tubules extend laterally through a capillary network and carry urine to the Wolffian duct. The capillary network is made up of vessels derived from the renal portal vein, which enters the posterior end of the kidney; blood leaves the kidney via the renal portal vein to the postcava. In males, the anterior kidney tubules usually receive the efferent tubules from the testes. The kidney tubules and glomeruli are essentially uniform in size throughout the length of the kidney in both sexes in caecilians, whereas in males of many salamanders and anurans the anterior nephric units are modified in that functional glomeruli and distal tubules are absent. In these males the tubules in the anterior part of the kidney function solely for sperm transport.

Gonads

Testes. The paired testes are attached to the kidneys by a membrane, the mesorchium, which supports the efferent ductules from the testes to the kidneys. The testes increase in size during the breeding season, and in some species of anurans they become pigmented. In anurans the testes usually are spheroid or ovoid structures that are ventral to the anterior half of the kidneys, but in some species the testes are much larger, especially in length, and extend nearly to the posterior end of the kidneys. The testes in anurans are not lobed as they are in many salamanders, in at least some of which lobes are added with successive annual breeding cycles (see Chapter 2). The testes in caecilians are greatly elongate and lobed; the lobes are connected by a longitudinal duct. The number of lobes varies from 11 to 20 in species of *Ichthyophis* to only one in *Idiocranium russeli* and some individuals of *Dermophis mexicanus* (M. Wake, 1968). In some species of caecilians the anterior lobes are largest; in others the posterior lobes are largest; and in still others the lobes are more or less uniform in size.

Spermatogenesis occurs in locules in the testes, and sperm are transported through collecting ducts into a longitudinal duct in the testes and then to the kidney via efferent ductules (vas efferentia). A longitudinal testicular duct is absent in some salamanders. The efferent ductules join nephric collecting tubules which empty into the Wolffian duct. The number of efferent ductules is highly variable and usually is correlated with the size of the testis and the number of lobes. For example, in caecilians there are usually 1 to 5 ductules per lobe, but some large anterior lobes may have more than 5 ductules. Salamanders and anurans usually have 4 to 12 ductules associated with each testis, but only 2 are present in proteid salamanders and discoglossid frogs (Noble, 1931b). Although sperm usually are transported to the cloaca in the Wolffian duct, the nephric collecting tubules pass directly into the cloaca in some primitive salamanders (Noble, 1931b). For example, in both sexes of *Andrias japonicus* and in male *Hynobius lichenatus* the collecting tubules empty independently into the cloaca; in female *H. lichenatus* some of the tubules enter into the cloaca and others into the Wolffian duct, whereas in male *Onychodactylus* some tubules form a common duct to the cloaca and others empty into the Wolffian duct.

In larval bufonids, the anterior end of each developing gonad has a growth of ovarian tissue. This is retained in adult male bufonids as the Bidder's organ, which may be a peripheral or lateral band or an anterior cap on the testis (Fig. 14-23).

Ovaries. The paired ovaries are suspended by a membrane, the mesovarium, from the mesial side of the kidneys. The ovary consists of a thin sheath of connective tissue, the ovisac, enclosing the ovarian follicles. Ovarian development is discussed in Chapter 2. Rupture of the ovisac releases the ripe ova into the coelom. The epithelium of the coelom is ciliated, and ciliary action moves the eggs anteriorly to the opening of the oviduct.

Urogenital Ducts

In addition to the kidney tubules and efferent ductules from the testes, two major longitudinal ducts are present in the urogenital system. The Wolffian duct originating on the lateral edge of the kidney carries urine (and in males, sperm) to the cloaca. Normally, each Wolffian duct enters the cloaca separately in salamanders, caecilians, and most anurans. However, the ducts unite and enter the cloaca through a single aperture in diverse kinds of anurans (e.g., *Eleutherodactylus, Heleophryne, Pachymedusa, Kassina,* and many species of *Bufo*). Sexual dimorphism in the fusion of the ducts was noted by Bhaduri (1953), who also noted the formation of a urogenital sinus upon fusion of the ducts in *Ascaphus truei* and *Rhinophrynus dorsalis.*

In some anurans the lower part of the Wolffian duct is expanded into a seminal vesicle; according to Bhaduri (1953) and Bhaduri and Basu (1957), the seminal vesicle may be seasonal in appearance. The portion of the Wolffian duct adjacent to the kidney is enlarged and has a glandular epithelium in species of *Rhacophorus, Polypedates,* and *Chiromantis* that have been examined. Bhaduri (1932) suggested that the glandular epithelium provided secretions that were used in the construction of arboreal or terrestrial foam nests (see Chapter 5). Iwasawa and Michibata (1972) found that sperm were stored in the coiled glandular part of the duct adjacent to the kidney in species of *Rhacophorus* that constructed foam nests.

The oviducts lie parallel and lateral to the kidneys; they are nearly straight in caecilians, slightly convoluted in salamanders, and greatly convoluted in anurans. The opening of the oviduct, the infundibulum (= ostium), is cil-

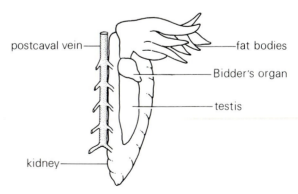

Figure 14-23. Ventral view of the left urogenital system of a male *Bufo woodhousii* showing the position of Bidder's organ.

iated and located in the vicinity of the lung. The walls of the oviduct contain a smooth muscle layer in a circular pattern of fibrous and elastic tissue. The lumen is lined with ciliated epithelium. During gestation in viviparous caecilians and anurans, the epithelial cells secrete substances that nourish the fetuses (see Chapter 2). Also, secretory glands in the lower part of the duct in oviparous species secrete mucoids that form the egg capsules (see Chapter 7).

Homologues of the oviducts, the Müllerian ducts, persist in males of a few species of anurans, but they apparently have no function. These ducts are comparatively well developed in male caecilians, in which the posterior part of each duct has glandular epithelium, the secretions of which apparently aid in sperm transport for internal fertilization (M. Wake,1981; see Chapter 3).

Urinary Bladder

The urinary bladder is a ventral outgrowth of the cloaca. Its single opening into the cloaca is controlled by a sphincter. The lining of the bladder consists of smooth epithelium separated by a submucosal layer from longitudinal smooth muscle. The latter lies inside bands of circular muscle. These muscle layers allow for the great distension of the bladder when it is filled with urine.

The bladder is cylindrical or bicornuate in salamanders, slightly bilobate in other salamanders and some anurans, and usually deeply bilobate in caecilians, a group in which the proportional sizes of the lobes is sexually dimorphic in some species. Other modifications of the bladder in caecilians, such as the degree of mesenteric attachment and presence of a m. rector cloacae, seem to be associated with the presence of a phallodeum and internal fertilization (M. Wake, 1970b).

Cloaca

The cloaca is the common receptacle for the alimentary canal, Wolffian ducts, oviducts, and the bladder. The alimentary canal enters the cloaca anteriorly, the bladder ventrally, and the ducts dorsally. A sphincter surrounds the external opening of the cloaca. Urogenital papillae are associated with the openings of the ducts in some species of caecilians and salamanders. The cloaca is a relatively simple structure in anurans and primitive salamanders. The lining of the cloaca is composed of ciliated, columnar epithelium, except cilia are lacking in pouches present in some caecilians. A submucosal layer is made up of fibrous connective tissue and is bounded by a layer of circular muscle and an outer layer of longitudinal muscle which is continuous with that of the intestine.

In contrast to the rather simple condition in anurans and primitive salamanders, the cloaca in those salamanders having internal fertilization is modified by the presence of sets of glands that are sexually dimorphic in structure and function; also, the cloaca in caecilians is sexually dimorphic in that a portion of the cloaca in males is eversible as a phallodeum. The structure and function of these glands and the associated structures are dealt with in the discussion of internal fertilization given in Chapter 3.

Fat Bodies

Fat bodies associated with the gonads are characteristic of all amphibians. In salamanders the fat bodies are in the form of longitudinal strips between the gonads and the kidneys. In anurans the fat bodies are in the form of many fingerlike projections aggregated at the anterior end of the gonads; the bodies are larger and more pointed in males than in females. Caecilians usually have numerous leaflike fat bodies that extend in a series on each side of the body from the liver to the cloaca. The fat bodies of anurans and caecilians are suspended from the body wall by a dorsal mesentery which is fused with the gonadal mesentery (mesovarium or mesorchium). The fat bodies in salamanders are suspended from the gonadal mesenteries. Fat bodies are composed of typical adipose tissue consisting of large cells, each with an oil vacuole. A thin, fibrous connective tissue surrounds each fat body; the individual coats of connective tissue fuse with the mesentery.

According to Noble (1931b), fat bodies are a source of nutrients for the gonads. The bodies are largest just before hibernation and smallest just after breeding.

DIGESTIVE SYSTEM

The alimentary canal and associated organs of amphibians commonly are the first aspects of internal anatomy viewed by students of biology. A general account of the digestive system in amphibians was given by Noble (1931b), and good descriptions of the system are available for *Rana esculenta* (Gaupp, 1896), *Salamandra salamandra* (Francis, 1934), and *Necturus maculosus* (I. Olsen, 1977). A comprehensive account of the microstructure and functional aspects of the system was provided by Reeder (1964). The larval gut and changes during metamorphosis are discussed in Chapter 7.

Structure

The basic structure of the system is fundamentally similar in all three groups of living amphibians, except that the organs are more compressed anteroposteriorly in anurans than they are in salamanders and they are attenuate in caecilians (Fig. 14-24).

Buccal Cavity. The mouth contains the teeth (absent in some anurans), tongue (absent in pipid frogs), and glands. The role of the teeth and tongue in obtaining food is discussed in Chapter 12. The buccal cavity is lined with oral mucosa variously elaborated as unicellular and multicellular glands. Nonsecretory areas of the palate, buccal floor, and walls of the pharynx are lined with ciliated epithelium.

Multicellular buccal glands are present in most am-

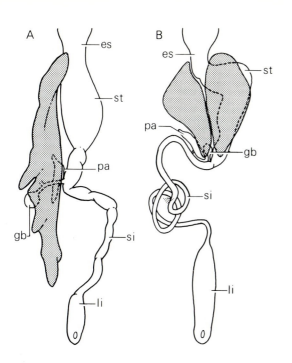

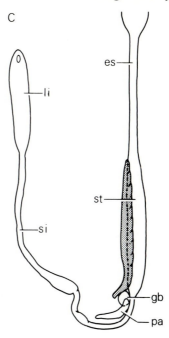

Figure 14-24. Semidiagrammatic ventral views of the digestive organs of amphibians. **A.** Salamander, *Necturus maculosus*. **B.** Anuran, *Rana catesbeiana*. **C.** Caecilian, *Siphonops annulatus*. Abbreviations: es = esophagus, gb = gall bladder, li = large intestine, pa = pancreas, si = small intestine, st = stomach. The liver is shaded.

phibians, but they are absent in some aquatic taxa. Presumably their absence in pipid frogs represents a loss of this feature, whereas their absence in some obligate neotenic salamanders (*Amphiuma, Siren*) seems to represent arrested development; buccal glands are absent in larval salamanders.

The intermaxillary gland is formed of alveoli or tubules within tissues between (and also posterior to) the nasal capsules; the collecting ducts open to the anterior palatal surface. In caecilians, the alveolar organs open separately, anterior and medial to the choanae. In salamanders and anurans, the glandular region is more extensive, and in anurans it extends nearly to the corner of the mouth. Furthermore, in anurans the secretory tubules form a single glandular system secreting fluid from a compact series of openings in the midline of the palatal surface. The secretion is sticky and when applied to the tongue seems to serve in the entrapment of prey.

Choanal glands in the palatal epithelium empty into the choanae. The glands are large in anurans and sometimes nearly occlude the lumen of the choanal canal. The choanal glands of caecilians open at the margin of the choanae, whereas those of salamanders open deep within the choanae at the margin of the olfactory epithelium.

Two main kinds of taste buds (gustatory organs) are present in the buccal cavity in anurans (C. Jaeger and D. Hillman, 1976). These include papillary organs on the apices of fungiform papillae on the dorsal surface of the tongue and nonpapillary organs imbedded in the ciliated epithelium throughout much of the buccal cavity and on the lateral surface of the tongue. Six types of cells in papillary organs are grouped into two classes— secretory and receptor cells. The latter extend throughout the disc-

like organs. Apically the receptor cells contain elaborate systems of intracellular membranes, and proximally the cells are in contact with afferent nerve fibers.

The pharynx is an expanded chamber lined with ciliated and mucus-secreting epithelium that lies posterior to the buccal cavity. A muscular sphincter separates the pharynx from the esophagus, and muscular actions open and close the glottis, the entryway to the lungs.

Esophagus.   The esophagus is a thin-walled tube extending from the pharynx to the stomach. It is a short structure that is broad in cross section in anurans, somewhat longer in salamanders, and long and slender in caecilians. At each end of the esophagus is a circular band of muscle that forms a sphincter. The lining of the esophagus is in six to eight longitudinal folds. The mucosal epithelium consists of cuboidal or columnar ciliated cells (cilia absent in *Proteus*) with interspersed goblet cells; the latter are most abundant anteriorly. Generally, four muscle layers are present. The innermost mucosal layer is represented by minute bundles of longitudinal smooth muscle, but this is reduced in some salamanders (single fibers in proteids and essentially absent in *Triturus*). This layer and the adjacent submucosal layer become better organized and developed near the stomach. The muscular tunic is composed of a well-developed layer of circular smooth muscle fibers. An outer layer of longitudinal fibers (when present) is sparse anteriorly and more robust posteriorly.

Glands in the mucosal lining secrete mucus and proliferate pepsinogen. The glands of the latter type are concentrated posteriorly and are absent in some salamanders (e.g., *Salamandra*) and anurans (e.g., *Bombina* and *Pipa*).

Stomach. The stomach usually lies to the left of the midline and is curved with the convex edge to the left. The stomach is broader, shorter, and more curved in anurans than in salamanders and caecilians. The mucosal layer consists of unciliated epithelium with many slender, spindle-shaped mucogenic cells, especially in the anterior three-fourths of the organ. The muscular layers consist of an inner, strong layer of circular muscle and a thinner, outer layer of longitudinal fibers. The posterior (pyloric) end of the stomach is separated from the duodenal portion of the small intestine by a distinct circular band of muscles, the pyloric sphincter.

Intestines. The intestine in amphibians is nearly uniform in diameter throughout its length, except for a broader, straight portion posteriorly, the large intestine. The intestine is nearly straight in caecilians, only slightly folded in salamanders, and more elongate (proportionately) and folded in anurans. The muscular layers of both large and small intestines are like those of the stomach.

The anterior portion of the small intestine, the duodenum, receives the bile and pancreatic ducts. The mucosa of the intestine is folded in interspecifically different patterns, all of which greatly increase the surface area of the canal. Surface area is increased further by myriads of tiny projections, microvilli. The epithelial surface is formed primarily by columnar cells interspersed with mucoid goblet cells. Elaborate multicellular digestive glands are unknown except in a few salamanders (e.g., *Salamandra*).

The large intestine is separated from the small intestine by a flaplike valve in some anurans; the valve is absent in salamanders, caecilians, and primitive anurans. The mucosal lining is composed of columnar epithelium interspersed with goblet cells, which become more numerous posteriorly. The terminal part of the tract is the cloaca, which receives ducts from the reproductive system and the urinary bladder. In salamanders in which fertilization is internal, the roof of the cloaca is modified into a spermatheca in females, and the walls contain modified mucous glands in males (see Chapter 3).

Associated Glands. Two glandular outgrowths of the embryonic midgut are the liver and pancreas. The liver is bilobate in anurans, elongate and sometimes emarginate in salamanders, and greatly elongate and slightly emarginate in caecilians. The gall bladder is attached to the liver and empties into the duodenum via the bile duct. The pancreas is enclosed in the hepato-gastric ligament and lies between the duodenum and the stomach. A single pancreatic duct leads to the duodenum in anurans; 2 or more ducts are present in caecilians and salamanders (up to 47 in *Proteus*). Differences exist in the mode of entrance of the pancreatic duct to the duodenum in anurans. Observations on European anurans by Dornesco et al. (1965) showed that the duct opens to the bile duct in the wall of the intestine in *Bombina* and *Pelobates* or in

its immediate vicinity in *Bufo* and *Hyla*, whereas the pancreatic duct joins the bile duct before the common duct leaves the pancreas in *Rana*.

Digestive Process

The realization of nutrients is a suite of complicated processes beginning with the capture of prey and terminating with the absorption of hydrolyzed components. Prey capture and nutritive values of prey are discussed in Chapter 9.

Passage of Food. Movement of the food through the digestive tract is by means of muscular and ciliary action. Food is forced from the mouth into the esophagus primarily by the swallowing action of the tongue; small fragments are moved by action of buccal and pharyngeal cilia. Food moves down the esophagus by peristaltic muscular contractions. It is held in the esophagus until the muscles of the sphincter at the gastric end relax and allow passage into the stomach, the anterior portion (fundus) of which is primarily a storage chamber. Slight muscle contractions in the wall of the stomach push the food into the pyloric end of the stomach. Passage of food from the stomach into the duodenum is controlled by the small intestine, where intermittent contractions of the muscular wall move the contents posteriorly in the lumen. Strong contractions of the stomach and concomitant relaxation of the sphincters at both ends of the esophagus permit regurgitation of the contents of the stomach. Mucus secreted by goblet cells in the pharynx, esophagus, and small intestine lubricates the food, thus permitting ease of passage through the alimentary canal and preventing mechanical damage to the lumen by sharp particles of chitin. Mucus secreted in the posterior part of the large intestine coats large concentrations of the contents for defecation.

Digestion. Ingested food is fragmented partially by the teeth in most amphibians. Consequently, the exterior surface, especially the chitin of insects, is subjected to mechanical breakdown which allows the entry of digestive enzymes into the soft tissues of the prey.

Digestive enzymes generally are considered to be absent in the buccal secretions, but low concentrations of diastatic amylase have been reported in the secretions of the intermaxillary, lingual, and pharyngeal glands in some European species of *Pelobates, Bufo,* and *Rana* (Reeder, 1964).

Pepsinogen and mucus secreted in the esophagus accrete around the food mass, but little or no mixture of secretions with the food takes place before the food reaches the stomach. The buccal and esophageal mucus, which is alkaline, prohibits proteolytic digestion before gastric acidification. Hydrochloric acid is secreted in the stomach. The acidic storage chamber inhibits bacterial activity, hastens the death of still-living prey, and begins the decalcification of bone. In the low pH of the pyloris, pepsinogen is transformed to pepsin, which attacks proteins.

Digestion is completed in the small intestine, in which the contents of the lumen are mixed with a variety of digestive enzymes by intermittent contractions of the muscular wall. Mucoid secretions in the duodenum neutralize the acidic material received from the stomach. Erepsin secreted by glands in the small intestine hydrolyzes peptones and proteases to amino acids. Secretin from the duodenal mucosa stimulates the release of pancreatic juices.

Bile salts from the gall bladder break down fats. Other digestive enzymes in the small intestine are secreted by the pancreas. Of these, trypsin hydrolyzes protein; amylase is active in the hydrolysis of glycogen and starches to simple sugars; and lipase facilitates hydrolysis of fats and glycerides to fatty acids and glycerol. No amphibians are known to possess enzymes that facilitate the breakdown of keratin, chitin, or cellulose.

Absorption.   Absorption commences in the small intestine, where nutrients are absorbed by the extensive capillary system in the walls of the intestine. Absorption of water and salts takes place in the large intestine.

ENDOCRINE GLANDS

The regulation and coordination of various organs is manifested either by electrochemical impulses transmitted by nervous tissue or by complex chemical substances, hormones, carried by the vascular system. Hormones are produced by the endocrine glands. Amphibians have all of the endocrine glands that are known in other tetrapods, and with few exceptions it seems that the endocrine secretions of amphibians resemble those of other vertebrates.

In this section the structure and function of the endocrine glands are described, and the sources and actions of their products are discussed. A summary of the endocrine glands and their products in amphibians is by Gorbman (1964). Much information on amphibians is included in texts on endocrinology, especially by C. Turner and Bagnara (1976), and a recent thorough account of the hormonal control of amphibian metamorphosis is provided by A. White and Nicoll (1981). The hormones produced by endocrine glands, their targets, and their actions are summarized in Table 14-2.

Pituitary

The pituitary is closely associated with the ventral surface of the diencephalon. It develops from a union of the distal end of a saclike diverticulum from the floor of the diencephalon called the infundibulum and a solid ectodermal dorsal protrusion from the buccal cavity. The infundibular part of the gland, the neurohypophysis, consists of two regions, the pars nervosa and the median eminence (Fig. 14-25). The part derived from the buccal protuberance, the adenohypophysis, consists of three regions—the median pars intermedia and pars distalis, and the bilateral pars tuberalis, which is absent in some salamanders.

Bilateral hypothalamo-hypophyseal neurosecretory fiber tracts extend posteriorly from the paired preoptic nuclei in the ventral wall of the hypothalamus. Some of these tracts terminate in the median eminence and others extend to the pars nervosa; some fibers terminate in the pars intermedia in *Triturus cristatus* and in some species of *Rana*. Blood is supplied to the neurohypophysis by the hypophyseal artery, and hypophyseal portal vessels extend from the median eminence into the pars distalis.

The functional capacity of the entire pituitary is dependent on its nervous and vascular association with the hypothalamus. These connections are responsible for the control of pituitary secretions in response to both exterior and endogenous stimuli integrated in the brain. The adenohypophysis is under neurosecretory regulation manifested by means of nerve fibers of the hypothalamo-hypophyseal tract or the hypophyseal portal vessels. The pituitary is an essential link in the neuroendocrine system, even though all of its secretions are controlled directly or indirectly by the brain.

The pars distalis produces five hormones. Two gonadotropic hormones (follicle-stimulating hormone and luteinizing hormone) are released cyclically in response to exterior stimuli mediated in the brain. Their effects on the gonads and the feedback mechanism are discussed in Chapter 2. Prolactin has a variety of effects (Bern and Nicoll, 1969): (1) stimulation of the water-drive and integumentary changes in efts of *Notophthalmus viridescens,* (2) secretion of oviducal jelly, (3) proliferation of melanophores, and (4) stimulation of larval growth (see Chapter 7). Thyrotropin stimulates the secretion of thyroxin, and adrenocorticotropin acts on the cortical cells of the adrenal glands to promote the output of adrenal steroids.

The pars intermedia secretes melanophore-stimulating hormone (intermedin, MSH) which affects integumentary chromatophores; MSH causes dispersal of melanosomes in melanophores and pigmentary organelles in xanthophores, and causes the aggregation of reflecting platelets in iridophores.

Neurohypophyseal hormones from the pars nervosa are important in regulating water loss and salt balance (see Chapter 8). Antidiuretic hormone (ADH) primarily causes an increase in the rate of reabsorption in the tubules of the kidney; secondarily it causes a decrease in the rate of glomerular filtration. Arginine vasotocin and the less effective oxytocin act on the skin and membranes of the urinary bladder and kidney tubules to increase passive permeability to water, salts, and urea and to stimulate active transport of sodium.

Thyroid

The thyroid glands are paired structures in the throat. The glands develop as a median growth from the ventral wall of the pharynx and then separate and move pos-

Table 14-2. Endocrine Glands, Their Hormones, Target Areas, and Actions

Gland/hormone	Target area	Action
Pituitary: pars distalis		
Follicle-stimulating hormone (FSH)	Germinal epithelium	Stimulates maturation of ovarian follicles
Luteinizing hormone (LH)	Testicular interstitial tissue	Stimulates production of testosterone
Prolactin	Lower oviducts	Production of oviducal jelly
	Integument	Glandular changes
	Integument	Proliferation of melanosomes
	Caudal and gill tissues	Growth
Thyrotropin (thyroid-stimulating hormone, TSH)	Thyroid	Stimulates thyroid secretions
Adrenocorticotropin (ACTH)	Adrenal cortex	Promotes output of adrenal steroids
Pituitary: pars intermedia		
Melanophore-stimulating hormone (MSH)	Integument	Color change
Pituitary: pars nervosa		
Antidiuretic hormone (ADH)	Kidneys	Concentration of urine
Arginine vasotocin	Skin, kidneys, urinary bladder	Increases permeability to water and salts
Oxytocin	Skin, kidneys, urinary bladder	Increases permeability to water and salts
Thyroid		
Thyroid hormones	Various tissues	Metamorphosis (see Table 7-2)
Parathyroids		
Calcitonin	Bones and kidneys	Metabolism of bone and minerals
Parathyroid hormone (PTH)	Bones and kidneys	Metabolism of bone and minerals
Ultimobranchial bodies		
Calcitonin	Bones and kidneys	Metabolism of bone and minerals
Thymus		
Thymosin	Lymphopoietic sites	Stimulates production of lymphocytes
Pineal body		
Melatonin	Integument	Aggregation of melanosomes
Pancreatic islets		
Insulin	Liver, muscles, adipose tissue	Facilitates assimilation of sugar
Adrenal: medulla		
Adrenalin	Cardiovascular system	Increases heart rate; vasodilation
	Skeletal muscle	Increases blood flow
	Liver and brain	Increases blood flow
	Kidneys	Decreases blood flow
Noradrenalin	Cardiovascular system	Increases heart rate; vasoconstriction
	Kidneys	Decreases blood flow
Adrenal: interrenal		
Corticosteroids	Intestine and skeletal muscles	Metamorphosis
Gonads: testes		
Testosterone	Germinal epithelium	Promotes spermatogenesis
	Integument	Development of secondary sex characteristics
Gonads: ovaries		
Estrogen	Germinal epithelium	Formation of primary follicles
Progesterone	Ovarian follicle cells	Initiates maturation of postvitellogenic ova

terolaterally to a point on the dorsal surface of the m. sternohyoideus in anurans. The glands are situated more laterally in salamanders and caecilians. Accessory thyroid follicles occur in the throat musculature. Each gland consists of a series of closed follicles innervated by the hypoglossal (C.N. XII). The glands are supplied by the thyroid branch of the external carotid artery and drained by the thyroid vein which carries blood to the external jugular vein.

The thyroid hormones, tetraiodothyronine (thyroxin,

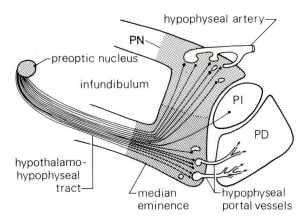

Figure 14-25. Diagrammatic sagittal section of the hypophyseal region of a frog, *Rana temporaria,* showing the relative positions of the components of the pituitary gland and the associated neurosecretory tracts. The parts of the pituitary are: PD = pars distalis, PI = pars intermedia, PN = pars nervosa. Adapted from Dierickx and van den Abeele (1959).

T_4) and triiodothyronine (T_3), have profound effects on morphological and functional changes during metamorphosis (see Chapter 9). Thyroid hormones in postmetamorphic amphibians have been implicated in (1) oxidative and other metabolism, (2) integumentary structure, and (3) nervous function. However, the experimental results in all of these areas are inconclusive (Gorbman, 1964).

Parathyroids

The parathyroids are small, spherical, encapsulated glands closely associated with the external jugular veins. The two pairs of glands arise from ventral growths of the third and fourth pharyngeal pouches. Parathyroids are absent in at least some obligate neotenic salamanders (e.g., *Necturus maculosus*). The activity of the glands seems to be seasonal at least in temperate species of anurans, in which the glands degenerate in winter.

The parathyroids secrete calcitonin and parathyroid hormone (PTH); both hormones are important in calcium metabolism (Bentley, 1984). Many species of amphibians seem to utilize PTH as a hypercalcemic hormone; the calcium stores in the bones and paravertebral "lime sacs" apparently are the primary sites for the effects of this hormone. Furthermore, PTH promotes the activation of vitamin D_3 to 1,25-dihydroxycholecaliferol, which also has a hypercalcemic effect resulting in increased absorption of calcium from the intestine and renal glomerular filtrate and enhanced resorption of calcium from bone. On the other hand, calcitonin has a hypocalcemic effect on body fluids because it is antagonistic to the resorptive process from bone and possibly enhances excretion of calcium in the urine.

Ultimobranchial Bodies

These small glands originate as epithelial growths from the sixth pharyngeal pouch. The glands are paired in adults and lie next to the larynx in anurans (absent in *Xenopus*) and caecilians. Only the gland on the left side persists in most salamanders, but in obligate neotenes such as *Amphiuma* and *Necturus* the glands are paired. The ultimobranchial bodies produce calcitonin (or a calcitonin-like substance) which affects metabolism of minerals. These glands are especially active during metamorphosis (see Chapter 7).

Thymus

The thymus gland originates as several paired thickenings on the dorsal side of the pharyngeal pouches. The first six pouches produce thymus buds in caecilians; the first and sixth buds are lost, and the others fuse into a single gland on each side. In salamanders the buds are associated with the first five pouches, but the first two are lost; this results in a trilobate gland on each side. In some anurans, buds originate only from the first and second pouches, and the first is lost (Noble, 1931b). In all adult amphibians the glands are located beneath the skin on either side of the throat. Secretions of the thymus gland, collectively known as thymosin, play major roles in immunity by stimulating lymphopoiesis (E. Cooper, 1976).

Pineal Body

The pineal body is a median outgrowth of the thalamus on the dorsal surface of the brain. This structure is sensitive to light, and prolonged darkness stimulates the release of melatonin, a hormone which aggregates melanosomes in melanophores in the skin, thereby resulting in a lightening of the color of the skin. Melatonin also may promote the release of prolactin by the pars distalis of the pituitary during larval development (Gutierrez et al., 1984).

Pancreatic Islets

In addition to secreting digestive enzymes, the pancreas contains masses of cells referred to as the Islets of Langerhans. These glands develop from pancreatic ducts in larvae and become functional at metamorphosis. The islets secrete insulin which is transported by the hepatic portal vein. Insulin is essential for carbohydrate metabolism by facilitating the assimilation of sugar by tissues.

Adrenals

The adrenal glands are composed of tissues of separate origins. Chromaffin cells are neuroectodermal, and the cortical (= steroidogenic) and Stilling cells are mesodermal. The chromaffin cells constitute the medullary part of the gland, whereas the cortical and Stilling cells form the interrenal portion; the latter is considered to be a separate gland by some workers. The function of Stilling cells is unknown. The adrenals are elongate structures on the ventromesial surface of each kidney in caecilians and salamanders. They are proportionately shorter structures on the midventral surface of each kidney in most anurans; are ventromesial in leiopelmatids, discoglossids, and pipids; medial in *Pelobates;* and lateral to the mid-section of the kidney in more advanced anurans (Grassi Milano and Accordi, 1983).

Two catecholamines are secreted by the chromaffin cells in the adrenal medulla. The principal hormone is adrenalin (= epinephrine) which chiefly affects the cardiovascular system and blood flow through the brain, liver, kidneys, and skeletal muscle (Table 14-2), as well as increases the rate of metabolism of blood sugars. The second hormone, noradrenalin (= norepinephrine), functions in much the same way as adrenalin, but the effects of the latter usually are much stronger than that of noradrenalin. The two hormones are antagonists in the vascular system in that adrenalin is a vasodilatator, whereas noradrenalin generally is a vasoconstrictor. Adrenalin also can cause melanosome aggregation in integumentary melanophores and increases in the activity of integumentary glands in anurans.

Adrenal cortical (= interrenal) secretions that have been identified are steroids—aldosterone, corticosterone, and cortisol; the circulating levels of these hormones change during metamorphosis, and they have been implicated in morphological changes occurring at metamorphosis (see Chapter 7).

The activity of the adrenal glands is controlled primarily by levels of the pituitary hormone adrenocorticotropin (ACTH) in the blood; ACTH stimulates adrenal activity.

Gonads

The development and structure of the gonads have been described in the foregoing section: Urogenital System. Although the gonads are primarily reproductive organs, they produce and secrete hormones that are important in the endogenous control of reproductive cycles and the development of secondary sex characters. The endocrine activity of the gonads is controlled by the pituitary gonadotropins. Luteinizing hormone influences the production of the male androgen, testosterone, in the interstitial cells of the testes. Testosterone facilitates spermatogenesis and promotes the development of secondary sex characters such as nuptial excrescences (see Chapter 3). The ovarian follicles produce estrogen which promotes the proliferation of the germinal epithelium in the ovary and the formation of primary follicles, but the maturation of the follicles depends on follicle-stimulating hormone from the pituitary. In at least one species, the viviparous anuran *Nectophrynoides occidentalis,* progesterone is secreted by the corpora lutea (see Chapter 2).

EVOLUTIONARY CONSIDERATIONS

It is commonly stated that amphibians are morphologically intermediate between fishes and amniotes. This is generally true for the gross morphology of the nervous, digestive, and urogenital systems. However, other systems are specialized and have characters that are unique to the amphibians. This is particularly true of the integument and the circulatory and respiratory systems which act in concert to provide an effective means of cutaneous respiration. The various combinations of branchial, pulmonary, and cutaneous respiration are unique to amphibians.

The integumentary stucture of amphibians is related not only to respiration but also to water balance. The rich supply of cutaneous capillaries is important in water and ion diffusion as well as gas exchange; these subjects are discussed at length in Chapter 8. The integument also contains the poison glands; these release combinations of toxins that are unique to amphibians and that are important in protection from predators (see Chapter 10).

The eyes of amphibians represent the first evolutionary step in vertebrate terrestrial vision, with powers of accommodation and generally with eyelids and associated glands and ducts. Depth perception and true color vision are present. Green rods in the retina are unique to amphibians and allow them to perceive a diverse range of wavelengths.

The auditory apparatus is uniquely amphibian, especially with the presence of papilla amphibiorum and a columellar-opercular complex, which, depending on the degree of modification of the component systems, allows for the effective reception or airborne and/or seismic signals.

Although the class Amphibia is characterized by a suite of features of the internal anatomy, each of the three living orders has certain characters that are different from the others. Salamanders are the most generalized, whereas anurans seem to have numerous derived characters. Caecilians have many specializations associated with their attenuate body form (e.g., reduced left lung, asymmetrical reduction of aortic arches) and fossorial existence (e.g., sensory tentacle, reduced eyes).

It is tempting to utilize some of the features of the internal systems in phylogenetic reconstruction. For example, caecilians, salamanders, and leiopelmatid frogs share the apparently primitive states of a simple patch of papilla amphibiorum and kinocilia of the auditory epithelium lacking terminal bulbs, whereas other anurans have an elongate patch of papilla amphibiorum and bulbed kinocilia. Likewise, the position of the adrenal gland in the presumed primitive families of anurans (leiopelmatids, discoglossids, pipids) is like that of salamanders and caecilians on the ventromesial side of the kidney, whereas in more advanced anurans the position of the gland is shifted laterally.

A major problem exists in the use of many of these features of soft anatomy in drawing phylogenetic conclusions. In contrast to osteological characters, the details of the internal organ systems are known for very few taxa, and there is virtually no knowledge of the intraspecific variation. Much more descriptive work needs to be done on many more taxa before characters of the internal systems can be employed with confidence in evolutionary studies.

PART 4

EVOLUTION

CHAPTER 15

But the great gulf within the vertebrata lies between Fishes and Amphibia. . . . On the side of the fishes only the Dipnoi and the Crossopterygii come into consideration.

Hans Gadow (1901)

Origin and Early Evolution

Humans, throughout recorded history, have attempted to explain the phenomena of nature that surround them. The study of evolutionary biology is merely the disciplined pursuit of the same end—a methodology by which scientists seek to explain the existence of organisms and the processes by which organisms change through time. Thus, it is entirely understandable that vertebrate biologists in general, and amphibian biologists in particular, long have been preoccupied with the question of the origin of the most primitive tetrapods, the amphibians. Many theories have been advanced and countless scenarios constructed to account for the appearance of the first amphibians in the Upper Devonian and the subsequent evolution of the group. The theories and the scenarios, like the organisms, have evolved as more and more evidence has accumulated and as we have become more perceptive in our understanding of the mechanisms of evolutionary change. The discussion that follows is a synthesis of our progress to date. Those who seek resolute solutions and incontrovertible fact may be dissatisfied, but hopefully the imagination of the perceptive reader will be challenged by the nature of the evidence and the conflicting emphases and interpretations of it that have led to substantially different views of the origin of amphibians.

All evolutionary biologists concede that the ancestor to amphibians is to be found among bony fishes of the class Osteichthyes, a group that appeared in marine waters and that, by the Devonian, inhabited marine and freshwater environments as well. Included in this class are three major groups of fishes—Actinopterygii (ray-finned fishes), Dipnoi (lungfishes), and lobe-finned crossopterygian fishes (Actinistia of some authors). From the actinopterygians arose the multitude of bony fishes that dominate marine and freshwater habitats today. This group is distinguished from both dipnoans and crossopterygians by its possession of (1) short-based, paired fins and (2) ganoid scales. In contrast to the actinopterygians, the dipnoans and crossopterygians are characterized by (1) paired fins having a pronounced, fleshy, lobed base that contains robust skeletal elements, and (2) cosmoid scales. The cosmoid scale is formed from thickened dermal bone composed of several layers—a lowermost, lamellar, bony layer, overlain by a highly canaliculate vascular layer, a typical dentine layer with a peculiar "pore-canal" system (dentine + pore-canal system + enamel = "cosmine"), and a thin superficial cover of enamel-like material. Ganoid scales differ in their lack of a pore-canal system and in their possession of multiple layers of enamel (= "ganoine").

The characters that distinguish dipnoans and crossopterygians from other bony fishes also ally them with the primitive tetrapods. The question of which of the two groups is related most closely to the tetrapods is equiv-

417

ocal, and likely will remain so for years to come, as will become evident in the discussions that follow.

NATURE OF A TETRAPOD

In seeking the origin of the tetrapods, we first must define them. Is the group monophyletic (i.e., including the most recent common ancestor and all of its descendants) or not? Although this question has been subject to considerable controversy during this century (see D. Rosen et al., 1981, for review), the majority of scientists today agree that the Tetrapoda represent a natural, monophyletic assemblage that is defined by a suite of characters described by Gaffney (1979) (for an alternative viewpoint, see Jarvik, 1980–81). Thus, all tetrapods, both fossil and Recent, are presumed to possess the characters described below, although some of these characters may have been modified or lost secondarily in derived taxa.

1. Solid braincase.—The braincase is that part of the skull that encloses the brain exclusive of those parts that house the sense organs (e.g., nasal and auditory capsules), and the dermal covering bones. The braincase is derived embryologically from the chondrocranium, a cartilaginous endoskeleton that is formed by developmental fusions of separate cartilage components (see Chapter 6). In tetrapods, the anterior (ethmosphenoid or ethmoidal + orbitotemporal) portion of the braincase is fused

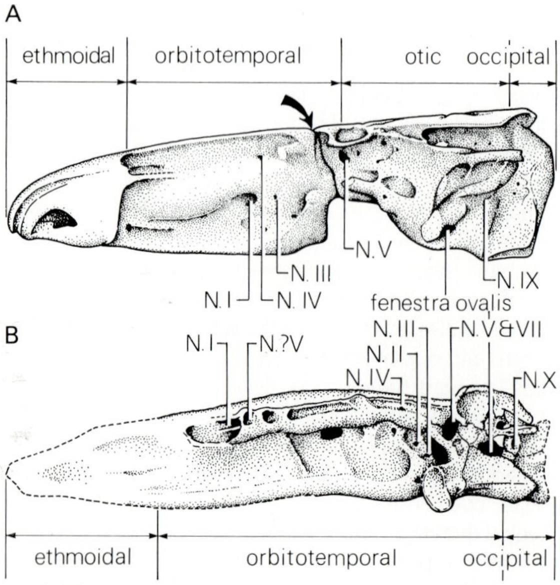

Figure 15-1. A. Braincase in lateral view of *Eusthenopteron foordi* (about ×1), an osteolepiform fish, redrawn from Jarvik (1980–81). **B.** *Eogyrinus attheyi* (about ×3), a labyrinthodont amphibian, redrawn from Panchen (1972). Note the presence of the intracranial joint (indicated by arrow) in *Eusthenopteron* and the differences in regional proportions of the skulls of these representatives of crossopterygians and primitive amphibians, respectively. The locations of major cranial nerve foramina are shown for each braincase.

with, or intimately united to, the posterior otico-occipital part of the braincase (Fig. 15-1).

2. Posterior (otico-occipital) region of skull longitudinally compact.—Clearly, this is a relative character, but in contrast to crossopterygians and some dipnoans, the posterior region of the braincase (i.e., that part posterior to the orbit) of tetrapods is relatively short compared with the facial region (Fig. 15-1; see Gaffney, 1979, for review of literature).

3. Jugular vein and truncus hyoideo-mandibularis of facial nerve (C.N. VII) pass across dorsal surface of hyomandibular bone and orbital artery runs through hyomandibular bone.—Classically, the possession of a bone lying between the auditory capsule and the cheek or otic region has been interpreted to be a middle-ear bone, i.e., the stapes or columella, that functionally is part of the impedance-matching system involved in sound transmission; as such, a middle-ear bone was thought to be a universal character of tetrapods (Gaffney, 1979). However, Carroll (1980) suggested that in the Lower Carboniferous labyrinthodont amphibian *Greererpeton* this bone braced the cheek region against the braincase, thereby providing internal cranial support as the skull became freely movable on the trunk and a more solid attachment between the dermatocranium and braincase evolved. Thus, the long-accepted distinction between the hyomandibular bone of fishes as a suspensory element and its homologue in tetrapods, the middle-ear bone (stapes or columella), as a sound-transmitting element is no longer appropriate. Smithson and Thomson (1982) reported that in the osteolepiform fish *Eusthenopteron foordi* the hyomandibular bone articulates with two discrete facets (the lateral commissure) that protrude from the lateral aspect of the auditory capsule. The jugular canal lies between these two facets and serves as the entrance into the head for the orbital (= stapedial) artery and the exit from the head of the jugular vein and truncus hyoideo-mandibularis of the facial nerve. From the jugular canal, the nerve passes through the hyomandibula via the hyomandibular canal. In contrast, in early tetrapods the lateral commissure and jugular canal are absent, and the truncus hyoideo-mandibularis does not pass through the "hyomandibula." Instead, this nerve, along with the jugular vein, passes across the dorsal surface of the hyomandibula and the orbital artery runs through the hyomandibula. Apparently, this is a primitive arrangement for all tetrapods and represents a fundamental distinction between fishes and amphibians. However, the arrangement is independent of any shift between suspensory and auditory functions. Following Smithson and Thomson (1982), the terms "stapes" and "columella" are associated here with the condition characteristic of tetrapods, in which the canal for the truncus hyoideo-mandibularis has been lost and a new canal has developed for the orbital (= stapedial) artery.

4. Presence of an otic notch.—The endoskeleton of the skull, the chondrocranium, is invested superficially by membrane bones that compose the dermatocranium. Topographically, these are arranged into the following regions: (1) *snout* anterior to orbits, (2) *margins of orbits*, (3) *skull table* covering the braincase and temporal fossae that house jaw-closing muscles, (4) *cheeks* that form the lateral walls of the temporal fossae, and (5) marginal *tooth-bearing bones*. The otic notch is a dorsolateral, V-shaped cleft in the skull roof; the notch is formed between the posterodorsal edge of the cheek and the posterolateral edge of the skull table (Figs. 15-2A, 15-2B, 15-17–19). The notch is presumed to have been present in all primitive amphibians except the lepospondyls, in which it is assumed to have been lost. Superficially, the otic notches of all amphibians and reptiles appear to be similar, and at one time they were assumed to be homologous structures that housed the eardrum or tympanum. In some primitive amphibians (e.g., *Greererpeton*), however, it has been found that the stapes attached distally to the cheek region; thus, it is questionable whether in these animals the otic notch actually housed an eardrum and therefore whether their so-called otic notch is homologous with those of other primitive amphibians (e.g., temnospondyls) and the reptiles. For the time being, the presence of an otic notch is accepted conditionally as a tetrapod feature with the realization that future findings may reveal that this character is not homologous in those animals in which it occurs.

5. *Single pair of nasal bones with or without a single median ossification (internasal).*—Nasals are dermal investing bones that roof the olfactory region on either side of the midline (Figs. 15-2A, 15-6A, 15-19A, and 15-20A). The nasals may be separated by a median ossification; occasionally they are fused or entirely lost, but they never are replaced by multiple, median ossifications (Figs. 15-10–12).

6. *Fenestra ovalis.*—The stapes (= columella) communicates with the cavum labyrinthicum of the inner ear via the fenestra ovalis, or oval window, an opening in the lateral wall of the auditory capsule (Fig. 15-21).

7. *Carpus, tarsus, and dactyly.*—Tetrapods bear fore- and hindlimbs with wrist and ankle joints, respectively, and digits on the manus and pes. Furthermore, it has been suggested that the possession of four digits on the manus and five digits on the pes is the primitive condition for tetrapods and that the prepollex (= precarpale *fide* Schaeffer, 1941) and postminimus (= postcarpale) do not represent the remains of additional digits (see Gaffney, 1979, for review of arguments).

8. *Pectoral skeleton free from skull; posttemporal, supracleithrum, gill cover, and anocleithrum absent; scapulocoracoid relatively larger than dermal shoulder elements.*—The posttemporal, supracleithrum, and anocleithrum are dorsodistal dermal bones of the pectoral girdle of crossopterygian fishes (Fig. 15-14). Because the posttemporal and gill cover (= operculum) unite the girdle to the skull, their loss marks the independence of these two units. The loss of all of these

dermal elements, together with the elaboration of the scapulocoracoid, is associated with the modification of the pectoral skeleton for terrestrial locomotion by means of fore- and hindlimbs in primitive tetrapods (Fig. 15-5).

9. *Well-developed pelvis with iliac blades that extend dorsally to articulate with an ossified sacral rib (ribs) of the vertebral column.*—The possession of limbs for terrestrial locomotion presupposes a structural link by which the support provided by the hindlimbs is transmitted to the body (Fig. 15-5). The tetrapod pelvis is composed of three endochondral elements on each side—the ilium, ischium, and pubis—which together form a cup-shaped depression, the acetabulum, that provides for the articulation of the head of the femur. The puboischiac plate surrounding the acetabulum provides a surface for muscle attachment. The robust median union of the two halves of the girdle, together with the iliac blades that articulate with the vertebral column, assures that support from the hindlimbs is transmitted to the body.

10. *Well-developed, ventrally oriented ribs.*—The possession of well-developed presacral ribs is associated with an elaboration of axial musculature and support of the body cavity (Fig. 15-5).

PRIMITIVE TETRAPODS

An understanding of the evolution of early tetrapods in general, and early amphibians in particular, necessitates a knowledge of certain fossil amphibians.

Labyrinthodont Amphibians

The most primitive tetrapods known are the labyrinthodont amphibians, which are known from Upper Devonian to Triassic fossils. Although these organisms represent a diverse morphological assemblage, they share the suite of characters listed above that are unique to tetrapods. Based on the fossil record, we are able to describe generally the basic structure of these ancient organisms—a step that is critical not only to our appreciation of the morphological changes that occurred as animals became better adapted to a terrestrial mode of existence, but to our understanding of the relationships among them, and between them and the crossopterygian and dipnoan fishes.

Skull. The skulls of labyrinthodont amphibians are massive and completely roofed by dermal investing bones (Figs. 15-2, 15-6A, 15-6C, 15-17A, and 15-17B). The snout (i.e., preorbital portion of the skull) tends to be long, whereas the otico-occipital portion is relatively short. The composition of the dermatocranium is relatively fixed. Thus, the skull roof is composed of nasals, frontals, and parietals. The upper jaw is made up of premaxillae and maxillae, both of which bear sharp, cone-shaped, labyrinthine teeth. The maxillary arch is united to the suspensorium by the quadratojugal. The orbit is enclosed by a circle of bones—prefrontal, postfrontal, jugal, and lacrimal. The temporal fossa, which accommodates the

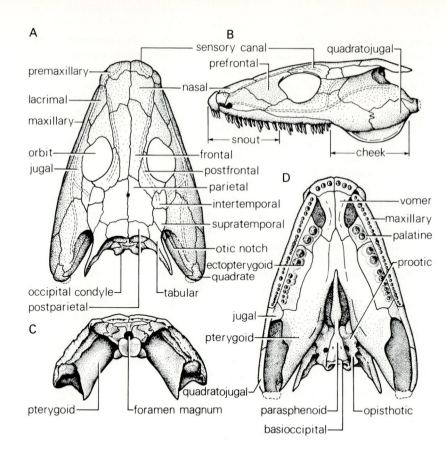

Figure 15-2. Skull of *Palaeoherpeton decorum*, a labyrinthodont amphibian (about × ⅓), redrawn from Panchen (1970). **A.** Dorsal view. **B.** Lateral view. **C.** Posterior view. **D.** Ventral view. For details of labyrinthodont teeth, see Figure 15-13.

jaw musculature, is roofed by one or two bones, the supratemporal and intertemporal; frequently, either one or both of these elements are absent. Laterally, the squamosal, quadratojugal, and part of the jugal enclose the temporal fossa, thereby forming a "cheek region." Because both the squamosal and quadratojugal articulate with the quadrate, they also are part of the suspensory apparatus. The posterior margin of the skull roof is bordered variably by a series of supraoccipital elements—the postparietals medially and the tabulars laterally. There is a single external narial opening, the external naris on each side of the skull; the naris usually is bordered by the premaxilla, maxilla, nasal, and lacrimal, and/or septomaxilla, if the latter is present.

An extensive palate is formed by dermal bones, many of which bear large teeth (Figs. 15-2D, 15-6B, 15-17B, and 15-17D). The vomers floor the nasal capsules anteriorly and form the anteromedial margin of each member of the single pair of internal narial openings, or choanae. The pterygoids lie posterior to the vomers and lateral to the braincase; they not only form a substantial part of the palate, but also brace the quadrate and maxilla against the central auditory and neurocranial regions of the skull. A pair of bracing elements parallel the maxilla and lie between this bone and the pterygoid and/or vomer. The most anterior of these, the palatine, forms the pos-

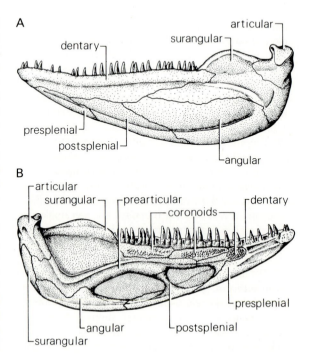

Figure 15-3. Jaw of labyrinthodont amphibian, *Eogyrinus attheyi* (× ⅓), redrawn from Panchen (1970). **A.** Lateral view. **B.** Lingual or medial view.

terior or posterolateral border of the choana. Posteriorly, the ectopterygoid articulates with the maxilla laterally and the pterygoid medially or posteromedially. The vomer, palatine, and ectopterygoid usually bear teeth. A median, longitudinal dermal investing bone, the parasphenoid, floors the braincase posterior to the vomers and between the pterygoids.

The fused braincase internal to the dermatocranium (Fig. 15-1B) is composed of several ossifications that are identifiable primarily by their general location owing to fusion of the elements in adults. The anterior braincase is formed by the sphenethmoid. Posteriorly, the opisthotic and prootic enclose the auditory region. The back of the braincase is composed primitively of up to four separate elements—the ventromedial basioccipital, dorsomedial supraoccipital, and paired exoccipitals. The basioccipital bears rounded, knoblike structures, occipital condyles, by which the skull articulates with the first, or cervical, vertebra.

The lower jaw of primitive amphibians is complex by comparison with more recent forms, being composed of as many as 10 elements (Figs. 15-3, 15-6D, and 15-6E). The primary tooth-bearing element of the mandible is the dentary. Laterally, this bone is supported by a series of four dermal bones; in an anterior to posterior sequence these are the splenial, postsplenial, angular, and surangular (= infradentaries 1–4 of Jarvik, 1980–81, and other works). Lingually, the dentary is supported by as many as three coronoid bones, which also bear teeth. The posterior portion of the mandible is composed of a large prearticular and a relatively smaller articular that articulates with the quadrate.

Little is known about the visceral skeleton of primitive amphibians, because these elements rarely were preserved as fossils. However, one component can be identified—the stapes or columella. Where preserved, this element extends from the auditory capsule to the cheek region or dorsolaterally from the auditory capsule to the region of the otic notch.

Axial Skeleton. The axial skeleton of primitive amphibians is well developed in order to support the weight of the body in terrestrial environments. The vertebral column, per se, is composed of a series of well-ossified vertebrae, each of which bears a neural arch enclosing the spinal cord dorsally and anterior and posterior processes, zygapophyses, that provide for articulation between adjacent vertebrae (Figs. 15-4 and 15-5). Ribs are associated with vertebrae between the neck and the proximal part of the tail. Anterior ribs are bicapitate, whereas more posterior ones are unicapitate. In the region of the pelvic girdle, the ribs are modified; these sacral ribs articulate with the iliac blades of the pelvic girdle.

Two distinct types of vertebrae characterize primitive amphibians. The difference involves the structure of the vertebral centrum, the cylindrical body of the vertebra that surrounds and replaces the notochord. The centrum

structure characteristic of labyrinthodonts (and all tetrapods except some amphibians) is the apsidospondylus, or "arch vertebra," in which the centrum region of each vertebra is composed of two sets of ossifications—the anteroventral intercentra and the posterodorsal pleurocentra. The lepospondylus, or "husk vertebra," characterizes small Paleozoic and some advanced amphibians (i.e., salamanders and caecilians), but the homology of these vertebrae is suspect in view of the many vertebral modifications observed among Paleozoic amphibians. The centrum of a lepospondylous vertebra is a single, spool-shaped structure that primitively was pierced by a lengthwise hole that accommodated the persistent notochord (Fig. 15-4D).

There are several subtypes of arch vertebrae. In the *rhachitomous* type (Fig. 15-4A), the intercentrum is median, ventral, wedge-shaped in lateral view, and crescent-shaped when viewed end-on. The pleurocentra are much smaller, paired blocks that are located dorsally between successive neural arches and intercentra. Depending on the relative contribution of the intercentrum and pleurocentrum to the development of the centrum, several other types of arch vertebrae can be distinguished. In the *stereospondylous* condition (Fig. 15-4B), the pleurocentrum is absent or reduced to such a point that the centrum is formed entirely by the paired intercentra that grow upward to form complete, or nearly complete, rings around the notochord. If both the intercentra and pleurocentra contribute to the centrum, the vertebra is called *embol-*

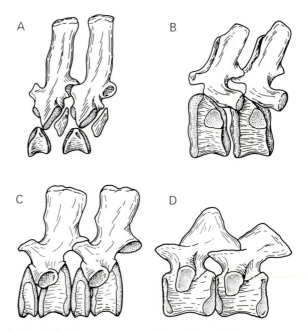

Figure 15-4. Two successive vertebrae of labyrinthodont amphibians in left lateral view. **A.** Rhachitomous, *Eryops.* **B.** Stereospondylus, *Mastodonsaurus.* **C.** Embolomerous, *Eogyrinus.* **D.** Lepospondylus, *Pantylus.* A–C redrawn from Panchen (1980); D from Panchen (1977).

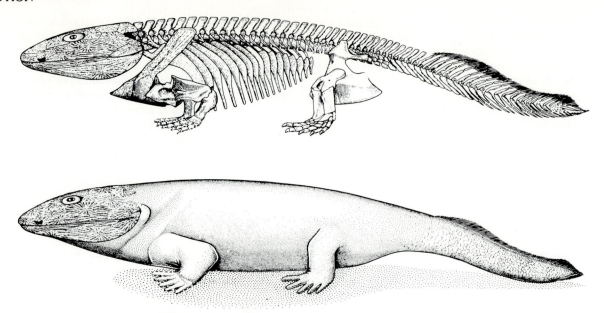

Figure 15-5. Restoration of *Icthyostega* sp. in lateral aspect from Jarvik (1980–81). Total length of specimen about 65 centimeters. Note massive pectoral girdle that is independent of the skull, broad ribs, and fusion of most posterior vertebrae into a rod. The dorsomedial tail fin supported by endoskeletal elements and dermal fin rays is atypical of other primitive tetrapods. Reproduced with permission of Academic Press.

omerous (Fig. 15-4C). In an alternative arrangement characteristic of one of the major groups of labyrinthodonts, the anthracosaurs, the intercentra are reduced, and the paired pleurocentra grow downward to form a ring around the notochord.

Pectoral Girdle. The primitive amphibian shoulder girdle is a robust structure that is independent of the skull and capable of supporting the anterior half of the body by providing expansive surfaces for the origin of massive muscles used to move the head and forelimbs (Figs. 15-5 and 15-7). The ventral portion of the girdle consists of two, flat, chest plates. The smaller anterior plate is formed by a single, median, longitudinally oriented interclavicle flanked on either side by the clavicles, whereas the posterior plate is composed of large paired coracoids. Dorsolaterally the plates articulate with the upper part of the pectoral girdle, the scapular plate, which incorporates the cleithrum along its leading edge. At the junction of the upper and lower portions of the girdle, an articular surface is formed for the humerus, the proximal bone of the forelimb.

Pelvic Girdle. The pelvic girdle is a massive structure providing for muscle attachments from the hindlimbs, and connecting the hindlimbs to the vertebral column via the sacrum (Figs. 15-5 and 15-8). The union of three bones on each side (pubis anteriorly, ischium posteriorly, and ilium dorsally) forms the acetabulum—the articular surface for the head of the femur, the proximal bone of the

hindlimb. Midventrally, the paired pubes and ischia form a broad plate. The upper part of the pelvic girdle is composed of dorsal or posterodorsally directed ilial blades that articulate with the sacral ribs.

Limbs. The basic structure of the fore- and hindlimbs is quite similar. Robust proximal elements, the humerus and femur, articulate with the pectoral and pelvic girdles, respectively (Fig. 15-5). Distally each of these elements articulates with paired longbones—the radius and ulna of forelimb, and tibia and fibula of hind limb. In each case, the inner bone of the pair (i.e., the radius and tibia, respectively) tends to rest directly under the proximal limb bone and, therefore, supports much of the weight of the body. Muscles pulling on the outer, or lateral, bone of each pair, the ulna and fibula, tend to extend the distal fore- and hindlimbs, respectively. The wrist and ankle are composed of a complex of small elements, the carpus of the forelimb and the tarsus of the hindlimb. Typically, the elements are arranged such that there is a proximal row of three or four relatively large elements lying between the lower limb bones and the remaining, smaller carpal or tarsal elements. The remaining elements can be divided into two groups. There is a series of four or five distal carpals and five tarsals, each of which is associated with the proximal head of a digit. The inner three distal carpal and tarsal elements (associated with Digits I–III) articulate proximally with three small elements known as the centralia.

The articulation of these short, robust limbs with massive girdles allows for anterior-posterior-ventral limb rotation. The structure of the limbs is such that there are two points of flexion—proximally at the elbow and knee, and distally at the wrist and ankle. Thus, the stocky, low-slung primitive amphibians probably were capable of lifting their bodies off the ground.

Ichthyostega: The Earliest Known Tetrapod

Ichthyostega is one of three genera of primitive amphibians that have been discovered from the Upper Devonian of eastern Greenland. Of the two other genera, *Ichthyostegopsis* is placed in the same family as *Ichthyostega*

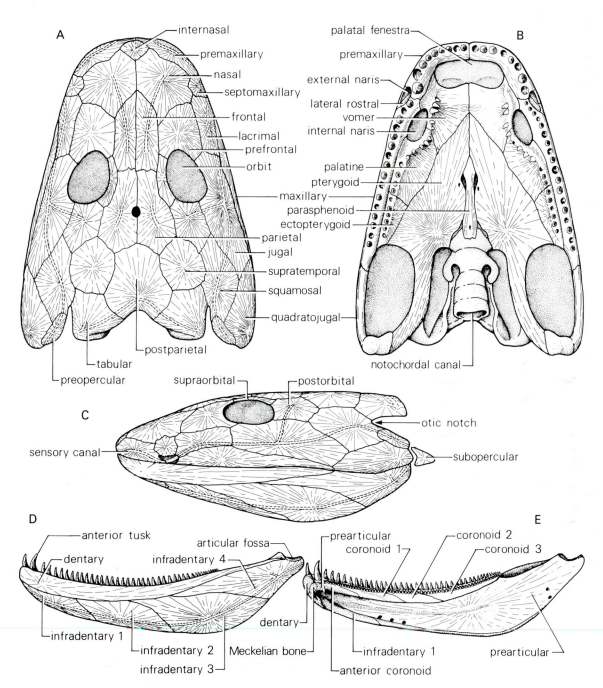

Figure 15-6. Skull and mandible of *Ichthyostega* sp. (about × ½), redrawn from Jarvik (1980–81). **A.** Skull in dorsal view, **B.** ventral view, and **C.** lateral view. **D.** Mandible in lateral view and **E.** lingual view. Note the remnant of a preoperculum (A), presence of a suboperculum (C), position of external nares (B, C), and incorporation of notochordal canal into posterior portion of braincase (B). Compare with Figure 15-2. Nomenclature of elements of lower jaw follows Jarvik (1980–81); thus, infradentaries 1–4 are equivalent to the presplenial, postsplenial, angular, and surangular, respectively, as illustrated in Figure 15-3.

(Ichthyostegidae), and *Acanthostega* in a separate family (Acanthostegidae). This material is represented only by partial skull tables, whereas complete skulls and post-cranial elements are assignable to *Ichthyostega* (Fig. 15-5). Thus, the following discussion centers on features of the best-known fossil material.

The discovery of *Ichthyostega* had profound effects on our characterization of tetrapods and description of their probable origins. Because *Ichthyostega* was stratigraphically older and anatomically more primitive than its Carboniferous relatives, it was anticipated that this organism would prove to be morphologically intermediate between the Carboniferous labyrinthodonts and the rhipidistian, lobe-finned fishes, which at that time were accepted almost universally as the closest relatives of primitive tetrapods. The position of *Ichthyostega* as the most primitive tetrapod is unassailable at present, but unfortunately, the animal did not conform to the preconceived model. For example, many features of the skull are primitive relative to those of other labyrinthodonts, but at the same time there are significant differences in proportions between the skull of *Ichthyostega* and those of osteolepiform fishes. Moreover, many structures are still unknown in *Ichthyostega* (e.g., the soft anatomy, structure of the manus, braincase, and detailed disposition of the sensory canals). It is the existence of apparently discordant characters and the lack of information about others that has prompted some recent authors (e.g., D. Rosen et al., 1981) to reinterpret morphological trends and reassess the phylogenetic relationships of primitive tetrapods. In view of the importance of *Ichthyostega*, a resume of its characters is presented below. Unless specifically stated otherwise, it can be assumed that the foregoing, generalized description of primitive tetrapods also applies to *Ichthyostega*.

Skull. The snout of *Ichthyostega* is similar in general aspect to that of other primitive amphibians (Fig. 15-6). The external nares are not visible in dorsal view because they are located low on the lateral margin of the maxillary arch, as they are in some Lower Carboniferous labyrinthodonts. The same bones participate in forming the margin of the nares, with the exception of the maxilla. The posteroventral margin of the naris is constituted by a slip of bone that has been interpreted as a slender process of the maxilla or a separate bone, the lateral rostral. In addition to the usual dermatocranial elements, *Ichthyostega* has a remnant of a preoperculum applied to the posterior margins of the squamosal and quadratojugal and a suboperculum that lies posteriorly adjacent to, but separate from, the quadratojugal. In contrast to all other primitive amphibians, a large notochordal canal is incorporated into the posterior braincase. With the exception of the jaws, the visceral skeleton of *Ichthyostega* is unknown.

Axial Skeleton. *Ichthyostega* is distinguished from other labyrinthodonts in possessing a dorsomedial tail fin that is supported by endoskeletal elements (radials) and dermal fin rays (lepidotrichia) characteristic of fishes (Fig. 15-5). The most posterior vertebrae are fused into a bony rod. The individual vertebrae are rhachitomous (Fig. 15-4A), and each presacral vertebra supports a pair of bicapitate ribs. The ribs are unusual in that each is composed of an anterior, curved rodlike portion, from which a posterior laminar plate arises. Successive ribs overlap one another to form a rigid armor that encloses the body cavity. The ribs diminish in length posteriorly. The condition of the sacral rib(s) is unknown; however, a few posterolaterally oriented postsacral ribs have been described.

Pectoral Girdle. Although the general architecture of the pectoral girdle is similar to that of other labyrinthodonts, there are significant differences in the components of the girdle. The upper portion is represented by a bladelike structure, the cleithrum (Fig. 15-7); the distinct scapular plate of other labyrinthodonts is absent. Moreover, the coracoid plate bears a posterior depression and supraglenoid process atypical of other primitive tetrapods.

Pelvic Girdle. The pelvic girdle of *Ichthyostega* (Fig. 15-8A, 15-8B) is represented by a single ossification, in contrast to the three, paired bones characteristic of other tetrapods. Despite this, distinct pubic, ischial, and ilial portions of the girdle can be identified, and the overall structural plan is nearly identical to that of other labyrinthodonts.

Limbs. The forelimb of *Ichthyostega* is known only from the proximal limb bones. The bones of the wrist are too disarticulated to be described, and the digits are unknown. The radius and ulna resemble the corresponding elements of other labyrinthodonts; however, the humerus is distinctive. In contrast to the robust bone of other labyrinthodonts, the main distal part of the humerus of *Ichthyostega* has three thin blades oriented in medial, lateral, and dorsal planes.

The hindlimb is shorter and stockier than that of other primitive amphibians (Fig. 15-7C). In particular, the tibia and fibula are short, broad elements that articulate medially throughout their lengths. The tarsus is composed of a broad but short tibiale, fibulare, and intermedium that articulate distally with 11 compact tarsal elements. The five digits are exceedingly short and stubby.

TETRAPOD AFFINITIES: LUNGFISHES OR LOBE-FINS?

At the time of this writing, there are two schools of thought regarding the closest relatives of fossil and Recent tetrapods. The debate is largely methodological—an expression of what is generally conceded to be the neontological viewpoint versus the paleontological. The paleontologist seeks to demonstrate changes in anatomical rela-

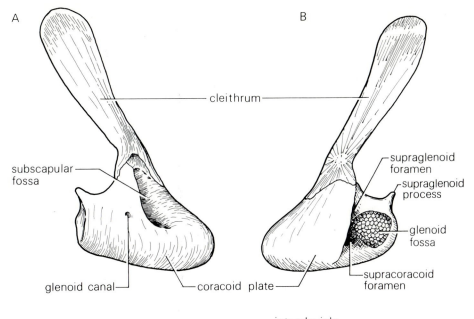

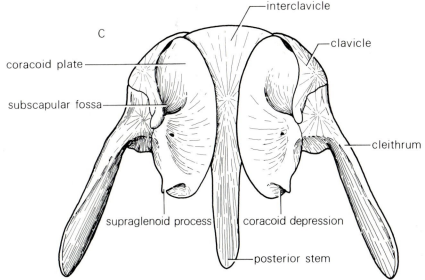

Figure 15-7. Pectoral girdle of *Ichthyostega* sp. **A.** Endoskeletal girdle and cleithrum of right half of girdle in medial view. **B.** Right side in lateral view. **C.** Restoration of entire girdle in dorsal view. Note the bladelike cleithrum and supraglenoid process atyical of other primitive tetrapods. Redrawn from Jarvik (1980–81).

tionships in the fossil record—a data matrix that is restricted by the fragmentary nature of most fossils, gaps in the fossil record, and a lack of knowledge of soft anatomical features. Neontologists, on the other hand, seek to demonstrate evolutionary changes by comparative morphological studies of extant species, deriving the evolutionary change in characters by comparisons with closely related forms not included in the group under study. Furthermore, neontologists seek to define homologies on the basis of ontogenetic changes of characters in the species under study; they also include features of soft anatomy, development, and physiology in their argument. Most paleontologists look for ancestors—an ancestor-descendant sequence in which ancestors are assumed to be more generalized in a particular character, and the descendants more specialized. Whereas proponents of both schools

of thought attempt to construct evolutionary trees (i.e., branching diagrams) based on nested sets of derived features, most neontologists do not seek to identify specific ancestors of Recent taxa or to define ancestor-descendant sequences. As a consequence of this methodological dichotomy, some biologists claim that lungfishes and tetrapods share a common ancestor that is not shared by any other groups, and therefore are related more closely to one another than either is to any other group (Fig. 15-9A). Those biologists who base their arguments only on features preserved in the fossil record favor a scheme in which the osteolepiform lobe-fin fishes (of which *Eusthenopteron foordi* is the best-known representative) are related most closely to primitive tetrapods (Fig. 15-9B). Evidence for both views is summarized below.

Dipnoans are known from marine habitats in the Early

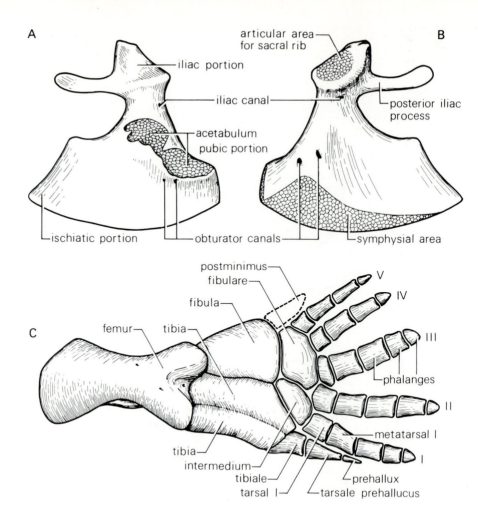

Figure 15-8. Pelvic girdle and hindlimb of *Ichthyostega* sp. **A.** Right side of pelvic bone in lateral view. **B.** Right side of pelvis in medial view. **C.** Left hindlimb in external view. Note that pelvis is composed of a single ossification rather than three separate bones as in other primitive tetrapods. Redrawn from Jarvik (1980–81).

Devonian. Although these specialized forms are moderately abundant and diverse in the fossil record, they are represented by only five species in three genera today—*Neoceratodus* (Australian lungfish), *Protopterus* (African lungfish), and *Lepidosiren* of South America. Lungfishes are elongate, round in cross section, and bear two pairs of lateral fins that are long, slim, fleshy structures with slightly webbed margins in *Protopterus* and *Lepidosiren*, but broader, fleshier structures in *Neoceratodus*. External nostrils are absent, but there are two pairs of narial openings (excurrent and incurrent) associated with the inside of the mouth. A spiracle is absent. Both lungs and gills are present.

Osteolepiform crossopterygians are also known from marine and freshwater habitats of the Devonian and Carboniferous, but they became extinct in the early Permian. The osteolepiforms bore two pairs of lateral fins which, in contrast to those of dipnoans, were short with a more robust, fleshy base. Only one pair of narial openings pierced the palate, and one pair of external nares was present on the dorsal aspect of the snout. A spiracle, lungs, and gills supposedly were present.

Comparative Morphology

Skull. In general proportions, the skulls of many dipnoans and all osteolepiforms are markedly different from those of primitive tetrapods in that the postorbital (i.e., otico-occipital) length is much shorter in tetrapods (compare Figs. 15-2, 15-10, and 15-11). Both dipnoans and osteolepiforms are characterized by a complex mosaic of dermal bones dorsally that bear questionable homologies to the relatively fixed pattern observed in primitive tetrapods, owing to the application of different criteria of homology (for a review of the arguments, see D. Rosen et al., 1981). Neither group has a pair of bones that can be designated as nasals; instead the snouts of each group are covered by an irregular mosaic of small bones. The posterior skull table (Fig. 15-12) is a special source of debate. If skull bones are defined relative to their position with respect to the eyes, then ichthyostegids are more similar to dipnoans than to osteolepiforms. On the other hand, if we assume (1) that the eyes and pineal foramen are capable of shifting their positions, but (2) that the lateral line canals occupy the same positions in the cranial

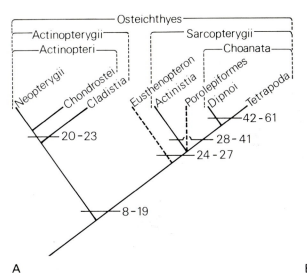

A

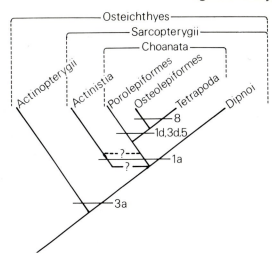

B

Figure 15-9. Character-state trees for major groups of Osteichthyes, after **A.** Rosen et al. (1981) and **B.** Schultze (1981). Broken lines indicate an unresolved cladistic position. Numbered characters refer to shared, derived features (synapomorphies). For cladogram A, the characters are:

    8. Dermal skull bones with internal processes attaching to endocranium and various toothed dermal bones on palate.

    9. Endochondral bone.

    10. Lepidotrichia and ceratotrichia in fins.

    11. Radials of fins never extending to fin margin.

    12. Two or fewer preaxial radials associated with first two metapterygial segments of pectoral fin endoskeleton.

    13. Dermal sclerotic ring of four plates.

    14. Marginal upper and lower jaw teeth on dermal bones lateral to palatoquadrate.

    15. Interhyal (= stylohyal) present.

    16. Infrapharyngobranchials with forward orientation.

    17. Suprapharyngobranchials present on first two gill arches.

    18. Gill arches 1 and 2 articulating on the same basibranchial.

    19. A pneumatic or buoyancy organ as an outpocketing of the anterior gut (lung, swimbladder).

    20. Absence of supramaxillary (jugal) canal joining infraorbital canal.

    21. Differentiated propterygium in pectoral fin.

    22. Modification of pelvic fin metapterygium to form part or all of pelvic girdle, and endoskeletal support of pelvic fin exclusively by preaxial pelvic radials.

    23. Acrodin caps on all teeth.

    24. An exclusively metapterygial pectoral and pelvic fin supported by a single basal element, and an anocleithrum in the shoulder girdle suspension.

    25. Absence of the connection between the preopercular and supratemporal lateral-line canal.

    26. Enamel on teeth.

    27. Sclerotic ring of more than four plates.

    28. Anocleithrum of dermal shoulder girdle sunken beneath dermis and lacking surface ornamentation.

    29. Clavicle large relative to cleithrum, and pectoral appendage insertion high as compared with those conditions in actinopterygians, cladistians, and *Eusthenopteron*.

    30. Both pectoral and pelvic appendages with long, muscular lobes that extend well below body wall and with structurally similar endoskeletal supports.

    31. Preaxial side of pectoral fin endoskeleton rotated to postaxial position.

    32. A series of canal-bearing bones (for supraorbital canal) lateral to large, paired, roofing bones between orbits.

    33. Absence of hyostyly in jaw suspension.

    34. Posterior margin of palatoquadrate erect or sloping backward rather than sharply forward from jaw articulation.

    35. Presence of a rostral organ.

    36. Basibranchial, single, broad, and triangular.

    37. Last gill arch articulating with base of preceding arch rather than with basibranchial.

    38. Reduction or loss of hypobranchials.

    39. Reduction or loss of pharyngobranchials.

    40. Inferior vena cava present.

    41. Pulmonary vein present.

    42. Choana present.

    43. Labial cavity present.

    44. Second metapterygial segment of paired appendages composed of paired subequal elements that are functionally joined distally.

    45. Two primary joints in each paired appendage, between endoskeletal girdle and unpaired basal element and between basal element and paired elements of second segment (in pectoral appendage, preaxial member of paired elements with ball-and-socket joint with basal and postaxial member articulating on dorsal—postaxial—margin of basal element).

    46. Reduction of ratio of dermal fin rays to endoskeletal supports in paired appendages.

    47. Tetrapodous locomotion in living representatives.

    48. Muscles in paired fins segmented.

    49. Fusion of right and left pelvic girdles to form pubic and ischial processes.

    50. Hyomandibula not involved in jaw suspension.

    51. Loss in interhyal (= stylohyal).

    52. Hyomandibula reduced and, at least in extant forms, joined dorsally by ligament and closely associated with otic recess in the braincase, and ventrally with quadrate.

    53. Loss of dorsal gill arch elements (pharyngobranchials).

    54. Opercular bone, in extant forms, reduced and joined posteriorly by a division of the epaxial musculature to the upper half of the primary shoulder girdle.

    55. Right and left pterygoids joined in midline, excluding the parasphenoid anteriorly from the roof of the mouth.

    56. Loss of autopalatine.

    57. Elongation of snout region.

    58. Eye somewhat posterior in skull, at about level of junction between two principal bones in skull roof.

    59. Pattern of five dermal bones covering otic and occipital regions of braincase.

    60. Resorption of calcified cartilage and subsequent deposition of bony tissue in vertebrae of Devonian *Griphognathus* (lungfish) is identical with the formation of bony tissue in uncalcified cartilage in Tetrapoda.

    61. Numerous features of soft anatomy, development, and physiology.

    For cladogram B, the characteristics are:

    1a. Teeth composed of true enamel.

    1d. Plicident teeth.

    3a. Prearticular present in lower jaw.

    3d. Three coronoid bones in lower jaw.

    5. One pair of choanae in roof of mouth.

    8. Endoskeleton of paired fins lacking in archipterygium.

Discussion of these characters may be found in Rosen et al. (1981) and Schultze (1981).

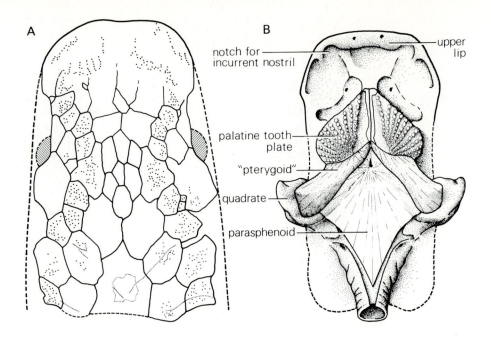

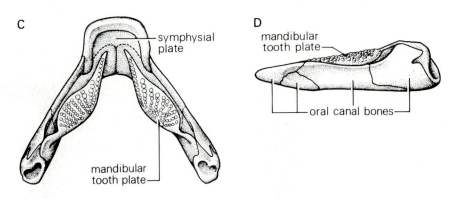

Figure 15-10. Skull and mandible of Devonian lungfish, *Dipterus valenciennesi*. **A.** Dorsal view of dermatocranium. **B.** Restoration of palate. **C.** Dorsal view of mandible. **D.** Lateral view of mandible. Note irregular mosaic of small bones that composes skull roof (position of eyes is hatched), presence of crushing tooth plates instead of plicident teeth, position of both excurrent and incurrent narial openings in roof of mouth, and relatively long otico-occipital portion of skull. The upper jaw lacks marginal bones (maxilla and premaxilla) typical of osteolepiforms and tetrapods. A and B redrawn from Jarvik (1980–81); C and D from Jarvik (1967).

bones of fishes and amphibians, then the posterior skull table of osteolepiforms is more similar to that of amphibians than that of dipnoans.

Both fossil and Recent lungfishes are distinct from osteolepiforms and ichthyostegids in their lack of the typical marginal jaw bones—i.e., maxillae and premaxillae (compare Figs. 15-6, 15-10, 15-11), and possession of crushing toothplates (Fig. 15-10) instead of cone-shaped teeth composed of folded dentine, or plicidentine (Fig. 15-13). Dipnoans are highly specialized in their possession of a toothed, bony preoral eminence instead of premaxillae, and lateral nasal toothplates instead of maxillae. Miles (1977) suggested that the preoral eminence and nasal toothplates were derived from the premaxillae and maxillae of gnathostome fishes. However, the histology of the preoral eminence and the toothplates is quite distinct from that of the premaxillae (Miles, 1977) and plicident teeth (Schultze, 1970) of osteolepiforms and primitive amphibians. Thus in these respects, the osteolepiforms

and primitive amphibians seem to resemble one another more closely than either group resembles lungfishes.

Dipnoans are unique in that there are no narial openings on the exterior of the skull. Rather, the incurrent opening lies on the lingual margin of the jaw and the excurrent opening in the roof of the mouth (Fig. 15-10B). This condition contrasts with that characterizing osteolepiforms and tetrapods in which there is an external naris (incurrent opening) on the snout and an internal palatal opening, the choana (Fig. 15-11B). The question of the homology of the dipnoan excurrent opening and the choanae of osteolepiforms and tetrapods is debated (see D. Rosen et al., 1981; Miles, 1977; and Jarvik, 1980–81, for reviews). In some actinopterygian fishes, there is a third opening in the palate region that looks similar to a choana. In these fishes, as well as dipnoans, there is no evidence that the nasal apparatus ever transmits air into the buccal cavity, as it does in tetrapods; instead it is purely an olfactory mechanism. The tetrapod choana de-

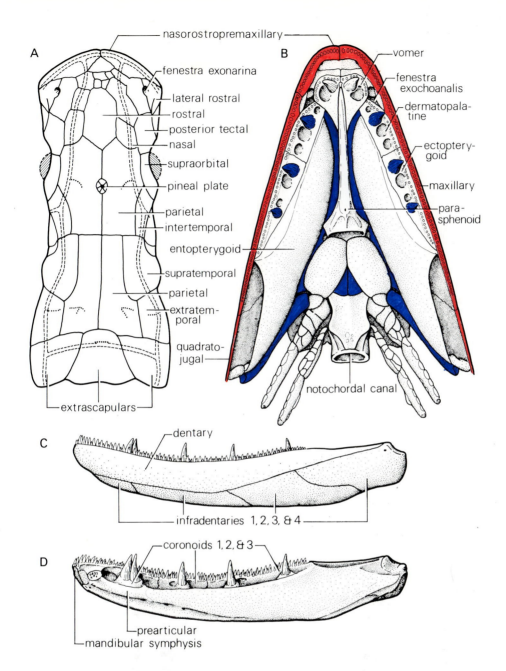

Figure 15-11. Skull and mandible of an osteolepiform fish, *Eusthenopteron foordi,* redrawn from Jarvik (1980–81). **A.** Dorsal view of dermatocranium. Note mosaic of small bones in nasal area, dorsal position of external nares, position of pineal foramen between eyes (which are hatched), and relative length of otico-occipital portion of skull. Sensory canals indicated by broken lines. **B.** Ventral view of skull. Note internal choanae, presence of marginal jaw bones (maxillae and premaxillae), and presence of true teeth. **C.** Lateral view of mandible. **D.** Medial view of mandible. The endocranium of *Eusthenopteron* is shown in Figure 15-1A. Terminology follows Jarvik (1980–81).

velops embryologically from the union of an internal process of the nasal sac and a small diverticulum from the gut—a morphogenetic process not observed in lungfishes. In the absence of information on the ontogeny of the choana in osteolepiforms, we can never be certain that this structure is homologous to that of tetrapods; however, its location in the palate and relationship with the external naris on the snout suggest that it is homologous (but see D. Rosen et al., 1981, for a different view).

The palate and mandible of osteolepiforms (Fig. 15-11B–D) largely correspond to those of tetrapods, whereas those of lungfishes (Fig. 15-10B–D) are reduced. The palates of some dipnoans lack both the palatine and ectopterygoid, and the lower jaw is composed of only six elements of disputed homologies (see Miles, 1977, for review). Among fossil dipnoans showing less reduction than Recent species, the lingual side of the mandible is composed of a large prearticular and a small, median adsymphysial plate. In lateral aspect there is a short, anterior dentary and a canal-bearing infradentary series consisting of a variety of bones of unknown homologies. Dipnoans apparently lack the coronoid bones and articular characteristic of osteolepiforms and primitive tetra-

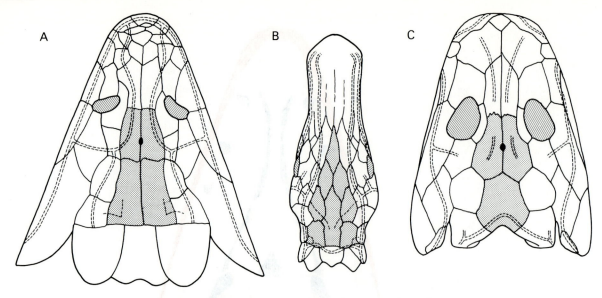

Figure 15-12. Comparison of skull tables (stippled bones) of **A.** an osteolepid fish, *Panderichthys,* **B.** a lungfish, *Griphognathus,* and **C.** a labyrinthodont amphibian, *Ichthyostega.* Pineal foramen (A, C) shown in black. Sensory canals indicated by broken lines and orbits by cross-hatching.

pods, and the mandible is equipped with crushing tooth-plates or denticles rather than teeth.

The endocrania or braincases of both lungfishes and tetrapods are considered to be fused in contrast to those of osteolepiforms, which are divided into an anterior ethmosphenoid portion and a posterior otico-occipital portion (Fig. 15-1). Dorsally, the dermal roofing bones form a transverse suture that coincides with the marginal abutment of the two halves of the braincase (Figs. 15-11A and 15-12A). The condition in osteolepiforms has been termed a hinged braincase. The so-called fused endocrania of lungfishes and tetrapods seem to be of two distinct types. In nearly all tetrapods the braincase is at least partially ossified; there is a single pair of anterior ossifications in the ethmosphenoid portion of the endocranium, whereas multiple centers of ossification compose the otico-occipital part of the braincase. In all tetrapods, except *Ichthyostega,* the anterior and posterior ossifications of the neurocranium are bridged dorsally by dermal roofing bones. In general, post-Devonian dipnoans have poorly ossified crania, with ossification being restricted to the occipital region and partial dermal ossification of the walls of the cranial cavity (Miles, 1977). The heavy and complete ossification of the endocranium of Devonian forms offers no clue to regional centers from which ossification proceeded. Based on the available evidence, the endocrania of osteolepiforms and tetrapods seem to be more nearly comparable than those of dipnoans and tetrapods.

Axial Skeleton. The vertebral skeleton of lungfishes is strikingly different from that of osteolepiforms. Among some fossil dipnoans, there is evidence that the noto-

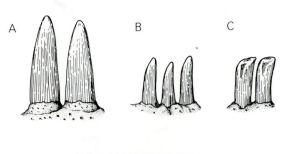

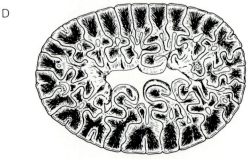

Figure 15-13. Maxillary teeth in lateral view of three labyrinthodont amphibians. **A.** Lanceolate teeth of *Anthracosaurus russelli* (natural size) and **B.** *Eogyrinus attheyi* (natural size) compared to chisel-shaped teeth of **C.** *Archeria crassidisca* (×2). Note prominent longitudinal ridges. **D.** Transverse section of palatine tusk of *Eogyrinus attheyi* at alveolar level, showing characteristic infolding of dentine (×4). Redrawn from Panchen (1970).

chordal sheath may have been invaded by sclerotomal cells to produce amphicoelous vertebral centra (with or without a notochordal canal) upon which cartilaginous neural and hemal (i.e., arcualia) arches rested. In some other fossils, the arcualia ossified. Recent lungfishes retain separate, cartilaginous arcualia around the notochord; cartilaginous vertebral bodies are found only in the tail. The single set of unicapitate pleural ribs is ventral—i.e., they are formed along the line of contact of the lining of the body cavity (somatopleure) with the myoseptum, in contrast to the dorsal rib of tetrapods that forms along the intersection of the horizontal septum and myoseptum.

In contrast, the vertebrae of osteolepiform fishes are composed of ossified arcualia that nearly surround the notochord in a rhachitomous fashion. The intercentra form the major part of the centrum with small posterodorsal components; it is uncertain whether the latter represent paired pleurocentra or nonhomologous, intercalary elements. The neural arch is well developed and ossified, but lacks the zygapophyses with adjacent neural arches that characterize tetrapods (Fig. 15-4). The ribs of *Eusthenopteron* are short, unicapitate, and dorsal.

Pectoral Girdle. A great deal remains to be learned about the homologies of the elements of the pisciform

and tetrapod shoulder girdles. Lungfishes and osteole-piforms are similar in sharing a connection of the dermal pectoral skeleton to the posterior margin of the skull. In *Eusthenopteron* (Fig. 15-14), the dermal pectoral skeleton consists of six elements; in a dorsal-ventral sequence these are: posttemporal, supracleithrum, anocleithrum, cleithrum, clavicle, and interclavicle. The posttemporal and supracleithrum bear the sensory canal connecting the lateral line of the body with the temporal canal of the head. The postcleithrum articulates with the temporal region of the skull and the cleithrum ventrally. The clavicles and interclavicle form an anteromedian breastplate. Little is known about the endoskeletal components, but it is suspected that there existed a dorsal scapular extension and an anteroventral and medial clavicular portion (= scapulocoracoid?), and a tuberosity providing an articular surface for the pectoral fin.

Lungfish pectoral girdles are best known in Recent taxa, and these are characterized by a reduced number of dermal components (Fig. 15-15A–C). The anocleithrum is the most dorsal element. It is reduced in size, is bifurcate, and lies within the epaxial musculature and within a liga-

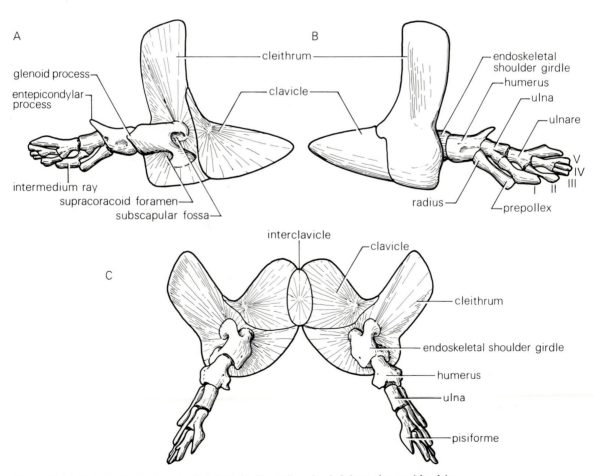

Figure 15-14. Ventral parts of exo- and endoskeletal shoulder girdle and endoskeleton of pectoral fin of the osteolepiform fish *Eusthenopteron foordi.* **A.** Right side, medial view. **B.** Right side, lateral view. **C.** Both halves, dorsal view. Redrawn from Jarvik (1980–81).

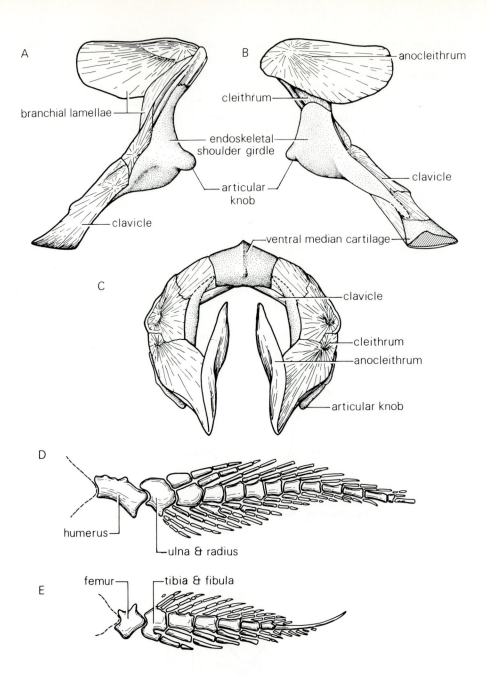

Figure 15-15. Appendicular elements of a lungfish, *Neoceratodus forsteri.* **A.** Endo- and exoskeletal components of pectoral girdle in left lateral, **B.** left medial, and **C.** complete dorsal views. **D.** Endoskeleton of left pectoral fin and **E.** pelvic fin in position of rest against body. A–C redrawn from Jarvik (1980–81); D–E redrawn from Rosen et al. (1981).

ment joining the posterior margin of the cranium to the girdle in *Protopterus* (Jollie, 1962), but is larger and not bifurcate in *Neoceratodus* (D. Rosen et al., 1981). Cleithrum-clavicle relationships are not clear. According to Jollie (1962), the cleithrum is much reduced and the clavicle extends from near the dorsal edge of the cleithrum and closely approaches the midline. In contrast, D. Rosen et al. (1981) claimed that the clavicle was not reduced in *Neoceratodus* and (based on Schmalhausen's, 1917, work) reported that the clavicle and cleithrum of *Protopterus* are fused to form a single element.

The endochondral skeleton of lungfish is represented by a pair of small scapulocoracoids that are joined midventrally and that bear a lateral tuberosity, against which the proximal bone of the pectoral fin articulates. According to Jollie (1962), the scapulocoracoid articulates with, and is partly supported by, a massive "rib" attached to the occipital region of the head—an observation not discussed by D. Rosen et al. (1981).

The variation observed in osteolepiform pectoral girdles, together with the conflicting and unresolved interpretations of the dipnoan girdle, suggests that much more needs to be known about this character complex to render it really useful in assessing phylogenetic relationships.

Pelvic Girdle. Unlike those of primitive tetrapods, the pelvic girdles of dipnoans and osteolepiforms are depressed, lacking a prominent dorsal iliac process. The two halves of the girdle are fused in lungfishes, whereas there is a median articulation in *Eusthenopteron.* Both bear prominent anterior pubic processes; in dipnoans the elements are long, slender, median, and fused throughout their lengths, whereas in *Eusthenopteron* the robust elements are oriented anteromedially and articulate at their anterior ends. The ilium of *Eusthenopteron,* together with the presumed posteromedial ischial region, forms a posterolaterally oriented articular surface for the femur; the ischium bears a posteromedially oriented ischiadic process. In contrast to *Eusthenopteron* and tetrapods, which bear a dorsal iliac process, the pelvic girdle of dipnoans is a long, slim, anterolaterally oriented structure. A posterolateral articular surface for the proximal fin element seems to be formed in the posterior ischium-ilia region, and each ischium bears short, slender posterior processes that are fused ventromedially. Clearly the pelvic girdles of dipnoans and osteolepiforms are as different from one another as each is from those of primitive tetrapods.

Limbs. The limbs of osteolepiforms and dipnoans are strikingly different (compare Figs. 15-14, 15-15D, 15-15E, and 15-16), but presumably both types of limbs evolved from the same primitive, finned ancestor. Two theories have been postulated to explain the mechanism by which discrete fins evolved; there is no conclusive evidence to support one over the other. According to the fin-fold theory, the ancestral vertebrate possessed a pair of continuous ventrolateral fin folds from which the paired fins arose by selective persistence of certain areas of the fin fold and elimination of others. The body-spine theory holds that early fishes possessed ventrolateral spines and that fins developed, first, as a flap of skin that extended from the spine to the body wall; subsequently the spine was elaborated into an endoskeletal framework supporting the fin. Regardless of the origin of the fins and their support, it is postulated that the endoskeleton might have

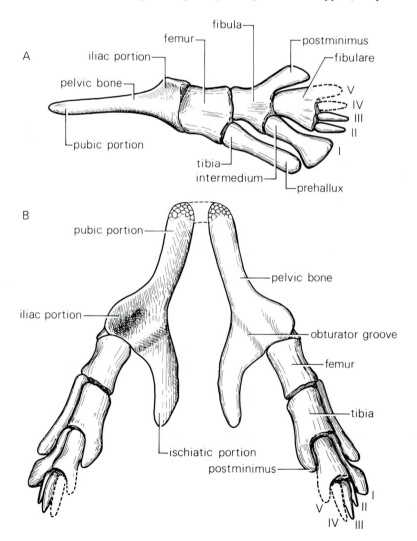

Figure 15-16. Restoration of the pelvic girdle and endoskeleton of the pelvic fins of the osteolepiform fish *Eusthenopteron foordi.* **A.** Lateral view. **B.** Dorsal view. Redrawn from Jarvik (1980–81).

434

consisted of a preaxial (i.e., leading-edge) spine with a posterior, longitudinal series of basal plates (pterygiophores); fin rays (dermatotrichia) may have extended laterally from the pterygiophores into the membranous fin. Loss of the preaxial spine and differentiation of the basal plates may have resulted in a fin composed of series of three large, longitudinally oriented basal plates associated with lateral rods (radials). The typical ray-fin of actinopterygians can be derived from this prototype through a constriction of the fin base by reduction in size of the basals and loss of some basals and most radials. In the primitive lobed or biserial fin, the basals form a longitudinal axis from which lateral rods radiate; short fin rays extend from the radials to the edge of the fin. Lungfishes retain the primitive biserial fin (Figs. 15-15D, 15-15E), whereas osteolepiforms have a more derived limb, in which the longitudinal basal axis of the fin has shifted to the posterior, postaxial border of the fin and the radials extend toward the preaxial and distal borders (Figs. 15-14, 15-16). The resulting limb is short, stout, and composed of a single proximal bone that articulates distally with a pair of robust elements. The latter, in turn, articulate with a series of asymmetrically arranged elements that have been homologized with carpal and tarsal elements of tetrapods (Jarvik, 1980–81; D. Rosen et al., 1981).

Other Characters

Some of the most persuasive arguments applied by those who seek to ally dipnoans and amphibians involve soft anatomical features, development, and physiology, the nature of which are unknown in fossil forms. These characteristics are discussed at some length by Schmalhausen (1968). For the purposes of this discussion it should be pointed out that Recent amphibians and lungfishes share the following characters: (1) lungs that are structurally similar internally and that are supplied with blood from the last pair of aortic arches; (2) a circulatory pattern in which blood is returned from the lungs via the pulmonary vein and the left side of the sinus venosus to the left part of the atrium; (3) presence of an elongate valve in the conus arteriosus that partially separates arterial and venous blood; (4) a venous system with an unpaired ventral vein; (5) well-developed blood vessels in the dermis; (6) telolecithal development of jelly-coated bipolar eggs; (7) ciliated larvae; and (8) presence of a glottis, epiglottis, flask glands, pituitary structure and a tetrapod neurohypophysial hormone, lens proteins, bile salts, and certain gill arch muscles.

Most fishes and most tetrapods have a genome size of 3–10 picograms of DNA per diploid nucleus (Morescalchi, 1977). The major exceptions to this generalization are salamanders and dipnoans. Most salamanders have 30–86 pg per nucleus, but members of the obligate neotenic families have 91–192 pg per nucleus, an amount exceeded only by lungfishes (160–284 pg per nucleus). However, there seems to be no phylogenetic significance in the amount of nuclear DNA within the neotenic families of salamanders or between salamanders and dipnoans. Instead, there is a close relationship between increased amounts of nuclear DNA and larger cell size in both groups (Thomson, 1972; Morescalchi, 1975). Szarski (1970) suggested that nuclear hypertrophy and associated low rates of cellular metabolism were physiological adaptations to stagnating aquatic habitats.

There are at least two significant features in which Recent amphibians and lungfishes differ. (1) All Recent amphibians and amniotes (with the possible exception of some marine hydrophiid snakes) possess Bowman's glands in the olfactory epithelium. These glands are absent in all fish, including the dipnoans (Parsons, 1959). (2) In amphibians, the testis is connected with some of the anterior kidney tubules, and the entire Wolffian duct is used for sperm transport; there is a strong tendency for the formation of accessory urinary ducts from the posterior part of the kidney. The reverse pattern characterizes lungfishes, in which the entire Wolffian duct is used for urine transport, and the testis is connected to the posterior end of the kidney, much as it is in actinopterygian fishes (Gerard, 1954; Parsons and E. Williams, 1963).

Discussion

The origin of primitive amphibians from crossopterygian ancestors is entrenched firmly in the literature of the past 50 years. Until recently, few have questioned seriously the premise that the closest relatives of primitive tetrapods were to be found among the osteolepiform fishes. But controversies have emerged in the face of changing methodologies involved in solving phylogenetic problems and the accumulation of more and diverse data. In assessing the relative merits of the two different phylogenetic schemes presented above (Fig. 15-9), it is important to note that two fundamentally different approaches have been involved. Thus, D. Rosen et al. (1931) and Gardiner (1982, 1983) in seeking to determine the closest relatives of the tetrapods, have identified patterns of morphological change by means of study of ontogeny and comparative anatomy—clearly an approach that must rely primarily on data gathered from extant organisms. Therefore, if we wish to identify the nearest living relatives of Recent amphibians, lungfishes probably are a justifiable choice. On the assumption that Recent amphibians are descended from labyrinthodonts, it follows that the nearest relatives of these fossil taxa are dipnoans also. On the other hand, if we restrict ourselves only to fossil taxa for the analysis of relationships in the manner of Schultze (1981) and others, we are asking a different question: What is the nearest relative of the most primitive known tetrapod, currently considered to be *Ichthyostega*? The paleontologist must rely on the fossil record with its acknowledged limitations, and the evidence to date (Schultze, 1981) suggests that osteolepiform fishes are more closely allied to labyrinthodont amphibians than are dipnoans.

Both phylogenetic schemes are hypotheses and, as such, they cannot be proven to be true, only shown to be incorrect. There are two ways in which to falsify any hypothetical scheme of genealogical relationships. The first involves demonstrating that one or more of the assumptions on which the scheme is based is incorrect. In this case, both phylogenies are based on the same set of assumptions (see D. Rosen et al., 1981, for list). The second way to invalidate a phylogenetic arrangement is to prove that the postulated sequence of character transformation has been misinterpreted—i.e., that characters considered to be homologous are not. This, in fact, accounts for the current controversy. A few examples will suffice. D. Rosen et al. (1981) considered the excurrent narial opening of lungfishes to be homologous with the internal choana of tetrapods; Schultze (1981) did not. The authors disagree about the homologies of the dermal bones of the tetrapod skull table, the tetrapod limb bones, and those of the maxillary arch in dipnoans, as well as the significance of tooth histology. Selection of one phylogenetic scheme in preference to the other becomes an exercise in deciding which author(s) interpreted the evolutionary sequence of character transformation more accurately. As new data are secured and old evidence reinterpreted, these phylogenetic arrangements possibly will be modified and perhaps even rejected in favor of alternative schemes. Thus, the question of the origin of amphibians remains a challenge to biologists.

DIVERSITY AND EVOLUTION OF EARLY TETRAPODS

Setting aside now the problematic issue of the origin of primitive tetrapods, we can address the amazing radiation of these ancient amphibians throughout the latter part of the Paleozoic (Carboniferous and Permian) and the Triassic. During these 120 million years, the primitive amphibians must have exploited the terrestrial environments within the bounds of their physiological limitations (moisture being a critical factor then, as it is for modern amphibians). Their first significant terrestrial competitors probably were reptiles, which are thought to have appeared near the middle of the Carboniferous. In the meantime, amphibians must have competed with a vast array of freshwater and marine fishes. Seemingly all primitive amphibians were predaceous; some must have preyed on fishes (both freshwater and marine), others on small amphibians, and some of the smaller types on aquatic and terrestrial invertebrates.

Adaptations to Terrestriality

The morphological features that distinguish tetrapods from their predecessors (see the earlier section: The Nature of a Tetrapod) can be interpreted as adaptations to increased terrestriality. The skull tended to become freely movable on the trunk, broad, flat, and rigid; the snout became elongate and the otico-occipital region relatively short compared with the facial region (Figs. 15-2, 15-6, and 15-17). A columella or stapes lay laterally adjacent to the auditory capsule in the region of the cheek or otic notch, and the skull articulated with the vertebral column by means of a double occipital condyle. Some of these changes can be related to a shift to terrestrial locomotion, air breathing, and the obvious premium that would have been placed on the development of sensory systems adapted to terrestrial rather than aquatic habitats. Although we cannot be sure, the shape of the skull suggests that primitive amphibians utilized a force-pump respiratory mechanism involving contractions of the mandibular musculature to draw air through the nostrils into the buccal cavity and thence into the lungs. A broad, flat, rigid skull would seem to be architecturally advantageous for this mechanism. Because the nostrils and associated olfactory organs served the dual purpose of air intake and olfaction, one would expect an elaboration of the snout region that might have been accomplished by a posterior shift in the orbits. Such a shift might have occasioned expansion of preorbital bones (e.g., prefrontal) and repression of postorbital bones (e.g., postorbital and postfrontal). Given the flattening of the head, the eyes came to be located dorsally. Once on land, the amphibians required a more sensitive sound-amplifying device. Hence, the stapes (derived from the hyomandibular bone of fishes) acted as a transmitter from the external surface of the head (presumably modified as a tympanic membrane or eardrum) in the region of the otic notch to the auditory capsule via the oval window (fenestra ovalis). The development of double occipital condyles would have allowed movement of the head in a dorsoventral plane; this, in combination with autostylic jaw suspension, would have facilitated a snap-and-grab mechanism of feeding.

Modifications of the axial and appendicular skeleton are associated with terrestrial rather than aquatic locomotor habits. The flexible notochord was supplemented, and ultimately replaced, by blocks of cartilage and bone along its length. The vertebrae formed by these cartilaginous and bony blocks took on a diversity of morphological types, ranging from "arch" to "husk" structures (Fig. 15-4). Regardless of the form, the function was similar—i.e., to provide an axial element strong enough to withstand resistance to the contraction of appendicular and trunk muscles in the terrestrial medium, which obviously provided much less support than the aquatic medium. Robust, bicapitate ribs were attached to the trunk vertebrae to form a thoracic basket, within which internal organs were protected (Fig. 15-5). Moreover, the well-developed, oblique ribs suggest that costal ventilation was a primitive feature of early amphibians. The pectoral girdle, freed of its bony attachment to the rear of the skull, provided a frame suspended by musculature with which the anterior limbs articulated. The pelvic girdle was suspended from the axial column via an articulation between the now prominent dorsal iliac processes and specially modified sacral ribs. The primitive finlike appendages were

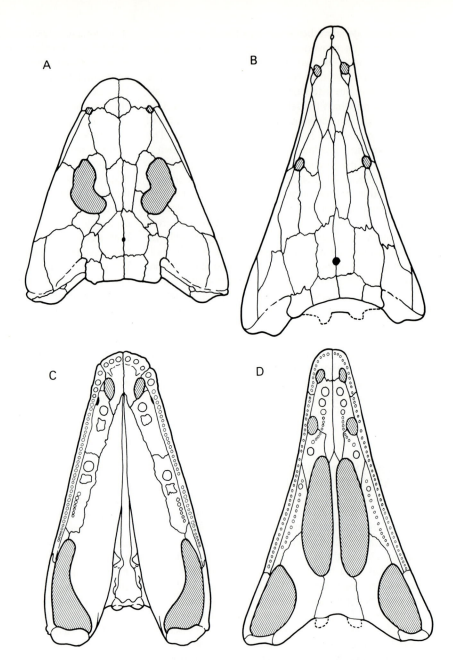

Figure 15-17. Diversity in cranial architecture among labyrinthodont amphibians.
A. *Loxomma*, dorsal view. **B.** *Trematosuchus*, dorsal view. **C.** *Eogyrinus*, ventral view.
D. *Trematosuchus*, ventral view. Orbits, nares, and palatal vacuities are hatched. Note positions and shapes of orbits in A and B, and interpterygoid vacuities in D. A and C redrawn from Panchen (1980); B and D redrawn from Romer (1947).

modified to include elbow and knee joints as torques were applied to the limbs in terrestrial locomotion. Resistance for forward thrust on land was provided by the pentadactyl hand and foot.

Although the fossil record provides no evidence of the soft anatomy of these primitive amphibians, we can assume that the transition to terrestrial habits must have occasioned some striking modifications. For example, in order to feed out of water, the development of a tongue would have helped to secure prey and manipulate and swallow it. Also, mucous-secreting intermaxillary glands would facilitate swallowing. Skin glands and a well-developed lymphatic system would have been important in keeping the skin moist for cutaneous respiration and for diminishing desiccation. The eye must have undergone some striking modifications, developing a convex cornea, flattened lens, and a mechanism to move the lens to accommodate vision in air. Similarly, removed from the aquatic medium, the eye must be protected; thus it is reasonable to assume that these organisms might have had eyelids, lubricating glands, and the ability to withdraw the eye at least partially into the head.

Groups of Primitive Amphibians

Classically, these tetrapods are divided into two subclasses, the Labyrinthodontia and the Lepospondyli, on the basis of the arch vertebrae of the former and husk vertebrae of the latter. The labyrinthodonts are common as Late Paleozoic and Triassic fossils and are represented by two orders, the Anthracosauria and the Temnospondyli. The primary distinction between these two groups lies in the structure of their arch vertebrae. In anthracosaurs the pleurocentrum tends to become the dominant element in the centrum, whereas in temnospondyls it is the intercentrum that dominates. Additionally, anthracosaurs are characterized by a moderately large tabular bone that articulates with the parietal, whereas in temnospondyls the bone is small and has no contact with the parietal. The anthracosaurs, which became extinct at the close of the Permian, were represented by two groups—the water-dwelling embolomeres (e.g., *Palaeoherpeton;* Fig. 15-2), and the more terrestrial seymouriamorphs that have a large otic notch and a single occipital condyle.

In contrast to the anthracosaurs, the temnospondyls persisted into the Triassic. It is in this latter group that we note a tendency for the skull to become flattened and reduced through the loss of bone (intertemporal lost; tendency for braincase to be cartilaginous; pterygoid reduced resulting in interpterygoid vacuities; tabular small), and to develop double occipital condyles (Fig. 15-17). The temnospondyls are represented by a variety of adaptive types ranging from specialized, long-snouted marine fish-eaters (e.g., *Trematosaurus*) to heavier-bodied, more generalized forms such as *Edops*. The more primitive temnospondyls are represented by the suborder Rhachitomi (e.g., *Eryops*), in which a pleurocentrum still persists along with the intercentrum. Among the rhachitomes was a group of small terrestrial animals, the dissorophids, from which some or all of the modern amphibians may have arisen. More advanced temnospondyls are represented by the stereospondyls (e.g., *Rhinesuchus*), in which pleurocentra and skulls are much reduced, and the palatal dentition is arranged in long rows of teeth smaller than the large tusks characteristic of more primitive temnospondyls. The third group of temnospondyls are the highly specialized plagiosaurs (e.g., *Plagiosaurus*), which are thought to be neotenic. These animals have broad, short skulls and peculiar, elongate vertebrae.

The second major group of primitive tetrapods is represented by two orders—the Aistopoda and Nectridea. Unlike the labyrinthodonts, these animals with husk-type vertebrae diversified into a variety of small forms, primarily in the Carboniferous; none is known later than the Permian. The aistopods (e.g., *Ophiderpeton*) are strange snakelike creatures with limbs reduced or lost and up to 200 vertebrae. Nectrideans are represented by two types—a limbless, or nearly limbless, eel-like animal with a long, pointed skull (e.g., *Urocordylus*), and the bizarre,

pond-dwelling animals represented by *Diplocaulus* with broad, flat bodies and "horned" skulls.

A third group, the microsaurs (e.g., *Euryodus*), were included formerly with the aistopods and nectrideans, but the microsaurs differ from these groups in having a small intercentrum. Furthermore, they are more generalized and characterized by an elongate trunk, weak limbs, three-digit manus, and a skull in which the supratemporal is retained but the intertemporal and tabular are lost. This group is important because it has been postulated by some authors to be ancestral to both salamanders and caecilians.

STATUS OF THE LISSAMPHIBIA

Since Gadow (1901) first proposed the infraclass Lissamphibia to include the three Recent amphibian orders—salamanders, caecilians, and anurans—the relationships of these groups to one another and to various fossil taxa have been the subject of continual, and at times, heated debate. A minority of scientists (e.g., Herre, 1935; Carroll and Currie, 1975; and Carroll and Holmes, 1980) have hypothesized separate origins for all three orders. Another group has suggested that although salamanders and caecilians share a common ancestor, anurans were derived independently; included here are Romer (1945), Holmgren (1952), von Huene (1956), J. Lehman (1956), and Jarvik (1942, 1960, 1980–81). Schmalhausen (1958, 1959) and Nieuwkoop and Sutasurya (1976) postulated independent origins of anurans and salamanders but did not comment on the position of the caecilians. Among those who believed salamanders and anurans share a common ancestor, with caecilians having been derived separately, are Haeckel (1866), Noble (1931b), Eaton (1959), and Reig (1964). Pusey (1943) and N. Stephenson (1951a, 1951b, 1955) supported the monophyly of salamanders and anurans, but did not comment on the status of caecilians. Finally, some authors—H. Parker (1956), Szarski (1962), Parsons and E. Williams (1963), Estes (1965), Jurgens (1971), Morescalchi (1973), Bolt (1977, 1979), Gardiner (1983)—supported the monophyletic origin of the three orders. To attempt a critical review of all of this literature would be cumbersome here. Instead, the reader is directed to the excellent summaries of pre-1962 papers in Szarski (1962) and Parsons and E. Williams (1963). The more recent contributions are reviewed here and integrated with the aforementioned syntheses.

Origin of the Lissamphibia

Among those authors who favor a monophyletic origin of the three orders or a common ancestor for anurans and salamanders, there is general agreement that this ancestor is to be found among the temnospondylous amphibians. Gardiner (1983) listed four synapomorphies of temnospondyls and Recent amphibians: (1) skull lacking

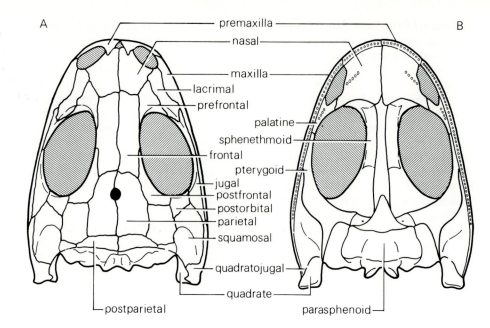

A

B

premaxilla

nasal

maxilla

lacrimal

prefrontal

palatine

sphenethmoid

frontal

pterygoid

jugal

postfrontal

postorbital

parietal

squamosal

quadratojugal

quadrate

postparietal

parasphenoid

Figure 15-18. Skull of the temnospondylous dissorophid amphibian *Doleserpeton annectens* in **A.** dorsal and **B.** ventral views. Redrawn from Bolt (1977).

an internasal bone; (2) possession of labyrinthodont teeth; (3) presence of small apical fossa with vomers that meet premaxillae anteriorly; and (4) infraorbital canal looped over lacrimal bone and continuous over jugal and lacrimal bones. Even among authors who favor a polyphyletic origin of the Lissamphibia, there is a general consensus that anurans are allied closely with temnospondyls of the family Dissorophidae that range from the Middle Pennsylvanian to the Lower Triassic. These amphibians were small, terrestrial organisms with a primitive amphibian biphasic life cycle (Bolt, 1979). The appendicular skeleton was well developed and the body relatively short (26 or fewer presacral vertebrae). Cranially, dissorophids lack an intertemporal bone and have a large orbit and an otic notch (Figs. 15-18, 15-19). The maxillary arch is complete, with the maxilla articulating with the quadratojugal. The occipital condyles are paired, and a hypoglossal foramen in the exoccipital presumably provided an exit for the eleventh and twelfth cranial nerves posterior to the skull.

Bolt (1977, 1979) suggested that lissamphibians may have arisen from dissorophids via progenesis, a heterochronic shift in the rate of ontogenetic development that results in paedomorphosis—an evolutionary mechanism in which larval and/or juvenile characters of the ancestor are retained in subadult and adult stages of the descendant. Progenesis involves precocious sexual maturity accompanied by an arrest of the rate of growth and change of body shape. The process should not be confused with a second heterochronic pattern, neoteny, that also results in paedomorphosis. Neoteny involves retardation of somatic development with respect to sexual maturation, or retardation of both sexual and somatic development.

Bolt (1977) argued for a paedomorphic origin of the lissamphibians from the dissorophids on the grounds that it is a recognized evolutionary mode among Recent salamanders and among some labyrinthodonts (Boy, 1972, 1974). Because of the small size of Recent amphibians, Bolt (1979) reasoned that progenesis is the most logical mechanism for their origin. Following S. Gould (1977), Bolt suggested further that a progenetic origin of lissamphibians from the terrestrially adapted dissorophids enabled them to reproduce rapidly in ephemeral aquatic environments and, as small-sized adults, exploit a variety of suitably moist terrestrial microhabitats—a strategy characteristic of many groups of Recent amphibians. Bolt's arguments are strengthened further by his observations that the juvenile dissorophid, *Doleserpeton,* possesses pedicellate palatal teeth, and that the earliest known dissorophid, *Amphibamus grandiceps* (Fig. 15-19), as an adult possesses *Doleserpeton*-like juvenile dentition. Moreover, their palatal tooth arrangement resembles that of lissamphibians. Bolt (1979) also reasoned that the ossified vertebral centra of *Doleserpeton* (consisting of a cylindrical pleurocentrum that may or may not be complete dorsally and a small crescentric intercentrum) may be ontogenetic precursors of the ossified rhachitomous centra of *Amphibamus* and other dissorophids (Fig. 15-19).

Nearly all proponents of polyphyletic origins of the Lissamphibia have sought the origins of salamanders and caecilians from one or more of the lepospondylous amphibians, owing principally to the superficial similarity between the husk-type vertebrae of these primitive amphibians and those of the modern salamanders and caecilians. Only the nectrideans and microsaurs have been

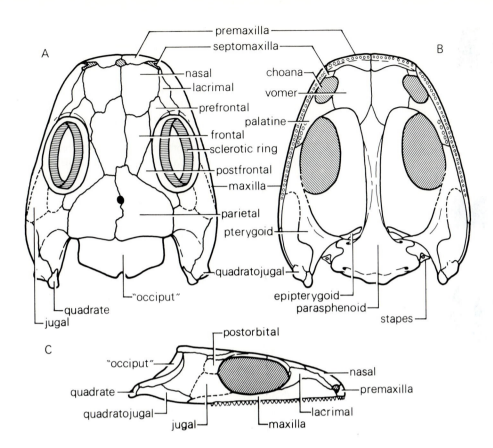

Figure 15-19. Skull of the temnospondylous dissorophid amphibian *Amphibamus grandiceps* in **A.** dorsal, **B.** ventral, and **C.** lateral views. Redrawn from Bolt (1979).

considered seriously as possible ancestors to salamanders and/or caecilians. Gregory et al. (1956) postulated that salamanders were derived from nectrideans; these is some evidence to support this (Gardiner, 1983), but there is some convincing counterevidence (Parsons and E. Williams, 1963). The primary characters that are contraindicative of a close relationship are the absence of: (1) pedicellate teeth, (2) operculum and otic notch, and (3) short, broad skull. As a group, nectrideans tend to have elongate bodies. The neural and haemal arches of the vertebrae possess unique striations unknown in modern amphibians, and the vertebrae tend to have unique articulating processes.

The microsaurs have been postulated to be ancestral to salamanders and caecilians most recently by Carroll and Currie (1975) and Carroll and Holmes (1980). Microsaurs resemble modern salamanders in possessing bicapitate ribs and in not having lost any of the dermal cranial elements typical of primitive Recent taxa. On the other hand, an otic notch is absent, as is an articulation between the maxilla and quadratojugal. On the basis of similarities of the skull roof, palate, and braincase in caecilians and the Paleozoic microsaur *Goniorhynchus*, Carroll and Currie (1975) suggested that caecilians were derived independently of salamanders and anurans, and possibly are allied to a *Goniorhynchus*-like microsaur.

Carroll and Holmes (1980) proposed that on the basis of the structure of the cheek and temporal region, microsaurs and salamanders share a similar pattern of adductor jaw muscles; thus, they suggested that the ancestors of anurans and salamanders diverged from one another in the early Carboniferous, with salamanders evolving from microsaurs and anurans from labyrinthodonts in the Late Permian and Triassic. The evidence for microsaurs or nectrideans as ancestors to any groups of modern amphibians is weak by comparison with the evidence supporting a dissorophid ancestor, because the latter evidence consists almost entirely of primitive resemblances.

Modern Amphibians

Parsons and E. Williams (1963) and Gardiner (1982, 1983) concisely interpreted the evidence for the monophyly of the three orders of living amphibians. Using Parsons and Williams's outline, we elaborate on the characters, incorporating and adding new or contradictory information that bears on the subject.

Characters Uniquely Linking the Three Recent Amphibian Orders. Several character complexes are common to all three living orders:

1. *Pedicellate teeth.*—In the majority of Recent am-

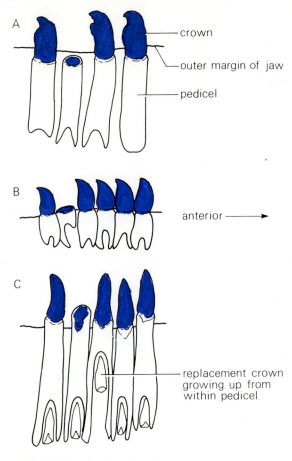

A
- crown
- outer margin of jaw
- pedicel

B
- anterior →

C
- replacement crown growing up from within pedicel

Figure 15-20. Pedicellate teeth in Lissamphibia. **A.** Salamander (*Amphiuma means*). **B.** Caecilian (*Dermophis mexicanus*). **C.** Anuran (*Caudiverbera caudiverbera*). Drawn from photographs in Parsons and E. Williams (1962).

phibians having teeth, the teeth consist of a basal pedicel and a distal crown (Fig. 15-20). Both are composed primarily of dentine, with the dentine of the pedicel and crown being divided by uncalcified dentine (some anurans) or a ring of fibrous connective tissue (salamanders, caecilians, other anurans). Generally the crown is shorter than the pedicel and is capped by enamel or an enamel-like material. The boundary between the crown and the pedicel, which is composed of cement, lies close to the gum line. Developmentally, both parts of the tooth arise as a continuous layer of tissue separated in the early stages from the bones of the jaw; the inner surfaces of both the crown and pedicel are lined with prominent odontoblasts (Parsons and E. Williams, 1963). Among the few amphibians that are known to lack pedicellate teeth are salamanders of the genus *Siren,* and frogs of the genera *Phyllobates* and *Ceratophrys.* The separation between the crown and the pedicel tends to be obscured in some specimens of salamanders of the genera *Necturus* and *Proteus,* in the anuran genus *Bombina* (Parsons and E. Williams, 1963), and in some paedomorphic

fossil salamanders (Estes, 1975). The significance of this variation is not entirely clear. In the frog *Ceratophrys,* J. Lehman (1968) demonstrated that the undivided teeth develop secondarily from divided teeth. However, Larsen (1963) noted that the larval salamanders that he examined had undivided teeth, and that divided teeth did not appear until the larvae transformed. Thus, the presence of undivided teeth in salamanders probably is a paedomorphic trait in contrast to their presence in anurans which seems to be a derived specialization.

Although the presence of this unique tooth structure has long been known in Recent amphibians (first noted by Leydig, 1867), it was not known to occur in any fossil groups until reported for the Lower Permian temnospondyl *Doloserpeton annectens* (Dissorophidae) by Bolt (1969). Subsequently, Bolt (1979) demonstrated that the palatal teeth of most adult dissorophids are conical and sharp-pointed—i.e., typical labyrinthodont fanglike teeth. However, juvenile *Doloserpeton* have pedicellate (and probably bicuspid) palatal teeth, and the Middle Pennsylvanian dissorophid *Amphibamus grandiceps* has pedicellate, bicuspid marginal teeth (palatal teeth unknown).

2. *Operculum-plectrum complex.*—Despite the statement of Carroll and Currie (1975) with regard to caecilians, it seems fairly certain that the majority of amphibians possess a columella (plectrum) and operculum to transmit sounds to the inner ear, although the two elements are fused in some taxa (see Chapter 13). The distal element, the columella, is derived phylogenetically from the hyoid arch and is invariably present in salamanders and caecilians. It is attached distally in cartilage, bone, or connective tissue with the squamosal or quadrate, or the hyoid. In some anurans, the columella is lost (Trueb, 1973, 1979), but in the majority that possess it, the columella is united to the external tympanum (absent in caecilians, salamanders, and some anurans) by the cartilaginous pars externa plectri derived from the palatoquadrate (Barry, 1956). The operculum develops in association with the fenestra ovalis in all amphibians, except obligate neotenic salamanders in which it presumably has been lost (see Chapter 6). In salamanders, the operculum and columella are separate or fused; in most anurans, they are syndesmotically united, and in caecilians they are thought to be fused synostotically into a single unit.

3. *Papilla amphibiorum.*—All amphibians possess a specialized and unique sensory area in the wall of the sacculus in the inner ear (see Chapter 14 for a description). The function of the papilla amphibiorum is to receive acoustic signals of less than 1,000 Hz, whereas a second sensory area, the papilla basilaris, receives sound frequencies of more than 1,000 Hz.

4. *Green rods.*—Both salamanders and anurans have a special type of visual cell in the retina, the "green rods," that are unique to these two groups (Walls, 1942). The function of these cells is unknown, and apparently they are absent in caecilians, which characteristically have greatly reduced eyes that, for all practical purposes, are non-functional as sight organs in adults.

5. *Structure of m. levator bulbi.*—Of the eight eye muscles, seven are innervated by branches of Cranial Nerves III, IV, and VI, whereas only one, the m. levator bulbi, is innervated by a branch of Cranial Nerve V. This muscle consists of a thin sheet that forms an elastic floor to the orbit, lying between the eye and the roof of the mouth. Its primary function seems to involve elevating the eye (an ability unique to amphibians), thereby enlarging the buccal cavity to facilitate respiration. The muscle is structurally similar in anurans and salamanders. Although the posterior part is reduced in caecilians, the anterior part is homologous to that in anurans and salamanders (Reig, 1964). The modification of this muscle in caecilians is not surprising in view of the reduction of the eye and complete dermal roofing of the skull.

6. *Fat bodies.*—All three orders are characterized by fat bodies associated with the gonads. Although their shape varies, the fat bodies similarly develop from the germinal ridge and therefore seem to be homologous in anurans, salamanders, and caecilians.

7. *Structure of skin glands.*—All Recent amphibians have two kinds of skin glands—mucous and granular (or poison) glands. The similarity of their structure in the three orders substantiates their homology.

8. *Respiratory mechanisms and attendant specializations.*—A peculiarity of all Recent amphibians is their reliance on cutaneous respiration facilitated by the maintenance of a moist skin surface by the numerous mucous glands for the transfer of oxygen. Presence of dermal skin coverings and reduced numbers of mucous glands preclude this mode of respiration in amniotes, which instead have perfected a respiratory mechanism that relies primarily on the action of intercostal muscles (among other specializations) to moderate the air pressure in the lungs and a sophisticated vascular system to distribute oxygenated blood to the tissues. This contrasts with the circulatory system in amphibians in which a three-chambered heart incompletely separates venous and arterial blood, and the organisms' reliance on a force-pump mechanism to inflate the lungs.

Whereas aquatic vertebrates that breathe with lungs use the pressure of the surrounding water to force air into the lungs, amphibians inspire air into the buccal cavity by lowering the floor of the mouth while the nostrils remain open. As the floor is raised, air is expelled. After several such oscillatory cycles, the nares are closed and the larynx opened, at which time some air from the lungs mixes with that in the buccal cavity. As the floor of the mouth is elevated when the nostrils are closed, some of the contents of the buccal cavity are forced by differential pressure into the lungs and trapped there by the closure of the larynx. Subsequent opening of the nostrils and movement of the floor of the mouth expels air from the buccal cavity. As the larynx opens and the body wall muscles contract, air flows from the lungs into the buccal

cavity. This force-pump mechanism characterizes all Recent amphibians and clearly is quite inefficient given the considerable amount of energy expended to secure a relatively small amount of oxygen, in contrast to the systems of amniotes and air-breathing fishes. The internal surfaces of the lungs of Recent amphibians are poorly developed, lacking the spongy surface characteristic of amniotes.

9. *Chromosomes and DNA content.*—Karyologically the modern groups of amphibians are characterized by (1) the tendency to acquire through evolution karyotypes composed of reduced numbers of chromosomes, all metacentric and differing little in size; (2) the tendency to increase the amount of DNA (genome size), especially in salamanders, but also in anurans and caecilians; and (3) notable interspecific variability in genome size even among related species having morphologically similar karyotypes (Morescalchi, 1973, 1980) (see Chapter 16 for details). These patterns are in marked contrast to all other groups of vertebrates.

10–14. *Other Characters.*—Among the synapomorphies listed by Gardiner (1983), the following are included here: (10) roofing bones in temporal region consisting of parietals only; (11) craniovertebral joints similar; (12) short ribs not encircling body; (13) musculocutaneous vein present; and (14) postfrontal bone absent.

Characters of Recent Amphibians that Occur in Other Tetrapods. Some characters that are shared by the three Recent groups of amphibians also occur in some other groups of tetrapods.

1. *Fenestration of the temporal region of the skull.*—In primitive amphibians the orbit is bounded ventrally and posteroventrally by the jugal and postorbital bones, respectively, that separate the orbit from the temporal region. Both the jugal and the postorbital are absent in all Recent amphibians. Salamanders and most anurans are alike in possessing a fenestrate temporal region in which the side of the skull ventral and posteroventral to the orbit is open but bounded ventrally to some degree by the maxillary arch. A number of anurans have elaborated dermal bone in the temporal region, thereby reducing the fenestration secondarily (Trueb, 1973). Among these is a wide array of casque-headed species of hylid and bufonid frogs that have elaborated the dermal roofing bones for purposes of protection and/or external support. In carnivorous anurans (of which there are representatives in the hylids, leptodactylids, and ranids), the elaboration of bone in the temporal region nearly covers the adductor jaw musculature. All of these are carnivores; therefore, as in the case of the casque-headed species, the elaboration of bone in the temporal region seems to be a derived feature associated with specialized habits. Likewise, the caecilians as a group lack temporal fenestration. This can be viewed as one of a suite of cranial modifications associated with the burrowing habits of the order. In the case of the caecilians, this specialization

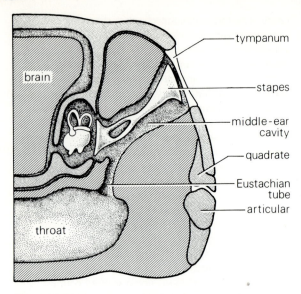

tympanum

stapes

middle-ear cavity

quadrate

Eustachian tube

articular

brain

throat

Figure 15-21. Cross section of half of an amphibian skull in the ear region showing the dorsal orientation of the stapes from the fenestra ovalis of the inner ear to the tympanum distally. Redrawn from Romer (1945).

(along with the others) is a feature common to all members of the group. Alternatively, Carroll and Currie (1975) suggested that the lack of temporal fenestration (along with some other cranial characters) allies caecilians more closely with the microsaur *Goniorhynchus* than with either salamanders or frogs. However, *Goniorhynchus* retains jugal, postorbital, and temporal bones, whereas caecilians do not; the ventral and posteroventral margins of the orbit are formed by the maxilla and squamosal, and the expanded squamosal covers most of the temporal region laterally.

2. *Loss of posterior skull bones.*—All Recent amphibians lack the supratemporal, intertemporal, tabular, and postparietal bones of the posterior skull table characteristic of primitive amphibians.

3. *Advanced type of palate.*—In primitive tetrapods the pterygoids are in close contact or approximate each other anteromedially. Posteromedially, they articulate (but do not fuse) with the braincase via a basipterygoid articulation. The medial part of the parasphenoid, the cultriform process, is a slender element, lies free dorsal to the pterygoids, and does not articulate with the vomers. In contrast, Recent amphibians are characterized by pterygoids that are separated widely and reduced, and that almost always articulate with the braincase. The cultriform process of the parasphenoid tends to be moderately broad to wide, never underlies the pterygoids, and occasionally articulates with the vomers (especially in salamanders and caecilians).

4. *Presence of double occipital condyles.*—In all modern amphibians the skull articulates with the vertebral column by means of two occipital condyles. The first

cervical vertebra, or atlas, characteristically bears double cotyles and lacks transverse processes or ribs.

5. *Morphology of nasal region.*—On the basis of detailed studies of the snout regions of anurans, salamanders, *Porolepis,* and *Eusthenopteron,* Jarvik (1942) postulated a basic dichotomy whereby porolepiforms were ancestral to salamanders that have widely separated nasal capsules and osteolepiforms (*Eusthenopteron*) gave rise to anurans characterized by medially adjacent nasal capsules. On the basis of an exhaustive study, Jurgens (1971) showed that the medial separation of the nasal capsules is variable in salamanders and anurans, depending on ontogenetic development. During development the forebrain is retracted from the internasal region; the more nearly complete the retraction, the closer the nasal sacs (and capsules) approximate one another medially. Retraction is most marked in caecilians and in advanced anurans, and least marked in primitive anurans (e.g., *Ascaphus* and *Leiopelma*) and salamanders, which resemble one another closely.

Jurgens (1971) also demonstrated that the three orders share other features in common. The ontogeny of the nasal sacs is the same, with the observed differences being expressions of the stage at which ontogenesis is terminated. The openings in the nasal capsule (i.e., foramen apicale of salamanders and caecilians, and fenestra nasobasalis of anurans) for the branches of the ramus ophthalmicus profundus nerve are homologous. Jacobson's organ is homologous in salamanders and anurans, and possibly in caecilians also, although in that group the association of the organ with the tentacular apparatus represents a specialization that obscures its primary condition. All three orders possess homologous intermaxillary glands.

6. *Position of stapes.*—Among temnospondyls for which there are data and all Recent amphibians, the stapes (= columella) is dorsolaterally directed from the fenestra ovalis (Fig. 15-21). The element is directed ventrolaterally in higher vertebrates and in osteolepiform fishes.

Equivocal features of modern amphibians. Some features of modern amphibians are insufficiently known to determine if they characterize the group as a whole or not.

1. *Vertebral column.*—Owing to the lack of fossil evidence, the homologies of vertebral centra in Recent amphibians (and tetrapods as a whole) are unknown (see D. Wake, 1970, for review of the literature and discussion). The vertebrae of the three orders of living amphibians are exclusively monospondylous; the neural arch usually is fused to the centrum, initial vertebral ossification appears in the intermyotomal recess, and some degree of ossification from the perichordal tube occurs in each order. Vertebral development in the three groups follows three quite distinct patterns (D. Wake, 1970). Thus in salamanders, the centrum is derived from hypertrophied intervertebral cartilage (formed in the perichondral tube surrounding the notochord) and the cartilage found within the notochord in midvertebral and intervertebral areas. In contrast, the majority of the centrum in caecilians is derived from membranous additions. Intervertebral cartilage is reduced; it forms a ligament joining adjacent centra and contributes bone to the ends of the centra. Notochordal tissue is limited to the intervertebral cartilage that underlies the cartilaginous rudiments of the neural pedicel. Anurans are characterized by two patterns of vertebral development, perichordal and epichordal. In the former mode, the cartilage vertebral model ossifies membranously around the notochord, reducing the size of the notochord and frequently obliterating it. Epichordal formation is characterized by ossification of the tissue dorsal to the notochord; the notochord itself, as well as the cells lateral and ventral to it, degenerate and disappear. With the exception of the primitive frogs, notochordal tissue does not persist in anurans.

2. *Mesoderm formation and formation of primordial germ cells.* —In the few species for which there are data (e.g., the salamander *Triturus* and the frogs *Bombina* and *Xenopus*), significant variation has been found in the mode of mesoderm formation. Nieuwkoop and Sutasurya (1976) reported that in the blastula–early gastrula stage the prospective mesoderm and adjacent suprablastoporal endoderm occupy the superficial cell layer in the marginal zone, which is external in *Triturus*. In contrast, the marginal zone in *Bombina* is exclusively internal. Because the blastula of *Triturus* is single-layered, the presence of surface mesoderm is associated with the occurrence of a rupture discontinuity in the superficial layer between the presumptive endoderm and mesoderm, as the mesoderm is brought into its definitive position between endoderm internally and ectoderm externally during gastrulation (R. E. Keller, 1976). In the double-layered blastula of *Bombina,* the superficial cells give rise to the ectodermal epithelial layer of the epidermis, the ependymal layer of the central nervous system, and the endodermal inner lining of the archenteron (i.e., the primitive gut); the inner layer of cells gives rise to the presumptive sensorial layer of the epidermis, most of the future nervous system, the entire chordal and prechordal mesoderm, and most of the endoderm (Nieuwkoop and Sutasurya, 1976). A third pattern of mesoderm formation was reported by R. E. Keller (1976) for the frog *Xenopus laevis*. In this species the mesoderm is double-layered, lies in the deep layer of the marginal zone (i.e., covered by the suprablastoporal endoderm—the prospective endodermal archenteron roof); as mesoderm is involuted over the lip of the blastopore, it moves along the inner surface of the deep layer of ectoderm toward the animal pole. At its upper extent the mesoderm, with the deep layer of the prospective neural and epidermal ectoderm, consists of the prospective notochord dorsally, flanked by prospective somite and lateral mesoderm. Further research on amphibians probably will yield further variation in the topography and morphogenetic movements of the primary anlagen, but to date too little is known to justify phylogenetic speculations on the significance of these differences.

Monophyly of the Lissamphibia.   Clearly, the monophyletic origin of the Recent amphibians cannot be defended unequivocally, although the accumulated evidence seems to support this hypothesis. The issue is obfuscated by the quality of the existing data. The fossil record is mediocre for salamanders and anurans and virtually nonexistent for caecilians. Many of the characters that unite the three orders are features of the soft anatomy that are not preserved in the fossils. And finally, there remains a great deal to be learned about the morphology and development of modern amphibians in general, and caecilians in particular. Progress, if it is to be made, lies in the pursuit of specific and detailed studies in these areas. And syntheses that address the phylogenetic relationships of amphibians are only relevant to the degree that they (1) consider the greatest number of characters possible, (2) establish the evolutionary polarities of the characters, (3) integrate features of fossil and Recent amphibians, and (4) justify the exclusion of contradictory evidence.

CHAPTER 16

Cytogenetic, Molecular, and Genomic Evolution

The Amphibia seem to be confronted by two contrasting genetic demands, namely to maintain a high degree of heterozygosity implying an adaptive function and to keep unaltered some relative linkage-groups, also of an adaptive value acquired over long evolutionary periods.

Alessandro Morescalchi (1979)

The ways in which genotypes are maintained within populations and species and the mechanisms by which changes occur in speciation and in the evolution of lineages are fundamental problems in evolutionary biology. Since about 1960, there have been great advances in the fields of cytogenetics and molecular genetics. A proliferation of new techniques and their continued refinement have permitted geneticists to make new kinds of observations, which have led to a much better understanding of the processes of genic evolution.

CYTOGENETICS

Amphibians are exceptionally good organisms for karyological studies because most have few, comparatively large chromosomes. Most of the work on amphibian cytogenetics has been with conventionally stained chromosomes; this kind of material allows the determination of size, centromeric position, secondary constrictions, and percentage lengths of chromosomes and their arms (see Morescalchi, 1973, for a review). Newly developed techniques, as used by O. Ward (1977), M. Schmid (1978a, b), M. Schmid et al. (1979), Veloso and Iturra (1979), and Vitelli et al. (1982), have provided an insight into the chromosomal location of constitutive heterochromatin, nucleolus organizer regions, and ribosomal RNA genes (see Birstein, 1982, for summary).

Chromosome Number and Structure

The karyological characteristics distinguishing amphibians from other classes of vertebrates are (1) a tendency toward genome hypertrophy, (2) a high degree of DNA spiralization, and (3) great interspecific differences in the amounts of nuclear DNA. The earlier ideas about relative conservativeness of chromosome morphology in the derived families in each order (e.g., Morescalchi, 1973) have been contradicted by more data on diverse taxa.

Gross morphological differences in chromosomes include size and centromeric position. Relative sizes generally are designated as microchromosomes and macrochromosomes. Microchromosomes are extremely small and possibly may be confused with so-called supernumerary or accessory chromosomes, which may be variable in their presence or number (Morescalchi, 1973; D. Green et al., 1980). Macrochromosomes commonly can be grouped into large or small chromosomes, but in some taxa there is a gradual change in size. Chromosomes are classified in relation to the position of the centromere along the length of the chromosome (Levan et al., 1964). Chromosomes having the centromere in the median region are termed metacentric. A submetacentric position denotes that the arms are unequal in length, and the shortest arm is above the centromere. A chromosome having the centromere in a terminal position is termed telocentric and one with the centromere near the end, subtelocentric. Centromeric position determines the number of arms on the chromosome (telocentrics have only one, whereas others have two). The number of arms sometimes is called the *nombre fundamental* (NF). Quantitative analytical procedures are being developed for karyotypic comparisons (D. Green et al., 1980).

In the following sections the karyotypes of the three living orders of amphibians are summarized. This survey is followed by discussions of sex chromosomes and polyploidy.

Caecilians. Karyological data are available for few species of caecilians (Table 16-1), and the absence of data on chromosomal banding precludes detailed comparisons. There is a general trend from a high number of chromosomes ($2N = 42$) and many microchromosomes (30) in primitive caecilians to fewer chromosomes ($2N = 20–24$) and no microchromosomes in advanced caecilians (Nussbaum, 1979a). However, some presumably derived karyotypes are associated with primitive morphological and life history traits among caeciliids (e.g., *Caecilia* and *Siphonops*). Additionally, some morphologically derived caeciliids have 4 or 5 pairs of microchromosomes (M. Wake et al., 1980), but none approaches the higher numbers (7–15 pairs) of microchromosomes of the ichthyophiids. Clearly, the paucity of data precludes any well-supported hypothesis on karyological evolution within caecilians, even though a general trend does seem to be apparent.

Salamanders. The extensive literature on the karyology of salamanders was summarized by Morescalchi (1975). The chromosomes of about 90% of the genera

are known (Table 16-2). The diploid number of chromosomes ranges from 66 in the hynobiids *Onychodactylus japonicus* and *Ranodon sibiricus* to 22 in New World salamandrids. With the exception of sirenids, which may be polyploid, the highest number of chromosomes and the greatest number of microchromosomes occur in the Cryptobranchoidea. Ambystomatids and plethodontids have only 13 or 14 pairs of chromosomes and completely lack microchromosomes. Salamandrids have 11 or 12 pairs that gradually grade from macro- to microchromosomes, as they do in amphiumids, which have 14 pairs. Proteids are intermediate between cryptobranchoids and other salamanders in having 19 pairs of chromosomes, of which 1 pair is classified as microchromosomes in *Necturus*.

Anurans. Several hundred species in diverse genera representing all families of anurans have been karyotypes (Table 16-3). Supposed microchromosomes have been found only in members of primitive families: *Ascaphus truei, Leiopelma hochstetteri,* and *Discoglossus pictus.* However, the small chromosomes in *Leiopelma* may be supernumerary chromosomes (Morescalchi, 1980), and those in *Ascaphus* may not be microchromosomes (D. Green et al., 1980). With the exception of *Xenopus,* the basic karyotype of other anurans seems to be 26 biarmed chromosomes. *Xenopus tropicalis* has only 20 chromosomes; the several species of *Xenopus* having 36 chromosomes may be the result of an ancient polyploidization (W. Müller, 1977).

Diverse lineages of anurans show a reduction from the basic number of 26 chromosomes. This is especially evident in the Leptodactylidae, Hylidae, and Ranidae, and

Table 16-1. Chromosomes of Caecilians

Species	Diploid number	Pairs of macro-/ microchromosomes	Reference
Ichthyophiidae			
Ichthyophis beddomei[a]	42	6/15	Seshacher (1937)
Ichthyophis glutinosus	42	10/11	Nussbaum and Treisman (1981)
Ichthyophis kohtaoensis	42	10/11	Nussbaum and Treisman (1981)
Ichthyophis orthoplicatus	42	10/11	Seto and Nussbaum (1976)
Uraeotyphlus menoni	36	11/7	Elayidom et al. (1963)
Uraeotyphlus narayani	36	8/10	Seshacher (1939)
Caeciliidae			
Caecilia occidentalis	24[b]	12/0	Barrio and Rinaldi de Chieri (1970a)
Dermophis mexicanus	26	8/5	M. Wake and Case (1975)
Gegeneophis carnosus	30	5/10	Seshacher (1944)
Geotrypetes seraphini	38[c]	15/4	Morescalchi (1973); Stingo (1974)
Grandisonia alternans	26	12/1	Blommers-Schlösser (1978)
Gymnopis multiplicata	24, 26	8/4, 5	M. Wake and Case (1975)
Hypogeophis rostratus	26	12/1	Nussbaum (1979a)
Siphonops paulensis	24	12/0	Barrio and Rinaldi de Chieri (1972)
Typhlonectidae			
Chthonerpeton indistinctum	20	10/0	Barrio et al. (1971)
Typhlonectes compressicauda	28	14/0	M. Wake et al. (1980)

[a]Reported as *Ichthyophis glutinosus*; see Seto and Nussbaum (1976).
[b]Also reported as 22 (M. Wake and Case, 1975).
[c]Also reported as 36 (M. Wake and Case, 1975).

Table 16-2. Chromosomes of Salamanders[a]

Taxonomic group	Diploid number	Pairs of macro-/ microchromosomes	Nuclear DNA (pg/N)[b]
Hynobiidae			
Onychodactylus japonicus	>66	21/>11	±100
Ranodon sibiricus	66	14/19	51
Batrachuperus mustersi	62	12/19	43
Salamandrella keyserlingi	62	19/12	42
Hynobius lichenatus	60	19/11	—
Hynobius (11 species)	56	18–20/8–10	33–41
Hynobius retardatus	40	20/0	38
Cryptobranchidae			
Andrias and *Cryptobranchus*	60	15/14–15	93–112
Sirenidae			
Pseudobranchus striatus (4N ?)	48/64	24–32/0	91
Siren lacertina (4N ?)	52	26/0	114
Siren intermedia (4N ?)	46	23/0	108
Salamandridae			
Old World (11 genera, 20 species)	24	12[c]	39–67
Notophthalmus viridescens	22	11[c]	63–86
Taricha (3 species)	22	11[c]	56–60
Proteidae			
Proteus anguinus	38	19/0	97
Necturus (5 species)	38	18/1	160
Amphiumidae			
Amphiuma (2 species)	28	14[c]	130–192
Dicamptodontidae			
Rhyacotriton	26	13/0	120
Dicamptodon	28	14/0	–
Ambystomatidae			
Ambystoma[d]	28	14/0	48–103
Plethodontidae			
Desmognathines (2 genera, 3 species)	28	14/0	30–40
Hemidactylines (3 genera, 5 species)	28	14/0	35–71
Plethodontines (3 genera, 8 species)	28	14/0	39–86
Hydromantes (5 species)	28	14/0	–
Bolitoglossines (7 genera, 17 species)	26	13/0	84[e]

[a]Based primarily on Morescalchi (1975) and Morescalchi et al. (1977, 1979).
[b]Diploid cells; picograms (10^{-12} g) per nucleus.
[c]Macrochromosomes gradually decreasing to microchromosomes.
[d]Exclusive of triploids.
[e]One species.

is characteristic of all bufonids. The reduction presumably has occurred, not through the loss of genomic material, but by the rearrangement of the material by centric fusion, especially of the smaller telocentric chromosomes (Morescalchi, 1973). Thus, there seems to be a general trend in some anuran lineages for reduction in the number of chromosomes and formation of bi-armed chromosomes. Reduction is extreme in some African ranids; there are eight pairs of chromosomes in some species of *Phrynobatrachus* and *Cardioglossa* and only seven pairs in *Arthroleptis* (Bogart and Tandy, 1981).

In some groups of frogs the basic number of 26 chromosomes is increased. For example, the primitive genera of hylids have 26 chromosomes, and although most *Hyla* and related genera have 24 chromosomes, many neotropical *Hyla* (the *H. leucophyllata* complex) have 30. The genus *Eleutherodactylus* has a great range (18–36) of chromosomes. Many of the 30-chromosome *Hyla* and *Eleutherodactylus* with high numbers of chromosomes have one or more pairs of telocentric chromosomes. Thus,

centric fission or dissociation of metacentric chromosomes is implicated in the formation of telocentric chromosomes. Fission or dissociation may be modified further by pericentric inversion and translocation (Bogart, 1973, 1981). Species in derived families having more than 26 chromosomes commonly have a corresponding number of telocentric chromosomes. The diploid number of chromosomes in most hylines, including *Osteopilus septentrionalis,* is 24. One species, *Osteopilus brunneus,* has 34, 20 of which are telocentric and compare with the 20 arms of metacentric chromosomes in *O. septentrionalis* (C. Cole, 1974). The extreme diploid number of 54 is in the African ranid *Astylosternus diadematus;* most of its chromosomes are telocentric (Bogart and Tandy, 1981).

Chromosomes and Sex Determination

There is no uniform type of genetic sex determination in amphibians. Sex reversal experiments showed female heterogamy in *Xenopus laevis* (M. Chang and Witschi, 1956), in *Pleurodeles poireti* and *P. waltl* (Gallien, 1954),

Table 16-3. Chromosomes of Anurans

Taxonomic group	Diploid number	Reference
Leiopelmatidae		
Ascaphus truei	46[a]	D. Green et al. (1980)
Leiopelma hochstetteri	22–30[a]	E. Stephenson et al. (1972, 1974)
Leiopelma archeyi and *hamiltoni*	18	E. Stephenson et al. (1972, 1974)
Discoglossidae		
Alytes obstetricans	38[a]	Morescalchi (1973)
Discoglossus pictus	28	Morescalchi (1973)
Bombina (3 species)	24	Morescalchi (1973)
Rhinophrynidae		
Rhinophrynus dorsalis	22	C. Cole (1971)
Pipidae		
Xenopus (6 species)[b]	36	Tymowska (1977)
Xenopus tropicalis	20	Tymowska (1973)
Hymenochirus boettgeri	24	Morescalchi (1981)
Pipa carvalhoi	20	Morescalchi (1981)
Pipa pipa	22	Morescalchi (1981)
Pipa parva	30	Olmo and Morescalchi (1978)
Pelobatidae		
All genera and species,	26	Morescalchi et al. (1977)
except *Leptolalax pelodytoides*	24	Morescalchi et al. (1977)
Pelodytidae		
Pelodytes punctatus	24	Morescalchi et al. (1977)
Myobatrachidae		
All genera and species,	24	Morescalchi and Ingram (1974, 1978)
except 4 species of *Limnodynastes*	22	Morescalchi and Ingram (1974, 1978)
Sooglossidae		
Nesomantis and *Sooglossus*	26	Nussbaum (1979b)
Heleophrynidae		
Heleophryne	26	Morescalchi (1981)
Leptodactylidae		
Ceratophryinae[b]	26	Barrio and Rinaldi de Chieri (1970c); Beçak et al. (1970)
Telmatobiinae		
Eupsophus	28, 30	Bogart (1970); Barrio and Rinaldi de Chieri (1971)
Other genera	26	J. D. Lynch (1978)[c]
Odontophrynini[b]	22	Saez and Brum-Zorrilla (1966)
Grypiscini	26	Beçak et al. (1970); Bogart (1970)
Eleutherodactylini		
Eleutherodactylus	18–36	Morescalchi (1979); Bogart (1981)
Sminthillus limbatus	32	Bogart (1981)
Syrrhophus (2 species)	26, 30	Bogart (1973)
Holoaden bradei	18	deLucca et al. (1974)
Other genera	22	J. D. Lynch (1971)[c]
Hylodinae		
Crossodactylus and *Hylodes*	26	Beçak (1968); Denaro (1972)
Leptodactylinae		
Limnomedusa (1 species)	26	Barrio (1971)
Adenomera (2 species)	26	Bogart (1974)
Adenomera marmorata	24	Bogart (1974)
Paratelmatobius lutzi	24	deLucca et al. (1974)
Pseudopaludicola (2 species)	18–22	Brum-Zorrilla and Saez (1968)
Lithodytes lineatus	18	Bogart (1974)
Other genera[b]	22	Morescalchi (1979)[c]
Bufonidae		
All genera and species,[b]	22	Bogart (1972)
except *Bufo regularis* group[b]	20	Bogart (1972)
Brachycephalidae		
Brachycephalus ephippium	22	Bogart (pers. comm.)
Rhinodermatidae		
Rhinoderma (2 species)	26	Formas (1976b)

[a] Part of the complement consists of pairs of microchromosomes: *Ascaphus*, 5/18 pairs of macro-/microchromosomes; *Leiopelma hochstetteri*, 11/0–8; *Alytes*, 11/8 (D. Green et al., 1980, offered a different explanation).

[b] In addition to the diploid numbers given, some species are polyploids.

[c] References to various genera and species included in these summaries.

[d] Several species of *Kaloula*, including *pulchra*, reported as having 28 chromosomes, but *K. pulchra* also reported to have only 24 by Bogart and C. Nelson (1976).

Taxonomic group	Diploid number	Reference
Pseudidae		
Pseudis paradoxa	24	Barrio and Pistol de Rubel (1970)
Hylidae		
Pelodryadines,	26	Menzies and Tippett (1976); Morescalchi (1979)
except *Litoria infrafrenata*	24	Menzies and Tippett (1976)
Phyllomedusines[b]	26	P. León (1970); Bogart (1973)
Hemiphractines		
Fritziana (3 species)	26–30	Bogart (1973)
Gastrotheca (12 species)	26, 28	Bogart and Duellman (unpublished)
Other genera and species	26	Bogart (1973); Duellman and Hoogmoed (1984)
Hylinae		
Osteopilus brunneus	34	C. Cole (1974)
Hyla "leucophyllata complex"	30	Bogart (1973); Duellman and Trueb (1983)
Acris crepitans	22	C. Cole (1966)
Other genera and species[b]	24	Morescalchi (1979)[c]
Centrolenidae		
Centrolenella	20	Bogart (1973)
Dendrobatidae		
Colostethus	24	Bogart (1973)
Dendrobates (6 species)	18–22	P. León (1970); Bogart (pers. comm.)
Ranidae		
Raninae[b]	26	Morescalchi (1979); Bogart and Tandy (1981)
except *Ptychadena* (5 species),	24	Bogart and Tandy (1981)
Rana (3 species),	24	Kobayashi (1963)
and *Rana kuhlii* and *namiyei*	22	Kuramoto (1972, 1980)
Petropedetinae		
Anhydrophryne and *Petropedetes*	26	Bogart and Tandy (1981)
Dimorphognathus africanus	24	Bogart and Tandy (1981)
Phrynobatrachus (6 species)	16–20	Bogart and Tandy (1981)
Mantellinae		
All genera and species,	26	Blommers-Schlösser (1978)
except some *Mantidactylus*	24	
Arthroleptinae		
Arthroleptis (3 species)	14	Bogart and Tandy (1981)
Cardioglossa (2 species)	16	Bogart and Tandy (1981)
Astylosterninae		
Astylosternus diadematus	54	Bogart and Tandy (1981)
Nyctibates corrugatus	28	Bogart and Tandy (1981)
Hemisinae		
Hemisus (1 species)	24	Bogart and Tandy (1981)
Hyperoliidae		
All genera and species,	24	Blommers-Schlösser (1978);
except *Leptopelis* (10 species)	22, 24, 30	Bogart and Tandy (1981)
Rhacophoridae		
All genera and species	26	Kuramoto (1977); Morescalchi (1981)
Microhylidae		
Asterophryinae	26	C. Cole and Zweifel (1971)
Genyophryninae	26	C. Cole and Zweifel (1971)
Phrynomerinae	26	Morescalchi (1981)
Dyscophinae	26	Blommers-Schlösser (1976)
Cophylinae	26	Blommers-Schlösser (1976)
Microhylinae		
Kaloula[d]	28	Kuramoto (1980)
Other Asian genera	26	Natarajan (1953)
Glossostoma and *Otophryne*	26	Bogart and C. Nelson (1976); Bogart et al. (1976)
Chiasmocleis	24	Bogart and C. Nelson (1976)
Other New World genera	22	Bogart and C. Nelson (1976)

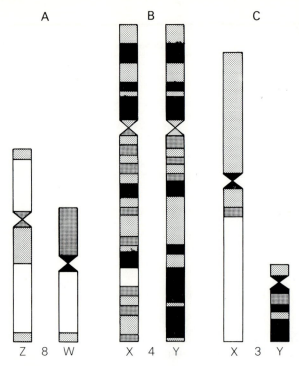

A   B   C

Z 8 W   X 4 Y   X 3 Y

Figure 16-1. Heteromorphic sex chromosomes in amphibians.
A. *Pyxicephalus adspersus,* ZZ/ZW type (M. Schmid, 1980).
B. *Rana esculenta,* XX/XY type (Schempp and M. Schmid, 1981).
C. *Necturus maculosus,* XX/XY type (Sessions, 1980). Different shading represents differentially stained bands; numbers refer to chromosome pair. All redrawn to approximately same scale.

Male heterogamy (XY/XX type) has been found in three anurans—*Rana esculenta* (Schempp and M. Schmid, 1981), *Eupsophus migueli* (Iturra and Veloso, 1981), and *Gastrotheca riobambae* (M. Schmid et al., 1983); several salamanders—five species of *Necturus* (Sessions and J. Wiley, 1985), *Triturus alpestris, T. helveticus,* and *T. vulgaris* (M. Schmid et al., 1979); and various species of bolitoglossine plethodontids (*Dendrotriton, Nototriton, Oedipina,* and *Thorius*) (P. León and Kezer, 1978).

Female heterogamy (ZZ/WZ type) has been noted for certain in one anuran, *Pyxicephalus adspersus* (M. Schmid, 1980), and possibly in *Discoglossus pictus* (Morescalchi, 1964), and in several salamanders: *Pleurodeles poireti* (Lacroix, 1970), *P. waltl* (Lacroix, 1968), *Triturus cristatus* (Callan and L. Lloyd, 1960), *T. marmoratus* (Mancino and Nardi, 1971), *Siren intermedia* (P. León and Kezer, 1974), *Ambystoma laterale* (Sessions, 1982), and *Aneides ferreus* (Kezer and Sessions, 1979).

No sex chromosomes have been identified in caecilians. Presumably the type of chromosomal heterogamy will be determined for many species of amphibians in the future through modern staining techniques and by gene linkage-group studies using gel electrophoresis. Possibly chromosomal heterogamy is not the mechanism for determining the sexes in all amphibians, for no sex chromosomes have been identified in several amphibians, including *Xenopus laevis,* which has been studied thoroughly (Tymowska, 1977). Although different morphologies and banding patterns (and therefore differential replicating DNA) have been identified, the causal factors for XY/XX and ZZ/WZ heterogamy have yet to be determined. However, it is now known that ribosomal RNA not only is a component of the nucleolus organizer regions but also occurs at other sites; the inheritance of these chromosomal sites follows simple Mendelian principles (Batistoni et al., 1978). Furthermore, in snakes having ZZ/WZ heterogamy (Singh et al., 1976), it has been shown that there is differential satellite DNA associated with the W and Z chromosomes. Possibly the origin of satellite DNA in the W chromosome is the first step in the differentiation of the sex chromosomes by generating asynchrony in the DNA replication pattern of Z and W chromosomes. Conceivably this reduces the frequency of crossing-over, which is the prerequisite of differentiation of sex chromosomes.

Polyploidy

The addition of one or more haploid chromosome complements to the normal diploid genome occurs naturally in several species of salamanders and anurans (Table 16-4). These polyploid species or populations generally are associated with their supposed ancestral diploid populations. With the possible exception of the sirenids, there are no known polyploid families, genera, or even species groups of amphibians (see Bogart, 1980, and Kawamura, 1984, for reviews). Polyploidy can be induced in eggs prior to the second meiotic division by temperature shock or elevated pressures in the laboratory (Ferrier and Jay-

in *Ambystoma mexicanum* and *A. tigrinum* (Humphrey, 1945), and in *Bufo bufo* (Ponse, 1942). On the other hand, similar experiments and investigations of parthenogenetically bred frogs indicated male heterogamy in *Bombina orientalis, Hyla japonica,* and four species of *Rana (brevipoda, japonica, nigromaculata, rugosa)* (Kawamura and Nishioka, 1977), and also in *R. pipiens* (C. Richards and Nace, 1978). Studies on the expression of the gene for the H-Y cell surface antigen have confirmed female heterogamy in *Xenopus laevis* and indicated male heterogamy in *Rana pipiens* (Wachtel et al., 1975). Sex-linked genes for enzymes have been detected in *Pleurodeles waltl* (Ferrier et al., 1980) and in hybrids of *Rana catesbeiana* and *R. clamitans* (Elinson, 1981). Sex-linked genetic loci have been identified in *R. pipiens.* In *Rana,* sex is determined by a locus or a small region of the chromosome; the rest of the "X" and "Y" chromosomes apparently are identical (D. Wright et al., 1983).

Relatively new techniques for the staining of constitutive heterochromatin, ribosomal proteins, and replicating chromosomal DNA have provided a way to identify sex chromosomes other than by gross morphology, as was done with *Discoglossus pictus* (Morescalchi, 1964). The cytological evidence for the few species in which sex chromosomes have been identified shows heteromorphic chromosomes by gross morphology and/or banding patterns; these fall into two types (Fig. 16-1).

Table 16-4. Occurrence of Polyploidy in Amphibians

Species	Zygote production	Ploidy	Reference
Salamanders			
Ambystoma platineum	Gynogenetic	$14 \times 3 = 42$	Uzzell (1963)
Ambystoma tremblayi	Gynogenetic	$14 \times 3 = 42$	Uzzell (1963)
Ambystoma texanum × laterale	Gynogenetic/ ?parthenogenetic	$14 \times 3 = 42$	Downs (1978)
Pseudobranchus striatus	Bisexual polyploid	$16 \times 4 = 64$	Morescalchi and Olmo (1974)
Siren lacertina	Bisexual polyploid	$13 \times 4 = 52$	Morescalchi and Olmo (1974)
Anurans			
Xenopus ruwenzoriensis	Bisexual polyploid	$18 \times 6 = 108$	Fischberg and Kobel (1978)
Xenopus vestitus	Bisexual polyploid	$18 \times 4 = 72$	Tymowska and Fischberg (1973)
Xenopus sp.	Bisexual polyploid	$18 \times 4 = 72$	Fischberg and Kobel (1978)
Neobatrachus sudelli	Bisexual polyploid	$12 \times 4 = 48$	Mahoney and Robertson (1980)
Neobatrachus sutor	Bisexual polyploid	$12 \times 4 = 48$	Mahoney and Robertson (1980)
Ceratophrys aurita	Bisexual polyploid	$13 \times 8 = 104$	Beçak et al. (1967)
Ceratophrys ornata	Bisexual polyploid	$13 \times 8 = 104$	Beçak et al. (1966)
*Odontophrynus americanus**	Bisexual polyploid	$11 \times 4 = 44$	Bogart (1967)
Pleurodema bibronii	Bisexual polyploid	$11 \times 4 = 44$	Barrio and Rinaldi de Chieri (1970b)
Pleurodema kriegi	Bisexual polyploid	$11 \times 4 = 44$	Barrio and Rinaldi de Chieri (1970b)
Bufo danatensis	Bisexual polyploid	$11 \times 4 = 44$	Pisanetz (1978)
*Bufo viridis**	Bisexual polyploid	$11 \times 4 = 44$	Mazik et al. (1976)
Bufo sp.	Bisexual polyploid	$10 \times 4 = 40$	Bogart and Tandy (1976)
Hyla versicolor	Bisexual polyploid	$12 \times 4 = 48$	Wasserman (1970)
*Phyllomedusa burmeisteri**	Bisexual polyploid	$13 \times 4 = 52$	Batistic et al. (1975)
Dicroglossus occipitalis	Bisexual polyploid	$13 \times 4 = 52$	Bogart and Tandy (1976)
*Rana esculenta**	Hybridogenetic	$13 \times 3 = 39$	R. Günther (1975a)
*Tomopterna delalandii**	Bisexual polyploid	$13 \times 4 = 52$	Bogart and Tandy (1976)

*Some populations are diploid and others polyploid.

let, 1978); also foreign or irradiated spermatozoa may activate development of gynogenetic diploid eggs that have been subjected to temperature or pressure shock (Nace et al., 1970; Volpe, 1970). Polyploidy in amphibians was reviewed by Bogart (1980).

Polyploidy in amphibians may be the result of hybridization of two or more species (allopolyploidy) or may have occurred spontaneously in a single species (autopolyploidy). Multivalent associations (more than two homologous chromosomes in synapsis) during meiosis have been used as evidence for chromosomal homology; thus, a polyploid having multivalents is assumed to be an autopolyploid. Because hybrid sets of chromosomes are not homologous, allopolyploids form few, if any, multivalents. However, multivalents can be expected only in a recent autopolyploid, for polyploid species probably go through stages of diploidization as the number of mutations accumulates; eventually the polyploid has fewer and fewer multivalents. Presumably most, if not all, polyploid species of amphibians are allopolyploids. In many cases the polyploids exist in at least partial sympatry with closely related diploid congeners (e.g., tetraploid *Hyla versicolor* with diploid *H. chrysoscelis;* octoploid *Ceratophrys ornata* with diploid *C. cranwelli*).

The hybridogenetic populations of *Rana esculenta* in Europe provide a fascinating natural experiment in polyploidy. The extensive literature on this complex of species has been reviewed by Berger (1977), Dubois (1878), and Hotz and Bruno (1980). *Rana ridibunda* and *R. lessonae*

are broadly sympatric with *R. esculenta,* a hybrid "species," diploids of which contain one set of chromosomes from each of the parental species. Ova of *R. esculenta* fall into distinct size classes; the large eggs develop into triploids. If these eggs are fertilized by *R. lessonae,* the genotypes of the offspring are composed of two sets of *R. lessonae* chromosomes and one set of *R. ridibunda* chromosomes. On the other hand, if the eggs are fertilized by *R. esculenta* or *R. ridibunda,* the genotypes of the offspring contain one set of *R. lessonae* chromosomes and two sets of *R. ridibunda* chromosomes. Presumably, diploid eggs are produced by diploid *R. esculenta,* but individual females may produce both haploid and diploid eggs (Uzzell et al., 1975). Crossing triploids results in phenotypes of all three taxa (Berger, 1977).

On the basis of the progeny from numerous matings (but without cytological documentation), the process of premeiotic endomitosis has been inferred to occur in *Rana esculenta* for the production of diploid ova (Uzzell et al., 1977). In this system in diploid *R. esculenta,* the genomes are segregated so that the *R. ridibunda* or *R. lessonae* genome ends up in the first polar body. The first polar body is eliminated, and the remaining *R. ridibunda* or *R. lessonae* genome passes through a second meiotic equational division and remains intact in the ovarian nucleus. Some multivalents and bridges occur in meiosis in male *R. esculenta,* thereby suggesting genetic recombination between nonsister homologues (R. Günther, 1975b).

Salamanders of the *Ambystoma jeffersonianum* com-

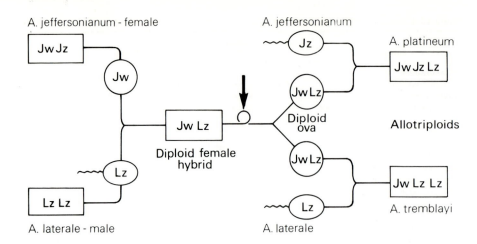

Figure 16-2. Hypothetical hybridization event in the origin of the triploid species in the *Ambystoma jeffersonianum* complex. J = *A. jeffersonianum* chromosome complement; L = *A. laterale* chromosome complement; w = female sex chromosome; z = male sex chromosome. Arrow designates chromosomal reduplication in oogenesis. Adapted from Sessions (1962).

plex occur in the Great Lakes region in North America; the complex consists of two bisexual diploid species (*A. jeffersonianum* and *A. laterale*) and two all-female triploid species (*A. platineum* and *A. tremblayi*) (Uzzell, 1964). Detailed cytological studies on these salamanders (Sessions, 1982) revealed that the triploid species are allotriploids with complementary karyotypes and identifiable sex chromosome heteromorphism of the WZ-female/ZZ-male type. The hybrid origin of the triploid species hypothesized by Sessions (1982) is one involving a female *A. jeffersonianum* and a male *A. laterale* that resulted in a diploid female hybrid, in which a prediplotene meiotic reduplication occurred during oogenesis. This resulted in the production of diploid ova. Such ova fertilized by sperm of *A. jeffersonianum* resulted in the allotriploid *A. platineum* having two complements of *A. jeffersonianum* chromosomes and one of *A. laterale;* fertilization by *A. laterale* resulted in the allotriploid *A. tremblayi* having one complement of *A. jeffersonianum* chromosomes and two of *A. laterale* (Fig. 16-2).

This model is parsimonious because it necessitates reduplication only once in the history of the complex. Furthermore, it explains the all-female populations of the triploid species, because sex determination in *Ambystoma* is the dominant-W (female heterogamy) type (Humphrey, 1945). The triploid species utilize the activation properties of sperm of diploid males to initiate zygote development; *A. platineum* uses sperm of *A. jeffersonianum,* and *A. tremblayi* uses sperm of *A. laterale.* The mechanism of sperm rejection is unknown, but because the triploid ova is in homologous balance chromosomally, a penetrating sperm nucleus, although required for activation of the egg, would be rejected as part of the physiological reaction to supernumerary sperm characteristic of most salamanders (Sessions, 1982). Breakdown of the sperm rejection mechanism results in tetraploids, as in female *A. tremblayi* inseminated by *A. laterale* males discovered by Sessions (1982), who also noted that apparent failure of oocyte chromosomes to reduplicate results in diploid offspring by triploid *A. pla-*

tineum; these offspring have karyotypes identical to those of *A. jeffersonianum.*

Mixed populations of all-female diploid and triploid *Ambystoma* occur on the Bass Islands in Lake Erie. These presumably are hybrids between *A. laterale* and *A. texanum,* with triploids having two sets of chromosomes of *A. texanum* (Downs, 1978). Because no males are known to occur on North Bass Island, the all-female *Ambystoma* on that island may be parthenogenetic.

Although experimental evidence is lacking, at least two species of sirenid salamanders may be tetraploids (Morescalchi and Olmo, 1974; Morescalchi, 1975). This hypothesis is based on chromosome structure and the absence of microchromosomes, but there is no published evidence for the formation of quadrivalents during meiosis.

Meiotic Chromosomal Structure

Cytological studies of meiotic processes have revealed some apparent differences in the morphological characteristics of the bivalents in different groups of amphibians. The lampbrush chromosomes (diplotene) are reasonably well known in salamanders, especially through the pioneering efforts of Kezer and Macgregor (1971), who identified centromeric heterochromatin and provided a foundation for investigations of DNA replication with respect to chromosome structure. Interspecific differences occur in the spiralization of the bivalents and in the position of the chiasmata, and in some salamandrids, differences exist in the frequency and position of chiasmata between the sexes (Morescalchi, 1973).

Within the salamanders the bivalents generally have more than two chiasmata, interstitial in position. Two patterns are evident in the anurans (Morescalchi, 1973):

In the Leiopelmatidae and Discoglossidae the diplotene stage of Late Prophase I is long with a short diakinesis; the bivalents have relatively little spiralization. There are more than two chiasmata in the large bivalents but only one in the small bivalents. Most chiasmata are interstitial, and at Metaphase I chiasmata terminalization is never total.

In the other families of anurans, the diplotene stage of Late Prophase I is short with a relatively long diakinesis; the bivalents are highly spiralized. Usually there are two chiasmata in both large and small bivalents, and usually the chiasmata are terminal. Exceptions include *Pipa parva* and some neotropical hylids having bivalents with interstitial (procentric) chiasmata, and some African ranoids having bivalents with proterminal chiasmata in late diplotene and diakinesis.

Variable numbers of chiasmata and chromosome morphology have been reported in two species of caecilians (Stingo, 1974; Seto and Nussbaum, 1976); available data are inadequate to make generalizations about caecilians. However, the morphology of meiotic chromosomes of salamanders and primitive families of anurans is similar, and different from that of the more advanced families of anurans.

MOLECULAR EVOLUTION

Recent technological advances have provided biologists with the opportunity to utilize macromolecules in evolutionary studies. These approaches include gel electrophoresis of proteins, microcomplement fixation of serum albumins and hemoglobin, immunodiffusion, and sequencing of nucleoenzymes, proteins, DNA, and RNA. Amphibians have figured prominently in these molecular studies, which have provided new insights into evolutionary mechanisms, as well as phylogenetic relationships.

Genome Size and Characteristics

The amount and replication sequences of nuclear DNA are highly variable among amphibians. Little is known about caecilians; three taxa have 7.4–27.9 picograms of nuclear DNA per diploid nucleus (Morescalchi, 1973). Anurans have 2–36 pg/N (Morescalchi, 1977), whereas salamanders have much greater amounts, 33–192 pg/N (Table 16-2). The salamanders fall into two distinct groups—normally metamorphosing, primarily terrestrial taxa having 33–86 pg/N, and obligate neotenic salamanders having 91–192 pg/N.

The modal genome size in anurans is 9 or 10 pg/N (K. Bachmann and Blommers-Schlösser, 1975). K. Bachmann et al. (1972) suggested that each group of organisms has a minimal amount of DNA representing the genetic information necessary for expressing the group-specific characteristics; the amount of DNA beyond this minimum codes for the species-specific characters. Furthermore, high values of DNA provide a reservoir of raw material for production of new genes. Generalized species of anurans usually have genome sizes near the mode, whereas highly specialized species tend to have extremely low or high amounts of DNA (K. Bachmann and Blommers-Schlösser, 1975). Another interpretation centers around the positive correlation between genome size and rate of embryonic development (K. Bachmann, 1972);

thus, anurans that have rapid embryonic development in temporary ponds tend to have the lowest amounts of nuclear DNA, and those that have prolonged development in cold water have large genomes. The genome size in species in the humid tropics is near or above the mode for anurans.

Within anurans and salamanders, there is a positive correlation between genome size and nuclear volume, cell volume, and cell surface area of erythrocytes (Olmo and Morescalchi, 1975, 1978), but there are differences between anurans and salamanders and between obligate neotenic salamanders and other salamanders. This is especially evident between genome size and relative cell surface area (Fig. 16-3). The values for anurans are lower than, but parallel to, those of non-neotenic salamanders, but there is great variation in large amounts of DNA in the large cells (with low surface-area/volume ratios) in the obligate neotenic salamanders. In anurans and non-neotenic salamanders, the correlation between genome size and relative cell surface area seems to be under the same mechanistic control. Thus, the genome size and cell volume/surface ratios seem to be indicative of physiological adaptations to various environmental conditions. However, qualitatively, the differences in cellular and nuclear sizes among amphibians seem to be associated with the more repetitive (nongenic) DNA fractions (Mizuno et al., 1976).

The fact that most salamanders have far more DNA than anurans may relate to different adaptive strategies in the two orders and certainly relates to the duration of embryonic development (see Chapter 5). According to Ohno (1970), the large quantities of DNA in salamanders, especially the obligate neotenes, may have been acquired through tandem duplication of the structural genes alone, which, by synthesizing great quantities of the same proteins, would lead to larger cell sizes. These large cells would require ever greater quantities of the same gene products and therefore the continuous activity of the duplicated genes. As a result, these salamanders cannot eliminate genetic redundancy. Ohno (1970) suggested that for this reason salamanders are "evolutionarily sterile."

Perhaps the obligate neotenic salamanders are evolutionary dead ends, but certainly this cannot be said for some other groups, especially the bolitoglossine plethodontids, which have relatively large amounts of DNA. Furthermore, the generalized quantification of genomes does not take into account the different components of DNA that have greatly different degrees of repetitiveness. As an example, DNA hybridization studies of 15 species of *Plethodon* (Mizuno and Macgregor, 1974) showed (1) salamanders in the same species group had 60–90% of observed repetitive DNA sequences in common; (2) two species groups in eastern North America shared 40–60% of the sequences; and (3) eastern and western North American species had less than 10% of the sequences in common.

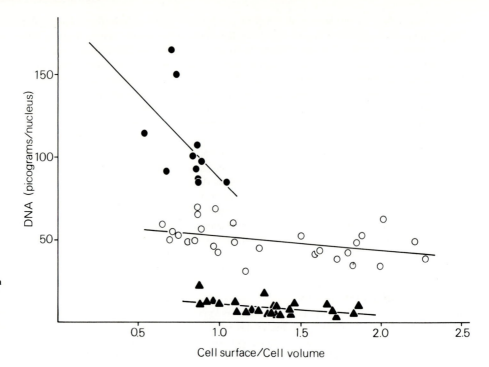

Figure 16-3. Relationship between the ratio of cell surface area to cell volume and nuclear DNA content. Triangles are anurans; open circles are non-neotenic salamanders, and solid circles are obligate neotenic salamanders. Adapted from Olmo and Morescalchi (1978).

Comparison of DNA reassociation and genome size in two anurans (*Xenopus laevis* and *Bufo bufo*) and two salamanders (*Necturus maculosus* and *Triturus cristatus*) by Baldari and Amaldi (1976) revealed that each of the species had about the same absolute amount of unique DNA. The differences in total nuclear DNA in these species were accounted for by quantitative variations of the repetitive sequence classes, at least in part because of changes in the numbers of copies of the various sequences. Moreover, these authors suggested that the great differences in amounts of nuclear DNA between salamanders and anurans involve all sequence classes in parallel.

The variation in the amount of nuclear DNA in closely related species is especially obvious in salamanders (Table 16-2). Moreover, among salamanders there seems to be no correlation between the diploid number of chromosomes and the genome size. For example, three species of *Taricha* have 22 chromosomes and 56–60 pg/N of DNA, whereas five species of desmognathines have 28 chromosomes but only 30–40 pg/N of DNA. On the other hand, interspecific differences in genome size are closely correlated with the number of chromosomes in *Xenopus* (Thiébaud and Fischberg, 1977). *Xenopus tropicalis* ($2N = 20$) has only 3.55 pg/N of DNA, whereas species having $2N = 36$ chromosomes have 6.35–8.45 pg/N. Two tetraploid species ($4N = 72$) have 12.57–12.83 pg/N, and one octoploid species ($8N = 108$) has 16.25 pg/N. Likewise, tetraploid populations of the frog *Odontophrynus americanus* have a nuclear DNA content of 7.1 pg/N, whereas diploid populations have 3.6 pg/N

(Schmidtke et al., 1976). The tetraploid *Hyla versicolor* has about twice the amount of DNA as its presumed diploid ancestor but has an equal amount of RNA (K. Bachmann and Bogart, 1975).

Although the amount of information accumulated on genome size and on DNA replication since the mid-1979s is impressive, patterns are only beginning to emerge. It seems that the DNA content is significant, not only in a genetic informational context, but also with respect to cellular metabolism and rate of embryonic development, both of which may be modified evolutionarily in response to the environment. Thus, genome size might increase as a protective adaptation to the higher mutation rate necessary for evolution, the higher information redundancy buffering the effect of somatic mutations. Therefore, both genome size and mutation rate would change under selective pressures.

Ribosomal RNA

The nucleolar organizer region (NOR) is the region of the chromosome that produces the nucleolus. In interphase through late prophase, these regions lack DNA but are rich in RNA. The nucleolar organizer is a differentiated region of chromatin (DNA), which, through transcription, produces the larger pieces of RNA—i.e., 18S and 28S ribosomal RNA (rRNA)—that are incorporated into the ribosomes. However, other regions of the genome produce the 5S rRNA and code for the ribosomal proteins.

Quantitative relationships exist between the amounts of chromosomal DNA and rDNA (the DNA sequences coding for 18S + 28S rRNA together with intervening spacer sequences). DNA-rRNA hybridization in three species of anurans and nine of salamanders revealed that the proportion of rDNA decreases with increasing DNA content (Vlad, 1977). Furthermore, the total amount of rDNA complementary to 18S and 28S rRNA is much less in anurans than in salamanders, all of which have much larger genome sizes than anurans. However, the interspecific variability in the proportion of the genome that is complementary in sequence to 18S and 28S rRNA suggests that factors other than the genome size may be significant in the transcription of RNA (see Vlad, 1977, for review).

The location of RNA genes has been determined for 12 species of anurans and several species and subspecies of salamanders (see Batistoni et al., 1980; and Vitelli et al., 1982, for review). Of the salamanders that have been examined, there is variation in the sites of 18S + 28S rDNA, and 5S DNA loci are found in different chromosomal positions. Among anurans, the 18S + 28S rRNA genes are clustered in one locus per haploid chromosome set; this locus is in an intercalary position proximal to the centromere or close to the telomere. The 5S rRNA genes occur at one to five loci per haploid complement. Each species has a distinctive pattern of 5S DNA loci, except that the two species of *Xenopus* studied have clusters of 5S DNA near the telomeres of probably all chromosomes. Furthermore, in primitive salamanders and anurans having microchromosomes, 5S DNA loci are present on the microchromosomes, which do not have detectable loci for 18S + 28S DNA. In more advanced groups of salamanders and anurans, microchromosomes are absent, and the 5S DNA loci are present in the macrochromosomes. This provides additional evidence for the incorporation of microchromosomes into the macrochromosomes in the karyological evolution of amphibians.

Gene amplification has been determined in various mononucleate amphibians and in the multinucleate *Ascaphus truei* and *Flectonotus pygmaeus* (Macgregor and Kezer, 1970; Macgregor and del Pino, 1982). Amplification is the multiplication of DNA sequences that code for 18S and 28S RNA (and the spacer sequences) within a nucleus to produce many copies of themselves that usually are not integrated physically into any chromosome. The possession of large numbers of ribosomal genes and intense nucleolar activity enables an oocyte to synthesize as much RNA in a few months as would be produced by another kind of cell in several hundred years. This RNA is incorporated into ribosomes that serve in protein synthesis from fertilization until feeding by the hatchling.

Measurements of amounts of DNA per nucleus reveal that in oocytes of *Xenopus laevis* each nucleus produces about 2000 copies of the genes for rDNA (Macgregor, 1968); approximately the same amount of replication is shared by eight nuclei in *Ascaphus truei* (Macgregor and Kezer, 1970). However, each oocyte of *Flectonotus pygmaeus* has in its early stages about 2500 nuclei, which produce about 280 times more rDNA than is known in any other amphibian (Macgregor and del Pino, 1982). This fantastically great amount of rDNA presumably is capable of synthesizing far more RNA than mononucleate oocytes of most amphibians. Thus, it is expected that the eggs of *Flectonotus* would be capable of synthesizing much greater quantities of protein at a faster rate than other eggs. This may account for the rapid development of *Flectonotus* through a nonfeeding larval stage.

Biochemical Genetics

Although genes are located on chromosomes and the loci for certain kinds of rDNA have been determined, among amphibians as well as most other organisms, the genetic factors responsible for characters observed in the phenotypes are mostly inferred, rather than known. Consequently, the determination of homogeneity and heterogeneity at loci for a variety of genes coding for certain proteins provides evidence for the genetic composition of organisms. Proteins subjected to electrophoresis can be identified chemically and different alleles determined. Estimates of genetic identity (I) and genetic distance (D) between samples can be calculated by the methods of Nei (1972) and Rogers (1972) (but see Hillis, 1984, for correction of calculations). Molecular divergence also can be measured by immunological distance (ID) by means of microcomplement fixation of serum albumins; one unit of immunological distance is approximately equivalent to a single amino acid difference between the samples compared (Maxson and A. Wilson, 1974).

Hybridization and Inheritance. Some of the earliest work dealing with proteins concerned the identification of hybrids with known or presumed parents (e.g., Guttman's, 1972, work on *Bufo*). Utilization of numerous proteins has permitted the determination of natural hybrids in numerous amphibians. Analysis of 30 proteins of two species of hylid frogs, *Pseudacris nigrita* and *P. triseriata,* in a narrow hybrid zone in the southern United States revealed that 4 proteins showed different patterns in parental and hybrid samples (Gartside, 1980). Likewise, 4 of 26 proteins in the salamanders *Desmognathus fuscus* and *D. ochrophaeus* reveal the occurrence of interspecific hybridization in these species (Karlin and Guttman, 1981). The European frog *Rana esculenta* is a hybridogenetic hybrid of *R. ridibunda* and *R. lessonae;* examination of six loci showed no instance in which *R. esculenta* appeared to lack one of its alleles derived from *R. lessonae* and the other from *R. ridibunda* (Uzzell and Berger, 1975).

In these and many other studies, the mode of inheritance of electrophoretic variants of proteins usually has been inferred from the resemblance of protein phenotypes to patterns predicted by simple Mendelian inheritance, by comparison with phenotypes for which the mode of inheritance is known, or by studies of natural or laboratory hybrids. Electrophoretic analysis of laboratory crosses of the Australian tree frog *Litoria ewingii* demonstrated that inheritance of transferrins is by a series of at least nine codominant alleles (Gartside and Watson, 1976). Only limited information is available concerning the chromosomal loci for specific proteins.

Electrophoretic patterns of extracts of seven proteins were examined with respect to the lampbrush chromosomes in oocytes of mature females produced from backcrosses between female reciprocal hybrids of *Rana nigromaculata* and *R. brevipoda* and males of those parental species (Nishioka et al., 1980). On the basis of the percentages of females whose genotypes agreed with a definite bivalent chromosome, the loci of the genes controlling the proteins were determined. Linkage maps were determined for *R. clamitans* (Elinson, 1983) and *R. pipiens* (D. Wright et al., 1983).

Laboratory production of interspecific hybrids of various anurans has demonstrated differential genetic compatibility in reciprocal crosses and in backcrosses, as well as different electrophoretic patterns of proteins. Extensive experiments involving many species of *Bufo* (W. Blair, 1972; Kawamura et al., 1980), members of the North American *Rana pipiens* complex (J. Frost, 1982a; J. Frost and Platz, 1983), and Japanese *Rana* (Kawamura and Nishioka, 1978) have revealed chromosomal, electrophoretic, developmental, morphological, and vocalization differences between hybrids and parental species. Moreover, similar kinds of differences were found among parental species and their natural hybrids in North American hylids—e.g., *Pseudacris* (Gartside, 1980) and *Hyla* (H. Gerhardt et al., 1980).

Anurans have proved to be especially useful in hybridization studies because many species that have external fertilization of aquatic eggs can be crossed in the laboratory. The results of such crosses have provided information about the degrees of genetic compatibility and are beginning to provide data on genetic markers that will permit the chromosomal localization of loci for certain genes (D. Wright et al., 1983).

Hybridization experiments have provided evidence for the inheritance of certain color pattern traits. In *Rana pipiens* the mottled "kandiyohi" and unspotted "burnsi" variants are expressed by two dominant nonallelic genes (Volpe, 1961); furthermore, the unspotted variant is a manifestation of genic interaction between a major pigmentary locus and a complex of modifying "minor-spotting" genes (Volpe and Dasgupta, 1962).

Comparison of crosses with Mendelian expectations indicates that the presence of a middorsal stripe in *Acris crepitans* is dominant in a single allele (Pyburn, 1961). In fact, in various kinds of amphibians that have pattern dimorphism of striped versus nonstriped individuals, the gene for the striped pattern is dominant—e.g., *Plethodon cinereus* (Highton, 1959), *Discoglossus pictus* (Lantz, 1947), *Eleutherodactylus planirostris* and some Jamaican species of *Eleutherodactylus* (Goin, 1947, 1950), and *Rana limnocharis* (Moriwaki, 1953).

Some genetic mutations in the *Rana pipiens* complex (Browder, 1975) and the *R. esculenta* complex (Dubois, 1979c) involve color pattern (including albinism and melanism), as well as other kinds of recessive anomalies, most of which are lethal. Albinism is a genetic recessive mutation in *Xenopus laevis* (Hoperskaya, 1975). Color mutants in laboratory-reared *Ambystoma mexicanum* provide an excellent opportunity for studying the nature of gene actions that only now is being realized (S. Frost and Malacinski, 1980).

Ecological and Population Genetics. The premises of ecological genetics are that natural populations are adapted to their physical and biological environments and that the genetic mechanisms respond to environmental change. There are many descriptive accounts of phenotypic differences among species of amphibians in different environments, but the genetic factors responsible for these differences are known in only a few cases.

The mottled "kandiyohi" and unspotted "burnsi" color morphs seem to have a selective advantage over the normal spotted morph of *Rana pipiens* in the north-central United States (Merrell, 1973). In the range of the unspotted morph, it and normal *R. pipiens* overwinter on the bottom of ponds. Comparisons of the numbers of individuals of the two morphs in spring and fall show that the unspotted morph has significantly higher survival during harsh winters, indicating that it has a physiological adaptive advantage over the spotted morph and may be maintained by a form of seasonal selection. The mottled and spotted morphs occur sympatrically in prairie habitats, where tadpoles of the mottled morph metamorphose significantly sooner than those of the spotted morph. Thus, the mottled morph presumably is maintained through selective advantage of more rapid larval development in prairie ponds that are subject to desiccation.

Geographic variation in proteins has been demonstrated in several species of amphibians. These patterns have been interpreted in three ways: (1) If the majority of electrophoretic variation is physiologically irrelevant, the geographic patterns may be the result of genetic drift and gene flow among populations. (2) Different allozymes at each locus are adapted to local environments and respond to selection. (3) The electrophoretic variants are physiologically neutral but are linked to loci that are under the influence of selection. In the newt, *Notophthalmus viridescens,* four of five loci examined showed correlations with environmental parameters (Tabachnick, 1977). Genetic variation is very high in *Bufo viridis;* 9–16 of 26 loci are polymorphic among populations of this toad in Israel (Dessauer et al., 1975). Frequencies of two alleles undergo clinal shifts corresponding to the rainfall gradient. The degree of isolation of populations of *B. viridis* in the Negev and Sinai deserts results in only slightly less polymorphism, but a population on Vis Island, in the Adriatic Sea, has low heterozygosity. As a rule, island populations may be less polymorphic than mainland populations, as is evident in *B. americanus* on islands in

Lake Michigan (Abramoff et al., 1964). Only 5 of 27 loci are monomorphic in *Hyla arborea* in Israel. The spatial patterns and environmental correlates and predictors of genic variation in this species suggest that protein polymorphisms are largely adaptive and are molded primarily by climatic selection rather than by stochastic processes or neutrality (Nevo and Yang, 1979). In contrast, only 1 of 32 loci is polymorphic in each of two species of *Pelobates*. These extremely homozygous species are fossorial, like other organisms displaying very low heterozygosity, which seems to be the result of selection by constant environments (Nevo, 1976).

The degree of relative heterogeneity in local populations (and the rate and amount of local differentiation) can be affected by the form of the postmetamorphic range (continuous, fragmented, linear, or two-dimensional), the relationship of the nonbreeding range to the breeding site, and the tendency to form breeding aggregations. Electrophoretic data on seven species of anurans in Malaysia indicate that those species that have the most restricted ranges and do not aggregate for breeding have the greatest homogeneity, whereas those with two-dimensional ranges and that aggregate for breeding (thereby resulting in the most interbreeding of individuals from throughout a large, local range) have the greatest heterogeneity (Inger et al., 1974).

In a review of the amounts of protein heterogeneity in animals, Nevo (1978) noted the high heterogeneity in lowland tropical anurans, as compared with temperate species. As a rule, anurans in the lowland humid tropics breed frequently, whereas those in the temperate regions usually breed only once or twice per year. Consequently, in tropical species there is more opportunity for genetic interchange among individuals in a given population and an expected higher amount of heterogeneity.

Speciation and Phylogenetics. The determination of genetic differences between species by electrophoretic assays of proteins has provided a new dimension to systematics. Electrophoretic studies on salamanders of the genera *Desmognathus* (Tilley et al., 1978; Tilley and Schwerdtfeger, 1981), *Taricha* (Hedgecock, 1976), *Triturus* (Kalezić and Hedgecock, 1980), and *Ambystoma* (Pierce and Mitton, 1980), among others, have provided biochemical data in support of morphological characters for the recognition of species. Likewise, similar studies on North American *Scaphiopus* (Sattler, 1980), *Rana* (Post and Uzzell, 1981), and *Hyla* (Case et al., 1975) and on Papuan *Litoria* (Dessauer et al., 1977) have supported previous systematic arrangements and, in some cases, have pointed out the existence of previously unknown differentiation. Assays of lactate dehydrogenase provided interfamilial comparisons of salamanders (Salthe and Kaplan, 1966).

The phylogenetic relationships among taxa have been hypothesized by measures of genetic distances of proteins based on electrophoretic data for a variety of plethodontid salamanders, notably *Batrachoseps* (Yanev,

1980) and *Plethodon* (Highton and Larson, 1979), and for various anuran taxa, the most extensive being the determination of genetic relationships on the basis of 50 loci among 20 species of the *Rana pipiens* complex (Hillis et al., 1983). Likewise, relationships of taxa have been hypothesized by immunological distances determined by microcomplement fixation of serum albumins. In this manner, relationships have been postulated among such diverse groups as *Leiopelma* (Daugherty et al., 1981), *Xenopus* (Bisbee et al., 1977), myobatrachines (Daugherty and Maxson, 1982), African and Eurasian *Bufo* (Maxson, 1981a, 1981b), and South American frogs of the genera *Leptodactylus* (Heyer and Maxson, 1982) and *Gastrotheca* (Scanlan et al., 1980). The same techniques have been applied to plethodontid salamanders (Maxson et al., 1979; Maxson and D. Wake, 1981) and caecilians (Case and M. Wake, 1977).

Both electrophoretic analysis of proteins and microcomplement fixation of serum albumins have provided congruent results in North American *Hyla* (Maxson and A. Wilson, 1975; Case et al., 1975) and *Rana* (Case, 1978), and in European and Californian species of salamanders of the genus *Hydromantes* (D. Wake et al., 1978). The most thorough analyses of genetic relationships have been with the genus *Plethodon,* in which results of electrophoretic analyses of 29 loci (Highton and Larson, 1979), immunological distances (Maxson et al., 1979), and DNA hybridization (Mizuno and Macgregor, 1974) yielded close comparisons (Maxson and Maxson, 1979). For the most part the biochemical data are highly congruent with morphological variation (Larson et al., 1981).

In several groups that have been studied, there are striking differences between the rates of molecular and morphological evolution. Measurements of molecular evolution are strictly estimations of divergence, whereas morphological convergence can give a false impression of relationships. Conversely, morphological divergence might be a rapid phenomenon in response to adaptive shifts, while molecular evolution proceeds at an apparently constant rate. Thus, the Middle American hylid frog *Anotheca spinosa* is much closer to hylines immunologically than it is to the more morphologically similar hemiphractines, and is an example of morphological convergence (Maxson, 1977). Some morphological similarities in populations of *Aneides flavipunctatus* are the result of independent paedomorphic changes, whereas protein divergence has been constant (Larson, 1980). Entering new adaptive zones may result in highly distinctive morphological divergence that belies the genetic similarities. For example, the semiaquatic hylid frogs of the genus *Acris* are highly divergent morphologically from other North American hylids; however, immunologically they are no more divergent than various groups of species of North American *Hyla* (Maxson and A. Wilson, 1975). Likewise, arboreal salamanders of the genus *Aneides* have a distinctive suite of morphological characters, but biochemically they are more closely related to species of *Pletho-*

don in western North America than the latter are to their eastern congeners (Larson et al., 1981). Some adaptive shifts in reproductive modes are relatively recent; for example, some species of Andean marsupial frogs (*Gastrotheca*) that have eggs that hatch as tadpoles are immunologically closer to species that have eggs that undergo direct development than they are to other tadpole-producing species (Scanlan et al., 1980). Although *Rheobatrachus* has a unique reproductive mode, its biochemical divergence is about the same as various other genera of myobatrachids that have generalized reproductive modes (Daugherty and Maxson, 1982).

Temporal Evolution. Subsequent to the discovery that albumin evolution proceeds in a clocklike fashion (Sarich and A. Wilson, 1967), there has been a rapidly growing body of evidence that protein evolution proceeds at an approximately constant rate and that the comparison of this rate with fossils of a known age and dated geological events provides a sound basis for dating the sequential times of divergences of lineages of living organisms (see A. Wilson et al., 1977, for review and Throckmorton et al., 1978, for application to phylogenetics). Although controversy has arisen (see Korey, 1981), the evidence seems to favor the regularity of evolutionary rates of homologous molecules; the discrepancies commonly noted between divergence times calculated on immunological distances (ID) and those on Nei distances (D) may be because neither (ID nor D) is in fact an accurate measure of time. Electrophoretic Nei distances are most sensitive for comparison of recently diverged proteins, and because albumin comparison encompasses a much greater range of phyletic distances, the measure of immunological distance is an excellent method for determining evolutionary relationships and divergence times (Maxson and Maxson, 1979); 100 units of immunological distance accumulate every 55–60 million years of lineage separation in amphibians (Carlson et al., 1978).

Dating of temporal sequences of molecular divergence in various groups of amphibians for the most part has been consistent with the dating of geological events and/or paleoclimatic changes that presumably were important to the diversification of separate phyletic lineages. Thus, the divergence of two lineages of egg-brooding hylid frogs, *Cryptobatrachus* and *Stefania,* in South America having an immunological distance of 155 units is timed to have occurred in the Middle Cretaceous, the time of uplift of the Guianan Highlands, an area where *Stefania* is endemic (Duellman and Hoogmoed, 1984). The antiquity of generic lineages of leptodactylid frogs inhabiting the ancient Brazilian Shield contrasts with the recent divergence times of species in lineages inhabiting the young Andes (Maxson and Heyer, 1982). The timing of the uplift of different parts of the Andes in the Cenozoic and Quaternary corresponds to the times of divergence among lineages of lowland species of marsupial frogs (*Gastrotheca*) on either side of the Andes and of the much more

recent divergence of the species living in high montane environments that did not exist prior to the end of the Pliocene (Scanlan et al., 1980).

Among the salamanders, the time of divergence of lineages of *Hydromantes,* as based on molecular analyses, corresponds well with the severance of the land connections between North America and Europe (D. Wake et al., 1978); however, the timing of divergence of holarctic pelobatid frogs seems to have been much earlier (Sage et al., 1982). Also, the time of divergence of eastern and western species groups of *Plethodon* corresponds with the discontinuity of forests across North America (Highton and Larson, 1979; Maxson et al., 1979). The pattern of speciation and distribution of salamanders of the genus *Batrachoseps* in California can be superimposed on a time-series of reconstructions of geological, climatic, and botanical history of the area for the past 10 million years (Yanev, 1980). The genetic distance between some Central and South American species of *Bolitoglossa* provides estimates of divergence time up to 18 million years ago, about 11 million years before the earliest estimated closure of the Panamanian Portal and the establishment of a continuous land connection between the American continents; thus, the divergence times are either grossly overestimated or a bolitoglossine salamander crossed the water gap and entered South America in the Pliocene (Hanken and D. Wake, 1982).

GENOMIC EVOLUTION

Morescalchi (1977, 1979, 1980) and Birstein (1982) reviewed evidence for evolution of karyotypes in amphibians; Morescalchi generalized that in all three living groups there are trends toward (1) a restricted number of chromosomes (all metacentric and differing little in size), (2) an increase in the amount of nuclear DNA, especially in salamanders, and (3) striking interspecific variability in genome size, even among related species having morphologically similar karyotypes.

Cytogeneticists have argued that centromeres may be lost but not gained, so karyotypic evolution has involved the incorporation of genetic material from a large number of telocentric chromosomes into a smaller number of metacentric chromosomes, a general trend apparent in amphibians. However, recent cytogenetic evidence suggests that centromeres may be gained and that telomeres may function as centromeres following chromosomal fission (Holmquist and Dancis, 1979). Multiplication of chromosomes by centric fission or centromeric dissociation presumably has occurred in several groups of frogs, especially *Eleutherodactylus* and some neotropical hylid frogs. Possibly this chromosomal rearrangement is significant in the rapid speciation in these groups. In contrast to salamanders, polyploidy is fairly common in anurans; this is another way to increase not only genetic heterogeneity but also genome size.

Superimposed on the general trends are other deviations, at least some of which seem to be highly adaptive. One of these deviations is the independent increase to very high levels of nuclear DNA in families of neotenic salamanders. At the cellular level these increases in nuclear DNA seem to parallel increases in nuclear and cellular volumes and in cell surface areas; these increases result in an inverse ratio of cell surface to cell volume, which can be considered as an index of the rate of oxidative metabolism. Lacking physiological mechanisms capable of controlling the rate of oxidative metabolism in the organism as a whole, possibly amphibians exercise this control at least partially at the cellular level, the modes and amounts depending on the adaptive strategies of the species. The genome size is implicated in these phenomena, but it is not clear whether the variations in the total amount of nuclear DNA are the cause or only the effects of the interspecific differences in the relative cell surfaces and therefore of general metabolism.

Considerable amounts of data support the hypothesis that there is a positive correlation between the total amount of nuclear DNA and duration of development. However, limited data suggest that increases in certain sequences of DNA might enhance the rate of development by more effective protein synthesis. Therefore, it is possible that some of the variations observed in developmental rates are influenced not only by the quantity, but more specifically by the quality, of the nuclear DNA. These differences, like those in genome size with respect to cellular volume and surface, must be viewed as adaptive variations that have evolved separately in different lineages and that are independent of the major evolutionary trends in the three orders of amphibians.

Recent suggestions (A. Wilson et al., 1974; Bush et al., 1977; among others) that molecular evolution is correlated more highly with karyotypic evolution than with structural gene evolution have resulted in more attention to changes in karyotypes by evolutionary biologists. Statistically significant correlations between estimates of genetic distance based on albumins, multiple proteins, and hybridization of nonrepetitive DNA in plethodontid salamanders (Maxson and Maxson, 1979) provided the molecular basis for comparisons of rates of molecular and chromosomal evolution in salamanders (Maxson and A. Wilson, 1979). Gross comparisons between estimated time of divergence (based on immunological distances) and pairs of species having the same karyotype provided an estimate of 0.006 point mutation per lineage per million years, a rate about half that estimated for anurans. The major difference is between amphibians and mammals; by comparison with amphibians, mammals have greatly diversified karyologically in a much shorter period of time. Thus, the conservativeness of the amphibian karyotype is evident. However, only gross morphology of the chromosomes has been considered. These karyotypic similarities may mask possible substructural differences that are being discovered in amphibian chromosomes. The answers to the relationships of molecular and karyotypic evolution lie in the determination of the positions of the loci for the various genes.

Finally, as emphasized by D. Wake (1981), molecular techniques have become an important new component in systematics, which traditionally has been based mostly on morphological data. The integration of molecular and traditional approaches greatly increases the potential for generating and testing hypotheses of phylogenetic relationships and temporal evolution of lineages.

CHAPTER 17

If we are to compare pattern with theories of process—as we must do to improve our very notions of process—we must have at the very least an accurate concept of evolutionary genealogy.

Niles Eldredge and Joel Cracraft (1980)

The evolutionary or phylogenetic relationships among the families of living amphibians are basic to an interpretation of their biogeography and to constructing a meaningful classification. Thus, the material presented in this chapter is fundamental to the biogeographic synthesis (Chapter 18) and the classification of the modern groups of amphibians (Chapter 19).

With the development of testable hypotheses of phylogenetic relationships based on shared derived character states as proposed by Hennig (see E. Wiley, 1981, for a recent synthesis), systematists have an explicit and objective methodology for determining phylogenetic relationships. This system is based on the identification of homologous structures and evolutionary direction (polarity) of transformation series from a primitive character (plesiomorphy) to a derived character. A theory of phylogenetic relationships is based on nested sets of derived character states (apomorphies) shared by two or more lineages, whereas primitive characters (plesiomorphies) shared by two or more taxa do not show relationships. Characters that are unique to a given lineage (autapomorphies) are useful in recognizing a particular lineage but not in determining the relationship of that lineage with any other one.

In the following analyses of phylogenetic relationships among the living groups of amphibians, hypothesized phylogenetic relationships were reconstructed by using the WAGNER78 computer program written by J. S. Farris. Depending on the number of convergences or reversals (homoplasies), alternative phylogenetic trees (cladograms) were generated. The preferred arrangement is the most parsimonious cladogram, that is, the one having the highest consistency index (minimal number of possible changes in character states/actual number of changes).

For each of the living orders of amphibians, the transformation series used in a phylogenetic reconstruction at the family level are described and their characters noted as primitive (0) or derived (1). In all cases the direction of evolutionary change is $0 \rightarrow 1$. In those cases in which there is more than one derived character, the characters are derived sequentially or serially (i.e., $0 \rightarrow 1 \rightarrow 2$, etc.) unless it is specified that certain characters are derived independently (i.e., $1' \leftarrow 0 \rightarrow 1 \rightarrow 2$). The direction (polarity) of evolutionary change is determined by the characters in an outgroup. For most characters the outgroup is other lissamphibians or tetrapods.

CAUDATA

Character States

The states of 30 characters that are variable within the families of salamanders are described below. The distribution of character states is given in Table 17-1. An ad-

Table 17-1. Distribution of Character States in Families of Salamanders[a]

Character[b]	Ambystomatidae	Amphiumidae	Cryptobranchidae	Dicamptodontidae	Hynobiidae	Plethodontidae	Proteidae	Salamandridae	Sirenidae	Batrachosauroididae	Karauridae	Prosirenidae	Scapherpetontidae
	Living families									**Extinct families**			
A. Fusion of premaxillae	0	1	0	0	0	0[c]	0	0[c]	0	0	0	0	0
B. Dorsal process of premaxilla	1	1	0	1	0	1	1	1	0	1	0	1	1
C. Maxilla	0	0	0	0	0	0[c]	1	0	1/1'	0	0	0	0
D. Septomaxilla	0	1	1	0	0	0[c]	1	1	1	?	?	?	?
E. Nasal ossification	1'	1'	0	1'[d]	0	1'	1"	1'	1'	?	?	?	?
F. Lacrimal	1	1	1	0	0	1	1	1	1	?	0	0	?
G. Quadratojugal	1	1	1	1	1	1	1	1	1	1	0	1	1
H. Otic-occipital ossification	1	1	0	0	0	1	0	1	0	1	0	1	0
I. Pterygoid	0	1	0	0[d]	0	2	0	0	1	0	0	0	0
J. Internal carotid foramen	0[c]	0	1	0	1	1	0	1	1	1	0	1	1
K. Opercular apparatus	1	1	0	0	0	2	0	1	0	?	0	?	?
L. Junction of periotic canal and cistern	2	2	1	2	2	2	1	2	0	?	?	?	?
M. Flexures of periotic canal	1	1	1	1[d]	1	2[e]	1	2[e]	0	?	?	?	?
N. Basilaris complex of inner ear	0	0	0	0	0	2	2	0[c]	2	?	?	?	?
O. Angular	1	1	0	1	0	1	1	1	1	0	0	0	0
P. First hypobranchial and first ceratobranchial	0	0	1	0	1	0	0	0[c]	0	?	?	?	?
Q. Second ceratobranchial	1	1	0	1	0	1	1	1	1	0	0	0	0
R. Number of larval gill slits	0	1	0	0	0	0/1	2	0	1/3	?	?	?	?
S. Palatal dentition	0	1	1	1""	0	1"	1	1'	1'"	?	1	?	1
T. Tooth structure	0	0	0	0	0	0	0	0	1	0	0	1	0
U. Scapulocoracoid	1	1	1	1	1	1	1	1	0	1	1	1	1
V. Vertebrae	0	0	0	0	0	1'	0	1	0	0/1	0	0	0
W. Ribs	0	0	1	0	1	0	0	0	0	0	0	0	0
X. Spinal nerves	3	1	0	2	0	3	0	4	4	0	0	0	2
Y. Ypsiloid cartilage	0	1	0	0	0	1	1	0	1	?	?	?	?
Z. Levator mandibulae muscle	1'	1'	1'	1'	1'	1'	1'	1'	1	1'	0	1'	1'
AA. Pubotibialis and puboischiotibialis muscles	0	0	1	0	1	0	0	0	0	0	0	0	0
BB. Kidney	1	1	1	1	1	1	1	1	0	?	?	?	?
CC. Mode of fertilization	1	1	0	1	0	1	1	1	0	?	?	?	?
DD. Chromosomes	3	2	0	3	0	3	1	2	4	?	?	?	?

[a] 0 = primitive; 1, 2, etc. = derived; ? = unknown. Autapomorphies not included.
[b] See text for definitions of states.
[c] Derived state in some taxa.
[d] *Rhyacotriton* differs: E = 1", I = 1, M = 2.
[e] Next most derived state in some taxa.

ditional 10 autapomorphic characters are listed and their unique taxa identified; these characters are not listed in Table 17-1.

A. *Fusion of Premaxillae.*—Primitively in tetrapods, the premaxillary bones are paired. Two premaxillae are considered to be primitive (0) and fused premaxillae derived (1). Fusion of the premaxillae is an ontogenetic phenomenon in some hynobiids and salamandrids, and in most plethodontids, although in some of the latter the premaxillae are fused in larvae (D. Wake, 1966). Thus, the derived state has evolved independently in each of these families, and in the Amphiumidae, which paedomorphically retains the condition in adults.

B. *Dorsal Process of Premaxilla.*—In primitive tetrapods and porolepiform fishes, the dorsal processes of the premaxillae do not separate the nasals; these processes extend posteriorly and separate the nasals in some families of salamanders. Short dorsal processes are considered to be primitive (0) and long processes separating the nasals derived (1).

C. *Maxilla.*—Maxillary bones are present in most gnathostomes. Presence of maxillae is primitive (0). Their loss is derived (1) independently in the Proteidae and in the paedomorphic *Pseudobranchus* (Sirenidae) and in *Haideotriton, Typhlomolge,* and some *Eurycea* and *Gyrinophilus* (Plethodontidae). Maxillae are the last dentigerous bones to ossify during ontogeny, and in many neotenic salamanders the maxillae are small. Therefore, absence of maxillae is a paedomorphic condition (Larsen, 1963). The absence of teeth on the maxillae (state 1′) is an independently derived state from the primitive condition and in sirenids is correlated with the presence of a horny beak (see Character EE).

D. Septomaxilla.—The small, paired septomaxillary bones associated with the nasal capsules are present primitively in tetrapods, but they are absent in several groups of salamanders, including all of the obligate neotenes. In salamanders that metamorphose, the septomaxillae are formed late in ontogeny. The presence of septomaxillae is considered to be primitive (0), and the paedomorphic loss of these elements is derived (1). Among the plethodontids, the derived state is found in the neotenic *Haideotriton, Typhlomolge,* and *Gyrinophilus palleucus,* in the paedomorphic species of *Eurycea,* and in some bolitoglossines (D. Wake, 1966).

E. Nasal Ossification.—In some salamanders and all other living lissamphibians, the nasals ossify from two cartilaginous anlagen (Jurgens, 1971). This is considered to be the primitive condition in salamanders (0). Independently derived states include ossification from only the median anlage (1), from only the lateral anlage (1′), or reduction or absence (1″) in *Rhyacotriton* (Dicamptodontidae), proteids, and some bolitoglossine plethodontids (*Nototriton* and *Thorius).*

F. Lacrimal.—Primitively, a lacrimal bone is present in the facial region of tetrapods. In salamanders, the presence of a lacrimal is considered to be primitive (0), and the loss of the bone is derived (1).

G. Quadratojugal.—Primitively in most tetrapods, this element is present in the maxillary arch. Its presence is considered to be primitive (0) and its absence derived (1).

H. Otic-Occipital Ossification.—Primitively in tetrapods, the exoccipital, prootic, and opisthotic are separate elements. This is considered to be the primitive state in salamanders (0), whereas the fusion of these elements into a single otic-occipital element is derived (1).

I. Pterygoid.—Paired pterygoid bones form part of the palate in primitive tetrapods. The presence of these elements is considered to be primitive (0), whereas sequentially derived states are reduction (1) and absence (2).

J. Internal Carotid Foramen.—Primitively in tetrapods, an internal carotid foramen is present in the lateral alae of the parasphenoid. This is considered to be the primitive state in salamanders (0); the absence of the foramen is derived (1).

K. Opercular Apparatus.—Primitively in tetrapods, the opercular apparatus consists of an ossified operculum and free, ossified columella; this is considered to be the primitive state in salamanders (0). A derived state is the fusion of the columella with the operculum (1); a secondarily derived state is the loss of the original operculum

and its functional replacement by the footplate of the columella (2) (Monath, 1965; Larsen, 1963).

L. Junction of Periotic Canal and Cistern.—In the inner ear, the periotic canal joins the periotic cistern dorsally at its posterior aspect in caecilians, anurans, and some salamanders; Lombard (1977) considered this to be the primitive state (0). Two sequentially derived states are the junction of the canal with the cistern slightly dorsal and posterior to the fenestra ovalis (1), and junction of the canal by a protrusion of the cistern into the fenestra ovalis (2). Most salamanders have state 2, but some obligate neotenes and larvae of dicamptodontids and ambystomatids have state 1 (Lombard, 1977).

M. Flexures of Periotic Canal.—In the inner ear, the periotic canal curves ventrally and medially from its junction with the periotic cistern in caecilians, anurans, and some salamanders. This is considered to be the primitive state in salamanders (0). A derived state is a relatively horizontal course of the canal (1). Lombard (1977) recognized four modifications of this derived state but could not demonstrate polarities convincingly, so only one secondarily derived state is recognized here—canal with one or more flexures (2). Reversals from state 2 to state 1 apparently have occurred in *Notophthalmus* (Salamandridae) and in *Batrachoseps* and *Thorius* (Plethodontidae).

N. Basilaris Complex of Inner Ear.—In anurans, primitive caecilians, and some salamanders, a recessus basilaris and papillae are present in the inner ear (0). Lombard (1977) indicated that sequentially derived states are the absence of papillae (1) and the absence of the entire complex (2). Some derived genera of salamandrids have state 1 or 2; state 1 is not characteristic of any family of salamanders.

O. Angular.—Primitively in tetrapods, an angular bone is present as a separate element in the lower jaw. In salamanders, the presence of a separate angular is considered to be primitive (0); its fusion with the prearticular is derived (1).

P. First Hypobranchial and First Ceratobranchial.—In most lissamphibians (at least larval forms), the first hypobranchial and first ceratobranchial (ceratobranchial and epibranchial, respectively, of some authors) in the hyoid arch are separate elements. This is considered to be the primitive state (0). The fusion of these two elements into a single cartilaginous rod is derived (1).

Q. Second Ceratobranchial.—The second ceratobranchial (epibranchial of some authors) persists in adults of primitive tetrapods. This is considered to be the primitive state (0). The loss of the second ceratobranchial during metamorphosis is derived (1).

R. Number of Larval Gill Slits.—Four pairs of gill slits are present in various primitive tetrapods and in most salamanders. This is the primitive state (0). In various neotenic salamanders, the number of gill slits is reduced; these presumably serially derived states are three pairs (1), two pairs (2), or one pair (3). Within the Sirenidae, two states are present—three pairs in *Siren* and one in *Pseudobranchus;* among plethodontids, the desmognathines have four pairs, and the others have three. Ontogenetic reduction in the number of slits occurs in cryptobranchids and amphiumids.

S. *Palatal Dentition.*—Based on larval and adult dentition patterns, Regal (1966) concluded that the pattern of transverse palatal dentition was primitive (0). Five states seem to be derived independently—teeth parallel to premaxillary and maxillary teeth (1), longitudinal extensions of teeth along the lateral edges of the vomers (1'), longitudinal extensions of teeth along the medial edges of the vomers (1"), teeth in large patches (1'''), and teeth in M-shaped pattern (1'''').

T. *Tooth Structure.*—Primitively, tetrapods have undivided teeth, whereas teeth that are divided into a distinct crown and pedicel are characteristic of most lissamphibians (Parsons and Williams, 1962). Within the Lissamphibia, pedicellate teeth must be considered as the primitive state (0), and the presence of undivided teeth is viewed as derived (1), either as a paedomorphic state or as a character reversal. An intermediate condition, termed subpedicellate by Estes (1981), occurs in the Batrachosauroididae and Proteidae.

U. *Scapulocoracoid.*—Primitively in tetrapods, a separate coracoid bone is present in the pectoral girdle; this condition is considered to be primitive (0), whereas the absence of a separate coracoid center of ossification is derived (1).

V. *Vertebrae.*—Primitively among tetrapods, the amphicoelous condition of vertebral centra is considered to be primitive (0). According to D. Wake and Lawson (1973), opisthocoely is derived in different ways in the Salamandridae (1) and Plethodontidae (1').

W. *Ribs.*—Primitively in many tetrapods, the ribs are bicapitate. This is the primitive condition in salamanders (0); unicapitate ribs are derived (1).

X. *Spinal Nerves.*—All spinal nerves exit intervertebrally from the vertebral column in primitive tetrapods (except the limbless aistopods). This is considered to be the primitive state in salamanders (0). Edwards (1976) defined several derived states in salamanders: only the posterior caudal nerves exiting through foramina in the vertebra (1), all postsacral nerves exiting intravertebrally (2), all but the first three nerves exiting intravertebrally (3), and all but the first two nerves exiting intravertebrally (4). These character states are derived sequentially.

Y. *Ypsiloid Cartilage.*—The ypsiloid cartilage, attached to an anterior process of the pubis, is associated with the presence of lungs in terrestrial salamanders, and it is absent in plethodontids and several neotenic groups. Presence of the cartilage is primitive (0), and its absence is derived (1).

Z. *Levator Mandibulae Muscle.*—The m. levator (= adductor) mandibulae anterior (= internus) superficialis originates on the skull roof in early tetrapods. Estes (1981) considered this to be the primitive state in sala-

manders (0). Independently derived states are an origin on the side of the skull (1) or an origin that includes the exoccipital (and, in some cases, the cervical vertebrae) (1').

AA. *Pubotibialis and Puboischiotibialis Muscles.*—These thigh muscles are separate in anurans and some salamanders. This is considered to be the primitive condition (0), whereas the fusion of the two muscles is derived (1).

BB. *Kidney.*—Glomeruli normally are well developed anteriorly in the kidney in lissamphibians. This might be considered the primitive state (0); reduction or absence of anterior glomeruli is the derived state (1).

CC. *Mode of Fertilization.*—External fertilization is the primitive state in tetrapods (0). Modified cloacal glands for the production of spermatophores and the presence of a spermatheca in females are derived characters for internal fertilization in salamanders (1).

DD. *Chromosomes.*—In primitive groups of the three living orders of amphibians, there is a large number of chromosomes that includes many microchromosomes. The presence of microchromosomes that constitute a distinct size class from the macrochromosomes, and of a diploid number of 56 or more chromosomes is considered to be primitive (0). Sequentially derived states are: diploid number of 38 chromosomes including one pair of microchromosomes (1), diploid number of 22 to 28 macrochromosomes gradually decreasing in size to microchromosomes (2), diploid number of 26 or 28 macrochromosomes with no microchromosomes (3). An independently derived state is 46 to 64 macrochromosomes and no microchromosomes (1'). See Table 16-2 for chromosome numbers.

Autapomorphies. Although they are not useful in determining relationships, uniquely derived character states are helpful in diagnosing some families.

EE. *Premaxillary Dentition.*—The pars dentalis of the premaxilla bears teeth in primitive tetrapods, but it is reduced in size and edentate in sirenids. Presence of premaxillary teeth is considered to be primitive (0) and absence of teeth derived (1). In sirenids, a horny beak covers the premaxillae and maxillae, which also are edentate; the presence of a horny beak is correlated absolutely with the absence of teeth and is not considered to be a separate character. The presence of a horny beak in place of teeth is an autapomorphy for sirenids.

FF. *Frontal.*—These roofing bones normally are paired (0); they are fused into a single element (1) in the Prosirenidae (Estes, 1981).

GG. *Fronto-squamosal Arch.*—Primitive salamanders lack an arch (0), which is present only in salamandrids as a derived state (1). The arch is reduced or absent in some salamandrids; these are considered by D. Wake and Ožeti (1969) to be secondarily derived states in that family.

HH. *Mandibular Symphysis.*—The union of the

mandibular rami is simple in most salamanders (0), but the rami have an interlocking symphysis (1) in prosirenids.

II. *Atlas-Axis Complex.*—In most amphibians the cervical vertebrae are unmodified (0), but these vertebrae are modified to form an analogue of the atlas-axis complex (1) in the Prosirenidae (Estes, 1981).

JJ. *Tuberculum Interglenoideum.*—An intercotylar process, the tuberculum interglenoideum, is present on the atlas of most salamanders. Estes (1981) considered this to be the primitive state (0) and the absence of the process in batrachosauroidids to be derived (1).

KK. *Pelvic Girdle.*—A pelvic girdle and hindlimbs are normal tetrapod characters (0). The loss of these structures in several groups of vertebrates, including sirenid salamanders, is an independently derived state (1).

LL. *Nasolabial Groove.*—The nasolabial region in most living amphibians lacks grooves (0); these sensory structures are derived in plethodontids (1).

MM. *Lungs.*—Lungs typically are present in metamorphosed salamanders (0); their absence in plethodontids and *Onychodactylus* (Hynobiidae) is independently derived (1). Lungs are reduced in *Rhyacotriton, Ranodon,* and several genera of salamandrids.

NN. *Interventricular Septum.*—The ventricle typically is a single chamber in primitive tetrapods (0), including all amphibians; an interventricular septum is present (1) in sirenids (J. Putnam, 1975).

Phylogeny

The major problem in reconstructing a phylogeny of salamanders is the large number of paedomorphic characters that result in similar character states in adults of some families and in larvae of presumed more primitive groups. Moreover, many of the characters are unknown in the extinct families; the characters of these and Recent groups have been reviewed most recently by Estes (1981). Hecht and Edwards (1977) discussed the familial characters of salamanders in relation to their phylogeny. In the most recent attempt at a phylogenetic reconstruction, Milner (1983) used only selected characters and misinterpreted the polarities of some of those characters.

Five data sets were used to generate cladograms:

1. Recent families using 37 characters (all characters except autapomorphies restricted to extinct families—FF, HH–JJ); consistency index = 62.6%.
2. All families using 23 characters (only those for which data are available for extinct families); consistency index = 65.9%.
3. Recent families using only those 23 characters available for all families; consistency index = 70.5%
4. Recent families using 27 characters (those that are not strongly paedomorphic—A–C, E–H,

K, 0–Q, T, U, W, X, Z, AA–GG, KK–NN); consistency index = 73%.

5. All families using 20 characters (those that are not strongly paedomorphic and for which data are available for extinct families—A–C, G, H, O, Q, T, U, W, X, Z, AA, EE–KK); consistency index = 72.5%.

In the cladogram based on 37 characters of Recent families, the paedomorphic families Amphiumidae, Proteidae, and Sirenidae are clustered. In all of the other analyses, except the one of non-paedomorphic characters of Recent families, the Salamandridae and Sirenidae share a stem. One shared derived state (Character X— all but the first two spinal nerves exiting intravertebrally) is responsible for this arrangement. Elimination of that character results in shifting the Sirenidae to a position between the Karauridae and the stem leading to all other living salamanders.

In all cladograms, the Cryptobranchidae and Hynobiidae have a common stem, and the Ambystomatidae, Salamandridae, and Plethodontidae have a common stem. In those cladograms including extinct families, the Scapherpetontidae and Dicamptodontidae and the Batrachosauroididae and Prosirenidae are clustered, and the Karauridae is always primitive. Depending on the cladogram, the positions of the Amphiumidae, Dicamptodontidae, and Proteidae change with respect to one another.

The placement of the Sirenidae is a major problem. Depending on the character set used, sirenids have 3–5 character reversals and 1–4 character convergences, plus a suite of seven autapomorphies. Obviously, sirenids have a peculiar combination of primitive and derived character states, not all of which are associated with paedomorphosis.

The preferred cladogram of Recent families is one in which strongly paedomorphic characters are excluded. This cladogram based on these 27 characters can be modified by assuming the states of some characters for extinct families (Fig. 17-1). The assumptions are based on association. For example, in all cladograms using only characters known for the extinct families, all extinct families except the Karauridae are placed within living families that have internal fertilization; therefore, internal fertilization is assumed for all extinct families except the Karauridae.

This phylogenetic arrangement has a slightly higher consistency index than any other cladogram generated. Moreover, the Sirenidae has only three reversals and one convergence, the lowest of any arrangement. However, there is an unresolved trichotomy involving the Proteidae and the stem leading to the Batrachosauroididae and Prosirenidae. Before a better phylogeny of salamanders can be generated, it is necessary to reevaluate certain characters (especially with respect to paedomorphosis) and to add new characters that pertain to all families.

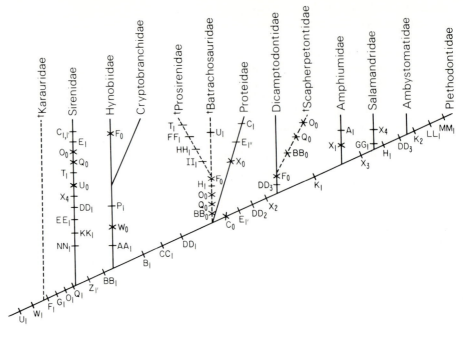

Figure 17-1. Hypothesized phylogenetic relationships among the families of salamanders based on nonpaedomorphic characters. Phylogeny of Recent families reconstructed by WAGNER78 program using 27 characters; consistency index = 73%. Approximate arrangement of extinct families (dashed lines) based on known character states and assumed states for characters E, F, K, P, BB, CC, LL, MM, and NN. See Table 17-1 for character states and text for descriptions of characters and polarities. Tick marks indicate places of shifts in characters to states indicated by subscripts; X's indicate reversals.

GYMNOPHIONA

Character States

The characters and their transformation series (Table 17-2) are based primarily on Nussbaum (1977, 1979a).

A. *Tail.*—A tail is present primitively in tetrapods and salamanders. The presence of a tail in caecilians is considered to be primitive (0); the absence of a tail is derived (1).

B. *Mouth Opening.*—Some caecilians have a terminal mouth like that of labyrinthodonts, whereas others have a projecting snout with a recessed mouth, a condition reflecting a specialization for burrowing. A terminal mouth is considered to be primitive (0). Serially derived states are subterminal (1) and recessed (2).

C. *Eye-Tentacle Relationship.*—The tentacle develops in the nasolacrimal duct and migrates varying distances anteriorly away from the eye during ontogeny. A tentacular opening adjacent to the anterior edge of the eye is considered to be primitive (0). A more anterior position is derived (1). A secondarily derived condition is the anterior translocation of the eye on the tentacle (2).

D. *Annulation.*—Caecilians have annular grooves. In some groups there are primary and secondary annuli throughout the length of the body, whereas in others secondary annuli are present only posteriorly or are absent. Also, in some caecilians having primary and secondary annuli, the annuli are orthoplicate (in the same plane around the body) throughout the length of the body; others are orthoplicate only posteriorly or not orthoplicate anywhere on the body. Nussbaum (1977) based the polarity of this character on the argument of cephalization. Accordingly, the presence of primary and sec-

ondary orthoplicate annuli throughout the length of the body is considered to be primitive (0). Sequentially derived states are primary and secondary annuli present throughout the length of the body but anterior annuli are not orthoplicate (1), secondary annuli are absent anteriorly or throughout the length of the body (2).

E. *Scales.*—Scales are present in the annular folds of many caecilians (E. Taylor, 1972). Using the argument of cephalization, Nussbaum (1977) considered the presence of scales in annular folds throughout the length of the body to be primitive (0). Reduction in size and number or complete absence of scales is derived (1).

F. *Premaxilla-Nasal.*—These bones are primitively paired, separate elements in amphibians. This is regarded as the primitive state in caecilians (0). The fusion of the nasals and premaxillae into paired nasopremaxillae is a derived state (1) that results in a more rigid tip of the snout as a specialization for burrowing.

G. *Septomaxilla.*—Primitively, these small bones are distinct, separate elements in lissamphibians. Within the caecilians, the presence of separate septomaxillae is primitive (0); their loss or fusion to adjacent bones is derived (1).

H. *Prefrontal.*—These paired bones characteristically are present primitively in tetrapods. This is the primitive state (0) in caecilians. The loss or fusion of the prefrontal with the maxillopalatine is a derived state (1).

I. *Squamosal-Frontal Articulation.*—Primitively in tetrapods, as well as nearly all vertebrates, the squamosal does not articulate with the frontal; this is the primitive state in caecilians (0). The articulation of the squamosal and frontal is a derived state (1) that increases skull rigidity as an adaptation for burrowing.

J. *Temporal Fossa.*—Nussbaum (1977) argued that

stegokrotaphy (complete skull roofing) is secondarily de-rived in caecilians; this conclusion was supported by the developmental studies of M. Wake and Hanken (1982). Thus, in caecilians, the presence of a temporal fossa be-tween the parietal and squamosal (zygokrotaphy) is prim-itive (0), whereas the juxtaposition of these elements is derived (1).

K. Vomer.—The vomers are separated by the cultri-form process of the parasphenoid portion of the basale in some caecilians. This is considered to be the primitive state (0). In other caecilians, the vomers are in contact for nearly their entire lengths; this lends rigidity to the skull and is considered to be the derived state (1).

L. Parasphenoid Architecture.—The sides of the parasphenoid portion of the basale in salamanders, anu-rans, and some caecilians are parallel. This is considered to be the primitive state (0). The anterior convergence of the sides of the parasphenoid region is derived (1).

M. Pterygoid.—These bracing bones are present primitively in tetrapods. Their presence as distinct ele-ments is primitive (0) in caecilians. Fusion of the ptery-goid with the maxillopalatine or quadrate is derived (1), and absence of pterygoids is secondarily derived (2).

N. Columellar Perforation.—Primitively in tetrapods, the columella (stapes) is pierced by the stapedial artery.

This is considered to be the primitive state (0); an un-perforated columella is derived (1).

O. Quadrate-Maxillopalatine Articulation.—The quadrate articulates with the maxillary via the jugal and quadratojugal (or simply the latter) primitively in tetra-pods. In some caecilians, the articulation is directly be-tween the quadrate and the maxillopalatine via an an-terior process of the quadrate, which may represent the quadratojugal. This is considered to be the primitive state (0). The absence of a bridge between, or articulation of, the quadrate and maxillopalatine is derived (1).

P. Retroarticular Process.—The retroarticular process of the pseudoangular is short and horizontal in some caecilians. This is the primitive state (0). A long process curving upward is a specialization for jaw closing and is derived (1).

Q. Larvae.—The presence of a larval stage is primi-tive for vertebrates. Thus, presence of larvae is primitive (0), whereas direct development is derived (1).

R. Body Shape.—Most caecilians have round bodies in cross section; this is considered to be the primitive state (0). Lateral compression of the body posteriorly in ty-phlonectids is an obvious aquatic specialization and is derived (1).

S. Eye.—The usual position of the eye in vertebrates

Table 17-2. Distribution of Character States in Families of Caecilians[a,b]

Character	Rhinatrematidae	Ichthyophiidae	Uraeotyphlidae	Scolecomorphidae	Typhlonectidae	Caeciliidae
A. Tail	0	0	0	1	1	1
B. Mouth opening	0	1	2	2	2	2
C. Eye-tentacle relationship	0	1	1	2	1	1
D. Annulation	0	1	1	2	2	2
E. Scales	0	0	1	1	1	1
F. Premaxilla-nasal	0	0	0	0	1	1
G. Septomaxilla	0	0	0	0	1	1
H. Prefrontal	1	0	0	0	1	1
I. Squamosal-frontal articulation	0	1	1	0	1	1
J. Temporal fossa	0	1	1	1	1	1
K. Vomer	0	1	1	1	1	1
L. Paraspenoid architecture	0	1	1	1	1	1
M. Pterygoid	0	0	0	2	1	1
N. Columellar perforation	0	0	0	0	1	1
O. Quadrate-maxillopalatine articulation	0	1	1	1	1	1
P. Retroarticular process	0	0	0	1	1	1
Q. Larvae	0	0	0	1	1	1
R. Body shape	0	0	0	0	1	0
S. Eye	0	0	0	1	0	0/1
T. Dorsolateral processes of basale	1	0	0	0	0	0
U. Columella	0	0	0	1	0	0
V. Anal claspers	0	0	0	0	1	0

[a]0 = primitive; 1, 2 = derived.
[b]See text for definitions of states.

is in a bony socket. This is the primitive condition (0), as contrasted with the derived state (1) of having the eye covered by bone as in scolecomorphids and some caeciliids.

T. **Dorsolateral Processes of Basale.**—These processes are absent in primitive tetrapods and most caecilians (0). Their presence (1) in an otherwise weak skull is a uniquely derived state in rhinatrematids.

U. **Columella.**—A columella is present primitively in tetrapods (0). The absence of this bone in scolecomorphids is derived (1).

V. **Anal Claspers.**—This type of modified anal region is unknown in tetrapods except in some typhlonectid caecilians. An unmodified vent is primitive (0), and the presence of anal "claspers" is derived (1).

Phylogeny

Nussbaum (1977, 1979a) demonstrated that the Rhinatrematidae is characterized by a suite of primitive character states and one autapomorphy. The ichthyophiids and uraeotyphlids possess a combination of primitive and derived character states; neither family has autapomorphies, so the historical reality of these groups is not assured. The other three families of caecilians form a group characterized by many derived character states. Three autapomorphies are present for the scolecomorphids and two for the typhlonectids. No autapomorphies characterize the Caeciliidae; although it is probably not a historical group, it is retained here. A phylogenetic reconstruction using 21 characters has a consistency index of 89.6% (Fig. 17-2). In this reconstruction, many characters used by Nussbaum (1977, 1979a) were omitted either because their states are unknown in many genera or be-

cause two or more characters seem to represent highly correlated changes in a single functional complex. Therefore, in the latter cases, the complex is treated as a single character.

The hypothesized phylogenetic relationships agree with Nussbaum's (1977) scenario that ancestral caecilians resembled rhinatrematids by having highly kinetic, zygokrotaphic skulls with a full complement of bony elements. The primitive caecilians had aquatic larvae. This mode of life history was maintained in ichthyophiids and uraeotyphlids, which are more active burrowers with stegokrotaphic skulls. Highly specialized burrowers with minimally kinetic skulls and terrestrial eggs undergoing direct development or viviparity evolved from uraeotyphlid-like ancestors. The aquatic typhlonectids have the burrowing specializations of caeciliids and presumably evolved from a caeciliid-like ancestor, a hypothesis not rejected by any autapomorphies of the Caeciliidae.

ANURA

For purposes of discussion, generally accepted suprafamilial categories are used, but with the clear understanding that such categories are not necessarily monophyletic; these categories are simply groupings of families. These descriptors are: (1) discoglossoid including the Leiopelmatidae and Discoglossidae; (2) pipoid including the Rhinophrynidae, Pipidae, and Palaeobatrachidae; (3) pelobatoid including the Pelobatidae and Pelodytidae; (4) microhylid containing only the Microhylidae; (5) ranoid including the Ranidae, Rhacophoridae, and Hyperoliidae; and (6) bufonoid containing all of the other families.

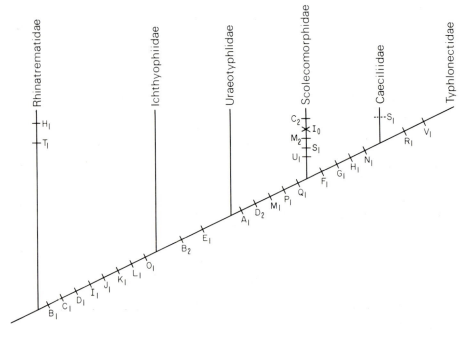

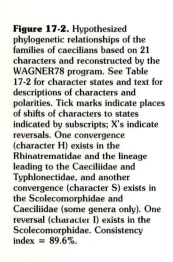

Figure 17-2. Hypothesized phylogenetic relationships of the families of caecilians based on 21 characters and reconstructed by the WAGNER78 program. See Table 17-2 for character states and text for descriptions of characters and polarities. Tick marks indicate places of shifts of characters to states indicated by subscripts; X's indicate reversals. One convergence (character H) exists in the Rhinatrematidae and the lineage leading to the Caeciliidae and Typhlonectidae, and another convergence (character S) exists in the Scolecomorphidae and Caeciliidae (some genera only). One reversal (character I) exists in the Scolecomorphidae. Consistency index = 89.6%.

Character States

A. *Vertebral Column.*—Noble (1922, 1931b) based his classification of anurans chiefly on the nature of the intervertebral joints, characters that were derived from the work of Nicholls (1916). The distribution of amphicoelous, anomocoelous, procoelous, and opisthocoelous vertebral joints (Table 17-3) suggests that these vertebral states are homoplasious. Mookerjee (1931) and Griffiths (1963) described patterns of vertebral development that resulted in different kinds of vertebral centra. Perichordal central are round in cross section, whereas epichordal centra are depressed in cross section. Griffiths described hollow perichordal centra as ectochordal and solid perichordal centra as holochordal. He designated epichordal centra as stegochordal and described two developmental pathways that resulted in indistinguishable stegochordal vertebrae in adult anurans. In their critique of Griffiths (1963), Kluge and Farris (1969) pointed out that the degree of epichordy as defined by Mookerjee (1931) and Mookerjee and Das (1939) is variable among the relatively few taxa of anurans that have been examined. Moreover, Griffiths (1963) defined two types of stegochordy (= epichordy) based on different developmental patterns. Owing to the incomplete knowledge of the developmental patterns and their distribution and variation among anurans, it is impossible to establish the polarities of the transformation series of the various vertebral types at this time. The foregoing characters are discussed in more detail in Chapter 13.

Many other vertebral characters have been used in phylogenetic reconstruction by various investigators (e.g., J. D. Lynch, 1973), but the distributions of many of these within family groups is inconsistent, and within nominal families there is variation in many of them (Table 17-3).

The only vertebral character included in the phylogenetic reconstruction offered herein is the reduction in the number of presacral vertebrae. In anurans, a greater number of presacral vertebrae is considered to be primitive because *Triadobatrachus* has 14 presacrals, and salamanders and caecilians have even more. Nine presacral vertebrae is considered to be primitive (0), and eight or fewer to be derived (1).

B. *Ribs.*—Ribs are characteristic of vertebrates. The presence of free dorsal ribs in adult anurans is considered to be primitive (0), and their absence derived (1).

C. *Basic Pectoral Girdle Architecture.*—Developmentally and structurally, anurans have either an arciferal or firmisternal pectoral girdle as explained in Chapter 13. Griffiths (1963) argued, probably correctly, that arcifery (characteristic of salamanders and most anurans) is primitive, and that firmisterny is a derived feature characteristic of ranoids, microhylids, and dendrobatids. In some developmentally arciferal anurans, the epicoracoid cartilages fuse medially to produce a pseudofirmisternal girdle; conversely, in a few firmisternal taxa, the epicoracoid cartilages are partially free, resulting in a so-called pseudoarciferal girdle. On the bases of ontogenetic and distributional evidence, it seems clear that both pseudofirmisterny and pseudoarcifery are derived, homoplasious features; thus, only firmisterny and arcifery are used in the phylogenetic reconstruction presented here. An arciferal girdle is considered to be primitive (0), whereas a firmisternal girdle is derived (1).

D. *Other Features of the Pectoral Girdle.*—In addition to the primary architecture, other features of the pectoral girdle that have been employed in anuran phylogenetic reconstructions include characters of the pre- and postzonal pectoral elements—presence or absence and degree of ossification of the omosternum and sternum (mesosternum and xiphisternum) (see J. D. Lynch, 1973, for discussion). The presence of a sternum in primitive tetrapods, salamanders, and most anurans suggests that its absence in *Rhinophrynus* and *Brachycephalus* is a derived feature. An omosternum is present or absent in arciferal anurans, and tends to be elaborated in firmisternal anurans that do not have reduced girdles (i.e., some microhylids). Because primitive arciferal anurans possess an omosternum, its presence is assumed to be primitive among anurans. Its loss among other arciferal anurans and some firmisternal frogs, as well as its elaboration among firmisternal frogs are presumed to be derived states.

Most of the anurans have a clavicle that articulates with the scapula anterior to the glenoid fossa. According to Kluge and Farris (1969), the distal end of the clavicle overlays the scapula anteriorly in primitive tetrapods. In anurans, this condition is considered to be primitive (0); nonoverlap of the scapula by the clavicle is derived (1).

E. *Cranium.*—There is considerable variation in the cranial elements of anurans, including reduction or loss of the vomers, palatines, quadratojugals, and columellae in diverse groups. The premaxillae and maxillae are dentate in most anurans, but edentate in rhinophrynids, bufonids, brachycephalids, rhinodermatids, and most microhylids; some taxa in other families also are edentate. The absence of teeth is considered to be a derived feature. Because palatines are present in salamanders and all extinct orders of amphibians, their absence in anurans is considered to be derived (1) and their presence primitive (0).

F. *Parahyoid.*—A parahyoid bone associated with the cartilaginous hyoid plate is present in discoglossoids, palaeobatrachids, *Rhinophrynus,* and *Pelodytes.* Although there is no record of its occurrence among other amphibians, De Beer (1937) suggested that the parahyoid in *Polypterus* and teleostean fishes is homologous with the same element in anurans. The nature of this ossification is highly variable and has not been investigated in detail. In some frogs it seems to be an irregularly shaped ossification associated with the cartilage of the hyoid plate and may be single and median (e.g., *Leiopelma hoch-*

Table 17-3. Vertebral Characteristics of Anuran Families[a]

Family	Number of presacral vertebrae	Presacrals I and II fused	Vertebral type[b]	Centrum type[c]	Neural arches imbricate	Atlantal cotyles juxtaposed	Free ribs	Sacral diapophyses	Sacro-coccygeal articulation	Transverse processes on coccyx
Brachycephalidae	7	+	P	H/?	+	−	−	Dilated	Bicondylar	−
Bufonidae	5–8	±	P	H/Pc	+	+	−	Dilated	Bicondylar	−
Centrolenidae	8	−	P	H/?	−	−	−	Dilated	Bicondylar	+
Dendrobatidae	8	−	P	H/?	−	−	−	Cylindrical	Bicondylar	+
Discoglossidae	8	−	0	S/Pc, Ep	+	+	+[d]	Expanded	Bicondylar	+
Heleophrynidae	8	−	A	E/?	±	+	−	Cylindrical	Bicondylar	+
Hylidae	8	−	P	H/Pc, Ep	±	±	−	Dilated[e]	Bicondylar	−
Hyperoliidae	8	−	P/D	H/?	−	−	−	Cylindrical	Bicondylar	+
Leiopelmatidae	9	−	Am	E/Pc	−	+	+	Dilated	Contiguous	±
Leptodactylidae	8	−	P	H/Pc, Ep	±	±	−	Cylindrical	Bicondylar	±
Microhylidae	8	±	P/D	H/Pc	±	−	−	Dilated	Bicondylar[f]	±
Myobatrachidae	8	+	A/P	H/?	±	±	+[g]	Dilated	Bicondylar	±
†Palaeobatrachidae	7–8	+	P	S/?	+	+	−	Dilated	Monocondylar[f]	+
Pelobatidae	8	−	A	S/?	+	+	−	Expanded	Monocondylar	+
Pelodytidae	8	+	A	S/?	+	+	−	Expanded	Fused	+
Pipidae	6–8	±	0	S/Ep	+	±	+[g]	Expanded	Fused	−
Pseudidae	8	−	P	H/Pc	−	+	−	Cylindrical	Bicondylar	−
Ranidae	8	±	P/D	H/Pc	±	−	−	Cylindrical	Bicondylar	−
Rhacophoridae	8	−	P/D	H/Pc, Ep	−	−	−	Cylindrical	Bicondylar	−
Rhinodermatidae	8	+	P	H/?	+	+	−	Dilated	Bicondylar	−
Rhinophrynidae	8	−	0	E/Pc	+	+	−	Expanded	Bicondylar	−
Sooglossidae	8	−	P	H/?	−	+	−	Dilated	Monocondylar	+

[a]Symbols are as follows:
+ = Presence of a structure in a family.
− = Absence of a structure in a family.
± = Variable in a family.
A = Amphicoelous or procoelous with free intervertebral bodies at some stage of development.
Am = Amphicoelous with contiguous intervertebral cartilage.
D = Diplasiocoelous.
E = Ectochordal.
Ep = Epichordal.
H = Holochordal.
P = Procoelous.
Pc = Perichordal.
S = Stegochordal.

[b]Sensu Noble (1922).
[c]Sensu Griffiths (1963)/sensu Kluge and Farris (1969).
[d]Ankylosed to transverse processes in *Bombina*.
[e]Cylindrical in some.
[f]Fused in some.
[g]Ankylosed to transverse processes in adults.

stetteri or paired and lateral (e.g., *Bombina variegata*). In *Rhinophrynus,* in contrast, the parahyoid is a transverse, shallowly V-shaped bone that extends across the width of the ventral surface of the hyoid plate. The function of the parahyoid bones is unknown, as are details of their development. Thus, at this time, it is not possible to make an unequivocal statement about their homologies. Based on the occurrence of a parahyoid in some fishes, the presence of this element in anurans is considered to be primitive (0) and its absence derived (1)

G. Cricoid Cartilage.—In most anurans, the cartilaginous cricoid ring of the larynx is complete in adults, and arises from paired cartilaginous structures. In myobatrachines and sooglossids, the ventral portions of the paired cartilages fail to unite, whereas in *Rhinophrynus* and pelobatoids, the dorsal portions of the paired cartilages do not unite. Assuming that the paired cartilaginous elements in early developmental stages of anurans are homologous with the lateral cartilages that support the laryngotracheal chamber in salamanders, paired cartilages as occur in early development are considered to be primitive in amphibians (0). A complete cricoid ring is derived (1). The failure of the cricoid cartilages to unite dorsally or ventrally is assumed to be a paedomorphic event that results in two independently derived states—ventral gap in the ring (0') and dorsal gap in the ring (0'').

H. Tongue.—Tongues are present in all amphibians except the pipid frogs, which retain vestiges of the lingual musculature. The presence of a tongue is primitive (0), and its absence is derived (1).

I. Astragalus and Calcaneum.—In salamanders and *Triadobatrachus,* the fibulare and tibiale (the astragalus and calcaneum, respectively, of Recent anurans) are separate tarsal elements. In anurans, these elements are elongated and fused proximally and distally in most taxa; the astragalus and calcaneum are fused throughout their lengths in only two families—the pelodytids and centrolenids. Incomplete fusion of the astragalus and calcaneum is assumed to be primitive (0), whereas complete fusion of these bones is derived (1).

J. Hands and Feet.—J. D. Lynch (1973) considered the number of tarsalia to be an important feature, with the presence of three tarsalia being primitive and the presence of two being derived. Salamanders have up to four free tarsalia, suggesting that the greater number of free elements in anurans is primitive. Fusion of Tarsalia 2, 3, and 4 has occurred to produce two tarsals (i.e., 1 + 2–4) in most anurans. In *Triadobatrachus,* discoglossoids, pelodytids, rhinodermatids, mantelline ranids, and hyperoliids, and some arthroleptine and astylosternine ranids, there are three tarsalia (i.e., 1 + 2 + 3–4) owing to the lack of fusion of Tarsal 2 with Tarsalia 3 and 4.

The normal phalangeal formulae in anurans is 2-2-3-3 (hand) and 2-2-3-4-3 (foot). Reduction in the number of phalanges occurs in a few taxa, and a reduction in the number of digits is characteristic of the Brachycephalidae. Such decreases in the phalangeal elements are interpreted as derived, paedomorphic events. An increase in the phalangeal formula by the addition of intercalary elements (usually short and cartilaginous) between the penultimate and terminal phalanges characterizes pseudids, hylids, centrolenids, rhacophorids, hyperoliids, phrynomerine microhylids and mantelline ranids. Absence of intercalary elements is considered to be a primitive state shared by salamanders and anurans (0), whereas their presence is derived (1).

K–L. Thigh Musculature.—As a result of Noble's (1922) study, characteristics of thigh musculature have been used widely in phylogenetic analyses of anurans. J. D. Lynch (1973) used only five features of the thigh musculature in his analysis: (1) the presence of the m. caudalipuboischitibialis, (2) the presence of an accessory tendon of the m. glutaeus magnus, (3) the presence of an accessory head of the m. adductor magnus, (4) the position of the insertion of the m. sartoriosemitendinosus relative to the m. gracilis, and (5) the condition of the m. semitendinosus-m. sartorius complex. Dunlap (1960) in his comparative study of the thigh musculature of several species of anurans documented the significant variation in the occurrence and sizes of accessory heads and extents of muscle insertions among anurans. This variation coupled with the fact that such information is available for relatively few species suggests that most of these characters are not amenable to phylogenetic interpretation at present. Although the occurrence of these characters insofar as they are known is listed in Table 17-4, only two are used in this analysis.

K. Caudalipuboischiotibialis muscle.—Noble (1922) concluded that the m. caudalipuboischiotibialis was homologous with the muscle of the same name in salamanders and that its presence only in leiopelmatids among all living anurans is primitive (0), and its absence is derived (1).

L. Semitendinosus-sartorius muscle complex.—The m. semitendinosus in anurans is homologous with the m. puboischiotibialis, an undivided thigh muscle in salamanders. In most anurans, a separate muscle, the m. sartorius, is differentiated from the m. semitendinosus. Kluge and Farris (1969) suggested that the differentiation of the m. sartorius from the m. semitendinosus represents a continuum and rejected the use of the character in phylogenetic analysis. The two muscles are only partially separated in *Discoglossus, Xenopus,* and *Limnodynastes.* Otherwise, in those anurans that have been examined only one muscle, the m. semitendinosus, is present or both muscles are discrete. Because of the single condition in salamanders, the absence of a discrete m. sartorius in anurans is considered to be primitive (0), whereas the presence of a discrete m. sartorius is derived (1).

M. Trigeminal and Facial Ganglia.—As explained by Sokol (1975) in his paper on the phylogeny of anuran larvae, two states pertain to the ganglia of the trigeminal and facial nerves (C.Nn. V and VII, respectively). In salamanders and all anurans with Type III larvae, the trigeminal and facial ganglia are separate, and the major rami of the facial nerve exit the chondrocranium via the palatine foramen, which lies lateral and slightly posterior to the prootic foramen; the cartilage separating the two foramina is termed the prefacial commissure. In all other anurans surveyed, the ganglia of the trigeminal and facial nerves are fused to form the single prootic ganglion. The rami of both nerves emerge via the single prootic foramen which is located immediately anterior to the otic capsule. Anurans having separate trigeminal and facial ganglia are primitive (0), whereas those in which the ganglia are fused to form a prootic ganglion are derived (1).

N. *Bidder's Organ.*—In all male bufonid larvae the anterior portion of each gonad becomes enlarged to form a Bidder's organ, which consists of ovarian tissue. In some genera (namely *Bufo, Pedostibes, Pseudobufo, Atelopus, Leptophryne, Dendrophryniscus, Nectophryne,* some species of *Nectophrynoides)*, Bidder's organ is retained in the adult males in association with the testis as either a peripheral, lateral band of ovarian tissue or a cap over the anterior pole of the testis (M. Wake, 1980a). Retention of Bidder's organ in adult bufonids seems to be a paedomorphic event (Griffiths, 1959b). Absence of this structure in anurans is considered to be primitive (0), and its presence in bufonids derived (1).

O. *Larval Types.*—As proposed by Orton (1957), modified by P. Starrett (1973), and elaborated by Sokol (1975), there are four types of anuran larvae. The morphological features of these types are discussed in more detail in Chapter 6. Type I is characteristic of the pipoidea, Type II the microhylids, Type III the discoglossoids, and Type IV all other anurans. Sokol (1975) suggested that Types III and IV were derived independently from a common ancestor. The opercular structure is derived in Types I and II; the m. interhyoideus posterior muscle is absent, and the ceratobranchial is fused with the hyobranchial plate. Because Types I, II, and IV share the derived feature of a single prootic ganglion (see discussion above), it is assumed that Types I and II are independent derivatives of larval Type IV. Larval Types I and II share many specialized morphological features in the structure of the chondrocranium, the filter apparatus, and the hyobranchial skeleton; moreover, neither type bears keratinized mouthparts.

However, Type I and Type II larvae are distinguished by the structures of the opercula, the modes of fusion of the hyobranchial apparatus, and the architecture of the suspensoria. Type I larvae also differ from Type II larvae in the absence of internal gills and the third interbranchial septum in the former. The coding of larval types follows the suggestion of Sokol (1975) wherein a hypothetical ancestral type is considered to be primitive (0). Types III and IV are independently derived and are coded as (1) and (1'), respectively. Types I and II are independently derived from Type IV and are coded as (2) and (2').

P. *Amplectic Position.*—J. D. Lynch (1973) argued convincingly that inguinal amplexus, as it occurs in all discoglossoids, pipoids, pelobatoids, heleophrynids, sooglossids, and myobatrachine myobatrachids (also in

Table 17-4. Characteristics of the Thigh Musculature in Anuran Families

Family	M. caudali-puboischiotibialis present	M. semitendinosus separate from m. sartorius	Insertion of tendon of m. semitendinosus*	Accessory tendon of m. glutaeus magnus	Accessory head of m. adductor magnus
Brachycephalidae	−	+	V	+	+
Bufonidae	−	+	V	+	+
Centrolenidae	−	+	V	−	+
Dendrobatidae	−	+	P	+	+
Discoglossidae	−	±	V	±	−
Heleophrynidae	−	+	V	+	+
Hylidae	−	+	V	−	+
Hyperoliidae	−	+	D	−	+
Leiopelmatidae	+	−	V	−	−
Leptodactylidae	−	+	P, V	+	+
Microhylidae	−	+	D	+	−
Myobatrachidae	−	+	D, P, V	+	+
Pelobatidae	−	−	V	+	−
Pelodytidae	−	−	V	+	−
Pipidae	−	±	P	+	−
Pseudidae	−	+	V	+	+
Ranidae	−	+	D	±	+
Rhacophoridae	−	+	D	−	+
Rhinodermatidae	−	+	V	+	−
Rhinophrynidae	−	+	P	−	−
Sooglossidae	−	+	D	+	−

*D = dorsal, P = penetrating, V = ventral to m. gracilis.

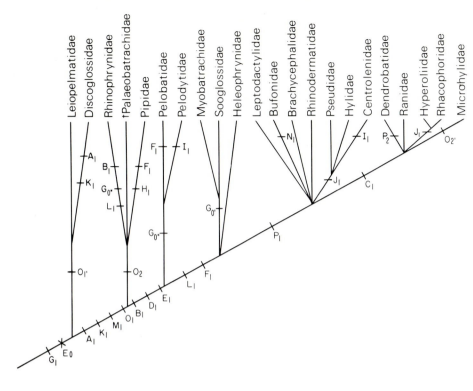

Figure 17-3. Hypothesized phylogenetic relationships of the families of anurans based on 16 characters and reconstructed by the WAGNER78 program. See Table 17-5 for character states and text for descriptions of characters and polarities. For purposes of analysis, the states of characters, G, L, M, and O of the extinct family Palaeobatrachidae were coded the same as those of Pipidae; also character N in the Brachycephalidae and Sooglossidae was coded the same as other bufonoids. Tick marks indicate places of shifts of characters to states indicated by subscripts. Two convergences exist in each of seven characters (A, B, G, I, J, K, and L), and three convergences occur in character F. Consistency index = 65.6%.

two genera of telmatobiine leptodactylids) is primitive (0). Sequentially derived states are axillary (1) and cephalic (2). In addition to these types of amplexus, there are deviations based on body morphs and behavior (see Chapter 3).

Other Characters

Numerous other characters have been used in phylogenetic reconstructions of anurans. However, they have not been used here because either (1) the direction of evolutionary change has not been determined, (2) the distribution of the character states among anurans is insufficiently known, or (3) the character states apparently have arisen so many times that the character cannot be used to show relationships. In addition to numerous characters that were rejected above, the following merit discussion.

Pupil Shape. As noted by J. D. Lynch (1973), anurans have four shapes of the pupil: (1) triangular (only in discoglossids), (2) round (only in pipids and some microhylids), (3) horizontal (most bufonoids, microhylids, and ranoids), and (4) vertically elliptical (some discoglossoids and pipoids, pelobatoids, heleophrynids, most hyperoliids, and some myobatrachids, leptodactylids, hylids, microhylids, and ranids). Although J. D. Lynch (1973) conceded that pupil shape might be adaptive, he concluded that the vertical pupil is primitive and the other shapes are independently derived.

Developmental Pattern. Reproductive modes are highly diverse in anruans. The presumed primitive mode is the deposition of eggs and development of larvae in ponds; 28 advanced modes are recognized (see Chapter 2). Although some families are characterized by derived modes (e.g., transportation of larvae in vocal sac in rhinodermatids, transportation of tadpoles on dorsum in dendrobatids, or arboreal eggs and stream tadpoles in centrolenids), other families have diverse modes (Table 2-3). It is evident that some of the derived reproductive modes, such as direct development of terrestrial eggs, have evolved independently in different lineages of anurans. Thus, developmental pattern is useful phylogenetically within lineages, but not for discerning relationships among anurans as a whole.

Chromosome Complement. Although karyotypes are known for a great variety of anurans representing all families (Table 16-3), few generalities can be made regarding chromosomal evolution in anurans. Microchromosomes occur only in discoglossoids. With the exception of *Xenopus,* the basic karyotype of other groups of anurans seems to be 2N = 26 bi-armed chromosomes. This number is reduced, presumably by centric fusion, in many lineages and increased by centric fission in a few groups (see Chapter 16).

Phylogeny

As emphasized in the foregoing discussion of characters, existing knowledge of the taxonomic distribution and the

Table 17-5. Distribution of Character States in Families of Anurans[a]

Character	Brachycephalidae	Bufonidae	Centrolenidae	Dendrobatidae	Discoglossidae	Heleophrynidae	Hylidae	Hyperoliidae	Leiopelmatidae	Leptodactylidae	Microhylidae	Myobatrachidae	†Palaeobatrachidae	Pelobatidae	Pelodytidae	Pipidae	Pseudidae	Ranidae	Rhacophoridae	Rhinodermatidae	Rhinophrynidae	Sooglossidae
A. Vertebral column	1	1	1	1	1	1	1	1	0	1	1	1	1	1	1	1	1	1	1	1	1	1
B. Ribs	1	1	1	1	0	1	1	1	0	1	1	1	0	1	1	0	1	1	1	1	1	1
C. Basic pectoral girdle architecture	0	0	0	1	0	0	0	1	0	0	1	0	0	0	0	0	0	1	1	0	0	0
D. Other features of the pectoral girdle	1	1	1	1	0	1	1	1	0	1	1	1	0	1	1	0	1	1	1	1	0	1
E. Cranium	0	0	0	0	1	0	0	0	1	0	0	0	1	0	0	1	0	0	0	0	1	0
F. Parahyoid	1	1	1	1	0	1	1	1	0	1	1	1	0	1	0	1	1	1	1	1	0	1
G. Cricoid cartilage	1	1	1	1	1	1	1	1	1	1	1	0'	?	0'	0'	1	1	1	1	1	1'	1'
H. Tongue	0	0	0	0	0	0	0	0	0	0	0	0	?	0	0	1	0	0	0	0	0'	0'
I. Astagalus and calcaneum	0	0	0	0	0	0	0	0	0	0	0	0	0	0	1	0	0	0	0	0	0	0
J. Hands and feet	0	0	1	0	0	0	0	0	0	0	0	0	0	0	0	0	0	0	0	0	0	0
K. Caudalipuboischio-tibialis muscle	1	1	1	1	1	1	1	1	0	1	0[c]	1	1	1	1	1	1	0[d]	1	1	1	1
L. Semitendinosus-sartorius muscle complex	1	1	1	1	0	0	1	1	0	1	1	1	?	0	0	0	1	1	1	1	1	1
M. Trigeminal and facial ganglia	1	1	1	1	0	0	1	1	0	1	1	1	?	1	1	1	1	1	1	1	1	1
N. Bidder's organ	0	1	0	0	0	0	0	0	0	0	0	0	?	0	0	0	0	0	0	0	0	0
O. Larval types	—	1'	1'	1'	1	1'	1'	1'	1	1[e]	2'	1'	2	1'	1'	2	1'	1'	1'	1'	2	—
P. Amplectic position	1	1	1	2	0	0	1	1	0	1	1	0[f]	?	0	0	0	1	1	1	1	0	0

[a] 0 = primitive; 1, 2, etc.; ? = unknown; — = not applicable.
[b] See text for definitions of states.
[c] Derived state in phrynomerines.
[d] Derived state in mantellines.
[e] Primitive state in some telmatobiines.
[f] Derived state (1) in limnodynastines.

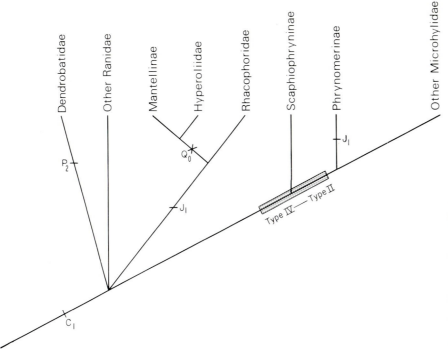

Figure 17-4. Hypothesized phylogenetic relationships among firmisternal anurans. Characters C, J, and P are the same as in Table 17-5 and Figure 17-3. Character Q is the number of tarsalia; according to J. D. Lynch (1973), the primitive state is three tarsalia (0), and the derived state (1) occurs in most firmisternal anurans. The tadpole of scaphiophrynines is intermediate between Type II of microhylids and Type IV of other firmisternal anurans (Wassersug, 1984).

direction of evolutionary change in many characters limits the number of characters that can be used in phylogenetic reconstruction. Consequently, only 16 characters were coded for phylogenetic analysis (Table 17-5). A cladogram generated from these character states (Figure 17-3) has eight homoplasious characters and a consistency index of 65.6%.

Several unresolved polytomies exist in this cladogram. If the exceptions in amplectic position (Character P) noted in Table 17-5 were shown on the cladogram, both groups of bufonoids would be rearranged. The limnodynastine myobatrachids would cluster with the leptodactylids, and two genera of leptodactylids, *Batrachyla* and *Pleurodema* (in part) would be associated with the myobatrachids. Thus, the bufonoids are a group of families that are distinguished from the ranoids and microhylids by the structure of the pectoral girdle. The elucidation of relationships among the bufonoid families is a prerequisite to a realistic phylogenetic reconstruction of anurans; certainly, no systematic problem dealing with amphibians is more deserving of intensive research.

An obvious difference between this cladogram and most phylogenetic arrangements is the placement of the dendrobatids with the ranids, as originally suggested by Griffiths (1959a). This association is based on the synapomorphy of the firmisternal pectoral girdle (Character C). Dendrobatids are like ranids in all characters coded except amplectic position; dendrobatids have a secondarily derived state of amplectic position. Dendrobatids also share with ranids round sacral diapophyses, but they are distinguished by the habit of carrying tadpoles on the dorsum.

It is evident that intercalary elements in the digits (Character J) evolved at least twice—once in an arciferal lineage and again in firmisternal frogs. The cladogram is over-simplified with respect to this character, for intercalary elements are present in mantelline ranids and phrynomerine microhylids. Also, not all microhylids have typical Type II tadpoles (see Chapter 6). Thus, if subfamilial groups are analyzed with respect to these characters, and some other characters, a somewhat different cladogram is generated (Fig. 17-4).

The distribution of some character states and the position of some families in the cladogram pose some other questions. A single synapomorphy unites the Rhinophrynidae with the Pipidae and Palaeobatrachidae, but this results in three convergences in the rhinophrynids and other lineages. Furthermore, one of these homoplasious character states (Character G) is the only synapomorphy uniting the Pelobatidae and the Pelodytidae. Additional characters are needed to resolve the relationships of the rhinophrynids with the pelobatids and pelodytids. There are some distinctive differences between the pelobatine and megophryine pelobatids (see account of Pelobatidae in Chapter 19). Resolution of the phylogenetic relationships of taxa included in the Pelobatidae may shed light not only on the relationships of the so-called primitive anurans but also between these and the myobatrachids. The Myobatrachidae contains two distinctive subfamilies, the Myobatrachinae and the Limnodynastinae. Possibly these are not sister groups.

Although not all branches on the cladogram are marked with apomorphies, characters do exist to define each of the families (see Chapter 19).

CHAPTER 18

Biogeography

The most striking feature of past and present distributions [of amphibians] is the fundamental and consistent association of distributions of each group with either Laurasia or Gondwanaland, and those supercontinent's Cretaceous fragments that by continental drift have come to form today's major land areas.

Jay M. Savage (1973)

Few scientific discoveries have influenced historical biogeography so significantly as the accumulating data on plate tectonics beginning in the early 1960s. Most syntheses of historical biogeography before the late 1960s were influenced by the arguments of Matthew (1915) that the evolution and distribution of mammals could be explained adequately by continental isostasy. Among Matthew's many influential disciples was Noble, who, in a series of papers culminating in his synthesis of amphibian biology (1931b), attempted to explain the distribution of families of amphibians by dispersal between static continents. With the advent of extensive geophysical evidence in support of continental drift, biogeographers began to reexamine earlier biogeographic arrangements. The results have been striking changes in biogeographic interpretations.

In order to address the biogeographic problems, one must formulate working principles and review the geologic and climatic changes that have taken place since the time of the origin of amphibians. This chapter discusses these subjects and then analyzes the historical and modern distributions of the three living orders of amphibians.

BIOGEOGRAPHIC PRINCIPLES

The documentation of the distribution of organisms in space and time is the raw material for biogeographic analysis. Although each taxon has its individual distribution because of its unique evolutionary history and particular ecological requirements, it is possible to determine patterns (generalized tracks) of coincident distributions of many monophyletic groups. This is the first step in biogeographic analysis. Second, it is necessary to determine disjunct clusters of distributions within the overall distribution of an inclusive taxonomic unit. These clusters commonly define the geographic limits of major modern biotas, have a high degree of endemism, and constitute centers of adaptive radiation. Third, it is desirable to identify the historical source units that contributed to the modern biotas, for the biota in any given region may have been derived from several historical source units at different times.

A major revitalization of historical biogeography has taken place in recent years with the formulation of vicariance biogeography (see G. Nelson and Platnick, 1981, and G. Nelson and D. Rosen, 1981, for reviews). Considerable controversy exists between adherents of the dispersal theory and the proponents of the vicariance theory, who argue that the vicariance approach provides testable hypotheses, whereas the dispersalist approach is untestable. J. Savage (1982) took a balanced view and outlined the conceptual framework of each approach, as given below.

Dispersal Theory
1. A monophyletic group arises at a center of origin.

2. Each group disperses from this center.
3. A generalized track corresponds to a dispersal route.
4. Each modern biota represents an assemblage derived from one to several historical source units.
5. Direction of dispersal may be deduced from tracks, evolutionary relationships, and past geologic and climatic history.
6. Climatic and/or physiographic change provides the major impetus and/or opportunity for dispersal.
7. Biotas are constituted by dispersal across barriers and subsequent evolution in isolation.
8. Dispersal is the key to explain modern patterns; related groups separated by barriers have dispersed across them when the barriers were absent or relatively ineffective, or less commonly by passing over or through existing barriers.
9. Dispersal is of primary significance in understanding current patterns; dispersal preceded barrier formation and vicariance, and occurs again when barriers subsequently are removed or become ineffective.

Vicariance Theory

1. Vicariants (allopatric taxa) arise after barriers separate parts of a formerly continuous population.
2. Substantial numbers of monophyletic groups are affected simultaneously by the same vicariating events (geographic barrier formation).
3. A generalized track estimates the biotic composition and geographic distribution of an ancestral biota before it subdivided (vicariated) into descendant biotas.
4. Vicariance after geographic subdivision produced modern biotas.
5. Each generalized track represents a historic source unit.
6. Sympatry of generalized tracks reflects geographic overlap of different biotas owing to dispersal.
7. The primary vicariating events are change in world geography that subdivided ancestral biotas.
8. Biotas evolve in isolation after barriers arise.
9. Vicariance is of primary importance in understanding modern patterns; related groups separated by barriers were fragmented by the appearances of barriers.

These two approaches differ mainly in their emphases. In the dispersal model, geographically associated taxa dispersed together so as to form a common pattern. In the vicariance model, original distributions are frag-

mented and the geographically associated taxa in each fragment evolved together.

The major patterns of amphibian distribution at the familial and subfamilial levels can be explained best by vicariance biogeography. Some facets of peripheral distributions definitely are the result of dispersal, but these are relatively minor in comparison with the overall distribution patterns, except for some widespread genera, such as *Bufo, Hyla,* and *Rana,* in which both phenomena seem to have been important. Any biogeographic scenario is only as good as the understanding of the phylogenetic relationships of the organisms involved. Unresolved phylogenetic relationships of many amphibian groups, especially some anurans, make some aspects of the biogeographic analysis tenuous at best.

Ideally, all biogeographic syntheses should be based on phylogenetic analyses of component taxa. This has not been the case, nor is it likely that this ever will be a reality. Instead, the methodology suggested by J. Savage (1982) has been used to a great extent, especially with the anurans. This method uses events in the history of the earth to predict general patterns of phylogenetic relationship. This approach implies a reciprocal relationship between the history of the earth and the history of the biota.

However, even this approach presents some problems, especially in the anurans, a group in which familial assignments of many taxa are open to question (see Chapter 17). Many assumptions are made in the following discussion, and in some cases alternatives are offered. Moreover, if the scenarios depicted are correct, many groups as now recognized are paraphyletic. These include the families Caeciliidae, Myobatrachidae, Leptodactylidae, Bufonidae, Hylidae, and Ranidae, the subfamily Microhylinae, and the genera *Eleutherodactylus, Bufo, Hyla,* and *Rana.*

The application of times of divergences of lineages derived from biochemical studies provides a data set independent of the phylogenies based on morphology and biogeography based solely on earth history. Although the evolutionary clock hypothesis of albumen changes has been criticized by some workers (see Chapter 16), the results are encouraging. In most cases in which phylogenetic analyses and earth history agree, there also is congruence of the molecular data.

The fossil record and the biochemical information emphasize the antiquity of many lineages of lissamphibians. As gaps are filled in the fossil record, more molecular data accumulated, and more cladistic studies completed, the biogeographic picture of amphibians should improve.

HISTORICAL SETTING

The fossil record of modern groups of amphibians extends back to the early Triassic (Table 18-1). Therefore, in order to interpret the distributional histories of the living groups, it is necessary to project the hypothesized phylogenetic relationships of each of the orders (see

Table 18-1. Major Geologic and Climatic Events Affecting the Distribution of Amphibians

Period or epoch[a]	Geologic events	Climatic events	Earliest known appearance of amphibian families[b]
Triassic, 220 m.y.	At Permo-Triassic boundary, east Asia consisted of several separate blocks south and east of major Asian continent. Otherwise, most if not all continents united in single land mass—Pangaea.	High-latitude humid belts separated from tropical humid belt by midlatitude arid zones; expansion of northern in Late Triassic.	Protobatrachidae
Jurassic, 190 m.y.	East Asian blocks unite with Pangaea. Breakup of Pangaea initiated about 180 m.y. when North America and Africa began to separate. By 160 m.y., Tethys Sea separated east Laurasia from east Gondwanaland; epeiric seas probably connected Tethys Sea with North Atlantic and possibly with East Pacific via Caribbean Basin. At about 140 m.y., Gondwanaland fragmented into three major blocks—South America–Africa, Antarctica–Australia, Madagascar–India.	Contraction of arid zones and expansion of high latitude and especially tropical humid belts.	Karauridae (U) Prosirenidae (M) Leiopelmatidae (L) Discoglossidae (U) Palaeobatrachidae (U)
Cretaceous, 135 m.y.	Turgai Sea separated east and west Eurasia. Midcontinental Sea separated east and west North America 100 to 75 m.y. Kolyma Block united with Asia 120 m.y. South Atlantic Ocean separated South America and Africa (±100 m.y.). Madagascar separated from Indian–Seychellean Plate. New Zealand separated from Australia. Possible connection between Central and South America in Late Cretaceous.	Temperate humid zones discontinuous in high latitudes. Tropical and subtropical climates dominating most land masses; arid zones small and discontinuous.	Sirenidae (U) Amphiumidae (U) Scapherpetontidae (U) Batrachosauroididae (U) Pipidae (L) Pelobatidae (L)
Paleocene, 65 m.y.	Turgai Sea separated east and west Eurasia. Seychelles separated from Indian Plate. Australia separated from Antarctica. Formation of Greater Antilles. DeGeer passage between Europe and North America. Beringia intermittent. Brief connection of South America with Central America.	Equable tropical and subtropical.	Cryptobranchidae Proteidae Dicamptodontidae Caeciliidae Rhinophrynidae Bufonidae Hylidae
Eocene, 54 m.y.	Turgai Sea separated east and west Eurasia. Thule connection of Europe and North America. Beringia intermittent.	Equable tropical and subtropical.	Salamandridae Pelodytidae Myobatrachidae
Oligocene, 36 m.y.	Turgai Sea subsided. Indian Plate collided with Asia. Japanese Archipelago separated from Asia. Southern edge of Oriental Plate formed proto-East Indies. Beringia intermittent.	Polar cooling and latitudinal zonation of climates.	Ambystomatidae Leptodactylidae Ranidae
Miocene, 23 m.y.	Australian Plate collided with Oriental Plate. Lesser Antilles began to form. Africa briefly connected with Eurasia. Beringia intermittent. Uplift of Andes and Sierra Nevada ranges.	Continued cooling; elimination of tropics in North America and Eurasia. Expansion of arid climates.	Plethodontidae Microhylidae
Pliocene, 10 m.y.	South America connected with Central America. Beringia submerged.	Continued polar cooling, latitudinal zonation, and aridity.	

[a]Time since beginning; m.y. = million years.　　[b]L = lower, M = middle, U = upper.

Chapter 17) on the patterns of changing continental configurations and climates during the past 200 million years. The continental configurations used here in reconstructing the biogeography of amphibians were taken from the paleogeographic maps prepared by Barron et al. (1981). The distribution of paleoclimates was synthesized from various sources, principally Axelrod (1960) and P. Robinson (1973). All dates are given in millions of years before the present (my).

Triassic

The earliest period of the Mesozoic extended from about 220 to 190 my.

Geologic Events. At the Permo-Triassic boundary, eastern Asia consisted of several separate blocks south and east of the major Asian land mass. Otherwise, most, if not all, continental masses were united into a single land mass—Pangaea.

Climatic Events. Latitudinal zonation of climates existed. A tropical (equatorial) humid zone was bordered by midlatitude arid belts. Humid temperate conditions existed at high latitudes. Toward the end of the Triassic, the northern humid zone expanded westward across central and western Laurasia.

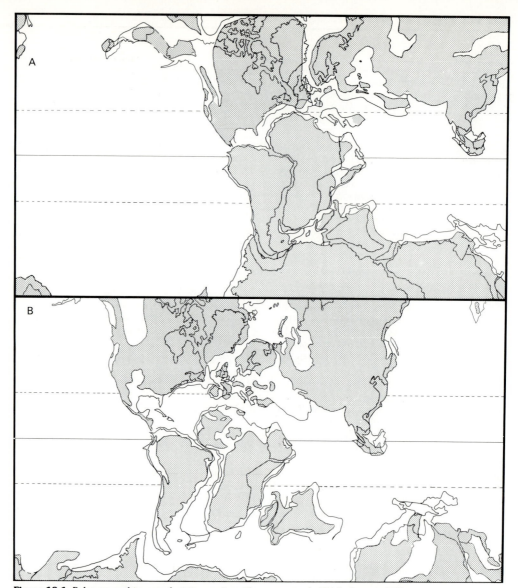

Figure 18-1. Paleogeographic maps depicting continental movements. **A.** Middle Jurassic (160 m.y.). **B.** Middle Cretaceous (100 m.y.). Edges of continental crusts are outlined. Shaded areas are emergent land. Adapted from Mercator projections of Barron et al. (1981).

Jurassic

The initial breakup of Pangaea was in this period, 190 to 135 my (Fig. 18-1A).

Geologic Events. At the beginning of the Jurassic the east Asian blocks united with Pangaea, the breakup of which was initiated at about 180 my by the opening of the North Atlantic Ocean and separation of North America from Africa. One plate (the Kolyma Block) rifted from northwestern North America about 180 my and drifted westward. By 160 my, the Tethys Sea separated eastern Laurasia to the north from eastern Gondwanaland to the south. Epeiric seas probably connected the Tethys Sea with the North Atlantic Ocean and possibly, by way of the Caribbean Basin, with the eastern Pacific Ocean. Extensive epeiric seas inundated North America and Eurasia from the Arctic Ocean and Asia from the Tethys Sea. By 140 my, that epeiric sea (now called the Turgai Sea) fragmented southern Europe and southwestern Asia into many large islands, and separated Europe from Asia. At about 140 my, the breakup of Gondwanaland also was initiated by fragmentation into three major land masses— South America-Africa, Antarctica-Australia, and Madagascar-Seychelles-India.

Climatic Events. Climatic zonation became less distinctive with an expansion of the humid zones, especially the tropics, with resulting contraction of mid-latitude arid zones.

Cretaceous

This is the longest period in the Mesozoic, 135 to 65 my.

Geologic Events. Epeiric seas fragmented many continents. Although parts of southern Europe and southwestern Asia were united temporarily with the rest of Europe about 120 my, and northern Europe with northwestern Asia about 100 my, the Turgai Sea persisted throughout the Cretaceous (Fig. 18-1B). The Midcontinental Sea separated eastern and western North America in the mid- to late Cretaceous (100 to 75 my), a time when epeiric seas fragmented northwestern Africa into at least two large islands and separated the western part of Australia from the Antarctic-Australian continent. The Kolyma Block collided with northeastern Asia about 120 my. The South Atlantic Ocean began to form between Africa and South America at about 125 my; during the ensuing 20 my, South America drifted westward, and the Atlantic Ocean became continuous. Volcanic activity in the Central American region may have provided an intermittent land connection between North and South America (Donnelly, 1985); this probably lasted into the Paleocene. At about 100 my, Madagascar terminated its northeastward drift, whereas the Seychelles-Indian continent continued drifting. The separation of the land mass now represented by New Zealand occurred at about 74 my.

Climatic Events. The climates throughout most of the Cretaceous were equable and tropical or subtropical. Temperate humid zones were discontinuous in the far north; arid zones were small and discontinuous.

Cenozoic

During the last 65 my the continents moved to their present positions and modern climatic patterns became established.

Geologic Events. The Turgai Sea persisted intermittently throughout the first half of the Cenozoic; continuous land connection between Europe and Asia has persisted since the end of the Eocene, about 35 my (Fig. 18-2). The Seychelles broke off from the Indian continent about 64 my, and India continued its northeastward arc to collide with Asia in the Oligocene (about 35 my). The collision resulted in the orogenic uplift of the Himalayas, which in time effectively separated the Indian subcontinent from the rest of Asia; an extensive embayment in Assam and Burma provided a barrier between India and southeastern Asia for much of the later Cenozoic. The land mass now represented by the Japanese Archipelago seems to have broken off from Asia at the Oligocene-Miocene boundary (23 my). The southern and eastern edge of the Oriental Plate became a series of islands in the Oligocene and Miocene. Australia separated from Antarctica about 55 my (late Paleocene). The northeastward arc of the Australian Plate resulted in its collision with the Oriental Plate in the Miocene with the consequent orogeny of the mountains of New Guinea. South America continued to drift westward and finally estab-

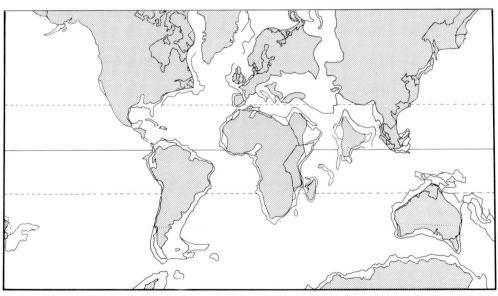

Figure 18-2. Paleogeographic map depicting the arrangement of the continents in the late Eocene (40 m.y.). Edges of continental crusts are outlined. Shaded areas are emergent land. Adapted from Mercator projections of Barron et al. (1981).

lished contact with the Central American appendage of North America in the Pliocene (3–6 my). Nuclear Central America was variously connected and separated from North America throughout most of the Cenozoic. The opposing movements of the Caribbean Plate (eastward) with respect to North America and South America (westward) resulted in the formation of the Greater Antilles, perhaps as early as the Cretaceous but certainly by the Paleocene (54–65 my), possibly with a continuous land connection with Central America. Beginning in the Miocene, the Lesser Antilles began to arise as oceanic islands along the arc of the Caribbean Plate to form the chain of islands between South America and the Greater Antilles. Africa had a restricted connection with Eurasia via Arabia from the late Miocene (about 8–10 my); with the rifting of the Red Sea this is now restricted to the Sinai region. Also in the late Miocene and/or early Pliocene there was a connection between Africa and the Iberian Peninsula. In the Northern Hemisphere there were two intermittent connections between Eurasia and North America. The Beringia land connection between North America and Asia was intermittent throughout most of the Cenozoic and finally submerged in the Pliocene (3–5 my). In the Paleocene-Eocene (50–60 my), two intermittent connections have been postulated to have existed between northern Europe and North America (McKenna, 1975)—(1) the DeGeer passage via Spitzbergen, northern Greenland, and Ellesmere Island, and (2) the Thule route via southern Greenland and Ellesmere Island.

Climatic Events. At the beginning of the Cenozoic most of the land masses of the world were under equable or subtropical climates; temperate climates existed only at high latitudes. Beginning in the Oligocene, polar cooling brought about a more distinctive latitudinal zonation of climates with a gradual elimination of tropical conditions and vegetation in North America and Eurasia, and with the restriction of tropical groups to the southern paleopeninsulas (Malay-Indonesian region of southeastern Asia and Central America) by the Miocene. Concomitant with the restriction of the tropics, there was an expansion of temperate climates into the lower latitudes of North America and Eurasia. During the northeastward drift of Australia in the Cenozoic, the continent changed latitudinal positions with the consequence that the climate changed from moist temperate to arid and semiarid over much of the continent in the latter part of the Cenozoic. Also at this time, most terrestrial life was eliminated from Antarctica. From the Miocene onward, there was an expansion of the arid and semiarid climates and vegetation over southwestern North America, southwestern Asia, western South America, and northern Africa. The development of arid conditions on western sides of continents was caused by cooling of high-latitude oceans and the patterns of cold currents from high to low latitudes along the west sides of continents. Also tectonic processes of the continental crusts of North and South America resulted in orogenies producing high mountains along the

western edges of the continents; the Andes and Sierra Nevada chains uplifted at various times during the Cenozoic, and by the time of the major uplifts in the Miocene and Pliocene they interrupted moisture-laden onshore winds and created rain shadows to the east. During the last 2 my, Pleistocene climatic fluctuations resulted in four or more major advances of polar and montane glaciers with concomitant latitudinal and altitudinal shifts in temperature belts and the restriction of humid tropical conditions during glacial phases and restrictions of the arid tropics during interglacials.

LISSAMPHIBIA

The fossil record of early lissamphibians is too poor to provide any meaningful information on the early distribution of the group. J. Savage (1973) emphasized that the early history of salamanders was associated with Laurasia, whereas caecilians and most anurans were restricted to Gondwanaland. If P. Robinson's (1973) interpretation of Permo-Triassic climatic zonation is correct, the distribution of lissamphibians at that time may have been divided by the midlatitude arid belt that isolated prosalamanders in the high-latitude humid zone and procaecilians and proanurans in the equatorial humid zone.

CAUDATA

The fossil history of the salamanders extends back to the Middle Jurassic, so the evolutionary geography of these amphibians is closely correlated with the breakup of Pangaea, especially Laurasia (essentially all fossil and living salamanders are associated with Laurasian land masses). Milner (1983) provided a geologically well-documented model for the biogeography of salamanders, but her phylogenetic arrangement is notably different from that proposed here (Chapter 17). Although Milner's emphasis on Laurasian cosmopolitanism of salamanders by the Middle Jurassic is correct, some of the details of the model do not fit the phylogenetic history.

The earliest known fossil salamander is the prosirenid *Albanerpeton* from the Middle Jurassic of Europe. If the hypothesized phylogeny of salamanders is correct, the four suborders were extant by the Middle Jurassic. However, the fossil record of early salamanders provides only limited support for this idea. The Karauroidea is known only from the Upper Jurassic of Asia, and the Sirenoidea and Salamandroidea (other than prosirenids) are unknown before the Late Cretaceous. Furthermore, the Cryptobranchoidea is unknown before the Paleocene. Nevertheless, the changing continental configurations and climates in the Mesozoic provide a basis for a biogeographic interpretation of the phylogenetic model.

If protosalamanders were distributed throughout the northern humid zone at the beginning of the Jurassic, the earliest fragmentation of Laurasia would have played an important role in their early evolution. Moreover, only

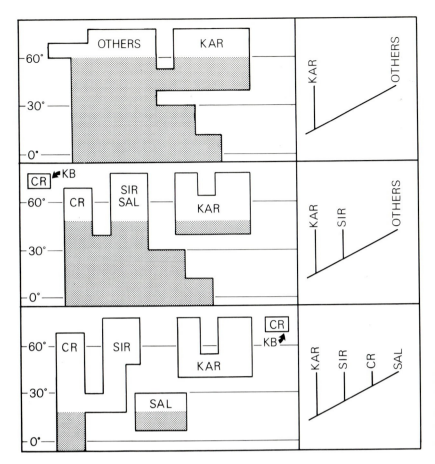

Figure 18-3. Diagrammatic representation of the sequential breakup of Laurasia in the Early and Middle Jurassic and corresponding vicariance events of the suborders of salamanders. Cross-hatched regions have unsuitable climates for salamanders. Abbreviations: CR = Cryptobranchoidea, KAR = Karauroidea, KB = Kolyma Block, SAL = Salamandroidea, SIR = Sirenoidea.

the northern fragmentation would have affected salamanders, because they were excluded from the middle and lower latitudes by the arid midlatitude climates. The combination of continental fragmentation (drift and epeiric seas) and expanding humid climates resulted in a series of vicariance events that could have given rise to the four suborders of salamanders by the Middle Jurassic. These geological and vicariance events are (Fig. 18-3):

1. Opening of the North Atlantic Ocean in the Early Jurassic (180 my) resulting in the separation of ancestral salamanders into two stocks along the northern margins of Asia and Euramerica. The stock in Asia gave rise to the Karauroidea and the one in Euramerica was the stock for all other salamanders.
2. Separation of the northern part of Euramerica by the Midcontinental Sea (160 my) resulting in the separation of sirenoids in aquatic habitats in eastern North America and cryptobranchoids and salamandroids in terrestrial habitats in western and eastern Euramerica, respectively. Cryptobranchoids also were present on the Kolyma Block, which subsequently rifted from western North America.

3. Fragmentation of Euramerica (150 my) resulting in the Sirenoidea surviving only in eastern North America and the Salamandroidea surviving only in Europe (then completely separated from Asia by the Turgai Sea).

Thus, by the Middle Jurassic, four stocks of salamanders were present on at least five land masses. From this point in time, the biogeography of each of the suborders can be treated separately.

The Karauroidea may have existed in parts of Asia east of the Turgai Sea until sometime in the Cenozoic, but the absence of fossils (other than the type) of this extinct suborder precludes any definitive biogeographic statements.

According to the vicariance events that isolated the suborders on separate continental blocks, the Sirenoidea was widespread east of the Midcontinental Sea in North America in the Upper Cretaceous and early Cenozoic. Presumably, limblessness and aquatic habits evolved early in the history of the suborder. Concomitant with the zonation of climates beginning in the Oligocene, the distribution of sirenids became restricted to southeastern North America.

Early in its history, the Cryptobranchoidea was restricted to North America. In the Early Jurassic, crypto-branchoids probably resembled hynobiids; such a stock remained relatively unchanged on the Kolyma Block as it drifted westward from North America and collided with eastern Asia in the Early Cretaceous (120 my), thereby introducing cryptobranchoids into Asia. This was the ancestral stock of the hynobiids. These salamanders probably did not reach their easternmost distribution until the Himalayan Orogeny and the disappearance of the Turgai Sea in the Oligocene. However, they probably were on the land mass that became the Japanese Archipelago before that block separated from Asia in the late Oligocene or early Miocene. The patterns of distribution of the living hynobiids suggest that lineages were isolated in the mesic montane areas by continental desiccation in the middle and late Cenozoic. The cryptobranchoid stock that remained in North America evolved through arrested development to become obligate neotenes, the crypto-branchids. Presumably, these aquatic salamanders were widespread throughout North America and Eurasia (via the DeGeer Passage) in the early Cenozoic. Latitudinal climatic zonation and continental desiccation in the Cenozoic resulted in the distributional relicts of *Cryptobranchus* in southeastern North America and *Andrias* in southeastern China and Japan.

The fragmentation of what now is Europe and southwestern Asia by the Tethys Sea probably resulted in salamandroids on several small land masses. Contraction of midlatitude arid zones in the Late Jurassic and Early Cretaceous would have allowed the expansion of the range of salamandroids into North America before the complete separation of Europe and North America in the early Cenozoic. The stocks of salamandroids that gave rise to the prosirenid-batrachosauroidid-proteid lineage, to the dicamptodontid-scapherpetontid lineage, and possibly to the amphiumids must have differentiated prior to the Late Cretaceous. All of these families are known from late Mesozoic or early Cenozoic deposits in both Europe and North America, except amphiumids and scapherpetontids, which are known only from North America. Therefore, the differentiation of these lineages of salamandroids seems to be associated with the complex fragmentation of Euramerica in the Middle Jurassic.

The prosirenids, batrachosauroidids, and scapherpetontids are extinct. Proteids survive as the subterranean *Proteus* in southern Europe and as five species of *Necturus* in eastern North America. The only living dicamptodontids are *Dicamptodon* and *Rhyacotriton* living in cold streams in northwestern North America. The only surviving amphiumid is *Amphiuma* in southeastern North America. All of these living salamanders are relicts of formerly more diverse and widespread groups of salamanders. The vicariance of the salamandrid and the ambystomatid-plethodontid lineage also may have occurred toward the end of the Mesozoic, when the last major land connections between Europe and North America were broken. According to Özeti and D. Wake (1969), there are three groups of salamandrids. *Pleurodeles* in Europe and *Tylototriton* and *Echinotriton* in eastern Asia share primitive characters and may represent relicts of a formerly widely distributed group of primitive salamandrids. *Salamandra* and its relatives are restricted to western Eurasia and presumably never existed east of the Turgai Sea; *Salamandra* is known in the fossil record of Europe since the late Eocene. The so-called *Triturus* group is holarctic in distribution. This group underwent its early differentiation in western Eurasia in the Cenozoic (fossil *Triturus* known as early as the Eocene in Europe) and apparently did not disperse into eastern Eurasia until the subsidence of the Turgai Sea at the beginning of the Oligocene. This timing is in accordance with this group reaching eastern Asia prior to the separation of the land mass that was destined to be the Japanese Archipelago and also for the dispersal of salamandrids into North America via Beringia (the first salamandrid fossils in North America are from the late Oligocene).

If the cladistic arrangement of the ambystomatids and plethodontids is correct, there is no major geologic event that could have separated these groups in North America after the Cretaceous, at which time the ancestral stock might have been split by the Midcontinental Sea. Ambystomatids do not appear in the fossil record until the Oligocene, and plethodontids are unknown as fossils prior to the Miocene. However, ages of separation of genera of plethodontids suggested by immunological distances are much older; some are placed in the Paleocene (Maxson et al., 1979). These data suggest that the separation of ambystomatids and plethodontids in the Cretaceous is reasonable. Ambystomatids seem to have adapted to subhumid climates better than any other North American salamanders. Their major centers of differentiation are in southeastern North America and along the southern edge of the Mexican Plateau.

The evolution of the plethodontids seems to have been associated with the Appalachian uplands of eastern North America. Generic differentiation between *Plethodon* and *Ensatina* took place in the Paleocene, and differentiation between the eastern and western groups of *Plethodon* occurred in the Eocene (dating based on immunological distances given by Maxson et al., 1979). Presumably *Plethodon* became separated into eastern and western groups as the result of climatic desiccation in midcontinental North America beginning in the Oligocene. The dispersal of the plethodontid genus *Hydromantes* from North America to Eurasia presumably took place via Beringia in the Oligocene; dating is based on immunological data (D. Wake et al., 1979). On the basis of that dating, it can be assumed that plethodontines of the tribe Bolitoglossini evolved prior to the Oligocene.

The supergenus *Bolitoglossa* contains 11 genera and 140 species in the tropical lowlands and the mountains of Mexico and Central America; two genera (*Bolitoglossa* and *Oedipina*) have representatives in South America (see section: Inter-American Interchange under Anura).

According to dates suggested by genic differentiation, *Bolitoglossa* entered South America in the late Miocene, prior to the establishment of the present continuous land connection in the Pliocene (Hanken and D. Wake, 1982). The greatest differentiation of genera of bolitoglossines is in the mountains of southern Mexico, and the greatest differentiation of species is in the highlands of southeastern Mexico (Oaxaca and Veracruz) and nuclear Central America (Guatemala and Chiapas, Mexico) and the highlands of Costa Rica and adjacent Panama (D. Wake and J. F. Lynch, 1976; D. Wake and P. Elias, 1983).

It might be expected that the differentiation of bolitoglossines in Mexico and Central America occurred in association with the orogenic events that took place principally in the Miocene and Pliocene. Immunological distances provide possible dates for differentiation of species of *Pseudoeurycea* from the Eocene to the Pliocene (8–50 my); differentiation of the genera *Chiropterotriton, Dendrotriton,* and *Pseudoeurycea* occurred in the Paleocene and Eocene according to immunological data (Maxson and D. Wake, 1981).

GYMNOPHIONA

With the exception of a few caeciliids in Central America and Mexico and a few ichthyophiids in southeastern Asia, all living caecilians occur on Gondwanan land masses. Moreover, the single fossil caecilian is from the Paleocene of Brazil. Therefore, the evolutionary history of caecilians must be associated with the history of the southern continents.

If the phylogeny proposed here (Fig. 17-2) is correct, the major vicariance events of the families of caecilians must have occurred prior to the breakup of Gondwanaland. The most primitive caecilians, the rhinatrematids, presently are restricted to the northern Andes and Guiana Shield in South America. Presumably rhinatrematids are relicts of a group that was widespread in Gondwanaland prior to the breakup of the continents in the Late Jurassic. Also, the ichthyophiids that survived on the Indian Plate as it drifted from Africa to Asia are relicts of a formerly more widely distributed group. Possibly the uraeotyphlids and scolecomorphids evolved in situ in peninsular India and tropical Africa, respectively. The caeciliids have a classic Gondwanan pattern—South America, Africa, and India, including the Seychelles Islands. The aquatic typhlonectids presumably evolved in situ in South America from a caeciliid-like ancestor.

The distributional data, in combination with the phylogenetic arrangement of caecilians, dictate an early divergence of most of the families—prior to the Late Jurassic, except for typhlonectids. The drift of the Indian Plate must have carried ichthyophiids, uraeotyphlids, and caeciliids to Asia; of these, only the ichthyophiids have extended beyond the Indian subcontinent. The presence of caeciliids on the India-Madagascar-Seychelles Plate is obvious because of their presence today in peninsular India and on the Seychelles. But why are there no caecilians on Madagascar?

The spread of ichthyophiids into southeastern Asia and adjacent islands must have occurred after the collision of the Indian Plate with Asia in Oligocene. Some caeciliids (*Dermophis* and *Gymnopis*) dispersed from South America into Central America during a brief connection in the Paleocene. Others (e.g., *Caecilia* and *Oscaecilia*) dispersed northward only after the closure of the Panamanian Portal in the Pliocene.

This hypothesized history of caecilians is supported (in part) by immunological data (Case and M. Wake, 1977). An estimated divergence time of *Dermophis* from *Caecilia* of 57 my coincides with the Paleocene separation of South and Central America. Estimated times of divergence of African (*Boulengerula* and *Geotrypetes*) and neotropical (*Dermophis*) caeciliids of 99 and 120 my are consistent with the separation of Africa and South America. An immunological distance of 210 units between *Ichthyophis* and *Dermophis* suggests an ancient separation of these taxa, but the limits of accurate measurement of immunological distance is at about 200 units. Thus it is possible to suggest only that divergence occured more than 120 my.

ANURA

J. Savage (1973) provided a lengthy discussion of the distribution of anurans, in which he showed that the histories of the family groups were intimately associated with the histories of the land masses that they occupied in the Mesozoic and Cenozoic. In some cases, Savage took unwarranted liberties with the classification of anurans. For example, he eliminated the distributional enigma of a dyscophine microhylid in the Oriental Region by assigning the genus *Calluela* to the Asterophryinae; otherwise, the Dyscophinae is restricted to Madagascar. Also, he split the melanobatrachine microhylids and placed *Melanobatrachus* in the Microhylinae and recognized the African genera in the Hoplophryninae. Moreover, he considered the Australo-Papuan hylids to be a separate family, the Pelodryadidae, having a history independent from the neotropical Hylidae. Savage's rearrangements make perfectly good sense biogeographically, and he may be correct evolutionarily; existing phylogenetic evidence neither supports nor refutes his changes. Savage's phylogeny of the suborders of anurans was based on P. Starrett's (1973) suggestion that the pipoid and microhyloid frogs were primitive sister groups. This idea was based on her interpretation of the evolution of larval characters. Starrett's phylogeny has been disputed by evidence from larvae provided by Sokol (1975) and Wassersug (1984).

As emphasized by J. Savage (1973), the historical biogeography of anurans is associated mainly with Gondwanaland. However, limited fossil evidence and present distributions of some families of anurans indicate that differentiation of some anuran stocks was associated with the initial breakup of Pangaea in the Early Jurassic (160–180 my). The Triassic *Triadobatrachus* from Madagascar generally is considered to be an early frog. The earliest known fossil that unquestionably is a frog is *Vieraella* from the Lower Jurassic of Argentina. By the Late Jurassic there are diverse anuran fossils from Europe, North America, and South America, so it may be assumed that frogs became widespread in the world during the Jurassic.

Leiopelmatids generally are considered to be the most primitive living anurans. The Jurassic *Vieraella* and *Notobatrachus* in Argentina and the living *Ascaphus* in North America and *Leiopelma* in New Zealand provide evidence that the primitive frogs grouped in the Leiopelmatidae were widely distributed prior to the breakup of Pangaea and that the living genera are relicts of this ancient group of anurans. The histories of the other families of anurans (with the possible exception of the pipids) are associated with either Laurasia or Gondwanaland.

Laurasia.　　Laurasian groups include the Discoglossidae, Palaeobatrachidae, Rhinophrynidae, Pelobatidae, and Pelodytidae.

Discoglossids presumably were associated with the humid temperate climates of Laurasia; the earliest fossils of the family are from the Late Jurassic of Europe and the Late Cretaceous of North America. Therefore, it seems likely that discoglossids evolved prior to the breakup of Laurasia in the Jurassic. Discoglossids seem to have diversified in Eurasia west of the Turgai Sea, where four genera survive. Subsequent to the subsidence of the Turgai Sea in the Oligocene, the European *Bombina* dispersed eastward. Ages of differentiation of species of *Bombina* determined from immunological distances by Maxson and Szymura (1979) show that the eastern Asian species *B. orientalis* differentiated in the Miocene, whereas *B. bombina* and *B. variegata* are late Pliocene or Pleistocene vicariants. Climatic deterioration in midcontinental Eurasia in the late Cenozoic and/or Pleistocene climatic fluctuations resulted in great discontinuities in the distribution of *Bombina*. However, *Barbourula* presumably was in Asia, where it became adapted to tropical conditions. As climatic cooling restricted tropical organisms to the Indo-Malay region, *Barbourula* survived in Borneo and dispersed to the Philippines.

Assuming that their unique larvae evolved only once, the pipoids (Rhinophrynidae, Palaeobatrachidae, and Pipidae) can be considered a natural group. Early fossil remains exist from Laurasia and Gondwanaland, and pipoids now occur in tropical North America, South America, and Africa. The palaeobatrachids are known from the uppermost Jurassic through the Pliocene of Europe, and from the late Cretaceous of North America. Rhinophrynids are known from the late Paleocene through the Oligocene of North America; the single living species is restricted to Mexico and Central America. Pipids are known from the Lower Cretaceous of Israel, Upper Cretaceous

of South America, and various Cenozoic ages in Africa and South America; living pipids occur in tropical South America and sub-Saharan Africa.

Protopipoids apparently were widely distributed in the humid tropical zone in Pangaea. The vicariance of rhinophrynids from other pipoids may have resulted from their isolation in North America after the initial opening of the North Atlantic Ocean in the early Jurassic (180 my). Subsequently, the vicariance of palaeobatrachids and pipids could have been associated with the separation of western Laurasia from western Gondwanaland by the Tethys Sea in the mid-Jurassic (160 my). Palaeobatrachids still had access to North America until the Eocene. In Europe at least, this family seems to have been the Laurasian counterpart to the Gondwanan pipids. The palaeobatrachids were widespread and diverse in Europe; their disappearance at the end of the Pliocene possibly was caused by the cold climates and glaciation in the Pleistocene. The history of the Pipidae is associated with the separation of Africa and South America and is discussed in the following section on Gondwanaland.

The pelobatoids include the pelobatids (Eopelobatinae, Pelobatinae, and Megophryinae) and the pelodytids in Laurasia. Estes (1970) considered the eopelobatines, which are known from the Late Cretaceous of North America and Asia, to be the most primitive group. Pelobatines are well represented in the fossil record beginning in the Eocene of Europe and in the Oligocene of North America; however, immunological dating of the living European *Pelobates* and North American *Scaphiopus* indicates divergence in the Cretaceous (Sage et al., 1982). Pelodytids first appear in the mid-Eocene of Europe, where the living *Pelodytes* survives; they also are known from the Miocene of North America, where the family is extinct. Living and fossil pelobatines have greatly enlarged metatarsal tubercles, and living species are fossorial. *Eopelobates* has only slightly enlarged metatarsal tubercles and may be a grade in the evolution of the fossorial pelobatines. Possibly these anurans evolved in the Laurasian arid zone and dispersed throughout xeric habitats in Laurasia prior to the separation of North America and Eurasia in the Early Jurassic and prior to the contraction of the arid zones in the Mid- and Late Cretaceous. The megophryines inhabit humid tropical and subtropical regions in southeastern Asia and adjacent archipelagos, and some taxa in the Himalayas; there are no fossils. Presumably they evolved from an eopelobatine-like ancestor (Estes, 1970). If pelodytids are a historical reality, they must have diverged from propelobatids prior to the mid-Jurassic; however, there is no fossil evidence for such an early vicariance.

Gondwanaland.　　The vicariance of the other family groups of anurans is associated primarily with the breakup of Gondwanaland. It is safe to assume that an ancestral stock of arciferal anurans was in Gondwanaland prior to the separation of that southern land mass from Laurasia

Table 18-2. Families of Anurans and Their Association with Gondwanan Continents in the Late Jurassic

Africa– South America	Madagascar- Seychelles-India	Australia- Antarctica
Leiopelmatidae	Myobatrachidae?	Leiopelmatidae
Pipidae	Bufonidae?	Myobatrachidae
Leptodactylidae	Microhylidae	Hylidae
Hylidae	Ranidae	
Bufonidae	Hyperoliidae	
Microhylidae	Rhacophoridae	
Ranidae		
Hyperoliidae		
Rhacophoridae		

in the mid-Jurassic. At that time, this group of anurans shared Gondwanaland with leiopelmatids and pipids. Prior to the initial breakup of Gondwanaland in the late Jurassic (140 my), this ancestral stock differentiated into three major groups that can be referred to as the bufonoids, ranoids, and microhyloids. The association of different lineages of these three major groups with different Gondwanan continents necessitates further differentiation within each group prior to the fragmentation of the continents (Table 18-2). The initial breakup of Gondwanaland resulted in three continental masses; the histories of the anuran faunas associated with each are discussed separately.

Antarctica-Australia.—The anuran fauna of the Antarctica-Australian continent definitely was composed of leiopelmatids and myobatrachids, and probably hylids. J. Savage (1973) suggested that microhylids reached the Oriental Region by being on Antarctica-Australia. As emphasized by Tyler (1979), there is no evidence for the presence of microhylids in Australia until the late Cenozoic, when a few species reached northern Australia from New Guinea. If the Australo-Papuan hylids represent a lineage independent from the neotropical hylids, the Hylidae (sensu stricto) was not present on Antarctica-Australia.

This continent had temperate and tropical climates; leiopelmatids apparently became restricted to the former and myobatrachids to the latter. In the Late Cretaceous, the land mass destined to become New Zealand fragmented from the temperate part of the continent. Leiopelmatid frogs survived as the only anurans on New Zealand and became extinct on Antarctica-Australia. Biochemical evidence suggests that the three species of *Leiopelma* diverged in the Miocene and Pliocene (Daugherty et al., 1981). Antarctica and Australia split apart in the Paleocene (55 my). Antarctica remained in its polar position and beginning in the Oligocene was subjected to extreme cold; the extensive polar icecap now conceals the fossils of the former biota. Australia drifted northeastward and late in the Cenozoic became increasingly arid.

According to dates derived from immunological data (Daugherty and Maxson, 1982), the differentiation of many

myobatrachine genera occurred in the mid-Cretaceous (*Assa*) or Late Cretaceous (*Arenophryne, Geocrinia, Myobatrachus, Paracrinia, Rheobatrachus,* and *Taudactylus* from *Crinia*); *Uperoleia* presumably diverged from *Crinia* in the late Eocene. On the other hand, hylid differentiation is a Cenozoic phenomenon (Maxson et al., 1982). In this view divergence of the *Cyclorana-Litoria aurea* lineage from other *Litoria* occurred in the late Eocene, and *Cyclorana* and the *Litoria aurea* group vicariated in the late Oligocene. Therefore, it is possible that most, if not all, of the autochthonous genera of Australian frogs, as well as some species groups, were in existence before Australia made contact with the Oriental Region.

The Australian Plate contacted the Oriental Plate in the Miocene and caused the complex uplift of New Guinea. This contact provided the first opportunity for interchange of biotas that had been separated for 120 million years since the initial fragmentation of Gondwanaland. At this time, hylids and myobatrachids from Australia became associated with Oriental microhylids in New Guinea, and one stock of Papuan hylids evolved into *Nyctimystes*. Although there have been brief periods of continuous land connection between New Guinea and Australia via the Torres Strait as recently as the Pleistocene, few Papuan taxa have dispersed southward into Australia. These include a few species of *Nyctimystes*, several species of two genera of microhylids (*Cophixalus* and *Sphenophryne*), and one species of *Rana*.

Madagascar-Seychelles-Australia.—The anuran fauna of the Madagascar-Seychelles-Indian continent that rifted from the rest of Gondwanaland about 140 million years ago contained only tropical groups. Present on this continent were ranids, hyperoliids, rhacophorids, and microhylids. Myobatrachids also are presumed to have been present, and probably bufonids were present. The ranids consisted of ranines and the stock that gave rise to the mantellines. The microhylids minimally consisted of melanobatrachines, microhylines, and a stock, perhaps much like living scaphiophrynines, that was to give rise to five subfamilies. If the Eocene *Indobatrachus* is indeed a myobatrachid, that family must have been represented on the continent. Also, the presence of myobatrachids is supported by evidence that myobatrachids and sooglossids are related. J. Savage (1973) suggested that the radiation of bufonids in southeastern Asia was a late Cenozoic event following the dispersal of *Bufo* into that region from North America via Beringia. The diversity of bufonid genera (e.g., *Ansonia* and *Pedostibes*) in southeastern Asia and adjacent islands strongly suggests an earlier arrival of a bufonid stock. This arrival could have been via the drifting continent. Unfortunately, there is no fossil evidence whatsoever. Savage also suggested that rhacoporids dispersed from Africa to Madagascar by waifing and to southeastern Asia by terrestrial dispersal via southwestern Asia, and that hyperoliids dispersed from Africa to Madagascar and the Seychelles. If these groups of

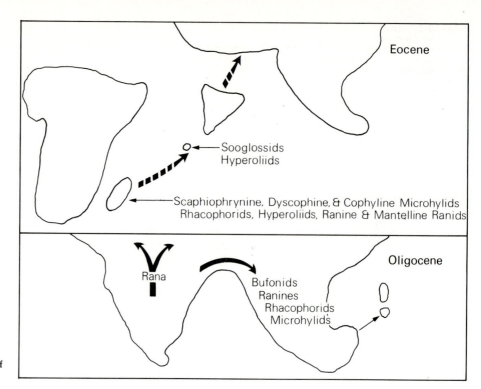

Eocene

Sooglossids
Hyperoliids

Scaphiophrynine, Dyscophine, & Cophyline Microhylids
Rhacophorids, Hyperoliids, Ranine & Mantelline Ranids

Oligocene

Rana

Bufonids
Ranines
Rhacophorids
Microhylids

Figure 18-4. Sequential tectonic movements of India and associated land masses during the early and middle Cenozoic, showing (top) the consequent isolation of anuran taxa on Madagascar and the Seychelles Islands and (bottom) the dispersal of taxa from India to Asia.

anurans were present on the drifting continent, these independent long-distance dispersals are not necessary.

During its drift from western Gondwanaland, the Madagascar-Seychelles-Indian continent fragmented. Madagascar split away from the rest of the continent in the mid-Cretaceous (100 my) and moved northward to its present position off the coast of Africa. As the Indian continent continued in its arc toward Asia, the small land mass that later became known as the Seychelles Islands broke off in the early Paleocene (64 my). India finally collided with Asia in the Oligocene (35 my). This drifting land mass provided transportation for several groups of Gondwanan anurans to the Oriental Region and resulted in the isolation of various groups of anurans on fragments left along its path.

The major part of the anuran fauna of Madagascar consists of scaphiophrynine, dyscophyne, and cophyline microhylids, mantelline ranids, rhacophorids, and hyperoliids. Ranines are represented by one species of *Tomopterna,* a genus that also has species in Africa and India. With the exception of *Tomopterna* and the dyscophine genus *Calluela,* which occurs in southeastern Asia and adjacent islands, all of the subfamilies of ranids and microhylids on Madagascar are endemic, as are the rhacophorid genera *Aglyptodactylus* and *Boophis,* and the hyperoliid genus *Heterixalus.* The subfamilies endemic to Madagascar presumably evolved in situ after the separation of the island from the rest of the drifting continent, which carried with it *Tomopterna* and an ancestor to *Calluela* (Fig. 18-4).

The Seychelles Islands have a small but significant anuran fauna. Except for *Ptychadena mascariensis,* a waif from Africa via Madagascar, the anuran fauna consists of three species of the endemic family Sooglossidae and the monotypic hyperoliid genus *Tachycnemis.* If sooglossids indeed are related to myobatrachids, as suggested by J. D. Lynch (1973) and Nussbaum (1979b), sooglossids can be viewed as isolated relicts, perhaps derivatives of an ancient lineage that is represented only by *Indobatrachus* from the Eocene of India. Most likely the anuran fauna of the Seychelles was much more diverse in the early Cenozoic than it is now. There is no reason to assume that microhylines, ranines, and rhacophorids did not exist there; those groups presumably met the fate of many island populations—extinction.

When India collided with Asia in the Oligocene, the subcontinent contained *Tomopterna* (also present today in Madagascar and Africa), *Melanobatrachus* (other melanobatrachine microhylids in Africa), ranines, rhacophorids, bufonids, microhylines, and an ancestor to the dyscophine *Calluela.* Once the land connection was effected, these groups (with the exception of *Tomopterna* and *Melanobatrachus*) dispersed eastward and thence southward into the area that fragmented in the late Oligocene and Miocene into the Greater Sunda Islands (Fig. 18-4). Most of this dispersal occurred prior to the marine transgression into the Assam-Burma region in the late Cenozoic. Bufonids, rhacophorids, and microhylids apparently waifed to the Philippines, which arose in the Oligocene.

The ancestral *Calluela* (Microhylidae) dispersed through this now insular region and differentiated into a stock that gave rise to the Genyophryninae, represented today by the widespread lowland genera *Cophixalus, Oreophryne,* and *Sphenophryne.* With the uplift of New Guinea resulting from the collision of the Australian Plate with the southern edge of the Oriental Plate in the Miocene, this microhylid stock differentiated into the diversity of genyophrynine and asterophryine microhylids known there today.

The early ranines in the Oriental Region proabably were the stocks that gave rise to two groups of ranids. One of these differentiated into several Oriental genera (e.g., *Amolops* and *Occidozyga*) that are distributed on the mainland (some in peninsular India) and in some cases also in the Greater Sunda Islands and the Philippines. The other group is the so-called platymantine ranids (*Batrachylodes, Ceratobatrachus, Discodeles, Palmatorappia,* and *Platymantis*). This group is widely distributed from the Philippines to Fiji but does not occur on the mainland; the greatest diversity is in the Solomon Islands. The genus *Rana* seems to have arrived in the Indo-Malayan region more recently.

Africa-South America.—The separation of South America from Africa was initiated in the mid-Cretaceous (100 my), but land connections between the continents may have persisted until 90 million years ago. Prior to the separation of the continents, the anuran fauna consisted of pipids, bufonids, leptodactylids, and microhylids (Fig. 18-5). Additionally, but apparently restricted to the African part of the continent, there were ranids, hyperoliids, and rhacophorids. Assuming that the dendrobatids and petropedetine ranids are sister groups, the immediate ancestor of these groups must have been present before the separation of the continents. Also, if the Australo-Papuan hylids are confamilial with the neotropical hylids, the Hylidae would have had to be present at least in the South American part of the continent.

Once South America and Africa were separated, the anuran faunas diversified independently on the two continents. In Africa, the leiopelmatids (and hylids, if they were there) became extinct, and the leptodactylid stock survived only as *Heleophryne* in cool streams in South Africa. Prior to the separation of the Madagascar-Seychelles-Indian continent, microhylids in Africa already had differentiated into melanobatrachines and microhylines. The former now is restricted to a few taxa in the mountains of East Africa. The latter differentiated into two lineages—phrynomerines and brevicipitines, both of which presently are widely distributed in sub-Saharan Africa.

In Africa, the pipids differentiated into numerous species; today, *Hymenochirus* and *Pseudhymenochirus* are restricted to tropical West Africa, whereas the more speciose genus *Xenopus* is widespread in sub-Saharan Africa. Among the tree frogs, the hyperoliids have differentiated into an array of 12 genera and nearly 200 species throughout sub-Saharan Africa, whereas the rhacophorids survive only as *Chiromantis* with three species in tropical Africa. Bufonids have diversified into a number of genera, and the genus *Bufo* is represented by many species. The presence of *Bufo* in the Paleocene of Brazil indicates that the genus was in existence before the separation of Africa and South America. Times of divergences based on immunological data corroborate the Cretaceous occurrence of *Bufo* (Maxson, 1981a); furthermore, her data indicated that *Schismaderma* differentiated in the Eocene and at least some species of African *Bufo* are Miocene in origin.

Africa is the site of the major radiation of ranids. A ranid stock represented by the Astylosterninae is restricted to humid habitats in tropical West Africa, and the Petropedetinae is widespread in sub-Saharan Africa. Terrestrial-breeding arthroleptines and fossorial hemisines represent two adaptive types in sub-Saharan Africa. The African ranines are highly diversified in nine genera, of which only *Rana, Ptychadena,* and *Tomopterna* occur outside of Africa.

Climatic deterioration in the latter part of the Cenozoic made much of Africa uninhabitable for many kinds of anurans. Humid forest refugia persisted in some lowland areas in West Africa and on ancient mountain masses; many anurans survived the vicissitudes of the Pleistocene

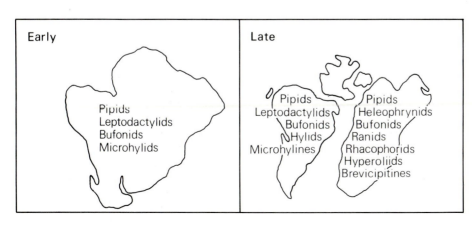

Figure 18-5. Separation of South America and Africa in the Cretaceous. Taxa of anurans listed are those presumed to have inhabited the major part of each continent.

in such refugia. These include bufonids such as *Necto-phrynoides,* hyperoliids such as *Chrysobatrachus,* and microhylids such as *Hoplophryne.*

In South America, the leiopelmatids became extinct. Several genera of pipids were extant in South America in the Cretaceous and Paleocene, including *Xenopus* (Estes, 1975). *Xenopus* survives only in Africa, and the only living pipids in South America are members of the genus *Pipa.* The major radiations among South American anurans took place in the leptodactylids and hylids.

Primitive leptodactylids, the telmatobiines, diversified in the southern, humid temperate region, where many primitive telmatobiine genera (e.g., *Caudiverbera* and *Eupsophus*) survive, as does an apparent early derivative, the Rhinodermatidae. Other lineages of leptodactylids differentiated and dispersed throughout South America. These are recognized now as ceratophryines and leptodactylines; the latter are especially diverse in the tropical lowlands east of the Andes. The hylodines are associated with the Brazilian Shield. The largest group of leptodactylids is the Telmatobiinae, which occurs throughout the tropical and subtropical parts of the continent, as well as in the humid temperate region. This subfamily contains diverse genera, such as the stream-dwelling *Telmatobius* in the Andes and the extremely speciose genus *Eleutherodactylus* that occurs throughout the humid tropical part of the continent.

The Hylidae is of unknown origin. Whether the Australo-Papuan hylids are closely related or the neotropical hylids evolved independently from a leptodactylid-like ancestor in South America, the family underwent a tremendous radiation in South America. Fossil hylids are known from the Paleocene of Brazil, but probably before the Late Cretaceous three lineages had differentiated— the arboreal forest-dwelling phyllomedusines, the egg-brooding hemiphractines, and the more generalized hylines. Presumably even earlier, two other groups with intercalary elements evolved from a prohylid ancestor; of these, the pseudids evolved into a specialized lowland aquatic group, and the centrolenids into a principally montane, arboreal group. Maxson's (1976) historical interpretation of immunological data supports an Early Cretaceous divergence of the neotropical subfamilies of hylids; her limited data also indicated smaller immunological distances between neotropical hylines and Australo-Papuan hylids than between neotropical phyllomedusines and hemiphractines.

Within South America, the Bufonidae evolved into various lineages of *Bufo* and some specialized, principally montane groups, recognized as separate genera (e.g., *Atelopus* and *Oreophrynella*). One presumed derivative of a bufonid stock, the Brachycephalidae, survives as two monotypic genera in the forests of eastern Brazil. Microhylines diversified into numerous genera and species; they are distributed throughout tropical South America.

The dendrobatids are widespread in South America but are especially speciose in the northwestern part of the continent, where all four genera occur.

During the Cenozoic, the humid temperate regions and humid tropical regions contracted because of climatic zonation. The elevation of the Andes interrupted wind currents and modified patterns of rainfall. The ancient highland areas—the Brazilian and Guianan shields— harbor presumed relicts of primitive groups (e.g., *Brachycephalus* and elosiines in Brazil, and *Oreophrynella* and *Otophryne* in the Guianas). Late Tertiary and Quaternary climatic changes are thought to have resulted in the contraction of lowland rainforests during arid phases correlated with glacial stages in the Pleistocene and contraction of non-forest habitats during humid phases correlated with interglacial stages. These changing conditions, together with correlated altitudinal fluctuations in climate, are responsible for many of the distributional patterns existing in South America. Also, patterns of speciation in some groups of anurans can be associated with Pleistocene refugia (Duellman, 1982a, 1982b), but the speciation of other groups is much older (Heyer and Maxson, 1982).

Determination of the time of differentiation by immunological distances suggests that many leptodactylid genera (e.g., *Caudiverbera, Ceratophrys, Cycloramphus, Leptodactylus, Odontophrynus, Proceratophrys, Telmatobius,* and *Thoropa*) date back at least to the Eocene (Maxson and Heyer, 1982). Furthermore, speciation in many leptodactylids, especially those associated with the Brazilian Shield, took place in the Paleocene to Miocene (Heyer and Maxson, 1982); also, many of the species in the widespread lowland genus *Leptodactylus* date from the Eocene. The differentiation among some genera of hylids seems to have occurred as long ago as the Late Cretaceous or early Cenozoic. For example, *Cryptobatrachus* in the northern Andes and *Stefania* in the Guiana Shield were estimated to have diverged in the Late Cretaceous (Duellman and Hoogmoed, 1984), and some lowland species of *Gastrotheca* differentiated in the Paleocene or Eocene (Scanlan et al., 1980), as did some groups of *Bufo* (Maxson, 1984). On the other hand, speciation in some old genera is relatively recent. For example, Andean species of *Telmatobius* differentiated in the Miocene to the Pleistocene (Maxson and Heyer, 1982). Similar recent dates of speciation were determined for Andean species of *Gastrotheca* (Scanlan et al., 1980). Although representing relatively few taxa, the immunological data strongly suggest that many of the genera and some of the species of South American anurans evolved early in the Cenozoic.

Inter-American Interchange.—The complex history of the Central American isthmus and the West Indies has received considerable attention from biogeographers. J. Savage (1982) provided a detailed analysis of the Central American herpetofauna. He proposed that a brief Late Cretaceous and/or early Paleocene connection between the Central American appendage of North America and South America allowed for the dispersal of taxa from one continent to another. There is no evidence for any North American amphibians having dispersed to South America in the Paleocene, but several groups dispersed northward (Fig. 18-6). These include caecilians, phyllomedusine hylids (ancestral stock of *Agalychnis* and *Pachymedusa*), microhylines (ancestral stock of *Gastrophryne* and *Hypopachus*), two stocks of *Bufo*, at least one stock of hylids (including *Hyla*), and at least one stock of leptodactylids (including *Eleutherodactylus*).

These Paleocene entrants into Central America were the stocks that evolved into several Mesoamerican groups of *Hyla*, *Bufo*, and *Eleutherodactylus*, plus many endemic genera (e.g., *Crepidophryne*, *Plectrohyla*, *Triprion*, and the eleutherodactyline derivatives—*Hylactophryne*, *Syrrhophus*, and *Tomodactylus*). Moreover, some of these stocks presumably were associated with the formation of the Greater Antilles, where hylids are respresented by three lineages of *Hyla*, plus *Osteopilus* and *Calyptahyla*.

Some West Indian *Eleutherodactylus* (including the Cuban *Sminthillus*) seem to have been derived from Central American groups, whereas others apparently represent the evolutionary results of the dispersal of *Eleutherodactylus* from South America via the Lesser Antilles to the Greater Antilles. The Bufonidae is represented in the Greater Antilles by the endemic *Peltophryne* (8 species), which may have been derived from a Central American bufonid stock.

The Paleocene separation of North American and South American stocks of some hylids is supported by immunological data, which used as an evolutionary clock, indicate times of divergence of *Agalychnis* from *Phyllomedusa* to have been no later than the Late Cretaceous (Maxson, 1976) and groups of North and South American *Hyla* to have been in the Paleocene (Maxson and A. Wilson, 1975). Moreover, distances between the West Indian hylid *Osteopilus septentrionalis* and various North American hylids indicate a divergence in the Paleocene (Maxson and A. Wilson, 1975).

With the closure of the Panamanian Portal in the Pliocene, a great interchange of South American and Central American taxa took place. Principal groups of anurans that dispersed northward include some *Eleutherodactylus*, *Leptodactylus*, *Physalaemus*, *Atelopus*, some *Bufo*, dendrobatids, centrolenids, some *Hyla*, *Phrynohyas*, and *Phyllomedusa*. Some South American taxa have dispersed no farther than Panama; this may be the result of either temporal or ecological limitations. Included in this group are *Pipa*, *Pleurodema*, *Rhamphophryne*, *Gastrotheca*, *Hemiphractus*, *Chiasmocleis*, and *Relictivomer*. At the same time, some Central American groups dispersed into South America. Some genera (e.g., the hylids *Agalychnis* and *Smilisca*) dispersed only into the northwestern part of the continent. *Rana* seems to be a recent invader from North America; it is represented in South America by a species that also occurs in Central America.

Laurasian Dispersal of Gondwanan Groups. With the exception of South American taxa that occur in Cen-

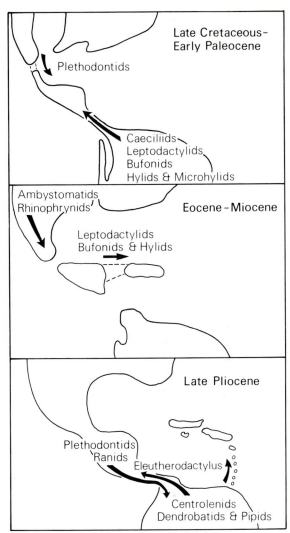

Figure 18-6. Dispersal of families of amphibians between North America, Central America, South America, and the West Indies from the Late Cretaceous through the Pliocene.

tral America, southern Mexico, and the West Indies, and the Gondwanan groups that occur in the Oriental tropics, there are only three genera of anurans that are Gondwanan in origin and widely distributed in the northern continents. Three other genera of hylids are endemic to North America.

Bufo presumably was extant before South America separated from Africa, and there is evidence that there was dispersal of South American *Bufo* back to Africa toward the end of the connection (Maxson, 1984). Subsequently, at least two stocks of *Bufo* entered North America from South America in the Paleocene. These dispersed into Eurasia via Beringia. The first of these was a tropical group that probably entered Eurasia in the Eocene and had a secondary radiation in southern Asia. The second was a temperate-adapted group that crossed Beringia in the Oligocene and became holarctic in distribution.

Tree frogs of the genus *Hyla* also dispersed from South America to North America in the Paleocene; they appear in the North American fossil record in the Oligocene. In North America, the hylid stock differentiated into a number of species, some of which are recognized as different genera—*Acris, Limnaoedus,* and *Pseudacris.* A temperate-adapted *Hyla* crossed Beringia probably in the Oligocene; the earliest Eurasian fossil *Hyla* are from the Miocene of Europe. From this species, the *Hyla arborea* group of species evolved in temperate habitats in Asia and Europe. Dating of times of divergence from immunological data shows the differentiation of hylids in North America to be a Cenozoic phenomenon and the divergence of the Eurasian *Hyla arborea* from North American hylids to be no less than 28 my in the Oligocene (Maxson and A. Wilson, 1975).

J. Savage (1973) suggested that *Rana* invaded Europe from Africa in the early Tertiary. However, after the formation of the Tethys Sea in the Jurassic, Africa was not connected with Eurasia until the end of the Miocene. *Rana* is known in the fossil record from the Oligocene through the Pleistocene of Europe. Therefore, it seems more likely that the ranine stock that reached Asia via drifting India was the source for the non-African members of the genus *Rana.* Beginning in the Oligocene, *Rana* dispersed and differentiated. Probably at least two stocks of *Rana* dispersed from Asia to North America via Beringia. At least one invasion occurred prior to the late Miocene, when *Rana* first appears in the fossil record of North America. Southward dispersal of *Rana* is limited. Only one species reaches South America, and only one reaches Australia. During the late Miocene and early Pliocene when a land connection existed between northwestern Africa and the Iberian Peninsula of Europe, *Rana* was able to disperse southward into mesic habitats in North Africa.

Timing of divergence of some lineages of holarctic *Rana* has been determined from immunological data. Uzzell (1982) noted that several European species of *Rana* differentiated in the Oligocene and Miocene (15–35 my). Divergence of the North American *R. catesbeiana* group from the Eurasian *R. temporaria* complex was in the Oligocene, and times of separation of the western North American *R. boylii* complex from the Eurasian *R. temporaria* complex vary from 33 to 17 million years (Oligocene and Miocene) (Post and Uzzell, 1981). Immunological distances between the European *R. perezi* and the North African *R. saharica* indicate a divergence time of about 7 million years, which is in accord with the time of the land connection between those continents (Uzzell, 1982). These data are not overly informative, but they do not refute the hypothesis of an Asian origin of holarctic *Rana.*

CHAPTER 19

The time has come to rid ourselves of the empirical methods which have necessarily prevailed so long in zootaxy, and endeavor to group species as far as possible, according to their phylogenetic relationships.

George A. Boulenger (1920)

Classification

Following is a classification of lissamphibians. In each account of an order, suborder, or family, information is provided in a hierarchical manner; that is, all statements in an ordinal account apply to all suborders and families in that order. Within each account, there is a definition containing a distinctive suite of morphological characters followed by a general description. The morphological characters of adults are described in detail in Chapters 13 and 14, and those of larvae are treated in Chapter 6. Subsequent sections in each account deal with distribution, fossil history, and life history. In the Remarks section, comments are made about the classification and relationships of the group under discussion. Under Content, the numbers of taxa at all levels down to the species are given. In the accounts of the families, all genera that are recognized currently are listed in alphabetical order (alphabetically within subfamilies in those families in which subfamilies are recognized). Each generic listing contains generic synonyms (including preoccupied senior synonyms but excluding emendations) in parentheses, followed by the number of species, geographic and geological distribution, and a reference to the most recent, comprehensive treatment of the genus or the most recent publication that provides an entree into the pertinent literature. The recognized living genera and number of species follow D. Frost (1985). Names of extinct taxa and synonyms based on fossils are preceded by a dagger (†).

The characters used in the definitions of the families are drawn from the character-state matrices in Chapter 17. All generic names, including synonyms, are listed in the Index.

Class AMPHIBIA Linnaeus, 1758

Definition.—Amphibians are ectothermic, gnathostome vertebrates having two pairs of limbs (lost in some groups). The skull is characterized by a closed otic notch, a large squamosal usually articulating with the parietal, post-temporal fossa and ectopterygoid absent, and septomaxilla (if present) internal. The mandible is composed of a single coronoid medially and three dermal elements laterally. The skull articulates with the vertebral column by means of a specialized vertebra, the atlas. This vertebra lacks ribs and has a pair of atlantal cotyles that articulate with a pair of medially directed occipital condyles of the skull (one condyle in some Paleozoic amphibians). The lepospondylous (husk-type) vertebrae are composed primarily of membrane bone. The centra are elongate with attached, interlocking neural arches; haemal arches (if present) are fused to the centra. Each vertebra bears a pair of projections on each side for the attachment of bicapitate ribs (ribs absent or attached to transverse processes in anurans). Lungs are present (secondarily absent in some salamanders), and the heart has three chambers. The skin is glandular and lacks epidermal scales, feathers, or hair. The eggs are anamniotic, and aquatic larvae in most groups metamorphose into adult forms.

Distribution.—Fossil and Recent amphibians have worldwide distributions. At least in the early Mesozoic, amphibians occurred in Antarctica. Living amphibians are absent from Antarctica and many oceanic islands.

Fossil history.—Amphibians first appeared in the Early Devonian; a great radiation took place in the Carboniferous, and only the Lissamphibia survived beyond the Jurassic.

Remarks.—The classification of the extinct amphibians is unresolved. There is little agreement about the recognition of subclasses and orders, even the time-honored Labyrinthodontia (see Gaffney, 1979; Panchen, 1980; and Gardiner, 1982, for recent discussions). Furthermore, because the Amphibia, as traditionally defined, is the group of tetrapods that lacks amniote eggs, some systematists (e.g., G. Nelson, 1969; E. Wiley, 1979) reject the Amphibia as a valid taxon, or restrict it to the Lissamphibia. However, Gardiner (1983) provided synapomorphies for the class Amphibia.

Subclass LISSAMPHIBIA Haeckel, 1866

Definition.—The vertebrae are monospondylous (i.e., lacking separate intercentra). The ribs (if present) are short and do not encircle the body cavity. Postfrontals and cranial roofing bones posterior to the parietals are absent. The surangular bone is absent in the mandible. The teeth are pedicellate (fang-like in some). A columella and operculum are present (secondarily absent in some taxa). Papilla amphibiorum are present in the inner ear, and green rods are present in the retina in taxa having fully functional eyes. Fat bodies are associated with the gonads (as they are in reptiles). Mucous and granular glands are present in the skin, and intermaxillary glands are present in the buccal cavity.

Distribution.—Lissamphibians occur throughout the tropical and temperate parts of the world, except for some oceanic islands, principally in the South Pacific Ocean, and the most extreme deserts.

Fossil history.—Lissamphibians are known from the Triassic to the Recent.

Remarks.—Gardiner (1983) considered temnospondyls to be the sister group of the Lissamphibia on the basis of three synapomorphies: (1) skull lacking internasal bone, (2) apical fossa small with vomers meeting premaxillae anteriorly, and (3) teeth labyrinthodont. A fourth character (infraorbital canal in relation to lacrimal and jugal bones) given by Gardiner is not applicable to most living Amphibia because they lack those bones. Also, of the temnospondyls, the Permian dissorophoids share the character of the pedicellate teeth with lissamphibians (Estes, 1965; Bolt, 1977).

Content.—The subclass is composed of three orders containing all living amphibians.

Order CAUDATA Oppel, 1811

Definition.—Salamanders have long tails and usually two pairs of limbs of about equal size (hindlimbs absent in Sirenidae). Their body form and structure show many similarities to Paleozoic amphibians. An otic notch and middle ear are absent. The columella has a large footplate and short stylus (absent in some taxa). The m. adductor mandibulae internus superficialis originates on the top and back of the skull (except *Karaurus*), and the m. levator (= adductor) mandibulae posterior is small. Postorbital, jugal, quadratojugal (except Karauridae), postfrontal, postparietal, tabular, supratemporal, supraoccipital, basioccipital, and ectopterygoid bones are absent. Ribs are present. The aquatic larvae (when present) have true teeth on both jaws, gill slits, and external gills.

Distribution.—Salamanders are principally holarctic. Eight living and three extinct families occur in North America (one living family extends into South America), and five living and three extinct familes occur in Eurasia.

Fossil history.—Salamanders are reasonably well represented in the fossil record beginning in the Upper Jurassic of North America and Eurasia and extending through the Pleistocene. The fossils were reviewed thoroughly by Estes (1981), who did not include the work of Nessov (1981). Three fossils are not assigned to families:

1. †*Comonecturoides* Hecht and Estes, 1960; 1 species; Upper Jurassic of Wyoming, U.S.A.
2. †*Galverpeton* Estes and Sanchíz, 1982; 1 species; Upper Cretaceous of Spain.
3. †*Hylaeobatrachus* Dollo, 1884; 1 species; Lower Cretaceous of Belgium.

Life history.—Salamanders have a wide range of courtship patterns. Fertilization is external in the Cryptobranchoidea and presumably in the Sirenoidea. In other living salamanders, internal fertilization is accomplished without copulation. Males have specialized cloacal glands that produce gelatinous pyramidal structures, spermatophores, which are capped with sperm. Females pick up the sperm cap in the cloaca, the roof of which is modified into a spermatheca, where sperm are stored. Eggs usually are fertilized as they pass through the cloaca. Salamanders of most families deposit their eggs singly or in clumps or strings in water; the eggs hatch into aquatic larvae. All members of the families Cryptobranchidae, Sirenidae, Amphiumidae, and Proteidae undergo incomplete metamorphosis; they are obligate neotenes. Most other salamanders undergo metamorphosis into terrestrial adults. Most plethodontids have direct development of terrestrial eggs, and some species of *Salamandra* and *Mertensiella* are ovoviviparous or viviparous.

Remarks.—With the exception of the three fossil genera that have not been allocated to families, the placement of salamanders in families poses few problems.

However, grouping of families into suborders is difficult.

The substitute ordinal name Urodela, dating from Latreille, 1825, commonly is used in place of Caudata.

Content.—Four suborders are recognized provisionally. In addition to the three monotypic fossil genera not assigned to families, these suborders include nine living and four extinct families containing 62 living genera with 352 living species. Sixty-seven extinct species are placed in some of the living genera and in 34 extinct genera.

Suborder †KARAUROIDEA Estes, 1981

The oldest known salamander has a unique combination of characters (see account of Karauridae for characters and discussion).

†KARAURIDAE Ivachnenko, 1978

Definition.—A single fossil from the Jurassic is defined by a suite of primitive character states. The dorsal processes of the premaxillae are short and do not separate the nasals. Lacrimals and quadratojugals are present. The angular is not fused with the prearticular, and a separate coracoid ossification is absent. The m. levator mandibulae internus superficialis originates on the skull roof only. The teeth are pedicellate, and the palatal dentition parallels the maxillary and premaxillary teeth. The vertebrae are amphicoelous, and all spinal nerves exit intervertebrally. The ribs are bicapitate. This small (120-mm snout-vent length) salamander has a large, flattened skull with pitted dermal sculpture.

Fossil history.—This family is represented by a single skeleton from the Upper Jurassic of southern Kazakhstan, U.S.S.R.

Remarks.—Estes (1981) noted the presence of many primitive characters in this ancient salamander and placed it in its own suborder.

Content.—A single monotypic genus:

1. †*Karaurus* Ivachnenko, 1978; 1 species. Upper Jurassic, southern Kazakhstan, U.S.S.R.

Suborder SIRENOIDEA Goodrich, 1930

A single family of aquatic, eel-like salamanders constitutes this distinctive suborder (see account of Sirenidae for characters and discussion).

SIRENIDAE Gray, 1825

Definition.—The pelvic girdle and hindlimbs are absent. The dorsal processes of the premaxillae are short and do not separate the nasals (Fig. 13-3G). Septomaxillae, coracoids, and second ceratobranchials are present. Maxillae are absent (*Pseudobranchus*) or free and edentate (*Siren*). The pterygoids are reduced, and the angular is fused with the prearticular. The exoccipital, prootic, and opisthotic are not fused, and the internal carotid foramen is absent. The columella is free from the operculum. The periotic canal joins the periotic cistern dorsally and

curves ventrally and medially from that junction. The teeth are nonpedicellate. The vertebrae are amphicoelous, and all but the first two spinal nerves exit intravertebrally. The ribs are bicapitate, and the ypsiloid cartilage is absent. Fertilization presumably is external. Sirens have several unique character states among salamanders; these are (1) nasals ossified from median anlagen; (2) palatal teeth in large patches, (3) m. adductor mandibulae internus superficialis originating on side of skull, (4) 46–64 macrochromosomes and no microchromosomes (possibly tetraploids), (5) premaxillary teeth absent, replaced by horny beaks, (6) interventricular septum present, and (7) glomeruli well developed in anterior part of kidney.

Sirenids exhibit several paedomorphic features, such as the absence of eyelids and presence of gill slits (one in *Pseudobranchus* and three in *Siren*) and external gills (Fig. 19-1). The forelimbs are greatly reduced; *Siren* has four digits on each forefoot, *Pseudobranchus* only three. The bodies are long and slender. *Siren lacertina* attains a length of 950 mm, whereas *Pseudobranchus* attains a length of only 250 mm.

Distribution.—Living sirenids are restricted to southeastern United States and northeastern Mexico (Fig. 19-2).

Figure 19-1. *Siren intermedia* from Louisiana, U.S.A. Photo by J. T. Collins.

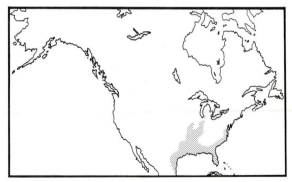

Figure 19-2. Distribution of living members of the family Sirenidae.

Fossil history.—Sirenids are well represented in the fossil record in North America with one extinct genus, *Habrosaurus,* in the Upper Cretaceous and Paleocene, *Siren* from the Eocene to Recent, and *Pseudobranchus* from the Pliocene to Recent.

Life history.—Because a spermatheca is absent in females and cloacal glands are absent in males, spermatophores presumably are not produced, and fertilization probably is external. The eggs are deposited singly or in small clumps attached to submerged vegetation in ponds and swamps.

Remarks.—The relationships of sirenids with other salamanders is problematical, because sirenids possess (1) a number of primitive characters shared with cryptobranchoids, (2) numerous derived characters shared with more advanced salamanders, (3) several paedomorphic characters shared with other neotenic families, and (4) a suite of unique primitive and derived characters. C. Goin and O. Goin (1962) placed sirenids in a separate order, Trachystomata, and suggested a relationship with the lepospondyls; this was rejected by Estes (1965), whose conclusions were followed by D. Wake (1966), Edwards (1976), and Hecht and Edwards (1977). Estes (1981) provisionally placed the sirenids and the salamandrids together in the Salamandroidea because of the number of shared derived characters. An analysis of the character states given in Table 17-1 shows only seven synapomorphies uniting sirenids and salamandrids; this is equal to the number uniting sirenids and plethodontids and one less than the number shared by sirenids and proteids and amphiumids. The paedomorphic nature of many of these character states weakens their usefulness in determining phylogenetic relationships. Based on characters not heavily influenced by paedomorphosis, it seems that sirenids are derived from a basal stock of post-karauroid salamanders.

Content.—Six fossil and three living species are placed in one extinct and two living genera:

1. †*Habrosaurus* Gilmore, 1928 (†*Adelphesiren* Goin and Auffenberg, 1958); 1 species. Up-per Cretaceous and upper Paleocene of north-central United States. Estes (1981).

2. *Pseudobranchus* Gray, 1825 (*Parvibranchus* Hogg, 1839); 1 species. Southeastern United States. Pliocene and Pleistocene of Florida, U.S.A. Martof (1972).

3. *Siren* Linnaeus, 1766; 2 species. Southeastern United States and northeastern Mexico. Middle Eocene of Wyoming, middle Miocene of Texas, lower Miocene and Pleistocene of Florida, U.S.A. Martof (1974).

Suborder CRYPTOBRANCHOIDEA Dunn, 1922

Definition.—The dorsal processes of the premaxillae are short and do not separate the nasals, which are ossified from two anlagen. The angular is not fused with the prearticular. The second ceratobranchials and the ypsiloid cartilage are present. The vertebrae are amphicoelous, and only the posterior caudal vertebrae exit intravertebrally. The ribs are unicapitate. Fertilization is external. The diploid number of chromosomes is 56 or more and consists of a few macrochromosomes and many microchromosomes. Cryptobranchoids have two unique structural features—the first hypobranchial and first ceratobranchial are fused into a single rod, and the m. pubotibialis and m. puboischiotibialis are fused.

The Cryptobranchoidea includes two rather different families—the relatively small, terrestrial or mountain-brook hynobiids of Asia and the largest living salamanders, the aquatic cryptobranchids, in North America and Asia.

Distribution.—Cryptobranchoids occur in eastern North America and in Asia eastward from Iran, Turkestan, and the Ural Mountains to China, Korea, and Japan.

Fossil history.—All fossil cryptobranchoids are referable to the Cryptobranchidae (see account of family).

Life history.—Aquatic eggs masses are enclosed in sacs (one from each oviduct) and fertilization is external.

Remarks.—The hynobiids and cryptobranchids usually have been grouped together. Although they share mainly plesiomorphic character states (Estes, 1981), their

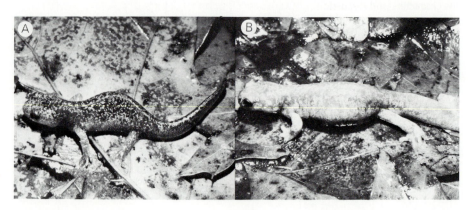

Figure 19-3. A. *Hynobius retardatus* from Japan. **B.** *Ranodon sibiricus* from the Soviet Union. Photos by J. T. Collins.

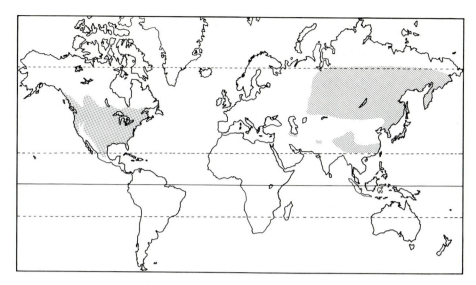

Figure 19-4. Distribution of the living members of the family Hynobiidae in Asia and of the family Ambystomatidae in North America.

association is based on three synapomorphies: (1) fusion of first hypobranchials and first ceratobranchials, (2) fusion of tibialis muscles, and (3) eggs enclosed in paired sacs.

Content.—Two living families, the Hynobiidae and Cryptobranchidae, are included in the suborder.

HYNOBIIDAE Cope, 1859

Definition.—Metamorphosis is complete. Adults have eyelids and no gill slits, and larvae have four pairs of gill slits. Lacrimals and septomaxillae are present (Fig. 13-3A). The palatal dentition pattern is transverse, not paralleling the maxillary and premaxillary teeth.

Hynobiids are small to moderate-sized salamanders. Several species of *Hynobius* attain maximum total lengths of no more than 100 mm, whereas *Ranodon sibiricus* attains a total length of more than 200 mm. Adults of most genera are terrestrial and have well-developed lungs (Fig. 19-3), but *Onychodactylus* lives in mountain streams and has no lungs. Larval hynobiids have external gills and caudal fins.

Distribution.—These Asian salamanders range from Siberia westward to the Ural Mountains and southwestward to Turkestan, Afghanistan, and Iran, and southward to China, Korea, and Japan (Fig. 19-4).

Fossil history.—No fossils are known.

Life history.—All hynobiids have aquatic eggs and larvae. The eggs are deposited in two spindle-shaped gelatinous sacs representing the eggs from each oviduct. The egg sacs are attached to stones or vegetation and subsequently are fertilized. *Hynobius* and some *Batrachuperus* deposit eggs in ponds; other *Batrachuperus, Onychodactylus,* and *Ranodon* deposit eggs in streams. The larvae of *Hynobius* hatch at a poorly developed stage and have balancers, whereas those of the stream-breeders hatch at a more advanced stage. Bannikov (1958) reported that *Ranodon sibiricus* deposits a spermato-

phore, and the female deposits eggs on top of it.

Remarks.—The only reviews of the hynobiid salamanders are by E. Dunn (1923), Thorn (1968), and Zhao and Q. Hu (1984). Tihen (1958), D. Wake (1966), and Regal (1966) suggested possible relationships with the Ambystomatoidea, but Edwards (1976) emphasized that such a relationship was based on symplesiomorphies.

Content.—Nine genera containing 32 species are recognized:

1. *Batrachuperus* Boulenger, 1878; 6 species. Western China, Tibet, Afghanistan, and Iran. Thorn (1968).
2. *Hynobius* Tschudi, 1838 (*Pseudosalamandra* Tschudi, 1838; *Molge* Bonaparte, 1839; *Hydroscopes* Gistel, 1848; *Ellipsoglossa* Duméril and Bibron, 1854; *Isodactylum* Strauch, 1870; *Turanomolge* Nikolski, 1918); 17 species. Japan; eastern Asia westward to Turkestan, U.S.S.R. Thorn (1968); Zhao and Q. Hu (1984).
3. *Liuia* Zhao and Hu, 1983; 1 species. North-central China. Zhao and Q. Hu (1983).
4. *Onychodactylus* Tschudi, 1838 (*Dactylonyx* Bibron, 1839; *Onychopus* Duméril, Bibron, and Duméril, 1854; *Geomolge* Boulenger, 1886); 2 species. Northeastern Asia; Honshu and Shikoku Islands, Japan. Thorn (1968).
5. *Pachyhynobius* Fei, Hu, and Wu, 1983; 1 species. Northeastern China. Zhao and Q. Hu (1984).
6. *Pachypalaminus* Thompson, 1912; 1 species. Japan. Thorn (1968).
7. *Paradactylodon* Risch, 1984; 1 species. North-central Iran. Risch (1984).
8. *Ranodon* Kessler, 1866 (*Ranidens* Boulenger, 1882; *Pseudohynobius* Fei and Ye, 1983); 2

species. Mountains of northern China and adjacent Russia. Zhao and Q. Hu (1984).

9. *Salamandrella* Dybowski, 1870; 1 species. Russian Turkestan through northern China and far eastern U.S.S.R. to Hokkaido, Japan. Zhao and Q. Hu (1984).

CRYPTOBRANCHIDAE Fitzinger, 1826

Definition.—Metamorphosis is incomplete. Adults lack eyelids and have one pair of gill slits (closed in *Andrias*). Lacrimals and septomaxillae are absent (Fig. 13-3B). The palatal teeth are in a curved row parallel to the maxillary and premaxillary teeth.

These huge, aquatic salamanders have depressed bodies and fleshy dermal folds (Fig. 19-5). *Andrias davidianus* attains a total length of 1520 mm, *A. japonicus* 1440 mm, and *Cryptobranchus alleganiensis* 750 mm. Larvae have caudal fins and short gills.

Distribution.—The range of the family includes eastern North America, central China, and Japan (Fig. 19-6).

Fossil history.—This family is known from the Paleocene, Miocene, and Pleistocene of North America, the Oligocene through the Pliocene of Europe, and the Pleistocene of Asia. Fossil *Andrias* attained total lengths of 2300 mm (Estes, 1981).

Life history.—Eggs are laid in paired, rosarylike strings, one from each oviduct, in depressions beneath stones in streams; fertilization is external. Several female *Cryptobranchus* may use the same nest site, and parental care of eggs occurs in *Andrias*.

Remarks.—The cryptobranchids seem to be derived from a hynobiid-like ancestor through the retention of larval characters in the adults. Estes (1981) reviewed fossil cryptobranchids and tentatively did not accept Naylor's (1981) placement of *Andrias* in the synonymy of *Cryptobranchus*.

Content.—Two genera contain three living and two extinct species:

1. *Andrias* Tschudi, 1837 (†*Proteocordylus* Cuvier, in Eichwald, 1831; †*Palaeotriton* Fitzinger, 1837; *Megalobatrachus* Tschudi, 1838; *Sieboldia* Gray, 1838; †*Hydrosalamandra* Leuckart, 1840; †*Tritogenius* Gistel, 1848; †*Tritomegas* Duméril and Bibron, 1854; *Megalobranchus* Van der Hoeven, 1855; *Hoplobatrachus* Mollendorff, 1877; †*Plicagnathus* Cook, 1917; †*Zaisanurus* Tschernov, 1959); 2 species. Japan and central China. Upper Oligocene to upper Pliocene of Europe; Miocene of North America and Pleistocene of Japan. Liu (1950); Zhao and Q. Hu (1984).

2. *Cryptobranchus* Leuckart, 1821 (*Urotropis* Rafinesque, 1822; *Protonopsis* LeConte, 1824;

Figure 19-5. *Cryptobranchus alleganiensis* from Missouri, U.S.A. Photo by J. T. Collins.

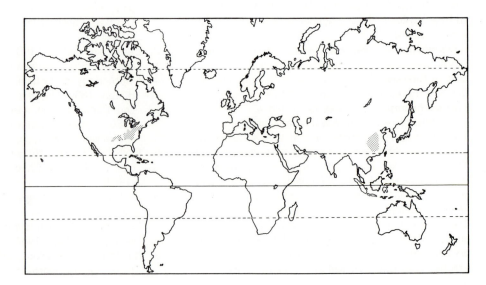

Figure 19-6. Distribution of living members of the family Cryptobranchidae.

Abranchus Harlan, 1825; *Menopoma* Harlan, 1825; *Salamandrops* Wagler, 1830); 1 species. Eastern United States. Upper Paleocene of Saskatchewan, Canada, and Pleistocene of Maryland, U.S.A. Nickerson and Mays (1973).

Suborder SALAMANDROIDEA Noble, 1931

Definition.—In this suborder, the dorsal processes of the premaxillae are long and separate the nasals, which ossify from lateral anlagen (nasals absent in proteids). The angular is fused with the prearticular in living families (not fused in extinct families). The ribs are bicapitate. Three other characters are shared by the living families, but their states are unknown in the fossil families: (1) second ceratobranchials absent, (2) diploid chromosome number 38 or less and with no more than one pair of microchromosomes, and (3) fertilization internal by means of spermatophores.

Most salamandroids are terrestrial and small to moderate in size, but the suborder contains two groups of large, neotenic salamanders that lack eyelids and have persistent gill slits.

Distribution.—This suborder occurs throughout the temperate holarctic region and enters the Neotropics into South America.

Fossil history.—An extensive fossil record begins in the Jurassic of Europe and the Cretaceous of North America and western Asia.

Life history.—Males have modified cloacal glands for the production of spermatophores, and females have a spermatheca for sperm storage; fertilization is internal.

Remarks.—The families herein grouped in the Salamandroidea were placed in six suborders by Estes (1981), who noted that his placement of several families was questionable. The shared derived states of the premaxillae, nasals, angulars, ribs, ceratobranchials, chromosomes, and fertilization indicate that the salamandroids are monophyletic. However, the relationships among the families included in the suborder are obfuscated by the paedomorphic nature of many characters used to separate the families and the absence of information concerning the characters of many of the extinct families.

The subordinal name Amphiumoidea Cope, 1889, antedates Salamandroidea, but because Amphiumoidea has been used only for the Amphiumidae and because the Law of Priority does not apply to ordinal names, the more commonly used Salamandroidea is employed here.

Content.—Six living and three extinct families comprise this suborder.

†PROSIRENIDAE Estes, 1969

Definition.—The premaxillae are paired, and lacrimals are present. The exoccipital, prootic, and opisthotic are fused, and the internal carotid foramen is absent. The vertebrae are amphicoelous, and all spinal nerves exit intravertebrally. Unique character states of the prosirenids are (1) teeth nonpedicellate, (2) frontals fused, (3)

mandibular rami with interlocking symphysis, and (4) cervical vertebrae modified to form an atlas-axis-like complex. These small, elongate salamanders may have been aquatic or even fossorial.

Fossil history.—Prosirenids are known from the Middle Jurassic to the middle Miocene of Europe, the Lower Cretaceous of North America, and the Upper Cretaceous of southwestern Asia.

Remarks.—Because of incomplete specimens, some important features cannot be determined. Moreover, there are some inconsistencies in the diagnostic characters (e.g., unicapitate ribs in *Albanerpeton,* according to Estes, 1981). The unique derived characters of prosirenids set them apart from other families of salamanders. Although the nonpedicellate structure of the teeth is shared with the Sirenidae, the abundance of characters unique to each family suggest that sirenids and prosirenids are not closely related.

Content.—Six extinct species are placed in four genera:

1. †*Albanerpeton* Estes and Hoffstetter, 1976; 3 species. Jurassic to Miocene of Europe; Upper Cretaceous of North America.
2. †*Nukusurus* Nessov, 1981; 1 species. Upper Cretaceous of Uzbekistan, U.S.S.R.
3. †*Prosiren* Goin and Auffenberg, 1958; 1 species. Lower Cretaceous of Texas, U.S.A.
4. †*Ramonellus* Nevo and Estes, 1969; 1 species. Lower Cretaceous of Israel.

†BATRACHOSAUROIDIDAE Auffenberg, 1958

Definition.—The premaxillae are paired. The exoccipital, prootic, and opisthotic are fused, and the internal carotid foramen is absent. The teeth are pedicellate. The vertebrae are opisthocoelous (amphicoely secondary in *Palaeoproteus* and *Peratosauroides*), and all spinal nerves exit intravertebrally. Among salamanders, batrachosauroidids are unique in lacking a tuberculum interglenoideum on the atlas. At least some of these large, paedomorphic salamanders had elongate bodies and reduced limbs; probably they were aquatic.

Fossil history.—Batrachosauroidids are known from the Upper Cretaceous to the lower Pliocene of North America, from the middle Eocene and possibly the Upper Cretaceous of Europe, and from the Upper Cretaceous of southwestern Asia.

Remarks.—The family seems to be most closely related to proteids; if the oldest members of the ancestral group to proteids and batrachosauroidids were opisthocoelous (as indicated by the oldest batrachosauroidid fossils), both proteids and later batrachosauroidids regained amphicoely. Both families are paedomorphic, but distinctive features (e.g., absence of maxillae in proteids) separate them. Estes (1981), who reviewed the family, noted the presence of subpedicellate teeth in *Palaeopro-*

teus and that the questionable batrachosauroidid fossil from the Late Cretaceous of France was not referred to a genus.

Content.—Eight extinct species are recognized in six genera:

1. †*Batrachosauroides* Taylor and Hesse, 1943; 2 species. Lower Eocene and Miocene of North America.
2. †*Mynbulakia* Nessov, 1981; 2 species. Upper Cretaceous of Uzbekistan, U.S.S.R.
3. †*Opisthotriton* Auffenberg, 1961; 1 species. Upper Cretaceous and Paleocene of North America.
4. †*Palaeoproteus* Herre, 1935; 1 species. Middle Eocene of Germany.
5. †*Peratosauroides* Naylor, 1981; 1 species. Lower Pliocene of California, U.S.A.
6. †*Prodesmodon* Estes, 1964 (*Cuttysarkus* Estes, 1964); 1 species. Upper Cretaceous and lower Paleocene of North America.

PROTEIDAE Gray, 1825

Definition.—The premaxillae are paired. Septomaxillae, lacrimals, ypsiloid cartilage, and the basilaris complex of the inner ear are absent. The opisthotic is not fused with the prootic and exoccipital, and the internal carotid foramen is present. The teeth are pedicellate, and the palatal teeth parallel the premaxillary teeth. Proteiids are unique in having (1) no maxillae, (2) the periotic canal horizontal from its posterodorsal junction with the periotic cistern, (3) two pairs of larval gill slits, and (4) a diploid chromosome number of 38.

These aquatic salamanders have large, filamentous gills and caudal fins (Fig. 19-7). *Proteus* has an elongate, slender body and reduced number of digits (three on forefeet, two on hind feet); in this subterranean salamander, pigment is absent in the skin, and the eyes are degenerate. *Proteus* attains a total length of about 300 mm, whereas *Necturus* reaches 400 mm and has a robust body, four digits on all feet, pigmented skin, and small, but normal, eyes.

Distribution.—The range of the family is disjunct. *Necturus* occurs in eastern North America, and *Proteus* is restricted to subterranean waters in southeastern Europe (Fig. 19-8).

Fossil history.—Although not abundant in the fossil record, proteids are known from the upper Paleocene and Pleistocene of North America, Miocene and Pleistocene of Europe, and Miocene of Asia.

Life history.—Courtship, mating, and oviposition take place in water (usually streams). The eggs are laid individually on the undersides of stones.

Remarks.—Some workers, principally Hecht and Edwards (1977), place *Proteus* and *Necturus* in separate families, but most evidence suggests that they are closely related (see Estes, 1981, for summary and references). *Comonecturoides,* formerly placed in the Proteidae, was removed by Estes (1981), who recognized the suborder Proteoidea containing the Proteidae and Batrachosauroididae.

Content.—Two genera contain six living species; four other species are extinct:

1. †*Mioproteus* Estes and Darevsky, 1978; 1 species. Middle Miocene of Caucasus Mountains, U.S.S.R.
2. *Necturus* Rafinesque, 1819 (*Exobranchia* Rafinesque, 1815; *Phanerobranchus* Leuckart, 1821; *Menobranchus* Harlan, 1825); 5 species. Eastern North America. Paleocene of Canada; Pleistocene of Florida, U.S.A. Hecht (1958).
3. †*Orthophyia* Meyer, 1845; 1 species. Upper Miocene of Germany.
4. *Proteus* Laurenti, 1768 (*Lavarius* Rafinesque, 1815; *Platyrhynchus* Leuckart, 1816; *Hypochthon* Merrem, 1820; *Caledon* Goldfuss, 1820; *Apneumona* Fleming, 1822; *Catedon* Duméril and Bibron, 1854); 1 species. Carniola Alps of Italy and Yugoslavia. Pleistocene of Germany. Thorn (1968).

DICAMPTODONTIDAE Tihen, 1958

Definition.—The premaxillae are paired. Septomaxillae, lacrimals, and the ypsiloid cartilage are present. The exoccipital, prootic, and opisthotic are not fused, and the internal carotid foramen is present. The nasals are ossified from lateral anlagen (nasals reduced or absent in *Rhyacotriton*). The teeth are pedicellate, and the palatal teeth are in an M-shaped pattern. The columella is free from the operculum; the pterygoid is reduced in *Rhyacotriton* (Fig. 13-3C). The periotic canal is horizontal from its junction with a protrusion of the periotic cistern into the fenestra ovalis (canal flexed in *Rhyacotriton*). The vertebrae are amphicoelous, and all postcranial nerves exit intravertebrally. The diploid number of chromosomes is 26 or 28.

Figure 19-7. *Necturus maculosus* from Missouri, U.S.A. Photo by J. T. Collins.

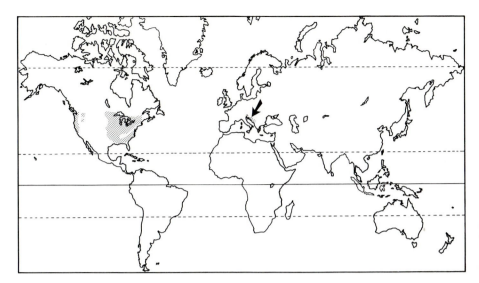

Figure 19-8. Distribution of living members of the family Proteiidae in eastern North America and southern Europe and of the family Dicamptodontidae in western North America.

Figure 19-9. *Dicamptodon ensatus* from Washington, U.S.A. Photo by J. T. Collins.

These generalized aquatic salamanders have well-developed limbs and eyelids; larvae have four pairs of gill slits and short, nonfilamentous gills (Fig. 19-9). *Dicamptodon* attains a total length of 351 mm, whereas *Rhyacotriton* is small (100 mm).

Distribution.—Pacific coastal region and mountains of northwestern United States from Washington (and adjacent Canada) to northern California, and in the northern Rocky Mountains in Idaho (Fig.19-8).

Fossil history.—Dicamptodontids are known from the Paleocene, lower Eocene and Pliocene of northwestern United States and from the Paleocene and upper Miocene of Europe.

Life history.—Eggs are deposited singly either free under stones or in cracks, or attached to undersides of stones in cold streams, where they may take up to 9 months to hatch. Larvae require 2 to 4.5 years to reach metamorphosis.

Remarks.—Until recently, the dicamptodontids usually were regarded as one or two subfamilies of the Am-

bystomatidae (Tihen, 1958). Edward's (1976) work on spinal nerves showed that dicamptodontids have a pattern shared only with the Scapherpetontidae, which along with other characters (e.g., presence of lacrimals and free columella), were regarded by Estes (1981) to be sufficient to give familial status to the dicamptodontids. All of the fossil taxa and the living *Dicamptodon* are placed in the subfamily Dicamptodontinae, characterized by: (1) teeth compressed, bladelike; (2) nasals and pterygoids well developed; (3) carpal and tarsal elements ossified in adults; (4) ypsiloid cartilage and lungs well developed; and (5) diploid chromosome number 28. *Rhyacotriton* is placed in its own subfamily, characterized principally by paedomorphic states: (1) teeth conical; (2) nasals reduced or absent and pterygoids reduced; (3) carpal and tarsal elements cartilaginous in adults; (4) ypsiloid cartilage and lungs reduced; and (5) diploid chromosome number 26. Some workers (e.g., Milner, 1983) have considered *Rhyacotriton* to be more closely related to plethodontids. However, *Dicamptodon* and *Rhyacotriton* share patterns of palatal dentition and spinal nerves. The similarities between *Rhyacotriton* and plethodontids are the result of convergence of paedomorphic characters, but the synapomorphies grouping *Rhyacotriton* and *Dicamptodon* are weak. The two genera may represent independent lineages, in which case the Dicamptodontidae is polyphyletic.

Content.—Three species in two living genera and five monotypic extinct genera are grouped into two subfamilies:

DICAMPTODONTINAE Tihen, 1958

1. †*Ambystomichnus* Peabody, 1954; 1 species. Paleocene of Montana, U.S.A.
2. †*Bargmannia* Herre, 1955; 1 species. Upper Miocene of Czechoslovakia.
3. †*Chrysotriton* Estes, 1981; 1 species. Lower Eocene of North Dakota, U.S.A.

4. *Dicamptodon* Strauch, 1870 (*Chondrotus* Cope, 1887); 2 species. Pacific coast of California to British Columbia; northern Idaho, U.S.A. Lower Pliocene of California. Nussbaum (1976).

5. †*Geyeriella* Herre, 1950; 1 species. Upper Paleocene of Germany.

6. †*Wolterstorffiella* Herre, 1950; 1 species. Upper Paleocene of Germany.

RHYACOTRITONINAE Tihen, 1958

7. *Rhyacotriton* Dunn, 1920; 1 species. Northwestern United States. J. Anderson (1968).

†SCAPHERPETONTIDAE Auffenberg and Goin, 1959

Definition.—The premaxillae are paired. The exoccipital, prootic, and opisthotic are not fused, and the internal carotid foramen is absent. The teeth are pedicellate, and the palatal dentition parallels the maxillary and premaxillary teeth. The vertebrae are amphicoelous, and all postsacral nerves exit intravertebrally. At least some of these presumably aquatic salamanders had reduced limbs.

Fossil history.—Scaperpetontids are known from the Upper Cretaceous of southwestern Asia and from the

Upper Cretaceous to the lower Eocene of northwestern United States and Canada north to Ellesmere Island.

Remarks.—On the basis of their shared pattern of spinal nerve foramina (nerves exit via foramina in postsacral vertebrae and between vertebrae presacrally), Edwards (1976) placed the scaperpetontids and dicamptodontids in a single family. However, Estes (1981) recognized the Scapherpetontidae, which differs from the Dicamptodontidae by lacking an internal carotid foramen and by having the angular separate from the prearticular and a different pattern of palatal dentition.

Content.—Five monotypic extinct genera are recognized:

1. †*Eoscapherpeton* Nessov, 1981; 1 species. Upper Cretaceous of Uzbekistan, U.S.S.R.

2. †*Horezmia* Nessov, 1981; 1 species. Upper Cretaceous of Uzbekistan, U.S.S.R.

3. †*Lisserpeton* Estes, 1965; 1 species. Upper Cretaceous and Paleocene of North America.

4. †*Piceoerpeton* Meszoely, 1967; 1 species. Upper Paleocene to lower Eocene of North America.

5. †*Scapherpeton* Cope, 1877 (*Hedronchus* Cope, 1877; *Hemitrypus* Cope, 1877); 1 species. Upper Cretaceous through Paleocene of North America.

AMPHIUMIDAE Gray, 1825

Definition.—The premaxillae are fused. Septomaxillae, lacrimals, and the ypsiloid cartilage are absent, and the pterygoids are reduced (Fig. 13-3F). The exoccipial, prootic, and opisthotic are not fused, and the internal carotid foramen is present. The nasals are ossified from lateral anlagen. The teeth are pedicellate, and the palatal teeth parallel the maxillary and premaxillary teeth. The columella is fused with the operculum. The periotic canal is horizontal from its junction with a protrusion of the periotic cistern into the fenestra ovalis. The vertebrae are amphicoelous, and only the posterior caudal nerves exit through foramina in the vertebrae. The pectoral and pelvic girdles are much reduced, and the limbs are vestigial. The diploid chromosome number is 28 with a gradual reduction from macrochromosomes to microchromosomes.

These large, aquatic salamanders retain some external larval features, such as one of the three larval gill slits (but no external gills), and have no eyelids (Fig. 19-10). These muscular, elongate salamanders attain total lengths of about 1 m.

Distribution.—Living amphiumids occur on the coastal plain of southeastern United States from Virginia to Louisiana and in the Mississippi River drainage northward to Missouri (Fig. 19-11).

Fossil history.—The family was widely distributed in North America from the Upper Cretaceous until the upper Miocene and restricted to southeastern United States in the Pleistocene.

Figure 19-10. *Amphiuma tridactylum* from Texas, U.S.A. Photo by J. T. Collins.

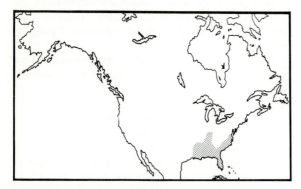

Figure 19-11. Distribution of living members of the family Amphiumidae.

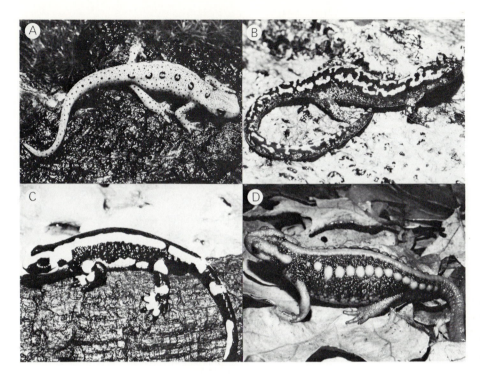

Figure 19-12. A. *Notophthalmus viridescens* from Indiana, U.S.A. **B.** *Mertensiella caucasica.* **C.** *Salamandra salamandra* from Europe. **D.** *Tylototriton verrucosus* from Asia. Photos by J. T. Collins.

Life history.—Long strings of up to 150 eggs are laid under shelter on mud near water; the eggs are guarded by the female. Hatchlings are about 65 mm long and have external gills.

Remarks.—Diverse opinions on the relationships of the amphiumids have been based on dentition patterns, vertebral structure, myology, immunology, and karyology (see Estes, 1981, for summary and references). The paedomorphic nature of most of the shared derived characters, as well as the unique derived characters, make absolute placement doubtful.

Content.—Three living and three extinct species are recognized in two genera:

1. *Amphiuma* Garden, 1821 (*Chrysodonta* Mitchill, 1822; *Sirenoidis* Fitzinger, 1843; *Muraenopsis* Fitzinger, 1843); 3 living and 2 extinct species. Southeastern United States. Upper Paleocene, Miocene, and Pleistocene of North America. Salthe (1973).
2. †*Proamphiuma* Estes, 1969; 1 species. Upper Cretaceous of North America.

SALAMANDRIDAE Gray, 1825

Definition.—The premaxillae are paired in primitive genera and fused in advanced genera (Fig. 13-3E). Septomaxillae, lacrimals, and the ypsiloid cartilage are present. The exoccipital, prootic, and opisthotic are fused, and the internal carotid foramen is absent. A frontosquamosal arch is present (reduced or absent as derived states in some genera). The columella is fused with the opercu-

lum. There are one or more flexures of the periotic canal after its junction with a protrusion of the periotic cistern into the fenestra ovalis (horizontal canal in *Notophthalmus*). The teeth are pedicellate, and the palatal dentition extends posteriorly on the lateral edges of the vomers. The vertebrae are opisthocoelous, and all but the first two spinal nerves exit intravertebrally. The diploid chromosome number is 22 or 24; in the latter, macrochromosomes gradually decrease to microchromosomes.

Salamandrids are highly variable in external appearance and size. Some *Salamandra* and *Pleurodeles* attain total lengths of more than 200 mm. All salamandrids have well-developed limbs, and many of the aquatic species have dorsal body and caudal fins (Fig. 19-12). All salamandrids have toxic skin secretions, and many genera have bright, aposematic colors that are displayed in defense postures. The larvae have four pairs of gill slits and large external gills; pond larvae have balancers.

Distribution.—The Salamandridae is distributed primarily in Europe and Asia, where it occurs from the British Isles and Scandinavia eastward to the Ural Mountains in Russia and southward into the Iberian Peninsula, Asia Minor, and some of the Grecian islands, as well as Corsica and Sardinia. In central and eastern Asia, salamandrids occur from northern India, Burma, Thailand, and Vietnam southeastward to Hong Kong and eastward through China and the Japanese Archipelago. Two European genera occur in extreme northwestern Africa, and two genera are endemic to North America (Fig. 19-13).

Fossil history.—Salamandrids are especially well represented in Cenozoic deposits in Europe, where they are

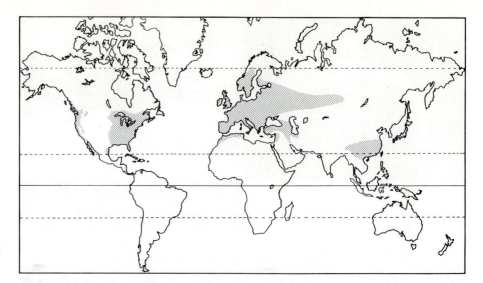

Figure 19-13. Distribution of living members of the family Salamandridae.

known from the Eocene to the Pleistocene. One extinct genus is known from the Miocene of Asia, and the living North American genera are known as fossils beginning in the Oligocene.

Life history.—Most of the genera are wholly or partially aquatic. Courtship and reproductive behavior is highly variable (Salthe, 1967). In *Notophthalmus*, there are usually three distinct life forms during ontogeny—an aquatic larval period of about 3 months, terrestrial sexually immature stage (eft) of 2 or 3 years, and aquatic adults. *Taricha* and *Triturus* have aquatic larvae and terrestrial adults, which return to water to breed. *Cynops, Notophthalmus, Paramesotriton, Pleurodeles, Triturus,* and *Tylototriton* breed in ponds; *Chioglossa, Euproctus, Salamandrina,* and *Taricha* breed in streams. Some *Salamandra* and *Mertensiella* produce living young. Individuals in some populations of *Notophthalmus, Pleurodeles,* and *Triturus* are facultatively neotenic.

Remarks.—Estes (1981) integrated data on fossil salamandrids with the phylogeny of the living genera presented by D. Wake and Özeti (1969). Brodie (1977) provided a phylogenetic assessment of antipredator behavior in salamandrids.

Content.—The 53 living and 15 fossil species are placed in 15 genera; eight extinct genera contain 10 species:

1. †*Archaeotriton* Meyer, 1860; 1 species. Upper Oligocene and lower Miocene of Czechoslovakia.
2. †*Brachycormus* Meyer, 1860; 1 species. Lower Miocene of Germany.
3. †*Chelotriton* Pomel, 1853 (†*Polysemia* Meyer, 1860; †*Heliarchon* Meyer, 1863; †*Grippiella* Herre, 1949; †*Palaeosalamandrina* Herre, 1949; †*Tischleriella* Herre, 1949; †*Epipolysemia* Brame, 1973); 3 species. Middle Eocene to middle Miocene of Europe.
4. *Chioglossa* Bocage, 1864; 1 species. North-western Spain and Portugal. Middle Miocene of France. Busack (1976).
5. *Cynops* Tschudi, 1839; 7 species. Central China and Japanese Archipelago. Zhao and Q. Hu (1984).
6. *Echinotriton* Nussbaum and Brodie, 1982; 2 species. Zhejiang and Hainan Island, China, and Ryukyu Islands. Nussbaum and Brodie (1982).
7. *Euproctus* Gene, 1838 (*Megapterna* Savi, 1838; *Phatnomatorhina* Bibron, in Bonaparte, 1839; *Pelonectes* Fitzinger, 1843; *Hemitriton* Dugés, 1852; *Calotriton* Gray, 1858); 3 species. Pyrenees mountains of Europe; Sardinia and Corsica. Pleistocene of Spain. Thorn (1968).
8. †*Koalliella* Herre, 1950; 1 species. Upper Paleocene of Europe.
9. †*Megalotriton* Zittel, 1890; 1 species. Eocene and Oligocene of Europe.
10. *Mertensiella* Wolterstorff, 1825 (*Exaeretus* Waga, 1876); 2 species. Western Caucasus Mountains of Georgian S.S.R., mountains of eastern Turkey, and island of Karpathos, Greece. Lower Miocene to upper Pliocene of Eastern Europe. Thorn (1968).
11. *Neurergus* Cope, 1862 (*Rhithrotriton* Nesterov, 1916); 4 species. Western Asia in Iran, Iraq, and Turkey. J. Schmidtler and F. Schmidtler (1975).
12. *Notophthalmus* Rafinesque, 1820 (*Tristella* Gray, 1850; *Diemyctylus* Hallowell, 1856); 3 species. Eastern North America. Miocene and Pleistocene of eastern United States. Mecham (1967a, 1967b, 1968).
13. †*Oligosemia* Navas, 1922; 1 species. Upper Miocene of Spain.
14. *Pachytriton* Boulenger, 1878 (*Pingia* Chang,

1936); 1 species. Mountains of southeastern China. Zhao and Q. Hu (1984).

15. †*Palaeopleurodeles* Herre, 1941; 1 species. Upper Oligocene of Germany.

16. *Paramesotriton* Chang, 1935 (*Mesotriton* Bourret, 1934; *Trituroides* Chang, 1936); 5 species. North Vietnam, western and southern China, and Hong Kong. Bischoff and Böhme (1980).

17. *Pleurodeles* Michahelles, 1830 (*Bradybates* Tschudi, 1839; *Glossoliga* Bonaparte, 1839); 2 species. Iberian Peninsula; Morocco, Tunisia, and Algeria in North Africa. Thorn (1968).

18. †*Procynops* Young, 1965; 1 species. Miocene of China.

19. *Salamandra* Laurenti, 1768 (†*Heteroclitotriton* de Stefano, 1903; †*Cryptobranchichnus* Huene, 1941; †*Palaeosalamandra* Herre, 1949; †*Voigtiella* Herre, 1949; †*Dehmiella* Herre and Lunau, 1950); 2 species. Middle and southern Europe, northwestern Africa, and western Asia. Upper Eocene to Pleistocene of Europe. Thorn (1968).

20. *Salamandrina* Fitzinger, 1826 (*Seiranota* Barnes, 1826); 1 species. Appennines mountains of Italy. Lower Miocene of Sardinia. Thorn (1968).

21. *Taricha* Gray, 1850 (†*Palaeotaricha* van Frank, 1955); 3 species. Pacific coastal region of North America. Oligocene to Pleistocene of western United States. Nussbaum and Brodie (1981).

22. *Triturus* Rafinesque, 1815 (*Triton* Laurenti, 1768; *Meinus* Rafinesque, 1815; *Oiacurus* Leuckart, 1821; *Geotriton* Bonaparte, 1832; *Lissotriton* Bell, 1839; *Lophinus* Rafinesque, in Gray, 1850; *Ommatotriton* Gray, 1850; *Hemisalamandra* Dugés, 1852; *Petraponia* Massalongo, 1854; *Pyronicia* Gray, 1858; *Pelonectes* Lataste, in Tourneville, 1879); 12 species. British Isles, Scandinavia, continental Europe, Asia Minor to Caspian Sea, eastward to Ural Mountains, U.S.S.R. Upper Eocene to Pleistocene of Europe; upper Miocene of U.S.S.R. Thorn (1968).

23. *Tylototriton* Anderson, 1871; 5 species. Northeastern India to southern China; Ryukyu Islands. Eocene of Germany. Zhao and Q Hu (1984).

AMBYSTOMATIDAE Hallowell, 1856

Definition.—The premaxillae are paired. Septomaxillae, pterygoids, and the ypsiloid cartilage are present, but lacrimals are absent (Fig. 13-3D). The exoccipital, prootic, and opisthotic are fused, and the internal carotid foramen is present. The teeth are pedicellate, and the palatal teeth are transverse. The nasals are ossified from lateral anla-

gen. The columella is fused with the operculum. The periotic canal is horizontal from its junction with a protrusion of the periotic cistern into the fenestra ovalis. The vertebrae are amphicoelous, and all but the first three spinal nerves exit intravertebrally. The diploid number of chromosomes is 28.

These moderate-sized salamanders (up to about 200 mm total length but up to 346 mm in *Ambystoma tigrinum*) have short, blunt heads and robust bodies and limbs (Fig. 19-14). Larvae have broad heads, caudal fins, four pairs of gill slits, and long filamentous gills; most have balancers.

Distribution.—Ambystomatids are widespread in North America from extreme southeastern Alaska and Labrador to the southern edge of the Mexican Plateau (Fig. 19-4).

Fossil history.—The family is known from the lower Oligocene through the Pleistocene of North America.

Life history.—In most *Ambystoma,* courtship and breeding take place in ponds in the spring, but some species breed in the autumn and deposit eggs on land near water, which subsequently floods the nests. Other *Ambystoma* lay eggs singly or in clumps in ponds or sluggish streams. *Rhyacosiredon* attaches large, unpigmented eggs singly on stones in mountain streams. Larvae of some species overwinter in ponds. Several species are obligate neotenes, whereas some others are facultatively neotenic (Table 7-4).

Remarks.—Ambystomatids share with plethodontids the most derived pattern of spinal nerves. Otherwise, they have many character states that are primitive in the Salamandroidea and have no unique derived characters. Osteologically and reproductively they are generalized. Therefore, the historical reality of the Ambystomatidae is questionable.

Two species are gynogenetic triploids (Table 16-4). This family includes the famous Mexican axolotl, *Ambystoma mexicanum,* which has been used extensively in experimental embryology and endocrinology (H. Smith and R. B. Smith, 1971).

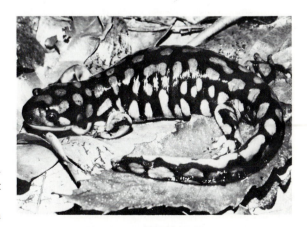

Figure 19-14. *Ambystoma tigrinum* from Lincoln County, Missouri, U.S.A. Photo by J. T. Collins.

Figure 19-15. A. *Desmognathus welteri* from Kentucky, U.S.A. **B.** *Gyrinophilus porphyriticus* from Kentucky, U.S.A. **C.** *Ensatina eschscholtzi* from California, U.S.A. **D.** *Pseudoeurycea cephalica* from Morelos, Mexico. A–C by J. T. Collins; D by W. E. Duellman.

Content.—Two living genera contain 30 species; 5 other species are known only as fossils, 1 in an extinct genus:

1. *Ambystoma* Tschudi, 1838 (*Gyrinus* Shaw and Nodder, 1789; *Axolotus* Jaroki, 1822; *Philhydrus* Brookes, 1828; *Siredon* Wagler, 1830; *Axolotl* Bonaparte, 1831; *Sirenodon* Wiegmann, 1832; *Stegoporus* Wiegmann, 1832; *Xiphonura* Tschudi, 1838; *Salamandroidis* Fitzinger, 1843; *Axolotes* Owen, 1844; *Amblystoma* Agassiz, 1844; *Heterotriton* Gray, 1845; *Limnarches* Gistel, 1848; *Xiphoctonus* Gistel, 1848; *Plagiodon* Duméril, Bibron, and Duméril, 1854; *Desmiostoma* Sager, 1858; *Camarataxis* Cope, 1859; *Pectoglossa* Mivart, 1867; *Linguaelapsus* Cope, 1887; †*Plioambystoma* Adams, 1929; *Bathysiredon* Dunn, 1939; †*Lanebatrachus* Taylor, 1941; †*Ogallalabatrachus* Taylor, 1941); 26 species. North America from southern Canada to central Mexico. Lower Oligocene through the Pleistocene of North America. Tihen (1969).

2. †*Amphitriton* Rogers, 1976; 1 species. Upper Pliocene of Texas, U.S.A.

3. *Rhyacosiredon* Dunn, 1928; 4 species. Mountains of central Mexico. Tihen (1958).

PLETHODONTIDAE Gray, 1850

Definition.—The premaxillae usually are paired (fused in many genera). Maxillae and premaxillae are present (secondarily reduced or absent in some genera; Fig. 13-

4). The exoccipital, prootic, and opisthotic are fused, and the internal carotid foramen is absent. The teeth are pedicellate, and the palatal teeth extend posteriorly along the medial edges of the vomers. The nasals are ossifed from lateral anlagen. Lacrimals, pterygoids, lungs, and the ypsiloid cartilage are absent, but pterygoids are present in larvae. The operculum is absent, and it is replaced functionally by the footplate of the columella. There are one or more flexures of the periotic canal from its junction with a protrusion of the periotic cistern into the fenestra ovalis (canal horizontal in *Batrachoseps* and *Thorius*). The vertebrae are opisthocoelous, and all but the first three spinal nerves exit intravertebrally. The diploid number of chromosomes is 26 or 28.

Plethodontids are highly variable in size and shape. Some species of *Thorius* have total lengths of no more than 27 mm, whereas the largest species are *Oedipina collaris* (253 mm) and *Pseudoeurycea bellii* (325 mm). Some plethodontids are slender and elongate (e.g., *Batrachoseps, Lineatriton,* and *Oedipina*), whereas others (e.g., desmognathines) are robust (Fig. 19-15). Some *Bolitoglossa* and *Chiropterotriton* have webbed feet, and *Aneides, Bolitoglossa,* and *Pseudoeurycea* have prehensile tails. Males of most genera have protuberances (cirri) on the upper lip associated with the nasolabial grooves and also have mental glands. Two genera (*Haideotriton* and *Typhlomolge*) are obligate neotenes.

Distribution.—Plethodontids occur in eastern and western North America from Nova Scotia and extreme southeastern Alaska southward, with some species in the central region (absent from the Great Plains, most of the

Rocky Mountains, and the Great Basin). A major center of differentiation is in Mexico and Central America, where the family occurs in all but the xeric regions. Two genera enter South America, where the family extends from Colombia to eastern Brazil and central Bolivia (Fig. 19-16). Two species of *Hydromantes* occur in southern Europe and on Sardinia; otherwise the genus is restricted to central California in North America.

Fossil history.—Six Recent genera are known from the lower Miocene to the Pleistocene of North America.

Life history.—Most desmognathines and the members of the tribe Hemidactyliini of the plethodontines have aquatic eggs and larvae, which have branched gills and no balancers. Other plethodontids have direct development of terrestrial eggs. Although the major evolutionary trend in life history of plethodontids has been from aquatic eggs and larvae to direct development of terrestrial eggs, some subterranean salamanders have remained in a larval state. This trend is seen in *Eurycea* and *Gyrinophilus*, in which some species metamorphose and others do not; extreme cases of paedomorphosis are exhibited by the obligate neotenes *Haideotriton* and *Typhlomolge*.

Remarks.—The evolutionary relationships among plethodontids were reviewed by Larson (1984). The two subfamilies were defined by D. Wake (1966), as follows: Desmognathinae—(1) four larval gill slits; (2) unique mouth-opening mechanism by means of which the mandibles are held rigid and the skull raised; (3) well-developed hypapophysial keels on anterior trunk vertebrae. Plethodontinae—(1) three larval or embryonic gill slits; (2) normal mouth opening mechanism by means of which the skull remains rigid and the mandibles are lowered; (3) no well-developed hypapophysial keels on vertebrae. D. Wake (1966) recognized three tribes in the Plethodontinae: (1) Hemidactyliini characterized by having aquatic larvae and containing eight genera (*Eurycea, Gyrinophilus, Haideotriton, Hemidactylium, Pseudotri-*ton, *Stereochilus, Typhlomolge,* and *Typhlotriton); (2)* Plethodontini characterized by lacking aquatic larvae and having large, ossified second basibranchial, and containing three genera (*Aneides, Ensatina,* and *Plethodon); and* (3) Bolitoglossini characterized by lacking aquatic larvae and second basibranchials, and containing all of the other plethodontine genera.

Content.—Two subfamilies contain 27 genera and 220 species:

DESMOGNATHINAE Cope, 1859

1. *Desmognathus* Baird, 1850; 11 species. Southeastern Canada and eastern United States west to Oklahoma and Texas. Pleistocene of Virginia and Texas. D. Wake (1966), Tilley et al. (1978), Tilley (1981).

2. *Leurognathus* Moore, 1899; 1 species. Southern Appalachian Mountains, U.S.A. Martof (1963).

3. *Phaeognathus* Highton, 1961; 1 species. Southern edge of Red Hills region, Alabama, U.S.A. Brandon (1966b).

PLETHODONTINAE Gray, 1850

4. *Aneides* Baird, 1849 (*Autodax* Boulenger, 1887); 5 species. Pacific coast of North America; Sacramento Mountains of New Mexico; Appalachian Mountains and associated piedmont of eastern U.S.A. Lower Miocene of Montana, U.S.A. D. Wake (1974).

5. *Batrachoseps* Bonaparte, 1841 (*Plethopsis* Bishop, 1937); 8 species. Western North America. Lower Pliocene of California, U.S.A. Yanev (1980).

6. *Bolitoglossa* Duméril, Bibron, and Duméril, 1854 (*Oedipus* Tschudi, 1838; *Eladinea* Miranda-Ribeiro, 1937; *Magnadigita* Taylor,

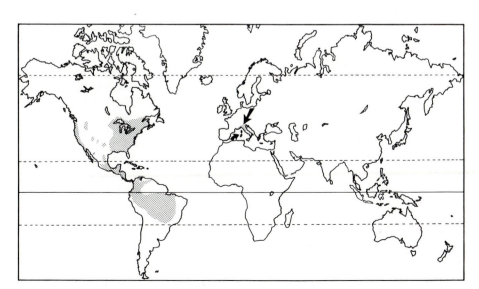

Figure 19-16. Distribution of living members of the family Plethodontidae.

1944; *Palmatotriton* Smith, 1945); 67 species. Northeastern Mexico to eastern Brazil and central Bolivia. D. Wake and J. F. Lynch (1976), D. Wake and P. Elias (1983).

7. *Bradytriton* Wake and Elias, 1983; 1 species. Sierra de los Cuchumatanes, Guatemala. D. Wake and P. Elias (1983).

8. *Chiropterotriton* Taylor, 1944; 9 species. Eastern Mexico. D. Wake and P. Elias (1983).

9. *Dendrotriton* Wake and Elias, 1983; 5 species. Southwestern Chiapas, Mexico, and western Guatemala. D. Wake and P. Elias (1983).

10. *Ensatina* Gray, 1850 (*Heredia* Girard, 1856; *Urotropis* Jiménez de la Espada, 1870); 1 species. Pacific coast and Sierra Nevada in western North America. Stebbins (1949b).

11. *Eurycea* Rafinesque, 1822 (*Spelerpes* Rafinesque, 1832; *Cylindrosoma* Tschudi, 1838; *Saurocercus* Fitzinger, 1843; *Manculus* Cope, 1869); 11 species. Eastern North America westward to Ozark uplift and to central Texas. D. Wake (1966).

12. *Gyrinophilus* Cope, 1869; 2 species. Appalachian uplift of eastern North America. Pleistocene of eastern United States. Brandon (1967a).

13. *Haideotriton* Carr, 1939; 1 species. Subterranean waters in southern Georgia and the Florida panhandle, U.S.A. Brandon (1967b).

14. *Hemidactylium* Tschudi, 1838 (*Cotobotes* Gistel, 1848; *Desmodactylus* Duméril, Bibron, and Duméril, 1854; *Dermodactylus* David, 1875); 1 species. Eastern North America. Neill (1963).

15. *Hydromantes* Gistel, 1848 (*Hydromantoides* Lanza and Vanni, 1981); 5 species. Mountains of central and northern California, U.S.A; northern Italy to southwestern France; Sardinia. D. Wake et al. (1978).

16. *Lineatriton* Tanner, 1950; 1 species. Eastern Mexico. D. Wake and P. Elias (1983).

17. *Nototriton* Wake and Elias, 1983; 6 species. Guatemala to Costa Rica. D. Wake and P. Elias (1983).

18. *Nyctanolis* Elias and Wake, 1983; 1 species. Mountains of northern Guatemala and adjacent Mexico. P. Elias and D. Wake (1983).

19. *Oedipina* Keferstein, 1868 (*Ophiobatrachus* Gray, 1868; *Haptoglossa* Cope, 1893; *Oedopinola* Hilton, 1946); 16 species. Chiapas, Mexico, to northwestern Ecuador. Brame (1968).

20. *Parvimolge* Taylor, 1944; 1 species. Eastern Mexico. D. Wake and P. Elias (1983).

21. *Plethodon* Tschudi, 1838 (*Sauropsis* Fitzinger, 1843); 26 species. Eastern and Western North America; Rocky Mountains in New Mexico, U.S.A. Highton and Larson (1979).

22. *Pseudoeurycea* Taylor, 1944; 25 species. Mexico and Guatemala. D. Wake and P. Elias (1983).

23. *Pseudotriton* Tschudi, 1838 (*Mycetoglossus* Bonaparte, 1839; *Batrachopsis* Fitzinger, 1843; *Pelodytes* Gistel, 1848); 2 species. Appalachian uplift of eastern United States. Martof (1975).

24. *Stereochilus* Cope, 1869; 1 species. Atlantic Coastal Plain from Virginia to Georgia, U.S.A. Pleistocene of Maryland and Georgia, U.S.A. G. Rabb (1966).

25. *Thorius* Cope, 1869; 9 species. Mountains of southern Mexico. D. Wake and P. Elias (1983).

26. *Typhlomolge* Stejneger, 1896; 2 species. Subterranean waters of central Texas, U.S.A. Potter and Sweet (1981).

27. *Typhlotriton* Stejneger, 1893; 1 species. Ozark uplift of south-central United States. Brandon (1970b).

Order GYMNOPHIONA Rafinesque, 1814

Definition.—Caecilians are elongate, limbless amphibians that are highly specialized for burrowing. The body is greatly elongate and segmented by annular grooves (containing scales in some species). The tail, if present, is short and pointed. The eyes are small and covered with skin or bone. The vertebrae are amphicoelous, and the ribs are bicapitate. Sternal elements, girdles, and limbs are absent. The skull is compact with fusion of some elements (e.g., maxilla and palatine into maxillopalatine, and the otic and occipital elements, and the parasphenoid into the basale). The columella (stapes) is massive or absent. The teeth generally are curved and are present on the premaxillae, maxillopalatines, vomers, dentaries, and usually on the splenials. The left lung usually is rudimentary. A protrusible, sensory tentacle is present between the eye and the nostril. Males have a single, median, protrusible copulatory organ (phallodeum). Aquatic larvae (if present) have gill slits but no external gills.

Distribution.—Caecilians are pantropical. Three families occur in southeastern Asia (one including the Oriental part of the Indo-Australian Archipelago eastward to Borneo and the Philippines). Two families (one endemic) are in tropical Africa, and three families (two endemic) occur in the American tropics. Three genera are endemic to the Seychelles islands in the Indian Ocean, but caecilians do not occur on other islands in the Indian Ocean, including Madagascar.

Fossil history.—The single recognized caecilian fossil is from the Paleocene of Brazil.

Life history.—Presumably all caecilians have internal fertilization. Primitive caecilians are oviparous and have aquatic larvae. Some advanced caecilians are oviparous;

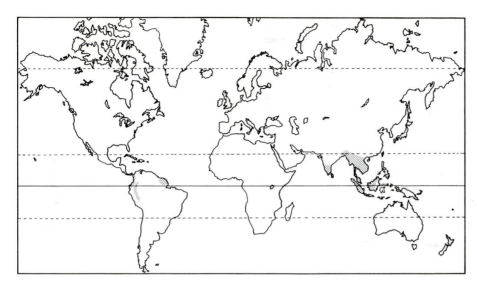

Figure 19-17. Distribution of living members of the family Rhinatrematidae in South America and of the family Ichthyophiidae in Asia.

their eggs undergo direct development into terrestrial young. Most advanced caecilians are viviparous. The foetuses have specialized teeth (shed at birth) with which they scrape the epithelial lining of the oviduct and obtain nutrients secreted by the oviducal cells (M. Wake, 1977a).

Remarks.—Caecilians are the least-known group of living amphibians. Although their morphology has long been of interest to anatomists (e.g., Wiedersheim, 1879; P. Sarasin and F. Sarasin, 1887–1890), only recently have comparative studies been undertaken. E. Taylor's (1968) monograph of caecilians was supplemented by his comparative studies of skulls (1969b), scales (1972), vertebrae (1977a), and mandibles (1977b). Nussbaum and Naylor (1982) reported on the trunk musculature. The urogenital system has been studied by M. Wake (1972 and papers cited therein). The teeth have been studied by M. Wake (1980d and papers cited therein), and vertebrae have been investigated by M. Wake (1980c). M. Wake and Hanken (1982) provided data on the ontogenetic development of the skull and summarized previous work on that subject. Nussbaum (1977, 1979a) has made the only attempts at phylogenetic reconstructions of caecilians.

The ordinal name Apoda sometimes used for caecilians was applied first to a group of eel-like fishes and is not available for caecilians.

Content.—Six families are recognized; these contain 34 living genera and 162 species and 1 extinct genus and species.

RHINATREMATIDAE Nussbaum, 1977

Definition.—The skulls of the most primitive family of caecilians are kinetic and zygokrotaphic (Fig. 13-10). The premaxillae are separate from the nasals; septomaxillae and postfrontals are present, but discrete prefrontals are absent. The squamosals do not articulate with the frontal,

and temporal fossae are present. The sides of the parasphenoid are parallel, and the vomers are separated by the cultiform process of the parasphenoid. The columella is pierced by the stapedial artery and is movably attached to the quadrate, which articulates with the maxillopalatine. The retroarticular process of the pseudoangular is short and horizontal. Dorsolateral processes are present on the basale.

Rhinatrematids are small caecilians (largest is *Epicrionops petersi* with a total length of 328 mm) and have a tail and a terminal mouth. The tentacular opening is adjacent to the anterior edge of the eye. Primary and secondary annuli are orthoplicate, present throughout the length of the body, and bear scales. *Rhinatrema* is slender and has yellow lateral stripes, like some species of *Epicrionops,* but some of the latter are unicolor and some others are thick-bodied. Larvae have obvious lateral-line systems and a single gill slit.

Distribution.—Rhinatrematids are restricted to South America where they occur in Caribbean, Amazonian, and Pacific drainages from Venezuela to Peru, and in the Guianan region (Fig. 19-17).

Fossil history.—None.

Life history.—Larvae are known for some species of *Epicrionops,* and *Rhinatrema* is presumed to have a larval stage. Larvae of *E. petersi* have been found in mud at the edge of a stream.

Remarks.—Nussbaum (1977) showed that rhinatrematids possess a suite of primitive characters that distinguish them from the more advanced ichthyophiids. Furthermore, rhinatrematids have a uniquely derived feature—paired dorsolateral processes of the basale that fit into notches in the posterior ends of the squamosals. These provide support to the cheek region and are important structural supports in an otherwise relatively weak, zygokrotaphic skull.

Content.—Two genera with nine species are recognized:

1. *Epicrionops* Boulenger, 1883; 8 species. Northwestern South America from Venezuela to Peru. E. Taylor (1968).
2. *Rhinatrema* Duméril and Bibron, 1841; 1 species. Guianan region of northeastern South America. Nussbaum and Hoogmoed (1979).

ICHTHYOPHIIDAE Taylor, 1968

Definition.—These Old World caecilians have a combination of primitive and derived characters that are intermediate between those of rhinatrematids and other caecilians. The premaxillae are separate from the nasals; septomaxillae and prefrontals are present, and discrete postfrontals usually are present (Fig. 13-11). The squamosals articulate with the frontal, and temporal fossae are absent. The pterygoids are not in contact with the parasphenoid portion of the basale. The sides of the parasphenoid are not parallel, and the vomers are in contact medially. The columella is pierced by the stapedial artery. There is no bridge between the quadrate and the maxillopalatine. The retroarticular process of the pseudoangular is long and curved.

These moderate-sized caecilians (total length to about 500 mm) have a tail and a subterminal mouth. The tentacular opening is midway between the eye and the nostril or closer to the eye. Primary and secondary annuli (2–4 secondaries per primary) are present throughout the length of the body, bear scales, and are orthoplicate posteriorly. Some ichthyophiids are unicolor gray or black; others have bold pale stripes laterally (Fig. 19-18). Larvae have well-developed lateral-line systems, one or two gill slits, and shallow caudal fins. The three pairs of embryonic gills apparently are absorbed at hatching.

Distribution.—The family is widespread in southeastern Asia, including the Indian subcontinent, Sri Lanka, Sumatra, Borneo, and the Philippines (Fig. 19-17).

Fossil history.—None.

Life history.—Eggs are deposited in mud near water; as many as 54 eggs are in a single clutch of *Ichthyophis glutinosus,* females of which guard the eggs. Free-swimming larvae live in ponds and streams.

Remarks.—Nussbaum (1979a) included the Uraeotyphlidae as a subfamily of the Ichthyophiidae. Although the two families have many characters in common, the uraeotyphlids are cladistically closer to the higher families of caecilians than to the ichthyophiids and are recognized herein as a separate family.

Content.—Two genera with 35 species are recognized:

1. *Caudacaecilia* Taylor, 1968; 5 species. Malaya, Sumatra, Borneo, and the Philippines. E. Taylor (1968).
2. *Ichthyophis* Fitzinger, 1826 (*Epicrium* Wagler, 1828); 30 species. India, Sri Lanka, southeastern Asia, southern Philippines, and western part of Indonesia. E. Taylor (1968).

URAEOTYPHLIDAE Nussbaum, 1979

Definition.—This family of caecilians shares many characters with the ichthyophiids, but uraeotyphlids are cladistically more closely related to the higher caecilian families than to the Ichthyophiidae. The premaxillae are separate from the nasals; septomaxillae, prefrontals, and postfrontals are present. The squamosals articulate with the frontal, and small temporal fossae are present. The

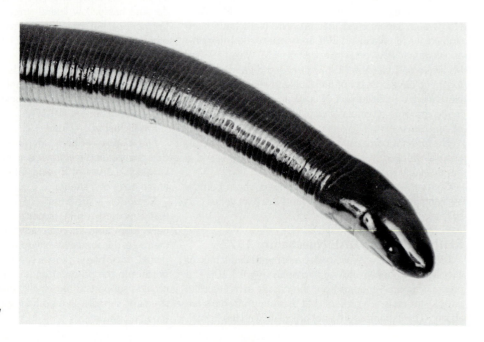

Figure 19-18. *Ichthyophis kohtaoensis* from Thailand. Photo by M. H. Wake.

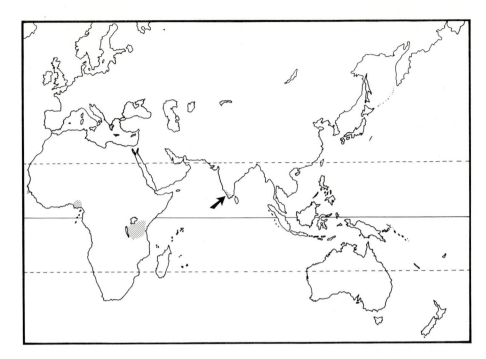

Figure 19-19. Distribution of living members of the family Uraeotyphlidae in India and of the family Scolecomorphidae in Africa.

pterygoids are in weak contact with the parasphenoid portion of the basale. The sides of the parasphenoid are not parallel, and the vomers are in contact medially. The columella is unperforated. There is no bridge between the quadrate and the maxillopalatine. The retroarticular process of the pseudoangular is long and curved.

These small caecilians (total length to about 300 mm) have a tail and a recessed mouth. The tentacular opening is below the nostril. Primary and secondary annuli are present throughout the length of the body; they bear scales, and they are not complete anteriorly. These cylindrical caecilians are dull gray to brown. The larvae are unknown.

Distribution.—This family is known only from southern peninsular India (Fig. 19-19).

Fossil history.—None.

Life history.—Presumably these caecilians are oviparous, possibly with direct development.

Remarks.—Nussbaum (1979a) showed that these caecilians are cladistically closer to higher caecilians than to ichthyophiids, but he regarded them as a subfamily of the Ichthyophiidae. The phylogenetic position of these caecilians is better shown by treating them as a separate family.

Content.—The single genus contains four species:

1. *Uraeotyphlus* Peters, 1879; 4 species. Southern India. Nussbaum (1979a).

SCOLECOMORPHIDAE Taylor, 1969

Definition.—These African caecilians have a suite of unique character states that set them apart from all other caecilians. The premaxillae are separate from the nasals;

Figure 19-20. *Scolecomorphus uluguruensis* from Africa. Photo by B. Fritzsch.

septomaxillae and prefrontals are present, but postfrontals, pterygoids, and columellae are absent. The squamosals do not articulate with the frontal. Temporal fossae are absent in West African species and present in East African species. The sides of the parasphenoid are not parallel, and the vomers are in contact medially. There is no bridge between the quadrate and the maxillopalatine. The retroarticular process of the pseudoangular is long and curved. The eye is covered with bone and protruded on the tentacle.

These are moderately large caecilians with a recessed mouth and no tail; *Scolecomorphus convexus* attains a total length of 448 mm. Secondary annuli and scales are absent. The dorsum is black or brown; in some species the venter is pale (Fig. 19-20).

Distribution.—The family has a discontinuous range in tropical, sub-Saharan Africa (Fig. 19-19); two species are known from Cameroon and three from Tanzania and Malawi.

Fossil history.—None.

Life history.—Embryos with branched gills are like those of species of *Dermophis* that are viviparous.

Remarks.—The skull of scolecomorphids seems to be adapted for burrowing in a different way than those of caeciliids. Although the skull of scolecomorphids is zygokrotaphic with no fusion or loss of roofing bones, it seems to be akinetic.

Content.—One genus contains seven species:

1. *Scolecomorphus* Boulenger, 1883 (*Bdellophis* Boulenger, 1895); 7 species. Tropical sub-Saharan Africa. Nussbaum (1981).

CAECILIIDAE Gray, 1825

Definition.—These terrestrial caecilians have many derived character states shared with other families. The premaxillae are fused with the nasals. Septomaxillae and prefrontals are absent, and postfrontals usually are absent. The squamosals articulate with the frontal, and temporal fossae are absent (except *Geotrypetes*). The pterygoids are fused with the maxillopalatines. The sides of the parasphenoid are not parallel, and the vomers usually are in contact medially (separated by the cultriform process of the parasphenoid in some genera). The columella is perforated or not by the stapedial artery and is firmly articulated with the quadrate. There is no bridge between the quadrate and the maxillopalatine. The retroarticular process of the pseudoangular is long and curved.

Caeciliids have a recessed mouth and no tail. The tentacular opening is anterior to the eye. Secondary annuli are absent anteriorly or throughout the length of the body; scales are present or absent. Although most caeciliids are dull gray or black, some are striped; *Boulengerula boulengeri* and *Microcaecilia albiceps* have pink heads, and *Schistometopum thomense* is bright yellow (Fig. 19-21). Many species are small; *Idiocranium russeli* and *Grandisonia brevis* attain lengths barely exceeding 100 mm, whereas some species grow to lengths of more than 1 m. The largest is *Caecilia thompsoni* with a total length of 1520 mm.

Distribution.—The family is distributed throughout the tropical regions of South and Central America (13 genera), sub-Saharan Africa (6 genera), and the Indian subcontinent (2 genera); 3 genera are endemic to the Seychelles islands in the Indian Ocean (Fig. 19-22).

Fossil history.—The single known fossil caecilian, *Apodops pricei* from the Paleocene of Brazil, tentatively is referred to this family. Estes and M. Wake (1972) indicated that the fossil vertebra is similar to those of the Recent African genus *Geotrypetes*.

Life history.—Some species lay eggs that undergo direct development; others are viviparous. Embryonic gills are triradiate; these and the lateral-line organs (present in some species) are resorbed before birth or hatching. The reproductive mode of too few species is known to draw any conclusions, but most of the New World species for which reproductive data are available are viviparous, and the Indian and Seychellean species are oviparous. Both oviparity and viviparity are known in African caeciliids.

Remarks.—All of the highly specialized burrowing caecilians with stegokrotaphic skulls are grouped in this family. Although most of the known genera and species were reviewed by E. Taylor (1968), the intrafamilial relationships remain obscure. Two subfamilies were proposed by Taylor (1969a) and their contents modified by M. Wake and Campbell (1983). Laurent (1984) suggested that the Caeciliidae should contain only *Caecilia* and *Oscaecilia* and that the other genera should be placed is the Dermophiidae with two subfamilies—the Dermophiinae in which splenial teeth are absent (except in *Gymnopis*) and containing all of the New World genera, and the Herpelinae in which splenial teeth are present (except in *Boulengerula*) and containing all of the Old World genera. However, the character of the fusion of the postfrontal used by Laurent to define the Caeciliidae is not consistent in the genus *Caecilia,* and the characters used to define the Herpelinae and Dermophiinae are not consistent within those subfamilies (as defined by Laurent). Herein two subfamilies are recognized: Dermophiinae with maxillary and premaxillary teeth not enlarged, and Caeciliinae with maxillary and premaxillary teeth enlarged.

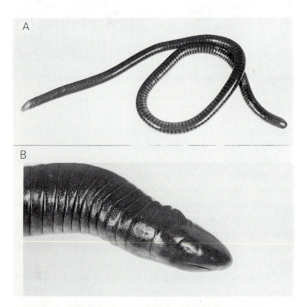

Figure 19-21. A. *Oscaecilia ochrocephala* **from Panama. B.** *Dermophis mexicanus* **from Chiapas, Mexico. Photos by M. H. Wake.**

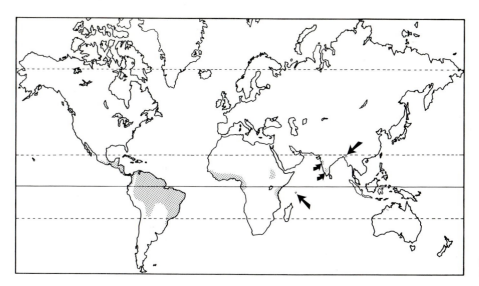

Figure 19-22. Distribution of living members of the family Caeciliidae.

Content.—Twenty-four living genera and one extinct genus contain 88 living and 1 extinct species are grouped into two subfamilies:

CAECILIINAE Gray, 1825

1. *Caecilia* Linnaeus, 1758 (*Amphiumophis* Werner, 1901); 31 species. Northern South America and eastern Panama. E. Taylor (1968).
2. *Microcaecilia* Taylor, 1968; 5 species. Northern South America. Nussbaum and Hoogmoed (1979).
3. *Minascaecilia* Wake and Campbell, 1983; 1 species. Guatemala. M. Wake and Campbell (1983).
4. *Oscaecilia* Taylor, 1968; 7 species. Panama and northern South America. E. Taylor (1968).
5. *Parvicaecilia* Taylor, 1968; 2 species. Northern Colombia. E. Taylor (1968).

DERMOPHIINAE Taylor, 1969.

6. *Afrocaecilia* Taylor, 1968; 3 species. Tanzania and Kenya. E. Taylor (1968).
7. †*Apodops* Estes and Wake, 1972; 1 species. Upper Paleocene of southeastern Brazil. Estes and M. Wake (1972).
8. *Boulengerula* Tornier, 1897; 1 species. Usamabara and Magrotto mountains, Tanzania. E. Taylor (1968).
9. *Brazilotyphlus* Taylor, 1968; 1 species. Amazon Basin, Brazil. E. Taylor (1968).
10. *Copeotyphlinus* Taylor, 1968; 1 species. ?Northern Honduras. Nussbaum (1979c).
11. *Dermophis* Peters, 1879; 3 species. Southern Mexico to northwestern Colombia. J. Savage and M. Wake (1972).

12. *Gegeneophis* Peters, 1879 (*Gegenes* Günther, 1875); 3 species. India. E. Taylor (1968).
13. *Geotrypetes* Peters, 1879; 4 species. Tropical West Africa and western Ethiopia. E. Taylor (1968).
14. *Grandisonia* Taylor, 1968; 5 species. Seychelles islands. E. Taylor (1968).
15. *Gymnopis* Peters, 1874 (*Cryptosophus* Boulenger, 1883); 1 species. Honduras to Panama. J. Savage and M. Wake (1972).
16. *Herpele* Peters, 1879; 2 species. Tropical West Africa. E. Taylor (1968).
17. *Hypogeophis* Peters, 1879; 1 species. Seychelles islands. E. Taylor (1968).
18. *Idiocranium* Parker, 1936; 1 species. Nigeria. E. Taylor (1968).
19. *Indotyphlus* Taylor, 1960; 1 species. India. E. Taylor (1968).
20. *Lutkenotyphlus* Taylor, 1968; 1 species. Southeastern Brazil. E. Taylor (1968).
21. *Mimosiphonops* Taylor, 1968; 1 species. Southeastern Brazil. E. Taylor (1968).
22. *Praslinia* Boulenger, 1909; 1 species. Seychelles islands. E. Taylor (1968).
23. *Pseudosiphonops* Taylor, 1968; 1 species. Brazil. E. Taylor (1968).
24. *Schistometopum* Parker, 1941; 5 species. Kenya, Tanzania, and islands in the Gulf of Guinea, West Africa. E. Taylor (1968).
25. *Siphonops* Wagler, 1830; 6 species. Tropical South America east of the Andes. E. Taylor (1968).

TYPHLONECTIDAE Taylor, 1968

Definition.—These aquatic caecilians have a suite of derived characters. The premaxillae are fused with the

Figure 19-23. *Typhlonectes compressicauda* from Leticia, Colombia. Photo by M. H. Wake.

are not parallel, and the vomers are in contact medially. The columella is unperforated and is firmly attached to the quadrate. There is no bridge between the quadrate and the maxillopalatine. The retroarticular process of the pseudoangular is long and curved.

Typhlonectids are completely aquatic (Fig. 19-23); the posterior part of the body is laterally compressed. There is no tail, and the mouth is recessed. Secondary annuli and scales are absent. The largest species, *Typhlonectes eiselti*, attains a total length of 725 mm. The dorsal color is gray to olive brown or bluish black, and the venter usually is a paler color. The choanae have well-developed valves, and the tongue has large narial plugs. The tentacle is small and usually protrudes just behind the nostrils. Males have modified anal regions that seem to serve for adhering the vent to the cloaca of the female during aquatic copulation.

Distribution.—The family has a discontinuous distribution in South America with the majority of the species in the northwestern part of the continent—Amazon, Orinoco, and Magdalena river drainages, but several species occur in the Río La Plata drainage in Argentina and Brazil (Fig. 19-24).

Fossil history.—None.

Life history.—Embryos of these viviparous caecilians have one pair of expanded, sheetlike external gills. These are resorbed, and the gill slits close before birth.

Remarks.—Nussbaum (1977) emphasized that the skulls of typhlonectids are like those of caeciliids specialized for burrowing; thus, he suggested that the aquatic typhlonectids evolved from a fossorial ancestor.

Content.—Four genera contain 19 species:

1. *Chthonerpeton* Peters, 1879; 6 species. Southern Brazil and northern Argentina. E. Taylor (1968).
2. *Nectocaecilia* Taylor, 1968; 5 species. Amazon Basin and Caribbean drainages in South America; ?Buenos Aires. E. Taylor (1968).
3. *Potomotyphlus* Taylor, 1968; 2 species. Amazon and Orinoco Basins, South America. E. Taylor (1968).
4. *Typhlonectes* Peters, 1879; 6 species. Northern South America. E. Taylor (1968).

Superorder SALIENTIA Laurenti, 1768

Definition.—Primitive salientians have a short tail; in anurans the caudal vertebrae are fused into a postsacral rod, the coccyx (or urostyle). The vertebral column contains no more than 14 presacral vertebrae. The ilia and proximal tarsal elements are elongated. The parasphenoid usually bears lateral alae posteriorly, and the pterygoid usually is triradiate. Teeth are absent on the dentary (except in one Recent species). Lacrimal, postorbital, jugal, postfrontal, postparietal, tabular, supratemporal, supraoccipital, basioccipital, and ectopterygoid bones are

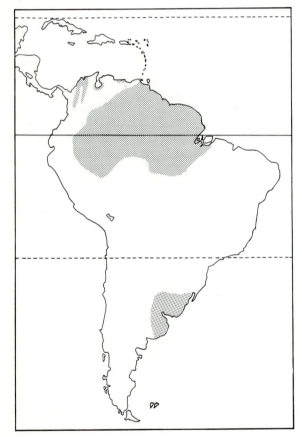

Figure 19-24. Distribution of living members of the family Typhlonectidae.

nasals; septomaxillae, prefrontals, and postfrontals are absent. The squamosals articulate with the frontal; temporal fossae are present. The pterygoids usually are fused with the maxillopalatines. The sides of the parasphenoid absent. Ribs are present in some taxa. The aquatic larvae (when present) lack true teeth, and most have internal gills with branchial baskets.

Content.—The superorder contains the Triassic frog-like *Triadobatrachus* and the anurans.

Order †PROANURA Romer, 1945

The oldest known salientian has many froglike features (see account of †Protobatrachidae for characters and discussion).

†PROTOBATRACHIDAE Piveteau, 1937

Definition.—A single fossil from the Triassic has a total length of about 100 mm, a broad head with large, paired (?) frontoparietals, triradiate pterygoids, and palatines present only laterally (?). There are 14 presacral vertebrae lacking transverse processes and bearing bicapitate ribs that presumably articulate in a manner similar to that of salamanders and caecilians; six postsacral (caudal) vertebrae are present. The ilial shaft is elongate and has a dorsal prominence. The proximal tarsal elements, the tibiale and fibulare (= astragalus and calcaneum) are elongate but not fused.

Fossil history.—This family is represented by a single nodule with dorsal and ventral impressions of the skeleton from the Lower Triassic of Madagascar.

Remarks.—According to Estes and Reig (1973), who summarized previous work on this fossil, the specimen probably represents a young individual of an aquatic animal that may be the sister group of anurans.

Content.—There is a single monotypic genus:

1. †*Triadobatrachus* Kuhn, 1962 (†*Protobatrachus* Piveteau, 1937); 1 species. Lower Triassic of Madagascar.

Order ANURA Rafinesque, 1815

Definition.—The frogs and toads are tailless amphibians with elongate hindlimbs; the foot is lengthened by the elongated proximal tarsal elements, the tibiale and fibulare (= astragalus and calcaneum), which are fused at least proximally and distally. The vertebral column consists of 5–9 (modally 8) presacral vertebrae. All vertebrae bear transverse processes, except the first (atlas) unless it is fused with Presacral II. Ribs are freely associated with, or fused to, the second, third, and fourth (also fifth and sixth in some) presacral vertebrae in some primitive families. The postsacral vertebrae are fused into a rodlike coccyx. The otic-occipital region is composed of prootics and exoccipitals (fused or unfused).

Distribution.—Anurans are cosmopolitan except for high latitudes in the Arctic, Antarctica, some oceanic islands, and some extremely xeric deserts. The greatest diversity of anurans is in the tropics. Nine families occur in South America, eight in Africa, and seven in tropical Asia, whereas only six occur in each of temperate North America and Eurasia. Four families occur in Australia, and four are on Madagascar; one family is endemic to the Seychelles islands in the Indian Ocean.

Fossil history.—Anurans are rather poorly represented in the fossil record beginning in the Jurassic of Europe, North America, and South America and extending through the Pleistocene. Six named fossil genera of anurans are not assignable to recognized families:

1. †*Comobatrachus* Hecht and Estes, 1960; 1 species. Late Jurassic of North America.
2. †*Eobatrachus* Moodie, 1912; 1 species. Late Jurassic of North America.
3. †*Eorubeta* Hecht, 1960; 1 species. Eocene of North America.
4. †*Montsechobatrachus* Fejérváry, 1923; 1 species. Late Jurassic or Early Cretaceous of Spain.
5. †*Theatonius* Fox, 1976; 1 species. Late Cretaceous of North America.
6. †*Tregobatrachus* Holman, 1975; 1 species. Lower Pliocene of North America.

Additionally, nine nominal genera are of unknown status; these are †*Asphaerion* Meyer, 1847; †*Baryboas* Gistel, 1848; †*Batrachulina* Kuhn, 1962; †*Batrachus* Pomel, 1853; †*Bufonopsis* Kuhn, 1941; †*Opisthocoelellus* Kuhn, 1941; †*Opisthocoelorum* Kuhn, 1941; †*Protophrynus* Pomel, 1853; and †*Ranavus* Portis, 1885.

Life history.—Anurans have a diversity of reproductive modes. Fertilization is external, except in *Ascaphus, Mertensophryne micranotis,* and some species of *Nectophrynoides* and *Eleutherodactylus.* The generalized (and presumably primitive) mode of life history involves aquatic eggs and larvae. Specialized modes include deposition of eggs out of water but aquatic tadpoles, terrestrial eggs undergoing direct development, ovoviviparity, and viviparity. Many kinds of anurans exhibit parental care by guarding or transporting eggs or tadpoles (for details, see Chapter 2).

Remarks.—The higher taxonomy of anurans is not well established. Present knowledge of many characters and the direction of their evolutionary change does not permit their utilization in the reconstruction of a phylogeny (Chapter 17) or the concomitant construction of a meaningful classification of anurans. Recent attempts at a classification of anurans by Duellman (1975), Laurent (1979), and Dubois (1983) have maintained paraphyletic groups. P. Starrett's (1973) classification based on larval characters was disputed by Sokol (1975) in his re-evaluation of larval characters. Moreover, the placement of some genera and subfamilies has shifted from one family to another. For example, are the Madagascaran mantellines ranids or rhacophorids? Or, are the Madagascaran scaphiophrynines ranids or microhylids? Some workers recognize the Myobatrachidae; others include those Austro-Papuan frogs in the Leptodactylidae. Are the South African frogs of the genus *Heleophryne* leptodactylids, myobatrachids, or neither? Are the relationships of the Sooglossidae with the megophryine pelobatids, myobatrachids, or ranids? Probably when a well-corroborated cladogram has been constructed these questions will be seen to have been the result of confusion between similarity based on retained primitive features and similarity based on shared-derived features.

Reig (1958) proposed the subordinal names Archaeobatrachia and Neobatrachia to include fundamentally those groups of anurans that had been referred to as archaic and advanced, respectively. Both Noble (1922, 1931b) and J. D. Lynch (1973) posited that some families could be regarded as transitional between these two categories. Duellman (1975) employed Reig's subordinal classification and recognized six superfamilies; these also were used by Laurent (1979) and with slight modification by Dubois (1983) (Table 19-1). Sokol (1977a) recognized two suborders, the Discoglossoidei and the Ranoidei, based on separate trigeminal and facial ganglia and free ribs in the former and fused ganglia and no ribs in the latter. As a compromise between the classifications of Duellman (1975) and Sokol (1977a), Laurent (1979) proposed the subordinal name Mesobatrachia to include part of the

archaic and transitional families. Based on apparent developmental differences of the frontoparietals, Roček (1981) proposed the order Archaeosalientia for *Pelobates,* pipids, palaeobatrachids, and rhinophrynids; the other anurans and *Triadobatrachus* were placed in the order Neosalientia.

The classification adopted here is rather traditional and generally follows that of the most recent checklist of anurans (D. Frost, 1985) in the recognition of families, except that arthroleptines and hemisines are regarded as subfamilies of the Ranidae rather than separate families. No superfamilies are recognized.

Content.—Twenty-one living and one extinct family are recognized. These contain 301 living genera with 3438 species, plus 98 extinct species. Including those fossil genera not assigned to family, there are 38 extinct genera with 64 species.

LEIOPELMATIDAE Mivart, 1869

Definition.—There are nine ectochordal, presacral vertebrae with cartilaginous intervertebral joints and nonimbricate neural arches. Presacrals I and II are not fused, and the atlantal cotyles of Presacral I are closely juxta-

Table 19-1. Comparison of Three Recent Classifications of Anurans

Duellman (1975)	Laurent (1979)	Dubois (1983)
Suborder Archaeobatrachia	Suborder Archaeobatrachia	Suborder Discoglossoidei
Superfamily Discoglossoidea	Superfamily Discoglossoidea	Superfamily Discoglossoidea
Family Leiopelmatidae	Family Leiopelmatidae	Family Discoglossidae
Discoglossidae	Discoglossidae	Leiopelmatidae
Superfamily Pipoidea	Suborder Mesobatrachia	Suborder Pipoidei
Family †Palaeobatrachidae	Superfamily Pipoidea	Superfamily Pipoidea
Pipidae	Family Pipidae	Family Pipidae
Rhinophrynidae	†Palaeobatrachidae	Rhinophrynidae
Superfamily Pelobatoidea	Rhinophrynidae	Superfamily Pelobatoidea
Family Pelobatidae	Superfamily Pelobatoidea	Family Pelobatidae
Pelodytidae	Family Pelobatidae	Pelodytidae
Suborder Neobatrachia	Pelodytidae	Superorder Ranoidei
Superfamily Bufonoidea	Suborder Neobatrachia	Superfamily Hyloidea
Family Myobatrachidae[a]	Superfamily Bufonoidea	Family Rheobatrachidae
Leptodactylidae	Family Rheobatrachidae	Myobatrachidae
Bufonidae	Myobatrachidae	Sooglossidae
Brachycephalidae	Sooglossidae	Leptodactylidae
Rhinodermatidae	Leptodactylidae	Dendrobatidae
Dendrobatidae	Phyllobatidae[b]	Bufonidae
Pseudidae	Bufonidae	Brachycephalidae
Hylidae[c]	Brachycephalidae	Rhinodermatidae
Centrolenidae	Rhinodermatidae	Pseudidae
Superfamily Microhyloidea	Pseudidae	Hylidae
Family Microhylidae	Hylidae	Centrolenidae
Superfamily Ranoidea	Centrolenidae	Pelodryadidae
Family Sooglossidae	Pelodryadidae	Superfamily Microhyloidea
Ranidae[d]	Superfamily Microhyloidea	Family Microhylidae
Hyperoliidae	Family Microhylidae	Superfamily Ranoidea
Rhacophoridae	Superfamily Ranoidea	Family Ranidae
	Family Hyperoliidae[f]	Rhacophoridae
	Ranidae	Arthroleptidae
	Hemisidae	Hyperoliidae
		Hemisidae

[a]Includes Rheobatrachidae. [d]Includes Arthroleptidae and Hemisidae.
[b]Equals Dendrobatidae. [e]Includes Rhacophoridae.
[c]Includes Pelodryadidae. [f]Includes Arthroleptidae.

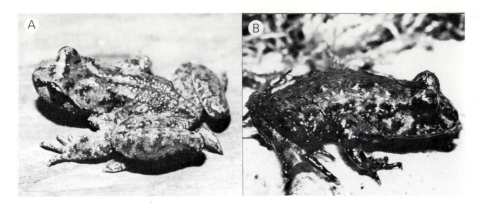

Figure 19-25. A. *Ascaphus truei* from Mount Ranier, Washington, U.S.A. (photo by J. T. Collins). **B.** *Leiopelma hochstetteri* from New Zealand (photo by J. V. Vindum).

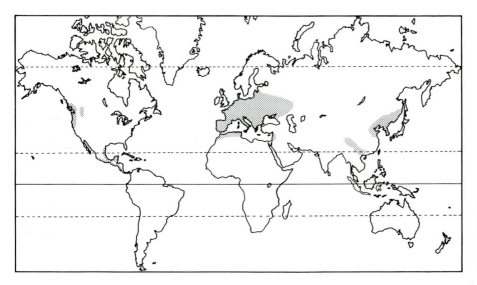

Figure 19-26. Distribution of living members of the family Leiopelmatidae (North America and New Zealand), Discoglossidae (Eurasia and North Africa), and Rhinophrynidae (North and Central America).

posed. Free ribs are present on Presacrals II–IV and occasionally on Presacral V in adults (on Presacrals II–V and occasionally on Presacral VI in *Notobatrachus*). The sacrum has narrowly dilated diapophyses and has a contiguous cartilaginous connection with the coccyx, which has transverse processes proximally. The pectoral girdle is arciferal and has a cartilaginous omosternum and sternum; the anterior end of the scapula is overlain by the clavicle in *Ascaphus* but not in *Leiopelma* or *Notobatrachus*. Palatines are absent; a parahyoid bone is present, and the cricoid ring is complete. The maxillae and premaxillae are dentate. The astragalus and calcaneum are fused only proximally and distally; there are three tarsalia, and the phalangeal formula is normal. The m. sartorius is not discrete from the m. semitendinosus, and the tendon of the latter inserts ventral to the m. gracilis; the m. glutaeus magnus lacks an accessory tendon, and the m. adductor magnus lacks an accessory head. The pupil is vertically elliptical. Amplexus is inguinal. Development is direct in *Leiopelma*. The aquatic Type III larvae of *Ascaphus* have beaks and many rows of denticles; a single median spiracle is formed by a hiatus in the operculum, and the trigeminal and facial ganglia are separate. The

diploid chromosome complement varies from 5 pairs of macrochromosomes and 18 pairs of microchromosomes (*Ascaphus*) to 11 pairs of macrochromosomes and 0–8 pairs of microchromosomes (*Leiopelma).*

Living leiopelmatids are small frogs attaining snout-vent lengths of no more than 50 mm. However, the Jurassic *Notobatrachus* attained 150 mm, and a subfossil *Leiopelma* had a snout-vent length of about 100 mm. The terrestrial *Leiopelma* and the aquatic *Ascaphus* are dull gray or brown and have little webbing on the feet (Fig. 19-25). Living leiopelmatids are unique among anurans in having vestigial tail-wagging muscles (m. caudaliopuboischiotibialis); *Ascaphus* is unique in having an intromittent organ formed from a cloacal extension in males, and *Leiopelma* is unique among amphibians in possessing cartilaginous inscriptional ribs.

Distribution.—Living leiopelmatids occur only in New Zealand, where they are the only native anurans, and in northwestern United States and extreme southwestern Canada (Fig. 19-26).

Fossil history.—The family is known from two extinct genera from the Jurassic of Patagonian Argentina.

Life history.—*Ascaphus* deposits unpigmented eggs in

strings adherent to undersides of rocks in mountain streams; the tadpoles develop in torrential streams and have an oral disc and up to 16 rows of denticles. *Leiopelma* deposits large, unpigmented eggs encased in a membrane in damp terrestrial situations; the eggs undergo direct development.

Remarks.—Some workers have used the familial name Ascaphidae dating from Fejérváry, 1923. J. Savage (1973) recognized both families, one for each of the living genera. Even though these genera are associated principally by primitive character states, their recognition as distributional relicts of a single formerly widespread group is supported by the presence of fossils in Jurassic formations in Argentina (Estes and Reig, 1973).

Content.—The two living genera contain four species; two extinct species are placed in two other genera:

1. *Ascaphus* Stejneger, 1899; 1 species. Northwestern United States and adjacent Canada. Metter (1968b).
2. *Leiopelma* Fitzinger, 1861; 3 species. New Zealand. B. Bell (1978).
3. †*Notobatrachus* Reig, 1957; 1 species. Late Jurassic of Argentina. Estes and Reig (1973).
4. †*Vieraella* Reig, 1961; 1 species. Early Jurassic of Argentina. Estes and Reig (1973).

DISCOGLOSSIDAE Günther, 1859

Definition.—There are eight stegochordal, opisthocoelous presacral vertebrae with imbricate neural arches. Presacrals I and II are not fused, and the atlantal cotyles of Presacral I are closely juxtaposed. Free ribs are present on Presacrals II–IV. The sacrum has expanded diapophyses and a bicondylar articulation with the coccyx (monocondylar in *Barbourula*), which has transverse processes proximally. The pectoral girdle is arciferal and has a cartilaginous omosternum (greatly reduced in *Bombina* and *Discoglossus*) and sternum; the anterior end of the scapula is overlain by the clavicle. Palatines are absent; a parahyoid bone (or bones) is present, and the cricoid ring is complete. The maxillae and premaxillae are dentate. The astragalus and calcaneum are fused only

proximally and distally; there are three tarsalia, and the phalangeal formula is normal. The m. sartorius is not discrete from the m. semitendinosus, and the tendon of the latter inserts ventral to the m. gracilis; the m. glutaeus magnus lacks an accessory tendon (present and fleshy in *Barbourula* and *Bombina*), and the m. adductor magnus lacks an accessory head. The pupil is vertically elliptical in *Alytes* and triangular in the others. Amplexus is inguinal. All have aquatic Type III larvae with beaks and denticles; a single median spiracle is formed by a hiatus in the operculum, and the trigeminal and facial ganglia are separate. The diploid chromosome complement varies from 22 to 28 macrochromosomes; 8 pairs of microchromosomes in *Alytes* give a total complement of 38.

Living discoglossids vary from the small (40–50 mm in snout-vent length) toadlike *Alytes, Baleaphryne,* and *Bombina* to the large (85-mm) aquatic *Barbourula* with webbed hands and feet (Fig. 19-27). The species of *Bombina* have black mottling on a bright orange or yellow venter.

Distribution.—The distribution of living discoglossids is disjunct in Eurasia and adjacent regions. The major distribution of the family includes Europe eastward through Turkey, Israel, and Syria to western U.S.S.R., plus North Africa. *Bombina* also occurs in eastern U.S.S.R., China, Vietnam, and Korea, and *Barbourula* is known from the Philippines and Borneo (Fig. 19-26).

Fossil history.—The family is comparatively well represented by fossils from Europe (Upper Jurassic through Quaternary) and North America (Upper Cretaceous and Paleocene). The family also is known from the upper Eocene of England and the middle Miocene of the Caucasus Mountains. Eight extinct genera are recognized; four Recent genera are represented in the fossil record.

Life history.—Insofar as is known, all discoglossids have aquatic eggs and larvae. *Bombina* lays pigmented eggs singly in ponds, and *Discoglossus* deposits clumps of pigmented eggs in ponds. *Barbourula* has unpigmented eggs and presumably deposits them in streams. *Alytes* mates on land. The eggs are exuded in strings; subsequent to fertilization, the amplectant male shifts to a cephalic embrace and pushes his legs among the eggs until they

Figure 19-27. A. *Alytes obstetricans,* male carrying eggs, from Provincia Oviedo, Spain. **B.** *Discoglossus pictus* from Provincia Cádiz, Spain. Photos by S. D. Busack.

adhere to his back and thighs. The male carries the eggs (into and out of water) until they are ready to hatch, at which time he enters the water. The tadpoles of *Barbourula* are unknown; otherwise, discoglossid tadpoles are a generalized pond-type with two upper and three lower rows of denticles.

Remarks.—The family is associated with the Leiopelmatidae on the basis of plesiomorphic characters and two synapomorphies of the larvae: (1) extensive fusions among hyobranchial elements, and (2) operculum greatly elongated posteriorly with a single midventral spiracular opening (Sokol, 1975). Lanza et at (1976) showed that *Discoglossus* was immunologically distant from *Bombina* and *Alytes* and suggested that the latter two genera should be placed in a separate family, the Bombinidae. (*Barbourula* was not compared, and *Baleaphryne* was unknown at the time.) Estes and Sanchíz (1982) discussed intrafamilial relations and retained all of the genera in one family.

Content.—Fourteen living species are placed in five genera. Eleven species are recognized in eight extinct genera:

1. *Alytes* Wagler, 1830 (*Obstetricans* Dugés, 1834; *Ammoryctis* Lataste, 1879); 2 species. Western, central, and southern Europe, and northwestern Africa. Upper Miocene and Pleistocene of western Europe. Crespo (1979).

2. *Baleaphryne* Sanchíz and Alcover, 1977; 1 species. Mallorca, Balearic islands, Spain. Pleistocene of Mallorca and Minorca, Spain. Hemmer and Alcover (1984).

3. †*Baranophrys* Kretzoi, 1956; 1 species. Pleistocene of Hungary.

4. *Barbourula* Taylor and Noble, 1924; 2 species. Palawan, Philippine Islands, and northern Borneo.

5. *Bombina* Oken, 1816 (*Bombinator* Merrem, 1820); 6 species. Europe, Turkey, and western U.S.S.R.; eastern Asia, including U.S.S.R., China, Korea, and Vietnam. Middle Miocene through Pleistocene of Europe.

6. *Discoglossus* Otth, 1837 (*Pseudes* Wagler, 1834; *Colodactylus* Tschudi, 1845); 3 species. Southern Europe, northwestern Africa, Israel, and Syria. Miocene through the Pleistocene of southern Europe.

7. †*Eodiscoglossus* Villada, 1957; 1 species. Upper Jurassic and Lower Cretaceous of Spain. Estes and Sanchíz (1982).

8. †*Latonia* Meyer, 1843 (†*Diplopelturus* Deperet, 1897; †*Miopelobates* Wettstein-Westersheimb, 1955); 4 species. Miocene of Europe.

9. †*Paradiscoglossus* Estes and Sanchíz, 1982; 1 species. Upper Cretaceous of Wyoming, U.S.A.

Figure 19-28. *Rhinophrynus dorsalis* from Campeche, Mexico. Photo by J. T. Collins.

10. †*Pelophilus* Tschudi, 1838; 1 species. Middle Miocene of Germany.

11. †*Prodiscoglossus* Friant, 1944; 1 species. Oligocene of France.

12. †*Scotiophryne* Estes, 1969; 1 species. Upper Cretaceous and middle Paleocene of Montana and Wyoming, U.S.A.

13. †*Spondylophryne* Kretzoi, 1956; 1 species. Pleistocene of Hungary.

RHINOPHRYNIDAE Günther, 1859

Definition.—There are eight, ectochordal, modified opisthocoelous presacral vertebrae (the intervertebral body tends to adhere to the anterior end of the centrum, but is not fused to it) with imbricate neural arches. Presacrals I and II are not fused, and the atlantal cotyles of Presacral I are closely juxtaposed. Free ribs are absent. The sacrum has expanded diapophyses and a bicondylar articulation with the coccyx, which lacks transverse processes. The pectoral girdle is arciferal and lacks an omosternum and sternum; the anterior end of the scapula is overlain by the clavicle. Palatines are absent; a parahyoid bone is present, and the cricoid ring is incomplete dorsally. The maxillae and premaxillae are edentate. The astragalus and calcaneum are fused only proximally and distally; there are two tarsalia, and the phalangeal formula is normal except for the loss of one phalange on the first toe. The m. sartorius is distinct from the m. semitendinosus, and the tendon of the latter penetrates the m. gracilis; the m. glutaeus magnus has no accessory tendon, and the m. adductor magnus has no accessory head. The pupil is vertical. Amplexus is inguinal. The aquatic Type I larvae have no beaks or denticles; paired, ventrolateral spiracles are formed as hiatuses in the operculum, and the trigeminal and facial ganglia are fused. The diploid chromosome complement is 22.

This fossorial, toadlike anuran has a robust body, short limbs, smooth skin, minute head, and a body length of about 75 mm (Fig. 19-28). The inner metatarsal tubercle is enlarged and spadelike; the frogs dig into soil rapidly by lateral movements of the feet. *Rhinophrynus* may be unique among anurans in having a tongue that is catapulted out of a small mouth; the small, pointed snout is calloused.

Distribution.—This family inhabits subhumid lowland areas from southern Texas, U.S.A., and Michoacán, Mexico, to Costa Rica (Fig. 19-26).

Fossil history.—Rhinophrynids are known from the late Paleocene and middle Eocene of Wyoming and the early Oligocene of Saskatchewan, Canada.

Life history.—*Rhinophrynus* spends most of its life underground. The frogs emerge only after heavy rains. Males call while floating on the surface of temporary ponds; the vocal sacs are paired and internal. Eggs are deposited in masses and subsequently float singly to the surface. The pelagic, filter-feeding tadpoles have 11 barbels (Fig. 6-14B).

Remarks.—Rhinophrynids are considered to be the sister group of the pipids and palaeobatrachids; this relationship is based mainly on larval characters of pipids and rhinophrynids (Sokol, 1975). However, on the basis of phenetic immunological distance, Maxson and Daugherty (1980) suggested that *Rhinophrynus* was more closely, albeit still distantly, related to *Ascaphus* (Leiopelmatidae).

Content.—A single living genus contains one living and one extinct species; another species is placed in an extinct genus:

1. †*Eorhinophrynus* Hecht, 1959; 1 species. Late Paleocene and middle Eocene of Wyoming, U.S.A.
2. *Rhinophrynus* Duméril and Bibron, 1841; 1 species. Rio Grande Embayment of Texas and Michoacán, Mexico, southward to Costa Rica. One fossil species from the early Oligocene of Saskatchewan, Canada. Fouquette (1969).

†PALAEOBATRACHIDAE Cope, 1865

Definition.—(Data incomplete). There are seven or eight stegochordal, procoelous presacral vertebrae with imbricate neural arches; the last two presacral vertebrae are fused with the sacrum in some specimens. Presacrals I and II are fused, and the atlantal cotyles of Presacral I are juxtaposed. Ribs are free in subadults and ankylosed to the transverse processes of Presacrals II–VI in adults. The sacrum has dilated diapophyses and a bicondylar articulation with the coccyx, which lacks transverse processes (present proximally in some subadults). The pectoral girdle is arciferal; the anterior end of the scapula is overlain by the clavicle. Palatines are absent; a parahyoid bone is present. The maxillae and premaxillae are dentate. The astragalus and calcaneum are fused only proximally and distally; there are two tarsalia, and the phalangeal formula is normal for the hand but increased in the foot by the addition of an extra phalange in the fifth toe. Aquatic Type I larvae had at least three pairs of

barbels and may have had paired spiracles (interpretations vary).

Palaeobatrachids were *Xenopus*-like aquatic frogs with fully webbed feet. Some species attained a snout-vent length of 120 mm. The teeth are elongate and nonpedicellate.

Fossil history.—Palaeobatrachids are well represented in the fossil beds from the Eocene through the Pliocene of Europe; specimens from the Upper Jurassic and the Pleistocene of Europe also are referred to this family. Upper Cretaceous specimens from North America formerly referred to the discoglossid genus *Barbourula* are palaeobatrachids (Estes and Sanchíz, 1982).

Remarks.—Palaeobatrachids apparently are the sister group of the Pipidae, from which they differ by having procoelous, instead of opisthocoelous, vertebrae and an extra phalange on the fifth toe (Estes and Reig, 1973). The family has been studied extensively by Špinar (1972), and much more material now is available from the Messel Quarry in Germany.

Content.—At least 17 species in five extinct genera are recognized:

1. †*Albionbatrachus* Meszoely, Špinar, and Ford, 1984; 1 species. Eocene of Isle of Wight, England.
2. †*Lithobatrachus* Parker, 1929; 1 species. Lower Miocene of Europe. Sanchíz (1981).
3. †*Neusibatrachus* Seiffert, 1972; 2 species. Jurassic-Cretaceous boundary of Spain and Miocene of Czechoslovakia.
4. †*Palaeobatrachus* Tschudi, 1838 (†*Palaeophrynos* Giebel, 1850; †*Pelobatinopsis* Kuhn, 1941; †*Quinquevertebron* Kuhn, 1941); 12 species. Eocene through Pliocene of Europe. Špinar (1972).
5. †*Pliobatrachus* Fejérváry, 1917; 1 species. Pleistocene of Germany. Sanchíz and Mlynarski (1979).

PIPIDAE Gray, 1825

Definition.—There are 6–8 epichordal, opisthocoelous, presacral vertebrae with imbricate neural arches. Presacrals I and II are fused (unfused in *Xenopus*), and the atlantal cotyles of Presacral I are juxtaposed (separate in *Pipa*). Presacral VIII is fused with the sacrum in some *Pipa*. The ribs are free in subadults of living genera and in adults of Early Cretaceous taxa, but are ankylosed to the transverse processes of Presacrals II–IV in adults of living taxa. The sacrum has expanded diapophyses and is fused with the coccyx, which usually lacks proximal transverse processes free of the sacrum. The pectoral girdle is pseudofirmisternal and lacks an omosternum. The sternum is greatly expanded, and the epicoracoid cartilages are elaborated posterior to the coracoids. The clavicle and scapula are fused, except in most *Pipa*, in which the anterior end of the scapula is overlain by the

Figure 19-29. A. *Xenopus gilli* from Cape Flats, South Africa (photo by J. Visser). **B.** *Pipa pipa* from Surinam (photo by K. T. Nemuras).

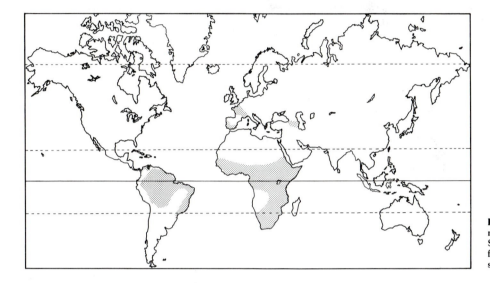

Figure 19-30. Distribution of living members of the family Pipidae in South America and Africa and the family Pelodytidae in Europe and southwestern Asia.

clavicle. Palatines are absent; a parahyoid is absent, and the cricoid ring is complete. The maxillae and premaxillae have nonpedicellate teeth in *Xenopus* and some species of *Pipa,* and they are edentate in other species of *Pipa, Hymenochirus,* and *Pseudhymenochirus.* The astragalus and calcaneum are fused only proximally and distally; there are two tarsalia, and the phalangeal formula is normal. The m. sartorius is not discrete from the m. semitendinosus (partially separate in *Xenopus*), and the tendon of the latter penetrates the m. gracilis; the m. gluteus magnus has an accessory tendon, and the m. adductor magnus lacks an accessory head. The pupil is round. Amplexus is inquinal. The aquatic Type I larvae lack beaks and denticles; paired, ventrolateral spiracles are formed as hiatuses in the operculum (spiracles absent in *Hymenochirus*), and the trigeminal and facial ganglia are fused. The diploid chromosome complement is 20–36; some species of *Xenopus* (2 N = 36) are polyploids.

These strictly aquatic frogs have long, unwebbed fingers (webbed in *Hymenochirus* and *Pseudhymenochirus*) and large, fully webbed feet; in all except *Pipa,* the toes terminate in clawlike, keratinized tips (Fig. 19-29).

Lateral-line organs are present (except in *Hymenochirus* and *Pseudhymenochirus);* the eyes are small and dorsal, and eyelids are poorly developed or absent. The range in size of living pipids is contained within the genus *Pipa*— 44 mm in *P. parva* to 171 mm in *P. pipa.* Pipids are unique among frogs in lacking a tongue.

Distribution.—The range of the family is disjunct; it occurs in tropical South America east of the Andes and in adjacent Panama and in sub-Saharan Africa (Fig. 19-30).

Fossil history.—Pipids are better represented in the fossil record than most families of anurans (see Báez, 1981, for review). They are known from the Lower Cretaceous of Israel, Upper Cretaceous through the Miocene of Africa, and the Upper Cretaceous and Paleocene of South America.

Life history.—African pipids deposit small, pigmented eggs on vegetation or as a surface film in quiet water; the tadpoles have a single pair of barbels (Fig. 6-14A) and are pelagic filter-feeders (except *Hymenochirus* which lacks barbels and is carnivorous). In *Pipa,* the eggs are imbedded in the dorsal skin of the female; in some species (e.g., *P. carvalhoi*) the eggs hatch into filter-feeding tadpoles, and in others (e.g., *P. pipa*) the eggs develop directly into froglets. *Hymenochirus* and *Pipa* have a complex courtship involving aquatic acrobatics (see Chapter 3).

Remarks.—Some authors (e.g., Dubois, 1983) recognize two subfamilies—the Pipinae for the South American *Pipa* and the Xenopinae (or the Dactylethrinae) for the African genera. Although larval African pipids share four synapomorphies, the adults of *Hymenochirus* are divergent from other pipids (Sokol, 1977b); moreover, the division of the Pipidae does not take into account the diverse fossil pipids, which include nominal *Xenopus* in South America.

Content.—Four extant genera contain 26 living species. Six extinct species are grouped into five genera, and six others are placed in the extant genus *Xenopus*:

1. †*Cordicephalus* Nevo, 1968; 2 species. Lower Cretaceous of Israel. Nevo (1968).
2. †*Eoxenopoides* Haughton, 1931; 1 species. Upper Eocene or Oligocene of South Africa. Estes (1977).
3. *Hymenochirus* Boulenger, 1896; 4 species. Equatorial western Africa. Perret (1966).
4. *Pipa* Laurenti, 1768 (*Piparia* Rafinesque, 1815; *Asterodactylus* Wagler, 1830; *Leptopus* Mayer, 1835; *Protopipa* Noble, 1925; *Hemipipa* Miranda-Ribeiro, 1937); 7 species. Northern South America east of the Andes; eastern Panama. Trueb (1984).
5. *Pseudhymenochirus* Chabanaud, 1920; 1 species. Western Africa in Guinea and Sierra Leone.
6. †*Saltenia* Reig, 1959; 1 species. Upper Cretaceous of Argentina. Báez (1981).
7. †*Shomronella* Estes, Špinar and Nevo, 1978; 1 species. Lower Cretaceous of Israel. Estes et al. (1978).
8. †*Thoraciliacus* Nevo, 1968; 1 species. Lower Cretaceous of Israel. Nevo (1968).
9. *Xenopus* Wagler, 1827 (*Dactylethra* Cuvier, 1829; *Silurana* Gray, 1864; †*Shelania* Casamiquela, 1961; †*Libycus* Špinar, 1980); 14 species. Sub-Saharan Africa. Two fossil species in South America (middle or upper Paleocene of Brazil, upper Paleocene of Argentina) and four species in Africa (Upper Cretaceous of Niger, Oligocene of Libya, Miocene of Morocco and South Africa) (Estes, 1975; Tinsley, 1981).

PELOBATIDAE Bonaparte, 1850

Definition.—There are eight stegochordal presacral vertebrae with imbricate neural arches. Ossified intervertebral discs are present; these fuse with the centrum to give a procoelous centrum in adults (discs remain free in megophryines). Presacrals I and II are not fused, and the atlantal cotyles of Presacral I are closely juxtaposed. Ribs are absent. The sacrum has greatly expanded diapophyses and is fused with the coccyx (monocondylar articulation with the coccyx in most megophryines and some eopelobatines). Transverse processes on the proximal part of the coccyx possibly are incorporated into a bony web between the coccyx and the sacral diapophyses in some taxa. The pectoral girdle is arciferal and has a cartilaginous omosternum and sternum (latter osseous in most taxa); the anterior end of the scapula is not overlain by the clavicle. Palatines are present, absent, or fused with adjacent elements; a parahyoid is absent, and the cricoid ring is incomplete dorsally. The maxillae and premaxillae are dentate. The astragalus and calcaneum are fused only proximally and distally; there are two tarsalia, and the phalangeal formula is normal. The m. sartorius is not discrete from the m. semitendinosus, and the tendon of the latter inserts ventral to the m. gracilis; the m. glutaeus magnus has an accessory tendon, and the m. adductor magnus lacks an accessory head. The pupil is vertically elliptical. Amplexus is inguinal. All have aquatic Type IV larvae with beaks and denticles; the spiracle is sinistral, and the trigeminal and facial ganglia are fused. The diploid number of chromosomes is 26 (24 in *Leptolalax pelodytoides*).

The holarctic pelobatines are short-legged, smooth-skinned fossorial toads with spadelike metatarsal tubercles; the largest attain a snout-vent length of about 85 mm. The Oriental megophryines are more diverse in external appearance; they are terrestrial or semifossorial, and some have fleshy dorsolateral folds and/or supraciliary processes (Fig. 19-31). The largest megophryines have a snout-vent length of about 125 mm.

Distribution.—Megophryines are distributed from Pakistan east to western China and through the Indo-Australian Archipelago to the Sunda Islands and the Philippine Islands. Pelobatines occur in Europe, western Asia, North Africa, and southern North America to southern Mexico (Fig. 19-32).

Fossil history.—Pelobatids have an extensive fossil history extending from the Late Cretaceous of North America and Asia and from the middle Eocene of Europe through the Pleistocene.

Life history.—All pelobatids have aquatic eggs and tadpoles. Pelobatines and some megophryines deposit pigmented eggs in temporary ponds and have generalized pond-type tadpoles. Other megophryines (*Leptobrachium, Leptolalax,* and *Scutiger*) have stream-adapted tadpoles, and the tadpoles of *Megophrys* are surface-feeders with upturned, funnel-shaped mouths (Figs. 6-12B, 6-13B).

Remarks.—The recognition of one extinct and two living subfamilies is based primarily on the work of Estes (1970). Some workers include the pelodytids as a subfamily of the Pelobatidae. Roček (1981) suggested that *Pelobates* and *Scaphiopus* evolved independently

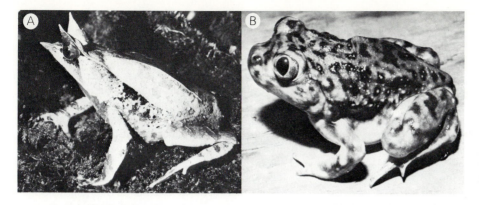

Figure 19-31. A. *Megophrys montana* from Asia (photo by K. T. Nemuras). **B.** *Scaphiopus bombifrons* from Comanche County, Kansas, U.S.A. (photo by J. T. Collins).

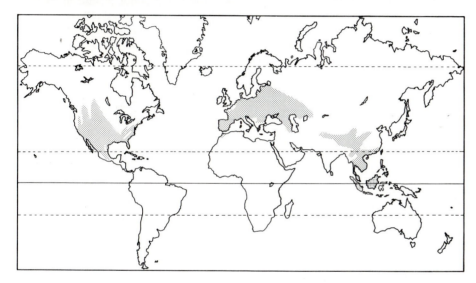

Figure 19-32. Distribution of living members of the family Pelobatidae.

and represented two families, but the immunological results of Sage et al. (1982) purport to show that the two genera were related but that their differentiation occurred in the Cretaceous.

Content.—Nine Recent genera containing 83 living species, are placed in two subfamilies, one of which contains a monotypic extinct genus. Three other extinct genera containing 12 species is placed in a third subfamily. Eight other fossil species are contained in one of the living genera.

†EOPELOBATINAE Špinar, 1972

1. †*Aralobatrachus* Nessov, 1981; 1 species. Late Cretaceous of Ubekistan, U.S.S.R.

2. †*Eopelobates* Parker, 1929 (†*Halleobatrachus* Kuhn, 1941; †*Eobufella* Kuhn, 1941; †*Parabufella* Kuhn, 1941; †*Palaeopelobates* Kuhn, 1941; †*Archaeopelobates* Kuhn, 1941; †*Amphignathodontoides* Kuhn, 1941; †*Germanobatrachus* Kuhn, 1941); 10 species. Late Cretaceous (?), early Eocene to early Oligocene of North America; middle Eocene to middle Miocene of Europe; Late

Cretaceous of Mongolia and southwestern Asia. Estes (1970); Roček (1981).

3. †*Kizylkuma* Nessov, 1981; 1 species. Late Cretaceous of Ubekistan, U.S.S.R.

MEGOPHRYINAE Noble, 1931

4. *Atympanophrys* Tian and Hu, 1983; 1 species. Sichuan, China. Tian and S. Hu (1983).

5. *Brachytarsophrys* Tian and Hu, 1983; 1 species. Southwestern China, Burma, and northern Thailand. Tian and S. Hu (1983).

6. *Leptobrachella* Smith, 1931 (*Nesobia* van Kampen, 1923); 6 species. Borneo and Natuna islands. Dring (1984).

7. *Leptobrachium* Tschudi, 1838 (*Septobrachium* Tschudi, 1838; *Pelobatrachus* Beddard, 1907; *Vibrissaphora* Liu, 1945); 11 species. Southern China and Indochina, Philippines, Sunda Islands to Bali.

8. *Leptolalax* Dubois, 1980 (*Carpophrys* Herpetol. Dept. Sichuan Biol. Res. Inst., 1977); 4 species. Southern China to Malaya and Borneo.

9. *Megophrys* Kuhn and van Hasselt, 1822

(*Megalophrys* Wagler, 1830; *Ceratophryne* Schlegel, in Günther, 1859; *Xenophrys* Günther, 1864; *Ophryophryne* Boulenger, 1883); 21 species. Southeastern Asia from India to China; Philippines, Sumatra, Java, Borneo, and Natuna.

10. *Scutiger* Theobold, 1868 (*Cophophryne* Boulenger, 1903; *Aelurophryne* Boulenger, 1919; *Oreolalax* Myers and Leviton, 1962); 29 species. Mountains of southwestern China to northern India.

PELOBATINAE Bonaparte, 1850

11. †*Macropelobates* Noble, 1924; 1 species. Middle Oligocene of Mongolia. Estes (1970).

12. *Pelobates* Wagler, 1830 (*Cultripes* Müller, 1832; *Didocus* Cope, 1866; †*Zaphrissa* Cope, 1866; †*Protopelobates* Bieber, 1880; *Pseudopelobates* Pasteur, 1958); 4 species. Europe, western Asia, and northwestern Africa. Middle Eocene to Pleistocene of Europe.

13. *Scaphiopus* Holbrook, 1836 (*Spea* Cope, 1866; †*Neoscaphiopus* Taylor, 1942); 6 species. North America. Early Oligocene through Pleistocene of North America (8 extinct species). Kluge (1966).

PELODYTIDAE Bonaparte, 1850

Definition.—There are eight stegochordal presacral vertebrae with procoelous centra and imbricate neural arches. The arches of Presacrals I and II are fused, and the atlantal cotyles of Presacral I are closely juxtaposed. Ribs are absent. The sacrum has broadly dilated diapophyses and has a bicondylar articulation with the coccyx, which bears transverse processes proximally. The pectoral girdle is arciferal and has a cartilaginous omosternum and osseous sternum; the anterior end of the scapula is not overlain by the clavicle. Palatines are present; a parahyoid bone is present, and the cricoid ring is incomplete dorsally. The maxillae and premaxillae are den-

Figure 19-33. *Pelodytes punctatus* from Provincia Cádiz, Spain. Photo by S. D. Busack.

tate. The astragalus and calcaneum are completely fused; there are three tarsalia, and the phalangeal formula is normal. The m. sartorius is not discrete from the m. semitendinosus, and the tendon of the latter inserts ventral to the m. gracilis; the m. glutaeus magnus has an accessory tendon, and the m. adductor magnus lacks an accessory head. The pupil is vertically elliptical. Amplexus is inguinal. The aquatic Type IV larvae have beaks and denticles; the spiracle is sinistral, and the trigeminal and facial ganglia are fused. The diploid number of chromosomes is 24.

Pelodytids are smooth-skinned, toadlike fossorial anurans. The maximum size is about 50 mm (Fig. 19-33).

Distribution.—The distribution is disjunct in western Europe and southwestern Asia (Fig. 19-30).

Fossil history.—Pelodytids are known from the middle Eocene through the Pleistocene of Europe (Sanchíz, 1978) and from the Miocene of North America.

Life history.—Pigmented eggs are laid in strings in ponds. The larvae are generalized pond-type tadpoles.

Remarks.—Pelodytids are placed as a subfamily of the Pelobatidae by some workers. Pelodytids differ from pelobatids in having Presacrals I and II fused, a parahyoid bone, fused astragalus and calcaneum, and three tarsalia.

Content.—Two Recent species are in one genus; two monotypic extinct genera are recognized:

1. †*Miopelodytes* Taylor, 1942; 1 species. Middle Miocene of Nevada, U.S.A.

2. *Pelodytes* Fitzinger, in Bonaparte, 1838 (*Pelodytopsis* Nikolski, 1896); 2 species. Western Europe and Caucasus Mountains of southwestern Asia, middle Eocene of Germany, middle Miocene of Spain, and Pleistocene of France.

3. †*Propelodytes* Weitzel, 1938; 1 species. Eocene of Germany.

MYOBATRACHIDAE Schlegel, 1850

Definition.—There are eight presacral vertebrae with a persistent notochord and free intervertebral discs in subadults (except free discs absent in *Lechriodus* and *Mixophys*) that tend to be fused to the posterior end of the sacrum in adults (procoely). The neural arches are imbricate in most limnodynastines and nonimbricate in most myobatrachines. Presacrals I and II are fused in limnodynastines (except *Lechriodus* and *Mixophys*) and are not fused in myobatrachines. The atlantal cotyles of Presacral I are juxtaposed in limnodynastines and widely separated in myobatrachines. Ribs are absent. The sacrum has dilated diapophyses and has a bicondylar articulation with the coccyx, which may or may not have transverse processes proximally. The pectoral girdle is arciferal and has a cartilaginous omosternum (absent in *Myobatrachus* and *Notaden*) and sternum. The anterior end of the scapula is not overlain by the clavicle. Palatines are present; a parahyoid is absent, and the cricoid

Figure 19-34. A. *Rheobatrachus silus* from Queensland, Australia. **B.** *Mixophys iteratus* from Queensland, Australia. **C.** *Limnodynastes terrareginae* from Queensland, Australia. **D.** *Notaden melanoscaphus* from Western Australia. Photos by W. E. Duellman.

ring is complete in limnodynastines and incomplete ventrally in myobatrachines. The maxillae and premaxillae are dentate in most genera (edentate in *Myobatrachus, Notaden, Pseudophryne,* and some *Uperoleia*). The astragalus and calcaneum are fused only proximally and distally; there are two tarsalia, and the phalangeal formula is normal. The m. sartorius usually is distinct from the m. semitendinosus, and the place of insertion of the tendon of the latter is variable (ventral to m. gracilis in most limnodynastines, penetrating m. gracilis in other limnodynastines and some myobatrachines, and dorsal to m. gracilis in other myobatrachines); the m. glutaeus magnus has an accessory tendon, and the m. adductor magnus has a small accessory head. The pupil usually is horizontal (vertically elliptical in *Heleioporus, Megistolotis, Mixophys,* and *Neobatrachus*). Amplexus is inguinal. In those species having aquatic larvae, they are Type IV with beaks and denticles; the spiracle is sinistral, and the trigeminal and facial ganglia are fused. The diploid chromosome complement is 24, except that four species of *Limnodynastes* have 22.

Myobatrachids are extremely variable in size; *Assa darlingtoni* attains a snout-vent length of only 20 mm, whereas *Mixophys iteratus* reaches 115 mm. Most myobatrachids are terrestrial, and some (notably *Arenophryne, Myobatrachus,* and *Notaden*) are fossorial. Most species of *Limnodynastes* inhabit marshes; *Taudactylus* lives along mountain streams, and the aquatic *Rheobatrachus* lives in mountain streams (Fig. 19-34).

Distribution.—All living genera inhabit Australia; three genera also occur on New Guinea and four on Tasmania (Fig. 19-35).

Fossil history.—The Eocene *Indobatrachus* tentatively was referred to this family by J. D. Lynch (1971). *Limnodynastes* is known from the Miocene, and it and two other genera are known from the Pleistocene of Australia.

Life history.—Eggs are laid on land by members of several genera; most of these develop into aquatic tadpoles, but nonfeeding tadpoles develop in the nests of *Kyarranus* and *Philoria* and in brood pouches in the male of *Assa,* and terrestrial eggs undergo direct development in *Arenophryne* and *Myobatrachus.* The eggs and tadpoles are brooded in the stomach of *Rheobatrachus.* Aquatic foam nests are characteristic of some limnodynastines, whereas other myobatrachids deposit their eggs in water; in both cases the larvae are aquatic. *Megistolotis* has tadpoles adapted for torrential streams.

Remarks.—Many authors (e.g., Tyler, 1979) include the myobatrachids in the Leptodactylidae. J. D. Lynch (1973) included the African *Helcophryne* (now recognized in its own family) as a subfamily of the Myobatrachidae, in which he recognized the Cycloraninae and Myobatrachinae. *Cyclorana* has been transferred to the Hylidae, so the next available family-group name for the other genera formerly placed in the Cycloraninae is Limnodynastinae. Heyer and S. Liem (1976) placed *Rheobatrachus* in its own subfamily, the Rheobatrachinae.

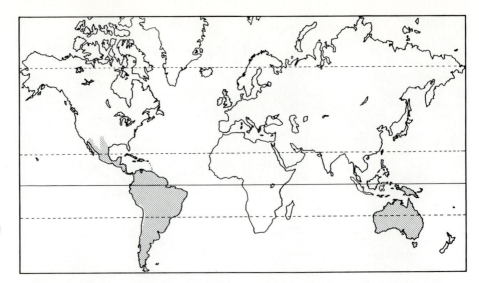

Figure 19-35. Distribution of living members of the family Myobatrachidae in Australia and New Guinea and of the family Leptodactylidae in the New World.

Laurent (1979) elevated this subfamily to the family level. Heyer and S. Liem's (1976) view of subfamilial relationships was rejected by Farris et al. (1982), whose reanalysis of Heyer and S. Liem's data set showed *Rheobatrachus* to be the sister taxon of the Limnodynastinae. However, on the basis of immunological evidence, Daugherty and Maxson (1982) placed *Rheobatrachus* in the Myobatrachinae. These different placements of *Rheobatrachus* reveal how little really is known about the relationships within the Myobatrachidae. Furthermore, the family possibly is paraphyletic. J. D. Lynch's (1973) morphological analysis showed that limnodynastines and the Heleophrynidae were similar to the leptodactylids, whereas myobatrachines and the Sooglossidae were more similar to ranids. Reviews of the literature and synonymies of the Australian myobatrachids were presented by Cogger et al (1983).

    Content.—The 20 living genera containing 99 species are grouped into two subfamilies:

LIMNODYNASTINAE Lynch, 1971

1. *Adelotus* Ogilby, 1907 (*Cryptotis* Günther, 1863); 1 species. Eastern Australia. Moore (1961).
2. *Heleioporus* Gray, 1841 (*Perialia* Gray, in Eyre, 1845; *Philocryphus* Fletcher, 1894); 6 species. Southwestern and southeastern Australia. A. Lee (1967).
3. *Kyarranus* Moore, 1958; 3 species. Mountains of eastern Australia. Ingram and Corben (1975).
4. *Lechriodus* Boulenger, 1882 (*Asterophrys* Doria, 1875; *Batrachopsis* Boulenger, 1882; *Phanerotis* Boulenger, 1890); 4 species. Eastern New Guinea, Aru Islands, and eastern Australia. Zweifel (1972b).

5. *Limnodynastes* Fitzinger, 1843 (*Wagleria* Girard, 1853; *Platyplectrum* Günther, 1863; *Opisthodon* Steindachner, 1867; *Heliorana* Steindachner, 1867; *Ranaster* MacCleay, 1878); 12 species. Australia, Tasmania, and southern New Guinea. Miocene and Pleistocene of South Australia.
6. *Megistolotis* Tyler, Martin, and Davies, 1979; 1 species. Northwestern Australia. Tyler et al. (1979).
7. *Mixophys* Günther, 1864; 4 species. Eastern Australia. Straughan (1968).
8. *Neobatrachus* Peters, 1863; 7 species. Southern and western Australia. Tyler et al. (1984).
9. *Notaden* Günther, 1873; 3 species. Northern and southeastern Australia.
10. *Philoria* Spencer, 1901; 1 species. Mount Baw Baw, Victoria, Australia.

MYOBATRACHINAE Schlegel, 1850

11. *Arenophryne* Tyler, 1976; 1 species. Coast of southern Western Australia. Tyler et al. (1980).
12. *Assa* Tyler, 1972; 1 species. Mountains of central eastern Australia. Ingram et al. (1975).
13. *Crinia* Tschudi, 1838 (*Ranidella* Girard, 1853; *Pternophrynus* Lutken, 1863; *Camariolius* Peters, 1863; *Australocrinia* Heyer and Liem, 1976); 13 species. Australia (except central part), Tasmania, and eastern New Guinea. Pleistocene of South Australia. Heyer et al. (1982).
14. *Geocrinia* Blake, 1973; 5 species. Southwestern and southeastern Australia; Tasmania. Pleistocene of South Australia. Blake (1973).

15. †*Indobatrachus* Noble, 1930; 1 species. Eocene of India.

16. *Myobatrachus* Schlegel, 1850 (*Chelydobatrachus* Günther, 1859); 1 species. Western Australia.

17. *Paracrinia*. Heyer and Liem, 1976; 1 species. Southeastern Australia. Heyer and S. Liem (1976).

18. *Pseudophryne* Fitzinger, 1843 (*Bufonella* Girard, 1853; *Metacrinia* Parker, 1940; *Kankanophryne* Heyer and Liem, 1976); 10 species. Eastern and western Australia; Tasmania.

19. *Rheobatrachus* Liem, 1973; 2 species. Mountains of Queensland, Australia. Tyler (1983); Mahony et el. (1984).

20. *Taudactylus* Straughan and Lee, 1966; 5 species. Mountains of Queensland, Australia.

21. *Uperoleia* Gray, 1841 (*Hyperolia* Cope, 1865; *Glauertia* Loveridge, 1933); 18 species. Australia, except central and southeastern part; southern New Guinea. Tyler et al. (1981).

HELEOPHRYNIDAE Noble, 1931

Definition.—There are eight ectochordal presacral vertebrae with cartilaginous intervertebral joints and a persistent notochord. The neural arches are imbricate, and Presacrals I and II are fused; the atlantal cotyles of Presacral I are closely juxtaposed. Ribs are absent. The sacrum has rounded diapophyses and has a bicondylar articulation with the coccyx, which has transverse processes proximally. The pectoral girdle is arciferal and has a cartilaginous omosternum and sternum; the anterior end of the scapula is not overlain by the clavicle. Palatines are present; a parahyoid is absent, and the cricoid ring is complete. The maxillae and premaxillae are dentate. The astragalus and calcaneum are fused only proximally and distally; there are two tarsalia, and the phalangeal formula is normal. The m. sartorius is distinct from the m. semitendinosus, and the tendon of the latter inserts ventral to the m. gracilis; the m. glutaeus magnus has an accessory tendon, and the m. adductor magnus has an accessory head. The pupil is vertically elliptical. Amplexus is inguinal. Type IV Larvae have denticles but no beaks; the spiracle is sinistral, and the trigeminal and facial ganglia are fused. The diploid chromosome complement is 26.

Heleophrynids are moderate-sized (35–65 mm snout-vent length) frogs that inhabit rocks in cascading mountain streams (Fig. 19-36). The tadpoles are unique in having large mouths lacking beaks.

Distribution.—The family is restricted to the highlands and areas of swiftly flowing streams in South Africa (Fig. 19-37).

Fossil history.—None.

Life history.—Large, unpigmented eggs are attached to rocks in streams. The torrent-adapted tadpoles have large mouths with 4 upper and 11–17 lower rows of denticles.

Remarks.—J. D. Lynch (1973) considered these frogs to be related to the limnodynastine myobatrachids. Heyer and S. Liem (1976) suggested that *Heleophryne* should be placed in its own family.

Content.—The single genus contains three species:

1. *Heleophryne* Sclater, 1898; 3 species. South Africa. Poynton (1964).

Figure 19-36. *Heleophryne purcelli* from Natal, South Africa. Photo by J. Visser.

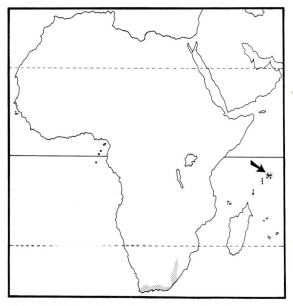

Figure 19-37. Distribution of living members of the family Heleophrynidae in South Africa and of the family Sooglossidae on the Seychelles Islands.

SOOGLOSSIDAE Noble, 1931

Definition.—There are eight presacral vertebrae with a persistent notochord and free intervertebral bodies in subadults; in adults the intercentral bodies are fused to give procoelous centra. The neural arches are not imbricate, and Presacrals I and II are not fused; the atlantal cotyles of Presacral I are widely separated. Ribs are absent. The sacrum has dilated diapophyses and a monocondylar articulation with the coccyx, which has small transverse processes proximally. The pectoral girdle is arciferal, but the epicoracoid cartilages are fused at their extreme anterior and posterior ends. A cartilaginous omosternum and bony sternum are present; the scapula is not overlain anteriorly by the clavicle. Palatines are present; a parahyoid is absent, and the cricoid ring is incomplete ventrally. The maxillae and premaxillae are dentate. The astragalus and calcaneum are fused only proximally and distally; there are two tarsalia, and the phalangeal formula is normal. The m. sartorius is discrete from the m. semitendinosus, and the tendon of the latter passes dorsal to the m. gracilis; the m. glutaeus magnus has an accessory tendon, and the m. adductor magnus has no accessory head. The pupil is horizontal. Amplexus is inguinal. Development is direct, or nonfeeding tadpoles lacking mouthparts and spiracles develop on the back of the adult. The diploid chromosome complement is 26.

These small (snout-vent length to 40 mm) terrestrial frogs have the digits terminating in small, pointed discs (Fig. 19-38).

Distribution.—Sooglossids are restricted to the Seychelles islands in the Indian Ocean (Fig. 19-37).

Fossil history.—None.

Life history.—The eggs are terrestrial; those of *Sooglossus gardineri* undergo direct development, whereas the eggs of *S. seychellensis* hatch as nonfeeding tadpoles that are carried on the back of the adult. These tadpoles lack a spiracle, internal gills, and mouthparts.

Remarks.—The relationships of the sooglossids are

Figure 19-38. *Nesomantis thomasseti* from Mahé, Seychelles Islands. Photo by E. D. Brodie, Jr.

unknown. Griffiths (1959a) proposed that these frogs should be regarded as a subfamily of ranids. J. D. Lynch (1973) considered them to be a sister group of the myobatrachines, a position supported by Nussbaum's (1979b) interpretation of the karyotype and the amplectic position (Nussbaum, 1980).

Content.—The three species are arranged in two genera:

1. *Nesomantis* Boulenger, 1909; 1 species. Mahé and Silhouette islands, Seychelles.
2. *Sooglossus* Boulenger, 1906; 2 species. Mahé and Silhouette islands, Seychelles.

LEPTODACTYLIDAE Werner, 1896

Definition.—There are eight presacral vertebrae with holochordal (stegochordal in some telmatobiines), procoelous centra. The neural arches are imbricate in ceratophryines and some telmatobiines and leptodactylines, and nonimbricate in hylodines, some telmatobiines, and most leptodactylines. Presacrals I and II are not fused (except in *Telmatobufo*); the atlantal cotyles of Presacral I are closely juxtaposed in ceratophryines and some telmatobiines, and widely separated in hylodines, leptodactylines, and other telmatobiines. Ribs are absent. The sacrum has rounded diapophyses (weakly dilated in ceratophrynines and some telmatobiines) and has a bicondylar articulation with the coccyx, which lacks transverse processes proximally (except in some telmatobiines). The pectoral girdle is arciferal (pseudofirmisternal in *Insuetophrynus*, *Sminthillus*, and *Phrynopus peruvianus*). A cartilaginous omosternum (absent in *Lepidobatrachus*, *Macrogenioglottus*, *Odontophrynus*, *Proceratophrys*, and some *Eleutherodactylus*) and cartilaginous sternum are present (also bony postzonal elements in leptodactylines). The anterior end of the scapula is not overlain by the clavicle. Palatines are present; a parahyoid is absent, and the cricoid ring is complete. The maxillae and premaxillae are dentate (edentate in *Batrachophrynus*, *Lynchophrys*, *Sminthillus*, and some *Physalaemus* and *Telmatobius*). The astragalus and calcaneum are fused only proximally and distally (completely fused in *Geobatrachus*); there are two tarsalia, and the phalangeal formula is normal (reduced in *Euparkerella* and *Phyllonastes*). The m. sartorius is distinct from the m. semitendinosus, and the tendon of the latter is ventral to the m. gracilis (penetrating m. gracilis in *Crossodactylus* and in some *Physalaemus*); the m. glutaeus magnus has an accessory tendon, and the m. adductor magnus has an accessory head. The pupil is horizontal in most genera (vertically elliptical in *Caudiverbera*, *Hydrolaetare*, *Hylorina*, *Lepidobatrachus*, *Limnomedusa*, and *Telmatobufo*). Amplexus is axillary (inguinal in *Batrachyla* and some *Pleurodema*). Aquatic Type IV larvae have denticles and beaks (except *Lepidobatrachus*); the spiracle is sinistral (paired, ventrolateral in *Lepidobatrachus*). The trigeminal and facial ganglia are fused. The diploid chromosome com-

Figure 19-39. A. *Ceratophrys calcarata* from South America. **B.** *Caudiverbera caudiverbera* from Provincia Valdivia, Chile. **C.** *Eleutherodactylus latidiscus* from Departamento Valle, Colombia. **D.** *Hylorina sylvatica* from Provincia Llanquihue, Chile. **E.** *Leptodactylus chaquensis* from Provincia Jujuy, Argentina. **F.** *Megaelosia goeldi* from Terezópolis, Brazil. A by K. T. Nemuras; B–E by W. E. Duellman; F. by J. P. Bogart.

plement varies from 18 to 36; in addition, some *Ceratophrys, Odontophrynus,* and *Pleurodema* are polyploids.

Leptodactylids are extremely variable in size (12–250 mm) and diverse in structure and appearance. Some are toadlike (*Odontophrynus*); some are large-headed carnivores (*Ceratophrys* and *Lepidobatrachus*), and some are strictly aquatic (*Batrachophrynus* and *Telmatobius* (Fig. 19-39).

Distribution.—Leptodactylids occur throughout most of South America, southern North America, and the West Indies (Fig. 19-35). Major centers of generic distribution are in the temperate forests of Chile and the southern Andes, highlands of southeastern Brazil, and the Patagonian-Chacoan region; secondary centers are in the northern Andes, Amazon Basin, and Mexico. Three gen-

era in Mexico barely enter southwestern United States, and two species of *Eleutherodactylus* have been introduced into Florida.

Fossil history.—The family has an extensive fossil history throughout the Cenozoic in South America, where two genera are known only as fossils. Two living genera are known from Pleistocene deposits in North America and one from the West Indies.

Life history.—Primitive telmatoblines have aquatic eggs and tadpoles; leptodactylines have foam nests and aquatic tadpoles, but the tadpoles complete their development in terrestrial nests in *Adenomera*. Others have terrestrial eggs that hatch into tadpoles that move to water (*Thoropa*) or hatch as advanced tadpoles that complete their development in the nest (*Crossodactylodes, Cycloramphus,* and *Zachaenus*). The species in at least nine genera, of which *Eleutherodactylus* is the most numerous and widespread, have direct development of terrestrial eggs. At least one species of *Eleutherodactylus (jasperi)* is viviparous and at least two (*E. coqui* and *E. jasperi*) have internal fertilization.

Remarks.—The leptodactylids were reviewed by J. D. Lynch (1971), who recognized four subfamilies. Heyer (1975) provided an alternative phylogenetic arrangement, and J. D. Lynch (1978) reviewed the lower telmatobiines. Some workers accord the ceratophryines familial status. Accounts and colored illustrations of Chilean and Argentine leptodactylids were provided by Cei (1962, 1980).

Content.—The 51 living and 2 fossil genera containing 710 living species are grouped into four subfamilies:

CERATOPHRYINAE Tschudi, 1838

1. *Ceratophrys* Wied, 1824 (*Stombus* Gravenhorst, 1825; *Phrynoceros* Bibron, in Tschudi, 1838; *Trigonophrys* Hallowell, 1856; *Chacophrys* Reig and Limeses, 1963); 6 species. Discontinuous in tropical and subtropical South America. Pliocene and Pleistocene of South America. J. D. Lynch (1982).

2. *Lepidobatrachus* Budgett, 1899; 3 species. Gran Chaco of Paraguay and Argentina. Cei (1980).

3. †*Wawelia* Casamiquela, 1963; 1 species. Upper Miocene of Argentina. J. D. Lynch (1971).

TELMATOBIINAE Fitzinger, 1843

4. *Adelophryne* Hoogmoed and Lescure, 1984; 2 species. Guiana Shield in northeastern South America. Hoogmoed and Lescure (1984).

5. *Alsodes* Bell, 1843 (*Hammatodactylus* Fitzinger, 1843; *Cacotus* Günther, 1868); 10 species. Austral forests of southern Argentina and Chile. J. D. Lynch (1978).

6. *Atelognathus* Lynch, 1978; 7 species. Patagonian Argentina and Isla Wellington, Chile. J. D. Lynch (1978).

7. *Barycholos* Heyer, 1969; 2 species. Pacific lowlands of Ecuador; central Brazil. J. D. Lynch (1980).

8. *Batrachophrynus* Peters, 1873; 1 species. Andean lakes in central Peru. J. D. Lynch (1978).

9. *Batrachyla* Bell, 1843; 3 species. Austral forests of southern Argentina and Chile. J. D. Lynch (1978).

10. *Caudiverbera* Laurenti, 1768 (*Calytocephalella* Strand, 1828; *Crossurus* Wagler, 1830; *Peltocephalus* Bibron, in Tschudi, 1838; *Calyptocephalus* Duméril and Bibron, 1841; †*Eophractus* Schaeffer, 1949; †*Gigantobatrachus* Casamiquela, 1959); 1 species. Aus-

tral forests of Chile. Upper Oligocene to upper Miocene of Patagonia; 1 fossil species from lower Eocene of Patagonia. J. D. Lynch (1978).

11. *Crossodactylodes* Cochran, 1938; 1 species. Southeastern Brazil. J. D. Lynch (1971).

12. *Cyclorhamphus* Tschudi, 1838 (*Pithecopsis* Günther, 1859; *Grypiscus* Cope, 1867; *Iliodiscus* Miranda-Ribeiro, 1920; *Craspedoglossa* Müller, 1922; *Niedenia* Ahl, 1923); 22 species. Southeastern Brazil. Heyer (1983).

13. *Dischidodactylus* Lynch, 1979; 1 species. Cerro Duida, southern Venezuela. J. D. Lynch (1979b).

14. *Eleutherodactylus* Duméril and Bibron, 1841 (*Cornufer* Tschudi, 1838; *Hylodes* Fitzinger, 1843; *Euhyas* Fitzinger, 1843; *Craugastor* Cope, 1862; *Strabomantis* Peters, 1863; *Leiyla* Keferstein, 1868; *Limnophys* Jiménez de la Espada, 1870; *Pristimantis* Jiménez de la Espada, 1870; *Cyclocephalus* Jiménez de la Espada, 1870; *Hypodictyon* Cope, 1885; *Basanitia* Miranda-Ribeiro, 1923; *Phrynanodus* Ahl, 1933; *Teletrema* Miranda-Ribeiro, 1937; *Microbatrachylus* Taylor, 1940; *Ctenocranius* Melin, 1941; *Pseudohyla* Andersson, 1945; *Amblyphrynus* Cochran and Goin, 1961; *Trachyphrynus* Cochran and Goin, 1963); 398 species. Mexico, Central America, and South America southward to northern Argentina and southeastern Brazil; West Indies; introduced into Florida. Pleistocene of West Indies. J. D. Lynch (1976); A. Schwartz and Thomas (1975).

15. *Euparkerella* Griffiths, 1959; 1 species. Southeastern Brazil. Heyer (1977).

16. *Eupsophus* Fitzinger, 1843 (*Borborocoetes* Bell, 1843); 5 species. Austral forests of southern Argentina and Chile. Lower Oligocene of Patagonia. J. D. Lynch (1978); Formas and Vera (1982).

17. *Geobatrachus* Ruthven, 1915; 1 species. Sierra Nevada de Santa Marta, northern Colombia. Ardila-Robayo (1979).

18. *Holoaden* Miranda-Ribeiro, 1920; 2 species. Southeastern Brazil. J. D. Lynch (1971).

19. *Hylactophryne* Lynch, 1968; 3 species. Mexico and southwestern United States. Pleistocene of Texas. J. D. Lynch (1971).

20. *Hylorina* Bell, 1843; 1 species. Austral forests of Chile. J. D. Lynch (1978).

21. *Insuetophrynus* Barrio, 1970; 1 species. Austral forests of Chile. J. D. Lynch (1978).

22. *Ischnocnema* Reinhardt and Lütken, 1862 (*Oreobates* Jiménez de la Espada, 1872); 3 species. Western Amazon Basin, eastern

slopes of Andes, and southeastern Brazil. J. D. Lynch (1971).

23. *Lynchophrys* Laurent, 1984; 1 species. Andes of central Peru.

24. *Macrogenioglottus* Carvalho, 1946; 1 species. Eastern Brazil. Reig (1972).

25. †*Neoprocoela* Schaeffer, 1949; 1 species. Lower Oligocene of Patagonia. J. D. Lynch (1971).

26. *Odontophrynus* Reinhardt and Lütken, 1862 (*Hyperoodon* Philippi, 1902); 5 species. Eastern Brazil to northern Argentina, southern Bolivia and Paraguay. Cei et al. (1982).

27. *Phrynopus* Peters, 1874 (*Noblella* Barbour, 1930; *Niceforonia* Goin and Cochran, 1963); 16 species. Andes from Colombia to Bolivia. Cannatella (1984).

28. *Phyllonastes* Heyer, 1977; 2 species. Upper Amazon Basin. Heyer (1977).

29. *Phyzelaphryne* Heyer, 1977; 1 species. Amazon Basin in Brazil. Hoogmoed and Lescure (1984).

30. *Proceratophrys* Miranda-Ribeiro, 1920; 10 species. Coastal Brazil to northern Argentina. J. D. Lynch (1971).

31. *Scythrophrys* Lynch, 1971; 1 species. Southeastern Brazil. J. D. Lynch (1971).

32. *Sminthillus* Barbour and Noble, 1920; 1 species. Cuba. J. D. Lynch (1971).

33. *Somuncuria* Lynch, 1978; 1 species. Patagonian Argentina. J. D. Lynch (1978).

34. *Syrrhophus* Cope, 1878 (*Epirhexis* Cope, 1866; *Malachylodes* Cope, 1879); 15 species. Texas to Guatemala and Belize. Pleistocene of Texas. J. D. Lynch (1970).

35. *Telmatobius* Wiegmann, 1835 (*Pseudobatrachus* Peters, 1873; *Cophaeus* Cope, 1889); 29 species. Andes from Ecuador to central Argentina and Chile. J. D. Lynch (1978).

36. *Telmatobufo* Schmidt, 1952; 3 species. South-central Chile. Formas and Veloso (1982).

37. *Thoropa* Cope, 1865; 3 species. Southeastern Brazil. Bokermann (1965b).

38. *Tomodactylus* Günther, 1901; 9 species. Western and southern Mexico. J. D. Lynch (1971).

39. *Zachaenus* Cope, 1866 (*Oocormus* Boulenger, 1905); 3 species. Southeastern Brazil. J. D. Lynch (1971).

HYLODINAE Günther, 1859

40. *Crossodactylus* Duméril and Bibron, 1841 (*Limnocharis* Bell, in Darwin, 1843; *Tarsopterus* Reinhardt and Lütken, 1862; *Calamobates* DeWitte, 1930); 5 species. Southeastern Brazil and northeastern Argentina. J. D. Lynch (1971).

41. *Hylodes* Fitzinger, 1826 (*Enydrobius* Wagler, 1830; *Elosia* Tschudi, 1838; *Scinacodes* Fitzinger, 1843); 13 species. Southeastern Brazil. Heyer (1982).

42. *Megaelosia* Miranda-Ribeiro, 1923; 1 species. Southeastern Brazil. J. D. Lynch (1971).

LEPTODACTYLINAE Werner, 1896

43. *Adenomera* Steindachner, 1867; 6 species. Cis-Andean tropical South America. Heyer (1974a).

44. *Edalorhina* Jiménez de la Espada, 1870 (*Bubonius* Cope, 1874); 2 species. Western Amazon Basin. J. D. Lynch (1971).

45. *Hydrolaetare* Gallardo, 1963; 1 species. Amazon Basin. J. D. Lynch (1971).

46. *Leptodactylus* Fitzinger, 1826 (*Cystignathus* Wagler, 1830; *Gnathophysa* Fitzinger, 1843; *Sibilatrix* Fitzinger, 1843; *Plectromantis* Peters, 1862; *Entomoglossus* Peters, 1870; *Pachypus* Lutz, 1930; *Cavicola* Lutz, 1930; *Parvulus* Lutz, 1930); 50 species. Tropical and subtropical America from southern Texas to central Argentina; Lesser Antilles and Hispaniola. Pleistocene of South America. Heyer (1970, 1978, 1979b).

47. *Limnomedusa* Fitzinger, 1843 (*Litopleura* Jiménez de la Espada, 1875); 1 species. Southern Brazil, northern Argentina, Uruguay. J. D. Lynch (1971).

48. *Lithodytes* Fitzinger, 1843; 1 species. Amazon Basin and Guianan region of South America. J. D. Lynch (1971).

49. *Paratelmatobius* Lutz and Carvalho, 1958; 2 species. Southeastern Brazil. J. D. Lynch (1971).

50. *Physalaemus* Fitzinger, 1826 (*Paludicola* Wagler, 1830; *Liupurus* Cope, 1860; *Gomphobates* Reinhardt and Lütken, 1862; *Eupemphix* Steindachner, 1863; *Nattereria* Steindachner, 1864; *Iliobates* Fitzinger, in Steindachner, 1867; *Engystomops* Jiménez de la Espada, 1872; *Microphryne* Peters, 1873; *Peralaimos* Jiménez de la Espada, 1875); 34 species. Tropical lowlands from Mexico to Argentina. Cannatella and Duellman (1984).

51. *Pleurodema* Tschudi, 1838 (*Chionopelas* Tschudi, 1838; *Leiuperus* Duméril and Bibron, 1841; *Physalaemus* Fitzinger, 1843; *?Metaeus* Girard, 1853; *Lystris* Cope, 1868); 12 species. Discontinuous from Panama to extreme southern Argentina and Chile. Duellman and Veloso (1977).

52. *Pseudopaludicola* Miranda-Ribeiro, 1926; 5 species. Cis-Andean tropical South America. J. D. Lynch (1971).

53. *Vanzolinius* Heyer, 1974; 1 species. Upper Amazon Basin. Heyer (1974b).

532

BUFONIDAE Gray, 1825

Definition.—There are 5–8 holochordal, procoelous presacral vertebrae with imbricate neural arches (intervertebral bodies not ossified in *Pseudobufo*). Variation in the number of presacral vertebrae is the result of the fusion of Preseacrals I and II (e.g., *Atelopus, Leptophryne, Oreophrynella,* and *Pelophryne*). The atlantal cotyles of Presacral I are juxtaposed. Ribs are absent. The sacrum has dilated diapophyses and a bicondylar articulation with the coccyx, except in those taxa in which there has been a forward shift of the sacral articulation; in these cases the original sacral vertebra is incorporated into the coccyx, and there is a monocondylar articulation or a fusion of the coccyx and the functional sacral vertebra (e.g., (*Didynamipus, Laurentophryne, Mertensophryne, Nectophryne, Pelophryne, Wolterstorffina,* and some *Rhamphophryne*). Transverse processes are absent on the coccyx. The pectoral girdle is arciferal or pseudofirmisternal by fusion of the epicoracoids (e.g., *Atelopus* and *Osornophryne*). The omosternum is absent (present in *Nectophrynoides, Werneria,* and some *Bufo*), and a bony sternum is present; the scapula is not overlain anteriorly by the clavicle. Palatines are present (absent in *Nectophryne* and *Pelophryne*); a parahyoid is absent, and the cricoid ring is complete. The maxillae and premaxillae are edentate. The astragalus and calcaneum are fused only proximally and distally; there are two tarsalia, and the phalangeal formula is normal in most genera

(reduced in *Crepidophryne, Didynamipus, Osornophryne, Pelophryne,* and some *Atelopus*). The m. sartorius is discrete from the m. semitendinosus, and the tendon of the latter passes ventral to the m. gracilis; the m. glutaeus magnus has an accessory tendon, and the m. adductor magnus has an accessory head. The pupil is horizontal. Amplexus is axillary (secondarily inguinal and dorsal in *Osornophryne;* inguinal and ventral in *Nectophrynoides malcolmi* and *N. occidentalis*). Aquatic Type IV tadpoles have beaks and denticles; the spiracle is sinistral, and the trigeminal and facial ganglia are fused. The diploid chromosome complement is 22 (except 20 in the *Bufo regularis* complex).

Toads and their allies generally have thick, glandular skin with or without pustular warts; *Bufo* and some other genera have parotoid glands, and some species have large glands on the limbs (Fig. 19-40). Most species are terrestrial or fossorial and have short limbs; the digits are reduced and shortened with a thick interdigital pad in *Osornophryne*. Bufonids vary in size from the minute *Oreophrynella* (20 mm) to the gigantic toad *Bufo blombergi* (250 mm). Most bufonids have extensively ossified skulls, and in most of these the skin is co-ossified with the skull. The quadratojugals are reduced or lost in *Ansonia, Laurentophryne, Nectophryne, Pelophryne,* and *Wolterstorffina;* palatines are absent in some *Dendrophryniscus* and *Melanophryniscus,* and the columella is absent in many genera and in some species of *Atelopus,*

Figure 19-40. A. *Bufo blombergi* from Departamento Valle, Colombia (photo by W. E. Duellman). **B.** *Atelopus varius* from Provincia Veraguas, Panama (photo by K. Nemuras). **C.** *Oreophrynella* sp. from Cerro Kukenan, Venezuela (photo by R. W. McDiarmid). **D.** *Nectophrynoides osgoodi* from Balé Province, Ethiopia (photo courtesy of the British Museum).

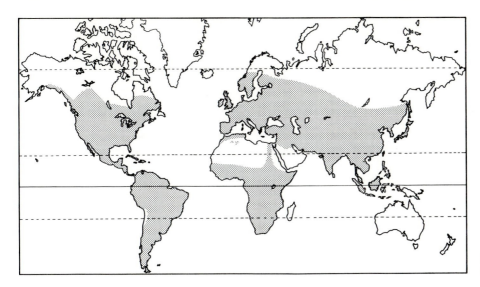

Figure 19-41. Distribution of living members of the family Bufonidae.

Bufo, and *Nectophrynoides.* The presence of a Bidder's organ is unique to the bufonids (absent in some *Dendrophryniscus);* this is a paedomorphic feature—the retention of a rudimentary ovary on the anterior end of the testis (Fig. 14-23).

Distribution.—The family is cosmopolitan in temperate and tropical regions, except for the Australo-Papuan, Madagascan, and Oceanic regions (Fig. 19-41). *Bufo marinus* has been introduced into Australia, and New Guinea and many other islands.

Fossil history.—The genus *Bufo* is known from the upper Paleocene of South America and from upper Tertiary and Quaternary deposits of North America, South America, Europe, and Africa.

Life history.—Most bufonids deposit strings of numerous small, pigmented eggs in water where generalized pond-type tadpoles develop. Peculiar crownlike structures are present on the head of tadpoles of *Mertensophryne* and *Stephopaedes* (Fig. 6-17F). The tadpoles of *Ansonia* and *Atelopus* develop in torrential streams and have large oral discs (Figs. 6-15C, 6-16C). *Oreophrynella, Osornophryne, Pelophryne, Rhamphophryne,* and some *Atelopus* have large, unpigmented eggs. *Pelophryne* has an abbreviated tadpole stage that survives on yolk; the same may be true for other bufonids with large, unpigmented eggs, or possibly they undergo direct development. Some species of *Nectophrynoides* produce tadpoles; others are ovoviviparous or viviparous. Fertilization is internal in some *Nectophrynoides* and in *Mertensophryne micranotis.*

Remarks.—Some of the genera that are now contained in the Bufonidae formerly were placed in the Atelopodidae. On the basis of the presence of a Bidder's organ all of the genera were placed in the Bufonidae, except *Brachycephalus* (Bidder's organ absent), which is now placed in the Brachycephalidae (McDiarmid, 1971). Toads of the genus *Bufo* were reviewed by W. Blair (1972).

Phylogenetic relationships among South American genera were discussed by McDiarmid (1971) and Trueb (1971), and among African genera by Grandison (1978, 1981).

Content.—Twenty-five genera contain 335 living and 20 extinct species:

1. *Ansonia* Stoliczka, 1870; 17 species. Southern India, Malay Peninsula, Tioman island, Borneo, and Mindanao, Philippines. Inger (1960b).

2. *Atelopus* Duméril and Bibron, 1841 (*Phrynidium* Lichtenstein and Martens, 1856; *Hylaemorphus* Schmidt, 1857; *Phirix* Schmidt, 1857); 43 species. Costa Rica to Bolivia; Guianan region and coastal eastern Brazil.

3. *Bufo* Laurenti, 1768; (*Batrachus* Rafinesque, 1814; *Bufotes* Rafinesque, 1815; *Oxyrhynchus* Spix, 1824; *Chascax* Oken, 1828; *Chaunus* Wagler, 1828; *Otilopha* Gray, 1831; *Phryniscus* Wiegmann, 1834; †*Palaeophrynos* Tschudi, 1838; *Sclerophrys* Bibron, in Tschudi, 1838; *Osilophus* Cuvier, in Tschudi, 1838; *Chilophryne* Fitzinger, 1843; *Incilius* Fitzinger, 1843; *Docidophryne* Fitzinger, 1843; *Eurhina* Fitzinger, 1843; *Phrynoidis* Fitzinger, 1843; *Phrynomorphus* Fitzinger, 1843; *Phryne* Oken, 1843; *Anaxyrus* Tschudi, 1845; *Trachycara* Tschudi, 1845; *Adenomus* Cope, 1860; *Rhaebo* Cope, 1862; *Epidalea* Cope, 1865; *Pegaeus* Gistel, 1868; *Nannophryne* Günther, 1870; *Cranopsis* Cope, 1876; *Ollotis* Cope, 1876; †*Platosphus* L'Isle, 1877; *Dromolectrus* Camerano, 1879; †*Bufavus* Portis, 1885; *Cranophryne* Cope, 1889; *Ancudia* Philippe, 1902; *Aruncus* Philippi, 1902; *Steno-*

dactylus Philippi, 1902); 205 species. Cosmopolitan except for Arctic regions, New Guinea, Australia, New Zealand, and South Pacific islands; *Bufo marinus* introduced in Australia, New Guinea, and on many tropical islands. Numerous Recent and extinct species known as fossils from the Paleocene, Miocene, Pliocene, and Pleistocene of South America, lower Miocene through Pleistocene of North America, upper Oligocene through Pleistocene of Europe, and Pliocene of North Africa. W. Blair (1972).

4. *Bufoides* Pillai and Yazdani, 1973; 1 species. Assam, India.

5. *Capensibufo* Grandison, 1980; 2 species. Mountains of Cape Province, South Africa. Grandison (1980a).

6. *Crepidophryne* Cope, 1889 (*Crepidius* Cope, 1876); 1 species. Mountains of western Panama and adjacent Costa Rica. J. Savage and Kluge (1961).

7. *Dendrophryniscus* Jiménez de la Espada, 1871; 3 species. Atlantic forests of Brazil, Guianas, upper Amazon Basin. McDiarmid (1971).

8. *Didynamipus* Andersson, 1903 (*Atelophryne* Boulenger, 1905); 1 species. Cameroon and Fernando Po island. Grandison (1981).

9. *Laurentophryne* Tihen, 1960; 1 species. Kiandjo, Zaire. Grandison (1981).

10. *Leptophryne* Fitzinger, 1843 (*Cacophryne* Davis, 1935); 2 species. Malay Peninsula and Greater Sunda Islands. Dubois (1982).

11. *Melanophryniscus* Gallardo, 1961; 8 species. Southern Brazil, Uruguay, Paraguay, and northern Argentina. McDiarmid (1971).

12. *Mertensophryne* Tihen, 1960; 2 species. Central Africa from Zaire eastward to Zanzibar. Grandison (1981).

13. *Nectophryne* Buchholz and Peters, 1875; 2 species. Western Africa from Nigeria to Zaire; Fernando Po island.

14. *Nectophrynoides* Noble, 1926; 8 species. Mountains of Central Africa in Liberia, Guinea, Ethiopia, and Tanzania. Grandison (1978, 1981).

15. *Oreophrynella* Boulenger, 1895; 2 species. Mountains of Guyana and southern Venezuela. McDiarmid (1971).

16. *Osornophryne* Ruíz and Hernández, 1976; 2 species. Andes of Colombia and northern Ecuador. Ruíz and Hernández (1976).

17. *Pedostibes* Günther, 1875; 6 species. Southern India; Malay Peninsula to Sumatra and Borneo. Inger (1966).

18. *Pelophryne* Barbour, 1938; 8 species. Malaya, Hainan island (China), Borneo, and the Philippines. Inger (1960a).

19. *Peltophryne* Fitzinger, 1843 (*Otaspis* Cope, 1868); 8 species. Greater Antilles. Pregill (1981).

20. *Pseudobufo* Tschudi, 1838 (*Pyleus* Gistel, 1848; *Nectes* Cope, 1865); 1 species. Malay Peninsula, Sumatra, Borneo. Inger (1966).

21. *Rhamphophryne* Trueb, 1971; 6 species. Mountains from western Panama to Ecuador; northeastern Brazil. Trueb (1971).

22. *Schismaderma* Smith, 1849; 1 species. Tanzania and Zaire to South Africa. Poynton (1964).

23. *Stephopaedes* Channing, 1978; 1 species. Southern Tanzania, western Mosambique, and Zimbabwe. Channing (1978).

24. *Werneria* Posch, 1903 (*Stenoglossa* Andersson, 1903); 4 species. Togo and Cameroon, West Africa. Amiet (1976).

25. *Wolterstorffina* Mertens, 1939; 2 species. Western Africa in Nigeria and Cameroon. Perret (1972).

BRACHYCEPHALIDAE Günther, 1859

Definition.—There are seven holochordal, procoelous presacral vertebrae with imbricate neural arches. Presacrals I and II are fused, and the atlantal cotyles of Presacral I are widely separated. Ribs are absent. The sacrum has dilated diapophyses and a bicondylar articulation with the coccyx, which lacks transverse processes. The pectoral girdle is arciferal, but the epicoracoids are completely ossified and articulating throughout most of their length. The omosternum and sternum are absent; the scapula is not overlain anteriorly by the clavicle. Palatines and prevomers are absent; a parahyoid is absent, and the cricoid ring is complete. The maxillae and premaxillae are edentate. The astragalus and calcaneum are fused only proximally and distally; there are two tarsalia, and the phalangeal formula is greatly reduced—1-2-3-1 and 0/1-2-3-4-1. The m. sartorius is distinct from the m. semitendinosus, and the tendon of the latter inserts ventral to the m. gracilis; the m. glutaeus magnus has an accessory tendon, and the m. adductor magnus has an accessory head. The pupil is horizontal. Amplexus is axillary. Aquatic tadpoles presumably are absent. The diploid chromosome complement is 22.

Brachycephalids have body lengths of less than 16 mm and greatly reduced phalanges (Fig. 19-42); there are only two functional digits on the hand and three on the foot. A dermal bony shield ossifies dorsal to the vertebrae in *Brachycephalus* (Fig. 14-5).

Distribution.—The family is restricted to the humid coastal region of southeastern Brazil (Fig. 19-43).

Fossil history.—No fossils are known.

Life history.—The presence of few, large, unpigmented ovarian eggs is indicative of direct development of terrestrial eggs.

Remarks.—Izecksohn (1971) described skeletal variation in *Brachycephalus,* and McDiarmid (1971) noted

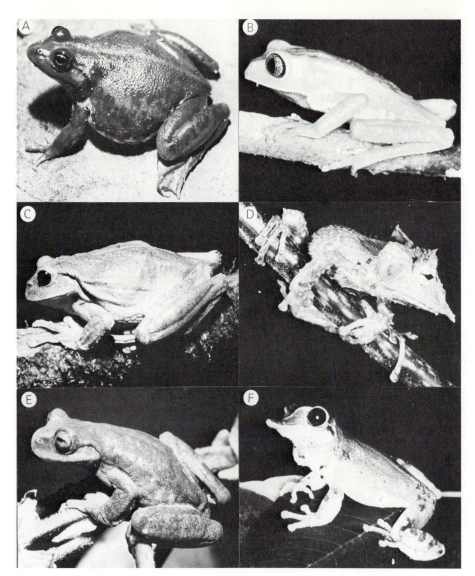

Figure 19-47. A. *Litoria dahlii* from Northern Territory, Australia. **B.** *Phyllomedusa tarsius* from Estado Bolívar, Venezuela. **C.** *Gastrotheca testudinea* from Provincia Ayacucho, Peru. **D.** *Hemiphractus bubalus* from Provincia Napo, Ecuador. **E.** *Hyla lindae* from Provincia Napo, Ecuador. **F.** *Triprion petasatus* from Yucátan, Mexico. Photos by W. E. Duellman.

and II are not fused, and the atlantal cotyles of Presacral I are widely separated. Ribs are absent. The sacrum has dilated diapophyses (round in *Acris* and some neotropical hylines) and has a bicondylar articulation with the coccyx, which lacks transverse processes. The pectoral girdle is arciferal and has a cartilaginous omosternum (absent in *Allophryne*) and sternum; the scapula is not overlain anteriorly by the clavicle. Palatines usually are present; a parahyoid is absent, and the cricoid ring is complete. The maxillae and premaxillae are dentate (edentate in *Allophryne*). The astragalus and calcaneum are fused only proximally and distally; there are two tarsalia, and the phalangeal formula is increased by the addition of a short, cartilaginous intercalary element between the penultimate and terminal phalanges (element cartilaginous, ossified, or absent in *Cyclorana*). The m. sartorius is discrete from the m. semitendinosus, and the tendon of the latter inserts ventral to the m. gracilis; the m. glutaeus magnus

has no accessory tendon, and the m. adductor magnus has an accessory head. The pupil is horizontal (vertically elliptical in phyllomedusines and *Nyctimystes*). Amplexus is axillary. Most have aquatic Type IV larvae with beaks and denticles (absent in some neotropical *Hyla*) and a sinistral spiracle varying in position from midlateral to nearly midventral; the trigeminal and facial ganglia are fused. Direct development of eggs carried by the female is characteristic of most hemiphractines. The diploid chromosome complement is 22–30.

Hylids are extremely variable in size (17–140 mm) and external appearance, but distinctive toe pads usually are present. Most hylids are arboreal, but some (*Acris*) are aquatic and others (*Cyclorana* and *Pternohyla*) are fossorial (Fig. 19-47).

Distribution.—The family occurs throughout temperate North America, Central America, the West Indies, and tropical South America; it also occurs throughout Aus-

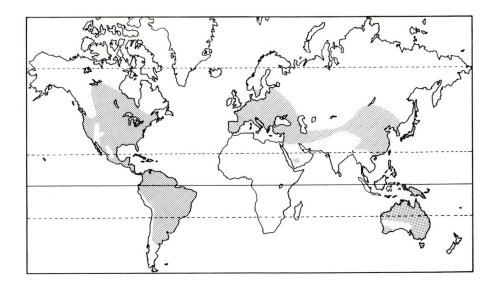

Figure 19-48. Distribution of living members of the family Hylidae.

tralia, Tasmania, New Guinea, and the Solomon Islands. The genus *Hyla* also occurs throughout most of temperate Eurasia, Japan, and extreme northern Africa (Fig. 19-48).

Fossil history.—Hylids are known from the Oligocene through the Pleistocene in North America, from the Miocene through the Pleistocene of Europe, and from the Miocene and Pleistocene of Australia. Hylids also are known from the Paleocene of Brazil (Estes and Reig, 1973). Two genera are known only as fossils.

Life history.—Hylines and pelodryadines normally have aquatic eggs and tadpoles, but some species of *Hyla* and *Litoria,* and all phyllomedusines deposit eggs on vegetation over ponds or streams, into which the hatching tadpoles drop. *Anotheca, Nyctimantis,* and *Phrynohyas resinifictrix* deposit their eggs in water-filled cavities in trees. The eggs and tadpoles of some *Hyla* develop in bromeliads. Hemiphractines brood the eggs on the dorsum (*Cryptobatrachus, Hemiphractus,* and *Stefania*) or in a dorsal brood pouch (other genera) of the females. The developing embryos have large, external gills and hatch as tadpoles in *Flectonotus, Fritziana,* and some *Gastrotheca* and as froglets in the other genera.

Remarks.—The relationships of the Australopapuan genera to the other hylids remains questionable. *Allophryne* is placed tentatively in the Hylidae (Duellman, 1975). J. Savage (1973) placed *Allophryne* in its own family, but because the family was not diagnosed, it has no taxonomic validity. The Australopapuan genera were reviewed by Tyler and M. Davies (1978a, 1979a), and the Middle American species were monographed by Duellman (1970). Accounts of Colombian species are available in Cochran and Goin (1970). The Brazilian species of *Hyla* were treated by B. Lutz (1973); the West Indian hylids were surveyed by Trueb and Tyler (1974), and the Argentinean species were treated by Cei (1980).

A checklist containing all of the taxa named through 1974 is available (Duellman, 1977).

Content.—Four subfamilies containing 630 species in 37 living genera are recognized, in addition to 2 monotypic fossil genera:

PELODRYADINAE Günther, 1859

1. †*Australobatrachus* Tyler, 1976; 1 species. Middle Miocene of South Australia. Tyler (1982).

2. *Cyclorana* Steindachner, 1867 (*Chiroleptes* Günther, 1859; *Phractops* Peters, 1867); 13 species. Australia. Tyler et al. (1978).

3. *Litoria* Tschudi, 1838 (*Ranoidea* Tschudi, 1838; *Lepthyla* Duméril and Bibron, 1841; *Euscelis* Fitzinger, 1843; *Pelobius* Fitzinger, 1843; *Polyphone* Gistel, 1848; *Pelodryas* Günther, 1859; *Chirodryas* Keferstein, 1867; *Fanchonia* Werner, 1893; *Mitrolysis* Cope, 1889); 106 species. New Guinea, Moluccan Islands, Lesser Sunda Islands, Timor, Bismarck Archipelago, Solomon Islands, Australia, and Tasmania; introduced into New Caledonia and New Zealand. Miocene and Pliocene of Australia. Tyler and M. Davies (1978a).

4. *Nyctimystes* Stejneger, 1916; 26 species. New Guinea, eastern Moluccan Islands, and northern Queensland, Australia. Tyler and M. Davies (1979a).

PHYLLOMEDUSINAE Günther, 1859

5. *Agalychnis* Cope, 1864; 8 species. Southern Mexico to Ecuador. Duellman (1977).

6. *Pachymedusa* Duellman, 1968; 1 species. Pacific lowlands of Mexico. Duellman (1970).

7. *Phyllomedusa* Wagler, 1830 (*Pithecopus*

Cope, 1866; *Hylomantis* Peters, 1872; *Phrynomedusa* Miranda-Ribeiro, 1923; *Bradymedusa* Miranda-Ribeiro, 1923); 33 species. Tropical South America to Costa Rica. Duellman (1977).

HEMIPHRACTINAE Peters, 1862

8. *Amphignathodon* Boulenger, 1882; 1 species. Andean slopes of Ecuador and southern Colombia.

9. *Cryptobatrachus* Ruthven, 1916; 3 species. Andean slopes of central and northern Colombia.

10. *Flectonotus* Miranda-Ribeiro, 1926; 2 species. Northern Venezuela, Trinidad, and Tobago. Duellman and Gray (1983).

11. *Fritziana* Mello-Leitao, 1937 (*Coelonotus* Miranda-Ribeiro, 1920; *Fritzia* Mello-Leitão, 1920; *Nototheca* Bokermann, 1950); 3 species. Mountains of southeastern Brazil. Duellman and Gray (1983).

12. *Gastrotheca* Fitzinger, 1843 (*Notodelphys* Lichtenstein and Weinland, 1854; *Nototrema* Günther, 1859; *Opisthodelphys* Günther, 1859); 37 species. Andean region of South America from Venezuela to northern Argentina; eastern Brazil; Panama.

13. *Hemiphractus* Wagler, 1830 (*Cerathyla* Jiménez de la Espada, 1871); 5 species. Northwestern South America; Panama. Trueb (1974).

14. *Stefania* Rivero, 1968; 7 species. Guianan highlands, northeastern South America. Duellman and Hoogmoed (1984).

HYLINAE Gray, 1825

15. *Acris* Duméril and Bibron, 1841; 2 species. Eastern North America. Lower Miocene through Pleistocene of North America. Duellman (1977).

16. *Allophryne* Gaige, 1926; 1 species. Guianan region of northeastern South America. Hoogmoed (1969).

17. *Anotheca* Smith, 1939; 1 species. Southern Mexico and Central America. Duellman (1970).

18. *Aparasphenodon* Miranda-Ribeiro, 1920; 2 species. Coastal southeastern Brazil; upper Orinoco Basin, Venezuela. Trueb (1970a).

19. *Aplastodiscus* Lutz, 1950; 1 species. Central and southeastern Brazil. Cochran (1955).

20. *Argenteohyla* Trueb, 1970; 1 species. Río Parana and Delta La Plata, Argentina and Uruguay. Trueb (1970b).

21. *Calyptahyla* Trueb and Tyler, 1974; 1 species. Jamaica. Trueb and Tyler (1974).

22. *Corythomantis* Boulenger, 1896; 1 species. Northeastern Brazil. Trueb (1970a).

23. *Hyla* Laurenti, 1768 (*Calamita* Schneider, 1799; *Hylaria* Rafinesque, 1814; *Boana* Gray, 1825; *Hypsiboas* Wagler, 1830; *Auletris* Wagler, 1830; *Hyas* Wagler, 1830; *Scinax* Wagler, 1830; *Dendrohyas* Wagler, 1830; *Lophopus* Tschudi, 1838; *Hypsipsophus* Fitzinger, 1843; *Lobipes* Fitzinger, 1843; *Phyllobius* Fitzinger, 1843; *Dendropsophus* Fitzinger, 1843; *Dryophytes* Fitzinger, 1843; *Centrotelma* Burmeister, 1856; *Hylomedusa* Burmeister, 1856; *Hylella* Reinhardt and Lütken, 1862; *Cinclidium* Cope, 1867; *Cincliscopus* Cope, 1870; *Cophomantis* Peters, 1870; *Exerodonta* Brocchi, 1879; *Hylonomus* Peters, 1882; *Hyloscirtus* Peters, 1882; *Epedaphus* Cope, 1885; *Hyliola* Mocquard, 1899; *Guentheria* Miranda-Ribeiro, 1926); 251 species. North, Central, and South America; Greater Antilles; Eurasia, except tropical southeastern Asia; Africa north of Sahara. Oligocene through Pleistocene of North America; Miocene through Pleistocene of Europe. Duellman (1977).

24. *Limnaoedus* Mittleman and List, 1953; 1 species. Southeastern United States. Franz and Chantell (1978).

25. *Nyctimantis* Boulenger, 1882; 1 species. Amazonian Ecuador. Duellman and Trueb (1976).

26. *Ololygon* Fitzinger, 1843 (*Garbeana* Miranda-Ribeiro, 1926); 54 species. Tropical America from Mexico to northern Argentina. Fouquette and Delahoussaye (1977).

27. *Osteocephalus* Steindachner, 1862; 6 species. Tropical South America east of the Andes. Trueb and Duellman (1971).

28. *Osteopilus* Fitzinger, 1843; 3 species. Greater Antilles, Bahamas, Florida. Trueb and Tyler (1974).

29. *Phrynohyas* Fitzinger, 1843 (*Acrodytes* Fitzinger, 1843; *Scytopis* Cope, 1862); 5 species. Tropical America from Mexico to northern Argentina. Duellman (1971).

30. *Phyllodytes* Wagler, 1830 (*Amphodus* Peters, 1872; *Lophyohyla* Miranda-Ribeiro, 1923); 4 species. Eastern Brazil; Trinidad. Bokermann (1966a).

31. *Plectrohyla* Brocchi, 1877 (*Cauphias* Brocchi, 1877); 13 species. Highlands of nuclear Central America. Duellman and Campbell (1984).

32. †*Proacris* Holman, 1961; 1 species. Miocene of Florida. Holman (1968).

33. *Pseudacris* Fitzinger, 1843 (*Chorophilus* Baird, 1854; *Helocaetes* Baird, 1854); 7 species. Eastern North America. Upper Miocene through the Pleistocene of North America. Duellman (1977).

Figure 19-49. A. *Centrolene geckoideum* from Provincia Pichincha, Ecuador. **B.** *Centrolenella prosoblepon* from Provincia Alajuela, Costa Rica. Photos by W. E. Duellman.

34. *Pternohyla* Boulenger, 1882; 2 species. Western Mexico; Arizona. Trueb (1969).

35. *Ptychohyla* Taylor, 1944; 6 species. Southern Mexico and northern Central America. Duellman and Campbell (1982).

36. *Smilisca* Cope, 1865; 6 species. Southern Texas to northwestern South America. Duellman (1970).

37. *Sphaenorhynchus* Tschudi, 1838 (*Dryomelictes* Fitzinger, 1843; *Hylopsis* Werner, 1894; *Sphoenohyla* Lutz and Lutz, 1948); 11 species. Tropical South America east of the Andes. Duellman (1977).

38. *Trachycephalus* Tschudi, 1838 (*Tetraprion* Stejneger and Test, 1891); 3 species. Eastern Brazil; coastal northwestern South America. Trueb (1970a).

39. *Triprion* Cope, 1866 (*Pharyngodon* Cope, 1865; *Diaglena* Cope, 1887); 2 species. Western Mexico and Yucatan Peninsula. Duellman (1970).

CENTROLENIDAE Taylor, 1951

Definition.—There are eight holochordal, procoelous presacral vertebrae with nonimbricate neural arches. Presacrals I and II are not fused, and the atlantal cotyles of Presacral I are widely separated. Ribs are absent. The sacrum has dilated diapophyses and a bicondylar articulation with the coccyx, which lacks transverse processes. The pectoral girdle is arciferal and has a sternum but no omosternum; the scapula is not overlain anteriorly by the clavicle. Palatines are present; a parahyoid is absent, and the cricoid ring is complete. The maxillae and premaxillae are dentate. The astragalus and calcaneum are fused throughout their lengths; there are two tarsalia, and the phalangeal formula is increased by the addition of a short, cartilaginous intercalary element between the penultimate and terminal phalanges. The m. sartorius is discrete from the m. semitendinosus, and the tendon of the latter inserts ventral to the m. gracilis; the m. glutaeus magnus lacks an accessory tendon, and the m. adductor magnus has an accessory head. The pupil is horizontal. Amplexus

is axillary. All have aquatic Type IV tadpoles with beaks and denticles; the spiracle is sinistral, and the trigeminal and facial ganglia are fused. The chromosome complement is 20.

Most centrolenids are small (30 mm) with transparent skin on the venter (Fig. 19-49); *Centrolene geckoideum* is much larger (77 mm). The terminal phalanges are T-shaped, and there is a medial protuberance on the third metatarsal.

Distribution.—The family occurs in humid regions from southern Mexico to Bolivia and northeastern Argentina (Fig. 19-50); the greatest diversity of species is on the slopes of the Andes in northwestern South America and secondarily in Costa Rica and Panama.

Fossil history.—No fossils are known.

Life history.—Small clutches of eggs are deposited on leaves (*Centrolenella*) or rocks (*Centrolene*) above streams and may be attended by territorial males. Elongate tadpoles (Fig. 6-15F) develop in gravel or detritus in flowing water.

Remarks.—Centrolenids are distinguished from hylids by the presence of a fused astragalus and calcaneum, T-shaped terminal phalanges, and a median protuberance on the third metacarpal.

Content.—Two genera containing 65 species are recognized:

1. *Centrolene* Jiménez de la Espada, 1872; 1 species. Andean slopes of Colombia and Ecuador. J. D. Lynch et al. (1983).

2. *Centrolenella* Noble, 1920 (*Cochranella* Taylor, 1951; *Teratohyla* Taylor, 1951); 64 species. Tropical America from Mexico to Bolivia and northeastern Argentina. Duellman (1977).

DENDROBATIDAE Cope, 1865

Definition.—There are eight holochordal, procoelous presacral vertebrae with nonimbricate neural arches. Presacrals I and II are not fused, but Presacral VIII is synostotically united with the sacrum in some *Dendrobates;* the atlantal cotyles of Presacral I are widely separated. Ribs are absent. The sacrum has rounded diapophyses and a bicondylar articulation with the coccyx, which usually has transverse processes proximally. The pectoral girdle is firmisternal; a cartilaginous omosternum and bony sternum are present, and the scapula is not overlain anteriorly by the clavicle. Palatines are present or absent; a parahyoid is absent, and the cricoid ring is complete. The maxillae and premaxillae are dentate or edentate. The astragalus and calcaneum are fused only proximally and distally; there are two tarsalia, and the phalangeal formula is normal. The m. sartorius is discrete from the m. semitendinosus, and the tendon of the latter pierces the m. gracilis; the m. glutaeus magnus has an accessory tendon, and the m. adductor magnus has an accessory head. The pupil is horizontal. Amplexus is cephalic or absent in some species. Aquatic Type IV tadpoles have beaks and denticles; the spiracle is sinistral, and the trigeminal and facial ganglia are fused. The diploid chromosome complement is 18–24.

Most dendrobatids are smaller than 50 mm. A pair of scalelike scutes is present on the dorsal surface of each terminal phalange (Fig. 19-51). Most known species of *Dendrobates* and *Phyllobates* are brightly colored and have toxic skin secretions. *Atopophrynus* and *Colostethus* tend to be dully colored and most seem to lack toxic skin secretions.

Distribution.—All genera occur in northwestern South America. The distribution of the family extends in humid tropical and subtropical regions from Nicaragua to southeastern Brazil and Bolivia (Fig. 19-52).

Fossil history.—No fossils are known.

Life history.—Small clutches of unpigmented eggs are deposited in humid terrestrial and arboreal situations. Either males or females remain with, or periodically visit, the nest and carry tadpoles on their backs to water, where the tadpoles complete their development. Females of some species of *Dendrobates* place individual tadpoles in water in the axils of bromeliads and then periodically return to the site of each tadpole and deposit unfertilized eggs, which are eaten by the tadpoles.

Remarks.—Griffiths (1959b) considered dendrobatids to be a subfamily of the Ranidae, whereas J. D. Lynch (1973) posited that dendrobatids were related to elosiine (= hylodine) leptodactylids. J. D. Lynch and Ruíz (1982) discussed the generic classification. The generic allocations of species to *Phyllobates* and *Dendrobates* by Silverstone (1975, 1976) was modified by Myers et al. (1978), who also summarized existing information on skin secretions and use of the skin toxins on poison darts.

Content.—Four genera containing 117 species are recognized:

1. *Atopophrynus* Lynch and Ruíz, 1982; 1 species. Andes of northern Colombia. J. D. Lynch and Ruíz (1982).
2. *Colostethus* Cope, 1866 (*Prostherapis* Cope,

Figure 19-50. Distribution of living members of the family Centrolenidae.

Figure 19-51. A. *Colostethus whymperi* from Provincia Pichincha, Ecuador. **B.** *Dendrobates leucomelas* from Estado Bolívar, Venezuela. Photos by W. E. Duellman.

Figure 19-52. Distribution of living members of the family Dendrobatidae.

1868; *Hyloxalus* Jiménez de la Espada, 1871 *Phyllodromus* Jiménez de la Espada, 1875); 63 species. Costa Rica to southeastern Brazil and Bolivia.

3. *Dendrobates* Wagler, 1830 (*Hylaplesia* Schlegel, in Boie, 1827; *Dendromedusa* Gistel, 1848); 48 species. Nicaragua to southeastern Brazil and Bolivia. Silverstone (1975, 1976); Myers et al. (1978).

4. *Phyllobates* Bibron, in de la Sagra, 1841; 5 species. Costa Rica to Pacific lowlands of northwestern South America. Silverstone (1976); Myers et al. (1978).

RANIDAE Gray, 1825

Definition.—There are eight holochordal, procoelous presacral vertebrae usually with nonimbricate neural arches (imbricate in astylosternines); in most taxa Presacral VIII is biconcave and the sacrum biconvex. Presacrals I and II are not fused in most taxa (fused in *Hemisus*), and the atlantal cotyles of Presacral I are widely separated. The sacrum has cylindrical diapophyses and a bicondylar ar-

ticulation with the coccyx, which lacks transverse processes. The pectoral girdle is firmisternal (arciferal in a few species of *Rana);* the omosternum usually is ossified, and the sternum is ossified in most taxa (usually cartilaginous in petropedetines). Postzonal sternal elements are present (except *Hemisus*), cartilaginous in arthroleptines and astylosternines, and bony in others; the scapula is not overlain anteriorly by the clavicle. Palatines are present; a parahyoid is absent, and the cricoid ring is complete. The maxillae and premaxillae are dentate in most groups (edentate in hemisines, mantellines, and some arthroleptines). The astragalus and calcaneum are fused only proximally and distally; there are two tarsalia (three in astylosternines and some petropedetines), and the phalangeal formula is normal (except in mantellines, in which it is increased by the addition of short, cartilaginous intercalary elements between the penultimate and terminal phalanges). The m. sartorius is discrete from the m. semitendinosus, and the tendon of the latter passes dorsal to the m. gracilis; the m. glutaeus magnus may or may not have an accessory tendon, and the m. adductor magnus has an accessory head. The pupil is horizontal in most taxa (vertically elliptical in astylosternines and hemisines). Amplexus is axillary (modified cephalic or absent in mantellines). Direct development occurs in arthroleptines and in some petropedetines and ranines; in all others, aquatic Type IV larvae have beaks, denticles, and a sinistral spiracle. The trigeminal and facial ganglia are fused. The diploid chromosome complement varies from 14 to 54; in addition, some species are polyploids.

Ranids are extremely variable in size and habitus. Many species are small (<50 mm snout-vent length) but *Conraua goliath,* the largest known frog, attains a length of 300 mm. Many ranids are riparian and have long legs and webbed feet (*Occidozyga, Ptychadena,* and some *Rana*), and some have robust bodies, extensive webbing, and live in and along mountain streams (*Amolops, Petropedetes, Staurois,* and some *Rana*). Others (*Pyxicephalus* and *Tomopterna*) are toadlike, and *Hemisus* is fossorial, whereas some *Platymantis* are arboreal (Figs. 19-53, 19-54).

Distribution.—The family is cosmopolitan except for southern South America, the West Indies, the Australian region, and most oceanic islands (Fig. 19-55). The range of the Raninae is the same as the family. Four subfamilies (Arthroleptinae, Astylosterninae, Hemisinae, and Pedropedetinae) are restricted to sub-Saharan Africa, and the Mantellinae (as used here) is endemic to Madagascar.

Fossil history.—Numerous Recent and extinct species of *Rana* are known from late Tertiary and Quaternary deposits in Europe and North America, and fossils referred to *Ptychadena* have been reported from the Miocene of Morocco.

Life history.—Most ranids deposit small, pigmented eggs in quiet water and have generalized pond-type tadpoles, but some (e.g., *Amolops*) have stream-adapted tadpoles. Direct development of terrestrial eggs occurs in

Figure 19-53. A. *Arthroleptis stenodactylus* from Chisambo, Malawi (photo by J. Visser). **B.** *Astylosternus batesi* from Cameroon (photo by J.-L. Perret). **C.** *Hemisus guttatum* from Natal, South Africa (photo by J. Visser). **D.** *Mantidactylus curtus* from Ankaratra Mountains, Madagascar (photo by R. M. Blommers-Schlösser).

Figure 19-54. A. *Cacosternum boettgeri* from Natal, South Africa (photo by W. E. Duellman). **B.** *Platymantis papuensis* from Lae, Papua New Guinea (photo by R. G. Zweifel). **C.** *Rana sylvatica* from Alabama, U.S.A. (photo by J. T. Collins). **D.** *Ptychadena anchietae* from Lake Bogoria, Kenya (photo by J. V. Vindum).

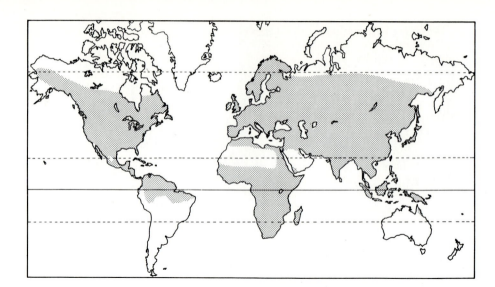

Figure 19-55. Distribution of living members of the family Ranidae.

various arthroleptines and petropedetines, and in some Asiatic ranines (*Ceratobatrachus, Discodeles, Palmatorappia,* and *Platymantis).*

Remarks.—Dubois (1981) considered the arthroleptines and astylosternines to represent a distinct family, the Arthroleptidae. Laurent (1979) recognized the hemisines as a separate family and included the rhacophorines and mantellines in the Ranidae, but placed the arthroleptines and astylosternines in the Hyperoliidae. These and other permutations discussed by Dubois (1981) reveal that the systematics of the ranoid frogs (Ranidae, Rhacophoridae, Hyperoliidae) is in a state of chaos. The only attempt at a phylogeny is B. Clarke's (1981) work on the African ranines. Some workers (e.g., Dubois, 1981) have recognized the nominal genus *Pseudophilautus* Laurent (Sri Lanka and Malabar coast of India) as a mantelline; evidence that this frog is distinct from *Philautus* (Rhacophoridae) is not compelling, and herein *Pseudophilautus* is considered to be a synonym of *Philautus.*

Content.—Different authors recognize various numbers of subfamilies (see B. Clarke, 1981, and Dubois, 1981). Herein six subfamilies are recognized containing 47 living genera with 667 species; an additional 50 species are known only as fossils. One generic name, *Dendrobatorana* Ahl, 1927, with one species, cannot be placed with certainty (Dubois, 1981).

ARTHROLEPTINAE Mivart, 1869
1. *Arthroleptis* Smith, 1849 (*Abroscaphus* Laurent, 1940; *Coracodichus* Laurent, 1940); 11 species. Sub-Saharan Africa.
2. *Cardioglossa* Boulenger, 1900; 16 species. Western and central sub-Saharan Africa.
3. *Schoutedenella* Witte, 1921 (*Arthroleptulus* Laurent, 1940); 20 species. Sub-Saharan Africa.

ASTYLOSTERNINAE Noble, 1927
4. *Astylosternus* Werner, 1898 (*Dilobates* Boulenger, 1900; *Gampsosteonyx* Boulenger, 1900); 11 species. Western Africa from Sierra Leon to Central African Republic and Zaire. Amiet (1977).
5. *Leptodactylon* Andersson, 1903 (*Bulua* Boulenger, 1904); 11 species. Western Africa from eastern Nigeria to southwestern Cameroon. Amiet (1980).
6. *Nyctibates* Boulenger, 1904; 1 species. Southwestern Cameroon. Amiet (1973).
7. *Scotobleps* Boulenger, 1900; 1 species. Eastern Nigeria to Zaire. Amiet (1973).
8. *Trichobatrachus* Boulenger, 1900; 1 species. Eastern Nigeria to Zaire.

HEMISINAE Cope, 1867
9. *Hemisus* Günther, 1859 (*Kakophrynus* Steindachner, 1863); 8 species. Tropical and subtropical sub-Saharan Africa. Laurent (1972).

MANTELLINAE Laurent, 1946
10. *Laurentomantis* Dubois, 1980 (*Microphryne* Methuen and Hewitt, 1913; *Trachymantis* Hewitt and Methuen, 1920); 3 species. Madagascar. Guibé (1978).
11. *Mantella* Boulenger, 1882; 4 species. Madagascar. Busse (1981).
12. *Mantidactylus* Boulenger, 1895 (*Gephyromantis* Methuen, 1920; *Hylobatrachus* Laurent, 1943); 53 species. Madagascar. Blommers-Schlösser (1979a).

PETROPEDETINAE Noble, 1931
13. *Anhydrophryne* Hewitt, 1919; 1 species. Amatola Mountains, South Africa. Poynton (1964).

14. *Arthroleptella* Hewitt, 1926; 2 species. Mountains of South Africa. Poynton (1964).

15. *Arthroleptides* Nieden, 1910; 2 species. Mountains of Kenya and Tanzania.

16. *Cacosterum* Boulenger, 1887; 5 species. Eastern and southern Africa.

17. *Dimorphognathus* Boulenger, 1906 (*Heteroglossa* Hallowell, 1858); 1 species. Western Africa (Cameroon, Gabon, Zaire). Perret (1966).

18. *Microbatrachella* Hewitt, 1926 (*Microbatrachus* Hewitt, 1926); 1 species. Cape Flats, South Africa. Poynton (1964).

19. *Natalobatrachus* Hewitt and Methuen, 1913; 1 species. Natal and Transkei, South Africa. Poynton (1976).

20. *Nothophryne* Poynton, 1963; 1 species. Mountains of Malawi and Mozambique. Poynton (1963).

21. *Petropedetes* Reichenow, 1874 (*Tympanoceros* Barboza du Bocage, 1895); 8 species. Sierra Leon to Cameroon; Fernando Po island. Amiet (1973).

22. *Phrynobatrachus* Günther, 1862 (*Stenorhynchus* Smith, 1849; *Hemimantis* Peters, 1863; *Leptoparius* Peters, 1863; *Hylarthroleptis* Ahl, 1923; *Pararthroleptis* Ahl, 1923; *Micrarthroleptis* Deckert, 1938; *Pseudoarthroleptis* Deckert, 1938); 63 species. Sub-Saharan Africa.

23. *Phrynodon* Parker, 1935; 1 species. Cameroon and Fernando Po island. Amiet (1981).

RANINAE Gray, 1825

24. *Altirana* Stejneger, 1927; 1 species. Tibet and Nepal. Dubois (1974).

25. *Amolops* Cope, 1865; 23 species. Northeastern India, Nepal, and southern China to the Greater Sunda Islands. Inger (1966).

26. *Aubria* Boulenger, 1917; 1 species. Gabon, western Africa. B. Clarke (1981).

27. *Batrachylodes* Boulenger, 1887; 8 species. Solomon Islands. W. Brown and F. Parker (1970).

28. *Ceratobatrachus* Boulenger, 1884; 1 species. Solomon Islands. W. Brown (1952).

29. *Conraua* Nieden, 1908 (*Pseudoxenopus* Barbour and Loveridge, 1927; *Gigantorana* Noble, 1931; *Paleorana* Scortecci, 1931; *Hydrobatrachus* Stadie, 1962); 6 species. Tropical sub-Saharan Africa. Lamotte and Perret (1968).

30. *Discodeles* Boulenger, 1918; 5 species. Admiralty, Bismarck, and Solomon islands. W. Brown (1952).

31. *Elachyglossa* Andersson, 1916; 1 species. Mountains of northern Thailand. E. Taylor (1962).

32. *Hildebrandtia* Nieden, 1907; 3 species. Tropical and subtropical sub-Saharan Africa. B. Clarke (1981).

33. *Lanzarana* Clarke, 1983; 1 species. Northern Somalia. B. Clarke (1983a).

34. *Micrixalus* Boulenger, 1888; 13 species. China, India, Sri Lanka, Borneo, and Philippines. Pillai (1978).

35. *Nannobatrachus* Boulenger, 1882; 3 species. Southern India.

36. *Nannophrys* Günther, 1869 (*Trachycephalus* Ferguson, 1875; *Fergusonia* Hoffmann, 1878); 3 species. Sri Lanka. B. Clarke (1983b).

37. *Nanorana* Günther, 1896 (*Montorana* Vogt, 1924); 1 species. Sichuan, China. Dubois (1981)

38. *Nyctibatrachus* Boulenger, 1882; 4 species. India.

39. *Occidozyga* Kuhl and van Hasselt, 1822 (*Houlema* Gray, 1831; *Oxyglossus* Tschudi, 1838; *Phrynoglossus* Peters, 1867; *Microdiscopus* Peters, 1877; *Oreobatrachus* Boulenger, 1896; *Osteosternum* Wu, 1929); 9 species. Southern China to India; Greater and Lesser Sunda Islands. Dubois (1981).

40. *Palmatorappia* Ahl, 1927 (*Hypsirana* Kinghorn, 1938); 1 species. Solomon Islands. W. Brown (1952).

41. *Platymantis* Günther, 1859 (*Halophila* Girard, 1853); 38 species. New Guinea, Philippines, Bismarck, Admiralty, Palau, Fiji, and Solomon Islands.

42. *Ptychadena* Boulenger, 1917 (*Limnophilus* Fitzinger, 1843; *Abrana* Parker, 1931; *Parkerana* Dubois, 1984); 38 species. Sub-Saharan Africa, Madagascar, Seychelles and Mascarene islands. Miocene of Morocco.

43. *Pyxicephalus* Tschudi, 1838 (*Maltzania* Boettger, 1881; *Phrynopsis* Pfeffer, 1883); 2 species. Sub-Saharan Africa.

44. *Rana* Linnaeus, 1768 (*Ranaria* Rafinesque, 1814; *Hylarana* Tschudi, 1838; *Limnodytes* Duméril and Bibron, 1841; *Lithobates* Fitzinger, 1843; *Pelophylax* Fitzinger, 1843; *Limnonectes* Fitzinger, 1843; *Hydrophylax* Fitzinger, 1843; *Euphlyctis* Fitzinger, 1843; *Phrynoderma* Fitzinger, 1843; *Zoodioctes* Gistel, 1848; †*Amphirana* Aymard, 1855; *Ranula* Peters, 1860; *Dicroglossus* Cope, 1860; *Hydrostentor* Fitzinger, 1861; *Hoplobatrachus* Peters, 1863; *Pohlia* Steindachner, 1867; *Trypheropsis* Cope, 1868; *Pachybatrachus* Mivart, 1869; *Clinotarsus* Mivart, 1869; *Crotaphitis* Schulze, 1891; *Baliopygus* Schulze, 1891; *Levirana* Cope, 1894; *Babina* Thompson, in van Denburgh,

1912; †*Fejervarya* Bolkay, 1915; *Ranosoma* Ahl, 1924; *Chaparana* Bourret, 1939; †*Anchylorana* Taylor, 1942; *Paa* Dubois, 1975); 258 species. Cosmopolitan except for southern South America and Australia. In addition to many Recent species being known from the Pliocene and Pleistocene, about 50 extinct species are recognized from the Oligocene through the Pleistocene of Europe, upper Miocene through the Pleistocene of North America, and the Pleistocene of El Salvador.

45. *Staurois* Cope, 1865 (*Simomantis* Boulenger, 1918); 3 species. Borneo and the Philippines. Inger (1966).

46. *Strongylopus* Tschudi, 1838; 5 species. South Africa northward in uplands to Tanzania. Greig et al. (1979).

47. *Tomopterna* Duméril and Bibron, 1841 (*Sphaerotheca* Günther, 1859); 12 species. Sub-Saharan Africa, Madagascar, and India. Dubois (1981).

HYPEROLIIDAE Laurent, 1943

Definition.—There are eight holochordal, procoelous presacral vertebrae with nonimbricate neural arches in most taxa (imbricate in *Cryptothylax, Kassina, Phlycti-* *mantis,* and *Tornierella);* Presacral VIII is biconcave and the sacrum biconvex in all genera except *Acanthixalus* and *Callixalus.* Presacrals I and II are not fused, and the atlantal cotyles of Presacral I are widely separated. The sacrum has cylindrical diapophyses and a bicondylar articulation with the coccyx, which lacks transverse processes. The pectoral girdle is firmisternal; a cartilaginous or bony omosternum and sternum are present, and the scapula is not overlain anteriorly by the clavicle. Palatines are present; a parahyoid is absent, and the cricoid ring is complete. The maxillae and premaxillae are dentate. The astragalus and calcaneum are fused only proximally and distally; there are three tarsalia, and the phalangeal formula is increased by the addition of short, cartilaginous intercalary elements between the penultimate and terminal phalanges. The m. sartorius is discrete from the m. semitendinosus, and the tendon of the latter passes dorsal to the m. gracilis; the m. glutaeus magnus lacks an accessory tendon, and the m. adductor magnus has an accessory head. The pupil is vertically elliptical in most genera (horizontal or round in *Acanthixalus, Chrysobatrachus,* and *Hyperolius*). Amplexus is axillary (inguinal in *Chrysobatrachus*). All have aquatic Type IV tadpoles with beaks and denticles; the spiracle is sinistral, and the trigeminal and facial ganglia are fused. The diploid chromosome complement is 22, 24, or 30.

Hyperoliids are mostly small to moderate-sized (15–82

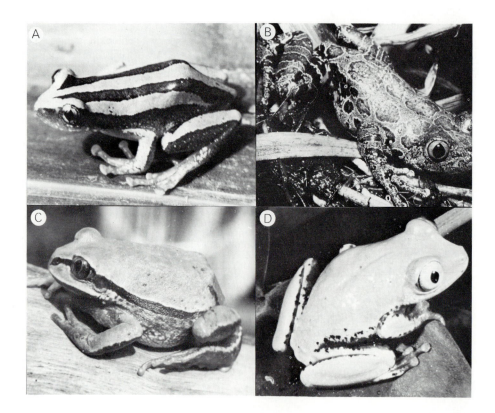

Figure 19-56. A. *Afrixalus quadrivittatus* from Lubao, Kenya (photo by R. C. Drewes). **B.** *Kassina maculata* from Ukunda, Kenya (photo by J. V. Vindum). **C.** *Leptopelis nordequatorialis* from Plateau Bamileka, Cameroon (photo by J.-L. Perret). **D.** *Tachycnemis seychellensis* from Praslin, Seychelles Islands (photo by J. V. Vindum).

mm snout-vent length) tree frogs with toe pads, but some (*Chrysobatrachus, Tornierella,* and some *Kassina*) are terrestrial (Fig. 19-56). With the exception of *Acanthixalus,* the skin is smooth. Except for *Leptopelis,* gular glands are present.

Distribution.—Most of the genera occur in sub-Saharan Africa; *Heterixalus* is endemic to Madagascar, and *Tachycnemis* is restricted to the Seychelles islands (Fig. 19-57).

Fossil history.—None.

Life history.—Many hyperoliids have small, pigmented, aquatic eggs, but *Afrixalus* and some *Hyperolius* deposit unpigmented (or pale green) eggs on vegetation above water (encased in folded leaf in *Afrixalus).* *Acanthixalus* lays unpigmented eggs in water in tree holes, and *Opisthothylax* has an arboreal foam nest. *Leptopelis* lays unpigmented eggs on the ground, and the tadpoles move to ponds. *Tachycnemis* deposits eggs on the ground or on stems of plants that are flooded before the tadpoles hatch.

Remarks.—S. Liem (1970) considered hyperoliids and rhacophorids to be derived independently from separate groups of ranids. Intrafamilial relationships were discussed by Drewes (1984), who provided diagnoses of the genera. Dubois (1981) recognized three subfamilies.

Content.—The 14 genera contain 206 species:

1. *Acanthixalus* Laurent, 1944; 1 species. Southern Nigeria and Cameroon to northeastern Zaire. Drewes (1984).
2. *Afrixalus* Laurent, 1944; 23 species. Sub-Saharan Africa. Laurent (1982); Drewes (1984).
3. *Callixalus* Laurent, 1950; 1 species. Highlands of eastern Zaire and western Rwanda. Drewes (1984).
4. *Chrysobatrachus* Laurent, 1951; 1 species. Itombwe Highlands in eastern Zaire. Drewes (1984).
5. *Cryptothylax* Laurent and Combaz, 1950; 2 species. Cameroon to Zaire. Drewes (1984).
6. *Heterixalus* Laurent, 1944; 8 species. Madagascar. Drewes (1984).
7. *Hyperolius* Rapp, 1842 (*Eucnemis* Tschudi, 1838; *Epipole* Gistel, 1848; *Crumenifera* Cope, 1863; *Rappia* Günther, 1865; *Nesionixalus* Perret, 1976); 109 species. Sub-Saharan Africa. Laurent (1983); Drewes (1984).
8. *Kassina* Girard, 1853 (*Eremiophilus* Fitzinger, 1843; *Hylambates* Duméril, 1853; *Paracassina* Peracca, 1907; *Cassinopsis* Monard, 1937; *Semnodactylus* Hoffmann, 1939); 12 species. Sub-Saharan Africa. Drewes (1984).
9. *Kassinula* Laurent, 1940; 1 species. Zaire and Zambia. Drewes (1984).
10. *Leptopelis* Günther, 1859 (*Pseudocassina* Ahl,

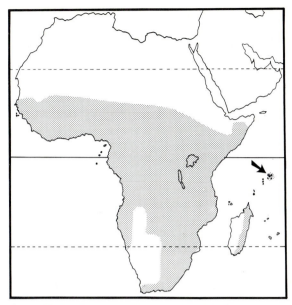

Figure 19-57. Distribution of living members of the family Hyperoliidae.

1924; *Elaphromantis* Laurent, 1941; *Heteropelis* Laurent, 1941; *Taphriomantis* Laurent, 1941; *Habrahyla* Goin, 1961); 41 species. Sub-Saharan Africa. Drewes (1984).
11. *Opisthothylax* Perret, 1966; 1 species. Southern Nigeria to Gabon. Drewes (1984).
12. *Phlyctimantis* Laurent and Combaz, 1950; 3 species. Southern Tanzania; western Africa. Drewes (1984).
13. *Tachycnemis* Fitzinger, 1843 (*Megalixalus* Günther, 1869); 1 species. Seychelles islands. Drewes (1984).
14. *Tornierella* Ahl, 1924 (*Rothschildia* Mocquard, 1905; *Mocquardia* Ahl, 1931); 2 species. Central Ethiopia. Drewes (1984).

RHACOPHORIDAE Hoffman, 1932

Definition.—There are eight holochordal, procoelous presacral vertebrae with nonimbricate neural arches; in some taxa, Presacral VIII is biconcave and the sacrum biconvex. Presacrals I and II are not fused, and the atlantal cotyles of Presacral I are widely separated. The sacrum has cylindrical diapophyses and a bicondylar articulation with the coccyx, which lacks transverse processes. The pectoral girdle is firmisternal; the omosternum, sternum, and postzonal elements are ossified, and the scapula is not overlain by the clavicle. Palatines are present; a parahyoid is absent, and the cricoid cartilage is complete. The maxillae and premaxillae are dentate. The astragalus and calcaneum are fused only proximally and distally; there are two tarsalia, and the phalangeal formula is increased by the addition of short, cartilaginous (ossified in some taxa) intercalary elements between the penultimate and terminal phalanges. The m. sartorius is discrete from the m. semitendinosus, and the tendon of the latter passes dorsal to the m. gracilis; the m. glutaeus magnus lacks an accessory tendon, and the m. adductor magnus has an accessory head. The pupil is horizontal. Aquatic Type IV tadpoles have beaks and denticles (absent in nonfeeding tadpoles of *Nyctixalus, Philautus,* and *Theloderma);* the spiracle is sinistral, and the trigeminal and facial ganglia are fused. The diploid chromosome complement is 26.

Most rhacophorids are arboreal frogs with enlarged toe pads, and some *Rhacophorus* have extensive webbing on the hands and feet, which gives them increased surface area for parachuting. Some rhacophorids (*Aglyptodactylus*) are terrestrial (Fig. 19-58). Size varies from 15 to 120 mm snout-vent length.

Distribution.—Rhacophorids are widely distributed in the Old World tropics (Fig. 19-59). Seven genera occur in the Asian tropics and subtropics from India and Sri Lanka to Japan, the Philippine Islands, and the Greater Sunda Islands. Two genera are endemic to Madagascar, and one is restricted to tropical Africa.

Fossil history.—None.

Life history.—The Madagascaran genera *Aglyptodactylus* and *Boophis* have small, aquatic eggs and tadpoles. *Buergeria, Chiromantis, Chirixalus, Polypedates,* and *Rhacophorus* have foam nests (usually on vegetation above water) and aquatic tadpoles. At least some species of *Nyctixalus, Philautus,* and *Theloderma* lay eggs in tree holes and have an abbreviated, nonfeeding larval stage.

Remarks.—The relationships of rhacophorid genera were discussed by S. Liem (1970). Blommers-Schlösser (1979a) moved the Mantellinae from the Rhacophoridae to the Ranidae. Dubois (1981) recognized two subfamilies.

Content.—Ten genera contain 186 species:

1. *Aglyptodactylus* Boulenger, 1919; 1 species. Madagascar. Blommers-Schlösser (1979a).
2. *Boophis* Tschudi, 1838 (*Elophila* Duméril and Bibron, 1841; *Buccinator* Gistel, 1848); 28 species. Madagascar. Blommers-Schlösser (1979b).
3. *Buergeria* Tschudi, 1838 (*Dendricus* Gistel, 1848); 4 species. Taiwan and Ryukyu Islands to Honshu, Japan. S. Liem (1970).
4. *Chirixalus* Boulenger, 1893; 7 species. Southeastern Asia. S. Liem (1970).
5. *Chiromantis* Peters, 1863; 3 species. Tropical Africa.
6. *Nyctixalus* Boulenger, 1882 (*Hazelia* Taylor, 1920; *Edwardtayloria* Marx, 1975); 3 species. India, Malaya, Philippines, and Greater Sunda Islands. S. Liem (1970).
7. *Philautus* Gistel, 1848 (*Orchestes* Tschudi, 1838; *Ixalus* Duméril and Bibron, 1841; *Pseudophilautus* Laurent, 1943); 63 spe-

Figure 19-58. A. *Aglyptodactylus madagascariensis* from Madagascar (photo by R. M. Blommers-Schlösser). **B.** *Boophis difficilis* from Perinet, Madagascar (photo by R. M. Blommers-Schlösser). **C.** *Chirixalus nongkhorensis* from Thailand (photo by K. Nemuras). **D.** *Chiromantis xerampelina* from Natal, South Africa (photo by W. E. Duellman).

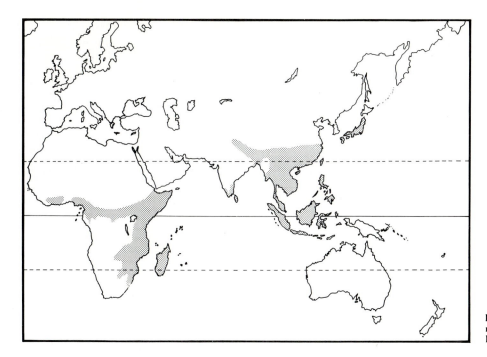

Figure 19-59. Distribution of living members of the family Rhacophoridae.

cies. India and Sri Lanka to China, the Philippines and Greater Sunda Islands. S. Liem (1970).

8. *Polypedates* Tschudi, 1838 (*Trachyhyas* Fitzinger, 1843); 11 species. Japan and eastern China throughout tropical Asia to Java, Borneo, and the Philippines. S. Liem (1970).

9. *Rhacophorus* Kuhl and van Hasselt, 1822 (*Leptomantis* Peters, 1867); 56 species. India and China to Japan and the Greater Sunda Islands. S. Liem (1970).

10. *Theloderma* Tschudi, 1838 (*Phrynoderma* Boulenger, 1893); 10 species. China and Burma to Malaya and Sumatra. S. Liem (1970).

MICROHYLIDAE Günther, 1859

Definition.—There are eight holochordal, procoelous presacral vertebrae with imbricate or nonimbricate neural arches; all vertebrae are procoelous in cophylines and genyophrynines, but Presacral VIII is biconcave and the sacrum biconvex in other subfamilies. Presacrals I and II are not fused, and the atlantal cotyles of Presacral I are widely separated. Ribs are absent. The sacrum has broadly dilated diapophyses and a bicondylar articulation with the coccyx (fused in some brevicipines), which lacks transverse processes. The pectoral girdle is firmisternal; the omosternum is absent in most taxa (present in brevicipines, cophylines, and some dyscophines and melanobatrachines). A cartilaginous sternum is present, and clavicles (if present) do not overlay the scapulae anteriorly (clavicles reduced, or absent in all but brevicipines).

Palatines are reduced or absent in most taxa; a parahyoid is absent, and the cricoid ring is complete. The maxillae and premaxillae are edentate in most taxa (dentate in dyscophines and some cophylines). The astragalus and calcaneum are fused only proximally and distally; there are two tarsalia, and the phalangeal formula is normal in most taxa (reduced in melanobatrachines and increased by the addition of short, cartilaginous intercalary elements between the penultimate and terminal phalanges in phrynomerines). The m. sartorius is discrete from the the m. semitendinosus, and the tendon of the latter passes dorsal to the m. gracilis; the m. glutaeus magnus has an accessory tendon, and the m. adductor magnus lacks an accessory head. The pupil is horizontal or round (vertically elliptical in dyscophines). Amplexus is axillary (males adherent to posterior part of female in some robust species). Many genera have direct development; of those having aquatic larvae, they are Type II tadpoles without beaks and denticles (except scaphiophrynines and *Otophryne*); the spiracle is single and median (an elongate, sinistral siphon in *Otophryne*), and the trigeminal and facial ganglia are fused. The diploid chromosome complement is 22–28.

Microhylids usually are small, but some attain snout-vent lengths of about 100 mm. The body shape varies from squat and small-headed to globular, toadlike animals and to arboreal frogs with expanded tips of the digits (Figs. 19-60, 19-61). The presence of two or three palatal folds is unique to this family, as is the fact that the nares remain closed in the tadpoles until shortly before metamorphosis.

Distribution.—The family is nearly cosmopolitan in

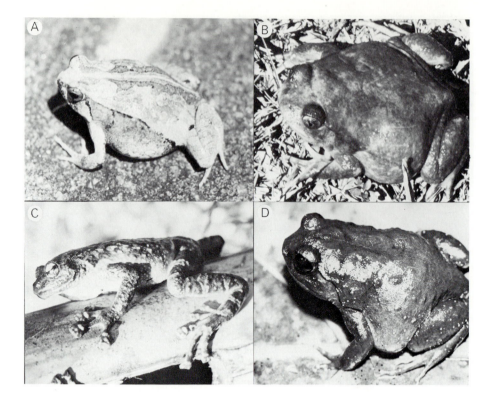

Figure 19-60. A. *Pseudohemisus granulosum* from Ampijoroa, Madagascar (photo by R. M. Blommers-Schlösser). **B.** *Dyscophus antongilii* from Antongil Bay, Madagascar (photo by R. M. Blommers-Schlösser). **C.** *Platypelis grandis* from Perinet, Madagascar (photo by R. M. Blommers-Schlösser). **D.** *Phrynomantis robusta* from Sempi, Papua New Guinea (photo by R. G. Zweifel).

Figure 19-61. A. *Cophixalus riparius* from Orumba, Papua New Guinea (photo by R. G. Zweifel). **B.** *Breviceps rosei* from Cape Province, South Africa (photo by J. Visser). **C.** *Phrynomerus bifasciatus* from Tasheni, Swaziland (photo by J. Visser). **D.** *Elachistocleis ovale* from Estado Táchira, Venezuela (photo by W. E. Duellman).

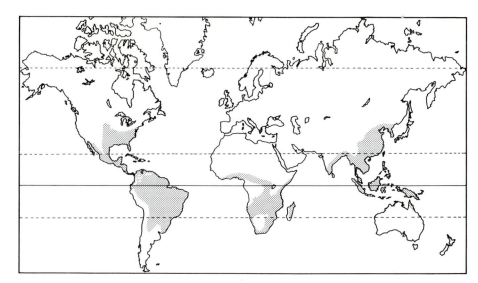

Figure 19-62. Distribution of the living members of the family Microhylidae.

temperate and tropical regions, except for the Palaearctic Region, most of Australia, the West Indies, and most oceanic islands (Fig. 19-62). The Asterophryinae is restricted to the Australo-Papuan region, where the Genyophryninae is most diverse, but also occurs in Celebes, Lesser Sunda Islands, and southern Philippine Islands. The Cophylinae and Scaphiophryninae are endemic to Madagascar, and the Dyscophinae occurs in Madagascar and southeastern Asia. The Microhylinae is widespread in the New World and southeastern Asia and adjacent islands; the Brevicipinae and Phrynomerinae are restricted to sub-Saharan Africa, a region also inhabited by the Melanobatrachinae, which also occurs in India.

Fossil history.—The only fossils referable to this family are those of *Gastrophryne* from the Miocene of Florida, U.S.A. (Holman, 1967).

Life history.—Most microhyline genera and phrynomerines have small, pigmented, aquatic eggs and free-swimming tadpoles with small terminal mouths lacking beaks and denticles. A dorsal funnel-shaped mouth is present in some Asiatic species *Microhyla* and *Kalophrynus*. Direct development of terrestrial eggs occurs in all asterophryines and genyophrynines and in some microhylines (*Myersiella* and presumably also in *Synapturanus*). In *Breviceps* and *Hoplophryne* terrestrial eggs hatch into nonfeeding tadpoles that complete their development within the nest. Knowledge of the life histories of many genera is lacking.

Remarks.—Both larval and adult morphology distinguish microhylids from other families of anurans. However, the relationships among the nine subfamilies are obscure. J. Savage (1973) combined the Asterophryinae and Genyophryninae (= Sphenophryninae) into one subfamily and made other changes in the contents of subfamilies; these changes were made mostly on geo-graphic grounds. Zweifel (1971) provided morphological evidence to support the recognition of the Asterophryinae and Genyophryninae. The Melanobatrachinae may be polyphyletic (J. Savage, 1973). Much of the basic information on microhylids is derived from H. Parker's (1934) monograph. More recent reviews are of South American microhylines (Carvalho, 1954), asterophryines (Zweifel, 1972a), and Madagascaran genera (Guibé, 1978).

Content.—Nine subfamilies contain 61 genera with 279 species:

SCAPHIOPHRYNINAE Laurent, 1946
1. *Pseudohemisus* Mocquard, 1895; 6 species. Madagascar. Guibé (1978).
2. *Scaphiophryne* Boulenger, 1882; 1 species. Madagascar. Guibé (1978).

DYSCOPHINAE Boulenger, 1882
3. *Calluela* Stoliczka, 1872 (*Colpoglossus* Boulenger, 1904; *Dyscophina* van Kampen, 1905; *Calliglutus* Barbour and Noble, 1916); 5 species. Southeastern Asia and Malay Archipelago to Borneo. Inger (1966).
4. *Dyscophus* Grandidier, 1872; 3 species. Madagascar. Guibé (1978).

COPHYLINAE Cope, 1889
5. *Anodonthyla* Müller, 1892; 3 species. Madagascar. Guibé (1978).
6. *Cophyla* Boettger, 1880; 1 species. Northern Madagascar. Guibé (1978).
7. *Madecassophryne* Guibe, 1974; 1 species. Madagascar. Guibé (1978).
8. *Mantipus* Peters, 1883 (*Mantiphrys* Mocquard, 1895); 7 species. Madagascar. Guibé (1978).

9. *Paracophyla* Millot and Guibe, 1951; 1 species. Eastern Madagascar. Guibé (1978).

10. *Platypelis* Boulenger, 1882 (*Platyhyla* Boulenger, 1889); 9 species. Madagascar. Guibé (1978).

11. *Plethodontohyla* Boulenger, 1882 (*Phrynocara* Peters, 1883); 7 species. Madagascar. Guibé (1978).

12. *Rhombophryne* Boettger, 1880; 1 species. Madagascar. Guibé (1978).

13. *Stumpffia* Boettger, 1881; 5 species. Madagascar. Guibé (1978).

ASTEROPHRYINAE Günther, 1859

14. *Asterophrys* Tschudi, 1838; 1 species. New Guinea. Zweifel (1972a).

15. *Barygenys* Parker, 1936; 7 species. Mountains of western Papua New Guinea and Louisiade Archipelago. Zweifel (1972a).

16. *Hylophorbus* Macleay, 1878 (*Metopostira* Mehely, 1901); 1 species. Papua New Guinea. Zweifel (1972a).

17. *Pherohapsis* Zweifel, 1972; 1 species. Papua New Guinea. Zweifel (1972a).

18. *Phrynomantis* Peters, 1867 (*Mantophryne* Boulenger, 1897; *Gnathophryne* Méhelÿ, 1901; *Pomatops* Barbour, 1910); 15 species. New Guinea, Moluccan islands, and Louisiade Archipelago. Zweifel (1972a).

19. *Xenobatrachus* Peters and Doria, 1878 (*Choanacantha* Méhelÿ, 1898); 9 species. New Guinea. Zweifel (1972a).

20. *Xenorhina* Peters, 1863 (*Callulops* Boulenger, 1888; *Pseudengystoma* Witte, 1930); 6 species. New Guinea and Louisiade Archipelago. Zweifel (1972a).

GENYOPHRYNINAE Boulenger, 1890

21. *Choerophryne* van Kampen, 1915; 1 species. New Guinea. Menzies and Tyler (1977).

22. *Cophixalus* Boettger, 1892 (*Phrynixalus* Boettger, 1895; *Aphantophryne* Fry, 1917); 23 species. New Guinea, Moluccas islands, and northeastern Queensland, Australia. Zweifel (1979); Cogger et al. (1983).

23. *Copiula* Méhelÿ, 1901; 3 species. New Guinea. Menzies and Tyler (1977).

24. *Genyophryne* Boulenger, 1890; 1 species. Eastern Papua New Guinea. Zweifel (1971).

25. *Oreophryne* Boettger, 1895 (*Mehelyia* Wandolleck, 1911); 24 species. Southern Philippine Islands, Celebes, Lesser Sunda Islands, New Guinea, and New Britain. Inger (1954); Zweifel (1956).

26. *Sphenophryne* Peters and Doria, 1878 (*Liophryne* Boulenger, 1897; *Microbatrachus* Roux, 1910; *Austrochaperina* Fry, 1912; *Oxydactyla* van Kampen, 1913); 17 species. New Guinea, New Britain, and extreme northern Australia. Cogger et al. (1983).

BREVICIPITINAE Bonaparte, 1850

27. *Breviceps* Merrem, 1820 (*Systoma* Wagler, 1830; *Engystoma* Fitzinger, 1843); 12 species. Southern Africa. Poynton (1964).

28. *Callulina* Nieden, 1910; 1 species. Mountains of Tanzania.

29. *Probreviceps* Parker, 1931; 3 species. Eastern Africa.

30. *Spelaeophryne* Ahl, 1924; 1 species. Eastern Tanzania.

MELANOBATRACHINAE Noble, 1931

31. *Hoplophryne* Barbour and Loveridge, 1928; 2 species. Mountains of Tanzania.

32. *Melanobatrachus* Beddome, 1878; 1 species. Southwestern India.

33. *Parhoplophryne* Barbour and Loveridge, 1928; 1 species. Usambara Mountains, Tanzania.

PHRYNOMERINAE Noble, 1931

34. *Phrynomerus* Noble, 1926 (*Brachymerus* Smith, 1847; *Fichteria* Scortecci, 1941); 4 species. Sub-Saharan Africa.

MICROHYLINAE Günther, 1859

35. *Arcovomer* Carvalho, 1954; 1 species. Southeastern Brazil. Carvalho (1954).

36. *Chaperina* Mocquard, 1892; 1 species. Malay Peninsula, Borneo, and the Philippines. Inger (1966).

37. *Chiasmocleis* Méhelÿ, 1904 (*Nectodactylus* Miranda-Ribeiro, 1924); 12 species. Cis-Andean South America and Panama.

38. *Ctenophryne* Mocquard, 1904; 1 species. Northern cis-Andean South America.

39. *Dasypops* Miranda-Ribeiro, 1924; 1 species. Coast of eastern Brazil.

40. *Dermatonotus* Méhelÿ, 1904; 1 species. Northeastern Brazil to Chacoan Argentina and Bolivia. Cei (1980).

41. *Elachistocleis* Parker, 1927; (*Microps* Wagler, 1828; *Stenocephalus* Tschudi, 1838); 4 species. Cis-Andean South America south to Argentina; Panama.

42. *Gastrophryne* Fitzinger, 1843; 5 species. Southern United States to Costa Rica. C. Nelson (1972).

43. *Gastrophrynoides* Noble, 1926; 1 species. Borneo. Inger (1966).

44. *Glossostoma* Günther, 1900; 2 species. Lowlands of Costa Rica to western Ecuador; Andes of Ecuador.

45. *Glyphoglossus* Günther, 1868; 1 species. Southeastern Asia. E. Taylor (1962).

46. *Hamptophryne* Carvalho, 1954; 1 species. Amazon Basin, South America. Duellman (1978).

47. *Hyophryne* Carvalho, 1954; 1 species. Northeastern Brazil.

48. *Hypopachus* Keferstein, 1867; 2 species.

Southern Texas, U.S.A., and Sonora, Mexico, to Costa Rica. C. Nelson (1973a).

49. *Kalophrynus* Tschudi, 1838 (*Calophryne* Fitzinger, 1843; *Berdmorea* Stoliczka, 1872); 9 species. Southern China to Borneo and the Philippines. Inger (1966).

50. *Kaloula* Gray, 1831 (*Hyladactylus* Tschudi, 1838; *Plectropus* Duméril and Bibron, 1841; *Calohyla* Peters, 1863; *Holonectes* Peters, 1863; *Callula* Günther, 1864; *Hylophryne* Fitzinger, in Steindachner, 1864; *Cacopoides* Barbour, 1908); 9 species. Korea and northern China to Lesser Sunda Islands, Philippines, and Sri Lanka.

51. *Metaphrynella* Parker, 1934; 2 species. Southern Malay Peninsula and Borneo. Inger (1966).

52. *Microhyla* Tschudi, 1838 (*Siphneus* Fitzinger, 1843; *Dendromanes* Gistel, 1848; *Diplopelma* Günther, 1859; *Scaptophryne* Fitzinger, 1861; *Copea* Steindachner, 1864; *Ranina* David, 1872); 21 species. Ryukyu Islands and China south through India to Sri Lanka, and southeastern Asia to Bali; one pur-

ported species from Madagascar.

53. *Myersiella* Carvalho, 1954; 1 species. Southeastern Brazil.

54. *Otophryne* Boulenger, 1900; 1 species. Guianan region of northern South America.

55. *Phrynella* Boulenger, 1887; 1 species. Malay Peninsula and Sumatra.

56. *Ramanella* Rao and Ramanna, 1925; 8 species. Southeastern India and Sri Lanka.

57. *Relictivomer* Carvalho, 1954; 1 species. Panama and northern Colombia.

58. *Stereocyclops* Cope, 1870 (*Emydops* Miranda-Ribeiro, 1920; *Ribeirina* Parker, 1934); 1 species. Coast of eastern Brazil. Cochran (1955).

59. *Synapturanus* Carvalho, 1954; 3 species. Colombia eastward to eastern Brazil.

60. *Syncope* Walker, 1973; 2 species. Amazon Basin in Ecuador and Peru.

61. *Uperodon* Duméril and Bibron, 1841 (*Hyperodon* Agassiz, 1846; *Cacopus* Günther, 1864; *Pachybatrachus* Keferstein, 1868); 2 species. India and Sri Lanka.

Literature Cited

Literature Cited

Abramoff, P., R. M. Darnell, and J. S. Balsano, 1964, "Serological relations of the toad populations of the Lake Michigan area," in C. A. Leone (ed.), *Taxonomic Biochemistry and Serology,* New York: Ronald Press, pp 515–525.

Abravaya, J. P., and J. F. Jackson, 1978, Reproduction in *Macrogenioglottus alipioi* Carvalho (Anura, Leptodactylidae), *Nat. Hist. Mus. Los Angeles Co. Contrib,* 298:1–9.

Adler, K., 1969, Extraoptic phase shifting of circadian locomotor rhythm in salamanders, *Science,* 164:1290–1292.

Adler, K., 1970, The role of extraoptic photoreceptors in amphibian rhythms and orientation: a review, *J. Herpetol.,* 4:99–112.

Adler, K., and D. H. Taylor, 1973, Extraocular perception of polarized light by orienting salamanders, *J. Comp. Physiol.,* 87:203–212.

Adler, W., 1901, Die Entwicklung der äusseren Körperform und des Mesoderms bei *Bufo vulgaris, Int. Monat. Anat. Physiol.,* 18:1–24.

Adolph, E. F., 1943, *Physiological Regulations,* Lancaster, Pennsylvania: Jacques Cattell Press.

Agar, W. E., 1910, The nesting habits of the tree-frog *Phyllomedusa sauvagii, Proc. Zool. Soc. London,* 1910:893–897.

Agarwal, S. K., and I. A. Niazi, 1977, Normal table of developmental stages of the Indian bull frog, *Rana tigerina* Daud. (Ranidae. Anura. Amphibia), *Proc. Natl. Acad. Sci. India,* 17(b):79–92.

Ahrenfeldt, R. H., 1960, Mating behavior of *Euproctus asper* in captivity, *British J. Herpetol.,* 2:194–197.

Alberch, P., 1981, Convergence and parallelism in foot evolution in the neotropical salamander genus *Bolitoglossa,* I. Function, *Evolution,* 35:84–100.

Alberch, P., 1983, Morphological variation in the neotropical salamander genus *Bolitoglossa, Evolution,* 37:906–919.

Alberch, P., and E. A. Gale, 1985, A developmental analysis of an evolutionary trend: digital reduction in amphibians, *Evolution,* 39:8–23.

Alcala, A. C., 1962, Breeding behavior and early development of frogs of Negros, Philippine Islands, *Copeia,* 1962:679–726.

Alcala, A. C., and W. C. Brown, 1956, Early life history of two Philippine frogs with notes on deposition of eggs, *Herpetologica,* 12:241–246.

Alexander, T. R., 1964, Observations on the feeding behavior of *Bufo marinus* (Linne), *Herpetologica,* 20:255-259.

Alley, K. E., and J. A. Cameron, 1983, Turnover of the anuran jaw muscles during metamorphosis (abstract), *Anat. Rec.,* 205:7.

Altig, R., and E. D. Brodie Jr., 1972, Laboratory behavior of *Ascaphus truei* tadpoles, *J. Herpetol.,* 6:21–24.

Altig, R., and P. C. Dumas, 1971, *Rana cascadae, Cat. Amer. Amphib. Rept.,* 105:1–2.

Alvarado, R. H., 1967, The significance of grouping on water conservation in *Ambystoma, Copeia,* 1967:667–668.

Amiet, J.-L., 1973, Voix d'amphibiens Camerounais I- *Astylosterninae:* genres *Leptodactylon, Scotobleps* et *Nyctibates, Ann. Fac. Sci. Cameroun,* 1973(12):79–100.

Amiet, J.-L., 1974, La ponte et la larve d'Opisthothylax immaculatus (Boulenger) (Amphibien anoure), *Ann. Fac. Sci. Cameroun,* 17:121–130.

Amiet, J.-L., 1976, Observations anatomiques et biologiques sur le genre *Werneria* Poche, 1903 (Amphibiens anoures, fam. Bufonidae), *Rev. Zool. Africains,* 90:33–45.

Amiet, J.-L., 1977, Les *Astylosternus* du Cameroun *(Amphibia Anura, Astylosterninae), Ann. Fac. Sci. Yaoundé,* 1977 (23–24):99–227.

Amiet, J.-L., 1980, Revision du genre *Leptodactylon* Andersson *(Amphibia, Anura, Astylosterninae), Ann. Fac. Sci. Yaoundé,* 1980(27):69–224.

Amiet, J.-L., 1981, Ecologie, éthologie et développement de *Phrynodon sandersoni* Parker, 1939 (Amphibia, Anura, Ranidae), *Amphib.-Rept.,* 2:1–13.

Andersen, M. L., 1978, *The Comparative Myology and Osteology of the Carpus and Tarsus of Selected Anurans,* Lawrence: Univ. Kansas, Ph.D. Dissertion.

Anderson, J. D., 1961, The life history and systematics of *Ambystoma rosaceum, Copeia,* 1961:371–377.

Anderson, J. D., 1967, A comparison of the life histories of coastal and montane populations of *Ambystoma macrodactylum* in California, *Amer. Midl. Nat.,* 77:323–355.

Anderson, J. D., 1968, *Rhyacotriton, R. olympicus, Cat. Amer. Amphib. Rept.,* 68:1–2.

Anderson, J. D., 1972, Phototactic behavior of larvae and adults of two subspecies of *Ambystoma macrodactylum, Herpetologica,* 28:222–226.

Anderson, J. D., and R. E. Graham, 1967, Vertical migration and stratification of larval *Ambystoma, Copeia,* 1967:371–374.

Anderson, J. D., D. D. Hassinger, and G. H. Dalrymple, 1971, Natural mortality of eggs and larvae of *Ambystoma t. tigrinum, Ecology,* 52:1107–1112.

Anderson, J. D., and P. J. Martino, 1966, The life history of *Eurycea l. longicauda* associated with ponds *Amer. Midl. Nat.,* 75:257–279.

Anderson, J. D., and G. K. Williamson, 1974, Nocturnal stratification in larvae of the mole salamander, *Ambystoma talpoideum Herpetologica,* 30:28–29.

Anderson, J. D., and G. K. Williamson, 1976, Terrestrial mode of reproduction in *Ambystoma cingulatum, Herpetologica,* 32:214–221.

Anderson, J. D., and R. D. Worthington, 1971, The life history of the Mexican salamander *Ambystoma ordinarium* Taylor, *Herpetologica,* 27:165–176.

Anderson, P. K., 1954, Studies in the ecology of the narrowmouthed toad, *Microhyla carolinensis carolinensis, Tulane Stud. Zool.,* 2:15–46.

Anderson, P. K., 1960, Ecology and evolution in island populations of salamanders in the San Francisco Bay region, *Ecol. Monog.,* 30:359–385.

Anderson, P. L., 1943, The normal development of *Triturus pyrrhogaster, Anat. Rec.,* 86:59–63.

Ando, T., M. Yamasaki, and K. Suzuki, 1973, *Protamines,* New York: Springer-Verlag.

Angel, F., 1947, *Vie et Moeurs des Amphibiens,* Paris: Payot.

Angle, J. P., 1969, The reproductive cycle of the northern ravine salamander *Plethodon richmondi richmondi,* in the Valley and Ridge Province of Pennsylvania and Maryland, *J. Washington Acad. Sci.,* 59:192–202.

Anstis, M., 1976, Breeding biology and larval development of *Litoria verreauxi* (Anura: Hylidae), *Trans. Roy. Soc. S. Australia,* 100:193–202.

Aplington, H. W. Jr., 1957, The insemination of body cavity and oviducal eggs of Amphibia, *Ohio J. Sci.,* 59:91–99.

Ardila-Robayo, M. C., 1979, Status sistemático del genero *Geobatrachus* Ruthven 1915 (Amphibia: Anura), *Caldasia,* 12:383–495.

Arnold, S. J., 1972, Species densities of predators and their prey, *Amer. Nat.,* 106:220–236.

Arnold, S. J., 1976, Sexual behavior, sexual interference and sexual defense in the salamanders *Ambystoma maculatum, Ambystoma tigrinum* and *Plethodon jordani, Zeit. Tierpsychol.,* 42:247–300.

Arnold, S. J., 1977, "The evolution of courtship behavior in New World salamanders with some comments on Old World salamandrids" in D. H. Taylor and S. I. Guttman (eds.), *The Reproductive Biology of Amphibians,* New York: Plenum Press, pp 141–183.

Arnold, S. J., 1982, A quantitative approach to antipredator performance. Salamander defense against snake attack, *Copeia,* 1982:247–253.

Arnold, S. J., and R. J. Wassersug, 1978, Differential predation on metamorphic anurans by garter snakes *(Thamnophis):* social behavior as a possible defense, *Ecology,* 59:1014–1022.

Arnoult, J., 1966, Ecologie et développement de *Mantella aurantiaca, Bull. Mus. Natl. Hist. Nat. Paris,* (2)37:931–940.

Arnoult, J., and M. Razarihelisoa, 1967, Contribution a l'étude des batraciens de Madagascar. Le genre *Mantidactylus* adultes et formes larvaires de *M. betsileanus* (Blgr.), *M. curtus* (Blgr.) et *M. alutus* (Peracca), *Bull. Mus. Natl. Hist. Nat. Paris,* (2)39:471–487.

Aronson, L. R., 1944, The sexual behavior of Anura. 6. The mating pattern of *Bufo americanus, Bufo fowleri,* and *Bufo terrestris, Amer. Mus. Novitat.,* 1250:1–15.

Ashby, K. R., 1969, The population ecology of a self-maintaining colony of the common frog *(Rana temporaria), J. Zool. London,* 158:453–474.

Ashley, H., P. Katti, and E. Frieden, 1968, Urea excretion in the bullfrog tadpole. Effect of temperature, metemorphosis and thyroid hormones, *Devel. Biol.,* 17:293–307.

Ashton, R. E. Jr., 1975, A study of movement, home range, and winter behavior of *Desmognathus fuscus* (Rafinesque), *J. Herpetol.,* 9:85–91.

Atkinson, B. G., 1981, "Biological basis of tissue regression and synthesis," in L. I. Gilbert and E. Frieden (eds.), *Metamorphosis. A Problem in Developmental Biology. 2nd Edition,* New York: Plenum Press, pp 397–444.

Atkinson, B. G., and J. J. Just, 1975, Biochemical and histological changes in the respiratory system of *Rana catesbeiana* larvae during normal and induced metamorphosis, *Devel. Biol.,* 45:151–165.

Atlas, M., 1935, The effect of temperature on the development of *Rana pipiens, Physiol. Zool.,* 8:290–310.

Atlas, M., 1938, The rate of oxygen consumption of frogs during embryonic development and growth, *Physiol. Zool.,* 11:278–291.

Atoda, K., 1950, Metamorphosis of the "non-aquatic frog" of the Palau Islands, Western Carolines, *Pacific Sci.,* 4:202–207.

Atz, J. W., 1952, Narial breathing in fishes and the evolution of internal nares, *Quart. Rev. Biol.,* 27:366–377.

Austin, C. R., and C. L. Baker, 1964, Spermatozoon of *Pseudobranchus striatus striatus, J. Reprod. Fertil.,* 7:123–125.

Awbrey, F. T., 1978, Social interaction among chorusing Pacific treefrogs, *Hyla regilla, Copeia,* 1978:208–214.

Axelrod, D. I., 1960, "The evolution of flowering plants," in S. Tax (ed.), *Evolution after Darwin, Vol. 1,* Chicago: Univ. Chicago Press, pp 227–305.

Axtell, R. W., 1958, Female reaction to the male call in two anurans (Amphibia), *Southwest. Nat.,* 3:70–76.

Bachmann, K., 1969, Temperature adaptations of amphibian embryos, *Amer. Nat.,* 104:115–130.

Bachmann, K., 1972, Nuclear DNA and developmental rate in frogs, *Quart. J. Florida Acad. Sci.,* 35:225–231.

Bachmann, K., and R. M. A. Blommers-Schlösser, 1975, Nuclear DNA amounts of frogs of Madagascar, *Zool. Anz.,* 194:13–21.

Bachmann, K., and J. P. Bogart, 1975, Comparative cytochemical measurements in the diploid-tetraploid species pair of hylid frogs *Hyla chrysoscelis* and *H. versicolor, Cytogenet. Cell. Genet.,* 15:186–194.

Bachmann, K., O. B. Goin, and C. J. Goin, 1972, Nuclear DNA amounts in vertebrates, *Brookhaven Symp. Biol.,* 23:419–447.

Bachmeyer, H., H. Michl, and B. Roos, 1967, "Chemistry of cytotoxic substances in amphibian toxins," in F. E. Russell and P. R. Saunders (eds.), *Animal Toxins,* Oxford: Pergamon Press, pp 395–399.

Badenhorst, A., 1978, The development and the phylogeny of the organ of Jacobson and the tentacular apparatus of Ichthyophis glutinosus (Linné), *Ann. Univ. Stellenbosch,* (A2)1:1–26.

Baer, J.-G., 1937, L'appareil respiratoire des gymnophiones, *Rev. Suisse Zool.,* 44:353–377.

Báez, A. M., 1981, Redescription and relationships of *Saltenia ibanezi,* a late Cretaceous pipid frog from northwestern Argentina, *Ameghiniana,* 18:127–154.

Bagnara, J. T., 1960, Pineal regulation of the body lightening reaction in amphibian larvae, *Science,* 132:1481–1483.

Bagnara, J. T., and W. Ferris, 1971, "Interrelationships of vertebrate chromatophores," in T. Kawamura, T. B. Fitzpatrick and M. Seiji (eds.), *Biology of Normal and Abnormal Melanocytes,* Tokyo: Univ. Tokyo Press, pp 57–76.

Bagnara, J. T., and W. Ferris, 1975, The presence of phyllomedusine melanosomes and pigments in Australian hylids, *Copeia,* 1975:592–595.

Bagnara, J. T., S. K. Frost, and J. Matsumoto, 1978, On the development of pigment patterns in amphibians, *Amer. Zool.,* 18:301–312.

Bagnara, J. T., and M. E. Hadley, 1969, The control of bright colored pigment cells of fishes and amphibians, *Amer. Zool.,* 9:465–478.

Bagnara, J. T., and M. E. Hadley, 1970, Endocrinology of the amphibian pineal, *Amer. Zool.,* 10:201–216.

Bagnara, J. T., and M. E. Hadley, 1973, *Chromatophores and Color Change,* Englewood Cliffs, New Jersey: Prentice-Hall, Inc.

Bagnara, J. T., M. E. Hadley, and J. D. Taylor, 1969, Regulation of bright-colored pigmentation of amphibians, *Gen. Comp. Endocrinol. Suppl.,* 2:425–438.

Bagnara, J. T., J. Matsumoto, W. Ferris, S. K. Frost, W. A. Turner Jr., T. T. Tchen, and J. D. Taylor, 1979, Common origin of pigment cells, *Science,* 201:410–415.

Bagnara, J. T., J. D. Taylor, and G. Prota, 1973, Color changes, unusual melanosomes, and a new pigment from leaf frogs, *Science,* 182:1034–1035.

Bagnara, J. T., W. A. Turner Jr., J. Rothstein, W. Ferris, and J. D. Taylor, 1979, Chromatophore organellogenesis, *Pigment Cell,* 4:13–27.

Bai A. R. K., 1956, Analysis of chromosomes in two genera of Microhylidae (Amphibia: Anura), *Proc. Natl. Inst. Sci. India,* 22(B):1–5.

Baird, I. L., 1951, An anatomical study of certain salamanders of the genus *Pseudoeurycea, Univ. Kansas Sci. Bull.,* 34:221–265.

Baker, C. L., L. C. Baker, and M. F. Caldwell, 1947, Observation of copulation in *Amphiuma tridactylum, J. Tennessee Acad. Sci.,* 22:87–88.

Baker, J. C., 1966, *Eurycea troglodytes, Cat. Amer. Amphib. Rept.,* 23:1–2.

Baker, L. C., 1937, Mating habits and life history of *Amphiuma tridactylum* Cuvier and effects of pituitary injections, *J. Tennessee Acad. Sci.,* 12:206–218.

Baldari, C. T., and F. Amaldi, 1976, DNA reassociation kinetics in relation to genome size in four amphibian species, *Chromosoma,* 59:13–22.

Baldauf, R. J., 1952, Climatic factors influencing the breeding migration of the spotted salamander, *Ambystoma maculatum* (Shaw), *Copeia,* 1952:178–181.

Baldwin, J., G. Friedman, and H. Lillywhite, 1977, Adaptation to temporary muscle anoxia in anurans: activities of glycolytic enzymes in muscles from species differing in their ability to produce lactate during exercise, *Australian J. Zool.,* 25:15–18.

Baldwin, R. A., 1974, The water balance response of the pelvic "patch" of *Bufo punctatus* and *Bufo boreas, Comp. Biochem. Physiol.,* 47(A):1285–1295.

Balinsky, B. I., 1960, *An Introduction to Embryology,* Philadelphia: W. B. Saunders Co.

Balinsky, B. I., 1969, The reproductive ecology of amphibians of the Transvaal high veld, *Zool. Africana,* 4:37–93.

Balinsky, B. I., and J. B. Balinsky, 1954, On the breeding habits of the South African bullfrog, *Pyxicephalus adspersus, South Africa J. Sci.,* 51:55–58.

Balinsky, J. B., 1970, "Nitrogen metabolism in amphibians," in J. W. Campbell (ed.), *Comparative Biochemistry of Nitrogen Metabolism. Vol. 2,* New York: Academic Press, pp 519–638.

Balinsky, J. B., S. M. Chemaly, A. E. Currin, A. R. Lee, R. L. Thompson, and D. R. Van Der Westhuizen, 1976, A comparative study of enzymes of urea and uric acid metabolism in different species of Amphibia, and the adaptation to the

environment of the tree frog *Chiromantis xerampelina* Peters, *Comp. Biochem. Physiol.,* 54(B):549–555.

Ballinger, R. E., and C. O. Mckinney, 1966, Developmental temperature tolerance of certain anuran species, *J. Exp. Zool.,* 161:21–28.

Bannikov, A. G., 1948, On the fluctuation of anuran populations (in Russian), *Dokl. Akad. Nauk. U. S. S. R.,* 61:131–134.

Bannikov, A. G., 1949, Notes on the biology of *Ranodon sibiricus* (in Russian), *Dokl. Akad. Nauk. Zool. U. S. S. R.,* 65:237–240.

Bannikov, A. G., 1950, Age distribution of a population and its dynamics in *Bombina bombina* L. (in Russian), *Dokl. Akad. Nauk. Zool. U. S. S. R.,* 70:101–103.

Bannikov, A. G., 1958, Die Biologie des Froschzahnmolches *Ranodon sibiricus* Kessler, *Zool. Jahrb. Syst.,* 86:245–249.

Barbault, R., 1974, Le régime alimentaire des amphibiens de la savane de Lamto (Côte d'Ivoire), *Bull. Inst. France Afrique Noire,* 36:952–972.

Barbault, R., and M. Trefaut Rodrigues, 1978, Observations sur la reproduction et la dynamique des populations de quelques anoures tropicaux. I. *Ptychadena maccarthyensis* et *Ptychadena oxyrhynchus, Terre et Vie,* 32:441–452.

Barbieri, F. D., 1976, Diffusible factors in anuran fertilization, *Acta Physiol. Latinoamer.,* 26:1–9.

Barbieri, F. D., and H. Salomón, 1963, Some experimental studies on glycogen and lactic acid in the developing eggs of *Bufo arenarum, Acta Embryol. Morphol. Exp.,* 6:304–310.

Barch, S. H., and J. R. Shaver, 1963, Regional antigenic differences in frog oviduct in relation to fertilization, *Amer. Zool.,* 3:157–165.

Barrio, A., 1969, Observaciones sobre *Chthonerpeton indistinctum* (Gymnophiona, Caecilidae) y su reproducción, *Physis,* 28:499–503.

Barrio, A., 1971, Sobre la conspecificidad de *Limnomedusa misiones* Schmidt y *Limnomedusa macroglossa* (Duméril et Bibron) (Anura, Leptodactylidae), *Physis,* 30:667–672.

Barrio, A., and D. Pistol de Rubel, 1970, Caracteristicas del cariotipo de los pseudidos (Amphibia, Anura), *Physis,* 29:505–510.

Barrio, A., and P. Rinaldi de Chieri, 1970a, Estudio chromosomico de *Caecilia occidentalis* (Gymnophiona, Caecilidae), *Physis,* 30:305–307.

Barrio, A., and P. Rinaldi de Chieri, 1970b, Estudios citogenéticos sobre el género *Pleurodema* y sus consecuencias evolutivas (Amphibia, Anura, Leptodactylidae) *Physis,* 30:309–319.

Barrio, A., and P. Rinaldi de Chieri, 1970c, Relaciones cariosistematicas de los Ceratophryidae de la Argentina (Amphibia, Anura), *Physis,* 30:321–329.

Barrio, A., and P. Rinaldi de Chieri, 1971, Contribución al esclaremcimiento de la posición taxofiletica de algunos batracios patagónicos de la familia Leptodactylidae mediante el análisis cariotípico, *Physis,* 30:673–685.

Barrio, A., and P. Rinaldi de Chieri, 1972, El complemento cromosómico de *Siphonops paulensis* (Gymnophiona, Caecilidae), *Physis,* 31:273–276.

Barrio, A., F. A. Saez, and P. Rinaldi de Chieri, 1971, The cytogenetics of *Chthonerpeton indistinctum* (Amphibia: Gymnophiona), *Caryologia,* 24:435–445.

Barron, E. J., C. G. A. Harrison, J. L. Sloan II, and W. W. Hay, 1981, Paleogeography, 180 million years ago to the present, *Ecol. Geol. Helveticae,* 74:443–470.

Barry, T. H., 1956, The antogenesis of the sound-conducting apparatus of Bufo angusticeps Smith, *Morphol. Jahrb.,* 97(4):477–544.

Barth, L. G., and L. J. Barth, 1954, *The Energetics of Development,* New York: Columbia Univ. Press.

Basinger, S., R. Hoffman, and M. Matthes, 1976, Photoreceptor shedding is initiated by light in the frog retina, *Science,* 194:1074–1076.

Batistic, R. F., M. Soma, M. L. Beçak, and W. Beçak, 1975,

Further study on polyploid amphibians. A diploid population of *Phyllomedusa burmeisteri, J. Heredity,* 66:160–162.

Batistoni, R., F. Andronico, J. Nardi, and G. Barsacchi-Pilone, 1978, Chromosome location of the ribosomal genes in *Triturus vulgaris meridionalis* (Amphibia Urodela). III. Inheritance of the chromosomal sites for 18s + 28s Ribosomal RNA, *Chromosoma,* 65:231–240.

Batistoni, R., S. de Lucchini, L. Vitelli, F. Andronico, J. Nardi, and G. Barsacchi-Pilone, 1980, Karyological analysis and distribution of ribosomal genes in *Hynobius keyserlingii* (Amphibia Urodela) and *Alytes obstetricans obstetricans* (Amphibia Anura), *Atti. Assoc. Genet. Italiano,* 25:31–35.

Bayley, I., 1950, The whistling frogs of Barbados, *J. Barbados Mus. Hist. Sci.,* 17:161–169.

Beattie, R. C., 1980, A physico-chemical investigation of the jelly capsules surrounding eggs of the common frog *(Rana temporaria temporaria), J. Zool. London,* 190:1–25.

Beaumont, J. de, 1933, La différenciation sexuelle dans l'appareil uro-genital du triton et son déterminisme, *Arch. Entwicklungsmech.,* 129:112–132.

Beçak, M. L., 1968, Chromosomal analysis of eighteen species of Anura, *Caryologia,* 21:191–208.

Beçak, M. L., W. Beçak, and M. N. Rabello, 1966, Cytological evidence of constant tetraploidy in the bisexual South American frog *Odontophrynus americanus, Chromosoma,* 19:188–193.

Beçak, M. L., W. Beçak, and M. N. Rabello, 1967, Further studies on polyploid amphibians (Ceratophrydidae). I. Mitotic and meiotic aspects, *Chromosoma,* 22:192–201.

Beçak, M. L., L. Denaro, and W. Beçak, 1970, Polyploidy and mechanisms of karyotypic diversification in Amphibia, *Cytogenetics* 9:225–238.

Beckenback, A. T., 1975, Influence of body size and temperature on the critical oxygen tension of some plethodontid salamanders, *Physiol. Zool.,* 48:338–347.

Becker, R. P., and R. E. Lombard, 1977, Structural correlates of function in the "opercularis" muscle, *Cell Tiss. Res.,* 175:499–522.

Bedriaga, J., 1882, Über die Begattung bei einigen geschwänzten Amphibien, *Zool. Anz.,* 5:265–268.

Beiswenger, R. E., 1975, Structure and function in aggregations of tadpoles of the American toad, *Bufo americanus, Herpetologica,* 31:222–233.

Beiswenger, R. E., 1977, Diel patterns of aggregative behavior in tadpoles of *Bufo americanus* in relation to light and temperature, *Ecology,* 58:98–108.

Beiswenger, R. E., 1981, Predation by gray jays on aggregating tadpoles of the boreal toad *(Bufo boreas), Copeia,* 1981:459–460.

Bêlehrádek, J., 1957, Physiological aspects of heat and cold, *Ann. Rev. Physiol.,* 19:59–82.

Bell, B. D., 1978, Observations on the ecology and reproduction of the New Zealand leiopelmid frogs, *Herpetologica,* 34:340–354.

Bell, G., 1975, The diet and dentition of smooth newt larvae *(Triturus vulgaris), J. Zool. London,* 176:411–424.

Bell, G., 1977, The life of the smooth newt *(Triturus vulgaris)* after metamorphosis, *Ecol. Monog.,* 47:279–299.

Bell, G., and J. H. Lawton, 1975, The ecology of the eggs and larvae of the smooth newt, *Triturus vulgaris* (Linn.), *J. Anim. Ecol.,* 44:393–424.

Bellis, E. D., 1957, The effects of temperature on salientian breeding calls, *Copeia,* 1957:85–89.

Bemis, W. E., K. Schwenk, and M. H. Wake, 1983, Morphology and function of the feeding apparatus in *Dermophis mexicanus* (Amphibia: Gymnophiona), *Zool. J. Linnaean Soc.,* 77:75–96.

Benbassat, J., 1970, Erythroid cell development during natural amphibian metamorphosis, *Devel. Biol.,* 21:557–583.

Bennett, A. F., 1974, Enzymatic correlates of activity metabolism in anuran amphibians, *Amer. J. Physiol.,* 226:1149–1151.

Bennett, A. F., 1978, Activity metabolism of the lower vertebrates, *Ann. Rev. Physiol.,* 400:447–469.

Bennett, A. F., and P. Licht, 1973, Relative contributions of anaerobic and aerobic energy production during activity in Amphibia, *J. Comp. Physiol.,* 87:351–360.

Bennett, A. F., and M. H. Wake, 1974, Metabolic correlates of activity in the caecilian *Geotrypetes seraphini, Copeia,* 1974:764–769.

Bennett, S. H., J. W. Gibbons, and J. Glanville, 1980, Terrestrial activity, abundance and diversity of amphibians in differently managed forest types, *Amer. Midl. Nat.,* 103:412–416.

Benson, D. G. Jr., 1968, Reproduction in urodeles. II. Observations on the spermatheca, *Experientia,* 24:853–854.

Bentley, P. J., 1966a, Adaptations of Amphibia to arid environments, *Science,* 152:619–623.

Bentley, P. J., 1966b, The physiology of the urinary bladder of Amphibia, *Biol. Rev.,* 41:275–316.

Bentley, P. J., 1974, "20. Actions of neurohypophyseal peptides in amphibians, reptiles, and birds," in *Handbook of Physiology. Section 8.*Endocrinology, New York: Academic Press, pp 545–563.

Bentley, P. J., 1984, Calcium metabolism in the Amphibia, *Comp. Biochem. Physiol.,* 79(A):1–5.

Bentley, P. J., A. K. Lee, and A. R. Main, 1958, Comparison of dehydration and hydration of two genera of frogs *(Heleioporus* and *Neobatrachus)* that live in areas of varying aridity, *J. Exp. Zool.,* 35:677–684.

Bentley, P. J., and A. R. Main, 1972, Zonal differences in permeability of the skin of some anuran Amphibia, *Amer. J. Physiol.,* 2:361–363.

Berger, L., 1977, "Systematics and hybridization in the *Rana esculenta* complex," in D. H. Taylor and S. I. Guttman (eds.), *The Reproductive Biology of Amphibians,* New York: Plenum Press, pp 367–388.

Berger, L., and J. Michalowski, 1963, Plazy, *Klucze Oznaczania Kregowców Polski,* 2:1–75.

Bern, H. A., and C. S. Nicoll, 1969, "The taxonomic specificity of prolactins," in M. Fontaine (ed.), *La Spécificité Zoologique des Hormones Hypophysaires et de Leurs Activités,* Paris: Centre Natl. Rech. Sci., pp 193–202.

Berry, P. Y., 1964, The breeding patterns of seven species of Singapore anura, *J. Anim. Ecol.,* 33:227–243.

Berry, P. Y., 1966, The food and feeding habits of the torrent frog, *Amolops larutensis, J. Zool. London,* 149:204–214.

Bertini, F., and J. M. Cei, 1960, Observaciones electroforeticas en seroproteinas de poblaciones Argentinas de *Bufo arenarum, Rev. Soc. Argentina Biol.,* 36:355–362.

Berven, K. A., 1981, Mate choice in the wood frog, *Rana sylvatica, Evolution,* 35:707–722.

Berven, K. A., D. E. Gill, and S. J. Smith-Gill, 1979, Countergradient selection in the green frog, *Rana clamitans, Evolution,* 33:609–623.

Besharse, J. C., and R. A. Brandon, 1973, Optomotor response and eye structure of the troglobitic salamander Gyrinophilus palleucus, *Amer. Midl. Nat.,* 89:463–467.

Besharse, J. C., and R. A. Brandon, 1974, Postembryonic eye degeneration in the troglobitic salamander *Typhlotriton spelaeus, J. Morph.,* 144:381–406.

Beshkov, V. A., and D. L. Jameson, 1980, Movement and abundance of the yellow-spotted toad *Bombina variegata, Herpetologica,* 36:365–370.

Beudt, E. L., 1930, Der Einfluss der Lichtes der Quarz-Quecksilber Lampe auf die Furschungs-und Larvenstadien verschieden Amphibien, *Zool. Jahrb. Syst.,* 47:623–684.

Beurden, E. van, 1979, Gamete development in relation to season, moisture, energy reserve, and size in the Australian waterholding frog *Cyclorana platycephalus, Herpetologica,* 35: 370–374.

Bhaduri, J. L., 1932, Observations on the urogenital system of the tree-frogs of the genus *Rhacophorus* Kuhl, with remarks on their breeding habits, *Anat. Anz.,* 74:336–343.

Bhaduri, J. L., 1953, A study of the urinogenital system of Salientia, *Proc. Zool. Soc. Bengal,* 6:1–111.

Bhaduri, J. L., and S. L. Basu, 1957, A study of the urinogenital system of Salientia. Part I. Ranidae and Hyperoliidae of Africa, *Ann. Mus. Royal Congo Belge. Sci. Zool.,* 55:1–56.

Bhati, D. P. S., 1969, Normal stages in the development of the larvae of *Rana tigerina* Daud and *Bufo andersonii* Bouleng., *Agra Univ. J. Res. (Sci.),* 18:1–13.

Birstein, V. J., 1982, Structural characteristics of genome organization in amphibians: differential staining of chromosomes and DNA structure, *J. Molec. Evol.,* 18:73–91.

Bisbee, C. A., M. A. Baker, A. C. Wilson, I. Hodji-Azimi, and M. Fischberg, 1977, Albumin phylogeny for clawed frogs *(Xenopus), Science,* 195:785–787.

Bischoff, W., and W. Böhme, 1980, Zur Kenntnis von *Paramesotriton caudopunctatus, Salamandra,* 16:137–148.

Bishop, S. C., 1926, Notes on the habits and development of the mudpuppy *Necturus maculosus, Bull. New York St. Mus.,* 268:1–60.

Bishop, S. C., 1941, The salamanders of New York, *Bull. New York St. Mus.,* 324:1–365.

Bishop, S. C., 1943, *Handbook of Salamanders,* Ithaca: Comstock Publ. Co.

Bizer, J. R., 1978, Growth rates and size at metamorphosis of high elevation populations of *Ambystoma tigrinum, Oecologia,* 34:175–184.

Black, J. H., 1970, A possible stimulus for the formation of some aggregations in tadpoles of *Scaphiopus bombifrons, Proc. Oklahoma Acad. Sci.,* 49:13–14.

Black, J. H., and R. B. Brunson, 1971, Breeding behavior of the boreal toad *(Bufo boreas boreas)* (Baird and Girard) in western Montana, *Gt. Basin Nat.,* 31:109–113.

Blair, A. P., 1942, Isolating mechanisms in a complex of four species of toads, *Biol. Symp.,* 6:235–249.

Blair, A. P., 1943, Population structure in toads, *Amer. Nat.,* 77:563–568.

Blair, A. P., 1946, The effects of various hormones on primary and secondary sex characters in juvenile *Bufo fowleri, J. Exp. Zool.,* 103:365–400.

Blair, A. P., 1950, Notes on Oklahoma microhylid frogs, *Copeia,* 1950:152.

Blair, W. F., 1953, Growth, dispersal and age at sexual maturity of the Mexican toad *(Bufo valliceps* Wiegmann), *Copeia,* 1953:208–212.

Blair, W. F., 1955, Mating call and stage of speciation in the *Microhyla olivacea-M. carolinensis* complex, *Evolution,* 9:469–480.

Blair, W. F., 1956, Call differences as an isolating mechanism in southwestern toads, *Texas J. Sci.,* 8:87–106.

Blair, W. F., 1958, Mating call and stage of speciation of anuran amphibians, *Amer. Nat.,* 92:27–51.

Blair, W. F., 1960, A breeding population of the Mexican toad *(Bufo valliceps)* in relation to its environment, *Ecology,* 41:165–174.

Blair, W. F., 1961, Calling and spawning seasons in a mixed population of anurans, *Ecology,* 42:99–110.

Blair, W. F., 1963, "Acoustic behavior of Amphibia," in R. G. Busnel (ed.), *Acoustic Behavior in Animals,* Amsterdam: Elsevier, pp 694–708, 803–804.

Blair, W. F., 1964, Evolution at populational and intrapopulational levels: isolating mechanisms and interspecies interactions in anuran amphibians, *Quart. Rev. Biol.,* 39:333–344.

Blair, W. F. (ed.), 1972, *Evolution in the Genus* Bufo, Austin: Univ. Texas Press.

Blair, W. F., and D. Pettus, 1954, The mating call and its significance in the Colorado River toad *(Bufo alvarius), Texas J. Sci.,* 6:72–77.

Blake, A. J. D., 1973, Taxonomy and relationships of myobatrachine frogs (Leptodactylidae): a numerical approach, *Australian J. Zool.,* 21:119–149.

Blanchard, F. N., 1934, Relation of the female *Hemidactylium scutatum* to her nest and eggs, *Copeia,* 1934:137–138.

Blanchard, F. N., and F. C. Blanchard, 1931, Size groups and their characteristics in the salamander *Hemidactylium scutatum* (Schlegel), *Amer. Nat.,* 65:149–164.

Blaustein, A. R., and R. K. O'Hara, 1981, Genetic control for sibling recognition?, *Nature,* 290:246–248.

Blaylock, L. A., R. Ruibal, and K. Platt-Aloia, 1976, Skin structure and wiping behavior of phyllomedusine frogs, *Copeia,* 1976:283–295.

Bles, E. J., 1905, The life history of *Xenopus laevis* Daud., *Trans. Roy. Soc. Edinburg,* 41:789–821.

Bles, E. J., 1907, "Notes on anuran development; Paludicola, Hemisus, and Phyllomedusa," in J. G. Kerr (ed.), *The Work of John Samuel Budgett,* Cambridge: Cambridge Univ. Press, pp 443–458.

Blommers-Schlösser, R. M. A., 1975a, A unique case of mating behaviour in a Malagasy tree frog, *Gephyromantis liber* (Peracca, 1893), with observations on the larval development (Amphibia, Ranidae), *Beaufortia,* 23:15–25.

Blommers-Schlösser, R. M. A., 1975b, Observations on the larval development of some Malagasy frogs, with notes on their ecology and biology (Anura: Dyscophinae, Scaphiophryninae and Cophylinae), *Beaufortia,* 24:7–26.

Blommers-Schlösser, R. M. A., 1976, Chromosomal analysis of twelve species of Microhylidae (Anura) from Madagascar, *Genetica,* 46:199–210.

Blommers-Schlösser, R. M. A., 1978, Cytotaxonomy of the Ranidae, Rhacophoridae, Hyperoliidae (Anura) from Madagascar with a note on the karyotype of two amphibians of the Seychelles, *Genetica,* 48:23–40.

Blommers-Schlösser, R. M. A., 1979a, Biosystematics of the Malagasy frogs. I. Mantellinae (Ranidae), *Beaufortia,* 29:1–77.

Blommers-Schlösser, R. M. A., 1979b, Biosystematics of the Malagasy frogs. II. The genus *Boophis* (Rhacophoridae), *Bij. Tot. Dierkunde (Zool.),* 49:261–312.

Bobka, M. S., R. G. Jaeger, and D. C. McNaught, 1981, Temperature dependent assimilation efficiencies of two species of terrestrial salamanders, *Copeia,* 1981:417–421.

Boell, E. J., P. Greenfield, and B. Higge, 1963, The respiratory function of gills in the larvae of *Amblystoma punctatum, Devel. Biol.,* 7:420–431.

Bogart, J. P., 1967, Chromosomes of the South American amphibian family Ceratophridae with a reconsideration of the taxonomic status of *Odontophrynus americanus, Canadian J. Genet. Cytol.,* 9:531–542.

Bogart, J. P., 1970, Systematic problems in the amphibian family Leptodactylidae (Anura) as indicated by karyotypic analysis, *Cytogenetics* 9:369–383.

Bogart, J. P., 1972, "Karyotypes," in W. F. Blair (ed.), *Evolution in the Genus* Bufo, Austin: Univ. Texas Press, pp 171–195.

Bogart, J. P., 1973, "Evolution of anuran karyotypes," in J. L. Vial (ed.), *Evolutionary Biology of the Anurans: Contemporary Research on Major Problems,* Columbia: Univ. Missouri Press, pp 337–349.

Bogart, J. P., 1974, A karyosystematic study of frogs in the genus *Leptodactylus* (Anura: Leptodactylidae), *Copeia,* 1974:728–737.

Bogart, J. P., 1980, "Evolutionary implications of polyploidy in amphibians and reptiles," in W. H. Lewis (ed.), *Polyploidy: Biological Relevance,* New York: Plenum Press, pp 341–378.

Bogart, J. P., 1981, Chromosome studies in *Sminthillus* from Cuba and *Eleutherodactylus* from Cuba and Puerto Rico (Anura: Leptodactylidae), *Life Sci. Contr. Royal Ontario Mus.,* 129:1–22.

Bogart, J. P., and C. E. Nelson, 1976, Evolutionary implications from karyotype analysis of frogs of the families Microhylidae and Rhinophrynidae, *Herpetologica,* 32:199-208.

Bogart, J. P., W. F. Pyburn, and C. E. Nelson, 1976, The karyotype of *Otophryne robusta* (Anura, Microhylidae), *Herpetologica,* 32:208–210.

Bogart, J. P., and M. Tandy, 1976, Polyploid amphibians: three more diploid-tetraploid species of frogs, *Science*, 193:334-335.

Bogart, J. P., and M. Tandy, 1981, Chromosome lineages in African ranoid frogs, *Monit. Zool. Italiano NS Suppl.*, 15:55–91.

Bogert, C. M., 1960, "The influence of sound on the behavior of amphibians and reptiles," in W. E. Lanyon and W. N. Tavolga (eds.), *Animal Sounds And Communication, Amer. Inst. Biol. Sci. Publ.*, 7:137–320.

Böhme, W., 1979, Zum Höchstalter des Feuersalamanders, *Salamandra salamandra* (Linnaeús, 1758): ein wiederentdecktes Dokument aus der Frühzeit der Terraristik. (Amphibia: Caudata: Salamandridae), *Salamandra*, 15:176–179.

Boice, R., and D. W. Witter, 1969, Hierarchical feeding behavior in the leopard frog *(Rana pipiens), Anim. Behav.*, 17:474–479.

Bokermann, W. C. A., 1962, Observações biológicas sobre *"Physalaemus cuvieri"* Fitz. 1826 (Amphibia, Salientia), *Rev. Brasil. Biol.*, 22:391–399.

Bokermann, W. C. A., 1963, Girinos de anfíbios Brasileiros - 1. (Amphibia - Salientia), *Ann. Acad. Brasil. Cien.*, 35:465–474.

Bokermann, W. C. A., 1965a, Field observations on the hylid frog *Osteocephalus taurinus* Fitz., *Herpetologica*, 20:252–255.

Bokermann, W. C. A., 1965b, Notas sobre as espécies de *Thoropa* Fitzinger (Amphibia, Leptodactylidae), *Ann. Acad. Brasil. Cien.*, 37:526–537.

Bokermann, W. C. A., 1966a, O gênero *Phyllodytes* Wagler, 1830 (Anura, Hylidae), *Ann. Acad. Brasil. Cien.*, 38:335–344.

Bokermann, W. C. A., 1966b, A new *Phyllomedusa* from southeastern Brasil, *Herpetologica*, 22:293–297.

Bokermann, W. C. A., 1978, Observações sobre hábitos alimentares do gavião *Geranospiza caerulescens* (Vieillot, 1817) (Aves, Accipitridae), *Rev. Brasil. Biol.*, 38:715–720.

Bolt, J. R., 1969, Lissamphibian origins: possible protolissamphibian from the Lower Permian of Oklahoma, *Science*, 166:888–891.

Bolt, J. R., 1977, Dissorophoid relationships and ontogeny, and the origin of the Lissamphibia, *J. Paleontol.*, 51:235–249.

Bolt, J. R., 1979, *"Amphibamus grandiceps* as a juvenile dissorophid: evidence and implications," in M. H. Nitecki (ed.), *Mazon Creek Fossils*, New York: Academic Press, pp 529–563.

Bond, A. N., 1960, An analysis of the response of salamander gills to changes in the oxygen concentration of the medium, *Devel. Biol.*, 2:1–11.

Bonebrake, J. E., and R. A. Brandon, 1971, Ontogeny of cranial ossification in the small-mouthed salamander, *Ambystoma texanum* (Matthes), *J. Morph.*, 133:189–204.

Borchers, H.-W., H. Burghagen, and J.-P. Ewert, 1978, Key stimuli of prey for toads *(Bufo bufo* L.): configuration and movement patterns, *J. Comp. Physiol.*, 128:189–192.

Bordzilovskaya, N. P., and T. A. Dettlaff, 1979, Table of stages of normal development of axolotl embryos and the prognostication of timing of successive developmental stages at various temperatures, *Axolotl Newslet.*, 7:2–22.

Boulenger, G. A., 1882a, *Catalogue of the Batrachia Salientia s. Ecaudata in the Collection of the British Museum, 2nd edition*, London: British Museum.

Boulenger, G. A., 1882b, *Catalogue of the Batrachia Gradientia s. Caudata and Batrachia Apoda in the* Collection of the British Museum, 2nd edition, London: British Museum.

Boulenger, G. A., 1884, Diagnoses of new reptiles and batrachians from the Solomon Islands, collected and presented to the British Museum by H. B. Guppy, Esq., M. B., H. M. S. 'Lark', *Proc. Zool. Soc. London*, 1884:210–213.

Boulenger, G. A., 1886, On the reptiles and batrachians of the Solomon Islands, *Trans. Zool. Soc. London*, 12:38–62.

Boulenger, G. A., 1897–1898, *The Tailless Batrachians of Europe*, London: Roy. Soc. London.

Boulenger, G. A., 1902, Further notes on the African batrachians, Trichobatrachus and Campsosteonyx, *Proc. Zool. Soc. London*, 1901:709–710.

Boulenger, G. A., 1906, (Untitled), *Proc. Zool. Soc. London*, 1(13):179.

Boulenger, G. A., 1920, A monograph of the South Asian, Papuan, Melanesian and Australian frogs of the genus *Rana, Rec. Indian Mus.*, 20:1–226.

Bourret, R., 1942, Les batraciens de l'Indochine, *Mem. Inst. Oceanograph. Indochine*, 6:1–547.

Bovbjerg, A. M., 1963, Development of the glands of the dermal plicae in *Rana pipiens, J. Morph.*, 113:231–243.

Bowker, R. G., and M. H. Bowker, 1979, Abundance and distribution of anurans in a Kenyan pond, *Copeia*, 1979:278–285.

Bowler, J. K., 1977, Longevity of reptiles and amphibians in North American collections, *Herpetol. Circ.*, 6:1–32.

Boy, J. A., 1972, Die Branchiosaurier (Amphibia) des saarpfälzischen Rotliegenden (Perm, SW-Deutschland), *Abh. Hess. L.-Amt Bodenforsch.*, 65:1–137.

Boy, J. A., 1974, Die Larven der rhachitomen Amphibien (Amphibia: Temnospondyli; Karbon-Trias), *Palaont. Zeit.*, 48:236–268.

Brachet, J., 1934, Étude du metabolisme de l'oeuf de grenouille *(Rana fusca)* au cours de développement. 1. - la respiration et la glycolyse de la segmentation à l'éclosion, *Arch Biol.*, 45:611–727.

Brachet, J., and J. Needham, 1935, Étude du metabolisme de l'oeuf de grenouille *(Rana fusca)* au cours de développement. IV. - La teneur en glycogéne de l'oeuf de la segmentation à l'éclosion, *Arch Biol.*, 46:821–835.

Bragg, A. N., 1940, Observations on the ecology and natural history of Anura. I. Habits, habitat and breeding of *Bufo cognatus* Say, *Amer. Nat.*, 74:424–438.

Bragg, A. N., 1942, Observations on the ecology and natural history of Anura. X. The breeding habits of Pseudacris streckeri Wright and Wright in Oklahoma including a description of the eggs and tadpoles, *Wasmann Coll.*, 5:47–62.

Bragg, A. N., 1945, The spadefoot toads in Oklahoma with a summary of our knowledge of the group II., *Amer. Nat.*, 79:52–72.

Bragg, A. N., 1962, Saprolegnia on tadpoles again in Oklahoma, *Southwest. Nat.*, 7:79–80.

Bragg, A. N., 1964, Lens action by jelly of frog's eggs, *Proc. Oklahoma Acad. Sci.*, 44:23.

Bragg, A. N., 1965, *Gnomes of the Night: The Spadefoot Toads*, Philadelphia: Univ. Pennsylvania Press.

Bragg, A. N., 1968, The formation of feeding schools in tadpoles of spadefoots, *Wasmann J. Biol.*, 26:11–26.

Brame, A. H. Jr., 1968, Systematics and evolution of the mesoamerican salamander genus *Oedipina, J. Herpetol.*, 2:1–64.

Branch, L. C., 1983, Social behavior of the tadpoles of *Phyllomedusa vaillanti, Copeia*, 1983:420–428.

Branch, L. C., and R. Altig, 1981, Nocturnal stratification of three species of *Ambystoma* larvae, *Copeia*, 1981:870–873.

Branch, L. C., and D. H. Taylor, 1977, Physiological and behavioural responses of larval spotted salamanders, *Comp. Biochem. Physiol.*, 58(A):269–274.

Branch, W. R., 1976, Two exceptional food records for the African bullfrog *Pyxicephalus adspersus* (Amphibia, Anura, Ranidae), *J. Herpetol.*, 10:266–268.

Brand, D. J., 1956, On the cranial morphology of *Scolecomorphus uluguruensis* (Barbour and Loveridge), *Ann. Univ. Stellenbosch*, 32(A):1–25.

Brandon, R. A., 1965, Morphological variation and ecology of the salamander *Phaeognathus hubrichti, Copeia*, 1965:67–71.

Brandon, R. A., 1966a, Systematics of the salamander genus *Gyrinophilus, Illinois Biol. Monog.*, 35:1–86.

Brandon, R. A., 1966b, *Phaeognathus, P. hubrichti, Cat. Amer. Amphib. Rept.*, 26:1–2.

Brandon, R. A., 1967a, *Gyrinophilus, Cat. Amer. Amphib. Rept.*, 31:1–2.

Brandon, R. A., 1967b, *Haideotriton, Cat. Amer. Amphib. Rept.*, 39:1–2.

Brandon, R. A., 1968, Structure of the eye of *Haideotriton wallacei,* a North American troglobitic salamander, *J. Morph.,* 124:345–352.

Brandon, R. A., 1970a, Size range, size at maturity, and reproduction of *Ambystoma (Bathysiredon) dumerilii* (Dugès), a paedogenetic Mexican salamander endemic to Lake Pátzcuaro, Michoacán, *Copeia,* 1970:385–388.

Brandon, R. A., 1970b, *Typhlotriton, T. spelaeus, Cat. Amer. Amphib. Rept.,* 84:1–2.

Brandon, R. A., 1976, Spontaneous and induced metamorphosis of *Ambystoma dumerilii* (Dugès), a paedogenetic Mexican salamander, under laboratory conditions, *Herpetologica,* 32:429–438.

Brandon, R. A., and R. G. Altig, 1973, Eggs and small larvae of two species of *Rhyacosiredon, Herpetologica,* 29:349–351.

Brandon, R. A., and D. J. Bremer, 1966, Neotenic newts, *Notophthalmus viridescens louisianensis,* in southern Illinois, *Herpetologica,* 22:213–217.

Brandon, R. A., and J. E. Huheey, 1981, Toxicity in the plethodontid salamanders *Pseudotriton ruber* and *Pseudotriton montanus* (Amphibia, Caudata), *Toxicon,* 19:25–31.

Brandon, R. A., G. M. Labanick, and J. E. Huheey, 1979, Learned avoidance of brown efts, *Notophthalmus viridescens louisianensis* (Amphibia, Urodela, Salamandridae), by chickens, *J. Herpetol.,* 13:171–176.

Brandon, R. A., J. Martan, J. W. E. Wortham, and D. C. Englert, 1974, The influence of interspecific hybridization on the morphology of the spermatozoa of *Ambystoma* (Caudata, Ambystomatidae), *J. Reprod. Fertil.,* 41:275–284.

Brattstrom, B. H., 1962, Thermal control of aggregation behavior in tadpoles, *Herpetologica,* 18:38–46.

Brattstrom, B. H., 1963, A preliminary review of the thermal requirements of amphibians, *Ecology,* 44:238–255.

Brattstrom, B. H., 1968, Thermal acclimation in anuran amphibians as a function of latitude and altitude, *Comp. Biochem. Physiol.,* 24:93–111.

Brattstrom, B. H., 1970, Thermal acclimation in Australian amphibians, *Comp. Biochem. Physiol.,* 35:69–103.

Brattstrom, B. H., and P. Lawrence, 1962, The rate of thermal acclimation in anuran amphibians, *Physiol. Zool.,* 35:148–156.

Brattstrom, B. H., and P. Regal, 1965, Rate of thermal acclimation in the Mexican salamander *Chiropterotriton, Copeia,* 1965:514–515.

Brattstrom, B. H., and R. M. Yarnell, 1968, Aggressive behavior in two species of leptodactylid frogs, *Herpetologica,* 24:222–228.

Brauer, A., 1897, Beiträge zur Kenntnis der Entwicklungsgeschichte und der Anatomie der Gymnophionen. Über die aussere Körperform. Beitrag 2, *Zool. Jahrb. Anat.,* 10:359–472.

Brauer, A., 1899, Beiträge zur Kenntniss der Entwicklung und Anatomie der Gymnophionen, II. Die Entwicklung der aussern Form, *Zool. Jahrb. Syst.,* 12:477–508.

Breckenridge, W. R., and S. Jayasinghe, 1979, Observations on the eggs and larvae of *Ichthyophis glutinosus, Ceylon J. Sci. (Biol. Sci.),* 13:187–202.

Breden, F., A. Lum, and R. Wassersug, 1982, Body size and orientation in aggregates of toad tadpoles *Bufo woodhousei, Copeia,* 1982:672–680.

Bridges, C. D. B., J. G. Hollyfield, P. Withovsky, and E. Gallin, 1977, The visual pigment and vitamin A of *Xenopus laevis* embryos, larvae, and adults, *Exp. Eye Res.,* 24:7–13.

Briegleb, W., 1962a, Zur Biologie und Ökologie des Grottenolms, *Zool. Anz.,* 166:87–91.

Briegleb, W., 1962b, Zur Biologie des Grottenolms *(Proteus anguineus* Laur. 1768) I., *Morphol. Oekol. Thier,* 51:271–344.

Briggs, J. L., and R. M. Storm, 1970, Growth and population structure of the Cascade frog, *Rana cascadae* Slater, *Herpetologica,* 26:283–300.

Brockelman, W. Y., 1969, An analysis of density effects and predation in *Bufo americanus* tadpoles, *Ecology,* 50:632–644.

Brodie, E. D. Jr., 1968, Investigations on the skin toxin of the adult rough-skinned newt, *Taricha granulosa, Copeia,* 1968:307–313.

Brodie, E. D. Jr., 1977, Salamander antipredator postures, *Copeia,* 1977:523–535.

Brodie, E. D. Jr., 1978, Biting and vocalization as antipredator mechanisms in terrestrial salamanders, *Copeia,* 1978:127–129.

Brodie, E. D. Jr., 1983, "Antipredator adaptations of salamanders: evolution and convergence among terrestrial species," in N. S. Margaris, M. Arianoutsou-Faraggitaki and R. J. Reiter (eds.), *Plant, Animal, and Microbial Adaptations to Terrestrial Environment,* New York: Plenum Publishing Corporation, pp 109–133.

Brodie, E. D. Jr., and E. D. Brodie III, 1980, Differential avoidance of mimetic salamanders by free-ranging birds, *Science,* 208:181–183.

Brodie, E. D. Jr., and D. R. Formanowicz Jr., 1981, Larvae of the predaceous diving beetle *Dystiscus verticalis* acquire an avoidance response to skin secretions of the newt *Notophthalmus viridescens, Herpetologica,* 37:172–176.

Brodie, E. D. Jr., D. R. Formanowicz Jr., and E. D. Brodie III, 1978, The development of noxiousness of *Bufo americanus* tadpoles to aquatic insect predators, *Herpetologica,* 34:302–306.

Brodie, E. D. Jr., J. L. Hensel Jr., and J. A. Johnson, 1974, Toxicity of the urodele amphibians *Taricha, Notophthalmus, Cynops* and *Paramesotriton* (Salamandridae), *Copeia,* 1974:506–511.

Brodie, E. D. Jr., R. T. Nowak, and W. R. Harvey, 1979, The effectiveness of antipredator secretions and behavior of selected salamanders against shrews, *Copeia,* 1979:270–274.

Brodie, E. D. Jr., and M. S. Tumbarello, 1978, The antipredator functions of *Dendrobates auratus* (Amphibia, Anura, Dendrobatidae) skin secretion in regard to a snake predator *(Thamnophis), J. Herpetol.,* 12:264–265.

Broman, I., 1900, Ueber Bau und Entwicklung der Spermien von Bombinator igneus, *Anat. Anz.,* 17:129–145.

Brooks, D. R., 1977, Evolutionary history of some plagiorchioid trematodes of anurans, *Syst. Zool.,* 26:277–289.

Brooks, D. R., 1984, "Platyhelminths," in G. L. Hoff, F. L. Frye and E. R. Jacobson (eds.), *Diseases of Amphibians and Reptiles,* New York: Plenum Publishing Corporation, pp 247–258.

Brooks, G. R., 1968, Natural history of a West Indian frog, *Leptodactylus fallax, Virginia J. Sci.,* 19:176.

Brophy, T. E., 1980, Food habits of sympatric larval *Ambystoma tigrinum* and *Notophthalmus viridescens, J. Herpetol.,* 14:1–6.

Browder, L. W., 1975, "Frogs of the genus *Rana,*" in R. C. King (ed.), *Handbook of Genetics, IV,* New York: Plenum Press, pp 19–33.

Brower, L. P., J. V. Z. Brower, and P. W. Westcott, 1960, Experimental studies of mimicry 5.The reactions of toads *(Bufo terrestris)* to bumblebees *(Bombus americanum)* and their robberfly mimics *(Mallophora bomboides),* with a discussion of aggressive mimicry, *Amer. Nat.,* 94:343–356.

Brown, B. C., 1967a, *Eurycea latitans, Cat. Amer. Amphib. Rept.,* 34:1–2.

Brown, B. C., 1967b, *Eurycea latitans nana, Cat. Amer. Amphib. Rept.,* 35:1–2.

Brown, C. W., 1968, Additional observations on the function of the nasolabial grooves of plethodontid salamanders, *Copeia,* 1968.728–731.

Brown, F. A. Jr., H. M. Webb, M. F. Bennett, and M. I. Sandeen, 1955, Evidence for an exogenous contribution to persistent diurnal and lunar rhythmicity under so-called constant conditions, *Biol. Bull.,* 109:238–254.

Brown, G. B., Y. H. Kim, H. Küntzel, H. S. Mosher, G. J. Fuhrman, and F. A. Fuhrman, 1977, Chemistry and pharmacology of skin toxins from the frog *Atelopus zeteki* (atelopidtoxin; zetekitoxin), *Toxicon,* 15:115–128.

Brown, H. A., 1967a, High temperature tolerance of the eggs

of a desert anuran, *Scaphiopus hammondii, Copeia,* 1967:365–370.

Brown, H. A., 1967b, Embryonic temperature adaptations and genetic compatability in two allopatric populations of the spadefoot toad, *Scaphiopus hammondi, Evolution,* 21: 742–761.

Brown, H. A., 1969, The heat resistance of some anuran tadpoles (Hylidae and Pelobatidae), *Copeia,* 1969:138–147.

Brown, H. A., 1975a, Temperature and development of the tailed frog, *Ascaphus truei, Comp. Biochem. Physiol.,* 50(A):397–505.

Brown, H. A., 1975b, Embryonic temperature adaptations of the Pacific treefrog, *Hyla regilla, Comp. Biochem. Physiol.,* 51(A):863–873.

Brown, H. A., 1976a, The time-temperature relation of embryonic development in the northwestern salamander, *Ambystoma gracile, Canadian J. Zool.,* 54:552–558.

Brown, H. A., 1976b, The status of California and Arizona populations of the western spadefoot toads (genus *Scaphiopus), Nat. Hist. Mus. Los Angeles Co. Contrib.,* 286:1–15.

Brown, H. A., 1977, Oxygen consumption of a large, cold-adapted frog egg *(Ascaphus truei* (Amphibia: Ascaphidae)), *Canadian J. Zool.,* 55:343–348.

Brown, L. E., and M. J. Littlejohn, 1971, "Male release call in the *Bufo americanus* group," in W. F. Blair (ed.), *Evolution in the Genus* Bufo, Austin: Univ. Texas Press, pp 310–323.

Brown, L. E., and J. R. Pierce, 1967, Male-male interactions and chorusing intensities of the Great Plains toad, *Bufo cognatus, Copeia,* 1967:149–154.

Brown, P. S., S. A. Hastings, and B. E. Frye, 1977, A comparison of water-balance response in five species of plethodontid salamander, *Physiol. Zool.,* 50:203–214.

Brown, W. C., 1952, The amphibians of the Solomon Islands, *Bull. Mus. Comp. Zool.,* 107:1–64.

Brown, W. C., and A. C. Alcala, 1961, Populations of amphibians and reptiles in the submontane and montane forests of Cuernos de Negros, Philippine Islands, *Ecology,* 42:628–636.

Brown, W. C., and A. C. Alcala, 1964, Relationship of the herpetofaunas of the non-dipterocarp communities to that of the dipterocarp forest on southern Negros Island, Philippines, *Sencken. Biol.,* 45:591–611.

Brown, W. C., and A. C. Alcala, 1970, Population ecology of the frog *Rana erythraea* in southern Negros, Philippines, *Copeia,* 1970:611–622.

Brown, W. C., and A. C. Alcala, 1983, "Modes of reproduction of Philippine Anurans," in A. G. J. Rhodin and K. Miyata (eds.), *Advances in Herpetology and Evolutionary Biology,* Cambridge, Massachusetts: Mus. Comp. Zool., pp 416–428.

Brown, W. C., and F. Parker, 1970, New frogs of the genus *Batrachylodes* (Ranidae) from the Solomon Islands, *Breviora,* 346:1–31.

Broyles, R. H., 1981, "Changes in the blood during amphibian metamorphosis," in L. I. Gilbert and E. Frieden (eds.), *Metamorphosis. A Problem in Developmental Biology. 2nd Edition,* New York: Plenum Press, pp 461–490.

Bruce, R. C., 1971, Life cycle and population structure of the salamander *Stereochilus marginatus* in North Carolina, *Copeia,* 1971:234–246.

Bruce, R. C., 1972a, Variation in the life cycle of the salamander *Gyrinophilus porphyriticus, Herpetologica,* 28:230–245.

Bruce, R. C., 1972b, The larval life of the red salamander, *Pseudotriton ruber, J. Herpetol.,* 6:43–51.

Bruce, R. C., 1975, Reproductive biology of the mud salamander, *Pseudotriton montanus,* in western South Carolina, *Copeia,* 1975:129–137.

Bruce, R. C., 1976, Population structure, life history and evolution of paedogenesis in the salamander *Eurycea neotenes, Copeia,* 1976:242–249.

Bruce, R. C., 1978a, Life-history patterns of the salamander *Gyrinophilus porphyriticus* in the Cowee Mountains, North Carolina, *Herpetologica,* 34:53–64.

Bruce, R. C., 1978b, Reproductive biology of the salamander *Pseudotriton ruber* in the southern Blue Ridge Mountains, *Copeia,* 1978:417–423.

Brum-Zorrilla, N., and F. A. Saez, 1968, Chromosomes of Leptodactylidae (Amphibia, Anura), *Experientia,* 24:969.

Bruner, H. L., 1896, Ein neuer Muskelapparat zum Schliessen und Öffnen der Nasenlöcher bei den Salamandriden, *Anat. Anz.,* 12:272–273.

Bruner, H. L., 1901, The smooth facial muscles of Anura and Salamandrina, a contribution to the anatomy and physiology of the respiratory mechanism of the amphibians, *Morphol. Jahrb.,* 29:317–364.

Bruner, H. L., 1914, Jacobson's organ and the respiratory mechanism of amphibians, *Morphol. Jahrb.,* 48:157–164.

Brunst, V. V., 1955, The axolotl *(Siredon mexicanum)* I. As material for scientific research, *Lab. Invest.,* 4:45–64.

Bucher, T. L., M. J. Ryan, and G. A. Bartholomew, 1982, Oxygen consumption during resting, calling, and nest building in the frog *Physalaemus pustulosus, Physiol. Zool.,* 55:10–22.

Budgett, J. S., 1899, Notes on the batrachians of the Paraguayan Chaco, with observations upon their breeding habits and development, especially with regard to *Phyllomedusa hypochondrialis* Cope. Also a description of a new genus, *Quart. J. Microsc. Sci. (N. S.),* 42:305–333.

Budtz, P. E., 1977, Aspects of moulting in anurans and its control, *Symp. Zool. Soc. London,* 39:317–334.

Bunnell, P., 1973, Vocalizations in the territorial behavior of the frog *Dendrobates pumilio, Copeia,* 1973:277–284.

Burghagen, H., and J.-P. Ewert, 1983, Influence of the background for discriminating object motion and self-induced motion in toads *Bufo bufo* (L.), *J. Comp. Physiol.,* 152(A): 241–249.

Burley, N., 1977, Parental investment, mate choice, and mate quality, *Proc. Natl. Acad. Sci. U. S. A.,* 74:3476–3479.

Burton, T. C., 1980, Phylogenetic and functional significance of cutaneous muscles in microhylid frogs, *Herpetologica,* 36:256–264.

Burton, T. C., 1983a, The musculature of the Papuan frog *Phrynomantis stictogaster* (Anura, Microhylidae), *J. Morph.,* 175:307–324.

Burton, T. C., 1983b, *The Phylogeny of the Papuan Subfamily Asterophryinae (Anura: Microhylidae),* Adelaide: Univ. Adelaide, Ph.D. Dissertion.

Burton, T. M., 1976, An analysis of the feeding ecology of the salamanders (Amphibia, Urodela) of the Hubbard Brook Experimental Forest, New Hampshire, *J. Herpetol.,* 10:187–204.

Burton, T. M., 1977, Population estimates, feeding habits and nutrient and energy relationships of *Notophthalmus v. viridescens,* in Mirror Lake New Hampshire, *Copeia,* 1977:139–143.

Burton, T. M., and G. E. Likens, 1975, Salamander populations and biomass in the Hubbard Brook Experimental Forest, New Hampshire, *Copeia,* 1975:541–546.

Bury, R. B., 1972, Small mammals and other prey in the diet of the Pacific giant salamander (Dicamptodon ensatus), *Amer. Midl. Nat.,* 87:524–526.

Busack, S. D., 1976, A review of the biology of the gold-striped salamander, *Chioglossa lusitanica* (Amphibia: Salamandridae), *Biol. Conserv.,* 10:309—319.

Bush, G. L., S. M. Case, A. C. Wilson, and J. L. Patton, 1977, Rapid speciation and chromosomal evolution in mammals, *Proc. Natl. Acad. Sci. U. S. A.,* 74:3942–3946.

Busse, K., 1981, Revision der Farbmuster-Variabilität in der Madagassischen Gattung *Mantella* (Salientia: Ranidae), *Amphib.-Rept.,* 2:23–42.

Byrne, J. J., and R. J. White, 1975, Cyclic changes in liver and muscle glycogen tissue lipid and blood glucose in a natural occurring population of *Rana catesbeiana, Comp. Biochem. Physiol.,* 50(A):709–715.

Cagle, F. R., 1948, Observations on a population of the salamander *Amphiuma tridactylum* Cuvier, *Ecology,* 29:479–491.

Calaby, J. H., 1956, The food habits of the frog, *Myobatrachus gouldii* (Gray), *West. Australian Nat.,* 5:93–96.

Caldwell, J. P., 1982, Disruptive selection: a tail color polymorphism in *Acris* tadpoles in response to differential predation, *Canadian J. Zool.,* 60:2817–2818.

Caldwell, J. P., J. H. Thorp, and T. O. Jervey, 1981, Predator-prey relationships among larval dragonflies, salamanders, and anurans, *Oecologia,* 46:285–289.

Calef, G. W., 1973, Natural mortality of tadpoles in a population of *Rana aurora, Ecology,* 54:741–758.

Callan, H. G., and L. Lloyd, 1960, Lampbrush chromosomes of crested newts *Triturus cristatus* (Laurenti), *Phil. Trans. Roy. Soc. London,* (B)243:135–219.

Calow, L. J., and R. McN. Alexander, 1973, A mechanical analysis of a hind leg of a frog *(Rana temporaria), J. Zool.,* 171:293–321.

Cambar, R., and J. P. Gipouloux, 1956, Table cronologique du développement embryonaire et larvaire du crapaud commun, *Bufo bufo* L., *Bull. Biol. France-Belgique,* 90:188–217.

Cambar, R., and B. Marrot, 1954, Table cronologique du développement de la grenouille agile *(Rana dalmatina* Bon.), *Bull. Biol. France-Belgique,* 88:168–177.

Cambar, R., and S. Martin, 1959, Table cronologique du développement embryonaire et larvaire du crapaud accoucheur *(Alytes obstetricans* Laur.), *Actes Soc. Lin. Bordeaux,* 98: 1–20.

Candelas, G. C., and M. Gomez, 1963, Nitrogen excretion in tadpoles of *Leptodactylus albilabris* and *Rana catesbeiana, Amer. Zool.,* 3:521–522.

Candelas, G. C., E. Ortiz, C. Vasquez, and L. Felix, 1961, Respiratory metabolism in tadpoles of *Leptodactylus albilabris, Amer. Zool.,* 1:348.

Cannatella, D. C., 1984, Two new species of the leptodactylid frog genus *Phrynopus* with comments on the phylogeny of the genus, *Occ. Pap. Mus. Nat. Hist. Univ. Kansas,* 113:1–16.

Cannatella, D. C., and W. E. Duellman, 1984, Leptodactylid frogs of the *Physalaemus pustulosus* group, *Copeia,* 1984:902–921.

Canning, E. V., E. Elkan, and P. I. Trigg, 1964, *Plistophora myotrophica* spec. nov. causing high mortality in the common toad *Bufo bufo* L. with notes on the maintenance of *Bufo* and *Xenopus* in the laboratory, *J. Protozool.,* 11:157–166.

Cannon, M. S., D. C. Brindley, and M. McGill, 1978, The paracnemid gland of *Bufo alvarius, Texas J. Sci.,* 30:133–143.

Capranica, R. R., 1965, The evoked vocal response of the bullfrog, *Massachusetts Inst. Tech. Res. Monog.,* 33:1–106.

Capranica, R. R., 1976, "The auditory system," in B. Lofts (ed.), *Physiology of the Amphibia, Vol. III,* New York: Academic Press, pp 443–466.

Capranica, R. R., 1977, "Auditory processing of vocal signals in anurans," in D. H. Taylor and S. I. Guttman (eds.), *The Reproductive Biology of Amphibians,* New York: Plenum Press, pp 337–355.

Capranica, R. R., L. S. Frishkopf, and E. Nevo, 1973, Encoding of geographic dialects in the auditory system of the cricket frog, *Science,* 182:1272–1275.

Cardellini, P., and M. Sala, 1979, Metamorphic variations in the hemoglobins of *Bombina variegata* (L.), *Comp. Biochem. Physiol.,* 64(B):113–116.

Cardoso, A. J., 1981, *Organização Espacial e Temporal na Reproducao e Vida Larvária em Uma Comunidade de Hilídeos no Sudeste do Brasil (Amphibia, Anura),* Inst. Biol. Univ. Estad. Campinas, Dissert.

Cardoso, A. J., and I. Sazima, 1977, Batracofagia fase adulta e larvária da rä pimenta, *Leptodactylus labyrinthicus* (Spix, 1824) Anura, *Ciencia Cultura,* 29:1130–1132.

Carey, C., 1978, Factors affecting body temperatures of toads, *Oecologia,* 35:197–219.

Cargo, D. G., 1960, Predation of eggs of the spotted salamander, *Ambystoma maculatum,* by the leech, *Macrobdella decora, Chesapeake Sci.,* 1:119–120.

Carlson, S. S., A. C. Wilson, and R. D. Maxson, 1978, Do albumin clocks run on time?, *Science,* 200:1183–1185.

Carpenter, C. C., 1953, An ecological survey of the herpetofauna of the Grand Teton-Jackson Hole area of Wyoming, *Copeia,* 1953:170–174.

Carr, A. F. Jr., 1940, A contribution to the herpetology of Florida, *Univ. Florida Publ. Biol. Sci.,* 3:1–118.

Carr, A. F. Jr., and C. J. Goin, 1943, Neoteny in Florida salamanders, *Proc. Florida Acad. Sci.,* 6:37–40.

Carr, A. H., R. L. Amborski, D. D. Culley Jr., and G. F. Amborski, 1976, Aerobic bacteria in the intestinal tracts of bullfrogs *(Rana catesbeiana)* maintained at low temperatures, *Herpetologica,* 32:239–244.

Carroll, R. L., 1980, "The hyomandibular as a supporting element in the skull of primitive tetrapods," in A. L. Panchen (ed.), *The Terrestrial Environment and Origin of Land Vertebrates,* London: Academic Press, pp 293–317.

Carroll, R. L., and P. J. Currie, 1975, Microsaurs as possible apodan ancestors, *Zool. J. Linn. Soc.,* 57:229–247.

Carroll, R. L., and R. Holmes, 1980, The skull and jaw musculature as guides to the ancestry of salamanders, *Zool. J. Linn. Soc.,* 68(1):1–40.

Carter, D. B., 1979, Structure and function of the subcutaneous lymph sacs in the anura (Amphibia), *J. Herpetol.,* 13:321–327.

Caruso, M. A., 1949, Sobre el ciclo sexual anual de algunos Hylidae del norte argentino *(Phyllomedusa sauvagii e Hyla raddiana), Acta Zool. Lilloana,* 8:83–103.

Carvalho, A. L. de, 1949, Notos sôbre os hábitos de "Dendrophryniscus brevipollicatus" Espada (Amphibia, Anura), *Rev. Brasil. Biol.,* 9:223–227.

Carvalho, A. L. de, 1954, A preliminary synopsis of the genera of American microhylid frogs, *Occ. Pap. Mus. Zool. Univ. Michigan,* 555:1–19.

Case, S. M., 1978, Biochemical systematics of members of the genus *Rana* native to western North America, *Syst. Zool.,* 27:299–311.

Case, S. M., P. G. Haneline, and M. F. Smith, 1975, Protein variation in several species of *Hyla, Syst. Zool.,* 24:281–295.

Case, S. M., and M. H. Wake, 1977, Immunological comparisons of caecilian albumins (Amphibia: Gymnophiona), *Herpetologica,* 33:94–98.

Catton, W. T., 1976, "Cutaneous mechanoreceptors," in R. Llinas and W. Precht (eds.), *Frog Neurobiology,* Berlin: Springer-Verlag, pp 629–642.

Cecil, S. G., and J. J. Just, 1979, Survival rate, population density and development of a naturally occurring anuran larvae *(Rana catesbeiana), Copeia,* 1979:447–453.

Cedrini, L., and A. Fasolo, 1971, Olfactory attractants in sex recognition of the crested newt. An electrophysiological research, *Monit. Zool. Italiano N.S.,* 5:223–229.

Cei, G., 1944, Analisi biogeographica e richerche biologiche e sperimenti sul cido sessuale annuo delle Rana rosse d'Europa, *Monit. Zool. Italiano N.S. Suppl.,* 54:1–117.

Cei, J. M., 1948, El ritmo estacional en los fenómenos cíclicos endocrinos sexuales de la rana criolla *Leptodactylus ocellatus* (L.) del norte argentino, *Acta Zool. Lilloana,* 6:283–331.

Cei, J. M., 1949a, Sobre la biología sexual de un batracio de gran altura de la region andina *(Telmatobius schreiteri* Vellard), *Acta Zool. Lilloana,* 7:467–488.

Cei, J. M., 1949b, El ciclo sexual y el predominio de la espermatogénesis anual continua en batracios chaquenos, *Acta Zool. Lilloana,* 7:527–544.

Cei, J. M., 1950, *Leptodactylus chaquensis* n. sp. y el valor sistemático real de la especie Linneana *Leptodactylus ocellatus* en la Argentina, *Acta Zool. Lilloana,* 9:395–423.

Cei, J. M., 1959, Ecological and physiological observations on polymorphic populations of the toad *Bufo arenarum* Hensel from Argentina, *Evolution,* 13:532–536.

Cei, J. M., 1961, Pleurodema bufonina Bell, anfibio austral con ciclo espermatogenetico discontinuo autoregulado, *Arch. Zool. Italia,* 46:167–180.

Cei, J. M., 1962, *Batracios de Chile,* Santiago: Univ. Chile.

Cei, J. M., 1963, Some precipitin tests and preliminary remarks on the systematic relationships of four South American families of frogs, *Serol. Mus. Bull.,* 30:4–6.

Cei, J. M., 1969, The patagonian telmatobiid fauna of the volcanic Somuncurá Plateau, *J. Herpetol.,* 3:1–18.

Cei, J. M., 1980, Amphibians of Argentina, *Monit. Zool. Italiano N.S. Monog.,* 2:1–609.

Cei, J. M., and L. F. Capurro, 1958, Biología y desarrollo de *Eupsophus taeniatus* Girard, *Invest. Zool. Chileno,* 4:150–182.

Cei, J. M., and V. Erspamer, 1966, Biochemical taxonomy of South American amphibians by means of skin amines and polypeptides, *Copeia,* 1966:74–78.

Cei, J. M., V. Erspamer, and M. Roseghini, 1972, "Biogenic amines," in W. F. Blair (ed.), *Evolution In The Genus* Bufo, Austin: Univ. Texas Press, pp 233–243.

Cei, J. M., I. R. G. Ruíz, and W. Beçak, 1982, *Odontophrynus barrioi,* a new species of anuran from Argentina, *J. Herpetol.,* 16:97–102.

Chaine, T., 1901, Anatomie compareé de certains muscles sushyoidiens, *Bull. Scient. France-Belgique,* 35:1–210.

Chang, C. Y., and E. Witschi, 1956, Genic control and hormonal sex reversal of sex differentiation in *Xenopus, Proc. Soc. Exp. Biol. Med.,* 93:140–144.

Chang, M. L. Y., 1936, *Contribution à l'Étude Morphologique, Biologique et Systématique des Amphibiens Urodèles de la Chine,* Paris: Picart Libr.

Channing, A., 1976, Life histories of frogs in the Namib Desert, *Zool. Africana,* 11:299–312.

Channing, A., 1978, A new bufonid genus (Amphibia: Anura) from Rhodesia, *Herpetologica,* 34:394–397.

Cherchi, M. A., 1958, Note su *Chiromantis petersi kelleri* Boettger e sui suoi nidi (Amphibien), *Atti Soc. Italiano Sci. Nat.,* 97:167–172.

Chester Jones, I., D. Bellamy, D. K. O. Chan, B. K. Follett, I. W. Henderson, J. G. Phillips, and R. S. Snart, 1972, "Biological actions of steroid hormones in nonmammalian vertebrates," in D. R. Idler (ed.), *Steroids in Nonmammalian Vertebrates,* New York: Academic Press, pp 414–480.

Chibon, P., 1962, Differenciation sexuelle de *Eleutherodactylus martinicensis* Tschudi, batracien anoure a développement direct, *Bull. Soc. Zool. France,* 87:509–515.

Christensen, C. N., 1974, Adaptations in the water economy of some anuran Amphibia, *Comp. Biochem. Physiol.,* 47(A):1035–1049.

Christian, K. A., 1982, Changes in the food niche during postmetamorphic ontogeny of the frog *Pseudacris triseriata, Copeia,* 1982:73–80.

Chu, C. P., and L. C. Sze, 1957, Normal stages in the development of *Rana nigromaculata* (in Chinese), *Acta Anat. Sinica,* 2:59–64.

Chugunov, J. D., and K. A. Kispoev, 1973, *The Respiration in Amphibia (in Russian),* Novosibirsk: Acad. Sci. U. S. S. R.. Nauka. Siberian Branch.

Chung, S.-H., A. Pettigrew, and M. Anson, 1978, Dynamics of the amphibian middle ear, *Nature,* 272:142–147.

Church, G., 1960a, Annual and lunar periodicity in the sexual cycle of the Javanese toad, *Bufo melanostictus* Schneider, *Zoologica,* 44:181–188.

Church, G., 1960b, The effects of seasonal and lunar changes on the breeding pattern of the edible Javanese frog, *Rana cancrivora* Gravenhorst, *Treubia,* 25:215–233.

Clarke, B. T., 1981, Comparative osteology and evolutionary relationships in the African Raninae (Anura, Ranidae), *Monit. Zool. Italiano N.S. Suppl.,* 15:285–331.

Clarke, B. T., 1983a, A new genus of ranine frog (Anura: Ranidae) from Somalia, *Bull. British Mus. Nat. Hist. (Zool.),* 43:179–183.

Clarke, B. T., 1983b, A morphological re-examination of the frog genus *Nannophrys* (Anura: Ranidae) with comments on

its biology, distribution and relationships, *Zool. J. Linnaean Soc. London,* 79:377–398.

Clarke, R. D., 1977, Postmetamorphic survivorship of Fowler's toad, *Bufo woodhousei fowleri, Copeia,* 1977:594–597.

Claussen, D. L., 1969, Studies of water-loss and rehydration in anurans, *Physiol. Zool.,* 42:1–14.

Claussen, D. L., 1977, Thermal acclimation in ambysotmatid salamanders, *Comp. Biochem. Physiol.,* 58(A):333–340.

Claussen, D. L., and J. R. Layne Jr., 1983, Growth and survival of juvenile toads, *Bufo woodhousei,* maintained on four different diets, *J. Herpetol.,* 17:107–112.

Cloete, S. E., 1961, The cranial morphology of Rhyacotriton olympicus olympicus (Gaige), *Ann. Univ. Stellenbosch,* 36:114–145.

Clyne, D., 1967, Prothalamion in a garden pool, *Victorian Nat.,* 84:232–235.

Cochran, D. M., 1941, The herpetology of Hispaniola, *Bull. U. S. Natl. Mus.,* 177:1–398.

Cochran, D. M., 1955, Frogs of southeastern Brazil, *Bull. U. S. Natl. Mus.,* 206:1–423.

Cochran, D. M., and C. J. Goin, 1970, Frogs of Colombia, *Bull. U. S. Natl. Mus.,* 288:1–655.

Coe, M. J., 1967, Co-operation of three males in nest construction by *Chiromantis rufescens* Günther (Amphibia: Rhacophoridae), *Nature,* 214:112–113.

Coe, M. J., 1974, Observations on the ecology and breeding biology of the genus *Chiromantis* (Amphibia: Rhacophoridae), *J. Zool. (London),* 172:13–34.

Cogger, H. G., E. E. Cameron, and H. M. Cogger, 1983, *Zoological Catalogue of Australia. Vol. 1. Amphibia and Reptilia,* Canberra: Australian Govt. Print. Serv.

Coghill, G. E., 1902, The cranial nerves of Amblystoma tigrinum, *J. Comp. Neurol.,* 12:205–289.

Cole, C. J., 1966, The chromosomes of *Acris crepitans blanchardi* Harper (Anura: Hylidae), *Copeia,* 1966:578–580.

Cole, C. J., 1971, Chromosomes of the rhinophrynid frog, *Rhinophrynus dorsalis* Duméril and Bibron, *Herpetol. Rev.,* 3:37–38.

Cole, C. J., 1974, Chromosome evolution in selected treefrogs, including casque-headed species *(Pternohyla, Triprion, Hyla,* and *Smilisca), Amer. Mus. Novitat.,* 2541:1–10.

Cole, C. J., and R. G. Zweifel, 1971, Chromosomes of a New Guinean microhylid frog, *Cophixalus riparius* Zweifel, *Herpetol. Rev.,* 3:15–16.

Cole, L. C., 1954, The population consequences of life history phenomena, *Quart. Rev. Biol.,* 29:103–137.

Collett, T., 1977, Stereopsis in toads, *Nature,* 267:349–351.

Collins, J. P., 1975, *A Comparative Study of the Life History Strategies in a Community of Frogs,* Ann Arbor: Univ. Michigan, Ph.D. Dissertion.

Collins, J. P., and J. E. Cheek, 1983, Effect of food and density on development of typical and cannibalistic salamander larvae in *Ambystoma tigrinum nebulosum, Amer. Zool.,* 23:77–84.

Commoner, B., 1964, DNA and the chemistry of inheritance, *Amer. Sci.,* 52:365–388.

Conaway, C. H., and D. E. Metter, 1967, Skin glands associated with breeding in *Microhyla carolinensis, Copeia,* 1967:672–673.

Connon, F. E., 1947, A comparative study of the respiration of normal and hybrid *Triturus* embryos and larvae, *J. Exp. Zool.,* 105:1–24.

Cooke, A. S., 1972, The effects of DDT, Dieldrin and 2,4-D on amphibian spawn and tadpoles, *Environ. Pollut.,* 3:51–68.

Cooke, A. S., 1974, Differential predation by newts on anuran tadpoles, *British J. Herpetol.,* 5:386–389.

Cooper, E. L., 1976, "Immunity mechanisms," in B. Lofts (ed.), *Physiology of the Amphibia. Vol. III.,* New York: Academic Press, pp 163–272.

Cope, E. D., 1864, On the limits and relations of the raniformes, *Proc. Acad. Nat. Sci. Philadelphia,* 16:181–184.

Cope, E. D., 1865, Sketch of the primary groups of Batrachia Salientia, *Nat. Hist. Rev.,* 5:97–120.

Cope, E. D., 1889, The Batrachia of North America, *Bull. U. S. Natl. Mus.*, 34:1–525.

Corben, C. J., G. J. Ingram, and M. J. Tyler, 1974, Gastric brooding: a unique form of parental care in an Australian frog, *Science*, 186:946–947.

Cornman, I., and N. Grier, 1941, Refraction of light by amphibian egg jelly, *Copeia*, 1941:180.

Cox, C. B., 1967, Cutaneous respiration and the origin of the modern Amphibia, *Proc. Linnean Soc. London*, 178:37–48.

Cragg, M. M., J. B. Balinsky, and E. Baldwin, 1961, A comparative study of nitrogen excretion in some Amphibia and reptiles. *Comp. Biochem. Physiol.*, 3:227–235.

Creed, K., 1964, A study of newts in the New Forest, *British J. Herpetol.*, 3:170–181.

Crespo, E. G., 1979, *Contribução para o Conhecimento da Biologia dos* Alytes *ibéricos,* Alytes obstetricans boscai *Lataste, 1879 e* Alytes cisternasii *Boscá, 1879 (Amphibia–Salientia):–A Problemática da Especiação de* Alytes cisternasii, Univ. Lisboa: Tese, Fac. Cienc.

Creusere, F. M., and W. G. Whitford, 1976, Ecological relationships in a desert anuran community, *Herpetologica*, 32:7–18.

Crump, M. L., 1971, Quantitative analysis of the ecological distribution of a tropical herpetofauna, *Occ. Pap. Mus. Nat. Hist. Univ. Kansas*, 3:1–62.

Crump, M. L., 1972, Territoriality and mating behavior in *Dendrobates granuliferus* (Anura: Dendrobatidae), *Herpetologica*, 28:195–198.

Crump, M. L., 1974, Reproductive strategies in a tropical anuran community, *Misc. Publ. Mus. Nat. Hist. Univ. Kansas*, 61:1–68.

Crump, M. L., 1979, Intra-population variation in energy parameters of the salamander *Plethodon cinereus*, *Oecologia*, 38:235–247.

Crump, M. L., 1982, "Amphibian reproductive ecology on the community level," in N. J. Scott Jr. (ed.), Herpetological Communities, *Wildlife Res. Rept.*, 13:1–239, pp 21–36.

Crump, M. L., and R. H. Kaplan, 1979, Clutch energy partitioning of tropical tree frogs (Hylidae), *Copeia*, 1979:626–635.

Culver, D. C., 1973, Feeding behavior of the salamander *Gyrinophilus porphyriticus* in caves, *Internat. J. Speleol.*, 5:369–377.

Cupp, P. V. Jr., 1980, Territoriality in the green salamander, *Aneides aeneus*, *Copeia*, 1980:463–468.

Czopek, J., 1962, Vascularization of respiratory surfaces in some caudata, *Copeia*, 1962:276–287.

Dalrymple, G. H., 1970, Caddis fly larvae feeding upon eggs of *Ambystoma t. tigrinum*, *Herpetologica*, 26:128–129.

Daly, J. W., 1982, "Alkaloids of Neotropical poison frogs (Dendrobatidae)," in W. Herz, H. Grisebach, and G. W. Kirby (eds.), *Progress in the Chemistry of Organic Natural Products. Vol. 41*, Vienna: Springer-Verlag, pp 205–340.

Daly, J. W., G. B. Brown, M. Mensah-Dwumah, and C. W. Myers, 1978, Classification of skin alkaloids from neotropical poison-dart frogs (Dendrobatidae), *Toxicon*, 16:163–188.

Daly, J. W., C. W. Myers, J. E. Warnick, and E. X. Albuquerque, 1980, Levels of batrachotoxin and lack of sensitivity to its action in poison-dart frogs *(Phyllobates)*, *Science*, 208:1383–1385.

Daly, J. W., and B. Witkop, 1971, "Chemistry and pharmacology of frog venoms," in W. Bücherl and E. E. Buckey (eds.), *Venomous Animals and their Venoms*, New York: Academic Press, pp 497–519.

Danstedt, R. T. Jr., 1975, Local geographic variation in demographic parameters and body size of *Desmognathus fuscus* (Amphibia: Plethodontidae), *Ecology*, 56:1054–1067.

Dash, M. C., and A. K. Hota, 1980, Density effects on the survival, growth rate, and metamorphosis of *Rana tigrina* tadpoles, *Ecology*, 61:1025–1028.

Daudin, F. M., 1802, *Histoire Naturelle des Rainettes, des Grenouilles et des Crapauds,* Paris: Lerrault.

Daudin, F. M., 1803, *Histoire Naturelle Générale et Particulière des Reptiles. Vol. 8.,* Paris: F. Dufart.

Daugherty, C. H., B. D. Bell, M. Adams, and L. R. Maxson, 1981, An electrophoretic study of genetic variation in the New Zealand frog genus *Leiopelma*, *New Zealand J. Zool.*, 8:543–550.

Daugherty, C. H., and L. R. Maxson, 1982, A biochemical assessment of the evolution of myobatrachine frogs, *Herpetologica*, 38:341–348.

Daugherty, C. H., and A. L. Sheldon, 1982a, Age-determination, growth, and life history of a Montana population of the tailed frog *(Ascaphus truei)*, *Herpetologica*, 38:461–468.

Daugherty, C. H., and A. L. Sheldon, 1982b, Age-specific movement patterns of the frog *Ascaphus truei*, *Herpetologica*, 38:468–474.

David, R. S., and R. G. Jaeger, 1981, Prey location through chemical cues by a terrestrial salamander, *Copeia*, 1981:435–440.

Davies, M., and T. C. Burton, 1982, Osteology and myology of the gastric brooding frog *Rheobatrachus silus* Liem (Anura: Leptodactylidae), *Australian J. Zool.*, 30:503–521.

Davies, N. B., and T. R. Halliday, 1977, Optimal mate selection in the toad *Bufo bufo*, *Nature*, 269:56–58.

Davis, D. D., 1965, Wallace's flying frog, *Malayan Nat. J.*, 19:149–151.

Davis, D. D., and C. R. Law, 1935, Gonadectomy and a new secondary sexual character in frogs, *Science*, 81:562–564.

Davis, J., 1952, Observations on the eggs and larvae of the salamander *Batrachoseps pacificus major*, *Copeia*, 1952:272–274.

Davis, J. R., and B. H. Brattstrom, 1975, Sounds produced by the California newt, *Taricha torosa*, *Herpetologica*, 31:409–412.

Davis, W. B., and E. T. Knapp, 1953, Notes on the salamander *Siren intermedia*, *Copeia*, 1953:119–121.

Davis, W. C., and V. C. Twitty, 1964, Courtship behavior and reproductive isolation in the species of *Taricha* (Amphibia, Caudata), *Copeia*, 1964:601–610.

Dawson, A. B., 1920, The integument of *Necturus maculosus*, *J. Morph.*, 34:467–589.

Dawson, A. B., 1936, Changes in the lateral line organs in the life of the newt, *Triturus viridescens*. A consideration of the endocrine factors involved in the maintenance of differentiation, *J. Exp. Zool.*, 74:221–237.

De Beer, G. R., 1937, *The Development of the Vertebrate Skull,* London: Oxford Univ. Press.

Deckert, K., 1963, Die Paarung des Beutelfrosches *(Gastrotheca marsupiata)*, *Zool. Garten (NF)*, 28:12–17.

Degani, G., and M. R. Warburg, 1978, Population structure and seasonal activity of the adult *Salamandra salamandra* (L.) (Amphibia, Urodela, Salamandridae) in Israel, *J. Herpetol.*, 12:437–444.

De Graaf, A. R., 1957, Investigations into the distribution of blood in the heart and aortic arches of *Xenopus laevis* (Daud.), *J. Exp. Biol.*, 34:143–172.

De Jager, E. F. J., 1938, A comparison of the cranial nerves and bloodvessels of Dermophis mexicanus and Dermophis gregorii, *Anat. Anz.*, 86:321–368.

De Jager, E. F. J., 1939a, Contributions to the cranial anatomy of the Gymnophiona. Further points regarding the cranial anatomy of *Dermophis, Anat. Anz.*, 88:193–222.

De Jager, E. F. J., 1939b, The cranial anatomy of *Coecilia ochrocephala* Cope (further contributions to the morphology of the Gymnophiona), *Anat. Anz.*, 88:433–469.

De Jongh, H. J., 1968, Functional morphology of the jaw apparatus of larval and metamorphosing *Rana temporaria* L., *Netherlands J. Zool.*, 18:1–103.

De Jongh, H. J., and C. Gans, 1969, On the mechanism of respiration in the bullfrog, *Rana catesbeiana*: a reassessment, *J. Morph.*, 127:259–290.

Del Conte, E., and J. L. Sirlin, 1952, Pattern series of the first embryonary stages in *Bufo arenarum, Anat. Rec.,* 112: 125–135.

De Lille, J., 1934, Nota preliminar acerca de la acción fisiológica del veneno de *Dermophis mexicanus, Ann. Inst. Biol. Univ. Nac. Mexico,* 5:323–326.

Del Pino, E. M., 1980a, Morphology of the pouch and incubatory integument in marsupial frogs (Hylidae), *Copeia,* 1980:10–17.

Del Pino, E. M., 1980b, El mantenimiento y aspectos del comportamiento en cautiverio del sapo marsupial *Gastrotheca riobambae* (Hylidae), *Rev. Univ. Catol. Ecuador,* 8:41–49.

Del Pino, E. M., and B. Escobar, 1981, Embryonic stages of *Gastrotheca riobambae* (Fowler) during maternal incubation and comparison of development with other marsupial frogs, *J. Morph.,* 167:277–295.

Del Pino, E. M., M. L. Galarza, C. M. de Abuja, and A. A. Humphries, Jr., 1975, The maternal pouch and development in the marsupial frog *Gastrotheca riobambae* (Fowler), *Biol. Bull.,* 149:480–491.

Del Pino, E. M., and A. A. Humphries Jr., 1978, Multiple nuclei during early oogenesis in *Flectonotus pygmaeus* and other marsupial frogs, *Biol. Bull.,* 154:198–212.

Del Pino, E. M., and G. Sanchez, 1977, Ovarian structure of the marsupial frog *Gastrotheca riobambae* (Fowler), *J. Morph.,* 153:153–162.

Delson, J., and W. G. Whitford, 1973a, Critical thermal maxima in several life history stages in desert and montane populations of *Ambystoma tigrinum, Herpetologica,* 29:352–355.

Delson, J., and W. G. Whitford, 1973b, Adaptations of the tiger salamander, *Ambystoma tigrinum,* to arid habitats, *Comp. Biochem. Physiol.,* 46(A):631–638.

De Lucca, E. J., J. Jim, and F. Foresti, 1974, Chromosomal studies in twelve species of Leptodactylidae and one Brachycephalidae, *Caryologia,* 27:183–192.

Dely, O. G., 1967, Neuere Angaben zur Kenntnis des neotenischen Teichmolches *(Triturus vulgaris), Acta. Zool. Acad. Sci. Hungary,* 13:253–270.

DeMar, R., 1968, The Permian labyrinthodont amphibian *Dissorophus multicinctus* and adaptations and phylogeny of the family Dissorophidae, *J. Paleontol.,* 42:1210–1242.

Dempster, W. T., 1930, The morphology of the amphibian endolymphatic organ, *J. Morph. Physiol.,* 50:71–126.

Denaro, L., 1972, Karyotypes of Leptodactylidae, *J. Herpetol.,* 6:71–74.

Dent, J. N., 1942, The embryonic development of Plethodon cinereus as correlated with the differentiation and functioning of the thyroid gland, *J. Morph.,* 71:577–598.

Dent, J. N., 1968, "Survey of amphibian metamorphosis," in W. Etkin and L. I. Gilbert (eds.), *Metamorphosis. A Problem in Developmental Biology,* New York: Appleton-Century-Crofts, pp 271–311.

Dent, J. N., 1970, The ultrastructure of the spermatheca in the red spotted newt, *J. Morph.,* 132:397–424.

Dent, J. N., and J. S. Kirby-Smith, 1963, Metamorphic physiology and morphology of the cave salamander *Gyrinophilus palleucus, Copeia,* 1963:119–130.

Dessauer, H. C., D. F. Gartside, and R. G. Zweifel, 1977, Protein electrophoresis and the systematics of New Guinean hylid frogs, *Syst. Zool.,* 26:426–436.

Dessauer, H. C., E. Nevo, and K.-C. Chuang, 1975, High genetic variability in an ecologically variable vertebrate, *Bufo viridis, Biochem. Genetics,* 13:651–661.

Detwiler, S. R., 1927, Die Morphogenese des peripheren und zentralen Nervensystems der Amphibien im Licht experimenteller Forschungen, *Naturwissenschaften,* 15:873–879.

Deuchar, E. M., 1975, Xenopus: *The South African Clawed Frog,* London: John Wiley & Sons.

De Villiers, C. G. S., 1922, Neue Beobachtungen über den Bau und die Entwicklung des Brust-Schulterapparates bei den Anuren, inbesondere bei Bombinator, *Acta Zool.,* 3:1–73.

De Villiers, C. G. S., 1932, Über das Gehörskelett der aglossen Anuren, *Anat. Anz.,* 71:305–331.

De Villiers, C. G. S., 1934, On the morphology of the epipubis, the Nobelian bones and the phallic organ of Ascaphus truei Stejneger, *Anat. Anz.,* 78:23–47.

DeVlaming, V. L., and R. B. Bury, 1970, Thermal selection in tadpoles of the tailed-frog, *Ascaphus truei, J. Herpetol.,* 4:179–189.

De Vos, C. M., 1938, The inscriptional ribs of Liopelma and their bearing upon the problem of abdominal ribs in Vertebrata, *Anat. Anz.,* 87:49–112.

Deyrup, I. J., 1964, "Water balance and kidney," in J. A. Moore (ed.), *Physiology of the Amphibia,* New York: Academic Press, pp 251–328.

Diakow, C., 1977, Initiation and inhibition of the release croak of *Rana pipiens, Physiol. Behav.,* 19:607–610.

Diaz, N. F., J. Valencia, and M. Sallaberry, 1983, Life history and phylogenetic relationships of *Insuetophrynus acarpicus* (Anura, Leptodactylidae), *Copeia,* 1983:30–37.

Dickerson, M. C., 1906, *The Frog Book,* New York: Doubleday, Page and Co.

Dierickx, K., and A. van den Abeele, 1959, On the relations between the hypothalamus and the anterior pituitary in *Rana temporaria, Zeit. Zellforsch. Mikroskop. Anat.,* 51:78–87.

DiGiovanni, M., and E. D. Brodie Jr., 1981, Efficacy of skin glands in protecting the salamander *Ambystoma opacum* from repeated attacks by the shrew *Blarina brevicauda, Herpetologica,* 37:234–237.

Dimmitt, M. A., and R. Ruibal, 1980, Exploitation of food resources by spadefoot toads *(Scaphiopus), Copeia,* 1980: 854–862.

Dixon, J. R., 1957, Geographic variation and distribution of the genus *Tomodactylus* in Mexico, *Texas J. Sci.,* 9:379–409.

Dixon, J. R., and W. R. Heyer, 1968, Anuran succession in a temporary pond in Colima, Mexico, *Bull. South. California Acad. Sci.,* 67:129–137.

Dixon, J. R., and M. A. Staton, 1976, Some aspects of the biology of *Leptodactylus macrosternum* Miranda-Ribeiro (Anura: Leptodactylidae) of the Venezuelan Llanos, *Herpetologica,* 32:227–232.

Dobrowolski, J., 1971, Influence of environmental changes in salinity and the pH on the development of Amphibia (in Russian), *Kosmos,* 5:445–457.

Dobzhansky, T., 1950, Evolution in the tropics, *Amer. Sci.,* 38:209–221.

Dodd, C. K. Jr., 1976, A bibliography of anuran defense mechanisms, *Smithsonian Herpetol. Info. Serv.,* 37:1–10.

Dodd, M. H. I., and J. M. Dodd, 1976, "The biology of metamorphosis," in B. A. Lofts (ed.), *Physiology of the Amphibia,* New York: Academic Press, pp 467–599.

Dodt, E., and E. Heerd, 1962, Mode of action of pineal nerve fibers in frogs, *J. Neurophysiol.,* 25:405–429.

Dodt, E., and M. Jacobson, 1963, Photosensitivity of a localized region of the frog diencephalon, *J. Neurophysiol.,* 26:752–758.

Dodt, E., and H. Meissl, 1982, The pineal and parietal organs of lower vertebrates, *Experientia,* 38:996–1000.

Dole, J. W., 1965, Spatial relations in natural populations of the leopard frog, *Rana pipiens* Schreber, in northern Michigan, *Amer. Midl. Nat.,* 74:464–478.

Dole, J. W., 1968, Homing in leopard frogs, *Rana pipiens, Ecology,* 49:386–399.

Dole, J. W., and P. Durant, 1974a, Movements and seasonal activity of *Atelopus oxyrhynchus* (Anura: Atelopodidae) in a Venezuelan cloud forest, *Copeia,* 1974:230–235.

Dole, J. W., and P. Durant, 1974b, Courtship behavior in *Colostethus collaris* (Dendrobatidae), *Copeia,* 1974:988–990.

Dole, J. W., B. B. Rose, and K. H. Tachiki, 1981, Western toads *(Bufo boreas)* learn odor of prey insects, *Herpetologica,* 37:63–68.

Donnelly, T., 1985, "Mesozoic and Cenozoic plate evolution of the Caribbean region", in F. Stehli and D. Webb (eds.), *The Great Continental Interchange,* New York: Plenum Press, in press.

Donner, K. O., and T. E. Reuter, 1976, "Visual pigments and photoreceptor function," in R. Llinas and W. Precht (eds.), *Frog Neurobiology,* Berlin: Springer-Verlag, pp 251–277.

Donoso-Barros, R., and J. León O., 1972, Desarrollo y evolución larval de *Hyla crepitans* (Amphibia-Salientia), *Bol. Soc. Biol. Concepcion,* 44:117–127.

Dornesco, G. T., V. Santa, and F. Zacharia, 1965, Sur les canaux hépatiques, cholésdoques et pancréatiques des anoures, *Anat. Anz.,* 116:239–257.

Douglas, R., 1948, Temperature and rate of development of eggs of British anura, *J. Anim. Ecol.,* 17:189–192.

Dowling, J. E., 1976, "Physiology and morphology of the retina," in R. Llinas and W. Precht (eds.), *Frog Neurobiology,* Berlin: Springer-Verlag, pp 278–296.

Downs, F. L., 1978, Unisexual *Ambystoma* from the Bass Islands of Lake Erie, *Occ. Pap. Mus. Zool. Univ. Michigan,* 685:1–36.

Drewes, R. C., 1984, A phylogenetic analysis of the Hyperoliidae (Anura): treefrogs of Africa, Madagascar, and the Seychelles Islands, *Occ. Pap. California Acad. Sci.,* 139:1–70.

Drewes, R. C., S. S. Hillman, R. W. Putnam, and O. M. Sokol, 1977, Water, nitrogen and ion balance in the African treefrog *Chiromantis petersi* Boulenger (Anura: Rhacophoridae), with comments on the structure of the integument, *J. Comp. Physiol.,* 116:257–267.

Drewes, R. C., and B. Roth, 1981, Snail-eating frogs from the Ethiopian highlands: a new anuran specialization, *Zool. J. Linnean Soc.,* 72(3):267–287.

Drewry, G. E., 1970, "The role of amphibians in the ecology of Puerto Rican rain forest," in *Puerto Rico Nuclear Center Rain Forest Project Annual Report,* San Juan, pp 16–85.

Drewry, G. E., W. R. Heyer, and A. S. Rand, 1982, A functional analysis of the complex call of the frog *Physalaemus pustulosus, Copeia,* 1982:636–645.

Drewry, G. E., and K. L. Jones, 1976, A new ovoviviparous frog, *Eleutherodactylus jasperi* (Amphibia, Anura, Leptodactylidae), from Puerto Rico, *J. Herpetol.,* 10:161–165.

Dring, J., 1984 ("1983"), Frogs of the genus *Leptobrachella* (Pelobatidae), *Amphib.-Rept.,* 4:89–102.

Drüner, L., 1901, Studien zur Anatomie des Zungebein-, Kiemenbogen- und Kehlkopfmuskels der Urodelen. I. Theil, *Zool. Jahrb. Abteil. Anat.,* 15:435–622.

Drüner, L., 1903, Über die Muskulatur des Visceralskeletts der Urodelen, *Anat. Anz.,* 23:545–571.

Drüner, L., 1904, Studien zur Anatomie des Zungebein-, Kiemenbogen- und Kehlkopfmuskulatur der Urodelen. II. Theil, *Zool. Jahrb. Abteil. Anat.,* 19:361–690.

Dubois, A., 1974, Liste commentée d'amphibiens recoltes au Nepal, *Bull. Mus. Natl. Hist. Nat. Paris,* 213(3):341–410.

Dubois, A., 1975, Un nouveau sous-genre *(Paa)* et tres nouvelles espèces du genre Rana. Remarques sur la phylogénie des ranidés (Amphibiens, Anoures), *Bull. Mus. Natl. Hist. Nat. Paris,* (3)324:1093–1115.

Dubois, A., 1978, "Les problémes de l'espèce chez les amphibiens anoures," in C. Bocquet, J. Genermont and M. Lamotte (eds.), *Les Problémes de l'Espèce dans le Régne Animal. II.,* Soc. Zool. France, pp 161–284.

Dubois, A., 1979a, Une espèce nouvelle de *Scutiger* (Amphibiens, Anoures) du nord de la Birmanie, *Rev. Suisse Zool.,* 86:631–640.

Dubois, A., 1979b, Neóténie et pédogenése. A propos d'une anomalie du développement chez *Bombina variegata* (Amphibiens, Anoures), *Bull. Mus. Natl. Hist. Nat. Paris,* (4)1(A):537–546.

Dubois, A., 1979c, Anomalies and mutations in natural populations of the *Rana "esculenta"* complex (Amphibia, Anura), *Mitt. Zool. Mus. Berlin,* 55:59–87.

Dubois, A., 1980, Notes sur la systematique et la repartition des amphibiens anoures de Chine et des regions avoisinantes. IV. Classification generique et subgenerique des Pelobatidae Megophryinae, *Bull. Soc. Linnéenne Lyon,* 49:469–482.

Dubois, A., 1981, Liste des genres et sous-genres nominaux de Ranoidea (amphibiens anoures) du monde, avec identification de leurs espèces-types: conséquences nomenclaturales, *Monit. Zool. Italiano N.S. Suppl.,* 15:225–284.

Dubois, A., 1982, *Leptophryne* Fitzinger, 1843, a senior synonym of *Cacophryne* Davis, 1935 (Bufonidae), *J. Herpetol.,* 16:173–174.

Dubois, A., 1983, Classification et nomenclature suprageneric des amphibiens anoures, *Bull. Men. Soc. Linnéenne Lyon,* 52:270–276.

Ducey, P. K., and E. D. Brodie Jr., 1983, Salamanders respond selectively to contacts with snakes: survival advantage of alternative antipredator strategies, *Copeia,* 1983:1036–1041.

Ducibella, T., 1974, The occurrence of biochemical metamorphic events without anatomical metamorphosis in the Axolotl, *Devel. Biol.,* 38:175–186.

Duellman, W. E., 1958, A monographic study of the colubrid snake genus *Leptodeira, Bull. Amer. Mus. Nat. Hist.,* 114:1–152.

Duellman, W. E., 1960, A distributional study of the amphibians and reptiles of the Isthmus of Tehuantepec, Mexico, *Univ. Kansas Publ. Mus. Nat. Hist.,* 13:19–72.

Duellman, W. E., 1966, Aggressive behavior in dendrobatid frogs, *Herpetologica,* 22:217–221.

Duellman, W. E., 1967a, Social organization in the mating calls of some neotropical anurans, *Amer. Midl. Nat.,* 77:156–163.

Duellman, W. E., 1967b, Courtship isolating mechanisms in Costa Rican hylid frogs, *Herpetologica,* 23:169–183.

Duellman, W. E., 1970, The hylid frogs of Middle America, *Monog. Mus. Nat. Hist. Univ. Kansas,* 1:1–753.

Duellman, W. E., 1971, A taxonomic review of South American hylid frogs, genus *Phrynohyas, Occ. Pap. Mus. Nat. Hist. Univ. Kansas,* 4:1–21.

Duellman, W. E., 1975, On the classification of frogs, *Occ. Pap. Mus. Nat. Hist. Univ. Kansas,* 42:1–14.

Duellman, W. E., 1977, Liste der rezenten Amphibien und Reptilien: Hylidae, Centrolenidae, Pseudidae, *Das Tierreich,* 95:1–225.

Duellman, W. E., 1978, The biology of an equatorial herpetofauna in Amazonian Ecuador, *Misc. Publ. Mus. Nat. Hist. Univ. Kansas,* 65:1–352.

Duellman, W. E., 1979, "The herpetofauna of the Andes: patterns of distribution, origin, differentiation, and present communities," in W. E. Duellman (ed.), *The South American Herpetofauna: Its Origin, Evolution, and Dispersal, Monog. Mus. Nat. Hist. Univ. Kansas,* 7:1–485.

Duellman, W. E., 1982a, "Quaternary climatic-ecological fluctuations in the lowland tropics: frogs and forests," in G. T. Prance (ed.), *Biological Diversification in the Tropics,* New York: Columbia Univ. Press, pp 389–402.

Duellman, W. E., 1982b, "Compresión climática cuaternaria en los andes: effectos sobre la especiación," in P. J. Salinas (ed.), *Zoologia Neotropical. Actas VIII,* Merida, Venezuela: Congr. Latinoamer. Zool., pp 177–201, 269, 271, 278.

Duellman, W. E., and J. A. Campbell, 1982, A new frog of the genus *Ptychohyla* (Hylidae) from the Sierra de las Minas, Guatemala, *Herpetologica,* 38:374–380.

Duellman, W. E., and J. A. Campbell, 1984, Two new species of *Plectrohyla* from Guatemala (Anura: Hylidae), *Copeia,* 1984:390–397.

Duellman, W. E., and M. L. Crump, 1974, Speciation in frogs of the *Hyla parviceps* group in the upper Amazon Basin, *Occ. Pap. Mus. Nat. Hist. Univ. Kansas,* 23:1–40.

Duellman, W. E., and P. Gray, 1983, Developmental biology and systematics of the egg-brooding hylid frogs, genera *Flectonotus* and *Fritziana, Herpetologica,* 39:333–359.

Duellman, W. E., and M. S. Hoogmoed, 1984, The taxonomy and phylogenetic relationships of the hylid frog genus *Stefania*, *Misc. Publ. Mus. Nat. Hist. Univ. Kansas*, 75:1–39.

Duellman, W. E., and J. Lescure, 1973, Life history and ecology of the hylid frog *Osteocephalus taurinus*, with observations on larval behavior, *Occ. Pap. Mus. Nat. Hist. Univ. Kansas*, 13:1–12.

Duellman, W. E., and J. D. Lynch, 1969, Descriptions of *Atelopus* tadpoles and their relevance to atelopodid classification, *Herpetologica*, 25:231–240.

Duellman, W. E., and S. J. Maness, 1980, The reproductive behavior of some hylid marsupial frogs, *J. Herpetol.*, 14:213–222.

Duellman, W. E., and R. A. Pyles, 1983, Acoustic resource partitioning in anuran communities, *Copeia*, 1983:639–649.

Duellman, W. E., and A. H. Savitzky, 1976, Aggressive behavior in a centrolenid frog, with comments on territoriality in anurans, *Herpetologica*, 32:401–404.

Duellman, W. E., and A. Schwartz, 1958, Amphibians and reptiles of southern Florida, *Bull. Florida St. Mus.*, 3:181–324.

Duellman, W. E., and L. Trueb, 1966, Neotropical hylid frogs, genus Smilisca, *Univ. Kansas Publ. Mus. Nat. Hist.*, 17:281–375.

Duellman, W. E., and L. Trueb, 1976, The systematic status and relationships of the hylid frog *Nyctimantis rugiceps* Boulenger, *Occ. Pap. Mus. Nat. Hist. Univ. Kansas*, 58:1–14.

Duellman, W. E., and L. Trueb, 1983, "Frogs of the *Hyla columbiana* group: taxonomy and phylogenetic relationships," in A. G. J. Rhodin and K. Miyata (eds.), *Advances in Herpetology and Evolutionary Biology*, Cambridge: Mus. Comp. Zool. Harvard Univ., pp 33–51.

Duellman, W. E., and A. Veloso M., 1977, Phylogeny of *Pleurodema* (Anura: Leptodactylidae): A biogeographic model, *Occ. Pap. Mus. Nat. Hist. Univ. Kansas*, 64:1–46.

Duellman, W. E., and J. T. Wood, 1954, Size and growth of the two-lined salamander, *Eurycea bislineata rivicola*, *Copeia*, 1954:92–96.

Dumas, P. C., 1956, The ecological relations of sympatry in *Plethodon dunni* and *Plethodon vehiculum*, *Ecology*, 37:484–495.

Duméril, A. M. C., and G. Bibron, 1841, *Erpétologie Générale ou Histoire Naturelle Complète des Reptiles. Vol. 8*, Paris: Librairie Roret.

Duméril, A. M. C., G. Bibron, and A. Duméril, 1854, *Erpétologie Générale ou Histoire Naturelle Complète des Reptiles. Vol. 9*, Paris: Librairie Roret.

Duncan, R., and R. Highton, 1979, Genetic relationships of the eastern large *Plethodon* of the Ouachita Mountains, *Copeia*, 1979:95–110.

Dundee, H. A., 1957, Partial metamorphosis induced in *Typhlomolge rathbuni*, *Copeia*, 1957:52–53.

Dundee, H. A., 1961, Response of the neotenic salamander *Haideotriton wallacei* to a metamorphic agent, *Science* 135:1060–1061.

Dundee, H. A., 1965a, *Eurycea multiplicata, Cat. Amer. Amphib. Rept.*, 21:1–2.

Dundee, H. A., 1965b, *Eurycea tynerensis, Cat. Amer. Amphib. Rept.*, 22:1–2.

Dunlap, D. G., 1960, The comparative myology of the pelvic appendage in the Salientia, *J. Morph.*, 106:1–76.

Dunn, E. R., 1923, The salamanders of the family Hynobiidae, *Proc. Amer. Acad. Arts Sci.*, 58:445–523.

Dunn, E. R., 1926a, The frogs of Jamaica, *Proc. Boston Soc. Nat. Hist.*, 38:111–130.

Dunn, E. R., 1926b, *The Salamanders of the Family Plethodontidae*, Northampton, Mass.: Smith College.

Dunn, E. R., 1937, The amphibian and reptilian fauna of bromeliads in Costa Rica and Panama, *Copeia*, 1937:163–167.

Dunson, W. A., 1977, Tolerance to high temperature and salinity by tadpoles of the Philippine frog, *Rana cancrivora*, *Copeia*, 1977:375–378.

Dunson, W. A., and J. Connell, 1982, Specific inhibition of hatching in amphibian embryos by low pH, *J. Herpetol.*, 16:314–316.

Durand, J., and A. Vandel, 1968, Proteus: an evolutionary relict, *Sci. J.*, 1968:44–49.

Durant, P., and J. W. Dole, 1975, Aggressive behavior in *Colostethus (Prostherapis) collaris* (Anura: Dendrobatidae), *Herpetologica*, 31:23–36.

Durham, L., and G. W. Bennett, 1963, Age, growth, and homing in the bullfrog, *J. Wildlife Manag.*, 27:107–123.

Dushane, G. P., and C. Hutchinson, 1944, Differences in size and developmental rate between eastern and midwestern embryos of *Ambystoma maculatum, Ecology*, 25:414–422.

Dyer, W. G., and R. Altig, 1976, Redescription of *Cosmocerca brasiliensis* Travassos 1925 (Nematoda: Cosmocercidae) from Ecuadorian frogs, *J. Parasitol.*, 62:262–264.

Dyer, W. G., and R. A. Brandon, 1973, Helminths of three sympatric species of cave-dwelling salamanders in southern Illinois, *Trans. Illinois State Acad. Sci.*, 66:23–29.

Dyrkacz, S., 1981, Recent incidences of albinism in North American amphibians and reptiles, *Herpetol. Circ.*, 11:1–31.

Eagleson, G. W., 1976, A comparison of the life histories and growth patterns of the salamander *Ambystoma gracile* (Baird) from permanent low-altitude and montane lakes, *Canadian J. Zool.*, 54:2098–2111.

Eagleson, G. W., and B. A. McKeown, 1978, Changes in thyroid activity of *Ambystoma gracile* (Baird) during different larval, transforming, and postmetamorphic phases, *Canadian J. Zool.*, 56:1377–1381.

Eakin, R. M., 1947, Stages in the normal development of *Hyla regilla*, *Univ. California Publ. Zool.*, 51:125–135.

Eakin, R. M., 1973, *The Third Eye*, Berkeley: University of California Press.

Eaton, T. H. Jr., 1933, The occurrence of streptostyly in the Ambystomatidae, *Univ. California Publ. Zool.*, 37:521–526.

Eaton, T. H. Jr., 1959, The ancestry of the modern Amphibia: a review of the evidence, *Univ. Kansas Publ. Mus. Nat. Hist.*, 12(2):155–180.

Ebbesson, S. O. E., 1976, "Morphology of the spinal cord," in R. Llinás and W. Precht (eds.), *Frog Neurobiology*, Berlin: Springer-Verlag, pp 679–706.

Edgeworth, F. H., 1935, *The Cranial Muscles of Vertebrates*, Cambridge: University Press.

Edwards, J. L., 1976, Spinal nerves and their bearing on salamander phylogeny, *J. Morph.*, 148:305–328.

Eibl-Eibesfeldt, I., 1956, Vergleichende Verhaltensstudien an Anuran; 2.Zur Paarungsbiologie der Gattungen *Bufo*, *Hyla*, *Rana*, und *Pelobates*, *Zool. Anz. Suppl.* 19:315–323.

Eigenmann, C. H., 1900, The eyes of the blind vertebrates of North America. II. The eyes of *Typhlomolge rathbuni* Stejneger, *Trans. Amer. Micros. Soc.*, 21:49–61.

Einem, G. E., and L. D. Ober, 1956, The seasonal behavior of certain Floridian Salientia, *Herpetologica*, 12:205–212.

Elayidom, N. B., S. Royan-Subramaniam, and M. K. Subramaniam, 1963, The chromosome number of *Uraetyphlus menoni* Annandale, *Curr. Sci. Bangalore*, 32:274–276.

Eldredge, N., and J. Cracraft, 1980, *Phylogenetic Patterns and the Evolutionary Process*, New York: Columbia Univ. Press.

Elias, H., and J. Shapiro, 1957, Histology of the skin of some toads and frogs, *Amer. Mus. Novit.*, 1819:1–27.

Elias, P., and D. B. Wake, 1983, "*Nyctanolis pernix*, a new genus and species of plethodontid salamander from northwestern Guatemala and Chiapas," in A. G. J. Rhodin and K. Miyata (eds.), *Advances in Herpetology and Evolutionary Biology*, Cambridge: Museum Of Comp. Zool., Harvard, pp 1–12.

Elinson, R. P., 1974, A comparative examination of amphibian sperm proteolytic activity, *Biol. Repro.*, 11:406–412.

Elinson, R. P., 1975, Site of sperm entry and a cortical contraction associated with egg activation in the frog *Rana pipiens*, *Devel. Biol.*, 47:257–268.

Elinson, R. P., 1977a, Amphibian hybrids: a genetic approach to the analysis of their developmental arrest, *Differentiation*, 9:3–9.

Elinson, R. P., 1977b, Fertilization of immature frog eggs: cleavage and development following subsequent activation, *J. Embryol. Exp. Morph.*, 37:187–201.

Elinson, R. P., 1981, Genetic analysis of developmental arrest in an amphibian hybrid (Rana catesbeiana, Rana clamitans), *Devel. Biol.*, 81:167–176.

Elinson, R. P., 1983, Inheritance and expression of sex-linked enzyme in the frog, *Rana clamitans*, *Biochem. Genet.*, 21:435–442.

Elinson, R. P., and E. M. Del Pino, 1982, Gastrulation in *Gastrotheca*: the formation of an embryonic disc in a frog, *Amer. Zool.*, 22:876.

Elinson, R. P., and M. E. Manes, 1978, Morphology of the site of sperm entry on the frog egg, *Devel. Biol.*, 63:67–75.

Elkan, E., 1976, "Pathology in the Amphibia," in B. Lofts (ed.), *Physiology of the Amphibia. Vol. 3*, New York: Academic Press, pp 273–312.

Ellinger, M. S., 1980, Genetic and experimental studies on a pigment mutation, "pale" (P_a), in the frog, *Bombina orientalis*, *J. Embryol. Exp. Morph.*, 56:125–137.

Elliott, A. B., and L. Karunakaran, 1974, Diet of *Rana cancrivora* in fresh water and brackish water environments, *J. Zool. (London)*, 174:203–215.

Emerson, E. T., 1905, General anatomy of *Typhlomolge rathbuni*, *Proc. Boston Soc. Nat. Hist.*, 32:43–76.

Emerson, S. B., 1979, The ilio-sacral articulation in frogs: form and function, *Biol. J. Linnean Soc.*, 11:153–168.

Emerson, S. B., 1982, Frog postcranial morphology: identification of a functional complex, *Copeia*, 1982:603–613.

Emerson, S. B., 1983, Functional analysis of frog pectoral girdles. The epicoracoid cartilages, *J. Zool.*, 201:293–308.

Emerson, S. B., 1984, Morphological variation in frog pectoral girdles: testing alternatives to a traditional adaptive explanation, *Evolution*, 38:376–388.

Emerson, S. B., and H. J. De Jong, 1980, Muscle activity in the ilio-sacral joint in frogs, *J. Morph.*, 166:129–144.

Emerson, S. B., and D. Diehl, 1980, Toe pad morphology and adhesive mechanisms in frogs, *Biol. J. Linnean Soc.*, 13:199–216.

Emlen, S. T., 1968, Territoriality in the bullfrog, *Rana catesbeiana*, *Copeia*, 1968:240–243.

Emlen, S. T., 1976, Lek organization and mating strategies in the bullfrog, *Behav. Ecol. Sociobiol.*, 1:283–313.

Emlen, S. T., and L. W. Oring, 1977, Ecology, sexual selection, and the evolution of mating systems, *Science*, 197:215–223.

Emmel, V. E., 1924, Studies on non-nucleated elements of blood. II. The occurrence and genesis of non-nucleated erythrocytes in vertebrates other than mammals, *Amer. J. Anat.*, 33:347–405.

Erdman, S., and D. Cundall, 1984, The feeding apparatus of the salamander *Amphiuma tridactylum*: morphology and behavior, *J. Morph.*, 181:175–204.

Erdmann, K., 1933, Zur Entwicklung des Knöchernen Skelets von *Triton* und *Rana* unterbesonderer Beruksichtigung der Zeitfulge der Ossifikationen, *Zeit. Anat. Entwgesch.*, 101:566–651.

Ernst, V. V., 1973a, The digital pads of the treefrog *Hyla cinerea*. I. The epidermis, *Tissue & Cell*, 5:83–96.

Ernst, V. V., 1973b, The digital pads of the treefrog *Hyla cinerea*. II. The mucous glands, *Tissue & Cell*, 5:97–104.

Erspamer, V., 1971, Bigenic amines and active polypeptides of the amphibian skin, *Ann. Rev. Pharmacol.*, 11:327–350.

Erspamer, V., G. Falconieri Erspamer, G. Mazzanti, and R. Endean, 1984, Active peptides in the skins of one hundred amphibian species from Australia and Papua New Guinea, *Comp. Biochem. Physiol.*, 77(C):99–108.

Erspamer, V., and P. Melchiorri, 1980, Active polypeptides: from amphibian skin to gastrointestinal tract and brain of mammals, *Trends Pharmacol. Sci.*, 1:391–395.

Estes, R., 1965, Fossil salamanders and salamander origins, *Amer. Zool.*, 5:319–334.

Estes, R., 1970, New fossil pelobatid frogs and a review of the genus *Eopelobates*, *Bull. Mus. Comp. Zool.*, 139:293–340.

Estes, R., 1975, Fossil *Xenopus* from the Paleocene of South America and the zoogeography of pipid frogs, *Herpetologica*, 31:263–278.

Estes, R., 1977, Relationships of the South African fossil frog *Eoxenopoides reuningi* (Anura, Pipidae), *Ann. South African Mus.*, 73:49–80.

Estes, R., 1981, Gymnophiona, Caudata, *Handb. Paläherpetol.*, 2:1–115.

Estes, R., and O. A. Reig, 1973, "The early fossil record of frogs: a review of the evidence," in J. L. Vial (ed.), *Evolutionary Biology Of The Anurans: Contemporary Research On Major Problems*, Columbia: Univ. Missouri Press, pp 11–63.

Estes, R., and F. B. Sanchíz, 1982, New discoglossid and palaeobatrachid frogs from the late Cretaceous of Wyoming and Montana, with a review of other frogs from the Lance and Hell Creek formations, *J. Vert. Paleo.*, 2:9–20.

Estes, R., Z. V. Špinar, and E. Nevo, 1978, Early Cretaceous pipid tadpoles from Israel (Amphibia: Anura), *Herpetologica*, 34:374–393.

Estes, R., and M. H. Wake, 1972, The first fossil record of caecilian amphibians, *Nature*, 239:228–231.

Etkin, W. E., 1932, Growth and resorption phenomena in anuran metamorphosis, I., *Physiol. Zool.*, 5:275–300.

Etkin, W. E., 1968, "Hormonal control of amphibian metamorphosis," in W. E. Etkin and L. I. Gilbert (eds.), *Metamorphosis. A Problem in Developmental Biology*, New York: Appleton-Century-Crofts, pp 313–348.

Etkin, W. E., and L. I. Gilbert (eds.), 1968, *Metamorphosis. A Problem in Developmental Biology*, New York: Appleton-Century-Crofts.

Ewer, R. F., 1952, The effects of posterior pituitary extracts on water balance in *Bufo carens* and *Xenopus laevis*, together with some general considerations of water economy, *J. Exp. Zool.*, 29:429–439.

Ewert, J.-P., 1976, "The visual system of the toad: behavioral and physiological studies on a pattern recognition system," in K. V. Fite (ed.), *The Amphibian Visual System: a Multidisciplinary Approach*, New York: Academic Press, pp 141–202.

Ewert, J.-P., H.-W. Borchers, and A. von Wietersheim, 1978, Question of prey feature detectors in the toad's *Bufo bufo* (L.) visual system: a correlation analysis, *J. Comp. Physiol.*, 126:43–47.

Eycleshymer, A. C., and J. M. Wilson, 1910, *Normal Plates of the Development of Necturus maculosus*, *Normentafeln zur Entwicklungsgeschichte der Wirbeltiere. II.*, Vienna: Gustav Fischer.

Fachbach, G., 1976, Biologie, Taxonomie und phylogenetische Beziehungen der verschiedenen Untergarten von *Salamandra salamandra* im Bereich der Iberischen Halbinsel. Teil II., *Zeit. Zool. Syst. Evolutionsforsch.*, 14:81–103.

Fain, A., 1962, Les acariens parasites nasicoles de batraciens: revision des Lawrencarinae Fain, 1957 (Ereynetidae, Trombidiformes), *Bull. Inst. Roy. Sci. Nat. Belge*, 38(25):1–69.

Fair, J. W., 1970, Comparative rates of rehydration from soil in two species of toads, *Bufo boreas* and *Bufo punctatus*, *Comp. Biochem. Physiol.*, 34:281–287.

Fankhauser, G., 1967, "Urodeles," in F. H. Wilt and N. K. Wessels (eds.), *Methods in Developmental Biology*, New York: Crowell, pp 85–99.

Fankhauser, G., and C. Moore, 1941, Cytological and experimental studies of polyspermy in the newt, *Triturus viridescens*. I. Normal fertilization, *J. Morph.*, 68:347–386.

Farrell, M. P., and J. A. MacMahon, 1969, An eco-physiological study of water economy in eight species of tree frogs (Hylidae), *Herpetologica*, 25:279–294.

Farris, J. S., A. G. Kluge, and M. F. Mickevich, 1982, Phylogenetic analysis, the monothetic group method, and myobatrachid frogs, *Syst. Zool.*, 31:317–327.

Fawcett, D. W., 1970, A comparative view of sperm ultrastructure, *Biol. Reprod., Supple.*, 2:90–127.

Feder, M. E., 1976, Lunglessness, body size, and metabolic rate in salamanders, *Physiol. Zool.*, 49:398–406.

Feder, M. E., 1977, Oxygen consumption and activity in salamanders: effect of body size and lunglessness, *J. Exp. Biol.*, 202:403–414.

Feder, M. E., 1978a, Environmental variability and thermal acclimation in Neotropical and temperate-zone salamanders, *Physiol. Zool.*, 51:7–16.

Feder, M. E., 1978b, Effect of temperature on post-activity oxygen consumption in lunged and lungless salamanders, *J. Exp. Zool.*, 206:179–190.

Feder, M. E., 1981, Effect of body size, trophic state, time of day, and experimental stress on oxygen consumption of anuran larvae: an experimental assessment and evaluation of the literature, *Comp. Biochem. Physiol.*, 70(A):497–508.

Feder, M. E., 1982a, Environmental variability and thermal acclimation of metabolism in tropical anurans, *J. Therm. Biol.*, 7:23–28.

Feder, M. E., 1982b, Thermal ecology of Neotropical lungless salamanders (Amphibia: Plethodontidae): environmental temperatures and behavioral responses, *Ecology*, 63:1665–1674.

Feder, M. E., 1982c, Effect of developmental stage and body size on oxygen consumption of anuran larvae: a reappraisal, *J. Exp. Zool.*, 220:33–42.

Feder, M. E., 1983a, Responses to acute aquatic hypoxia in larvae of the frog *Rana berlandieri, J. Exp. Biol.*, 104:79–95.

Feder, M. E., 1983b, Integrating the ecology and physiology of plethodontid salamanders, *Herpetologica*, 39:291–310.

Feder, M. E., and S. J. Arnold, 1982, Anaerobic metabolism and behavior during predatory encounters between snakes *(Thamnophis elegans)* and salamanders *(Plethodon jordani)*, *Oecologia*, 53:93–97.

Feder, M. E., and J. F. Lynch, 1982, Effects of latitude, elevation, and microhabitat on field body temperatures of neotropical and temperate zone salamanders, *Ecology*, 63:1657–1664.

Feder, M. E., J. F. Lynch, H. B. Shaffer, and D. B. Wake, 1982, Field body temperatures of tropical and temperate zone salamanders, *Smithsonian Herpetol. Infor. Serv.*, 52:1–23.

Feder, M. E., and L. E. Olsen, 1978, Behavioral and physiological correlates of recovery from exhaustion in the lungless salamander *Batrachoseps attenuatus* (Amphibia: Plethodontidae), *J. Comp. Physiol.*, 128:101–107.

Feder, M. E., and F. H. Pough, 1975, Increased temperature resistance produced by ionizing radiation in the newt *Notophthalmus v. viridescens, Copeia*, 1975:658–661.

Feldhoff, R. C., 1971, Quantitative changes in plasma albumin during bullfrog metamorphosis, *Comp. Biochem. Physiol.*, 40(B):733–739.

Fellers, G. M., 1979a, Aggression, territoriality, and mating behaviour in North American treefrogs, *Anim. Behav.*, 27:107–119.

Fellers, G. M., 1979b, Mate selection in the gray treefrog, *Hyla versicolor, Copeia*, 1979:286–290.

Ferguson, D. E., 1967, "Sun-compass orientation in anurans," in R. M. Storm (ed.), *Animal Orientation and Navigation*, Corvallis: Oregon State Univ. Press, pp 21–34.

Ferrier, V., 1974, Cronologie du développement de l'amphibien urodèle *Tylototriton verrucosus* Anderson (Salamandridae), *Ann. Embryol. Morph.*, 7:407–416.

Ferrier, V., and A. Jaylet, 1978, Induction of triploidy in the newt *Pleurodeles waltlii* by heat shock or hydrostatic pressure. Interpretation of the different types of ploidy using a chromosomal marker, *Chromosoma*, 69:47–63.

Ferrier, V., A. Jaylet, C. Cayrol, and F. Gasser, 1980, Electro-phoretic study on red blood cell peptidases in the newt *Pleurodeles waltlii:* evidence for a sex-linked locus, *Compt. Rend. Acad. Sci. Paris*, 290:571–574.

Finkenstädt, T., and J.-P. Ewert, 1983, Visual pattern discrimination through interactions of neural networks: a combined electrical brain s timulation, brain lesion, and extracellular recording study in *Salamandra salamandra, J. Comp. Physiol.*, 153(A):99–110.

Firschen, I. L., 1951, A peculiar behavior pattern in a Mexican toad, *Bufo nayaritensis*, during amplexus, *Copeia*, 1951:73–74.

Fischberg, M., 1948, Experimentelle Auslösung von Heteroploidie durch Kältebehandlung der Eier von *Triton alpestris* aus verscheidenen Populationen, *Genetica*, 24:213–329.

Fischberg, M., and H. R. Kobel, 1978, Two new polyploid *Xenopus* species from western Uganda, *Experientia*, 34:1012–1014.

Fischer, H. G., and H. Hartwig, 1938, Vergleichende Messungen der Atmung des Amphibienkeimes und semer Teile während der Entwicklung, *Biol. Zentralbl.*, 58:567–589.

Fitch, H. S., 1956, A field study of the Kansas ant-eating frog, *Gastrophryne olivacea, Univ. Kansas Publ. Mus. Nat. Hist.*, 8:275–306.

Fitch, H. S., 1965, The University of Kansas Natural History Reservation in 1965, *Misc. Publ. Mus. Nat. Hist. Univ. Kansas*, 42:1–60.

Fite, K. V., 1976, *The Amphibian Visual System: a Multidisciplinary Approach*, New York: Academic Press.

Fitzinger, L., 1843, *Systema Reptilium*, Vienna.

Fitzpatrick, L. C., 1973a, Energy allocation in the Allegheny Mountain salamander, *Desmognathus ochrophaeus, Ecol. Monog.*, 43:43–58.

Fitzpatrick, L. C., 1973b, Influence of seasonal temperatures on the energy budget and metabolic rates of the northern two-lined salamander, *Eurycea bislineata bislineata, Comp. Biochem. Physiol.*, 45(A):807–818.

Fitzpatrick, L. C., and A. V. Brown, 1975, Metabolic compensation to temperature in the salamander *Desmognathus ochrophaeus* from a high elevation population, *Comp. Biochem. Physiol.*, 50(A):733–737.

Flier, J., M. W. Edwards, J. W. Daly, and C. W. Myers, 1980, Widespread occurrence in frogs and toads of skin compounds interacting with the ovabain site of Na+, K+-ATPase, *Science*, 208:503–505.

Florkin, M., and E. Schoffeniels, 1965, "Euryhalinity and its concept of physiological radiation," in K. A. Munday (ed.), *Studies in Comparative Biochemistry*, New York: Pergamon Press, pp 6–40.

Flower, S. S., 1936, Further notes on the duration of life in animals.–II. Amphibians, *Proc. Zool. Soc. London*, 1936:369–394.

Follett, B. K., and M. R. Redshaw, 1974, "The physiology of vitellogenesis," in B. Lofts (ed.), *Physiology of the Amphibia, II.*, New York: Academic Press, pp 219–308.

Forbes, M. S., R. A. Zaccaria, and J. N. Dent, 1973, Developmental cytology of chromatophores in the red-spotted newt, *Amer. J. Anat.*, 138:37–72.

Force, E. R., 1933, The age of attainment of sexual maturity of the leopard frog, *Rana pipiens* (Schreber), in northern Michigan, *Copeia*, 1933:128–131.

Forester, D. C., 1973, Mating call as a reproductive isolating mechanism between *Scaphiopus bombifrons* and *S. hammondii, Copeia*, 1973:60–67.

Forester, D. C., 1979, The adaptiveness of parental care in *Desmognathus ochrophaeus* (Urodela; Plethodontidae), *Copeia*, 1979:332–341.

Formanowicz, D. R. Jr., and E. D. Brodie Jr., 1982, Relative palatabilities of members of a larval amphibian community, *Copeia*, 1982:91–97.

Formanowicz, D. R. Jr., M. M. Stewart, K. Townsend, F. H. Pough, and P. Brussard, 1981, Predation by giant crab spiders on the Puerto Rican frog *Eleutherodactylus coqui, Herpetologica*, 37:125–129.

Formas, J. R., 1976a, Descriptions of *Batrachyla* (Amphibia, Anura, Leptodactylidae) tadpoles, *J. Herpetol.*, 10:221–225.

Formas, J. R., 1976b, New karyological data of *Rhinoderma*: the chromosomes of *Rhinoderma rufum, Experientia, 32*: 1000–1002.

Formas, J. R., and E. Pugín, 1978, Tadpoles of *Hylorina sylvatica, Eupsophus vittatus,* and *Bufo rubropunctatus* in southern Chile, *Herpetologica,* 34:355–358.

Formas, J. R., E. Pugín, and B. Jorquera, 1975, La identidad del batracio chileno *Heminectes rufus* Philippi, 1902, *Physis,* 34:147–157.

Formas, J. R., and A. Veloso, 1982, Taxonomy of *Bufo venustus* Philippi, 1899 (Anura: Leptodactylidae) from central Chile, *Proc. Biol. Soc. Washington, 95*:688–693.

Formas, J. R., and M. I. Vera, 1980, Reproductive patterns of *Eupsophus roseus* and *E. vittatus, J. Herpetol., 14*:11–14.

Formas, J. R., and M. I. Vera, 1982, The status of two frogs of the genus *Eupsophus* (Anura: Leptodactylidae), *Proc. Biol. Soc. Washington,* 95:594–601.

Foster, M. S., and R. W. McDiarmid, 1982, Study of aggregative behavior of *Rhinophrynus dorsalis* tadpoles: design and analysis, *Herpetologica,* 38:395–404.

Fouquette, M. J. Jr., 1960, Isolating mechanisms in three sympatric tree frogs in the Canal Zone, *Evolution,* 14:484–497.

Fouquette, M. J. Jr., 1969, *Rhinophrynus, R. dorsalis, Cat. Amer. Amphib. Rept.,* 78:1–2.

Fouquette, M. J. Jr., 1975, Speciation in chorus frogs. I. Reproductive character displacement in the *Pseudacris nigrita* complex, *Syst. Zool.,* 24:16–23.

Fouquette, M. J. Jr., and A. J. Delahoussaye, 1977, Sperm morphology in the *Hyla rubra* group (Amphibia, Anura, Hylidae), and its bearing on generic status, *J. Herpetol.,* 11:387–396.

Fox, H., 1963, The amphibian pronephros, *Quart. Rev. Biol.,* 38:1–25.

Fox, H., 1981, "Cytological and morphological changes during amphibian metamorphosis," in L. I. Gilbert and E. Frieden (eds.), *Metamorphosis. A Problem in Developmental Biology.* 2nd Edit., New York: Plenum Press, pp 327–362.

Fox, H., 1983, The skin of *Ichthyophis* (Amphibia: Caecilia): an ultrastructural study, *J. Zool.,* 199:223–248.

Fox, H., 1984, *Amphibian Morphogenesis,* Clifton, New Jersey: Humana Press.

Foxon, G. E. H., 1964, "Blood and respiration," in J. A. Moore (ed.), *Physiology of the Amphibia,* New York: Academic Press, pp 151–209.

Franchi, L. L., A. M. Mandl, and S. Zuckerman, 1962, "The development of the ovary and the process of oogenesis," in S. Zuckerman (ed.), *The Ovary. Vol. 1,* New York: Academic Press, pp 1–88.

Francis, E. T. B., 1934, *The Anatomy of the Salamander,* London: Oxford Univ. Press.

Franz, R., 1960, The eggs of the long-tailed salamander from a Maryland cave, *Herpetologica,* 20:216.

Franz, R., and C. J. Chantell, 1978, *Limnaoedus, L. ocularis, Cat. Amer. Amphib. Rept.,* 209:1–2.

Fraser, D. F., 1980, On the environmental control of oocyte maturation in a plethodontid salamander, *Oecologia,* 46:302–307.

Frazzetta, T. H., 1975, *Complex Adaptations in Evolving Populations,* Sunderland, Massachusetts: Sinauer Associates, Inc.

Freed, A. N., 1980, Prey selection and feeding behavior of the green treefrog (*Hyla cinerea*), *Ecology,* 61:461–465.

Freeman, F. B., 1968, A study of the jelly envelopes surrounding the egg of the amphibian *Xenopus laevis, Biol. Bull.,* 135:501–513.

Frieden, E., 1961, Biochemical adaptation and anuran metamorphosis, *Amer. Zool.,* 1:115–149.

Frieden, E., 1968, "Biochemistry of amphibian metamorphosis," in W. Etkin and L. I. Gilbert (eds.), *Metamorphosis. A*

Problem in Developmental Biology, New York: Appleton-Century-Crofts, pp 349–398.

Frieden, E., A. E. Heiner, L. Fish, and E. J. C. Lewis, 1957, Changes in serum proteins in amphibian metamorphosis, *Science,* 126:559–560.

Frishkopf, L. S., R. R. Capranica, and M. H. Goldstein, 1968, Neural coding in the bullfrog's auditory system—a teleological approach, *Proc. Inst. Elec. Electron. Engr.,* 56:969–980.

Frishkopf, L. S., and M. H. Goldstein Jr., 1963, Responses to acoustic stimuli from single units in the eighth nerve of the bullfrog, *J. Acoust. Soc. Amer.,* 35:1219–1228.

Fritzsch, B., 1981, The pattern of lateral line afferents in urodeles. A horseradish-peroxidase study, *Cell Tissue Res.,* 218:581–594.

Fritzsch, B., and U. Wahnschaffe, 1983, The electroreceptive ampullary organs of urodeles, *Cell Tissue Res.,* 229:483–503.

Fromm, P. O., 1956, Heat production of frogs, *Physiol. Zool.,* 29:234–240.

Frost, D. (ed.), 1985, *Amphibian Species of the World,* Lawrence, Kansas: Assoc. Syst. Coll.

Frost, J. S., 1982a, Functional genetic similarity between geographically separated populations of Mexican leopard frogs (*Rana pipiens* complex), *Syst. Zool.,* 31:57–67.

Frost, J. S., 1982b, A time-efficient, low cost method for the laboratory rearing of frogs, *Herpetol. Rev.,* 13:73–77.

Frost, J. S., and J. E. Platz, 1983, Comparative assessment of modes of reproductive isolation among four species of leopard frogs (*Rana pipiens* complex), *Evolution,* 37:66–78.

Frost, S. K., and J. T. Bagnara, 1979a, Allopurinol-induced melanism in the tiger salamander (*Ambystoma tigrinum nebulosum*), *J. Morph.,* 209:455–466.

Frost, S. K., and J. T. Bagnara, 1979b, The effects of allopurinol on pteridine pigments during leaf frog development, *Pigment Cell,* 4:203–209.

Frost, S. K., F. Briggs, and G. M. Malacinski, 1984, A color atlas of pigment genes in the Mexican axolotl (*Ambystoma mexicanum*), *Differentiation,* 26:182–188.

Frost, S. K., and G. M. Malacinski, 1980, The developmental genetics of pigment mutants in the Mexican axolotl, *Develop. Genet.,* 1:271–294.

Frost, S. K., and S. J. Robinson, 1984, Pigment cell differentiation in the fire-bellied toad, *Bombina orientalis.* I. Structural, chemical, and physical aspects of the adult pigment pattern, *J. Morph.,* 179:229–242.

Frye, B. E., P. S. Brown, and B. W. Snyder, 1972, Effects of prolactin and somatotropin on growth and metamorphosis of amphibians, *Gen. Comp. Endocrinol., Suppl.,* 3:209–220.

Funkhouser, D., and L. Goldstein, 1973, Urea response to pure osmotic stress in the aquatic toad, *Xenopus laevis, Amer. J. Physiol.,* 224:524–529.

Furieri, P., 1975, The peculiar morphology of the spermatozoan of *Bombina variegata* (L.), *Monit. Zool. Italiano (N.S.),* 9:185–201.

Gabrion, J., and P. Sentein, 1972, Diminution de l'activité thyroidienne chez les individus néoténiques de *Triturus helveticus,* Raz. Étude cytologique et autoradiographique, *Compt. Rendu Soc. Biol.,* 166:146–150.

Gabrion, J., P. Sentein, and C. Gabrion, 1977, Les populations néoténiques de *Triturus helveticus* des causses et du Bas-Languedoc. I. Répartition et caractéristiques, *Terre et Vie,* 31:489–506.

Gadow, H., 1901, *Amphibia and Reptiles, The Cambridge Natural History, Vol. 8,* London: Macmillan.

Gadow, H., 1908, *Through Southern Mexico,* London: Witherby and Co.

Gaffney, E. S., 1979, Tetrapod monophyly: a phylogenetic analysis, *Bull. Carnegie Mus. Nat. Hist.,* 13:92–105.

Gallardo, J. M., 1961, On the species of Pseudidae, *Bull. Mus. Comp. Zool.,* 125:108–134.

Gallien, L., 1952, Élevage et comportement du pleurodèle au laboratoire, *Bull. Soc. Zool. France,* 77:456–461.

Gallien, L., 1954, Démostration de l'homogamétie du sexe male chez le triton *Pleurodeles waltlii* Michah. par l'étude de la descendance d'animaux à sexe physiologique inversé, après un traitement hormonal gynogène (bezoate d'oestradiol)., *Compt. Rend. Acad. Sci. Paris*, 238:402–404.

Gallien, L., 1958, *Problèmes et Concepts de l'Embryologie Expérimentale*, Paris: Galinard.

Gallien, L., and O. Bidaud, 1959, Table chronologique du développement chez *Triturus helveticus* Razoumowsky, *Bull. Soc. Zool. France*, 84:22–31.

Gallien, L., and M. Durocher, 1957, Table cronologique du développement chez *Pleurodeles waltii* Michad., *Bull. Biol. France-Belgique*, 9:97–114.

Gallien, L., and C. Houillon, 1951, Table cronologique de développement chez *Discoglossus pictus*, *Bull. Biol. France-Belgique*, 85:373–375.

Gambs, R. D., and M. J. Littlejohn, 1979, Acoustic behavior of males of the Rio Grande leopard frog (*Rana berlandieri*) an experimental analysis through field playback trials, *Copeia*, 1979:643–650.

Gans, C., 1961, A bullfrog and its prey, *Nat. Hist.*, 1961 (Feb.):26–37.

Gans, C., 1973a, Locomotion and burrowing in limbless vertebrates, *Nature*, 242:414–415.

Gans, C., 1973b, Sound production in the Salientia: mechanism and evolution of the emitter, *Amer. Zool.*, 13:1179–1194.

Gans, C., 1974, *Biomechanics*, Philadelphia: J. B. Lippincott Co.

Gans, C., and G. C. Gorniak, 1982a, How does the toad flip its tongue? Test of two hypotheses, *Science*, 216:1335–1337.

Gans, C., and G. C. Gorniak, 1982b, Functional morphology of lingual protrusion in marine toads (*Bufo marinus*), *Amer. J. Anat.*, 163:195–222.

Gans, C., and R. Pyles, 1983, Narial closure in toads: which muscles?, *Respiration Physiol.*, 53:215–223.

Gardiner, B. G., 1982, Tetrapod classification, *Zool. J. Linnaean Soc.*, 74:207–232.

Gardiner, B. G., 1983, Gnathostome vertebrae and the classification of the amphibia, *Zool. J. Linnaean Soc.*, 79:1–59.

Garland, H. O., and I. W. Henderson, 1975, Influence of environmental salinity on renal and adrenocortical function in the toad, *Bufo marinus*, *Gen. Comp. Endocrinol.*, 27:136–143.

Garlick, R. L., B. J. Davis, M. Farmer, H. J. Fyhn, W. E. H. Fyhn, R. W. Noble, D. A. Powers, A. Riggs, and R. E. Weber, 1979, A fetal-maternal shift in the oxygen equilibrium from the viviparous caecilian, *Typhlonectes compressicauda*, *Comp. Biochem. Physiol.*, 62(A):239–244.

Garton, J. S., and R. A. Brandon, 1975, Reproductive ecology of the green treefrog, *Hyla cinerea*, in southern Illinois (Anura: Hylidae), *Herpetologica*, 31:150–161.

Garton, J. S., and H. R. Mushinsky, 1979, Integumentary toxicity and unpalatability as a defensive mechanism in *Gastrophryne carolinensis*, *Canadian J. Zool.*, 57:1965–1973.

Gartside, D. F., 1980, Analysis of a hybrid zone between chorus frogs of the *Pseudacris nigrita* complex in the southern United States, *Copeia*, 1980:56–66.

Gartside, D. F., and G. F. Watson, 1976, Inheritance of transferrins in progeny of in vitro crosses involving the tree frog *Litoria ewingi* (Anura: Hylidae), *Comp. Biochem. Physiol.*, 53(B):431–434.

Gasche, P., 1939, Beiträge zur Kenntnis der Entwicklungsgeschichte von *Salamandra salamandra* L. mit besonderer Berücksichtigung der Winterpass, der Metamorphose und des Verhaltens der Schildrüse, *Rev. Suisse Zool.*, 46:403–548.

Gasco, F., 1881, Les amours des axolotls, *Bull. Soc. Zool. France*, 6:151–164.

Gasser, F., 1964, Observations sur les stades initiaux du développoppement de l'urodèle Pyrènèen *Euproctus asper*, *Bull. Soc. Zool. France*, 89:423–428.

Gatz, A. J. Jr., 1971, Critical thermal maxima of *Ambystoma maculatum* (Shaw) and *Ambystoma jeffersonianum* (Green) in relation to time of breeding, *Herpetologica*, 27:157–160.

Gatz, A. J. Jr., 1973, Intraspecific variation in critical thermal maxima of *Ambystoma maculatum*, *Herpetologica*, 29:264–268.

Gaudin, A. J., 1965, Larval development of the tree frogs *Hyla regilla* and *Hyla californiae*, *Herpetologica*, 21:117–130.

Gaupp, E., 1896, *A. Ecker's und R. Wiedersheim's Anatomie des Frosches. 2 Vols.*, Braunschweg: Friedrich Vieweg Und Sohn.

Gaupp, E., 1904, *Anatomie des Frosches. Pt. 3. 2nd Edit.*, Braunschweg: Friedrich Vieweg Und Sohn.

Gaupp, E., 1906, "Die Entwicklung des Kopfskelettes," in D. Hertwig (ed.), *Handbuch der Vergleichenden und Experimentellen Entwicklungslehre der Werbeltiere, Vol. 3, Pt. 2*, Vienna: Gustav Fischer, pp 573–890.

Gehlbach, F. R., 1967, *Ambystoma tigrinum, Cat. Amer. Amphib. Rept.*, 52:1–4.

Gehlbach, F. R., 1968, Evolution of tiger salamanders (*Ambystoma tigrinum*) on the Grand Canyon rims, Arizona, *Amer. Philos. Soc. Yearb.*, 1967:266–269.

Gehlbach, F. R., R. Gordon, and J. B. Jordan, 1973, Aestivation of the salamander, *Siren intermedia*, *Amer. Midl. Nat.*, 89:455–463.

Gehlbach, F. R., J. R. Kimmel, and W. A. Weems, 1969, Aggregations and body water relations in tiger salamanders (*Ambystoma tigrinum*) from the Grand Canyon rims, Arizona, *Physiol. Zool.*, 42:173–182.

Gehlbach, F. R., and B. Walker, 1970, Acoustic behavior of the aquatic salamander, *Siren intermedia*, *Bioscience*, 20:1107–1108.

Geisselmann, B., R. Flindt, and H. Hemmer, 1971, Studien zur Biologie, Ökologie und Merkmalsvariabilität der beiden Braunfroscharten, *Rana temporaria* L. und *Rana dalmatina* Bonaparte, *Zool. Jahrb. Syst.*, 98:521–568.

Gentry, G., 1968, Notes on the availability of eggs of the *Ambystoma* species of salamanders in Tennessee, *J. Tennessee Acad. Sci.*, 43:53. Gerard, P., 1954, "Organes uro-genitaux," in P. P. Grasse (ed.), *Traite de Zoologie. Vol. 12*, Paris: Masson, pp 974–1043.

Gerhardt, E., 1932, Die Kiemenentwicklung bei Anuren (*Pelobates fuscus, Hyla arborea*) und Urodelen (*Triton vulgaris*), *Zool. Jahrb. Syst.*, 55:173–220.

Gerhardt, H. C., 1974a, The vocalizations of some hybrid treefrogs: acoustic and behavioral analyses, *Behaviour*, 49:130–151.

Gerhardt, H. C., 1974b, The significance of spectral features in mating call recognition in the green treefrog (*Hyla cinerea*), *J. Exp. Biol.*, 61:229–241.

Gerhardt, H. C., 1975, Sound pressure levels and radiation patterns of the vocalizations of some North American frogs and toads, *J. Comp. Physiol.*, 102:1–12.

Gerhardt, H. C., 1978, Temperature coupling in the vocal communication system of the gray tree frog, *Hyla versicolor*, *Science*, 199:992–994.

Gerhardt, H. C., S. I. Guttman, and A. A. Karlin, 1980, Natural hybrids between *Hyla cinerea* and *Hyla gratiosa* morphology, vocalization and electrophoretic analysis, *Copeia*, 1980:577–584.

Gesteland, R. C., 1976, "Physiology of olfactory reception," in R. Llinás and W. Precht (eds.), *Frog Neurobiology*, Berlin: Springer-Verlag, pp 234–250.

Gewolf, S., 1923, Die Kehlkopf bei *Hypogeophis*, *Zeit. Anat. Entwgesch.*, 68:433–454.

Gilbert, L. I., and E. Frieden (Eds.), 1981, *Metamorphosis. A Problem in Developmental Biology. 2nd Edit.*, New York: Plenum Press.

Gill, D. E., 1978, The metapopulation ecology of the red-spotted newt, *Notophthalmus viridescens* (Rafinesque), *Ecol. Monog.*, 48:145–166.

Gillette, R., 1955, The dynamics of continuous succession of teeth in the frog (Rana pipiens), *Amer. J. Anat.,* 96:1–36.

Gislén, T., and H. Kauri, 1959, Zoogeography of the Swedish amphibians and reptiles with notes on their growth and ecology, *Acta Vert.,* 1:195–397.

Gitlin, D., 1944, The development of *Eleutherodactylus portoricensis, Copeia,* 1944:91–98.

Glaesner, L., 1925, *Normentafel zur Entwicklung des Gemeinen Wassermolchs (Molge vulgaris).* Normentafeln zur Entwicklungsgeschichte der Wirbeltiere. 14., Vienna: Gustav Fischer.

Glücksohn, S., 1931, Aussere Entwicklung der Extremitaten und Stadieneinteilung der Larvenperiode von *Triton taeniatus* und *T. cristatus, Arch. Entwicklungsmech.,* 125:341–365.

Godwin, G. J., and S. Roble, 1983, Mating success in male treefrogs, *Hyla chrysoscelis* (Anura: Hylidae), *Herpetologica,* 39:141–146.

Goeldi, E., 1899, Uber die Entwicklung von *Siphonops annulatus, Zool. Jahrb. Syst.,* 12:170–173.

Goff, L. J., and J. R. Stein, 1978, Ammonia: basis for algal symbiosis in salamander egg masses, *Life Sci.,* 22:1463–1468.

Goin, C. J., 1947, Studies on the life history of *Eleutherodactylus ricordii planirostris* (Cope) in Florida, *Univ. Florida Publ. Biol. Sci.,* 4(2):1–56.

Goin, C. J., 1950, Color pattern inheritance in some frogs of the genus *Eleutherodactylus, Bull. Chicago Acad. Sci.,* 9:1–15.

Goin, C. J., 1960, Amphibians, pioneers of terrestrial breeding habits, *Smithsonian Rept.,* 1959:427–455.

Goin, C. J., and O. B. Goin, 1962, *Introduction to Herpetology,* San Francisco: Freeman.

Goin, C. J., O. B. Goin, and G. R. Zug, 1978, *Introduction to Herpetology,* 3rd Edit., San Francisco: Freeman.

Goin, C. J., and M. Hester, 1961, Studies on the development, succession and replacement of teeth in the frog, *Hyla cinerea, J. Morph.,* 109:279–287.

Goin, C. J., and L. H. Ogren, 1956, Parasitic copepods (Argulidae) on amphibians, *J. Parasitol.,* 42:154.

Goin, O. B., C. J. Goin, and K. Bachmann, 1968, DNA and amphibian life history, *Copeia,* 1968:532–540.

Goldstein, L., 1972, "Adaptation of urea metabolism in aquatic vertebrates," in J. W. Campbell and L. Goldstein (eds.), *Nitrogen Metabolism and the Environment,* New York: Academic Press, pp 55–77.

Good, G. M., and J. F. Daniel, 1943, Fertilization of coelomic eggs of *Triturus torosus, Univ. California Publ. Zool.,* 15:149–158.

Goodman, D. E., 1971, Territorial behavior in a Neotropical frog, *Dendrobates granuliferus, Copeia,* 1971:365–370.

Goodyear, C. P., and R. Altig, 1971, Orientation of bullfrogs *(Rana catesbeiana)* during metamorphosis, *Copeia,* 1971:362–364.

Goos, H. J., 1978, Hypophysiotropic centers in the brain of amphibians and fish, *Amer. Zool.,* 18:401–410.

Gorbman, A., 1964, "Endocrinology of the Amphibia," in J. A. Moore (ed.), *Physiology of the Amphibia,* New York: Academic Press, pp 371–425.

Gordon, J., and D. C. Hood, 1976, "Anatomy and physiology of the frog retina," in K. V. Fite (ed.), *The Amphibian Visual System,* New York: Academic Press, pp 29–86.

Gordon, M. S., 1962, Osmotic regulation in the green toad *(Bufo viridis), J. Exp. Biol.,* 39:261–270.

Gordon, M. S., K. Schmidt-Nielsen, and H. M. Kelly, 1961, Osmotic regulation in the crab-eating frog *(Rana cancrivora), J. Exp. Biol.,* 38:659–678.

Gordon, M. S., and V. Tucker, 1968, Further observations on the physiology of salinity adaptation in the crab-eating frog *(Rana cancrivora), J. Exp. Biol.,* 49:185–193.

Gordon, R. E., 1952, A contribution to the life history and ecology of the plethodontid salamander *Aneides aeneus* (Cope and Packard), *Amer. Midl. Nat.,* 47:666–701.

Gordon, R. E., 1966, Some observations on the biology of *Pseudotriton ruber schencki, J. Ohio Herpetol. Soc.,* 5:163–164.

Gordon, R. E., J. A. MacMahon, and D. B. Wake, 1962, Relative abundance, microhabitat, and behavior of some southern Appalachian salamanders, *Zoologica,* 47:9–14.

Gorgees, N. S., A. Y. Yacob, and L. J. Rashan, 1977, Observations on the lateral-line sense organs of the salamander *Neurergus crocatus crocatus* Cope (Amphibia: Urodela), *Gegenbaurs Morphol. Jahrb.,* 123:621–637.

Gorman, J., 1956, Reproduction in the plethodontids of the genus *Hydromantes, Herpetologica,* 12:249–259.

Gorzula, S. J., 1977, Foam nesting in leptodactylids: a possible function, *British J. Herpetol.,* 5:657–659.

Gorzula, S. J., 1978, An ecological study of Caiman crocodilus crocodilus inhabiting savanna lagoons in the Venezuelan Guyana, *Oecologia,* 35:21–34.

Gosner, K. L., 1960, A simplified table for staging anuran embryos and larvae with notes on identification, *Herpetologica,* 16:183–190.

Gosner, K. L., and D. A. Rossman, 1959, Observations on the reproductive cycle of the swamp chorus frog *Pseudacris nigrita, Copeia,* 1959:263–266.

Gosner, K. L., and D. A. Rossman, 1960, Eggs and larval development of the treefrogs *Hyla crucifer* and *Hyla ocularis, Herpetologica,* 16:225–232.

Gould, S. J., 1977, *Ontogeny and Phylogeny,* Cambridge: Harvard Univ. Press.

Gradwell, N., 1968, The jaw and hyoidean mechanism of the bullfrog tadpole during aqueous ventilation, *Canadian J. Zool.,* 46(5):1041–1052.

Gradwell, N., 1969, The function of the internal nares of the bullfrog tadpole, *Herpetologica,* 25:120–121.

Gradwell, N., 1970, The function of the ventral velum during gill irrigation in *Rana catesbeiana, Canadian J. Zool.,* 48(6):1179–1186.

Gradwell, N., 1971, *Xenopus* tadpole: on the water pumping mechanism, *Herpetologica,* 27:107–123.

Gradwell, N., 1972a, Gill irrigation in *Rana catesbeiana* Part I. On the anatomical basis, *Canadian J. Zool.,* 50:481–499.

Gradwell, N., 1972b, Gill irrigation in *Rana catesbeiana.* Part II. On the musculoskeletal mechanism, *Canadian J. Zool.,* 50:501–521.

Gradwell, N., 1973, On the functional morphology of suction and gill irrigation in the tadpole of *Ascaphus,* and notes on hibernation, *Herpetologica,* 29:84–93.

Graeff, D., and R. Schulte, 1980, Neue Erkenntnisse zur Brutbiologie von *Dendrobates pumilio, Herpetofauna,* 2(7):17–22.

Grandison, A. G. C., 1978, The occurrence of *Nectophrynoides* (Anura Bufonidae) in Ethiopia. A new concept of the genus with a description of a new species, *Monit. Zool. Italiano (N.S.) Suppl.,* 11:119–172.

Grandison, A. G. C., 1980a, A new genus of toad (Anura: Bufonidae) from the Republic of South Africa with remarks on its relationships, *Bull. British Mus. Nat. Hist. (Zool.),* 39:293–298.

Grandison, A. G. C., 1980b, Aspects of breeding morphology in *Mertensophryne micranotis* (Anura: Bufonidae): secondary sexual characters, eggs and tadpoles, *Bull. British Mus. Nat. Hist. (Zool.),* 39:299–304.

Grandison, A. G. C., 1981, Morphology and phylogenetic position of the west African *Didynamipus sjoestedti* Andersson, 1903 (Anura: Bufonidae), *Monit. Zool. Italiano N.S. Suppl.,* 15:187–215.

Grandison, A. G. C., and S. Ashe, 1983, The distribution, behavioral ecology and breeding strategy of the pygmy toad, *Mertensophryne micronotus* (Lov.), *Bull. British Mus. Nat. Hist. (Zool.),* 45:85–93.

Grant, D., O. Anderson, and V. C. Twitty, 1968, Homing orientation by olfaction in newts *(Taricha rivularis), Science,* 160:1354–1355.

Grant, M. P., 1930a, Diagnostic stages of metamorphosis in *Amblystoma jeffersonianum* and *Amblystoma opacum, Anat. Rec.,* 51:1–15.

Grant, M. P., 1930b, Diagnostic stages of urodele metamorphosis with reference to *Amblystoma punctatum* and *Triturus viridescens, Anat. Rec.,* 45:1–25.

Grant, P., 1953, Phosphate metabolism during oogenesis in *Rana temporaria, J. Exp. Zool.,* 124:513–543.

Grassi Milano, E., and F. Accordi, 1983, Comparative morphology of the adrenal gland of anuran Amphibia, *J. Anat.,* 136:165–174.

Green, D. M., 1979, Treefrog toepads: comparative surface morphology using scanning electron microscopy, *Canadian J. Zool.,* 57:2033–2046.

Green, D. M., 1981, Adhesion and the toe-pads of treefrogs, *Copeia,* 1981:790–796.

Green, D. M., and P. Alberch, 1981, Interdigital webbing and skin morphology in the neotropical salamander genus *Bolitoglossa* (Amphibia; Plethodontidae), *J. Morph.,* 170:273–282.

Green, D. M., J. P. Bogart, E. H. Anthony, and D. L. Genner, 1980, An interactive, microcomputer based karyotype analysis system for phylogenetic cytotaxonomy, *Comput. Biol. Med.,* 10:219–227.

Green, D. M., C. H. Daugherty, and J. P. Bogart, 1980, Karyology and systematic relationships of the tailed frog *Ascaphus truei, Herpetologica,* 36:346–352.

Green, N. B., 1938, The breeding habits of *Pseudacris brachyphona* (Cope) with a description of the eggs and tadpoles, *Copeia,* 1938:79–82.

Green, T. L., 1931, On the pelvis of the anura: a study in adaptation and recapitulation, *Proc. Zool. Soc. London,* 1931:1259–1291.

Greenberg, B., 1942, Some effects of testosterone on the sexual pigmentation and other sex characters of the cricket frog *(Acris gryllus), J. Exp. Zool.,* 91:435–446.

Greer, B. J., and K. D. Wells, 1980, Territorial and reproductive behavior of the tropical American frog *(Centrolenella fleischmanni), Herpetologica,* 36:318–326.

Gregory, J. T., F. E. Peabody, and L. I. Price, 1956, Revision of the Gymnarthridae American Permian microsaurs, *Peabody Mus. Nat. Hist. Yale Univ.,* 10:1–77.

Greig, J. C., R. C. Boycott, and A. L. De Villiers, 1979, Notes on the elevation of *Rana fasciata montana* Fitzsimons, 1946 to specific rank and on the identity of *Rana fasciata* sensu Burchell, 1824 (Anura: Ranidae), *Ann. Cape Prov. Mus. (Nat. Hist.),* 13:1–30.

Griffiths, I., 1959a, The phylogenetic status of the Sooglossinae, *Ann. Mag. Nat. Hist.,* (13)2:626–640.

Griffiths, I., 1959b, The phylogeny of *Sminthillus limbatus* and the status of the Brachycephalidae (Amphibia, Salientia), *Proc. Zool. Soc. London,* 132:457–487.

Griffiths, I., 1961, The form and function of the fore-gut in anuran larvae (Amphibia, Salientia) with particular reference to the manicotto glandulare, *Proc. Zool. Soc. London,* 137:249–283.

Griffiths, I., 1963, The phylogeny of the Salientia, *Biol. Rev.,* 38:241–292.

Griffiths, I., and A. L. de Carvalho, 1965, On the validity of employing larval characters as major phyletic indices in Amphibia Salientia, *Rev. Brasil. Biol.,* 25:113–121.

Grobbelaar, C. S., 1924, Beiträge zu einer anatomischen Monographie von Xenopus laevis (Daud.), *Zeit. Ges. Anat. München,* 72:131–168.

Gromko, M. H., F. S. Mason, and S. J. Smith-Gill, 1973, Analysis of the crowding effect in *Rana pipiens* tadpoles, *J. Exp. Zool.,* 186:63–72.

Gross, M. R., and R. Shine, 1981, Parental care and mode of fertilization in ectothermic vertebrates, *Evolution,* 35:775–793.

Grubb, J. D., 1972, Differential predation by Gambusia affinis on the eggs of seven species of anuran amphibians, *Amer. Midl. Nat.,* 88:102–108.

Grüsser, O.-J., and U. Grüsser-Cornehls, 1976, "Neurophysiology of the anuran visual system," in R. Llinás and W. Precht (eds.), *Frog Neurobiology,* Berlin: Springer-Verlag, pp 297–385.

Grüsser-Cornehls, W., and W. Himstedt, 1976, "The urodele visual system," in K. V. Fite (ed.), *The Amphibian Visual System, a Multidisciplinary Approach,* New York: Academic Press, pp 203–266.

Guibé, J., 1978, Les batraciens de Madagascar, *Bonner Zool. Monog.,* 11:1–140.

Guimond, R. W., and V. H. Hutchinson, 1972, Pulmonary, branchial and cutaneous gas exchange in the mud puppy, *Necturus maculosus maculosus* (Rafinesque), *Comp. Biochem. Physiol.,* 42(A):367–392.

Guimond, R. W., and V. H. Hutchinson, 1976, "Gas exchange of the giant salamanders of North America," in G. M. Hughs (ed.), *Respiration of Amphibious Vertebrates,* New York: Academic Press, pp 313–338.

Gundernatsch, J. F., 1912, Feeding experiments on tadpoles. I. The influence of specific organs given as food on growth and differentiation. A contribution to the knowledge of organs with internal secretion, *Wilhelm Roux Arch. Entwicklungsmech. Organismen,* 35:457–483.

Günther, A. C. L. G., 1859, *Catalogue of the Batrachia Salientia in the Collection of the British Museum,* London: British Museum.

Günther, R., 1975a, Zum natürlichen Vorkommen und zur Morphologie triploider Teichfrosche, *Rana "esculenta"* L. in der D.D.R. (Anura, Ranidae), *Mitt. Zool. Mus. Berlin,* 51:145–158.

Günther, R., 1975b, Untersuchungen der Meiose bei Männchen von *Rana ridibunda* Pall., *Rana lessonae* Cam. und der Bastardform *Rana "esculenta"* L. (Anura), *Biol. Zentralbl.,* 94:277–294.

Gurdon, J. B., 1960, The effects of ultraviolet irradiation on uncleaved eggs of *Xenopus laevis, Quart. J. Microsc. Sci.,* 101:299–305.

Gutierrez, P., M. J. Delgado, and M. Alonso-Bedate, 1984, Influence of photoperiod and melatonin administration on growth and metamorphosis in *Discoglossus pictus* larvae, *Comp. Biochem. Physiol.,* 79(A):255–260.

Guttman, S. I., 1972, "Blood proteins," in W. F. Blair (ed.), *Evolution in the Genus* Bufo, Austin: Univ. of Texas Press, pp 265–278.

Hadfield, S., 1966, Observations on body temperature and activity in the toad *Bufo woodhousei fowleri, Copeia,* 1966:581–582.

Hadley, M. E., and J. T. Bagnara, 1969a, Integrated nature of chromatophore responses in the *in vitro* frog skin bioassay, *Endocrinology,* 84:69–82.

Haeckel, E., 1866, *Generelle Morphologie der Organismen, 2 Vols.,* Berlin: Reimer.

Häfeli, H. P., 1971, Zur Fortpflanzungsbiologie des Alpensalamanders *(Salamandra atra* Laur.), *Rev. Suisse Zool.,* 78:235–293.

Hailman, J. P., and R. G. Jaeger, 1974, Phototactic responses to spectrally dominant stimuli and use of colour vision by adult anuran amphibians: a comparative survey, *Anim. Behav.,* 22:757–795.

Hailman, J. P., and R. G. Jaeger, 1976, A model of phototaxis and its evaluation with anuran amphibians, *Behaviour,* 56:215–249.

Hairston, N. G., 1949, The local distribution and ecology of the plethodontid salamanders of the southern Appalachians, *Ecol. Monog.,* 19:47–73.

Hairston, N. G., 1980, Species packing in the salamander genus *Desmognathus:* what are the interspecific interactions involved?, *Amer. Nat.,* 115:354–366.

Hairston, N. G., 1981, An experimental test of a guild: salamander competition, *Ecology,* 62:65–72.

Hairston, N. G., 1983a, Growth, survival and reproduction of *Plethodon jordani:* trade-offs between selective pressures, *Copeia,* 1983:1024–1035.

Hairston, N. G., 1983b, Alpha selection in competing salamanders: experimental verification of an a priori hypothesis, *Amer. Nat.,* 122:105–113.

Hall, R. J., 1976, Summer foods of the salamander, *Plethodon wehrlei* (Amphibia, Urodela, Plethodontidae), *J. Herpetol.,* 10:129–131.

Hall, R. J., and D. P. Stafford, 1972, Studies in the life history of Wehrle's salamander, *Plethodon wehrlei, Herpetologica,* 28:300–309.

Halliday, T. R., 1977, "The courtship of European newts: an evolutionary perspective," in D. H. Taylor and S. I. Guttman (eds.), *The Reproductive Biology of Amphibians,* New York: Plenum Press, pp 185–232.

Hamburger, V., 1936, The larval development of reciprocal species hybrids of *Triton taeniatus* Leyd. (and *Triton palmatus* Dugés) X *Triton cristatus* Laur., *J. Exp. Zool.,* 73:319–364.

Hamilton, W. J. Jr., 1934, The rate of growth of the toad *(Bufo americanus americanus* Holbrook) under natural conditions, *Copeia,* 1934:88–90.

Hamilton, W. J. Jr., 1955, Notes on the ecology of the oak toad in Florida, *Herpetologica,* 11:205–210.

Hanken, J., 1979, Egg development time and clutch size in two Neotropical salamanders, *Copeia,* 1979:741–744.

Hanken, J., 1982, Appendicular skeletal morphology in minute salamanders, genus *Thorius* (Amphibia: Plethodontidae): growth regulation, adult size determination and natural variation, *J. Morph.,* 174:57–77.

Hanken, J., 1983, High incidence of limb skeletal variants in a peripheral population of the red-backed salamander, *Plethodon cinereus* (Amphibia: Plethodontidae), from Nova Scotia, *Canadian J. Zool.,* 61:1925–1931.

Hanken, J., and D. B. Wake, 1982, Genetic defferentiation among plethodontid salamanders (genus *Bolitoglossa)* in Central and South America: implications for the South American invasion, *Herpetologica,* 38:272–287.

Hanlin, H. G., and R. H. Mount, 1978, Reproduction and activity of the greater siren, *Siren lacertina* (Amphibia: Sirenidae) in Alabama, *J. Alabama Acad. Sci.,* 49:31–39.

Hansen, K. L., 1958, Breeding pattern of the eastern spadefoot toad, *Herpetologica,* 14:57–67.

Hanson, J. A., and J. L. Vial, 1956, Defensive behavior and effects of toxins in *Bufo alvarius, Herpetologica,* 12:141–149.

Hara, K., and E. C. Boterenbrood, 1977, Refinement of Harrison's normal table for the morula and blastula of the axolotl, *Wilhelm Roux Arch. Entwicklungsmech. Organismen,* 181: 89–93.

Harding, K. A., 1982, Courtship display in a Bornean frog, *Proc. Biol. Soc. Washington,* 95:621–624.

Hardy, L. M., and L. R. Raymond, 1980, The breeding migration of the mole salamander, *Ambystoma talpoideum,* in Louisiana, *J. Herpetol.,* 14:327–335.

Harlow, H. J., 1978, Seasonal aerobic and anaerobic metabolism at rest and during activity in the salamander *Taricha torosa, Comp. Biochem. Physiol.,* 61(A):177–182.

Harris, J. P., 1956, A review of the pertinent literature on the thyroid of the urodela, with special reference to *Necturus, Field Lab.,* 24:21–36.

Harris, R. N., 1981, Intrapond homing behavior in *Notophthalmus viridescens, J. Herpetol.,* 15:355–356.

Harris, R. N., and D. E. Gill, 1980, Communal nesting, brooding behavior, and embryonic survival of the four-toed salamander *Hemidactylium scutatum, Herpetologica,* 36:141–144.

Harris, R. T., 1975, Seasonal activity and microhabitat utilization in *Hyla cadaverina* (Anura: Hylidae), *Herpetologica,* 31:236–239.

Harrison, J. R., 1967, Observations on the life history, ecology, and distribution of *Desmognathus aeneus aeneus* Brown and Bishop, *Amer. Midl. Nat.,* 77:356–370.

Harrison, J. R., 1973, Observations on the life history and ecology of *Eurycea quadridigittata* (Holbrook), *H. I. S. S. News-Jour.,* 1:57–58.

Harrison, R. G., 1969, "Harrison stages and description of the normal development of the spotted salamander, *Amblystoma punctatum* (Linn.)," in R. G. Harrison (ed.), *Organization and Development of the Embryo,* New Haven: Yale Univ. Press, pp 44–66.

Hasegawa, K., 1960, Quantitative studies on the nucleic acids of toad embryos, *J. Sci. Hiroshima Univ.,* (B)19:117–162.

Hassinger, D. D., 1970, Notes on the thermal properties of frog eggs, *Herpetologica,* 26:49–51.

Hassinger, D. D., J. D. Anderson, and G. H. Dalrymple, 1970, The early life history and ecology of Ambystoma tigrinum and Ambystoma opacum in New Jersey, *Amer. Midl. Nat.,* 84:474–495.

Haubrich, R., 1961, Hierarchical behavior in the South African clawed frog *Xenopus laevis* Daudin, *Anim. Behav.,* 9:71–76.

Hayes, M. P., 1983, Predation on the adults and prehatching stages of glass frogs (Centrolenidae), *Biotropica,* 15:74–76.

Healy, W. R., 1974, Population consequences of alternative life histories in *Notophthalmus v. viridescens, Copeia,* 1974: 221–229.

Heath, A. G., 1975, Behavioral thermoregulation in high altitude tiger salamanders, *Ambystoma tigrinum, Herpetologica,* 31: 84–93.

Heatwole, H., 1960, Burrowing ability and behavioral responses to desiccation of the salamander, *Plethodon cinereus, Ecology,* 41:661–668.

Heatwole, H., 1961, Rates of desiccation and rehydration of eggs in a terrestrial salamander, *Plethodon cinereus, Copeia,* 1961:110–112.

Heatwole, H., 1982, A review of structuring in herpetofaunal assemblages, *U. S. Fish And Wildlife Res. Rept.,* 13:1–19.

Heatwole, H., E. Cameron, and G. J. W. Webb, 1971, Studies on anuran water balance. II. Evaporative water loss, vital limit, and behavioral responses to desiccation in *Notaden bennetti,* Herpetologica, 27:365–378.

Heatwole, H., S. S. DeAustin, and R. Herrero, 1968, Heat tolerances of tadpoles of two species of tropical anurans, *Comp. Biochem. Physiol.,* 27:807–815.

Heatwole, H., and A. Heatwole, 1968, Motivational aspects of feeding behavior in toads, *Copeia,* 1968:692–698.

Heatwole, H., and K. Lim, 1961, Relation of substrate moisture to absorption and loss of water by the salamander, *Plethodon cinereus, Ecology,* 42:814–819.

Heatwole, H., N. Mercado, and E. Ortiz, 1965, Comparison of critical thermal maxima of two species of Puerto Rican frogs of the genus Eleutherodactylus, *Physiol. Zool.,* 38:1–8.

Heatwole, H., and R. C. Newby, 1972, Interaction of internal rhythm and loss of body water in influencing activity levels of amphibians, *Herpetologica,* 28:156–162.

Heatwole, H., and O. J. Sexton, 1966, Herpetofaunal comparisons between two climatic zones in Panama, *Amer. Midl. Nat.,* 75:45–60.

Heatwole, H., F. Torres, S. B. de Austin, and A. Heatwole, 1969, Studies on anuran water balance-I. Dynamics of evaporative water loss in the coqui, *Eleutherodactylus portoricensis, Comp. Biochem. Physiol.,* 28:245–269.

Hecht, M. K., 1958, A synopsis of the mud puppies of eastern North America, *Proc. Staten Island Inst. Arts Sci.,* 2:4–38.

Hecht, M. K., and J. L. Edwards, 1977, "The methodology of phylogenetic inference above the species level," in M. K. Hecht, P. Goody and B. M. Hecht (eds.), *Major Patterns in Vertebrate Evolution,* New York: Plenum Press, pp 3–51.

Hedeen, S. E., 1971, Growth of the tadpoles of the mink frog, *Rana septentrionalis, Herpetologica,* 27:160–165.

Hedeen, S. E., 1972, Postmetamorphic growth and reproduction of the mink frog, *Rana septentrionalis* Baird, *Copeia,* 1972:169–175.

Hedgecock, D., 1976, Genetic variation in two wide spread species of salamanders, *Taricha granulosa* and *Taricha torosa, Biochem. Genetics,* 14:561–576.

Heinzmann, U., 1970, Untersuchen zur Bio-Akustik und Ökologie der Geburtshelferkröte, *Alytes o. obstetricans* (Laur.), *Oecologia*, 5:19–55.

Helling, H., 1938, Das Geruchsorgan der Anuren, vergleichend-morphologisch betrachtet., *Zeit. Ges. Anat.*, 108:587–643.

Hemmer, H., and J. A. Alcover (eds.), 1984, *Història Biològica del Ferreret (Life History of the Mallorcan Midwife Toad)*, Mallorca: Editorial Moll, Monogr. Cien. 3.

Henderson, B. A., 1973, The specialized feeding behavior of *Ambystoma gracile* in Marion Lake, British Columbia, *Canadian Field-Nat.*, 87:151–154.

Hendrickson, J. R., 1954, Ecology and systematics of salamanders of the genus *Batrachoseps*, *Univ. California Publ. Zool.*, 54:1–46.

Hensel, J. L. Jr., and E. D. Brodie Jr., 1976, An experimental study of aposematic coloration in the salamander *Plethodon jordani*, *Copeia*, 1976:59–65.

Herre, W., 1935, Die Schwanzlurche den mitteleocänen (oberlutetischen) Braunkohle des Geiseltales und die Phylogenie der Urodelen unter Einschluss der fossilen Formen, *Zoologica*, 33(87):1–85.

Herreid, C. F. II., and S. Kinney, 1966, Survival of Alaskan woodfrog *(Rana sylvatica)* larvae, *Ecology*, 47:1039–1041.

Herreid, C. F. II., and S. Kinney, 1967, Temperature and development of the woodfrog, *Rana sylvatica*, in Alaska, *Ecology*, 48:579–590.

Herrick, C. J., 1948, *The Brain Of The Tiger Salamander* Ambystoma tigrinum, Chicago: Univ. Chicago Press.

Hertwig, O., 1898, Über den Einfluss der Temperatur auf die Entwicklung von *Rana fusca* und *Rana esculenta*, *Arch. Mikr. Anat.*, 51:319–381.

Hetherington, T. E., and R. E. Lombard, 1982, Opercularis muscle effects on vibration sensitivity in the bullfrog *Rana catesbeiana*, *Amer. Zool.*, 22:887.

Hetherington, T. E., and M. H. Wake, 1979, The lateral line system in larval *Ichthyophis* (Amphibia: Gymnophiona), *Zoomorphologie*, 93:209–225.

Heusser, H., 1958, Zum geruchlichen Beutefinden und Gähnen der Kreuzkröte *(Bufo calamita* Laur.), *Zeit. Tierpsychol.*, 15:94–98.

Heusser, H., 1960, Über die Beziehungen der Erdkröte *(Bufo bufo* L.) zu ihrem Laichplatz. II., *Behaviour*, 16:93–109.

Heusser, H., 1961, Die Bedeutung der äusseren Situation im Verhalten einiger Amphibienarten, *Rev. Suisse Zool.*, 68:1–39.

Heusser, H., 1963, Die Ovulation des Erdkrötenweibchens im Rahmen der Verhaltensorganisation von *Bufo bufo* L., *Rev. Suisse Zool.*, 70:741–758.

Heusser, H., 1968, Die Lebensweise der Erdkrote, *Bufo bufo* (L.); Wanderungen und Sommerquartiere, *Rev. Suisse Zool.*, 75:927–982.

Heusser, H., 1969, Die Lebensweise der Erdkrote, *Bufo bufo* (L.); das Orientierungsproblem, *Rev. Suisse Zool.*, 76:443–518.

Heusser, H., 1970a, Laich-Fressen durch Kaulquappen als mögliche Ursache spezifischer Biotoppraferenzen und kurzer Laichzeiten bei europäischen Froschlurchen (Amphibia, Anura), *Oecologia*, 4:83–88.

Heusser, H., 1970b, Ansiedlung, Ortstreue und Populationsdynamik des Grasfrosches (Rana temporaria) an einem Gartenweiher, *Salamandra*, 6:80–87.

Heusser, H., 1970c, Die Lebensweise der Erdkröte, *Bufo bufo* (L.), *Mitt. Naturfors. Gesell. Schaffhausen*, 29:1–29.

Heusser, H., 1971, Differenzierendes Kaulquappen-Fressen durch Molche, *Experientia*, 27:475.

Heusser, H., 1972a, Intra- und interspezifische Crowding-Effekte bei Kaulquappen der Kreuzkröte, *Bufo calamita* Laur., *Oecologia*, 10:93–98.

Heusser, H., 1972b, Intra- und interspezifische Crowding-Effekte bei Kaulquappen einheimischer Anuren-Arten, *Viertel. Naturf. Gesell. Zurich*, 2:121–128.

Heusser, H., and H. J. Blankenhorn, 1973, Crowding-Experimente mit Kaulquappen aus homo- und heterotypischen

Kreuzungen der Phänotypen *esculenta, lessonae* und *ridibunda (Rana esculenta-* Komplex, Anura, Amphibia), *Rev. Suisse Zool.*, 80:543–569.

Heusser, H., and K. Meisterhans, 1969, Zur Populationsdynamik der Kreuzkröte, *Bufo calamita* Laur., *Viertel. Naturf. Gesell. Zurich*, 114:269–277.

Heyer, W. R., 1969, The adaptive ecology of the species groups of the genus *Leptodactylus* (Amphibia, Leptodactylidae), *Evolution*, 23:421–428.

Heyer, W. R., 1970, Studies on the frogs of the genus *Leptodactylus* (Amphibia: Leptodactylidae), VI: Biosystematics of the melanonotus group, *Contrib. Sci. Los Angeles Co. Mus. Nat. Hist.*, 191:1–48.

Heyer, W. R., 1971, Mating calls of some frogs from Thailand, *Fieldiana Zool.*, 58:61–82.

Heyer, W. R., 1973, Ecological interactions of frog larvae at a seasonal tropical location in Thailand, *J. Herpetol.*, 7:337–361.

Heyer, W. R., 1974a, Relationships of the *marmoratus* species group (Amphibia; Leptodactylidae) within the subfamily Leptodactylinae, *Contrib. Sci. Los Angeles Co. Mus. Nat. Hist.*, 253:1–46.

Heyer, W. R., 1974b, *Vanzolinius*, a new genus proposed for *Leptodactylus discodactylus* (Amphibia, Leptodactylidae), *Proc. Biol. Soc. Washington*, 87:81–90.

Heyer, W. R., 1974c, Niche measurements of frog larvae from a seasonal tropical location in Thailand, *Ecology*, 55:651–656.

Heyer, W. R., 1975, A preliminary analysis of the intergeneric relationships of the frog family Leptodactylidae, *Smithsonian Contr. Zool.*, 199:1–55.

Heyer, W. R., 1976, Studies in larval amphibian habitat partitioning, *Smithsonian Contr. Zool.*, 242:1–27.

Heyer, W. R., 1977, Taxonomic notes on frogs from the Madeira and Purus rivers, Brasil, *Pap. Avul. Zool.*, 31:141–162.

Heyer, W. R., 1978, Systematics of the *fuscus* group of the frog genus *Leptodactylus* (Amphibia, Leptodactylidae), *Sci. Bull. Los Angeles Co. Mus. Nat. Hist.*, 29:1–85.

Heyer, W. R., 1979a, Annual variation in larval amphibian populations within a temporary pond, *J. Washington Acad. Sci.*, 69:65–74.

Heyer, W. R., 1979b, Systematics of the *pentadactylus* species group fo the frog genus *Leptodactylus* (Amphibia: Leptodactylidae), *Smithsonian Contr. Zool.*, 301:1–43.

Heyer, W. R., 1982, Two new species of the frog genus *Hylodes* from Caparaó, Minas Gerais, Brasil (Amphibia: Leptodactylidae), *Proc. Biol. Soc. Washington*, 95:377–385.

Heyer, W. R., 1983, Variation and systematics of frogs of the genus *Cycloramphus* (Amphibia, Leptodactylidae), *Arq. Zool. Mus. Zool. Univ. São Paulo*, 30:235–339.

Heyer, W. R., and R. I. Crombie, 1979, Natural history notes on *Craspedoglossa stejnegeri* and *Thoropa petropolitana* (Amphibia: Salientia, Leptodactylidae), *J. Washington Acad. Sci.*, 69:17–20.

Heyer, W. R., C. H. Daugherty, and L. R. Maxson, 1982, Systematic resolution of the genera of the *Crinia* complex (Amphibia: Anura: Myobatrachidae), *Proc. Biol. Soc. Washington*, 95:423–427.

Heyer, W. R., and D. (=S.) S. Liem, 1976, Analysis of the intergeneric relationships of the Australian frog family Myobatrachidae, *Smithsonian Contr. Zool.*, 233:1–29.

Heyer, W. R., R. W. McDiarmid, and D. L. Weigmann, 1975, Tadpoles, predation and pond habitats in the tropics, *Biotropica*, 7:100–111.

Heyer, W. R., and L. R. Maxson, 1982, "Distributions, relationships, and zoogeography of lowland frogs: the *Leptodactylus* complex in South America, with special reference to Amazonia," in G. T. Prance (ed.), *Biological Diversification in the Tropics*, New York: Columbia Univ. Press, pp 375–388.

Heyer, W. R., and P. A. Silverstone, 1969, The larva of the frog *Leptodactylus hylaedactylus* (Leptodactylidae), *Fieldiana Zool.*, 51:141–145.

Higgins, C., and C. Sheard, 1926, Effects of ultraviolet radiation on the early larval development of *Rana pipiens, J. Exp. Zool.,* 46:333–343.

Highton, R., 1956, The life history of the slimy slalamander, *Plethodon glutinosus,* in Florida, *Copeia,* 1956:75–93.

Highton, R., 1959, The inheritance of the color phases of *Plethodon cinereus, Copeia,* 1959:33–37.

Highton, R., 1962, Geographic variation in the life history of the slimy salamander, *Copeia,* 1962:597–613.

Highton, R., and A. Larson, 1979, The genetic relationships of the salamanders of the genus *Plethodon, Syst. Zool.,* 28:579–599.

Highton, R., and T. Savage, 1961, Functions of the brooding behavior in the female red-backed salamander, *Plethodon cinereus, Copeia,* 1961:95–98.

Hillis, D. M., 1984, Misuse and modification of Nei's genetic distance, *Syst. Zool.,* 33:238–240.

Hillis, D. M., J. S. Frost, and D. A. Wright, 1983, Phylogeny and biogeography of the *Rana pipiens* complex: a biochemical evaluation, *Syst. Zool.,* 32:132–143.

Hillis, D. M., and R. Miller, 1976, an instance of overwintering of larval *Ambystoma maculatum* in Maryland, *Bull. Maryland Herpetol. Soc.,* 12:65–66.

Hillman, S. S., and P. C. Withers, 1979, an analysis of respiratory surface area as a limit to activity metabolism in amphibians, *Canadian J. Zool.,* 57:2100–2105.

Hillyard, S. D., 1976a, The movement of soil water across the isolated amphibian skin, *Copeia,* 1976:314–320.

Hillyard, S. D., 1976b, Variation in the effects of antidiuretic hormone on the isolated skin of the toad, *Scaphiopus couchi, J. Exp. Zool.,* 195:196–200.

Hilton, W. A., 1902, A structural feature connected with mating in *Diemyctylus viridescens, Amer. Nat.,* 36:643–647.

Hilton, W. A., 1945, The skeleton of Hydromantes, *J. Entomol. Zool.,* 37:98–102.

Hilton, W. A., 1946a, Skeletons of Mexican and Central American salamanders of the family Plethodontidae, *J. Entomol. Zool.,* 38:1–8.

Hilton, W. A., 1946b, A preliminary study of skeletons of Amblystomidae, *J. Entomol. Zool.,* 38:29–36.

Hilton, W. A., 1947, The hyobranchial skeleton of Plethodontidae, *Herpetologica,* 3:191–194.

Hilton, W. A., 1948, The vertebrae of salamanders, *J. Entomol. Zool.,* 40:47–65.

Himstedt, W., 1972, Untersuchungen zum Farbensehen von Urodelen, *J. Comp. Physiol.,* 81:229–274.

Himstedt, W., J. Kopp, and W. Schmidt, 1982, Electroreception guides feeding behavior in amphibians, *Naturwissenschaften,* 69:552–553.

Hing, L. K., 1959, The breeding habits and development of Rana chalconota (Schleg.) (Amphibia), *Treubia,* 25:89–111.

Hinsche, G., 1928, Kampfreaktionen bei einheimschen Anuren, *Biol. Zentralbl.,* 48:577–617.

Hock, R. J., 1967, Temperature effect on breeding of the toad, *Bufo variegatus,* in southern Chile, *Copeia,* 1967:227–230.

Hödl, W., 1977, Call differences and calling site segregation in anuran species from central Amazonian floating meadows, *Oecologia,* 28:351–363.

Hodler, F., 1958, Untersuchungen über den Crowd-Effekt an Kaulquappen von *Rana temporaria* L., *Rev. Suisse Zool.,* 65:350–359.

Hoff, G. L., F. L. Frye, and E. R. Jacobson (eds.), 1984, *Diseases of Amphibians and Reptiles,* New York: Plenum Publishing Corporation.

Hoff, J. G., and S. A. Moss, 1974, A distress call in the bullfrog, *Rana catesbeiana, Copeia,* 1974:533–534.

Hoffmann, C. K., 1873–1878, *Dr. H. G. Bronn's Klassen und Ordnungen der Amphibien,* Leipzig: C. F. Winter'sche Verlagshandlung.

Holland, C. A., and J. N. Dumont, 1975, Oogenesis in *Xenopus laevis* (Daudin). IV. Effects of gonadotropin, estrogen and starvation on endocytosis in developing oocytes, *Cell Tiss. Res.,* 162:177–184.

Holloway, W. R., and R. W. Dapson, 1971, Histochemistry of the integumentary secretions of the narrow-mouth toad, *Gastrophryne carolinensis, Copeia,* 1971:351–353.

Holman, J. A., 1967, Additional Miocene anurans from Florida, *Quart. J. Florida Acad. Sci.,* 30:121–140.

Holman, J. A., 1968, A small Miocene herpetofauna from Texas, *Quart. J. Florida Acad. Sci.,* 29("1966"):267–275.

Holmgren, N., 1952, an embryological analysis of the mammalian carpus and its bearing upon the question of the origin of the tetrapod limb, *Acta Zool.,* 33:1–115.

Holmquist, G. P., and B. Dancis, 1979, Telomere replication, kinetochore organizers, and satellite DNA evolution, *Proc. Nat. Acad. Sci. U. S. A.,* 76:4566–4570.

Holomuzki, J. R., 1980, Synchronous foraging and dietary overlap of three species of plethodontid salamanders, *Herpetologica,* 36:109–115.

Holomuzki, J. R., 1982, Homing behavior of *Desmognathus ochrophaeus* along a stream, *J. Herpetol.,* 16:307–309.

Honegger, R. E., 1981, *Threatened Amphibians and Reptiles in Europe,* Wiesbaden: Akad. Verlagsges.

Hoogmoed, M. S., 1967, Mating and early development of *Gastrotheca marsupiata* (Duméril and Bibron) in captivity (Hylidae, Anura, Amphibia), *British J. Herpetol.,* 4:1–7.

Hoogmoed, M. S., 1969, Notes on the herpetology of Surinam II.-On the occurrence of *Allophryne ruthveni* Gaige (Amphibia, Salientia, Hylidae) in Surinam, *Zool. Mededel., Leiden,* 44:75–81.

Hoogmoed, M. S., and S. J. Gorzula, 1979, Checklist of the savanna inhabiting frogs of the El Manteco region with notes on their ecology and the description of a new species of treefrog (Hylidae, Anura), *Zool. Mededel.,* 54:183–216.

Hoogmoed, M. S., and J. Lescure, 1984, A new genus and two new species of minute leptodactylid frogs from northern South America, with comments upon *Phyzelaphryne* (Amphibia: Anura: Leptodactylidae), *Zool. Mededel., Leiden,* 58:85–115.

Hoperskaya, O. A., 1975, The development of an animal homozygous for a mutation causing a periodic albinism (a^p) in *Xenopus laevis, J. Embryol. Exp. Morph.,* 34:253–264.

Hopkins, H. S., and S. W. Handford, 1943, Respiratory metabolism during development in two species of *Amblystoma, J. Exp. Zool.,* 93:403–414.

Hoppe, D. M., 1978, Thermal tolerance in tadpoles of the chorus frog *Pseudacris triseriata, Herpetologica,* 34:318–321.

Horton, P., 1982a, Precocious reproduction in the Australian frog *Limnodynastes tasmaniensis, Herpetologica,* 38:486–489.

Horton, P., 1982b, Diversity and systematic significance of anuran tongue musculature, *Copeia,* 1982:595–602.

Hotz, H., and S. Bruno, 1980, Il problema delle rane verdi e l'Italia (Amphibia, Salientia), *Accad. Naz. Sci. Mem. Sci. Fisic. Nat.,* 98:49–112.

Houck, L. D., 1977a, Reproductive biology of a Neotropical salamander, *Bolitoglossa rostrata, Copeia,* 1977:70–82.

Houck, L. D., 1977b, "Life history patterns and reproductive biology of Neotropical salamanders," in D. H. Taylor and S. I. Guttman (eds.), *The Reproductive Biology of Amphibians,* New York: Plenum Press, pp 43–71.

Houck, L. D., 1982, Growth rates and age at maturity for the plethodontid salamander *Bolitoglossa subpalmata, Copeia,* 1982:474–478.

Howard, R. D., 1978a, The evolution of mating strategies in bullfrogs, *Rana catesbeiana, Evolution,* 32:850–871.

Howard, R. D., 1978b, The influence of male-defended oviposition sites on early embryo mortality in bullfrogs, *Ecology,* 59:789–798.

Howard, R. D., 1980, Mating behaviour and mating success in woodfrogs, *Rana sylvatica, Anim. Behav.,* 28:705–716.

Howard, R. R., and E. D. Brodie Jr., 1973, Experimental study of Batesian mimicry in the salamanders *Plethodon jordani* and *Desmognathus ochrophaeus, Amer. Midl. Nat.,* 60:38–46.

Hoyt, D. L., 1960, Mating behavior and eggs of the plains spadefoot, *Herpetologica,* 16:199–200.

Hsiao, S. D., 1933–1934, A comparative study of the pectoral region of some typical Chinese Salientia, *Peking Nat. Hist. Bull.,* 8:169–204.

Hubbs, C., T. Wright, and O. Cuellar, 1963, Developmental temperature tolerances of central Texas populations of two anuran amphibians, *Bufo valliceps* and *Pseudacris streckeri, Southwest. Nat.,* 8:142–149.

Hudl, L., and H. Schneider, 1979, Temperature and auditory thresholds: bioacoustic studies of the frogs *Rana r. ridibunda, Hyla a. arborea* and *Hyla a. savignyi* (Anura, Amphibia), *J. Comp. Physiol.,* 130(A):17–27.

Huey, R. B., and M. Slatkin, 1976, Costs and benefits of lizard thermoregulation, *Quart. Rev. Biol.,* 51:363–384.

Hulse, A. C., 1979, Notes on the biology of *Pleurodema cinerea* (Amphibia, Anura, Leptodactylidae) in northwestern Argentina, *J. Herpetol.,* 13:153–156.

Humphrey, R. R., 1945, Sex determination in ambystomid salamanders: a study of the progeny of females experimentally converted into males, *Amer. J. Anat.,* 76:33–66.

Humphries, A. A. Jr., 1955, Observations on the mating behavior of normal and pituitary-implanted *Triturus viridescens, Physiol. Zool.,* 28:73–79.

Humphries, A. A. Jr., 1966, Observations on the deposition, structure, and cytochemistry of the jelly envelopes of the newt, *Triturus viridescens, Devel. Biol.,* 13:214–230.

Humphries, A. A. Jr., 1970, Incorporation of ^{35}S-sulphur into the oviducts and egg jelly of the newt, *Notophthalmus viridescens, Exp. Cell Res.,* 59:157–160.

Humphries, R. B., 1981, The structure of a temperate frog community, *Proc. Melbourne Herpetol. Symp.,* p 159.

Hurlbert, S. H., 1969, The breeding migrations and interhabitat wandering of the vermilion-spotted newt *Notophthalmus viridescens* (Rafinesque), *Ecol. Monog.,* 39:465–488.

Hurlbert, S. H., 1978, The measurement of niche overlap and some relatives, *Ecology,* 59:67–77.

Husting, E. L., 1965, Survival and breeding structure in a population of *Ambystoma maculatum, Copeia,* 1965:352–362.

Hutchinson, C., and D. Hewitt, 1935, A study of larval growth in *Amblystoma, J. Exp. Zool.,* 71:465–480.

Hutchinson, V. H., 1961, Critical thermal maxima in salamanders, *Physiol. Zool.,* 34:92–125.

Hutchinson, V. H., 1971, "Oxygen consumption. Part IV. Amphibians," in P. L. Altman and D. S. Dittmer (eds.), *Respiration and Circulation, Biological Handbooks,* Bethesda, Maryland: Amer. Fed. Exp. Biol., pp 481–485.

Hutchinson, V. H., H. B. Haines, and G. Engbretson, 1976, Aquatic life at high altitude: respiratory adaptations in the Lake Titicaca frog, *Telmatobius culeus, Respiration Physiol.,* 27:115–129.

Hutchinson, V. H., and M. A. Kohl, 1971, The effect of photoperiod on daily rythms of oxygen consumption in the tropical toad, *Bufo marinus, Zeit. Vergl. Physiol.,* 75:367–382.

Hutchinson, V. H., and S. D. Rowlan, 1975, Thermal acclimation and tolerance in the mudpuppy, *Necturus maculosus, J. Herpetol.,* 9:367–368.

Hutchinson, V. H., W. G. Whitford, and M. Kohl, 1968, Relation of body size and surface area to gas exchange in anurans, *Physiol. Zool.,* 41:65–85. Ichikawa, M., 1931, On the development of the green frog *Rhacophorus schlegelii arborea, Mem. Coll. Sci. Kyoto Imp. Univ.,* (B)7:17–38.

Ideker, J., 1976, Tadpole thermoregulatory behavior facilitates grackle predation, *Texas J. Sci.,* 27:244–245.

Ifft, J. D., 1942, The effect of environmental factors on the sperm cycle of *Triturus viridescens, Biol. Bull.,* 33:111–128.

Iga, T., and J. T. Bagnara, 1975, An analysis of color change phenomena in the leaf frog *Agalychnis dacnicolor, J. Exp. Zool.,* 192:331–342.

Inger, R. F., 1954, Systematics and zoogeography of Philippine Amphibia, *Fieldiana Zool.,* 33:181–531.

Inger, R. F., 1956a, Morphology and development of the vocal sac apparatus in the African clawed frog *Rana (Ptychadena) porosissima* Steindachner, *J. Morph.,* 99:57–72.

Inger, R. F., 1956b, Some amphibians from the lowlands of North Borneo, *Fieldiana Zool.,* 34:389–424.

Inger, R. F., 1960a, Notes on toads of the genus *Pelophryne, Fieldiana Zool.,* 39:415–418.

Inger, R. F., 1960b, A review of the Oriental toads of the genus *Ansonia, Fieldiana Zool.,* 39:473–503.

Inger, R. F., 1966, The systematics and zoogeography of the Amphibia of Borneo, *Fieldiana Zool.,* 52:1–402.

Inger, R. F., 1967, The development of a phylogeny of frogs, *Evolution,* 21:369–384.

Inger, R. F., 1969, Organization of communities of frogs along small rain forest streams in Sarawak, *J. Anim. Ecol.,* 38:123–148.

Inger, R. F., 1980a, "Abundances of amphibians and reptiles in tropical forests of south-east Asia," in A. G. Marshall (ed.), *Trans. Sixth Aberdeen-Hull Symp. Malesian Ecology, Univ. Hull Dept. Geography Misc. Ser.,* 22:93–110.

Inger, R. F., 1980b, Densities of floor-dwelling frogs and lizards in lowland forests of southeast Asia and Central America, *Amer. Nat.,* 115:761–770.

Inger, R. F., and J. P. Bacon Jr., 1968, Annual reproduction and clutch size in rain forest frogs from Sarawak, *Copeia,* 1968:602–606.

Inger, R. F., and R. K. Colwell, 1977, Organization of contiguous communities of amphibians and reptiles in Thailand, *Ecol. Monog.,* 47:229–253.

Inger, R. F., and B. Greenberg, 1956, Morphology and seasonal development of sex characters in two sympatric African toads, *J. Morph.,* 99:549–574.

Inger, R. F., and B. Greenberg, 1963, The annual reproductive pattern of the frog Rana erythraea in Sarawak, *Physiol. Zool.,* 36:21–33.

Inger, R. F., and B. Greenberg, 1966, Ecological and competitive relations among three species of frog (genus *Rana), Ecology,* 47:746–759.

Inger, R. F., and H. Marx, 1961, The food of amphibians, *Exploration du Parc National de l'Upemba, Fasc.,* 64:1–86.

Inger, R. F., H. K. Voris, and H. H. Voris, 1974, Genetic variation and population ecology of some southeast Asian frogs of the genera *Bufo* and *Rana, Biochem. Genetics,* 12:121–145.

Ingle, D., 1976, "Spatial vision in anurans," in K. V. Fite (ed.), *The Amphibian Visual System,* New York: Academic Press, pp 119–140.

Ingle, D., and D. McKinley, 1978, Effects of stimulus configuration on elicited prey catching by the marine toad *(Bufo marinus), Anim. Behav.,* 26:885–891.

Ingram, G. J., M. Anstis, and C. J. Corben, 1975, Observations on the Australian leptodactylid frog, *Assa darlingtoni, Herpetologica,* 31:425–429.

Ingram, G. J., and C. J. Corben, 1975, A new species of *Kyarranus* (Anura: Leptodactylidae) from Queensland, Australia, *Mem. Queensland Mus.,* 17:335–339.

Ireland, M. P., 1973, Studies on the adaptation of *Xenopus laevis* to hyperosmotic media, *Comp. Biochem. Physiol.,* 46(A):469–476.

Ireland, M. P., and I. M. Simons, 1977, Adaptation of the axolotl *(Ambystoma mexicanum)* to a hyperosmotic medium, *Comp. Biochem. Physiol.,* 56(A):415–417.

Ireland, P. H., 1976, Reproduction and larval development of the gray-bellied salamander *Eurycea multiplicata grisegaster, Herpetologica,* 32:233–238.

Iturra, P., and A. Veloso M., 1981, Evidence for heteromorphic sex chromosomes in male amphibians (Anura: Leptodactylidae), *Cytogenet. Cell. Genet.,* 31:108–110.

Iwasawa, H., and N. Kawasaki, 1979, Normal stages of development of the Japanese green frog *Rhacophorus arboreus* (Okada and Kawano)(in Japanese, English summary), *Japanese J. Herpetol.,* 8:22–35.

Iwasawa, H., and Y. Kera, 1980, Normal stages of development of the Japanese lungless salamander, *Onychodactylus japonicus* (Houttuyn)(in Japanese, English summary), *Japanese J. Herpetol.,* 8:73–89.

Iwasawa, H., and H. Michibata, 1972, Comparative morphology of sperm storage portion of Wolffian duct in Japanese anurans, *Annot. Zool. Japonenses,* 45:218–233.

Iwasawa, H., and Y. Morita, 1980, Normal stages of development in the frog, *Rana brevipoda porosa* (in Japanese, English summary), *Zool. Mag. (Tokyo),* 89:65–75.

Izecksohn, E., 1971, Novo genero e nova especie de Brachycephalidae do Estado do Rio de Janeiro, Brasil (Amphibia, Anura), *Bol. Mus. Nac. Rio de Janeiro Zool.,* 280:1–12.

Izecksohn, E., J. Jim, S. Tenorio de Albuquerque, and W. Furtado de Mendoca, 1971, Observações sobre o desenvolimento e os hábitos de *Myersiella subnigra* (Miranda-Ribeiro), *Arq. Mus. Nac. Rio de Janeiro,* 54:69–72. Jackman, R., S. Nowicki, D. J. Aneshansley, and T. Eisner, 1983, Predatory capture of toads by fly larvae, *Science,* 222:515–516.

Jackson, A. W., 1952, The effect of temperature, humidity, and barometric pressure on the rate of call in *Acris crepitans* Baird in Brazos County, Texas, *Herpetologica,* 8:18–20.

Jaeger, C. B., and D. E. Hillman, 1976, "Morphology of gustatory organs," in R. Llinás and W. Precht (eds.), *Frog Neurobiology,* Berlin: Springer-Verlag, pp 588–606.

Jaeger, R. G., 1971, Moisture as a factor influencing the distributions of two species of terrestrial salamanders, *Oecologia,* 6:191–207.

Jaeger, R. G., 1976, Possible prey-call window in anuran auditory perception, *Copeia,* 1976:833–834.

Jaeger, R. G., 1978, Plant climbing by salamanders: periodic availability of plant-dwelling prey, *Copeia,* 1978:686–691.

Jaeger, R. G., 1980a, Fluctuations in prey availability and food limitation for a terrestrial salamander, *Oecologia,* 44:335–341.

Jaeger, R. G., 1980b, Density-dependent and density-independent causes of extinction of a salamander population, *Evolution,* 34:617–621.

Jaeger, R. G., 1980c, Microhabitats of a terrestrial forest salamander, *Copeia,* 1980:265–268.

Jaeger, R. G., 1981a, Birds as inefficient predators on terrestrial salamanders, *Amer. Nat.,* 117:835–837.

Jaeger, R. G., 1981b, Dear enemy recognition and the costs of aggression between salamanders, *Amer. Nat.,* 117:962–974.

Jaeger, R. G., and D. E. Barnard, 1981, Foraging tactics of a terrestrial salamander: choice of diet in structurally simple environments, *Amer. Nat.,* 117:639–664.

Jaeger, R. G., D. E. Barnard, and R. G. Joseph, 1982, Foraging tactics of a terrestrial salamander: assessing prey density, *Amer. Nat.,* 119:885–890.

Jaeger, R. G., and W. F. Gergits, 1979, Intra- and interspecific communication in salamanders through chemical signals on the substrate, *Anim. Behav.,* 27:150–156.

Jaeger, R. G., and J. P. Hailman, 1976, Ontogenetic shift of spectral phototactic preferences in anuran tadpoles, *J. Comp. Physiol. Psychol.,* 10:930–945.

Jameson, D. L., 1950, Development of *Eleutherodactylus latrans, Copeia,* 1950:44–46.

Jameson, D. L., 1955a, The population dynamics of the cliff frog, *Syrrhophus marnocki, Amer. Midl. Nat.,* 54:342–381.

Jameson, D. L., 1955b, Evolutionary trends in the courtship and mating behavior of Salientia, *Syst. Zool.,* 4:105–119.

Jameson, D. L., 1956, Growth, dispersal and survival of the Pacific tree frog, *Copeia,* 1956:25–29.

Jameson, D. L., 1957, Population structure and homing responses in the Pacific tree frog, *Copeia,* 1957:221–228.

Jarvik, E., 1942, On the structure of the snout of crossopterygians and lower gnathostomes in general, *Zool. Bidrag,* 21:235–675.

Jarvik, E., 1960, *Théories de l'Évolution des Vertébrés Reconsidérées à la Lumiere des Rècentes Découvertes sur les Vertébrés Inférieurs.* (Translated by J. P. Lehman), Paris: Masson.

Jarvik, E., 1967, On the structure of the lower jaw in dipnoans: with a description of an early Devonian dipnoan from Canada, *Melanognathus canadensis* gen. et sp. nov., *J. Linnaean Soc. (Zool.),* 47(311):155–183.

Jarvik, E., 1980–1981, *Basic Structure and Evolution of Vertebrates. 2 Vols.,* New York: Academic Press.

Jaslow, A. P., 1979, Vocalization and aggression in *Atelopus chiriquiensis* (Amphibia, Anura, Bufonidae), *J. Herpetol.,* 13:141–145.

Jaussi, R., and P. A. Kunz, 1978, Isolation of the major toxic protein from the skin of the crested newt, *Triturus cristatus, Experientia,* 34:503–504.

Johansen, K., and A. S. F. Ditada, 1966, Double circulation in the giant toad, Bufo paracnemis, *Physiol. Zool.,* 39:140–150.

Johansen, K., and C. Lenfant, 1972, "A comparative approach to the adaptability of O_2-Hb affinity," in P. Astrup and M. Rorth (eds.), *Oxygen Affinity of Hemoglobin and Red Cell Acid Base Status,* Copenhagen: Munksgaard, pp 750–780.

Johnson, B. K., and J. L. Christiansen, 1976, The food and food habits of Blanchard's cricket frog, *Acris crepitans blanchardi* (Amphibia, Anura, Hylidae) in Iowa, *J. Herpetol.,* 10:63–64.

Johnson, C. R., 1969, Aggregation as a means of water conservation in juvenile *Limnodynastes* from Australia, *Herpetologica,* 25:275–276.

Johnson, C. R., and J. Lowrey, 1968, Observations on the breeding behavior of *Rhacophorus leucomystax* (Kuhl) from the Republic of Viet Nam, *Herpetologica,* 24:336–338.
Johnson, C. R., and C. B. Schreck, 1969, Food and feeding of larval *Dicamptodon ensatus* from California, *Amer. Midl. Nat.,* 81:280–281.

Jollie, M., 1962, *Chordate Morphology,* New York: Reinhold Publ. Co.

Joly, J., 1960a, La conservation des spermatozoides et les particularités histophysiologiques du réceptacle séminale chez la salamandre *Salamandra salamandra taeniata, Compt. Rend. Acad. Sci. Paris,* 250:2269–2271.

Joly, J., 1960b, Le cycle sexuel de la salamandre tachetee *Salamandra salamandra quadri-virgata* dans l'oueste de la France, *Compt. Rend. Acad. Sci. Paris,* 251:2594–2596.

Joly, J., 1961, Le cycle sexuel biennial chez la femelle de *Salamandra salamandra quadri-virgata* dans les hautes-Pyrénées, *Compt. Rend. Acad. Sci. Paris,* 252:3145–3147.

Joly, J., 1966, Sur l'ethologie sexuelle de *Salamandra salamandra* L., *Zeit. Tierpsychol.,* 23:8–27.

Joly, J., 1971, Les cycles sexueles de *Salamandra* (L.). I., *Ann. Sci. Nat. Zool. Biol. Anim.,* 13:451–504.

Jones, E. I., 1933, The variability of the musculature in relation to the reduction of the clavicle, procoracoid, and episternum, *Ann. Mag. Nat. Hist.,* 12:403–420.

Jones, K. L., 1982, Prey patterns and trophic niche overlap in four species of Caribbean frogs, *U. S. Fish And Wildlife Res. Rept.,* 13:49–55.

Jones, R. E., A. M. Gerrard, and J. J. Roth, 1973, Estrogen and brood pouch formation in the marsupial frog *Gastrotheca riobambae, J. Exp. Zool.,* 184:177–184.

Jones, R. M., and S. S. Hillman, 1978, Salinity adaptation in the salamander *Batrachoseps, J. Exp. Biol.,* 76:1–10.

Jordan, M., G. Luthardt, C. Meyer-Naujoks, and G. Roth, 1980, The role of eye accomodation in depth perception of common toads, *Zeit. Naturforsch.,* 35(C):851–852.

Jørgensen, C. B., 1974, "Integrative functions of the brain," in B. Lofts (ed.), *Physiology of the Amphibia, II,* New York: Academic Press, pp 1–51.

Jorquera, B., and L. Izquierdo, 1964, Tabla de desarrollo normal de *Calyptocephalella gayi* (Rana chilena), *Biologica,* 36:43–53.

Jorquera, B., E. Pugín, and O. Goicoechea, 1972, Tabla de desarrollo normal de *Rhinoderma darwini, Arch. Med. Veter.,* 4:1–15.

Jorquera, B., E. Pugín, and O. Goicoechea, 1974, Tabla de desarrollo normal de *Rhinoderma darwini* (Concepción), *Bol. Soc. Biol. Concepción,* 48:127–146.

Joubert, P. J., 1961, Contributions to the cranial morphology of Pseudotriton ruber ruber (Sonnini), *Ann. Univ. Stellenbosch,* 36(A):389–418.

Judd, F. W., 1977, Toxicity of monosodium methanearsonate herbicide to Couch's spadefoot toad, *Scaphiopus couchi, Herpetologica,* 33:44–46.

Jungreis, A. M., 1976, Minireview. Partition of excretory nitrogen in Amphibia, *Comp. Biochem. Physiol.,* 53(A):133–141.

Jurgens, J. D., 1971, The morphology of the nasal region of Amphibia and its bearing on the phylogeny of the group, *Ann. Univ. Stellenbosch,* (A)46(2):1–146.

Jurgens, J. D., 1978, Amplexus in *Breviceps* adspersus—who's the sticky partner?, *J. Herpetol. Assoc. Africa,* 18:6.

Just, J. J., 1972, Protein-bound iodine and protein concentration in plasma and pericardial fluid of metamorphosing anuran tadpoles, *Physiol. Zool.,* 45:143–152.

Just, J. J., R. Sperka, and S. Strange, 1977, A quantitative analysis of plasma osmotic pressure during metamorphosis of the bullfrog, *Rana catesbeiana, Experientia,* 33:1503–1505.

Justis, C. S., and D. H. Taylor, 1976, Extraocular photoreception and compass orientation in larval bullfrogs, *Rana catesbeiana, Copeia,* 1976:98–105.

Justus, J. T., M. Sandomir, T. Urquhart, and B. O. Ewan, 1977, Developmental rates of two species of toads from the desert southwest, *Copeia,* 1977:592–594.

Kalezić, M. L., and D. Hedgecock, 1980, Genetic variation and differentiation of three common European newts *(Triturus)* in Yugoslavia, *British J. Herpetol.,* 6:49–57.

Kambara, S., 1953, Role of jelly envelope of toad eggs in fertilization, *Annot. Zool. Japan,* 26:78–84.

Kampen, P. N. van, 1923, *The Amphibians of the Indo-Australian Archipelago,* Leiden: E. J. Brill, Ltd..

Kaplan, R. H., 1979, Ontogenetic variation in "ovum" size in two species of *Ambystoma, Copeia,* 1979:348–350.

Kaplan, R. H., 1980a, The implications of ovum size variability for offspring fitness and clutch size within several populations of salamanders *(Ambystoma), Evolution,* 34:51–64.

Kaplan, R. H., 1980b, Ontogenetic energetics in *Ambystoma, Physiol. Zool.,* 53:43–56.

Kaplan, R. H., and M. L. Crump, 1978, The non-cost of brooding in *Ambystoma opacum, Copeia,* 1978:99–103.

Kaplan, R. H., and S. N. Salthe, 1979, The allometry of reproduction: an empirical view in salamanders, *Amer. Nat.,* 113:671–689.

Kaplan, R. H., and P. W. Sherman, 1980, Intraspecific oophagy in California newts, *J. Herpetol.,* 14:183–185.

Karlin, A. A., and S. I. Guttman, 1981, Hybridization between *Desmognathus fuscus* and *Desmognathus ochrophaeus* (Amphibia: Urodela: Plethodontidae) in northeastern Ohio and northwestern Pennsylvania, *Copeia,* 1981:371–377.

Karlstrom, E. L., 1962, The toad genus Bufo in the Sierra Nevada of California. Ecological and systematic relationships, *Univ. California Publ. Zool.,* 62:1–104.

Kasinsky, H. E., S. Y. Huang, S. Kwauk, M. Mann, M. A. J. Sweeney, and B. Yee, 1978, On the diversity of sperm histones in the vertebrates III. Electrophoretic variability of testis-specific histone patterns in Anura contrasts with relative constancy in Squamata, *J. Exp. Zool.,* 203:109–126.

Kasinsky, H. E., M. Mann, L. Pickerill, L. Gutovich, and E. W. Byrd Jr., 1981, Sperm histone diversity in the vertebrates: an evolutionary trend, *J. Cell Biol.,* 91:187.

Katagiri, C., 1963, Fertilizability of the egg of *Hyla arborea japonica,* with special reference to the change of jelly envelopes, *Zool. Mag.,* 72:23–28.

Katow, H., 1979, Structure and formation of ankylosis in *Xenopus laevis, J. Morph.,* 162:327–341.

Katz, L. C., M. J. Potel, and R. J. Wassersug, 1981, Structure and mechanisms of schooling in tadpoles of the clawed frog, *Xenopus laevis, Anim. Behav.,* 29:20–33.

Kawamura, T., 1953, Studies on hybridization in amphibians. V. Physiological isolation among four *Hynobius* species, *J. Sci. Hiroshima Univ. (Zool.),* 14:93–116.

Kawamura, T., 1984, Polyploidy in amphibians, *Zool. Sci.,* 1:1–15.

Kawamura, T., and M. Nishioka, 1977, "Aspects of the reproductive biology of Japanese anurans," in D. H. Taylor and S. I. Guttman (eds.), *The Reproductive Biology of Amphibians,* New York: Plenum Press, pp 103–139.

Kawamura, T., and M. Nishioka, 1978, Descendants of reciprocal hybrids between two Japanese pond-frog species, *Rana nigromaculata* and *Rana brevipoda, Sci. Rept. Lab. Amphib. Biol. Hiroshima,* 3:399–419.

Kawamura, T., M. Nishioka, and M. Kuramoto, 1972, Reproduction of the Oriental fire-bellied toad, *Bombina orientalis,* with special reference to the superiority of this species as a laboratory animal, *Sci. Rept. Lab. Amphib. Biol. Hiroshima,* 1:303–317.

Kawamura, T., M. Nishioka, and H. Ueda, 1980, Inter- and intraspecific hybrids among Japanese, European and American toads, *Sci. Rept. Lab. Amphib. Biol. Hiroshima,* 4:1–126.

Kawamura, T., and S. Sawada, 1959, On the sexual isolation among different species and local races of Japanese newts, *J. Sci. Hiroshima Univ. (Zool.),* (B)18(1):17–31.

Keen, W. H., and E. E. Schroeder, 1975, Temperature selection and tolerance in three species of *Ambystoma* larvae, *Copeia,* 1975:523–530.

Kelleher, K. E., and J. R. Tester, 1969, Homing and survival in the Manitoba toad, *Bufo hemiophrys* in Minnesota, *Ecology,* 50:1040–1048.

Keller, R., 1946, Morphogenetische Untersuchungen und Skelett von *Siredon mexicanus* Shaw mit besonderer Berucksichtigung des Ossifikationsmodus beim neotenen Axolotl, *Rev. Suisse Zool.,* 53:329–426.

Keller, R. E., 1976, Vital dye mapping of the gastrula and neurula of *Xenopus laevis.* II. Prospective areas and morphogenetic movements of the deep layer, *Devel. Biol.,* 51:118–137.

Kelly, D. B., 1980, Auditory and vocal nuclei in the frog brain concentrates sex hormones, *Science,* 207:553–555.

Kelly, D. E., 1971, "Developmental aspects of amphibian pineal systems," in G. E. Wolstenholme and J. Knight (eds.), *The Pineal Gland,* Edinburgh: Churchill-Livingston, pp 53–74.

Kenny, J. S., 1966, Nest building in Phyllomedusa trinitatus Mertens, *Caribbean J. Sci.,* 6:15–22.

Kenny, J. S., 1968, Early development and larval natural history of Phyllomedusa trinitatus Mertens, *Caribbean J. Sci.,* 8:35–45.

Kenny, J. S., 1969a, The Amphibia of Trinidad, *Stud. Fauna Curaçao Caribbean Isl.,* 29:1–78.

Kenny, J. S., 1969b, Feeding mechanisms in anuran larvae, *J. Zool. London,* 157:225–246.

Kenny, J. S., 1969c, Pharyngeal mucous secreting epithelia of anuran larvae, *Acta Zool.,* 50:143–153.

Kerbert, C., 1904, Zur Fortpflanzung der *Megalobatrachus maximus* Schlegel, *Zool. Anz.,* 27:305–316.

Kerr, J. G., 1919, *Text Book of Embryology, II. Vertebrata with the Exception of Mammalia,* New York: MacMillan.

Kezer, J., 1952, Thyroxin induced metamorphosis of the neotenic salamanders *Eurycea tynerensis* and *Eurycea neotenes, Copeia,* 1952:234–237.

Kezer, J., and H. C. Macgregor, 1971, A fresh look at meiosis and centromeric heterochromatin in the red-backed salamander, *Plethodon cinereus cinereus* (Green), *Chromosoma,* 33:146–166.

Kezer, J., and S. K. Sessions, 1979, Chromosome variation in the plethodontid salamander, *Aneides ferreus, Chromosoma,* 71:65–80.

Khan, M. S., 1965, A normal table of *Bufo melanostictus* Schneider, *Biologia,* 11:1–39.

Khan, M. S., 1969, A normal table of *Rana tigrina* Daudin I. Early development (stages 1-27), *Pakistan J. Sci.,* 21:36–50.

Khmelevskaya, N. V., and T. O. Duelina, 1971, On the role of the sense of smell in the life of anura, *Zool. Zhur.,* 51:764–767.

Kiester, A. R., 1971, Species density of North American amphibians and reptiles, *Syst. Zool.,* 20:127–137.

Kim, Y. H., G. H. Brown, H. S. Mosher, and F. H. Fuhrman, 1975, Tetrodotoxin: occurrence in atelopodid frogs of Costa Rica, *Science,* 189:151–152.

King, O. M., 1960, Observations on Oklahoma toads, *Southwest. Nat.,* 5:103.

Kingsbury, B. G., and H. D. Reed, 1909, The columella auris in Amphibia, *J. Morph.,* 20:549–628.

Kirschner, L. B., T. Kerstetter, D. Porter, and R. H. Alvarado, 1971, Adaptation of larval *Ambystoma tigrinum* to concentrated environments, *Amer. J. Physiol.,* 220:1814–1819.

Kirtisinghe, P., 1957, *The Amphibia of Ceylon,* Colombo: (Priv. Publ.).

Kistler, A., K. Yoshizato, and E. Frieden, 1977, Preferential binding of tri-substituted thyronine analogs by bullfrog tadpole tail fin cytosol, *Endocrinology,* 100:134–137.

Kleeberger, S. R., and J. K. Werner, 1982, Home range and homing behavior of *Plethodon cinereus* in northern Michigan, *Copeia,* 1983:409–415.

Kleeberger, S. R., and J. K. Werner, 1983, Post-breeding migration and summer movement of *Ambystoma maculatum, J. Herpetol.,* 17:176–177.

Klopfer, P. H., and R. H. MacArthur, 1961, On the causes of tropical species diversity: niche overlap, *Amer. Nat.,* 95:223–226.

Kluge, A. J., 1966, A new pelobatine frog from the lower Miocene of South Dakota with a discussion of the evolution of the *Scaphiopus-Spea* complex, *Contrib. Sci. Los Angeles Co. Mus. Nat. Hist.,* 113:1–65.

Kluge, A. G., 1981, The life history, social organization, and parental behavior of *Hyla rosenbergi* Boulenger, a nest-building gladiator frog, *Misc. Publ. Mus. Zool. Univ. Michigan,* 160:1–170.

Kluge, A. G., and J. S. Farris, 1969, Quantitative phyletics and the evolution of anurans, *Syst. Zool.,* 18:1–32.

Knight, F. C. E., 1938, Die Entwicklung von *Triton alpestris* bei verscheidenen Temperaturen, mit Normentafel, *Arch. Entwicklungsmech.,* 137:461–473.

Knoepffler, L.-P., 1962, Contribution a l'étude de genre *Discoglossus* (Amphibiens, Anoures), *Vie Milieu,* 13:1–94.

Kobayashi, H., 1954, Hatching mechanism in the toad, *Bufo vulgaris formosus.* 3.Extrusion of embryos from the jelly string and colloidal nature of the jelly, *J. Fac. Sci. Tokyo Univ.,* (4)7:97–105.

Kobayashi, M., 1963, Studies on reproductive isolating mechanisms in brown frogs. I. Development and inviability of hybrids, *J. Sci. Hiroshima Univ. (Zool.),* 20:147–165.

Kollros, J. J., 1981, "Transitions in the nervous system during amphibian metamorphosis," in L. I. Gilbert and E. Frieden (eds.), *Metamorphosis: a Problem in Developmental Biology. 2nd Edit.,* New York: Plenum Press, pp 445–459.

Konishi, M., 1970, Evolution of design features in the coding of species-specificity, *Amer. Zool.,* 10:67–72.

Kopsch, F., 1952, *Die Entwicklung des Braunen Grasfrosches Rana fusca Roesl.,* Stuttgart: George Thieme.

Korey, K. A., 1981, Species number, generation length, and the molecular clock, *Evolution,* 35:139–147.

Kourany, M., C. W. Myers, and C. R. Schneider, 1970, Panamanian amphibians and reptiles as carriers of *Salmonella, Amer. J. Trop. Med. Hyg.,* 19:632–638.

Koyama, H., E. R. Lewis, E. L. Leverenz, and R. A. Baird, 1982, Acute seismic sensitivity in the bullfrog ear, *Brain Res.,* 250:168–172.

Kozlowska, M., 1971, Differences in the reproductive biology of mountain and lowland common frogs, *Rana temporaria* L., *Acta Biol. Cracoviensia, Zool.,* 14:2–32.

Kraft, A. V., 1968, Larvengestalt und Eingeveide-situs beim Alpenmolch *(Triturus alpestris)* nach Halbseiter UV-bestrahlung von Neurula- und Nachneurula-keime, *Arch. Entwicklungsmech.,* 160:259–297.

Kramek, W. C., 1976, Feeding behavior of *Rana septentrionalis* (Amphibia, Anura, Ranidae), *J. Herpetol.,* 10:249–251.

Krebs, J. R., 1978, "Optimal foraging: decision rules for predators," in J. R. Krebs and N. B. Davies (eds.), *Behavioral Ecology: an Evolutionary Approach,* Sunderland, Mass.: Sinauer, pp 23–63.

Krug, E. C., K. V. Honn, J. Battista, and C. S. Nicoll, 1978, Corticosteroid and thyroid hormone (TH) levels in serum of bullfrog tadpoles during development and metamorphosis, *Amer. Zool.,* 18:614.

Krzysik, A. J., 1979, Resource allocation, coexistence, and the niche structure of a streambank salamander community, *Ecol. Monog.,* 49:173–194.

Krzysik, A. J., 1980, Trophic aspects of brooding behavior in *Desmognathus fuscus fuscus, J. Herpetol.,* 14:426–428.

Kudo, T., 1938, *Normentafel zur Entwicklungsgeschichte des Japanischen Reisensalamanders* (Megalobatrachus japonicus *Temminck). Normentafeln zur Entwicklungsgeschichte der Wirbeltiere 16,* Vienna: Gustav Fischer.

Kuhlenbeck, H., 1922, Zur Morphologie des Gymnophionengehirns, *Jena Zeit. Naturw.,* 58:453–484.

Kuhlenbeck, H., T. D. Malewitz, and A. B. Beasley, 1966, "Further observations on the morphology of the forebrain in gymnophiona, with reference to the topologic vertebrate forebrain pattern," in R. Hassler and H. Stephan (eds.), *Evolution of the Forebrain,* Stuttgart: Georg Thieme Verlag, pp 9–19.

Kumar, S., 1975, *The Amphibian Heart,* New Delhi: S. Chand & Co.

Kunz, A., 1924, Anatomical and physiological changes in the digestive system during metamorphosis in *Rana pipiens* and *Amblystoma tigrinum, J. Morph.,* 38:581–598.

Kuramoto, M., 1972, Karyotypes of six species of frogs (genus *Rana*) endemic to the Ryukyu Islands, *Caryologia,* 25:547–559.

Kuramoto, M., 1975, Adaptive significance in oxygen consumption in frog embryos in relation to the environmental temperature, *Comp. Biochem. Physiol.,* 52(A):59–62.

Kuramoto, M., 1977, A comparative study of karyotypes in the treefrogs (family Rhacophoridae) from Japan and Taiwan, *Caryologia,* 30:333–342.

Kuramoto, M., 1978a, Correlations of quantitative parameters of fecundity in amphibians, *Evolution,* 32:287–296.

Kuramoto, M., 1978b, Thermal tolerance of frog embryos as a function of developmental stage, *Herpetologica,* 34:417–422.

Kuramoto, M., 1980, Karyotypes of several frogs from Korea, Taiwan and the Philippines, *Experientia,* 36:826–827.

Labanick, G. M., 1976, Prey availability, consumption and selection in the cricket frog, *Acris crepitans* (Amphibia, Anura, Hylidae), *J. Herpetol.,* 10:293–298.

Labanick, G. M., and R. A. Brandon, 1981, An experimental study of Batesian mimicry between the salamanders *Plethodon jordani* and *Desmognathus ochrophaeus, J. Herpetol.,* 15:275–281.

Lacroix, J.-C., 1968, Étude descriptive des chromosomes en écouvillon dans le genre *Pleurodeles* (Amphibien, Urodèle), *Ann. Embryol. Morph.,* 1:179–202.

Lacroix, J.-C., 1970, Mise en évidence sur les chromosomes en écouvillon de *Pleurodeles poireti* Gervais, amphibien urodèle, d'une structure liée au sexe, identifiant le bivalent sexual et marquant le chromosome W, *Compt. Rend. Acad. Sci. Paris,* 271(D):102–104.

Lagerspetz, K. Y. H., 1977, Interactions of season and temperature acclimation in the control of metabolism in Amphibia, *J. Therm. Biol.,* 2:223–231.

Lamotte, M., 1959, Observations ecologiques sur les populations naturelles de *Nectophrynoides occidentalis* (fam. Bufonidés), *Bull. Biol. France Belgique,* 43:355–413.

Lamotte, M., and J. Lescure, 1977, Tendances adaptatives a l'affranchissement du milieu aquatique chez les amphibiens anoures, *Terre et Vie,* 30:225–312.

Lamotte, M., and J.-L. Perret, 1963, Contribution à l'étude des batraciens de l'ouest africain. XV.-Le développement direct de l'espece *Arthroleptis poecilonotus* Peters, *Bull. Inst. France Afrique Noire,* 25(A):277–284.

Lamotte, M., and J.-L. Perret, 1968, Révision du genre *Conrava* Nieden, *Bull. Inst. Fond. Afrique Noire,* (A)30:1603–1644.

Lamotte, M., and P. Rey, 1954, Existence de corpora lutea chez un batracien anoure vivipare, *Nectophrynoides occidentalis* Angel: leur evolution morphologique, *Compt. Rend. Acad. Sci. Paris,* 283:393–395.

Lamotte, M., P. Rey, and M. Vogeli, 1964, Recherches sur l'ovaire de *Nectophrynoides occidentalis,* batracien anoure vivipare, *Arch. Anat. Micro. Morph. Exp.,* 53:179–224.

Lamotte, M., and F. Xavier, 1972a, Les amphibiens anoures a développement direct d'Afrique. Observations sur la biologie de *Nectophrynoides tornieri* (Roux), *Bull. Soc. Zool. France,* 97:413–428.

Lamotte, M., and F. Xavier, 1972b, Recherches sur le développement embryonnaire de *Nectophrynoides occidentalis* Angel, amphibien anoure vivipare. I-Les principaux traits morphologiques et biométriques du développement, *Ann. Embryol. Morph.,* 10:315–340.

Landreth, H. F., and D. E. Ferguson, 1966, Evidence of suncompass orientation in the chorus frog, *Pseudacris triseriata, Herpetologica,* 22:106–112.

Landreth, H. F., and D. E. Ferguson, 1967, Newts: sun-compass orientation, *Science,* 158:1459–1461.

Lannoo, M. J., and M. D. Bachmann, 1984a, Aspects of cannibalistic morphs in a population of *Ambystoma t. tigrinum* larvae, *Amer. Midl. Nat.,* 112:103–110.

Lannoo, M. J., and M. D. Bachmann, 1984b, On flotation and air breathing in *Ambystoma tigrinum* larvae: stimuli for and the relationship between these behaviors, *Canadian J. Zool.,* 62:15–18.

Lantz, L. A., 1947, Note (Appendix to article by Bruce and Parkes, Observations on *Discoglossus pictus* Otth), *Proc. Royal Soc. London,* 134(B):52–56.

Lanza, B., J. M. Cei, and E. G. Crespo, 1976, Further immunological evidence for the validity of the family Bombinidae (Amphibia, Salientia), *Monit. Zool. Italiano,* 10:311–314.

Largen, M. J., P. A. Morris, and D. W. Yalden, 1972, Observations on the caecilian *Geotrypetes grandisonae* Taylor (Amphibia Gymnophiona) from Ethiopia, *Monit. Zool. Italiano N.S. Suppl.,* 4(8):185–205.

Larsen, J. H. Jr., 1963, *The Cranial Osteology of Neotenic and Transformed Salamanders and its Bearing on Interfamilial Relationships,* Seattle: Univ. Washington, Ph.D. Dissertation.

Larsen, J. H. Jr., and D. J. Guthrie, 1975, The feeding mechanism of terrestrial tiger salamanders *(Ambystoma tigrinum melanostictum* Baird), *J. Morph.,* 147:137–154.

Larson, A., 1980, Paedomorphosis in relation to rates of morphological and molecular evolution in the salamander *Aneides flavipunctatus* (Amphibia, Plethodontidae), *Evolution,* 34:1–17.

Larson, A., 1984, "Neontological inferences of evolutionary pattern and process in the salamander family Plethodontida e," in M. K. Hecht, B. Wallace and G. T. Prance (eds.), *Evolutionary Biology, Vol. 17,* New York: Plenum Publishing Corporation, pp 119–217.

Larson, A., D. B. Wake, L. R. Maxson, and R. Highton, 1981, A molecular phylogenetic perspective on the origins of morphological novelties in the salamanders of the tribe Plethodontini (Amphibia, Plethodontidae), *Evolution,* 35:405–422.

Laurent, R. F., 1964, Adaptive modifications in frogs of an isolated highland fauna in central Africa, *Evolution,* 18:458–467.

Laurent, R. F., 1972, Tentative revision of the genus *Hemisus* Günther, *Ann. Mus. Royal Afrique Cent. (8-Zool.),* 194:1–67.

Laurent, R. F., 1979, Esquisse d'une phylogenèse des anoures, *Bull. Soc. Zool. France,* 104:397–422.

Laurent, R. F., 1982, Le genre *Afrixalus* Laurent (Hyperoliidae) en Afrique centrale, *Ann. Mus. Royal Afrique Cent. (8-Zool.),* 235:1–58.

Laurent, R. F., 1983, La superespèce *Hyperolius viridiflavus* (Duméril and Bibron, 1841) (Anura Hyperoliidae) en Afrique centrale, *Monit. Zool. Italiano N.S. Suppl.,* 15:1–93.

Laurent, R. F., 1984, Heterogeneidad de la familia Caeciliidae (Amphibia-Apoda), *Acta Zool. Lilloana,* 37:199–200.

Lawson, R., 1963, The anatomy of *Hypogeophis rostratus* Cuvier. Part I. The skin and skeleton, *Proc. Univ. Durham Philos. Soc.,* 13(A):254–273.

Lawson, R., 1965, The anatomy of *Hypogeophis rostratus* Cuvier (Amphibia: Apoda or Gymnophiona). Part II. The musculature, *Proc. Univ. Newcastle Upon Tyne Philos. Soc.,* 1:52–63.

Lawson, R., 1966, The anatomy of the heart of *Hypogeophis rostratus* (Amphibia, Apoda) and its possible mode of action, *J. Zool.,* 149:320–336.

Lawson, R., D. B. Wake, and N. Beck, 1971, Tooth replacement in the red-backed salamander, *Plethodon cinereus, J. Morph.,* 134:259–270.

Layne, J. R. Jr., and D. L. Claussen, 1982, Seasonal variation in the thermal acclimation of critical thermal maxima (CTMax) and minima (CTMin) in the salamander *Eurycea bislineata, J. Therm. Biol.,* 7:29–33.

Lebedkina, N. S., 1960, Development of the bones of the palatal arch in the caudate Amphibia (Biol. Sci. Sec. translation), *Doklady. Akad. Nauk. S.S.S.R.,* 131:218–220.

Lebedkina, N. S., 1968, "The development of bones in the skull roof of Amphibia," in T. Ørvig (ed.), *Current Problems of Lower Vertebrate Phylogeny,* Stockholm: Almqvist and Wiksell, pp 317–329.

Lebedkina, N. S., 1979, *Evolution of the Amphibian Skull* (in Russian), Moskow: Nauka.

Ledford, B. E., and E. Fieden, 1973, Albumin synthesis during induced and spontaneous metamorphosis in the bullfrog *Rana catesbeiana, Devel. Biol.,* 30:187–197.

Lee, A. K., 1967, Studies in Australian Amphibia II. Taxonomy, ecology, and evolution of the genus *Helioporus* (Gray) (Anura: Leptodactylidae), *Australian J. Zool.,* 15:367–439.

Lee, A. K., 1968, Water economy of the burrowing frog, *Heleioporus eyrei* (Gray), *Copeia,* 1968:741–745.

Lee, A. K., and E. H. Mercer, 1967, Cocoon surrounding desert-dwelling frogs, *Science,* 157:87–88.

Lee, J. C., 1980, An ecogeographic analysis of the herpetofauna of the Yucatan Peninsula, *Misc. Publ. Mus. Nat. Hist. Univ. Kansas,* 67:1–75.

Lee, J. C., and M. L. Crump, 1981, Morphological correlates of male mating success in *Triprion petasatus* and *Hyla marmorata* (Anura: Hylidae), *Oecologia,* 50:153–157.

Lee, T. W., 1964, Maintenance of the unswollen state of the egg jelly in the *Rana pipiens* reproductive tract, *J. Elisha Mitchell Sci. Soc.,* 80:1–8.

Lehman, J. P., 1956, L'évolution des dipneustes et l'origine des urodèles. Probl. actuel paleontol., *Cent. Natl. Rech. Sci. Colloq. Intern.*, 60:69–76.

Lehman, J. P., 1968, "Remarques concernant la phylogénie des amphibiens," in T. Ørvig (ed.), *Current Problems of Lower Vertebrate Phylogeny,* Stockholm: Nobel Symposium 4, pp 307–315.

Leloup, J., and M. Buscaglia, 1977, La triiodothyronine, hormone de la métamorphose des Amphibiens, *Compt. Rend. Acad. Sci. Paris,* 284(D):2261–2263.

Lenfant, C., and K. Johansen, 1967, Respiratory adaptations in selected amphibians, *Respiration Physiol.,* 2:247–260.

Leon, P. E., 1970, Report of the chromosome numbers of some Costa Rican anurans, *Rev. Biol. Trop.,* 17:119–124.

León, P. E., and J. Kezer, 1974, The chromosomes of *Siren intermedia nettingi* (Goin) and their significance to comparative salamander karyology, *Herpetologica,* 30:1–11.

León, P. E., and J. Kezer, 1978, Localization of 5S RNA genes on chromosomes of plethodontid salamanders, *Chromosoma,* 65:213–230.

León O., J., and R. Donoso-Barros, 1970, Desarrollo embrionario y metamorphosis de *Pleurodema brachyops* (Cope) (Salientia-Leptodactylidae), *Bol. Soc. Biol. Concepción,* 42:355–379.

Le Quang Trong, Y., 1966, Histogenèse et histochimie des glandes cutanées de l'Axolotl *(Ambystoma tigrinum* Green), *Arch. Zool. Exp. Gen.,* 108:49–73.

Le Quang Trong, Y., 1967, Structure et développement de la peau et des glandes cutanées de *Nectophrynoides occidentalis* Angel, *Arch. Zool. Exp. Gen.,* 108:589–610.

Le Quang Trong, Y., 1971, Étude de la peau et des glandes cutanées de quelques amphibiens du genre *Phrynobatrachus, Bull. Inst. Fond. Afrique Noire,* 33:987–1025.

Le Quang Trong, Y., 1975a, La peau et les glandes cutanées de *Dicroglossus occipitalis* Günther, *Ann. Univ. Abidjan,* (E)8:15–29.

Le Quang Trong, Y., 1975b, Étude de la peau et des glandes cutanées de quelques amphibiens du genre *Ptychadena, Ann. Univ. Abidjan,* (E)8:31–52.

Le Quang Trong, Y., and Y. Bouligand, 1976, Les desmosomes et l'orientation des tonofilaments dans le tégument des anoures, *Bull. Soc. Zool. France, 101:637–645.*

Lescure, J., 1968, Le comportement social des batraciens, *Rev. Comport. Anim.,* 2:1–33.

Lescure, J., 1977, "Le comportement de défense chez les amphibiens," in Y. Leroy (ed.), *Ethno-écologie des Communications chez les Amphibiens, Bull. Soc. Zool. France,* 102(2):27–36.

Lescure, J., 1979, Étude taxonomique et éco-éthologique d'un amphibien des petites Antilles *Leptodactylus fallax* Müller, 1926 (Leptodactylidae), *Bull. Mus. Natl. Hist. Nat. Paris,* 1(4): 757–774.

Lettvin, J. Y., H. R. Maturana, W. S. McCulloch, and W. H. Pitts, 1959, What the frog's eye tells the frog's brain, *Proc. Inst. Radio Eng.,* 47:1940–1951.

Levan, A., K. Fredga, and A. A. Sandberg, 1964, Nomenclature for centromeric position of chromosomes, *Hereditas,* 52: 201–220.

Lewis, E. R., 1978, Comparative studies of the anuran auditory papillae, *Scan. Elec. Micros.,* 2:633–642.

Lewis, E. R., 1981, Evolution of the inner-ear apparatus in the frog, *Brain Res.,* 219:149–155.

Lewis, E. R., 1985, On the frog amphibian papilla, *Scan. Elec. Micros.,* 4:1899–1913.

Lewis, E. R., and E. L. Leverenz, 1983, Morphological basis for tonotopy in the anuran amphibian papilla, *Scan. Elec. Micros.,* 1983:198–200.

Lewis, E. R., E. L. Leverenz, and H. Koyama, 1982, The tonotopic organization of the bullfrog amphibian papilla, an auditory organ lacking a basilar membrane, *J. Comp. Physiol.,* 145(A):437–445.

Lewis, E. R., and C. W. Li, 1973, Evidence concerning the morphogenesis of saccular receptors in the bullfrog *(Rana catesbeiana), J. Morph.,* 139:351–361.

Lewis, E. R., and P. M. Narins, 1985, Do frogs communicate with seismic signals?, *Science,* 227:187–189.

Leydig, F., 1867, Uber die Molche (Salamandrina) der Wurttembergischen Fauna, *Arch. Naturgesch. Jahrg.,* 33(1): 163–282.

Li, C. W., and E. R. Lewis, 1974, Morphogenesis of auditory receptor epithelia in the bullfrog, *Scan. Elec. Micros.,* 1974:791–798.

Licht, L. E., 1967, Growth inhibition in crowded tadpoles: intraspecific and interspecific effects, *Ecology,* 48:736–745.

Licht, L. E., 1968, Unpalatability and toxicity of toad eggs, *Herpetologica,* 24:93–98.

Licht, L. E., 1969, Comparative breeding biology of the red-legged frog *(Rana aurora aurora)* and the western spotted frog *(Rana pretiosa pretiosa)* in southwestern British Columbia, *Canadian J. Zool.,* 47:505–509.

Licht, L. E., 1973, Behavior and sound production by the northwestern salamander, *Ambystoma gracile, Canadian J. Zool.,* 51:1055–1056.

Licht, L. E., 1974, Survival of embryos, tadpoles, and adults of the frogs *Rana aurora aurora* and *Rana pretiosa pretiosa* sympatric in southwestern British Columbia, *Canadian J. Zool.,* 52:613–627.

Licht, L. E., 1975, Comparative life history features of the western spotted frog, *Rana pretiosa,* from low- and high-elevation populations, *Canadian J. Zool.,* 53:1254–1257.

Licht, L. E., 1976, Sexual selection in toads *(Bufo americanus), Canadian J. Zool.,* 54:1277–1284.

Licht, P., and A. G. Brown, 1967, Behavioral thermoregulation and its role in the ecology of the red-bellied newt, *Taricha rivularis, Ecology,* 48:598–611.

Lieberkind, I., 1937, *Vergleichende Studien über die Morphologie und Histogenese der Larvalen Haftorgane bei den Amphibien,* Copenhagen: C. A. Reitzels Forlag.

Liebmann, P. A., and G. Entine, 1968, Visual pigments of frog and tadpole *(Rana pipiens), Vision Res.,* 8:761–775.

Liem, K. F., 1961, On the taxonomic status and the granular patches of the Javanese frog *Rana chalconota, Herpetologica,* 17:69–71.

Liem, K. F., 1977, "Musculoskeletal system," in A. G. Kluge (ed.), *Chordate Structure and Function, Edit. 2,* New York: Macmillan Publ. Co., pp 179–269.

Liem, S. (= D.) S., 1970, The morphology, systematics, and evolution of the Old World treefrogs (Rhacophoridae and Hyperoliidae), *Fieldiana Zool.,* 57:1–145.

Lillie, F. R., and F. P. Knowlton, 1897, On the effect of temperature on the development of animals, *Zool. Bull.,* 1: 179–193.

Lillywhite, H. B., 1970, Behavioral thermoregulation in the bullfrog, *Rana catesbeiana, Copeia,* 1970:158–168.

Lillywhite, H. B., 1971a, Thermal modulation of cutaneous mucus discharge as a determinant of evaporative water loss in the frog, *Rana catesbeiana, Zeit. Vergl. Physiol.,* 73:84–104.

Lillywhite, H. B., 1971b, Temperature selection by the bullfrog, *Rana catesbeiana, Comp. Biochem. Physiol.,* 40(A):213–227.

Lillywhite, H. B., and P. Licht, 1974, Movement of water over toad skin: functional role of epidermal sculpturing, *Copeia,* 1974:165–171.

Lillywhite, H. B., P. Licht, and P. Chelgren, 1973, The role of behavioral thermoregulation in the growth energetics of the toad, *Bufo boreas, Ecology,* 54:375–383.

Limbaugh, B. A., and E. P. Volpe, 1957, Early development of the Gulf Coast toad, *Bufo valliceps* Wiegmann, *Amer. Mus. Novitat.,* 1842:1–32.

Limerick, S., 1980, Courtship behavior and oviposition of the poison-arrow frog *Dendrobates pumilio, Herpetologica,* 36:69–71.

Limeses, C. E., 1965, La musculatura mandibular en los ceratofrinidos y formas afines (Anura, Ceratophrynidae), *Physis,* 25:41–58.

Lindemann, B., and C. Voûte, 1976, "Structure and function of the epidermis," in R. Llinás and W. Precht (eds.), *Frog Neurobiology,* Berlin: Springer-Verlag, pp 169–210.

Lindquist, S. B., and M. D. Bachmann, 1982, The role of visual and olfactory cues in the prey catching behavior of the tiger salamander, *Ambystoma tigrinum, Copeia,* 1982:81–90.

Ling, J. K., 1972, Adaptive function of vertebrate molting cycles, *Amer. Zool.,* 12:77–93.

Linnaeus, C., 1758, *Systema Naturae, Edit. 10, Tom. 1, Pt. 1,* Upsala.

Littlejohn, M. J., 1959, Call differentiation in a complex of seven species of *Crinia, Evolution,* 13:452–468.

Littlejohn, M. J., 1963, The breeding biology of the Baw Baw frog *Philoria frosti* Spencer, *Proc. Linnean Soc. New S. Wales,* 88:273–276.

Littlejohn, M. J., 1969, "The significance of isolating mechanisms," in *Systematic Biology,* Washington: Nat. Acad. Sci. U. S. A., pp 459–482.

Littlejohn, M. J., 1977, "Long range acoustic communication in anurans: an integrated and evolutionary approach," in D. H. Taylor and S. I. Guttman (eds.), *The Reproductive Biology of Amphibians,* New York: Plenum Press, pp 263–294.

Littlejohn, M. J., and P. A. Harrison, 1981, "Acoustic communication in *Geocrinia victoriana* (Anura: Leptodactylidae)," in C. B. Banks and A. A. Martin (eds.), *Proc. Melbourne Herpetological Symposium,* Melbourne, p 6.

Littlejohn, M. J., and A. A. Martin, 1969, Acoustic interaction between two species of leptodactylid frogs, *Anim. Behav.,* 17:785–791.

Littlejohn, M. J., and T. C. Michaud, 1959, Mating call discrimination by females of Strecker's chorus frog *(Pseudacris streckeri), Texas J. Sci.,* 11:86–92.

Littlejohn, M. J., and G. F. Watson, 1974, Mating call discrimination and phonotaxis by females of the *Crinia laevis* complex (Anura: Leptodactylidae), *Copeia,* 1974:171–175.

Littlejohn, M. J., and G. F. Watson, 1976, Effectiveness of a hybrid mating call in eliciting phonotaxis by females of the *Geocrinia laevis* complex (Anura: Leptodactylidae), *Copeia,* 1976:76–79.

Liu, C. C., 1935a, The "linea masculina," a new secondary sex character in Salientia, *J. Morph.,* 57:131–145.

Liu, C. C., 1935b, Types of vocal sac in the Salientia, *Proc. Boston Soc. Nat. Hist.,* 41:19–40.

Liu, C. C., 1936, Secondary sex characters of Chinese frogs and toads, *Zool. Ser. Field Mus. Nat. Hist.,* 22:115–156.

Liu, C. C., 1950, Amphibians of western China, *Fieldiana Zool. Mem.,* 2:1–400.

Liu, C. C., and S. Hu, 1961, *Tailless Amphibians Of China* (in Chinese), Beijing: Science Press.

Livezey, R. L., and A. H. Wright, 1947, A synoptic key to the salientian eggs of the United States, *Amer. Midl. Nat.,* 37:179–222.

Llinás, R., and W. Precht, 1976, *Frog Neurobiology,* Berlin: Springer-Verlag.

Lloyd, M., R. F. Inger, and F. W. King, 1968, On the diversity of reptile and amphibian species in a Bornean rain forest, *Amer. Nat.,* 102:497–515.

Lock, A., and T. Collett, 1980, The three-dimensional world of a toad, *Proc. Royal Soc. London,* B206:481–487.

Lofts, B., 1974, "Reproduction," in B. Lofts (ed.), *Physiology of the Amphibia, Vol. 2,* New York: Academic Press, pp 107–218.

Lofts, B. (ed.), 1974, *Physiology of the Amphibia. Vol. 2,* New York: Academic Press.

Lofts, B. (ed.), 1976, *Physiology of the Amphibia. Vol. 3,* New York: Academic Press.

Loftus-Hills, J. J., 1973, Comparative aspects of auditory function in Australian anurans, *Australian J. Zool.,* 21:353–367.

Loftus-Hills, J. J., 1974, Analysis of an acoustic pacemaker in Strecker's chorus frog, *Pseudacris streckeri* (Anura: Hylidae), *J. Comp. Physiol. Psychol.,* 90:75–87.

Loftus-Hills, J. J., and B. M. Johnstone, 1970, Auditory function, communication and brain-evoked response in anuran amphibians, *J. Acoust. Soc. Amer.,* 47:1131–1138.

Loftus-Hills, J. J., and M. J. Littlejohn, 1971a, Mating-call sound intensities of anuran amphibians, *J. Acoust. Soc. Amer.,* 49:1327–1329.

Loftus-Hills, J. J., and M. J. Littlejohn, 1971b, Pulse repetition rate difference as the basis for mating call discrimination by two sympatric species of hylid frogs, *Copeia,* 1971:154–156.

Logier, E. B. S., 1952, *The Frogs, Toads and Salamanders of Eastern Canada,* Toronto: Clarke Irwin.

Lombard, R. E., 1977, Comparative morphology of the inner ear in salamanders (Caudata: Amphibia), *Contr. Vert. Evol.,* 2:1–140.

Lombard, R. E., 1980, "The structure of the amphibian auditory periphery: a unique experiment in terrestrial hearing," in A. N. Popper and R. R. Fay (eds.), *Comparative Studies of Hearing in Vertebrates,* New York: Springer-Verlag, pp 121–138.

Lombard, R. E., R. R. Fay, and Y. L. Werner, 1981, Underwater hearing in the frog, *Rana catesbeiana, J. Exp. Biol.,* 91:57–71.

Lombard, R. E., and I. R. Straughan, 1974, Functional aspects of anuran middle ear structures, *J. Exp. Biol.,* 61:71–93.

Lombard, R. E., and D. B. Wake, 1976, Tongue evolution in the lungless salamanders, family Plethodontidae. I. Introduction, theory and a general model of dynamics, *J. Morph.,* 148:265–286.

Lombard, R. E., and D. B. Wake, 1977, Tongue evolution in the lungless salamanders, family Plethodontidae. II. Function and evolutionary diversity, *J. Morph.,* 153:39–80.

Lopez, C. H., and E. D. Brodie Jr., 1977, The function of costal grooves in salamanders (Amphiuma, Urodela), *J. Herpetol.,* 11:372–374.

Lörcher, K., 1969, Vergleichende bioakustiche Untersuchungen an der Rot- und Gelbbauchunke, *Bombina bombina* (L.) und *Bombina variegata* (L.), *Oecologia,* 3:84–124.

Lovejoy, T. E., 1982, "Designing refugia for tomorrow," in G. T. Prance (ed.), *Biological Diversification in the Tropics,* New York: Columbia Univ. Press, pp 673–680.

Loveridge, J. P., 1970, Observations on nitrogenous excretion and water relations of *Chiromantis xerampelina* (Amphibia, Anura), *Arnoldia,* 5:1–6.

Loveridge, J. P., and G. Crayé, 1979, Cocoon formation in two species of southern African frogs, *South Africa J. Sci.,* 75:18–20.

Loveridge, J. P., and P. C. Withers, 1981, Metabolism and water balance of active and cocooned African bullfrogs, *Pyxicephalus adspersus, Physiol. Zool.,* 54:203–214.

Løvtrup, S., and A. Pigón, 1969, Observations on the gill development in frogs, *Ann. Embryol. Morph.,* 2:3–13.

Løvtrup, S., and B. Werdinius, 1957, Metabolic phases during amphibian embryogenesis, *J. Exp. Zool.,* 135:203–220.

Low, B. S., 1972, "Evidence from parotoid-gland secretions," in W. F. Blair (ed.), *Evolution In The Genus* Bufo, Austin: Univ. Texas Press, pp 244–264.

Low, B. S., 1976, "The evolution of amphibian life histories in the desert," in D. W. Goodall (ed.), *Evolution of Desert Biota,* Austin: Univ. Texas Press, pp 149–195.

Low, K. L., T. W. Chen, and C. K. Tan, 1976, The acquisition of egg jelly and its effect on fertilizability and hatchability in *Bufo melanostictus, Copeia,* 1976:684–689.

Lubosch, W., 1913, Die Kaumuskulatur der Amphibien, verglichen mit der Sauropsiden und Säugetiere, *Verhand. Anat. Gesell.,* 27:67–76.

Lubosch, W., 1915, Vergleichende Anatomie der Kaumuskeln

der Wirbeltiere, in funf Teilen. I. Die Kaumuskeln der Amphibi en, Jena Zeit. Naturw., 53:51–188.

Lucas, E. A., and W. A. Reynolds, 1967, Temperature selection by amphibian larvae, Physiol. Zool., 40:159–171.

Lucké, B., 1934, A neoplastic disease of the kidney of the leopard frog, Amer. J. Cancer, 20:352–379.

Luddecke, H., 1976, Einige Ergebnisse aus Feldbeobachtungen an Phyllobates palmatus (Amphibia, Ranidae) in Kolumbien, Mitt. Inst. Colombo-Aleman Invest. Cien, 8:157–163.

Lue, G.-Y., and S.-H. Chen, 1982, Amphibians of Taiwan (in Chinese), Taiwan: Zhang Zheng Xiong.

Luthardt, G., and G. Roth, 1979, The relationship between stimulus orientation and stimulus movement pattern in the prey catching behavior of Salamandra salamandra, Copeia, 1979:442–447.

Luther, A., 1914, Über die vom N. trigeminus versorgte Muskulatur der Amphibien mit einem vergleichenden Ausblick über der Adductor mandibulae der Gnathostomen und einem Beitrag zum Verständnis der Organisation der Anuren Larven, Acta Soc. Sci. Fennica, 44:1–151.

Lutz, B., 1954, Anfibios anuros do Distrito Federal, Mem. Inst. Oswaldo Cruz, 52:155–238.

Lutz, B., 1960, Fighting and incipient notion of territoriality in male tree frogs, Copeia, 1960:61–63.

Lutz, B., 1973, Brazilian Species of Hyla, Austin: Univ. Texas Press.

Lutz, B., and G. Orton, 1946, Hyla claresignata Lutz & B. Lutz, 1939. Aspects of the life history and description of the rhyacophilous tadpole. (Salientia-Hylidae), Bol. Mus. Nac. Rio de Janeiro, 70:1–20.

Lynch, J. D., 1970, A taxonomic revision of the leptodactylid frog genus Syrrhophus Cope, Univ. Kansas Publ. Mus. Nat. Hist., 20:1–45.

Lynch, J. D., 1971, Evolutionary relationships, osteology, and zoogeography of leptodactyloid frogs, Misc. Publ. Mus. Nat. Hist. Univ. Kansas, 53:1–238.

Lynch, J. D., 1973, "The transition from archaic to advanced frogs," in J. L. Vial (ed.), Evolutionary Biology of the Anurans: Contemporary Research on Major Problems, Columbia: Univ. Missouri Press, pp 133–182.

Lynch, J. D., 1976, The species groups of South American frogs of the genus Eleutherodactylus (Leptodactylidae), Occ. Pap. Mus. Nat. Hist. Univ. Kansas, 61:1–24.

Lynch, J. D., 1978, A re-assessment of the telmatobiine leptodactylid frogs of Patagónia, Occ. Pap. Mus. Nat. Hist. Univ. Kansas, 72:1–57.

Lynch, J. D., 1979a, "The amphibians of the lowland tropical forests," in W. E. Duellman (ed.), The South American Herpetofauna: Its Origin, Evolution, and Dispersal, Monog. Mus. Nat. Hist. Univ. Kansas, 7:189–215.

Lynch, J. D., 1979b, A new genus for Elosia duidensis Rivero (Amphibia, Leptodactylidae), Amer. Mus. Novit., 2680:1–8.

Lynch, J. D., 1980, A new species of Barycholos from Estado Goiás, Brasil (Amphibia, Anura, Leptodactylidae) with remarks on related genera, Bull. Mus. Natl. Hist. Nat., Ser. 4, 2, A, 1:289–302.

Lynch, J. D., 1982, Relationships of the frogs of the genus Ceratophrys (Leptodactylidae) and their bearing on the hypothesis of Pleistocene forest refugia in South America and punctuated equilibria, Syst. Zool., 31:166–179.

Lynch, J. D., and P. M. Ruíz-C., 1982, A new genus and species of poison-dart frog (Amphibia: Dendrobatidae) from the Andes of northern Colombia, Proc. Biol. Soc. Washington, 95: 557–562.

Lynch, J. D., P. M. Ruíz-C., and J. V. Rueda, 1983, Notes on the distribution and reproductive biology of Centrolene geckoideum Jiménez de la Espada in Colombia and Ecuador (Amphibia: Centrolenidae), Stud. Neotrop. Fauna Envir., 18:239–243.

Lynch, K., 1984, Growth and metamorphosis of the rectus abdominis muscle in Rana pipiens, J. Morph., 182:317–337.

Lynn, W. G., 1942, The embryology of Eleutherodactylus nubicola, an anuran which has no tadpole stage, Carnegie Inst. Washington Contr. Embryo, 30:27–59.

Lynn, W. G., 1961, Types of amphibian metamorphosis, Amer. Zool., 1:151–161.

Lynn, W. G., and C. Grant, 1940, The herpetology of Jamaica, Inst. Jamaica, 1:1–148.

Lynn, W. G., and B. Lutz, 1946a, The development of Eleutherodactylus guentheri Stdnr. 1864, Bol. Mus. Nac. Rio de Janeiro, N.S. Zool., 71:1–46.

Lynn, W. G., and B. Lutz, 1946b, The development of Eleutherodactylus nasutus Lutz, Bol. Mus. Nac. Rio de Janeiro, N.S. Zool., 79:1–30. MacArthur, R. H., and E. O. Wilson, 1967, Theory of Island Biogeography, Princeton, New Jersey: Princeton Univ. Press.

McAuliffe, J. R., 1978, Biological Survey and Management of Sport-hunted Bullfrog Populations in Nebraska, Lincoln: Nebraska Game Parks Com., Rept.

McClanahan, L. L., 1964, Osmotic tolerance of the muscles of two desert inhabiting toads, Bufo cognatus and Scaphiopus couchi, Comp. Biochem. Physiol., 12:501–508.

McClanahan, L. L., 1967, Adaptations of the spadefoot toad, Scaphiopus couchii, to desert environments, Comp. Biochem. Physiol., 20:73–99.

McClanahan, L. L., 1972, Changes in body fluids in burrowed spadefoot toads as a function of soil water potential, Copeia, 1972:209–216.

McClanahan, L. L., 1975, "Nitrogen excretion in arid-adapted amphibians," in N. F. Hadley (ed.), Environmental Physiology of Desert Organisms, Stroudsburg, Pennsylvania: Dowden, Hutchinson & Ross, Inc., pp 106–116.

McClanahan, L. L., and R. Baldwin, 1969, Rate of water uptake through the integument of the desert toad, Bufo punctatus, Comp. Biochem. Physiol., 28:381–390.

McClanahan, L. L., R. Ruibal, and V. H. Shoemaker, 1983, Rate of cocoon formation and its physiological correlates in a ceratophryd frog, Physiol. Zool., 56:430–435.

McClanahan, L. L., V. H. Shoemaker, and R. Ruibal, 1976, Structure and function of the cocoon of a ceratophryd frog, Copeia, 1976:179–185.

McCoid, M. J., and T. H. Fritts, 1980, Observations of feral populations of Xenopus laevis (Pipidae) in southern California, Bull. South. California Acad. Sci., 79:82–86.

McCurdy, H. M., 1931, Development of the sex organs in Triturus torosus, Amer. J. Anat., 47:367–403.

McDiarmid, R. W., 1971, Comparative morphology and evolution of frogs of the Neotropical genera Atelopus, Dendrophryniscus, Melanophryniscus, and Oreophrynella, Nat. Hist. Mus. Los Angeles Co. Sci. Bull., 12:1–66.

McDiarmid, R. W., 1975, Glass frog romance along a tropical stream, Nat. Hist. Mus. Los Angeles Co. Terra, 13(4):14–18.

McDiarmid, R. W., 1978, "Evolution of parental care in frogs," in G. M. Burkhardt and M. Bekoff (eds.), The Development of Behavior: Comparative and Evolutionary Aspects, New York: STPM Press, pp 127–147.

McDiarmid, R. W., and K. Adler, 1974, Notes on territorial and vocal behavior of Neotropical frogs of the genus Centrolenella, Herpetologica, 30:75–78.

McDiarmid, R. W., and R. D. Worthington, 1970, Concerning the reproductive habits of tropical plethodontid salamanders, Herpetologica, 26:57–70.

McDonald, K. R., and M. J. Tyler, 1984, Evidence of gastric brooding in the Australasian leptodactylid frog Rheobatrachus vitellinus, Trans. Royal Soc. South Australia, 108:226.

Macgregor, H. C., 1968, Nucleolar DNA in oocytes of Xenopus laevis, J. Cell Sci., 3:437–444.

Macgregor, H. C., and E. M. Del Pino, 1982, Ribosomal gene amplification in multinucleate oocytes of the egg brooding hylid frog Flectonotus pygmaeus, Chromosoma, 85:475–488.

Macgregor, H. C., and J. Kezer, 1970, Gene amplification in oocytes with 8 germinal vesicles from the tailed frog, *Ascaphus truei* Stejneger, *Chromosoma,* 29:189–206.

Macgregor, H. C., and M. H. Walker, 1973, The arrangement of chromosomes in nuclei of sperm from plethodontid salamanders, *Chromosoma,* 40:243–262.

McKenna, M. C., 1975, Fossil mammals and early Eocene North Atlantic land continuity, *Ann. Missouri Bot. Gard.,* 62:335–353.

Mackenzie, D. S., P. Licht, and H. Papkoff, 1978, Thyrotropin from amphibian *(Rana catesbeiana)* pituitaries and evidence for heterothyrotropic activity of bullfrog luteinizing hormone in reptiles, *Gen. Comp. Endocrinol.,* 36:566–574.

McLaren, I. A., 1965, Temperature and frog eggs: a reconsideration of metabolic control, *J. Gen. Physiol., (Suppl.),* 48:1071–1079.

McLaren, I. A., and J. M. Cooley, 1972, Temperature adaptation of embryonic development rate among frogs, *Physiol. Zool.,* 45:223–228.

McLaughlin, E. W., and A. A. Humphries Jr., 1978, The jelly envelopes and fertilization of eggs of the newt, *Notophthalmus viridescens, J. Morph.,* 158:73–90.

Maclean, N., and R. D. Jurd, 1971, Electrophoretic analysis of the haemoglobins of *Ambystoma mexicanum, Comp. Biochem. Physiol.,* 40(B):751–755.

McManus, M. I., 1937, A cytological study of the skin glands of the dusky salamander, *J. Elisha Mitchell Sci. Soc.,* 53:101–113.

McMullen, E. C., 1938, The morphology of the aortic arches in four genera of plethodontid salamanders, *J. Morph.,* 62:559–597.

MacNamara, M. C., 1977, Food habits of terrestrial adult migrants and immature red efts of the red-spotted newt *Notophthalmus viridescens, Herpetologica,* 33:127–132.

McVey, M. E., R. G. Zahary, D. Perry, and J. MacDougal, 1981, Territoriality and homing behavior in the poison dart frog *(Dendrobates pumilio), Copeia,* 1981:1–8.

Madison, D. M., 1969, Homing behaviour of the red-cheeked salamander, *Plethodon jordani, Anim. Behav.,* 17:25–39.

Madison, D. M., 1977, "Chemical communication in amphibians and reptiles," in D. Müller-Schwarze and M. M. Mozell (eds.), *Chemical Signals in Vertebrates,* New York: Plenum Publishing Corporation, pp 135–168.

Madison, D. M., and C. R. Shoop, 1970, Homing behavior, orientation, and home range of salamanders tagged with tantalum-182, *Science,* 168:1484–1487.

Magimel-Pelonnier, O., 1924, *La Langue des Amphibiens. Thèse, Fac. Sci. Paris,* Bordeaux: A. Saugnac Et E. Provillard.

Mahoney, J. J., and V. H. Hutchinson, 1969, Photoperiod acclimation and 24-hour variations in the critical thermal maxima of a tropical and temperate frog, *Oecologia,* 2:143–161.

Mahony, M., M. J. Tyler, and M. Davies, 1984, A new species of the genus *Rheobatrachus* (Anura: Leptodactylidae) from Queensland, *Trans. Royal Soc. South Australia,* 108:155–162.

Mahony, M. J., and E. S. Robinson, 1980, Polyploidy in the Australian leptodactylid frog genus *Neobatrachus, Chromosoma,* 81:199–212.

Main, A. R., 1968, "Ecology, systematics and evolution of Australian frogs," in J. B. Cragg (ed.), *Advances in Ecological Research, Vol.5,* New York: Academic Press, pp 37–86.

Main, A. R., and P. J. Bentley, 1964, Water relations of Australian burrowing frogs and tree frogs, *Ecology,* 45:379–382.

Maiorana, B. C., 1978, Behavior of an unobservable species: diet selection by a salamander, *Copeia,* 1978:664–672.

Maiorana, V. C., 1976a, Size and environmental predictability for salamanders, *Evolution,* 30:599–613.

Maiorana, V. C., 1976b, Predation, submergent behavior, and tropical diversity, *Evol. Theory,* 1:157–177.

Maller, J., D. Poccia, D. Nishioka, P. Kidd, J. Gerhart, and M. Hartman, 1976, Spindle formation and cleavage in *Xenopus* eggs injected with centriole-containing fractions from sperm, *Exp. Cell Res.,* 99:285–294.

Mancino, G., and I. Nardi, 1971, Chromosome heteromorphism and female heterogamety in the marbled newt *Triturus marmoratus* (Latreille), *Experientia,* 27:821–822.

Manes, M. E., and F. D. Barbieri, 1976, Symmetrization in the amphibian egg by disrupted sperm cells, *Devel. Biol.,* 53:138–141.

Manes, M. E., and F. D. Barbieri, 1977, On the possibility of sperm aster involvement in dorsoventral polarization and pronuclear migration in the amphibian egg, *J. Embryol. Exp. Morph.,* 40:187–198.

Manion, J. J., and L. Cory, 1952, Winter kill of Rana pipiens in shallow ponds, *Herpetologica,* 8:32.

Mann, K. H., and M. J. Tyler, 1963, Leeches as endoparasites of frogs, *Nature,* 197:1224–1225.

Manz, R., 1975, Die Fusionsfrequenzen der Kehlkopfmuskeln und eines Beinmuskels in Abhängigkeit von der Temperatur bei europäischen Froschlurchen (Anura), *Zool. Jbuch. Physiol.,* 79:221–245.

Marangio, M. S., 1975, Phototaxis in larvae and adults of the marbled salamander, *Ambystoma opacum, J. Herpetol.,* 9:293–297.

Marche, C., and J. P. Durand, 1983, Recherches comparatives sur l'ontogénèse et l'évolution de l'appareil hyobranchial de *Proteus anguinus* L., proteidae aveugle des eaux souterraines, *Amphib.-Rept.,* 4:1–16.

Marchisin, A., and J. D. Anderson, 1978, Strategies employed by frogs and toads (Amphibia, Anura) to avoid predation by snakes (Reptilia, Ser pentes), J. Herpetol., 12:151–155.

Marcus, H., 1908, Beiträge zur Kenntnis der Gymnophionen, II. Über intersegmentale Lymphherzen nebst Bemerkungen uber das Lymphsystem, *Morph. Jahrb.,* 38:590–607.

Marcus, H., 1909, Beiträge zur Kenntnis der Gymnophionen. III. Zur Entwickslungsgeschichte des Kopfes, *Morphol. Jahrb.,* 40:105–183.

Marcus, H., 1910, Beiträge zur Kenntnis der Gymnophionen. IV. Zur Entwickslungsgeschichte des Kopfes. II. Theil., *Festschr. R. Hertig.,* 2:375–462.

Marcus, H., 1922, Beiträge zur Kenntnis der Gymnophionen. V. Die Kehlkopf bei *Hypogeophis, Anat. Anz.,* 1:188–222.

Marcus, H., 1935, Zur Entstehung der Stapesplatte bei *Hypogeophis, Anat. Anz.,* 80:142–146.

Marcus, H., 1939, Beiträge zur Kenntnis der Gymnophionen 31. Über Keimbahn, Keimdrusen, Fettkorper u. Urogenitalverbindung bei *Hypogeophis, Bio-Morphosis,* 1:360–384.

Marcus, H., E. Stimmelmayr, and G. Porsch, 1935, Beiträge zur Kenntnis der Gymnophionen. XXV. Die Ossifikation des Hypogeophisschädels, *Morphol. Jahrb.,* 76:375–420.

Marcus, H., O. Winsauer, and A. Hueber, 1933, Beitrage zur Kenntnis der Gymnophionen. XVIII. Der kinetische Schadel von *Hypogeophis* und die Gehörknöchelchen, *Zeit. Anat. Entwicug.,* 100:149–193.

Marcus, L. C., 1981, *Veterinary Biology and Medicine of Captive Amphibians and Reptiles,* Philadelphia: Lea & Febiger.

Margolis, S. E., 1976, Influence of olfactory stimuli on the efficiency of visual stimuli in the behavior of newts *(Triturus vulgaris, T. cristatus)* (in Russian, English summary), *Zool. Zhur.,* 55:1201–1205.

Marshall, E., and G. Grigg, 1980, Lack of metabolic acclimation to different thermal histories by tadpoles of Limnodynastes peroni (Anura: Leptodactylidae), *Physiol. Zool.,* 53:1–7.

Martan, J., and E. Wortham, 1972, A tail membrane on the spermatozoa of some ambystomatid salamanders, *Anat. Rec.,* 172:460.

Martin, A. A., 1967, "Australian anuran life histories: some evolutionary and ecological aspects," in A. H. Weatherley (ed.), *Australian Inland Waters and Their Fauna,* Canberra: Nat. Univ. Press, pp 175–191.

Martin, A. A., 1968, The biology of tadpoles, *Australian Nat. Hist.,* 15:326–330.

Martin, A. A., 1970, Parallel evolution in the adaptive ecology of leptodactylid frogs of South America and Australia, *Evolution*, 24:643–644.

Martin, A. A., and A. K. Cooper, 1972, The ecology of terrestrial anuran eggs, genus *Crinia* (Leptodactylidae), *Copeia*, 1972:163–168.

Martin, A. A., M. J. Tyler, and M. Davies, 1980, A new species of *Ranidella* (Anura: Leptodactylidae) from northwestern Australia, *Copeia*, 1980:93–99.

Martin, J. B., N. B. Witherspoon, and M. H. A. Keenleyside, 1974, Analysis of feeding behavior in the newt *Notophthalmus viridescens*, *Canadian J. Zool.*, 52:277–281.

Martin, W. F., 1972, "Evolution of vocalization in the toad genus *Bufo*," in W. F. Blair (ed.), *Evolution in the Genus* Bufo, Austin: Univ. Texas Press, pp 279–309.

Martof, B. S., 1953, Home range and movements of the green frog, *Rana clamitans*, *Ecology*, 34:529–543.

Martof, B. S., 1956, Growth and development of the green frog, *Rana clamitans*, under natural conditions, *Amer. Midl. Nat.*, 55:101–117.

Martof, B. S., 1962a, Some observations on the feeding of Fowler's toad, *Copeia*, 1962:439.

Martof, B. S., 1962b, Some observations on the role of olfaction among salientian amphibia, *Physiol. Zool.*, 35:270–272.

Martof, B. S., 1962c, Some aspects of the life history and ecology of the salamander *Leurognathus*, *Amer. Midl. Nat.*, 67:1–35.

Martof, B. S., 1963, *Leurognathus, L. marmoratus, Cat. Amer. Amphib. Rept.*, 3:1–2.

Martof, B. S., 1972, *Pseudobranchus, P. striatus, Cat. Amer. Amphib. Rept.*, 118:1–4.

Martof, B. S., 1974, Sirenidae, *Cat. Amer. Amphib. Rept.*, 151:1–2.

Martof, B. S., 1975, *Pseudotriton, Cat. Amer. Amphib. Rept.*, 165:1–2.

Martof, B. S., and R. L. Humphries, 1959, Variation in Rana sylvatica, *Amer. Midl. Nat.*, 61:350–389.

Martof, B. S., and D. C. Scott, 1957, The food of the salamander *Leurognathus*, *Ecology*, 38:494–501.

Martof, B. S., and E. F. Thompson, 1958, Reproductive behavior of the chorus frog *Pseudacris nigrita*, *Behaviour*, 13:243–258.

Maslin, T. P., 1950, The production of sound in caudate amphibia, *Univ. Colorado Stud. Biol. Ser.*, 1:29–45.

Mason, J. R., M. D. Rabin, and D. A. Stevens, 1982, Conditioned taste aversions: skin secretions used for defense by tiger salamanders, *Ambystoma tigrinum*, *Copeia*, 1982:667–671.

Matthes, E., 1934, Bau und Funktion der Lippensäume wasserlebender Urodelen, *Zeit. Morph. Okol. Thiere*, 28:155–169.

Matthew, W. D., 1915, Climate and evolution, *Ann. New York Acad. Sci.*, 24:171–318.

Mattison, C., 1982, *The Care of Reptiles and Amphibians in Captivity*, Poole, Dorset: Blandford Press.

Maturana, H. R., W. S. McCulloch, J. Y. Lettvin, and W. H. Pitts, 1960, Anatomy and physiology of vision in the frog (*Rana pipiens*), *J. Gen. Physiol.*, (Suppl.), 43:129–175.

Maurer, F., 1892, Der Aufbau und die Entwicklung der ventralen Rumpfmuskulatur bei den urodelen Amphibien und deren Beziehung zu den gleichen Muskelnder Selachier und Teleostier, *Morphol. Jahrb.*, 18:76–179.

Maurer, F., 1911, Die ventralen Rumpfmuskulatur von Menobranchus, Menopoma und Amphiuma, vergleichen mit der gleichen Muskelnanderer Urodelen, *Jena Zeit. Naturw.*, 47:1–42.

Maxson, L. R., 1976, The phylogenetic status of phyllomedusine frogs (Hylidae) as evidenced from immunological studies of their serum albumins, *Experientia*, 32:1149–1150.

Maxson, L. R., 1977, Immunological detection of convergent evolution in the frog *Anotheca spinosa* (Hylidae), *Syst. Zool.*, 26:72–76.

Maxson, L. R., 1981a, Albumin evolution and its phylogenetic implications in African toads of the genus *Bufo, Herpetologica*, 37:96–104.

Maxson, L. R., 1981b, Albumin evolution and its phylogenetic implications in toads of the genus .*Bufo* II. Relationships among Eurasian *Bufo, Copeia*, 1981:579–583.

Maxson, L. R., 1984, Molecular probes of phylogeny and biogeography in toads of the widespread genus *Bufo, Mol. Biol. Evol.*, 1:345–356.

Maxson, L. R., and C. H. Daugherty, 1980, Evolutionary relationships of the monotypic toad family Rhinophrynidae: a biochemical perspective, *Herpetologica*, 36:275–280.

Maxson, L. R., and W. R. Heyer, 1982, Leptodactylid frogs and the Brazilian Shield: an old and continuing adaptive relationship, *Biotropica*, 14:10–15.

Maxson, L. R., R. Highton, and D. B. Wake, 1979, Albumin evolution and its phylogenetic implications in the plethodontid salamander genera *Plethodon* and *Ensatina*, *Copeia*, 1979:502–508.

Maxson, L. R., and R. D. Maxson, 1979, Comparative albumin and biochemical evolution in plethodontid salamanders, *Evolution*, 33:1057–1062.

Maxson, L. R., and J. M. Szymura, 1979, Quantitative immunological studies of the albumins of several species of fire bellied toads, genus *Bombina, Comp. Biochem. Physiol.*, 63(B):517–519.

Maxson, L. R., M. J. Tyler, and R. D. Maxson, 1982, Phylogenetic relationships of *Cyclorana* and the *Litoria aurea* species-group (Anura: Hylidae): a molecular perspective, *Australian J. Zool.*, 30:643–651.

Maxson, L. R., and D. B. Wake, 1981, Albumin evolution and its phylogenetic implications in the plethodontid salamander genera *Pseudoeurycea* and *Chiropterotriton, Herpetologica*, 37:109–117.

Maxson, L. R., and A. C. Wilson, 1974, Convergent morphological evolution detected by studying proteins of tree frogs in the *Hyla eximia* species group, *Science*, 185:66–68.

Maxson, L. R., and A. C. Wilson, 1975, Albumin evolution and organismal evolution in tree frogs (Hylidae), *Syst. Zool.*, 24:1–15.

Maxson, L. R., and A. C. Wilson, 1979, Rates of molecular and chromosomal evolution in salamanders, *Evolution*, 33: 734–740.

Mazik, E. Y., B. K. Kadyrova, and A. T. Toktosunov, 1976, Peculiarities of the karyotype of the green toad (*Bufo viridis*) of Kirghizia (in Russian, English summary), *Zool. Zhur.*, 55:1740–1742.

Means, D. B., 1975, Competitive exclusion along a habitat gradient between two species of salamanders (*Desmognathus*) in western Florida, *J. Biogeog.*, 2:253–263.

Mecham, J. S., 1960, Introgressive hybridization between two southeastern tree frogs, *Evolution*, 14:447–457.

Mecham, J. S., 1967a, *Notophthalmus perstriatus, Cat. Amer. Amphib. Rept.*, 38:1–2.

Mecham, J. S., 1967b, *Notophthalmus viridescens, Cat. Amer. Amphib. Rept.*, 53:1–4.

Mecham, J. S., 1968, *Notophthalmus meridionalis, Cat. Amer. Amphib. Rept.*, 74:1–2.

Mecham, J. S., 1971, Vocalizations of the leopard frog, *Rana pipiens*, and three related Mexican species, *Copeia*, 1971: 505–516.

Méhelÿ, L. V., 1901, Beiträge zur Kenntniss der Engystomatiden von Neu-Guinea, *Termész. Füz.*, 24:169–271.

Meisterhans, K., and H. Heusser, 1970, Lucilia Befall an vier Anuren Arten, *Mitt. Schweizerischen Entomol. Gesell.*, 43: 41–44.

Mendes, E. G., 1945, Contribução para a fisïologica dos sistemas respiratório e circulatório de *Siphonops annulatus* (Amphibia-Gymnophiona), *Bol. Fac. Filos. Cienc. Letras Univ. São Paulo, Zool.*, 9:25–64.

Menzies, J. I., and J. Tippett, 1976, Chromosome numbers of

Papuan hylid frogs and the karyotype of *Litoria infrafrenata* (Amphibia, Anura, Hylidae), *J. Herpetol.,* 10:167–173.

Menzies, J. I., and M. J. Tyler, 1977, The systematics and adaptations of some Papuan microhylid frogs which live underground, *J. Zool. (London),* 183:431–464.

Merchant, H. M., 1972, Estimated population size and home range of the salamanders *Plethodon jordani* and *Plethodon glutinosus, J. Washington Acad. Sci.,* 62:248–257.

Merrell, D. J., 1973, "Ecological genetics of anurans as exemplified by *Rana pipiens,*" in J. L. Vial (ed.), *Evolutionary Biology of the Anurans: Contemporary Research on Major Problems,* Columbia: Univ. Missouri Press, pp 329–335.

Mertens, R., 1957, Zur Naturgeschichte des venezolanischen Reisen-Beutelfrosches, *Gastrotheca ovifera, Zool. Garten (NF),* 23:110–133.

Metcalf, M. M., 1923a, The opalinid ciliate infusorians, *Bull. U. S. Natl. Mus.,* 120:1–471.

Metcalf, M. M., 1923b, The origin and distribution of the Anura, *Amer. Nat.,* 57:385–411.

Metter, D. E., 1963, Stomach contents of Idaho larval *Dicamptodon, Copeia,* 1963:435–436.

Metter, D. E., 1964a, A morphological and ecological comparison of two populations of the tailed frog, *Ascaphus truei* Stejneger, *Copeia,* 1964:181–195.

Metter, D. E., 1964b, On breeding and sperm retention in *Ascaphus, Copeia,* 1964:710–711.

Metter, D. E., 1968a, The influence of floods on population structure of *Ascaphus truei* Stejneger, *J. Herpetol.,* 1:105–106.

Metter, D. E., 1968b, *Ascaphus, A. truei, Cat. Amer. Amphib. Rept.,* 69:1–2.

Michael, J., 1981, A normal table of early development in *Bombina orientalis* (Boulenger) in relation to rearing temperature, *Develop. Growth. Differ.,* 23:149–155.

Michl, H., and E. Kaiser, 1963, Chemie und Biochemie der Amphibiengifte, *Toxicon,* 1:175–228.

Michniewska-Predygier, Z., and A. Pigón, 1957, Early developmental stages of *Rana temporaria* L., *R. terrestris* Andrz., *R. esculenta* L., and *Bufo bufo* (L.), *Studia Soc. Sci. Torunensis,* 3(E):147–157.

Miganti, A., and G. Azzolina, 1955, Attivita proteolitica dell'enzima della schiusa di *Bufo e Discoglossus, Ric. Sci.,* 25:2103–2108.

Miles, R. S., 1977, Dipnoan (lungfish) skulls and the relationships of the group: a study based on new species from the Devonian of Australia, *Zool. J. Linnean Soc.,* 61:1–328.

Millard, N., 1941, The vascular anatomy of Xenopus laevis (Daudin), *Trans. Royal Soc. S. Africa,* 28:387–489.

Miller, K., and G. C. Packard, 1977, An altitudinal cline in critical thermal maxima of chorus frogs *(Pseudacris triseriata), Amer. Nat.,* 111:267–277.

Milner, A. R., 1983, "The biogeography of salamanders in the Mesozoic and early Caenozoic: a cladistic-vicariance model," in R. W. Simms, J. H. Price and P. E. S. Whalley (eds.), *Evolution, Time and Space: the Emergence of the Biosphere,* London: Academic Press, pp 431–468.

Miranda-Ribeiro, A. de, 1926, Notas para servirem ao estudo dos gymnobatrachos (Anura) Brasileiros, *Arq. Mus. Nac. Rio de Janeiro,* 27:1–227.

Misuraca, G., G. Prota, J. T. Bagnara, and S. K. Frost, 1977, Identification of the leaf-frog melanophore pigment, rhodomelanochrome, as pterorhodin, *Comp. Biochem. Physiol.,* 57(B):41–43.

Miyamoto, M. M., and J. H. Cane, 1980a, Notes on the reproductive behavior of a Costa Rican population of *Hyla ebraccata, Copeia,* 1980:928–930.

Miyamoto, M. M., and J. H. Cane, 1980b, Behavioral observations on noncalling males in Costa Rican *Hyla ebraccata, Biotropica,* 12:225–227.

Mizuno, S., C. Andrews, and H. C. Macgregor, 1976, Interspecific 'common' repetitive DNA sequences in salamanders of the genus *Plethodon, Chromosoma,* 58:1–31.

Mizuno, S., and H. C. Macgregor, 1974, Chromosomes, DNA sequences, and evolution in salamanders of the genus *Plethodon, Chromosoma,* 48:239–296.

Mohanty-Hejmadi, P., and S. K. Dutta, 1981, Effects of some pesticides on the development of the Indian bull frog *Rana tigerina, Environ. Pollut.,* 24:145–161.

Mohanty-Hejmadi, P., S. K. Dutta, and S. C. Mallick, 1979, Life history of Indian frogs II. The marbled balloon frog *Uperodon systoma* Schneider, *J. Zool. Soc. India,* 31:65–72.

Mohanty-Hejmadi, P., S. K. Dutta, and S. C. Parida, 1979, Life history of the Indian frogs: 1. The burrowing frog *Rana breviceps* Schneider, *J. Zool. Soc. India,* 31:29–37.

Mohneke, R., and H. Schneider, 1979, Effect of temperature upon auditory thresholds in two anuran species, *Bombina v. variegata* and *Alytes o. obstetricans* (Amphibia, Discoglossidae), *J. Comp. Physiol.,* 130(A):9–16.

Monath, T., 1965, The opercular apparatus of salamanders, *J. Morph.,* 116:149–170.

Moodie, G. E. E., 1978, Observations on the life history of the caecilian *Typhlonectes compressicaudus* (Duméril and Bibron) in the Amazon basin, *Canadian J. Zool.,* 56:1005–1008.

Mookerjee, H. K., 1931, On the development of the vertebral column of Anura, *Philos. Trans. Royal Soc. London,* 219(B):165–196.

Mookerjee, H. K., and S. K. Das, 1939, Further investigation on the development of the vertebral column in Salientia (Anura), *J. Morph.,* 3:167–209.

Moore, J. A., 1939, Temperature tolerance and rates of development in the eggs of Amphibia, *Ecology,* 20:459–478.

Moore, J. A., 1940, Adaptive differences in the egg membranes of frogs, *Amer. Nat.,* 74:89–93.

Moore, J. A., 1942, The role of temperature in speciation of frogs, *Biol. Symp.,* 6:189–213.

Moore, J. A., 1949, Geographic variation of adaptive characters in *Rana pipiens* Schreber, *Evolution,* 3:1–24.

Moore, J. A., 1952, An analytical study of the geographic distribution of *Rana septentrionalis, Amer. Nat.,* 86:5–22.

Moore, J. A., 1961, The frogs of eastern New South Wales, *Bull. Amer. Mus. Nat. Hist.,* 121:149–386.

Moore, J. A. (ed.), 1964, *Physiology of the Amphibia,* New York: Academic Press.

Morescalchi, A., 1964, Il corredo cromosomico di *Discoglossus pictus* Otth: cromosomi sessuali, spiralizzazione cromosomica e zone eterocromatiche, *Caryologia,* 17:327–345.

Morescalchi, A., 1973, "Amphibia," in A. B. Chiarelli and E. Capanna (eds.), *Cytotaxonomy and Vertebrate Evolution,* New York: Academic Press, pp 233–348.

Morescalchi, A., 1975, Chromosome evolution in the caudate amphibia, *Evol. Biol.,* 8:339–387.

Morescalchi, A., 1977, "Phylogenetic aspects of karyological evidence," in M. K. Hecht, P. C. Goody and B. M. Hecht (eds.), *Major Patterns in Vertebrate Evolution,* New York: Plenum Press, pp 149–167.

Morescalchi, A., 1979, New developments in vertebrate cytotaxonomy I. Cytotaxonomy of the Amphibians, *Genetica,* 50:179–193.

Morescalchi, A., 1980, Evolution and the karyology of the amphibians, *Bull. Zool., (Suppl.),* 47:113–126.

Morescalchi, A., 1981, Karyology of the main groups of African frogs, *Monit. Zool. Italiano NS Suppl.,* 15:41–53.

Morescalchi, A., and G. J. Ingram, 1974, New chromosome numbers in Australian Leptodactylidae (Amphibia, Salientia), *Experientia,* 30:1134–1135.

Morescalchi, A., and G. J. Ingram, 1978, Cytotaxonomy of the myobatrachid frogs of the genus *Limnodynastes, Experientia,* 34:584–585.

Morescalchi, A., G. Odierna, and E. Olmo, 1977, Karyological relationships between the cryptobranchid salamanders, *Experientia,* 33:1579–1581.

Morescalchi, A., G. Odierna, and E. Olmo, 1979, Karyology of the primitive salamanders, family Hynobiidae, *Experientia*, 35:1434–1435.

Morescalchi, A., and E. Olmo, 1974, Sirenids: a family of polyploid urodeles?, *Experientia*, 30:491–492.

Morescalchi, A., E. Olmo, and V. Stingo, 1977, Trends of karyological evolution in pelobatoid frogs, *Experientia*, 33:1577–1578.

Morin, P. J., 1981, Predatory salamanders reverse the outcome of competition among three species of anuran tadpoles, *Science*, 212:1284–1286.

Morin, P. J., 1983a, Competitive and predatory interactions in natural and experimental populations of *Notophthalmus viridescens dorsalis* and *Ambystoma tigrinum*, *Copeia*, 1984:628–639.

Morin, P. J., 1983b, Predation, competition, and the composition of larval anuran guilds, *Ecol. Monog.*, 53:119–138.

Moriwaki, T., 1953, The inheritance of the dorso-median stripe in *Rana limnocharis* Wiegmann, *J. Sci. Hiroshima Univ.*, (B)14:159–164.

Moser, H., 1950, Ein Beiträg zur Analyse der Thyroxineinwirkung im Kaulquappenversuch und zur Frage nach dem Zustandekommen der Frübereitschaft des Metamorphosis-Reactionsystems, *Rev. Suisse Zool.*, 57(2):1–144.

Mosher, H. S., F. A. Fuhrman, H. D. Buchwald, and H. G. Fisher, 1964, Tarichatoxin-tetrodotoxin: a potent neurotoxin, *Science*, 144:1100–1110.

Moulton, J. M., A. Jurand, and H. Fox, 1968, A cytological study of Mauthner's cells in *Xenopus laevis* and *Rana temporaria* during metamorphosis, *J. Embryol. Exp. Morph.*, 19:415–431.

Muhse, E. F., 1909, The cutaneous glands of the common toads, *Amer. J. Anat.*, 9:321–359.

Mullally, D. P., 1952, Habits and minimum temperature of the toad *Bufo boreas halophilus*, *Copeia*, 1952:274–276.

Mullally, D. P., 1953, Observations on the ecology of the toad, *Bufo canorus*, *Copeia*, 1953:182–183.

Mullen, T. L., and R. H. Alvarado, 1976, Osmotic and ionic regulation in amphibians, *Physiol. Zool.*, 49:11–23.

Müller, J., 1835, Über die Kiemenlöcher der jungen *Caecilia hypocyanea*, *Arch. Anat. Phys. Wiss. Med.*, 1835:391–398.

Müller, K., and J. Kiepeheuer, 1976, Olfactory orientation in frogs, *Naturwissenschaften*, 63:49–50.

Müller, W. P., 1977, Diplotene chromosomes of *Xenopus* hybrid oocytes, *Chromosoma*, 59:273–282.

Munroe, A. F., 1953, The ammonia and urea excretion of different species of Amphibia during their development and metamorphosis, *Biochem. J.*, 54:29–36.

Muntz, W. R. A., 1962, Effectiveness of different colors of light in releasing the positive phototactic behavior of frogs, and a possible function of the retinal projection of the diencephalon, *J. Neurophysiol.*, 25:712–720.

Muntz, W. R. A., 1963a, Phototaxis and green rods in urodeles, *Nature*, 199:620.

Muntz, W. R. A., 1963b, The development of phototaxis in the frog *(Rana temporaria)*, *J. Exp. Biol.*, 40:371–379.

Münz, H., B. Claas, and B. Fritzsch, 1982, Electrophysiological evidence of electroreception in the axolotl *Siredon mexicanum*, *Neuro. Lett.*, 28:107–111.

Murphy, J. B., 1976, Pedal luring in the leptodactylid frog, *Ceratophrys calcarata* Boulenger, *Herpetologica*, 32:339–341.

Murphy, J. B., H. Quinn, and J. A. Campbell, 1977, Observations on the breeding habits of the aquatic caecilian *Typhlonectes compressicaudus*, *Copeia*, 1977:66–69.

Muskhelishvili, T. A., 1964, New findings about reproduction of the Caucasus salamander *(Mertensiella caucasica)* (in Russian), *Soobshch. Akad. Nauk Gruz. SSR.*, 36:183–185.

Muto, Y., and M. Kawai, 1960, Increase for the tolerance of high temperature with the development of toad embryos, *Bull. Aichi Univ. Educ.*, 9:137–145.

Myers, C. W., 1966, The distribution and behavior of a tropical horned frog, *Cerathyla panamensis* Stejneger, *Herpetologica*, 22:68–71.

Myers, C. W., 1969, The ecological geography of cloud forest in Panama, *Amer. Mus. Novitat.*, 2396:1–52.

Myers, C. W., and J. W. Daly, 1976, Preliminary evaluation of skin toxins and vocalizations in taxonomic and evolutionary studies of poison-dart frogs (Dendrobatidae), *Bull. Amer. Mus. Nat. Hist.*, 157:173–262.

Myers, C. W., and J. W. Daly, 1979, A name for the poison frog of Cordillera Azul, eastern Peru, with notes on its biology and skin toxins (Dendrobatidae), *Amer. Mus. Novitat.*, 2674:1–24.

Myers, C. W., and J. W. Daly, 1983, Dart-poison frogs, *Sci. Amer.*, 248(2):120–133.

Myers, C. W., J. W. Daly, and B. Malkin, 1978, A dangerously toxic new frog *(Phyllobates)* used by Emberá Indians of western Colombia, with discussion of blowgun fabrication and dart poisoning, *Bull. Amer. Mus. Nat. Hist.*, 161:307–366.

Myers, C. W., and A. S. Rand, 1969, Checklist of amphibians and reptiles of Barro Colorado Island, Panama, with comments on faunal change and sampling, Smithsonian Contr. Zool., 10:1–11.

Nace, G. W., C. M. Richards, and J. H. Asher Jr., 1970, Parthenogenesis and genetic variability. I. Linkage and inbreeding estimations in the frog, *Rana pipiens*, *Genetics*, 66:349–368.

Nadamitsu, S., 1957, Fertilization of coelomic and oviducal eggs of *Triturus pyrrhogaster*, *J. Sci. Hiroshima Univ.*, (B)17:1–3.

Nagel, J. W., 1979, Life history of the ravine salamander *(Plethodon richmondi)* in northeastern Tennessee, *Herpetologica*, 35:38–43.

Nakajima, T., 1981, Active peptides in amphibian skin, *Trends Pharmacol. Sci.*, 2:202–205.

Narins, P. M., and R. R. Capranica, 1976, Sexual difference in the auditory system of the treefrog *Eleutherodactylus coqui*, *Science*, 192:378–380.

Narins, P. M., and R. R. Capranica, 1978, Communicative significance of the two-note call of the treefrog *Eleutherodactylus coqui*, *J. Comp. Physiol.*, 127(A):1–9.

Narins, P. M., and R. R. Capranica, 1980, Neural adaptations for processing the two-note call of the Puerto Rican treefrog, *Eleutherodactylus coqui*, *Brain Behav. Evol.*, 17:48–66.

Narins, P. M., and D. D. Hurley, 1981, The relationship between call intensity and function in the Puerto Rican coqui (Anura: Leptodactylidae), *Herpetologica*, 38:287–295.

Natarajan, R., 1953, A note on the chromosomes of *Cacopus systoma* Cunth. [sic], *Proc. 40th Indian Sci. Congr. Lucknow*, 1953:180–181.

Naylor, B. G., 1978a, The frontosquamosal arch in newts as a defence against predators, *Canadian J. Zool.*, 56:2211–2216.

Naylor, B. G., 1978b, *The Systematics of Fossil and Recent Salamanders (Amphibia: Caudata), with Special Reference to the Vertebral Column and Trunk Musculature*, Edmonton: Univ. Alberta, Ph.D. Dissertation.

Naylor, B. G., 1981, Cryptobranchid salamanders from the Paleocene and Miocene of Saskatchewan, *Copeia*, 1981:76–86.

Naylor, B. G., and R. A. Nussbaum, 1980, The trunk musculature of caecilians (Amphibia: Gymnophiona), *J. Morph.*, 166:259–273.

Nei, M., 1972, Genetic distance between populations, *Amer. Nat.*, 106:283–292.

Neill, W. T., 1952, Remarks on salamander voices, *Copeia*, 1952:195–196.

Neill, W. T., 1963, Hemidactylium, *Cat. Amer. Amphib. Rept.*, 1:1.

Neill, W. T., 1968, Predation on *Bufo valliceps* tadpoles by the predaceous diving beetle *Acilius semisulcatus*, *Bull. Ecol. Soc. Amer.*, 49:169.

Nel, N. E., 1970, The anatomy of the heart of the plethodontid salamander Ensatina eschscholtzii eschscholtzii Gray, *Ann. Univ. Stellenbosch,* A45(2):1–18.

Nelson, C. E., 1972, Systematic studies of the North American microhylid genus *Gastrophryne, J. Herpetol.,* 6:111–137.

Nelson, C. E., 1973a, Systematics of the Middle American upland populations of *Hypopachus* (Anura: Microhylidae), *Herpetologica,* 29:6–17.

Nelson, C. E., 1973b, Mating calls of the Microhylinae: descriptions and phylogenetic and ecological considerations, *Herpetologica,* 29:163–176.

Nelson, C. E., and R. R. Humphrey, 1972, Artificial interspecific hybridization among *Ambystoma, Herpetologica,* 28:27–32.

Nelson, C. E., and G. A. Miller, 1971, A possible case of mimicry in frogs, *Herpetol. Rev.,* 3:109.

Nelson, G. J., 1969, Gill arches and the phylogeny of fishes, with notes on the classification of vertebrates, *Bull. Amer. Mus. Nat. Hist.,* 141:477–552.

Nelson, G. J., and N. I. Platnick, 1981, *Systematics and Biogeography,* New York: Columbia Univ. Press.

Nelson, G. J., and D. E. Rosen (Eds.), 1981, *Vicariance Biogeography: a Critique,* New York: Columbia Univ. Press.

Nessov, L. A., 1981, Cretaceous salamanders and frogs of Kizylkum Desert (in Russian, English summary), *Trudy Zool. Inst. Leningrad,* 101:57–88.

Neuwirth, M., J. W. Daly, C. W. Myers, and L. W. Tice, 1979, Morphology of the granular secretory glands in skin of poison-dart frogs (Dendrobatidae), *Tissue & Cell,* 11:755–771.

Nevo, E., 1968, Pipid frogs from the early Cretaceous of Israel and pipid evolution, *Bull. Mus. Comp. Zool.,* 136:255–318.

Nevo, E., 1969, "Discussion on the systematic significance of isolating mechanisms," in *Systematic Biology,* Washington, D. C.: Natl. Acad. Sci., pp 485–489.

Nevo, E., 1976, Genetic variation in constant environments, *Experientia,* 32:858–859.

Nevo, E., 1978, Genetic variation in natural populations: patterns and theory, *Theoret. Pop. Biol.,* 13:121–177.

Nevo, E., and H. Schneider, 1976, Mating call pattern of green toads in Israel and its ecological correlates, *J. Zool. (London),* 178:133–145.

Nevo, E., and S. Y. Yang, 1979, Genetic diversity and climatic determinants of tree frogs in Israel, *Oecologia,* 41:47–63.

Nicholls, G. C., 1916, The structure of the vertebral column in anura phaneroglossa and its importance as a basis of classification, *Proc. Linnean Soc. London,* 128:80–92.

Nickerson, M. A., and C. E. Mays, 1973, The hellbenders: North American "giant Salamanders," *Milwaukee Publ. Mus. Publ. Biol. Geol.,* 1:1–106.

Nielsen, H. I., 1978a, Ultrastructural changes in the dermal chromatophore unit of *Hyla arborea* during color change, *Cell Tissue Res.,* 194:405–418.

Nielsen, H. I., 1978b, The effect of stress and adrenaline on the color of *Hyla cinerea* and *Hyla arborea, Gen. Comp. Endocrinol.,* 36:543–552.

Nielsen, H. I., 1979, Chromatophores and adaptation to coloured backgrounds in two colour types of the edible frog, *Rana esculenta, J. Zool.,* 189:349–358.

Nielsen, H. I., and J. Dyck, 1978, Adaptation of the tree frog, *Hyla cinerea,* to colored backgrounds, and the role of the three chromatophore types, *J. Exp. Zool.,* 205:79–94.

Nietfeldt, J. W., S. M. Jones, D. L. Droge, and R. E. Ballinger, 1980, Rate of thermal acclimation in larval *Ambystoma tigrinum, J. Herpetol.,* 14:209–211.

Nieuwenhuys, R., and P. Opdam, 1976, "Structure of the brain stem," in R. Llinás and W. Precht (eds.), *Frog Neurobiology,* Berlin: Springer-Verlag, pp 811–855.

Nieuwkoop, P. D., and J. Faber, 1967, *Normal Table Of Xenopus laevis (Daudin). 2nd Edit.,* Amsterdam: North Holland Publ. Co.

Nieuwkoop, P. D., and L. A. Satasurya, 1976, Embryological evidence for a possible polyphyletic origin of recent amphibians, *J. Embryol. Exp. Morph.,* 35:159–167.

Nigrelli, R. F., 1954, Some longevity records of vertebrates, *Trans. New York Acad. Sci.,* 16(2):296–299.

Nilsson, S. E. G., 1964, An electron microscopic classification of the retinal receptors of the leopard frog *(Rana pipiens), J. Ultrastruct. Res.,* 10:390–416.

Nishi, S., 1916, Zur vergleichenden Anatomie der eigentlichen Ruckenmuskeln, *Morphol. Jahrb.,* 50:167–318.

Nishi, S., 1938, "Muskeln des Rumpfes," in E. Göppert (ed.), *Handbuch der Vergleichenden Anatomie der Wirbeltiere,* Berlin: Urban and Schwarzenberg, pp 351–466.

Nishioka, M., H. Ohtani, and M. Sumida, 1980, Detection of chromosomes bearing the loci for seven kinds of proteins in Japanese pond frogs, *Sci. Rept. Lab. Amphib. Biol. Hiroshima Univ.,* 4:127–184.

Noble, G. K., 1922, The phylogeny of the Salientia. I. The osteology and the thigh musculature; their bearing on classification and phylogeny, *Bull. Amer. Mus. Nat. Hist.,* 46:1–87.

Noble, G. K., 1925a, The integumentary, pulmonary, and cardiac modifications correlated with increased cutaneous respiration in the Amphibia: a solution of the "hairy frog" problem, *J. Morph. Physiol.,* 40:341–416.

Noble, G. K., 1925b, The evolution and dispersal of the frogs, *Amer. Nat.,* 59:265–271.

Noble, G. K., 1926, The "buccal brooding habits" of the African tree frog *Leptopelis brevirostris, Copeia,* 154:134–135.

Noble, G. K., 1927a, The plethodontid salamanders; some aspects of their evolution, *Amer. Mus. Novitat.,* 249:1–26.

Noble, G. K., 1927b, The value of life history data in the study of the evolution of the Amphibia, *Ann. New York Acad. Sci.,* 30:31–128.

Noble, G. K., 1929a, The adaptive modifications of the arboreal tadpoles of *Hoplophryne* and the torrent tadpoles of *Staurois, Bull. Amer. Mus. Nat. Hist.,* 58:291–334.

Noble, G. K., 1929b, The relation of courtship to the secondary characters of the two-lined salamander, *Eurycea bislineata* (Green), *Amer. Mus. Novitat.,* 362:1–5.

Noble, G. K., 1931a, The hedonic glands of the plethodontid salamanders and their relations to the sex hormones, *Anat. Rec.,* 48:57–58.

Noble, G. K., 1931b, *The Biology of the Amphibia,* New York: McGraw-Hill Book Co.

Noble, G. K., and M. K. Brady, 1933, Observations on the life history of the marbled salamander *Ambystoma opacum* Gravenhorst, *Zoologica,* 11:89–132.

Noble, G. K., and B. C. Marshall, 1929, The breeding habits of two salamanders, *Amer. Mus. Novitat.,* 347:1–12.

Noble, G. K., and B. C. Marshall, 1932, The validity of *Siren intermedia* LeConte, with observations on its life history, *Amer. Mus. Novitat.,* 532:1–17.

Noble, G. K., and R. C. Noble, 1923, The Anderson tree frog *(Hyla andersonii* Baird). Observations on its habits and life history, *Zoologica,* 11:414–455.

Noble, G. K., and S. H. Pope, 1929, The modification of the cloaca and teeth of the adult salamander, *Desmognathus,* by testicular transplants and by castration, *British J. Exper. Biol.,* 6:399–411.

Noble, G. K., and P. G. Putnam, 1931, Observations on the life history of *Ascaphus truei* Stejneger, *Copeia,* 1931:97–101.

Noble, G. K., and L. B. Richards, 1932, Experiments on the egg-laying of salamanders, *Amer. Mus. Novitat.,* 513:1–25.

Noble, G. K., and J. A. Weber, 1929, The spermatophores of *Desmognathus* and other plethodontid salamanders, *Amer. Mus. Novitat.,* 351:1–15.

Noland, R., and G. R. Ultsch, 1981, The role of temperature and dissolved oxygen in microhabitat selection by the tadpoles of a frog *(Rana pipiens)* and a toad *(Bufo terrestris), Copeia,* 1981:645–652.

Norris, D. O., and J. E. Platt, 1973, Effects of pituitary hormones, melatonin, and thyroidal inhibitors on radioiodide uptake by the thyroid glands of larval and adult tiger salamanders, *Ambystoma tigrinum* (Amphibia: Caudata), *Gen. Comp. Endocrinol.*, 21:368–376.

Norris, D. O., and J. E. Platt, 1974, T_3 and T_4 induced rates of metamorphosis in immature and sexually mature larvae of *Ambystoma tigrinum* (Amphibia: Caudata), *J. Exp. Zool.*, 189:303–310.

Norris, H. W., 1908, The cranial nerves of *Amphiuma means*, *J. Comp. Neurol. Psych.*, 18:527–568.

Norris, H. W., 1913, The cranial nerves of *Siren lacertina*, *J. Morph.*, 24:245–338.

Norris, H. W., and S. P. Hughes, 1918, The cranial and anterior spinal nerves of the caecilian amphibians, *J. Morph.*, 31: 490–557.

Norris, K. S., and C. H. Lowe, 1964, An analysis of background color-matching in amphibians and reptiles, *Ecology*, 45: 565–580.

Novak, R. M., and D. C. Robinson, 1975, Observations on the reproduction and ecology of the tropical montane toad, *Bufo holdridgei* Taylor in Costa Rica, *Rev. Biol. Trop.*, 23:213–237.

Nussbaum, R. A., 1969a, Nest and eggs of the Pacific giant salamander, *Dicamptodon ensatus* (Eschscholtz), *Herpetologica*, 25:257–261.

Nussbaum, R. A., 1969b, A nest site of the Olympic salamander, *Rhyacotriton olympicus* (Gaige), *Herpetologica*, 25:277–278.

Nussbaum, R. A., 1974, Changes in serum proteins associated with metamorphosis in salamanders of the family Ambystomatidae, *Comp. Biochem. Physiol.*, 53(B):569–573.

Nussbaum, R. A., 1976, Geographic variation and systematics of salamanders of the genus *Dicamptodon* Strauch (Ambystomatidae), *Misc. Publ. Mus. Zool. Univ. Michigan*, 149:1–94.

Nussbaum, R. A., 1977, Rhinatrematidae: a new family of caecilians (Amphibia: Gymnophiona), *Occ. Pap. Mus. Zool. Univ. Michigan*, 682:1–30.

Nussbaum, R. A., 1979a, The taxonomic status of the caecilian genus *Uraeotyphlus* Peters, *Occ. Pap. Mus. Zool. Univ. Michigan*, 687:1–20.

Nussbaum, R. A., 1979b, Mitotic chromosomes of Sooglossidae (Amphibia: Anura), *Caryologia*, 32:279–298.

Nussbaum, R. A., 1979c, The status of *Copeotyphlinus syntremus* (Amphibia: Gymnophiona), *J. Herpetol.*, 13:121–123.

Nussbaum, R. A., 1980, Phylogenetic implications of amplectic behavior in sooglossid frogs, *Herpetologica*, 36:1–5.

Nussbaum, R. A., 1981, *Scolecomorphus lamottei*, a new caecilian from West Africa (Amphibia: Gymnophiona: Scolecomorphidae), *Copeia*, 1981:265–269.

Nussbaum, R. A., 1982, Heterotopic bones in the hindlimbs of frogs of the families Pipidae, Ranidae, and Sooglossidae, *Herpetologica*, 38:312–320.

Nussbaum, R. A., 1983, The evolution of a unique dual jaw-closing mechanism in caecilians (Amphibia: Gymnophiona) and its bearing on caecilian ancestry, *J. Zool. (London)*, 199:545–554.

Nussbaum, R. A., and E. D. Brodie Jr., 1981, *Taricha, Cat. Amer. Amphib. Rept.*, 271:1–2.

Nussbaum, R. A., and E. D. Brodie Jr., 1982, Partitioning of the salamandrid genus *Tylototriton* Anderson (Amphibia: Caudata) with a description of a new genus, *Herpetologica*, 38:320–332.

Nussbaum, R. A., and G. W. Clothier, 1973, Population structure, growth, and size of larval *Dicamptodon ensatus* (Eschscholtz), *Northwest Sci.*, 47:218–227.

Nussbaum, R. A., and M. S. Hoogmoed, 1979, Surinam caecilians, with notes on *Rhinatrema bivittatum* and the description of a new species of *Microcaecilia* (Amphibia, Gymnophiona), *Zool. Mededel., Leiden*, 54:217–235.

Nussbaum, R. A., and B. G. Naylor, 1982, Variation in the trunk musculature of caecilians (Amphibia: Gymnophiona), *J. Zool. London*, 198:383–398.

Nussbaum, R. A., and C. K. Tait, 1977, Aspects of the life history and ecology of the Olympic salamander, Rhyacotriton olympicus (Gaige), *Amer. Midl. Nat.*, 98:176–199.

Nussbaum, R. A., and G. Treisman, 1981, Cytotaxonomy of *Ichthyophis glutinosus* and *I. kohtaoensis*, two primitive caecilians from southeast Asia, *J. Herpetol.*, 15:109–113.

Obert, H. J., 1977, "Hormonal influences on calling and reproductive behavior in anurans," in D. H. Taylor and S. I. Guttman (eds.), *The Reproductive Biology of Amphibians*, New York: Plenum Press, pp 357–366.

O'Hara, R. K., and A. R. Blaustein, 1981, An investigation of sibling recognition in *Rana cascadae* tadpoles, *Anim. Behav.*, 29:1121–1126.

Ohno, S., 1970, *Evolution by Gene Duplication*, Berlin: Springer-Verlag.

Okada, Y., 1966, *Fauna Japonica: Anura (Amphibia)*, Tokyo: Biogeog. Soc. Japan.

Okada, Y. K., and M. Ichikawa, 1947, A new normal table for the development of *Triturus pyrrhogaster, Exp. Morph.*, 1:3–16.

Oksche, A., 1965, Survey of the development and comparative anatomy of the pineal organ, *Progr. Brain Res.*, 10:3–29.

Oksche, A., and M. Ueck, 1976, "The nervous system," in R. Llinás and W. Precht (eds.), *Frog Neurobiology*, Berlin: Springer-Verlag, pp 313–419.

Oldham, R. S., 1967, Orienting mechanisms in the green frog, *Rana clamitans, Ecology*, 48:477–491.

Oldham, R. S., 1977, Terrestrial locomotion in two species of amphibian larva, *J. Zool. (London)*, 181:285–295.

Olmo, E., and A. Morescalchi, 1975, Evolution of the genome and cell sizes in salamanders, *Experientia*, 31:804–806.

Olmo, E., and A. Morescalchi, 1978, Genome and cell sizes in frogs: a comparison with salamanders, *Experientia*, 34:44–46.

Olsen, I. D., 1977, "Digestion and nutrition," in A. G. Kluge (ed.), *Chordate Structure and Function*, New York: MacMillan Publishing Co., Inc., pp 270–305.

Oordt, P. G. W. J. van, 1956, The role of temperature in regulating the spermatogenic cycle in the common frog, *(Rana temporaria), Acta Endocrinol.*, 23:251–264.

Oordt, P. G. W. J. van, 1960, The influence of internal and external factors in the regulation of the spermatogenetic cycle in Amphibia, *Symp. Zool. Soc. London*, 2:29–52.

Oordt, P. G. W. J. van, 1961, The gonadotrophin producing and other cell types in the distal lobe of the pituitary of the common frog, *Rana temporaria, Gen. Comp. Endocrinol.*, 1:364–374.

Organ, J. A., 1961, Studies of the local distribution, life history, and population dynamics of the salamander genus *Desmognathus* in Virginia, *Ecol. Monog.*, 31:189–220.

Organ, J. A., 1968, Time of courtship activity of the slimy salamander, *Plethodon glutinosus*, in New Jersey, *Herpetologica*, 24:85–86.

Organ, J. A., and L. A. Lowenthal, 1963, Comparative studies of macroscopic and microscopic features of spermatophores of some plethodontid salamanders, *Copeia*, 1963:659–669.

Organ, J. A., and D. J. Organ, 1968, Courtship behavior of the red salamander *Pseudotriton ruber, Copeia*, 1968:217–223.

Orton, G. L., 1953, The systematics of vertebrate larvae, *Syst. Zool.*, 2:63–75.

Orton, G. L., 1954, Dimorphism in larval mouthparts in spadefoot toads of the *Scaphiopus hammondi* group, *Copeia*, 1954:97–100.

Orton, G. L., 1957, The bearing of larval evolution on some problems in frog classification, *Syst. Zool.*, 6:79–86.

Osaki, S., G. T. James, and E. Frieden, 1974, Iron metabolism of bullfrog tadpoles during metamorphosis, *Devel. Biol.*, 39:158–163.

Oshima, K., and A. Gorbman, 1969, Evidence for a doubly innervated secretory unit in the anuran pars intermedia. I. Electrophysiologic studies, *Gen. Comp. Endocrinol.*, 13: 98–107.

Özeti, N., 1979, Reproductive biology of the salamander *Mertensiella luschani antalyana, Herpetologica*, 35:193–197.

Özeti, N., and D. B. Wake, 1969, The morphology and evolution of the tongue and associated structures in salamanders and newts (family Salamandridae), *Copeia*, 1969:91–123.

Pace, A. E., 1974, Systematic and biological studies of the leopard frogs (*Rana pipiens* complex) of the United States, *Misc. Publ. Mus. Zool. Univ. Michigan*, 148:1–140.

Packer, W. C., 1963, Dehydration, hydration and burrowing behaviour in *Heleioporus eyrei* (Gray)(Leptodactylidae), *Ecology*, 44:643–651.

Packer, W. C., 1966, Embryonic and larval development of *Heleioporus eyrei* (Amphibia: Leptodactylidae), *Copeia*, 1966:92–97.

Paillette, M., 1971, Communication acoustique chez les amphibiens anoures, *J. Psychol. Norm. Pathol.*, 1971:327–351.

Paillette, M., 1976, Étude experimentale des interactions sonores dans les choeurs de rainettes *Hyla meridionalis* (Amphibien Anoure) par stimulation avec des signaux sonores periodiques de synthese, *Terre et Vie*, 30:89–120.

Panchen, A. L., 1970, Batrachosauria, Part A. Anthracosauria, *Handb. Palaoherpetol.*, 5:1–84.

Panchen, A. L., 1972, The skull and skeleton of *Eogyrinus attheyi* Watson (Amphibia: Labyrinthodontia), *Phil. Trans. Roy. Soc. London*, (B)263(851):279–326.

Panchen, A. L., 1977, "The origin and early evolution of tetrapod vertebrae," in S. M. Andrews, R. S. Miles and A. D. Walker (eds.), *Problems in Vertebrate Evolution, Linnean Soc. Symp. Ser.*, 4:289–318.

Panchen, A. L., 1980, "The origin and relationships of the anthracosaur Amphibia from the Late Palaeozoic," in A. L. Panchen (ed.), *The Terrestrial Environment and Origin of Land Vertebrates*, London: Academic Press, pp 319–350.

Panse, K., 1942, Sur la diagametie du crapaud hermaphrodite, *Rev. Suisse Zool.*, 49:185–189.

Papendieck, H. I. C. M., 1954, Contributions to the cranial morphology of Ambystoma macrodactylum Baird, *Ann. Univ. Stellenbosch*, 30:151–178.

Parâtre, R., 1894, Notes sur *Salamandra maculosa*; sa présence aux environs immédiats de Paris; remarques sur sa réproduction; époque de sa parturition; développement de la larve, *Mem. Soc. Zool. France*, 10:132–160.

Parker, G. E., 1967, The influence of temperature and thyroxin on oxygen consumption in *Rana pipiens* tadpoles, *Copeia*, 1967:610–616.

Parker, H. W., 1934, *A Monograph of the Frogs of the Family Microhylidae*, London: British Museum (Natural History).

Parker, H. W., 1956, Viviparous caecilians and amphibian phylogeny, *Nature*, 178:250–252.

Parker, W. K., 1877, On the structure and development of the skull in urodelous Amphibia, *Philos. Trans.*, 167:529–597.

Parker, W. K., 1882, On the morphology of the skull in the Amphibia Urodela, *Trans. Linnean Soc. London (2, Zool.)*, 2:165–209.

Parsons, T. S., 1959, Nasal anatomy and the phylogeny of reptiles, *Evolution*, 13:175–187.

Parsons, T. S., and E. E. Williams, 1962, The teeth of Amphibia and their relation to amphibian phylogeny, *J. Morph.*, 110(3):375–389.

Parsons, T. S., and E. E. Williams, 1963, The relationships of the modern Amphibia: a re-examination, *Quart. Rev. Biol.*, 38:26–53.

Pasqualini, R.-Q., and J. C. Riseau, 1951, Action de la désoxycorticotérone sur l'absorption cutanée chez le crapaud, *Compt. Rendu Soc. Biol.*, 146:604–606.

Passmore, N. I., 1977, Mating calls and other vocalizations of five species of *Ptychadena* (Anura: Ranidae), *South Africa J. Sci.*, 73:212–214.

Passmore, N. I., 1981, Sound levels of mating calls of some African frogs, *Herpetologica*, 37:166–171.

Passmore, N. I., and V. C. Carruthers, 1979, *South African Frogs*, Johannesburg: Witwatersrand Univ. Press.

Pastisson, C., 1963, Evolution de la gonade juvénile et cycles sexuels chez le triton *Pleurodeles walti* Michah, *Bull. Soc. Exp. Biol. Med.*, 25:218–225.

Paterson, N. F., 1939, The head of *Xenopus laevis*, *Quart. J. Micro. Soc.*, 81:161–234.

Pavelka, L. A., Y. H. Kim, and H. S. Mosher, 1977, Tetrodotoxin and tetrodotoxin-like compounds from the eggs of the Costa Rican frog *Atelopus chiriquiensis*, *Toxicon*, 15:135–139.

Peacock, R. L., and R. A. Nussbaum, 1973, Reproductive biology and population structure of the western red-backed salamander, *Plethodon vehiculum*, *J. Herpetol.*, 7:215–224.

Pearson, O. P., and D. F. Bradford, 1976, Thermoregulation of lizards and toads at high altitudes in Peru, *Copeia*, 1976:155–170.

Pearson, P. G., 1955, Population ecology of the spadefoot toad, *Scaphiopus h. holbrooki* (Harlan), *Ecol. Monog.*, 25:233–267.

Peck, S. B., 1973, Feeding efficiency in the cave salamander *Haideotriton wallacei*, *Internat. J. Speleol.*, 5:15–19.

Peet, R. K., 1975, Relative diversity indices, *Ecology*, 56:496–498.

Péfaur, J. E., and W. E. Duellman, 1980, Community structure in high Andean herpetofaunas, *Trans. Kansas Acad. Sci.*, 83:45–65.

Pemberton, C. E., 1934, Local investigations on the introduced tropical American toad *Bufo marinus*, *Hawaiian Planters' Rec.*, 38:186–192.

Pengilley, R. K., 1971, Calling and associated behaviour of some species of *Pseudophryne* (Anura: Leptodactylidae), *J. Zool. (London)*, 163:73–92.

Penn, A., and B. L. Glenhill, 1972, Acrosomal proteolytic activity of amphibian sperm. A direct demonstration, *Exp. Cell Res.*, 74:285–288.

Penna, M. V., and A. Veloso M., 1981, Acoustical signals related to reproduction in the *spinulosus* group of *Bufo* (Amphibia, Bufonidae), *Canadian J. Zool.*, 59:54–60.

Perret, J.-L., 1962, La biologie d'*Acanthixalus spinosus (Amphibia salientia)*, *Rech. Etudes Cameroun*, 1(1961):90–101.

Perret, J.-L., 1966, Les amphibiens du Cameroun, *Zool. Jahrb. Syst.*, 93:289–464.

Perret, J.-L., 1972, Les espèces des genres *Wolterstorffina* et *Nectophrynoides* d'Afrique (Amphibia, Bufonidae), *Ann. Fac. Sci. Cameroun*, 11:93–119.

Perret, J.-L., 1979, Moyens de chez les anoures, *Mus. Genève*, 191:15–18.

Perrill, S. A., and R. E. Daniel, 1983, Multiple egg clutches in *Hyla regilla*, *H. cinerea* and *H. gratiosa*, *Copeia*, 1983:513–516.

Perrill, S. A., H. C. Gerhardt, and R. Daniel, 1978, Sexual parasitism in the green tree frog *(Hyla cinerea)*, *Science*, 200:1179–1180.

Peter, K., 1898, Die Entwicklung und Funktionen-Gestaltung des Schädels von *Ichthyophis glutinosus*, *Morphol. Jahrb.*, 25:554–628.

Peterson, C. L., R. F. Wilkinson Jr., M. S. Topping, and D. E. Metter, 1983, Age and growth of the Ozark Hellbender *(Cryptobranchus alleganiensis bishopi)*, *Copeia*, 1983:225–231.

Petranka, J. W., 1983, Fish predation: a factor affecting the spatial distribution of a stream-breeding salamander, *Copeia*, 1983:624–628.

Petranka, J. W., J. J. Just, and E. C. Crawford, 1982, Hatching of amphibian embryos: the physiological trigger, *Science*, 217:257–259.

Pettigrew, A., S.-H. Chung, and M. Anson, 1978, Neurophysiological basis for directional hearing in Amphibia, *Nature*, 272:138–142.

Pettus, D., and G. M. Angleton, 1967, Comparative reproductive biology of montane and piedmont chorus frogs, *Evolution*, 21:500–507.

Pflaumer, C., 1936, Observaciones biologicas acerca de la *Rhinoderma darwinii* D. & B., *Rev. Chilena Hist. Nat. Pura Apl.*, 39:28–30.

Philibosian, R., R. Ruibal, V. H. Shoemaker, and L. L. Mc-Clanahan, 1974, Nesting behavior and early larval life of the frog, *Leptodactylus bufonius, Herpetologica,* 30:381–386.

Pianka, E. R., 1966, Latitudinal gradients in species diversity: a review of concepts, *Amer. Nat.,* 100:33–46.

Pianka, E. R., 1970, On "r" and "K" selection, *Amer. Nat.,* 104:592–597.

Pianka, E. R., 1977, "Reptilian species diversity," in C. Gans and D. W. Tinkle (eds.), *Biology of the Reptilia, Vol. 7,* New York: Academic Press, pp 1–34.

Pierce, B. A., and J. A. Mitton, 1980, Patterns of allozyme variation in *Ambystoma tigrinum mavortium* and *A. t. nebulosum, Copeia,* 1980:594–605.

Pierce, B. A., J. A. Mitton, and F. L. Rose, 1981, Allozyme variation among large, small and cannibal morphs of the tiger salamander inhabiting the Llano Estacado of west Texas, *Copeia,* 1981:590–595.

Pierce, B. A., and H. M. Smith, 1979, Neoteny or paedogenesis?, *J. Herpetol.,* 13:119–121.

Piiper, J., R. N. Gatz, and E. C. Crawford Jr., 1976, "Gas transport characteristics in an exclusively skin-breathing salamander, Desmognathus fuscus (Plethodontidae)," in G. M. Hughs (ed.), *Respiration of Amphibious Vertebrates,* New York: Academic Press, pp 339–356.

Pikulik, M. M., 1977, Experimental study of growth and development of *Rana temporaria* larvae under natural conditions (in Russian), *Soviet J. Ecol.,* 8:275–278.

Pillai, R. S., 1978, A new frog of the genus *Micrixalus* Boul. from Wynad, s. India, *Proc. Indian Acad. Sci.,* (B)87:173–177.

Pisanetz, Y. M., 1978, New polyploid species of *Bufo danatensis* Pisanetz, sp. nov., from the Turkmen SSR (in Russian), *Sopov. Akad. Nauk. Ukr. Rsp., Heol. Biol. Nauky,* 3(B):277–282.

Pisano, A., and A. G. Del Río, 1968, New biological properties in the foamy jelly of amphibians, *Arch. Zool. Italia,* 53:189–201.

Polder, W. N., 1974, Pflege und Fortpflanzung von *Dendrobates azureus* und anderer Dendrobatiden II., *Aquarien Terrarien Zeit.,* 27:28–32.

Polder, W. N., 1976, *Dendrobates, Phyllobates en Colostethus, Het Aquarium,* 46:260–266.

Pollister, A. W., and J. A. Moore, 1937, Tables for the normal development of *Rana sylvatica, Anat. Rec.,* 68:489–496.

Pope, C. H., 1924, Notes on North Carolina salamanders with special reference to the egg-laying habits of *Leurognathus* and *Desmognathus, Amer. Mus. Novitat.,* 153:1–15.

Pope, C. H., 1931, Notes on amphibians from Fukien, Hainan, and other parts of China, *Bull. Amer. Mus. Nat. Hist.,* 61:397–611.

Porter, K. R., 1972, *Herpetology,* Philadelphia: W. B. Saunders Co.

Porter, K. R., and D. E. Hakanson, 1976, Toxicity of mine drainage to embryonic and larval boreal toads (Bufonidae: *Bufo boreas), Copeia,* 1976:327–331.

Post, T. J., and T. M. Uzzell Jr., 1981, The relationships of *Rana sylvatica* and the monophyly of the *Rana boylei* group, *Syst. Zool.,* 30:170–180.

Potter, F. E. Jr., and S. S. Sweet, 1981, Generic boundaries in Texas cave salamanders, and a redescription of *Typhlomolge robusta* (Amphibia: Plethodontidae), *Copeia,* 1981:64–75.

Pough, F. H., 1971, Leech-repellant property of eastern red-spotted newts, *Notophthalmus viridescens, Science,* 174:1144–1146.

Pough, F. H., M. M. Stewart, and R. G. Thomas, 1977, Physiological basis of habitat partitioning in Jamaican *Eleutherodactylus, Oecologia,* 27:285–293.

Pough, F. H., T. L. Taigen, M. M. Stewart, and P. F. Brussard, 1983, Behavioral modification of evaporative water loss by a Puerto Rican frog, *Ecology,* 64:244–252.

Pough, F. H., and R. E. Wilson, 1970, Natural daily temperature stress, dehydration, and acclimation in juvenile *Ambystoma maculatum* (Shaw) (Amphibia: Caudata), *Physiol. Zool.,* 43:194–205.

Powders, V. N., and W. L. Tietjen, 1974, The comparative food habits of sympatric and allopatric salamanders, *Plethodon glutinosus* and *Plethodon jordani* in eastern Tennessee and adjacent areas, *Herpetologica,* 30:167–175.

Poynton, J. C., 1963, Descriptions of southern African amphibians, *Ann. Natal Mus.,* 15:319–332.

Poynton, J. C., 1964, The amphibia of southern Africa, *Ann. Natal Mus.,* 17:1–334.

Poynton, J. C., 1976, Classification and the Arthroleptinae (Amphibia), *Rev. Zool. Africa,* 90:215–220.

Poynton, J. C., and S. Pritchard, 1976, Notes on the biology of *Breviceps* (Anura: Microhylidae), *Zool. Africana,* 11:313–318.

Prance, G. T., 1982, *Biological Diversification in the Tropics,* New York: Columbia Univ. Press.

Pregill, G., 1981, Cranial morphology and the evolution of West Indian toads (Salientia: Bufonidae): resurrection of the genus *Peltophryne Fitzinger, Copeia,* 1981:273–285.

Preusser, H. J., G. Habermehl, M. Sablofski, and D. Schmall-Haury, 1975, Antimicrobial activity of alkaloids from amphibian venoms and effects on the ultrastructure of yeast cells, *Toxicon,* 13:285–289.

Prudhoe, S., and R. A. Bray, 1982, *Platyhelminth Parasites of the Amphibia,* London: Oxford Univ. Press.

Punzo, F., 1976, The effects of early experience on habitat selection in tadpoles of the Malayan painted frog *Kaloula pulchra* (Anura: Microhylidae), *J. Bombay Nat. Hist. Soc.,* 73:270–277.

Pusey, H. K., 1943, On the head of the liopelmid frog, *Ascaphus truei.* I. The chondrocranium, jaws, arches, and muscles of a partly grown larva, *Quart. J. Microsc. Sci.,* 84:105–185.

Putnam, J. L., 1975, Septation in the ventricle of the heart of *Siren intermedia, Copeia,* 1975:773–774.

Putnam, J. L., and J. F. Dunn, 1978, Septation in the ventricle of the heart of *Necturus maculosus, Herpetologica,* 34:292–297.

Putnam, J. L., and D. L. Kelly, 1978, A new interpretation of interatrial septation in the lungless salamander, *Plethodon glutinosus, Copeia,* 1978:251–254.

Putnam, J. L., and B. N. Sebastian, 1977, The fifth aortic arch in *Amphiuma,* a new discovery, *Copeia,* 1977:600–601.

Putnam, R. W., and S. S. Hillman, 1977, Activity responses of anurans to dehydration, *Copeia,* 1977:746–749.

Pyburn, W. F., 1958, Size and movements of a local population of cricket frogs *(Acris crepitans), Texas J. Sci.,* 10:325–342.

Pyburn, W. F., 1961, "The inheritance and distribution of vertebral stripe color in the cricket frog," in W. F. Blair (ed.), *Vertebrate Speciation,* Austin: Univ. Texas Press, pp 235–261.

Pyburn, W. F., 1963, Observations on the life history of the treefrog *Phyllomedusa callidryas* (Cope), *Texas J. Sci.,* 15:155–170.

Pyburn, W. F., 1966, Breeding activity, larvae and relationship of the treefrog *Hyla phaeota cyanosticta, Southwest. Nat.,* 11:1–18.

Pyburn, W. F., 1967, Breeding and larval development of the hylid frog *Phrynohyas spilomma* in southern Veracruz, Mexico, *Herpetologica,* 23:184–194.

Pyburn, W. F., 1970, Breeding behavior of the leaf-frogs *Phyllomedusa callidryas* and *Phyllomedusa dacnicolor* in Mexico, *Copeia,* 1970:209–218.

Pyburn, W. F., 1975, A new species of microhylid frog of the genus *Synapturanus* from southeastern Colombia, *Herpetologica,* 31:439–443.

Pyburn, W. F., 1980a, The function of eggless capsules and leaf in nests of the frog *Phyllomedusa hypochondrialis* (Anura: Hylidae), *Proc. Biol. Soc. Washington,* 93:153–167.

Pyburn, W. F., 1980b, An unusual anuran larva from the Vaupés region of southeastern Colombia, *Pap. Avul. Zool. São Paulo,* 33:231–238.

Pyke, G. H., H. R. Pulliam, and E. L. Charnov, 1977, Optimal foraging: a selective review of theory and tests, *Quart. Rev. Biol.,* 52:137–154.

Quay, W. B., 1972, Integument and the environment: glandular composition, function, and evolution, *Amer. Zool.,* 12:95–108.

Rabb, G. B., 1956, Some observations on the salamander, *Stereochilus marginatus, Copeia,* 1956:119.

Rabb, G. B., 1960, On the unique sound production of the Surinam toad *(Pipa pipa), Copeia,* 1960:368–369.

Rabb, G. B., 1966, *Stereochilus, S. marginatus, Cat. Amer. Amphib. Rept.,* 25:1–2.

Rabb, G. B., 1969, Fighting frogs, *Brookfield Bandarlog,* 37:4–5.

Rabb, G. B., 1973, "Evolutionary aspects of the reproductive behavior of frogs," in J. L. Vial (ed.), *Evolutionary Biology of the Anurans: Contemporary Research on Major Problems,* Columbia: Univ. Missouri Press, pp 213–227.

Rabb, G. B., and M. S. Rabb, 1961, On the mating and egg-laying behavior of the Surinam toad, *Pipa pipa, Copeia,* 1960:271–276.

Rabb, G. B., and M. S. Rabb, 1963a, On the behavior and breeding biology of the African pipid frog *Hymenochirus boettgeri, Zeit. Tierpsychol.,* 20:215–241.

Rabb, G. B., and M. S. Rabb, 1963b, Additional observations on breeding behavior of the Surinam toad, *Pipa pipa, Copeia,* 1963:636–642.

Rabb, G. B., and R. Snedigar, 1960, Observations on breeding and development of the Surinam toad, *Pipa pipa, Copeia,* 1960:40–44.

Rabl, H., 1931, "Integument der Anamnier," in L. E. Bolk, E. Göppert, E. Kallius and W. Lubosch (eds.), *Handbuch der Vergleichenden Anatomie der Wirbeltiere, Vol. I,* Berlin, pp 271–374.

Radinsky, L., 1979, "The comparative anatomy of the muscular system," in M. Wake (ed.), *Hyman's Comparative Vertebrate Anatomy, Edit. 3,* Chicago: Univ. Chicago Press, pp 327–377.

Ralin, D. B., 1968, Ecological and reproductive differentiation in the cryptic species of the *Hyla versicolor* complex (Hylidae), *Southwest. Nat.,* 13:283–299.

Ralin, D. B., and J. S. Rogers, 1972, Aspects of tolerance to desiccation in *Acris crepitans* and *Pseudacris streckeri, Copeia,* 1972:519–525.

Ramaswami, L. S., 1944, An account of the heart and associated vessels in some genera of Apoda (Amphibia), *Proc. Zool. Soc. London,* 114:117–138.

Ramaswami, L. S., 1948, The chondrocranium of *Gegenophis* (Apoda: Amphibia), *Proc. Zool. Soc. London,* 118:752–760.

Ramaswami, L. S., and A. B. Lakshman, 1959, The skipper-frog as a suitable embryological animal and an account of the action of mammalian hormones on spawning of same, *Proc. Natl. Inst. Sci. India,* 25(B):68–79.

Ramer, J. D., T. H. Jenssen, and C. J. Hurst, 1983, Size-related variation in the advertisement call of *Rana clamitans* (Anura: Ranidae), and its effect on conspecific males, *Copeia,* 1983:141–155.

Rand, A. S., and M. J. Ryan, 1981, The adaptive significance of a complex vocal repertoire in a Neotropical frog, *Zeit. Tierpsychol.,* 57:209–214.

Rand, A. S., M. J. Ryan, and K. Troyer, 1983, A population explosion in a tropical tree frog: *Hyla rufitela* on Barro Colorado Island, Panama, *Biotropica,* 15:72–73.

Raney, E. H., and W. M. Ingram, 1941, Growth of tagged frogs (Rana catesbeiana Shaw and Rana clamitans Daudin) under natural conditions, *Amer. Midl. Nat.,* 26:201–206.

Rapola, J., 1963, The adrenal cortex and metamorphosis of *Xenopus laevis* Daudin, *Gen. Comp. Endocrinol.,* 3:412–421.

Rastogi, R. K., and G. Chieffi, 1970, A cytological study of the pars distalis of pituitary gland of normal, gonadectomized, and

gonadectomized steroid hormone-treated green frog, *Rana esculenta* L., *Gen. Comp. Endocrinol.,* 15:247–263.

Ray, C., 1958, Vital limits and rates of desiccation in salamanders, *Ecology,* 39:75–83.

Redshaw, M. R., 1972, The hormonal control of the amphibian ovary, *Amer. Zool.,* 12:289–306.

Reeder, W. G., 1964, "The digestive system," in J. A. Moore (ed.), *Physiology of the Amphibia,* New York: Academic Press, pp 99–149.

Regal, P. J., 1966, Feeding specializations and the classification of terrestrial salamanders, *Evolution,* 20:392–407.

Regal, P. J., and C. Gans, 1976, Functional aspects of the evolution of frog tongues, *Evolution,* 30:718–734.

Reichenbach-Klinke, H., and E. Elkan, 1965, *The Principal Diseases of Lower Vertebrates,* New York: Academic Press.

Reig, O. A., 1958, Proposiciones para una nueva macrosistematica de los anuros. Nota preliminar, *Physis,* 21:109–118.

Reig, O. A., 1964, El problema del origen monofiletico or polifiletico de los anfibios, con consideraciones sobre las relaciones entre anuros, urodelos y apodos, *Ameghiniana,* 3:191–211.

Reig, O. A., 1972, "*Macrogenioglottus* and the South American bufonid toads," in W. F. Blair (ed.), *Evolution In The Genus Bufo,* Austin: Univ. Texas Press, pp 14–36.

Reinbach, W., 1950, Über den schalleitenden Apparat der Amphibien und Reptilien (zur schmalhausenshen Theorie der Gehörnknochelchen), *Zeit. Anat. Entwgesch.,* 114:611–639.

Rengel, D., 1950, Acción de la temperatura elevada sobre la espermatogenesis de dos formas de *Leptodactylus ocellatus* L., *Acta Zool. Lilloana,* 9:425–438.

Reno, H. W., F. R. Gehlbach, and R. A. Turner, 1972, Skin and aestivational cocoon of the aquatic amphibian, *Siren intermedia* Le Conte, *Copeia,* 1972:625–631.

Reno, H. W., and H. H. Middleton, 1973, Lateral line system of *Siren intermedia* Le Conte (Amphibia: Sirenidae), during aquatic activity and aestivation, *Acta Zool.,* 54:21–29.

Reuter, T. E., R. H. White, and G. Wald, 1971, Rhodopsin and porphyropsin fields in the adult bullfrog retina, *J. Gen. Physiol.,* 58:351–371.

Reyes Campos, N. B., 1971, Observaciones sobre la conducta del coqui, *Eleutherodactylus coqui, Caribbean J. Sci.,* 11: 209–210.

Rheinlaender, J., H. C. Gerhardt, D. D. Yager, and R. R. Capranica, 1979, Accuracy of phonotaxis by the green treefrog *(Hyla cinerea), J. Comp. Physiol.,* 133(A):247–255.

Richards, C. M., 1958, The inhibition of growth in crowded *Rana pipiens* tadpoles, *Physiol. Zool.,* 31:138–151.

Richards, C. M., 1977, Reproductive potential under laboratory conditions of *Hyperolius viridiflavus* (Amphibia, Anura, Hyperoliidae), a Kenyan reed frog, *J. Herpetol.,* 11:426–428.

Richards, C. M., 1982, The alteration of chromatophore expression by sex hormones in the Kenyan reed frog, *Hyperolius viridiflavus, Gen. Comp. Endocrinol.,* 46:59–67.

Richards, C. M., and G. C. Lehman, 1980, Photoperiod stimulation of growth in postmetamorphic *Rana pipiens, Copeia,* 1980:147–149.

Richards, C. M., and G. W. Nace, 1978, Gynogenetic and hormonal sex reversal used in tests of the XX-XY hypothesis of sex determination in *Rana pipiens, Growth,* 42:319–331.

Richards, C. M., and G. W. Nace, 1983, Dark pigment variants in anurans: classification, new descriptions, color changes and inheritance, *Copeia,* 1983:979–990.

Richmond, N. D., 1947, Life history of *Scaphiopus holbrooki holbrooki* (Harlan). Part I. Larval development and behavior, *Ecology,* 28:53–67.

Richmond, N. D., 1964, The green frog *(Rana clamitans melanota)* developing in one season, *Herpetologica,* 20: 132.

Ridewood, W. G., 1897, On the structure and development of

the hyobranchial skeleton and larynx in *Xenopus* and *Pipa; with remarks on the affinities of the Aglossa, Zool. J. Linnaean Soc.*, 26:53–128.

Ridewood, W. G., 1900, On the hyobranchial skeleton and larynx of a new aglossal toad, *Hymenochirus boettgeri, Zool. J. Linnaean Soc.*, 27:454–460.

Riemer, W. J., 1958, Variation and systematic relationships within the salamandrid genus *Taricha, Univ. California Publ. Zool.*, 56:47–124.

Risch, J.-P., 1984, Breve diagnose de *Paradactylon*, genre nouveau d'urodele de l'Iran (Amphibia, Caudata, Hynobiidae), *Alytes*, 3:44–46.

Ritland, R. M., 1955, Studies on the post-cranial morphology of Ascaphus truei. II. Myology, *J. Morph.*, 97:215–282.

Ritter, W. E., and L. Miller, 1899, A contribution to the life history of *Autodax lugubris*, a Californian salamander, *Amer. Nat.*, 33:691–704.

Rivero, J. A., 1961, Salientia of Venezuela, *Bull. Mus. Comp. Zool.*, 126:1–207.

Rivero, J. A., 1978, *Los Anfibios y Reptiles de Puerto Rico,* San Juan: Educ. Universitaria Puerto Rico.

Rivero, J. A., and A. E. Esteves, 1969, Observations on the agonistic and breeding behavior of *Leptodactylus pentadactylus* and other amphibian species in Venezuela, *Breviora*, 321:1–14.

Roberts, J. D., 1981, Terrestrial breeding in the Australian leptodactylid frog *Myobatrachus gouldii* (Gray), *Australian Wildl. Res.*, 8:451–462.

Roberts, J. D., 1984, Terrestrial egg deposition and direct development in *Arenophryne rotunda* Tyler: a myobatrachid frog from coastal sand dunes at Shark Bay, Western Australia, *Australian Wildl. Res.*, 11:191–200.

Robertson, J. G. M., 1981, "Sexual selection and spacing in *Uperoleia rugosa* (red-groined toadlet) (Anura: Leptodactylidae)," in C. B. Banks and A. A. Martin (eds.), *Proc. Melbourne Herpetological Symp.*, Melbourne, pp 4–5.

Robinson, P. L., 1973, "Paleoclimatology and continental drift," in D. H. Tarling and S. K. Runcorn (eds.), *Implications of Continental Drift to the Earth Sciences, Vol. 1,* London: Academic Press, pp 451–476.

Roček, Z., 1974, Beitrag zur Erkennung der Neotenie des Alpenmolches *Triturus alpestris* (Laurenti, 1768), *Vest. Ceskosl. Spol. Zool. Ceskosl.*, 38:285–294.

Roček, Z., 1981, Cranial anatomy of frogs of the family Pelobitidae Stannius, 1856, with outlines of their phylogeny and systematics, *Acta Univ. Carolinae, Biol.*, 1980:1–164.

Rogers, J. S., 1972, Measures of genetic similarity and genetic distance, *Univ. Texas Publ.*, 7213:145–153.

Romer, A. S., 1945, *Vertebrate Paleontology,* Chicago: Univ. Chicago Press.

Romer, A. S., 1947, Review of the Labyrinthodontia, *Bull. Mus. Comp. Zool.*, 99:1–368.

Romspert, A. P., 1976, Osmoregulation of the African clawed frog, *Xenopus laevis* in hypersaline media, *Comp. Biochem. Physiol.*, 54(A):207–210.

Rose, F. L., 1966, Homing to nests by the salamander *Desmognathus auriculatus, Copeia*, 1966:251–253.

Rose, F. L., and D. Armentrout, 1976, Adaptive strategies of *Ambystoma tigrinum* (Green) inhabiting the Llano Estacado of west Texas, *J. Anim. Ecol.*, 45:713–729.

Rose, G., and R. R. Capranica, 1983, Temporal selectivity in the central auditory system of the leopard frog, *Science*, 219:1087–1089.

Rose, S. M., 1960, A feedback mechanism of growth control in tadpoles, *Ecology*, 41:188–198.

Rose, W., 1962, *The Reptiles and Amphibians of Southern Africa,* Capetown: Maskew Miller.

Roseghini, M., V. Erspamer, and R. Endean, 1976, Indole-, imidazole-, and phenylalkylamines in the skin of one hundred amphibian species from Australia and New Guinea, *Comp. Physiol. Biochem.*, 54(C):31–43.

Rösel von Rosenhof, A. J., 1753–1758, *Historia naturalis Ranarum nostratium,* Nurenberg.

Rosen, D., P. L. Forey, B. G. Gardiner, and C. Patterson, 1981, Lungfishes, tetrpods, paleontology, and plesiomorphy, *Bull. Amer. Mus. Nat. Hist.*, 167:161–275.

Rosen, M., and R. E. Lemon, 1974, The vocal behavior of spring peepers, *Hyla crucifer, Copeia*, 1974:940–950.

Ross, R. J., and J. J. B. Smith, 1980, Detection of substrate vibrations by salamanders: frequency sensitivity of the ear, *Comp. Biochem. Physiol.*, 65(A):167–172.

Rossi, A., 1959, Tavole cronologiche dello sviluppo embrionale e larval del *Bufo bufo* (L.), *Monit. Zool. Italiano*, 66:1–11.

Rossi, J. V., 1983, The use of olfactory cues by *Bufo marinus, J. Herpetol.*, 17:72–73.

Roth, G., 1976, Experimental analysis of the prey catching behavior of *Hydromantes italicus* Dunn (Amphibia, Plethodontidae), *J. Comp. Physiol.*, 109:47–58.

Roth, G., 1978, The role of stimulus movement patterns in the prey catching behavior of *Hydromantes genei* (Schlegel), *J. Comp. Physiol.*, 123:261–264.

Roth, G., W. Grunwald, R. Linke, G. Rettig, and B. Rotlauff, 1983, Evolutionary patterns in the visual system of lungless salamanders (Plethodontidae), *Arch. Biol. Med. Exp.*, 16:329–341.

Roth, J. J., 1973, Vascular supply to the ventral pelvic region of anurans as related to water balance, *J. Morph.*, 140:443–460.

Rotmann, E., 1940, Die Bedeutung der Zellgrösse für die Entwicklung der Amphibienlinse, *Arch. Entwicklungsmech.*, 140:124–147.

Roughgarden, J., 1983, Competition and theory in community ecology, *Amer. Nat.*, 122:583–601.

Rugh, R., 1951, *The Frog, its Reproduction and Development,* New York: McGraw-Hill Book Co.

Rugh, R., 1962, *Experimental Embryology,* Minneapolis: Burgess Publ. Co.

Ruibal, R., 1955, A study of altitudinal races in *Rana pipiens, Evolution*, 9:322–338.

Ruibal, R., 1962a, The ecology and genetics of a desert population of *Rana pipiens, Copeia*, 1962:189–195.

Ruibal, R., 1962b, The adaptive value of bladder water in the toad, *Bufo cognatus, Physiol. Zool.*, 35:218–223.

Ruibal, R., and S. Hillman, 1981, Cocoon structure and function in the burrowing hylid frog, *Pternohyla fodiens, J. Herpetol.*, 15:403–408.

Ruibal, R., and V. Shoemaker, 1984, Osteoderms in anurans, *J. Herpetol.*, 18:313–328.

Ruibal, R., L. Tevis Jr., and V. Roig, 1969, The terrestrial ecology of the spadefoot toad *Scaphiopus hammondii, Copeia*, 1969:571–584.

Ruíz-C., P. M., and J. I. Hernández-C., 1976, *Osornophryne*, género nuevo de anfibios bufonidos de Colombia y Ecuador, *Caldasia*, 11:93–148.

Runkova, G. G., Z. L. Stepanova, and L. A. Koval'chuk, 1974, Organ specificity in the action of metabolites of amphibian larvae on their endogenous metabolism under condition of increased population density. The role of protein in the regulating influence of metabolites (in Russian), *Akad. Nauk. SSR Doklady Biol. Sci. Sec.*, 217:328–330.

Russell, I. J., 1976, "Amphibian lateral line receptors," in R. Llinas and W. Precht (eds.), *Frog Neurobiology,* Berlin: Springer-Verlag, pp 513–550.

Ryan, M. J., 1977, Parental care in salamanders, *Bull. New York Herpetol. Soc.*, 13:23–27.

Ryan, M. J., 1978, A thermal property of the *Rana catesbeiana* (Amphibia, Anura, Ranidae) egg mass, *J. Herpetol.*, 12:247–248.

Ryan, M. J., 1980a, Female mate choice in a Neotropical frog, *Science,* 209:523–525.

Ryan, M. J., 1980b, The reproductive behavior of the bullfrog *(Rana catesbeiana), Copeia,* 1980:108–114.

Ryan, M. J., and M. D. Tuttle, 1983, The ability of the frog-eating bat to discriminate among novel and potentially poisonous frog species using acoustic cues, *Anim. Behav.,* 31:827–833.

Ryan, M. J., M. D. Tuttle, and A. S. Rand, 1982, Bat predation and sexual advertisement in a Neotropical anuran, *Amer. Nat.,* 119:136–139.

Ryan, M. J., M. D. Tuttle, and L. K. Taft, 1981, The costs and benefits of frog chorusing behavior, *Behav. Ecol. Sociobiol.,* 8:273–278.

Ryan, R. A., 1953, Growth rates of some ranids under natural conditions, *Copeia,* 1953:73–80.

Rÿke, P. A. J., 1950, Contributions to the cranial morphology of the Asiatic urodele Onychodactylus japonicus (Houttuijn), *Ann. Univ. Stellenbosch,* 26:2–21.

Saez, F. A., and N. Brum-Zorrilla, 1966, Karyotype variation in some species of the genus *Odontophrynus* (Amphibia-Anura), *Caryologia,* 19:55–63.

Sage, R. D., E. M. Prager, and D. B. Wake, 1982, A Cretaceous divergence time between pelobatid frogs *(Pelobates and Scaphiopus):* immunological studies of serum albumin, *J. Zool.,* 198:481–494.

Saint-Aubain, M. L. de, 1981, Amphibian limb ontogeny and its bearing on the phylogeny of the group, *Zeit. Zool. Syst. Evol.,* 19:175–194.

Salibián, A., 1977, Transporte de chloro y de sodio a través de la piel *in situ* de anfibios sudamericanos, *Bol. Mus. Nac. Hist. Nat. Chile,* 35:121–163.

Salomatina, N. I., 1982, "Morphological analysis of the mandibular apparatus of caudate and noncaudate Amphibia," in E. I. Vorob'eva and N. N. Iordanskj (eds.), *Morphofunctional Transformations of Vertebrates in the Process of Occupying Dry Land* (in Russian), Ann. SSR Inst. Evol. Morf. Ehkol. Zhiv. Nauk., pp 102–124.

Salthe, S. N., 1963, The egg capsules in the Amphibia, *J. Morph.,* 113:161–171.

Salthe, S. N., 1965, Increase in volume of the perivitelline chamber during development of *Rana pipiens* Schreber, *Physiol. Zool.,* 38:80–98.

Salthe, S. N., 1967, Courtship patterns and phylogeny of the urodeles, *Copeia,* 1967:100–117.

Salthe, S. N., 1969, Reproductive modes and the number and sizes of ova in the urodeles, *Amer. Midl. Nat.,* 81:467–490.

Salthe, S. N., 1973, Amphiumidae, *Amphiuma, Cat. Amer. Amphib. Rept.,* 147:1–4.

Salthe, S. N., and W. E. Duellman, 1973, "Quantitative constraints associated with reproductive mode in anurans," in J. L. Vial (ed.), *Evolutionary Biology of the Anurans: Contemporary Research on Major Problems,* Columbia: Univ. Missouri Press, pp 229–249.

Salthe, S. N., and N. O. Kaplan, 1966, Immunology and rates of enzyme evolution in the Amphibia in relation to the origins of certain taxa, *Evolution,* 20:603–616.

Salthe, S. N., and J. S. Mecham, 1974, "Reproductive and courtship patterns," in B. Lofts (ed.), *Physiology of the Amphibia, Vol. II,* New York: Academic Press, pp 309–521.

Samollow, P. B., 1980, Selective mortality and reproduction in a natural population of *Bufo boreas, Evolution,* 34:18–39.

Sanchíz, F. B., 1978, Nuevos restos fósiles de la familia Pelodytidae (Amphibia, Anura), *Estudios Geol.,* 34:9–27.

Sanchíz, F. B., 1981, Registro fósil y antigüedad de la familia Hylidae (Amphibia, Anura) en Europa, *Ann. Cong. Latino-Amer. Paleo. Porto Alegre,* pp 757–764.

Sanchíz, F. B., and M. Mlynarski, 1979, Remarks on the fossil anurans from the Polish Neogene, *Acta Zool. Cracoviense,* 24:153–174.

Sanderson, I. T., 1932, *Animal Treasure,* New York: Viking Press.

Sarasin, P., and F. Sarasin, 1887–1890, *Ergebnisse Naturwissenschaftlichen. Forschungen auf Ceylon in den Jahren 1884-1886. Zur Entwicklungsgeschichte u. Anat. der Ceylonische Blindwuhle Ichthyophis glutinosus,* Wiesbaden: Keidel's Verlag.

Sarich, V. M., and A. C. Wilson, 1967, Immunological time scale for hominid evolution, *Science,* 158:1200–1203.

Sasaki, M., 1924, On a Japanese salamander, in Lake Kuttarush, which propagates like the axolotl, *J. Coll. Agricul. Hokkaido Imp. Univ.,* 15:1–36.

Sato, A., and I. Kawakami, 1976, The fine structure of the lateral line organ of larvae of the newt, Triturus pyrrhogaster, *Annot. Zool. Japan,* 49:131–141.

Sato, I., 1943, *The Tailed Batrachia of Japan (in Japanese),* Tokyo.

Sattler, P. W., 1980, Genetic relationships among selected species of North American *Scaphiopus, Copeia,* 1980:605–610.

Savage, J. M., "1966" (1967), An extraordinary new toad *(Bufo)* from Costa Rica, *Rev. Biol. Trop.,* 14:153–167.

Savage, J. M., 1973, "The geographic distribution of frogs: patterns and predictions," in J. L. Vial (ed.), *Evolutionary Biology of the Anurans: Contemporary Research on Major Problems,* Columbia: Univ. Missouri Press, pp 352–445.

Savage, J. M., 1982, The enigma of the Central American herpetofauna: dispersals or vicariance?, *Ann. Missouri Bot. Gard.,* 69:464–547.

Savage, J. M., and A. L. de Carvalho, 1953, The family position of the neotropical frogs currently referred to the genus *Pseudis, Zoologica,* 38:193–200.

Savage, J. M., and A. G. Kluge, 1961, Rediscovery of the strange Costa Rican toad, *Crepidius epioticus* Cope, *Rev. Biol. Trop.,* 9:39–51.

Savage, J. M., and M. H. Wake, 1972, Geographic variation and systematics of the Middle American caecilians, genera *Dermophis* and *Gymnopis, Copeia,* 1972:680–695.

Savage, R. M., 1932, The spawning, voice, and sexual behaviour of *Bombina variegata variegata, Proc. Zool. Soc. London,* 1932:889–898.

Savage, R. M., 1952, Ecological, physiological and anatomical observations on some species of anuran tadpoles, *Proc. Zool. Soc. London,* 122:467–514.

Savage, R. M., 1961, *The Ecology and Life History of the Common Frog* (Rana temporaria temporaria), London: Pitman.

Savage, R. M., 1965, External stimulus of the natural spawning of *Xenopus laevis, Nature,* 205:618–619.

Sawaya, P., 1940, Sobre o veneno das glandulas cutaneas, a secreção e o coração do Siphonops annulatus, *Bol. Fac. Filos. Cienc. Letras Univ. São Paulo Ser. Zool.,* 19:207–270.

Saxén, L., and S. Toivonen, 1962, *Primary Embryonic Induction,* London: Academic Press.

Sayler, A., 1966, The reproductive ecology of the red-backed salamander, *Plethodon cinereus,* in Maryland, *Copeia,* 1966:183–193.

Sazima, I., 1972, The occurrence of marine invertebrates in the stomach contents of the frog Thoropa miliaris, *Ciencia Cultura,* 23:647–648.

Sazima, I., 1975, Distress call in newly metamorphosed smith frog, *Hyla faber* Wied., *Herpetologica,* 31:471–472.

Sazima, I., 1978, Convergent defense behavior of two leaf-litter frogs in southeastern Brasil, *Biotropica,* 10:158.

Scalia, F., 1976a, "Structure of the olfactory and accessory olfactory systems," in R. Llinás and W. Precht (eds.), *Frog Neurobiology,* Berlin: Springer-Verlag, pp 213–233.

Scalia, F., 1976b, "The optic pathway of the frog: nuclear organization and connections," in R. Llinás and W. Precht (eds.), *Frog Neurobiology,* Berlin: Springer-Verlag, pp 386–406.

Scanlan, B. E., L. R. Maxson, and W. E. Duellman, 1980, Albumin evolution in marsupial frogs (Hylidae, *Gastrotheca*), *Evolution,* 34:222–229.

Schaeffer, B., 1941, The morphological and functional evolution of the tarsus in amphibians and reptiles, *Bull. Amer. Mus. Nat. Hist.,* 78:395–472.

Scheel, J. J., 1970, Notes on the biology of the African tree-toad, *Nectophryne afra* Buchholz and Peters, 1875, (Bufonidae, Anura) from Fernando Po, *Rev. Zool. Africa,* 81:225–236.

Scheer, B. T., and R. P. Markel, 1962, The effect of osmotic stress and hypophysectomy on blood and urine urea levels in frogs, *Comp. Biochem. Physiol.,* 7:289–297.

Schempp, W., and M. Schmid, 1981, Chromosome banding in Amphibia. VI. BrdU-replication patterns in Anura and demonstration of XX/XY sex chromosomes in *Rana esculenta, Chromosoma,* 83:697–710.

Schiøtz, A., 1963, The amphibians of Nigeria, *Vidensk. Medd. Dansk. Naturh. Foren.,* 125:1–92.

Schiøtz, A., 1967, The treefrogs (Rhacophoridae) of West Africa, *Spol. Zool. Mus. Haun. (Copenhagen),* 25:1–346.

Schiøtz, A., 1973, "Evolution of anuran mating calls. Ecological aspects," in J. L. Vial (ed.), *Evolutionary Biology of the Anurans: Contemporary Research On Major Problems,* Columbia: Univ. Missouri Press, pp 311–319.

Schiøtz, A., 1975, *The Treefrogs of Eastern Africa,* Copenhagen: Steenstrupia.

Schlampp, K. W., 1892, Das Auge des Grottenolms *(Proteus anguineus), Zeit. Wissen. Zool.,* 53:537–557.

Schlisio, V. W., K. Jurss, and L. Spannhof, 1973, Osmo- und Ionenregulation von *Xenopus laevis* Daud. nach Adaptation in verschiedenen osmotisch wirksamen Losungen, *Zool. Jahrb. Physiol.,* 77:275–290.

Schluter, A., 1979, Bio-akustische Untersuchen an Hylidan in einem begrenzten Gebiet des tropischen Regenwaldes von Peru, *Salamandra,* 15:211–236.

Schmalhausen, I. I., 1917, On the dermal bones of the shoulder-girdle of the Amphibia, *Revue Zool. Russe,* 2:84–110.

Schmalhausen, I. I., 1958, Die Entstehung der Amphibien im Verlauf der Erdgeschichte, *Naturwiss. Beitrage (Sowjetwiss.),* 9:941–961.

Schmalhausen, I. I., 1959, Concerning monophyletism and polyphyletism in relation to the problem of the origin of land vertebrates (in Russian), *Byul. Mosk. Obshchestva. Ispytatelei Prirody, Otd. Biol.,* 64(4):16–33.

Schmalhausen, I. I., 1968, *The Origin of Terrestrial Vertebrates,* New York: Academic Press.

Schmid, M., 1978a, Chromosome banding in Amphibia. I. Constitutive heterochromatin and nucleolus organizer regions in *Bufo* and *Hyla, Chromosoma,* 66:361–388.

Schmid, M., 1978b, Chromosome banding in Amphibia. II. Constitutive heterochromatin and nucleolus organizer regions in Ranidae, Microhylidae and Rhacophoridae, *Chromosoma,* 68:131–148.

Schmid, M., 1980, Chromosome banding in Amphibia. V. Highly differentiated ZW/ZZ sex chromosomes and exceptional genome size in *Pyxicephalus adspersus* (Anura, Ranidae), *Chromosoma,* 80:69–96.

Schmid, M., T. Haaf, B. Geile, and S. Sims, 1983, Chromosome banding in Amphibia VIII. An unusual XY/XX-sex chromosome system in *Gastrotheca riobambae* (Anura, Hylidae), *Chromosoma,* 88:69–82.

Schmid, M., J. Olert, and C. Klett, 1979, Chromosome banding in Amphibia. III. Sex chromosomes in *Triturus, Chromosoma,* 71:29–55.

Schmid, W. D., 1965, Some aspects of the water economies of nine species of amphibians, *Ecology,* 46:261–269.

Schmid, W. D., 1982, Survival of frogs in low temperature, *Science,* 215:697–698.

Schmidt, K. P., and R. F. Inger, 1959, Amphibians exclusive of the genera *Afrixalus* and *Hyperolius, Expl. du Parc National de l'Upemba, Fasc.,* 56:1–264.

Schmidt, R. S., 1966, Hormonal mechanisms of frog mating calling, *Copeia,* 1966:637–644.

Schmidt, R. S., 1970, Auditory receptors of two mating call-less anurans, *Copeia,* 1970:169–170.

Schmidt, R. S., 1971, A model of the central mechanisms of male anuran acoustic behavior, *Behaviour,* 39:288–317.

Schmidt, R. S., 1973, Central mechanisms of frog calling, *Amer. Zool.,* 13:1169–1177.

Schmidtke, J., W. Beçak, and W. Engel, 1976, The reduction of genic activity in the tetraploid amphibian *Odontophrynus americanus* is not due to loss of ribosomal DNA, *Experientia,* 32:27–28.

Schmidtler, J. J., and J. F. Schmidtler, 1975, Untersuchungen an westpersischen Bergbachmolchen der Gattung *Neurergus, Salamandra,* 11:84–98.

Schmidt-Nielsen, K., and P. Lee, 1962, Kidney function in the crab-eating frog *(Rana cancrivora), J. Exp. Biol.,* 39:166–177.

Schneider, C. W., 1968, Avoidance learning and the response tendencies of the larval salamander *Amblystoma punctatum* to photic stimulation, *Anim. Behav.,* 16:492–495.

Schneider, H., 1977, "Acoustic behavior and physiology of vocalization in the European tree frog, *Hyla arborea* (L.)," in D. H. Taylor and S. I. Guttman (eds.), *The Reproductive Biology of Amphibians,* New York: Plenum Press, pp 295–335.

Schnurbein, A. F. von, 1935, Der Bewegungsapparat von *Hypogeophis.* Beitrag zur Kenntnis der Gymnophionen XXIII., *Morphol. Jahrb.,* 75:315–330.

Schoener, T. W., 1983, Field experiments on interspecific competition, *Amer. Nat.,* 122:240–285.

Schreckenberg, G. M., and A. G. Jacobson, 1975, Normal stages of development of the axolotl, *Ambystoma mexicanum, Devel. Biol.,* 42:391–400.

Schuierer, F. W., 1962, Remarks upon the natural history of *Bufo exul* Myers, the endemic toad of Deep Springs Valley, Inyo County, California, *Herpetologica,* 17:260–266.

Schulte, R., 1980, *Frösche und Kröten,* Stuttgart: Verlag Eugen Ulmer.

Schultze, H.-P., 1970, Folded teeth and the monophyletic origin of tetrapods, *Amer. Mus. Novitat.,* 2408:1–10.

Schultze, H.-P., 1981, Hennig und der Ursprung der Tetrapoda, *Palaont. Zeit.,* 55:71–86.

Schwalm, P. A., P. H. Starrett, and R. W. McDiarmid, 1977, Infrared reflectance in leaf-sitting neotropical frogs, *Science,* 196:1225–1227.

Schwartz, A., and R. Thomas, 1975, A checklist of West Indian amphibians and reptiles, *Carnegie Mus. Nat. Hist. Spec. Publ.,* 1:1–216.

Schwartz, J. J., and K. D. Wells, 1983, An experimental study of acoustic interference between two species of neotropical treefrogs, *Anim. Behav.,* 3:181–190.

Scott, N. J. Jr., 1976, The abundance and diversities of the herpetofauna of tropical forest litter, *Biotropica,* 8:41–58.

Scott, N. J. Jr., 1982, The herpetofauna of forest litter plots from Cameroon, Africa, *U. S. Fish And Wildlife Res. Rept.,* 13:145–150.

Scott, N. J. Jr., and A. Starrett, 1974, An unusual breeding aggregation of frogs, with notes on the ecology of *Agalychnis spurrelli* (Anura: Hylidae), *Bull. South. California Acad. Sci.,* 73:86–94.

Sealander, J. A., and B. W. West, 1969, Critical thermal maxima of some Arkansas salamanders in relation to thermal acclimation, *Herpetologica,* 25:124–125.

Seale, D. B., 1980, Influence of amphibian larvae on primary production, nutrient flux, and competition in a pond ecosystem, *Ecology,* 6:1531–1550.

Sedra, S. N., 1950, The metamorphosis of the jaws and their muscles in the toad, *Bufo regularis* Reuss, correlated with changes in the animal's feeding habits, *Proc. Zool. Soc. London,* 120:405–449.

Sedra, S. N., and M. I. Michael, 1961, Normal table of the Egyptian toad *Bufo regularis* Reuss, with an addendum on the standardization of the stages considered in previous publications, *Ceskoslovenská Morfd.*, 9:333–351.

Seibel, R. V., 1970, Variables affecting the critical thermal maximum of the leopard frog, *Rana pipiens* Schreber, *Herpetologica*, 26:208–213.

Semlitsch, R. D., 1980, Geographic and local variation in population parameters of the slimy salamander *Plethodon glutinosus, Herpetologica*, 17:6–16.

Semlitsch, R. D., 1981, Terrestrial activity and summer home range of the mole salamander (Ambystoma talpoideum), *Canadian J. Zool.*, 59:315–322.

Semlitsch, R. D., 1983, Structure and dynamics of two breeding populations of the eastern tiger salamander, *Ambystoma tigrinum, Copeia*, 1983:608–616.

Semlitsch, R. D., and J. P. Caldwell, 1982, Effects of density on growth, metamorphosis, and survivorship in tadpoles of *Scaphiopus holbrooki, Ecology*, 63:905–911.

Senfft, W., 1936, Das Brutgeschäft des Baumsteigerfrosches (Dendrobates auratus Girard) in Gefangenschaft, *Zool. Garten*, 8:122–131.

Sergeev, A. M., and K. S. Smirnov, 1939, The color of eggs of Amphibia, *Vop. Ekol. Biotzenol.*, 5:319–324.

Seshachar, B. R., 1937, The chromosomes of *Ichthyophis glutinosus* (Linn.), *Cytologia*, 8:327–331.

Seshachar, B. R., 1939, The spermatogenesis of Uraetyphlus narayani Seshachar, *La Cellule*, 48:63–76.

Seshachar, B. R., 1944, The chromosomes of *Gegenophis carnosus, Half Yearly J. Mysore Univ., Ns*, 5(B):251–253.

Sessions, S. K., 1980, Evidence for a highly differentiated sex chromosome heteromorphism in the salamander *Necturus maculosus* (Rafinesque), *Chromosoma*, 77:157–168.

Sessions, S. K., 1982, Cytogenetics of diploid and triploid salamanders of the *Ambystoma jeffersonianum* complex, *Chromosoma*, 84:599–621.

Sessions, S. K., P. E. León, and J. Kezer, 1982, Cytogenetics of the Chinese giant salamander, *Andrias davidianus* (Blanchard): the evolutionary significance of cryptobranchoid karyotypes, *Chromosoma*, 86:341–357.

Sessions, S. K., and J. E. Wiley, 1985, Chromosome evolution in salamanders of the genus *Necturus, Brimelyana*, 10:37–52.

Seto, T., and R. A. Nussbaum, 1976, Mitotic and meiotic chromosomes of *Ichthyophis orthoplicatus* Taylor (Amphibia: Gymnophiona), *Caryologia*, 29:317–331.

Sever, D. M., 1976, Induction of secondary sexual characters in *Eurycea quadridigitata, Copeia*, 1976:830–833.

Severtzov, A. S., 1968, The evolution of the hyobranchial apparatus in the larvae of Amphibia (English translation of thesis abstract), *Smithsonian Herpetol. Infor. Serv.*, 21:1–8(1970).

Severtzov, A. S., 1969, Food-seizing mechanisms in anuran larvae (in Russian), *Dokl. Akad. Nauk. SSR Ser. Biol.*, 187:530–532.

Severtzov, A. S., 1971, The mechanism of food capture in tailed amphibians (in Russian, English translation), *Dokl. Akad. Nauk. SSR Ser. Biol.*, 154:34–37.

Severtzov, A. S., 1972, Mechanism of movements of the sublingual system and possible causes for reduction of lungs in Urodela (in Russian), *Zool. Zhur.*, 51:94–112.

Sexton, O, J., 1960, Some aspects of the behavior and of the territory of a dendrobatid frog, *Prostherapis trinitatis, Ecology*, 41:107–115.

Sexton, O. J., 1962, Apparent territorialism in *Leptodactylus insularum, Herpetologica*, 18:212–214.

Seymour, R. S., 1972, Behavioral thermoregulation by juvenile green toads, *Bufo debilis, Copeia*, 1972:572–575.

Seymour, R. S., 1973a, Physiological correlates of forced activity and burrowing in the spadefoot toad, *Scaphiopus hammondii, Copeia*, 1973:103–115.

Seymour, R. S., 1973b, Energy metabolism of dormant spadefoot toads *(Scaphiopus), Copeia*, 1973:435–445.

Seymour, R. S., 1973c, Gas exchange in spadefoot toads beneath the ground, *Copeia*, 1973:452–460.

Shannon, C. E., and W. Weaver, 1949, *The Mathematical Theory of Communication*, Urbana: Univ. Illinois Press.

Shaver, J. R., S. Barch, and C. C. Umpierre, 1970, Interspecific relationships of oviducal materials as related to fertilization in Amphibia, *J. Embryol. Exp. Morph.*, 24:209–225.

Shaw, J. P., 1979, The time scale of tooth development and replacement in *Xenopus laevis* (Daudin), *J. Anat.*, 129:232–242.

Shelton, G., 1976, "Gas exchange, pulmonary blood supply, and the partially divided amphibian heart," in P. S. Davies (ed.), *Perspectives in Experimental Biology. Vol. 1. Zoology*, Oxford: Pergamon Press, pp 247–259.

Shelton, P. M. J., 1970, The lateral line system at metamorphosis in *Xenopus laevis* (Daudin), *J. Embryol. Exp. Morph.*, 24:511–524.

Shine, R., 1979, Sexual selection and sexual dimorphism in the Amphibia, *Copeia*, 1979:297–306.

Shinn, E. A., and J. W. Dole, 1978, Evidence for a role for olfactory cues in the feeding response of leopard frogs, *Rana pipiens, Herpetologica*, 34:167–172.

Shoemaker, V. H., 1964, The effects of dehydration on electrolyte concentrations in a toad, *Bufo marinus, Comp. Biochem. Physiol.*, 13:261–271.

Shoemaker, V. H., R. Balding, R. Ruibal, and L. L. McClanahan Jr., 1972, Uricotelism and low evaporative water loss in a South American frog, *Science*, 175:1018–1020.

Shoemaker, V. H., and L. L. McClanahan Jr., 1973, Nitrogen excretion in the larvae of a land-nesting frog *(Leptodactylus bufonius), Comp. Biochem. Physiol.*, 44(A):1149–1156.

Shoemaker, V. H., and L. L. McClanahan Jr., 1975, Evaporative water loss, nitrogen excretion, and osmoregulation in phyllomedusine frogs, *J. Comp. Physiol.*, 100:331–345.

Shoemaker, V. H., and L. L. McClanahan Jr., 1980, Nitrogen excretion and water balance in amphibians of Borneo, *Copeia*, 1980:446–451.

Shoemaker, V. H., L. L. McClanahan Jr., and R. Ruibal, 1969, Seasonal changes in body fluids in a field population of spadefoot toads, *Copeia*, 1969:585–591.

Shoemaker, V. H., and K. Nagy, 1977, Osmoregulation in amphibians and reptiles, *Ann. Rev. Physiol.*, 39:449–471.

Shoop, C. R., 1960, The breeding habits of the mole salamander in southeastern Louisiana, *Tulane Stud. Zool.*, 8:65–82.

Shoop, C. R., 1965a, Orientation of *Ambystoma maculatum* movements to and from breeding ponds, *Science*, 149:558–559.

Shoop, C. R., 1965b, Aspects of reproduction in Louisiana Necturus populations, *Amer. Midl. Nat.*, 74:357–367.

Shoop, C. R., 1968, Migratory orientation of Ambystoma maculatum: movements near breeding ponds and displacements of migrating individuals, *Biol. Bull.*, 135:230–238.

Shoop, C. R., 1974, Yearly variation in larval survival of *Ambystoma maculatum, Ecology*, 55:440–444.

Shumway, W., 1940, Stages in the normal development of *Rana pipiens*. I. External form, *Anat. Rec.*, 78:139–144.

Siboulet, R., 1971, Table chronologique du développement embryonnaire et larvaire du crapaud de Mauretanie *Bufo mauritanicus* Schlegel, 1841, a differentes temperatures, *Vie Milieu*, 21(C):179–197.

Siebert, E. A., H. B. Lillywhite, and R. J. Wassersug, 1974, Cranial coossification in frogs: relationships to rates of evaporative water loss, *Physiol. Zool.*, 47:261–265.

Siedlecki, M., 1909, Zur Kenntniss der javanischen Flugfrosches, *Biol. Zentralbl.*, 29:704–737.

Silverstone, P. A., 1973, Observations on the behavior and ecology of a Colombian poison-arrow frog, kokoe-pa *(Dendrobates histrionicus* Berthold), *Herpetologica*, 29:295–301.

Silverstone, P. A., 1975, A revision of the poison-arrow frogs of the genus *Dendrobates* Wagler, *Nat. Hist. Mus. Los Angeles Co. Sci. Bull.*, 21:1–55.

Silverstone, P. A., 1976, A revision of the poison-arrow frogs of the genus *Phyllobates* Bibron *in* Sagra (Family Dendrobatidae), *Nat. Hist. Mus. Los Angeles Co. Sci. Bull.,* 27:1–53.

Simberloff, D., 1983, "Sizes of coexisting species," in D. J. Futuym and M. Slatkin (eds.), *Coevolution,* Sunderland, Massachusetts: Sinauer Assoc., pp 404–430.

Simms, C., 1968, Crested newt, *Triturus cristatus* Laurentus, double brooded in an indoor aquarium, *British J. Herpetol.,* 4:43.

Simon, M. P., 1983, The ecology of parental care in a terrestrial breeding frog from New Guinea, *Behav. Ecol. Sociobiol.,* 14:61–67.

Simons, J. R., 1959, The distribution of the blood from the heart in some amphibians, *Proc. Zool. Soc. London,* 132:51–64.

Singh, L., I. F. Purdom, and K. W. Jones, 1976, Satellite DNA and evolution of sex chromosomes, *Chromosoma,* 59:43–62.

Sites, J. W. Jr., 1978, The foraging strategy of the dusky salamander, *Desmognathus fuscus* (Amphibia, Urodela, Plethodontidae): an empirical approach to predation theory, *J. Herpetol.,* 12:373–383.

Sivak, J. G., and M. R. Warburg, 1980, Optical metamorphosis of the eye of *Salamandra salamandra, Canadian J. Zool.,* 58:2059–2064.

Sivak, J. G., and M. R. Warburg, 1983, Changes in optical properties of the eye during metamorphosis of an anuran, *Pelobates syriacus, J. Comp. Physiol.,* 150(A):329–332.

Slater, P., and A. R. Main, 1963, Notes on the biology of *Notaden nichollsi* Parker (Anura, Leptodactylidae), *West. Australian Nat.,* 8:163–166.

Smith, A. K., 1977, Attraction of bullfrogs (Amphibia: Ranidae) to distress calls of immature frogs, *J. Herpetol.,* 11:234–235.

Smith, B. G., 1907, The life history and habits of *Cryptobranchus alleganiensis, Biol. Bull.,* 13:5–39.

Smith, C. C., 1959, Notes on the salamanders of Arkansas, 1. Life history of a neotenic, stream-dwelling form, *Proc. Arkansas Acad. Sci.,* 13:66–74.

Smith, C. L., 1955, Reproduction in female Amphibia, *Mem. Soc. Endocrinol.,* 4:39–56.

Smith, D. C., 1983, Factors controlling tadpole populations of the chorus frog *(Pseudacris triseriata)* on Isle Royale, Michigan, *Ecology,* 64:501–510.

Smith, G. C., 1976, Ecological energetics of three species of ectothermic vertebrates, *Ecology,* 57:252–264.

Smith, H. M., and R. B. Smith, 1971, *Synopsis of the Herpetofauna of Mexico. I. Analysis of the Literature on the Mexican Axolotl,* Augusta, West Virginia: Lundberg.

Smith, H. M., and E. H. Taylor, 1948, An annotated checklist and key to the Amphibia of Mexico, *Bull. U. S. Natl. Mus.,* 194:1–118.

Smith, R. E., 1941, Mating behavior in *Triturus torosus* and related newts, *Copeia,* 1941:255–262.

Smith-Gill, S. J., and V. Carver, 1981, "Biochemical characterization of organ differentiation and maturation," in L. I. Gilbert and E. Frieden (eds.), *Metamorphosis. A Problem in Developmental Biology. 2nd Edit.,* New York: Plenum Press, pp 491–544.

Smithson, T. R., and K. S. Thomson, 1982, The hyomandibular of *Eusthenopteron foordi* Whiteaves (Pisces: Crossopterygii) and the early evolution of the tetrapod stapes, *Zool. J. Linnean Soc.,* 74:93–103.

Snyder, G. K., and W. W. Weathers, 1975, Temperature adaptation in amphibians, *Amer. Nat.,* 109:93–101.

Snyder, W. F., and D. L. Jameson, 1965, Multivariable geographic variation of mating calls in populations of the Pacific tree frog *(Hyla regilla), Copeia,* 1965:129–142.

Sokol, O. M., 1962, The tadpole of *Hymenochirus boettgeri, Copeia,* 1962:272–284.

Sokol, O. M., 1969, Feeding in the pipid frog *Hymenochirus boettgeri* (Tornier), *Herpetologica,* 25:9–24.

Sokol, O. M., 1975, The phylogeny of anuran larvae: a new look, *Copeia,* 1975:1–23.

Sokol, O. M., 1977a, A subordinal classification of frogs (Amphibia: Anura), *J. Zool.,* 182:505–508.

Sokol, O. M., 1977b, The free swimming *Pipa* larvae, with a review of pipid larvae and pipid phylogeny (Anura: Pipidae), *J. Morph.,* 154:357–426.

Sotelo, C., 1976, "Morphology of the cerebellar cortex," in R. Llinás and W. Precht (eds.), *Frog Neurobiology,* Berlin: Springer-Verlag, pp 864–891.

Sotelo, C., and I. Grofova, 1976, "Ultrastructural features of the spinal cord," in R. Llinás and W. Precht (eds.), *Frog Neurobiology,* Berlin: Springer-Verlag, pp 707–727.

Spight, T. M., 1967a, The water economy of salamanders: exchange of water with soil, *Biol. Bull.,* 132:126–132.

Spight, T. M., 1967b, Population structure and biomass production by a stream salamander, *Amer. Midl. Nat.,* 78:437–447.

Špinar, Z. V., 1972, *Tertiary Frogs from Central Europe,* Prague: Academia, Czechoslovak Acad. Sci.

Spirito, A., 1939, Il significato dell'anaerobiosi negli embrioni di anfibi anuri, *Bol. Soc. Italiano Biol. Sper.,* 13:920–932.

Spotila, J. R., 1972, Role of temperature and water in the ecology of lungless salamanders, *Ecol. Monog.,* 42:95–125.

Spray, D. C., 1976, "Pain and temperature receptors of anurans," in R. Llinás and W. Precht (eds.), *Frog Neurobiology,* Berlin: Springer-Verlag, pp 607–628.

Sprules, W. G., 1974a, The adaptive significance of paedogenesis in the North American species of *Ambystoma* (Amphibia: Caudata): an hypothesis, *Canadian J. Zool.,* 52: 393–400.

Sprules, W. G., 1974b, Environmental factors and the incidence of neoteny in *Ambystoma gracile* (Baird) (Amphibia: Caudata), *Canadian J. Zool.,* 52:1545–1552.

Spurway, H., 1953, Genetics of specific and subspecific differences in European newts, *Symp. Soc. Exp. Bio.,* 7:200–238.

Stadtmüller, F., 1924, Studien am Urodelenschadel. I. Zur Entwicklungsgeschicte der Kopfskelette der *Salamandra maculosa, Zeit. Anat. Entwgesch.,* 75:149–225.

Starrett, P. H., 1960, Descriptions of tadpoles of Middle American frogs, *Misc. Publ. Mus. Zool. Univ. Michigan,* 110:1–37.

Starrett, P. H., 1967, Observations on the life history of the frogs of the family Atelopodidae, *Herpetologica,* 23:195–204.

Starrett, P. H., 1968, *The Phylogenetic Significance of the Jaw Musculature in Anuran Amphibians,* Ann Arbor: Univ. Michigan, Ph.D. Dissertion.

Starrett, P. H., 1973, "Evolutionary patterns in larval morphology," in J. L. Vial (ed.), *Evolutionary Biology of the Anurans: Contemporary Research on Major Problems,* Columbia: Univ. Missouri Press, pp 251–271.

Stearns, S. C., 1976, Life-history tactics: a review of the ideas, *Quart. Rev. Biol.,* 51:3–47.

Stebbins, R. C., 1949a, Observations on the laying, development, and hatching of the eggs of *Batrachoseps wrighti, Copeia,* 1949:161–168.

Stebbins, R. C., 1949b, Speciation in salamanders of the plethodontid genus *Ensatina, Univ. Calif. Publ. Zool.,* 48:377–526.

Stebbins, R. C., 1951, *Amphibians of Western North America,* Berkeley: Univ. California Press.

Stebbins, R. C., 1954, Natural history of the salamanders of the plethodontid genus *Ensatina, Univ. California Publ. Zool.,* 54:377–512.

Stebbins, R. C., and J. R. Hendrickson, 1959, Field studies of amphibians in Colombia, South America, *Univ. California Publ. Zool.,* 56:497–540.

Steinke, J. H., and D. G. Benson Jr., 1970, The structure and polysaccharide chemistry of the jelly envelopes of the egg of the frog, *Rana pipiens, J. Morph.,* 130:57–66.

Steinwascher, K., 1978, Interference and exploitation competition among tadpoles of *Rana utricularia, Ecology,* 59: 1039–1046.

Steinwascher, K., 1979, Host-parasite interaction as a potential population-regulating mechanism, *Ecology,* 60:884–890.

Stejneger, L., 1907, Herpetology of Japan and adjacent territory, *Bull. U. S. Natl. Mus.*, 58:1–577.

Stepanova, Z. L., 1974, The chemical nature of the products of metabolism of amphibian larvae, excreted into the water (in Russian), *Soviet J. Ecol.*, 5:148–149.

Stephens, L. B., 1965, The influence of thyroxin upon Rohon-Beard cells of *Rana pipiens* larvae, *Amer. Zool.*, 5:222.

Stephenson, E. M., E. S. Robinson, and N. G. Stephenson, 1972, Karyotype variation within the genus *Leiopelma* (Amphibia: Anura), *Caldasia*, 14:691–702.

Stephenson, E. M., E. S. Robinson, and N. G. Stephenson, 1974, Interspceific relationships of *Leiopelma* (Amphibia: Anura): further karyological evidence, *Experientia*, 30:1248–1250.

Stephenson, E. M., and N. G. Stephenson, 1957, Field observations on the New Zealand frog, *Leiopelma* Fitzinger, *Trans. Roy. Soc. New Zealand*, 84:867–882.

Stephenson, N. G., 1951a, On the development of the chondrocranium and visceral arches of *Leiopelma archeyi*, *Trans. Zool. Soc. London*, 27:203–253.

Stephenson, N. G., 1951b, Observations on the development of the amphicoelous frogs, *Leiopelma* and *Ascaphus*, *Zool. J. Linnaean Soc.*, 42:18–28.

Stephenson, N. G., 1955, On the development of the frog *Leiopelma hochstetteri* Fitzinger, *Proc. Zool. Soc. London*, 124:785–795.

Stephenson, N. G., and H. R. de Beer, 1951, Observations on the development of the amphicoelous frogs *Leiopelma* and *Ascaphus*, *Zool. J. Linnaean Soc.*, 42:18–28.

Steward, J. W., 1970, *The Tailed Amphibians of Europe*, New York: Taplinger Publ. Co.

Stewart, M. M., 1958, Seasonal variation in the teeth of the two-lined salamander, *Copeia*, 1958:190–196.

Stewart, M. M., and F. H. Pough, 1983, Population density of tropical forest frogs: relation to retreat sites, *Science*, 221:570–572.

Stiffler, D. F., and R. H. Alvardo, 1974, Renal function in response to reduced osmotic load in larval salamanders, *Amer. J. Physiol.*, 266:1243–1249.

Stingo, V., 1974, Karyology of *Geotrypetes seraphini* (Amphibia, Apoda), *Caryologia*, 27:485–492.

Storez, R. A., 1969, Observations on the courtship of *Ambystoma laterale*, *J. Herpetol.*, 3:87–95.

Storm, R. M., 1960, Notes on the breeding biology of the red-legged frog *(Rana aurora aurora)*, *Herpetologica*, 16:251–259.

Straughan, I. R., 1968, A taxonomic review of the genus *Mixophys* (Anura: Leptodactylidae), *Proc. Linnean Soc. New South Wales*, 93:52–59.

Straughan, I. R., 1973, "Evolution of anuran mating calls," in J. L. Vial (ed.), *Evolutionary Biology of the Anurans: Contemporary Research on Major Problems,* Columbia: Univ. Missouri Press, pp 321–327.

Straughan, I. R., 1975, An analysis of the mechanisms of mating call discrimination in the frogs *Hyla regilla* and *H. cadaverina*, *Copeia*, 1975:415–424.

Straughan, I. R., and W. R. Heyer, 1976, A functional analysis of the mating calls of the Neotropical frog genera of the *Leptodactylus* complex (Amphibia, Leptodactylidae), *Pap. Avulsos Zool.*, 29:221–245.

Straughan, I. R., and A. R. Main, 1966, Speciation and polymorphism in the genus *Crinia* Tschudi (Anura, Leptodactylidae) in Queensland, *Proc. Roy. Soc. Queensland*, 78:11–28.

Strong, D. R., L. A. Syska, and D. I. Simberloff, 1979, Tests of community-wide character displacement against null hypotheses, *Evolution*, 33:897–913.

Stuart, L. C., 1951, The distributional implications of temperature tolerance and hemoglobin values in the toads *Bufo marinus* (Linnaeus) and *Bufo bocourti* Brocchi, *Copeia*, 1951:220–221.

Stuart, L. C., 1961, Some observations on the natural history of tadpoles of *Rhinophrynus dorsalis* Duméril and Bibron, *Herpetologica*, 17:73–79.

Subtelny, S., and O. Bradt, 1961, Transplantation of blastula nuclei into activated eggs from the body cavity and from the uterus of *Rana pipiens*, *Devel. Biol.*, 3:96–114.

Sughrue, M., 1969, Underwater acrobats, *Brookfield Bandarlog*, 37:6–10.

Svinkin, V. B., 1962, The heat resistance of the oocytes of the frog in early stages of cleavage (in Russian; English translation by Consultants Bureau), *Dokl. Akad. Nauk. SSR*, 145:913–916.

Swammerdam, J., 1737–1738, "Of historie der insecten," in H. Boerhave (ed.), *Bybel der Natuure* (2 vols., 53 pls.), Leiden: I. Severin and P. van der Aa.

Sweet, S. S., 1977a, Natural metamorphosis in *Eurycea neotenes*, and the generic allocation of the Texas *Eurycea* (Amphibia: Plethodontidae), *Herpetologica*, 33:364–375.

Sweet, S. S., 1977b, *Eurycea tridentifera*, *Cat. Amer. Amphib. Rept.*, 199:1–2.

Szarski, H., 1948, On the blood-vascular system of the Salientia, *Bull. Acad. Polonaise Sci. Ser. B*, 1947:146–211.

Szarski, H., 1962, The origin of the Amphibia, *Quart. Rev. Biol.*, 37:189–241.

Szarski, H., 1970, Changes in the amount of DNA in cell nuclei during vertebrate evolution, *Nature*, 226:651–652.

Szarski, H., and G. Czopek, 1966, Erythrocyte diameter in some amphibians and reptiles, *Bull. Acad. Polonaise Ser. Sci. Biol.*, 14:433–437.

Tabachnick, W. J., 1977, Geographic variation of five biochemical polymorphisms in *Notophthalmus viridescens*, *J. Heredity*, 68:117–122.

Tago, K., 1929, Notes on the habits and life history of *Megalobatrachus japonicus*, *Proc. 10th Internat. Congr. Zool. Budapest, 1927*, 4:828–838.

Tahara, Y., 1959, Table of the normal developmental stages of the frog, Rana japonica. 1. Early development (stages 1-25), *Japan. J. Exp. Morph.*, 13:49–60.

Tahara, Y., 1974, Table of normal developmental stages of the frog .Rana japonica 2.Late development (stages 26-40), *Mem. Osaka Kyoiku Univ. (Nat. Sci. Appl. Sci.)*, 23:33–53.

Taigen, T. L., 1981, "Water balance of the eggs of *Eleutherodactylus coqui*: importance of parental brooding," in *Annual Meeting S.S.A.R./H.L.*, Memphis, Tennessee, p 72.

Taigen, T. L., S. B. Emerson, and F. H. Pough, 1982, Ecological correlates of anuran exercise physiology, *Oecologia*, 52:49–56.

Taigen, T. L., and F. H. Pough, 1981, Activity metabolism of the toad *(Bufo americanus)*: ecological consequences of ontogenetic change, *J. Comp. Physiol.*, 144:247–252.

Taigen, T. L., and F. H. Pough, 1983, Prey preference, foraging behavior, and metabolic characteristics of frogs, *Amer. Nat.*, 122:509–520.

Tamini, E., 1947, Effetti della temperatura sullo sviluppo di alcuni anfibi, *Rend. Ist. Lomb. Cl. Sci. Mat. Nat.*, 80:59–71.

Tandy, M., and R. Keith, 1972, "*Bufo* of Africa," in W. F. Blair (ed.), *Evolution in the Genus* Bufo, Austin: Univ. Texas Press, pp 119–170.

Tandy, M., and J. Tandy, 1976, Evolution of acoustic behavior of African *Bufo*, *Zool. Africana*, 11:349–368.

Tanner, W. W., 1953, Herpetological notes, *Herpetologica*, 9:139–140.

Taurog, A., 1974, The effect of TSH and long acting thyroid stimulator on the thyroid ^{131}I metabolism and metamorphosis in the Mexican axolotl *(Ambystoma mexicanum)*, *Gen. Comp. Endocrinol.*, 24:257–266.

Taurog, A., C. Oliver, R. L. Eskay, J. C. Porter, and J. M. McKenzie, 1974, The role of TRH in the neoteny of the Mexican axolotl *(Ambystoma mexicanum)*, *Gen. Comp. Endocrinol.*, 24:267–279.

Taylor, A. C., and J. J. Kollros, 1946, Stages in the normal development of *Rana pipiens* larvae, *Anat. Rec.*, 94:7–23.

Taylor, D. H., 1972, Extra-optic photoreception and compass orientation in larval and adult salamanders *(Ambystoma tigrinum)*, *Anim. Behav.*, 20:233–236.

Taylor, D. H., and D. E. Ferguson, 1970, Extraoptic celestial orientation in the southern cricket frog *Acris gryllus, Science,* 168:390–392.

Taylor, D. H., and S. I. Guttman (eds.), 1977, *The Reproductive Biology of Amphibians,* New York: Plenum Press.

Taylor, E. H., 1920, Philippine Amphibia, *Philippine J. Sci.,* 16:213–359.

Taylor, E. H., 1952, A review of the frogs and toads of Costa Rica, *Univ. Kansas Sci. Bull.,* 35:577–942.

Taylor, E. H., 1954, Frog-egg eating tadpoles of *Anotheca coronata* (Stejneger) (Salientia, Hylidae), *Univ. Kansas Sci. Bull.,* 36:589–596.

Taylor, E. H., 1962, The amphibian fauna of Thailand, *Univ. Kansas Sci. Bull.,* 43:265–599.

Taylor, E. H., 1968, *The Caecilians of the World,* Lawrence: Univ. Kansas Press.

Taylor, E. H., 1969a, A new family of African Gymnophiona, *Univ. Kansas Sci. Bull.,* 48:297–305.

Taylor, E. H., 1969b, Skulls of Gymnophiona and their significance in the taxonomy of the group, *Univ. Kansas Sci. Bull.,* 48:585–687.

Taylor, E. H., 1972, Squamation in caecilians, with an atlas of scales, *Univ. Kansas Sci. Bull.,* 49:986–1164.

Taylor, E. H., 1977a, Comparative anatomy of caecilian anterior vertebrae, *Univ. Kansas Sci. Bull.,* 51:219–231.

Taylor, E. H., 1977b, The comparative anatomy of caecilian mandibles and their teeth, *Univ. Kansas Sci. Bull.,* 51:261–282.

Taylor, J., 1983, Size-specific associations of larval and neotenic northwestern salamanders, *Ambystoma gracile, J. Herpetol.,* 17:203–209.

Taylor, J. D., 1969, The effects of intermedin on the ultrastructure of amphibian iridophores, *Gen. Comp. Endocrinol.,* 12:405–416.

Test, F. H., and B. A. Bingham, 1948, Census of a population of the red-backed salamander *(Plethodon cinereus), Amer. Midl. Nat.,* 39:362–372.

Tester, J. R., and W. J. Breckenridge, 1964, Population dynamics of the Manitoba toad, *Bufo hemiophrys,* in northwestern Minnesota, *Ecology,* 45:592–601.

Theis, A., 1932, Histologische Untersuchen über die Epidermis im Individualcyclus von Salamandra maculosa Laur., *Zeit. Wissen. Zool.,* 140:356–420.

Theron, J. G., 1952, On the cranial morphology of Ambystoma maculatum (Shaw), *South African J. Sci.,* 48:343–365.

Thesleff, S., and K. Schmidt-Nielsen, 1962, Osmotic tolerance of the muscles of the crab-eating frog, *Rana cancrivora, J. Cell. Comp. Physiol.,* 59:31–34.

Thexton, A. J., D. B. Wake, and M. H. Wake, 1977, Tongue function in the salamander *Bolitoglossa occidentalis, Arch. Oral Biol.,* 22:361–366.

Thiébaud, C. H., and M. Fischberg, 1977, DNA content in the genus *Xenopus, Chromosoma,* 59:253–257.

Thomson, K. S., 1972, An attempt to recontruct evolutionary changes in the cellular DNA content of lungfish, *J. Exp. Zool.,* 180:363–372.

Thorn, R., 1962, Protection of the brood by a male salamander, *Hynobius nebulosus, Copeia,* 1962:638–640.

Thorn, R., 1963, Contribution à l'étude d'une salamandre japonaise l'Hynobius *nebulosus* (Schlegel). Comportement et reproduction en captivité, *Arch. Inst. Grand-Duc. Luxembourg, Sec. Sci. Nouv. Ser.,* 29:201–215.

Thorn, R., 1967, Nouvelles observations sur l'éthologie sexuelle de l'Hynobius *nebulosus* (Temminck et Schlegel), *Arch. Inst. Grand-Duc. Luxembourg, Sec. Sci. Nouv. Ser.,* 32:267–271.

Thorn, R., 1968, *Les Salamandres d'Europe, d'Asie, et d'Afrique du Nord,* Paris: Ed. Paul Lechevalie.

Thornton, W. A., 1960, Population dynamics in *Bufo woodhousei* and *Bufo valliceps, Texas J. Sci.,* 12:176–200.

Thorson, T. B., 1964, The partitioning of body water in Amphibia, *Physiol. Zool.,* 37:395–399.

Throckmorton, L. H., 1978, "Molecular phylogenetics," in J. A. Romberger, R. H. Foote, L. Knutson and P. L. Lentz (eds.),

Biosystematics in Agriculture, Montclair, New Jersey: Allanheld, Osmum And Co., pp 221–239.

Thurow, G. R., 1976, Aggression and competition in eastern *Plethodon* (Amphibia, Urodela, Plethodontidae), *J. Herpetol.,* 10:277–291.

Thurow, G. R., and H. J. Gould, 1977, Sound production in a caecilian, *Herpetologica,* 33:234–237.

Tian, W., and S. Hu, 1983, Taxonomic study on genus *Megophrys,* with descriptions of two new genera, *Acta Herpetol. Sinica,* 2(2):45–48.

Tihen, J. A., 1958, Comments on the osteology and phylogeny of ambystomatid salamanders, *Bull. Florida St. Mus. Biol. Sci.,* 3:1–50.

Tihen, J. A., 1965, Evolutionary trends in frogs, *Amer. Zool.,* 5:309–318.

Tihen, J. A., 1969, *Ambystoma, Cat. Amer. Amphib. Rept.,* 75:1–4.

Tilley, S. G., 1964, A quantitative study of the shrinkage in the digestive tract of the tiger salamander (*Ambystoma tigrinum* Green) during metamorphosis, *J. Ohio Herpetol. Soc.,* 4:81–85.

Tilley, S. G., 1968, Size-fecundity relationships and their evolutionary implications in five desmognathine salamanders, *Evolution,* 22:806–816.

Tilley, S. G., 1972, Aspects of parental care and embryonic development in *Desmognathus ochrophaeus, Copeia,* 1972:532–540.

Tilley, S. G., 1973, Life histories and natural selection in populations of the salamander *Desmognathus ochrophaeus, Ecology,* 54:3–17.

Tilley, S. G., 1977, "Studies of life histories and reproduction in North American plethodontid salamanders," in D. H. Taylor and S. I. Guttman (eds.), *The Reproductive Biology of Amphibians,* New York: Plenum Press, pp 1–41.

Tilley, S. G., 1981, A new species of *Desmognathus* (Amphibia: Caudata: Plethodontidae) from the southern Appalachian Mountains, *Occ. Pap. Mus. Zool. Univ. Michigan,* 695:1–23.

Tilley, S. G., R. B. Merritt, B. Wu, and R. Highton, 1978, Genetic differentiation in salamanders of the *Desmognathus ochrophaeus* complex (Plethodontidae), *Evolution,* 32:93–115.

Tilley, S. G., and P. M. Schwerdtfeger, 1981, Electrophoretic variation in Appalachian populations of the *Desmognathus fuscus* complex (Amphibia: Plethodontidae), *Copeia,* 1981:109–119.

Tinsley, R. C., 1981, Interactions between *Xenopus* species (Anura Pipidae), *Monit. Zool. Italiano N.S. Suppl.,* 15:133–150.

Toft, C. A., 1980a, Feeding ecology of thirteen syntopic species of anurans in a seasonal tropical environment, *Oecologia,* 45:131–141.

Toft, C. A., 1980b, :Seasonal variation in populations of Panamanian litter frogs and their prey comparison of wetter and drier sites, *Oecologia,* 47:34–38.

Toft, C. A., 1982, Community structure of litter anurans in a tropical forest, Makokov, Gabon: a preliminary analysis in the minor dry season, *Terre et Vie,* 36:223–232.

Toft, C. A., 1985, Resource partitioning in amphibians and reptiles, *Copeia,* in press.

Toft, C. A., and W. E. Duellman, 1979, Anurans of the lower Río Llullapichis, Amazonian Peru: a preliminary analysis of community structure, *Herpetologica,* 35:71–77.

Tomson, O. H., and D. E. Ferguson, 1972, Y-axis orientation in larvae and juveniles of three species of *Ambystoma, Herpetologica,* 28:6–9.

Townes, R. L., 1953, Effects of proteolytic enzymes on the fertilization membrane and jelly layers of the amphibian embryo, *Exp. Cell Res.,* 4:96–101.

Townsend, D. S., and M. M. Stewart, 1985, Direct development in *Eleutherodactylus coqui:* a staging table, *Copeia,* 1985:423–436.

Townsend, D. S., M. M. Stewart, and F. H. Pough, 1984, Male parental care and its adaptive significance in a neotropical frog, *Anim. Behav.,* 32:421–431.

Townsend, D. S., M. M. Stewart, F. H. Pough, and P. F. Brussard, 1981, Internal fertilization in an oviparous frog, *Science,* 212:469–471.

Tracy, C. R., 1973, Observations on social behavior in immature California toads *(Bufo boreas)* during feeding, *Copeia,* 1973:342–345.

Tracy, C. R., 1975, "Water and energy relations of terrestrial amphibians: insights from mechanistic modeling," in D. M. Gates and R. Schmerl (eds.), *Perspectives in Biophysical Ecology,* New York: Springer-Verlag, pp 325–346.

Tracy, C. R., 1976, A model of the dynamic exchanges of water and energy between a terrestrial amphibian and its environment, *Ecol. Monog.,* 46:293–326.

Tracy, C. R., and J. W. Dole, 1969, Orientation of displaced California toads, *Bufo boreas,* to their breeding sites, *Copeia,* 1969:693–700.

Travis, J., 1983, Variation in development patterns of larval anurans in temporary ponds. I. Persistent variation within a *Hyla gratiosa* population, *Evolution,* 37:496–512.

Trewavas, E., 1933, The hyoid and larynx of the Anura, *Phil. Trans. Roy. Soc. London,* 222(B):401–527.

Trivers, R. L., 1972, "Parental investment and sexual selection," in B. G. Campbell (ed.), *Sexual Selection and the Descent of Man,* Chicago: Aldine Press, pp 136–179.

Trowbridge, M. S., 1941, Studies on the normal development of *Scaphiopus bombifrons* Cope. I. The cleavage period, *Trans. Amer. Micros. Soc.,* 60:508–526.

Trowbridge, M. S., 1942, Studies on the normal development of *Scaphiopus bombifrons* Cope. II. The later embryonic and larval periods, *Trans. Amer. Micros. Soc.,* 61:66–83.

Trueb, L., 1966, Morphology and development of the skull in the frog *Hyla septentrionalis, Copeia,* 1966:562–573.

Trueb, L., 1968, Cranial osteology of the hylid frog, Smilisca baudini, *Univ. Kansas Publ. Mus. Nat. Hist.,* 18:11–35.

Trueb, L., 1969, *Pternohyla, P. dentata, P. fodiens, Cat. Amer. Amphib. Rept.,* 77:1–4.

Trueb, L., 1970a, Evolutionary relationships of casque-head tree frogs with co-ossified skulls (Family Hylidae), *Univ. Kansas Publ. Mus. Nat. Hist.,* 18:547–716.

Trueb, L., 1970b, The generic status of *Hyla siemersi* Mertens, *Herpetologica,* 26:254–267.

Trueb, L., 1971, Phylogenetic relationships of certain Neotropical toads with the description of a new genus (Anura: Bufonidae), *Contrib. Sci. Los Angeles Co. Mus. Nat. Hist.,* 216:1–40.

Trueb, L., 1973, "Bones, frogs, and evolution," in J. L. Vial (ed.), *Evolutionary Biology of the Anurans: Contemporary Research on Major Problems,* Columbia: Univ. Missouri Press, pp 65–132.

Trueb, L., 1974, Systematic relationships of Neotropical horned frogs, genus *Hemiphractus* (Anura: Hylidae), *Occ. Pap. Mus. Nat. Hist. Univ. Kansas,* 29:1–60.

Trueb, L., 1979, Leptodactylid frogs of the genus *Telmatobius* in Ecuador with the description of a new species, *Copeia,* 1979:714–733.

Trueb, L., 1984, Description of a new species of *Pipa* (Anura: Pipidae) from Panama, *Herpetologica,* 40:225–234.

Trueb, L., 1985, A summary of osteocranial development in anurans with notes on the sequence of cranial ossification in *Rhinophrynus dorsalis* (Anura: Pipoidea: Rhinophrynidae), *S. African J. Sci.:,* 81:181–185.

Trueb, L., and P. Alberch, 1985, "Miniaturization and the anuran skull: a case of heterochrony," in H.-R. Dunker and G. Fleischer (eds.), *International Symposium on Vertebrate Morphology, Fortsch. Zool.,* in press.

Trueb, L., and D. C. Cannatella, 1982, The cranial osteology and hyolaryngeal apparatus of *Rhinophrynus dorsalis* (Anura: Rhinophrynidae) with comparisons to Recent pipid frogs, *J. Morph.,* 171:11–40.

Trueb, L., and W. E. Duellman, 1971, A synopsis of Neotropical hylid frogs, genus *Osteocephalus, Occ. Pap. Mus. Nat. Hist. Univ. Kansas,* 1:1–47.

Trueb, L., and C. Gans, 1983, Feeding specializations of the Mexican burrowing toad, *Rhinophrynus dorsalis* (Anura: Rhinophrynidae), *J. Zool. London,* 199:198–208.

Trueb, L., and M. J. Tyler, 1974, Systematics and evolution of the Greater Antillean hylid frogs, *Occ. Pap. Mus. Nat. Hist. Univ. Kansas,* 24:1–60.

Trufell, G. T., 1954, A macroscopic and microscopic study of the mental hedonic gland clusters of some plethodontid salamanders, *Univ. Kansas Sci. Bull.,* 36:3–39.

Tschudi, J. J., 1838, *Classification der Batrachier,* Neuchatel.

Tsutsui, Y., 1931, Notes on the behavior of the common Japanese newt, *Diemyctylus pyrrhogaster* Boie. 1) Breeding habits, *Mem. Coll. Sci. Kyoto Imp. Univ.,* 7(B):159–167.

Tuff, D. W., and D. G. Huffman, 1977, An index to the genera of hosts in Yamaguti's Systema Helminthum, *Texas J. Sci.,* 28:161–191.

Tupa, D. D., and W. K. Davis, 1976, Population dynamics of the San Marcos salamander, *Eurycea nana* Bishop, *Texas J. Sci.,* 27:179–195.

Turner, C. D., and J. T. Bagnara, 1976, *General Endocrinology, 6th Edition.* Philadelphia: W. B. Saunders Co.

Turner, F. B., 1958, Life history of the western spotted frog in Yellowstone National Park, *Herpetologica,* 14:96–100.

Turner, F. B., 1959, An analysis of the feeding habits of Rana p. pretiosa in Yellowstone Park, Wyoming, *Amer. Midl. Nat.,* 61:403–413.

Turner, F. B., 1960a, Postmetamorphic growth in anurans, *Amer. Midl. Nat.,* 64:327–338.

Turner, F. B., 1960b, Population structure and dynamics of the western spotted frog, *Rana pretiosa pretiosa,* in Yellowstone Park, Wyoming, *Ecol. Monog.,* 30:251–278.

Turner, F. B., 1962, The demography of frogs and toads, *Quart. Rev. Biol.,* 37:303–314.

Turney, L. D., and V. H. Hutchinson, 1974, Metabolic scope, oxygen debt and the diurnal oxygen consumption cycle of the leopard frog, *Rana pipiens, Comp. Biochem. Physiol.,* 49(A):583–601.

Tuttle, M. D., and M. J. Ryan, 1981, Bat predation and the evolution of frog vocalizations in the tropics, *Science,* 214:677–678.

Tuttle, M. D., and M. J. Ryan, 1982, The role of synchronized calling, ambient light, and ambient noise in anti-bat-predator behavior of a treefrog, *Behav. Ecol. Sociobiol.,* 11:125–131.

Tuttle, M. D., L. K. Taft, and M. J. Ryan, 1981, Acoustical location of calling frogs by philander opossums, *Biotropica,* 13:233–234.

Tuttle, M. D., L. K. Taft, and M. J. Ryan, 1982, Evasive behaviour of a frog in response to bat predation, *Anim. Behav.,* 30:393–397.

Twitty, V. C., 1955, Field experiments on the biology and genetic relationships of the California species of *Triturus, J. Exp. Zool.,* 129:129–148.

Twitty, V. C., 1961, "Experiments on homing behavior and speciation in Taricha," in W. F. Blair (ed.), *Vertebrate Speciation,* Austin: Univ. Texas Press, pp 415–459.

Twitty, V. C., 1966, *Of Scientists and Salamanders,* San Francisco: Freeman & Co.

Twitty, V. C., and D. Bodenstein, 1948, *"Triturus torosus,"* in R. Rugh (ed.), *Experimental Embryology,* Minneapolis: Burgess Pub. Co., p 94.

Twitty, V. C., D. Grant, and O. Anderson, 1967, Long distance homing in the newt *Taricha rivularis, Proc. Nat. Acad. Sci. U. S. A.,* 50:51–58.

Tyler, M. J., 1963a, A taxonomic study of amphibians and reptiles of the central highlands of New Guinea, with notes on their ecology and biology. I. Anura: Microhylidae, *Trans. Roy. Soc. S. Australia,* 86:11–29.

Tyler, M. J., 1963b, A taxonomic study of amphibians and reptiles of the central highlands of New Guinea, with notes on their ecology and biology. II. Anura: Ranidae and Hylidae, *Trans. Roy. Soc. S. Australia,* 86:105–130.

Tyler, M. J., 1967, Microhylid frogs of New Britain, *Trans. Roy. Soc. S. Australia,* 91:187–190.

Tyler, M. J., 1971a, The phylogenetic significance of vocal sac structure in hylid frogs, *Univ. Kansas Publ. Mus. Nat. Hist.,* 19:319–360.

Tyler, M. J., 1971b, Observations on anuran myo-integumental attachments associated with vocal sac apparatus, *J. Nat. Hist.,* 5:225–231.

Tyler, M. J., 1972, Superficial mandibular musculature, vocal sacs and the phylogeny of Australo-Papuan leptodactylid frogs, *Rec. South Australian Mus.,* 16:1–20.

Tyler, M. J., 1974, Superficial mandibular musculature and vocal sac structure of the mexican burrowing toad, *Rhinophrynus dorsalis, Herpetologica,* 30:313–316.

Tyler, M. J., 1976, *Frogs,* Sydney: Collins, Ltd.

Tyler, M. J., 1979, "Herpetofaunal relationships of South America with Australia," in W. E. Duellman (ed.), *The South American Herpetofauna: its Origin, Evolution, and Dispersal, Monog. Mus. Nat. Hist. Univ. Kansas,* 7:1–485.

Tyler, M. J., 1982, Tertiary frogs from South Australia, *Alcheringa,* 6:101–103.

Tyler, M. J. (ed.), 1983, *The Gastric Brooding Frog,* London: Croom Helm.

Tyler, M. J., and D. B. Carter, 1981, Oral birth of the young of the gastric brooding frog *Rheobatrachus silus, Anim. Behav.,* 29:280–282.

Tyler, M. J., and M. Davies, 1978a, Species-groups within the Australopapuan hylid frog genus *Litoria* Tschudi, *Australian J. Zool.,* 63:1–47.

Tyler, M. J., and M. Davies, 1978b, Phylogenetic relationships of Australian hyline and neotropical phyllomedusine frogs of the family Hylidae, *Herpetologica,* 34:219–224.

Tyler, M. J., and M. Davies, 1979a, Redefinition and evolutionary origin of the Australopapuan frog genus *Nyctimystes* Stejneger, *Australian J. Zool.,* 27:755–772.

Tyler, M. J., and M. Davies, 1979b, Foam nest construction by Australian leptodactylid frogs (Amphibia, Anura, Leptodactylidae), *J. Herpetol.,* 13:509–510.

Tyler, M. J., M. Davies, and M. King, 1978, The australian frog *Chiroleptes dahlii* Boulenger: its systematic position, morphology, chromosomes and distribution, *Trans. Royal Soc. S. Australia,* 102:17–24.

Tyler, M. J., M. Davies, and A. A. Martin, 1981, Australian frogs of the leptodactylid genus *Uperoleia* Gray, *Australian J. Zool. Suppl. Ser.,* 79:1–64.

Tyler, M. J., A. A. Martin, and M. Davies, 1979, Biology and systematics of a new limnodynastine genus (Anura: Leptodactylidae) from north-western Australia, *Australian J. Zool.,* 27:135–150.

Tyler, M. J., J. D. Roberts, and M. Davies, 1980, Field observations on *Arenophryne rotunda* Tyler, a leptodactylid frog inhabiting coastal sandhills, *Australian Wildl. Res.,* 7:295–304.

Tyler, M. J., L. A. Smith, and R. E. Johnstone, 1984, *Frogs of Western Australia,* Perth: Western Australian Mus.

Tymowska, J., 1973, Karyotype analysis of *Xenopus tropicalis* Gray, Pipidae, *Cytogenet. Cell. Genet.,* 12:297–304.

Tymowska, J., 1977, A comparative study of the karyotypes of eight *Xenopus* species and subspecies possessing a 36-chromosome complement, *Cytogenet. Cell. Genet.,* 18:165–181.

Tymowska, J., and M. Fischberg, 1973, Chromosome complements of the genus *Xenopus, Chromosoma,* 44:335–342.

Ueck, M., M. Vaupel-von Harnack, and Y. Morita, 1971, Weitere experimentelle und neuroanatomische Untersuchungen an den Nervenbahnen des Pinealkomplexes der Anuren, *Zeit. Zellforsch.,* 116:250–274.

Ultsch, G. R., 1973, Observations on the life history of *Siren lacertina, Herpetologica,* 29:304–305.

Ultsch, G. R., 1974, Gas exchange and metabolism in the sirenidae (Amphibia: Caudata). I. Oxygen consumption of submerged sirenids as a function of body size and respiratory surface area, *Comp. Biochem. Physiol.,* 47(A):485–498.

Ultsch, G. R., 1976, "Eco-physiological studies of some metabolic and respiratory adaptations of sirenid salamanders," in G. M. Hughs (ed.), *Respiration of Amphibious Vertebrates,* New York: Academic Press, pp 287–312.

Underhill, J. C., 1960, Breeding and growth in Woodhouse's toad, *Herpetologica,* 16:237–242.

Ushakov, B., 1964, Thermostability of cells and proteins and its significance in speciation, *Physiol. Rev.,* 44:518–560.

Usui, M., and M. Hamsaki, 1939, Illustration of stages of development of *Hynobius nigrescens* (in Japanese), *Zool. Mag. (Tokyo),* 51:195–207.

Utsunomiya, Y., and T. Utsonomiya, 1977, On the development of *Tylotriton andersoni* (in Japanese, English summary), *J. Fac. Fish. Anim. Husb. Hiroshima Univ.,* 16:65–76.

Uzzell, T. M. Jr., 1963, Natural triploidy in salamanders related to *Ambystoma jeffersonianum, Science,* 139:113–115.

Uzzell, T. M. Jr., 1964, Relations of the diploid and triploid species of the *Ambystoma jeffersonianum* complex (Amphibia, Caudata), *Copeia,* 1964:257–300.

Uzzell, T. M. Jr., 1982, Immunological relationship of western palearctic water frogs (Salientia: Ranidae), *Amphib.-Rept.,* 3:135–143.

Uzzell, T. M. Jr., and L. Berger, 1975, Electrophoretic phenotypes of *Rana ridibunda, Rana lessonae,* and their hybridogenetic associate, *Rana esculenta, Proc. Acad. Nat. Sci. Philadelphia,* 127:13–24.

Uzzell, T. M. Jr., L. Berger, and R. Günther, 1975, Diploid and triploid progeny from a diploid female *Rana esculenta* (Amphibia, Salientia), *Proc. Acad. Nat. Sci. Philadelphia,* 127:81–91.

Uzzell, T. M. Jr., R. Günther, and L. Berger, 1977, *Rana ridibunda* and *Rana esculenta:* a leaky hybridogenetic system (Amphibia, Salientia), *Proc. Acad. Nat. Sci. Philadelphia,* 128:147–171.

Valdivieso, D., and J. R. Tamsitt, 1965, Reproduction in a Neotropical salamander *Bolitoglossa adspersa* (Peters), *Herpetologica,* 21:228–236.

Valdivieso, D., and J. R. Tamsitt, 1974, Thermal relations of the Neotropical frog *Hyla labialis* (Anura: Hylidae), *Life Sci. Occ. Pap. Royal Ontario Mus.,* 26:1–10.

Valentine, B. D., and D. M. Dennis, 1964, A comparison of the gill-arch system and fins of three genera of larval salamanders, *Rhyacotriton, Gyrinophilus,* and *Ambystoma, Copeia,* 1964:196–201.

Valett, B. B., and D. L. Jameson, 1961, The embryology of *Eleutherodactylus augusti latrans, Copeia,* 1961:103–109.

Van Berkum, F. H., F. H. Pough, M. M. Stewart, and P. F. Brussard, 1982, Altitudinal and interspecific differences in the rehydration abilities of Puerto Rican frogs *(Eleutherodactylus), Physiol. Zool.,* 55:130–136.

Van Beurden, E. K., 1979, Gamete development in relation to season, moisture, energy reserve, and size in the Australian water-holding frog, *Cyclorana platycephalus, Herpetologica,* 35:370–374.

Van Beurden, E. K., 1980, Energy metabolism of dormant Australian water-holding frogs *(Cyclorana platycephalus), Copeia,* 1980:787–799.

Van de Kamer, J. C., 1965, Histological structure and cytology of the pineal complex in fishes, amphibians and reptiles, *Progr. Brain Res.,* 10:30–48.

Vandel, A., and M. Bouillon, 1959, La réproduction du protée *(Proteus anguineus), Compt. Rend. Acad. Sci. Paris,* 248:1267–1272.

Van Dijk, D. E., 1955, The "tail" of Ascaphus: a historical résumé and new histological-anatomical details, *Ann. Univ. Stellenbosch,* 31:1–71.

Van Dijk, D. E., 1959, On the cloacal region of Anura in particular of larval Ascaphus, *Ann. Univ. Stellenbosch,* 35:169–249.

Van Dijk, D. E., 1972, The behaviour of southern African anuran tadpoles with particular reference to their ecology and related external morphological features, *Zool. Africana,* 7: 49–52.

Vaz-Ferreira, R., and A. Gehrau, 1975, Comportamiento epimeletico de la rana comun, *Leptodactylus ocellatus* (L.) (Amphibia, Leptodactylidae). I. Atencion de la cria y actividades alimentarias y agresivas relacionados, *Physis,* 34:1–14.

Veloso M., A., 1977, Aggressive behavior and the generic relationships of *Caudiverbera caudiverbera* (Amphibia: Leptodactylidae), *Herpetologica,* 33:434-442.

Veloso M., A., and P. Iturra C., 1979, Posibilidades del análisis citogenético en un estudio de bandeo cromosómico en dos especies de anfibios (Anura-Leptodactylidae), *Arch Biol. Med. Exper.,* 12:91–96.

Vernberg, F. J., 1952, The oxygen consumption of two species of salamanders at different seasons of the year, *Physiol. Zool.,* 25:243–249.

Vial, J. L., 1968, The ecology of the tropical salamander, *Bolitoglossa subpalmata,* in Costa Rica, *Rev. Biol. Trop.,* 15: 13–115.

Vial, J. L., and F. B. Prieb, 1966, Antibiotic assay of dermal secretions from the salamander, *Plethodon cinereus, Herpetologica,* 22:284–286.

Vial, J. L., and F. B. Prieb, 1967, An investigation of antibiosis as a function of brooding behavior in the salamander, *Plethodon cinereus, Trans. Missouri Acad. Sci.,* 1:37–40.

Vigny, C., 1979, The mating calls of 12 species and sub-species of the genus *Xenopus* (Amphibia: Anura), *J. Zool.,* 188: 103–122.

Vijayakumar, S., C. B. Jørgensen, and K. Kjaer, 1971, Regulation of the ovarian cycle in the toad *Bufo bufo bufo* (L.): effects of autografting pars distalis of the hypophysis, of extirpating gonadotropic hypothalamic region, and of parietal ovariectomy, *Gen. Comp. Endocrinol.,* 17:432–443.

Villa, J., 1979, Two fungi lethal to frog eggs in Central America, *Copeia,* 1979:650–655.

Villa, J., 1980, "Frogflies" from Central and South America with notes on other organisms of the amphibian egg microhabitat, *Brenesia,* 17:49–68.

Villa, J., R. W. McDiarmid, and J. M. Gallardo, 1982, Arthropod predators of leptodactylid frog foam nests, *Brenesia,* 19/20:577–589.

Villa, J., and D. S. Townsend, 1983, Viable frog eggs eaten by phorid fly larvae, *J. Herpetol.,* 17:278–281.

Vilter, V., and A. Lugand, 1959, Trophisme intrautérin et croissance embryonnaire chez le *Nectophrynoides occidentalis* Ang., crapaud totalement vivipare du Mont Nimba (Haut Guinee), *Compt. Rend. Soc. Biol. Paris,* 153:29–32.

Vilter, V., and A. Vilter, 1960, Sur la gestation de la salamandre noir des Alpes, *Salamandra atra* Laur., *Compt. Rend. Soc. Biol. Paris,* 154:290–291.

Vilter, V., and A. Vilter, 1963, Mise en évidence d'un cycle reproducteur biennial chez le tritron alpestre de montagne, *Compt. Rend. Soc. Biol. Paris,* 157:464–469.

Vilter, V., and A. Vilter, 1964, Sur l'evotion des corps jaunes ovariens chez *Salamandra atra* Laur. des Alpes vaudoises, *Compt. Rend. Hebd. Sean. Soc. Biol.,* 158:457–461.

Viparina, S., and J. J. Just, 1975, The life period, growth and differentiation of *Rana catesbeiana* larvae occurring in nature, *Copeia,* 1975:103–109.

Visser, J., 1971, Hunting the eggs of the ghost frog, *African Wild Life,* 25:22–24.

Visser, J., J. M. Cei, and L. S. Gutierrez, 1982, The histology of dermal glands of mating *Breviceps* with comments on their possible functional value in microhylids (Amphibia: Anura), *South Africa J. Sci.,* 17:24–27.

Visser, M. H. C., 1963, The cranial morphology of *Ichthyophis glutinosus* (Linné) and *Ichthyophis monochrous* (Bleeker), *Ann. Univ. Stellenbosch,* 38A:67–102.

Vitelli, L., R. Batistoni, F. Andronico, I. Nardi, and G. Barsacchi-Pilone, 1982, Chromosomal localization of 18S + 28S and 5S ribosomal RNA genes in evolutionarily diverse anuran amphibians, *Chromosoma,* 84:475–491.

Vlad, M., 1977, Quantitative studies of rDNA in amphibians, *J. Cell Sci.,* 24:109–118.

Voitkevich, A. A., 1963, The effect of temperature on the function of the preoptic nucleus in the amphibian hypophysis, *Bull. Exp. Biol. Med. U. S. S. R.,* 53:199–204.

Volpe, E. P., 1952, Physiological evidence for natural hybridization of *Bufo americanus* and *Bufo fowleri, Evolution,* 6:393–406.

Volpe, E. P., 1953, Embryonic temperature adaptations and relationships in toads, *Physiol. Zool.,* 26:344–354.

Volpe, E. P., 1957a, Embryonic temperature tolerance and rate of development in *Bufo valliceps, Physiol. Zool.,* 30:164–176.

Volpe, E. P., 1957b, Embryonic temperature adaptations in highland *Rana pipiens, Amer. Nat.,* 9:303–310.

Volpe, E. P., 1957c, The early development of *Rana capito sevosa, Tulane Stud. Zool.,* 5:207–225.

Volpe, E. P., 1961, "Polymorphism in anuran populations," in W. F. Blair (ed.), *Vertebrate Speciation,* Austin: Univ. Texas Press, pp 221–234.

Volpe, E. P., 1970, Chromosome mapping in the leopard frog, *Genetics,* 64:11–21.

Volpe, E. P., and S. Dasgupta, 1962, Effects of different doses and combinations of spotting genes in the leopard frog, *Rana pipiens, Devel. Biol.,* 5:264–295.

Volpe, E. P., and J. L. Dobie, 1959, The larva of the oak toad, *Bufo quercicus* Holbrook, *Tulane Stud. Zool.,* 7:145–152.

Volpe, E. P., M. A. Wilkens, and J. L. Dobie, 1961, Embryonic and larval development of *Hyla avivoca, Copeia,* 1961: 340–349.

Von Huene, F., 1956, *Paläontologie und Phylogenie der Niederen Tetrapoden,* Jena: Fischer.

Voss, W. J., 1961, Rate of larval development and metamorphosis of the spadefoot toad, *Scaphiopus bombifrons, Southwest. Nat.,* 6:168–174.

Wachtel, S. S., G. C. Koo, and E. A. Boyse, 1975, Evolutionary conservation of H-Y (male) antigen, *Nature,* 254:270–272.

Wager, V. A., 1965, *The Frogs of South Africa,* Capetown: Purnell & Sons.

Wahl, M., 1969, Untersuchungen zur Bio-Akustik des Wasserfrosches *Rana esculenta* (L.), *Oecologia,* 3:14–15.

Wahlert, G. von, 1953, Eileiter, Laich und Kloake der Salamandriden, *Zool. Jahrb. Syst.,* 73:276–310.

Waite, E. R., 1925, Field notes on some Australian reptiles and a batrachian, *Rec. S. Australian Mus.,* 3:17–32.

Wake, D. B., 1963, Comparative osteology of the plethodontid salamander genus *Aneides, J. Morph.,* 113:77–118.

Wake, D. B., 1966, Comparative osteology and evolution of the lungless salamanders, family Plethodontidae, *Mem. S. California Acad. Sci.,* 4:1–111.

Wake, D. B., 1970, Aspects of vertebral evolution in the modern Amphibia, *Forma et Functio,* 3:33–60.

Wake, D. B., 1974, *Aneides, Cat. Amer. Amphib. Rept.,* 157:1–2.

Wake, D. B., 1981, "The application of allozyme evidence to problems in the evolution of morphology," in G. G. E. Scudder and J. L. Reveal (eds.), *Evolution Today,* Proc. 2nd Internat. Cong. Syst. Evol. Biol., pp 257–270.

Wake, D. B., 1982, "Functional and developmental constraints and opportunities in the evolution of feeding systems in urodeles," in D. Mossakowski and G. Roth (eds.), *Environmental Adaptation and Evolution,* Stuttgart: Gustav Fischer, pp 51–66.

Wake, D. B., and A. H. Brame Jr., 1969, Systematics and evolution of neotropical salamanders of the *Bolitoglossa helmrichi* group, *Contrib. Sci. Los Angeles Co. Mus. Nat. Hist.,* 175:1–40.

Wake, D. B., and I. G. Dresner, 1967, Functional morphology and evolution of tail autotomy in salamanders, *J. Morph.,* 122:265–306.

Wake, D. B., and P. Elias, 1983, New genera and a new species of Central American salamanders, with a review of the tropical genera (Amphibia, Caudata, Plethodontidae), *Contrib. Sci. Los Angeles Co. Mus. Nat. Hist.,* 345:1–19.

Wake, D. B., and R. Lawson, 1973, Developmental and adult morphology of the vertebral column in the plethodontid salamander *Eurycea bislineata,* with comments on vertebral evolution in the Amphibia, *J. Morph.,* 139:251–300.

Wake, D. B., and J. F. Lynch, 1976, The distribution, ecology, and evolutionary history of plethodontid salamanders in tropical America, *Sci. Bull. Los Angeles Co. Mus. Nat. Hist.,* 25:1–65.

Wake, D. B., L. R. Maxson, and G. Z. Wurst, 1978, Genetic differentiation, albumin evolution, and their geographic implications in plethodontid salamanders of California and southern Europe, *Evolution,* 32:529–539.

Wake, D. B., and N. Özeti, 1969, Evolutionary relationships in the family Salamandridae, *Copeia,* 1969:124–137.

Wake, M. H., 1968, Evolutionary morphology of the caecilian urogenital system, Part I. The gonads and fat bodies, *J. Morph.,* 126:291–332.

Wake, M. H., 1969, Gill ontogeny in embryos of *Gymnopis* (Amphibia: Gymnophiona), *Copeia,* 1969:183–184.

Wake, M. H., 1970a, Evolutionary morphology of the caecilian urogenital system. Part II. The kidneys and urogenital ducts, *Acta Anat.,* 75:321–358.

Wake, M. H., 1970b, Evolutionary morphology of the caecilian urogenital system. Part III. The bladder, *Herpetologica,* 26:120–128.

Wake, M. H., 1972, Evolutionary morphology of the caecilian urogenital system. IV. The cloaca, *J. Morph.,* 136:353–366.

Wake, M. H., 1975, Another scaled caecilian (Gymnophiona: Typhlonectidae), *Herpetologica,* 31:134–136.

Wake, M. H., 1976, The development and replacement of teeth in viviparous caecilians, *J. Morph.,* 148:33–64.

Wake, M. H., 1977a, "The reproductive biology of caecilians: an evolutionary perspective," in D. H. Taylor and S. I. Guttman (eds.), *The Reproductive Biology of Amphibians,* New York: Plenum Press, pp 73–101.

Wake, M. H., 1977b, Fetal maintenance and its evolutionary significance in the Amphibia: Gymnophiona, *J. Herpetol.,* 11:379–386.

Wake, M. H., 1978, The reproductive biology of *Eleutherodactylus jasperi* (Amphibia, Anura, Leptodactylidae), with comments on the evolution of live-bearing systems, *J. Herpetol.,* 12:121–133.

Wake, M. H., 1980a, The reproductive biology of *Nectophrynoides malcolmi* (Amphibia: Bufonidae), with comments on the evolution of reproductive modes in the genus *Nectophrynoides, Copeia,* 1980:193–209.

Wake, M. H., 1980b, Reproduction, growth, and population structure of the caecilian *Dermophis mexicanus, Herpetologica,* 36:244–256.

Wake, M. H., 1980c, Morphometrics of the skeleton of *Dermophis mexicanus* (Amphibia: Gymnophiona). Part I. The vertebrae, with comparisons to other species, *J. Morph.,* 165:117–130.

Wake, M. H., 1980d, Fetal tooth development and adult replacement in *Dermophis mexicanus* (Amphibia: Gymnophiona): fields vs. clones, *J. Morph.,* 166:203–216.

Wake, M. H., 1981, Structure and function of the male Müllerian gland in caecilians, with comments on its evolutionary significance, *J. Herpetol.,* 15:17–22.

Wake, M. H., 1982, "Diversity within a framework of contraints. Amphibian reproductive modes," in D. Mossakowski and G. Roth (eds.), *Environmental Adaptation and Evolution,* Stuttgart: Gustav Fischer, pp 87–106.

Wake, M. H., and J. A. Campbell, 1983, A new genus and species of caecilian from the Sierra de las Minas of Guatemala, *Copeia,* 1983:857–863.

Wake, M. H., and S. M. Case, 1975, The chromosomes of caecilians, *Copeia,* 1975:510–516.

Wake, M. H., J. C. Hafner, M. S. Hafner, L. L. Klosterman, and J. L. Patton, 1980, The karyotype of *Typhlonectes compressicauda* (Amphibia: Gymnophiona) with comments on chromosome evolution in caecilians, *Experientia,* 36:171–172.

Wake, M. H., and J. Hanken, 1982, Development of the skull of *Dermophis mexicanus* (Amphibia: Gymnophiona), with comments on skull kinesis and amphibian relationships, *J. Morph.,* 173:203–223.

Wake, M. H., and G. Z. Wurst, 1979, Tooth crown morphology in caecilians (Amphibia: Gymnophiona), *J. Morph.,* 159:331–341.

Wake, T. A., D. B. Wake, and M. H. Wake, 1983, The ossification sequence of *Aneides lugubris,* with comments on heterochrony, *J. Herpetol.,* 17:10–22.

Waldman, B., 1981, Sibling recognition in toad tadpoles: the role of experience, *Zeit. Tierpsychol.,* 56:341–358.

Waldman, B., 1982a, Adaptive significance of communal oviposition in wood frogs *(Rana sylvatica), Behav. Ecol. Sociobiol.,* 10:169–174.

Waldman, B., 1982b, Sibling association among schooling toad tadpoles: field evidence and implications, *Anim. Behav.,* 30:700–713.

Waldman, B., and K. Adler, 1979, Toad tadpoles associate preferentially with siblings, *Nature,* 282:611–613.

Walker, R. F., and W. G. Whitford, 1970, Soil water absorption capabilities in selected species of anurans, *Herpetologica,* 26:411–418.

Walker, W. F. Jr., 1967, *Dissection of the Frog,* San Francisco: W. H. Freeman and Co.

Wallace, R. A., D. W. Jared, and B. L. Welson, 1970, Protein incorporation by isolated amphibian oocytes. I. Preliminary studies, *J. Exp. Zool.,* 175:259–270.

Walls, G. L., 1942, The vertebrate eye and its adaptive radiation, *Bull. Cranbrook. Inst. Sci.,* 19:1–785.

Walter, F., 1887, Das Visceralskelett und seine Muskulatur bei den einheimischen Amphibien und Reptilien, *Jena Zeit. Naturw.,* 21:1–45.

Walters, B. L., 1975, Studies of interspecific predation within an amphibian community, *J. Herpetol.,* 9:267–280.

Ward, D., and O. J. Sexton, 1981, Anti-predator role of salamander egg membranes, *Copeia,* 1981:724–726.

Ward, O. G., 1977, Dimorphic nucleolar organizer regions in the frog *Rana blairi, Canadian J. Genet. Cytol.,* 19:51–57.

Wartemberg, H., and W. Schmidt, 1961, Elektronenmikroskopische Untersuchungen der strukturellen Veränderungen im Rindenbereich des Amphibieneies im Ovar und nach der Befruchtung, *Zeit. Zellforsch.,* 54:118–146.

Wasserman, A. O., 1970, Polyploidy in the common tree toad, *Hyla versicolor* LeConte, *Science,* 167:385–386.

Wassersug, R. J., 1972, The mechanism of ultraplanktonic entrapment in anuran larvae, *J. Morph.,* 137:279–288.

Wassersug, R. J., 1973, "Aspects of social behavior in anuran larvae," in J. L. Vial (ed.), *Evolutionary Biology of the Anurans: Contemproary Research on Major Problems,* Columbia: Univ. Missouri Press, pp 273–297.

Wassersug, R. J., 1975, The adaptive significance of the tadpole stage with comments on the maintenance of complex life cycles in anurans, *Amer. Zool.,* 15:405–417.

Wassersug, R. J., 1976, Oral morphology of anuran larvae: terminology and general description, *Occ. Pap. Mus. Nat. Hist. Univ. Kansas,* 48:1–23.

Wassersug, R. J., 1980, Internal oral features of larvae from eight anuran families: functional, systematic, evolutionary and ecological considerations, *Misc. Publ. Mus. Nat. Hist. Univ. Kansas,* 68:1–146.

Wassersug, R. J., 1984, The *Pseudohemisus* tadpole: a morphological link between microhylid (Orton Type 2) and ranoid (Orton Type 4) larvae, *Herpetologica,* 40:138–149.

Wassersug, R. J., and W. E. Duellman, 1984, Oral structures and their development in egg-brooding hylid frog embryos and larvae: evolutionary and ecological implications, *J. Morph.,* 182:1–37.

Wassersug, R. J., and M. E. Feder, 1983, The effects of aquatic oxygen concentration, body size and respiratory behavior on the stamina of obligate aquatic *(Bufo americanus)* and facultative air-breathing *(Xenopus laevis* and *Rana berlandieri)* anuran larvae, *J. Exp. Biol.,* 105:173–190.

Wassersug, R. J., K. J. Frogner, and R. F. Inger, 1981, Adaptations for life in tree holes by rhacophorid tadpoles from Thailand, *J. Herpetol.,* 15:41–52.

Wassersug, R. J., and C. M. Hessler, 1971, Tadpole behaviour: aggregation in larval *Xenopus laevis, Anim. Behav.,* 19: 386–389.

Wassersug, R. J., and W. R. Heyer, 1983, Morphological correlates of subaerial existence in leptodactylid tadpoles associated with flowing water, *Canadian J. Zool.,* 61:761–769.

Wassersug, R. J., and K. Hoff, 1979, A comparative study of the buccal pumping mechanism of tadpoles, *Biol. J. Linnean Soc.,* 12(3):225–259.

Wassersug, R. J., A. M. Lum, and M. J. Potel, 1981, An analysis of school structure for tadpoles (Anura: Amphibia), *Behav. Ecol. Sociobiol.,* 9:15–22.

Wassersug, R. J., and E. A. Seibert, 1975, Behavioral responses of amphibian larvae to variation in dissolved oxygen, *Copeia,* 1975:86–103.

Wassersug, R. J., and D. G. Sperry, 1977, The relationship of locomotion to differential predation on *Pseudacris triseriata* (Anura: Hylidae), *Ecology,* 58:830–839.

Watkins, W. A., E. R. Baylor, and A. T. Bowen, 1970, The call of *Eleutherodactylus johnstonei,* the whistling frog of Bermuda, *Copeia,* 1970:558–561.

Watson, G. F., and A. A. Martin, 1973, Life history, larval morphology and relationships of Australian leptodactylid frogs, *Trans. Roy. Soc. S. Australia,* 47:33–45.

Weathers, W. W., and G. K. Snyder, 1977, Relation of oxygen consumption to temperature and time of day in tropical anuran amphibians, *Australian J. Zool.,* 25:19–24.

Weber, E., 1978, Distress calls of *Bufo calamita* and *B. viridis* (Amphibia: Anura), *Copeia,* 1978:354–356.

Weber, J. A., 1944, Observations on the life history of *Amphiuma means, Copeia,* 1961:61–62.

Weigmann, D. L., and R. Altig, 1975, Anoxic tolerances of three species of salamander larvae, *Comp. Biochem. Physiol.,* 50(A):681–684.

Weisz, P. B., 1925, The normal stages of development of the South African clawed toad, *Xenopus laevis, Anat. Rec.,* 93:161–170.

Wells, K. D., 1976, Multiple egg clutches in the green frog *(Rana clamitans), Herpetologica,* 32:85–87.

Wells, K. D., 1977a, The social behaviour of anuran amphibians, *Anim. Behav.,* 25:666–693.

Wells, K. D., 1977b, "The courtship of frogs," in D. H. Taylor and S. I. Guttman (eds.), *The Reproductive Biology of Amphibians,* New York: Plenum Press, pp 233–262.

Wells, K. D., 1977c, Territoriality and male mating success in the green frog *(Rana clamitans), Ecology,* 58:750–762.

Wells, K. D., 1978a, Courtship and parental behavior in a Panamanian poison-arrow frog *(Dendrobates auratus), Herpetologica,* 34:148–155.

Wells, K. D., 1978b, Territoriality in the green frog *(Rana clamitans):* vocalizations and agonistic behaviour, *Anim. Behav.,* 26:1051–1063.

Wells, K. D., 1979, Reproductive behavior and male mating success in a Neotropical toad, *Bufo typhonius, Biotropica,* 11:301–307.

Wells, K. D., 1980a, Behavioral ecology and social organization of a dendrobatid frog *(Colostethus inguinalis), Behav. Ecol. Sociobiol.,* 6:199–209.

Wells, K. D., 1980b, Social behavior and communication of a dendrobatid frog *(Colostethus trinitatis), Herpetologica,* 36:189–199.

Wells, K. D., 1980c, Evidence for growth of tadpoles during parental transport in *Colostethus inguinalis, J. Herpetol.,* 14:426–428.

Wells, K. D., 1981a, "Parental behavior in male and female frogs," in D. R. Alexander and D. W. Tinkle (eds.), *Natural Selection and Social Behavior: Recent Research and New Theory,* Newton, Massachusetts: Chiron Press, pp 184–197.

Wells, K. D., 1981b, Territorial behavior of the frog *Eleutherodactylus urichi* in Trinidad, *Copeia,* 1981:726–728.

Wells, K. D., and B. J. Greer, 1981, Vocal responses to conspecific calls in a Neotropical hylid frog, *Hyla ebraccata, Copeia,* 1981:615–624.

Wells, K. D., and J. J. Schwartz, 1982, The effect of vegetation on the propagation of calls in the Neotropical frog *Centrolenella fleischmanni, Herpetologica,* 38:449–455.

Werner, C., 1970, "On the development and structure of the head and neck in urodele sperm," in B. Baccetti (ed.), *Comparative Spermatology,* New York: Academic Press, pp 85–92.

Werner, J. K., 1969, Temperature-photoperiod effects on spermatogenesis in the salamander *Plethodon cinereus, Copeia,* 1969:592–602.

West, L. B., 1960, The nature of growth inhibitory material from crowded *Rana pipiens* tadpoles, *Physiol. Zool.,* 33:232–239.

West, N. H., and W. W. Burggren, 1982, Gill and lung ventilatory responses to steady-state aquatic hypoxia and hyperoxia in the bullfrog tadpole, *Respiration Physiol.,* 47:165–176.

Wever, E. G., 1973, The ear and hearing in the frog, *Rana pipiens, J. Morph.,* 141:461–478.

Wever, E. G., 1975, The caecilian ear, *J. Exp. Zool.,* 191:63–72.

Wever, E. G., 1978, Sound transmission in the salamander ear, *Proc. Natl. Acad. Sci. U. S. A.,* 75:529–530.

Wever, E. G., 1979, Middle ear muscles of the frog, *Proc. Natl. Acad. Sci. U. S. A.,* 76:3031–3033.

Wever, E. G., and C. Gans, 1976, The caecilian ear: further observations, *Proc. Natl. Acad. Sci. U. S. A.,* 73:3744–3746.

Wever, E. G., and J. A. Vernon, 1960, The problem of hearing in snakes, *J. Aud. Res.,* 1:77–83.

Weygoldt, P., 1976a, Beobachtung zur Biologie und Ethologie von *Pipa (Hemipipa) carvalhoi* Mir. Rib. 1937 (Anura, Pipidae), *Zeit. Tierpsychol.,* 40:80–99.

Weygoldt, P., 1976b, Beobachtung zur Fortpflanzungsbiologie der Wabenkröte *Pipa carvalhoi* Miranda Ribeiro, *Zeit. Kolner Zoo,* 19:77–84.

Weygoldt, P., 1980, Complex brood care and reproductive behavior in captive poison-arrow frogs, *Dendrobates pumilio, Behav. Ecol. Sociobiol.,* 7:329–332.

Weygoldt, P., 1981, Beobachtungen zur Fortpflanzungsbiologie von *Phyllodytes luteolus* (Wied 1824) im Terrarium, *Salamandra,* 17:1–11.

White, B. A., and C. S. Nicoll, 1981, "Hormonal control of amphibian metamorphosis," in L. I. Gilbert and E. Frieden (eds.), *Metamorphosis. A Problem in Developmental Biology,* New York: Plenum Press, pp 363–396.

White, R. L. II, 1977, Prey selection by the rough skinned newt *(Taricha granulosa)* in two pond types, *Northwest Sci.,* 51:114–118.

Whitear, M., 1977, A functional comparison between the epidermis of fish and of amphibians, *Symp. Zool. Soc. London,* 39:291–313.

Whitford, W. G., 1973, The effects of temperature on respiration in the Amphibia, *Amer. Zool.,* 13:505–512.

Whitford, W. G., and V. H. Hutchinson, 1963, Cutaneous and pulmonary gas exchange in the spotted salamander, *Ambystoma maculatum, Biol. Bull.,* 124:344–354.

Whitford, W. G., and V. H. Hutchinson, 1965, Gas exchange in salamanders, *Physiol. Zool.,* 38:228–242.

Whitford, W. G., and V. H. Hutchinson, 1967, Body size and metabolic rate in salamanders, *Physiol. Zool.,* 40:127–133.

Whitford, W. G., and R. E. Sherman, 1968, Aerial and aquatic respiration in axolotl and transformed *Ambystoma tigrinum, Herpetologica,* 24:233–237.

Whiting, H. P., 1961, Pelvic girdle in anuran locomotion, *Symp. Zool. Soc. London,* 5:43–57.

Whitney, C. L., 1981, The monophasic call of *Hyla regilla* (Anura: Hylidae), *Copeia,* 1981:230–233.

Whitney, C. L., and J. R. Krebs, 1975, Mate selection in Pacific tree frogs, *Hyla regilla, Nature,* 255:325–326.

Wiedersheim, R., 1877, Das Kopfskelet der Urodelen, *Gegen. Morph. Jahrb.,* 3:352–548.

Wiedersheim, R., 1879, *Die Anatomie der Gymnophionen,* Vienna: Gustav Fischer Verlag.

Wiens, J. A., 1970, Effects of early experience on substrate pattern selection in *Rana aurora* tadpoles, *Copeia,* 1970: 543–548.

Wiens, J. A., 1972, Anuran habitat selection: early experience and substrate selection in *Rana cascadae* tadpoles, *Anim. Behav.,* 20:218–221.

Wiest, J. A. Jr., 1982, Anuran succession at temporary ponds in a post oak-savanna region of Texas, *U. S. Fish And Wildlife Res. Rept.,* 13:39–47.

Wiewandt, T. A., 1969, Vocalization, aggressive behavior, and territoriality in the bullfrog, *Rana catesbeiana, Copeia,* 1969: 276–285.

Wiewandt, T. A., 1971, Breeding biology of the Mexican leaf-frog, *Fauna,* 2:29–34.

Wilbur, H. M., 1972, Competition, predation, and the structure of the *Ambystoma-Rana sylvatica* community, *Ecology,* 53: 3–21.

Wilbur, H. M., 1977a, Propagule size, number, and dispersion pattern in *Ambystoma* and *Asclepias, Amer. Nat.,* 111:43–68.

Wilbur, H. M., 1977b, Density-dependent aspects of growth and metamorphosis in *Bufo americanus, Ecology,* 58:196–200.

Wilbur, H. M., 1977c, Interactions of food level and population density in *Rana sylvatica, Ecology,* 58:206–209.

Wilbur, H. M., and J. P. Collins, 1973, Ecological aspects of amphibian metamorphosis, *Science,* 182:1305–1314.

Wilbur, H. M., D. I. Rubenstein, and L. Fairchild, 1978, Sexual selection in toads: the roles of female choice and male body size, *Evolution,* 32:264–270.

Wilbur, H. M., D. W. Tinkle, and J. P. Collins, 1974, Environmental certainty, trophic level, and resource availability in life history evolution, *Amer. Nat.,* 108:805–817.

Wilder, H. H., 1894, Lungenlosen Salamandriden, *Anat. Anz.,* 9:216–220.

Wilder, I. W., 1925, *The Morphology of Amphibian Metamorphosis,* Northampton, Massachusetts: Smith College.

Wiley, E. O., 1979, Ventral gill arch muscles and the interrelationships of gnathostomes, with a new classification of the vertebrata, *Zool. J. Linnaean Soc.,* 67:149–179.

Wiley, E. O., 1981, *Phylogenetics. The Theory and Practice of Phylogenetic Systematics,* New York: John Wiley and Sons.

Wiley, R. H., and D. G. Richards, 1978, Physical constraints on acoustic communication in the atmosphere: implications for the evolution of animal vocalizations, *Behav. Ecol. Sociobiol.,* 3:69–94.

Willem, L., 1924, Recherches sur la respiration aérienne des amphibiens, *Bull. Acad. Royale Belgique, Cl. Sci.,* 10:31–47.

Williams, E. E., 1959, Gadow's arcualia and the development of tetrapod vertebrae, *Quart. Rev. Biol.,* 34:1–32.

Williams, G. C., 1975, *Sex and Evolution,* Princeton, New Jersey: Princeton Univ. Press.

Wills, L. A., 1936, The respiratory rate of developing Amphibia with special reference to sex differentiation, *J. Exp. Zool.,* 73:481–510.

Wilson, A. C., S. S. Carlson, and T. J. White, 1977, Biochemical evolution, *Ann. Rev. Biochem.,* 46:573–639.

Wilson, A. C., V. M. Sarich, and L. R. Maxson, 1974, The importance of gene arrangement in evolution. Evidence from studies on rate of chromosomal, protein, and anatomical evolution, *Proc. Nat. Acad. Sci. U. S. A.,* 71:3028–3030.

Wilson, L. D., and L. Porras, 1983, The ecological impact of man on the South Florida herpetofauna, *Spec. Publ. Mus. Nat. Hist. Univ. Kansas,* 9:1–89.

Winpenny, R. S., 1951, The effect of vegetation on the breeding of newts, *Molge cristata* and *Molge vulgaris, J. Anim. Ecol.,* 20:98–100.

Withers, P. C., 1978, Acid-base regulation as a function of body temperature in ectothermic toads, a heliothermic lizard, and a heterothermic mammal, *J. Therm. Biol.,* 3:163–171.

Withers, P. C., 1980, Oxygen consumption of plethodontid salamanders during rest, activity and recovery, *Copeia,* 1980: 781–787.

Withers, P. C., S. S. Hillman, R. C. Drewes, and O. M. Sokol,

1982, Water loss and nitrogen excretion in sharp-nosed reed frogs (*Hyperolius nasutus:* Anura, Hyperoliidae), *J. Exp. Biol.,* 97:335–343.

Witschi, E., 1924, Die Entwicklung der Keimzellen der *Rana temporaria* L. I. Urkeimzellen und Spermatogenese, *Zeit. Zellen Gewebelehre,* 1:532–561.

Wood, J. T., 1951, Protective behavior and photic orientation in aquatic adult and larval two-lined salamanders, *Eurycea b. bislineata X cirrigera, Virginia J. Sci.,* 2:113–121.

Wood, J. T., and O. K. Goodwin, 1954, Observations on the abundance, food, and feeding behavior of the newt, *Notophthalmus viridescens viridescens* (Rafinesque) in Virginia, *J. Elisha Mitchell Sci. Soc.,* 70:27–30.

Wood, S. C., 1971, Effects of metamorphosis on blood respiratory properties and erythrocyte ATP levels in the salamander, *Dicamptodon ensatus, Respiration Physiol.,* 12:53–65.

Wood, S. C., R. E. Weber, G. M. L. Maloiy, and K. Johansen, 1975, Oxygen uptake and blood respiratory properties of a caecilian, *Boulengerula taitanus, Respiration Physiol.,* 24: 255–263.

Woodruff, D. S., 1976a, Courtship, reproductive rates, and mating system in three Australian *Pseudophryne* (Amphibia, Anura, Leptodactylidae), *J. Herpetol.,* 10:313–318.

Woodruff, D. S., 1976b, Embryonic mortality in *Pseudophryne* (Anura: Leptodactylidae), *Copeia,* 1976:445–449.

Woodruff, D. S., 1977, Male postmating brooding behavior in three Australian *Pseudophryne* (Anura: Leptodactylidae), *Herpetologica,* 33:296–303.

Woodward, B. D., 1982a, Local intraspecific variation in clutch parameters in the spotted salamander (*Ambystoma maculatum), Copeia,* 1982:157–160.

Woodward, B. D., 1982b, Tadpole competition in a desert anuran community, *Oecologia,* 54:96–100.

Woodward, B. D., 1982c, Tadpole interactions in the Chihuahuan Desert at two experimental densities, *Southwest. Nat.,* 27:119–122.

Wortham, J. W. E. Jr., R. A. Brandon, and J. Martan, 1977, Comparative morphology of some plethodontid salamander spermatozoa, *Copeia,* 1977:666–680.

Wortham, J. W. E. Jr., J. A. Murphy, J. Martan, and R. A. Brandon, 1982, Scanning electron microscopy of some salamander spermatozoa, *Copeia,* 1982:52–60.

Worthington, R. D., 1971, Postmetamorphic changes in the vertebrae of the marbled salamander *Ambystoma opacum* Gravehorst (Amphibia, Caudata), *Univ. Texas El Paso Sci. Ser.,* 4:1–74.

Worthington, R. D., and D. B. Wake, 1972, Patterns of regional variation in the vertebral column of terrestrial salamanders, *J. Morph.,* 137:257–278.

Wright, A. H., and A. A. Wright, 1949, *Handbook of Frogs and Toads of the United States and Canada,* Ithaca, N. Y.: Comstock Publ. Co.

Wright, D. A., C. M. Richards, J. S. Frost, A. M. Camozzi, and B. J. Kunz, 1983, "Genetic mapping in amphibians," in *Isozymes: Current Topics Biol. Med. Res., Genetics and Evolution,* 10:287–311.

Wu, W. H., and T. H. Wang, 1948, On the occurrence and significance of the antiproteolytic substance in the embryos of fishes and frogs near hatching, *Sinensia,* 19:6–11.

Wunderer, H., 1910, Die Entwicklung der äusseren Körperform des Alpensalamanders (*Salamandra atra* Laur.), *Zool. Jahrb. (Anat. Ontog. Tiere),* 29:267–414.

Wyman, R. L., and J. H. Thrall, 1972, Sound production by the spotted salamander, *Ambystoma maculatum, Herpetologica,* 28:210–212.

Xavier, F., 1970, Action modératrice de la progestérones sur la croissance des embryons chez *Nectophrynoides occidentalis* Angel, *Compt. Rend. Acad. Sci. Paris,* (D)270:2115–2117.

Xavier, F., 1973, Le cycle des voies génitales femelles de *Nectophrynoides occidentalis* Angel, amphibien anoure vivipare, *Zeit. Zellforsch.,* 140:509–534.

Xavier, F., 1977, "An exceptional reproductive strategy in Anura: *Nectophrynoides occidentalis* Angel (Bufonidae), an example of adaptation to terrestrial life by viviparity," in M. K. Hecht, P. C. Goody and B. M. Hecht (eds.), *Major Patterns in Vertebrate Evolution,* New York: Plenum Press, pp 545–552.

Xavier, F., M. Zuber-Vogeli, and Y. Le Quang Trong, 1970, Recherches sur l'activity endocrine de l'ovaire de *Nectophrynoides occidentalis* Angel (Amphibien anoure vivipare). I. Etude histochimique, *Gen. Comp. Endocrinol.,* 15:425–431.

Yager, D. D., 1982, A novel mechanism for underwater sound production in *Xenopus borealis, Amer. Zool.,* 22:887.

Yamaguti, S., 1959–1963, *Systema Helminthum,* New York: Interscience Publ. Co.

Yamaguti, S., 1971, *Synopsis of Digenetic Trematodes of Vertebrates,* Tokyo: Keigaku Publ. Co.

Yanev, K. P., 1980, "Biogeography and distribution of three parapatric salamander species in coastal and borderland California," in D. M. Power (ed.), *The California Islands: Proceedings of a Multidisciplinary Symposium,* Santa Barbara, Calif.: Santa Barbara Mus. Nat. Hist., pp 531–550.

Yorke, C. D., 1983, Survival of embryos and larvae of the frog *Polypedates leucomystax* in Malaysia, *J. Herpetol.,* 17: 235–241.

Young, A. M., 1967, Predation in the larvae of *Dytiscus marginalis* Linnaeus (Coleoptera: Dytiscidae), *Pan-Pacific Ent.,* 43:113–117.

Zhao, E., and Q. Hu, 1983, Taxonomy and evolution of Hynobiidae in western China, with description of a new genus (in Chinese, English summary), *Acta Herpetol. Sinica,* 2(2): 29–35.

Zhao, E., and Q. Hu, 1984, *Studies on Chinese Tailed Amphibians* (in Chinese, English summary), Chengdu: Sichuan Sci. And Tech. Publ. House.

Zimmerman, B., and W. Hödl, 1983, Distinction of *Phrynohyas resinifictrix* (Goeldi, 1907) from *Phrynohyas venulosa* (Laurenti, 1768) based on acoustical and behavioral parameters (Amphibia, Anura, Hylidae), *Zool. Anz.,* 211:341–352.

Zimmermann, H., and E. Zimmermann, 1981, Sozialverhalten, Fortpflanzungsverhalten und Zucht der Färberfrösche *Dendrobates histrionicus* und *D. lehmanni* sowie einiger anderer Dendrobatiden, *Zeit. Köhlner Zoo,* 24:83–99.

Zuber-Vogeli, M., 1968, Les variations cytologiques de l'hypophyse distale des femelles de *Nectophrynoides occidentalis, Gen. Comp. Endocrinol.,* 11:495–514.

Zug, G. R., E. Lindgren, and J. R. Pippet, 1975, Distribution and ecology of the marine toad, *Bufo marinus,* in Papua New Guinea, *Pacific Sci.,* 29:31–50.

Zug, G. R., and P. B. Zug, 1979, The marine toad, *Bufo marinus:* a natural history resume of native populations, *Smithsonian Contr. Zool.,* 284:1–58.

Zweifel, R. G., 1956, Results of the Archbold Expeditions. No. 72. Microhylid frogs from New Guinea, with descriptions of new species, *Amer. Mus. Novitat.,* 1766:1–49.

Zweifel, R. G., 1958, Results of the Archbold Expeditions. No. 78. Frogs of the Papuan hylid genus *Nyctimystes, Amer. Mus. Novitat.,* 1896:1–51.

Zweifel, R. G., 1959, Effect of temperature on call of the frog, *Bombina variegata, Copeia,* 1959:322–327.

Zweifel, R. G., 1968a, Effects of temperature, body size, and hybridization on mating calls of toads, *Bufo a. americanus* and *Bufo woodhousei fowleri, Copeia,* 1968:269–285.

Zweifel, R. G., 1968b, Reproductive biology of anurans of the arid southwest, with emphasis on adaptation of embryos to temperature, *Bull. Amer. Mus. Nat. Hist.,* 140:1–64.

Zweifel, R. G., 1971, Results of the Archbold Expeditions. No. 96. Relationships and distribution of *Genyophryne thomsoni,* a microhylid frog of New Guinea, *Amer. Mus. Novit.,* 2469:1–13.

Zweifel, R. G., 1972a, Results of the Archbold Expeditions. No. 97.A revision of the frogs of the subfamily Asterophryinae, Family Microhylidae, *Bull. Amer. Mus. Nat. Hist.,* 148:411–546.

Zweifel, R. G., 1972b, A review of the frog genus *Lechriodus* (Leptodactylidae) of New Guinea and Australia, *Amer. Mus. Novit.,* 2507:1–41.

Zweifel, R. G., 1977, Upper thermal tolerances of anuran embryos in relation to stage of development and breeding habits, *Amer. Mus. Novitat.,* 2617:1–21.

Zweifel, R. G., 1979, A new cryptic species of microhylid frog (genus *Cophixalus)* from Papua New Guinea, with notes on related forms, *Amer. Mus. Novit.,* 2678:1–14.

Zylberberg, L., J. Castanet, and A. de Ricqles, 1980, Structure of the dermal scales in Gymnophiona (Amphibia), *J. Morph.,* 165:41–54.

Index

Index

The first page reference to all Recent and fossil genera of anurans, caecilians, and salamanders is to the listing of the genera and their synonyms in Chapter 19: Classification. Boldface numbers refer to pages on which taxa, structures, or processes are illustrated; boldface numbers immediately following a specific name refer to photographs in Chapter 19.

A

Abramoff, P.: population genetics, 457
Abrana, 545
Abranchus, 499
Abravaya, J. P.: anuran reproduction, 34, 73
Abroscaphus, 544
Acanthixalus, 547
    absence of advertisement call, 105
    reproduction, 547
    structure, 546–547
Acanthixalus spinosus: defensive behavior, 253
    reproductive mode, 24
    secondary sex characters, 56, **58**
    sexual dimorphism, 56
Acathocephalus ranae: parasitism, 243
Acanthostega: osteology, 424
Accordi, F.: adrenal glands in anurans, 414
Acheta domestica: in diet of *Bufo*, **264**
Acilius: predation, 244
Acris, 539
    biogeography, 492
    geographic variation in advertisement call, 98
    escape behavior, 247
    habits, 457, 537
    structure, 537
    water absorption, 199
Acris crepitans: age at first reproduction, 37
    breeding season, 278

Acris crepitans—cont.
    call rate and temperatures, 104
    chromosome complement, 449
    concealing coloration, 247
    geographic variation in advertisement call, 96
    inheritance of color pattern, 456
    molecular versus morphological evolution, 457
    movements, 266
    prey selection, 230
    rate of food consumption, 239
    thermoregulation, 215
Acris gryllus: celestial orientation, 52
    pineal photoreception, 52, 384
Acrodytes, 539
Activity: bursts and anaerobic metabolism, 224
    cycles regulated by environment, 226
    foraging, 238–239
    levels and rates of oxygen consumption, 223–224
    times and water conservation, 204
Adelphesiren, 496
Adelophryne, 530
Adelotus, 526
    odontoids, 319
    reproductive mode, 25
Adelotus brevis: mandibular tusks, 55–56
    parental care, 40, 46
Adenohypophysis: control of gametogenesis, 14–15
    hormones produced, 175–178, 210
    structure, 411, **413**

Adenohypophysis—*cont.*
    types of cells affecting reproductive activity, 16
Adenomera, 531
    chromosome complement, 448
    reproductive mode, 24–25, 41, 529
Adenomera marmorata: chromosome complement, 448
Adenomus, 533
Adhesive organs: development, 126
    function, 126–**127**
    phagocytosis, 185
    structure, **126**
Adler, K.: anuran courtship and mating, 80–81, 101
    celestial orientation and extraoptic photoreception, 52, 383–384
    larvae, 170
    research, 6
Adler, W.: development, 129
Adolph, E. F.: water economy, 198
Adrenal glands: structure and function, 413–414
Advertisement calls (anurans): abiotic factors affecting, 104–105
    acoustic interference, 105–106
    choruses, 102, 106
    convergence, 107
    genetic basis, 98, 103
    inhibitory effects, 107
    predator attraction, 102
    species specificity, 98–101
    territorial calls as part of, 101–102
    variation, 98

613

Centrolenella griffithsi: larval structure, **160**
  territoriality, 81
Centrolenella prosoblepon, **540**
Centrolenella valerioi: mating success, 84
  parental care, 41
  territoriality, 81
Centrolenidae: definition, 540
  fusion of astragalus and calcaneum, 540
  reproductive mode, 28
Centrotelma, 539
Cerathyla, 539
Ceratobatrachus, 545
  biogeography, 489
  cranial osteology, 318
  cryptic structure, 248
  dentition, 55, 319
  reproduction, 24, 544
Ceratophryinae: chromosome complement, 448
  content, 530
  structure, 528
Ceratophryne, 524
Ceratophrys, 530
  biogeography, 490
  defensive behavior, 257
  dentition, 319, 440
  dermal shield, 373
  metamorphosis of gut, 186
  odontoids, 237
  polyploidy, 529
  predation by: adults, 102, 245, 529
   larvae, 162, 273
  prey attraction, 238
  rate of food consumption, 239
Ceratophrys aurita: polyploidy, 451
Ceratophrys calcarata, **529**
Ceratophrys cornuta: larvae feeding on tadpoles, 244
  structure of larvae, **158, 161**
  trophic partitioning, 279
Ceratophrys cranwelli: chromosome complement, 451
Ceratophrys ornata: carnivory, 229
  longevity, 265
  metamorphosis of gonads, 188
  polyploidy, 451
  reproduction, 15
  waterproofing, 204
Chacophrys, 530
Chaine, T.: anuran hyobranchium, 237
Chang, C. Y.: sex reversal, 447
Chang, M. L. Y.: salamander reproduction, 17
Channing, A.: anuran vocalization, 99
  Bufonidae, 534
  larvae, 162, 169–171
Chantell, C. J.: Hylidae, 539
Chaparana, 546
Chaperina, 552
Charchesium: parasitism, 242
Chascax, 533
Chaunus, 533
Cheek, J. E.: larvae, 166
Chelotriton, 504
Chelydobatrachus, 527
Chen, S.-H.: Taiwanese amphibians, 4
Cherchi, M. A.: development, 125
Chester Jones, I.: renal function, 210

Chiasmocelis, 552
  biogeography, 491
  chromosome complement, 449
Chibon, P.: anuran reproduction, 21, 37
Chieffi, G.: reproduction, 15
Chilophryne, 533
Chioglossa, 504
  antipredator mechanisms, 250
  courtship, 61
  lungs, 235
  reproduction, 504
  tail autotomy, 325
Chioglossa lusitanica: tail autotomy, 260
  throat muscles and hyobranchium, **303**
Chionopelas, 531
Chirixalus, 548
  reproduction, 548
Chirixalus nongkhorensis, **548**
  reproductive mode, 23
Chirodryas, 538
Chiroleptes, 538
Chiromantis, 548
  amplexus, 69
  biogeography, 489
  osmoregulation, 209, 375
  reproduction, 25–26, 548
  Wolffian ducts, 407
Chiromantis petersi: duration of development, 35
  early development, 125
  evaporative water loss, 201
  fecundity, 35
  foam nest, **76**
  nitrogen excretion, 207
  osmoregulation, 208
Chiromantis rufescens: oviposition, 77
Chiromantis xerampelina, **548**
  evaporative water loss, 201
  nitrogen excretion, 207
  osmoregulation, 209
  parental care, 42
Chironius: predation on anurans, 245
Chironomidae: parasitism, 243
Chiropterotriton, 508
  antipredator mechanisms, 251
  biogeography, 485
  defensive behavior, 252
  structure, 506
Chiropterotriton multidentatus: thermal acclimation, 213–214
Chlamydocephalus: parasitism, 242
Chlamydomonas: occurrence in salamander eggs, 120
Choanacantha, 551
Choanenschleimbeutel (caecilians), 385–386
Choerophryne, 552
Chondrocranium: of anurans, 151–152
  of caecilians, 145–147
  components, **143**–145
  embryonic origin, 143
  of salamanders, **143**, 148–149
  sequence of ossification, 147, 149–150, 152
Chondrotus, 502
Chorophilus, 539
Christensen, C. N.: water economy, 200, 239
Christian, K. A.: prey selection, 230

Chromatophores: changes in during metamorphosis, 181, 184
  origin, 376
  possible function in evaporative water loss, 201, 375
  structure and function, 374, **375–376**
Chromosomes:
  characteristics: anurans, 446–449
   caecilians, 446
   salamanders, 446–447
  evolution, 458–459, 464, 473
  meiotic, 452–453
Chrysobatrachus, 547
  biogeography, 490
  structure, 546–547
Chrysobatrachus cupreonitens: amplexus, 69
Chrysodonta, 503
Chrysotriton, 501
Chthonerpeton, 514
  aortic arches, 399
  copulation, 53
Chthonerpeton indistinctum: chromosome complement, 446
  courtship, 61
Chu, C. P.: development, 129
Chugunov, J. D.: respiration, 217
Chung, S.-H.: sound reception, 95–96, 389
Church, G.: anuran reproduction, 16, 19
Cinclidium, 539
Cincliscopus, 539
Circulation: aortic arches, 399
  gas transport, 219
  gills, 399–400
  heart, 400
  lungs, 405
Cladosporium: infections, 242
Clarke, B. T.: Ranidae, 544–545
Clarke, R. D.: survivorship, 269
Classification: Anura, 514–553
  Caudata, 495–508
  Gymnophiona, 508–514
Claussen, D. L.: thermal biology, 212–214, 264
  water economy, 203
Cleavage, 125
Clinotarsus, 545
Cloaca: glands, 53, 79
  modifications, 53, 59, 77–78, 468
  origin, 145
  structure, 408
Cloete, S. E.: salamander osteology, 296, 299, 302
Clothier, G. W.: survivorship of larvae, 268
Clyne, D.: anuran reproduction, 81
Cochran, D. M.: Brachycephalidae, 535
  Hylidae, 538–539
  Microhylidae, 553
  tropical anurans, 5
Cochranella, 540
Coe, M. J.: anuran reproduction, 25–26, 35, 77
  eggs, 115
Coelonotus, 539
Cogger, H. G.: Microhylidae, 552
  Myobatrachidae, 526
Coghill, G. E.: cranial nerves, 393
Cole, C. J.: anuran chromosomes, 447–449
Cole, L.: reproductive strategies, 47
Collett, T.: visual perception, 383

625

D

F

H

647

N

Q

R

S

V

W